Operating Systems

Taken from:

Operating Systems: A Systematic View, Sixth Edition
by William S. Davis and T.M. Rajkumar

Operating Systems for Technicians 2004
by Todd Meadors and Cheryl A. Schmidt

PEARSON CUSTOM PUBLISHING
501 Boylston Street, Suite 900, Boston, MA 02116
A Pearson Education Company

To Cathy

Contents

4   Linking the Hardware Components   69

PART 2: BASIC OPERATING SYSTEM CONCEPTS 91

PART 3: COMMUNICATING WITH THE OPERATING SYSTEM   145

7   MS-DOS Commands   147

8   The Microsoft Windows User Interface   177

9   The UNIX/Linux User Interface   211

PART 4: OPERATING SYSTEM INTERNALS   249

10 The Intel Architecture   251

13 UNIX and Linux Internals 315

14 Macintosh OS X Internals   343

21   Novell NetWare   541

APPENDIX C: Summary of UNIX Commands 593

APPENDIX D: IBM OS/JCL   603

Preface

■ Philosophy and Perspective

The first edition of *Operating Systems: A Systematic View* was published in 1977. In those days, one company, IBM, dominated the computer industry. The first edition reflected that reality, but times have changed. Today, a typical computing environment consists of multiple computers from multiple vendors linked to form a network, and that new reality is a key driving force behind this sixth edition.

Although numerous changes have been made, *Operating Systems: A Systematic View* remains an *applied* introduction to operating systems. This is not a theoretical text. It is aimed at those who are interested in using (rather than designing) computers, operating systems, and networks. The intent is to show *why* operating systems are needed and *what,* at a functional level, they do.

The early editions of this book looked at operating systems from the perspective of an application programmer. Like the fifth edition, this edition expands that perspective a bit to include experienced users who may or may not know how to program. As before, the book assumes little or no mathematics beyond high school algebra. The only prerequisites are a reasonable understanding of basic computer concepts and a sincere interest in knowing what goes on beneath the surface of a computer application.

■ Changes from the Fifth Edition

In addition to technological updates throughout the text, a chapter on Macintosh OS X (14) has been added to the sixth edition, the Windows chapters (8, 12, and 19) have been updated to reflect the most current versions of this popular operating system, additional coverage of Linux has been integrated into the UNIX/Linux chapters (9, 13, and 20), and Part 5 has been substantially rewritten to incorporate the evolving communication infrastructure and network principles (Chapter 16), the Internet (Chapter 17), and the client/server model and security implications (Chapter 18).

Gone from the new edition is the fifth edition chapter on virtual machines (19), although key virtual machine concepts have been incorporated into other chapters. Additionally, the chapters on OS/JCL (11 and 12) have been merged and streamlined to form a new Appendix D, and the contents of fifth edition Chapters 17 (Principles of Operation) and 18 (IBM MVS) have been merged to form a new Chapter 15 on MVS. For interested instructors, fifth edition Chapters 11, 12, 17, 18, and 19 are available for downloading on the book's companion Web site.

◼ Sixth Edition Contents

The new edition retains the pace, level, and writing style of the earlier editions. As before, numerous illustrations closely follow the narrative and visually reinforce the concepts. The book also retains such chapter-level pedagogical features as learning objectives, summaries, key word lists, and review questions, and adds a set of thought-provoking exercises designed to encourage the student to think beyond the book.

Part 1 (Chapters 2-4) reviews essential computer concepts. The primary purpose of these three chapters is to ensure that all students start with a consistent technical base before moving on. Some students might find at least some of this material familiar.

Part 2 presents an overview of key operating system concepts. Chapter 5 discusses the user interface, the file system, and device management. Chapter 6 moves inside the operating system and introduces the more transparent memory and processor management functions. The intent of this section is to present a high-level, generic map of an operating system's primary functions. Later in the text when you begin reading about the internals of several different operating systems, these two chapters will help you make sense of the details.

Users and programmers communicate with an operating system through a user interface, the subject of Part 3. The primary focus of this section is using an interface or a command language to create and manipulate files. Chapters 7, 8, and 9 are presented as interactive tutorials on MS-DOS, Windows XP, and UNIX/Linux respectively. If possible, they should be read while you are sitting in front of a computer and following along, step by step.

Part 4 moves inside the computer. Chapter 10 introduces the Intel Pentium architecture, useful (though not essential) preparation for Chapters 11 (MS-DOS) and 12 (Windows XP). The material in Chapter 13 (UNIX and Linux Internals) is independent of the underlying hardware architecture. Chapter 14 is a new chapter on Macintosh OS X internals. Chapter 15 introduces selected principles underlying the traditional IBM mainframe architecture and describes the IBM MVS dispatching process.

Part 5 covers network operating systems. Chapter 16 introduces the communication infrastructure and key networking concepts, Chapter 17 describes the Internet and the World Wide Web, and Chapter 18 covers key client/server network concepts and explores security implications of networks. Chapters 19, 20, and 21 show how the concepts introduced in Chapter 18 are implemented using Windows 2003, Linux, and Novell NetWare respectively.

◼ Supplements

The following supplementary materials are available to assist instructors and students:

▶ *Online Instructor's Manual:* Lecture/discussion suggestions and solutions to textbook review questions and exercises.
▶ *Test Bank:* Sample examination questions.
▶ *Online PowerPoint presentations:* An average of 27 slides per chapter, including virtually all the textbook figures.
▶ *Online, downloadable copies of selected fifth edition chapters:* Chapters 11 and 12 (IBM's OS/JCL), Chapter 17 (Traditional IBM Mainframe Operating Principles), Chapter 18 (IBM MVS), and Chapter 19 (Virtual Machines).

The Instructor's Manual, Test Bank, and PowerPoint presentations are available only to instructors through your Addison-Wesley sales representative, or e-mail Addison-Wesley (aw.cse@aw.com) for information on how to access them.

◼ Acknowledgements

We'd like to thank our editor, Michael Hirsch, and our project editor, Katherine Harutunian. Juliet Silveri managed the production process. Elizabeth Hopwood was our primary contact at the production subcontractor, Dartmouth Publishing, Inc., Mary Alice Richardson, our copy editor, asked many excellent questions, and Shoreh Hashemi of the University of Houston prepared the instructor's manual. Additionally, we would like to acknowledge the following reviewers for their many valuable insights and suggestions:

William T. Anderson, *Northwood University, Midland Campus*
Francis Kofi Andoh-Baidoo, *Virginia Commonwealth University*
Peter de Luca, *DeVry Institute of Technology*
Shohreh Hashemi, *University of Houston, Downtown*
K. Niki Kunene, *Virginia Commonwealth University*
Michael Kusheba, *Kilgore College*
Nipul Patel, *Purdue University Calumet*
Michael Stanton, *ITT Technical Institute*

We're excited about this new edition, and we sincerely hope it meets your needs.

WSD, Sarasota, Florida
TMR, Oxford, Ohio

CHAPTER 1

What Is an Operating System?

When you finish reading this chapter you should be able to:

▶ Define the term operating system.

▶ Identify an operating system's interfaces.

▶ Define the term service.

▶ Explain how the operating system serves as a platform for constructing and running application programs.

▶ Describe an operating system's environment in terms of layers of abstraction.

▶ Relate the black box concept to the layering concept.

▶ List and briefly describe the primary services provided by a modern operating system.

▶ Explain how a complex system can be constructed by plugging together a set of layers.

▶ Distinguish between open source and proprietary.

■ Basic Operating System Functions

An **operating system** is a set of system software routines that sits between the application program and the hardware (Figure 1.1). It defines a set of standard interface rules, provides numerous services, and serves as a platform for running and developing application programs.

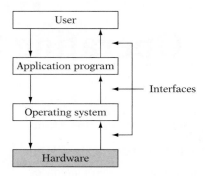

FIGURE 1.1
The operating system sits between the application program and the hardware.

The Interface Function

An **interface** is a point of connection or linkage between two components. Note that there are three interfaces pictured in Figure 1.1: The user communicates with the application program, the application program communicates with the operating system, and the operating system communicates with the hardware. The operating system incorporates logic that supports interfaces with both the application program and the hardware. All application programs access the hardware *through* the operating system following rules imposed *by* the operating system. A modern computer literally cannot function without an operating system in place.

Services

The operating system's internal routines can be viewed as small, single-function programs that perform key support **services** such as communicating with peripheral devices and accepting and carrying out such user commands as launch a program, copy a file, create a directory, open a file, save a file, and so on. A service is a software routine that runs in support of another program.

For example, imagine using a word processing application to write a paper. Most of the time you are working directly with the application logic, but occasionally you encounter a need to perform an input or output operation such as saving a file. Although such tasks seem simple, they are in reality deceptively complex. They are also common to virtually all applications, and it makes little sense to duplicate them in each and every program. The operating system's central position makes it an ideal repository for these common, shared system services because all application programs access the hardware through the operating system. Thus, when you tell your application (via the user interface) to save a file, your application program calls the operating system's file save routine. The application program resumes processing after the requested service is completed.

Platforms

At the hardware level, computers distributed by different manufacturers are often incompatible, perhaps using different rules for communicating with peripherals and other hardware components. Consequently, a program written for one brand of computer might not work on a competitive machine. However, if both computers support the same operating system they can probably run the same application software. Because different brands often imply different hardware, the operating system routines that communicate directly with the hardware might be quite different, but the routines that interface with the application program present a consistent **platform** (Figure 1.2) to the programs running on both machines. Because all communication with the hardware goes through the operating system, the programmer can ignore the hardware differences and the software developer can market the same application program to users of numerous computer brands.

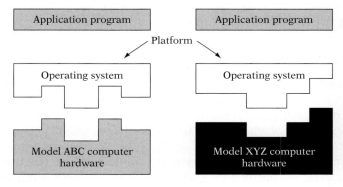

FIGURE 1.2

The operating system is a platform for executing application programs.

Sidebars

Throughout this book, you will encounter numerous sidebars like this one. They are designed to supplement the primary narrative, providing historical background, tips, different perspectives, related issues, and similar information. We hope you find them interesting.

◼ Layers of Abstraction

Figure 1.1 shows the user, the application program, the operating system, and the hardware as four linked layers. Each of those layers represents an **abstraction,** a simplified view of an object that ignores the internal details. (For example, standardized controls make it possible for an experienced driver to operate virtually any automobile.) The advantage of using layers of abstraction is that you can focus on the details of any given layer without losing sight of the other layers.

The idea behind viewing a system as a set of layers of abstraction is derived from an old architectural concept called **layering.** For example, imagine that a major retailer has decided to construct a new superstore. Given a choice between locating the new store near a major interstate highway interchange and developing a more remote site, the retailer is likely to choose the former because tapping into the existing transportation infrastructure (the interstate highway system) is far less expensive than building new access roads to bring customers to an outlying site. Moving on to the construction phase, rather than creating new electric power generation, communication, water, and sewer systems, the contractor will almost certainly adopt the standards documented in the local building codes and tap into the existing infrastructures provided by the local electric, communication, water, and sewer utilities. Creating a new building would be prohibitively expensive without layering.

Black Boxes

An operating system's environment can conveniently be viewed as a set of layers of abstraction. Think of the user, application program, operating system, and hardware layers from Figure 1.1 as **black boxes** (Figure 1.3). The contents of a black box are unknown to the other boxes, so each layer is functionally **independent.** Two black boxes communicate with each other only through a shared interface or point of linkage (Figure 1.4). Generally, the interface is defined by a set of rules or standards, such as a list of parameters. Black box A follows those standards to deliver content to the interface. Black box B follows those same standards to accept that content from the interface.

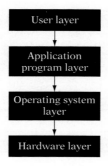

FIGURE 1.3
View each layer of abstraction as a black box.

Viewing each layer of abstraction as an independent black box is useful because it allows you to work with the layers one at a time. Because the other layers are independent of the user, anyone who understands the application program's user interface can access the system. Because the application program layer is independent, the program can be modified, updated, and patched transparently. Because the operating system layer is independent, it is possible to upgrade the operating system without affecting the other layers. Because the hardware layer is independent, it is possible for the top three layers to run, almost literally without change, on a new computer. The only requirement is that the rules imposed by the interfaces must be followed. That is why modern information systems are designed as a series of independent layers of abstraction linked by clearly defined interfaces.

FIGURE 1.4
Two black boxes communicate through a shared interface.

A Modern Operating System's Primary Services

Another advantage of the layered approach is that it gives you the ability to focus on the contents of a given layer while essentially ignoring the other layers. For example, by exploding (adding detail to) the application program layer, you can clearly show that an operating system can support multiple application programs (Figure 1.5).

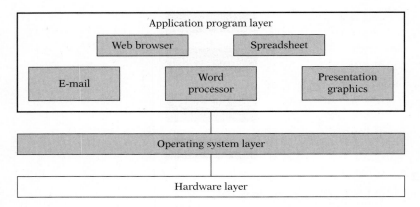

FIGURE 1.5

An operating system can support many application programs.

Similarly, it is possible to explode the operating system layer and identify the operating system's primary services (Figure 1.6). The **user interface**, sometimes called the **shell**, provides a mechanism for the user and application programs to communicate with the operating system and request operating system support. An operating system's file management and device management functions are closely related. The **file management** function, sometimes called the **file system**, incorporates routines that allow the user or programmer to create, delete, modify, and manipulate files logically, by name. The **device management** function is responsible for controlling communications with the system's physical peripheral devices, such as the keyboard, the display screen, the printer, and secondary storage.

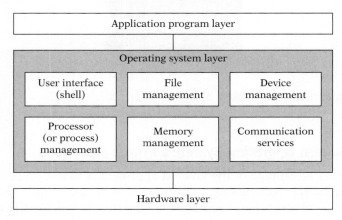

FIGURE 1.6

A modern operating system contains these primary components.

An operating system's processor and memory management functions are more transparent to the user. **Processor** (or **process**) **management** is concerned with efficiently managing the processor's time. **Memory management** is concerned with managing the system's memory resources as the computer runs, allocating space to applications as needed and ensuring that those applications do not interfere with each other.

Inter-layer and Intralayer Communication

You can also show how logic flows between layers and within a layer. For example, Figure 1.7 shows the steps required to carry out a user request to open a file. When the user clicks on the *Open* icon, the application program responds by calling the open routine in the operating system's shell. The shell passes the open file request down to the file management layer, which determines exactly where the requested file is located. If the file is on the local computer, the file management layer passes the request down to the device management layer, which communicates with the hardware layer.

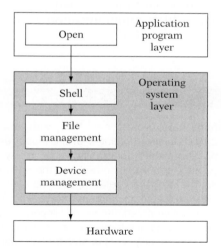

FIGURE 1.7
Opening a file.

Intercomputer Communication

In today's distributed computing environments, applications are often spread over two or more computers, with each computer performing part of the application task. Intercomputer communication is enabled by

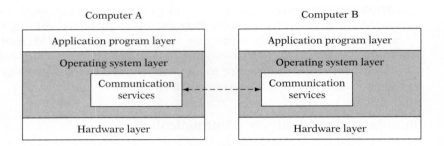

FIGURE 1.8
Intercomputer communication is enabled by communication services installed on both machines.

communication services software installed on both machines (Figure 1.8). Note that each of the two interconnected computers has its own operating system with its own shell, file management, device management, memory management, and processor management services. Note also that the same (or at least compatible) communication services must be installed on both computers.

Operating System Evolution

Operating systems have evolved over time, with new features constantly being added to reflect technological change. Often, those features begin as application programs, demonstrate their applicability to a variety of application and system tasks, gain popularity, and are absorbed into the operating system.

For example, the very first operating systems consisted of little more than collections of device management routines that supported input and output operations. Over time, creative programmers developed file management routines, and other programmers, recognizing the value of those routines, incorporated them into their own programs. Eventually, a set of standard file management routines emerged and joined the device management routines in the evolving operating system.

The evolutionary process continues today. Windows got its start as a shell that ran on top of MS-DOS, in effect as an application program. Today, the shell, Windows, has *become* the operating system, effectively absorbing MS-DOS. Similarly, Web browsers and communication support software started as application programs. Today the distinction between those routines and the operating system is hazy at best. Perhaps over the next several years, voice input will become commonplace. If that happens, voice recognition software is likely to migrate from application routine to operating system feature.

Assembling Systems

Breaking a given layer into sublayers helps to simplify system maintenance. Going the other way, plugging a given layer into higher-level layers is an excellent way to construct a complex system. For example, you have probably copied a spreadsheet into a slide presentation or copied a paragraph from an e-mail message into a word processing document. Such copy operations work because several application programs can run concurrently on the same operating system. Similarly, if you have ever exchanged e-mail messages or viewed a Web page, you know that your system can be plugged into other systems, literally worldwide. The layering concept is the key to understanding how systems are assembled and how they interact. Because each layer is functionally independent, stacking layers is like stacking building blocks. Understand layering and you understand the context in which the individual components and subassemblies operate.

◼ Open Source and Proprietary Operating Systems

Throughout the balance of this book, you will study several different operating systems. Some, like UNIX and Linux, are **open source;** in other words, they are based on open, published source code that can be modified and improved by anyone. Many open source operating systems can run on virtually any computer. At the other extreme are **proprietary** operating systems such as the one that supports Apple's Macintosh computers. Proprietary operating systems are closed. For example, OS X is designed specifically to run on Macintosh computers and most of the underlying source code is accessible only to Apple's programmers.[1] Microsoft Windows is a bit of a hybrid; it runs on computers supplied by numerous vendors, but the operating system's source code is proprietary. The strengths and weaknesses of the open source and proprietary philosophies will be explored in subsequent chapters.

◼ A Look Ahead

This book is divided into five parts. Part 1 (Chapters 2 through 4) covers a computer's basic hardware, software, and data resources, essentially exploring the contents of the application program and hardware layers. For

---

[1]OS X has one open source routine called darwin, but the rest of the operating system is proprietary.

some students, these three chapters will be largely review. Part 2 (Chapters 5 and 6) explains the essential functions performed by a modern operating system by exploding the operating system layer. Part 3 (Chapters 7 through 9) introduces the user interfaces and command languages for three well-known operating systems: MS-DOS, Windows XP, and UNIX/Linux. Part 4 (Chapters 10 through 15) explains how those three operating systems plus Macintosh OS X and IBM's traditional mainframe operating systems work internally. Finally, Part 5 (Chapters 16 through 21) investigates modern networks and intercomputer communication. Think of layering as the common thread that ties together all these topics.

▄ Summary

An operating system is a set of software routines that sits between the application program and the hardware and serves as a hardware/application software interface, acts as a repository for shared services, and defines a platform for constructing and executing application software. The operating system's environment can conveniently be viewed as a set of layers of abstraction, where each layer is an independent black box. A modern operating system incorporates a user interface or shell, file management routines (sometimes called the file system), device management routines, memory management routines, processor management routines, and communication services. Some operating systems are open source; others are proprietary; others are a hybrid of open source and proprietary.

▄ Key Words

abstraction	memory management
black box	open source
communication services	operating system
device management	platform
file management	processor or process management
file system	proprietary
independent	service
interface	shell
layering	user interface

▌Review Questions

1. Briefly, what is an operating system? What is an interface? Identify the operating system's interfaces.

2. What is a service?

3. The operating system is a convenient repository for common, shared routines. Why?

4. An operating system serves as a platform for constructing and running application programs. What does this mean and why is it important?

5. What is an abstraction? What is layering? How can viewing an information system as a set of layers of abstraction help you to better understand operating systems?

6. Describe Figure 1.1 as a set of independent layers of abstraction.

7. What is a black box? Relate the black box concept to the layering concept. Why is functional independence important?

8. List and briefly describe the primary services provided by a modern operating system.

9. What are communication services and why are they important?

10. Explain how a complex system can be constructed by plugging together a set of layers.

11. Distinguish between open source and proprietary.

▌Exercises

1. Identify the operating system that runs on your computer.

2. Study the application programs you use regularly and look for shared features. For example, it is likely that most if not all of the application programs that run on your system interpret such basic mouse operations as click, double click, and drag identically, include essentially the same set of commands on any of the drop down menus, and so on. Such common functions are likely to be performed by the operating system. Why does that make sense?

3. In your opinion, what multimedia applications or tasks, if any, might be candidates for inclusion in a near-future operating system?

4. Imagine that we really do learn how to inexpensively beam people and products from place to place as they do on Star Trek. How would that breakthrough affect the established transportation infrastructure? How would the resulting changes affect population patterns?

5. One factor that stands in the way of the widespread acceptance of such transportation alternatives as electric-powered automobiles is the established infrastructure for distributing gasoline. Explain why.

System Resources

This section overviews a computer's basic resources. Chapter 2 is an overview of a stand-alone computer's key hardware components, Chapter 3 discusses software and data, and Chapter 4 focuses on how those basic resources are linked. For some readers, at least of the material in Part 1 will be review. The intent of this section is to ensure that all readers begin with a strong technical foundation.

CHAPTER 2

Hardware

When you finish reading this chapter you should be able to:

▶ Relate the terms bit, byte, and word.

▶ Explain how a computer's memory is addressed.

▶ Identify the key components of a processor.

▶ Explain what happens during a computer's basic machine cycle.

▶ Describe several common input and output devices and media.

▶ Briefly explain the process of reading data from or writing data to disk.

▶ Explain the purpose of a disk's directory.

▶ Distinguish between a simple microcomputer interface and the channels and control units used on mainframes.

▶ Explain the purpose of a buffer.

▪ Memory

This chapter focuses on key hardware layer components (Figure 2.1). We begin with memory.

A computer's **main memory** (henceforth, just **memory**) holds currently active programs and data. A program must be stored in memory before it can be executed. Data must be stored in memory before the computer can manipulate them, and all data input to and output from a computer must pass through memory.

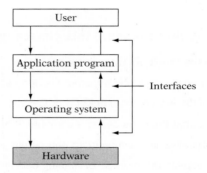

FIGURE 2.1
This chapter focuses on key hardware layer components.

Physical Memory Devices

A computer's memory holds binary digits, or **bits** (see Appendix A for a review of number system concepts). Almost any device that can assume either of two states (on, off) can serve as computer memory, but most computers use integrated circuit chips.

When you **read** memory, you extract the contents but you do not change them. When you **write** memory, in contrast, you record new values and thus destroy the old contents. Write is a "destructive" operation. Read is not destructive.

Most computer memory is random access memory (RAM). The programmer (through a program, of course) can read or write RAM; its contents are easy to change. Usually, this flexibility is an advantage. Sometimes, however, it makes sense to record key software or data in more permanent, read-only memory (ROM). As the name implies, ROM can be read, but not written.

Bytes and Words

A single bit can hold either a 0 or a 1. Generally, however, the contents of memory are envisioned as groups of bits called bytes and words. A **byte** contains enough bits (usually eight) to represent a single character. For example, the ASCII code for a capital A is 01000001. Within memory, the letter A would be stored by recording that bit pattern in a single byte (8 bits).

Bytes are fine for storing characters, but are too small to hold a meaningful number. Most computers are able to manipulate a group of bytes called a **word.** Some small computers have 8-bit words, but 16-bit (2-byte), 32-bit (4-byte), and even 64-bit word computers are more common.

Thus we have a memory hierarchy (Figure 2.2). The basic unit of storage is the bit. Bits are grouped to form bytes, which in turn are grouped to form words. In one application, a given word might hold a binary number. In another, that word's bytes might hold individual characters or a program instruction.

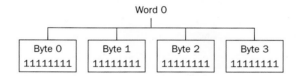

FIGURE 2.2

In a computer's memory, bits are grouped to form bytes, which in turn are grouped to form words.

Addressing Memory

Memory capacity is typically measured in megabytes (millions of bytes) or gigabytes (billions of bytes). To distinguish them, each byte (more generally, each physical storage unit) is assigned a unique **address.** On most computers, the bytes (or words) are numbered sequentially—0, 1, 2, and so on. The processor accesses a specific memory location by referencing its address.

For example, if the processor (the component that manipulates the data) needs the data stored in byte 1048, it asks memory for the contents of byte 1048. Since there is only one byte 1048, the processor gets the right data. Depending on the computer, bytes or words are the basic *addressable* units of memory. Data move between the processor and memory one byte or one word at a time.

Cache Memory

One way to increase processing speed is to move program instructions and data from memory to the processor more quickly. To help accomplish this objective, many computers contain a block of high-speed **cache** (pronounced "cash") **memory**. Think of cache as a staging area for the processor (Figure 2.3). The program is stored in standard RAM. As the program executes, the active instructions and the active data are transferred to high-speed cache memory. Subsequently, the individual instructions and the data referenced by those instructions move from cache to the processor. Thus, the processor waits for high-speed cache instead of slower RAM, and that increases processing speed.

If the relationship between main memory, cache, and the processor reminds you of layering, good.

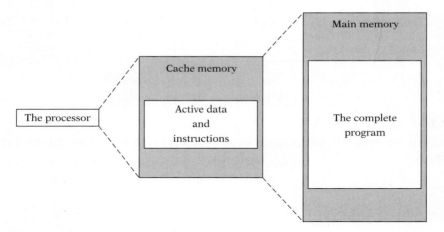

FIGURE 2.3
Think of cache memory as a staging area for the processor.

■ The Processor

The **processor,** often called the central processing unit (CPU) or main processor, is the component that manipulates data. A processor can do nothing without a program to provide control; whatever intelligence a computer has is derived from software, not hardware. The processor manipulates data stored in memory under the control of a program stored in memory (Figure 2.4).

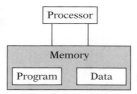

FIGURE 2.4

The processor manipulates data stored in memory under the control of a program stored in memory.

Program Instructions

A **program** is a series of **instructions** each of which tells the computer to perform one of its basic functions: add, subtract, multiply, divide, compare, copy, start input, or start output. Each instruction has an operation code and one or more operands (Figure 2.5). The operation code specifies the function to be performed, and the operands identify the memory locations or data that are to participate in the operation. For example, the instruction in Figure 2.5 tells the computer to add the contents of memory locations 1000 and 1004.

Operation code	Operands
ADD	*1000, 1004*

FIGURE 2.5

Each instruction has an operation code and one or more operands.

The Processor's Components

The processor contains four key components (Figure 2.6). The **instruction control unit** (ICU) fetches instructions from memory. The **arithmetic and logic unit** (ALU) holds or activates the computer's instruction set (the circuits that add, subtract, multiply, and so on) and executes instructions. **Registers** are temporary storage devices that hold control information, key data, and intermediate results. The **clock** (which typically occupies a separate chip of its own) generates precisely timed electronic pulses that synchronize the other components.

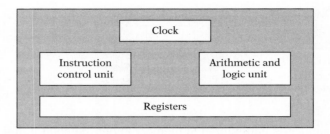

FIGURE 2.6
The processor contains four key components.

Machine Cycles

A good way to understand how a computer's internal components work together to execute instructions is to use a model of a simple computer system (Figure 2.7a) to illustrate a few **machine cycles.** Start with the processor. In addition to the clock, it contains an instruction control unit, an arithmetic and logic unit, and several registers, including an instruction counter, an instruction register, and a work register called the accumulator. The computer's other major component, memory, holds program instructions and data values. Note that each memory location is assigned an address.

The process starts when the clock generates a pulse of current that activates the instruction control unit (ICU). The ICU's job is to decide what the machine will do next. The computer is controlled by program instructions, which are stored in memory. The address of the next instruction to be executed is always found in the instruction counter (Figure 2.7a). (*Note:* The operating system places the address of a program's first instruction in the instruction counter when the program is launched or started.) The instruction control unit checks the instruction counter, finds the address, fetches the next instruction, and puts it into the instruction register (Figure 2.7b). Fetching an instruction from memory takes time, giving the instruction control unit an opportunity to increment the instruction counter to point to the next instruction (Figure 2.7b, again).

Once the fetch operation is complete, the instruction control unit activates the arithmetic and logic unit, which executes the instruction (in this case, a copy instruction) found in the instruction register (Figure 2.7c). Following execution of the instruction, a data value is copied from memory to the accumulator register.

Once again, the clock "ticks," activating the instruction control unit and starting the next machine cycle (Figure 2.7d). Referring to the instruction counter, the instruction control unit fetches the next instruction and copies it into the instruction register (Figure 2.7e). Once again, note that the instruction register now points to the *next* instruction.

The arithmetic and logic unit gets control and executes the instruction found in the instruction register (Figure 2.7f). As a result, a data value from memory is added to the accumulator. The next clock pulse once again activates the instruction control unit. As before, the instruction counter points to the next instruction. As before, this instruction is fetched into the instruction register. As before, the instruction control unit then activates the arithmetic and logic unit, which executes the instruction.

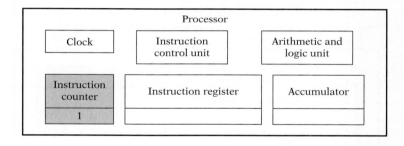

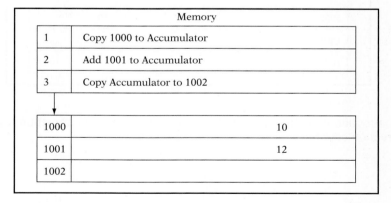

FIGURE 2.7

A computer executes instructions by following a basic machine cycle.

a. As the example begins, memory holds both program instructions and data. The instruction counter points to the first instruction to be executed.

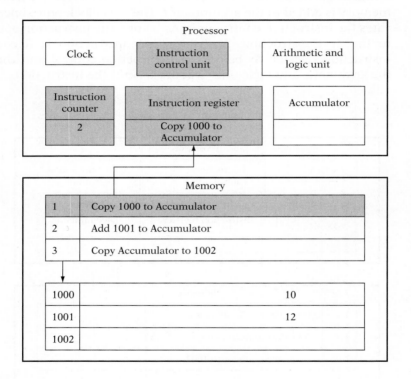

FIGURE 2.7

b. The first instruction is fetched from memory and stored in the instruction register. Note that the instruction counter points to the *next* instruction.

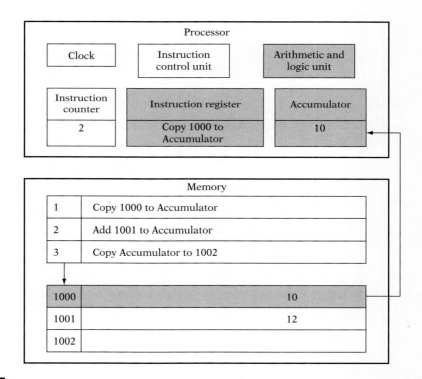

FIGURE 2.7

c. The arithmetic and logic unit executes the instruction in the instruction register.

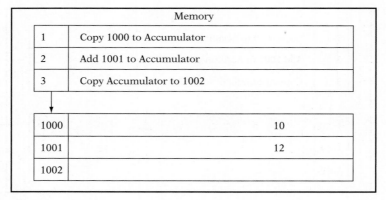

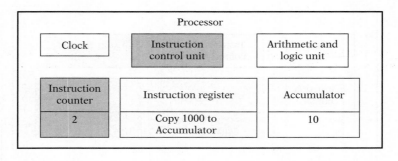

FIGURE 2.7

d. The instruction control unit once again looks to the instruction counter for the address of the next instruction.

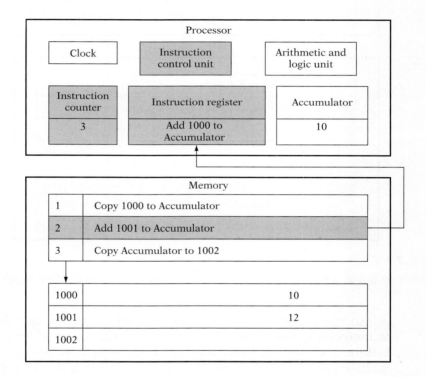

FIGURE 2.7

e. The next instruction is fetched into the instruction register. Note that the instruction counter points to the *next* instruction.

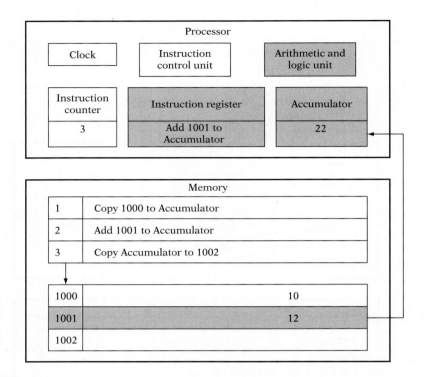

FIGURE 2.7

f. The arithmetic and logic unit executes the instruction in the instruction register.

An instruction is fetched by the instruction control unit during **I-time** or **instruction time** and executed by the arithmetic and logic unit during **E-time** or **execution time.** Together, both steps make up a single machine cycle (Figure 2.8). This process is repeated over and over again until the program is finished. The clock drives the process by generating pulses at precisely timed intervals. The rate at which those clock pulses are generated determines the computer's operating speed. Clock speed is typically expressed in megahertz (MHz) (millions of cycles per second) or gigahertz (GHz) (billions of instructions per second). For example, a 1.5 gigahertz processor is driven by a 1.5 gigahertz clock that "ticks" 1.5 billion times per second and thus is theoretically capable of executing 1.5 billion instructions per second. Actual processing speed is typically less than this theoretical limit, however, because many instructions need more than a single machine cycle to execute.

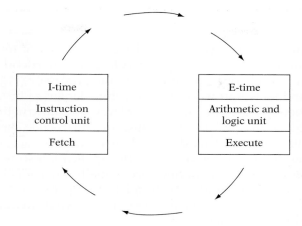

FIGURE 2.8

During a single machine cycle, an instruction is fetched by the instruction control unit during I-time and executed by the arithmetic and logic unit during E-time.

Coprocessors

Some computers contain more than one processor. A **coprocessor** is a special-purpose processor that assists the main processor on certain operations. For example, a math coprocessor performs floating-point computations, and a graphics coprocessor manipulates graphic images.

Moore's Law

In 1965, Gordon Moore, cofounder of Intel Corporation, observed that the number of transistors on an integrated circuit chip doubled roughly every eighteen months. Because the speed of a processor chip and the storage capacity of a memory chip are directly related to the number of transistors on the chip, his observation, which has become known as Moore's Law, suggested that both processing speed and memory capacity would double every eighteen months, and that's pretty much what happened. Most experts expect Moore's Law to hold true for at least the near future.

◼ Microcode

Computer hardware is typically designed as a set of interconnected layers. For example, on many computers a layer of **microcode,** sometimes called firmware, lies between memory and the processor (Figure 2.9). The arithmetic and logic unit works with machine-language instructions, which are subsequently translated into lower-level microinstructions before they are executed by the processor. Because the microcode insulates the software from the hardware, hardware changes can be accommodated without affecting the operating system or the application software. In some cases, key operating system routines are actually implemented in microcode to improve efficiency. Additionally, microcode is relatively difficult to "clone," and that can give a company with a successful architecture a significant competitive advantage.

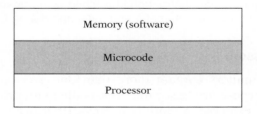

FIGURE 2.9
A layer of microcode lies between memory and the processor.

◼ Input and Output Devices

Input and output devices provide a means for people to access a computer. The basic **input** devices on most personal computer systems are a keyboard and a mouse. As characters are typed, they are stored in memory and then copied from memory to the basic **output** device, a display screen. In effect, the screen serves as a window on memory, allowing the user to view selected contents. Traditionally, display units have relied on cathode ray tube (CRT) technology, but flat-panel LCD (liquid crystal display) screens are becoming increasingly popular as they drop in price.

The image displayed on a screen is temporary; it fades as soon as the power is cut. By routing the output to a printer, a permanent copy (called a hard copy) is obtained. Computers are not limited to displaying characters, of course; graphic output is possible, too. Laser and ink jet printers are popular tools for generating hard copy text and graphic output in both color and black and white.

Several common input media rely on magnetic properties. For example, the characters on the bottom of most checks are printed with a type of magnetic ink called MICR (magnetic ink character recognition) that can be read electronically. On a magnetic strip card, the strip of magnetic tape holds such data as a customer's account number and credit limit, and is read much like sound recording tape. A smart card uses an embedded integrated circuit chip to hold data.

Other media are read optically. For example, consider standardized test forms. Students use a black pencil to mark their answers. The white paper reflects light; the black spots reflect much less; and variations in the intensity of the reflected light can be converted to an electronic pattern. OCR (optical character recognition) equipment uses the same principle to read typed or even handwritten material. Bar codes, such as the Universal Product Code (UPC) printed on most retail items, can be scanned at a checkout station. General-purpose scanners are used to convert a hard copy to a bit pattern that can be manipulated by a computer. Special software can be used to convert the bit patterns that represent a printed page into discrete characters.

Perhaps the most natural way of communicating with a computer is by voice. Voice response (output) is already common. Because of the tremendous variety of human speech patterns, voice recognition (input) is much more difficult to achieve, but increased processing speeds have already moved applications featuring limited voice recognition into the mainstream.

Many modern computer applications utilize multimedia, mixing text, graphics, sound, animations, and other elements to form an integrated, interactive environment. Not too many years ago, such processor- and memory-intensive applications would have been impossible, but increased processing speeds and memory capacities have made them common. Today, most computers are sold with sophisticated sound systems, advanced graphics features, and other multimedia tools, and electronic gamers often enhance their systems with special joysticks and even tactile feedback devices. In many ways, multimedia represent the state of the information technology art.

■ Secondary Storage

There are numerous problems with RAM. For one thing, although cost continues to decline, it is relatively expensive and the supply on most machines, though substantial, is limited. The big problem, however, is volatility; RAM loses its contents when the power is cut.

Secondary storage is a fast, accurate, inexpensive, high-capacity, non-volatile extension of main memory. Note, however, that a computer cannot execute a program on secondary storage unless it is first copied into memory, nor can it manipulate the data stored on a secondary medium until they have been copied into memory. Main memory holds the current program and the current data. Secondary storage is long-term storage. The input and output devices described earlier in this chapter provide human access to the computer system; taken together, they are sometimes called the computer's front end. Secondary storage is a machine-readable medium. Data are stored in a form convenient to the computer, and can be read and written only by the machine. Taken together, a computer's secondary storage devices form its back end. The only way people can access the data stored on secondary storage is by instructing the computer to read the data into memory and then write the data to the screen (or some other output device).

Magnetic Disk

Most computers incorporate a **disk,** or **hard disk,** for storing software and data. The storage capacity of a hard disk is typically measured in gigabytes (billions of bytes). The data on a disk are recorded on a series of concentric circles called tracks (Figure 2.10). The tracks are subdivided into sectors,

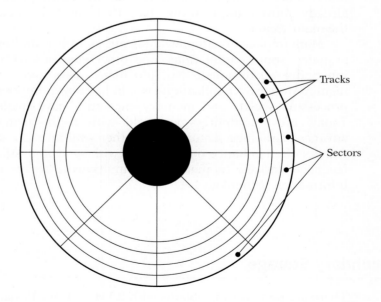

FIGURE 2.10

The data on a disk are recorded on a series of concentric circles called tracks. The tracks are subdivided into sectors.

and it is the contents of a sector that move between the disk's surface and memory. To distinguish the sectors, they are addressed by numbering them sequentially—0, 1, 2, and so on.

When a *read disk* instruction is executed, the processor sends a control signal to the drive. In response, the access mechanism is moved to the track that holds the desired data (Figure 2.11a). The time required to position the access mechanism is called seek time. Data are transferred between the diskette and memory a sector at a time, and the desired sector may be anywhere on the track. The time required for the sector to rotate to the access mechanism (Figure 2.11b) is called rotational delay. The time that elapses between the processor's initial request for data and the actual start of data transfer (in effect, the sum of seek time and rotational delay) is called latency.

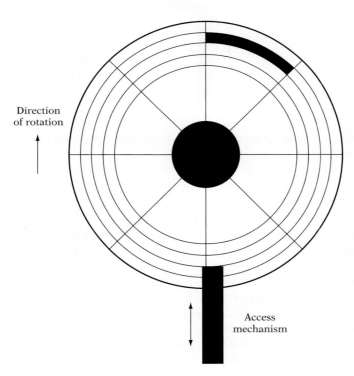

Direction
of rotation

Access
mechanism

FIGURE 2.11

Reading a sector from disk.

a. During seek time the access mechanism is positioned over the track that holds the desired data.

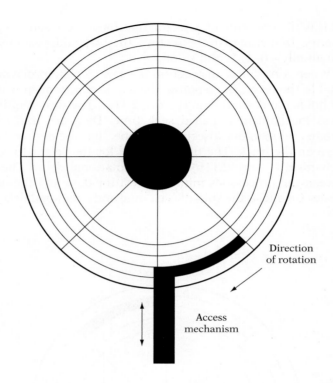

Direction
of rotation

Access
mechanism

FIGURE 2.11

b. The system waits while the sector rotates to the read/write head (rotational delay) and the data are transferred into memory.

Most hard disks store data on both the upper and lower surface, and disk packs consisting of two or more recording surfaces stacked on a common drive shaft (Figure 2.12) are also available. Typically, each surface has its own read/write head. The heads are arrayed on a single, comblike access mechanism, so they all move together. Imagine, for example, that the access mechanism is positioned over track 30. The top read/write head will access track 30 on surface 0. Moving down, surface by surface, the second head will be over track 30 on surface 1, the third over track 30 on surface 2, and so on. One position of the access mechanism corresponds to one track on each surface. This set of tracks is called a cylinder.

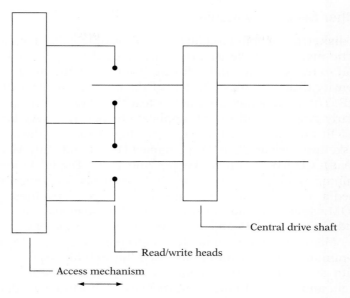

Central drive shaft

Read/write heads

Access mechanism

FIGURE 2.12
Each surface on a disk pack has its own read/write head.

Usually, the tracks are divided into fixed-length sectors. Data move between the disk's surface and the computer's memory a sector at a time. However, some hard disks, particularly on large mainframes, are track addressed, with tracks subdivided into physical records or blocks. A physical record can be any length, from a single byte to a full track; the physical record length (or block size) is chosen to fit the application. On such systems, data are transferred between secondary storage and memory a block at a time.

Backup

Given the tremendous capacity of a hard disk, losing one, through human error, fire, flood, or similar disaster, can destroy a great deal of important data. Consequently, it is crucial that the contents of a disk be regularly backed up, usually by copying them to some other secondary medium. Should a disk be lost, the **backup** copy is used to restore its contents.

Other Secondary Media

A **diskette** is a thin circular piece of flexible polyester coated with a magnetic material. Diskettes are typically used to store backup copies of files and to transfer data and software from one computer to another. A double density diskette holds 720 KB of data; a high-density diskette holds 1.44 MB. These capacities are fine for text files, but modern multimedia (particularly graphics and sound) applications generate very large files that may not fit on a diskette. Consequently, high-capacity alternatives to standard diskettes, such as CD-ROM (Compact Disk, Read-Only Memory), CD-R (CD-Read), CD-RW (CD-Read/Write), and DVD (Digital Video Disk) disks, are gaining popularity. Jaz disks and zip disks are removable, diskette-like media with considerably greater storage capacities. Except for CD-ROM, which is a read-only medium, all these media can be used for backup and to transfer data and software between computers.

Magnetic tape (similar to reel-to-reel or cassette recording tape) is a common backup medium. Accessed through high-speed drives, tape is fast, with data transfer rates comparable to disk. Its storage capacity is quite high, and a reel of tape is inexpensive. Unfortunately, data can be read or written only in a fixed sequence, which limits tape to a few applications.

Longevity

Sumerian cuneiform and Egyptian hieroglyphics have existed in readable form for millennia. The Gutenberg Bible was printed in the mid-1400s, and readable copies still exist over five hundred years later. Unfortunately, not all electronic storage media have exhibited such longevity.

In the early 1980s, a mere two decades ago, 5.25-inch floppy disks were the de facto personal computer secondary storage standard. As we enter the twenty-first century, try finding a computer that can read, much less interpret the contents of, a 5.25-inch floppy disk. Floppy disks were replaced by 3.5-inch diskettes, but not all computers can read a 3.5-inch diskette anymore. Today's personal computers store information on CD-ROM, CD-R, CD-RW, and DVD. How confident are you that you will be able to read those media twenty years from now?

The Directory

Because of its storage capacity, a typical hard disk holds thousands of programs and/or the data for hundreds of different applications. If you are a computer user, however, you want a particular program, and you want to access a particular data file. How does the computer find the right program or the right data?

Start by reviewing how data are stored on disk. The surface is divided into tracks, which in turn are divided into sectors or blocks. The tracks are numbered sequentially. The outer track is 0. Moving toward the disk's center, the next track is 1, then 2, and so on. The sectors (or blocks) on a track are also numbered sequentially starting with 0. Track 5, sector 8 is a particular sector; track 5, sector 9 is a different sector; and track 6, sector 8 is yet another one. Each sector has a unique track/sector address.

Depending on the operating system, when a file is stored on disk it is either recorded in consecutive sectors (or blocks) or its sectors are in some way linked sequentially. Consequently, if the computer can find the file's first sector, it can find the entire file. To record the starting address of each of its files, a portion of the disk's first track is set aside to hold a **directory** (Figure 2.13). When the file is first written to disk, it is assigned a name. The file's name is then recorded in the directory, along with the track and sector (or track and block) address where it begins. Later, to retrieve the file, a user enters the file's name. Given a name, the computer reads the directory, searches the directory for the file name, extracts the file's start address, and reads the file.

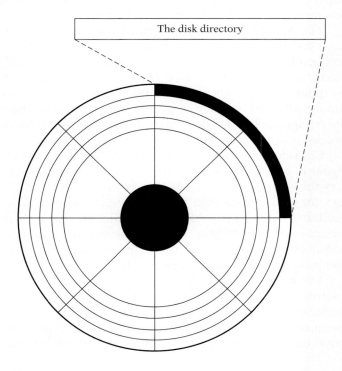

FIGURE 2.13

The programs and data files stored on a disk are listed in the disk's directory.

◼ Communication Hardware

Given the emergence of e-mail, Web browsing, and other online activities, most modern computers come equipped with communication hardware. Perhaps the most familiar device is a **modem** that allows the computer to communicate over standard telephone lines. Access to high-speed communication lines (such as cable) often calls for a **cable modem** or a network interface card (NIC). Typically, a modem, cable modem, or NIC is the computer's point of access to a network such as the Internet. You will examine networks and the Internet in depth in Part 5 of this text.

◼ Linking the Components

Data are stored in memory as patterns of bits. Within a given machine, the patterns are consistent; for example, if the code for the letter A is 01000001, this pattern, and only this pattern, will be used to represent an A.

The rule does not apply to input, output, or secondary storage devices, however. On a keyboard, each key generates one character. A laser printer represents characters as patterns of dots. An optical device reads light intensity, while a disk drive records and reads magnetized spots. Each peripheral device represents or interprets data in its own unique way, and the signals used by a device may or may not match the signals stored inside the computer. If these dissimilar devices are to communicate, translation is necessary. That is the function of an **interface** board.

Consider, for example, a keyboard. When a key is pressed, an electronic signal is sent to the keyboard's interface. In response, the interface generates the code that represents the character inside the computer, and transfers the coded data into memory (Figure 2.14a). Change the device to a printer (Figure 2.14b). As output begins, the data are stored in memory as binary-coded characters. Assume the printer requires a dot pattern. The coded characters are sent to the printer's interface, which translates the computer's binary codes to printer form.

The printer and the keyboard are different; the signals that physically control them and the electronic patterns they use to represent data are device-dependent. However, because the device-dependent tasks are assigned to the respective interface boards, both can be attached to the same computer. On input, an interface translates external signals into a

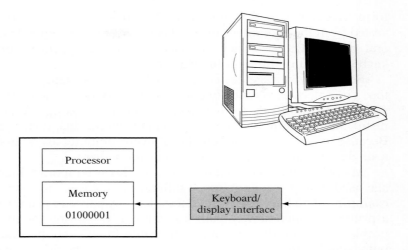

FIGURE 2.14

The functions of an interface board.

a. Input from the keyboard is converted to the computer's internal form by the keyboard/display interface.

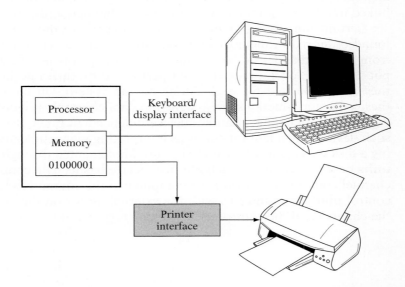

b. Data stored in memory are sent to the printer interface, converted to printer form, and output.

form acceptable to the computer. Output signals are electronically converted from the computer's internal code to a form acceptable to the peripheral device. Because they are electronically different, a printer and a keyboard require different interface boards.

Secondary storage devices are linked to the system through interfaces, too. The interface physically controls the disk drive, accepting seek, read, and write commands from the processor, positioning the access mechanism, and managing the flow of data between the disk surface and memory. Because the disk drives attached to a given computer are virtually identical, a single interface often controls two or more drives.

Many interfaces contain buffers. A **buffer** is temporary memory or storage used to adjust for the speed differential between adjacent devices. For example, if you have ever waited for a lengthy paper to print, you know that a printer is much slower than a computer. If waiting for the printer is a problem, add a buffer to your printer interface. Then, instead of the computer sending the contents of memory directly to the printer, it can send the information to the buffer at computer speed. Subsequently, as the characters are dumped from the buffer to the printer at printer speed, you can use the computer for some other task.

Assigning one interface to each device is reasonable on a microcomputer system. However, on a large system with hundreds of peripherals, this approach is simply unworkable. Instead, input and output devices are linked to a large computer system through channels and control units.

Certain functions (for example, deciding where the next byte can be found or stored in memory and counting the characters transferred to or from an external device) are common to almost all types of input and output. On a microcomputer, they are performed by each interface; in effect, they are duplicated for each device on the system. On larger machines, these common functions are assigned to data **channels** (Figure 2.15).

Note that a channel handles device-independent functions. What about such device-dependent functions as interpreting magnetic patterns or moving a disk's access mechanism? They are implemented through **I/O control units** or interface units. Each physical device has its own control unit. The channel communicates with the computer in the computer's language; the control unit communicates with the external device on the device's terms; the channel and the control unit, working together, translate.

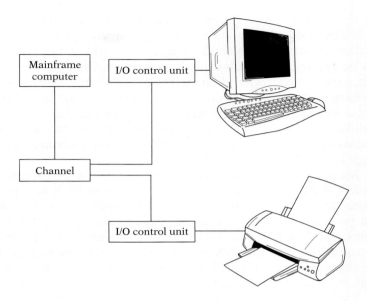

FIGURE 2.15

On a mainframe, peripheral devices are linked to the system through a channel and an I/O control unit.

▌ Summary

A computer's memory holds active programs and data. Memory is grouped into bytes, or words, or both, and each basic storage unit is assigned an address. Using this address, the processor can read or write selected bytes or words. High-speed cache memory serves as a staging area for the processor.

The processor consists of a clock, an instruction control unit, an arithmetic and logic unit, and registers. During I-time, the instruction control unit fetches an instruction from memory; during E-time, the arithmetic and logic unit executes that instruction. Precisely timed electronic pulses generated by the clock drive this basic machine cycle. Some computers contain coprocessors.

People access a computer through its input and output devices. The chapter briefly reviewed several common input and output devices and media.

Data are stored on a disk's surface on a series of concentric circles called tracks. The tracks are subdivided into sectors. On input, the contents of one sector are copied from disk to memory; on output, one sector is copied from memory to the disk's surface. To access disk, it is first necessary to move the access mechanism over the track containing the desired data (seek time). Additional time is lost waiting for the desired sector to rotate to the read/write head (rotational delay). Often, several surfaces are stacked on a single drive shaft to form a disk pack.

Because data are so valuable, disks are normally backed up. Diskettes, CD-R, CD-RW, and DVD disks are used to store backup copies of files and to transfer data and software from one computer to another. Magnetic tape is a common backup medium. A single disk can contain numerous programs and data files. The disk's directory identifies the programs and data files and indicates the disk address where each one begins. Most modern computers incorporate such communication devices as a modem, a cable modem, or a network interface card.

Each peripheral device is electronically different, but internally the computer always deals with a common code. An interface serves to bridge this gap. A buffer can help to adjust for the speed differential between adjacent devices. On larger computers, each peripheral device is linked to a control unit, the control units are plugged into channels, and the channels are connected to the computer.

▌ Key Words

address	instruction
arithmetic and logic unit	instruction control unit
backup	interface
bit	I-time (instruction time)
buffer	machine cycle
byte	main memory
cable modem	memory
cache memory	microcode
channel	modem
clock	output
control unit (I/O)	processor
coprocessor	program
directory	read (memory)
disk	register
diskette	secondary storage
E-time (execution time)	word
hard disk	write (memory)
input	

◼ Review Questions

1. Distinguish between reading and writing memory. Distinguish between ROM and RAM.
2. Distinguish between physical memory and its contents.
3. Distinguish bits, bytes, and words.
4. How is a computer's memory addressed? Why is addressing memory important?
5. What is cache memory? Why is cache memory used?
6. Explain what happens during a computer's basic machine cycle.
7. What is a coprocessor? Why are coprocessors needed?
8. What is microcode?
9. How are input/output and secondary storage devices similar? How are they different?
10. Why is secondary storage necessary?
11. Distinguish cylinders, tracks, and sectors.
12. Briefly explain the process of reading data from or writing data to disk.
13. Why is it so important to back up the contents of a disk?
14. Identify several secondary storage media other than hard disk.
15. What is the purpose of a disk's directory? Why is it needed?
16. What is the purpose of an interface? Why are interfaces needed?
17. What is a buffer? Why are buffers used?
18. Distinguish between a microcomputer interface and the channel/control unit architecture used on mainframes. How are they similar? How are they different?
19. Why do computer manufacturers use channels and control units instead of simple interface boards on large computer systems?

◼ Exercises

1. Draw a sketch showing the key components of a processor. Add blocks representing memory, a program, and data.
2. Open a computer and investigate its internal contents. Compare your observations to the sketch you drew in Exercise 1.
3. Exercise 1 asked you to sketch a computer's internal components. Add channels, control units, I/O devices, and secondary storage devices to your sketch.
4. Compile a list of the I/O devices, secondary storage devices, and other peripherals on your computer.
5. A computer is a binary machine. What does that statement mean?
6. Investigate how typical processor speeds have changed over the past decade. Do your results confirm or conflict with Moore's Law?

7. Relate microcode to the layering concept.

8. Why do you suppose that modern secondary storage media have such a short shelf life? Can you think of strategies you might try to overcome that problem?

9. If you have access to a computer running Microsoft Windows, double-click the *My Computer* icon and view the contents of selected folders. Where do you suppose the computer finds the information it displays?

10. There are 35 key words at the end of Chapter 2, and you will find subsequent chapters to be equally rich in terminology. If you are tempted to look up the definitions of each of those key words and memorize all those definitions, you will quickly exceed the capacity of your short-term memory. A better strategy is to visualize the terms in the context of a two-dimensional model; for this chapter, Figure 2.7a is a good candidate. Once you have selected a diagram, go through the list of key terms and write each one where it best fits. Skip unfamiliar terms on the first pass. Then go back for a second pass; you'll be surprised how many of the remaining terms seem to fall into place, effectively defined by related terms. If a term is still unfamiliar, reread the relevant text discussion. When you finish, your diagram will give you a context for understanding the technology. Use the same strategy to structure the key terms at the end of subsequent chapters.

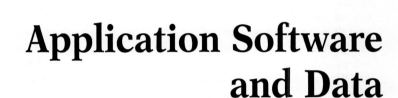

CHAPTER 3

Application Software and Data

When you finish reading this chapter you should be able to:

▶ Explain how an assembler, a compiler, an interpreter, and a nonprocedural language differ and how they are similar.

▶ Distinguish between traditional structured software and object-oriented software.

▶ Define the terms object, method, encapsulation, signal, and operation.

▶ Define the terms source code, object module, and load module.

▶ Explain the purpose of an application programming interface (API).

▶ Define data element and data structure. Identify a list, a linked list, a stack, and a queue.

▶ Relate characters, fields, records, and files.

▶ Explain the relative record concept.

▶ Distinguish between sequential and direct (or random) access.

▶ Discuss the advantages derived from using a database.

▪ Hardware, Software, and Data

A computer is a machine (hardware) that processes data under control of a stored program (software). All three elements—hardware, data, and software—must be present or the system cannot function. This chapter focuses on application software and the data processed by that software within the application program layer (Figure 3.1). Hardware (Chapter 2) is physical. Software and data, in contrast, are logical; they consist of nothing more substantial than electronic patterns stored on the hardware in binary form. One pattern of bits might represent a machine-level instruction (software). Another might hold an ASCII coded character, a binary integer, or a floating-point number (data). Thus, it makes sense to group software and data together.

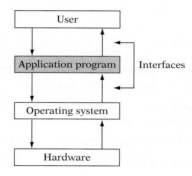

FIGURE 3.1
This chapter focuses on the application program layer.

▪ Software

A **program** is a series of instructions that guides a computer through a process. Each **instruction** tells the machine to perform one of its basic functions: add, subtract, multiply, divide, compare, copy, request input, or request output. The processor fetches and executes a single instruction during each machine cycle. A typical instruction (Figure 3.2) contains an operation code that specifies the function to be performed and one or more operands that specify the memory locations or registers that hold the data to be manipulated. For example, the instruction

AR 3,4

tells a hypothetical computer to add the contents of registers 3 and 4.

Operation code	Operands
AR	3,4

FIGURE 3.2

A typical instruction contains an operation code and one or more operands.

Because a computer's instruction set is so limited, even simple logical operations call for multiple instructions. For example, imagine two data values stored in memory. To add them on many computers, both values are first loaded (or copied) into registers, the registers are added, and then the answer is stored (or copied) back into memory. That's four instructions: LOAD, LOAD, ADD, and STORE. If four instructions are needed to perform a simple add operation, imagine the number of instruction in a complex program.

A computer runs under the control of a program stored in its own memory. Because memory stores bits, it follows that a program stored in memory must be in binary form. Figure 3.3 shows the binary, machine-level instructions needed to load two numbers into registers, add them, and store the answer in memory. If programmers had to write in **machine language** there would be very few programmers.

```
0101100000110000
1100000000000000
0101100001000000
1100000000000100
0001101000110100
0101000000110000
1100000000001000
```

FIGURE 3.3

The binary, machine-level instructions needed to add two numbers.

Absolute and Relative Addressing

A computer's memory is addressed by numbering the bytes sequentially—0, 1, 2, and so on up to the total number of bytes in memory. Hardware works with these **absolute addresses,** fetching and storing the contents of individual bytes by referencing their byte numbers.

Absolute addresses are not convenient for software, however. A program that references absolute addresses must be loaded in exactly the same place in memory every time it runs. Additionally, absolute addresses tend to be lengthy. For example, a 32-bit word computer might use 32-bit addresses. A typical instruction contains an operation code plus two addresses (for example, the locations of the two data values to be added), and if those addresses are expressed in absolute terms, a single instruction on a 32-bit word computer would be over 64 bits long. Such lengthy instructions tend to produce huge programs.

An alternative is to use relative addresses. A **relative address** is an address expressed relative to some base location. For example, a program routine might be written as though its first byte (usually, its entry point) is address 0, with every other location in the routine expressed as an offset or **displacement** from that starting point. When the routine is subsequently loaded into memory, the absolute address of its entry point is stored in a register, thus establishing a **base address** for the routine. Before a given instruction is executed, hardware (during the I-time portion of each machine cycle) adds each relative address (the displacement) to the base address (which is stored in a register) to get the equivalent absolute address. The process of converting a relative address to an absolute address is called **dynamic address translation.**

Relative addressing achieves two objectives. First, it allows a routine to be relocated in memory—in other words, to be loaded into a different location in memory each time it runs. Because every location in the routine is expressed relative to the entry point and the actual entry point address is stored in a base register, it is always possible to compute a given byte's absolute address by adding the entry point address to the displacement. Second, because only the displacement portion of the address must be stored in the instruction, fewer bits are required to hold each address, yielding smaller instructions and, hence, smaller programs.

Programming Languages

One option to writing programs in machine language is to use an **assembler language**. For example, Figure 3.4 shows how two numbers might be added using an IBM mainframe assembler language. The programmer writes one mnemonic (memory aiding) instruction for each machine-level instruction. AR (for add registers) is much easier to remember than the equivalent binary operation code: 00011010. L (for load) is much easier to remember than 01011000. The operands use labels (such as A, B, and C) instead of numbers to represent *symbolic* memory addresses, and that simplifies the code, too. The assembler program assigns numeric relative addresses to the labels as part of the assembly process.

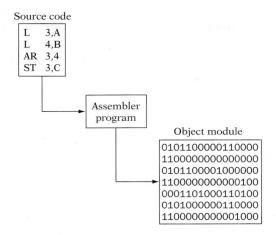

FIGURE 3.4
An assembler converts each source statement to a single machine-level instruction.

There are no computers that can directly execute assembler language instructions. Writing mnemonic codes may simplify the programmer's job, but computers are still binary machines and require binary instructions. Thus, translation is necessary. An assembler program (Figure 3.4) reads a programmer's **source code,** translates the source statements to binary, and produces an **object module.** Because the object module is a machine-level version of the programmer's code, it can be loaded into memory and executed.

An assembler language programmer writes one mnemonic instruction for each machine-level instruction. Because of this one-to-one relationship between the source code and the object code, assemblers are machine dependent, and a program written for one type of computer will not run on another. On a given machine, assembler language generates the most efficient programs possible, and thus an assembler often used to write operating systems and other system software routines. However, when it comes to application programs, machine dependency is a high price to pay for efficiency, so application programs are rarely written in assembler.

A computer needs four machine-level instructions to add two numbers because that's the way a computer works. Human beings should not have to think like computers. Why not simply allow the programmer to indicate addition and assume the other instructions? For example, one way to view addition is as an algebraic expression:

$$C = A + B$$

Why not allow a programmer to write statements in a form similar to algebraic expressions, read those source statements into a program, and let the program generate the necessary machine-level code (Figure 3.5)? That's exactly what happens with a **compiler.** Compare the binary instructions in Figures 3.4 and 3.5. They are identical.

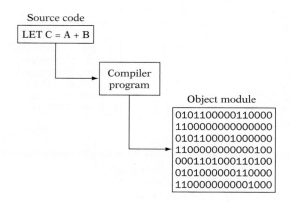

FIGURE 3.5

A compiler converts each source statement to one or more machine-level instructions.

Many compiler languages are algebraically based. In contrast, COBOL (Common Business Oriented Language) statements resemble brief English-language sentences. Note, however, that no matter what language is used, the objective is the same. The programmer writes source code. The assembler or compiler reads the source code and generates a machine-level object module.

With an assembler, each source statement is converted to a single machine-level instruction. With a compiler, a given source statement may be converted to any number of machine-level instructions. Note, however, that both assemblers and compilers read a complete source program and generate a complete object module. An **interpreter,** in contrast, works with one source statement at a time, reading it, translating it to machine-level, executing the resulting binary instructions, and then moving on to the next source statement. Each language has its own syntax, punctuation, and spelling rules, so a C source program is meaningless to a COBOL compiler or a BASIC interpreter. However, no matter what language is used, the objective is the same: defining a series of steps to guide the computer through a process.

With assemblers, compilers, and interpreters, the programmer defines a "procedure" that tells the computer exactly how to solve a problem.

However, with a nonprocedural language (sometimes called a fourth-generation or declarative language), the programmer simply defines the logical structure of the problem and lets the language translator figure out how to solve it. Examples include Prolog, Focus, Excel, and many others.

Layers of Abstraction

A machine language programmer writes binary object code, so the object code itself is the only possible source of application layer errors. In contrast, the compilation process adds at least two new layers of abstraction to the process of creating object code (Figure 3.6). Think of each of those layers as a possible source of error. In a compiled application, a programmer error might add a bug to the source code, the compiler might introduce an error by misinterpreting a source statement, and an electronic error of some kind might change a few object code bits.

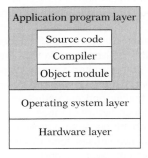

FIGURE 3.6

The compilation process adds two layers of abstraction to the application program layer.

If the source code and the compiler are potential sources of error, why not code in machine language? To answer that question, look back at Figure 3.5 and compare the source code to the string of binary digits that represent the equivalent object code. Then grab a sheet of paper and copy the bits. Are you really sure you got every bit right? Get one bit wrong and the program fails, so precision is crucial. The point is that writing binary machine language code is extremely difficult, very time consuming, and highly error prone.

Programmers find it much easier to write source statements such as LET C = A + B than the equivalent bit strings. As a result, they write their programs much more quickly and are much less likely to introduce errors into the source code. Ironically, in spite of the extra layers of abstraction, compiled object code almost always contains fewer bugs than the equivalent code written directly in machine language. Add significant productivity gains to improved quality and you can clearly see why most programs are written at the source code level.

Layers and Vulnerability

Imagine you are using an application program when an error occurs. Your first impulse is probably to assume that you did something wrong. Perhaps you selected the wrong option. Maybe you forgot to click the appropriate icon. Often, if you undo the operation and try it again you get the correct result.

Blaming yourself is a good strategy because it usually works, but what if redoing the task doesn't help? What if you are absolutely certain you did everything correctly but you still get that same error? Where else might the problem lie? To answer that question, just look at the layers summarized in Figure 3.6. The programmer might have overlooked a bug in the source code. If the source code is correct, an error could have been inserted into the object code by the compiler or by a hacker. The program might harbor a bad macro. There could be a bug in the operating system. Although they are extremely rare, errors are even possible down in the hardware layer.

Implementing software as a set of independent layers simplifies the task of correcting errors within a given layer. In fact, the ability to isolate errors to a single module or object is properly cited as a major advantage of layered approaches to program development. On the other hand, however, layering can significantly complicate the task of finding and correcting an error when the responsible layer is unknown, and the hidden nature of those "other" layers makes a computer system more vulnerable to attack because it gives the attacker places to hide. For example, the most destructive viruses tend to enter a system through the macro layer or the operating system layer, in part because the typical user is essentially unaware of what happens in those layers.

Structured Software

A **structured program** consists of a series of logical modules linked by a control structure (Figure 3.7). The idea is to achieve module independence by:

1. designing each module to perform a single, cohesive function,
2. assigning each module its own local data (data values known only within the module), and
3. linking the modules by passing between them the minimum number of global data elements (data known to all modules) necessary.

The existence of a pool of shared, global data serves to limit module independence, however, because an error that affects a global data value can ripple though numerous modules.

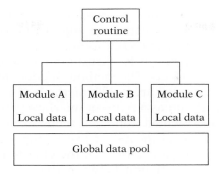

FIGURE 3.7

A structured program.

Object-Oriented Software

The basic idea of the **object-oriented** approach to software development is to design and write the software as a set of independent objects linked by signals. Many modern operating systems are object-oriented. Common object-oriented programming languages include C++, Java, and many others.

An **object** is a thing about which data are stored and manipulated. An object contains both data and **methods** (Figure 3.8). A method is a process that accesses and manipulates the object's data. The data form the core of the object. The only way other objects can access the object's data is through one of its methods. That makes the object highly independent. Hiding implementation details in this way is called encapsulation.

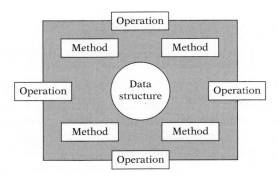

FIGURE 3.8

An object contains both data and methods.

Objects communicate by transmitting and responding to **messages,** where a message might contain a **signal** (information about an event or occurrence) or data. The messages are sent and received by entities called **operations.** An operation is an external view of the object that can be accessed by other objects. The methods hidden inside the object are private. Operations, in contrast, are public methods. Think of the object as a black box and the operation as a point of interface with other objects.

The objected-oriented approach tends to produce higher quality software because it reduces the risk of errors propagated throughout a program by erroneous global data. However, the object-oriented metaphor adds yet another layer of abstraction between the source code and the compiler (Figure 3.9).

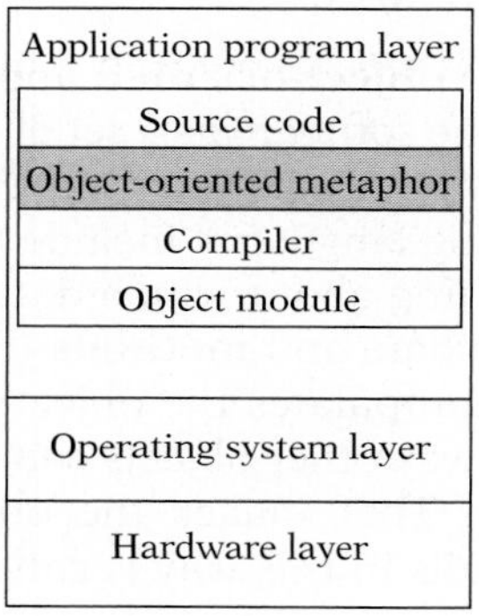

Application program layer
Source code
Object-oriented metaphor
Compiler
Object module
Operating system layer
Hardware layer

FIGURE 3.9

The object-oriented metaphor adds another layer of abstraction.

Libraries

Picture a programmer writing a large routine. As source statements are entered, they are manipulated by an editor program and stored on disk. Because large programs are rarely written in a single session, the programmer will eventually stop working and close the source file. Later, when work resumes, the source file is reopened and new source statements are added to the old ones. That same disk might hold other source programs and even routines written by other programmers. It's a good example of a source statement **library** (Figure 3.10).

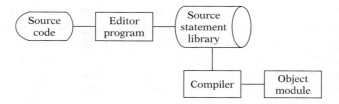

FIGURE 3.10

Source code is stored on a source statement library.

Eventually, the source program is completed and compiled. The resulting object module might be loaded directly into memory, but more often, it is stored on an object module library (Figure 3.11). Because object modules are binary, machine-level routines, there is no inherent difference between one produced by an assembler, one produced by a COBOL compiler, and one produced by a C++ compiler, so object modules generated by different source languages can be stored on the same library.

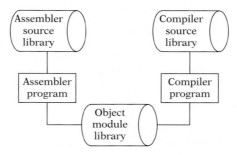

FIGURE 3.11

Object modules are stored on an object module library.

Some object modules can be loaded into memory and executed. Others, however, include references to subroutines that are not part of the object module. For example, imagine a program that simulates a game of cards. If, some time ago, another programmer wrote an excellent subroutine to deal cards, it would make sense to reuse that logic.

Picture the new program after it has been written, compiled, and stored on the object module library (Figure 3.12). The subroutine that deals cards is stored on the same library. Before the program is loaded, the two routines must be combined to form a **load module** (Figure 3.13). An object module is a machine-language translation of a source module that may include references to other (external) subroutines that are not part of the object module. A load module is a complete, ready to execute program with all subroutines in place. Combining object modules to form a load module is the job of the **linkage editor** (Figure 3.14). A linkage editor prepares a complete load module and copies it to a load module library for immediate or eventual loading and execution.

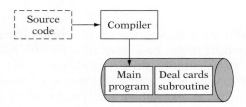

FIGURE 3.12
Object modules can contain references to external subroutines.

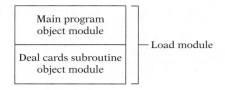

FIGURE 3.13
Before a program can be executed, the object modules for the main program and any external subroutines must be combined to form a load module.

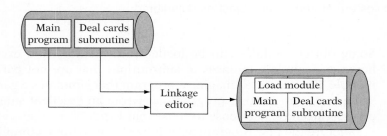

FIGURE 3.14
The linkage editor combines object modules to form a load module.

Reentrant Code

Many programs modify themselves as they run, changing key data values and even executable instructions. Imagine two users concurrently accessing the same program. Any attempt to share the code would be doomed because changes made by one user could have unforeseen consequences for the other. If the program can modify itself, there must be one copy in memory for each concurrent user.

A **reentrant** program or program module does *not* modify itself. Consequently, since the code does not change, two or more users can share the same logic. Often, the secret to creating reentrant code is breaking the program into two components: a logic segment and a data segment (Figure 3.15). The data segment belongs to an individual user, and can be modified as the program runs. The logic segment, on the other hand, consists of reentrant program instructions that cannot be changed. Given such segmentation, it is possible to assign each of several users their own data segments and allow them to share a single logic segment. Avoiding duplication of program logic can save a great deal of memory space.

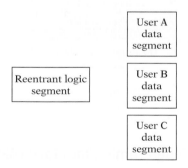

FIGURE 3.15
Using reentrant code, it is possible for several users to share the same logic segment.

An operating system is composed of system software modules that support application programs. On a large system, several applications might execute concurrently. It makes little sense to include multiple copies of the same support logic, so (almost by definition) an operating system contains a great deal of shared, reentrant code.

An Application Program's Interfaces

An application program sits between the user and the operating system (Figure 3.16). It communicates with the user through a user interface. For example, a word processing program's user interface allows you to enter data and manipulate icons, menus, and windows to request such services as open, create, edit, save, and print. The application program also communicates with the operating system through an operating system interface. In between the two interfaces is an application logic layer, sometimes called the business logic layer.

Almost by definition, you cannot effectively use an application program unless you are familiar with its user interface layer; in fact, learning a new application essentially means learning the program's user interface. The business logic and operating system interface layers are hidden, however, responding transparently, black box-like, to commands and data entered through the user interface.

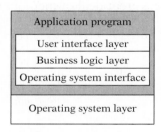

FIGURE 3.16
An application program's interfaces.

The Application Programming Interface (API)

An application program's user interface and application (or business) logic lie outside the scope of this book, but the program's interface with the operating system does not. Often, the interface with the operating system is implemented through an **application programming interface** or **API** (Figure 3.17). An API is a set of source-level functions and calling conventions. When the source code is compiled, each API reference is translated into a call to the appropriate operating system service. The API allows the programmer to view the various operating system services as black boxes and essentially ignore the details of how the service is performed, which simplifies programming and enhances **portability,** the ability to run the application program on multiple platforms.

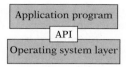

FIGURE 3.17
The application programming interface (API).

◼ Data

Like software, data are stored on hardware as patterns of bits. Simply storing the data is not enough, however. A typical computer system, even a small one, can have multiple disks each holding data for dozens of different applications, and for any given application, one and only one set of data will do. Additionally, data are often processed selectively, a few elements at a time, so it must be possible to distinguish the individual data elements, too. These are the primary concerns of data management.

Data Elements

A **data element** is a single, meaningful unit of data, such as a name, a social security number, or a temperature reading. Most computers can store and manipulate pure binary integers, floating-point numbers, decimal numbers, and character or string data. See Appendix A for a review of these data types.

Data Structures

The key to retrieving data is remembering where they are stored. If the data elements are stored according to a consistent and well understood structure, it is possible to retrieve them by remembering that data structure. The most basic **data structure** is a list (Figure 3.18). Each entry in the list is called a node, and each node holds a single data element. Lists are frequently used by operating systems.

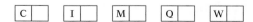

FIGURE 3.18
The most basic data structure is a list.

In a **linked list** (Figure 3.19), each node contains data plus a pointer to the next node. Note that the data items need not be stored in adjacent memory locations because the pointers define the list's logical order. To insert a node into a linked list, locate the prior node, change its pointer to the new node, and set the new node's pointer to the next node (Figure 3.20). To delete a node from a linked list, change the appropriate pointer to "jump over" the deleted node (Figure 3.21).

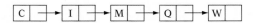

FIGURE 3.19

A linked list.

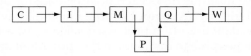

FIGURE 3.20

Inserting a node into a linked list.

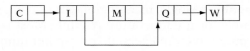

FIGURE 3.21

Deleting a node from a linked list.

A **stack** (Figure 3.22) is a type of linked list in which all insertions and deletions occur at the top. Access to the stack is controlled by a single pointer. Because insertions and deletions occur only at the top, the last item added to the stack is the first item removed from the stack (last in, first out).

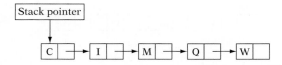

FIGURE 3.22

A stack is a type of linked list in which all insertions and deletions occur at the top.

A **queue** is a type of linked list in which insertions occur at the rear and deletions occur at the front. Access to a queue is controlled by two pointers (Figure 3.23), and the first item added to a queue is the first item removed (first in, first out).

Most programming languages support a more complex, spreadsheet-like data structure called an array. Each array element holds one data value. Each element is assigned a unique identifying number (or numbers), and individual data elements can be inserted, extracted, or manipulated by referencing those numbers.

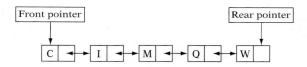

FIGURE 3.23

A queue is a type of linked list in which insertions occur at the rear and deletions occur at the front.

Data Files

Consider a program that generates name and address labels. Each label requires a name, a street address, a city, a state, and a zip code. A list structure might be adequate for a few labels, but separating the elements would soon become tedious. An option is setting up an array of names and addresses, with each row holding the data for a single label. The only problem is that the entire array must be in memory before the individual elements can be accessed, and memory space is limited.

A better solution is to organize the data as a **file** (Figure 3.24), perhaps the most familiar type of data structure. On a file, the data elements are called fields, a group of related fields forms a record, and the file is a set of related records. For example, in a name and address file, an individual's name is a field, each record holds a complete set of data for a single individual (a name, a street address, and so on), and the file consists of all the records.

The data in a file are typically processed record by record. Normally, the file is stored on a secondary medium such as disk. Programs are written to read a record, process its fields, generate the appropriate output, and then read and process another record. Because only one record is in memory at a time, relatively little memory is needed. Because many records can be stored on a single disk, a great deal of data can be processed in this limited space.

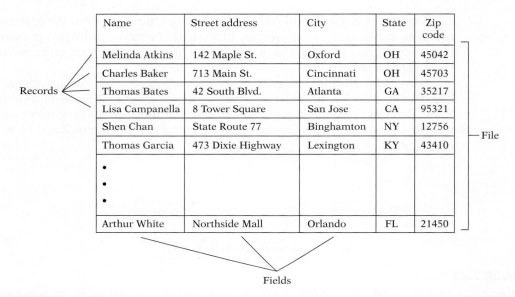

FIGURE 3.24
Fields are grouped to form records. A file is a set of related records.

Multimedia Files

Not all files are broken into records and fields. For example, multimedia files (sounds, pictures, graphic images) often contain a single logical entity such as a photograph or a sound track; see Appendix A for a list of common multimedia file formats. When an image file or an MP3 file is loaded from disk into memory, the entire file is transferred. In effect, the image or the sound track can be viewed as the file's only record.

The Relative Record Concept

Normally, however, the contents of a traditional data file are processed one record at a time. Often, the key to finding the correct record is the **relative record number.** Imagine a string of 100 records. Number the first one 0, the second 1, the third 2, and so on. The numbers indicate a given record's position relative to the first record in the file. The file's first record (relative record 0) is at "start of file plus 0," its second record is at "start of file plus 1," and so on.

Now, store the records on disk (Figure 3.25), one per sector. Number the sectors relative to the start of the file—0, 1, 2, and so on. Note that the relative record number (a logical concept) and the relative sector number (a physical location) are identical. Given a relative record number, it is possible to compute a relative sector number. Given a relative sector number, it is possible to compute a physical disk address.

| Relative record 0 | Relative record 1 | Relative record 2 | Relative record 3 | Relative record 4 |

Relative sector   0   1   2   3   4

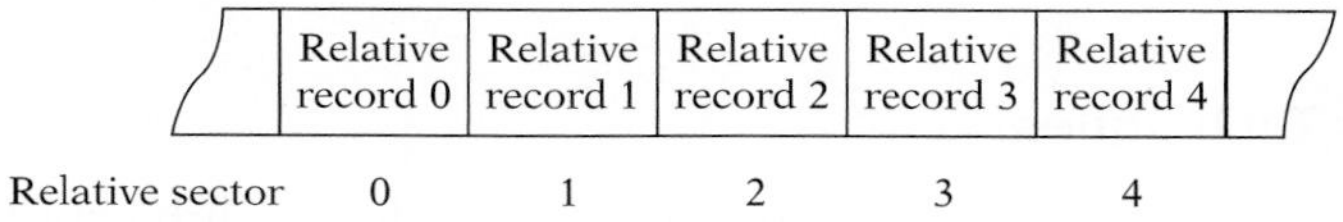

FIGURE 3.25

A relative record number indicates a record's position relative to the first record in the file.

Assume a file begins at track 30, sector 1, and that one logical record is stored in each sector. As Figure 3.26 shows, relative record 0 is stored at track 30, sector 1, relative record 1 is at track 30, sector 2, and so on. Note that the relative record number indicates how many sectors away from the beginning of the file the record is stored. The file starts at track 30, sector 1. Relative record 10 is stored 10 sectors away at track 30, sector 11. The one record per sector assumption is not realistic, but even with multiple records per sector it is possible to develop a simple algorithm to compute a record's physical location given its relative record number.

Relative record number	Actual disk address	
	Track	Sector
0	30	1
1	30	2
2	30	3
3	30	4
4	30	5
5	30	6
6	30	7
7	30	8
... and so on		

FIGURE 3.26

Given the start of file address and a relative record number, a physical disk address can be computed.

Not all data access techniques rely on relative record numbers; in fact, some computer experts consider the very concept of a record an unnecessary anachronism left over from punched card days. On many modern operating systems, most notably UNIX, there are no records. Instead, data stored on disk are treated as a simple strings of bytes, and no other structure is imposed. On such systems, programmers address data by relative byte number, the same way they address memory.

Access Techniques

Imagine preparing meeting announcements for a club. You need a set of mailing labels, and each member's name and address is recorded on an index card. Probably the easiest way to generate the labels is to pick up the first card and copy the data, turn to the second card and copy its data, and so on, processing the records sequentially, from the beginning of the file to the end.

Magazine publishers face the same problem with each new issue, but need mailing labels for tens of thousands of subscribers. Rather than using index cards, they store customer data on a secondary storage medium, one record per subscriber. The easiest way to ensure that all the labels are generated is to process the records in the order in which they are stored, proceeding sequentially from the first record in the file to the last. To simplify handling, the records might be presorted (by zip code or a mailing zone, for example), but the basic idea of processing the data in physical order still holds. A relative record number indicates a record's position relative to the start of the file. With **sequential access,** processing begins with relative record 0, then moves to relative record 1, 2, and so on. In other words, accessing data sequentially involves little more than counting.

Processing records in sequence is not always acceptable. For example, when a subscriber moves, his or her address must be changed. Searching for that subscriber's record sequentially is like looking for a telephone number by reading the telephone book line by line. That is not how you use a telephone book. Instead, knowing that the records are stored in alphabetical order, you use the index at the top of the page to quickly narrow your search to a portion of a single page and then begin reading the entries, ignoring the bulk of the data. The way you use a telephone book is a good example of **direct,** or **random, access.**

A disk drive reads or writes one sector at a time. To randomly access a specific record, all the programmer must do is remember the address of the sector that holds the record, and ask for it. The problem is remembering all those disk addresses. One solution is maintaining an index of the records. As a file is created, records are written to disk one at a time in relative record number order. Additionally, as each record is written, the record's key (a field that uniquely identifies the record) and the associated relative record number are recorded in an array or index (Figure 3.27). After the last record has been written to disk and its position recorded on the index, the index is itself stored on disk.

Key	Relative record
Melinda Atkins	0
Charles Baker	1
Thomas Bates	2
Lisa Campanella	3
Shen Chan	4
Thomas Garcia	5
•	
•	
•	

FIGURE 3.27
An index can be used to convert a logical key to a relative record number.

Once the index has been created, it can be used to find individual records. Imagine, for example, that Sarah Smith has changed her address. Assuming that the customer name has been used as a key, a program could change her address on the file by:

1. reading the file index into memory,
2. searching the index for her name,
3. finding her relative record number,
4. computing the disk address and reading her record,
5. changing her address, and
6. rewriting the record to the same place on disk.

Note that only Sarah Smith's record is accessed, and that no other records in the file are involved.

The basic idea of direct access is assigning each record an easy-to-remember, logical key, and then converting that key to a relative record number. Given this relative location, a physical address can be computed and the record accessed. Using an index is one technique for converting keys to physical addresses. Another option is passing a numeric key to a hashing algorithm and computing a relative record number.

Data Redundancy

Not too long ago, one of this book's authors received a telephone call from a former student. The young woman expressed regret at having missed an on-campus seminar she'd wanted to attend because, even though she'd graduated more than a decade earlier, her invitation had been sent to her parent's old address and by the time the letter found its way to her, the seminar date had passed. In contrast, the alumni office always seemed to know exactly where she lived no matter how often she moved. How, she wondered, was that possible?

The answer, most likely, was data redundancy. Simply put, her former academic department and the alumni office kept track of her name and address independently, and they did not share their information. While she was in school, her department maintained current information about all its majors, including her. When she graduated, however, the department stopped updating information about her because it had no reason to do so. That's why the department office sent the seminar announcement to the wrong address. When she graduated she became an alumnus. Fund raising is a major part of the alumni association's job, so they have a reason to keep alumni mailing addresses current, and that is why she consistently received her annual contribution request. Any time there are two (or more) values for the same data element (or elements), at least one of those values must be wrong. A central database can help by eliminating redundant data and allowing everyone to share the most current information available.

Database Management

There are problems with traditional data management. Many result from viewing applications independently. For example, consider payroll. Most organizations prepare their payrolls by computer because using a machine instead of a small army of clerks saves money. Thus, the firm develops a payroll program to process the data on the payroll file. Inventory, accounts receivable, accounts payable, and general ledger are similar applications, so the firm develops an inventory program to process the data in an inventory file, an accounts receivable program to process the data in an accounts receivable file, and so on. Each program is independent, and each processes its own independent data file.

The problem is that different applications often need the same data elements. For example, schools generate both bills and student grade reports. View the applications independently. The billing program reads a file of billing data and the grade report program reads an independent file of grade data. The outputs of both programs are mailed to the students' homes, so student names and addresses must be redundantly recorded on both files.

What happens when a student moves? Unless both files are updated, at least one will be wrong. Redundant data are difficult to maintain.

Data dependency is a more subtle problem. There are many different file organizations, each has its own rules for storing and retrieving data, and certain "tricks of the trade" can significantly improve the efficiency of a given program. If the programmer takes advantage of these efficiencies, the program's logic can become dependent upon the physical structure of the data. When a program's logic is tied to its physical data structure, changing that structure will almost certainly require changing the program. As a result, programs using traditional access methods can be difficult to maintain.

The solution to both problems is organizing the data as a single, integrated **database.** The task of controlling access to all the data can then be concentrated in a centralized database management system (Figure 3.28). On a centralized database, all data are collected and stored in a single place, so there is one and only one copy of any given data element. When a new value for a data element such as an address is received, the change is noted on the database. Subsequently, any program requiring access to this data element gets the same value, because there is only one value. Additionally, since the responsibility for accessing the physical data rests with the database management system, the programmer can ignore the physical data structure, so programs tend to be much less dependent upon their data and are generally easier to maintain. Note, however, that a database management system adds another layer of abstraction to the process of manipulating data.

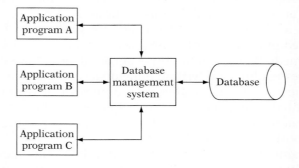

FIGURE 3.28

Many of the problems associated with traditional data access techniques can be solved by using a database.

▋ Summary

A program is a series of instructions that guides a computer through a process. An assembler translates each mnemonic instruction into a single machine-level instruction. Hardware works with absolute addresses. Software generally references addresses that are expressed relative to a base location. A compiler reads source statements, translates each one into one or more machine-level instructions, and combines them to form an object module. An interpreter reads and executes one source statement at a time. Using a compiler adds two layers of abstraction to the process of creating a program.

A structured program consists of a series of logical modules linked by a control structure. The basic idea of the object-oriented approach is to design and write the software as a set of independent objects linked by signals. An object contains both data and methods. Objects communicate by transmitting and responding to signals that are sent and received by entities called operations. Hiding implementation details in this way is called encapsulation.

Source code is stored on a source statement library; an object module is stored on an object module library. A linkage editor or loader combines object modules to form a load module. A reentrant program does *not* modify itself. An application program incorporates a user interface and an interface with the operating system. An application programming interface is a set of source-level functions and calling conventions that are compiled to operating system calls.

A data element is a single, meaningful unit of data. The simplest data structure is a list. In a linked list, each node contains data plus a pointer to the next node. A stack is a type of linked list in which all insertions and deletions occur at the top. A queue is a type of linked list in which insertions occur at the rear and deletions occur at the front.

In a file, individual characters are grouped to form fields, fields are grouped to form records, and a set of related records forms the file. Many multimedia files contain only a single record. Accessing the data on a file involves reading and writing individual records. Often, the key to finding a specific record is its relative record number or relative byte number. With sequential access, data are stored and retrieved in a fixed order. With direct or random access, individual records can be retrieved without regard for their positions on the physical file.

Traditional data files often exhibit data redundancy and data dependency. With a database, there is only one copy of each data element, so the data redundancy problem is minimized. Because every program must access data through a database management system, programs are insulated from the physical data structure, thus reducing data dependency.

▪ Key Words

absolute address	machine language
application programming interface (API)	message
	method
assembler language	object
base address	object module
compiler	object-oriented
database	operation
data element	portability
data structure	program
direct access	queue
displacement	random access
dynamic address translation	reentrant
file	relative address
instruction	relative record number
interpreter	sequential access
library	signal
linkage editor	source code
linked list	stack
load module	structured program

▪ Review Questions

1. Identify the components of a machine language instruction.

2. Distinguish between an absolute address and a relative address.

3. What is dynamic address translation?

4. How do an assembler, a compiler, an interpreter, and a nonprocedural language differ? What do they have in common?

5. Using a compiler adds two layers of abstraction to the process of creating an application program. What does that mean? If the statement is true, why do programmers use compilers?

6. Distinguish between traditional structured software and object-oriented software.

7. Define the terms object, method, encapsulation, message, and operation.

8. What is a library? Why are libraries useful?

9. Distinguish among source code, an object module, and a load module.

10. What does a linkage editor do?

11. What is reentrant code? Why is reentrant code important?

12. Identify an application program's interfaces.

13. What is an application programming interface (API)?

14. What is a data element? Describe several different types of data elements.

15. What is a data structure? Why are data structures important?

16. Describe a list, a linked list, a stack, and a queue.

17. Relate the terms character, field, record, and file. Distinguish between a traditional data file and a multimedia file.

18. Explain the relative record concept.

19. Distinguish between sequential and direct (or random) access. Relate both techniques to the relative record concept.

20. What is a database? Why are databases useful?

◼ Exercises

1. Without a program to provide control, a computer is little more than an expensive calculator. Do you agree? Why, or why not?

2. Relate the idea of an instruction to a computer's basic machine cycle from Chapter 2.

3. Why are programming languages necessary?

4. Manually copy the bit string pictured in Figure 3.3 to a sheet of paper. Check the accuracy of your copy and correct any errors you might have made. Then copy the equivalent BASIC instruction, LET A = B + C, to the same sheet of paper. When you finish, write a few paragraphs comparing your impressions of the relative coding efficiency and accuracy of machine-level programming and compiler-level programming.

5. Explain how software layering can make a system more vulnerable to attack.

6. Students who change their address with the university often find that correspondence is sent to their old address long after they report the change. Why do you suppose that happens?

7. If a student changes his or her address during an academic term, that term's grade report is often sent to the old address, but the next term's bill is almost always sent to the correct address. How do you explain that?

8. Some modern operating systems do not recognize records, treating data stored on disk as simple strings of bytes. What advantages might you expect from such an approach? What disadvantages?

9. Figures 3.6 and 3.18 are useful templates for organizing many of this chapter's key terms, although traditional file and database terms do not fit either model very well.

CHAPTER 4

Linking the Hardware Components

When you finish reading this chapter you should be able to:

▶ Identify several common bus types.

▶ Relate a computer's word size to its processing speed, memory capacity, precision, and instruction set size.

▶ Illustrate how a computer's internal components interact by outlining the steps in a complete machine cycle.

▶ Explain how a single-bus architecture computer's internal components are physically linked.

▶ Distinguish between single-bus architecture and multiple-bus architecture.

▶ Explain how channels and control units are used to link peripheral devices to a multiple-bus architecture computer.

▶ Define primitive operation.

▶ Explain what happens when a file is opened.

▶ Distinguish between logical I/O and physical I/O.

▶ Distinguish between an access method and a device driver.

◼ Linking Hardware

This chapter focuses on how the hardware layer components are physically connected to each other and how the operating system layer communicates with the hardware layer (Figure 4.1). We begin with the hardware layer.

The Bus

A computer's internal components are physically linked by a **bus,** a ribbon-like set of electrical lines (or wires) that carries several bits at a time, in parallel. Some of those lines transmit power. Others carry instructions, data, addresses, or commands.

Modern computers incorporate different types of buses to perform different functions. A processor bus delivers information to and from the processor, while a memory bus carries information between memory and the processor, and a cache bus, sometimes called a backside bus, links the system cache and the processor. On many computers, a single system bus combines the functions of both the processor bus and the memory bus. The local I/O bus links high-speed peripherals, such as a disk, to the system, while slower devices such as the keyboard and the mouse are linked through a standard I/O bus. For example, many personal computers feature a local I/O bus that follows the **PCI (Peripheral Component Interconnect)** standard and a slower **ISA (Industry Standard Architecture)** bus.

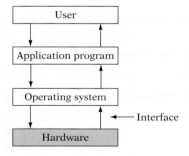

FIGURE 4.1

This chapter focuses on how the hardware layer components are physically connected and how the operating system layer communicates with the hardware layer.

Word Size

Communication between components is greatly simplified if they are electronically similar. Thus, on most systems the internal components are designed around a common **word** size. For example, on a 32-bit computer, the processor manipulates 32-bit numbers, memory and the registers store 32-bit words, and data and instructions move over a 32-bit bus.

A computer's word size affects its processing speed, memory capacity, precision, instruction set size, and cost. Consider speed first. A 32-bit bus contains 32 parallel lines that can carry 32 bits at a time. A 16-bit bus has only 16 parallel lines and thus can carry only 16. Because the wider bus moves twice as much data in the same amount of time, the 32-bit machine is clearly faster. Generally, the bigger the word size, the faster the computer.

Memory capacity is also a function of word size. To access memory, the processor must transmit over a bus the address of a desired instruction or data element. On a 32-bit machine, a 32-bit address can be transmitted. The biggest 32-bit number is roughly 4 billion in decimal terms, so the processor can access as many as 4 billion different memory locations. A 16-bit computer, in contrast, transmits a 16-bit address, limiting it to roughly 64,000 memory locations. Generally, the bigger its word size, the more memory a computer can address.

There are 16-bit microcomputers that access considerably more than 64 K bytes of memory. How is that possible? A 16-bit machine can access more than 64 KB if addresses are broken into two or more parts and transmitted during successive machine cycles. Each machine cycle takes time, however, so memory capacity is gained at the expense of processing speed.

Next, consider precision, the number of significant digits a machine can manipulate. Registers generally hold one word, and the processor's internal circuitry is usually most efficient when manipulating words. A 64-bit processor adds 64-bit numbers; a 32-bit processor adds 32-bit numbers; clearly, the machine with the bigger word size is more precise. While the 32-bit machine may be able to add two 64-bit numbers, it will need several machine cycles to do so, sacrificing speed for precision.

Like data, instructions move from memory to the processor over a bus, and a 32-bit bus can carry a bigger instruction than a 16-bit bus. The bigger instruction size means more bits are available for the operation code, and that means (potentially) a bigger instruction set.

Word size also influences a system's cost because a larger word size complicates production. Generally, a bigger word size means a faster, more precise machine with greater memory capacity, a larger, more varied instruction set, and a higher price tag.

Obsolescence

The very first personal computers were built around 8-bit processor chips. By the early 1980s, the standard word size was 16 bits. Today, 32-bit machines are the norm and 64-bit processors are common.

As word size increases, we tend to assume that older, obsolete processors fade quietly into oblivion, but that is simply not the case. In fact, the number of 8-bit (and even 4-bit) processors currently in use is staggering. Where do you find such "obsolete" electronic components? Inside virtually any consumer electronics product you can imagine, including cameras, receivers, cell phones, pagers, watches, automobiles, calculators, CD players, camcorders, and on and on. Why? Because those so-called "obsolete" processors are perfectly adequate for such applications and they are very inexpensive.

Machine Cycles

Perhaps the easiest way to envision how the various components of a computer are linked is to follow the steps in a typical **machine cycle.** Consider the computer pictured in Figure 4.2a. Memory holds a program and some data. In the processor, some of the registers hold key control information and other work registers are used by the programmer for computations or addressing. A single bus links the processor, the registers, and memory.

During instruction time or I-time, the instruction control unit fetches the next instruction from memory. The address of the next instruction is found in the instruction counter. The instruction control unit extracts this address and sends it (as part of a fetch command) over the bus to the memory controller (Figure 4.2a). The memory controller accepts the command, reads the requested memory location, and copies its contents onto the bus (Figure 4.2b). This takes time, giving the instruction control unit an opportunity to increment the instruction counter to point to the next instruction. Meanwhile, the current instruction moves over the bus and into the instruction register (Figure 4.2c).

During execution time or E-time, the instruction control unit activates the arithmetic and logic unit, which executes the instruction in the instruction register (Figure 4.2d). Assume the instruction calls for loading the contents of a word stored in memory into a work register. In response, the arithmetic and logic unit issues, again over the bus, a command to fetch the contents of the specified memory location (Figure 4.2e). As before, the memory controller reads the requested word and copies the contents onto the bus. Once on the bus, the data flows to a work register (Figure 4.2f).

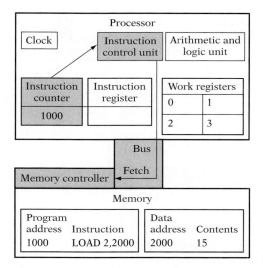

FIGURE 4.2
A machine cycle. **a.** The instruction control unit sends a fetch command to memory.

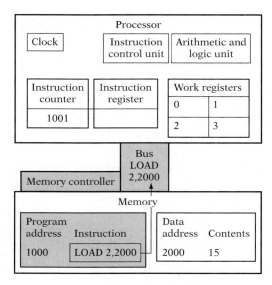

b. The memory controller copies the contents of the requested memory location onto the bus.

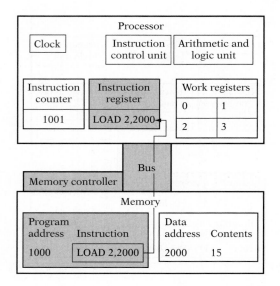

FIGURE 4.2

c. The instruction moves over the bus and into the instruction register.

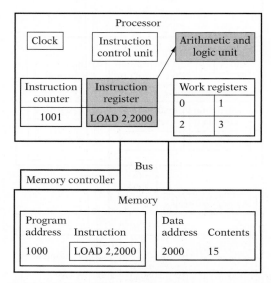

d. The arithmetic and logic unit executes the instruction in the instruction register.

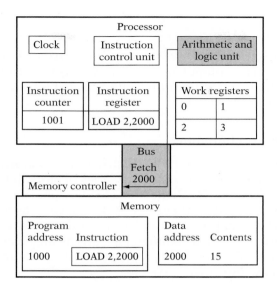

FIGURE 4.2

e. The arithmetic and logic unit sends a fetch command to memory.

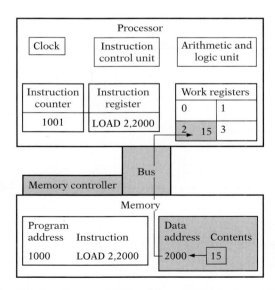

f. The memory controller copies the contents of the requested memory location onto the bus and the data value flows into a work register.

◾ Architectures

Computer scientists use the term **architecture** to describe the interconnections that link a computer's components. As you read the next several topics, note how computer architecture resembles the layering concept you read about in Chapter 1.

Single-Bus Architecture

Most microcomputers are constructed around a **motherboard** (Figure 4.3), a metal framework that contains a series of **slots** linked through a bus to a processor (Figure 4.4). Memory is added by plugging a memory board into one of the open slots (Figure 4.5). Interface boards are used to connect external buses and peripheral devices to the system. Because all the components are linked to a common bus, this arrangement is called **single-bus architecture** (Figure 4.6). At some point, all communication between components flows over this single bus.

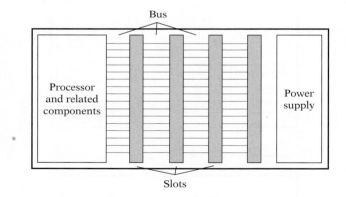

FIGURE 4.3

Most microcomputers are constructed around a motherboard.

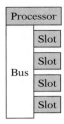

FIGURE 4.4

A schematic drawing of a motherboard highlighting the slots.

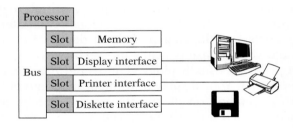

FIGURE 4.5

Memory, peripherals, and secondary storage devices are added to the system by plugging the appropriate board into an open slot.

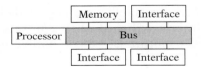

FIGURE 4.6

With single-bus architecture all the components are linked by a common bus.

Interfaces

Because the electronic signals controlling a keyboard, a display, a printer, and a disk drive are different, each peripheral device must have its own. One side of the **interface** communicates with the computer and uses internal codes (Figure 4.7). The other side is device-dependent and communicates with the external device in the peripheral's external form. The interface translates.

For example, outside the computer the letter A is represented physically both as a key on a keyboard and as a dot pattern on a laser printer. When a user types the letter A, an electronic pulse enters the keyboard interface where it is translated to the binary code that represents A inside the computer. Later, on output, this same code is sent to a printer interface where it is translated to the electronic signals needed to form the proper dot pattern. Note that the computer always uses the same binary code no matter what peripheral device is involved. To the processor all peripherals look the same.

If you turn to the back of a personal computer, you will see several **device ports** for plugging peripheral devices into the system. Your keyboard and your mouse typically use **serial ports** that transmit one bit at a time. A printer is usually plugged into a **parallel port** that transmits several bits in parallel. Your display unit might plug into either a serial or a parallel port, depending on its specifications. A peripheral is plugged into its interface through a device port. The interface, in turn, plugs directly into the bus. Thus, there is an unbroken path leading from the peripheral device, through a cable, to a **port**, to an interface, to the bus, to the processor and memory.

Controllers

The act of transferring data from a bus to a peripheral device or from a peripheral device to a bus involves such logical tasks as counting and synchronization. The necessary intelligence is provided by a **controller,** a chip mounted on the interface board that controls the transfer process. Obviously, a controller chip must be compatible with the underlying bus and the peripheral device.

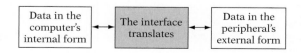

FIGURE 4.7

An interface translates between internal and external data forms.

Earlier in this chapter, in the narrative that accompanied the multiple steps in Figure 4.2, you read about a memory controller. Much as an interface controller controls the transfer of data between a peripheral device and a bus, the memory controller provides the intelligence needed to transfer information from memory to the system bus and from the system bus into memory.

External Buses

On a single-bus architecture system, the number of available slots limits the number of peripheral devices that can be connected to the system. One solution to this limitation is to use an **external bus** to connect several peripheral devices through a single port. For example, it is possible to plug a printer, a scanner, a mouse, a modem, and other serial devices into a **USB (Universal Serial Bus)** hub and then plug the USB hub into a single USB port that connects all those devices to the system. On some systems, printers, external disk drives, and similar parallel devices are connected to the system through a **SCSI (Small Computer System Interface)** bus that plugs into a SCSI (pronounced "skuzzy") port. USB and SCSI connections are beginning to replace traditional serial and parallel ports. Incidentally, a port is typically used to connect one device or one external bus to the system, while a bus can (potentially) link numerous devices.

Channels and Control Units

Microcomputers are designed for a few users, so single-bus architecture is reasonable. A mainframe is much more powerful and expensive, however, so mainframes generally support multiple concurrent users. A mainframe's processor still fetches and executes one instruction at a time, however. How is it possible to support multiple concurrent users when the processor executes only one instruction at a time?

One key is freeing the main processor from responsibility for input and output. Controlling input and output involves such logical functions as selecting the path over which the data are to flow, counting characters, and computing memory addresses. Because the main processor is the only source of logic on a microcomputer system, it must perform these common tasks for every input or output operation. While it is controlling input and output, the processor is not available to execute application program instructions, but given the nature of a microcomputer system, the resulting inefficiency is a minor problem.

Most mainframes assign the task of controlling input and output to **channels** (Figure 4.8). A channel is an independent, special-purpose computer with its own processor, so it can perform logical functions in parallel with the mainframe's main processor. That frees the main processor to do other things.

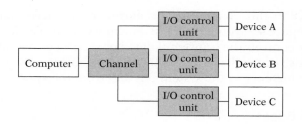

FIGURE 4.8

On a mainframe, device-independent functions are assigned to a channel and device-dependent functions are assigned to an I/O control unit.

Some input and output functions are device-dependent; for example, controlling the movement of an access arm is a disk problem, while a laser printer requires that characters be converted to a dot pattern. Other tasks, such as selecting a data path, counting characters, and computing memory addresses, are common to all input and output operations no matter what peripheral device is involved. The channel handles these device-independent functions. The device-dependent functions are assigned to an input/output **control unit.** Each physical device has its own control unit.

Multiple-Bus Architecture

Single-bus architecture creates a number of problems on a multiple-user system. Channel communication is one of the easiest to visualize. A channel moves data between memory and a peripheral device. The computer's processor manipulates data in memory. Allowing a channel and a processor to simultaneously access memory will not work on a microcomputer system because the single-bus architecture provides only one physical data path. Simultaneous access requires independent data paths, so most mainframes use **multiple-bus architecture** (Figure 4.9).

Start with a channel. Typically, two buses link it to the computer (Figure 4.9a)—one for commands and one for data. As an input or output operation begins, the main processor sends a *start I/O* command over the command bus to the channel's processor. In response, the channel assumes responsibility for the I/O operation, establishing a link with the external device and controlling the transfer of data into memory over the data bus (Figure 4.9b). Note that the *channel's* memory serves as a buffer between the peripheral device and the computer's memory. Because the channel manages the I/O operation, the main processor can turn its attention to another program.

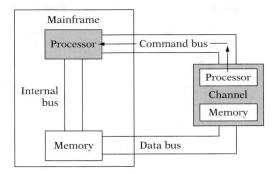

FIGURE 4.9

Most mainframes use multiple-bus architecture.

a. The main processor starts an I/O operation by sending a signal to the channel.

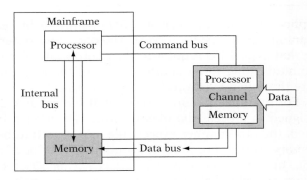

b. The channel assumes responsibility for the I/O operation and the processor turns its attention to another program.

The channel is an independent, asynchronous computer with its own processor and memory. It controls the I/O operation. Because the channel and the computer are independent, the main processor has no way of knowing when the I/O operation is complete unless the channel tells it. Thus as the last character of data flows across the channel, the channel processor sends the main processor an electronic signal called an interrupt (Figure 4.9c). When it receives the **interrupt,** the main processor knows the requested I/O operation has been completed and the program that requested that operation can resume processing. The interrupt process will be discussed in detail in later chapters.

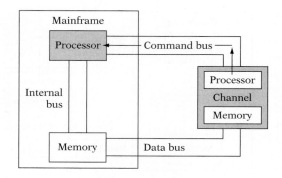

FIGURE 4.9

c. The channel sends an interrupt to the processor to signal the end of the I/O operation.

■ The Hardware/Software Interface

Application programs perform I/O operations by sending a logical request to an operating system service. The operating system responds by converting that logical I/O request to the appropriate physical I/O commands and communicating those commands from the operating system to the hardware through a hardware/software interface.

For example, picture a sequential file on disk and imagine a program designed to process the file's records. Whenever a READ statement is executed, the programmer expects the next record to be copied from disk into memory. Think about that for a minute. The "next" record is a logical concept. In effect, the programmer is saying, "Get me the next record in sequence, and I don't care what physical steps are involved." It's not that easy.

Primitives

The interface (or control unit) that controls a peripheral device is limited to a few **primitive** operations. For example, a disk interface (more accurately, a disk controller) can send the disk drive one of the following three commands:

1.   move the access mechanism to a specific track (seek),
2.   read a specific sector, or
3.   write a specific sector.

Because printers, disk drives, and display screens are so different, they are controlled by different sets of primitive operations and thus by different interfaces. Interfaces and control units execute special programs that consist of primitive commands.

Open

Because computers and their peripherals are physically independent, their electronic signals must be carefully synchronized before they can begin communicating. Often, an initial electronic link is established by exchanging a set of prearranged signals at **open** time. An operating system service initiates and interprets those signals. After a device is officially opened, the operating system knows it exists and knows how to communicate with it.

The open operation might involve more than simply establishing communication with a peripheral device, however. For example, a single disk can hold hundreds of programs and data files. For a given application, only one program and only one set of data will do. How does the system select the right program or the right data file?

The files stored on a disk are identified by name in the disk's directory (see Chapter 2). On a given system, the directory is always stored in the same place (for example, track 0 sector 2). Once initial contact with the disk drive has been established, the open logic (an operating system service) can issue the primitive commands to read the directory (seek track 0, read sector 2). Once the directory is in memory, the open logic can search it for the file's name. Recorded along with the file name is the disk address of the file's first sector. Given the address of a file's first sector, the location of its other sectors can be computed.

Logical and Physical I/O

A disk's interface or control unit is (essentially) limited to three primitive functions:

1. seek to a track,
2. read a sector, or
3. write a sector.

The concept of the "next" record is meaningless at this level. To find data physically on disk, you must specify a track and issue a seek command and then, subsequently, specify a sector and issue a read command. The programmer is concerned with **logical I/O.** The act of physically transferring a unit of data between memory and a peripheral device is called **physical I/O.** Note that logical I/O is performed by software and physical I/O is performed by hardware.

The process of bridging this gap begins when the application program issues a logical I/O request. The problem is converting this logical request into a series of primitive physical I/O operations. Often, the key is the relative record number.

A relative record number indicates a record's position relative to the beginning of a file. How does the system know where the file begins? One function of the open logic is reading the disk's directory, searching it for the file's name, and extracting the file's start address. In general, once a file is opened, its start address is known and the location of any record on that file can be computed by using the appropriate relative record number.

Imagine a program that reads data sequentially. When the file is opened, the disk address of its first record is known. The file's first record is relative record 0; its second record is relative record 1, and so on, so accessing individual records involves little more than counting them. For example, imagine that relative record 5 has just been read. Clearly, the "next" record is relative record 6. Where is it physically located? Given the start of file address (from open), and knowing that the desired record is at "start of file plus 6," its disk address can be computed and the necessary primitive commands issued.

Now, picture a direct access application. A program needs data for student number 123456. In some way, that student number must be converted to a relative record number. One option is using a hashing algorithm. Another is reading an index of student numbers and their associated relative record numbers and doing a table look-up. The start of file address is known from open, so once the student number has been converted to a relative record number, the process of computing its disk address is easy. Given the disk address, the necessary primitive commands can be issued.

Most students are surprised to learn that a task as apparently simple as reading data from disk can be so complex. In fact, the complexity associated with physical I/O is one of the major reasons why operating systems and systems software came into being. Even today, input/output control services form the core of most modern operating systems.

Access Methods

Few programmers communicate directly with peripheral devices at a primitive level. Generally, the responsibility for translating a programmer's logical I/O requests to physical commands is assigned to an operating system service (Figure 4.10). Because there are so many data access techniques available, some mainframe computers assign application-dependent portions of this translation process to special subroutines called **access methods** (Figure 4.11), keeping only application-independent logic in the operating system. The linkage editor adds the access method to the load module at load time (Figure 4.12), so application-dependent I/O logic occupies memory only when the application program occupies memory. Another option is assigning responsibility for all database access to a database management system.

FIGURE 4.10
A programmer's logical I/O request is converted to the appropriate physical I/O operations by the operating system.

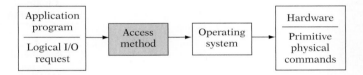

FIGURE 4.11
Some mainframes assign application-dependent portions of the logical-to-physical translation process to access methods.

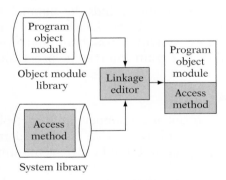

FIGURE 4.12
The access method is added to the load module at load time.

Once a record's physical location has been determined, the process of communicating with the peripheral device can begin (Figure 4.13). Typically, the access method identifies the necessary primitive commands, sets up a channel program, and calls the operating system. The operating system then sends a *start I/O* signal to the channel. The channel,

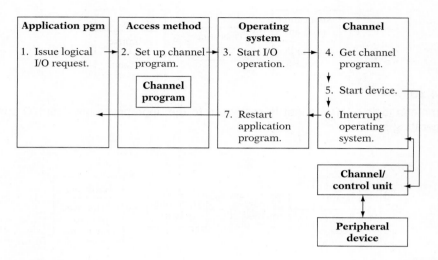

FIGURE 4.13

The process of converting a logical I/O request to primitive physical commands on a mainframe.

subsequently, accesses memory, finds the channel program, and transfers it to the I/O control unit. Once the data have been transferred, the channel notifies the operating system (through an interrupt) that the I/O operation is complete, and the program can resume processing.

Device Drivers

Microcomputers do not use channels and control units. With single-bus architecture, each peripheral device is plugged into an interface board, which in turn is plugged into the bus. It seems simple, but there are complications.

For example, imagine that your printer is attached to your computer by a cable that runs from the printer to the parallel port. What happens when you change printers? Assume, for example, that you want to take your black-and-white laser printer offline and hook up your color printer so you can print some color images. You should be able to unplug the parallel cable from the laser printer and plug it into the color printer with no problem because everything fits. But even though the physical connection remains intact, the color printer is unlikely to work unless you also make some logical (software) changes.

Although they can all be plugged into the parallel port, laser printers, ink jet printers, color printers, and even functionally similar printers manufactured by different companies are different. (The same problem occurs with other peripheral devices such as display units, scanners, and so on.) Providing a custom port and/or interface for each manufacturer's peripheral is not a reasonable solution to this problem. Instead, the responsibility for performing unique, device-specific tasks is assigned to a software routine called a **device driver.** Many common device drivers are preinstalled into the operating system. When you purchase a new peripheral, it typically comes with an installation disk. Among other things, the disk usually contains the latest device driver for the peripheral. During the installation process, the device driver is installed on the system's hard disk.

Assume the peripheral device is a printer and you have just clicked on an application program's *Print* icon. In response, the program passes a print request to the operating system (Figure 4.14). The operating system, in turn, finds the appropriate device driver on disk and launches it. The device driver communicates with the interface card, which passes the request to the printer. If a subsequent input or output operation calls for communicating with a different peripheral device, the operating system selects a different device driver appropriate for that peripheral. Note how Figure 4.14 reflects the layering concept.

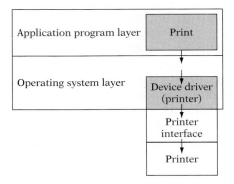

FIGURE 4.14

Microcomputers use device drivers as part of the logical-to-physical I/O conversion process.

Updating Device Drivers

If you purchase a new computer or install a new operating system, there is a very good chance that one or more previously working peripherals will no longer operate. Often, the problem is an incompatible device driver, and the solution is to install an updated device driver. A good starting point is the peripheral manufacturer's Web site; for example, if you have a Canon printer, go to *www.canon.com* and if you have a Hewlett-Packard printer go to *www.hp.com*. Once you reach the Web site, look for a link to *Downloads, Software,* or a similar term that seems to make sense or, if the site supports a search feature, search on *device drivers.* You'll probably need such information as the peripheral's make and model, the version of your operating system, and, perhaps, the manufacturer and model of your computer system, so be prepared. Other possible sources of downloadable device drivers include your operating system supplier, your computer's manufacturer, or any of a number of independent Web sites that specialize in software downloads and patches.

◗ Summary

A computer's internal components communicate over a bus. Modern computers incorporate different types of buses. On most computers, the internal components are designed around a common word size. The communication between internal components was illustrated by following a single machine cycle.

Computer scientists use the term architecture to describe the interconnections that link a computer's components. Typically, each peripheral device requires its own interface board. A peripheral is plugged into its interface via a device port, and a controller provides the interface's intelligence. Multiple peripherals can be attached to a system through a single port by using an external bus.

Mainframes often support multiple concurrent users and assign responsibility for controlling input and output to a channel and a control unit. When a channel completes an I/O operation, it notifies the main processor by sending it an electronic signal called an interrupt. Most mainframes use multiple-bus architecture.

An I/O control unit and an interface execute primitive commands to physically control a peripheral device. The first step in accessing a peripheral device is opening it. Few programmers actually deal with physical I/O operations. Instead, they assign responsibility for translating logical I/O requests to physical form to the operation system, an access method, or a database management system. On many single-bus architecture systems, the responsibility for performing unique, device-specific tasks is assigned to a software routine called a device driver.

◼ Key Words

access method

architecture

bus

channel

control unit (I/O)

controller

device driver

device port

external bus

interface

interrupt

ISA (Industry Standard
    Architecture)

logical I/O

machine cycle

motherboard

multiple-bus architecture

open

parallel port

PCI (Peripheral Component Interconnect)

physical I/O

port

primitive

SCSI (Small Computer System Interface)

serial port

single-bus architecture

slot

USB (Universal Serial Bus)

word

◼ Review Questions

1. Explain how a computer's internal components are physically linked.

2. What functions are performed by a processor bus, a memory bus, a local I/O bus, and a standard I/O bus? Distinguish between a PCI bus and an ISA bus.

3. Discuss the purpose of a processor bus, a memory bus, an I/O bus, and a standard bus.

4. On most computers, all internal components are designed around a common word size. Why?

5. Explain how a computer's word size affects its processing speed, memory capacity, precision, and instruction set size.

6. Illustrate how a computer's internal components interact by outlining the steps in a complete machine cycle.

7. What is meant by a computer's architecture?

8. Relate the terms motherboard, slot, and bus.

9. On a typical microcomputer system, each input, output, and secondary storage device has its own interface. Why?

10. What is a device port? Distinguish between a serial port and a parallel port.

11. What is the function of a controller?

12. What is the purpose of an external bus? Distinguish between a USB bus and an SCSI bus.

13. Trace the electronic path that links a peripheral device to a single-bus architecture computer's internal components.

14. Distinguish between single-bus architecture and multiple-bus architecture.

15. On a mainframe computer, peripheral devices are linked to the internal components through channels and control units instead of simple interfaces. How? Why?

16. What is a primitive operation?

17. Explain what happens when a file is opened.

18. Distinguish between logical I/O and physical I/O.

19. What is a device driver? Why are device drivers necessary?

20. Distinguish between an access method and a device driver.

◀ Exercises

1. Identify several current uses for apparently obsolete 8- and 16-bit processors.

2. Find a computer that is no longer in use. Remove the cover and identify the processor, memory, the bus, and the various interface boards. Prepare a sketch showing how the internal components are linked. Compare your sketch to the generic architecture diagrams in the book.

3. Disassemble the computer from Exercise 2 and study the components. Then reassemble the computer.

4. Relate the idea of a disk's directory to a library catalog.

5. Relate computer architecture to the layering concept.

6. Identify at least three potential sources for device drivers for each of the peripheral devices attached to your computer.

7. Figures 4.2, 4.6 and 4.13 are useful templates for organizing many of this chapter's key terms.

PART 2

Basic Operating System Concepts

Chapters 5 and 6 focus on essential operating system concepts and principles. If you understand these basic ideas, you will find it much easier to grasp the content of subsequent chapters.

CHAPTER 5

The User Interface, the File System, and the IOCS

When you finish reading this chapter you should be able to:

▶ Identify the basic functions performed by an operating system's user interface.

▶ Distinguish a command interface, a menu interface, a graphical user interface, a voice-actuated interface, and a Web-form interface.

▶ Identify the primary functions performed by the file system.

▶ Distinguish between logical I/O and physical I/O.

▶ Distinguish between directory management and disk space management.

▶ Identify the primary functions performed by the input/output control system.

▶ Distinguish between the input/output control system and the file system.

▶ Distinguish between a resident routine and a transient routine.

▶ Outline the boot process.

◼ An Operating System's Basic Functions

As you learned in Chapter 1, most modern operating systems incorporate the functions summarized in Figure 5.1. The user interface provides a mechanism for the system operator and the user to communicate with the operating system and request operating system services. The file system incorporates routines that allow the user or programmer to create, delete, modify, and manipulate files by name. The device management function is responsible for controlling communications with the system's peripheral devices. Processor management is concerned with efficiently managing the processor's time. Memory management is concerned with managing the system's memory resources, allocating space to applications as needed and ensuring that those applications do not interfere with each other. Finally, as the name implies, communication support makes it possible for one computer to communicate with another.

Memory management and processor management are largely transparent to the user. They will be covered in Chapter 6. Communication is the subject of Part V, Chapters 16-21. This chapter discusses the shell, the file system, and device management.

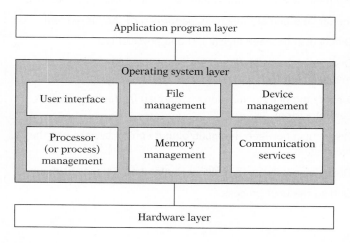

FIGURE 5.1

The components of a modern operating system.

The User Interface

Most of the time, a user communicates with a computer through an application program's user interface (Figure 5.2). The application program, in turn, transparently requests operating system services through an application programming interface (API).

Before a user can begin to access an application program's user interface, however, the operating system must first be told to launch the program. A system operator or a user identifies the program to be launched by issuing one or more **commands** directly to the operating system. The operating system's **user interface** accepts, interprets, and carries out the commands. Each command tells the operating system to perform a single service, such as log a user onto the system, start an application program, allocate a peripheral device, and so on. The user interface interprets each command and requests support from other operating system layers as appropriate.

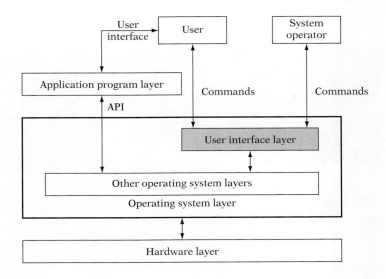

FIGURE 5.2
The user interface accepts, interprets, and carries out commands.

User Interfaces

A user communicates with a **command line interface** or **shell** by typing brief, cryptic commands, such as

COPY file-A file-B

MS-DOS line commands are a good example. Cryptic commands can save a sophisticated user a great deal of time, but command line interfaces require considerable user training.

A **menu interface** presents the user with a list of available options. The user selects the desired option by highlighting it and pressing enter, by typing the option's identifying letter or number, or by pointing to the option and clicking the mouse. Often, selecting one option leads to a second menu listing suboptions, so the user might have to work through a hierarchy of related menus. Compared to commands, menus are easier to use and easier to learn, but traversing multiple menus can be time consuming.

The Apple Macintosh and Microsoft Windows both feature a **graphical user interface** (GUI) that presents the user with a selection of windows, icons, and menus (Figure 5.3). The user points to the desired element and

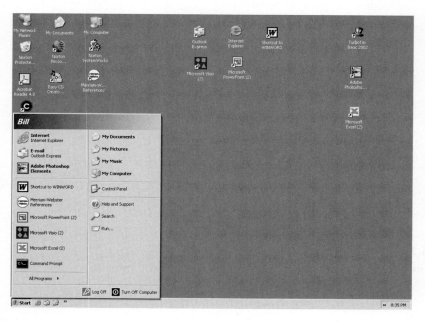

FIGURE 5.3

A graphical user interface.

clicks a mouse button to trigger the associated action. Graphical user interfaces are relatively easy to understand, learn, and use. Compared to commands and simple menus, however, they consume considerable processor time and memory. A graphical user interface is sometimes called an object-oriented interface or an icon-based interface.

A **voice-activated interface** utilizes such natural language processing elements as voice recognition, voice data entry, and voice response. Keyboards, pointing devices, and microphones are the primary input devices, and speakers provide audio output. Natural language processing requires a powerful computer with a great deal of memory and a fast processor. The current state of the art can be observed in sophisticated multimedia applications and online games.

A **Web-form interface** follows the metaphor established by the Internet and the World Wide Web. Because so many people use the Web, adopting Web rules to support a non-Web interface minimizes the need for additional training.

Because the user interface is implemented as an independent layer, its contents can be changed without affecting the other layers. As a result, several different user interfaces can coexist on the same computer. For example, imagine that your operating system supports a command line interface and a voice-activated interface in addition to the default graphical user interface (Figure 5.4). Normally you use the GUI, but the command line interface is convenient for certain file management tasks and the voice-activated interface is an excellent choice for certain computer games. Clearly, the rules the user must follow to communicate with the three interfaces are different, but as long as all three interfaces pass the same parameters down to lower operating system layers, those lower layers have no need to know how the user interface works.

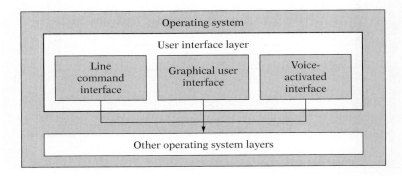

FIGURE 5.4

The user interface layer can support several different interfaces.

The Command Language

Although the rules for using different types of interfaces can vary considerably, they all do basically the same thing. The user interface allows the user to issue a command by typing it, selecting it, speaking it, or taking some other action. The command is then interpreted and passed on to another layer for processing.

Inside the user interface layer are links to a number of routines, each of which performs a single service (Figure 5.5). For example, one routine contains the instructions that guide the computer through the process of loading a program from disk into memory and launching it, while another contains the instructions to open a file, and so on. The user tells the user interface which service to perform by issuing a command such as *Open*, *Copy*, or *Save*. The user interface interprets the command and calls the appropriate service routine. The set of available commands and their syntax rules forms a **command language.**

For example, consider the task of launching a program. It is the user's responsibility to specify or otherwise select the program or routine to be executed by typing the program name, double-clicking on the program's icon, or selecting the program's name from a menu. In response to the user's action, the command flows into memory (Figure 5.6a). The user interface then interprets the command and calls the routine that loads the requested program (Figure 5.6b). Once the program is loaded into memory, the user interface starts it (Figure 5.6c).

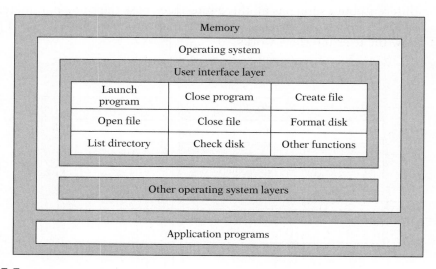

FIGURE 5.5

The user interface layer links to a number of routines, each of which performs a single service.

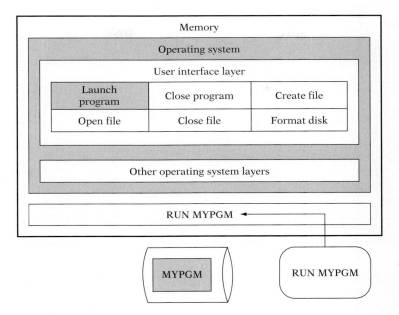

FIGURE 5.6
Launching an application program. **a.** The user selects the program.

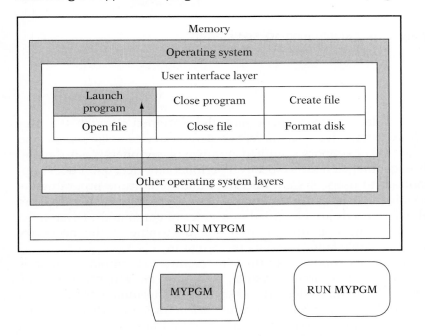

b. The user interface calls the *launch program* routine.

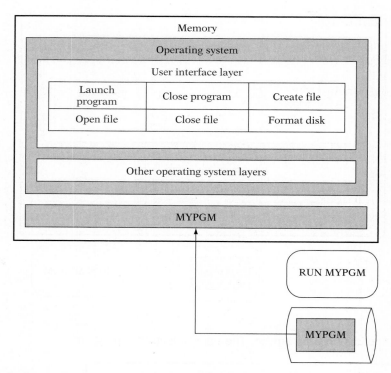

c. The application program is loaded into memory and started.

Peripheral device requirements are also specified through the user interface. Most interactive systems rely on default device assignments, and personal computers support a limited number of peripherals, so the end user rarely encounters a need to specify a peripheral device, but it does happen. In contrast to users, system operators and mainframe programmers specify peripheral devices on a regular basis. Typically, each program's peripheral device needs are identified in a series of commands. Given a list of device needs, the operating system can determine if the necessary resources are available before loading the program.

Other commands support run-time intervention. A simple example is rebooting a personal computer system. If a program stops functioning properly and locks up the system, the user can often terminate the program by simultaneously pressing *control, alt,* and *delete* (or some other combination of keys). Run-time intervention can be considerably more complex on a multiple user system.

Batch Commands

Imagine a payroll application in which input data are verified by a program named VERIFY, sorted (SORT), and processed (PAYCHECK) before the checks are printed (PAYPRINT). The commands to perform these functions might include:

VERIFY TIMEDATA
SORT TIMEDATA
PAYCHECK
PAYPRINT

Payroll is run weekly, so the same four commands must be typed (or selected) once a week.

Computers are much better than people at repetitive tasks, so most operating systems support **batch files.** To create a batch file, the programmer types a set of commands and saves them in a file. Given the batch file, the application can subsequently be run by typing (or selecting) the batch file name, for example,

payroll

The command processor responds by searching the system disk for a batch file named *payroll,* reading the file, and then carrying out the commands stored in the file.

A Human Perspective

Sometimes a human perspective can help clarify a technical concept. For example, the evolution of the user interface can be explained (at least in part) by the amount of work a computer can perform in an "instant." An instant is a brief, almost imperceptible period of time. If something happens instantly, it happens immediately, and you, as a human being, are unaware that time has passed. Few people are capable of actually sensing anything that happens in less then 0.001 seconds, so let's use 0.001 seconds as a working definition of an instant. If a computer is to respond instantly, it must be capable of accepting all relevant input data, processing the data, and outputting the results within 0.001 seconds.

Back in the late 1970s and early 1980s the first personal computers were capable of processing about one line of data (80 characters) within 0.001 seconds. In those days, a line command could be executed "instantly," but processing more data (such as a full screen) took considerably longer, so line command interfaces made sense. By the middle 1980s, faster processors were able to "instantly" support monochrome screens (80 characters by 25 lines), making menu interfaces viable. A few years later, processors were capable of supporting low-resolution graphics (320 by 200 pixels) screens, and the first graphical user interfaces appeared. Eventually, when processor speeds increased to the point where they could handle the computations necessary to compute 786,432 (1024 x 768) pixel settings within an instant, SVGA graphics (1024 by 768 pixels) became the standard. Note the common denominator. The de facto standard interface is defined by the amount of processing a computer can do within a human instant.

◼ The File System

The user interface allows the user to communicate with the operating system. The **file system** occupies a lower operating system layer (Figure 5.7) and helps keep track of the data and programs stored on disk and other secondary storage devices.

Directory Management

A disk can hold hundreds of different files and programs, but if you want to load a particular program, only that program will do, and if the program needs data from a particular file, only that file will do. As you learned in Chapter 2, the location (the start address) of every file stored on a disk can be found by searching the disk's directory (Figure 5.8). (*Note:* A program is a type of file.) The file system manages the directory.

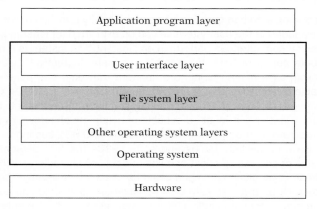

FIGURE 5.7

The file system layer.

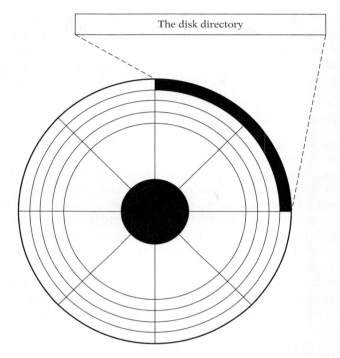

FIGURE 5.8

The location of every file stored on a disk can be found by searching the disk's directory.

For a given operating system the directory is always stored at the same location on every disk, so the file system can always find it. When a program is first installed or a data file is first created, its name and physical location are recorded in the directory by the file system. To retrieve the program or open the file, the file system reads the directory, searches it for the program or file name, and extracts the program or file's disk address. When a program or file is deleted, the file system removes its entry from the directory.

Launching a Program

For example, the process of launching a program begins when a user types a command such as SPACEWAR or clicks on the *Spacewar* icon. The user interface interprets the command and passes the program name to the file system, which reads the directory. Once the directory is in memory, the file system searches it. Each program is identified by name, and following the program's name is its physical location on disk—the track and sector address of its first instructions. The file system extracts the program's disk address and passes it to the device management layer, which physically loads a copy of the program into memory. Once the program is loaded, the file system notifies the user interface, which starts the program.

Opening and Closing Data Files

Programs are normally installed and launched in response to operator or user commands. Data files, on the other hand, are created and accessed through application programs. To create a new file, the user enters some data through an application routine and then saves the file. When a file is saved for the first time the file system creates a directory entry, allocates disk space to hold the file, and notes the file's start address in the directory.

To find an existing file, the user issues an **open** command. When a file is opened, the file system reads the directory, finds the file's directory entry, extracts the file's start address, and (sometimes) reads all or part of the file. Generally, when a program is finished processing a file, it closes the file. In response to a **close** command, the file system updates the directory to indicate such information as the file's length and ending address.

Logical I/O and Physical I/O

A similar process supports reading and writing data records from a file. The process begins after the file is opened. The program issues a **logical I/O** request such as "get the next record" or "get the record for student 123456." Note that the logical I/O request asks for a specific logical unit of data but does not indicate where (or how) the data are physically stored.

The act of physically transferring a unit of data between a peripheral device and memory is called **physical I/O.** Physical I/O is the responsibility of a lower operating system layer, the device management layer. The file system accepts the logical I/O request from the application program layer and converts it into a physical I/O request by reading the directory and finding the record's physical address. The file system then transfers the request to the device management layer which communicates with the physical device. Incidentally, the file system relies on the device management layer to physically read and write the directory.

Logical and Physical Records

A **physical record** is the unit of data (for example, a sector) that is transferred between a peripheral device and memory. A **logical record** is the unit of data processed by a single iteration of an application program. They are not necessarily the same, and that can complicate things.

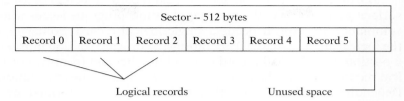

FIGURE 5.9
Blocking.

For example, imagine a program that processes a series of 80-byte (single line) logical records stored on disk. A disk, as you know, transfers one sector at a time into memory, so the physical record is a sector. Assume that each sector holds 512 bytes. Storing one 80-byte logical record in each 512-byte physical sector means wasting 432 bytes per sector, which is clearly unacceptable. One solution is to **block** the data, storing several logical records in each sector (Figure 5.9); for example, six 80-byte records can be stored in a single 512-byte sector leaving 32 bytes of unused space. Note that one physical record (one sector) holds six logical records.

Some applications involve lengthy records. For example, the academic history of a college senior might not fit in a single 512-byte sector (Figure 5.10), so the logical record (a single student's grade history), is bigger than the physical record (a single sector). Thus, assembling the data to support a single logical read calls for two or more physical input operations, while a single logical write implies two or more physical writes. A single logical record that extends over two or more physical records is called a **spanned record.**

Sector 0		
Personal data	Freshman year	Sophomore year

Sector 1		
Junior year	Senior year	

FIGURE 5.10
A single logical record that extends over two or more physical records is called a spanned record.

Hardware transfers a single physical record (a sector) between the disk's surface and memory. When an application program issues a logical read command, however, it needs a single logical record. Somewhere between the logical and physical I/O operations, a software routine must either select a portion of a physical record or combine the data from two or more physical records to form the logical record required by the application program. Depending on the system, that task might be performed by an access method, an application program routine, the file system, or a database management system.

Disk Space Management

The file system is also responsible for allocating space on disk. Ideally, when a file is created its data are stored in a series of consecutive sectors, but because many different files share the same disk, that is not always possible. For example, imagine that a file is created on Wednesday and updated on Thursday. Wednesday's data might occupy consecutive sectors, but data belonging to some other file might lie between Wednesday's data and Thursday's data. The file system bridges this gap.

Often, a linked list of sector numbers (or cluster numbers, where a cluster is a set of sectors) called a file allocation table is maintained on disk (Figure 5.11). When a file is created, the file system records the number of the file's first sector in the directory. When that first sector is filled, the file allocation table is searched and the next available free sector is allocated to the program. (In this example, free sectors are identified by a 0 table value.) Note that the next free sector might not be physically adjacent to the first one.

To link the sectors, the second sector's number is recorded in the first sector's file allocation table entry. Follow the chain of pointers (the linked list) in Figure 5.11. The directory indicates that file A starts in sector 6. The file allocation table entry for sector 6 points to sector 7, sector 7's entry points to sector 9, and sector 9's file allocation table entry points to sector 12. Because sector 12's file allocation table entry holds a sentinel value, it marks the end of the file. Of course, not all file systems use 0 to mark free sectors and -1 as a sentinel value, but this example gives you a sense of how disk allocation techniques work.

Directory Management and Disk Space Management

Note carefully the difference between the file system's directory management and disk space management functions. Directory management

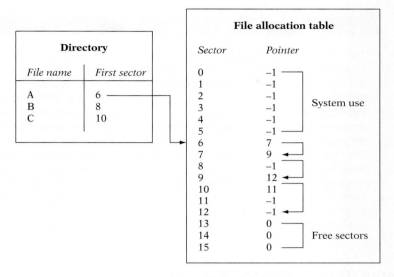

FIGURE 5.11

Many operating systems maintain a linked list of sectors to help manage disk space.

works with the directory. When a file is created, directory management establishes a directory entry. When a file is opened, directory management finds the file's physical address by reading and searching the directory. When a file is deleted, directory management deletes the associated directory entry.

Disk space management, in contrast, works with the file allocation table. When a file is created, the disk space management routine finds the first available free sector, marks it as no longer free, and passes the physical address of that sector back to the directory management routine, which notes it on the file's directory entry. As the file grows, the disk space management routine finds the necessary free space, assigns it to the file, and notes the assignment in the file allocation table. The directory and the file allocation table are tightly linked, with each directory entry pointing to the start of a linked list on the file allocation table. They are separate entities, however. Together, directory management and disk space management represent an interesting example of layering.

Early Operating Systems

The very first operating systems were developed back in the late 1950s and early 1960s primarily to support physical I/O. In those days, program instructions were prepared on a keypunch, one instruction per card, and the deck of cards was submitted to the computer operator for eventual processing. Standard input and output operations such as read a card or print a line appeared in virtually every program, so many computer centers prepared stacks of prepunched I/O routines for programmers to insert into their card decks. Eventually, someone came up with the idea of writing the I/O routines as a set of macros, storing them on disk, and allowing an assembler or a compiler to insert the code into the object module in response to a macro reference. Over time, those macros split into two components: a set of application-dependent routines called access methods and a smaller set of physical I/O routines. Those physical I/O routines evolved into a primitive IOCS that formed the core of many early operating systems.

▌ The Input/Output Control System

As you learned in the previous section, following a logical I/O request from an application program, the file system searches the directory and finds the appropriate physical address. The file system then passes the physical address to the operating system's device management layer. On many operating systems, the device management routine that generates primitive physical I/O commands and communicates directly with the peripherals is called the **input/output control system** or **IOCS** (Figure 5.12).

Consider, for example, the process of reading a sector from disk. A disk drive is limited to a few primitive operations, including:

1. seek to a track,
2. read a sector from that track,
3. write a sector to that track.

The only way to read a program or a set of data from disk into memory is to send the drive a series of primitive commands asking it to seek and read the contents of one or more sectors. Note that the disk drive must be told exactly where to position the access mechanism and exactly which sectors to read. If your program needs the data stored on track 20, sectors 8 and 9, the IOCS would have to tell the hardware to:

SEEK 20
READ 8
SEEK 20
READ 9

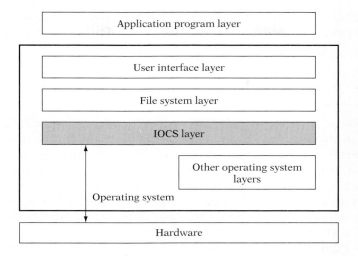

FIGURE 5.12
The IOCS generates the primitive commands that control a peripheral device.

All the application program wants, of course, is the data.

Quickly review the process. The input/output process starts when an application program passes a logical I/O request to the file system. The file responds by translating the logical I/O request into a physical I/O request, which it passes to the IOCS. The IOCS then generates the appropriate primitive commands that control the physical peripheral device. In other words, the application program performs logical I/O, the IOCS performs physical I/O, and the file system translates—another example of layering.

◼ Resident and Transient Routines

In addition to its primary layers, most operating systems incorporate a set of **utility** routines such as linkage editors, loaders, line editors, disk formatting routines, sort routines, debugging features, library management routines, and so on. Other utilities designed to recover lost data, convert data from one format to another, optimize the way data are stored on a disk, make backup copies of files or disks, check a file for viruses, and perform similar support services can be purchased from independent sources. As such third-party utilities gain popularity their functions are often absorbed into a future release of the operating system.

Utilities are needed only occasionally, so most are treated as **transient** routines that are stored on disk and loaded into memory only when necessary.

In contrast, the file system and the IOCS support application programs in real time as they execute and thus must be **resident** in memory at all times.

◾ The Boot

Because it performs essential support services, the operating system must be in memory before any application program can be executed. On some systems, the operating system resides in read-only memory. ROM is permanent. It keeps its contents even when power is lost, so a ROM-based operating system is always there. The main memory of most computers is composed of RAM, however. RAM is volatile; it loses its contents when power is cut. Consequently, the operating system must be loaded into memory each time the computer is restarted.

Typically, the operating system is stored on disk, and the program that loads the operating system into memory, the **boot,** is stored on the first sector (or two) of the same disk (Figure 5.13). Hardware is designed to read the boot automatically whenever the power is turned on or the system is restarted (Figure 5.13a), often by executing a small, ROM-based routine. The boot consists of only a few instructions, but they are sufficient to read the resident portion of the operating system into memory (Figure 5.13b); note how it is seemingly "pulled in by its own bootstraps." Once the operating system is in memory, a user can issue the commands to launch application programs.

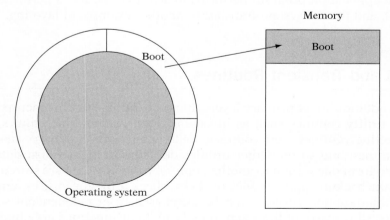

FIGURE 5.13

The boot.

a. Hardware automatically reads the boot when power is turned on.

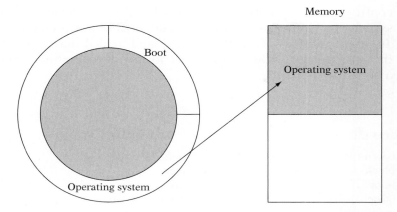

FIGURE 5.13

b. The boot reads the rest of the operating system into memory.

Loading the operating system from scratch is called a cold boot or cold start. If the computer is already running, it is often possible to warm boot or warm start the operating system by pressing a specific key combination such as *ctrl, alt,* and *delete*. Because key control information is already in place, a warm boot can bypass certain preliminary tasks, and that saves time. Note that on many modern operating systems, pressing *ctrl, alt,* and *delete* opens a window that gives you several options.

Summary

People communicate directly with the operating system through the user interface by issuing commands. There are several different types of user interfaces, including a command interface or shell, a menu interface, a graphical user interface or GUI, a voice-activated interface, and a Web-form interface. The set of available commands and their syntax rules forms a command language. Often, a batch file is used to simplify issuing repetitive commands.

Files and programs are accessed by name through the file system. Each file name is recorded in a disk directory. The file system manages the directory and also manages disk space. Programs are launched or closed in response to commands. Data files are opened and closed and data is read and written in response to program instructions. Blocking and spanned records complicate the task of reading and writing data. The input/output control system communicates with the physical devices. Most operating systems include utility routines. Resident routines are stored in memory. Transient routines are stored on disk and loaded into memory only when they are needed. The routine that loads the operating system is called a boot.

Key Words

batch file	menu interface
block	open
boot	physical I/O
close	physical record
command	resident
command line interface	shell
command language	spanned record
file system	transient
graphical user interface	user interface
input/output control system	utility
(IOCS)	voice-activated interface
logical I/O	Web-form interface
logical record	

Review Questions

1. Identify the basic functions performed by an operating system's user interface.
2. Distinguish a command interface or shell, a menu interface, a graphical user interface, a voice-activated interface, and a Web-form interface.
3. What is a command? What is a command language? How are commands used to communicate with the user interface?
4. What is a batch command file? Why are batch files used?
5. What functions are performed by the file system?
6. What happens when a program is launched?
7. What happens when a data file is opened? What happens when a data file is closed?
8. Distinguish between launching a program and opening a data file. How are these processes similar? How do they differ?
9. Distinguish between logical I/O and physical I/O.
10. Distinguish between a physical record and a logical record.
11. What is blocking? What is a spanned record?
12. Distinguish between directory management and disk space management.
13. Identify the primary functions performed by the input/output control system.

14. Distinguish between the input/output control system and the file system.
15. What is a utility?
16. Distinguish between a resident routine and a transient routine.
17. What is a boot? Why is a boot necessary? What happens during the boot process?

▮ Exercises

1. Explain the relationship between the evolution of the user interface and the amount of work a computer can perform within a single instant.

2. Do you think a voice-activated user interface will ever become the standard? Why, or why not?

3. Many old-time programmers are happy to talk about their experiences writing code back in the batch processing days before personal computers and interactive user interfaces became the norm. Many are retired or rapidly approaching retirement age, so you might not be able to talk to one of the old timers, but if you can, ask about what programming was like back in the (not so) good old days.

4. Why does it make sense to shift the details associated with opening and closing files, physical I/O, and disk space management down into the operating system? Can you think of any possible dangers that might arise from this approach?

5. Identify several utility programs that are marketed independently of the operating system.

6. Figure 5.12 is a useful template for organizing many of this chapter's key terms.

CHAPTER 6

Resource Management

When you finish reading this chapter you should be able to:

▶ Define several common measures of computer performance.

▶ Distinguish between resident and transient routines.

▶ Distinguish among fixed-partition memory management, dynamic memory management, segmentation, paging, and segmentation *and* paging.

▶ Explain dynamic address translation.

▶ Explain how virtual memory works.

▶ Discuss the role of control blocks and interrupts in the dispatching process.

▶ Explain how the queuing routine and the scheduler work together to load application programs.

▶ Distinguish between multiprogramming and time-sharing.

▶ Explain the virtual machine concept.

▶ Explain why deadlock is a problem.

◨ Measures of Effectiveness

On most modern computers, the operating system serves as the primary resource manager, allocating and managing processor time, memory space, peripheral devices, secondary storage space, and data and program libraries. A well-designed operating system attempts to optimize the utilization of all the system resources.

The first step in achieving optimization is to define precisely what you mean by optimum. Consider an analogy. What is the optimum automobile? Are you primarily interested in speed or safety? Do you prefer fuel efficiency or interior space and a comfortable ride? Are you interested in low cost transportation or high status? Until you define your criteria, you cannot *begin* to discuss the precise meaning of the word optimum because the criteria conflict. What is best for you is not necessarily *best* for me because best is a relative term.

Several criteria are commonly used to measure a computer system's performance (Figure 6.1). The perfect system would maximize throughput while minimizing both turnaround and response time. The system would be available on demand, and would be remarkably easy to use. Security would, of course, be absolute, system reliability would approach 100 percent, and the system would quickly recover on its own from the occasional error. All this would be accomplished at very low cost, of course. Unfortunately, such perfection is impossible to achieve because the measures of effectiveness conflict.

Resource management is a key operating system function. The operating system's job is to manage the computer system's resources as efficiently as possible, but the precise definition of efficiency depends on the computing environment. Your personal computer, a corporate mainframe, and a network computer that manages machine-to-machine communications perform very different functions and emphasize different criteria, so their operating systems will differ. Keep those differences in mind as you read this chapter and study the various operating systems discussed in the balance of this book.

◨ Memory Management

Chapter 5 discussed the shell, the file system, and the IOCS, three major operating system components that directly support an application program's input and output operations. This chapter focuses primarily on memory management and processor management. **Memory management** is concerned with managing the computer's available pool of memory, allocating space to application routines and making sure that they do not

Criterion	Meaning
Throughput	Generally, total execution time (for all programs) divided by total elapsed time, often expressed as a percentage. Higher is better.
Turnaround	The elapsed time between job submission and job completion. Shorter is better.
Response time	The elapsed time between a request for the computer's attention and the computer's response. Shorter is better.
Availability	A measure of a user's ability to gain access to a computer system. Expressed variously as the ration of free time to elapsed time (higher is better), the ratio of unavailable time to elapsed time (lower is better), or wait time to gain access (lower is better). Availability is concerned with getting on the system in the first place. Throughput, turnaround, and response time are relevant only after access is gained.
Security	A measure of a system's ability to avoid being compromised. Difficult to measure precisely. See Chapter 18.
Reliability	The probability that a system will perform as expected for a specified period of time. Higher is better.
Robustness	The ability of the system to recover quickly from errors or unusual circumstances.
Cost	The system's cost. Lower is better.
Ease of use	A subjective measure, sometimes expressed negatively as the time required to learn how to use a system. Quicker is better.

FIGURE 6.1
Some commonly used measures of computer system effectiveness.

interfere with each other. **Processor management** is concerned with managing the processor's time. Unlike the topics of Chapter 5, these resource management tasks are largely hidden from the user's view.

We begin with memory management.

Resident and Transient Routines

The operating system is a collection of software routines. Some routines, such as the ones that control physical I/O, directly support application programs as they run and thus must be **resident.** Others, such as the routine that formats diskettes, are used only occasionally. These **transient** routines are stored on disk and read into memory only when needed.

Generally, the operating system occupies low memory beginning with address 0 (Figure 6.2). System control information comes first, followed by the various resident operating system routines. The remaining memory, called the **transient area,** is where application programs and transient operating system routines are loaded.

Concurrency

Given the speed disparity between a computer and its peripherals, input and output operations significantly impact efficiency. For example, picture a computer with a single program in memory. The program cannot process data it does not yet have, and success cannot be assumed until an output operation is finished, so the program waits for input or output. Since the program controls the computer, the computer waits, too. Typically, given the speed disparity between the processor and its peripheral devices, a program spends far more time waiting for I/O than processing data.

Why not put two programs in memory and allow them to execute concurrently? Then, when program A is waiting for data, the processor can turn its attention to program B. And why stop at two programs? With three concurrent programs, even more otherwise wasted time is utilized (Figure 6.3). Generally, the more programs in memory, the greater the utilization of the processor.

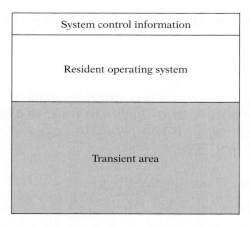

FIGURE 6.2

The operating system occupies low memory. Application programs and transient operating system routines are loaded into the transient area.

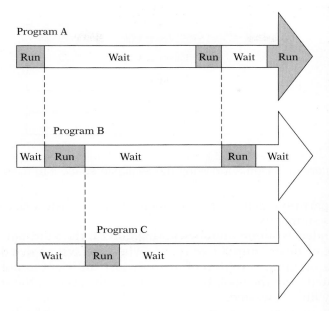

FIGURE 6.3
Multiple programs can be loaded into memory and executed concurrently.

Partitions and Regions

The simplest approach to managing memory for multiple, concurrent programs, **fixed-partition memory management** (Figure 6.4), divides the available space into fixed-length **partitions** each of which holds one program. Partition sizes are generally set when the system is initially started, so the memory allocation decision is made before the actual amount of space needed by a given program is known. Because the size of a partition must be big enough to hold the largest program that is likely to be loaded,

---

Concurrent and Simultaneous

The processor fetches and executes a single instruction during each machine cycle. Clearly, if the processor can execute only one *instruction* at a time, it cannot possibly execute two or more programs at a time. Thus, although multiple programs can share memory, only one can be active at any given time. Simultaneous means "at the same instant." No single processor can execute two or more *programs* simultaneously. Concurrent means "over the same time period." A processor can certainly execute two or more programs concurrently.

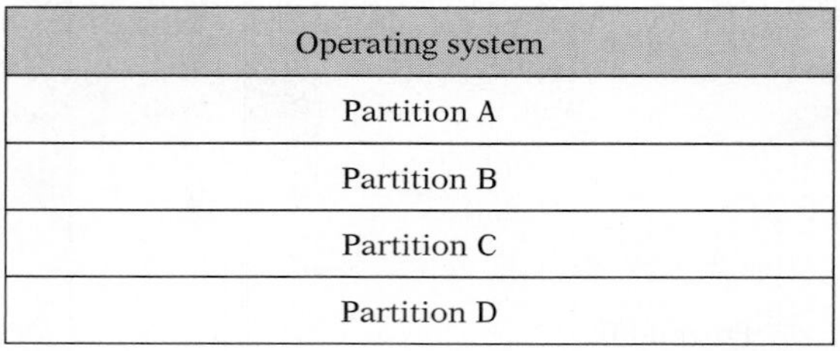

Operating system
Partition A
Partition B
Partition C
Partition D

FIGURE 6.4

Fixed-partition memory management divides the available space into fixed-length partitions.

fixed partition memory management tends to waste space. Its major advantage is simplicity.

Under **dynamic memory management,** the transient area is treated as a pool of unstructured free space. When the system decides to load a particular program, a **region** of memory just sufficient to hold the program is allocated from the pool. Because a program gets only the space it needs, relatively little is wasted.

Dynamic memory management does not completely solve the wasted space problem, however. Assume, for example, that a 64MB program has just finished executing (Figure 6.5). If there are no 64MB programs available, the system might load a 25MB program and a 30MB program, but note that 9MB remains unallocated. If no 9MB or smaller programs are available, the space will simply not be used. Over time, little chunks of unused space will be spread throughout memory, creating a **fragmentation** problem.

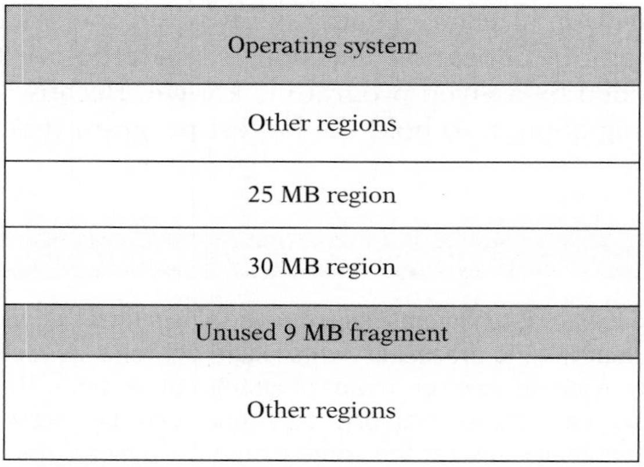

Operating system
Other regions
25 MB region
30 MB region
Unused 9 MB fragment
Other regions

FIGURE 6.5

Under dynamic memory management, the transient area is treated as a pool of unstructured free space. Fragmentation is a possible problem.

Segmentation

One reason for the fragmentation problem is that both fixed-partition and dynamic memory management assume that a given program must be loaded into *contiguous* memory. With **segmentation,** programs are divided into independently addressed segments and stored in *noncontiguous* memory (Figure 6.6).

Segmentation requires adding a step to the address translation process. When a program is loaded into memory, the operating system builds a segment table listing the (absolute) entry point address of each of the program's segments (Figure 6.7). (Note that there is one segment table for each active program.) Later, when the operating system starts a given program, it loads the address of that program's segment table into a special register.

As the program runs, addresses must be translated from relative to absolute form because programmers still write the same code and compilers still generate base-plus-displacement addresses. After fetching an instruction, the instruction control unit expands each operand address by adding the base register and the displacement. Traditionally, the expanded address was an absolute address. On a segmented system, however, the expanded address consists of two parts: a segment number and a displacement (Figure 6.7).

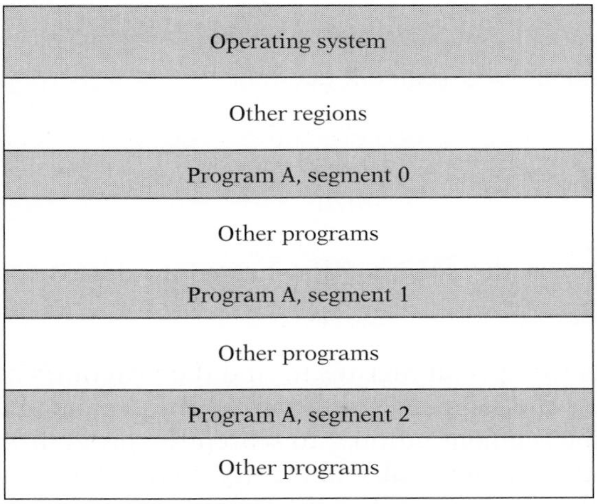

Operating system
Other regions
Program A, segment 0
Other programs
Program A, segment 1
Other programs
Program A, segment 2
Other programs

FIGURE 6.6

With segmentation, independently addressed segments are stored in noncontiguous memory.

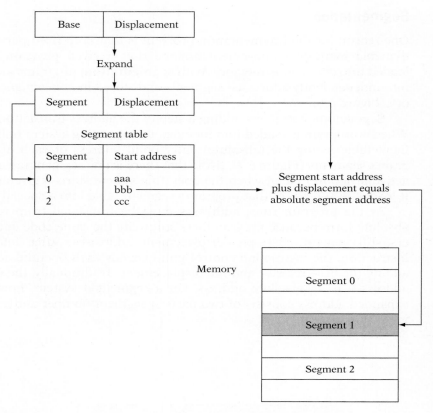

FIGURE 6.7
Dynamic address translation of a segment address.

To convert the segment/displacement address to an absolute address, hardware:

1. checks the special register to find the program's segment table,
2. extracts the segment number from the expanded address,
3. uses the segment number to search the program's segment table,
4. finds the segment's absolute entry point address,
5. adds the displacement to the entry point address to get an absolute address.

The process outlined in Figure 6.7 is called **dynamic address translation.**

Paging

A program's segments can vary in length. Under **paging,** in contrast, a program is broken into *fixed-length* pages. Page size is generally small and chosen with hardware efficiency in mind.

Like segments, a program's pages are loaded into noncontiguous memory. Addresses consist of two parts (Figure 6.8), a page number in the high-order positions and a displacement in the low-order bits. Addresses are dynamically translated as the program runs. When an instruction is fetched, its base-plus-displacement addresses are expanded to absolute addresses by hardware. Then the page's base address is looked up in a program page table (like the segment table, maintained by the operating system) and added to the displacement.

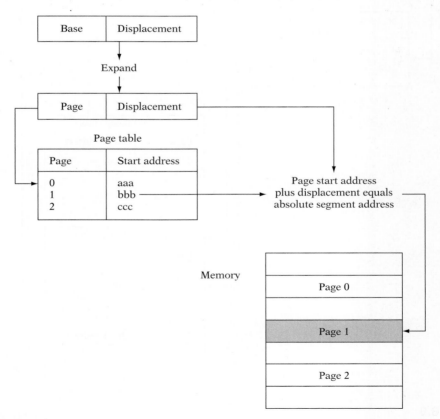

FIGURE 6.8
Dynamic address translation of a page address.

Segmentation *and* Paging

With **segmentation *and* paging,** addresses are divided into a segment number, a page number within that segment, and a displacement within that page (Figure 6.9). After the instruction control unit expands the relative address, dynamic address translation begins. First, the program's seg-

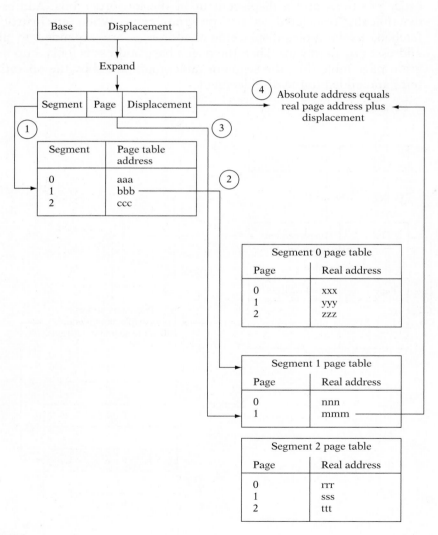

FIGURE 6.9

Under segmentation *and* paging, addresses are divided into three parts: a segment, a page, and a displacement.

ment table is searched for the segment number, which yields the address of the segment's page table. The page table is then searched for the *page's* base address, which is added to the displacement to get an absolute address.

Memory Protection

The contents of RAM are easily changed. With multiple programs sharing memory, it is possible for one program to destroy the contents of memory space belonging to another, so the active programs must be protected from each other. Generally, the operating system keeps track of the space assigned to each program. If a program attempts to modify (or, sometimes, even to read) the contents of memory locations that do not belong to it, the operating system's **memory protection** routine intervenes and (usually) terminates the program.

◼ Virtual Memory

If a processor can execute only one instruction at a time, why is it necessary for *every* instruction in a program to be in memory before that program can begin executing? It isn't. Loading only currently active pages is the underlying principle behind modern **virtual memory** systems.

Overlay Structures

The computers of the 1950s and early 1960s contained relatively little main memory. For example, imagine a second generation programmer faced with the problem of running a 32K program on a 16KB (yes, kilobyte) machine. One solution was to use overlay structures.

The idea was to break the program into logically independent modules. For example, imagine a program with four 8K modules (Figure 6.10a). Module 1 holds the main control logic and key data common to the entire program. Module 2 processes valid input data. Occasionally, errors or unusual data values call for the logic in module 3. Module 4 generates end-of-program statistics, so it is needed only when the program terminates.

Clearly, module 1 must remain in memory at all times. If no errors are encountered, there is no need for module 3. On the other hand, if an error occurs, module 3's logic must be executed, but modules 2 and 4 are superfluous. Thus, the program begins with modules 1 and 2 in memory (Figure 6.10b). When an error occurs, module 3 overlays module 2 (Figure 6.10c) and stays in memory until the next valid set of data is read, at which time module 2 replaces it. Finally, just before the program ends, module 4 overlays 2 or 3 (Figure 6.10d) and generates its statistics.

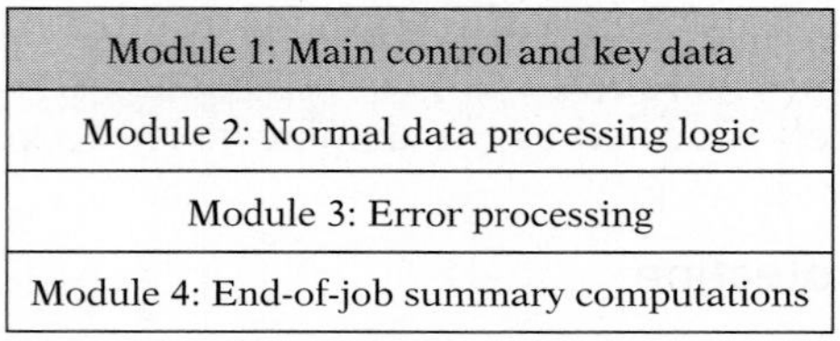

Module 1: Main control and key data
Module 2: Normal data processing logic
Module 3: Error processing
Module 4: End-of-job summary computations

FIGURE 6.10

With overlay structures, only the active portions of a program are loaded into memory.

a. The complete program consists of four modules.

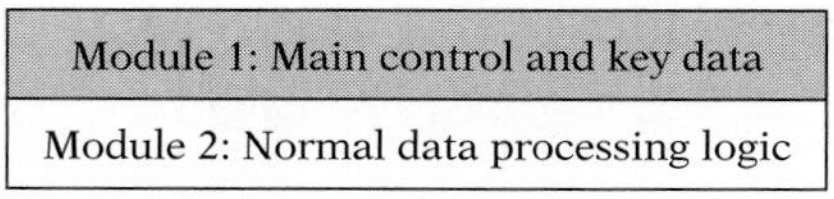

Module 1: Main control and key data
Module 2: Normal data processing logic

b. Under normal conditions, only modules 1 and 2 are in memory.

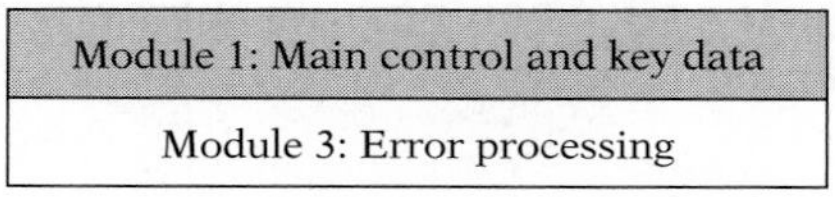

Module 1: Main control and key data
Module 3: Error processing

c. When errors occur, module 3 overlays module 2.

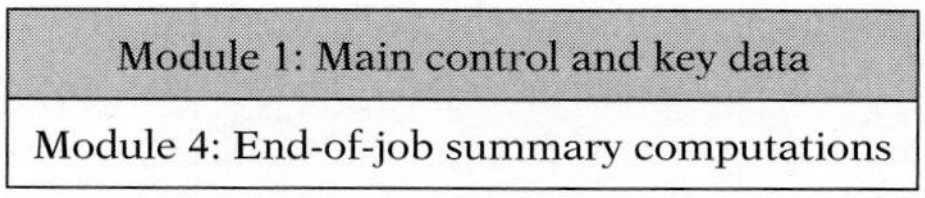

Module 1: Main control and key data
Module 4: End-of-job summary computations

d. At end-of-job, only modules 1 and 4 are needed.

Modern computers have much more memory than their second generation ancestors, but overlay structures are still used. More significantly, the idea of loading only a program's active modules into memory lives today in modern virtual memory systems.

Implementing Virtual Memory

Figure 6.11 illustrates a common approach to implementing virtual memory. It shows three levels of storage—virtual memory, the **external paging device,** and **real memory.** Real memory is good, old-fashioned main memory, directly addressable by the processor. The external paging device is usually disk. Virtual memory is a model that simplifies address translation. It "contains" the operating system and all the application programs, but it does not physically exist anywhere. Instead, its contents are physically stored in real memory and on the external paging device.

Virtual memory is divided into two components. The first part is exactly equal to the amount of real memory on the system and is physically stored in real memory. It holds the resident operating system and the transient program area (called the page pool). The second component of virtual memory consists of space over and above real memory's capacity. It is physically stored on the external paging device and holds application programs and transient operating system routines. The resident operating system is loaded into real memory. Application programs and transients are loaded onto the external paging device. Selected pages are then swapped between the real memory page pool and the external paging device (Figure 6.12).

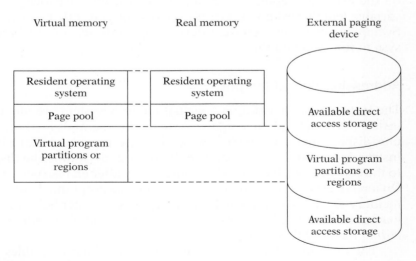

FIGURE 6.11
Virtual memory.

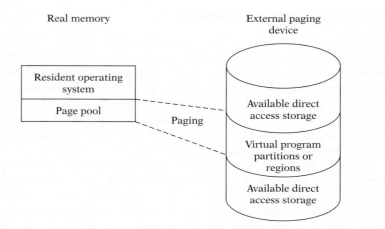

FIGURE 6.12

Pages are swapped between the external paging device and the real-memory page pool.

Traditionally, the operating system's memory management routine was concerned with allocating real memory space. On a virtual memory system, an equivalent module allocates space on the external paging device. Space on the external paging device can be divided into fixed-length partitions, variable-length regions, segments, pages, or any other convenient unit. Swapping pages between the external paging device and real memory is a system function and thus is transparent to the user.

Addressing Virtual Memory

The instructions that run on a virtual memory system are identical to the instructions that run on a regular system. The operands hold relative (base-plus-displacement) addresses. As is the case on non-virtual systems, the instruction control unit expands each address by adding the displacement to the contents of a base register immediately after an instruction is fetched. On a regular system, the base register holds the program's load point in real memory. On a virtual system, however, the base register holds the program's load point in *virtual* memory, so the computed address reflects the page's *virtual* memory location.

The dynamic address translation process (which resembles segmenta-tion *and* paging addressing; see Figure 6.9) starts when the program is loaded into virtual memory. The operating system allocates space on the external paging device and notes the virtual addresses of the program's seg-ments and pages in the program's segment and page tables. Later, when a given page is swapped into real memory, the page's *real* address is noted in the page table.

Note that a page must be in real memory for the processor to execute its instructions. When an instruction executes, the instruction control unit (in its usual way) adds the base register and the displacement to get an address in virtual memory. To convert a virtual address to a real address, hardware then:

1. accesses the program's segment table using the high-order bits of the virtual address as a key,
2. locates the program's page table using the pointer in the segment table,
3. accesses the page table to find the page's *real* base address using the middle bits in the virtual address as a key,
4. adds the displacement found in the low-order bits of the virtual address to the page's real memory base address.

On most systems, the process is streamlined through the use of special registers and other hardware.

Page Faults

When a virtual address points to a page that is not in real memory, a **page fault** is recognized and a page-in (or swap-in) operation begins. If no real memory is available for the new page, some other page must be swapped out. Often the "least currently accessed" or "least currently used" page (the page that has gone the longest time without being referenced) is selected.

Bringing pages into memory only when they are referenced is called **demand paging.** An option called **pre-paging** involves predicting the demand for a new page and swapping it into memory before it is actually needed. Many pre-paging algorithms assume that segments hold logically related code, so if the instructions on page 1 are currently executing the chances are that the instructions on page 2 will be executed next. While far from perfect, such techniques can significantly speed up program execution.

Thrashing

When real memory is full, a demand for a new page means that another page must be swapped out. If this happens frequently, the system can find itself spending so much time swapping pages into and out from memory that little time is left for useful work.

This problem is called **thrashing,** and it can seriously degrade system performance. The short-term solution is removing a program or two from real memory until the system settles down. The long-term solution is to improve the real-to-virtual ratio, usually by adding more real memory.

Memory Mapping

Memory mapping is a technique for minimizing the number of physical I/O operations. The idea is to map an image of the target file into the program's virtual memory address space, in effect storing the file in virtual memory. Once a file is mapped, data can be transferred between memory and disk by taking advantage of the system's paging mechanism, which is considerably more efficient than physical I/O.

▌ Multiprogramming

Multiprogramming is a common approach to processor management when two or more programs occupy memory and execute concurrently. Originally developed to support batch-processing applications, multiprogramming takes advantage of the extreme speed disparity between a computer and its peripheral devices. Traditionally, the key measures of multiprogramming effectiveness are throughput (run time divided by elapsed time) and turnaround (the time between job submission and job completion).

The Serial Batch Era

Back in the 1950s and early 1960s, most computers operated in serial batch mode. Programs were submitted, usually in punched card form, to a human operator who scheduled the computer. When the time came to run a given program, the operator cleared the computer of all residual settings from the last program; set up the new job by loading the necessary disk packs, tape volumes, special printer forms, and other media; and started the program. As it ran, the program had exclusive use of all the computer's resources. Only when the program finished processing was the next program set up and run.

As you might imagine, the serial batch process resulted in lengthy wait times, and 24-hour turnaround (the elapsed time between submitting a job and getting the results) was considered normal. By the mid-1960s, multiprogramming, with its ability to concurrently support several application programs, had significantly reduced average turnaround time to a matter of hours. Today, we consider a delay of more than a few seconds to be intolerably long. It is interesting to note how our perspective of time has changed over the years.

The Dispatcher

Imagine two programs concurrently occupying memory. Some time ago, program A requested data from disk (Figure 6.13). Because program A was unable to continue until the input operation was completed, it dropped into a **wait state** and the processor turned to program B.

Assume program A's input operation has just been completed. Both programs are now in a **ready state;** in other words, both are ready to resume processing. Which one goes first? Computers are so fast that a human operator cannot effectively make such real-time choices. Instead, the decision is made by a processor management routine called the **dispatcher.**

Consider a system with two partitions: foreground and background. The dispatcher typically checks the program in the foreground partition first. If the program is ready, the dispatcher restarts it. Only if the foreground program is still in a wait state does the dispatcher check the background partition. The foreground has high priority; the background has low priority.

This idea can be extended to larger systems with multiple concurrent programs in memory. The dispatcher checks partitions in a fixed order until a ready state program is found. The first partition checked has highest priority; the last has lowest priority. The only way the low-priority program can execute is if all the higher-priority partitions are in a wait state.

Control Blocks

There are several control fields that must be maintained in support of each active program. On many systems, a **control block** is created to hold a partition's key control flags, constants, and variables (Figure 6.14). The control blocks (one per partition) form a linked list. The dispatcher typically determines which program to start next by following the chain of pointers from control block to control block. A given control block's relative position in the linked list might be determined by its priority or computed dynamically, perhaps taking into account such factors as program size, time in memory, peripheral device requirements, and other measures of the program's impact on system resources.

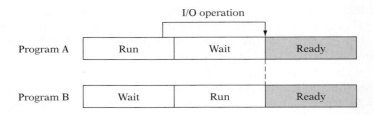

FIGURE 6.13

When two or more programs are in a ready state, the dispatcher decides which one executes first.

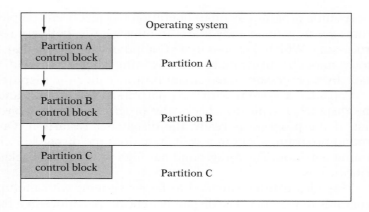

FIGURE 6.14

The dispatcher determines which program to start next by following a linked list of control blocks.

Interrupts

A program normally surrenders control of the processor when it requests an I/O operation and is eligible to continue processing when that I/O operation is completed. Consequently, the key to multiprogramming is recognizing when input or output operations begin or end. The operating system knows when these events occur because they are marked by **interrupts.**

An interrupt is an electronic signal. Hardware senses the signal, saves key control information for the currently executing program, and starts the operating system's **interrupt handler** routine. At that instant, the interrupt ends. The operating system then processes the interrupt and calls the dispatcher, which starts an application program. Eventually, the program that was executing at the time of the interrupt resumes processing.

Interrupts can originate with either hardware or software. A program issues an interrupt to request the operating system's support (for example, to start an I/O operation). Hardware issues an interrupt to notify the processor that an asynchronous event (such as the completion of an I/O operation or a hardware failure) has occurred. Other types of interrupts might signal an illegal operation (a zero divide) or the expiration of a preset time interval.

For example, follow the steps in Figure 6.15. When an application program needs data, it issues an interrupt (Figure 6.15a). In response, hardware starts the interrupt handler routine, which saves key control information, drops the application program into a wait state (Figure 6.15b), and calls the input/output control system to start the I/O operation. Finally, control flows to the dispatcher, which starts a different program (Figure 6.15c).

Later, when the I/O operation is finished, the channel issues an interrupt (Figure 6.15d). Once again the interrupt handler routine begins executing (Figure 6.15e). After verifying that the I/O operation was successfully completed, it resets the program that initially requested the data (program A) to a ready state. Then it calls the dispatcher, which starts the highest priority "ready" application program (Figure 6.15f). In this example, note that program A, the higher priority program, goes next even though program B was running at the time the interrupt occurred.

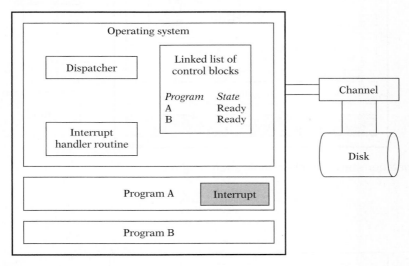

FIGURE 6.15

The dispatching process.

a. The program issues an interrupt.

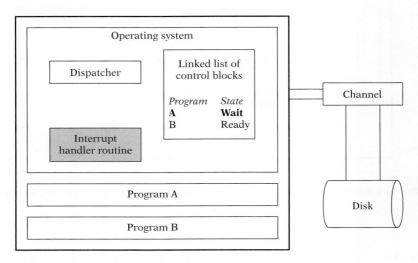

b. The interrupt handler routine sets the program to a wait state.

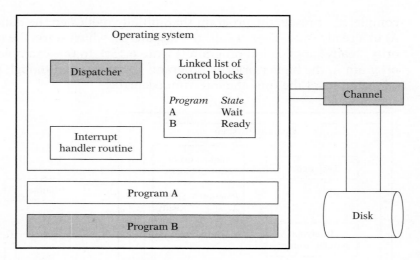

c. The dispatcher starts another application program.

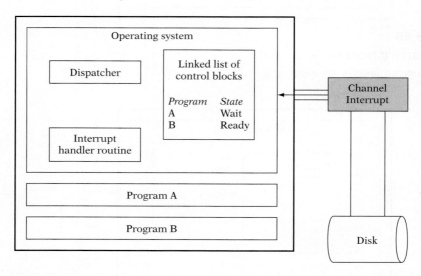

d. The channel signals the end of the I/O operation by sending the processor an interrupt.

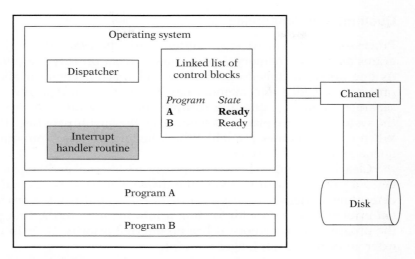

e. The interrupt handler routine resets program A to a ready state.

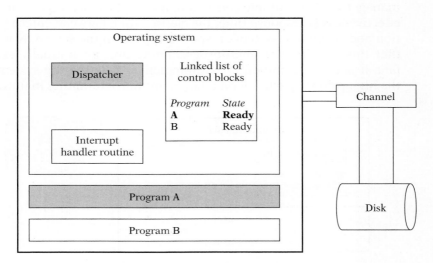

f. The dispatcher selects an application program and starts it.

Queuing and Scheduling

Processor management is concerned with the *internal* priorities of programs already in memory. A program's *external* priority is a different issue. As one program finishes processing and space becomes available, which program is loaded into memory next? This decision typically involves two separate modules, a **queuing routine** and a **scheduler.** As programs enter the system, they are placed on a queue by the queuing routine (Figure 6.16). When space becomes available, the scheduler selects a program from the queue and loads it into memory.

Clearly distinguish between a program's internal and external priorities. Once a program is in memory, the dispatcher uses its *internal* priority to determine its right to access the processor. In contrast, the program's *external* priority has to do with loading it into memory in the first place. Until the program is in memory, it has no internal priority. Once in memory, its external priority is no longer relevant.

◼ Time-Sharing

Time-sharing is a more interactive approach to processor and memory management for multiple concurrent users. The most important measure of effectiveness is response time, the elapsed time between entering a transaction and seeing the system's response appear on the screen. Note, however, that time-sharing and multiprogramming are not mutually exclusive. In fact, it is not uncommon for an interactive, time-sharing system to run in the high priority partition on a large, multiprogramming mainframe.

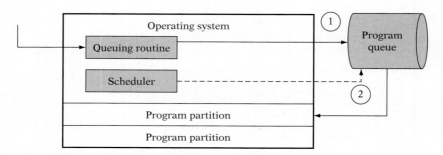

FIGURE 6.16
Queuing and scheduling.

Roll-In/Roll-Out

Picture a typical time-sharing application. A series of brief transactions (single program statements, single lines of input data, single commands) are typed through a keyboard. In most cases, very little actual processing is required to support each transaction. Typing is (relatively speaking) slow, perhaps two transactions per minute.

To the computer, each user represents a string of brief, widely spaced processing demands. Consequently, as a given transaction is processed, the system knows that considerable time will pass before that user's next transaction arrives, so the workspace can be rolled out to secondary storage, making room for another application in memory. Later, when the first user's next transaction arrives, his or her workspace is rolled back in. Most time-sharing systems use such **roll-in/roll-out** techniques to manage memory space.

Time-Slicing

Imagine that you have just spent twenty minutes typing the data for a statistical analysis program. Each line of data was one brief transaction; your work to this point is a typical time-sharing application. Your last transaction is different, however. It is a command that tells the system to process the data, and that command initiates a computational routine that can easily run for several minutes. While your transaction is being processed, the other users on the system will have to wait, and given the objective of maintaining good response time, that is unacceptable.

The solution is **time-slicing.** Each program is restricted to a maximum "slice" of time, perhaps 0.001 second. Once a program begins executing, it runs until one of two things happens. If the program requires input or output before exhausting its time slice, it calls the operating system and "voluntarily" drops into a wait state, much like a multiprogramming application. If, however, the program uses up its entire time slice, a timer interrupt transfers control to the operating system and the time-sharing dispatcher starts the next program.

Polling

Often, a time-shared system uses a **polling** algorithm to determine which program to start next. Imagine a table of program control blocks (Figure 6.17). Starting at the top of the table, the dispatcher checks program 1's status. If program 1 is ready, the dispatcher starts it. If not, program 2's status is checked. Assume that program 2 is ready and the dispatcher starts it.

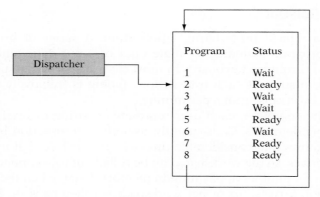

FIGURE 6.17
Some time-sharing dispatchers rely on a polling algorithm.

One time slice later, program 2 is forced to surrender control of the processor. Because the last program executed was number 2, the dispatcher resumes polling with the *third* table entry; note that program 2 is now at the end of the line. Eventually, the dispatcher works its way through the entire table, returns to the top, and repeats the process. Program 2 will get another shot only after every other program has a chance.

There are alternatives to simple round robin polling. Two (or even more) tables can be maintained, with high priority programs on the first one and background or low priority routines on the second. Another option is to place multiple references to a crucial program on the table, thus giving it several shots at the processor on each polling cycle. Some systems use a priority scheme and recompute priorities every second or two. A common priority algorithm is dividing actual run time by elapsed residency time. The limit of this computation is 1, which is considered low priority. The more processor time a program uses, the worse its priority becomes, so compute-bound tasks tend to drop to the end of the line.

■ The Virtual Machine Concept

Start with a full-featured mainframe. Share its resources among several concurrent users. If those users occupy partitions, regions, or workspaces, you have a traditional multiprogramming or time-sharing system.

Now take the idea a step further. Instead of simply allocating each application routine some memory and running it directly under the operating system, simulate several imaginary computers on that **real computer** (Figure 6.18). Assign each **virtual machine** its own virtual operating system and its own virtual peripherals. Traditionally, multiprogramming and time-sharing imply running several *application routines* concurrently. The virtual machine concept calls for multiprogramming or time-sharing at the *operating system* level.

Each virtual machine has its own virtual operating system, its own virtual memory, and its own virtual peripherals. Because all the virtual machines run on the same real computer, their access to facilities is limited only by the facilities of the real machine. Thus, each virtual machine has access to gigabytes of storage and scores of peripherals, and can execute billions of instructions per second. Because they share a single real computer, program development can take place on one virtual machine in interactive mode, while production applications run on another virtual machine under a traditional multiprogramming operating system.

To the user, the virtual machine is *the* computer. The details associated with the real machine are transparent, hidden by the facilities of the "real" operating system. Thus, much as a time-sharing user can ignore other, concurrent users and imagine that he or she directly controls the computer, a virtual machine user can ignore other virtual machines.

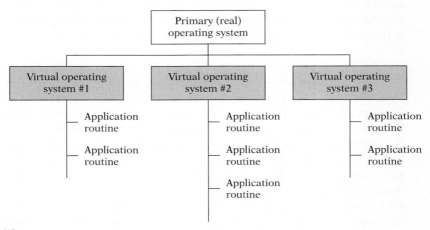

FIGURE 6.18

The virtual machine concept implies multiprogramming at the operating system level.

◼ Peripheral Device Management

In addition to memory and the processor, most computer systems also have numerous peripheral devices, and only a few of those peripherals can be shared by multiple concurrent users. For example, consider a printer. Once you start a print operation, you expect the entire document or report to print contiguously as a single entity, and if output data from some other program is interspersed with your data, the printout is useless. The operating system incorporates routines that manage peripheral device allocation and ensure that device assignments to multiple concurrent applications do not conflict.

Spooling

Imagine a program that generates payroll for 10,000 employees. Printing 10,000 checks takes several minutes. Why not write the checks to disk and print them later, in the background? That way, the memory allocated to the payroll program is freed for another program much more quickly.

That is the essential idea behind **spooling.** Even with multiprogramming, it is common for all application programs to be waiting for I/O. During these idle periods, the operating system's spooling module reads data from such slow devices as terminal keyboards and stores them on a high-speed medium such as disk. Later, when the program is loaded, its input data can be read from high-speed disk. On output, data are spooled to disk and later dumped to the printer during idle periods. Because the application program deals only with high-speed I/O, it finishes processing and thus frees space for another program much more quickly. Because output is spooled before it is printed, the various programs' printouts are kept separate.

Deadlock

Deadlock is one possible consequence of poor resource management. Imagine, for example, that two programs need data from the same disk. Program A issues a seek command and drops into a wait state. Subsequently, program B begins executing and issues its own seek command. Eventually, the first seek operation is completed and the dispatcher starts program A, which issues a read command. Unfortunately, the second seek command has moved the access mechanism, so A must reissue the seek command and once again drop into a wait state. Soon B issues its read command, discovers that the access mechanism is in the wrong place, and reissues its own seek command.

Consider the outcome of this nightmare. Program A positions the access mechanism. Program B moves it. Program A repositions it; program B repositions it again. Picture the access mechanism moving rapidly back and forth across the disk's surface. No data are read or written. Neither program can proceed. The result is deadlock.

Deadlock is not limited to peripheral devices. It happens when two (or more) programs each control any resource needed by the other. Neither program can continue until the other program releases its resource. If neither program is willing to give in, the system, almost literally, "spins its wheels." At best, that leads to inefficiency. At worst, it can bring the entire system to a halt. One solution is prevention; some operating systems will not load a program unless all its resource needs can be guaranteed. Other operating systems allow some deadlocks to occur, sense them, and take corrective action.

▌ Summary

The chapter opened with a brief discussion of various measures of computer system effectiveness. Memory management is concerned with managing the computer's available pool of memory. Some operating system routines directly support application programs as they run and thus must be resident. Other transient routines are stored on disk and read into memory only when needed.

Many modern operating systems support multiple concurrent programs. Fixed-partition memory management divides memory into fixed-length partitions. Greater efficiency can be achieved by using dynamic memory management. Under segmentation, a program is broken into variable-length segments that are independently loaded into noncontiguous memory. Segmented addresses are converted to absolute form through a process called dynamic address translation. Paging is similar to segmentation except that pages are fixed in length. With segmentation *and* paging, programs are broken into logical segments and the segments subdivided into pages. Most operating systems incorporate memory protection features.

With overlay structures, a program is broken into logically independent modules, and only those modules that are actually active are loaded into memory. On a virtual memory system, programs are loaded on the external paging device and individual pages are paged-in to real memory as needed. Virtual memory is a logical model that supports dynamic address translation. If a referenced page is not in real memory, a page fault is recognized and the needed page is swapped in. Excessive paging can lead to thrashing, which degrades system performance.

Multiprogramming is a processor management technique that relies on the speed disparity between a computer and its peripherals. Typically, interrupts mark the beginning and end of each input and output operation. Following an interrupt, the dispatcher finds the highest priority ready state program on a linked list of control blocks and starts it.   When a program first enters a system, it might be stored on a queue by a queuing routine. Later, when space becomes available, a scheduler selects the next program from the queue and loads it into memory. Time-sharing supports multiple concurrent interactive applications using roll-in/roll-out techniques for memory management and time-slicing for processor management. Often, the dispatcher follows a polling algorithm to determine which program to start next. The virtual machine concept calls for multiprogramming or time-sharing at the operating system level.

The operating system incorporates routines that manage peripheral device allocation. With spooling, slow output operations are shifted to the background. Deadlock occurs when two programs each control a resource needed by the other but neither is willing to give up its resource.

▌ Key Words

control block	processor management
deadlock	queuing routine
demand paging	ready state
dispatcher	real computer
dynamic address translation	real memory
dynamic memory management	region
external paging device	resident
fixed-partition memory	roll-in/roll-out
management	scheduler
fragmentation	segmentation
interrupt	segmentation *and* paging
interrupt handler	spooling
memory management	thrashing
memory mapping	time-sharing
memory protection	time-slicing
multiprogramming	transient
page fault	transient area
paging	virtual machine
partition	virtual memory
polling	wait state
pre-paging	

▌ Review Questions

1. Define throughput, turnaround, response time, availability security, reliability, and robustness. Explain why these measures of effectiveness conflict.

2. Distinguish between resident and transient routines. What is the transient area?

3. Distinguish between fixed-partition memory management and dynamic memory management.

4. Segmentation and/or paging can help to minimize fragmentation because programs are loaded into noncontiguous memory. Briefly explain what that means.

5. Distinguish between segmentation and paging. Explain segmentation *and* paging.

6. Explain dynamic address translation.

7. Why is memory protection necessary?

8. What is an overlay structure? Why are overlay structures used?

9. How does a virtual memory system work? Distinguish between virtual memory, the external paging device, and real memory.

10. What is a page fault? Distinguish between demand paging and pre-paging. Explain thrashing.

11. What is multiprogramming?

12. What are control blocks and why are they necessary?

13. What is an interrupt? What is the interrupt handler routine?

14. Explain how a multiprogramming system's dispatcher relies on control blocks and interrupts to manage the processor.

15. Explain how the queuing routine and the scheduler work together to load application programs. Distinguish between a program's internal and external priorities.

16. Distinguish between multiprogramming and time-sharing. Explain roll-in/roll out, time-slicing, and polling.

17. Explain the virtual machine concept.

18. What is spooling? Why is spooling used?

19. What is deadlock? Why is deadlock a problem?

▋ Exercises

1. Why do you suppose there are so many different operating systems?

2. Distinguish between concurrent and simultaneous. A single processor can execute two or more programs concurrently but not simultaneously. Why?

3. A student can concurrently study and watch television, but he or she cannot simultaneously study and watch television. Explain.

4. Overlay structures can be viewed as precursors to modern virtual memory systems. Explain why.

5. During the serial batch era, 24 hours was considered a normal turnaround time. In contrast, modern microcomputer users expect the computer to respond almost instantaneously. Would you consider using a computer if you had to wait 24 hours for feedback? Why, or why not?

6. Most personal computer systems spool printed output. Consequently, you can usually perform other work while your document prints. Explain how spooling makes that possible.

7. Identify several noncomputer examples of the deadlock principle. For example, imagine that you have a CD player, your friend has a favorite CD, and neither one of you is willing to give up your resource. How would you solve that deadlock?

8. Figures 6.9, 6.11, and 6.15a are useful templates for organizing many of this chapter's key terms.

Communicating with the Operating System

This section focuses on the user interfaces for three popular operating systems: MS-DOS (Chapter 7), Windows XP (Chapter 8), and UNIX/Linux (Chapter 9). The material is presented from a user's perspective. Think of the user or the application program as one layer and the operating system as the next lower layer. The interface between them defines the rules for layer-to-layer communication.

CHAPTER 7

MS-DOS Commands

When you finish reading this chapter you should be able to:

▶ Describe the structure of an MS-DOS command.

▶ Set the default drive and format a diskette.

▶ Define a valid MS-DOS file name, including an extension.

▶ Describe the MS-DOS hierarchical directory structure and define a path name.

▶ Use a directory command to view the contents of a directory.

▶ Create a directory.

▶ Distinguish between the root directory and the current working directory, and use a change directory command to change the working directory.

▶ Use copy commands to create a file from the console and to copy an existing file.

▶ Use wild card characters to copy several files with a single operation.

▶ Explain redirection, filters, and pipes.

▉ MS-DOS

Given the availability of Windows and other more intuitive interfaces, **MS-DOS** is rarely used today, so why bother to learn about MS-DOS? Basically, there are two reasons:

1. Windows and other, more sophisticated operating systems sometimes do a bit too much for the user, effectively hiding what is really happening inside the computer. MS-DOS is much more basic and direct. Consequently, if you can understand what is happening in MS-DOS, you may find it easier to understand what is happening in Windows.
2. Should your computer fail or become infected with a virus, many utility and virus protection programs include a special recovery diskette. Often, the recovery diskette uses MS-DOS commands to support the recovery process.

MS-DOS Commands

Typically, a user accesses a computer through an application program's interface and the program communicates with the operating system through an application programming interface (Figure 7.1). At times, however, the user must communicate directly with the operating system to perform such functions as launching a program. This chapter focuses on the MS-DOS user interface.

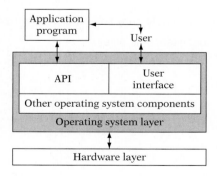

FIGURE 7.1

A user communicates with the operating system through a user interface.

MS-DOS and Microsoft

When IBM entered the personal computer marketplace in the fall of 1981, respon-sibility for creating an operating system was subcontracted to a company named Microsoft recently formed by two young men named Bill Gates and Paul Allen. The result, originally called PC-DOS, was a command-driven operating system that allowed users to issue cryptic, single-line commands through a command inter-face. Rechristened MS-DOS, Gates and Allen's operating system quickly became an industry standard and established a stable platform that served as a launching pad for the personal computer industry. MS-DOS also laid the financial base on which the founders built today's Microsoft.

Under MS-DOS, a user communicates with the operating system by issuing **commands.** The general form of an MS-DOS command is shown in Figure 7.2. The **default drive** and the system **prompt** are displayed by the operating system. The user responds to an active prompt by typing a com-mand name followed by any necessary **parameters.** A **delimiter,** usually a space, separates the command from the parameters and (if there are sev-eral) the parameters from each other.

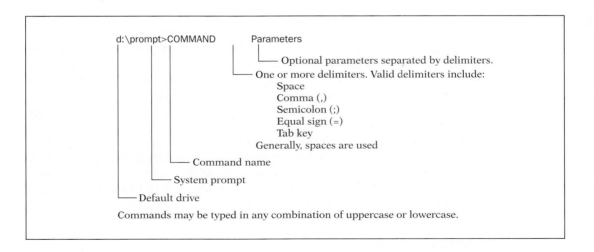

FIGURE 7.2

The general form of an MS-DOS command.

The Chapter Tutorial

This introduction to MS-DOS is presented as a tutorial. Do not simply read it. Instead, find a personal computer that runs Microsoft Windows, open your book, and follow along. As you read about a command, enter it and see for yourself how the computer responds. You will need a blank diskette. Later, you may find Appendix B a useful reference.

MS-DOS error messages tend to be rather cryptic and (often) not very useful. Common mistakes include misspelling a command or file name, failing to type a space between a command and its parameters (or between parameters), and adding extra, unnecessary parameters. If you type a command, press enter, and see an error message, simply retype the command after the next MS-DOS prompt.

◼ Getting Started

The easiest (and safest) way to access MS-DOS through Microsoft Windows is to select the *MS-DOS Prompt* from the *All Programs* or *Programs* menu. Click on the *Start* button. If you are using Windows XP, move the mouse pointer to *All Programs,* then *Accessories*. On the *Accessories* menu, you should find an entry labeled *Command Prompt* (Figure 7.3). On some earlier versions of Windows, the *Accessories* menu entry might read *MS-DOS Prompt,* and you might find the *MS-DOS Prompt* or *Command Prompt* entry on the *All Programs* menu rather than on the *Accessories* sub-menu.

In any event, click on *Command Prompt* or *MS-DOS Prompt* and the initial MS-DOS screen (or window) will appear (Figure 7.4). If you are using Windows XP, the system prompt should read *C:\Documents and Settings\default>*. On earlier versions of Windows, the prompt is likely to read *C:\>* or *C:\Windows>*. The precise wording of the prompt is not significant to the rest of this tutorial.

For future reference, there are at least two other ways to access MS-DOS. One is to boot the system from an MS-DOS system diskette. Alternatively, when you shut down a pre-XP version of Windows, one option on the shut down menu is *Restart,* or *Restart the computer* in MS-DOS mode. Stay with the *Command Prompt* or *MS-DOS Prompt* for now, however.

Selecting the Default Drive

The last line on the screen (Figure 7.4) holds the MS-DOS prompt

```
C:\Documents and Settings\default>
```

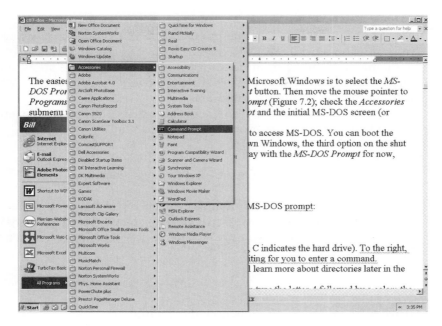

FIGURE 7.3
Accessing the command prompt through the Windows *Start* menu.

FIGURE 7.4
The initial MS-DOS prompt.

The C: indicates that C is the current default drive. (On most systems, C indicates the hard drive.) *Documents and Settings\\default>* (or *Windows>*) is the name of the current directory; you will learn more about directories later in this chapter. The greater than (>) symbol indicates that **MS-DOS** is waiting for you to enter a command.

Insert a blank diskette into the diskette drive. Then type the letter A followed by a colon (:); the prompt line should read

C:\Documents and Settings\default>A:

In this tutorial, sample commands will be typed uppercase, but you can type commands in uppercase, lowercase, or mixed case because **MS-DOS** is not case sensitive. After you press enter, a new prompt will appear (Figure 7.5)

A:\>

Drive A (the diskette drive) is now the default.

Experiment a bit. Type the letter C followed by a colon and the initial C prompt will reappear. Type A: and you'll return to the A:\> prompt.

FIGURE 7.5
Changing the default drive to A.

Generally, type any drive letter followed by a colon and that drive becomes your default drive.

Make sure the prompt reads A:\> before you move on to the next step.

Formatting a Diskette

Later in the chapter you will need a work diskette. Before a diskette can be used, it must be formatted. The formatting process writes a pattern of sectors on the disk surface, records a copy of the boot routine on the first sector, and initializes control information.

The **FORMAT command** (Figure 7.6) is used to format a disk[1]. The simplest form of the command consists of a single word: FORMAT. If you issue such a command, MS-DOS will format the disk in the default drive to that drive's default density (for a diskette, usually 1.44 MB or high density). Several optional parameters are summarized in Figure 7.6. If you type more than one parameter, insert spaces to separate them.

A note of caution: *be careful*. FORMAT is a destructive command. When you format a disk, you erase whatever data might be stored on it. *If your default drive is a hard drive (for example, drive C), do not under any circumstances format that disk.* You could destroy your system.

Before you move on to the next step in this tutorial, make sure your default drive is your diskette drive (usually, drive A). If not, type A: and press the enter key.

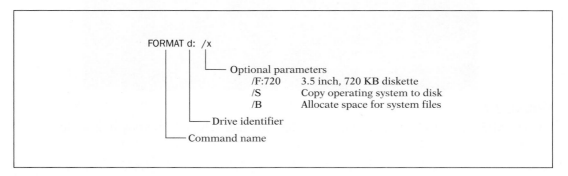

FIGURE 7.6
The FORMAT command.

---

[1]Most diskettes are purchased pre-formatted, so it may be unnecessary to format a new diskette. Using a **FORMAT** command to re-format a previously used diskette is common, however.

Even with the default drive set correctly, it is a good idea to specify the target drive as part of your command. For example, type the command

FORMAT A:

(Figure 7.7). The A: parameter identifies drive A as the target drive. A message will tell you to insert the diskette to be formatted into drive A and press the enter key[2]. After you press enter, a series of messages will track the format routine's progress as it formats the diskette. In response to the *Volume label* prompt you can optionally specify an identifying label that will be

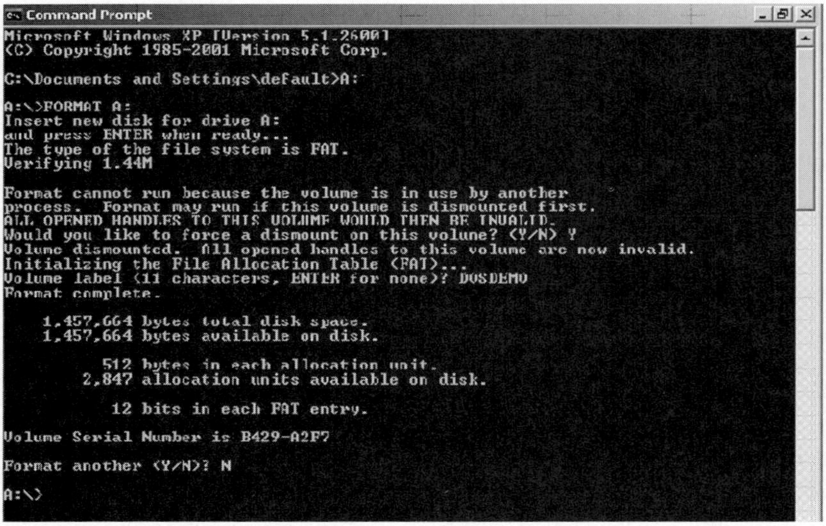

FIGURE 7.7
The FORMAT command guides the user through the process of formatting a diskette.

---

[2]Windows XP users might get a *Format cannot run ...* message, as shown in Figure 7.7. If the message appears, type *Y* and press enter in response to the *... force a dismount ...* query. Users of other versions of Windows should not get this message.

stored electronically on the disk. Type DOSDEMO. The format routine then summarizes the space available on the diskette, assigns a volume serial number, and asks if you would like to format another diskette. Type N (for no) and press the enter key.

◼ The File System

The MS-DOS **file system** allows a user to identify, save, and retrieve files by name. Note that a program is a type of file.

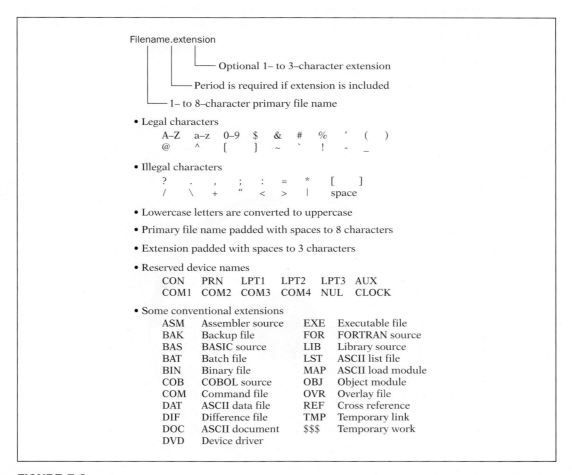

FIGURE 7.8

The rules for defining a file name.

File Names

A **file name** (Figure 7.8) is composed of the name itself and an optional **extension.** The name consists of from 1 to 8 characters. A few file names are reserved by the system, and delimiter characters may not be used in a file name. Otherwise, just about any combination of characters you can type is legal. Incidentally, most Windows users can issue line commands that reference long file names (Chapter 8), but the traditional MS-DOS 8-character limit featured throughout this chapter is valid no matter what version you might be using.

The file name is separated from its optional, 1- to 3-character extension by a period. Some extensions have special meaning to the operating system; they are summarized near the end of Figure 7.8. The extension is sometimes used to identify a version of a program or data file; for example, VITA.1, VITA.2, and so on.

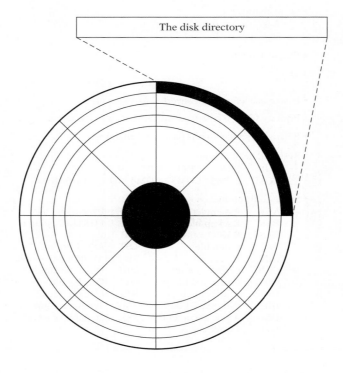

FIGURE 7.9

A file's name and starting address are recorded in the disk directory.

Directories

Directory management is a key MS-DOS file system function. The first time a file is written to disk, its name, disk address, creation date, and other information are recorded in the disk's **directory** (Figure 7.9). Later, when the file is retrieved, the operating system reads the directory and searches it for the file name. When a file is modified, the file system updates its directory entry. When the file is deleted, its directory entry is marked as deleted.

Subdirectories

When a disk is first formatted, a single **root directory** is created by the format routine. Using a single directory is fine for a few files, but as the number of files increases, distinguishing them becomes increasingly difficult.

For example, imagine a work disk that holds several different types of files. To simplify keeping track of the files, MS-DOS allows the user to create special files called **subdirectories.** For example, Figure 7.10 shows the root directory and three subdirectories. LETTERS holds letters and other correspondence. A book's chapters are stored under subdirectory BOOK. Finally spreadsheets are grouped in subdirectory WS. Think of a subdirectory as a file folder that allows you to group related files and thus organize the disk.

Path Names

When subdirectories are used, you need more than a simple file name to find a file. For example, it is possible to have files named PAY stored in two different subdirectories. A reference to PAY would thus be ambiguous—which PAY do you mean?

To fully identify a file you need a complete **path name** (Figure 7.11). For example,

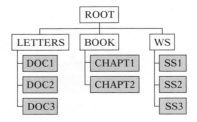

FIGURE 7.10

Subdirectories help to organize the data stored on a disk.

\LETTERS\PAY

and

\WS\PAY

are two different files. The first one is stored in subdirectory LETTERS. The second one is stored in subdirectory WS.

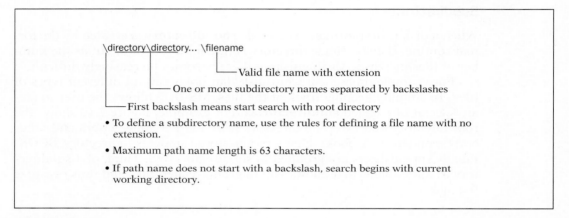

FIGURE 7.11
The rules for defining a path name.

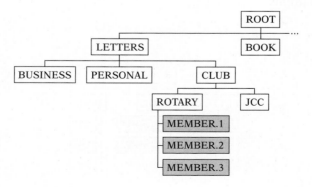

FIGURE 7.12
Directories can be subdivided into lower-level subdirectories.

Study the first path names listed above. The first backslash references the root directory. The second backslash separates the subdirectory name from the file name. The first path name shown above tells MS-DOS to start with the root directory, find a subdirectory named LETTERS, and search the subdirectory for a file named PAY. The second path name tells MS-DOS to start with the root directory, find a subdirectory named WS, and search the subdirectory for a file named PAY.

It is possible to divide a subdirectory into lower-level subdirectories. For example, Figure 7.12 shows LETTERS broken into three subdirectories. One, CLUB, is further subdivided into ROTARY and JCC. To retrieve a document named MEMBER.3 from the ROTARY subdirectory, the path name would be

\LETTERS\CLUB\ROTARY\MEMBER.3

Note how the path name leads from directory to directory until you reach the desired file.

At first glance, subdirectories may seem to complicate rather than simplify the task of accessing files. In practice, however, people rarely use such lengthy path names. Instead, they select a working directory and allow the operating system to keep track of the subdirectories needed to complete a path name. Later in the chapter you will learn how to select a working directory.

The Backslash

Why did Microsoft decide to use a backslash (\) as a separator in an MS-DOS path name? A good way to answer that question is with another question: When is the last time you typed a backslash other than in a path name? Simply put, the backslash character is almost never used, so adopting it as a path name field separator was unlikely to create confusion.

Viewing a Directory

Before you begin creating and manipulating directories, it might be wise to look through an existing one. Following the A-prompt, type

C:

and press the enter key. The new prompt (Figure 7.13) should read

FIGURE 7.13
Make the C drive your default drive.

> C:\Documents and Settings\default>

or

> C:\Windows>

It tells you that drive C is your default drive and it identifies the **current directory.**

No matter what the default directory, all versions of Windows contain a directory named *Windows* that holds numerous system files. To list the contents of the *Windows* directory, type a **directory (DIR) command** (Figure 7.14).

> DIR \WINDOWS

Figure 7.13 shows the command as typed. DIR is the command name and \WINDOWS (note the initial backslash) is the path name of the *Windows* directory. Press the enter key, and a list of file names and other information will scroll rapidly across your screen[3]. Figure 7.15 shows the last screen followed by a new prompt.

---

[3]If necessary, ask your instructor to help you find the WINDOWS directory on your system.

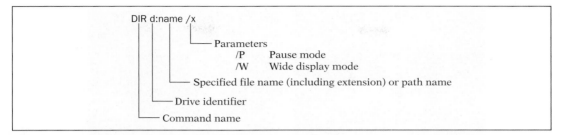

FIGURE 7.14
The directory (DIR) command displays a directory's contents.

As entered, the directory command was not very useful because the list of files in directory Windows is much too big to fit on a single screen. Try adding a pause parameter. Type the command

DIR \WINDOWS /P

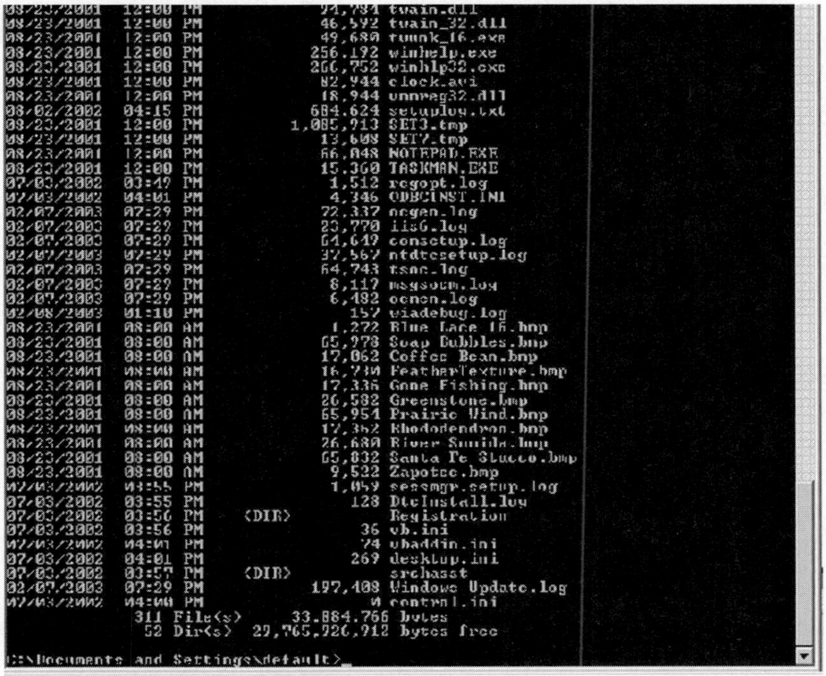

FIGURE 7.15
The last page of a directory list.

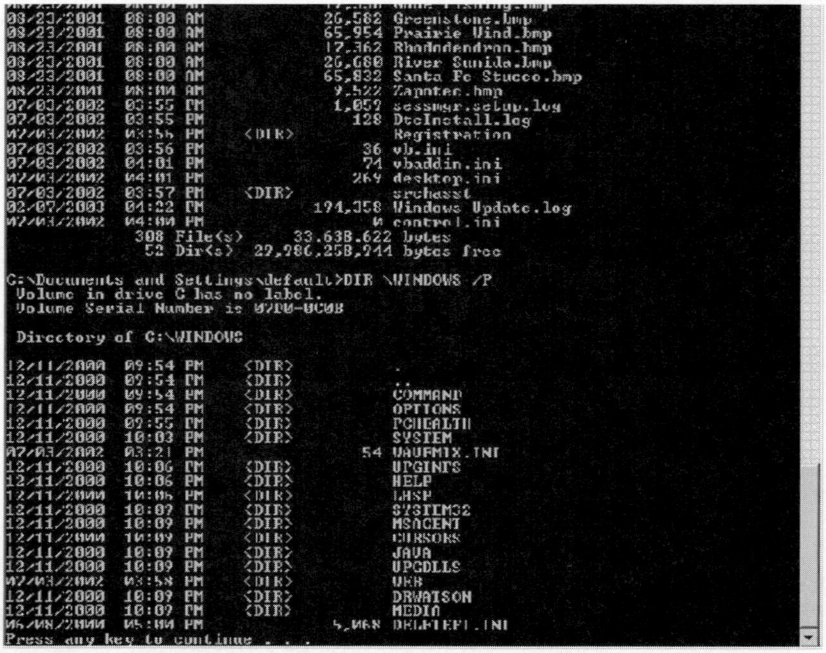

FIGURE 7.16

A directory command with a pause option.

A space separates the command from the parameter, and the slash is a regular slash, not a backslash. Press the enter key, and a single page of information will appear on your screen (Figure 7.16). Reading from left to right, each Windows XP line displays a file's creation date and time, either <DIR> (for a directory) or the file length, and the file name. On non-XP versions of Windows, the file name comes first.

The last line on Figure 7.16 reads *Press any key to continue*. Press the space bar, and a new screen of file names will appear. Continue pressing the space bar to step through the directory one screen at a time.

The wide mode display is another useful option. When the next prompt appears, type the command

DIR \WINDOWS /W

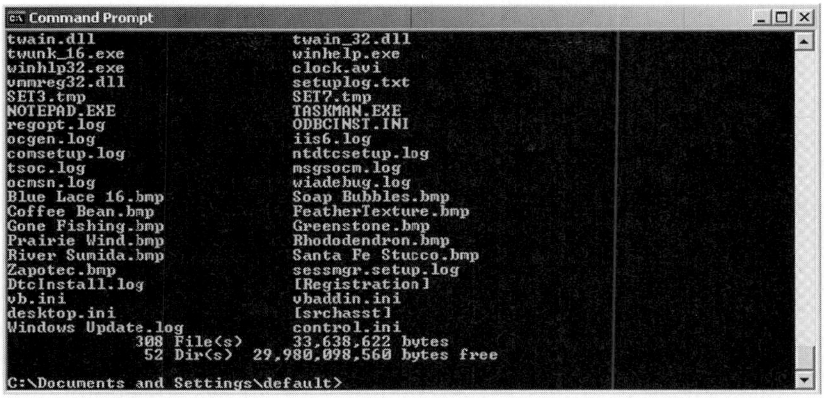

FIGURE 7.17
A wide mode directory list.

and press enter. The resulting screen (Figure 7.17) lists only file names, two across on Windows XP and between two and five across on earlier versions of Windows. The *Windows* directory contains so many files that not even a wide mode list will fit on a single screen.

Creating Directories

Before you move on to the next task, make sure the diskette you formatted is in the drive. Then change your default drive back to the diskette drive by typing

A:

and pressing enter. You are about to create three new directories and several files on your diskette.

Use the **make directory (MKDIR, or MD) command** (Figure 7.18) to create a directory. For example, type the command

MKDIR \LETTERS

(Figure 7.19) and press enter. The backslash indicates that LETTERS is a subdirectory of the root directory. Use similar MKDIR commands to create

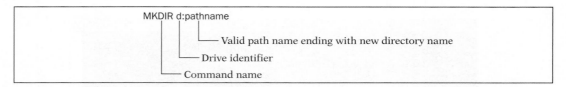

FIGURE 7.18

The make directory (MKDIR) command creates a new directory.

two more directories: BOOK and WS. When you finish creating the directories, type a DIR command with no parameters. A DIR command with no parameters will list the contents of the current directory, which is your diskette's root directory. As Figure 7.19 shows, three subdirectories have been added to the diskette's root directory.

A MKDIR command is used to create a subdirectory. To remove or delete a directory, issue a remove directory (RMDIR, or RD) command.

Creating Files

Most files are created by application programs such as a word processor, a spreadsheet, a database manager, and so on, but you can also copy an existing file. When MS-DOS carries out a **COPY command** (Figure 7.20), it reads the file specified in the first parameter (the source file) and copies it to the file specified in the second parameter (the destination file).

A simple way to create a short file is to copy it from the console (your system's keyboard and display). For example, type the command

```
Command Prompt                                              _ □ ×

C:\Documents and Settings\default>A:

A:\>MKDIR LETTERS

A:\>MKDIR BOOK

A:\>MKDIR WS

A:\>DIR
 Volume in drive A is DOSDEMO
 Volume Serial Number is 7C50-C9BD

 Directory of A:\

02/07/2003  04:37 PM    <DIR>          LETTERS
02/07/2003  04:37 PM    <DIR>          BOOK
02/07/2003  04:37 PM    <DIR>          WS
               0 File(s)              0 bytes
               3 Dir(s)       1,456,128 bytes free

A:\>_
```

FIGURE 7.19

The commands to create and list three subdirectories.

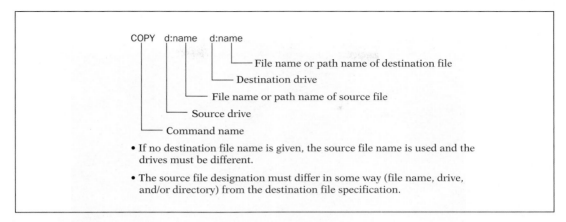

FIGURE 7.20
The COPY command copies one or more files from a source to a destination.

COPY CON A:\LETTERS\JIM

(Figure 7.21). The first (source) file name, CON, stands for the console. The second (destination) file name specifies a path name. (Read the command from left to right.) The destination file will be stored on drive A, subdirectory LETTERS and assigned the file name JIM.

If you haven't already done so, press enter to issue the COPY command. The cursor will appear directly under the command line (you will see no prompt). At this point you can type whatever you want. (If you'd like your file's

```
A:\>COPY CON A:\LETTERS\JIM
Looking forward to spring break!
Will I see you in Florida?
^Z
        1 file(s) copied.

A:\>COPY CON A:\LETTERS\SALLY
Sorry, Jim.
I'm going skiing in Utah!
^Z
        1 file(s) copied.

A:\>COPY CON A:\LETTERS\TOM
Note:
Math assignment.
Chapter 8, problems 10-14.
^Z
        1 file(s) copied.

A:\>
```

FIGURE 7.21
Copy these three files from the console to directory LETTERS.

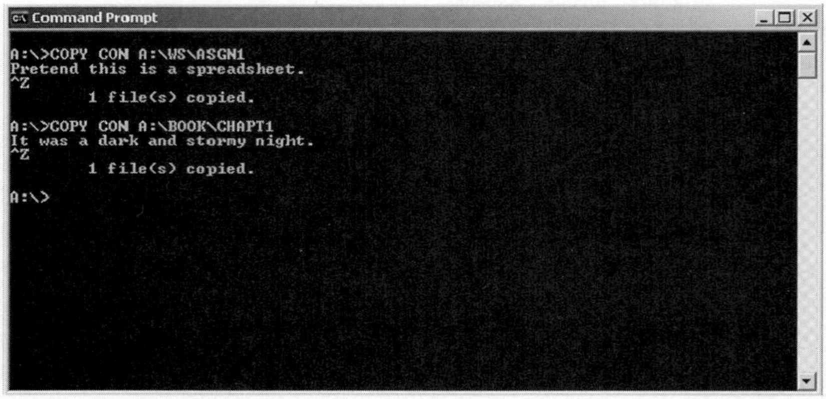

FIGURE 7.22
Copy this pretend spreadsheet to WS and this opening sentence to BOOK.

contents to match subsequent examples, refer to Figure 7.21 and type what you see.) When you reach the end of a line, press the enter key. When you have typed all your lines, press function key F6 or simultaneously press *ctrl-Z* (either generates the COPY command's sentinel value) and then press enter.

Copy the three files you see in Figure 7.21 (or substitute your own content) to directory LETTERS. Then refer to Figure 7.22, copy a line that represents a pretend spreadsheet to directory WS, and copy the first line of Chapter 1 to directory BOOK.

Changing Directories

Now that your diskette holds some directories and files, investigate it. Start by typing the command

DIR A:

and pressing enter. Only the three directories (the contents of the root directory) are listed (Figure 7.23). To view the contents of the LETTERS directory, type

DIR A:\LETTERS

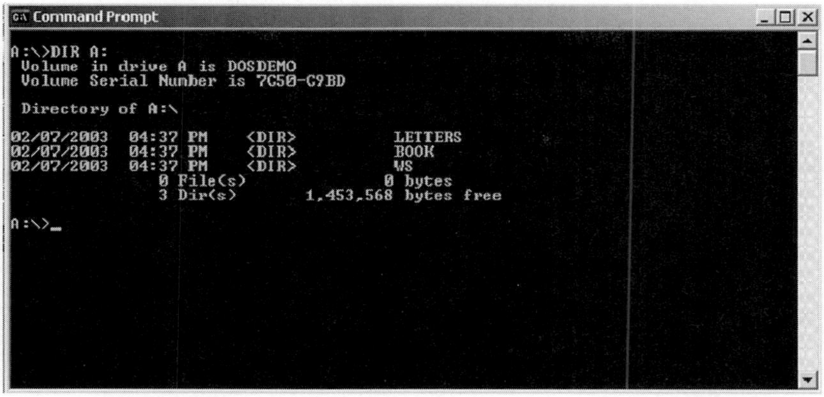

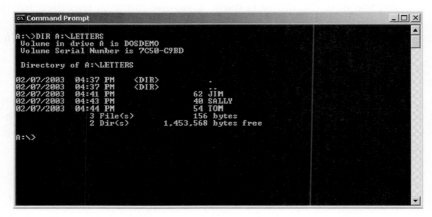

FIGURE 7.23
Your diskette's root directory.

and press enter. Note that the three files you just created are listed (Figure 7.24).

Look carefully at Figure 7.24. Directory LETTERS contains two unusual files: (**.**) and (**..**). The single dot refers to the directory itself. The double dot is a reference to its parent, in this case, the root directory.

The root directory is the current **working directory.** To shift to a different working directory, type a **change directory (CHDIR,** or **CD) command** (Figure 7.25)

FIGURE 7.24
The contents of subdirectory LETTERS.

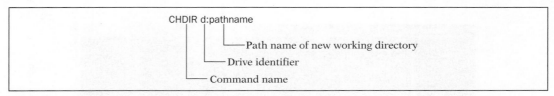

FIGURE 7.25
Use a change directory command to change the working directory.

CHDIR A:\LETTERS

and press enter. Then type the command

DIR A:

with no parameters and press enter again. The output should match Figure 7.24. If no directory is specified, MS-DOS assumes the current working directory. The change directory command allows you to specify a new working directory.

Manipulating Files

Earlier, you copied some text from the console to create a file on diskette. More generally, any existing file can be copied. The COPY command's first parameter specifies a source file and its second parameter specifies a destination file. If drive designators are prefixed to a parameter, a file on one disk can be copied to another. If a file name is specified for the destination file, the new file name is used. If no file name is specified for the destination file, the source file name is used.

For example, make sure your diskette is in the drive and type the command

COPY A:\LETTERS\TOM A:\LETTERS\TAMMY

(Figure 7.26). Note that a space separates the two parameters. Press the enter key. MS-DOS will read the file named TOM from the LETTERS directory on drive A, make a copy, and store the new copy on the LETTERS directory.

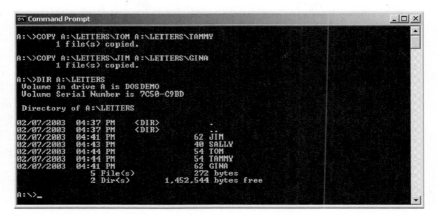

FIGURE 7.26
Some copy commands.

Wild Card Characters

Consider a few generic examples before you resume the tutorial. Special **wild card** characters allow a user to generalize the parameters. A question mark (?) represents any single character; for example, the file name

TERM.?

identifies TERM.1, TERM.2, TERM.C, and any other file named TERM with a 1-character extension. An asterisk (*) represents multiple characters; for example,

TERM.*

stands for every file named TERM with a 1-, 2-, or 3-character extension, including TERM.1, TERM.V6, and TERM.ABC.

Imagine you have been working on a BASIC program named MYPGM. By convention, your source module uses the extension BAS and your object module uses the extension OBJ. You want to copy both. You can, of course, issue two COPY commands, but you can copy both with a single command if you reference MYPGM.* or MYPGM.??? as your source file. Seeing the wild card characters, MS-DOS will look for all files that fit, so the single COPY command

COPY MYPGM.* A:\PROGRAMS

(which you should not issue) will copy both **MYPGM.BAS** and **MYPGM.OBJ** to a subdirectory named **PROGRAMS** on the A drive using the source file names.

Consider one more example before you resume the tutorial. Wild card characters are particularly useful for making backup copies of selected files or an entire disk. For example, the command

COPY C:\PAYROLL*.* A:

(which you should not issue) copies all the files from a directory named **PAY-ROLL** on the C drive to the diskette in the A drive. Similarly, the command

COPY C:\PROGRAMS*.BAS A:

(which you should not issue) copies all the files with the extension **BAS** from a directory named **PROGRAMS** on the C drive to the diskette in the A drive.

Now, back to the tutorial. Type the command

COPY A:\LETTERS\JIM A:\LETTERS\GINA

(Figure 7.26) and press enter. MS-DOS will retrieve a copy of the file named JIM from subdirectory LETTERS, rename it GINA, and store the copy on subdirectory LETTERS. To verify the copy operation, type the directory command

DIR A:\LETTERS

and press enter. Note the file named GINA on Figure 7.26. (You created the file named TAMMY earlier.)

Next, type the command

COPY A:\LETTERS\T* A:\WS

and press enter. It copies every file on subdirectory LETTERS that begins with the letter T to the directory named WS. To verify the copy operation, type the directory command

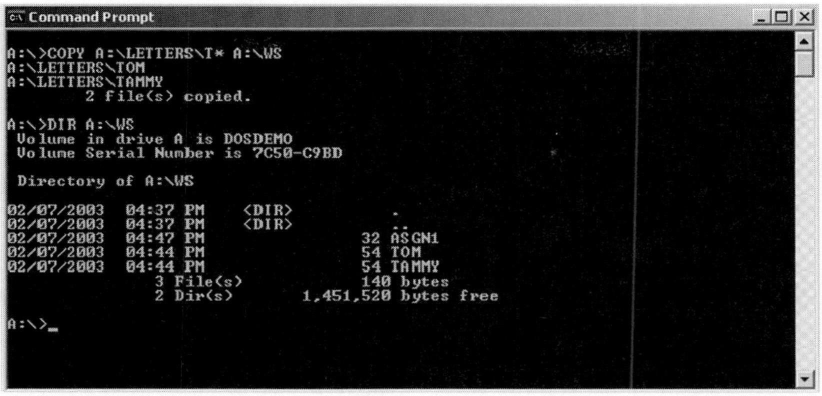

FIGURE 7.27

This copy command uses wild card characters.

DIR A:\WS

and press enter. As you can see in Figure 7.27, files named TOM and TAMMY have been stored on subdirectory WS.

Incidentally, many people who learned MS-DOS in the pre-Windows era still switch to the command prompt to take advantage of wild card characters for certain file manipulation tasks. Wild cards are very useful.

Batch Files

A **batch file** is a file of precoded MS-DOS commands. You can assign any file name to a batch file, but the extension must be .BAT. If you type the batch file's name and press enter, MS-DOS will execute the commands in sequence. For example, if it exists, a file named AUTOEXEC.BAT is automatically executed each time the system is booted.

Program Files

A program is a special type of file. By convention, executable programs are assigned the extension COM or EXE. To load and execute a program, simply type its file name (with or without its extension) as though it was a command. If no extension is given, MS-DOS will look for a command with the specified file name and a .COM extension, then search for a .EXE file, and finally for a .BAT file.

▪ Pipes, Filters, and Redirection

Many MS-DOS commands assume a standard input or output device; for example, by default the directory command sends its output to the screen. By using **redirection** parameters (Figure 7.28) the user can change those defaults. For example, the command

DIR > PRN

sends the output directory listing to the printer instead of to the display screen.

Parameter	Meaning	Example
<	Change source to a specified device or file	<MYFILE.DAT
>	Change destination to a specified device or file	>PRN
>>	Change destination (usually) to an existing file and append output to it.	>>HOLD.DAT
|	Pipe standard output to another command or to a filter	DIR | MORE

FIGURE 7.28
Many MS-DOS commands and filters utilize the standard input and output devices. Redirection parameters allow a user to change to a specified file or device.

A **filter** is a special type of command. It accepts input from the standard input device, modifies (or filters) the data in some way, and sends the results to the standard output device. For example, the SORT filter, (Figure 7.29) accepts data from the keyboard, sorts the data into alphabetical or numerical sequence, and outputs the sorted data to the screen. You can add

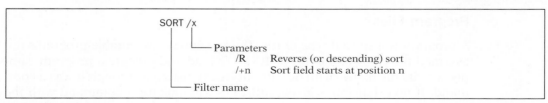

FIGURE 7.29
The SORT filter.

redirection parameters to override or change the standard input device, output device, or both.

For example, consider the command

SORT <A:\LETTERS\JIM

Because of the redirection parameter (<), this SORT filter accepts its input from the file named JIM. The output, the lines of text that you typed when you created JIM sorted into alphabetical order, should appear on your screen[4]. For future reference, to sort and store the output on a different file, code something like

SORT <MYFILE >RESULT

Note that both source and destination redirection parameters are included.

MORE is another useful filter (Figure 7.30). It sends output to the terminal one screen at a time. MORE is often used with pipes. A **pipe** causes one command's standard output to be used as the standard input to another command. Pipes are designated by a vertical line (|); you will find this character on the right of most alphanumeric keyboards, often just below the *Backspace* key.

For example, type

C:

and press enter to make drive C your default drive. Then type

DIR /WINDOWS

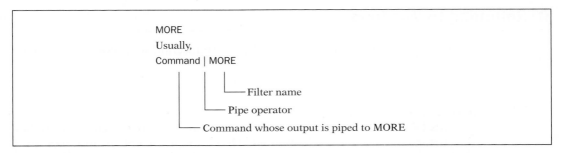

FIGURE 7.30
The MORE filter.

---

[4]The SORT filter may not be supported by all versions of Windows

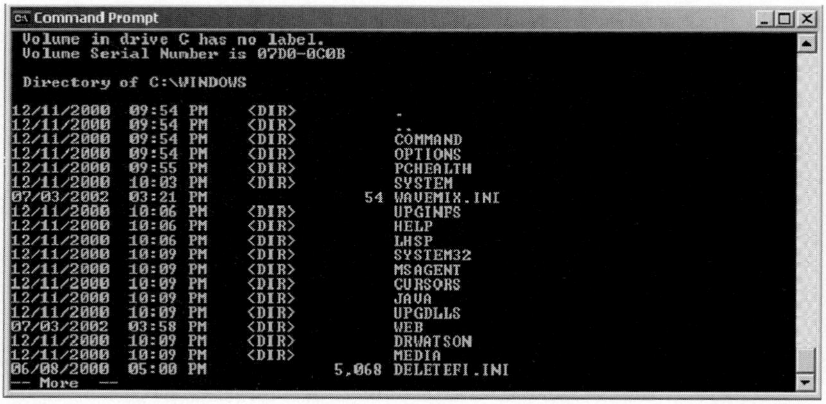

```
Command Prompt                                          _ □ X
Volume in drive C has no label.
Volume Serial Number is 07D0-0C0B

Directory of C:\WINDOWS

12/11/2000  09:54 PM    <DIR>          .
12/11/2000  09:54 PM    <DIR>          ..
12/11/2000  09:54 PM    <DIR>          COMMAND
12/11/2000  09:54 PM    <DIR>          OPTIONS
12/11/2000  09:55 PM    <DIR>          PCHEALTH
12/11/2000  10:03 PM    <DIR>          SYSTEM
07/03/2002  03:21 PM              54   WAVEMIX.INI
12/11/2000  10:06 PM    <DIR>          UPGINFS
12/11/2000  10:06 PM    <DIR>          HELP
12/11/2000  10:06 PM    <DIR>          LHSP
12/11/2000  10:09 PM    <DIR>          SYSTEM32
12/11/2000  10:09 PM    <DIR>          MSAGENT
12/11/2000  10:09 PM    <DIR>          CURSORS
12/11/2000  10:09 PM    <DIR>          JAVA
12/11/2000  10:09 PM    <DIR>          UPGDLLS
07/03/2002  03:58 PM    <DIR>          WEB
12/11/2000  10:09 PM    <DIR>          DRWATSON
12/11/2000  10:09 PM    <DIR>          MEDIA
06/08/2000  05:00 PM           5,068   DELETEFI.INI
-- More  --
```

FIGURE 7.31

The MORE filter displays data one screen at a time.

Press enter and watch the file names scroll by too quickly to read. Now type the command

DIR /WINDOWS | MORE

The directory command's standard output will be routed to the **MORE** filter rather than directly to the screen. The filter will display one screen and then wait until you press the enter key before it displays the next screen (Figure 7.31).

▇ Returning to Windows

That completes the chapter tutorial. To return to Windows, type the command

EXIT

and press the enter key.

MS-DOS is a powerful operating system and you have barely scratched the surface of its command language. However, given a clear understanding of the commands in this brief tutorial, you should be able to read a reference manual and determine how to use additional commands on your own.

◗ Summary

MS-DOS is a command-driven operating system that allows users to issue cryptic, single-line commands through a command interface. The default drive and the system prompt are displayed by the operating system. The user types a command name followed by necessary parameters.

You can access MS-DOS or the command prompt through Microsoft Windows. The FORMAT command is used to format a disk. The MS-DOS file system allows a user to identify, save, and retrieve files by name. Directory management is a key function of the MS-DOS file system. When a disk is first formatted, a single root directory is created by the format routine. When subdirectories are used, you need a complete path name to fully identify a file.

The system prompt identifies the default drive and the current working directory. To list the contents of a directory, type a directory (DIR) command. Use the make directory (MKDIR, MD) command to create a directory. To shift to a different working directory, type a change directory (CHDIR, CD) command.

Use a COPY command to copy an existing file. When you issue a COPY command, special wild card characters allow a user to generalize the parameters and copy several files with a single operation. A batch file is a file of precoded MS-DOS commands. A program is a special type of file.

Many MS-DOS commands assume a standard input or output device. By using redirection parameters the user can change those defaults. A filter accepts input from the standard input device, modifies (or filters) the data in some way, and sends the results to the standard output device. A pipe causes one command's standard output to be used as the standard input to another command. To return to Windows from the MS-DOS prompt, type the command EXIT.

◗ Key Words

batch file
change directory (CHDIR, CD)
     command
command
COPY command
current directory
default drive
delimiter
directory
directory (DIR) command
extension
file name
file system
filter

FORMAT command
make directory (MKDIR, MD) command
MS-DOS
parameters
path name
pipe
prompt
redirection
root directory
subdirectory
wild card
working directory

◼ Review Questions

1. Given that Microsoft Windows has largely supplanted MS-DOS, why is it still useful to learn about MS-DOS commands?

2. Describe the general structure of an MS-DOS command. What are parameters? What are delimiters?

3. What is the significance of the default drive? How do you set the default drive?

4. Why must a disk be formatted before use?

5. Briefly describe the rules for defining a file name. What is the significance of the file name extension?

6. Briefly describe a hierarchical directory structure. What advantages does a hierarchical directory structure offer over using a single directory to hold all files?

7. Distinguish between a path name and a file name.

8. What is the purpose of a directory command?

9. Distinguish between a directory and a file. How are they similar? How are they different?

10. Briefly explain how to use a copy command to create a file and enter the data from the keyboard.

11. Distinguish between the root directory and the current working directory.

12. What are wild card characters? Why are they useful? Why can they not be part of a file's legal name?

13. What is a batch file? Why are batch files useful?

14. Explain redirection.

15. What are filters? What are pipes? Explain how they work together.

◼ Exercises

1. If you have not already done so, work through the chapter tutorial.

2. Create a set of directories to help keep track of your data files or programs. Add your existing files to the new directory structure by copying them.

3. MS-DOS established Microsoft as an industry leader, and Windows solidified the company's status as the owner of the de facto personal computer operating system standard. In your opinion, was that a good thing or a bad thing?

4. Do some research into the origin of MS-DOS and write a paper based on your results. You'll find appropriate material in numerous sources.

5. The most effective way to learn this chapter's key terms is to complete the chapter tutorial.

The Microsoft Windows User Interface

When you finish reading this chapter you should be able to:

▶ Describe the standard Windows desktop.

▶ Identify two ways to execute a program under Windows and explain how to switch between active programs.

▶ Maximize, minimize, and restore a window to its original size.

▶ Exit a program and shut down Windows.

▶ Describe the functions performed by the Windows file system.

▶ Distinguish between a regular file name and a long file name.

▶ Distinguish between the *My Computer* and *Explorer* views.

▶ Copy and rename a file. Copy multiple files. Copy an entire folder.

▶ Search for a file by name, by type, or by contents.

▶ Explain how the recycle bin allows you to recover a file you deleted by accident.

Windows XP

Typically, a user accesses a computer through an application program and the application logic communicates with the operating system through an application programming interface. At times, however, it is necessary to communicate directly with the operating system to perform such functions as launching a program. This chapter presents an overview of the Microsoft **Windows XP** graphical user interface (GUI) (Figure 8.1). The Windows XP GUI incorporates a command line shell comparable to the MS-DOS user interface (Chapter 7).

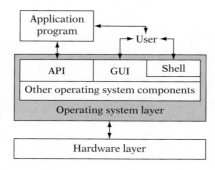

FIGURE 8.1

The standard Windows XP user interface is a GUI.

The Graphical User Interface

By most accounts, the first operational graphical user interface (GUI) was developed at Xerox Corporation's Palo Alto Research Center (PARC) in the 1970s, but Xerox was unable to convert the research into a marketable product. The first widely available computer that featured a GUI was Apple's Lisa, which reached the marketplace in 1983. Lisa faded quickly, but Apple's Macintosh platform proved a breakout product, effectively defining the look and feel of a modern GUI. Perhaps you have seen the company's famous "Big Brother" advertisement that was featured during the 1984 Super Bowl. Microsoft responded with its own GUI, Windows 1.0, a shell that ran as a separate layer on top of MS-DOS, but Windows didn't really catch on until Release 3.1 hit the market in 1992. Today, Windows is by far the dominant personal computer operating system. Apple's OS X is a significant competitor, but the Macintosh is a proprietary platform, which limits its potential market.

If possible, read this material while sitting in front of a computer and following along with the chapter tutorial. The screen captures were created using Windows XP Professional version running on an HP Pavilion computer, so your screens might not precisely match the text figures even if you are using XP. Although the screens will look different, you should be able to complete much of the tutorial using Windows 95, 98, ME, or 2000.

The User Interface

The standard Windows user interface is called the **desktop** (Figure 8.2). A single *Recycle Bin* **icon** that represents a subdirectory or folder that holds deleted files is displayed at the bottom right of the default desktop. However, users typically customize their desktops by adding icons for programs and files they access frequently. For example, the icons at the top left of Figure 8.2 represent *Internet Explorer*, a browser program, and the *Hummingbird Neighborhood*, a network frequently accessed by one of the authors.

Three key elements are found at the bottom of the desktop: the Start button, the taskbar, and the notification area. The ***Start*** **button** allows you to access a series of menus that lead to your system's application programs, key data folders, and numerous support functions. The **taskbar** holds a button for each currently active program. The **notification area** displays

Start button   Taskbar   Notification area

FIGURE 8.2
The desktop interface.

important information such as the current time. When an event such as the arrival of an e-mail message occurs, Windows notifies you by placing the appropriate icon in notification area.

The desktop is manipulated by using a mouse. Moving the mouse pointer (typically an arrow) to touch an icon or button is called pointing. If you point to an item and click the left mouse button you select that item; for example, if you click on *Start,* the *Start* menu appears (Figure 8.3). On the *Start* menu, frequently used programs are listed on the left side and frequently used folders (such as *My Documents*) are listed on the right side. Near the bottom of the right column are a Hewlett-Packard logo and a brief message asking the user to *Keep in touch with HP*. If you are not running an HP computer, you might see a different computer manufacture's logo or nothing at all in that space.

Launching or Starting a Program

Perhaps the easiest way to launch or start a program whose icon appears on the desktop is to double click the icon (point to the icon and rapidly click the left mouse button twice). For example, if the *Internet Explorer* icon appears on your desktop, double click it[1]. If you are not connected to the Internet, you might get a warning that the Web page is unavailable while offline. Respond by clicking *Stay Offline*.

Another way to start a program is from the Start menu (Figure 8.3). For example, if the *Internet Explorer* icon is not on your desktop look for *Internet Explorer* near the top left of the Start menu and click on it. More generally, to launch any program from the *Start* menu, click *All Programs* (lower left) and then select the program from the *All Programs* **menu** (Figure 8.4). The *All Programs* menu is organized hierarchically, so the program you need might be hidden within a submenu. Look for an arrow to the right of an All Programs menu item, point to that item, and the submenu will open. For example, *Notepad,* a text editor, is listed in a submenu of *Accessories*. To start *Notepad,* click the sequence *Start/All Programs/Accessories/Notepad*. Try it.

---

[1] If the icon is not on your desktop, you'll learn how to launch Internet Explorer in the next paragraph.

Later in this chapter, you will learn that you can also start a program by clicking on its taskbar button, searching for it using *Explorer* or *My Computer,* or issuing a command in MS-DOS mode. Additionally, if you double click most data file icons, the appropriate program will open; for example, if you double click a Word document icon, Word will open. Although some methods are better suited for certain tasks, how you choose to launch your programs is largely up to you.

FIGURE 8.3

The *Start* menu.

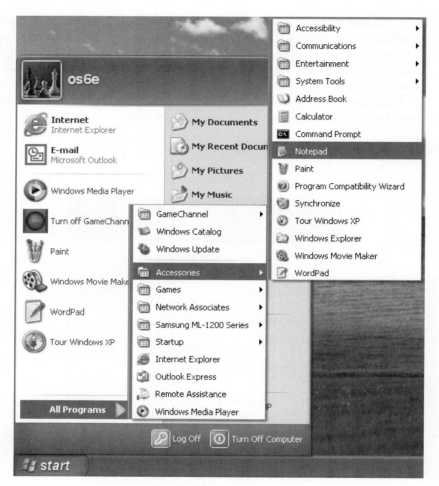

FIGURE 8.4
The *Start/All Programs* menu.

Switching Between Active Programs

At this point you should have two active programs: *Internet Explorer* and *Notepad*. (If you don't, go back to the previous paragraph.) Note that icons for both programs appear on the taskbar. To switch between them, simply click the taskbar icon that represents the program you want to run. Since *Notepad* was the last program you launched, it is probably the one you see on your screen. To switch to *Internet Explorer,* click the *Internet Explorer* taskbar icon. Running two or more programs concurrently is called **multitasking**.

Maximizing and Minimizing a Window

Each active program runs in its own **window.** You can enlarge a window to occupy the entire screen by clicking on the *maximize* button (the middle or square button) at the window's upper right (Figure 8.5). Once a window is maximized, the *maximize* button is replaced by the *restore down* button (two overlapping squares). If you click on *restore down* the window will return to its original size. You can also minimize a window by clicking on the *minimize* button (the leftmost or -sign button). When you minimize a window, it disappears from the screen but its icon remains on the taskbar.

The Menu Bar

If you haven't already done so, minimize *Notepad* and maximize *Internet Explorer.* Note the **menu bar** at the top left of the window (Figure 8.6). To open any menu, click on the appropriate key word. For example, click on *File* and the *File* menu drops down. You have probably accessed similar menus in a word processing or spreadsheet program.

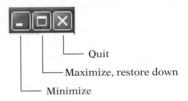

FIGURE 8.5

The maximize, minimize, and quit buttons.

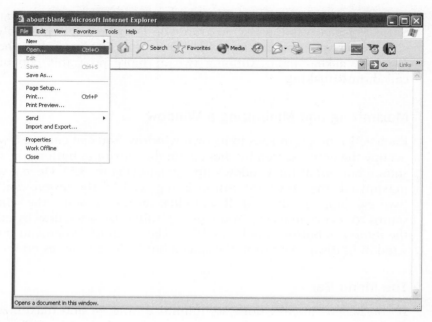

FIGURE 8.6

Selecting an entry on the menu bar pulls down a menu.

Quitting a Program

You can quit a program by opening the *File* menu and selecting *Exit* or by clicking on the *X* button (the rightmost button) at the window's upper right.

Look and Feel

You may have noticed that the drop down menus accessed from the menu bar in *Excel, Internet Explorer, Outlook, PowerPoint, Word,* and many other application programs are virtually identical. Such consistency is enabled by implementing the underlying menu functions in the Windows operating system rather than in the individual application programs. The result is a highly predictable interface in which the distinction between *Save* and *Save as* or *Cut* and *Copy* is clearly defined no matter what application program you might be using. Implementing common or shared functions in the operating system contributes to a consistent look and feel across applications. That consistency helps to reduce errors and simplifies the task of learning a new application.

For example, *Internet Explorer* should be the active program. (If not, click on its taskbar icon to activate it.) Close *Internet Explorer* by clicking on its close (X) button. Then activate *Notepad,* pull down its *File* menu, and click on *Exit* to close *Notepad*.

Shutting Down

When you are finished working on your computer, you normally shut it down[2]. Although you should not shut down now because the tutorial is just getting started, you might find it necessary to quit before you finish the chapter. For future reference, the process is simple. Click on *Start*. Then click *Turn off Computer*. A window should open listing your options. For now (if you already started the process) click the *Cancel* button at the lower right. Normally you click *Turn off*. You might be prompted to save your work in other active programs. Eventually, either your computer shuts down or a message appears informing you that you can safely exit the system.

▪ Working with the Windows File System

The Windows **file system** allows a user to identify, save, and retrieve files by name. (A program is a type of file). The file allocation table is a table maintained by Windows XP to identify the disk segments occupied by the various files. Windows XP supports three different file systems. FAT was the original MS-DOS file system and it works well for small disks up to 2GB in size. FAT32 is an enhancement of FAT that allocates the disk space in smaller units, creating a more efficient file system. NTFS not only manages files, handles large disk spaces, and so on, but also incorporates additional robustness features required by corporations and businesses.

At this point, you need not worry about which file system your computer uses because your operating system will automatically default to the correct one. You will learn more about FAT in Chapter 11 and FAT32 and NTFS in Chapter 12.

---

[2]*Note:* In many microcomputer labs, students never shut down the computer. Check with your instructor.

Formatting a Diskette

Later in the chapter you will need a work diskette, and before a diskette can be used, it must be formatted³. The formatting process writes a pattern of sectors on the diskette surface, may record a copy of the boot routine on the first sector, and initializes control information. A boot routine contains instructions that are read automatically on startup. Those instructions, in turn, read the rest of the operating system into memory.

Please be careful before you carry out the instructions in the next paragraph because the format operation is a destructive command; it erases all the data on the disk. In particular, make sure that you do *not* try to format your C drive.

To **format** a diskette, insert a blank diskette into the diskette drive (usually drive A). Click *Start/My Computer*. Right click (click the *right* mouse button) on the *3 1/2 Floppy* (A:) icon and then click *Format* (Figure 8.7). A

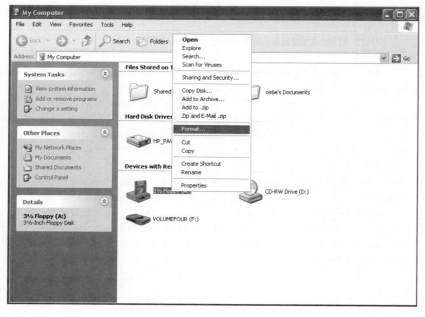

FIGURE 8.7

Using *My Computer* to format a diskette.

---

³Most diskettes are purchased preformatted, but reformatting does not hurt anything. The formatting process is useful for reinitializing a previously used diskette.

window will open (Figure 8.8). Type a *volume label* (such as the word CLASS) in the Volume label subwindow and click on Start. The system will respond by formatting your diskette to the drive's default capacity at 512 bytes per sector. (You might have to say *OK* if the diskette was previously formatted.)

After your diskette is formatted, a format results window is displayed. Click OK to close this window. Then click *Close* to close the formatting window.

File Names

As the term implies, a **file name** is the name you assign to a file. A file name is composed of the name itself and an optional extension. The FAT file system supports file names up to eight characters long with a 1- to 3-character

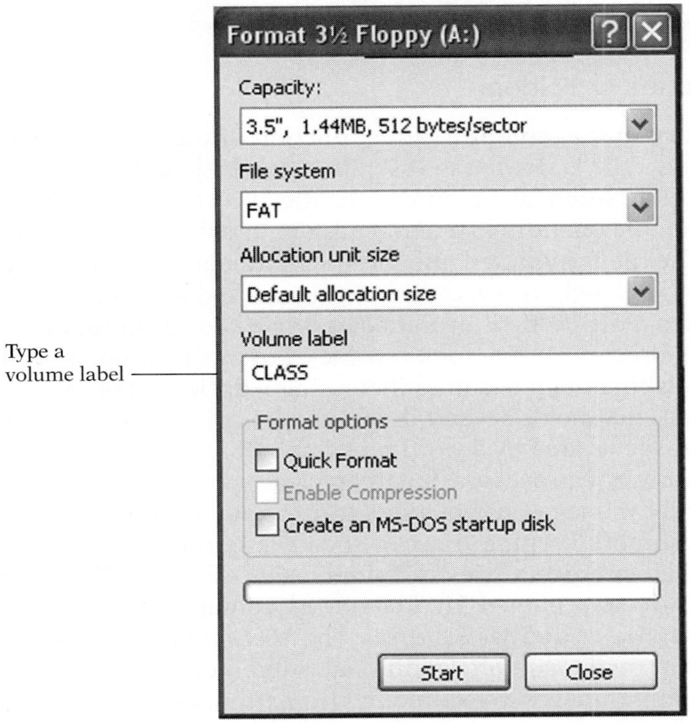

Type a
volume label

FIGURE 8.8
The format window.

extension (see MS-DOS file names in Chapter 7). The file name is separated from its extension by a period.

Windows XP supports FAT file names but also allows long file names. **Long file names** can be up to 255 characters long but cannot contain any of the following characters:

$$/ : * ? " < > | \backslash$$

Windows XP automatically translates the long file names to FAT file names for Windows 3.1 and DOS users. The extension in a long file name is used to identify an associated program that can open the file. For example, in a file named *resume.doc,* the extension *(.doc)* is used to associate the file with *Microsoft Word.* When a user double clicks on a file name with the extension *.doc,* the file is opened using Word.

Note that Windows is *not* case sensitive, so you can type a file name all lowercase, all uppercase, or mixed case. For example, *myfile, MYFILE,* and *MyFile* are all legal versions of the same file name.

Directories or Folders

Directory management is a key function of the Windows file system. The first time a file is written to disk, its name, disk address, creation date, and other information are recorded in the directory. Later, when the file is retrieved, the operating system reads the directory and searches it by name. When the file is modified, the file system updates the directory entry. When the file is deleted, its directory entry is marked as deleted.

When a disk is first formatted, a single **root directory** is created. Using a single directory is fine for a few files, but as the number of files increases, distinguishing them becomes increasingly difficult. For example, imagine a work disk that holds several different types of files. Letters and correspondence are generated by a word processor. Chapters for a book are output by the same word processor, but they clearly represent a separate group of files. Finally, images and pictures form another group of files.

To simplify keeping track of such file groups, the user creates special files called **subdirectories** or **folders.** For example, Figure 8.9 shows that the subdirectory named *My Documents* contains two lower-level subdirectories: *My Music* and *My Pictures.* (The *My Documents* subdirectory on your computer might contain additional subdirectories.) As the subdirectory names imply, images are stored in *My Pictures,* and music files are stored in *My Music.* Think of a subdirectory as a folder that is used to group related files and thus organize a disk. Given the sheer number of files on a hard disk, it is essential to create subdirectories or folders to organize the files. Later in the chapter you will learn to create your own folders.

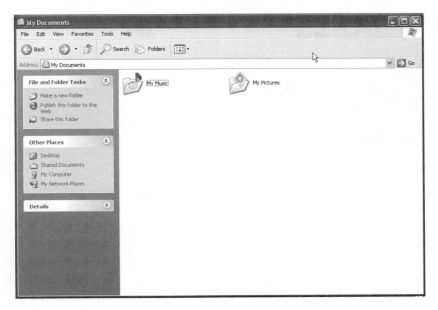

FIGURE 8.9
By default, *My Documents* contains two subdirectories or subfolders.

The Windows *Explorer*

Before you begin creating and manipulating directories, it might be wise to look through some existing examples. Windows ***Explorer*** provides a hierarchical view of the directories on your system. To access *Explorer* from Windows XP, click on *Start,* select *Programs,* select *Accessories,* and then click on *Windows Explorer.* To access *Explorer* from Windows 95, right click (using the right mouse button) the *Start* button and then select *Explore.*

The *Explorer* window (Figure 8.10) is organized into two panes. The left pane lists the folders on your C drive and, depending on your system settings, possibly your other drives. The right pane displays the contents of the selected folder, in this example the *My Documents* folder. Your screen might look different.

Any icon in the left pane with a + sign to its left contains subfolders. For, example, note in Figure 8.10 the + to the left of the *My Computer* folder. Click on the + next to *My Computer* to reveal your disk drives; note once again that your screen might look different. Next, click on the *3 1/2 Floppy(A:)* icon to view the contents of the diskette in drive A (Figure 8.11). You have not yet added any folders or files to the diskette you just formatted, so it should be empty.

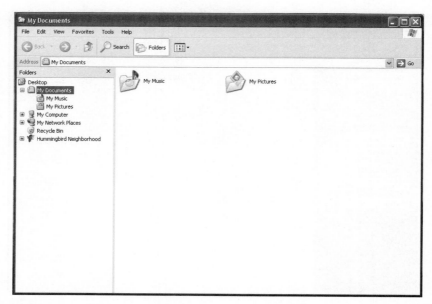

FIGURE 8.10

Explorer shows a hierarchical view of a system's directory structure.

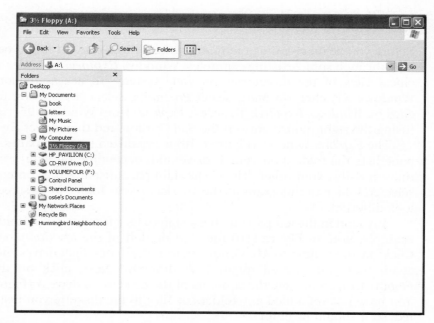

FIGURE 8.11

The diskette you just formatted should be empty.

Some of the disk drives shown under *My Computer* in Figure 8.11 are unique to the authors' installation; ignore them. Click on the C drive icon to view the contents of your local hard disk drive[4] (Figure 8.12). On the authors' system, the icon reads HP_PAVILION (C:) but your system's icon might read *Local Disk (C:)* or it might reference your computer's manufacturer. In any event, your C drive will contain numerous subdirectories. The contents of your C drive probably won't match Figure 8.12, but it will contain three key subdirectories—*Documents and Settings, Program Files,* and *Windows.* Respectively, they hold key documents, your computer's program files, and the system files required by Windows.

Click on the minus sign (-) to the left of the C drive icon to collapse the subdirectories. A plus sign (+) should appear to take its place. Clicking on a plus sign displays the list of subdirectories. Clicking on a minus sign collapses the list.

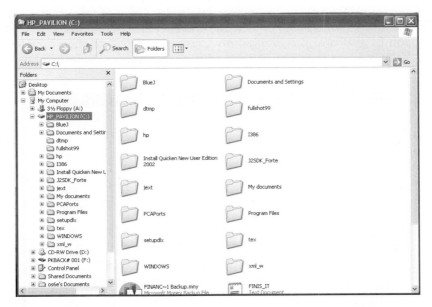

FIGURE 8.12

The C Drive.

---

[4]If the resulting screen reads *These files are hidden,* click on *Show the contents of this folder.*

Look down the list of folders under *My Computer* and click on the + sign to the left of *Control Panel* to reveal its subfolders. Click on *Fonts,* and you should see displayed in the right pane a set of icons for the type fonts that are installed on your computer (Figure 8.13). Move the mouse pointer to the menu bar, pull down the *View* menu, and click on *Details* to switch from icons to a list view that shows such details as file name, size, date last modified and so on (Figure 8.14). Click *View/List* to get a list of file names without the details. Then click *View/Icons* to go back to the icons. Once again, click the negative sign (–) icon on *Control Panel* to collapse or hide the subfolders.

My Computer

Close *Explorer* by clicking the X box at the window's upper right. Then click *Start* and select *My Computer* from the *Start* menu's left pane to open a different view of your computer's peripherals and subfolders (Figure 8.15). You may recognize the **My Computer** view from Figure 8.7 where you accessed it to format a diskette, but you can also use it to view the contents of any single device or folder. For example, look under *Other Places* on the left pane and click on *Control Panel* to view the control panel's contents. Click the *Back* button to return to the original *My Computer* view, and then double click the C drive icon on the right panel to view the contents of your local drive.

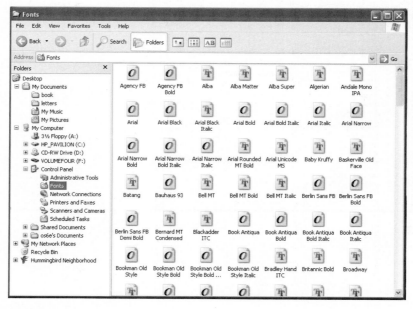

FIGURE 8.13
The Control Panel.

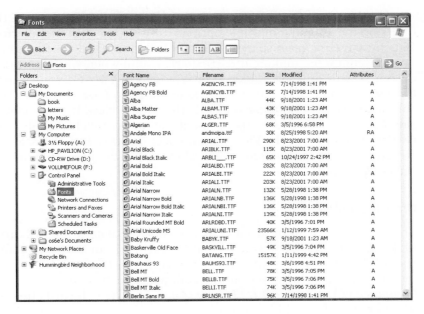

FIGURE 8.14

The *View* menu allows you to control the appearance of the right pane.

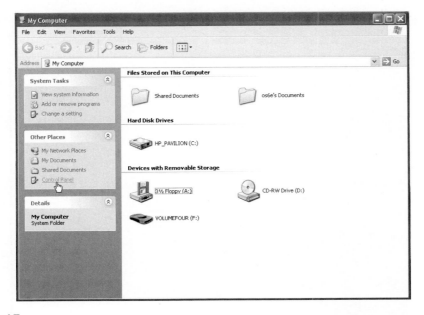

FIGURE 8.15

The *My Computer* View.

The *My Computer* view focuses on one device or folder at a time and offers on the left pane multiple options for working with the selected entity. In contrast, *Explorer* displays a hierarchical view of all the files and folders on your computer, making it particularly useful when you are working concurrently with multiple folders. On Windows XP, *My Computer* appears on the *Start* menu's right panel while launching *Explorer* requires negotiating submenus, so *My Computer* is clearly the default view. If you prefer to make the *Explorer* view your (permanent or temporary) default, open *My Computer*, pull down the View menu, select *Explorer Bar*, and select *Folders*. To return to the *My Computer* view, click on *View/Explorer Bar* and uncheck the *Folders* option.

Creating Folders

The next step in the tutorial calls for you to create a few subdirectories. Make sure the diskette you formatted earlier is in drive A. Your screen should display the *My Computer* view shown in Figure 8.15. (If it doesn't, return to the previous section and follow the instructions to return to *My Computer*.) Click on the *3 1/2 Floppy (A:)* icon to view the diskette's contents. At this point, it should be empty.

To create a new folder, look under *File and Folder Tasks* on the left pane and click on *Make a new Folder* (Figure 8.16). A new folder icon with its

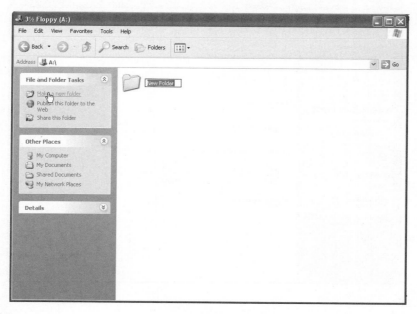

FIGURE 8.16
Creating a new folder.

default name highlighted will appear in the right pane. Type *Letters* to replace the default name and press enter. Then repeat the process to create two more folders named *Books* and *My Pictures* (Figure 8.17).

Creating Files

Most files are created by compilers, interpreters, word processors, spreadsheet programs, database managers, and other application routines. Because the *Notepad* editor is available on virtually all versions of Windows, use *Notepad* to create a few files.

Click on *Start,* point to *All Programs,* and then select *Accessories.* Select *Notepad* from the *Accessories* menu to start the *Notepad* editor. Position the cursor within the *Notepad* window and type the following:

Looking forward to spring break!
See you in Florida!

Pull down the *File* menu and click on *Save.* Because the file was just created, the *Save as* window will open (Figure 8.18). Click on the downward pointing arrow to the right of the *Save in* line near the top of the window and choose the A drive and the folder *Letters* from the drop down menu. Then move down to the *File name* line near the bottom of the window, name your file *Jim,* and click the *Save* button. When you finish, click on the X box at the upper right of the window to close *Notepad.*

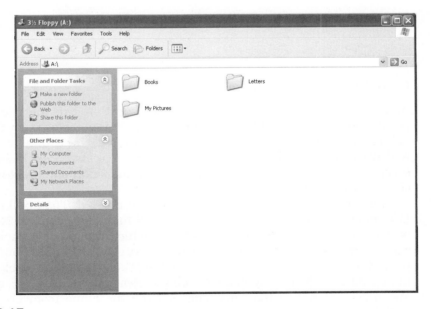

FIGURE 8.17

The diskette now holds three folders.

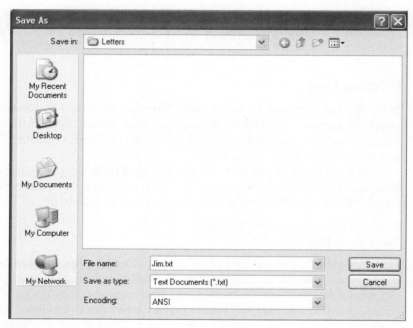

FIGURE 8.18
Saving a *Notepad* file.

Copying and Renaming Files

Another option for creating a file is to copy an existing file. At this point, your screen should resemble Figure 8.17. (If you closed *My Computer* before you opened Notepad, reopen *My Computer* and double click the A drive icon.) Switch to *Explorer* view *(View/Explorer Bar/Folders),* click on the + sign to the left of *3 1/2 Floppy (A:),* and select subdirectory *Letters* (Figure 8.19).

Click on *Jim* to highlight the file you just created. Then pull down the *Edit* menu and select *Copy* to store a copy of the file in memory. Next, click on *Edit* and then *Paste* to paste a copy of the file from memory back into the same folder. An icon for a file named *Copy of Jim* will appear on the right pane. Click on *Copy of Jim* to select the file. Then right click (click the *right* mouse button) the highlighted icon, choose *Rename* (Figure 8.20), type *Sally* and press enter. You have just changed the file name from *Copy of Jim* to *Sally*.

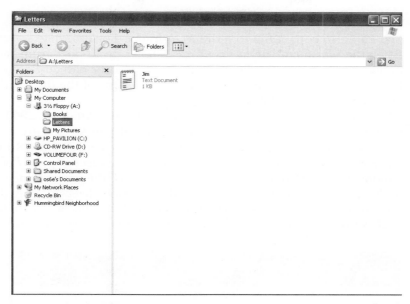

FIGURE 8.19

Selecting a subfolder.

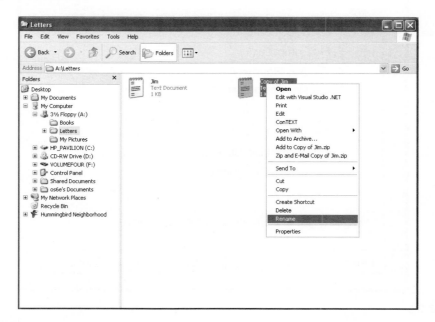

FIGURE 8.20

Renaming a file.

Copying to a Different Folder

You can also copy a file to a different folder. For example, select *Jim,* pull down the *Edit* menu, and select *Copy.* Then select *Books* from the left pane under *3 1/2 Floppy* and the currently empty folder named *Books* will open. Pull down the *Edit* menu, select *Paste,* and a copy of the file named *Jim* will appear in the *Books* folder.

There is a new option in Windows XP and Windows 2000 called the *Copy to Folder*[5] that is particularly valuable if you are unsure of the target folder's name. Reselect the folder *Letters* under *3 1/2 Floppy (A:)* on the left pane. Select *Jim,* pull down the *Edit* menu, and select *Copy to Folder.* A new window will open that allows you to browse for the target folder. Click on + to the left of *My Computer* to display the available drives (Figure 8.21). Click on + to the left of the A drive and then click on the *Books* folder. Finally, click on the *Copy* button to select *Books* and make the copy. If you already

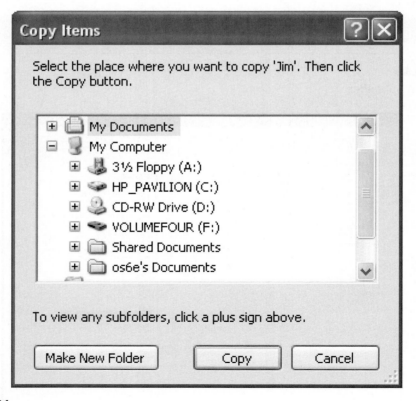

FIGURE 8.21

Browsing for a folder using the *Copy to Folder* option.

---

[5]This option is not available under Windows 95/98.

copied the file to the *Books* folder using the previous paragraph's technique, click on the *Yes* prompt to replace the file.

Copying Multiple Files

To copy multiple files, select the first file name or icon in the usual way. Then hold down the control *(Ctrl)* key while you select additional files. Once you have selected all the desired files, you can do an *Edit/Copy* to copy them into memory and a subsequent *Edit/Paste* to paste them into the target folder.

Make sure you are in the *Letters* folder by clicking on *Letters* in the left pane of the *Explorer* view. Click on *Jim* to select the file. Hold the control key and click on *Sally,* and both files will be highlighted. To create copies of both files, click on *Edit/Copy*. Then click on *Edit/Paste* to make copies of both files in the same folder. When you finish, four files will appear in the Letters folder: *Jim, Copy of Jim, Sally,* and *Copy of Sally*.

Copying Entire Subfolders

You can use *Explorer* (or *My Computer*) to copy an entire subfolder by high-lighting the subfolder, performing an *Edit/Copy,* and then performing an *Edit/Paste* at the new location. Click on the A drive icon in the left pane to display the three folders in the right pane (Figure 8.22). Click on *Letters* to highlight the folder, pull down the *Edit* menu, and click on *Copy*. Then go

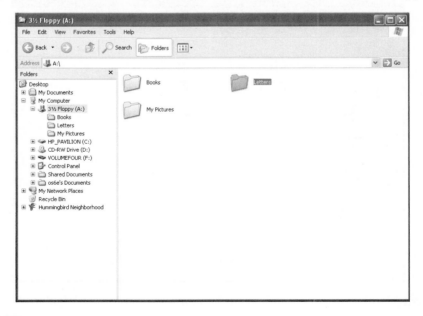

FIGURE 8.22
Copying an entire subfolder.

back to the left pane, click on *Books,* pull down the *Edit* menu, and click on *Paste*. The entire *Letters* folder will be copied to the *Books* folder. Note on the left pane that the *Books* folder now has a + to its left to indicate that it contains a subfolder.

Manipulating Files

Notepad creates simple text files with a .txt extension. *WordPad,* another standard Windows accessory, creates rich text format *(.rtf)* files in XP and WINDOWS 2000, and *.doc* files in earlier versions of Windows. To illustrate how Windows can distinguish different types of files, use *WordPad* to create a simple file with a different extension.

Launch *WordPad* by clicking *Start/All/Programs/Accessories/WordPad* and enter the following data as your first *WordPad* document:

Sorry Jim.
I am going skiing.

Save the file as *tom* in the *A:\Letters* subfolder and close *WordPad*. Copy and paste the file named *tom* to create another file named *Copy of tom* in the *Letters* folder and then rename the file *bob*. Your *Explorer* view of the *Letters* subfolder in the A drive should resemble Figure 8.23. Note that the first four

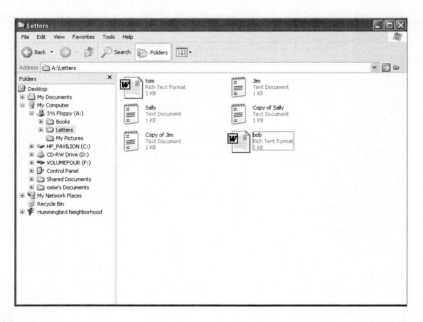

FIGURE 8.23
The *a:\letters* folder.

files you created are simple text documents, but *tom* and *bob* are rich text (or *.doc*) format documents.

Searching for Files

You can use either the *Explorer* view or the *My Computer* view to select just the *Notepad* files or just the *WordPad* files from subfolder *Letters* because their extensions, *.rtf* and *.txt,* provide a basis for distinguishing them. If you have been following along with the tutorial, your screen should resemble Figure 8.23 with the *Explorer* view active. Just for variety, return to the *My Computer* view by closing *Explorer* and clicking on *Start/My Computer*. Then click on the *Search* icon on the toolbar and the *Search Companion* will appear in the left pane (Figure 8.24).

Choose *All files and folders* from the *Search Companion* and a search criteria window will open (Figure 8.25). Assuming you are using Windows XP or Windows 2000, enter **.rtf* [6] in the text box labeled *All or part of the file*

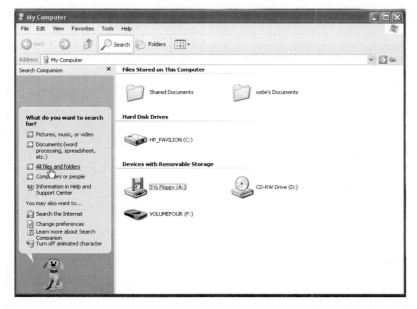

FIGURE 8.24

Search companion.

---

[6]Substitute *.doc* if you are using an earlier version of Windows.

name:. The asterisk (*) is a wild card character that represents one or more file name characters. The *rtf* indicates that the extension must be *rtf*. In this example, the * is the lone file name character, so this search criterion will match *bob.rtf, tom.rtf,* and any other *rtf* file name (of any length) in the target folder or folders. If you refine the search to *b*.rtf,* however, only file names that start with the letter *b* followed by any character or characters will match, so *bob* will be selected from the *Letters* subfolder but *tom* will not.

You can also use a question mark (?) as a wild card character to represent any single character. For example, the search criterion *bo?* identifies all file names that start with *bo* and contain exactly one additional character, such as *bob, boy, boa,* and so on. The wild card characters can be used anywhere in the name, including the extension. For example, the search criterion *bob.** would find *bob.txt, bob.rtf,* and *bob.doc*.

Use the downward pointing arrow to the right of the *Look in* box to select the A drive from a pull down menu (Figure 8.25). Then click on the *Search* button at the bottom right of the *Search Companion* to find all the *WordPad* files (more generally, the *rtf* files) on the A drive. When the search is finished, all the files that match the search criterion will be listed on the right pane (Figure 8.26).

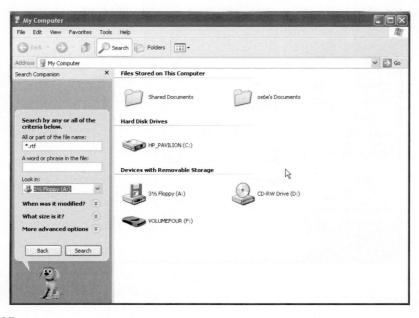

FIGURE 8.25
Search for files.

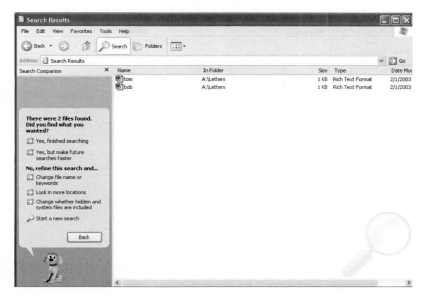

FIGURE 8.26
Search results.

In addition to the files themselves, you can also search for a string of text contained in one or more files. For example, click the *X* box just to the right of *Search Companion* to close the current *search*. Then start a new search by clicking the *Search* icon on the toolbar. Enter the word *Florida* in the text box labeled *A word or phrase in the file* and choose the A drive for *Look in*. Click on the *Search* button. The search results should list *Jim, Sally,* and all copies of the *Jim* and *Sally* files.

Sorting Files

In either the *My Computer* view or the *Explorer* view you can sort the file names shown on the right pane based on a variety of attributes. Close *Search Companion*. Then display the contents of the A drive's *Letters* sub-folder on the right pane. Pull down the *View* menu and choose *Details*. Then click on *View/Arrange Icons* to sort the files based on name, date, size, or type. For example, if you click on *name,* the entries will rearrange themselves into alphabetical order by file name. You can also click on *View/Choose Details* to select the columns (or attributes) you want to see in

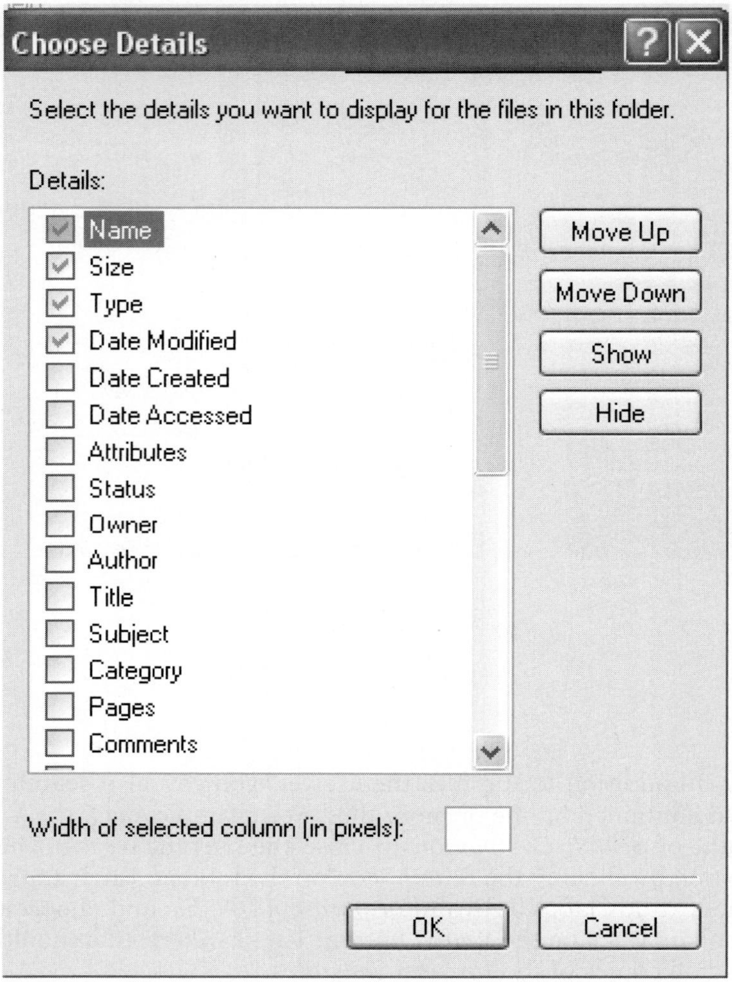

FIGURE 8.27
Column Settings control file details.

a detail view (Figure 8.27). A checkmark in a checkbox indicates that the selected attribute will be displayed in the right pane whenever *Details* is selected.

Shortcuts to Files

It is often useful to create **shortcuts** to files that you access frequently. A shortcut is a link to the file's original location, not a copy of the file. If you delete the shortcut, you delete only the link and not the file.

Try creating a shortcut on your diskette. Start *My Computer* (either view) and display the *A:\Letters* subdirectory. Select the file *tom* and right click the mouse. Choose *Create Shortcut,* (Figure 8.28) to create a shortcut to the file. Highlight the shortcut and click *Edit/Copy*. Then return to the diskette's root directory (click the *Back* button in *My Computer* view or click *3 1/2 Floppy (A:)* on the left pane in *Explorer* view) and click *Edit/Paste*. The shortcut will appear on the diskette's root directory. Normally, shortcuts are created for frequently used programs and files stored on your system's C drive. The shortcuts are then copied to the desktop to simplify the task of launching those frequently used programs. Basically, that is how you customize your desktop.

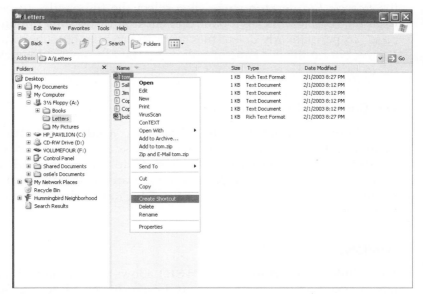

FIGURE 8.28
Creating a shortcut.

◾ Other Features

That ends the chapter tutorial. You may shut down your system or follow the appropriate laboratory procedures for exiting now. The material that follows is not part of the tutorial but is intended for future reference.

The Recycle Bin

To delete a file or a folder, select the file in the *Explorer* or *My Computer* view and either select *File/Delete* from the menu bar or press the delete key. Deleted files or folders are not permanently removed from the computer, however. Instead, when you delete a file from the hard disk, its directory entry is transferred from its folder to the **recycle bin.** The file is permanently removed from the system only when you empty the recycle bin, so as long as the file name remains in the recycle bin, the file can be recovered. Note that files deleted from the A drive (more generally, any removable drive or network drive) are not sent to the recycle bin and thus cannot be recovered.

For future reference, to recover a file deleted from the C drive, click on the *Recycle Bin* desktop icon. Then select the file or files to be recovered from the recycle bin's right pane and click on the *Restore* option on the left pane. To permanently delete files from the recycle bin, click on *Empty the Recycle bin* on the left pane or pull down the *File* menu and click on *Empty the Recycle bin.*

The Command Line Interface

In addition to its graphical user interface, Windows XP also supports a **command line** interface that provides access to most if not all the features of MS-DOS. Almost everything that can be done from the GUI can be done from the command line. Additionally, you can create and run batch files to automate repetitive tasks. See Chapter 7 for more information on the command line interface.

Windows Scripting Host

The **Windows Scripting Host (WSH)** allows users to launch scripts written in scripting languages such as JavaScript or VBScript. Such scripts exploit the functionality of a modern Windows operating system much more effectively than do command line batch files. Scripts can be run from the command prompt or launched directly from the desktop by clicking on a script file icon. In addition to running repetitive tasks like batch files, the Windows Scripting Host lets you access and control applications such as Word and Excel, allowing you to write a single script that integrates features from diverse applications.

Multimedia Support

The switch from Windows 2000 to Windows XP brought a number of enhancements to Microsoft's multimedia support. For example, XP makes it easy to write to a CD, in effect treating a CD drive much like a hard disk drive. Additionally, the option to write to a CD is now associated with the *My Pictures* and *My Music* folders. XP also allows you to download images from a digital camera via a USB port, do some simple image editing, publish an image on the Web, or write an image to a CD. The Windows media player can play audio, video, and movies. The media player also supports ripping audio files and writing them to CD, but it does not support the popular *mp3* format. A video software moviemaker allows for simple video tape capture, edit, and write back. Microsoft also sells a modified version of Windows XP Professional called Windows XP Media Center Edition that lets you seamlessly capture, organize, and play back TV shows, DVD movies, music, photos, and other types of digital content.

■ The Macintosh User Interface

The Apple Macintosh was the first commercially successful graphical user interface, and the authors seriously considered adding a chapter on the Macintosh interface. Although there are important differences between the Macintosh and Windows platforms, their GUIs are similar, and a separate chapter on the Mac interface is difficult to justify given the nature of this book. The internal differences are more dramatic, however, so Part Four features independent chapters on Windows XP internals (Chapter 12) and Macintosh OS X internals (Chapter 14).

▋ Summary

The desktop is the standard Windows user interface. To start a program, you double click its icon or select it from the *Start/All Programs* menu. Each program runs in its own window. You switch between active programs by clicking on the taskbar icon that represents the program you want to run. To enlarge a window, you maximize it. When you minimize a window, it disappears from the screen but its icon remains on the taskbar. To quit a program, open the *File* men and select *Exit* or click on the *X* button at the upper right of the window.

The file system allows a user to identify, save, and retrieve files by name. A file name is composed of the name itself and an optional extension. Windows XP supports both FAT file names and long file names up to 255 characters long. Directory management is a key function of the Windows file system. To simplify keeping track of multiple files, the user creates special files called subdirectories or folders. Both Windows *Explorer* and *My Computer* are used to view and manipulate folders and files. You can copy a file to the same folder or to a different folder, copy multiple files, and copy the contents of a complete folder. The *Search* feature allows you to search for files by file name, by partial file name using wild card characters, or by file contents.

Deleted files or folders are stored in the recycle bin. A file is permanently removed from the system when you empty the recycle bin. Windows XP provides a command line interface that allows the user to access all the features of MS-DOS. The Windows Scripting Host (WSH) allows users to launch scripts written in such scripting languages such as JavaScript or VBScript. Windows XP incorporates enhanced multimedia support.

Key Words

command line	multitasking
desktop	*My Computer*
directory management	notification area
Explorer	recycle bin
file name	root directory
file system	shortcut
folder	*Start* button
format	subdirectory
icon	taskbar
long file name	window
menu	Windows XP
menu bar	Windows Scripting Host (WSH)

Review Questions

1. Describe the standard Windows desktop and briefly explain how to manipulate the desktop.
2. Describe at least two different ways to execute a program under Windows. What is multitasking?
3. Explain how to switch between two active programs.
4. Explain how to maximize, minimize, and restore a window to its original size.
5. Explain how to exit a program. Explain how to shut down the system.
6. What does the file system do?
7. What does the formatting process do?
8. What is the difference between a regular file name and a long file name?

9. Briefly describe the Windows hierarchical directory structure. What is the root directory? What are subdirectories or folders?

10. Distinguish between the Windows *Explorer* and *My Computer* views.

11. How is *My Computer* used to create new folders?

12. Explain how to copy and rename a file. Explain how to copy a file from one folder to another, how to copy multiple files with a single command, and how to copy an entire folder.

13. Explain how the *Search* feature can be used to search for a file by name, by type, or by contents.

14. What is a shortcut? Why are shortcuts useful?

15. Explain how the recycle bin allows you to recover a file you deleted by accident.

16. Why is the command line interface useful?

17. What is the Windows Scripting Host?

18. Describe several enhancements to Microsoft's multimedia support that were implemented in Windows XP.

▉ Exercises

1. If you have not already done so, work through the chapter tutorial.

2. Use the Internet to find an archived copy of Apple's 1984 Super Bowl ad for the Macintosh and view it. From the perspective of two decades, describe your reaction.

3. Implementing common functions such as *Save* and *Save as* in Windows helps to promote a consistent look and feel from application to application. Explain this concept in terms of layering.

4. Create a set of directories to help keep track of your data files or programs. Add your existing files to the new directory structure by copying or renaming them.

5. What advantages does a hierarchical directory structure offer over using a single directory to hold all files?

6. Create a file on your C drive. Delete the file and then recover it from the recycle bin.

7. Why do you suppose Microsoft chose *not* to support the *mp3* file format on Windows XP?

8. Given a choice between a command line interface and a GUI, most people prefer the GUI. There are, however, people who prefer the command line interface. Why do you suppose anyone would prefer a command line interface?

9. The most effective way to learn this chapter's key terms is to complete the chapter tutorial.

CHAPTER 9

The UNIX/Linux User Interface

When you finish reading this chapter you should be able to:

▶ Describe the components of a UNIX/Linux path name.

▶ View a directory using both *Konqueror* and UNIX/Linux line commands.

▶ Create a directory using both *Konqueror* and UNIX/Linux line commands.

▶ Create a file using both KDE and UNIX/Linux line commands.

▶ List a file's contents using both *Konqueror* and UNIX/Linux line commands.

▶ Copy a file using both *Konqueror* and UNIX/Linux line commands.

▶ Search for a file using both KDE and UNIX/Linux line commands.

▶ Explain redirection, filters, and pipes.

◪ UNIX

UNIX was developed at Bell Laboratories, a division of AT&T, in the 1970s. Largely the work of two individuals, Ken Thompson and Dennis Ritchie, the system's main thrust was providing a convenient working environment for writing programs. Almost from its inception, UNIX has been an open source operating system, a decision that in no small way has contributed to its development. Today, UNIX is an important standard that has influenced the design of many modern operating systems. Experienced programmers consider UNIX simple, elegant, and easy to learn. Beginners, on the other hand, sometimes find it terse and not very friendly.

Linux

In 1991, Linus Torvald, then a student at the University at Helsinki, created an open source version of UNIX called **Linux** designed to run on the Intel 386 chip, the precursor to today's Pentium family of chips. The complete source code is freely available on the Internet, and over the years Linux has been refined and modified to incorporate contributions from hundreds of software developers throughout the world. Today, versions of Linux are available for most platforms including most personal computers.

The **kernel** is the core of the operating system that communicates directly with the hardware. Applications such as the shell, utilities, compilers and other programs run on the kernel. Version 1.0, the initial stable version of the Linux kernel, was released in 1994. Subsequently, commercial vendors such as RedHat, Mandrake, and SuSe and open source distributions such as Debian and Gentoo have packaged the software for easy installation on a wide variety of personal computers and added enhancements that make Linux more useful. The sample screens in this chapter were created under Debian's stable woody version, which uses Linux kernel 2.4.18. Your screens will probably look a bit different.

The Hacker's Creed

In the late 1960 and early 1970s, the term hacker was used to describe a highly skilled programmer with a knack for writing tight, efficient, elegant code. Many of those early hackers shared a common set of values that were reflected in an often unpublished hacker's creed. Although there are many versions of the hacker's creed, most agree that a hacker should do no harm and should not benefit financially from his or her hacking. Another common principle was that information should be free, an idea consistent with open source software. The people who developed (and continue to develop) UNIX were hackers in the original sense of the word, and the hacker's creed still influences today's UNIX and Linux operating systems.

The User Interface

Typically, a user accesses a computer through an application program's interface and the application logic communicates with UNIX through an application programming interface such as **POSIX,** Portable Operating System Interface for UNIX. At times, however, it is necessary to communicate directly with the operating system to perform such functions as launching a program.

UNIX line commands are processed by a command processor or **shell** that lies between the user and the kernel (Figure 9.1). The shell is not really part of the operating system so it can be changed; in fact, the idea of implementing the command processor in its own independent layer was an important UNIX innovation. In UNIX terminology, the shell is the command line interface, but the term shell is sometimes used to refer more broadly to the user interface layer.

Beginners often find a command line interface a bit intimidating and prefer such alternatives as a menu interface, a graphical user interface, or voice commands. Many UNIX systems incorporate a standard graphical user interface called X-Windows. Most Linux systems provide either the **K-Desktop Environment (KDE)** or the GNOME interface, both of which are built on top of X-Windows and resemble the Windows interface (Chapter 8). KDE is the more popular of the two.

Because UNIX/Linux actively supports both line commands and a GUI, a key focus of this chapter is to compare and contrast these two types of interfaces. Much of the material is presented in the form of a tutorial. If possible, find a Linux or UNIX system and, as you read about a command, issue it and see for yourself how the computer responds. You will need a user name and a password; if necessary, see your instructor or your system's super user. Later, you may find Appendix C a useful reference.

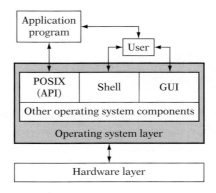

FIGURE 9.1
A UNIX user has several options for communicating with the operating system.

Logging On

Every UNIX session begins with a request for a **login name** and a **password.** If your system starts in command line mode, type your login name and press enter in response to the first prompt (Figure 9.2). Next, you'll be asked for your password. Type it and press enter. (For security reasons, passwords are never displayed.) If your system starts at the graphical user interface, the screen will look different but it should request the same information.

If you started with the graphical user interface, the KDE desktop should appear immediately after a successful login and you can simply read the rest of this paragraph. If you successfully logged in via the command line interface or shell, you will see on the last line a **prompt** consisting of your login name followed by a dollar sign ($), a percent sign (%), or a colon (:) (Figure 9.2). The precise format of the prompt depends on which UNIX shell is your system's default. At the prompt, type

startx

to start the KDE desktop.

The KDE Desktop

Like Windows (Chapter 8), the standard KDE 3.1 interface features a **desktop** metaphor (Figure 9.3); if you are following along on your own computer, your desktop might look different. On the left side of the desktop is a set of icons that represent programs or files. For example, the *Home* icon near the top left of Figure 9.3 represents a program named *Konqueror*, the KDE file manager. If you click the *Home* icon, *Konqueror* displays the contents of your home folder or directory.

```
Debian GNU/Linux 3.0 os6 tty3
os6 login: rajkumar
Password:
Last login: Sun Feb 9 21:00:55 2003 on tty3
Linux os6 2.4.18–bf2.4 #1 Sun Apr 14 09:53:28 EST 2002
i686 unknown

rajkumar@os6:~$ startx
```

FIGURE 9.2

A log on sequence.

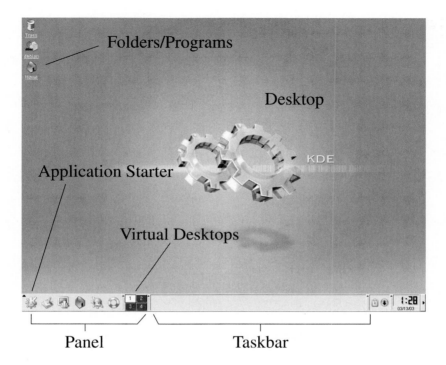

Folders/Programs

Desktop

KDE

Application Starter

Virtual Desktops

Panel   Taskbar

FIGURE 9.3
The KDE user interface.

The KDE desktop's **panel** is found at the bottom left. The first (or leftmost) panel entry, an iconic *K*, represents the ***Application Starter***. Click on the *Application Starter* and a set of menu options for launching programs appears (Figure 9.4). Click any spot outside the application menu to return to the desktop (Figure 9.3). KDE supports multiple concurrent desktops called **virtual desktops.** You can select the active desktop by clicking on one of the numbered buttons to the right of the panel; for example, the current screen is virtual desktop number 1.

The **taskbar** lies to the right of the virtual desktop buttons. It displays an icon for each active program. To switch to a different program, simply click the new program's taskbar icon. The system date and time are displayed at the lower right, and the icon that resembles a clipboard with a lowercase k represents (as you might expect) the clipboard.

FIGURE 9.4
The KDE application menu.

Command Line Utilities

The third icon from the left on the panel resembles a shell; the program it represents is called *Konsole*. Click the *Konsole* icon to switch to the command line interface or **shell mode** (Figure 9.5). If a window displaying a *Konsole* tip pops up, click *Close*. At this point your screen should resemble Figure 9.5. Note that the shell runs in its own window and that an icon labeled *Shell—Konsole* appears on the taskbar. Note also that your prompt will start with your login name rather than *rajkumar*.

Figure 9.6 shows the format of a UNIX **line command.** Command names are generally terse (ed for editor, cp for copy a file), but meaningful. One or more spaces separate the command name from the options. If they are included, the options are usually preceded by a minus sign to

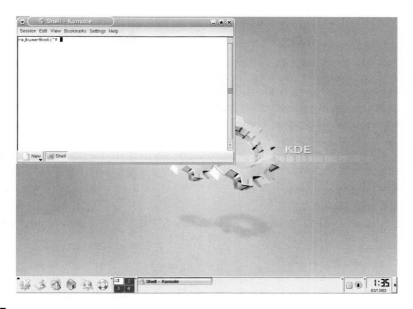

FIGURE 9.5

The command line shell.

distinguish them from the arguments. Most options are designated by a single lowercase letter, and multiple options can be coded. One or more spaces separate the options from the arguments, which usually consist of one or more file names.

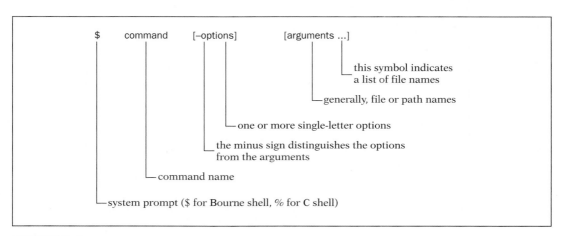

FIGURE 9.6

A UNIX line command.

Use the **passwd** utility to change your password. Type

passwd

The system will prompt for your current password and the new password; Figure 9.7 shows the contents of the shell window. Respond by typing the corresponding passwords into the system. After verifying the new password, UNIX will notify you that it has changed your password, but it will not display the new password.

Three more line commands are shown in Figure 9.8. The **date** utility displays the system date and time. Simply type

date

and press enter. Use the **who** utility to identify all the users who are currently logged onto your system by typing

who

A user working on more than one project might have two or more login names, and that can be confusing. The command

whoami

(no spaces) displays the user's current login name.

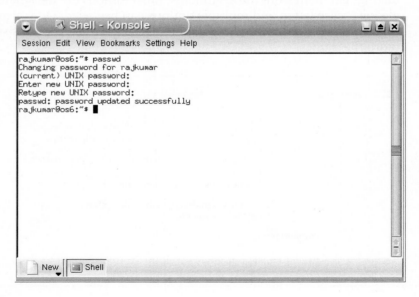

FIGURE 9.7

Use the passwd utility to change your password.

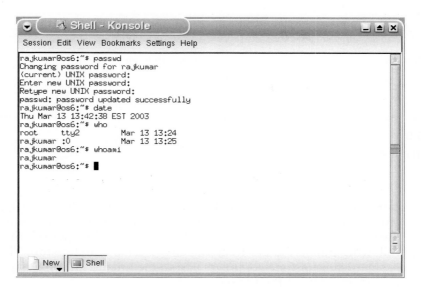

FIGURE 9.8
The date and who utilities.

Many other utilities are available. For example, the mail utility sends and receives e-mail, and most UNIX systems feature an on-line reference manual. To obtain a description of any utility, code man followed by the utility name. For example,

man who

displays a description of the who utility.

▪ The File System

The **file system** is a key UNIX component that allows a user to identify, save, and retrieve files by name. (A program, remember, is a type of file.) Before you begin using the UNIX file system, however, you must first understand a few underlying concepts.

File Names

A UNIX **file name** (Figure 9.9) consists of from 1 to 255 characters. Do not use slashes (/), and avoid starting a file name with a minus sign or hyphen;

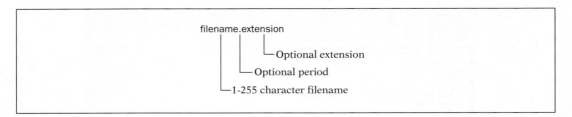

FIGURE 9.9
UNIX file names.

otherwise, virtually any combination of characters you can type is legal. Note that UNIX is case sensitive—it distinguishes between uppercase and lowercase, so A and a are different. If you include a period, the characters following the period are treated as the file name **extension.** The extension is significant to some compilers and to the linkage editor, but generally it is considered part of the file name.

Directories

Imagine a user who maintains several different types of files. Letters and other correspondence are generated by a text editor, chapters for a book are output by a word processor, and C programs form a third group. Dozens, perhaps even hundreds of different users will have similar needs. Keeping track of all those files in a single directory is virtually impossible. Instead, UNIX uses a flexible hierarchical **directory** structure (Figure 9.10).

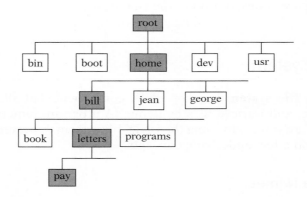

FIGURE 9.10
UNIX uses a hierarchical directory structure.

The structure begins with a **root directory**. Several "children" grow from the root. Some hold references to utilities and other system routines. One directory, *home*, holds all the user's directory names[1]. Note that *bill* is a child of *home* and a grandchild of the root directory. Under *bill* come subdirectories to hold letters, book chapters, and programs. Incidentally, a directory is a special type of file, so the rules for naming directories and files are identical.

Path Names

With all those directories, you need more than a simple name to find a file. For example, it is possible to have files named *pay* recorded under two different directories. A reference to *pay* would thus be ambiguous—which *pay* do you mean? To uniquely identify a file, you need a complete **path name** (Figure 9.11). For example,

/home/bill/letters/pay

defines the path to a file named pay on the *bill/letters* directory. Look at Figure 9.10, and follow the path name. The first slash[2] (/) indicates the root directory. Move down through the hierarchical directory structure to *home*, then *bill*, then *letters*, and finally to the file *pay*.

At first glance, subdirectories seem to complicate rather than simplify accessing files. In practice, however, you will rarely use such lengthy path names. Instead, when you log on, UNIX selects your **home directory** (its name usually matches your login name) as your initial **working directory**.

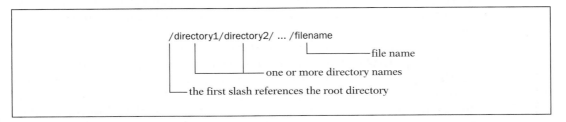

FIGURE 9.11
You must specify a complete path name to uniquely identify a file.

---

[1]Note that *home* is a generic directory name. The actual name of your home directory usually matches your login ID, which explains why the author's home directory is named *rajkumar*.

[2]Note: NOT a backslash (\). The backslash is an MS-DOS separator (Chapter 7).

Unless it is told otherwise, the operating system searches for files starting with your working directory. Thus, if bill is the working directory,

letters/pay

is all you need to find file *pay*. Later in the chapter, you'll see how to change working directories.

■ Working with the File System

Both KDE and the shell allow a user to work with the UNIX file system. The material that follows switches back and forth between the two interfaces and asks you to perform essentially the same tasks under both, giving you an opportunity to compare and contrast a GUI and a line command interface.

Viewing a Directory

Konqueror is KDE's file manager. Like the Windows file manager (Chapter 8), *Konqueror* uses folders to represent directories. Your most recent commands were issued at the line command prompt (Figure 9.8) within the Konsole window, so click anywhere on the desktop to switch back to the KDE desktop (Figure 9.3).

There are two ways to open *Konqueror*. One is to click the *Home* icon at the KDE desktop's upper left. The second option is to click the application starter, an iconic *K* icon at the lower left, and then select *Home (Personal files)* from the program menu (Figure 9.12). Choose either option to start the file manager.

Konqueror displays two panels (Figure 9.13). (If you do not see two panels, click on *Window/Show Navigation Panel*.) The left panel, called the **navigation panel,** lists the folder's contents as a hierarchical directory structure. By default, *Konqueror* starts with your home directory; note that the path name of your home directory folder is displayed in the location toolbar just above the panels. The right panel displays the folders and files stored in the directory. Note that there are three folders and no files visible in the *Konqueror* window in Figure 9.13.

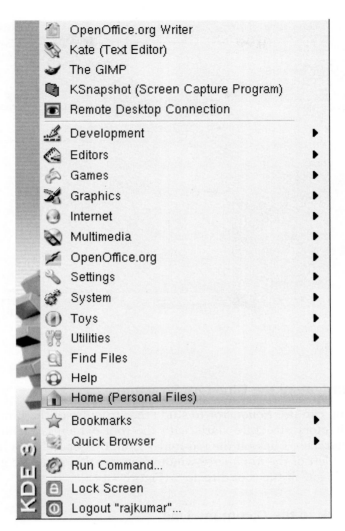

FIGURE 9.12

The *Konqueror* file manager.

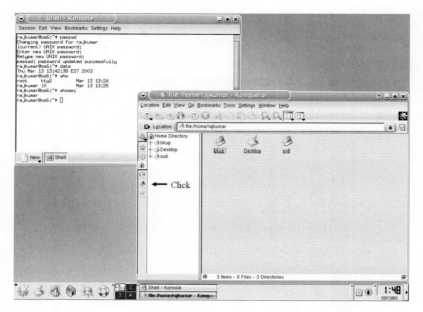

FIGURE 9.13
Konqueror panels.

Navigating the Directory Structure

You can use *Konqueror* to study the structure of the Linux file system. The directory structure starts with the root, which is identified by a / (slash) character. Click on the red folder icon, the second icon from the bottom to the left of the *Konqueror* window's navigation panel, to get a full hierarchical view of the root directory (Figure 9.14).

Back to the Command Line

Click on the Shell icon in the taskbar to switch back to the command line interface. Then clear the existing contents on the screen by typing the command

clear

and print or display your working directory by issuing the command

pwd

Your author's working directory appears on the second line of Figure 9.15. Your working directory's name will be different, of course. By default, it should be your home directory.

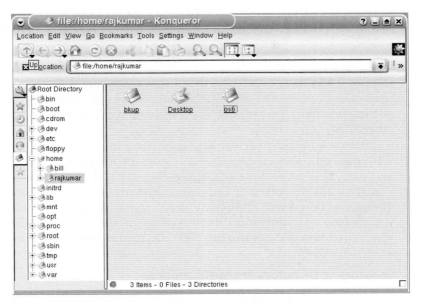

FIGURE 9.14

The directory structure.

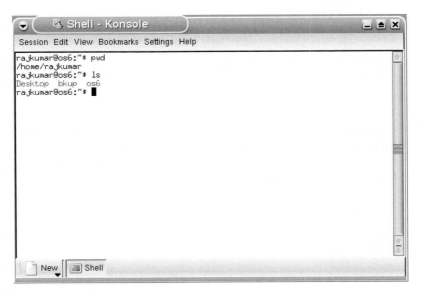

FIGURE 9.15

The pwd and ls line commands.

Even if this is the first time you have logged on, your home directory should contain a few files. To view their names, type an **ls** (list directory) command

ls

(Figure 9.15). As you can see, the author's working directory contains three files: *Desktop*, *bkup*, and *os6*. Your working directory will probably not include *bkup* or *os6*, but it should contain Desktop and perhaps some other files.

Before you move on, quickly compare Figures 9.14 and 9.15. In Figure 9.14, the right *Konqueror* panel shows icons for three files—*bkup*, *Desktop*, and *os6*. The same three file names appear just above the last prompt in Figure 9.15. In other words you just used two different interfaces, *Konqueror* and *Shell*, to display the same information. Under *Konqueror*, you clicked on your home directory name in the left panel. Under the *Shell*, you issued two line commands. But the results were identical.

Creating a Directory from *Konqueror*

The next step is to create a subdirectory under your home directory. Click the *Konqueror* icon on the taskbar to activate the KDE file manager. Click *Edit/New Directory*, enter *Books* for the directory name (Figure 9.16), and click on *OK* to create the folder *Books*. To open the new subdirectory *Books*, click on its icon in the left panel. To move back to your home directory, click on *Home Directory*.

Creating a Directory from the Command Line

Activate the shell by clicking on the *Shell* icon in the taskbar, issue a clear command to clear the previous topic, and then type the command

mkdir Letters

(Figure 9.17). From the command line, you use the **mkdir** (make directory) utility to create a directory and rmdir (remove directory) to remove or delete one.

To make the subdirectory *Letters* your working directory, issue a **cd** (change directory) command by typing

cd Letters

Type pwd to verify that the *Letters* subdirectory is your working directory, and then type

ls -a

to list the files (Figure 9.17).

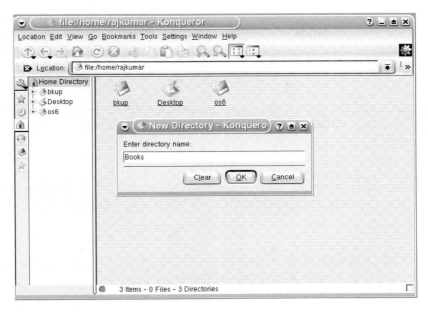

FIGURE 9.16
Creating a directory.

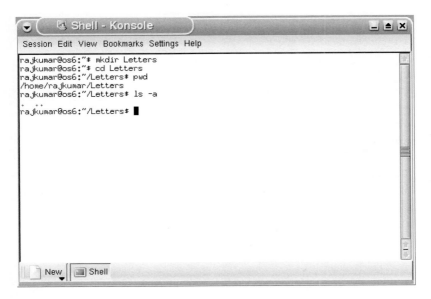

FIGURE 9.17
The mkdir utility and the cd line command.

Note the two files named (.) and (..) because they are significant. The single period stands for the working directory, and the double period is a synonym for its parent. They are useful shorthand for writing path names. Type

cd ..

to make the parent of *Letters* (your home directory) the working directory. Then try some other variations. For example, in the command

cd /

the slash identifies the root directory. Although UNIX displays no confirmation message, the root directory will be your new working directory. Now type

ls

and press enter. The output (on the author's system) appears in Figure 9.18. Finally, to return to your home directory, type

cd

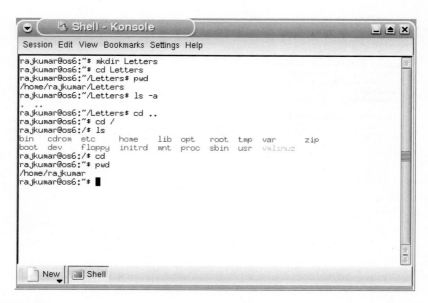

FIGURE 9.18
The contents of the author's root directory and home directory.

Then type

pwd

to verify that your home directory is your working directory.

Creating Files from the Command Line

Most user files are created by application programs such as editors, compilers, word processors, spreadsheet programs and database managers. Different systems feature different applications, but most UNIX systems incorporate a full screen visual editor called **vi** that you can use to create a few simple files.

First, however, change the working directory to *Letters*. *Letters* is a subdirectory of your home directory, which, if you've been following the tutorial, is your current working directory. Unless you specify otherwise, UNIX always assumes a file reference starts with the current working directory, so

cd Letters

changes the working directory to *Letters* (Figure 9.19).

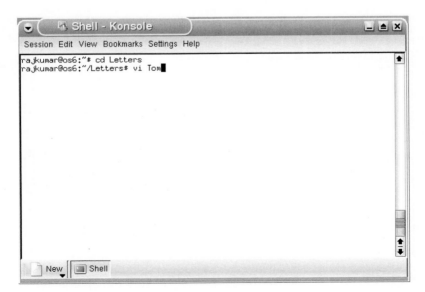

FIGURE 9.19
Starting the visual editor.

To launch the visual editor and use it to create (in the working directory) a file named *Tom,* issue the command

vi Tom

(Figure 9.19, second line). Except for a message at the bottom, the vi window should go blank. The visual editor has two operating modes: command and insert. As you begin, you are in command mode by default. To switch to insert mode, press *I.* You'll get no confirmation, but you should be able to begin entering text.

Type the following two lines:

Looking forward to spring break!
See you in Florida!

When you are finished, exit insert mode by pressing the escape key. (On some systems, you must press a function key—see your instructor.) Then type :wq, for write quit (Figure 9.20). (Some systems accept a pair of capital Zs as a command to exit vi.) You should see a system prompt indicating that you're back in the shell.

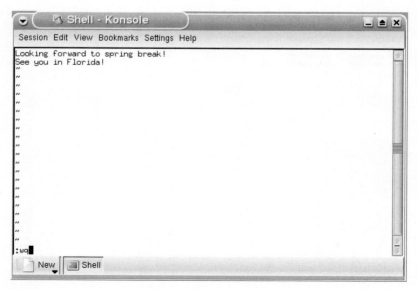

FIGURE 9.20
Exiting vi.

Type the command

ls –l

to verify that the file is on disk; the l option indicates long form. Then type a cd command to return to your home directory and issue another

ls –l

command to list the contents of your home directory in long form (Figure 9.21).

The first ten characters in a long form directory listing indicate the file type and its access permissions (Figure 9.22). The file can be an ordinary file (data or a program), a directory, or a special file that corresponds to an input or output device; note in Figure 9.21 that *Tom* is an ordinary file (type –) and the subdirectories on your home directory are all file type *d*. Three sets of permissions are included: one for the file's owner, a second for users in the owner's group, and a third for all other users. Based on the recorded values, a given user or group can be granted read *(r)*, write *(w)*, and/or execute *(x)* permission. A minus sign indicates no permission. Use the chmod utility to change a file's access permissions.

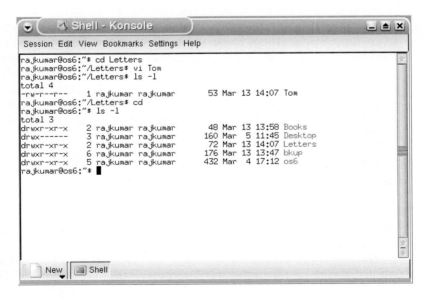

FIGURE 9.21
A long form directory listing.

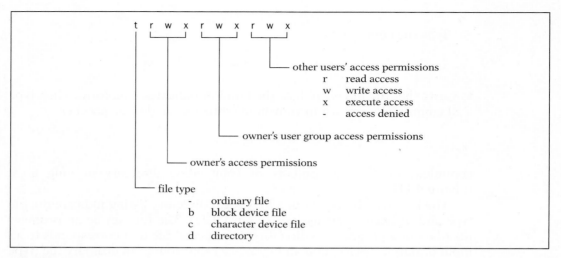

FIGURE 9.22

File type and access permissions.

Creating Files from KDE

Click on the *Konqueror* icon on the taskbar to activate the KDE file manager. One way to start a program from within KDE is to click on the *Application Starter* (the *K* icon) and then select the program you want to run from the menu (Figure 9.23). The menus are organized hierarchically and you might find the program you need in a subfolder; for example, *Kwrite*, a text editor, is in a subfolder called *Editors*. To start *Kwrite*, click the sequence *K/Editors/Kwrite*. (Check with your instructor if *Kwrite* is not in the *Editors* subfolder.) Then position the cursor within the *Kwrite* window's top right panel and type

Sorry Tom.
I am going skiing!

Click on *File/Save* to save the file (Figure 9.24). Choose the subdirectory *Letters*, give your file the name *Jim* and click *Save*. Then click on *File/Quit* to close *Kwrite*.

Note that the subdirectory *Letters* was created by a line command, but you just created a file under KDE and saved that file in *Letters*. The point is it doesn't matter whether you use the shell or the graphical user interface to create a subdirectory or a folder, because those two interfaces are simply different ways of doing essentially the same thing.

You can also use *Konqueror* to view the new file's permissions, much as you did with a long form list directory option in the previous section. Select the file *Jim* by holding down *Ctrl* and clicking the left mouse button. (Under KDE, just clicking on the file name opens the file.) Then right click on *Jim* and choose *Properties*. A new window will open. If necessary, click on the *Permissions* tab to access a set of check boxes that allow you to change the file's permission settings (Figure 9.25). For example, to allow everyone to modify the file Jim, give them Write permission by checking the *Write* box to the right of *Others*. For now, simply click on *Cancel* and return to *Konqueror*.

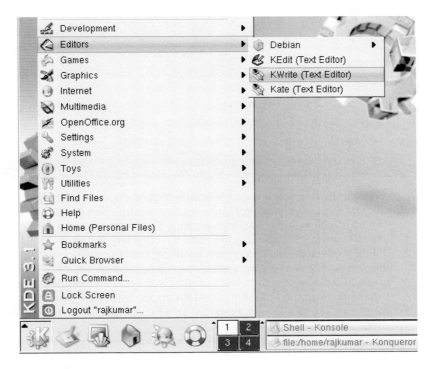

FIGURE 9.23
The Editor submenu.

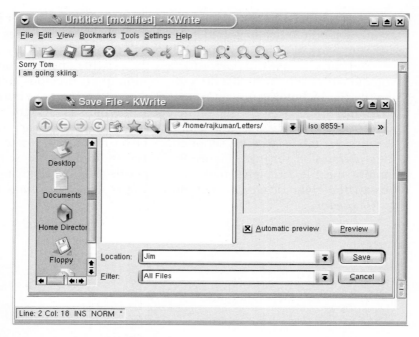

FIGURE 9.24
Saving a file.

The Ease-of-Use/Efficiency Tradeoff

A typical user begins a work session by logging on and launching an application program such as a word processor, a spreadsheet, or an e-mail program. Logging on and launching a program are operating system tasks, but once the application starts, subsequent communication with the operating system takes place indirectly (through the application program's interface) until the time comes to log off. The user might be an expert in manipulating the application interface, but the need to issue commands directly to the operating system is so rare that the efficiency of those interactions is irrelevant. Given the choice between a terse, non-intuitive line command interface and a relatively easy-to-use graphical user interface, most users prefer the GUI.

A system operator or sysop looks at the ease-of-use/efficiency tradeoff differently, however. The sysop works with the operating system, not with application programs. A GUI might be intuitive and easy to use, but working through a hierarchy of screens and menus is not very efficient when the process must be repeated frequently. To a sysop, those terse, nonintuitive line commands save time. Given a choice between navigating the multiple screens and menus of a graphical user interface and issuing relatively efficient line commands, most sysops prefer the line command interface.

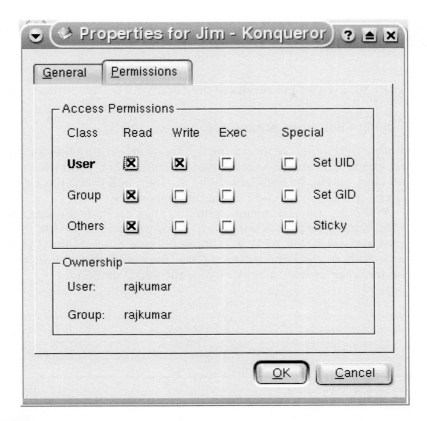

FIGURE 9.25

File properties.

Listing File Contents from Konqueror

Now that you've created some files, you can manipulate them. To display a file's contents from *Konqueror*, simply click on the file within *Konqueror*. For example, to view the contents of the file *Tom*, navigate to the *Letters* sub-directory and click on *Tom* to start the *Kwrite* editor. The contents of the file *Tom* will be displayed on screen and can be modified if desired. Click on *File/Quit* to close *Kwrite*.

Listing File Contents from the Command Line

Click on the *Shell Konsole* icon on the taskbar to activate the shell. Make sure that your current directory is *Letters* by typing

```
cd
cd Letters
pwd
```

Then use the *more* utility to display the contents of the file *Tom*. Type

more Tom

Figure 9.26 shows the results of the command on the author's system.

Copying Files from Konqueror

Another option for creating a file is to copy an existing file. Start *Konqueror* and choose the subdirectory *Letters* (Figure 9.27). Hold down the *ctrl* key and click on *Jim* to highlight the icon. Then pull down the *Edit* menu and select *Copy* to store a copy of the file in memory.

Pull down the *Edit* menu again and click on *Paste* to paste the file back to the same directory. A window will pop up to indicate the file name *Jim* exists and ask if you want to rename the new copy (Figure 9.28). Type the name *Sally* in the window (to replace *Jim*), and click the *Rename* button. You have just created a copy of your file and renamed it.

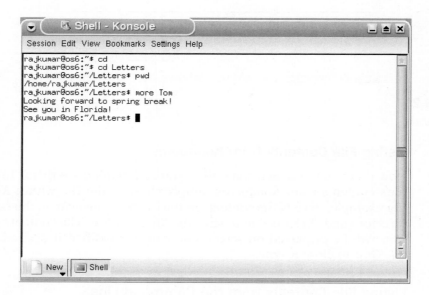

FIGURE 9.26
Viewing a file's contents with the more utility.

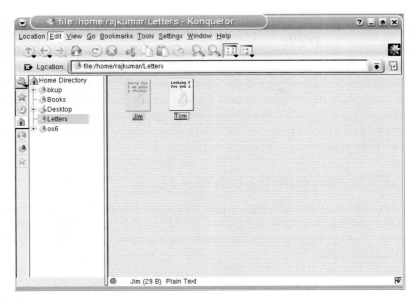

FIGURE 9.27
Copying a file.

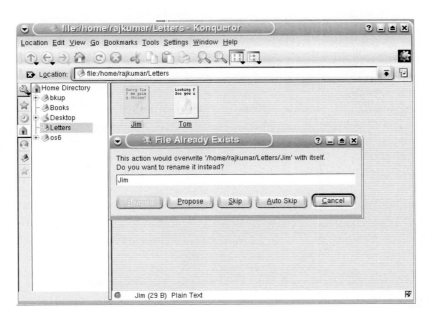

FIGURE 9.28
Rename on paste.

You can also copy a file to a different folder. Hold down *Ctrl* and click the file *Jim* to select it. Then simply drag its icon to the folder *Books* on the left pane. When you release the mouse button, *Konqueror* displays a menu (Figure 9.29). Choose *Copy Here,* and the file named *Jim* is copied into the *Books* folder. There are three other options listed in the pop-up window in Figure 9.29. *Move Here* copies the file to the new folder and deletes it from the original folder. *Link Here* neither copies nor moves the file. Instead it creates a reference to the file in the new directory. *Cancel,* of course, cancels the operation.

Copying Files from the Command Line

You can use the copy (**cp**) utility to copy a file from the command line. For example, click the *Shell* icon to switch to the line interface and make sure your home directory is the working directory (Figure 9.30). Then issue the command

cp Letters/Tom Books/Tom

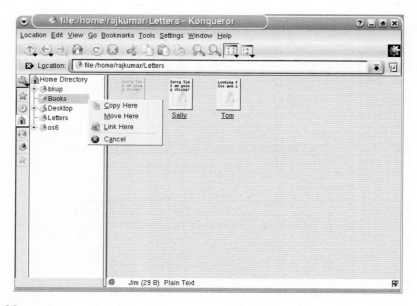

FIGURE 9.29
Copying to a different folder.

followed by

ls Books

to verify that the copy took place. Next, use the ln command to create a link by typing

ln -s Letters/Sally Books
ls -l Books

You can see the results in Figure 9.30. Note that *Sally,* the second entry in directory list, is file type *l,* for link.

Searching for Files from KDE

Kfind is a KDE utility that helps find a file when you know either a part of its file name or a specific string of text within the file. Switch to KDE and start *Kfind* by choosing *K(Application Starter)/Find Files*.

Assume you know you have a file whose name starts with *Sa* (note the uppercase S), but you do not remember the full file name. Enter *Sa** in the

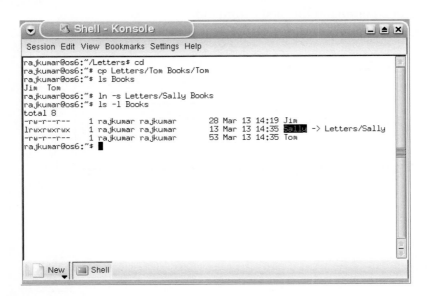

FIGURE 9.30
Copying and linking files at the command line.

Named box (Figure 9.31). The * (asterisk) is a **wild card** character that represents one or more characters in the file name. Since the search string you entered starts with Sa*, it will match *Sally, Saturday, Sam,* and any other file name that starts with Sa. After you enter *Sa** in the location box, click on *Find* and *Kfind* will return the *Sally* files in both the *Books* and *Letters* folders.

In addition to the * character, you can also use a question mark (?) as a wild card character. A question mark represents a single character; for example, the file name *Sa?* matches *Sam, Sat, Say,* and any other file name that starts with Sa and ends with any other single character. The wild card characters can be used anywhere in the search name.

Searching for Files from the Command Line

Use the *find* utility (Figure 9.32) to find files from the command line. Activate the shell by clicking on the *shell* icon on the taskbar. To search for files starting with Sa*, type

find . -name "Sa*"

and press enter. The single period (.) tells find to start the search from the current directory and its subdirectories, and the operator -name followed by the option "Sa*" identifies the search string. Figure 9.33 displays the results of a command line find command.

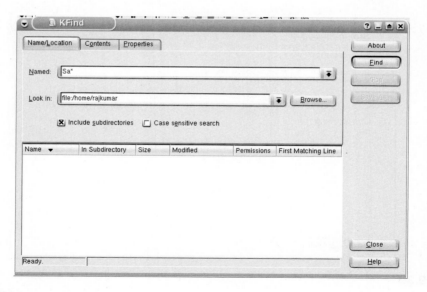

FIGURE 9.31

Finding files based on name.

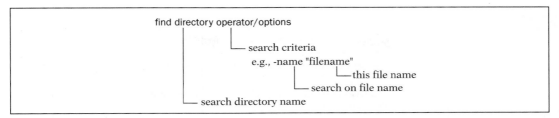

FIGURE 9.32
The find utility.

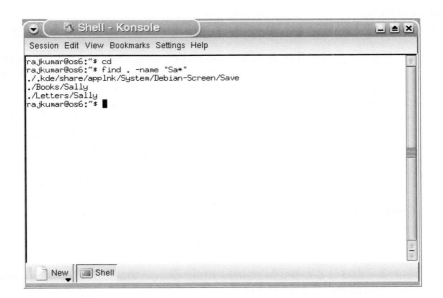

FIGURE 9.33
Using find.

■ Pipes, Filters, and Redirection

Many UNIX utilities and commands assume a standard input or output device; for example, find sends its output to the screen, while vi gets its input from the keyboard. By using **redirection** operators (Figure 9.34), a user can instruct the shell to change those defaults.

Operator	Meaning	Example
<	change source to a specified device or file	<myfile
>	change destination to a specified device or file	>tempfile
>>	change destination to an existing file and append new data	>>master.pay
|	pipe standard output to another command or to a filter	cat file1 | sort

FIGURE 9.34

Redirection operators.

Use the find utility to illustrate redirection. You already know that a find command followed by a directory name and a search string returns a list of file names that match the search string and that the ls command displays the contents of a file. Since no inputs or outputs are specified, the shell assumes the standard input and output devices (the keyboard and the screen). That is why the command results are displayed on the screen.

Redirect the output. Type

> find . -name "Sa*" >Letters/findSally.txt

Then list your directory

> ls -a Letters

You should see a new file named findSally.txt that contains the results of the find operation (Figure 9.35).

A **filter** accepts input from the standard input device, modifies (or filters) the data in some way, and sends the results to the standard output device. For example, the **sort** utility (Figure 9.36) reads input from the specified file or files (or the standard input device), sorts them into alphabetical or numerical sequence, and outputs the sorted data to the screen.

A **pipe** causes one utility's standard output to be used as another utility's standard input. Pipes are designated by a vertical line (|). For example, earlier in the chapter, you issued the command

> find . -name "Sa*"

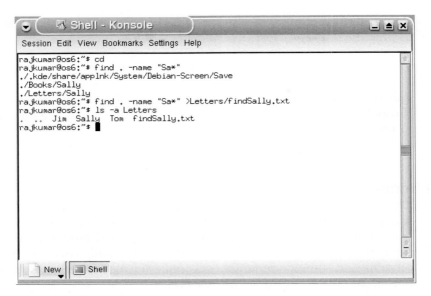

FIGURE 9.35

Redirecting output.

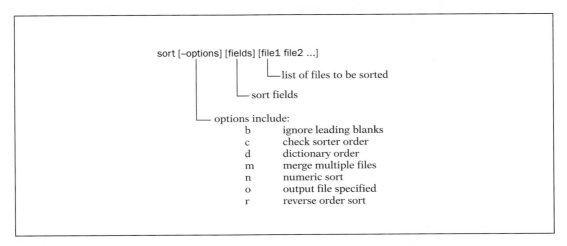

FIGURE 9.36

The sort utility.

Retype that command, but do not press enter. Instead, add a pipe operator to pipe the output to sort

find . -name "Sa*" | sort -r

and then press enter. As Figure 9.37 shows, the output has been routed through sort and, because of the r option the file names are now displayed in reverse alphabetical order.

Shell Scripts

Many computer applications are run daily, weekly, or at other regular intervals. Others, such as a program test, are repeated numerous times. Each time such applications are run, a set of commands must be issued, and retyping the same commands over and over again is annoying and error prone. An option is to write a **shell script.**

A shell script is a file that consists of a series of commands. (It resembles an MS-DOS BAT file—see Chapter 7.) The shell is actually a highly

FIGURE 9.37
Using a pipe.

sophisticated, interpretive programming language with its own variables, expressions, sequence, decision, and repetitive structures. Writing shell scripts is beyond the scope of this book, but it is a powerful UNIX feature that you will eventually want to learn more about.

UNIX utilities, filters, and shell scripts are powerful command line features. View them as tools. Each one performs a single function. Instead of writing a massive program to perform a series of functions, it makes sense to use the existing tools and link them with pipes, filters, and redirection operators. As you become more experienced with UNIX, you will find many uses for them.

This marks the end of the chapter tutorial. To log off the system from *Konqueror,* click on *K/Logout.* To log off the system from the command line, type logout and press enter.

◼ The Command Line and GUI Layers

Throughout this chapter, you used both the shell and KDE to communicate with UNIX. One way to grasp the differences between these two interfaces is to view them as layers (Figure 9.38). When you issue a line command, you communicate *directly* with the operating system; in other words, each command activates a specific operating system routine that carries out the requested operation. When you work through a graphical user interface, however, you communicate with a GUI interface such as the KDE desktop metaphor. Your mouse clicks and menu selections are essentially interpreted by the GUI to obtain the functional equivalent of line commands, and those command equivalents are, in turn, passed down to UNIX. The GUI is easier to use because it presents a visual picture of the available options, but communicating through a GUI is relatively inefficient because the commands must be processed by an extra layer. Typing line commands can seem intimidating to a beginner, but they are more efficient because they reduce the number of layers separating the user from the operating system.

	The desktop metaphor	
Shell	KDE	
UNIX		

FIGURE 9.38

View the shell and a GUI as layers.

◼ Summary

Linux is an open source version of UNIX. The user of a modern Linux system can often choose between the traditional line command interface or shell and a graphical user interface such as KDE. The UNIX file system allows a user to store, retrieve, and manipulate files by name. The KDE file manager is called *Konqueror*. Because UNIX uses a hierarchical directory structure, a path name must be specified to completely identify a file.

The chapter tutorial switched back and forth between KDE and the command line shell. In the context of that tutorial, you viewed the contents of a directory, created a directory, created some files, displayed the contents of those files, copied files, and searched for files by file name.

Many UNIX utilities and commands assume the standard input or output device. Redirection tells the shell to change the defaults. A filter accepts data from the standard input device, modifies them in some way, and sends the results to the standard output device. Pipes allow a user to link utilities and other programs, treating the standard output generated by one as the standard input for another. A shell script is a file that consists of a series of commands. A graphical user interface is more user friendly but less efficient than a command line interface.

◼ Key Words

Application Starter	panel
cd	passwd
cp	password
date	path name
desktop	pipe
directory	POSIX
extension	prompt
file name	redirection
file system	root directory
filter	shell
home directory	shell mode
KDE (K-Desktop Environment)	shell script
kernel	sort
Konqueror	taskbar
Konsole	UNIX
line command	vi
Linux	virtual desktop
login name	who
ls	wild card
mkdir	working directory
navigation panel	

■ Review Questions

1. Discuss the origins of UNIX and Linux.
2. Describe the KDE desktop interface.
3. Describe the general form of a UNIX line command.
4. Distinguish between the root directory, your home directory, and your working directory.
5. Describe the components of a UNIX path name, including any intermediate directories and the file name.
6. View the contents of a directory using *Konqueror*.
7. View the contents of a directory using UNIX line commands.
8. Explain the significance of the (.) and (..) file names. What do they mean? Why are they useful?
9. Create a directory using *Konqueror*.
10. Create a directory using UNIX line commands.
11. Create a file using KDE.
12. Create a file using UNIX line commands.
13. View the contents of a file using *Konqueror*.
14. View the contents of a file using UNIX line commands.
15. Copy a file using *Konqueror*.
16. Copy a file using UNIX line commands.
17. Search for a file using KDE.
18. Search for a file using UNIX line commands.
19. Explain how wild card characters can enhance the search process.
20. Explain redirection, filters, and pipes.
21. What is a shell script? Why are shell scripts useful?
22. Compare and contrast a graphical user interface and a line command interface. What are the strengths and weaknesses of each?

■ Exercises

1. If you haven't already done so, work through the chapter tutorial.
2. Relate the UNIX shell and the KDE graphical user interface to the command processor introduced in Chapter 5.
3. Go online, find a version of the hacker's creed, and read it. Do you agree or disagree with the principles stated in that creed? Why?
4. Briefly describe a hierarchical directory structure. What advantages does it offer over a simple linear directory structure?

5. When you log on, your home directory is your working directory. Why would you want to change that?

6. Why is it that some people prefer the UNIX line command interface and other people prefer a graphical user interface such as KDE?

7. Relate pipes, filters, and redirection to the layering concept.

8. Compare a UNIX shell script to an MS-DOS batch file (Chapter 7).

9. Figures 9.1 and/or 9.38 are useful templates for organizing many of this chapter's key terms, but the most effective way to learn the key terms is to complete the chapter tutorial.

Operating System Internals

This section drops inside the operating system, discusses the Intel architecture (Chapter 10), and explains how several popular operating systems, including MS-DOS (Chapter 11), Windows XP (Chapter 12), Macintosh OS X (Chapter 13), UNIX/Linux (Chapter 14), and IBM's traditional mainframe operating system (Chapter 15), work internally. In Part 5, the stand alone systems discussed in this section will be treated as layers that can be plugged together to form complex distributed systems.

CHAPTER 10

The Intel Architecture

When you finish reading this chapter you should be able to:

▶ Explain how the Intel Pentium family of processors fetches and executes instructions.

▶ Describe the Intel architecture's execution environment.

▶ Distinguish between a logical address and a physical address.

▶ Distinguish between a flat memory model and a segmented memory model.

▶ Describe the process of translating a logical segment address into a physical address.

▶ Describe the components of an Intel task.

▶ Discuss the Intel architecture's memory protection features.

▶ Describe the Intel Pentium interrupt handling process.

▶ Explain pipelining.

▶ Distinguish between Intel's 32-bit architecture and Intel's 64-bit Itanium architecture.

▣ Introduction

Chapters 7, 8, and 9 focused on the operating system's user interface. This chapter is concerned with the Intel hardware environment and the operating system's hardware interface (Figure 10.1). Initially established with the release of the Intel 4004 in early 1971 and the Intel 8086 in the early 1980s, the Intel architecture (IA) remains the foundation of the processors that power most of the personal computers in operation today, including the Pentium family and the Celeron family. This chapter introduces the Intel architecture and its principles of operation. Chapters 11 and 12 describe two operating systems, MS-DOS and Windows XP, designed to work in the context of the Intel architecture.

▣ Intel Architecture Overview

A simplified block diagram of the Intel architecture that supports the Pentium family of processors is shown in Figure 10.2. The processor is responsible for fetching instructions and decoding those instructions into a series of micro-operations. The processor then executes the micro-operations.

Cache is an area of high-speed memory that sits between the processor and primary memory. Frequently accessed instructions and data are copied from memory to cache to speed up the processor because transfers from cache are faster than transfers from primary memory. The memory subsystem of the Pentium processor consists of primary memory and two integrated caches, a primary cache (L1) and a secondary cache (L2).

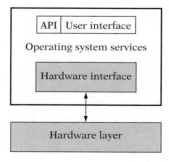

FIGURE 10.1

This chapter is concerned with the Intel hardware environment and the operating system's hardware interface.

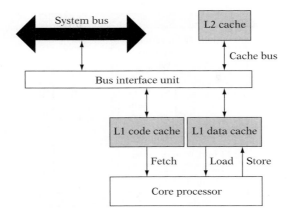

FIGURE 10.2

A simplified block diagram of the Pentium architecture.

Instructions are fetched into the L1 code cache. The L1 *data* cache holds frequently accessed data. A cache hit occurs when the processor requests data already present in the L1 data cache. A miss occurs when the data requested are not in the cache. In the event of a miss, the L1 data cache hands the operation off to the L2 cache, which requests the data from the system bus. In addition to distinguishing between the L1 and L2 caches, the Pentium processor also distinguishes between data and instruction (or code) caches. Consequently, the instruction fetch operation can proceed in parallel with the data access operation, which enhances cache read and write speed.

Intel Execution Environment

Inside an Intel architecture processor are eight 32-bit general-purpose registers, six 16-bit segment registers, and two status and control registers: EIP (the instruction pointer register), and EFLAGS (Figure 10.3). The general-purpose registers are used as storage areas for the results of arithmetic and logical operations, for address calculations, and for memory pointers. The six 16-bit segment registers—CS, DS, SS, ES, FS, and GS—hold pointers to segment locations in memory. The instruction pointer (EIP) register contains the offset (or displacement) in the current code segment for the next instruction to be executed. The EFLAGS register stores the status of most instructions. For example, several arithmetic status flags indicate the results (carry, parity, sign, overflow, and so on) of arithmetic instructions.

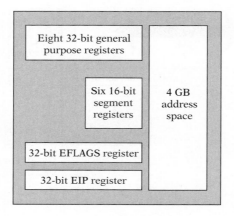

FIGURE 10.3

The Pentium's execution environment.

Architectures and Micro Architectures

When a company (such as Intel) designs a new processor, the engineers start by defining an architecture, defining a micro architecture, and selecting a clock speed. The architecture is intended to be stable for perhaps ten to twenty-five years; Intel's 32-bit architecture is a good example. Micro architectures, in contrast, change every few years; for example, the Intel 32-bit architecture supports the 486, Pentium I, Pentium II, Pentium III, Pentium IV, and P6 processors, but each of those processors has a different micro architecture. Clock speed, of course, changes very frequently—perhaps as often as several times a year.

Intel has defined a new architecture to support the company's 64-bit Itanium processors. The Itanium is targeted for the lucrative, $25 billion a year server market currently dominated by IBM and Sun. Intel's interest in the 64-bit server market is understandable when you look at the revenue numbers. Although 64-bit machines account for only about five percent of the total server units sold worldwide, they account for roughly sixty five percent of worldwide server revenue[1].

[1]Kirkpatrick, David. February 17, 2003. "See This Chip?" *Fortune:* 78-88.

Execution Mode

The Intel architecture supports four modes of operation. **Real address mode** is for systems that still run older 8086 programs. In this mode the processor is treated as a high speed 8086. MS-DOS operates in real address mode. After reset or power up, the processor goes into the real mode before most operating systems (except MS-DOS) switch into **protected mode.**

Operating systems such as Windows XP and Linux run in protected mode. Protected mode provides the code and data protection that allows multiple programs to run concurrently without interfering with each other. **Virtual 8086 mode** runs under protected mode. Under virtual 8086 mode, an 8086 processor is simulated in a separate protected region of memory, thus allowing 8086 applications to execute while still enjoying the full benefits of the protection mechanism. The primary purpose of this mode is to provide compatibility with old MS-DOS programs while allowing the concurrent execution of Windows XP or Linux applications. When a user opens an MS-DOS window in Windows 95, Windows 98, or Windows 2000, the processor is running in virtual 8086 mode. Finally, **system management mode** is used primarily for system security and power management.

◼ Memory Addressing

In Intel usage, real memory is called physical memory and is organized as a sequence of bytes. Each byte is assigned a unique **physical address** by counting the bytes sequentially starting with zero (0). The processor can reference physical addresses from 0 to a maximum 4 GB, but a typical microcomputer system contains far less physical memory.

Program instructions (software) specify **logical addresses.** A logical address consists of a base address and an offset from the base address. Note that a logical address is *relative* to some reference location and need not be associated with a *specific* physical address. For example, a logical address can refer to a location in virtual memory, and the translation from a logical virtual address to a real physical address can be postponed until execution time.

Address Translation

In a **flat memory model,** (Figure 10.4) the program sees a single continuous, byte addressable address space called the **linear address space.** The addresses run from 0 to 4 GB, and the base address is always 0. Hence, the offset is the actual physical address and is called a **linear address.**

In a **segmented model,** memory is pictured not as a continuous address space but as a group of independent address spaces called segments. In a segmented logical address (Figure 10.5), the **segment selector** identifies the segment. The segment selector, in turn, points to the **segment descriptor** (Figure 10.6) which holds the segment's base address. The actual logical address is an offset within this segment. At execution time, the processor translates the logical address to a linear address by adding the offset to the segment's base address. The segment descriptors for all the segments are stored in a **descriptor table.**

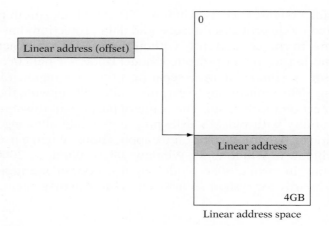

FIGURE 10.4
A flat memory model.

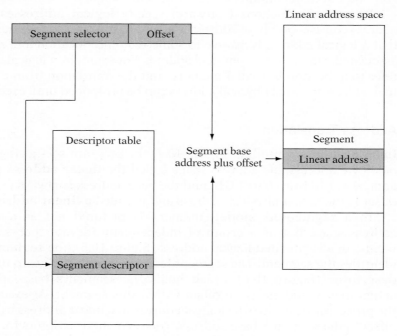

FIGURE 10.5
A logical, segmented address.

FIGURE 10.6
Segment address translation.

Paging

On a virtual memory system, the computed linear address refers to a location in virtual memory and not to a real physical address. Generally, virtual memory is divided into fixed length, 4 KB pages, and programs and data are swapped between virtual and real memory a page at a time. Consequently, additional address translation is required before the instruction can be executed.

On an Intel machine, when a program references a logical address, the processor's segmentation mechanism translates it into a physical address. First, the address is translated into a linear (virtual) address as described above. The linear address is then broken into three parts (Figure 10.7). The high-order bits (22 to 31) contain an offset to an entry in the **page directory** table. (The address of the page directory table is found in a system register.) The page directory entry points to a **page table** and bits 12 to 21 of the linear address contain an offset to an entry in the page table. The page table entry, in turn, points to a page, and bits 0 through 11 of the linear address contain an offset to the actual byte on this page. Since the page directory and page table offsets are 10 bits each, they can address 1024 times 1024 pages of 4 KB each, yielding a maximum address space of 4 GB.

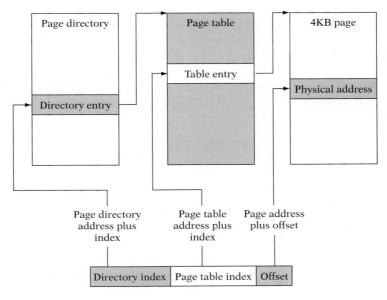

FIGURE 10.7

Linear-to-physical address translation.

Bit 0 of the page table or page directory entry contains the P or present flag. The P flag indicates if the page (or the page-table) pointed to by the entry is in physical memory. If the flag is 1, the page is already in physical memory and address translation is carried out. If the flag is zero (0), a page fault occurs and the referenced page is swapped into real memory. In order to speed up page translation, the processor stores the most recently accessed page directory and page table entries in the translation lookaside buffer (TLB).

Task Management

A **task** is a unit of work that the processor can dispatch, execute, and suspend, such as a program, a process, an interrupt handler, or an operating system process. Under the Intel architecture, a task (Figure 10.8) consists of a **task execution space** and a **task state segment (TSS).** The task execution space holds the code, stack, and data segments. The task state segment points to the segments in the task execution space. It also provides a storage space for the processor's state information (such as the contents of the registers). When a user switches to a new task, the processor saves the state of the current task by storing all the registers in the task state segment before the new task starts executing.

Memory Protection

Memory protection helps to prevent one task from accidentally or intentionally changing the contents of memory assigned to another task. Any vio-

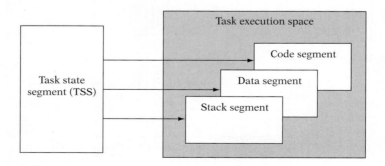

FIGURE 10.8
A task consists of a task execution space and a task state segment (TSS).

lation of a protection mechanism results in a general protection fault and, usually, the termination of the responsible task. Limit checking ensures that a given memory access is not beyond the segment's boundaries. For example, if a segment is defined to be 50 bytes long, the offset cannot not be greater than or equal to 50 because such an offset would result in a memory access beyond the segment's boundary. Type checking ensures that only code, data, or stack segment descriptors are used and that they are used as intended. The processor examines the segment descriptor to determine its type. It then ensures that the segment descriptor is used properly. For example, a code segment cannot be written into.

The processor's segment protection feature assigns one of four **privilege levels** (numbered 0 through 3) to each active task (Figure 10.9). Level 0 has the highest privilege and level 3 has the lowest privilege. A task executing at a lower privilege level cannot access a segment or page associated with a higher privilege task. Usually, the operating system runs at level 0 and applications run at level 3, which prevents applications from accessing operating system objects.

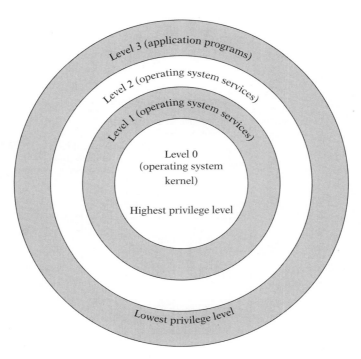

FIGURE 10.9
Segment protection privilege levels.

◧ Interrupt Handling

An interrupt is an electronic signal that results in the forced transfer of control to an interrupt handling routine. Interrupts can originate with either hardware or software. They are asynchronous; in other words, an interrupt can occur at any time and need not be timed to match the processor's clock pulses. In contrast, an **exception** is a synchronous event that is generated when the processor detects a predefined condition such as division by 0. Note that an exception occurs during the machine cycle when the predefined condition is detected. Because machine cycles are driven by the clock, exceptions occur in response to a clock pulse and thus are synchronized with the processor. The processor handles interrupts and exceptions similarly by halting execution of the current task and switching to an interrupt handling procedure. If possible, the interrupted program or task resumes processing upon completion of the interrupt handling procedure.

Associated with every interrupt (Figure 10.10) is an identification number (0 through 255) called a **vector.** The processor maintains an **interrupt descriptor table (IDT)** that associates each interrupt vector with an

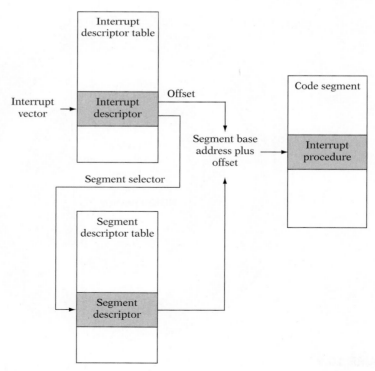

FIGURE 10.10

Interrupt procedure calls.

interrupt descriptor. (The address of the interrupt descriptor table is found in a system register.) The interrupt descriptor points to the base address of the executable code segment that holds the interrupt handling code. Adding the segment's base address and the offset (from the interrupt descriptor) yields the address of the first instruction in the interrupt handling procedure.

▣ Improving the Performance of the Intel Architecture

Intel uses a variety of techniques to enhance processing speed and functionality with each processor chip upgrade.

Pipelining and Superpipelining

Pipelining is a technique that allows a single processor to simultaneously process multiple instructions. The underlying idea is to break the machine cycle into multiple stages, with each stage representing a portion of the cycle. For example, on many computers each machine cycle is broken into four discrete stages: fetch, decode, execute, and write-back. During fetch the instruction control unit retrieves the next instruction from memory (or cache) and moves it into the processor. During the decode stage, the processor translates the instruction into one or more simple instructions called micro-operations. During the execute stage, the micro-operations are dispatched and executed. Finally, the results are written back to memory.

A nonpipelined processor fetches a single instruction, decodes it, executes it, writes the results to memory, and then fetches the next instruction. A pipelined processor, in contrast, fetches the first instruction and then fetches the second instruction while the first instruction is being decoded. Thus, at any given time there are four instructions in the pipeline (Figure 10.11), with one instruction at each machine cycle phase. Pipelining increases the microprocessor's throughput.

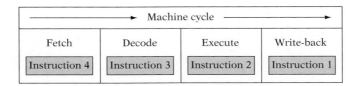

FIGURE 10.11
Pipelining.

The machine cycle on a **superpipelining** chip is broken into more than four stages, allowing a faster clock cycle than is possible with a normal pipelined processor. The Pentium II and Pentium Pro chips use a super-pipeline with twelve-stage instructions, and the Pentium IV chip features a twenty-stage machine cycle.

A **scalar** processor is a chip that uses a single pipeline. **Superscalar** chips use more than one pipeline and thus allow more than one instruction to be executed simultaneously. For example, the Pentium chip uses two integer pipelines and a floating-point pipeline and thus can execute as many as three instructions simultaneously.

Hyperthreading

The growing gap between processor speed and memory speed results in a latency problem as the processor waits for data to be transferred from memory. The result is processor underutilization. One solution is to utilize the idle latency time associated with a given task by performing computations related to a different task. Executing tasks (as opposed to instructions) in parallel is called **hyperthreading.**

Hyperthreading achieves thread-level parallelism by allowing the operating system to see two logical processors instead of just one. The system maintains copies of both logical processors' states (the contents of their general purpose registers and key control registers), and the logical processors share the remaining physical execution resources (Figure 10.12). From the real processor's perspective, instructions from the logical processors execute simultaneously on the shared execution resources, so the operating system can schedule tasks across the two logical processors. Intel has already implemented hyperthreading in their Pentium IV processors

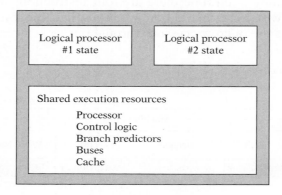

FIGURE 10.12

Hyperthreading presents the operating system with two logical processors.

operating at 3.06 GHz and above and estimates potential performance gains of as much as 25 percent. Those performance gains are far from guaranteed, however, because programs must be written specifically to take advantage of hyperthreading and few such programs exist today.

Out-of-Order Execution and Branch Prediction

Normally, the instructions in a program are executed sequentially, but if there are no dependencies among the instructions it is sometimes possible to execute them out of order. For example, consider the set of instructions outlined in Figure 10.13. Note that instruction B is dependent on instruction A because instruction B cannot be executed until the value of R1 is known. Consequently, instructions A and B must be executed in sequence. However, instructions C and D are independent of A and B and of each other, so they can be executed in any order.

If you assume that each instruction is executed in a single machine cycle and that the instructions are executed sequentially, the routine outlined in Figure 10.13 will finish processing in four machine cycles. However, if instructions A, C, and D are executed in parallel during a first clock cycle and B (which depends on A) is executed during a second clock cycle, the total time to execute the routine is cut in half. Note that the instructions are retired (written back to memory) in their original order to maintain data integrity.

A branch instruction is any instruction that causes a break in the sequential execution of instructions. Examples include branch, jump, procedure call, return, and interrupts. The Pentium processor attempts to identify the target instruction for the program's next jump, pre-fetches the instruction, decodes it, and speculatively executes it. If the prediction is correct, processor throughput is increased. If the prediction is incorrect, the processor must flush the speculative execution, fetch the correct instruction, and execute it instead. The Pentium chip tries to predict up to the next branch. The P6 chip goes a step further and predicts multiple branches and returns. The Pentium IV generates fewer incorrect branch predictions than the P6 by keeping a detailed history of its past branches in a buffer and using an improved branch prediction algorithm.

A	R1 = Mem(x)
B	R2 = R1 – R3
C	R4 = 100
D	R5 = R5 – 10

FIGURE 10.13

Out-of-order instruction execution.

MMX Technology

MMX (Multimedia Extensions) **technology** is a set of extensions built on top of the Intel architecture that enhance the performance of multimedia applications such as video, audio, and 3D graphics. The extensions include new registers, data types, and additional instructions to support multimedia.

With a normal instruction, the processor works on one piece of data at a time. In contrast, with the new MMX instructions the processor simultaneously manipulates many data values in parallel. For example, multiplying all the elements in an array by a constant is a common operation in image processing and graphical analysis. On a non-MMX processor, the multiplication is performed repetitively on every element in the array. With MMX, new data types are supported for these applications and all the multiplication is done in parallel, which enhances processor speed.

The L2 cache (Figure 10.2) is useful only if the data are reused frequently by the processor. However, when you play back a streaming video (such as an MPEG file or an MP3 audio file), you process the data only once. The new MMX instructions remove the L2 cache from the data transfer path, writing and reading directly from memory instead. The result is better multimedia performance.

The PowerPC

The PowerPC is the processor that drives Apple's Macintosh computers and runs in 64-bit mode on the Nintendo and Sony PlayStation 2. The Apple G4 uses the PowerPC 7450 and 7455 processors, both of which deliver good performance relative to comparable Pentium processors. Much like an MMX-enhanced Pentium processor, the PowerPC supports single instruction multiple data (SIMD) processing which enables the acceleration of multimedia operations. The SIMD instructions are executed in a separate functional unit within the processor, allowing the system to crunch data while simultaneously performing extensive multimedia operations. The PowerPC instruction set is not compatible with the Intel platform, however, which helps to explain the difference between Intel and Apple multimedia data formatting standards.

◼ Intel's 64-Bit Itanium Architecture

The Intel 64-bit **Itanium** architecture is a radical departure from the Intel 32-bit Pentium architecture, although the Itanium chip is designed to run existing Pentium code by emulating Intel's 32-bit architecture in hardware.

The Itanium chip can address up to 16 exabytes (10^{18} bytes) of logical memory and 8 exabytes of physical memory and has 128 general purpose registers, 128 floating-point registers, 64 predicate registers, and 8 branch registers. Additionally, because a 64-bit processor runs significantly faster than a 32-bit processor, the Itanium architecture enables an order of magnitude improvement in application performance. Today, 64-bit chips based on the IBM Power chip are an evolving standard in the highly demanding electronic game industry, where they power the Nintendo 64 and the Sony PlayStation 2.

There are two ways to increase a chip's throughput. One is to do things more quickly by, for example, increasing clock speed. Intel achieves this objective by implementing enhanced out-of-order execution and branch prediction capabilities in the Itanium chip.

A second option is to make the chip do more things in parallel. Intel increases parallelism by incorporating a technique called explicitly parallel instructional computing (EPIC) in its new Itanium architecture. The key to this technique is to bundle instructions. The Itanium fetches a 128-bit (2-word) instruction bundle that contains up to three 41-bit instructions and a 5-bit template that tells the processor how to handle the instructions (Figure 10.14). Sometimes the instructions must be executed in sequence, so the bundle holds only one instruction. In other cases, however, two or even all three instructions can be executed in parallel, so the bundle holds two or three instructions. With Intel's Itanium architecture, the compiler explicitly determines which instructions should share a bundle, an approach that distinguishes the Itanium architecture from other bundling systems such as Transmeta.

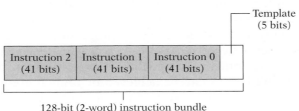

FIGURE 10.14
An Itanium instruction bundle.

▌Summary

The processor is responsible for fetching instructions and decoding those instructions into a series of micro-operations. The Intel architecture relies on a set of caches to streamline the data and instruction fetch processes. The processor runs in one of four modes: real address mode, protected mode, virtual 8086 mode, or system management mode.

Each byte of physical memory is assigned a unique physical address. A logical address is made up of a base address and an offset from the base address. In a flat memory model, the program sees a single continuous address space called the linear address space. In the segmented model, the program sees memory as a group of independent address spaces called segments. When a program or task references a logical address, the processor's segmentation mechanism translates it to a physical address. First, the logical address is converted to a linear address. Then the linear address is broken into three parts: an index to a page directory, an index to a page table, and an offset on the page.

A task is a unit of work that the processor can dispatch, execute, and suspend. An Intel architecture task consists of a task execution space and a task state segment. The task execution space holds the code, stack, and data segments. Memory protection helps to prevent one task from changing the contents of memory assigned to another task. The processor assigns each task one of four privilege levels to support memory protection.

The processor handles interrupts and exceptions similarly by halting execution of the current task and switching to an interrupt handling procedure. Associated with every interrupt is an identification number called a vector. The processor maintains an interrupt descriptor table (IDT) that associates each interrupt vector with an interrupt descriptor that is used to service the interrupt.

Pipelining allows multiple instructions to be processed simultaneously, thus enhancing processor throughput. A superpipelining chip uses more than four stages to complete an instruction. Superscalar chips use more than one pipeline and thus allow more than one instruction to be executed simultaneously. Executing tasks in parallel is called hyperthreading. Normally, the instructions in a program are executed sequentially, in the order they are received, but if there are no dependencies among the instructions it is sometimes possible to execute them out of order. Additional throughput gains can be achieved by branch prediction. MMX technology is a set of extensions built on top of the Intel architecture that enhance the performance of multimedia applications. The Intel 64-bit Itanium architecture is a radical departure from Intel's 32-bit Pentium architecture.

◼ Key Words

cache	privilege level
descriptor table	protected mode
exception	real address mode
flat memory model	scalar
hyperthreading	segment descriptor
interrupt descriptor table (IDT)	segment selector
Itanium	segmented model
linear address	superpipelining
linear address space	superscalar
logical address	system management mode
memory protection	task
MMX technology	task execution space
page directory	task state segment (TSS)
page table	vector
physical address	virtual 8086 mode
pipelining	

◼ Review Questions

1. Explain how the Intel Pentium family of processors fetches and executes instructions.
2. Describe the Intel architecture's execution environment.
3. Identify an Intel processor's four operating modes.
4. Distinguish between a logical address and a physical address.
5. Distinguish between a flat memory model and a segmented memory model.
6. Distinguish between a segment selector and a segment descriptor.
7. Describe the process of translating a logical segment address into a physical address.
8. Identify the components of an Intel architecture task.
9. Explain how a Pentium system switches to a new task.
10. Explain how limit checking, type checking, and privilege levels support memory protection.
11. Distinguish between an interrupt and an exception.
12. Explain how a Pentium system processes an interrupt.
13. Explain pipelining. Distinguish between pipelining and superpipelining.
14. Distinguish between a scalar processor and a superscalar processor.
15. What is hyperthreading? How does Intel implement hyperthreading?

16. Explain how a processor can execute instructions out of sequence.

17. Explain how branch prediction can help to enhance processor throughput.

18. What are some advantages of MMX technology?

19. Distinguish between Intel's 32-bit architecture and Intel's 64-bit Itanium architecture.

◼ Exercises

1. Identify the processor that powers your computer.

2. Read an advertisement for a state-of-the art personal computer system and interpret the specifications.

3. Why do you suppose companies like Intel distinguish between an architecture and a micro architecture?

4. Why is memory protection necessary?

5. Distinguish between the standard PC platform and the computer gaming platform operating environments.

6. Figures 10.2, 10.7, and 10.8 are useful templates for organizing many of this chapter's key terms.

MS-DOS Internals

When you finish reading this chapter you should be able to:

▶ Distinguish between resident and transient modules.

▶ Relate the functions of COMMAND.COM to the general functions of a command processor or shell as described in Chapter 5.

▶ Identify the functions performed by IO.SYS and MSDOS.SYS and explain why it makes sense to split these sets of functions.

▶ Relate the functions performed by IO.SYS and MSDOS.SYS to the basic concepts of logical and physical I/O.

▶ Sketch the contents of an MS-DOS disk.

▶ Explain how a disk file's clusters are linked through the file allocation table.

▶ Explain how MS-DOS processes interrupts.

▶ Sketch the contents of memory immediately after MS-DOS has been booted.

◼ MS-DOS

MS-DOS was once the world's most commonly used microcomputer operating system. In fact, the earliest versions of Windows ran on top of MS-DOS, much like an application program. By the late 1990s, however, Windows had become an operating system in its own right and MS-DOS was relegated to the Windows *Accessories* submenu. Today, MS-DOS has essentially disappeared inside Windows, but you can still execute MS-DOS line commands from the Windows XP command line.

This chapter discusses the internal structure of MS-DOS before its functions were absorbed into Windows.

Resident and Transient Routines

Every operating system contains a set of **resident** routines that must be in memory at all times. Sometimes called the **nucleus,** the **kernel,** or the **supervisor,** the resident core typically contains an **input/output control system** or **IOCS,** a **file system,** various interrupt handling routines, and resource management routines (Figure 11.1). The **command processor** or **shell** is not generally considered part of the kernel, but it too must be resident. Also resident are a number of system constants, parameters, and

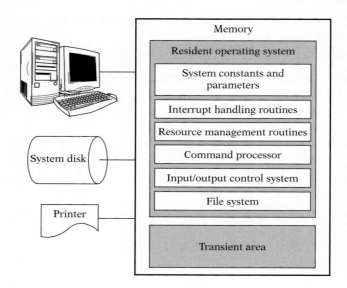

FIGURE 11.1

The components of a typical operating system.

control fields. These routines and parameters reside in memory and provide real-time support to active application and system programs.

Not all operating routines must be resident, however. Consider, for example, formatting a disk. Because the routine that performs this task is needed only when a disk is actually being formatted, it resides on disk and is loaded into memory on demand. The free area or **transient area** of memory (Figure 11.1), which contains all the space not allocated to the resident operating system, holds these **transient** modules and active application programs.

The Shell

MS-DOS is a command-driven operating system; you studied its command language in Chapter 7. Users request operating system services by typing commands in response to a system prompt. When the enter key is pressed, an operating system component called **COMMAND.COM** (the shell) interprets the command and calls the appropriate lower level routine or program. COMMAND.COM consists of a command interpreter and a number of resident operating system routines that remain in memory at all times (Figure 11.2). Other COMMAND.COM routines are transient and are read into memory on demand. Generally, the resident routines support active programs as they run.

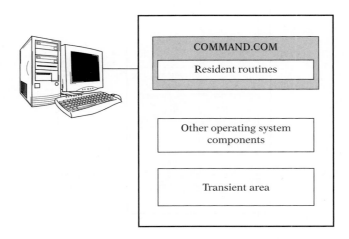

FIGURE 11.2
The MS-DOS command processor is called COMMAND.COM.

Accessing Peripherals

The task of accessing peripheral devices is divided between two operating system components: IO.SYS and MSDOS.SYS (Figure 11.3). **IO.SYS** is a hardware dependent module that issues *physical* data transfer commands. IO.SYS interacts with the basic input/output system (BIOS), which is usually implemented in read-only memory. Logical I/O is supported by a hardware *independent* module called **MSDOS.SYS.** MSDOS.SYS accepts logical I/O requests from application programs or other operating system modules, translates them into physical I/O commands, and passes the physical commands to IO.SYS. Note that only IO.SYS, the machine *dependent* module, communicates *directly* with peripheral devices. A version of MS-DOS written for a COMPAQ computer and one written for a Dell computer will differ only in their IO.SYS; other operating system modules should be the same.

Each physical device attached to the computer is described in a special file called a **device driver** (Figure 11.4). Character drivers control such devices as the keyboard, the screen, and the printer. Block drivers control disk and similar block-oriented devices and transfer data in 512-byte blocks. The device driver is used by MSDOS.SYS to translate logical I/O requests to physical form. Certain standard device drivers, such as COM1 (the first serial printer or modem), CON (the console), and PRN (the first parallel printer) are built into the operating system. Additional devices can be defined by adding a description to a special file called CONFIG.SYS.

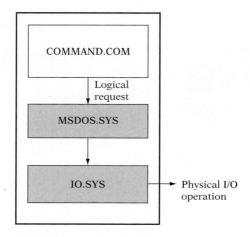

FIGURE 11.3

IO.SYS and MSDOS.SYS share responsibility for communicating with peripheral devices.

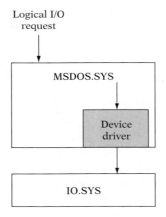

FIGURE 11.4

MSDOS.SYS uses a device driver to translate logical I/O requests to physical form.

Layering

If you look carefully at Figure 11.3, you'll see an excellent example of the layering concept introduced in Chapter 1. COMMAND.COM initiates an I/O operation (often in response to an application program request), MSDOS.SYS performs the necessary logical I/O functions, IO.SYS takes care of physical I/O, and those three modules communicate by passing parameters back and forth. Because the responsibility for I/O is divided among three independent routines, it is possible to enhance any one of those routines without affecting the others. Perhaps the most dramatic example of functional independence affected COMMAND.COM. The first releases of Microsoft Windows essentially replaced the traditional command processor with a GUI that passed commands down to the same MSDOS.SYS and IO.SYS routines that COMMAND.COM once called. Today's Windows incorporates enhanced logical and physical I/O support, but the modular design of MS-DOS allowed Microsoft to get a head start on the transition from command lines to a GUI.

The File System

MSDOS.SYS is the MS-DOS file system. In addition to translating logical I/O requests to physical form, it is also responsible for directory management. Chapter 7 introduced the MS-DOS directory structure; if you completed the chapter tutorial, you know how to create and delete directories with operating system commands. For example, when a make directory command, such as

MKDIR LETTERS

is accepted by COMMAND.COM, the shell calls MSDOS.SYS (Figure 11.5a), which, in turn, calls IO.SYS to read the directory (Figure 11.5b). MSDOS.SYS then inserts the new directory entry (Figure 11.5c), and calls IO.SYS to rewrite the modified directory back to disk (Figure 11.5d). Generally, MSDOS.SYS creates, deletes, and modifies directory entries in response to requests from COMMAND.COM (or an application routine), and relies on IO.SYS to perform the actual data transfer operations.

MSDOS.SYS also supports application program I/O. When a disk file is first opened, MSDOS.SYS calls IO.SYS to read the directory. MSDOS.SYS then extracts the location of an existing file or creates a directory entry for a new one and, if necessary, calls IO.SYS to rewrite the directory. As the program runs, each logical input and output operation implies a transfer of control to MSDOS.SYS. Using the start of file address from open, the operating system computes the physical address of the data and then passes the address to IO.SYS.

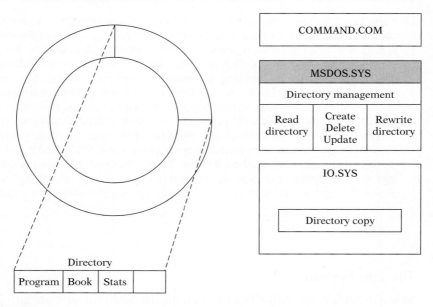

FIGURE 11.5

MSDOS.SYS is responsible for directory management.

a. Following a MKDIR command, COMMAND.COM calls MSDOS.SYS.

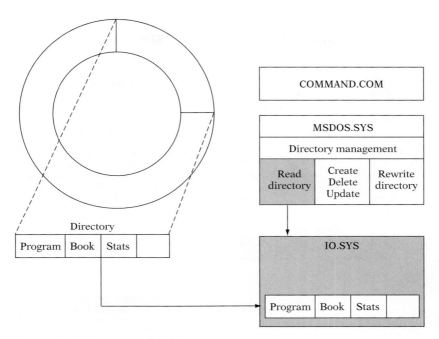

b. MSDOS.SYS calls IO.SYS to read the directory.

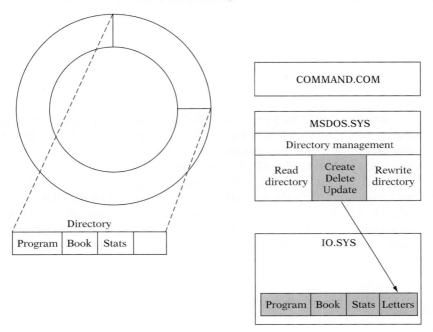

c. MSDOS.SYS adds a new directory entry.

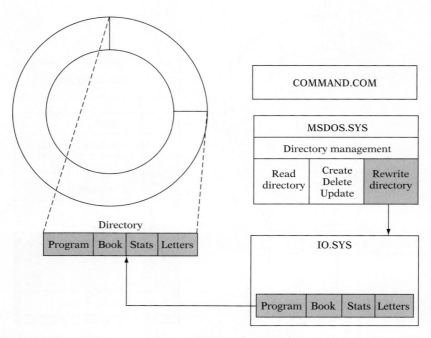

d. MSDOS.SYS calls IO.SYS to rewrite the directory to disk.

Another MSDOS.SYS responsibility is allocating space on disk. Quickly overview a disk's format (Figure 11.6). Track 0, sector 0 (the first sector on the disk) holds the boot routine. Next, in sectors 1 and 2 are two copies of the file allocation table (FAT); more about it later. The root directory begins with track 0, sector 5. On system disks, the various components of the operating system follow the root directory and the rest of the disk is used to hold files. If a disk does not contain a copy of the system, all the space after the root directory is used to hold files. Note that a file might contain software, data, or a directory.

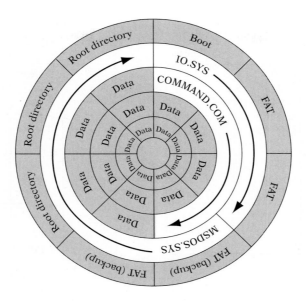

FIGURE 11.6
The format of a typical MS-DOS system disk.

The File Allocation Table (FAT)

Disk space is allocated in **clusters.** For example, on a diskette, each cluster holds 1024 bytes (two sectors) and the clusters are numbered sequentially starting with zero. The **file allocation table** contains an entry for each cluster on the disk.

When a file is created, the number of its first cluster is stored in the directory. As data are added to the file, the second cluster is assigned dynamically by recording its number in the first cluster's FAT entry; note that the first cluster points to the second one (Figure 11.7). As additional data are added, the third cluster's number is recorded in the second cluster's FAT entry, and so on. If you follow the chain of pointers from the directory, through the file allocation table, to the end of file marker, you step cluster by cluster through the file. Note that the clusters belonging to a file need not be contiguous.

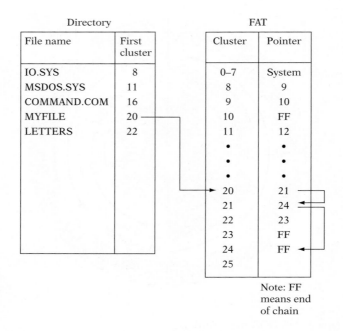

FIGURE 11.7
A file's clusters are linked by a chain of pointers in the file allocation table.

MS-DOS views the data stored in a disk file as a continuous stream of bytes. Logical I/O operations request data by relative *byte* (rather than by relative record or relative sector). A file's first cluster holds relative bytes 0 through 1023, its second cluster holds relative bytes 1024 through 2047, and so on. As part of its blocking and deblocking functions, MS-DOS.SYS calls IO.SYS to perform whatever physical I/O operations are necessary to access the requested string. Logically, data on disk are addressed just like data in memory.

Interrupt Processing

The Intel processor at the heart of most MS-DOS systems relies on **interrupts** to establish communication with its peripheral devices. As you may recall from Chapter 6, an interrupt is an electronic signal. Hardware senses the signal, saves key control information for the currently executing program, and starts the operating system's interrupt handling routine. At that instant, the interrupt ends. The operating system then processes the interrupt. Processing interrupts is an important MS-DOS function.

The key to MS-DOS interrupt processing is an **interrupt vector table** that occupies the first 1K bytes of memory. This table holds interrupt vectors, the addresses of up to 256 different interrupt processing routines, most of which are found in MSDOS.SYS or IO.SYS. Two special registers are also crucial. The instruction counter is found in the IP (instruction pointer) register, and another key register points to a memory stack.

The interrupt itself consists of an electronic pulse and the address of an interrupt vector. When an interrupt occurs, hardware immediately copies the contents of the IP register (along with a few other registers) to the stack (Figure 11.8a), and loads the specified interrupt vector into the IP register. (Figure 11.8b). With the next machine cycle, the first instruction in the interrupt processing routine is fetched (Figure 11.8c). Once the interrupt is processed, the contents of the stack are copied back into the IP register and the original program resumes processing (Figure 11.8d).

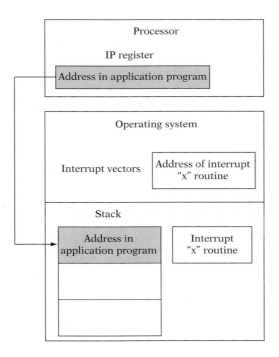

FIGURE 11.8

MS-DOS interrupt processing.

a. The contents of the instruction pointer (IP) register are copied to the stack.

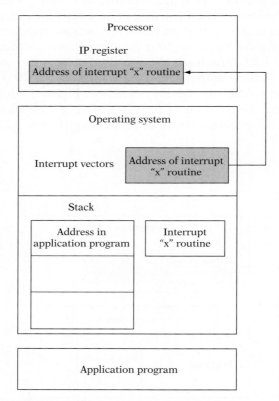

b. The specified interrupt vector is loaded into the instruction pointer.

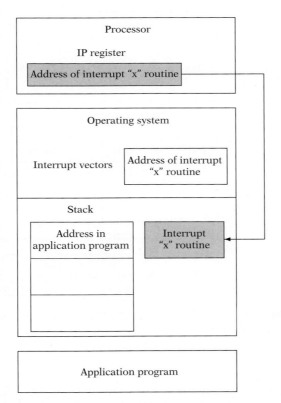

c. The first instruction in the interrupt processing routine is fetched.

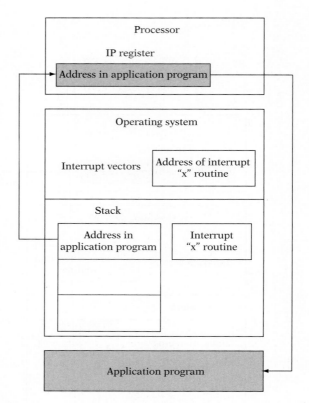

d. The contents of the stack are loaded back into the instruction pointer register and the application program resumes processing.

Interrupts are much more common than you might imagine. For example, an interrupt is generated each time you press a key on the keyboard. In response to the interrupt, the operating system copies a single character from the keyboard buffer into memory and then waits for the next interrupt to herald the arrival of the next character. A few keys, such as return and escape, signal the operating system to take a different action. Interrupts also allow the printer, a disk drive, and other peripherals to communicate with the processor.

Not all interrupts originate with hardware, however. Although it is legal for an application program to communicate directly with IO.SYS, most rely on MSDOS.SYS to translate their logical I/O requests to physical form. Branching to or calling an operating system module implies knowledge of MS-DOS internals that few people possess. Thus, by convention, an assembler language programmer who wants to perform I/O loads descriptive information into a few registers and then executes an interrupt instruction that references interrupt vector 33 (21 hex).

Hardware responds to a software generated interrupt exactly as if the source had been hardware, copying the IP register to the stack and loading the contents of the specified vector into the IP register. The address in vector 33 points to an MSDOS.SYS module that analyzes register contents and determines which I/O operation was requested. In compiler languages, the instructions to set registers and interrupt the operating system are generated for you.

Why Are Interrupts Necessary?

The telephone rings. How do you respond? Chances are, you stop what you're doing, pick up the telephone, and say "Hello." Think of the ring as an interrupt; note that it literally interrupts your train of thought. Think of "Hello" as the first step in processing the interrupt and you have a pretty good mental image of what an interrupt is.

But why are interrupts necessary? The answer, if you think about it, is pretty obvious—you had no idea someone was going to call you until the phone rang. You and your caller are independent. You function asynchronously. Unless you are incredibly psychic, you have no way of knowing precisely when someone might call, so you rely on the interrupt (in this case a ring, a buzz, or some other signal) to alert you when that asynchronous event occurs.

Inside a computer, such components as the processor, memory, and the bus are synchronized by the processor's clock, and intercomponent communication depends on precise timing. The peripheral devices in contrast operate asynchronously. For example, the processor has no way of predicting when you will press the next key on your keyboard. For all practical purposes, to the processor the timing of a keystroke is a random event comparable to the arrival of a telephone call.

When you press a key, the associated character is copied into a memory buffer and an interrupt is generated. In effect, the interrupt tells the system to "start accepting one character now." The process of transferring the character from the keyboard's memory buffer to the appropriate location in memory involves only internal components and thus can be synchronized by the processor's clock. In effect, the interrupt announces that a random event requiring processing has just occurred, giving the system a starting point for precisely timing its response to that event.

Much the same thing happens when an application program issues an interrupt to start an I/O operation. The processor and the peripheral are asynchronous. When the processor sends an interrupt to the peripheral, the electronic signal establishes a starting point for the two devices to synchronize their signals long enough to exchange the information the peripheral needs to carry out the operation. Simply put, interrupts are necessary because the computer and its peripherals are asynchronous and they must communicate with each other.

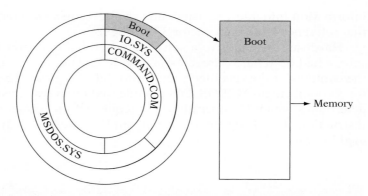

FIGURE 11.9
Hardware reads the boot routine from the first sector on the system disk.

Booting MS-DOS

Memory is volatile; it loses its contents when the computer loses power. Consequently, the operating system must be loaded into memory each time the computer is started. Under MS-DOS, the **boot** routine is stored on the first sector of each disk. Flipping the power switch (or simultaneously pressing *Ctrl, Alt,* and *Delete*) causes hardware to read into memory the first sector from the disk in the system drive (Figure 11.9). The boot then reads IO.SYS, which, in turn, initializes key system tables, reads MSDOS.SYS, and, finally, reads COMMAND.COM (Figure 11.10).

The COMMAND.COM modules that immediately follow MSDOS.SYS are resident. Other COMMAND.COM modules are stored at the high end of memory following the transient area. While technically resident, this second group of routines can be overlaid if necessary by a large application program. If they are overlaid, they must be restored after the program is finished.

Interrupt vectors (first 1K)
IO.SYS
MSDOS.SYS
COMMAND.COM (resident)
Transient area
COMMAND.COM (overlay)

FIGURE 11.10
The contents of memory after MS-DOS is booted.

Running MS-DOS

Once the operating system is booted, MS-DOS controls literally everything that happens on the computer. First, COMMAND.COM is activated and, by calling IO.SYS, displays a system prompt on the screen. As the user types a command, each character generates an interrupt. Responding to the interrupt, the operating system reads the character, stores it in memory, and, again using IO.SYS, displays it on the screen.

Eventually, the user presses enter. Like any other key, the enter key generates an interrupt. The interrupt handling routine recognizes the enter key as a special case, however, and calls the COMMAND.COM module that interprets commands. This module, in turn, either displays an error message or takes whatever action is necessary to carry out the command.

For example, imagine the user has typed a resident command such as DIR. Since the appropriate routine is already in memory, COMMAND.COM simply calls it. When the resident routine finishes carrying out the command, it calls COMMAND.COM, which displays a prompt and waits for the next command.

What if the command refers to a transient module or to an application program? Because these routines are not yet in memory, they must be loaded before they can execute. Thus, COMMAND.COM calls MSDOS.SYS and passes it the requested routine's name. MSDOS.SYS, in turn, reads (by calling IO.SYS) the disk directory, searches it, finds the referenced routine, and instructs IO.SYS to load it into the transient area. Once the requested routine is in memory, control is returned to COMMAND.COM. At this point, with the transient module in memory, there is no real difference between calling it and calling a resident routine.

The basic workflow is simple. A prompt is displayed. The user types a command or a program name and MS-DOS calls the appropriate operating system module or application program. As the program runs, the operating system supports it by processing interrupts. Eventually, the program returns control to COMMAND.COM and the process is repeated, again and again until the machine is shut down. MS-DOS is command driven.

■ Summary

The MS-DOS command processor is called COMMAND.COM. Physical I/O is controlled by IO.SYS. Logical I/O is the responsibility of MSDOS.SYS. The boot occupies the first sector of a disk. Next come two copies of the file allocation table, the root directory, the operating system (on a system disk), and, finally, file storage. Space on disk is allocated in clusters. The clusters are numbered sequentially, and an entry for each one is recorded in the file allocation table. The number of a file's first cluster is recorded in the directory. A file's clusters are linked by a series of pointers through the file allocation table.

The processor relies on interrupts to control communication with its peripherals, so interrupt processing is an important MS-DOS function. The first 1K bytes of memory hold up to 256 interrupt vectors. When an interrupt occurs, the contents of the instruction pointer are copied to the stack, the contents of the designated interrupt vector are loaded into the instruction pointer, and the interrupt processing routine begins running. After the interrupt is processed, the contents of the stack are loaded back into the instruction pointer and the original program resumes processing. Some interrupts originate with hardware; others originate with software.

The MS-DOS boot routine is stored on the first sector of each disk. When the computer is turned on, hardware reads the boot, which loads the rest of the operating system. The chapter's last section, *Running MS-DOS*, summarizes the operating system's primary features.

▆ Key Words

boot	IO.SYS
cluster	kernel
command processor	MS-DOS
COMMAND.COM	MSDOS.SYS
device driver	nucleus
file allocation table (FAT)	resident
file system	shell
input/output control system	supervisor
(IOCS)	transient
interrupt	transient area
interrupt vector table	

▆ Review Questions

1. Distinguish between resident and transient modules. Why does it make sense to have some modules transient? Why must other operating system modules be resident?

2. Relate the functions of COMMAND.COM to the general functions of a command processor or shell as described in Chapter 5.

3. The task of accessing physical devices is divided between IO.SYS and MSDOS.SYS. Briefly explain the functions performed by these two modules. Why does it make sense to split these sets of functions?

4. What is a device driver?

5. Relate the functions performed by IO.SYS and MSDOS.SYS to the basic concepts of logical and physical I/O.

6. Sketch the contents of an **MS-DOS** disk.

7. Explain how a disk file's clusters are linked through the file allocation table.

8. What is an interrupt? Explain how **MS-DOS** processes interrupts.

9. Why is a boot routine necessary?

10. Sketch the contents of memory immediately after **MS-DOS** has been booted.

▌ Exercises

1. Microcomputer operating systems generally contain a command processor, an input/output control system, and a file system; why *these* components?

2. Relate the modular design of **MS-DOS** to the layering concept you read about in Chapter 1.

3. Why are interrupts necessary?

4. Some interrupts originate with hardware. Others originate with software. Why?

5. Relate the process of communicating by telephone to the interrupt concept.

6. Figures 11.1 and 11.8a are useful templates for organizing many of this chapter's key terms.

CHAPTER 12

Windows XP Internals

When you finish reading this chapter you should be able to:

▶ Explain client/server mode.

▶ Discuss the relationship between the application program interface (API) and the dynamic link library (DLL).

▶ Identify the functions performed by the primary kernel mode components.

▶ Explain how the process manager creates a new process.

▶ Explain how the virtual memory manager implements paging.

▶ Describe the contents of a Windows XP 32-bit address and explain how a virtual address is translated into a physical (real) address.

▶ Discuss the organization of an NTFS disk.

▶ Explain how NTFS enables the smooth recovery of the file system following a system crash or disk failure.

▶ Explain how Windows XP uses caching.

▶ Explain the purpose of the registry.

◼ Windows XP

Windows XP is an update of Windows 2000, a multipurpose operating system that evolved from Windows NT and Windows 98. Windows NT was designed to run on several different types of processors and to support applications written for numerous environments such as MS-DOS, Windows, OS/2, and POSIX (a UNIX application programming interface), making it highly portable. Windows XP merges the best features of Windows 98 and Windows NT, but XP runs only on Intel architecture processors and no longer supports OS/2 or POSIX. Windows XP is available in 32-bit and 64-bit versions, and both home and professional versions are available. This chapter focuses on the 32-bit professional version's internal services that lie between the user interface and the hardware interface (Figure 12.1).

Client/Server Mode

In Windows usage, a module is a software component that provides a set of services to the rest of the system. Some Windows modules are configured in a hierarchical layered mode much like MS-DOS and UNIX. Other modules work in **client/server mode** (Figure 12.2). In client/server mode, each server module performs a single service such as a file service, a memory service, and so on. A client module requests a service by sending a message to the server module. The server module executes the request and sends the reply to the client module.

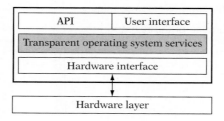

FIGURE 12.1

This chapter focuses on the 32-bit professional version's internal contents that lie between the user interface and the hardware interface.

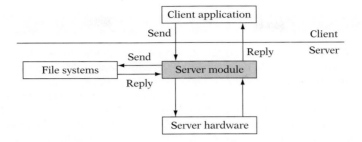

FIGURE 12.2
Client/server mode.

The client/server architecture offers several advantages over a hierarchy of layered modules[1]. It improves reliability because each service runs in its own process with its own memory that is protected from other processes. It provides a simple and uniform mechanism for processes to communicate with each other. Finally, it allows for new functionality to be added to the operating system by simply incorporating new service modules.

Reliability

Windows XP incorporates features that make it considerably more reliable than previous versions of Windows. For example, if you update a device driver and it does not function properly, XP allows you to roll back to a previous version. Additionally, the **system restore** feature allows you to roll back your entire system in the event of a problem. XP monitors changes to the system data and automatically creates system restore points at least daily. Restore points are also created whenever a device driver is updated or some other system change takes place. If a system failure occurs, the restore feature allows the system to be reset to the most recent restore point. Note that system restore does not monitor changes to your data, but Windows XP does include facilities that help to implement data monitoring.

---

[1]Note that it is still useful to view the client and the server as independent layers, but they are not linked to form a hierarchy.

Robustness

A system that recovers gracefully from errors is said to be robust. Earlier versions of Windows, particularly Windows 98 and Windows ME, were not known for their robustness because they tended to crash whenever an application misbehaved. In fact, system crashes were so common that the standard crash report, the so-called "Blue Screen of Death" or BSOD, has become a bit of a cliché. Windows XP evolved to a large degree from Windows NT, a much more stable operating system, and it is quite robust. For example, when your author was using Windows ME, his system typically crashed at least once a week. Since he upgraded to Windows XP, however, he has experienced zero (0) system crashes.

▰ Windows XP Architecture

A simple block diagram of the Windows architecture is shown in Figure 12.3. The system operates in either **user mode** or **kernel mode.** User applications and a collection of subsystems run in user mode. The primary kernel mode modules include the hardware abstraction layer (HAL), the kernel, and executive services. In contrast to user mode, kernel mode processes have access to the entire system memory and all processor instructions and can bypass Windows security to access objects. As you learned in Chapter 10, the Pentium architecture defines four privilege levels to protect system code and data from being inadvertently overwritten. The kernel processes run at level 0, while user processes run at level 3.

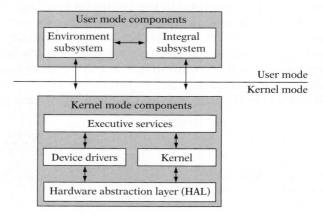

FIGURE 12.3

A block diagram of the Windows architecture.

User Mode

Application programs run in user mode within the **environment subsystem.** Because they are applications, they run at a lower priority than the kernel processes. Application programs are not allowed to directly access the hardware or the device drivers, so when a user issues a command (through the user interface) that requires operating system support, the program communicates with the kernel through an **application programming interface** or **API** (Figure 12.4). The API is a set of routines, protocols, and other tools that programmers, writing in a variety of languages, can use to build applications consistent with the underlying operating environment.

Rather than incorporating the API's routines and protocols into each application program, key functions and data are stored on the **dynamic link library (DLL).** From the programmer's perspective, the application program interface defines the rules for calling the dynamic link library's functions, and the DLL provides the necessary link with the operating system. Some DLL functions are written to support a specific application and are loaded statically when the program is launched. Most DLL functions are application independent, however. An application-independent function stored on the DLL can be accessed dynamically (as needed) and used simultaneously by numerous applications.

The 32-bit version of Windows XP is designed primarily to run 32-bit Windows (Win32) applications, but XP can also run MS-DOS applications and other 16-bit (Win16) applications (Figure 12.5), and you can optionally add the Interix subsystem to run UNIX applications. The Win32 subsystem is responsible for native Windows applications and screen-oriented I/O. Win16 and MS-DOS applications run on virtual DOS machines (VDMs) that understand the 16-bit calls.

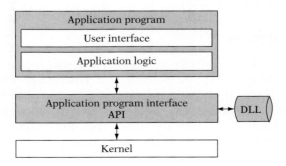

FIGURE 12.4

The application programming interface.

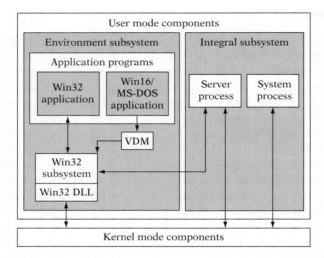

FIGURE 12.5
User mode components.

The other user mode component, the **integral subsystem,** is made up of server and system processes that provide protection and system services. A **service** is a program or process that performs a specific system function to support other programs. **Server processes** are Win32 services (such as event log, spooler, and so on) that are run automatically at startup. Server processes start up or shut down without user interaction, and many server processes are launched even before the user logs on. **System processes,** in contrast, do not run as services and require an interactive login. For example, the interactive login facility that accepts user logons and authenticates them is a system process.

Kernel Mode

One way to view the kernel mode processes is as a layered hierarchy (Figure 12.6). Starting at the bottom, the **Hardware Abstraction Layer (HAL)** hides the underlying hardware and provides a virtual machine interface to the other processes. Because such processor-specific functions as interrupt controllers and I/O interfaces are implemented in the hardware abstraction layer, the higher-level layers can be easily ported to different hardware environments.

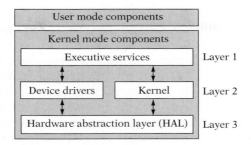

FIGURE 12.6
View the kernel mode processes as a layered hierarchy.

The second layer holds the device drivers and the kernel. The device drivers are responsible for translating logical I/O calls to specific physical I/O hardware primitives. The kernel (or microkernel) manages the microprocessor by coordinating dispatching and multiprocessor synchronization and handling asynchronous procedure calls such as interrupts, power notify, and power status functions (useful in laptops). Additionally, it provides the base kernel objects that are utilized by the executive.

The top layer consists of a set of modules collectively called the **executive** or **executive services** (Figure 12.7). Windows XP is an object-oriented system that uses objects for all its services and entities. Files, directories, processes, threads, and ports are all objects in Windows XP, and the **object manager,** pictured as the largest executive service, is responsible for creating, destroying, and granting access to an object's services or data. Access is provided to objects through a handle, a pointerlike reference to the object generated by the object manager.

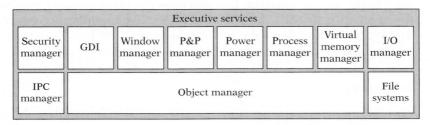

FIGURE 12.7
The top layer in kernel mode is the executive.

Moving clockwise from the object manager (Figure 12.7), the inter-process communication (IPC) manager is responsible for client/server communication, including local procedure calls that link a server and a client on the same computer and remote procedure calls that link server and client modules on different computers. The security manager is responsible for the security of the local computer's objects. Security information is associated with an object via a security descriptor, and the security manager uses the security descriptor to support run-time object protection and auditing. The graphical device interface (GDI) supports the graphical user interface and incorporates functions for drawing and manipulating graphics. The window manager controls the creation, display, and destruction of windows and is also responsible for receiving input from the keyboard and the mouse and routing the data to the appropriate application. The plug and play (P&P) manager deals with plug and play devices, communicating with the device drivers to add and start the devices. The power manager manages power functions. The process manager, the virtual memory manager, the I/O manager, and the various file systems are discussed in detail in the balance of this chapter.

◼ Process Management

A Windows XP **process** is an object that consists of an executable program. A program contains initial code and data, private memory address space, access to system resources (such as files, ports, and windows), and one or more threads. A **thread** is a unit of work that can execute sequentially and is interruptible.

The Windows XP **process manager** is responsible for providing services for creating and deleting processes and threads. For example, when a Windows application must create a process (Figure 12.8), it sends a message to the Win32 subsystem, which calls the process manager. The process manager in turn calls the object manager, which creates a process object and returns a handle to the process manager. The handle is then returned to the application.

Multithreading

A process contains one or more threads, and Windows XP can concurrently execute those threads using a technique called **multithreading.** Each thread has its own unique identifier, thread context (basically, its register contents), user mode and kernel mode stacks, and storage space for subsystems, dynamic link libraries, and run-time libraries. Additionally, the threads can exchange information via the common address space and other shared resources.

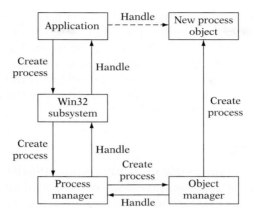

FIGURE 12.8
Process creation.

Multitasking

Windows XP also supports **multitasking,** the concurrent execution of two or more processes, which allows threads in different processes to execute concurrently. If the system has more than one processor, threads in the same process can run concurrently on different processors.

Multitasking is accomplished by **context switching.** With context switching a thread executes until it is interrupted by the operating system or must wait for resources (such as a file to be opened). When a thread is interrupted, the system saves the context of the thread (its register settings and so on), loads the context of another thread, and executes the new thread.

Windows XP is a **preemptive multitasking** operating system. Each thread or process is given a set amount of time called a quantum to access the processor. Once the quantum has expired, Windows XP interrupts the thread and starts another thread with the same priority. If a second thread with a higher priority is ready to execute, Windows XP interrupts the current thread to let the higher priority thread run.

Windows XP recognizes 32 different **priority** levels numbered 0 through 31. (Note that these priority levels are different from the Intel processor's privilege levels, which are concerned with memory protection.) Levels 16-31 are reserved for kernel processes and levels 0-15 are reserved for user processes.

Each user process has a base priority, but the priority of a given thread can be adjusted to help ensure quick response for interactive user threads without starving the background processes. For example, assume a process has a base priority of 8. A thread running within that process and waiting for user input might get a boost of 6, yielding a new thread priority of 14.

The kernel determines the magnitude of the priority boost dynamically; for example, a thread waiting for user input might get a priority boost of 6, while a thread waiting for a disk operation might have its priority boosted by only 1. To prevent compute-intensive threads from dominating, a thread's priority is adjusted for only a single quantum or time slice, and it falls by one priority level following each subsequent quantum until it reaches the process's base priority.

Multiprocessing

Windows XP is a **symmetric multiprocessing (SMP)** system. SMP systems run system and application processes on any available processor, ensuring that all available microprocessor resources are used efficiently. Windows XP combines **multiprocessing** and multitasking by dispatching a ready state thread to the next available microprocessor or (to take advantage of the memory caches from its previous execution) to the last microprocessor it ran on.

▣ Memory Management

Windows XP implements a flat linear 32-bit memory model. Addresses are 32 bits long, so the biggest possible address is 4 GB. Consequently, 4 GB of virtual address space is available to each process (Figure 12.9). Windows XP uses the top 2 GB for kernel mode threads and the bottom 2 GB for user mode threads.

Windows XP uses a **virtual memory manager (VMM)** to allocate and manage system memory. The VMM maintains a memory map table and is responsible for paging. When a process requests access to memory, it references an address in the process's virtual address space. The VMM translates the virtual address to the actual physical memory location and then transfers the data to the process.

FIGURE 12.9
Each process has up to 4 GB of virtual address space.

Paging

Paging is the process of swapping the contents of memory between physical (main) memory and disk. The virtual address space is made up of 4 KB pages that are designated as valid or invalid (Figure 12.10). A **valid page** resides in physical memory. An **invalid page** does not reside in physical memory because it has either been swapped out to disk or has not yet been loaded into memory.

When a process or thread references the contents of a virtual address on an invalid page, a **page fault** occurs. The system responds by reading (or swapping) the requested data (or code) from disk into the first available physical memory location. When physical memory is full and a thread subsequently references data or code not yet in memory, the VMM follows a first-in-first-out policy to clear space, swapping out to disk the page that was read into memory first. The code or data requested by the thread is then swapped into the freed memory. Swapping in response to a page fault is called demand paging.

The VMM combines demand paging with a technique called clustering. When a process reads in a specific page, it is likely that it will access adjacent pages in the near future. Thus, when a page fault occurs the VMM swaps in both the requested page and a few adjacent pages. Clustering tends to reduce the number of future page faults.

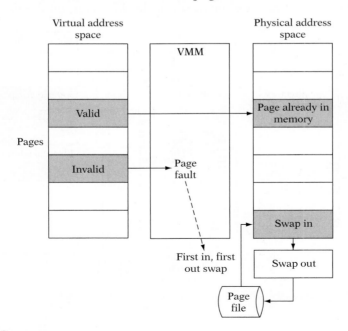

FIGURE 12.10

Valid and invalid pages.

Reserve and Commit

Every byte (real or virtual) in a process's address space exists in one of three states: free, reserved, or committed. Initially, the entire address space is free, or unallocated. When the program is launched, the virtual memory manager (VMM) **reserves** a range of virtual address space. Because no physical storage space is allocated either in memory or on the paging file, this task can be accomplished very quickly. The act of reserving virtual space before the space is actually needed is useful because a continuous range of addresses can be allocated to the process and, because a program typically executes sequentially, the virtual address space it occupies must be contiguous. The reserved memory does not count against the process's 2 GB limit until it is **committed** and actual physical pages are stored in memory and on the page file.

Address Translation

A 32-bit virtual address is split into three parts (Figure 12.11). The first 10 bits hold an index to the **page directory,** where a page directory entry (PDE) specifies the address of the appropriate page table. The second 10 bits hold an index to the **page table,** where a page table entry (PTE) points to the actual physical address of the page that holds the referenced code or data. The last 12 bits are the offset or displacement on the page.

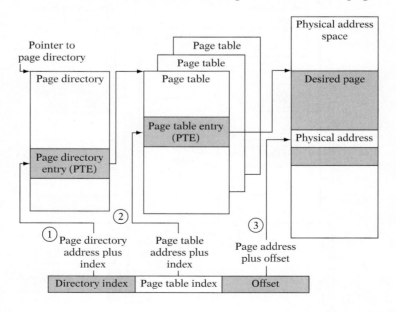

FIGURE 12.11
A 32-bit virtual address is split into three parts.

◼ Disk Management

Windows XP incorporates several features that enhance disk management. For example, the **dynamic storage** feature allows a user to resize a disk without restarting Windows. A disk that is initialized for dynamic storage is called a dynamic disk. The dynamic storage feature creates a single partition that includes the entire disk.

You can divide a dynamic disk into volumes, where each volume consists of a portion or portions of one or more physical disks. The system's need for **fault tolerance** (the ability of the computer to recover data in case of errors) dictates the type of volume selected. A simple volume contains space from a single hard disk and is not fault tolerant. A spanned volume combines space from multiple hard drives. Data are written first to the first hard disk, then to the second hard disk, and so on. A spanned volume is not fault tolerant because if a hard disk fails, all data stored on it are lost. A mirrored volume contains disk space from two separate hard disks and keeps identical (duplicate) copies on both. A striped volume in contrast combines disk space from multiple hard drives into one logical volume and adds data to all the volumes at the same rate. A striped volume is not fault tolerant because the failure of a disk leads to a complete loss of information stored on the disk. A RAID-5 volume is a fault tolerant striped volume because a parity information stripe is added to each disk partition in the volume, and when a physical disk fails the parity information is used to reconstruct the data.

◼ File Management

Windows XP supports FAT, FAT32, and its native NTFS file system. FAT, the MS-DOS file system, was discussed in Chapter 11. FAT32 is an enhanced version of FAT that allows long file names and supports access to larger disk drives. FAT and FAT32 do not offer many of the features supported by NTFS such as file- and folder-level security, encryption, enforcement of disk quotas for multiple users, and so on, so FAT and FAT32 should be avoided on a Windows XP system. Windows XP supports FAT32 on DVD-RAM devices such as CD, DVD, and rewriteable disks, but NTFS is the preferred file system.

NTFS

NTFS (the Windows NT file system) allocates a disk volume's space in **clusters,** where a cluster is one or more (generally, a power of 2) contiguous sectors. The cluster size is defined when the disk is formatted. NTFS uses logical cluster numbers as disk addresses. Multiplying the logical cluster number by the cluster size yields a physical disk (or volume) address.

Partition boot sector	Master file table	System files	File area

FIGURE 12.12

Each volume is organized into four regions.

Each volume is organized into four regions (Figure 12.12). The first few sectors contain the partition boot sector. Next comes the **master file table (MFT),** essentially the volume's master directory. Following the MFT is a system area that holds a partial copy of the MFT, log files to support recoverability, and other system information. The rest of the volume is the file area where larger files are stored.

The master file table, which is used by NTFS to access files, consists of an array of variable length records. The first 16 records describe the master file table (MFT) itself. Subsequent master file table records provide access to each file or directory on the volume. Small files (less than 1200 bytes) are written directly in the MFT. For larger files, the MFT entry contains index pointers to the clusters that hold the actual data.

Windows XP differs from MS-DOS (Chapter 11) and UNIX (Chapter 13) in the way it handles files. Both DOS and UNIX consider the file to be a string of bytes. In contrast, a Windows XP file is an object, and NTFS stores the file's attributes inside the object itself. Each file attribute is stored as a separate stream of bytes within the file.

A file's attributes are recorded in the master file table as an independent byte string that can be created, read, written, and deleted (Figure 12.13). As a minimum, certain standard information such as read-only, archive, time stamps, and so on must be associated with every file. The file name is the name associated with the file, and a file can have multiple names including an NTFS long file name and a short MS-DOS file name. The security descriptor specifies who owns the file and who can access the file; it

Standard information	File name or directory name	Security descriptor	Data or index to data

FIGURE 12.13

Certain attributes are associated with every file.

protects the file from unauthorized access. The data or the index to the data tells Windows XP where to find the contents of the file.

Because files are objects, not all files must have the same attributes, and a user can design a file to meet his or her particular needs. For example, a Macintosh file can have attributes corresponding to its data fork and resource fork, and a multimedia file (such as an AVI file) can have separate audio and video streams.

A directory is a file of indexes to the other files within the directory (Figure 12.14). When a directory cannot fit in a master file table (MFT) record, its attributes are stored in a separate run of **virtual cluster numbers (VCNs).** These VCNs are mapped to their logical cluster numbers (LCNs) to identify the file on disk. For large directories, the file indexes are stored in index buffers that are organized as a B+ tree, where each entry points to a series of lower-level entries with lesser index values. For example, in Figure 12.14, the reference to file F4 points to an index buffer with file names less than itself. Conceptually, the files in this index buffer can point to another, still lower-level index buffer, and so on. With a B+ tree organization, the time to look up any particular file in the directory is fast and is the same for all files.

NTFS also has the capability to compress a file or a folder of files if necessary. If a compressed file is accessed by an application, NTFS decompresses the file before making it available. When the file is later saved by the application, NTFS converts it back to compressed form. Windows XP also supports file encryption.

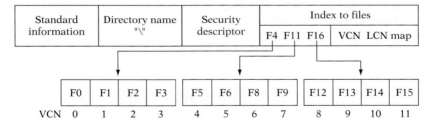

FIGURE 12.14
A directory is a file of indexes to the files stored or referenced in the directory.

File System Recovery

NTFS enables the smooth recovery of the file system following a system crash or disk failure. All changes to the master file table and file system structure are carried out using transactions. Before any changes are made, the change is written to a log. Subsequently, in the event of a system crash, the log can be used to undo partially completed transactions and redo (or recover) completed transactions. The key to file system recovery is a series of checkpoint records that are periodically (every 5 seconds) written to a log. Because earlier checkpoints are unneeded, all log entries prior to the checkpoint are discarded, which keeps the log file's size within reasonable bounds.

It should be noted that a transaction changes only the metadata (the data *about* the data), so although the file system can be recovered, NTFS does not guarantee the recovery of the file contents. In other words, you must still do your own backups.

▪ Input Output Manager

The **input output manager or I/O manager** manages the system's device drivers, works with the virtual memory manager (VMM) to provide memory-mapped file I/O, and manages the file system buffers (Figure 12.15). Using buffers hides the speed disparity between the computer's internal components and slower I/O devices. Each request for service to the I/O manager is translated and formatted as a standard **I/O request packet (IRP),** and the IRP is forwarded to the appropriate device driver for processing. On completion of the request, the device driver sends a message to the I/O manager which, in turn, notifies the requesting process that that the service has been completed.

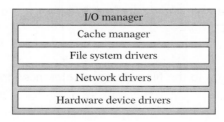

FIGURE 12.15
The I/O manager.

Device Drivers

A device driver is a software routine that allows the operating system to communicate with a specific piece of hardware. The Windows XP I/O manager supports four different types of drivers (Figure 12.15). All hardware devices (scanners, modems, printers, and so on) require hardware device drivers that manipulate the hardware to retrieve input from or write output to the physical device or network. File system drivers are device drivers that accept file-oriented I/O requests and translate them to the appropriate primitive I/O commands for the physical device. A network driver is a file system driver that redirects the I/O request to the appropriate machine on the network and receives data from the remote machine.

Windows XP device drivers meet a new standard called the Windows driver model (WDM) that enables Windows XP to share drivers with other Windows operating systems. WDM also incorporates features that enhance real time streaming media by processing the data in kernel mode rather than user mode.

Caching

Caching is a major I/O manager service that enhances performance by holding information in memory (rather than simply on disk) in case the information is needed again. File updates are written to the cache, not directly to disk. Later, when demand is low, the data are written to the disk by a background process. In most operating systems, caching is handled by the file system. In contrast, Windows XP implements caching as a centralized facility that provides service not only to the file system but also to all the components (such as the network components) under the control of the I/O manager. The size of the cache varies with the amount of free physical memory available in the system. Up to half the space in the system memory area (Figure 12.9) is allocated to cache by the virtual memory manager. The cache manager maps a file into this address space and uses the capabilities of the VMM to handle file I/O.

When a process requests an I/O service such as access to a file (Figure 12.16, step 1), the I/O manager passes an I/O request packet (IRP) to the cache manager (2). If the file is already in cache, the cache manager locates the information and copies it to the process's buffer via the virtual memory manager (3), which notifies the process that the requested I/O operation has been completed (4).

The process is a bit more complex if the file is not already in cache. As before, the process requests a service (Figure 12.17, step 1) and the I/O manager sends an IRP to the cache manager (2). Because the file is not in cache, the cache manager generates a page fault (3) and the virtual memory manager responds by sending a noncached service request back to the I/O

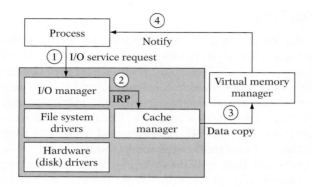

FIGURE 12.16

A cached I/O service request.

manager (4). The I/O manager then issues an IRP (5) to the file system driver. The file system driver, in turn, passes the IRP to the device driver (6) one or more times, depending on the size of the file. After the data (7) are read into the cache (8), the file is copied to the process's buffer (9) as if it had been in the cache when the initial I/O request was issued. The virtual memory manager then notifies the process that the I/O service request has been completed (10).

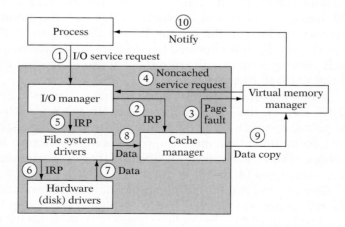

FIGURE 12.17

A non-cached I/O service request.

Whenever possible, Windows XP handles I/O requests in asynchronous mode. With asynchronous mode, the request is handed off to the I/O manager and the process or thread that made the request continues to execute while the I/O operation is being processed. Asynchronous mode execution helps to optimize application performance.

■ The Registry

The **registry** is a hierarchical database that Windows XP uses to keep track of hardware and software settings within the computer. The registry holds information on the system's hardware (the processor, the bus type, the amount of system memory, and so on), its available device drivers, the network adapter (settings, network protocols), user and hardware profiles, and so on.

The registry is used by the kernel, administrative programs, the device drivers, and setup programs (Figure 12.18). On startup, the Windows XP bus driver (a software driver that services a bus controller) collects the list of installed hardware components and passes it to the kernel for inclusion in the registry. During the boot process, the kernel reads information about the devices and their load order from the registry, and starts the device drivers and services. The device drivers read from and write to the registry their configuration parameters. Application setup programs use the registry to determine whether the required components are already installed, and they add configuration information as necessary. When applications run, they use the registry to determine the system configuration. When multiple users use the system or when different hardware configurations exist on the computer, the appropriate data are stored in the registry.

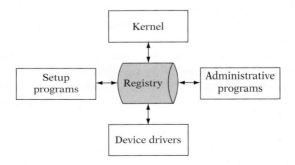

FIGURE 12.18
The registry.

Microsoft's Market Dominance

Imagine your software company is about to announce a major upgrade to your best-selling application program. Assuming the market responds positively, you plan to release versions for the Macintosh, UNIX, and Windows platforms, but which version should you release first? A rational decision maker would probably choose the version that has the greatest sales potential. By most accounts, Windows users represent at least 90 percent of the potential market, so the choice is obvious: you release the Windows version first. In fact, the decision to fully develop and release the Macintosh and UNIX versions will probably depend on how the marketplace responds to the Windows version.

Expand your viewpoint from a single company to the entire software industry and imagine numerous CEOs making equally rational decisions. That is why, with the exception of certain niche markets, the Windows version of a new software product or upgrade is almost always released first and versions for other platforms follow later, if at all. Walk into any retail software outlet and you will quickly discover that, except perhaps for games, Windows applications dominate the shelves, and a closer examination will probably reveal that many Windows titles are simply not available for other platforms. As a result, a Windows user can choose from more (and more recently updated) applications than can a Macintosh or a UNIX user. Although it may seem like circular reasoning, Microsoft's continuing market dominance is at least in part a function of Microsoft's continuing market dominance.

Multimedia Support

Windows XP incorporates several useful multimedia features. For example, DirectX is an application programming interface (API) that supports the capture and playback of audio, full-color video, and 3-D graphics and such multimedia peripheral devices as a joystick. DirectX provides a hardware abstraction layer between the hardware and software, which enables device-independent applications to be developed. Windows XP also includes support for DVD playback using either hardware or software decoders. The kernel provides streaming drivers using the Windows driver model and also provides support for reading (but not for writing) the DVD universal disk format (UDF) file system. Also, you can write to DVD-RAM using the FAT32 file system.

Windows XP's Windows Media feature provides several special purpose audio and video codecs (compressor/decompressor routines) that achieve better compression ratios than MP3 and MPEG4, the industry's video standard. Windows XP also provides a media player for playback, media tools to develop content, a movie maker to transfer video into a computer, and services for distributing content. A Windows media file can be encrypted using Windows Media digital rights management to secure against unauthorized distribution.

Windows Media uses a content-independent container format called advanced streaming format (ASF) to store and distribute digital media (Figure 12.19). An ASF file begins with a header that describes the metadata (the data about the data) and defines the relationships between and configurations of the various data streams. The body of the container holds the interleaved data streams; for example, a multimedia file might consist of an audio stream, a video stream, and so on. The container ends with an optional index that holds pointers (such as frame numbers or time based coding) to the data to simplify retrieval.

The 64-Bit Version

The 64-bit version of Windows XP runs on the Intel Itanium chip and supports up to 16 GB of physical memory and up to 16 TB (terabytes) of virtual memory. In contrast, the 32-bit version is limited to 4 GB and 16 GB respectively. The way the virtual address space is laid out is also different. As you learned earlier in the chapter, the 32-bit version allocates 2 GB for user space and 2 GB for system space, but the 64-bit version uses 7,152 GB (less than .00005 % of total available virtual memory) per user process and allocates the rest of the 16 TB to system processes and managing data. As a result, a 32-bit program running under the 64-bit version of Windows XP can exceed the old 2 GB memory limit, and applications with large data sets, such as computer-aided design and financial applications, can run faster.

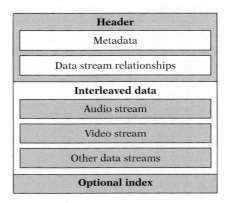

FIGURE 12.19
An ASF file container.

Thunking

Windows XP was designed for the IA64 Itanium chip and executes 64-bit applications in native mode. Running a 32-bit application on the IA64 architecture requires a **thunking**[2] layer (Figure 12.20) to convert the 32-bit calls into corresponding 64-bit calls; note how closely Figure 12.20 resembles Figure 12.5. The Windows on Windows (WOW64) subsystem provides this thunking layer and helps isolate the 64-bit applications from collisions with the 32-bit applications. Cut and paste and similar interoperability features can be used to pass information between 32- and 64-bit applications, however.

Disk Partitioning

The IA64 (Itanium) chip replaces the traditional BIOS firmware interface with the extensible firmware interface (EFI). EFI contains some platform specific information and provides consistent boot and run-time services across all platforms. The EFI specification also defines a new disk partitioning scheme called the Globally Unique Identifier Partition Table or GPT. GPT supports up to 128 primary partitions (up from 4) and very large disks with up to 18 exabytes of storage capacity, where one exabyte is 2^{60} bytes. GPT also enhances partition security and helps to ensure data integrity by using such measures as error checking and recording a redundant backup copy of partition information at the end of the disk. Windows XP supports the EFI interface in its 64-bit edition.

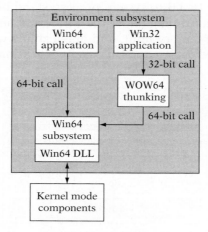

FIGURE 12.20
Thunking.

---

[2]According to the online *Jargon Dictionary,* a thunk is "a piece of coding which provides an address." See *http://info.astrian.net/jargon/terms/t.html#thunk*.

▌ Summary

Some Windows XP modules operate in hierarchical layered mode and others operate in client/server mode. The Windows XP system is divided into the user mode and the kernel mode. User applications and a collection of subsystems run in user mode. The user mode components include the environment subsystem and the integral subsystem. An application program communicates with the operating system by calling an application programming interface, which translates the call to kernel form by accessing the dynamic link library. Win32 applications communicate directly with the Win32 subsystem. Win16 and MS-DOS applications run on virtual DOS machines (VDMs). On the integral subsystem, server processes are run as services and system processes require an interactive logon.

One way to view the kernel mode processes is as a layered hierarchy that includes the hardware abstraction layer (HAL), the device drivers, the kernel, and the executive. The object manager is responsible for creating, destroying, and granting access to an object's services or data. The process manager creates and deletes processes and threads. Windows XP supports multithreading, preemptive multitasking, and symmetric multiprocessing.

Windows XP uses a virtual memory manager (VMM) to allocate memory to processes and to manage system memory. When a process or thread references a virtual address on an invalid page, a page fault occurs. The system responds by reading (or swapping) the requested data (or code) from disk into the first available physical memory location. Allocating memory in Windows is a two-step process: reserve and commit. A 32-bit virtual address is divided into three parts: an index to the page directory, an index to the page table, and the displacement on the page.

Dynamic storage is a feature that allows a user to resize a disk without restarting Windows XP. You can divide a dynamic disk into volumes. Fault tolerance is the ability of the computer to recover data in case of errors. Windows XP supports FAT, FAT 32, and its native NTFS file system. NTFS enables the smooth recovery of the file system in case of a system crash or disk failure.

The input output manager (I/O manager) manages cache and the file system, device, and network drivers. Each request to the I/O manager for service is translated and formatted to a standard I/O request packet (IRP). Caching increases performance by holding the information in memory in case the information is needed a second time. The registry is a hierarchical database used by Windows XP to keep track of hardware and software settings within the computer.

Windows XP incorporates several new multimedia features. The 64-bit version of Windows XP runs on the Intel Itanium chip and supports up to 16 GB of memory and 16 TB (terabytes) of virtual memory.

◼ Key Words

application programming
   interface (API)
caching
client/server mode
cluster
commit
context switching
dynamic link library (DDL)
dynamic storage
environment subsystem
executive, or executive services
fault tolerance
Hardware Abstraction Layer
   (HAL)
input output manager (I/O
   manager)
integral subsystem
invalid page
I/O request packet (IRP)
kernel mode
master file table (MFT)
multiprocessing
multitasking

multithreading
NTFS
object manager
page directory
page fault
page table
preemptive multitasking
priority
process
process manager
registry
reserve
server process
service
symmetric multiprocessing (SMP) system
system process
system restore
thread
thunk
user mode
valid page
virtual cluster number (VCN)
virtual memory manager (VMM)

◼ Review Questions

1. Explain client/server mode.
2. Distinguish between user mode and kernel mode.
3. Distinguish between user mode's environmental and integral subsystems.
4. What is an application program interface (API)? What is a dynamic link library (DLL)? How are an API and a DDL related?
5. Distinguish between server processes and system processes.
6. Identify the functions performed by the primary kernel mode components.
7. List the primary modules that make up executive services.
8. Define the terms module, process, and thread.
9. Explain how the process manager creates a new process.
10. Define multithreading, multitasking, and multiprocessing.

11. Explain how the virtual memory manager implements paging.

12. Distinguish between memory reserve and memory commit. Why is that distinction important?

13. Describe the contents of a Windows XP 32-bit address. Explain how a virtual address is translated into a physical (real) address.

14. What is dynamic storage and why is it considered important?

15. Why are mirrored and RAID-5 volumes considered fault tolerant while simple, spanned, and striped volumes are not?

16. Describe the organization of an NTFS disk.

17. Explain how Windows XP uses virtual cluster numbers to find files on disk.

18. How does NTFS enable the smooth recovery of the file system following a system crash or disk failure?

19. Explain how Windows XP uses caching.

20. What is the purpose of the Windows XP registry?

21. Identify several Windows XP multimedia support features.

22. Discuss several key differences between the 32-bit and 64-bit versions of Windows XP.

Exercises

1. According to your text, some Windows modules are configured in a hierarchical layered mode, but other modules work in client/server mode. However, a footnote in the same section stated that it is still useful to view the client and the server as independent layers. How do you explain that apparent contradiction?

2. Why is it so difficult to compete directly with a company like Microsoft that dominates its marketplace?

3. From the 1960s through most of the 1980s, IBM dominated the information technology marketplace. Although the company is still a major player, it is no longer the dominant player, however. Do a little research and see if you can find out why.

4. Why is robustness an important operating system criterion?

5. Relate fault tolerance to robustness.

6. If you are experienced with multimedia applications, review the new multimedia features bundled with XP and indicate why you might (or might not) find them useful.

7. Figures 12.3, 12.11, and 12.16 (without the numbers) are useful templates for organizing many of this chapter's key terms.

CHAPTER 13

UNIX and Linux Internals

When you finish reading this chapter you should be able to:

▶ Explain the significance of the UNIX kernel.

▶ Distinguish an image from a process.

▶ Differentiate a user's text, data, stack, and system data segments.

▶ Explain how processes are created under UNIX.

▶ Discuss UNIX dispatching.

▶ Explain how UNIX links a peripheral device and an application process.

▶ Sketch the contents of a UNIX disk.

▶ Explain how UNIX converts a file name to the file's location on disk.

▶ Explain how the buffer pool supports asynchronous I/O.

▶ Identify several unique features of Linux.

◼ The UNIX System

A UNIX user communicates with the system indirectly through an application programming interface such as **POSIX** (Portable Operating System Interface for UNIX, a standard application programming interface) or directly through a shell or a graphical user interface (Figure 13.1). The shell and the GUI are treated much like application programs and are technically not part of the operating system, an important UNIX innovation that makes it relatively easy to replace the standard use interface with a custom user interface. For example, a professional programmer might consider the rather terse commands associated with the command line shell easy to use, while a nontechnical user might find the same commands intimidating and prefer a GUI.

Among its resident modules, the focus of this chapter, UNIX contains an input/output control system, a file system, and routines to swap segments, handle interrupts, schedule the processor's time, manage memory space, and allocate peripheral devices. Additionally, the operating system maintains several tables to track the system's status. Routines that communicate directly with the hardware are concentrated in a relatively small **kernel** (Figure 13.1). The kernel is (at least in part) hardware-dependent and varies significantly from system to system. However, the interface to the kernel is consistent across implementations.

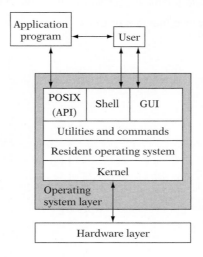

FIGURE 13.1

Hardware-dependent UNIX/Linux logic is concentrated in the kernel.

UNIX is a time-sharing system, with program segments swapped in and out of memory as required. To ensure reasonable response time, processor access is limited by time-slicing. Segmentation is the most common addressing scheme, and most UNIX systems implement virtual memory techniques.

Portability

Significant parts of most operating systems are written in assembler language and thus are limited to a single platform or a single architecture. In contrast, only a small portion of the UNIX kernel is written in assembler. The rest of the operating system is written primarily in a high-level language (C), making it highly portable. As a result, UNIX can run on virtually any platform, an extremely valuable attribute in today's distributed computing environment.

Images and Processes

The pseudocomputer concept is an important UNIX innovation. A user's routine is viewed as an **image,** defined by Ritchie and Thompson as an "execution environment" that consists of program and data storage, the contents of general-purpose registers, the status of open files, the current directory, and other key elements. To the user, it *appears* that this image is executed on a private pseudocomputer under control of a command-driven operating system. In reality, UNIX is a multiple user, time-sharing system.

An image consists of three segments (Figure 13.2). Starting at virtual address 0 is a program **text segment** followed by a **data segment.** The image ends with a **stack segment.** Between the data and the stack segments is a free area. As the program runs, the data segment grows toward high memory (down in Figure 13.2), and the stack segment grows toward low memory.

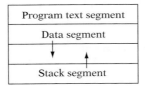

FIGURE 13.2

An image consists of a program text segment, a data segment, and a stack segment.

The execution of an image is called a **process.** As a process executes, the image's text, data, and stack segments must be in memory. (Note: they need not occupy contiguous memory.) Thus, the image is not *really* executed on a pseudocomputer. Instead, the image and the pseudocomputer serve as virtual models of the user's environment.

The program text segment is reentrant, and thus it can be shared. UNIX, remember, is a multiple user system. If two or more users access the same program, only one text segment is physically stored in memory. Both users have their independent images. Both *imagine* that they and they alone have access to their program code. Physically, however, they share a single text segment (Figure 13.3).

The data and stack segments, on the other hand, are private; for example, if two users are executing the same code, memory will hold one text segment, two data segments, and two stack segments. Additionally, each process has its own **system data segment** containing data needed by the operating system when the process is active. This system data segment is not part of the user's image, and the user cannot access it. When the user calls the operating system (for example, to request an input or output service), the process switches from a user state to a system state, making the system data segment available to UNIX.

Process Creation

A process is created when an executing process calls the *fork* routine (a system primitive). In response, UNIX duplicates the executing process, creating two identical copies. Because both copies contain the system data segment, they share open files and other key data. The operating system distinguishes between the parent and the child by giving them different return codes. Thus, although the parent and the child are identical, they can take different actions based on their return codes.

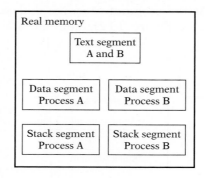

FIGURE 13.3

The text segment is reentrant. The data and stack segments are private.

The parent starts the process by calling *fork*. It is a system call, so a return address is stored in the process's system data area and UNIX gets control of the processor. After the duplicate process is created, UNIX returns control to the parent, which checks the return code. By convention, the parent gets the process number (called the **process id** or **pid**) of the child (a positive integer), while the child gets a return code of 0. (A negative return code indicates an error.) Because the return code is positive, the parent normally calls *wait,* and waits for the child to die[1] or finish processing (Figure 13.4a).

Eventually, the child is launched and begins to execute. Because it is a duplicate of the parent, the return address in its system data area points to the instruction immediately following *fork* (addresses are virtual). Thus, the child begins by checking the return code (Figure 13.4b). Because the return code is 0, the child calls another system primitive, *exec.* The *exec* routine responds by overlaying the child's text and data segments with the contents of a new file (Figure 13.4c). Technically, the resulting image is still the same process, but its contents are different. Later, when the child dies, the parent can resume processing (Figure 13.4d).

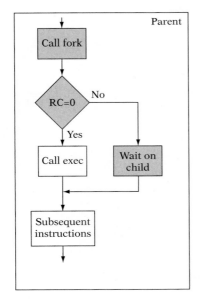 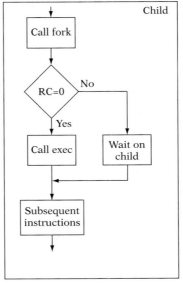

FIGURE 13.4

UNIX process creation.

a. The parent calls *fork* and drops into a wait state.

---

[1] UNIX terminology is sometimes a bit morbid.

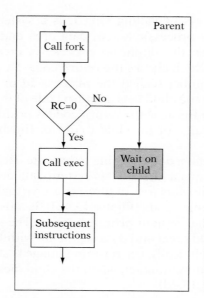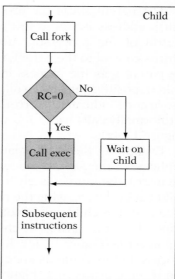

b. Because its return code is 0, the child calls *exec.*

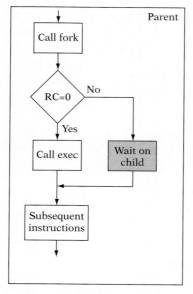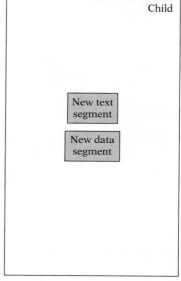

c. The exec routine overlays the child's text and data segments.

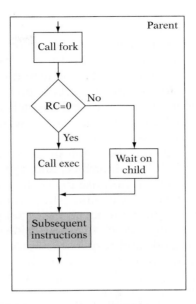

d. When the child dies, the parent resumes processing.

Briefly review the process creation sequence, because it is important. The parent calls *fork*. In response, UNIX duplicates the process, and returns control to the parent. Because the return code is a positive integer (the child's process number), the parent calls *wait*, and "goes to sleep" until the child dies.

Eventually, the child, a duplicate of the parent, is launched. When the parent called *fork*, the address of its next instruction was recorded in the system data area, so the child's system data area contains the same (virtual) return address. Thus, the instruction following *fork* is executed. Typically, this instruction checks the return code. Because the return code is 0, *exec* is called and a new program overlays the child. Following *exec*, the first instruction in this new program is executed. Eventually, the new program calls ***exit*** and the child dies. Consequently, the parent is awakened and, eventually, begins executing again.

Some applications call for parallel parent and child processes. As before, the child is created when the parent calls *fork*, but instead of calling *wait*, the parent executes regular instructions so both the parent and the child are active. With most operating systems, radically different commands or parameters are used to define parallel and serial processes. UNIX, in contrast, supports serial and parallel processes with remarkable consistency, one reason why professional programmers find it so elegant.

Initialization

When UNIX is booted, a process named ***init*** is activated. This "original ancestor" creates one logon process for each potential user; for example, if the system supports up to twenty concurrent users, twenty logon processes are created. A user logs on to one of these processes. The logon process then (normally) launches *(exec)* the shell, which overlays the logon process. Later, when the shell dies (in other words, when the user logs off), *init* creates a new logon process.

When a user logs on, the logon process scans a table of login names, identifies the user's default interface, and, typically, executes either a command line shell or a GUI. Because the shell is treated as a process, it's relatively easy to substitute a custom shell. Another option is no shell. In response to a particular login name, the logon process can start an *application* routine, effectively placing the user inside the shell and thus restricting that user to commands and responses appropriate to that application routine. The logon process overlays itself with the user's primary system interface. When that interface dies, *init* spawns another logon process, which waits for another user to log on.

The image described earlier allows a user to visualize a program. Real memory is a bit more complex, however. Imagine a UNIX system supporting four concurrent users (Figure 13.5). Three are active, so memory holds three shells. Running under each shell are user processes; note that two or more parallel processes can be associated with a single shell. A fourth potential user has not yet logged on, so the logon process is still active.

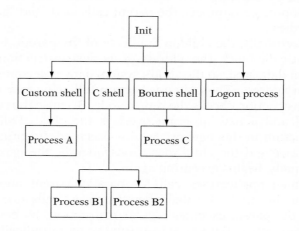

FIGURE 13.5

The possible contents of memory on a UNIX system supporting four concurrent users.

The user sees the image of a *single process* and can imagine that process running all by itself on a private pseudocomputer. The details associated with time-slicing, swapping, real memory allocation, and physical device access are buried in UNIX and thus are transparent to the user.

Process Management

UNIX is a multiple user operating system, with several concurrent programs occupying memory. It is inevitable that two or more programs will want to access the processor at the same time, so the operating system must carefully schedule them. The UNIX dispatcher is responsible for process scheduling.

The UNIX dispatcher relies on a **process table** that holds one entry for each process (Figure 13.6). The entry is allocated when the process is created *(fork)* and freed when the process dies. Each entry contains all the data needed by UNIX when the process is *not* active. Among other things, the process table entry indicates whether the process is ready (awake) or waiting (asleep).

For example, imagine the shell (the parent) has just received a command that requires a new process. The shell responds by calling *fork*. In response, the kernel creates the new process, assigns a process number (a positive integer), adds a new entry to the process table, and returns to the shell. The shell then (typically) calls *wait* and "goes to sleep" until the newly created child dies.

```
One entry per process.

Each entry contains:
        Process number
        Process state (ready, waiting)
        Process priority
        Event number process is waiting on
        Text table address
        Data segment address
        Stack segment address
        System data segment address
```

FIGURE 13.6

The process table contains one entry per process.

Meanwhile, the child is launched, calls *exec*, and carries out the command. Later, when it finishes processing, it calls exit and dies. The death of a process generates an **event** that produces a **signal**. The event is reported to the operating system's *event-wait* routine as a positive integer—the event number or process number. UNIX responds by searching the process table and waking (setting to a ready state) every process waiting for that event.

Each user process has a priority. Priorities are recomputed frequently by dividing execution time by elapsed real time (the smaller the number, the higher the priority). When an event signal is sensed, the operating system's *event-wait* routine is called. First, *event-wait* awakens all processes waiting for that event. Then, it searches the process table, selects the highest priority "ready" process, and starts it.

Events occupy no memory; they are represented by electronic signals. When a signal is sensed, *event-wait* scans the process table and awakens all processes waiting for the associated event. Then the system forgets that the event ever happened. What if time passes between the decision to wait and the implementation of the wait state? For example, imagine a process calls *fork*, performs some calculations, and *then* calls *wait*. What if, between *fork* and *wait*, the new process is launched and dies? By the time the parent calls *wait*, the event it plans to wait for has already happened. Because the child process has already died, it will not appear in the process table. When the UNIX *wait* routine gets control, it checks the process table and, if the calling routine has no children, returns an error code. A programmer should be prepared for this sequence of events any time parallel processes are activated.

Getting Started

When *init* creates a logon process, it opens the standard input, output, and error files, thus allowing the logon process to accept user input from the terminal and display both normal output and error messages. When a user logs on, typically by entering a user ID and a password, a copy of the shell or a GUI is loaded into memory and overlays the logon process's text and data segments. The system data segment is not affected, however, so the standard input, output, and error files are still open. Consequently, the user can begin issuing commands without opening these standard files.

In response to a command, the shell sets up an *exec*, calls *fork*, and then waits for the child process to carry out the command. If the command is followed by an ampersand (&), the shell does not wait. Instead, it spawns a new process to carry out the command in parallel and immediately displays a prompt for the next command.

Time-Slicing and Interrupts

Under UNIX, the operating system schedules processes by responding to event signals. For example, an event occurs when a process dies. If the process is compute-bound, however, considerable time can pass between events, and that, in turn, can negatively impact response time. To minimize the risk that a single process will monopolize the system's time, time-slicing is imposed.

Programs are generally limited to a brief interval of processor time. If, during that time interval, the process voluntarily surrenders control, fine; normal dispatching rules are adequate. If, however, a process exceeds its allotted time interval, a special event (perhaps, a timer interrupt) is signaled and *event-wait* is called. After recomputing priorities (thus lowering the offending process's priority), *event-wait* searches the process table and selects the highest priority ready process.

Interrupt handling routines are located in the UNIX kernel. (Because UNIX is supported on a variety of computers, each of which might implement interrupts differently, the hardware details are not covered in this text.) When an interrupt occurs, control of the processor is transferred to the kernel. Once the interrupt is handled, *event-wait* awakens any processes waiting for the interrupt and then schedules the next process.

Memory Management

UNIX relies on virtual memory and segmentation techniques to manage memory space. The user's image is a virtual model of a pseudocomputer. The text, data, and stack segments that make up that image are independently loaded into real memory. As necessary, segments (and even complete images) are swapped out to secondary memory to free space for active processes.

Swapping (or Paging)

Consider swapping in more detail. When a process first enters real memory, the entire image is loaded. As the process grows, new primary memory is allocated, the process is copied to the new space, and the process table is updated. If sufficient memory is not available, the growing process is allocated space on secondary memory and swapped out. At this point, the process is ready to be swapped back in. Over time, several processes can reside on secondary memory.

The swapping process is part of the kernel (Figure 13.7) and thus can be activated each time UNIX gets control of the processor. It scans the process table looking for a ready process that has been swapped out. If it finds one, it allocates primary memory and swaps in the process. If sufficient memory space is not available, the swapping routine selects a process to be swapped out, copies the selected process to secondary storage, frees the memory space, and then swaps in the ready process.

The swap-in decision is based on secondary storage residency time—the longer a process resides on disk, the higher its priority. Generally, processes waiting for slow events are primary swap-out candidates. If there are several such processes, age in primary memory is a secondary criterion, and a slight penalty is imposed on large programs. To help minimize thrashing, processes do not become candidates for swapping out until they have achieved at least a minimum age in primary memory.

Early versions of UNIX swapped segments. Newer versions designed to run on page-oriented hardware subdivide segments into pages and swap pages.

Memory Space and Reentrant Code

Text segments contain reentrant code, and that has memory management implications. On the one hand, because several processes can physically share a single text segment the total amount of space that must be allocated to support all those processes is reduced. On the other hand, if several processes share the same text segment, that segment's space cannot be released until all the processes using it have died.

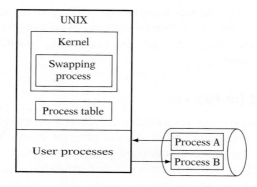

FIGURE 13.7
The swapping process is part of the kernel.

To keep track of active text segments, UNIX maintains a **text table** that lists each current text segment, its primary and secondary addresses, and a count of the number of processes sharing it (Figure 13.8). As a process dies, the count is decremented. Although the space associated with the data, stack, and system data segments can immediately be freed when a process dies, the text segment must remain in memory until its count reaches zero.

■ The File System

According to its designers, the **file system** is the key to UNIX. It offers compatible device, file, and interprocess I/O; in essence, the user simply sends and receives data. All data are treated as strings of bytes and no physical structure is imposed by the system. Instead, the user's program overlays its own data structure. The result is considerable freedom from any concern for physical I/O.

Block (structured) devices (normally, disk) hold files. A hierarchical directory structure maps the entire file system and allows the operating system to create, retrieve, and update data files by name. The information associated with a directory is itself kept in a file (another important UNIX innovation). Disk I/O will be discussed in some detail a bit later.

Character devices include printers and other nonblock peripherals. They operate through a simple queuing process. For example, to output data to a printer, UNIX places bytes, one by one, on the printer's output queue. The printer's controller subsequently retrieves them, one by one.

Character devices, block devices, and data files are all treated as files and are accessed by a common set of system calls (*open, read, write,* and so on). Data files are called **ordinary files.** Files that represent a block or character device are called **special files.** Once again, consistency makes the operating system easier to use.

> Each text table entry contains:
>   The text segment's identification
>   The text segment's primary memory address
>   The text segment's secondary memory address
>   A count of the number of processes using this text segment

FIGURE 13.8
UNIX maintains a text table to keep track of active segments.

Inside the operating system, each physical device is controlled by a **device driver** (Figure 13.9). All devices attached to the system are listed in a **configuration table** and identified by a major **device number** and a minor device number. When UNIX receives a request to start I/O, it uses the major device number to search the configuration table, finds the address of the appropriate device driver, and then activates the device driver. The minor device number is passed to the device driver. It might designate a specific disk drive on a multiple drive system, a specific peripheral on a channel, or, depending on the device, some other detail. As a system changes, device drivers and configuration table entries can be added or deleted, usually by the system's super user.

Accessing Disk Files

Disk is the standard block device. The disk surface is divided into four regions (Figure 13.10). The boot block, as the name implies, holds a boot routine. Next comes a **super block** that identifies the disk, defines the sizes of the disk's regions, and tracks free blocks. The third region holds the **i-list.** Each entry on the i-list is an **i-node,** a 64-byte file definition that lists the disk addresses of blocks associated with a single ordinary file. A special file describes a physical device, and a special file's i-node holds the device's major and minor device numbers. The i-nodes are numbered sequentially. An i-node's offset from the beginning of the i-list is its **i-number.** The

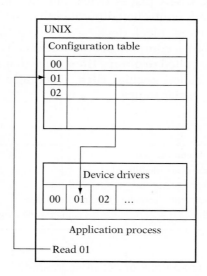

FIGURE 13.9

A configuration table lists all the device drivers.

combination of a device number and an i-number defines a specific file. Following the i-list, the remaining space on disk is divided into 1 KB blocks that hold data and/or directories.

A known i-node (often, i-number 2) points to the root directory. When a user logs on, UNIX reads the root directory, finds the user's home directory, and records the home directory's i-number in the process's system data area. In response to a change directory command, UNIX replaces the recorded i-number with the new directory's i-number.

When a program opens an ordinary file (Figure 13.11), UNIX uses the working directory's i-number to begin its search for the requested file. Each directory entry consists of a file name and an i-number. Once the file name is found in the directory, the associated i-number is extracted. The i-number points to the file's i-node. That i-node, in turn, holds the disk address of the file's first block and starts a chain of pointers that link all the file's blocks.

- Boot block
- Super block
  - Region sizes
  - Disk identification
  - Free block list
- i-list
  - i-nodes (file definitions)
- File and directory blocks

FIGURE 13.10
A UNIX disk is divided into four regions.

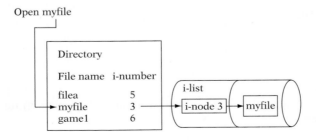

FIGURE 13.11
Associated with each file name on the directory is an i-number that points to a specific i-node.

UNIX, remember, is a multiple user system. Thus, at any given time, numerous devices and files will be open, and it is likely that two or more processes will try to concurrently access the same disk (or even the same file). To avoid conflicts, the operating system maintains a **system file table,** sometimes called the **i-node table** (Figure 13.12). When the file is opened, its i-node is copied into the system file table.

To the user's process, an open file is identified by a **file descriptor,** a small, nonnegative integer number. Within the process's system data area, the file is listed in a **process file table.** The process file table entry points, in turn, to an i-node in the system file table, so the process is only aware of its own open files. UNIX, on the other hand, can track every open file, no matter what process it might be associated with.

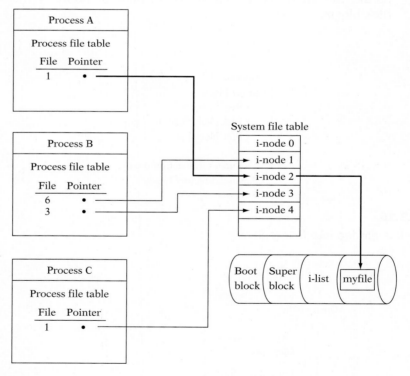

FIGURE 13.12

A process file table entry points to a system file table entry which, in turn, points to the file's location on disk.

Later, when the user process calls *read* or *write*, UNIX uses the *process* file table's pointer to locate the file's i-node in the *system* file table. That i-node, in turn, provides a start of file address. Because the file is viewed as a simple string of bytes, individual substrings can be accessed by using relative byte numbers. The UNIX file system assumes responsibility for converting relative byte addresses into physical disk addresses and reading or writing the appropriate block or blocks. The application program makes sense of the data by overlaying its own data structure.

Managing Disk Space

UNIX is also responsible for managing disk space. When a file is created or an existing file grows, the operating system scans the free block list in the super block and allocates space to the file. The free block list is a series of pointers that link unused disk blocks. After allocating space, UNIX updates the pointers.

Note that space is allocated dynamically. When a file is first created, it might be assigned several contiguous blocks, but subsequent requests for space are filled by allocating blocks located anywhere on the disk's surface. In addition to pointing to the start-of-file address, the i-node starts a list of pointers that link all a file's blocks, including the noncontiguous ones.

Buffering

All block I/O takes place through a buffer pool located in the operating system (no system buffers are found in the user's image). A *read* command implies a buffer search. If the requested block is already in memory, no physical input operation is needed. If physical I/O is necessary, the "least currently accessed" buffer is renamed and the block is read into it. Additionally, whenever UNIX must physically read a block, it automatically prereads the next one. Consequently, given the nature of most programs, the data are often already in memory when the next *read* command is issued.

Normally, when UNIX selects the least currently accessed buffer and renames it, the contents of that buffer are lost. To avoid destroying valid output data residing in a buffer, UNIX responds to a *write* command by marking the appropriate buffer **dirty** (basically, the operating system sets a switch). No physical output occurs at write time, however. Instead, when the buffer is later identified as least currently accessed, its contents are physically copied to disk before the buffer space is reassigned. Delaying the physical data transfer until a buffer is no longer active also tends to reduce physical I/O.

UNIX implements pipes by taking advantage of its buffering scheme. When data are sent to the standard output device, they are first copied to a buffer, and then output. Likewise, when data are read from the standard input device, they flow from the device into a buffer and are subsequently made available to the process. With pipes, the standard output is transferred to a buffer and simply held. The next process then gets its input directly from the first process's output buffer.

By reducing physical I/O operations, UNIX dramatically improves system efficiency. There are, however, disadvantages to the dynamic buffering approach. For one thing, although physical I/O may *appear* synchronous, it is really asynchronous (in other words, physical data transfers and logical read or write commands do not necessary occur in a predictable time sequence). This makes real-time error reporting or user error handling difficult to implement. Because of the delayed write described earlier, valid output data can be lost if UNIX crashes unexpectedly. Finally, the sequence of logical and physical I/O operations can differ, which can cause serious problems for applications that rely on data sequence. UNIX does allow a user to open a file in raw mode. Such files maintain a logical/physical correspondence. In spite of these problems, however, the UNIX I/O model has been adopted by a number of modern operating systems.

■ UNIX Internals

One of the best ways to get an overview of an operating system is to follow the pointers that link the system's components. Figure 13.13 summarizes the key UNIX tables. Start with the process table. For each process, the process table holds pointers to the process's data segment, stack segment, and system data segment. Additionally, the process table entry points to a text table entry which, in turn, points to the process's text segment. Thus, the process table and the text table link all the process's segments.

Each process has a system data segment. The i-number of the user's working directory is stored here. Physical devices are linked to the process through a list of open files. Each open file reference points to a configuration table entry which in turn points to a device driver. The files themselves are identified through pointers (in the process file table) to the system file table. Each system file table entry is an i-node that holds a file's disk address.

At first glance, Figure 13.13 appears complex, but compared to other operating systems, its use of tables and pointers to link a system's components is remarkably elegant, one reason why UNIX is so popular with computer professionals.

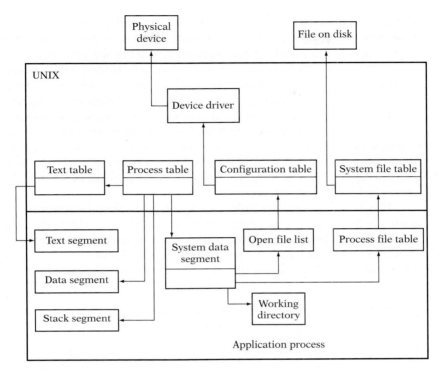

FIGURE 13.13

A summary of key UNIX system tables.

Linux

Linux is a POSIX-compliant clone of UNIX. This section notes some variations from standard UNIX and some unique features of Linux.

Linux Architecture

Linux features a layered architecture that resembles UNIX and Windows (Figure 13.14). While Linux is widely used on the Intel 32-bit architecture, it has been ported to many different hardware architectures including Intel's Itanium 64-bit architecture, the PowerPC, and the Alpha processor. Linux concentrates the architecture-dependent code at its lowest layer. Resting on the architecture-dependent layer is the kernel. The kernel processes are broadly classified as input/output-related (file systems, networking, and device drivers) and process-related (scheduling, memory management, and interprocess communication). On top of the process-related and input/output-related processes is the system call interface (the application program interface) that the kernel exposes to user processes. Even though user processes can make direct kernel calls using the system level interface, more often they do so using a user-level system library, such as *libc*, a standard C language application programming interface library. Referencing an intermediate system library simplifies the task of calling the kernel.

The architecture-independent services can be viewed as modules rather than layers. Each module, such as the scheduler, provides a core service. These modules can independently call each other, which is more efficient than calling a process in a higher or lower layer. For example, if the memory manager wants to swap the contents of a portion of memory to disk, it can call the file system directly.

The Linux kernel includes device drivers that communicate directly with the hardware layer's peripheral devices. Rather than including *all* the device drivers by default, Linux loads and unloads specific components (or modules) of kernel code as necessary, which allows the system to operate with a minimal kernel and frees up more memory for user programs.

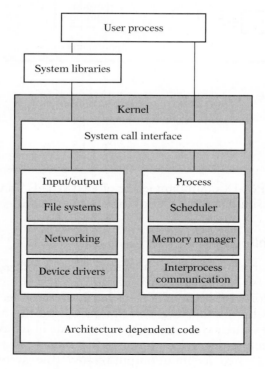

FIGURE 13.14

Linux system architecture.

The Profit Motive

One reason the Linux kernel is modular has to do with licensing. The Linux kernel is distributed under the Gnu license, which requires anyone who modifies the source code with the intent of selling or making money from their innovation to make the modified source code publicly available. Although making the source public was consistent with UNIX's open-source legacy, it discouraged business entities (who almost by definition are profit motivated) from contributing to the development of Linux. Linus Torvalds, the creator of the original open source Linux kernel, saw an elegant way out of this licensing straightjacket, providing hooks into the kernel and giving the kernel the ability to load and unload modules. Consequently, commercial enterprises were free to develop their own kernel-level enhancements without releasing their source code.

Linux Processes

The Linux process model closely resembles the UNIX process model, but it can call either a *fork* or a ***clone*** to create a process. The Unix/Linux *fork* routine calls *exec* to give the process its new context. In contrast, a clone gives the process a new identity but does not call *exec*. The clone can share both the text and data segments with the parent if needed. Associated with each Linux process is a property called a **personality identifier.** Personality allows Linux to emulate the behavior of other versions of UNIX (such as System V Release 4) and allows programs from these other versions to run under Linux without modification.

A Linux process can be divided into multiple threads, where a **thread** is a basic unit of work that can be executed and is interruptible. Linux uses *clone* primarily to create threads. Threads run concurrently within the associated process's memory space; in other words, all the threads within a process share the same memory space.

The Linux Task Scheduler

The Linux scheduler is thread based and distinguishes between normal threads and real-time threads. Each process is assigned a priority between +20 and -20. Associated with each thread in a process is a goodness value equal to the process's base priority for a normal thread and the base priority plus 1000 for a real-time thread. The scheduler schedules the next ready state thread with the highest goodness value, so real-time threads always run ahead of normal threads.

Real-time threads are further classified as first-in/first-out or round robin. A first-in/first out real-time thread either runs to completion or is unable to proceed because it is waiting for an I/O operation. A round robin real-time thread, in contrast, runs for a single time slice and then yields to the next ready state real-time thread.

A normal thread resembles a first-in/first-out real-time thread, but its goodness value is decremented by 1 following every quantum or time slice. The thread continues to run until its goodness value reaches 0, until the thread is unable to proceed because it is waiting for an I/O operation, or until a wait state thread with a higher goodness reverts to a ready state. When all ready-state threads have reached a goodness value of 0, the goodness values for all threads (both waiting and ready) are dynamically recalculated by the scheduler using the algorithm goodness/2 + priority. By setting the priority for background or compute-intensive process to low, Linux automatically gives higher priority to interactive or I/O bound processes for which a quick response is necessary.

Linux, like UNIX, can run on multiprocessor machines and supports symmetric multiprocessing (SMP). When the SMP version of Linux is used, the scheduler normally runs all threads that belong to the same process within the same processor. Under many UNIX and Linux systems, however, the administrator can assign a given process to a specific processor.

Linux Memory Management

Linux assigns every process 4 GB of virtual address space (Figure 13.15). The high order 1 GB is reserved for kernel space and can be addressed only in kernel mode. The remaining 3 GB is allocated to user space, which enables large programs to run.

Linux is designed to run on several different architectures, so it uses an architecture independent three-level set of page tables for translating virtual addresses to physical addresses (Figure 13.16). A linear (virtual) address contains a page directory index, a page middle directory index, a page table index, and an offset. The page directory index points to one of several page middle directories. Each entry in the page middle directory points to one of several page tables in the page table array. The page table entry, in turn, points to a specific page in physical memory. The page's entry point address is added to the page offset to calculate the actual physical address. In contrast, Windows uses a two-level addressing scheme (Figure 12.11) consistent with the Intel Architecture. When Linux runs on a 32-bit Intel architecture machine, the size of the page middle directory is set to one (1) by the memory manager, so the page middle directory essentially disappears.

Linux uses demand paging to load executable images into memory. When a user executes a command, the executable file is opened and its contents are mapped into the process's virtual memory address space. Pages belonging to other processes might be swapped out to create room for the new process. Linux uses a least recently used page aging technique to

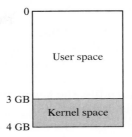

FIGURE 13.15
Linux virtual address space.

decide which pages to swap out. A page that was accessed recently is considered young. In contrast, a page that has not been accessed for some time is stale and is considered old. The oldest pages are swapped out first.

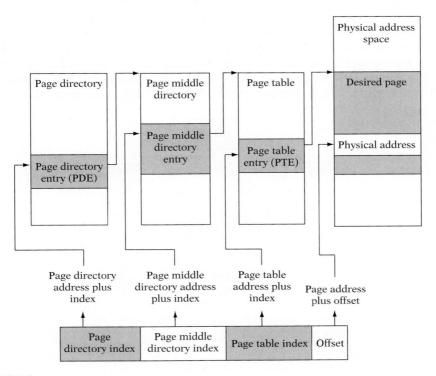

FIGURE 13.16
Linux supports three levels of page tables.

The Linux File System

The native Linux file system, **ext2fs,** resembles the standard UNIX model and can support additional file systems such as Fat32 (Windows) and HFS+ (Macintosh). The kernel maintains a layer called **virtual file system (VFS)** that allows processes to access all file systems uniformly (Figure 13.17). When a process accesses a file, the kernel directs the request to VFS, which calls the appropriate file system.

Like the standard UNIX file systems, ext2fs uses a block-based allocation mechanism. The file contains two logical units: a metadata block and the file's data. The metadata block keeps track of the i-node structure, i-node maps, free block allocation maps, and so on. When data are added to a file they are written in new blocks, so both the metadata and the data must be written to disk. The metadata are written asynchronously, so changes to the data might be written to disk before the metadata. If a system crashes before the metadata are written, the file system can become unstable and, because there is no redundant copy of the i-node table, the data loss can be substantial.

Journaling file systems use a log to keep track of changes to the metadata in an effort to compensate for such problems and provide improved consistency and recoverability. A copy of the metadata is written to the log when the metadata changes. If the system should crash before the metadata are written to disk, the log can be used to undo any partially completed task that would leave the system in any unstable state. ReiserFs, a journaling file system, comes standard with Linux. Other journaling file systems, such as XFS from Silicon Graphics and JFS from IBM, are also available.

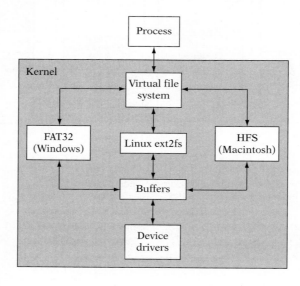

FIGURE 13.17

The virtual file system allows the various processes to access all file systems uniformly.

The Logical Volume Manager

Linux 2.4 incorporates a logical volume manager to support a layer of logical volumes between the physical peripherals and the kernel's I/O interfaces. The **logical volume manager** allows a user to combine two or more physical disks to create a volume group, a virtual disk that can be partitioned into logical volumes upon which file systems can be built. File systems are mounted on these logical volumes instead of on the physical disks.

For example, consider Figure 13.18. At the top are two physical disks, A and B. Disk A is divided into two physical partitions numbered 1 and 2, while disk B contains only partition 3. Using the logical volume manager, it is possible to logically reallocate those three physical partitions into two logical volume groups (Figure 13.18, middle layer). Logical volume group 1 encompasses disk A's physical partition 1 and disk B's physical partition 3. Logical volume group 2 corresponds to disk A's physical partition 2.

Once the logical volume groups are defined, it is possible to reallocate them into logical volumes (Figure 13.18, bottom layer). For example, logical volume group1 might be renamed logical volume 1, allowing the file system to reference the information on physical partitions 1 and 3 as though they occupied a single logical partition. At the same time, logical volume group 2, which holds only a single physical partition, might be divided into logical volume 2 and logical volume 3, effectively simulating a two-partition disk. Note that the physical volumes on which the data are actually stored and the logical volumes referenced by the file system can be quite different from each other.

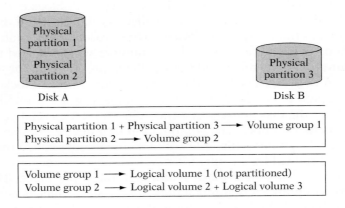

FIGURE 13.18

The logical volume manager allows a user to combine two or more physical disks to create a volume group that can be partitioned into logical volumes.

Multimedia Support

Linux supports many sound cards either directly (by the kernel) or by using technology such as Alsa (Advanced Linux Sound Architecture) that provides the appropriate drivers. On multiuser, multiprocess systems such as Linux, numerous application programs require access to the sound card, and sound servers such as aRts (analog real time synthesizer) fulfill this need. aRts is currently integrated into the KDE environment (Chapter 9) and is scheduled to be integrated into the Linux kernel. Support for video is also available within Linux, although it is less standardized than sound. Drivers for popular hardware acceleration cards are available and can be used effectively by X-Windows, the Linux window manager. Application software for playing back video is packaged with many Linux distributions and includes such software as *xine* and *mplayer* that can play back *mpeg* files, *avi* files, and so on.

◼ Summary

Under UNIX, key resident operating system services are concentrated in a relatively small kernel. To a user, an executing program image appears to be running on a personal pseudocomputer. The image consists of a text segment, a data segment, and a stack segment. The execution of an image is called a process. Processes are created by the *fork* system primitive. The death of a process creates an event signal.

UNIX manages memory space by swapping or paging processes between primary and secondary memory. The process table contains pointers that link each process's segments. The text segment is reentrant, so text segments are tracked in a text table. UNIX supports both block and character devices. Files that represent devices are called special files, and data files are called ordinary files. A system's device drivers are listed in a configuration table. An I/O operation references a device number which is used to search the configuration table for the address of the appropriate device driver.

A UNIX disk is divided into four regions: a boot block, a super block, an i-list, and a data area. The i-list contains a series of i-nodes, each of which defines the disk address of a file. A given i-node's relative position on the i-list is its i-number. The combination of a device number and an i-number uniquely defines a file. A list of open file i-nodes called the system file table is maintained by the operating system. UNIX manages disk space by maintaining a list of free block pointers in the super block. The i-node starts a series of pointers that link a file's blocks, so the blocks need not be contiguous. Block I/O takes place through a system buffer pool. Logical and physical I/O operations are asynchronous. Figure 13.13 is a useful summary of UNIX tables and pointers.

Linux features a layered architecture that resembles UNIX and Windows. Linux can call either a *fork* or a *clone* to create a process. The Linux scheduler is thread based and distinguishes between normal threads and real-time threads. Linux assigns every process 4 GB of virtual address space. The Linux logical volume manager allows a user to combine two or more physical disks to create a volume group that can be partitioned into logical volumes. The native Linux file system, ext2fs, resembles the standard UNIX model and can support additional file systems. The kernel maintains a layer called virtual file system (VFS) that allows processes to access all file systems uniformly. Linux provides considerable multimedia support.

▊ Key Words

clone	kernel
configuration table	logical volume manager
data segment	ordinary file
device driver	personality identifier
device number	POSIX
dirty	process
event	process file table
exec	process id (pid)
exit	process table
ext2fs	signal
file descriptor	special file
file system	stack segment
fork	super block
i-list	system data segment
image	system file table
init	text segment
i-node	text table
i-node table	thread
i-number	virtual file system (VFS)
journaling file system	*wait*

▊ Review Questions

1. What is the UNIX kernel?
2. Briefly explain the pseudocomputer concept. Relate the pseudocomputer concept to the ease-of-use criterion.
3. Describe (or sketch) a UNIX user program image.
4. Distinguish an image from a process.

5. A user's text segment is reentrant and thus can be shared. Data and stack segments, on the other hand, are private. What does this mean? Why is it significant?

6. Why is the system data segment necessary? It is not part of the user's image. Why?

7. Explain how processes are created under UNIX.

8. The *fork* primitive creates two *identical* processes, yet those processes can yield very different results. Explain how.

9. Explain UNIX dispatching. Distinguish between an event and a process. How do time-slicing and interrupts affect the dispatching process?

10. Describe the UNIX swapping process.

11. Why does UNIX need a text table?

12. Explain how UNIX links a peripheral device and an application process.

13. Sketch the contents of a UNIX disk.

14. Explain how UNIX converts a file name to the file's location on disk. Why is the system file table necessary?

15. All block I/O takes place through a buffer pool. Explain.

16. Under UNIX, logical I/O and physical I/O are asynchronous. What does this mean? Why is it significant?

17. Explain how UNIX links the various segments that make up a process. Explain how that process is linked to its physical devices and files.

18. Sketch the Linux architecture.

19. Describe how the Linux task scheduler works.

20. Describe how Linux manages memory.

21. Discuss the Linux file system.

22. Briefly describe Linux multimedia support.

▪ Exercises

1. UNIX is highly portable. What is portability? What makes UNIX so portable? Why is portability important?

2. Under UNIX, a user can visualize his or her image running on a private pseudocomputer. Why is that visualization valuable?

3. Why do you suppose professional programmers find the consistency and elegance of UNIX so appealing?

4. How did the profit motive influence the design of Linux?

5. Figures 13.4, 13.13, and 13.14 are useful templates for organizing many of this chapter's key terms.

CHAPTER 14

Macintosh OS X Internals

When you finish reading this chapter you should be able to:

▶ Identify the four primary layers in the functional view of OS X.

▶ Distinguish between the functional and system software views of OS X.

▶ Identify Darwin's two basic layers.

▶ Define the terms task, thread, message, and message port from an OS X perspective.

▶ Explain the OS X thread scheduling process.

▶ Explain how OS/X manages memory.

▶ Explain how the virtual file system (VFS) allows OS X to support multiple file systems.

▶ Distinguish between HFS+ and UFS and describe the contents of an HFS+ volume.

▶ Distinguish between a user-space device driver and a kernel-space device driver.

▶ Explain how the services provided by I/O Kit support writing device drivers and populating the I/O registry.

Introduction

When Apple introduced the Macintosh in 1984, it was the first system to feature an affordable graphical user interface (GUI). Today's Mac, powered by a 32-bit PowerPC chip manufactured by Motorola, represents the most successful non-Intel personal computer system in the marketplace and enjoys cultlike status within segments of the PC community. With its impressive graphic applications and its legendary ease of use, the Mac has long been a favorite of artistically oriented users, particularly for such applications as desktop publishing and multimedia, and many Mac devotees simply refuse to work with any other platform.

Over the years, Apple has steadily upgraded Mac OS, the Macintosh operating system, assigning each new release a different system number. An improved file system named HFS appeared with the release of OS System 3, cooperative multitasking was added to System 4, Internet and multimedia support were key features of System 7, and System 9 brought support for the PowerPC chip and some multiuser capability. Following the release of System 9, Apple decided to significantly change the Macintosh operating system's internals to keep up with developments in information technology, particularly enhanced hardware capabilities. In 1996, Apple rehired Steven Jobs, one of the company's founders, acquired his NeXT Corporation, and began to integrate features from OpenStep, the NeXT operating system, into the Mac. The end result, **Mac OS X,** combines the stability of UNIX with the Mac's legendary ease of use, incorporating such key features such as preemptive multitasking, memory protection, and symmetric multiprocessing while continuing to support classic Macintosh applications.

OS X Architecture

OS X can be viewed from two different perspectives: a functional view that focuses on the functions the operating system provides to users and a system software view that focuses on the internal services the operating system provides.

The Functional View

From the functional or user-oriented point of view, OS X consists of four layers: Darwin, the graphics subsystem, the application environments, and the Aqua user interface (Figure 14.1).

Darwin, the lowest layer, is the open source UNIX base on which OS X is built; it represents the core of the operating system. Darwin is responsible for kernel and operating system services, memory protection, memory management, high performance file systems, networking, preemptive multitasking, symmetric multiprocessing, multi-threading, network kernel extensions, and device driver support.

The **graphics subsystem** is responsible for screen rendering; in other words, it controls what appears on the display and ensures that type fonts are smooth and not jagged. Within the graphics subsystem, Open GL is a widely adopted application programming interface (API) standard for developing interactive 2D and 3D applications, and Quartz is a 2D graphics environment that supports the portable document format (PDF). QuickTime, another graphics subsystem component, makes available such multimedia applications as creating, editing, and playing back video, audio, animation, graphics, and text and also supports a real-time streaming Web protocol that allows users to view both live and on-demand movies[1]. The graphics subsystem also provides the OS X window server, making windows and event routing services available to the application environments, assigning each application its own window, and routing input from the keyboard and the mouse to the appropriate application.

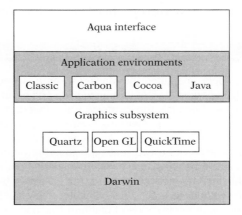

FIGURE 14.1
A functional view of OS X.

---

[1]QuickTime is available as a plug-in application for Windows and other operating environments.

Under OS X, an application program runs in one of four **application environments.** Existing System 9 applications run natively (rather than in emulation mode) within the Classic environment. Carbon makes it relatively easy to migrate System 9 applications to the OS X environment by providing nearly 70 percent of System 9's application programming interfaces, thus allowing older applications to take advantage of such OS X features as the Aqua interface, protected memory, and multiprocessing, often without modification. Cocoa supports native OS X applications and provides an object-oriented framework for rapidly developing those applications. The Java environment adds to Java programs a look and feel consistent with the Aqua user interface.

Aqua is the Mac OS X graphical user interface. It uses the windowing and 2D technology features provided by the graphical subsystem to create attractive controls and menus, photo-quality 128-pixel icons, windows, and drop shadows for menu bars, thus enhancing ease of use. Aqua manages the screen real estate and avoids modal windows to the extent possible. An example of a modal window is a warning message in a dialog box that requires the user to click on an option before the program continues. Aqua improves the user experience by providing nonmodal windows called sheets that attach themselves to the title bar of the document window like sticky notes. At first glance, a nonmodal window resembles a modal window, but a nonmodal window does not interfere with or interrupt the user work flow because the user can perform other tasks before responding.

Open and Closed Standards

Traditionally, Apple marketed the Macintosh as a closed platform, never publishing its flagship operating system's source code and never licensing its system software to anyone. Because the platform was closed, Apple was able to control virtually every aspect of its operating environment, a key factor in the company's ability to provide the user-friendly interface for which the Macintosh is famous. However, many experts believe that this closed environment explains at least in part why the Macintosh has such a limited market share while Microsoft's Windows (a comparable but, at least according to Mac devotees, technically inferior product) has become the dominant personal computer operating system.

In a break with Apple's closed platform tradition, OS X has multiple features that tap into the open source movement. For example, Darwin draws extensively from such open-source environments as Mach and FreeBSD, Apple has released Darwin under an open-source license, and there is a version of Darwin that runs on Intel platforms. OS X also supports other open source licensed software such as the Apache Web server, and Safari, the new OS X browser, is built on Konqueror's (KDE) code base (Chapter 9). The graphics subsystems, the application environments, and the Aqua interface are still proprietary, however, which protects the Macintosh look and feel.

The System Software View

OS X can also be viewed from a system perspective as a set of layers (Figure 14.2). At the top are the Classic, Carbon, Cocoa, and Java application environments you read about in the previous section. To the right of Figure 14.2 is the BSD (Berkeley Software Design) UNIX shell that supports a command line environment. (Because most users prefer a graphical user interface, BSD does not appear in the functional view.) Note that BSD interacts directly with the kernel and the Classic environment interacts directly with each of the other three layers. In contrast, Carbon, Cocoa, and Java interact exclusively with application services.

The **application services** layer provides graphical and windowing services to Classic, Carbon, Cocoa, and Java. Clearly distinguish between an application environment and an application service. Application programs run in an application environment. An application service is an operating system service that supports an application program. Note in Figure 14.2 that QuickTime bridges both layers. QuickTime is a hybrid—it requires a host environment (such as a browser) so it resembles an application service but it offers multimedia services that are found only in an application environment.

The **core services** layer provides all nonwindowing and nongraphical services that are common to all the application environments except BSD, giving OS X the ability to share code and data across environments. The core services layer also provides functions for managing lists, queues, and stacks, programming interfaces for managing processes and threads, and functions for creating and managing interprocess messages. Other core services enable a program to communicate with software running on remote machines using architecture-independent Internet and Web services (Chapter 17).

The bottom layer is the kernel environment provided by Darwin, the subject of the next section.

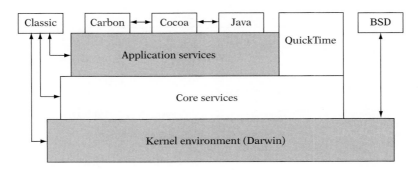

FIGURE 14.2

A system software view of OS X.

▪ Darwin

Darwin, the OS X kernel, is divided into two layers (Figure 14.3). **Mach 3.0,** the kernel's lowest layer, is a microkernel, a compact version of a kernel that implements a limited number of specific tasks and serves as a base for supporting any of several operating systems. The OS X process management services, memory management subsystem, device driver subsystem, and interprocess messaging services are implemented in Mach 3.0. **BSD** (Berkeley Software Design) **UNIX** is a popular open-source version of UNIX that represents Darwin's second layer. BSD incorporates the OS X networking services, file systems, and user management policies such as security.

Mach 3.0

Mach 3.0 assigns an address space (virtual memory) and the rights to access selected resources to a **task,** the basic OS X resource allocation unit. Each task has access to 4 GB of protected virtual address space. A task is a container for many **threads,** where a thread is the basic unit that Mach schedules for execution on the processor. For example, within a word processing task, spell checking, printing, and editing might be performed by different threads. The function of an OS X task is to manage memory, the virtual address space, and other resources and to provide a framework within which its threads run. The term process (from earlier chapters) typically implies a Mach task and one or more threads.

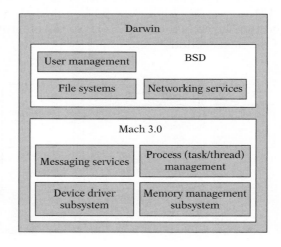

FIGURE 14.3
Darwin, the OS X kernel.

Client tasks access resources by sending **messages** to a **message port**, a secure channel for intertask or interprocess communication. Think of a message port as a protected mailbox or communication channel with its access rights managed by the kernel; in other words, a given task must have the kernel's permission to access a given port. In addition to interprocess communication, Mach's messaging feature also supports remote procedure calls to, as the term implies, procedures stored and executed on another machine. The threads within a task share resources, ports, and the address space. Mach also supports real-time services, provides a scheduler for symmetric multiprocessing (SMP), manages memory, and communicates with peripheral devices through the device driver subsystem. Mach and BSD services run in kernel mode. All other processes run in user mode.

BSD

One of Mach's design goals was portability. Systems designed with portability in mind often take a performance hit because of the need for constant communication and translation between the user mode and the kernel mode processes. To help improve performance, OS X adds a layer of BSD (Berkeley Software Design) UNIX services to the kernel and directly links Mach and BSD. The BSD layer is based primarily on FreeBSD, an open-source implementation of 4.4 BSD[2].

BSD views an active program as a process. Each process maps to a single Mach task and one or more Mach threads. Process management and file systems support are key BSD responsibilities, and because the Internet's underlying protocols (Chapter 17) were created on BSD UNIX systems, it makes sense to assign network services to the BSD layer. Additionally, OS X is a multiuser operating system and such security procedures as verifying user IDs and group IDs and controlling access to shared printers and other shared network resources are implemented in the BSD layer. BSD provides the OS X startup (boot), shutdown, and accounting procedures. Darwin also supports POSIX (the de facto standard portable operating system interface), adding much of the POSIX application programming interface (API) to the FreeBSD base.

---

[2] UC Berkeley's style places the release level first, as in 4.4 BSD, rather than last, as in OS X.

Processor Scheduling

BSD implements processes on top of Mach's task management facility. A task provides a framework for running threads, so a thread represents the basic OS X computational unit.

Thread Scheduling

Mach provides thread support and schedules threads preemptively. A fixed priority thread runs for a fixed quantum of time and then moves to the end of the queue of threads with the same priority. To improve response time for interactive tasks, an alternative is to use a time-sharing policy to raise or lower a thread's priority based on its resource needs. For example, the priority of a thread waiting for input might be raised, while the priority of a compute-bound thread might be lowered.

A given thread is classified into one of four **priority bands** (Figure 14.4). Normal application threads are assigned normal priority. If a thread's priority has been raised by a time-sharing policy, it is assigned system high priority. Kernel mode priority is assigned to threads running in the kernel space. Real time threads are threads that consume a significant fraction of the available clock cycles; for example, an audio-playback program's thread might consume 2,500 of the next 10,000 clock cycles. If a real-time thread were allowed to run continuously it would prevent other threads from running, so real-time threads are typically limited to a percentage of the available clock cycles. Because of the time-sharing scheduling policy enforced by OS X, a given thread can move from one priority band to another, but most threads stay within a single band. For example, if a real-time thread

Priority bands	Characteristics
Normal	Normal application threads
System high priority	Threads whose priority has been raised above normal
Kernel mode threads	Threads created in the kernel that run at a higher priority than all user space threads.
Real-time threads	Threads that need a significant fraction of available clock cycles

FIGURE 14.4

Thread priority bands.

requests a reasonable number of clock cycles, it stays in the real-time band. However, if the real-time thread exhibits compute-bound behavior, its priority might be reduced to a normal thread level.

Multiprocessor Scheduling

Mach and OS X support multiple processors. Processors are grouped into processor sets, with a given processor assigned to only one processor set. A given task is allocated to a specific processor set, and all threads associated with that task execute within the assigned processor set. Each processor schedules its threads as described above.

◼ Memory Management

OS X relies on Mach for memory management. A machine-dependent physical mapping module runs in the kernel and is responsible for managing the PowerPC's processor by coordinating the processor's memory cache and address translation operations. A machine independent virtual memory (VM) module also runs in the kernel and is responsible for processing page faults, managing address maps, and swapping pages.

A Mach task sees a large, sparsely populated, nonlinear, noncontiguous 4 GB virtual address space. The virtual address space is divided into text, data, stack, and mapped file regions that are separated by undefined, unallocated address spaces (Figure 14.5). The regions are themselves divided into pages, and it is the pages that are swapped between virtual memory and physical memory. If a thread accesses a region not currently in physical memory, Mach creates a page fault and swaps the appropriate address space into physical memory.

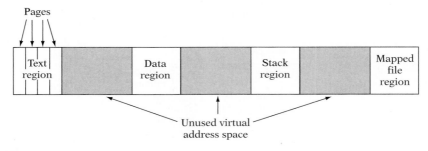

FIGURE 14.5
Virtual address space.

The kernel associates a **VM object** with each region in the virtual address space. The VM object is used to track and manage the resident (in physical memory) and nonresident portions of the memory region. Each VM object is managed by a **pager,** a task that is used to move data between the backing store (usually disk) and physical memory. Implicitly, each VM object is associated with a given pager through its memory object. A **memory object** is a specific source of data, such as a file. Logically, you can think of the memory object as a repository for data upon which various operations (read and write) can be performed.

The pager is the task that has the right to access the memory object's port. When a process needs data in its virtual address space, the VM object sends to the memory object a message requesting that the address be populated with data. The pager reads this request, and transfers the data to the address. When Mach needs to reclaim the page, it notifies the pager to transfer it back to disk.

OS X supports two pagers: a default pager and a vnode pager (Figure 14.6). The default pager is a system manager that maps nonresident virtual memory pages to the swap space and fetches them when requested. The default pager handles nonpersistent memory that exists only during the life of the task. The role of the default pager is swap space management. It stores dirty pages (pages with modified data) and finds the dirty pages when they are needed again.

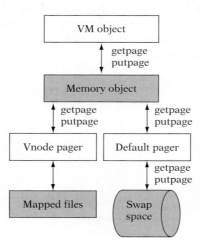

FIGURE 14.6

VM objects and pagers.

The vnode pager handles VM objects that map files accessed via a file system. When a page request is received, the pager loads the physical memory page with the file contents. When a vnode pager is asked to save a page, it simply writes the page back to the file. Thus, the vnode pager allows the task (or the process) to read and write the contents of the file as though it were reading and writing memory (Figure 14.6). You will read more about vnodes in the next section.

When a new task (or process) is created, it is cloned (or copied) from a parent. The underlying memory address space is cloned as well, so the new task inherits and either shares or copies the address space. Mach uses **copy-on-write,** a form of delayed copy, to speed up this process. Copy-on-write is done via protected sharing; in other words, both tasks are granted read-only access to the shared memory (Figure 14.7a). If either task modifies a portion of shared memory, Mach makes another copy of the modified range and gives the initiating task write access (Figure 14.7b).

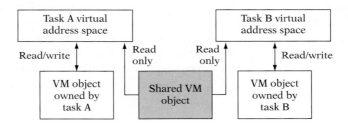

FIGURE 14.7

Copy on write.

a. When a new task is created, it is cloned (or copied) from a parent.

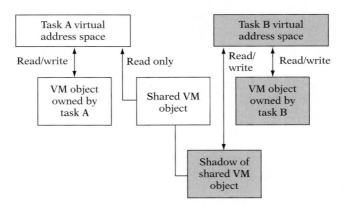

b. If a task modifies a portion of shared memory, Mach makes another copy and gives the task write access.

▪ File Systems

Before OS X was released, the standard Mac OS file system was called **hierarchical file system plus (HFS+),** also known as the extended file system (efs). OS X supports as its primary file systems both HFS+ and the BSD **UNIX file system (UFS).** Additionally, OS X supports several file systems that enable file sharing over a network, including network file system (NFS), a Microsoft Windows standard called server message block (SMB), and a proprietary Macintosh standard called AppleTalk filing protocol (AFP). Finally, two multimedia file systems are supported: ISO9660 for CD-ROM and universal disk format (UDF) for DVD.

OS X supports multiple file systems through a kernel layer **virtual file system** or **VFS** that separates file-system generic operations from specific implementations (Figure 14.8). VFS uses a file representation structure called a **vnode.** A vnode operation or VOP call is used to perform operations on a file within the file system (read, write, and so on); note that there is a unique vnode for each active file or folder. An operation or a request by a task to read from or write to a file is translated to a corresponding I/O request on the specific file system and the results are returned to the task. A VFS vnode resembles a UNIX i-node, but vnode ids are unique network wide while UNIX i-nodes are unique only within a specific file system.

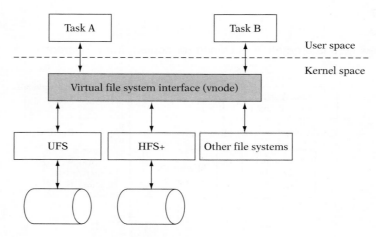

FIGURE 14.8

The virtual file system (VFS).

HFS+

An HFS file has two forks, a data fork and a resource fork, either or both of which can be empty (Figure 14.9). The data fork contains the same information as a regular file in UNIX or Windows. The resource fork contains Macintosh resources (data in a special format) that describe the menus, dialog boxes, icons, and so on associated with the file. The advantage of using a resource fork is that it enables such features as displaying menu items in the appropriate local language (English, French, Italian, Arabic...).

HFS+ specifies how a volume is stored on a disk by using a number of structures to manage the organization of data in the volume (Figure 14.10). Starting to the left of Figure 14.10, the first two sectors on every Macintosh volume are boot blocks. These blocks contain instructions and information essential to boot (start up) a system. The **volume header** is stored in sector 3 and contains information about the entire volume, including the number of files stored on the volume, the date and time the volume was created, and the location of other key structures. A copy of the volume header called the alternate volume header is stored in the next to last sector, 1024 bytes from the volume's end. The remaining structures can appear anywhere between the volume header and the alternate volume header.

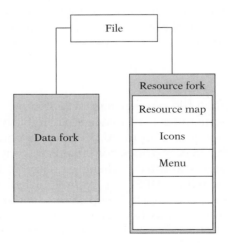

FIGURE 14.9

An OS X file has two forks.

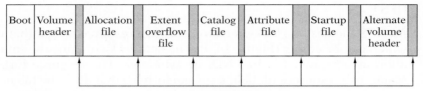

FIGURE 14.10

The contents of an HFS+ volume.

HFS+ allocates sectors in groups called allocation blocks. Typically, each allocation block holds 4 KB of storage space. The **allocation file** uses a bitmap (a bit for every block on disk) to indicate whether each block has or has not been used. An extent is a contiguous range of allocation blocks that is allocated to a fork. The first eight extents of a user file associated with a given fork are stored in the volume's catalog. The remaining extents are stored in an extent overflow file, another HFS+ volume structure. Defective portions of the medium (usually disk) are listed in a bad block file within the extent overflow file and not allocated.

The **catalog file** describes the volume's folder/file hierarchy, holds vital information about those files and folders in the files' data and resource forks, and enables quick searches for files in the hierarchy. Each file or folder name consists of up to 255 Unicode characters[3]. The attribute file contains additional data for a file or folder and is meant for future use for storing information about new forks. Finally, the startup file facilitates booting of non-Macintosh operating systems from an HFS+ plus volume.

UFS

HFS+ is the default file system on most Macintosh systems, but UFS (UNIX file system) is sometimes used instead, particularly in client/server environments. HFS+ stores data in multiple forks. In contrast, UFS stores only a single data fork. OS X provides commands to copy and move files between the two file systems and tries whenever possible to preserve the resource fork information within UFS. For example, when you move a file from an HFS+ to a UFS file system, OS X copies the data fork and resource fork separately and stores them as two separate files in the UFS system, using the same name for both but prefixing a dot underscore (._) to the resource fork name to distinguish them.

---

[3]Unicode is a 16-bit character set that can represent as many as 65,536 unique characters including the characters used in numerous foreign languages.

Other key differences involve file names and path names. UFS is case sensitive, so *Letters, LETTERS,* and *letters* are three different files. HFS+, in contrast, is case insensitive, so *Letters, LETTERS,* and *letters* are simply versions of the same file name. Within a path name, HFS+ uses a colon as a separator while UFS uses a slash (/). OS X can translate between the two as necessary.

Aliases and symbolic links are used to maintain references to files within a file system and allow you to refer to a file using a different name. In HFS+ an alias refers to both the path name and the unique file name, while UFS uses only the path name to store a symbolic link. If you move a UFS file from its original location you change the path name, so USF can no longer find the file. In contrast, HFS+ tries the path name first. If the file cannot be found, HFS+ uses the file's unique name and then updates the path name.

One advantage UFS enjoys is the ability to store sparse files efficiently. Space is allocated in 4 KB blocks, so a file that contains fewer than 4 KB will not fill the first allocation block. UFS can store the data without storing the unused space, but HFS+ fills the unused space and uses the entire 4 KB.

■ Device Drivers

A device driver provides an abstract view of a hardware device to the software layers above it. OS X supports two types of device drivers (Figure 14.11). As the names imply, a **user-space driver** runs in an application program's virtual address space and a **kernel-space driver** runs in the kernel's

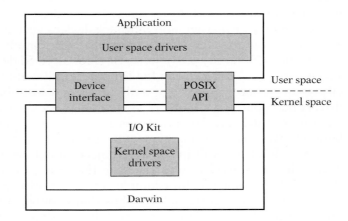

FIGURE 14.11

OS X supports user-space and kernel-space device drivers.

address space. User-space drivers are preferred because kernel-space drivers are difficult to write and if something goes wrong they can crash the system, but both types are used. For example, security considerations sometimes rule out direct user space access to a particular hardware device, and if multiple user programs frequently access the same device it makes more sense to use a shared kernel-space driver than it does to replicate a user-space driver in each application.

A user space driver communicates with the kernel either by calling a BSD POSIX procedure or by accessing a device interface that allows a program in user space to communicate with the kernel to control a specific device (Figure 14.11). For example, if an application wants to communicate with an SCSI (small computer system interface or "skuzzy") compatible scanner, the application calls the device interface which sends the request to the SCSI device driver via a communication channel called a nub (Figure 14.12). Nubs are more fully defined in the next section.

I/O Kit

The device files and device interfaces that support the OS X file systems are made available by **I/O Kit,** the OS X device driver subsystem. Device drivers are difficult to write. Not only do they require the programmer to know how to control a specific peripheral device, but other hardware components, such as buses, call for hardware-specific code, too. I/O Kit is an object-oriented framework (similar to an application programming interface) that simplifies the process of creating device drivers.

I/O Kit supports three major types of entities. **Family** is an object that provides a software abstraction common to all devices of a particular type. Think of a family as a library of methods and data associated with a particular class of device such as a type of bus, a class of disk devices, network services such as Ethernet, and interface devices such as the mouse and the keyboard. Note that the support provided by a family is generic; in other words, the SCSI family provides services for all SCSI devices but not for any specific device. A **driver** is an I/O Kit object that communicates with a specific piece of hardware such as a disk drive or a scanning device. Except for drivers that control a specific physical device, each driver is associated with a family. A **nub** is an object that acts as a bridge or communication channel between two drivers (hence two families).

Using I/O Kit's built-in software objects simplifies the task of writing a device driver. A good way to visualize the process is as a series of layers (Figure 14.13). Imagine, for example, an ink jet printer that is connected to the computer via an external USB bus that is plugged into an internal PCI bus. The top layer, which holds the ink jet printer driver and the ink jet printer family, is specific to the device—it drives the printer. The USB driver/USB family layer is more generic, holding methods and data that

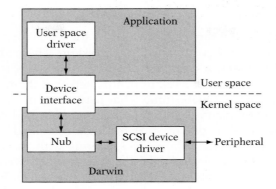

FIGURE 14.12

Accessing a device through the device interface.

apply to any USB connection, including the scanner, an ink jet printer, a mouse, and so on. At the bottom layer, the PCI bus driver and the PCI family are methods and data that apply to any PCI connection but not to the attached buses. Those three layers are connected by nubs. Rather than writing an ink jet printer driver that incorporates code to communicate with the printer, the USB bus controller, *and* the PCI bus driver, the programmer using I/O Kit writes only the printer-specific code and uses the USB and PCI code from the lower layers.

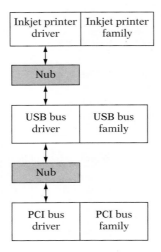

FIGURE 14.13

I/O Kit's objects as a series of layers.

I/O Registry

Inside OS X, the services provided by I/O Kit are used to provide an abstraction for each device attached to the system. These abstractions are stored in the **I/O registry,** a dynamic database that keeps track of active nubs and drivers and tracks the relationships between them. Active programs check the I/O registry to determine what peripheral devices are available.

The I/O registry is stored only in memory and is not archived when the computer is shut down, so it must be recreated each time the system is booted or restarted. The process begins with the I/O registry's root node, which starts the platform driver. The platform driver responds by creating a nub for each bus on the system (Figure 14.14). Each of those nubs then searches the **I/O catalog,** a library of the system's available device drivers, and loads the driver and associated family for each bus type. Each bus driver checks its bus and generates a nub for each peripheral or external bus card plugged into it; for example, the USB bus driver identifies each device attached to the USB bus and creates a nub for each one. Each of those nubs, in turn, loads the appropriate device driver and its associated family. The result resembles an inverted tree, with each lower level child driver/family linked to its parent driver/family by a nub.

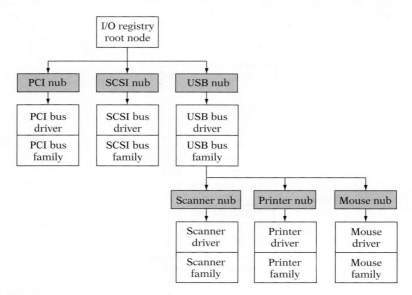

FIGURE 14.14
Building the I/O registry.

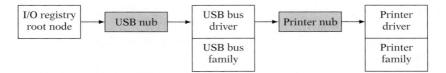

FIGURE 14.15
Adding a new device to the I/O registry.

After the system is running, if a peripheral is added to or removed from the system the registry is immediately updated with the new configuration. For example, imagine that the user plugs an ink jet printer into a USB port. Following a process that resembles the boot process, the printer's device driver is linked by nubs to the intermediate driver/family objects (Figure 14.15), and that path is stored in the I/O registry.

Windows Compatibility

In spite of its legendary ease of use and technically impressive architecture, sales of the Macintosh platform have consistently lagged behind Windows, accounting for less than five percent of personal computer sales. The reasons most often cited for the Mac's relatively poor market showing include Apple's closed platform strategy and the limited availability of Mac-compatible application software, but those issues are beginning to fade. Today, there are Mac-compatible versions of many popular applications including the Microsoft Office suite, Internet Explorer, and Quicken, and those programs use the same file formats on both the Windows and Macintosh platforms so file exchange is not a problem. More important, however, is the Mac's compatibility with such open source standards as the Internet (Chapter 17), the universal serial bus (USB), and Apple's own FireWire bus (a trademarked name for Apple's version of the IEEE 1394 standard). Such standards make it relatively easy for a Macintosh system and a Windows system to communicate and allow a Macintosh computer to operate transparently on a network designed with Windows platforms in mind. Networks are the subject of Part Five.

◼ QuickTime

QuickTime is the OS X multimedia component that allows a user to play back audio, video, graphics, and animation. QuickTime supports most of the major file formats used for audio, video, and animation and it is portable across different environments, including Windows and Java.

QuickTime consists of a set of managers (Figure 14.16). Starting on the left, the Movie Toolbox provides functions that an application program can use to store, retrieve, edit, and play back movies. QuickTime provides a number of built-in components such as image processors, media handlers, and other utilities that enable multimedia to be played back and provide services to the managers and applications; for example, the sound manager can be used to play back audio tracks such as a movie's soundtrack. These components are registered with the component manager. Application programs access the various components through the component manager. Components are extensible; in other words, QuickTime makes it possible to develop new component processes and register them with the component manager. The image compression manager provides a set of device and driver independent functions to compress and decompress images. Most applications access and use QuickTime by calling functions in the Movie Toolbox.

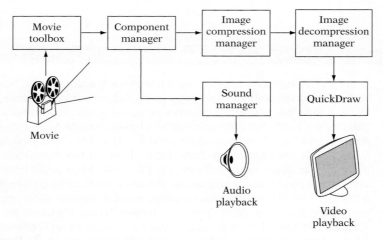

FIGURE 14.16
The QuickTime architecture.

▣ Summary

The four primary layers in the functional view of OS X are Darwin, the graphics subsystems, the application environments, and the Aqua interface. The application environments include Classic, Carbon, Cocoa, and Java. OS X can also be viewed from a system software perspective, with the application environments communicating with core services and Darwin via an application services layer.

Darwin is the OS X open source kernel. Within Darwin, Mach 3.0 is responsible for process, task, and thread management, memory management, intertask messaging services, and the device driver subsystem. BSD adds file systems, user management services, and networking services to Darwin, including the virtual file system (VFS), that allows OS X to support multiple file systems such as HFS+ and UFS. Device drivers can reside in user space or kernel space. The services provided by I/O Kit support writing device drivers and populating the I/O registry. QuickTime is the OS X multimedia component

▣ Key Words

allocation file
application environment
application services
Aqua
BSD (Berkeley Software Design) UNIX
catalog file
copy-on-write
core services
Darwin
driver
family
graphics subsystem
HFS+ (hierarchical file system plus)
I/O catalog
I/O Kit
I/O registry
kernel-space driver
Mac OS X
Mach 3.0
memory object
message
message port
nub
pager
priority bands
QuickTime
task
thread
UFS (UNIX file system)
user-space driver
virtual file system (VFS)
VM object
vnode
volume header

▪ Review Questions

1. Identify the four primary layers in the functional view of OS X.
2. What functions are performed by the OS X graphic subsystems?
3. Differentiate the Classic, Carbon, Cocoa, and Java application environments.
4. Distinguish between the functional and system software views of OS X.
5. What is Darwin? Identify Darwin's two basic layers.
6. Why is Darwin broken into two layers?
7. Define the terms task, thread, message, and message port from an OS X perspective.
8. Explain the OS X thread scheduling process.
9. Explain how OS/X manages memory.
10. How does the virtual file system (VFS) allow OS X to support multiple file systems?
11. Describe the contents of an HFS+ volume.
12. Distinguish between HFS+ and UFS.
13. Distinguish between a user-space device driver and a kernel-space device driver. User-space device drivers are preferred. Why? Under what conditions is a kernel-space driver considered a better choice?
14. Explain how the services provided by I/O Kit support writing device drivers.
15. Explain how the services provided by I/O Kit support populating the I/O registry.
16. What is QuickTime? What does QuickTime do?

▪ Exercises

1. How do you suppose a closed platform helped Apple maintain the Macintosh's user friendly interface?
2. Talk to a committed Macintosh user and ask why he or she prefers the Mac over such alternatives as a Windows platform. If you are not already aware, you might be surprised about how strongly Mac users feel about their platform of choice.
3. How does a closed platform help to explain the Macintosh's limited market success?
4. Relate I/O Kit families to the object-oriented inheritance principle.
5. What are the marketing implications of Apple's decision to adopt open source standards for OS X?
6. Looking beyond marketing, what factors do you suppose might have influenced Apple to adopt open standards for OS X? Note your initial thoughts now, and return to this question after you have completed Part Five.
7. Figures 14.2, 14.3, 14.10, and 14.14 are useful templates for organizing many of this chapter's key terms.

MVS Internals

When you finish reading this chapter you should be able to:

▶ Identify the key fields in a traditional IBM mainframe's PSW.

▶ Describe how physical I/O is performed on a traditional IBM mainframe.

▶ Explain how the interrupt concept is implemented on a traditional IBM mainframe.

▶ Describe the relationship between software-generated interrupts and privileged instructions.

▶ Distinguish between a job and a task.

▶ Describe the functions performed by job management.

▶ Describe the functions performed by task management.

▶ Identify the key control blocks that support the dispatching process.

▶ Discuss the traditional IBM mainframe dispatching process.

■ Traditional Mainframes

To this point, you have focused on personal computer operating systems[1]. Mainframes are different. This chapter is concerned with the internal workings of a traditional mainframe; more specifically on an early 1980s IBM mainframe running under an operating system called **MVS.** The intent is to give you a sense of how the dispatching process works on such a machine. In the days before PCs and the Internet, IBM's mainframes dominated the information technology marketplace. Initially, the mainframe operating systems were designed to concurrently process several batch applications. Over time, the number of concurrent applications increased and eventually such innovations as virtual memory, multiple virtual machines, time sharing, and interactivity enhanced the operating environment, but the underlying architecture of the operating system still reflected its batch processing roots.

In contrast, today's dominant distributed information technology environment (the subject of Part 5) is highly interactive, with a myriad of personal computers and workstations simultaneously communicating with a variety of remote service providers via the Internet and similar networks. Clearly, the operating systems that function in such a complex, distributed environment have outgrown their batch roots. Traditional batch-oriented operating systems still exist, however, running primarily as virtual machines under a higher-level operating system.

Although they represent old technology, traditional mainframe operating systems such as MVS do, however, offer one significant advantage—relative simplicity. A modern distributed system is incredibly complex and is best studied by focusing on the interrelated layers rather than on the contents of any given layer. It is, however, possible to understand the internal logic of an MVS operating system, and what happens within a stand-alone computer is a pretty good reflection of what happens inside one of those complex, distributed system's independent layers.

---

[1]Although UNIX can be scaled to run on virtually any platform, Chapters 9 and 13 were written from a microcomputer perspective.

IBM's Traditional Mainframes

To many experts, the modern computer era began in 1964 when IBM released the System/360 family of computers. For the first time, customers were presented with a set of architecturally compatible machines that allowed the organization to start small and upgrade to a more powerful mainframe without rewriting existing software or reformatting existing data. By the early 1970s, when the System/370 family replaced the System/360, IBM was clearly the dominant force in information technology, and its products defined a set of de facto standards that shaped the industry until the microcomputer revolution of the 1980s changed the landscape.

The first System/360 computers ran one of three batch-oriented, multiprogramming operating systems: DOS (*not* MS-DOS), OS/MFT, and OS/MVT. DOS was an entry level system that initially supported only two concurrent application programs and was not fully compatible with the other two operating systems. OS/MFT supported up to fifteen concurrent applications in fixed partitions, while OS/MVT supported up to fifteen applications in dynamically allocated regions. DOS evolved into DOS/VSE and, eventually, VSE. Over time, OS/MVT evolved into MVS, a sophisticated operating system that controlled multiple virtual systems. Although the batch processing era is clearly over, IBM's traditional mainframe operating systems helped to set the stage for today's interactive environments.

◼ Traditional IBM Mainframe Operating Principles

Before you consider MVS internals, you must understand a few basic IBM mainframe operating principles. These principles reflect the mechanism by which the operating system layer communicates with the hardware layer.

The Program Status Word

A computer executes one instruction during each machine cycle. The instruction control unit looks to the instruction counter for the address of its next instruction. An IBM mainframe's instruction counter is called the **program status** word or **PSW** (Figure 15.1).

Three PSW fields are particularly relevant to this chapter. Bits 8-11 hold the **protection key.** Each partition is assigned its own unique protection key, and the operating system's memory management function uses the protection key to ensure that one task does not attempt to modify the space assigned to another task. Bits 14 and 15 indicate the task's state—more about that later. The last 31 bits hold the **instruction address,** the address of the next instruction to be executed. In generic terms, those 31 bits are the instruction counter.

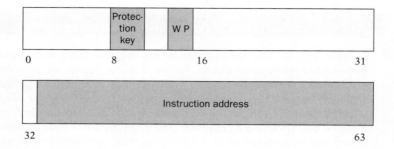

FIGURE 15.1
The program status word.

Physical I/O

External devices are attached to a traditional IBM mainframe through channels. A channel is a special-purpose computer. Because it has its own, independent processor, the channel can function in parallel with the main processor, thus freeing the mainframe to do other work.

Like any computer, a channel executes instructions. The channel's instructions are stored in a **channel program.** The channel's function is to transfer a certain number of bytes from a peripheral device into memory (or from memory to a peripheral device), so among the key parameters that must be included in the channel program are a byte count and a memory address. The channel program is stored in the main computer's memory and passed to the channel when the I/O operation begins.

A channel program consists of one or more **channel command words** (Figure 15.2). Each **CCW** contains a command code that specifies the operation to be performed (e.g., read, write, or seek), a data address, a byte count, and several flags. Programmers can write their own channel programs, but rarely do. Instead, the channel program is typically part of an access method.

Just before it starts a physical I/O operation, the mainframe operating system places the address of the channel program's first CCW in the **channel address word (CAW)** (Figure 15.3). Note that the CAW also holds the requesting partition's protection key. The protection key, remember, uniquely identifies the partition that originated the I/O request. Refer to Figure 15.4. When the channel's processor receives a start I/O (SIO) command from the main processor (1), it copies the channel address word into the channel's instruction counter (2). Then the channel fetches and executes the first channel command word (3).

The channel and the computer are asynchronous; in other words, they function independently. Consequently, the main processor has no way of knowing when the channel has completed its work unless the channel tells it. Thus, when the I/O operation is finished, the channel signals the main processor and reports its status to the operating system through the **channel status word** or **CSW** (Figure 15.5). Note again that the requesting partition's protection key occupies the first four bits in the channel status word.

FIGURE 15.2

The format of a channel command word (CCW).

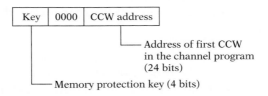

FIGURE 15.3

The channel address word (CAW).

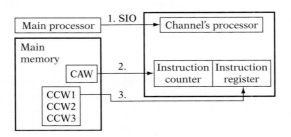

FIGURE 15.4

The channel's processor looks to the channel address word to find the first channel command word.

Key		Command address	Status	Byte count

FIGURE 15.5

The channel status word (CSW).

Interrupts

The signal that flashes from a channel to the processor is called an **interrupt.** A traditional IBM mainframe's hardware responds to an interrupt signal by switching PSWs. Three fields are involved: the **current PSW,** an **old PSW,** and a **new PSW.** The current PSW is the special register that holds the address of the next instruction to be executed. The old PSW is located in memory. The new PSW (also found in memory) holds the address of an interrupt handling routine in the operating system.

When an interrupt occurs, hardware stores the current program status word in the old PSW field and then loads the new PSW into the current PSW register (Figure 15.6). Note that following the interrupt, the current PSW points to the interrupt handling routine. Thus, as the processor begins its next machine cycle, it fetches the instruction whose address is in the program status word and starts the interrupt handling routine. Note also that the old PSW holds the address of the next instruction in the original application program, so after the interrupt is processed, the application program can be resumed.

Traditional IBM mainframes recognize six different interrupt types. Because the channels and the main processor work independently, the channel must signal the processor when an I/O operation is completed by sending it an **input/output (I/O) interrupt.** A **restart interrupt** allows an operator or another processor to intervene and start a program. An **external interrupt** comes from the operator's console, another processor, or the timer. A **machine check interrupt** occurs when the computer's self-checking circuitry detects a hardware failure.

Not all interrupts originate with hardware. A **supervisor call (SVC) interrupt** is issued when a program executes an SVC instruction, such as

SVC 17

The operand, in this case 17, requests a particular supervisor routine. An SVC interrupt is generated by a valid instruction. In contrast, a **program interrupt** is the result of an illegal or invalid instruction. Consequently, SVC and program interrupts are mutually exclusive because a given instruction cannot possibly be simultaneously valid and invalid.

Permanent Storage Assignments

The old and new PSWs, the channel status word, and the channel address word are stored in the same fixed memory locations on every traditional IBM mainframe (Figure 15.7). They, along with the computer's control registers, represent the primary interface between hardware and software.

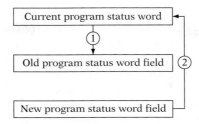

FIGURE 15.6

Switching PSWs.

Program States and Privileged Instructions

The computer, at any given time, is either executing an application program or a supervisor routine; in other words, it is either in the **problem state** or the **supervisory state.** PSW bit 15 indicates the computer's state—1 means problem and 0 means supervisory.

Address		Purpose
Decimal	Hexadecimal	
0	0	Restart new PSW
8	8	Restart old PSW
16	10	Unused
24	18	External old PSW
32	20	Supervisor call old PSW
40	28	Program old PSW
48	30	Machine check old PSW
56	38	Input/output old PSW
64	40	Channel status word
72	48	Channel address word
76	4C	Unused
80	50	Timer
84	54	Unused
88	58	External new PSW
96	60	Supervisor call new PSW
104	68	Program new PSW
112	70	Machine check new PSW
120	78	Input/output new PSW

FIGURE 15.7

Fixed memory locations.

Privileged instructions can be executed only in supervisory state. For example, because the instructions that directly control physical I/O are privileged, an application program must issue an SVC to request the operating system's support to perform an I/O operation. As you learned in Chapter 6, activating the operating system at the beginning and the end of each I/O operation is an important key to multiprogramming.

Additionally, a given program is either ready to resume processing or waiting for the completion of some event such as an I/O operation; in other words, it is either in a **ready state** or a **wait state.** A 0 in PSW bit 14 means ready; a 1 means wait.

Operating System Functions

In addition to key principles of operation, you must also understand the functions performed by several operating system routines.

Job and Task Management

To a programmer, a test run is a single job that generates a listing and a set of results. To the computer, this job involves three distinct steps or tasks: compile, link edit, and execute. A **task** is a single program or routine that has been loaded on the computer and is ready to run. A **job** consists of one or more related tasks. The programmer visualizes a job. The computer loads and executes tasks.

Within the operating system, the routines that dispatch, queue, schedule, load, initiate, and terminate jobs or tasks are part of **job management.** Note that job management is concerned with job-to-job and task-to-task *transitions*. Once a program or routine has been loaded into memory and started, **task management** supports it as it runs by handling interrupts.

The Master Scheduler

The **master scheduler** (Figure 15.8), a key job management routine, is the MVS dispatcher. With several application tasks sharing memory, it is inevitable that two or more will be ready to use the processor at the same time. The master scheduler resolves this conflict by following an algorithm to select the next task to run. The operator can issue an external interrupt to communicate with the master scheduler and thus override standard system action, perhaps improving the priority of a "hot" routine or canceling a task locked in an endless loop.

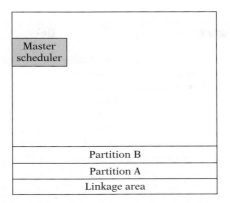

FIGURE 15.8
The master scheduler is the dispatcher.

The Initiator/Terminator

The **initiator/terminator** is a transient module that occupies memory only when needed (Figure 15.9). When a partition becomes available, the initiator/terminator reads the next job step from a queue and loads it into memory. Once the job step enters memory, it becomes a task. Later, the terminator cleans up the partition when the task ends. Because the initiator/terminator starts and ends tasks (two obvious transition points), it is part of job management.

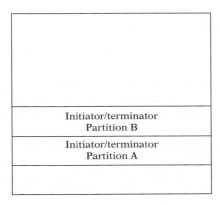

FIGURE 15.9
Each partition has its own initiator/terminator.

Job Control Language

IBM's traditional mainframe operating systems were designed to support a batch processing environment. In a batch environment, the complete job, including all the related programs or job steps and their peripheral device requirements, must be specified in advance and submitted to a computer operator or an operating system scheduler routine so it can be placed in a queue for eventual processing. The specifications are defined in a series of job control language (JCL) statements.

An OS/JCL job stream consists of three types of JCL statements. Every job begins with a JOB statement that defines such things as accounting parameters and the job's class or external priority. Each job step is defined by an EXEC (execute) statement that identifies the program to be loaded and executed. For example, a compile, link edit, and execute job would have three EXEC statements—one for the compiler, one for the linkage editor, and one for the load module. The peripheral devices needed to support a given job step are specified in a series of DD (data definition) statements that follow the step's EXEC statement. Think of each JCL statement as a single line command and a job's complete job stream as a batch file or a script.

Initially, the JCL statements were keypunched and a job was submitted to the computer center as a deck of punched cards. Over time, terminals replaced the keypunches, the JCL statements were typed with each card becoming one line, the complete job stream was stored as a file, and the file was submitted to the mainframe for processing. Although using a terminal was more convenient than punching cards, the JCL line command interface could hardly be called user friendly. In fact, the JCL statements were typically prepared and submitted by computer professionals and ordinary users rarely if ever worked with them. Today's graphical user interfaces can seem intimidating at times, but they are orders of magnitude more user friendly than batch JCL.

You will find a brief introduction to MVS JCL in Appendix D.

Task Management

Task management supports a program as it runs. A task management interrupt handling routine is activated following an interrupt. After the interrupt has been processed, task management calls job management's master scheduler, which selects the next task to be executed.

On a traditional IBM mainframe, interrupts are implemented by switching program status words, so the old PSW field provides a link back to the task that was executing at the time the interrupt occurred. Call the active task X. Following the interrupt, the master scheduler might start some other higher priority task before it restarts task X. Thus, the contents of the old PSW must be stored, because if another task is activated first, the link back to task X might be destroyed by a subsequent interrupt. Task management is responsible for saving the old PSW.

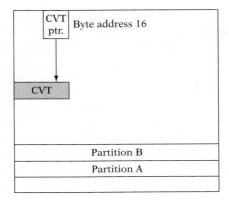

FIGURE 15.10

The communication vector table holds the addresses of key system control blocks.

Control Blocks

Job management, task management, and application program routines are linked through a series of **control blocks** that hold key control information in memory. The **communication vector table** or **CVT** (Figure 15.10) holds system constants and pointers. Each partition has its own **task control block** or **TCB** (Figure 15.11). The communication vector table points to the first partition's TCB, which points to the second partition's TCB, which points to the third, and so on, forming a linked list called a TCB queue.

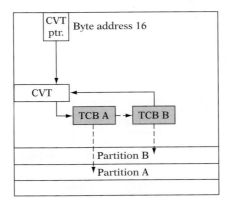

FIGURE 15.11

The TCBs are linked by pointers.

The contents of a given partition are described in a series of **request blocks** spun off the partition's task control block (Figure 15.12). The existence of a **program request block** or **PRB** indicates that the partition holds an active task. If a supervisor call interrupt is being processed in support of the partition, this fact is indicated by a **supervisor request block** or **SVRB,** so each TCB can have several request blocks attached to it. Note that each request block identifies one active task executing in or in support of the partition. Following any interrupt, task management stores the interrupted task's old PSW plus other key control fields in the appropriate request block. If the request block queue is empty, so is the partition. The terminator deletes no longer needed request blocks following task completion.

■ The Dispatching Process

At this point, you have enough information to following the MVS dispatching process through a few nanoseconds of system time. Quickly review the essential concepts before you begin.

The master scheduler is activated after any interrupt. It selects the next task by following the pointers through the task control block queue (or linked list). The communication vector table points to the high priority partition's task control block. If the task in the first partition is ready, the master scheduler starts it. If the task in the first partition is waiting, however, the master scheduler looks to the second partition's task control block. One by one, it follows the pointers from TCB to TCB, starting the first ready task it finds. Thus, on a system with fifteen active partitions, the task at the end of the TCB queue is allowed to execute only if the fourteen higher priority tasks are *all* in a wait state.

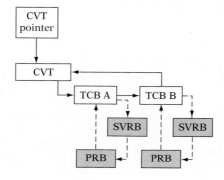

FIGURE 15.12

A request block queue is linked to each task control block.

Starting the First Task

As the example begins, the computer's two partitions, A and B, are both empty and the master scheduler is executing. The communication vector table points to the first (highest priority) task control block, which has no active request blocks (Figure 15.13). Because this first partition is empty, the master scheduler creates a program request block, loads the initiator/terminator into partition A, and starts it (Figure 15.14). The initiator/terminator, in turn, reads the first task from the job queue and loads it into the partition. For simplicity, ignore the time delay inherent in loading the task.

Soon, the application routine finds itself in need of input data, so it executes a supervisor call (SVC) instruction (Figure 15.15). The resulting SVC interrupt starts the SVC interrupt handling routine (Figure 15.16). The interrupt handler stores the old SVC PSW in the Class A partition's program request block and attaches a supervisor request block to the queue (Figure 15.17). After storing the channel program address in the channel address word, the interrupt handling routine executes a privileged start I/O instruction and then waits until the channel reports its status through the channel status word. Finally, the wait state bit in the original task's PSW (which is stored in the program request block) is set to 1 (wait state), and the master scheduler is called.

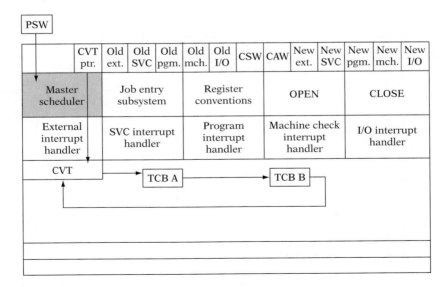

FIGURE 15.13

The master scheduler finds an open partition.

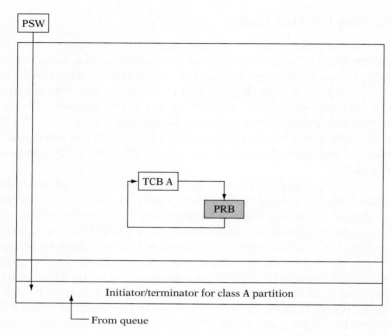

FIGURE 15.14

The initiator/terminator loads a task.

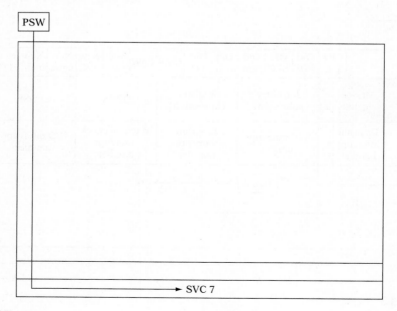

FIGURE 15.15

The application task executes an SVC instruction.

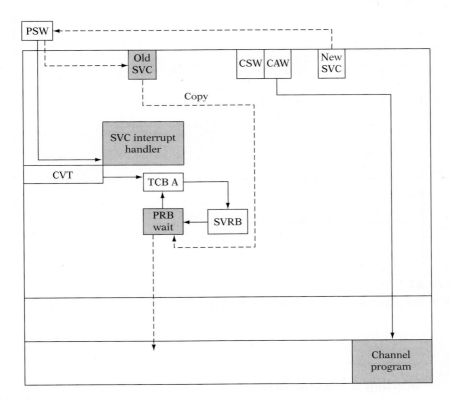

FIGURE 15.16

The interrupt handling routine starts the I/O operation.

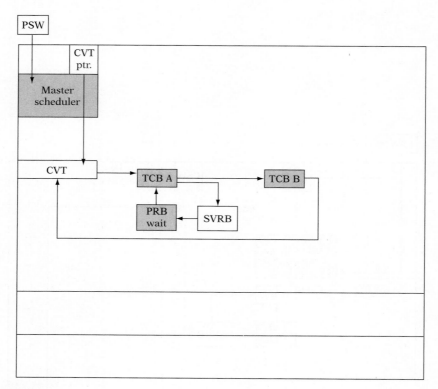

FIGURE 15.17

The task in the class A partition is in a wait state.

Starting a Second Task

Once again, the master scheduler searches the TCB queue. The communication vector table points to partition A's task control block. The partition is active (there are request blocks present), but the PSW field in the program request block indicates a wait state (Figure 15.17). Since the first partition's task is waiting, the master scheduler follows the pointer to the second task control block. Because no request blocks are chained off this second TCB, the master scheduler knows the partition is empty, so it loads the initiator/terminator into partition B (Figure 15.18) and the initiator/terminator subsequently loads a task (Figure 15.19).

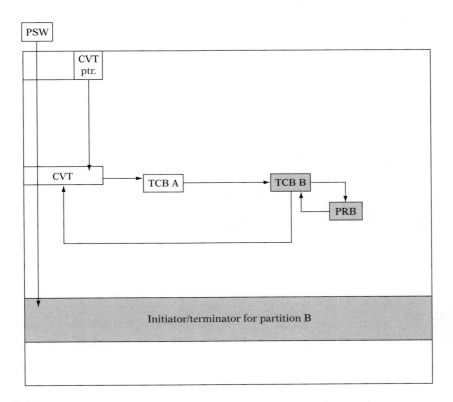

FIGURE 15.18

The master scheduler loads the initiator/terminator into partition B.

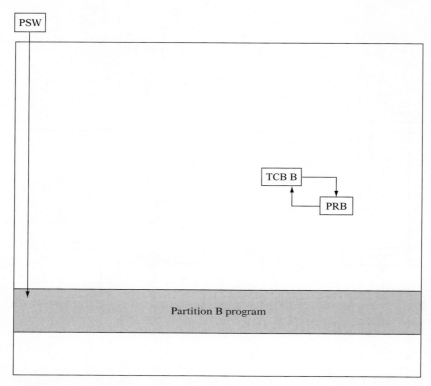

FIGURE 15.19
A second task begins executing.

Restarting a Task

Suddenly, the I/O operation that was started earlier is completed and an I/O interrupt occurs. After the PSWs are switched, the I/O interrupt handler, a task management routine, takes over (Figure 15.20). The old I/O PSW field, don't forget, still points to the program in partition B, and this program is in a ready state. Even so, the old PSW is copied to partition B's program request block.

The interrupt handling routine then checks the protection key in the channel status word, which uniquely identifies the partition that requested the I/O operation. By following the CVT/TCB/RB chain, the interrupt handling routine locates that partition's program request block, which holds the active task's most current program status word and resets its wait state bit to a ready state (Figure 15.21).

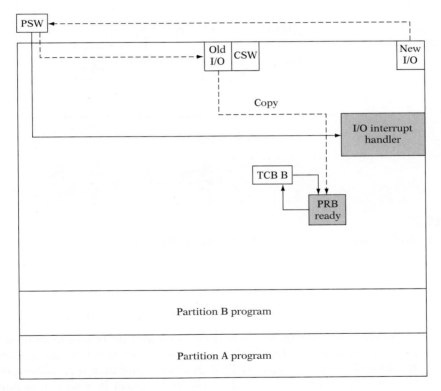

FIGURE 15.20

An I/O interrupt occurs.

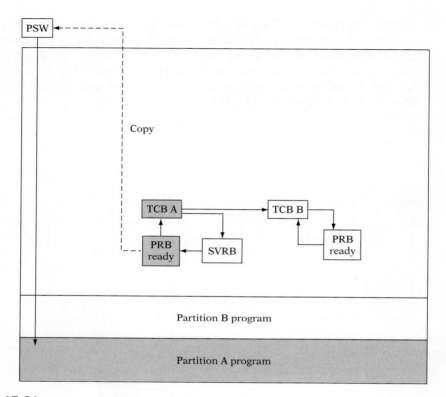

FIGURE 15.21

The I/O interrupt handling routine calls the master scheduler.

Once again, the master scheduler is called and begins searching the task control block queue. The first TCB is associated with the task in partition A. Because the task is ready, its PSW is loaded and task A resumes processing (Figure 15.21), even though the task in partition B, which was running at the time of the interrupt, is also ready.

Restarting a Second Task

Soon, the task in partition A is ready to output data to the printer, so it executes an SVC instruction. As a result, the SVC interrupt handling routine is activated (Figure 15.22). The SVC interrupt handler stores the old SVC PSW in the program request block, creates another SVRB, starts the output operation, sets the application task's PSW to a wait state, and calls the master scheduler (Figure 15.23).

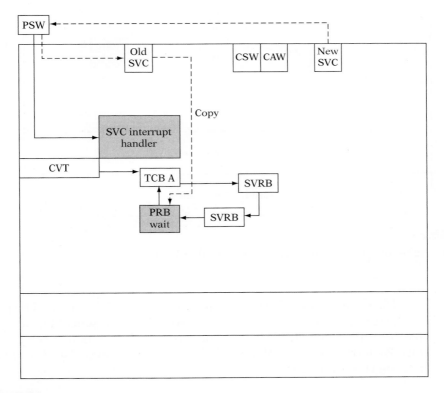

FIGURE 15.22

Another supervisor call interrupt occurs.

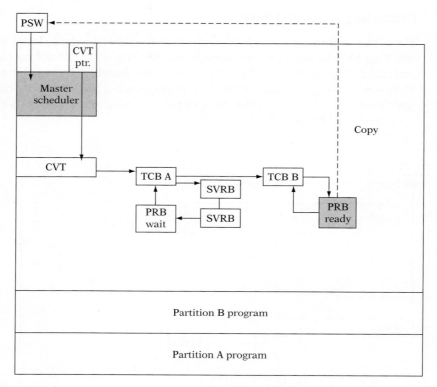

FIGURE 15.23
The master scheduler loads the PSW for the partition B task.

The master scheduler once again searches the TCB queue. The program in the first partition is in a wait state, so the master scheduler moves on to partition B's task control block. The partition B task is in a ready state, so task B's most current PSW is loaded from the PRB and task B resumes processing (Figure 15.24).

The Process

Note how predictable and repetitive the dispatching process is. Following any interrupt, the master scheduler is activated. It finds the address of the first task control block in the communication vector table. That first or high priority TCB marks the beginning of a linked list that ties together all the TCBs. The master scheduler follows the chain of TCB pointers and starts the first ready task it finds. That basic dispatching cycle is repeated over and over again from the instant the operating system is booted until it is shut down.

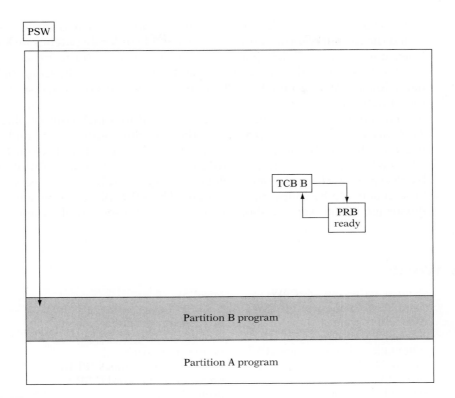

FIGURE 15.24
The partition B task begins executing.

▎Summary

A traditional IBM mainframe's instruction counter is called the program status word. An application program starts an I/O operation by executing an SIO operation. The operating system responds by storing the address of the first channel command word in the channel address word and issuing a privileged start I/O instruction. When the I/O operation is completed, the channel notifies the processor by sending an interrupt and reporting its status through the channel status word. A traditional IBM mainframe responds to an interrupt by storing the current PSW in the old PSW field and loading the new PSW into the current PSW. Six types of interrupts are supported: external, I/O, machine check, restart, program, and SVC.

A task is a routine that is loaded into memory and ready to run. A job is a set of related tasks. Job management is concerned with job-to-job and task-to-task transitions. Task management supports the tasks as they run.

Job management includes the master scheduler and a transient routine called the initiator/ terminator. The master scheduler dispatches tasks, identifies empty or available partitions, loads the initiator/terminator in an empty partition, and communicates with the operator. The initiator/terminator loads tasks into memory. Task management is composed of interrupt handling routines.

The contents of each partition are defined in a task control block. The TCBs are linked in a fixed order, with the communication vector table pointing to the first TCB, the first TCB pointing to the second, and so on. The specific tasks active in a given partition are described by a chain of request blocks spun off the task control block. The master scheduler selects the next task to activate by following this chain. The MVS dispatching scheme was illustrated by an example showing a fraction of a second of computer time.

▪ Key Words

channel address word (CAW)
channel command word (CCW)
channel program
channel status word (CSW)
communication vector table (CVT)
control block
current PSW
external interrupt
initiator/terminator
input/output (I/O) interrupt
instruction address
interrupt
job
job management
machine check interrupt
master scheduler
MVS

new PSW
old PSW
privileged instruction
problem state
program interrupt
program request block (PRB)
program status word (PSW)
protection key
ready state
request block
restart interrupt
supervisor call (SVC) interrupt
supervisor request block (SVRB)
supervisory state
task
task control block (TCB)
task management
wait state

▪ Review Questions

1. Identify the key fields in a traditional IBM mainframe's PSW and explain the purpose of those key fields.

2. Explain how physical I/O is performed on a traditional IBM mainframe. Include in your response the access method, the channel program, the channel command word, the channel address word, the operating system, and the channel status word.

3. Explain how the interrupt concept is implemented on a traditional IBM mainframe.

4. List the types of interrupts recognized on a traditional IBM mainframe and identify the source of each type.

5. What are permanent storage assignments? Why are they necessary on a traditional IBM mainframe?

6. Describe the relationship between software-generated interrupts and privileged instructions.

7. Distinguish between a job and a task.

8. Distinguish between job management and task management.

9. What functions are performed by job management?

10. The initiator/terminator is a transient module. Why? What does transient mean?

11. What functions are performed by task management?

12. Identify the key control blocks that support the dispatching process.

13. How does the master scheduler discover if a partition is free or busy? Identify all the tables, control blocks, and pointers involved in this process.

14. How does the master scheduler determine which task to start next?

15. How does the master scheduler know when to start a new task?

▪ Exercises

1. IBM's traditional mainframe operating systems were initially designed to support batch processing applications. Why?

2. IBM's mainframes dominated information technology until well into the 1980s. Why do you suppose IBM lost that dominant position? Or did they?

3. For those who might be interested in studying JCL in greater depth, appropriate material from earlier editions can be found on this textbook's companion Web site.

4. Describe the MVS dispatching process in terms of layering.

5. Figure 15.13 is a useful template for organizing many of this chapter's key terms.

6. An excellent way to gain a deeper understanding of this chapter's underlying concepts is to start with Figure 15.13, add a third partition to the example developed in the text, and explain how this third partition might change the flow of control through the system.

Distributed Systems

This section focuses on distributed operating systems and the software that controls inter-computer communication. Chapter 16 discusses basic communication and networking concepts. Chaper 17 focuses on the Internet, the evolving standard platform for intercomputer communications, and Chapter 18 presents client/server operating system concepts, principles, and security implications. Chapter 19, 20, and 21 introduce the user interface and key internal operating principles for three real-world network operating systems: Windows XP Server, Linux, and Novell NetWare.

CHAPTER 16

Data Communication and Networks

When you finish reading this chapter you should be able to:

▶ List and define the basic elements essential to data communication.

▶ Identify several common data communication media.

▶ Distinguish between a message and a signal and explain modulation and demodulation.

▶ Distinguish between analog and digital data communication.

▶ Explain packet switching.

▶ Distinguish between wired and wireless communication services and explain the last mile problem.

▶ Distinguish between a LAN and a WAN.

▶ Distinguish among polling, collision detection, token passing, and routing.

▶ Define internetworking and distinguish between a bridge and a gateway.

▶ Explain how a client/server network works.

▐ Layers

Many of today's information systems are spread over multiple computers that communicate with each other and share responsibility for information processing, storage, and retrieval. A good way to view such distributed systems is as a set of layers (Figure 16.1). The individual computers are linked by a communication infrastructure. The computers physically communicate via the underlying infrastructure following the rules imposed by a set of network protocols that reside in each computer's operating system. Each computer hosts a portion of the multiple-computer application, and those partial applications communicate with each other via their operating systems, their network protocols, and the data communication infrastructure. This chapter focuses on the communication infrastructure and key network principles.

▐ Data Communication

Data communication is the process of transferring data, information, or commands between two computers or between a computer and a terminal. Successful communication requires a message, a transmitter, a receiver, a medium, and a protocol (Figure 16.2). The **message** is the information being sent. The **transmitter** or sender is the source of the message and the **receiver** is the destination. The **medium,** sometimes called a line, a channel, or informally a pipe, is the path over which the message flows. A data

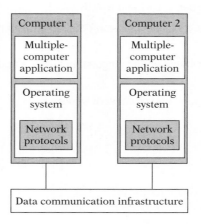

FIGURE 16.1

View multicomputer applications as a series of layers.

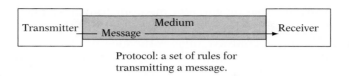

FIGURE 16.2
Communication requires a message, a transmitter, a receiver, a medium, and a protocol.

communication **protocol** is an agreed upon format or procedure (in effect, a set of rules) for transmitting a message over a communication medium. There are many different protocols, but the transmitter and the receiver must both use the same one. A protocol can be implemented in hardware, software, or both. Key issues include delivering messages efficiently and detecting and/or correcting errors.

Connectivity

Connectivity refers to the ability of a device or a program to communicate with other devices or software. *Physical* connectivity is achieved by establishing a connection between the transmitter and the receiver via some medium. *Logical* connectivity is achieved by using a common set of protocols to ensure that both the transmitter and the receiver follow the same rules and speak the same language. For example, when you answer the telephone, you say "hello." You and the caller then identify yourselves, and the conversation begins. Without really thinking about it, you both use the same language and you exchange information by taking turns. Finally, you say "goodbye" and hang up. Those informal telephone etiquette rules represent a primitive communication protocol. In this example, the telephone line is the medium. Combining a medium and a protocol enables connectivity.

Data Communication Media

There are two types of data communication media: cable and wireless. A **cable** medium physically links the transmitter and the receiver; examples include a twisted pair of wires, a coaxial cable, a fiber-optic cable, and so on. There is no physical connection when **wireless** media, such as radio, television, cellular telephone, Wi-Fi[1], microwave links, satellite links, and infrared beams, are used. A dedicated line is a permanent link between a sender and a receiver. A **switched line,** in contrast, links the sender and the receiver only while the message or a series of related messages are being exchanged.

---

[1]Intel's new Centrino mobile laptop technology comes with built-in Wi-Fi connectivity.

A given cable or wireless medium transmits messages in either base-band or broadband mode. A **baseband** line carries one message at a time. **Broadband,** in contrast, divides the medium into distinct channels that act much like independent wires and transmit simultaneous messages in paral-lel. For example, your cable television service allows you to select from many different stations all of which are transmitted over the same cable. Some sources use the term broadband as a synonym for high-speed com-munication, perhaps because most high-speed lines are broadband.

The speed of a communication line is a function of its **bandwidth,** the number of bits the line can transmit in a fixed amount of time. Bandwidth is usually expressed in bits per second (bps) or bytes per second (Bps). Each byte holds 8 bits, so 2,400 Bps is equivalent to 19,200 bps. Prefixes such as K (1000), M (1 million), or G (1 billion) are used to indicate order of mag-nitude; for example, 5 Mbps means 5 *million* bits per second. Figure 16.3 summarizes the communication speeds of several common media.

Compression

Line speed is a significant bottleneck in many applications. There are two ways to transmit a message more quickly. One is to increase the bandwidth of the connecting medium by switching to a faster line. The second, less obvious solution is to transmit fewer bits.

Connection type	Bandwidth
Local telephone line	56 Kbps

Wireless
    2G digital cellular
    2.5G digital cellular
    3G digital cellular
    Bluetooth
    Wi-Fi (802.11b)
	
	19.2 Kbps
	144 Kbps
	2 Mbps
	1 Mbps
	Up to 11 Mbps

Home satellite service	400 Kbps
DSL	1.44 Mbps
Cable service	2 to 10 Mbps
Leased line (T-1, T-3)	1.5 to 43 Mbps
Fiber optic cable	Up to 10 Gbps

FIGURE 16.3

Bandwidth is a measure of the amount of data a line can transmit in a given period of time.

One way to reduce the size of a message is to use a **compression** algorithm. For example, Figure 16.4 shows a long form directory listing of two files. The first file is a 633 KB bitmap *(bmp)* of a digital photograph of a sunset. The second file is a compressed 70 KB *jpg* version of the same image. Compression typically reduces file size by 50 to 75 percent (or more), and smaller files mean fewer bits to transmit.

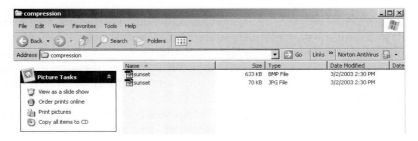

FIGURE 16.4

Compression.

Messages and Signals

A message consists of a header, a body, and a trailer (Figure 16.5). The header holds such system information as the source address and the receiving address. The body contains the message content; from the user's point of view the body is the message. The trailer, when present, holds additional system information such as an end-of-message marker. The precise format of the header and the trailer depends on the protocol.

A message moves over a communication line in the form of a **signal;** for example, the signal might consist of a fluctuating electric current or a flashing light. Variations in the signal represent coded information. The sending device creates the signal variations, and the receiving device interprets them.

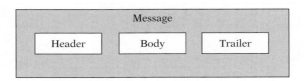

FIGURE 16.5

A message consists of a header, a body, and a trailer.

Modulation and Demodulation

A direct link between two devices that are in close proximity to each other is called a local connection. For example, a sales associate might transfer the week's sales activity from his or her laptop to the office desktop by stringing a cable between the two machines and running a file transfer program. Communication over such local connections is similar to sending output data from a computer to a printer. Incidentally, most local connections are baseband.

Remote communication between two devices that are separated by more than a mile or two is much more complex, however. When data are transmitted over a distance, the signal attenuates (or loses intensity) and picks up electronic interference called noise. The further the signal moves from its source, the weaker it becomes until eventually it is overwhelmed by the noise. If you have ever tuned your vehicle's radio to a local FM station and driven away from town, you have experienced both attenuation and noise.

Messages are typically transmitted over a distance in the context of a carrier signal such as the sine wave pictured in Figure 16.6. One complete S-on-its-side pattern is called a cycle, the height of the wave is its amplitude, and the number of cycles per second (usually expressed in hertz) is its frequency. Because the carrier signal's frequency and amplitude are known, equipment can be designed to filter and boost it.

The task of transmitting a message in the context of a carrier signal is performed by a device called a **modem** (an acronym for modulator/demodulator) placed at both ends of the communication line (Figure 16.7). At the transmitter's end the modem adds the data (or the intelligence) to the carrier signal in a process called modulation. At the other end of the line, the receiver's modem demodulates the signal by subtracting out the carrier signal, leaving only the data.

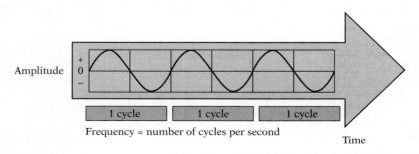

FIGURE 16.6
A carrier signal.

FIGURE 16.7
Modems are placed at both ends of the communication line.

Analog and Digital Data Transmission

A sine wave is a continuous analog signal, and analog signals are boosted by amplifying them. The problem is that when you amplify the signal, you also amplify the noise. As a result, an analog signal accumulates noise as it travels along a line, which makes it difficult to maintain signal quality. An option is to use digital technology.

Superficially, there is little difference between transmitting analog and digital data. In both cases, the transmitting modem adds the data to the carrier signal and the receiving modem subtracts the carrier signal to recover the data. What happens in between the modems, however, is what distinguishes analog from digital data transmission. An analog signal is boosted by amplifying it. A digital signal, in contrast, is electronically captured, reconstructed, and retransmitted, so most of the noise is automatically filtered from the signal. Just as a digital compact disk yields a clearer, sharper sound than an analog cassette or a vinyl LP, digital data transmission means better quality than analog data transmission.

Analog and Digital Sound

For many years, such analog media as vinyl LP and magnetic tape dominated the sound recording industry. Over the past decade, however, those analog media have been largely supplanted by digital media such as CD and DVD. Given that both the analog and digital recording processes start with the same analog sound patterns (a rhythm track, a lead guitar track, a lead vocalist track, and so on), why the change?

The analog process records a continuous signal. Play back the recording and you reproduce the original signal. The digital process, in contrast, samples the source signal, converts each sample to a pattern of digits, and records a series of discrete digital pulses. Imagine flipping a microphone on and off thousands of times a second and you have a pretty good mental image of the digital recording process. Note that in between samples, the digital process records absolutely

(continued)

Analog and Digital Sound *(continued)*

nothing, but if you sample frequently enough, when you play back the digital signal the listener hears what seems to be a continuous signal.

The problem with analog is that you record the *entire* signal, warts and all, and when you amplify the signal to play it back you also amplify any noise it might have picked up. That is why the background hiss gets louder when you crank up the volume on a cassette player, and that is why sound quality tends to deteriorate when you copy an analog recording.

Digital recording tends to produce a higher quality sound because any noise that occurs in between samples is ignored and the discrete digital pulses that are captured can be screened and filtered to remove unwanted sounds. Also, because the digital signal consists of a string of numbers, it can be stored and reproduced with no loss in quality (a fact that concerns the sound recording industry).

Are there any advantages associated with analog recording? Actually, there are. Many audiophiles prefer older analog recordings because they find digital sound a bit too cold and precise. Imagine a singer holding a note for several seconds. The sound waves produced by the singer are a continuous analog signal. The sampling process chops the signal into very brief digital pulses, but by its very nature the process misses any sounds that occur in between samples. Those inter-sample periods are not silent, of course. On most recordings, most listeners do not consciously notice the on/off nature of a digital signal, but a true audiophile might sense the enhanced warmth of the analog version.

Packet Switching

For any given sender, the typical data communication pattern consists of occasional bursts of activity separated by lengthy quiet times. The high bandwidth lines used for remote communication are quite expensive, so efficiency is a priority. Local lines are relatively inexpensive so low utilization is not a concern, but there is a risk that a single user might dominate a line. **Packet switching** achieves efficient message delivery by allowing numerous messages to share the line while preventing any single user from dominating it.

With packet switching, a message is divided into a set of small blocks called packets. Picture the communication line as a continuously moving escalator-like matrix of slots, each of which can hold one packet (Figure 16.8). Some of the slots hold packets from other messages. Some are empty. The first packet from the new message is dropped into the first available slot, the second packet goes into the next available slot, and so on; note how packets from numerous messages are intermixed. At the receiving end, the packets are reassembled to form the original message. Should transmission errors occur, only lost or erroneous packets must be retransmitted, which is much more efficient than resending the entire message.

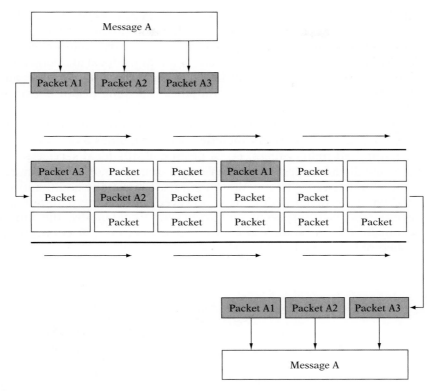

FIGURE 16.8
Packet switching.

■ The Public Communication Infrastructure

Think of a simple device-to-device link as the communication infrastructure's base layer. More complex communication systems are created by combining one or more of those basic links. A **common carrier** is an organization that provides the public communication services that define the higher levels of the communication infrastructure.

Plain Old Telephone Service

Today's best-known common carriers are the companies that provide **plain old telephone service (POTS).** The process of placing a call begins when the sender (a person or a computer) dials a number. The act of dialing generates a signal that travels from the originator's telephone over a wire (or cable) to the local telephone service provider's central office (Figure 16.9). Local calls are connected directly by the local provider. Long distance calls, however, are routed over a high-speed line to the destination telephone's central office, which completes the call. Think of the local and long distance segments as two independent layers. The local layer transmits the call between the sender and the sender's central office. The long distance layer transmits the message between the two central offices. The receiver's central office then passes the message to the receiver's local layer and on to the receiver.

Long distance carriers include such companies as AT&T, MCI, Sprint, Verizon, and many others. For a given call, the local service provider and the long distance service provider might or might not be the same company, and a long distance connection might use almost any combination of cable and wireless media. To the user, however, the specific path assigned to the connection is transparent and irrelevant. Incidentally, the long distance connection is an example of a switched line because the connection is established only for the length of the call.

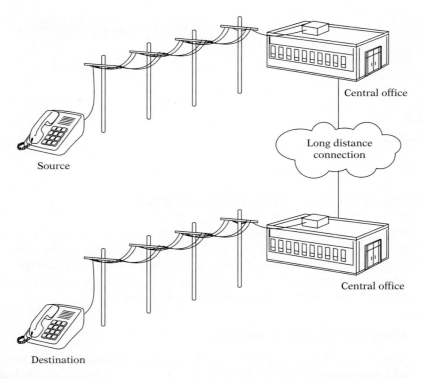

FIGURE 16.9
Plain old telephone service (POTS).

Perhaps you noticed that the long distance layer is visualized as a cloud in Figure 16.9. The cloud image suggests that the underlying infrastructure acts like a black box, an independent layer that can be used without fully understanding what happens inside the box. For example, when you call a friend, your voices flow between the two telephones and you could care less about what happens in between. As far as you are concerned, the call disappears into a cloud and emerges at the other end. Implementing the telephone system in layers allows you to ignore the underlying technology and makes mass telephone communication possible.

Communication Pricing

In the 1960s, the cost of a long distance telephone call was a function of time and distance. To help control costs, many homes (and even a few businesses) kept a three-minute egg timer next to the telephone, and cross-country calls were reserved for special occasions.

Today, the major telephone service providers offer rates as low as 7 cents per minute to anywhere in the United States, and in most parts of the country the local (free) calling area has expanded from a single community to a much larger region. Expect that trend to continue, with the "local" calling area expanding until, eventually, the pricing model resembles cable TV's, with unlimited calls anywhere within the country for a fixed monthly fee, plus additional charges for extra services such as call waiting, call forwarding, voice messaging, teleconferencing, and so on.

Why the trend toward fixed fee pricing? Monitoring the length of individual phone calls and printing multipage monthly bills is expensive. Shifting to fixed fee pricing significantly reduces administrative costs, leading to increased profits for the company and often lower bills for the customer—a classic win-win scenario.

Wireless Communication

In contrast to POTS, cellular telephones rely on wireless communication. When the originator dials a number on his or her mobile phone, an antenna picks up the signal and transmits it to a base station (Figure 16.10), which forwards the signal to a mobile switching center. If the receiving cell phone is in the same service area, the call is completed by the mobile switching center in much the same way a POTS central office completes a local call. If the call is to a wire-based telephone, it is transferred to the appropriate POTS central office, which makes the final connection. If the call is long distance, the mobile switching center routes it to a long distance carrier,

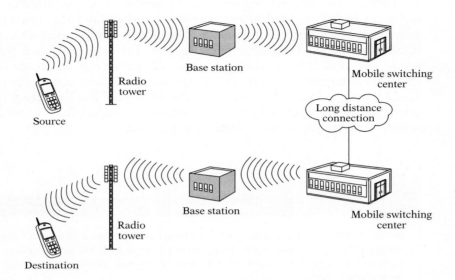

FIGURE 16.10
Wireless communication.

often one of the same companies that transmit traditional, wire-based telephone calls. Note that on a long distance call, both wire-based and wireless service providers access the same long distance infrastructure (Figure 16.11). Think of POTS and wireless services as independent layers that plug into the long distance layer.

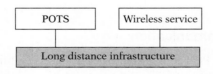

FIGURE 16.11
POTS and wireless are alternative access paths to the long distance communication infrastructure.

The Last Mile Problem

Using a modem, the current de facto standard for transmitting a message over a local telephone line is 56 Kbps. Wireless cell phones support comparable transmission rates, but quality is a problem and retransmitting errors cuts the effective speed. Once the message is transferred to a long distance service provider, however, it is sent on its way over high-speed (Mbps or Gbps) lines. The enormous speed disparity between a local line and a long distance line is called the **last mile problem,** where the "last mile" is the link between a home or office and the telephone service provider's local central office.

There are promising broadband alternatives for plugging into the long distance layer; several of them were summarized in Figure 16.3. First-generation cellular phones and second-generation digital cellular services are not quite fast enough or reliable enough for serious data communication, but third-generation wireless technology should be, and new wireless options such as Bluetooth and Wi-Fi are gaining users. Another wireless option, home satellite service, is widely available today.

A digital subscriber line (DSL) enables high-speed data communication on existing local telephone lines. Cable service bypasses the telephone company, offering connectivity from the subscriber's home or office via high bandwidth cable. Business, government, educational, and other large organizations sometimes bypass the last mile problem by leasing a high-speed (T-1 or T-3) line that links them directly to a central office or a long distance carrier, and fiber-optic cable looks very promising.

◼ Networks

As individuals, we tend to see the act of communication (a phone call or an e-mail message) as a two-party process involving a sender and a receiver. On many modern information systems, however, a given computer or workstation often must communicate with many other computers or workstations. Imagine stringing separate lines linking every computer in the company to every other computer in the company. In addition to looking ugly and costing a fortune, the resulting spaghetti-like jumble of wires would be virtually impossible to manage and maintain.

The solution is to create a network. A **network** is composed of two or more (usually more) computers or other intelligent devices linked by communication lines in a way that allows them to communicate effectively.

Each device on the network is called a **node.** For a given message, one node is the transmitter or sender and another node (or set of nodes) is the receiver. The rules for sending the message from the transmitting node to the receiving node are defined in a communication protocol. In effect, networks are constructed on top of the communication infrastructure described earlier in this chapter.

LANs and WANs

A group of interconnected computers or workstations located in close proximity (for example within the same building or adjacent buildings) form a **local area network** or **LAN.** Each node has a unique address that distinguishes it from all the other nodes. The message header typically carries information for delivering the message, including the addresses of the source and the receiving nodes.

A **wide area network** or **WAN,** in contrast, links computers or LANs that are geographically disbursed. Most WANs utilize (at least in part) high-speed, broadband public communication services such as those provided by the telephone company and other common carriers.

Topologies

A LAN's topology describes its shape or form and defines its (typically baseband) connections or data paths (Figure 16.12). In a bus network, all the nodes share a common communication line called a bus. In a star network, all the nodes are linked to a central star node and all communications flow through the star node. For example, a local telephone service provider operates a star network with the central office computer as the star and your telephone as one of the other nodes. In a ring network, the nodes form a ring or loop and messages move around the ring from node to node.

Some local area networks transmit messages directly from the transmitting node to the receiving node. Others **broadcast** messages, sending every message to every node on the network. When a message reaches a given node on a broadcast network, the appropriate protocol checks the header, accepts (or receives) any messages addressed to it, and ignores messages addressed to some other node.

LAN Protocols

The nodes on a local area network are asynchronous; in other words, they operate independently. Consequently, it is possible for two (or more) nodes to transmit data simultaneously (or nearly simultaneously) over the same line. When that happens, the messages interfere with each other and both are rendered unreadable. Such interference is called a **collision.**

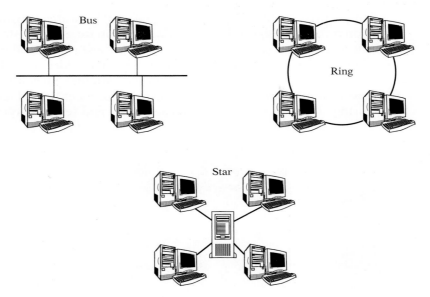

FIGURE 16.12
Some common LAN topologies.

One solution to the interference problem is to use a collision avoidance protocol that prohibits simultaneous message transmission. For example, on a **token passing** (or token ring) network, an electronic signal called the token moves continuously around the network and a node is allowed to transmit only when it holds the token. Since only one node can transmit at any given time, collisions cannot happen. Token passing is common on ring networks.

Polling is another collision avoidance protocol. On a star network, the primary or star node starts the polling process by sending a polling signal to node A. If node A is ready to transmit a message, it does so. If not, the star computer sends a polling signal to node B, then node C, and so on in round-robin fashion. Only one polling signal is active at any given time, and a node can transmit only when polled, so collisions are impossible.

On a **collision detection** network, in contrast, a given node can transmit whenever the line is clear. Because it takes time for a signal to traverse a line, however, two nodes might both sense a clear line and transmit simultaneously (or nearly simultaneously), so collisions *are* possible. When a collision occurs, it is detected electronically and the affected messages are retransmitted. Token passing and polling are most effective on a heavily loaded LAN. Collision detection is often a better option on a lightly loaded LAN, because fewer messages mean fewer collisions.

Ethernet is a popular, inexpensive, high-speed local area network collision detection protocol designed by Xerox Corporation for a bus or star topology. An Ethernet adapter card or network interface card is installed in each network node and assigned a unique (within the LAN) address. Each station is linked to a central wiring closet. For example, Miami University's School of Business Administration LAN has one wiring closet per floor (Figure 16.13). The wiring closets are connected to each other and (eventually) to the rest

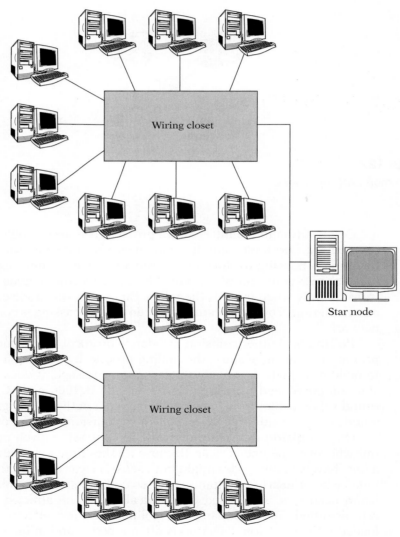

FIGURE 16.13

An Ethernet network.

of the network by coaxial or fiber optic cables that stretch from floor to floor and between buildings.

Routing

Most WANs lack an easily defined topology. For example, the Internet, a worldwide network of networks, is so vast that nobody knows exactly what it looks like. Lacking obvious connection paths, such networks (including some LANs) rely on point-to-point transmission, passing the message from node to node across the network in a series of hops (Figure 16.14). The intermediate nodes might be computers or routers, hardware devices that accept a message, examine the header, and forward the message to the next node without regard for the message's content.

The process of selecting the next node or set of nodes is called **routing.** For example, consider node 5 in the middle of Figure 16.14 and imagine that it just received a message from node 4. In addition to node 4 (which, we'll assume, cannot be the next target), node 5 has links to nodes 3, 6, and 7. How does it select the next node? The decision is often made by consulting a routing table; in effect, a list of routing rules. Static routing uses preset paths; for example, whenever node 5 receives a message from node 4 it might always forward the message to node 6. Sometimes the routing node is given a bit more flexibility. For example, node 5 might direct the message to node 7 if the path to node 6 is busy, or alternate between nodes 6 and 7 to achieve better load balancing. With dynamic or adaptive routing, the best path is computed based on real-time data such as the candidate destination nodes' utilization rates or failure rates.

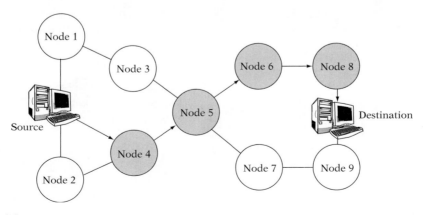

FIGURE 16.14

With point-to-point transmission, a signal is routed node-by-node across the network.

Internetworking

The process of linking two or more networks (LANs, WANs, or both) is called **internetworking.** A number of hardware devices are used to control and coordinate internetwork communication. A bridge is a node that links two or more similar networks (Figure 16.15). A gateway is a node that links dissimilar networks; for example, a local area network might be connected to a wide area network through a gateway. Note that the term Internet is an acronym for *internet*working.

Client/Server Networks

In addition to their physical configuration, most networks also have a logical configuration that defines the role played by each node. For example, on a **client/server network** (Figure 16.16), specialized computers called **servers** control access to all the network's shared resources, and the other nodes act as **clients.** When a client logs onto a network, the client node establishes a connection to a server and, subsequently, asks the server for help when it needs a shared resource. The server provides **services,** specific tasks (often system tasks) that support other programs.

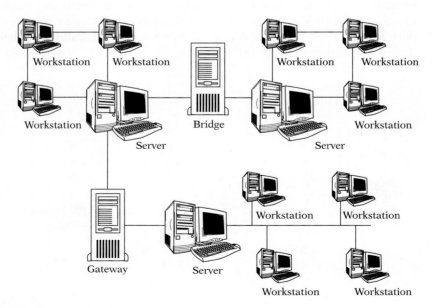

FIGURE 16.15

A bridge links two or more similar networks. A gateway links dissimilar networks.

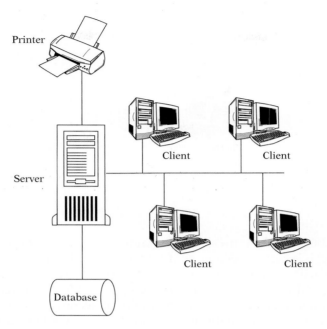

FIGURE 16.16
A client/server network.

A client/server network is an implementation of the more general client/server model. The basic idea of the client/server model is to assign a resource to the most appropriate computer or software routine (the server) and require other components (the clients) to access that resource through the server. For example, imagine that a mainframe controls access to a database and a microcomputer controls access to a high-speed laser printer (Figure 16.17). If the microcomputer needs information from the database, it is the client and the mainframe is the server. If, on the other hand, the mainframe generates a report that must be printed on the laser printer, the mainframe becomes the client and the microcomputer becomes the server. Note that the terms *client* and *server* relate to the function and not to the machine. A client requests support. A server fills the request.

Note also that the terms *client* and *server* do not necessarily refer to hardware. Consider, for example, the system pictured in Figure 16.18. There are two programs in memory. The user interface communicates with the user through the console and the database server manages access to the database. If a user requests information from the database, the user interface routine acts as the client and requests the data from the database server routine, which acts as the server.

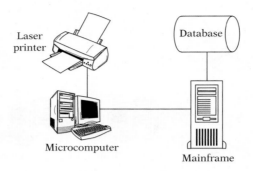

FIGURE 16.17
The client/server model.

Because the term server is commonly applied to both hardware and software, it is easy to become confused, particularly when you see advertisements for Dell's server hardware and Microsoft's server software. A computer designed to be a server (hardware) typically has a powerful processor, considerable memory, and vast amounts of secondary storage, but it is still a computer and, given the appropriate software, could be used as a client workstation. Server software, on the other hand, is an application program that allocates shared resources and provides services on request. Install a server software routine on any computer, and that computer becomes a server.

Peer-to-Peer Networks

In a peer-to-peer network (Figure 16.19) there is no dedicated server. Every computer on the network can be a server and a client, and each user can decide to share his or her files or printer resources with any other user. If

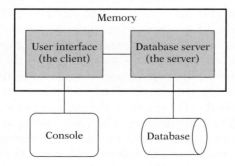

FIGURE 16.18
Software clients and servers.

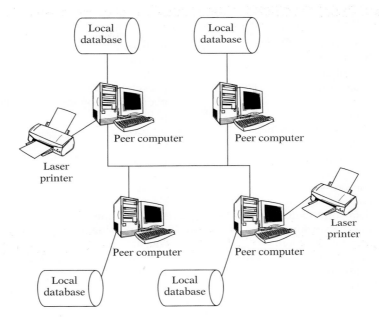

FIGURE 16.19
A peer-to-peer network.

you have ever accessed a Napster-like file sharing network, you have used a peer-to-peer network.

Summary

Data communication requires a message, a transmitter, a receiver, a protocol, and a medium. Today's best-known connectivity options are plain old telephone service (POTS) and wireless. Broadband options such as DSL, cable service, home satellite services, and leased high-speed lines help to solve the last mile problem.

Each device on a network is called a node. A local area network's topology defines the communication links that connect its nodes. Token passing and collision detection are two options for ensuring successful message delivery on a LAN. Ethernet is a popular LAN protocol. Many wide area networks (WANs) rely on point-to-point transmission and routing. Internetworking uses bridges, gateways, and routers to link LANs and WANs. On a client/server network, the servers control access to various services and the clients request the services they need. On a peer-to-peer network, there is no central server.

◼ Key Words

bandwidth	modem
baseband	network
broadband	node
broadcast	packet switching
cable	plain old telephone service (**POTS**)
client	polling
client/server network	protocol
collision	receiver
collision detection	routing
common carrier	server
compression	service
connectivity	signal
data communication	switched line
internetworking	token passing
last mile problem	transmitter
local area network (**LAN**)	wide area network (**WAN**)
medium	wireless
message	

◼ Review Questions

1. List and define the basic elements essential to data communication.
2. Identify several common data communication media. How is the speed of a data communication medium expressed?
3. What is compression? Why is compression valuable?
4. Distinguish between a message and a signal.
5. If you want to transmit data over a distance, you must boost and filter the signal. Why?
6. What are modulation and demodulation and why are they necessary?
7. Distinguish between analog and digital data.
8. Explain packet switching.
9. Distinguish between wired and wireless communication services and explain the last mile problem.
10. What is a network?
11. Distinguish between a local area network and a wide area network.
12. Briefly describe a bus network, a star network, and a ring network.
13. Distinguish among polling, collision detection, and token passing.
14. Define routing.
15. Define internetworking.

16. Distinguish between a bridge and a gateway.

17. Explain how a client/server network works.

18. Distinguish between server hardware and server software.

◼ Exercises

1. Take a digital picture or scan a photograph. Store the image on your hard disk as a bitmap file and again in the same folder as a *jpg* file. Then compare the sizes of the two files.

2. Listen to a recording on vinyl LP and then listen to the digital (CD or DVD) version of the same recording. Do you sense any differences? Note your impressions.

3. Why do you suppose the sound recording industry is so concerned about digital file sharing?

4. A chapter sidebar suggested that communication pricing may be moving toward the cable TV model, with a base price for standard service and additional fees for premium services. Do you agree or disagree? Why?

5. Do a little research and find out what broadband connectivity options are available in your town or on your campus.

6. Figure 16.1, perhaps supplemented by Figure 16.11, and Figure 16.15 are useful templates for organizing many of this chapter's key terms.

CHAPTER 17

The Internet and the World Wide Web

When you finish reading this chapter you should be able to:

▶ Describe the structure of the Internet's backbone and the services that link a user to the backbone.

▶ Read and understand a domain name and an IP address.

▶ Explain how the domain name system (DNS) maps a domain name to an IP address.

▶ Explain how the address resolution protocol (ARP) maps an IP address to a MAC (media access control) address.

▶ List the layers in the TCP/IP model and explain what happens at each layer.

▶ Explain the difference between an application program and an application layer protocol.

▶ Explain how a logical messaging port number establishes a link to a specific application protocol.

▶ Distinguish between a Web page, a home page, and a Web site.

▶ Explain how a browser and a Web server work together to transfer a Web page from a Web site to a client.

▶ Read and understand a Uniform Resource Locator (URL).

▪ The Internet's Infrastructure

The **Internet** is a vast network of networks layered on top of the global data communication network described in Chapter 16 (Figure 17.1). Accessible from virtually anywhere in the world, the Internet has effectively reshaped modern information technology. As a result, almost without exception modern operating systems are Internet enabled.

FIGURE 17.1

The Internet is layered on top of the global data communication network.

Internet Service Providers

Most users and many business concerns access the Internet through an **Internet service provider (ISP)** such as America Online, MSN, or one of thousands of others (Figure 17.2). The ISP, in turn, connects the user to the Internet much as a POTS central office or a mobile switching center links a caller to a long distance connection. Most ISPs offer additional services such as e-mail, data access, training, chat rooms, news, and so on. These services are implemented on host computers, where a **host** (or end system) is a computer attached to the Internet that runs (or hosts) application programs such as server software.

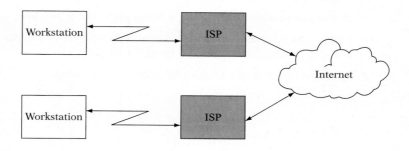

FIGURE 17.2

Most users access the Internet through an Internet service provider (ISP).

The Backbone

The **backbone** is a network of high-speed communication lines that carries the bulk of the traffic between major segments of the Internet (Figure 17.3). In the United States, backbone service is provided by a number of commercial **network service providers (NSPs),** and the major ISPs lease service from and access the Internet though one of the NSPs. Among the primary NSPs are many long distance telephone service providers.

Each NSP operates its own (national) wide area network of high-speed communication lines. Because those WANs are independently owned and operated, it is often necessary to transfer a message from one NSP to another. The network service providers are interconnected and exchange data through **network access points (NAPs).** Some major Internet service

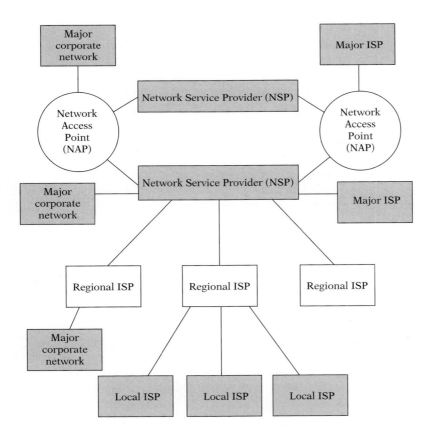

FIGURE 17.3

The backbone.

providers and a few large organizations such as universities, research centers, and corporations connect directly to a network access point, but most access the Internet through an ISP or a regional ISP.

A **regional ISP** operates a statewide or regional backbone and (typically) connects to the Internet by leasing bandwidth from a network service provider. Many local ISPs access the Internet through a regional ISP, and large organizations sometimes lease a direct broadband connection to a regional ISP or even an NSP.

Local Networks

At Miami University, each division (Arts & Science, Business, Education, Engineering...) has its own local area network (Figure 17.4). The divisional LANs are all linked to a university host named *muohio* that serves as a

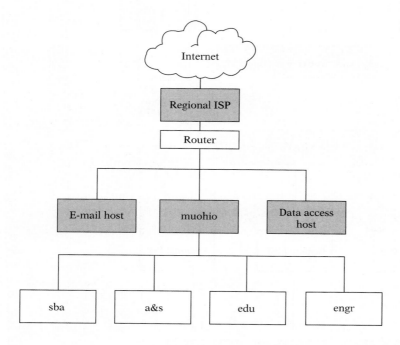

FIGURE 17.4
Miami University's network structure.

LAN-to-LAN bridge or gateway. Other university hosts support e-mail and data access. Access to the Internet (pictured as a cloud) is through a router connected to a high-speed leased line that links Miami to a regional ISP.

Note that the divisional LANs and their workstations are not directly connected to the Internet. Instead, much as a home user accesses the Internet through an ISP, they access the Internet through a host *(muohio)* that serves as a gateway to the Internet. Because the host is the only node known to the Internet, anything that happens behind the host is the responsibility of the local network and not the Internet. In other words, the Internet delivers the message to the host, and the local network forwards the message to the receiving node.

Internet Addressing

Your school's network might link hundreds, perhaps even thousands of computers, and a large company's network links even more. Even the biggest corporate network appears insignificant when compared to the Internet, however. In order to route a message across the Internet (or any network for that matter), each connected device must have a unique address that distinguishes it from all the other nodes. The Internet could not function without an effective system for assigning, maintaining, and retrieving those addresses.

Domain Names

A **domain** is a set of nodes that are administered as a unit; for example, all the networked computers belonging to Miami University form one domain and all the networked computers belonging to Microsoft Corporation form another. A **domain name** consists of two to four words separated by dots (Figure 17.5). Starting at the right is a top-level domain name such as *edu* for an educational institution, *com* for a commercial entity, *org* for a non-profit group, *gov* for a government service, and so on. Moving to the left are the entities within the domain. For example, in the domain name *sbaserver1.sba.muohio.edu*, *edu* is the top-level domain, *muohio* is Miami University's domain (part of the edu domain), *sba* is the School of Business Administration subnet (a network that forms a part of a larger network) within the *muohio* domain, and *sbaserver1* is a server within the *sba* subnet. Note how the various elements of the domain name correspond to the network structure pictured in Figure 17.4.

The top-level domain names are assigned by the Internet Corporation for Assigned Names and Numbers (ICANN); Figure 17.6 lists several. An organization's domain name (for example, *muohio* or *aol*) is assigned to a

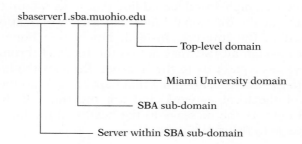

FIGURE 17.5
A domain name.

host computer that is linked to the Internet 24 hours a day. To the left of the domain name, the subnet and server names are assigned by the domain and consequently have meaning only within the domain. For example, the Internet can deliver a message to *muohio,* but it is *muohio's* responsibility to pass the message to *sba,* and *sba's* responsibility to pass the message to *sbaserver1.*

Domain	Signifies
aero	Air-transport industry
biz	Business organization
com	US commercial
coop	Cooperatives
edu	US educational
info	Unrestricted
gov	US government
mil	US military
museum	Museums
name	Individuals
net	US network
org	US non-profit
pro	Professionals

Domain	Signifies
au	Australia
br	Brazil
ca	Canada
cn	China
de	Germany
fi	Finland
fr	France
gb	Great Britain
in	India
it	Italy
jp	Japan
ru	Russia
za	South Africa

FIGURE 17.6
Some top-level domain names.

Domain Name Registration

To avoid duplication, domain names are registered with a central authority and kept in a central registry. In the United States, responsibility for top-level *com, net,* and *org* domain name registration rests with the Internet Corporation for Assigned Names and Numbers (ICANN). Together with Network Solutions, Inc. (NSI), ICANN accredits the organizations that perform the actual registration process, usually for a fee. Other governments are responsible for allocating domain names in their own domains; for example, Japan controls the top-level domain *jp,* Germany controls *de,* and Italy controls *it.* Because the supply of unique names is limited, an organization's domain name is a valuable piece of intellectual property that can be bought and sold, often through a domain name brokerage. For example, a few years ago Delta Airlines purchased the rights to *delta.com* from the insurance company that previously (and legitimately) owned it, and if your local television station has a domain name ending in *tv,* the station (directly or indirectly) purchased the name from the tiny South Pacific country of Tuvalu. Such new top-level domains as *biz, coop,* and *pro* should help increase the supply of appropriate domain names.

The IP Address

An **IP address** is a number that uniquely identifies a specific node. The Internet uses this number to route packets to the node. An IP address consists of four numbers separated by dots (Figure 17.7). For example, in the address 134.53.40.2, the first number, 134, is the top-level domain *(edu);* 53 designates Miami University's domain; 40 is the School of Business Administration subnet; and 2 is a server within this subnet.

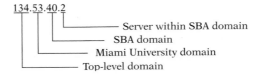

FIGURE 17.7

An IP address.

The Domain Name System

The actual physical transmission of a message across the Internet requires an IP address, not a domain name. Fortunately, a given node's domain name and IP address convey exactly the same information (Figure 17.8), and the **domain name system (DNS)** takes advantage of that relationship to convert domain names to IP addresses. The domain name system is implemented by a DNS protocol and by a hierarchy of DNS servers that store tables of domain-name-to-IP-address mappings that allow each layer to find the IP addresses for the next higher and next lower layers.

Imagine, for example, sending a message to *service.microsoft.com* from within the Miami University School of Business network *(sbaserver1.sba.muohio.edu)*. The search begins with the *sba* DNS server (Figure 17.9, step 1). The *sba* DNS server knows the next higher layer's IP address so the request is sent to *muohio* (2). The *muohio* DNS server knows the IP addresses of its next higher layer (the top level domains) so it sends the request to *com* at IP address 207 (3). The top level DNS server knows *microsoft's* IP address (207.46) because *microsoft* is at the next lower level, but it does not know *service* because *service* is two levels down. Thus, *com* sends Microsoft's numeric IP address (207.46) back to *muohio* (4). Miami's DNS server then sends a request to Microsoft (5). *Microsoft.com* knows the IP address for *service* (one level down) and completes the address translation (6). The IP address (207.46.140.71) is then returned to the originating server *(sba)* (7), which (finally) sends the message.

Following the initial address translation, the participating domain name systems cache or save the domain name and its matching IP address. Consequently, the next time a user in the SBA lab types the domain name *service.microsoft.com*, a cached copy is in *sba* and the address translation is done immediately rather than being forwarded up the ladder. Similarly, if another Miami user not on the SBA subdomain requests *service.microsoft.com*, another cached copy is available on *muohio,* so the university computer's DNS does the address translation.

FIGURE 17.8

A domain name and an IP address convey the same information.

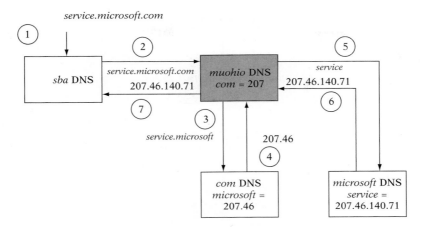

FIGURE 17.9
The domain name system.

The Media Access Control Address

An IP address points to a specific computer, router, or (more generally) node on the Internet. However, the ultimate destination of most messages lies *off* the Internet within a local domain. The IP address of any node not directly connected to the Internet (for example, a user workstation on a subnet) is assigned by and has meaning only within the local domain. As a result, physically transmitting a message to its final destination node (the last hop) requires the physical **media access control (MAC)** address of that node. For example, in an Ethernet LAN an Ethernet card is installed in each workstation and each card has a unique MAC address that is hard-coded by the card's manufacturer. To cite another example, if the last hop from an ISP to a client workstation is via a dial-up telephone line, the physical address of the modem is the MAC address. On the final hop from the destination server to the destination computer, the **address resolution protocol (ARP)** translates the workstation's IP address to a MAC address. The message is then routed to the destination computer.

Address Translation

Quickly review the relationship between the three types of Internet addresses (Figure 17.10). The task of transmitting a message begins when a user identifies the destination node's domain name by typing it, selecting it

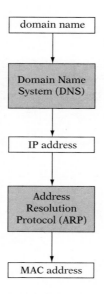

FIGURE 17.10
Internet address translation.

from a list, or clicking on a hyperlink. The Internet uses numeric IP addresses to route packets from node to node, so the domain name system (DNS) converts the domain name to an IP address.

At the other end of the connection, the final hop takes the packet from a server to the destination node. Because the destination node is inside the local domain, its IP address is assigned by and has meaning only within the domain. Thus the server's address resolution protocol (ARP) maps the final node's IP address (which means nothing to the Internet) to a physical media access control (MAC) address. Note that the address translation process starts with a relatively easy to remember logical name and ends with the numeric physical address of a specific device.

■ TCP/IP, the Internet's Protocols

As you learned in Chapter 16, if two devices are to communicate, both the transmitter and the receiver must use the same protocols. Although it links *millions* of computers worldwide, messages still move over the Internet in a series of node-to-node hops, and the common protocol rule applies to each of those hops. The Internet simply could not exist without a set of widely accepted standard protocols.

The TCP/IP (Internet) Model

The **TCP/IP** or **Internet model** (Figure 17.11) specifies a set of layered packet switching protocols that define the rules for communicating over the Internet. (In fact, the Internet is sometimes defined as the set of interconnected computers that use TCP/IP.) The top two layers deal with the complete message and the bottom two layers work with individual packets. As you are about to learn, Internet access only *seems* easy; an incredible number of tasks are hidden beneath the surface. Because of TCP/IP's layered architecture, however, the underlying complexity is largely transparent, making Internet access available even to nontechnical users. As you read about the TCP/IP protocols, note how each protocol layer builds on the standards implemented in the layer below it. That is the essence of layering.

The TCP/IP model resembles the International Organization for Standardization's seven-layer Open Systems Interconnect (OSI) reference model for packet switching, computer-to-computer communication (Figure 17.12). Although rarely implemented precisely as specified, the OSI model is a useful blueprint for designing and creating networking hardware and software. In the OSI reference model, the top three layers deal with the complete message. The fourth layer, transport, breaks the message into packets on the sending computer and reassembles the packets to reform the complete message on the receiving computer. The bottom three layers route, format, deliver, and receive the packets.

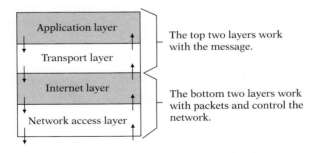

FIGURE 17.11
The TCP/IP model.

OSI layer	Responsibilities
The top three layers work with the message.	
Application	Provides a logical link between an application program and the lower-level protocols.
Presentation	Performs necessary data representation and/or syntax conversions; e.g., encryption/decryption.
Session	Establishes, maintains, and terminates a connection.
The transport layer breaks the message into packets and reassembles the packets at the receiving end.	
Transport	Breaks the message into packets. Ensures error free, end-to-end delivery of the complete message.
The bottom three layers work with packets.	
Network	Determines the best route for sending a packet from the source node to the destination node.
Data-link	Formats a packet for transmission to the next node.
Physical	Interfaces with the physical communication medium.

FIGURE 17.12

The Open Systems Interconnect (OSI) model.

The Application Program

A typical Internet transaction begins and ends with an application program. For example, if you use an e-mail program to send a message to a friend, your friend on the other end of the line must use a compatible e-mail program to read that message. Similarly, if you use an FTP program to transfer a file from a file server, you can safely assume that you are communicating with a compatible FTP program because if you aren't, the file transfer will not work. Basically, the user initiates a transaction through the application program's user interface, and the application program calls and passes parameters down to the appropriate application layer protocol.

For example, imagine using the FTP protocol to download a file from a file server to your computer. After launching the FTP application program, you indicate the file server's domain name address, identify the file to be transferred, and start the file transfer process. The FTP program responds by calling the application layer's FTP protocol and passing it the target domain name and file path name.

The Application Layer

The TCP/IP **application layer** holds protocols that directly support application programs (Figure 17.13). Several well-known application layer protocols, including the FTP protocol, are summarized in Figure 17.14. On the sending computer, an application layer protocol accepts the parameters passed down from an application program and creates the parameters needed by the next layer down. At the other end of the line, the application layer protocol accepts information from the next layer down and passes it up to an equivalent application program on the receiving machine.

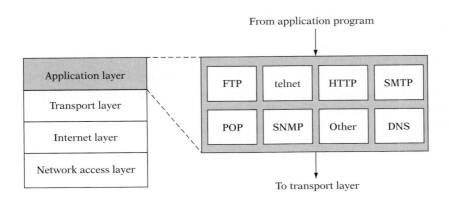

FIGURE 17.13

The application layer protocols directly support application programs.

Acronym	Name	Function
DNS	Domain name system	Translate a domain name to an IP address.
FTP	File transfer protocol	Download a file from or upload a file to another computer.
HTTP	Hypertext transfer protocol	Request and download a web page. HTTP is the standard Web surfing protocol.
POP	Post office protocol	Deliver accumulated mail from a mail server to the recipient's computer.
SMTP	Simple mail transfer protocol	Send an e-mail message from the originator's computer to the recipient's mail server.
SNMP	Simple network managment protocol	Monitor the activity of a network's hardware and software components.
Telnet	Terminal emulation protocol	Log into a remote computer. System operators use telnet to remotely control a server.

FIGURE 17.14

Some common application layer protocols.

The lower TCP/IP layers require IP addresses, not domain names. The responsibility for translating the domain name passed down from the application program into an equivalent IP address is assigned to the application layer's DNS protocol. The DNS protocol relies on the domain name system pictured in Figure 17.9 to accomplish its task.

The IP address allows the FTP message to be transmitted to the correct node, in this example to the file server host. At the receiving end, the message is passed to the correct application program by referencing a port number. As you know from Chapter 4, a device port is a physical interface or plug; for example, you plug your printer into a printer port. In the TCP/IP model, a **port** is also the endpoint of a *logical* connection (a program-to-program link), and every application layer protocol is associated with a logical **messaging port** number. Often, the word port is used without qualification and the type of port referenced is implied by context. A device port links physical hardware components such as a network access line and an Ethernet card. A messaging port links logical software routines such as the transport layer's TCP protocol and the application layer's FTP protocol.

TCP/IP supports up to 64K unique messaging ports, but port numbers below 1024 are assigned by the Internet Assigned Numbers Authority (IANA) and are considered well-known ports. Figure 17.15 lists several well-known port assignments.

Port	Used for:	
5	RJE	Remote job entry
20	FTP	File transfer protocol data
21	FTP	File transfer protocol control
23	Telnet	Terminal emulator
25	SMTP	Simple mail transfer protocol
79	Finger	Given e-mail address, identify user
80	HTTP	Hypertext transfer protocol
110	POP3	Post office protocol, version 3
119	NNTP	Network news transfer protocol

FIGURE 17.15

Some well-known port assignments.

For example, the telnet protocol connects port 23 on the sending computer to port 23 on the receiving computer (Figure 17.16). A file transfer protocol (FTP) exchange uses two ports: 20 for the data and 21 for control signals (Figure 17.17). Using FTP is more efficient than attaching a file to an e-mail message because the FTP data and control signals simultaneously travel over separate connections in parallel. Superficially, e-mail seems like a simple application, perhaps because mail programs like *Outlook* and *Eudora* are so familiar, but transferring an e-mail message is actually a relatively complex two-step operation (Figure 17.18). First, the simple mail transfer protocol (SMTP) transfers a single message from port 25 on the sending computer to port 25 on the recipient's e-mail server. Subsequently, the recipient uses a post office protocol such as POP3 to transfer accumulated e-mail from port 110 on the e-mail server to port 110 on his or her own workstation.

Getting back to the FTP application, the application layer's FTP protocol adds to the message passed down from the application program a header that contains information needed by the receiving node's FTP protocol (Figure 17.19) and passes the header, the FTP request, the IP address, and the port number (20 or 21) down to the transport layer. At the other end of the line, when the message reaches the receiving node (the file server), the receiving application layer's FTP protocol strips off the header, uses the header contents, and passes the request up to the FTP application program.

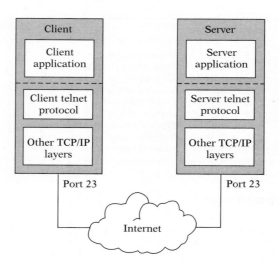

FIGURE 17.16

The *telnet* protocol uses port 23.

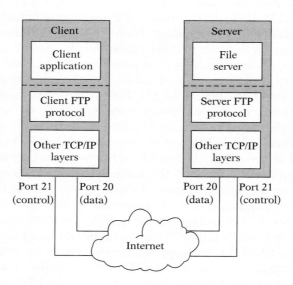

FIGURE 17.17

The *FTP* protocol uses ports 20 and 21.

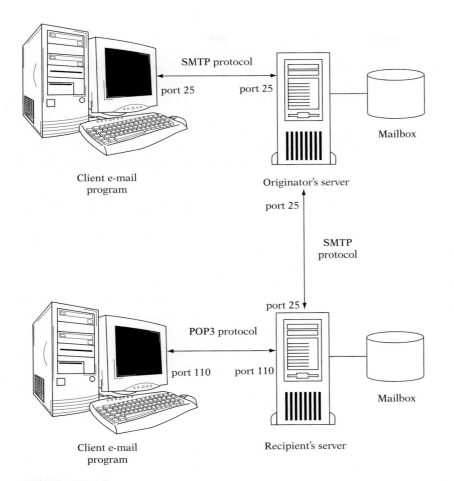

FIGURE 17.18

Sending an e-mail message is a two-step process.

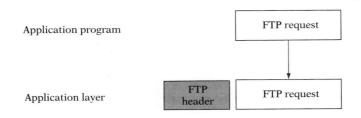

FIGURE 17.19

The application layer *FTP* protocol adds a header to the FTP request.

The Transport Layer

The next layer down, the **transport layer**, also known as the host-to-host transport layer (Figure 17.20), is responsible for ensuring successful end-to-end delivery of the complete message from an application layer protocol on the sending node to the same application layer protocol on the receiving node. For example, a message passed down to the transport layer by the application layer FTP protocol will be passed up to the receiving node's FTP protocol. Several transport layer protocols (including UDP, the user datagram protocol) can be used, but the **transmission control protocol (TCP)** is by far the most common.

The "message" passed down to the transport layer consists of the application layer's header plus the message created by the user. TCP breaks the message into packets (note that only the first packet contains the FTP header) and adds a TCP header to each packet (Figure 17.21). The TCP header (Figure 17.22) holds the source port number, the destination port number, and a sequence number. The port number, remember, is linked to a specific application layer protocol—in this example, the header to a packet carrying FTP data would reference port 20 and a packet carrying all or part of an FTP control signal would reference port 21. The sequence number is assigned by TCP to indicate the proper sequence of the packets.

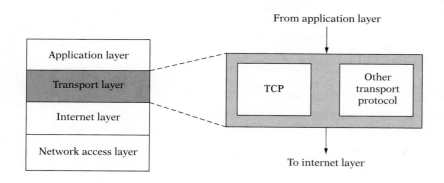

FIGURE 17.20

The next layer down is the transport layer.

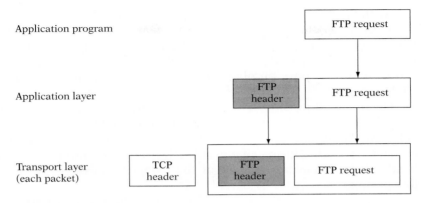

FIGURE 17.21

TCP adds its own header.

Byte	Contents
00 01	Source port number
02 03	Destination port number
04 05 06 07	Sequence number
08 09 10 11	Acknowledgement number
12	Header length
13	Control bits
14 15	Window size
16 17	TCP checksum
18 19	Pointer

FIGURE 17.22

The format of a TCP header.

At the receiving end, the destination computer's transmission control protocol (TCP) checks each packet for errors and uses the sequence numbers to reassemble the packets in the proper order. When the message is fully assembled, TCP passes it up to the application layer protocol associated with the port number in the TCP header, in this example, the FTP protocol.

On the sending side, TCP guarantees error free message delivery by waiting to receive from the destination computer's transport layer an acknowledgement for every packet sent and resending individual packets as necessary. On the receiving side, the sequence numbers in the TCP header help to ensure delivery of the *complete* message by highlighting lost packets.

Note that the application and transport layers deal with the entire message. Below the transport layer, the Internet and network access layers work with the packets created in the transport layer.

The Internet Layer

The **Internet** or **network layer,** the second layer from the bottom (Figure 17.23), uses the **Internet protocol (IP)** to route packets by selecting the next node on the path that leads (eventually) to the receiving node. The Internet layer accepts a packet from the transport layer (the next higher layer) and adds its own IP header (Figure 17.24) which holds the IP addresses of the source and destination nodes (Figure 17.25). Note that each packet contains an IP header that identifies the sending and receiving IP addresses and a TCP header that identifies the sending and receiving ports, so the path from an application protocol on the sending node to an application protocol on the receiving node is fully defined.

Once the Internet layer has added its header to the packet, it passes the packet down to the network access layer. At each of the intermediate nodes (and there may be many), the IP protocol selects the next node, replaces the old IP header with a new one, and passes the packet down to the network access layer. Once the packet reaches the destination node, it is passed up to the transport layer, where TCP reassembles the packets.

Note that the address resolution protocol (ARP) is an Internet layer protocol, because each packet must be routed to its final destination before the packets are reassembled at the transport layer. Note also that IP routes packets; it does not deliver them. Packet delivery is the responsibility of the next layer down, the network access layer. Finally, note that the source computer's IP protocol does not receive an acknowledgement from the receiving node. Guaranteeing delivery is TCP's job.

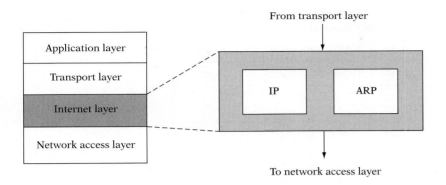

FIGURE 17.23
The Internet layer uses the Internet protocol (IP).

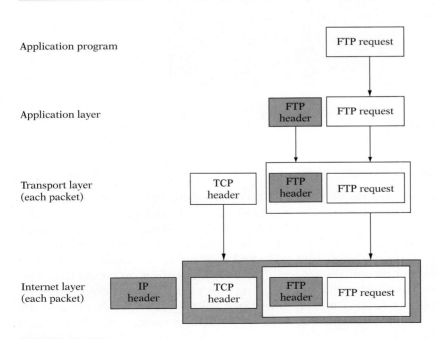

FIGURE 17.24
IP adds its own header.

Byte	Contents
00	Version/Header leader
01	Type of service
02 03	Length (bytes)
04 05	Identification
06	Flags/Offset address
07	Offset address
08	Time to live
09	Protocol
10 11	Header checksum
12 13 14 15	Source IP address
16 17 18 19	Destination IP address

FIGURE 17.25

The format of an IP header.

The Network Access Layer

The **network access** or **physical layer** is where packets are transferred from a node to the physical communication line and sent on to the next node. Like the other layers, the network access layer accepts a message from its immediate upper layer (Internet) and adds its own header containing the address of the current node and the next node (Figure 17.26). The TCP/IP model recognizes several data communication protocols that support numerous technologies (including Ethernet, collision detection, and token ring) for routing messages within a subnetwork (or subnet), and the precise content of a network access layer header varies with the physical network structure. Because the interface with the physical network is fully contained within the network access layer, however, the upper layers are independent of the physical network structure.

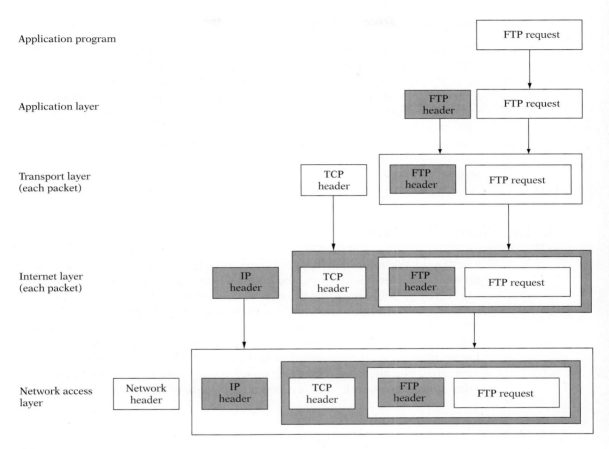

FIGURE 17.26

The network access layer adds another header.

Note in Figure 17.26 that each packet moving from one node to the next node over a communication line carries three headers, one each for the transport, Internet, and network access layers. (Generally, only a message's first packet carries an application layer header.) Each header holds control information appropriate to its layer. When the message reaches the destination node, the network access layer uses the information from the network header; the Internet layer uses the information from the IP header, and so on. Once the message is reassembled at the transport layer and passed up to the application layer, the application protocol (in this case, FTP) uses the application header embedded in the message. That is how each layer communicates with its peer layer on the other node.

The User Datagram Protocol

UDP (user datagram protocol) is an alternative transport protocol to TCP. UDP is not so accurate or reliable as TCP, primarily because it skips much of TCP's error checking, but it is significantly faster. The extra speed makes UDP particularly attractive for multimedia applications. For example, if one video frame out of every 30 fails to arrive or arrives out of order, you probably won't even notice the missing frame. In contrast, one missing piece renders a spreadsheet unusable, so the more reliable TCP protocol is a better choice for transmitting spreadsheets and similar nonmultimedia, nonstreaming files.

■ The World Wide Web

The **World Wide Web,** or **Web** for short, is a client/server application layered on top of the Internet that provides simple, standardized protocols for naming, linking, and accessing virtually everything on the Internet. The basic unit of information on the Web is a **Web page.** A **Web site** is a set of closely related Web pages that are interconnected by logical pointers called **hyperlinks** (Figure 17.27). Generally, one page is designated as the Web site's **home page,** a starting point that serves as a table of contents or index for navigating the site, and most Web pages incorporate hyperlinks to pages on other Web sites as well. The result is a vast, global "Web" of *billions* of pages.

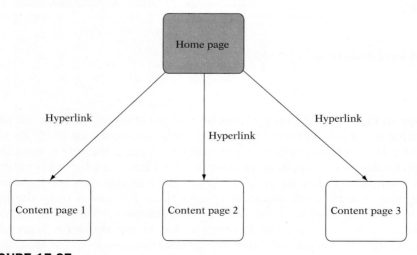

FIGURE 17.27
A Web site consists of a set of related Web pages.

Browsers and Web Servers

The World Wide Web supports communication between a browser and a Web server (Figure 17.28). A **browser** is an application program such as Internet Explorer or Netscape that runs on the client computer and requests and displays Web pages. A **Web server** is a server-side application program that runs on a host computer and manages the Web pages stored on the Web site's database.

Typically, the browser requests an initial home page from the Web server and displays the page. Once the initial home page is displayed, the user can begin surfing the Web. Hidden behind each hyperlink is the address of another Web page. Clicking on a hyperlink sends a page request from the browser (the client) to the desired page's Web server. The Web server responds by returning a copy of the requested page to the client's browser. The browser then displays the page.

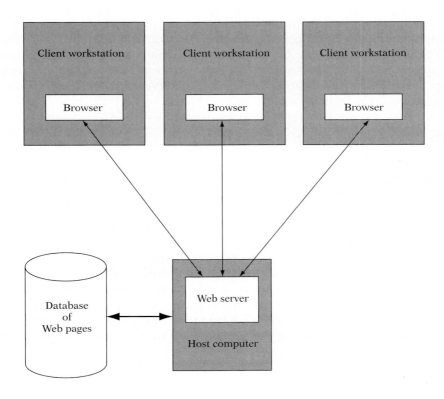

FIGURE 17.28
The World Wide Web links a browser and a Web server.

For example, imagine requesting a Web page from a major corporation like Microsoft (Figure 17.29). The client workstation resides on a LAN and is running a browser program (1). The user clicks on a hyperlink to Microsoft and the browser responds by generating a page request. The page request then flows from the workstation to the LAN server[1] (2), crosses the Internet, and makes its way to Microsoft's host computer (3). On Microsoft's host (hardware), a Web server (software) retrieves the requested page from a database of Web pages (4) and returns it via the Internet (5) to the LAN server (6) and on to the client workstation (7), where the browser displays the page.

The term "Web server" is sometimes used to refer collectively to an organization's Internet host and its hardware, software, and data components, but you will find the Web much easier to understand if you clearly distinguish between server hardware and server software. When you think of server hardware, picture a computer system designed and marketed to perform the server role in a client/server network. When you think of server software, picture an application program that runs on a server or a host computer and provides the requested service. The name of a server software application usually reflects its function; for example, a Web server returns Web pages, a file server retrieves files, an e-mail server manages e-mail, a database server controls access to a database, and so on. Unless the authors specify otherwise, the word server implies server software throughout the balance of this book.

The Uniform Resource Locator (URL)

Every page on the World Wide Web is assigned a unique address called a **uniform resource locator (URL)** (Figure 17.30); this is the Web page address that hides behind a hyperlink. Starting at the left, the first parameter names the access method or protocol to be used. **Hypertext transfer protocol (HTTP)** is the standard TCP/IP application layer protocol for requesting and transmitting Web pages between a client browser and a Web server via port 80. The colon is a separator, and the double slash indicates that a system address (rather than a file address) follows. The host computer's domain name comes next. To the right of the domain name is the path name of the host file that holds the requested Web page. The path name is a list of subdirectories that lead to the file. Note that a URL follows the UNIX standard, using regular slashes (rather than backslashes) to separate fields.

---

[1]Technically, there should be a gateway host or a router (or both) between the LAN server and the Internet in Figure 17.29, but for simplicity we'll ignore them.

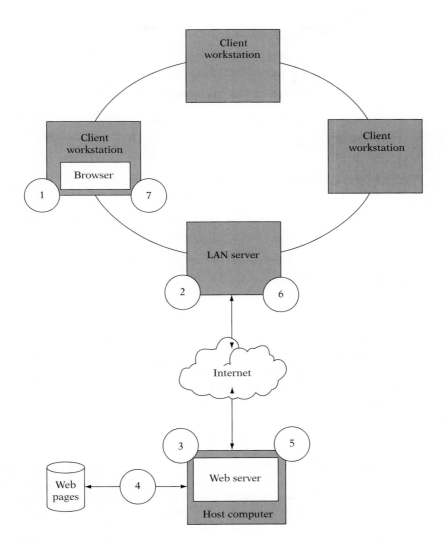

FIGURE 17.29
Downloading a Web page.

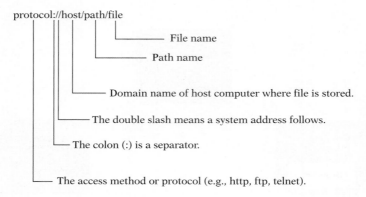

FIGURE 17.30
A URL.

For example, in the URL

http://www.anyco.com

http is the protocol, *www* (a conventional name for a publicly accessible Web server) is the name of Web server application program that runs on the host computer that holds the desired Web page, *anyco* is the local domain, *com* is the top-level domain, and dots or periods are used to separate the parts of the domain name. In the URL

http://employees.anyco.com/help.html

employees is a different *anyco* Web server (perhaps a private, password protected server for employees only) and *help.html* is the name of a Web page stored on the host. By default, if no file name is specified the server assumes an initial page (or home page) named *index.html, index.htm, default.html,* or *default.htm*.

Although most URLs begin with *http,* other protocols can be referenced. For example, the URL

ftp://archives.anyco.com/myfile

uses FTP, the file transfer protocol, to initiate a request for a file named *myfile* from *archives,* an *anyco* file server. Once again, the leftmost parameter in a URL defines the access method or protocol that supports the transaction.

Downloading a Web Page

The task of downloading a Web page from a server to a client is accomplished by the standard TCP/IP protocols. The process starts with the client's browser (Figure 17.31). The user identifies the desired page by clicking on a hyperlink, selecting a link from a bookmark or a *Favorites* file, a list of recently accessed URLs, or a history file, or by typing a URL on the address line. The request is passed to the TCP/IP application layer via port 80, where the HTTP protocol prepares a request for the selected page, calls on the application layer's domain name system (DNS) to convert the domain name specified in the URL to an equivalent IP address, adds a header, and passes the request down to the transport layer. The transport layer establishes a connection with the destination host, breaks the request into packets, and passes the first packet to the Internet layer. The Internet layer then adds its header, routes the packet to the next node, and passes the packet down to the network access layer, which adds a final header and drops the packet on the communication line.

The packet is routed through numerous intermediate nodes as it moves across the Internet. Once it reaches the target host, the network access layer removes it from the communication line and passes it up to the Internet layer, which checks the packet and passes it up to the transport layer. At the transport layer, the packets are collected and the message (a page request) is reassembled and passed, via port 80, through the application layer to the Web server, an application program. The Web server then retrieves the requested page and passes it down through the application, transport, Internet, and network access layers for transmission back to the client. When the packets that make up the requested Web page reach the client node, the client's network access layer takes each packet off the line and passes it up to the Internet layer. Subsequently, the transport layer assembles the packets and passes the message to the application layer via port 80, where HTTP passes it to the browser. Finally, the browser displays the page.

Note that the link between the client and the server is temporary. It is established when the client sends a page request to the host server and is terminated when the requested page is returned to the client. To the user there appears to be no difference (ignoring time delays) between loading a page from a local hard disk, another computer on the same local area network, or a remote host located halfway around the world because the various lower-level protocols operate transparently (and very quickly).

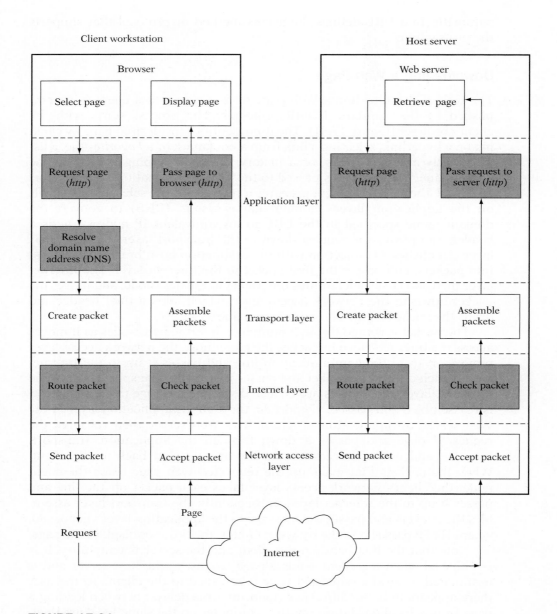

FIGURE 17.31

Using TCP/IP protocols to download a page.

Bottlenecks

Although it is convenient to think of each Internet and Web layer as an independent black box that performs its assigned task instantly, the reality is quite different. In Chapter 16 and this chapter you learned about the numerous intermediate computers and routers that participate in transmitting packets across the Internet and the TCP/IP protocols that run on each of those machines. Note that delays are possible within any layer on any device. An unacceptably long response time might be traced to the client's browser, one or more of the client's TCP/IP layers, the client's hardware, the client's local Internet service provider, backbone congestion, an intermediate router, the server's local Internet access provider, the server's hardware, the server's TCP/IP layers, the server software, and so on.

It is important to remember that the infrastructure is a complex, integrated system of many parts. What good is a super-fast computer if excessive traffic clogs the backbone? What good is a beautifully designed, highly interactive Web page if the user's underpowered computer (or modem, or local service provider) slows the page display process to such an extent that the user abandons the download? Layering makes it possible to deal with a complex system by allowing people to focus on one layer at a time, but those layers are still interconnected, and at some point they must function together or the system will not work well.

Web Page Contents

A basic Web page is a text file of **hypertext markup language (HTML)** tags (Figure 17.32) and embedded text that tells the client's browser how to display the page elements. HTML is a standard formatting language that all browsers understand. Consequently, any browser can display any Web page written in standard HTML.

HTML was originally designed to support text, but plain text can be boring. To make a page more interesting, hyperlinks to image, animation, sound, and multimedia files can be inserted into the HTML. For example, imagine a real estate agency's Web site that features photographs of available properties, one per page. The HTML for each page consists of several lines of text that describe the property and a hyperlink to an image file. When a customer selects the property by clicking on a hyperlink, the browser responds by requesting the appropriate page and the Web server returns an HTML file. The browser then maps the file's contents to the screen (Figure 17.33), scans the HTML for any embedded files, extracts the hyperlink, and sends another request to the Web server. The Web server responds by returning the image file, and the browser displays it (Figure 17.34).

Tag	Description	Tag	Description
<APPLET>	Java applet	<HEAD>	Document header
<B>	Bold	<HTML>	HTML document
<BIG>	Big text	<I>	Italics
<BODY>	Body of document	<IMG>	Image file
 	Line break	<LINK>	Hyperlink
<CENTER>	Center element	<MENU>	Menu list
<EMBED>	Embed a plug-in	<META>	Metatag
<FIG>	Figure (gif or jpeg)	<P>	Paragraph break
<FONT>	Define type font	<SCRIPT>	Insert script
<FRAME>	Define a frame	<SMALL>	Small text
<FRAMESET>	Define a frameset	<Tab>	Insert tab
<H1>	Level 1 heading	<TABLE>	Table of data
<H2>	Level 2 heading	<TITLE>	Page title
<H3>	Level 3 heading	<U>	Underline

FIGURE 17.32
HTML tags.

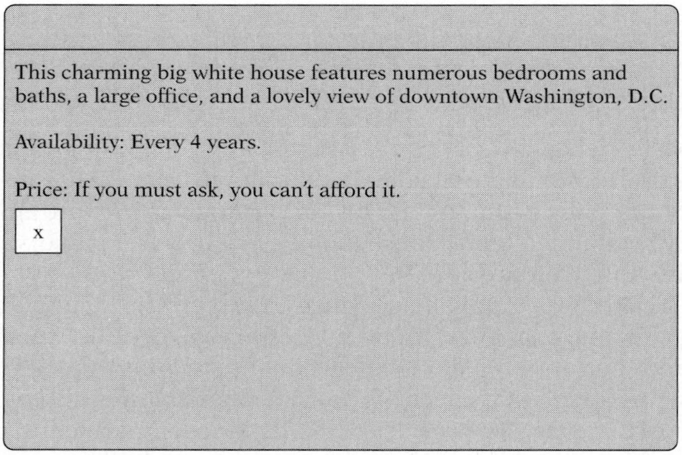

This charming big white house features numerous bedrooms and baths, a large office, and a lovely view of downtown Washington, D.C.

Availability: Every 4 years.

Price: If you must ask, you can't afford it.

x

FIGURE 17.33
The text is displayed first.

This charming big white house features numerous bedrooms and baths, a large office, and a lovely view of downtown Washington, D.C.

Availability: Every 4 years.

Price: If you must ask, you can't afford it.

Source: http://www.whitehouse.gov/history/tours/

FIGURE 17.34
The browser requests the embedded file and displays its contents.

Page Load Time

Page load time is the elapsed time between the act of clicking on the first hyperlink and the appearance of the finished page on the client's screen. Because downloading each embedded file takes time, page load time increases as the number and size of the embedded files increases. One consequence is that the Internet's default is to transfer only compressed files using such formats as *jpg* and *gif*.

Another way to speed up the page loading process is to use a **proxy server,** an intermediate server located on the client side of the connection that accepts a transaction from a user, forwards it to the appropriate server, and returns the response to the originator. To the real client, the proxy server appears to be the server. To the real server, the proxy server appears to be the client. Thus, the proxy server performs an intermediate role.

A proxy server can be used to perform such functions as screening transactions, maintaining a log, and performing virus and security checks, but in the context of the current topic, its most valuable function is caching pages to reduce page load time. The first time a given page is requested by a client, the proxy server forwards the request to the Web server and then caches (or saves) the returned page. Subsequently, should any client on the local network request the same page, the proxy server responds by returning the cached copy, thus bypassing the time delays inherent in transmitting the page across the Web.

■ An Expanded Layered View

As you learned in the first part of this chapter, the Internet is a worldwide network of networks layered on top of the global communication network (Figure 17.35). The World Wide Web is a client/server application layered on top of the Internet, and Web-based systems, the subject of Chapter 18, are built on top of that base. Each of those layers can be expanded to multiple sublayers, of course, but such high-level views help to clarify the relationships between the layers.

■ Summary

Internet connectivity is achieved through an Internet service provider (ISP). The Internet's backbone is maintained by a number of network service providers (NSPs) who lease bandwidth to regional ISPs. NSPs exchange messages at network access points (NAPs).

A domain is a set of nodes that are administered as a unit. Each domain is assigned a domain name. The domain name system (DNS) converts domain names to the numeric IP addresses used by the Internet. The address resolution protocol matches the IP address to a physical MAC (media access control) address.

The TCP/IP or Internet model defines a set of standard packet switching protocols. The application layer protocols directly support application programs. The transport layer uses TCP and ensures successful end-to-end delivery of the complete message. The Internet or network layer uses IP to route packets. The network access or physical layer transfers packets to and from the physical network.

The basic unit of information on the World Wide Web is a Web page. A Web site consists of a set of related Web pages. Web pages and page requests are transferred between a client-side browser and a server-side Web server by following the standard TCP/IP protocols. Every page on the World Wide Web is assigned a unique address called a Uniform Resource Locator

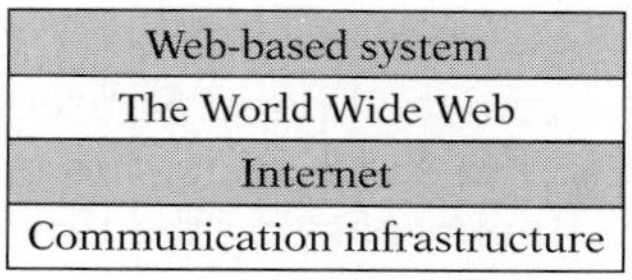

Web-based system
The World Wide Web
Internet
Communication infrastructure

FIGURE 17.35

An expanded layered view.

(URL). The hypertext transfer protocol (HTTP) is the standard protocol for requesting a Web page from a server. Web pages are created using HTML. Hyperlinks to image, animation, sound, and multimedia files can be inserted into the HTML. Page load time increases with the number and size of embedded files.

Key Words

address resolution protocol (ARP)
application layer
backbone
browser
domain
domain name
domain name system (DNS)
home page
host
HTML (hypertext markup language)
HTTP (hypertext transfer protocol)
hyperlink
Internet
Internet layer
Internet model
Internet protocol (IP)
Internet service provider (ISP)
IP address

media access control (MAC) address
messaging port
network access layer
network access point (NAP)
network layer
network service provider (NSP)
physical layer
port (logical)
proxy server
regional ISP
TCP/IP model
transmission control protocol (TCP)
transport layer
UDP (user datagram protocol)
uniform resource locator (URL)
Web page
Web server
Web site
World Wide Web, or Web

Review Questions

1. What is the Internet?
2. What functions does an Internet service provider (ISP) perform?
3. What is the Internet's backbone? Who maintains the backbone? How does a user gain access to the backbone?
4. How is a workstation on a local network linked to the Internet?
5. What is a domain? Explain what each part of your school or organization's domain name means.
6. What is an IP address? Explain what each of the numbers in an IP address means.
7. Explain how the domain name system (DNS) maps a domain name to an IP address.

8. Explain how the address resolution protocol (ARP) maps an IP address to a MAC (media access control) address.

9. List the layers in the TCP/IP model and explain what happens at each layer.

10. What is a protocol? What functions are performed by TCP (transmission control protocol)? What functions are performed by IP (Internet protocol)?

11. What is UDP? Why is UDP used?

12. Explain the difference between an application program and an application layer protocol.

13. Explain how a logical messaging port number establishes a link to a specific application layer protocol.

14. Identify at least five application layer protocols and their port assignments.

15. Distinguish between a Web page, a home page, and a Web site.

16. What is a browser? How does a browser work?

17. What is a Web server? Explain how a Web server and a browser work together to download a page from a Web site.

18. Explain each element in the URL *http://www.muohio.edu/admissions.html*.

19. Describe the process of downloading a Web page in terms of the TCP/IP layers.

20. Explain how page load time is affected by the number and size of the files referenced on a page.

▌ Exercises

1. Access the Web site *www.thelist.com* and identify several nearby Internet service providers and the types of services they offer.

2. Cybersquatting is the act of registering a domain name someone else might want with the intent of selling it rather than using it. Why would anyone want to do that?

3. Use a dial-up line to access a Web site that features numerous graphical images. Watch as the images appear one by one, and explain what is happening.

4. If you are using Windows, investigate the Internet by issuing the following commands at the MS-DOS prompt. Look for *Command Prompt* on the *Accessories* menu if you are using Windows 2000 or Windows XP or MS-DOS *Prompt* on the *Programs* menu if you are using Windows 98.

   a. Find your computer's IP address by issuing the command *ipconfig/all*. Explain what the various parts of the IP address mean.

   b. If you are using Windows XP, issue the command *nslookup domain.top* (for example, *nslookup muohio.edu*) to find the equivalent IP address. Substitute your school or employer's domain name.

   c. To determine if a remote host is active, issue the command *ping domain.top* (for example, *ping muohio.edu*).

   d. Trace the path of a packet as it travels over the Internet by issuing the command *tracert www.muohio.edu*. Feel free to substitute another domain name of interest to you.

5. To view source information for an e-mail message, launch your mail program and select the message you want to read. Then pull down the *File* menu and click on *Properties*. The *General* tab summarizes key information about the message's source. Click on the *Details* tab to view source information in greater detail, and click on the *Message Source* button at the bottom of the *Details* window to see an enlarged view of the information. You might not understand everything listed, but much of it will make sense.

6. To view source information on a Web page, first launch your browser. When your initial home page appears, pull down the *File* menu and click on *Properties*. The contents of the *Properties* window should make sense. To see the source HTML, pull down the *View* window and click on *Source*. Even if your experience with HTML is limited, you should be able to connect at least portions of the HTML stream with the content displayed on the Web page.

7. Figures 17.3, 17.9, 17.26, and 17.31 are useful templates for organizing many of this chapter's key terms.

CHAPTER 18

Client/Server Information Systems

When you finish reading this chapter you should be able to:

▶ Define the term Web information system.

▶ Explain the concept of partitioning a Web information system's logic.

▶ Identify several different types of services.

▶ Explain how middleware enables complex Web applications.

▶ Define security. List and define seven key security criteria.

▶ Identify several common network vulnerabilities.

▶ Explain how antivirus software works.

▶ Describe the functions performed by a firewall.

▶ Distinguish between symmetric and asymmetric cryptography. Distinguish a public key, a private key, and a secret key.

▶ Discuss the need for security services.

■ Web Information Systems

Today's state of the art in information technology features sophisticated interactive **Web information systems,** also known as **client/server information systems,** that rely on communication between asynchronous client-side and server-side application routines. A **Web-based** application is designed and built specifically to take advantage of the Internet and the World Wide Web. A **Web-enabled** application is a non-Web application, often a legacy application, to which a Web interface has been added, thus enabling a level of Web interactivity.

Web information systems follow the client/server model. Visualize a set of interconnected layers (Figure 18.1). The client platform and the server platform are linked by the underlying data communication infrastructure, the Internet, and the World Wide Web. An operating system and a Web application program run on both the client platform and the server platform. Those two Web applications, linked by the underlying infrastructure, form the Web information system.

Most operating systems (including Windows, UNIX, and Linux) can be used to support a client/server network, and the client and the server do not necessarily have to run the same operating system. However, if they are to communicate, both the client operating system and the server operating system must use the same set of communication protocols, and for Web applications the TCP/IP protocol suite is by far the most common choice (Figure 18.2). Most server operating systems come with the TCP/IP protocols preinstalled, and for a home computer user (the client), the installation program on an Internet service provider's activation CD typically installs and/or activates the TCP/IP protocols. The odds are very good that you have seen one of those ubiquitous AOL CDs, and most ISPs provide a comparable self-installation option.

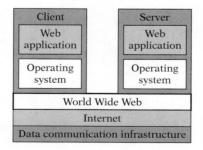

FIGURE 18.1

Web information systems are built on the infrastructure defined by the Internet and the World Wide Web.

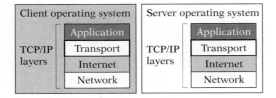

FIGURE 18.2
The client and the server both use the TCP/IP protocols.

Services

By definition, a Web information system incorporates at least two computers—a client and a server. Consequently, applications can be **partitioned** so that some of the logic is executed on the client and some on the server. On the client side, the logic is typically performed by an application program such as a browser. On the server side, the logic is typically implemented as one or more services, where a **service** is a routine that performs a single task, such as returning a Web page or downloading a file, in support of another program. Several common services are described below.

Web Services

A Web server is a server-side application program that provides **Web services,** such as retrieving Web pages in response to a request from a client (Figure 18.3) or supporting the ability to run scripts[1] on both the client side and the server side. When you browse the Web, you use a client-side browser program to communicate with a server-side Web server.

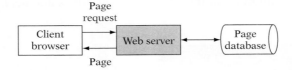

FIGURE 18.3
A Web server.

---

[1]A script is a programlike set of precoded commands.

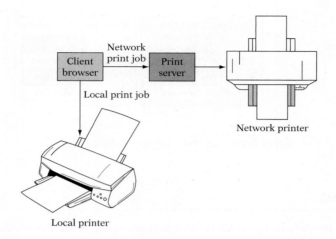

FIGURE 18.4

Print services.

Print Services

On many local area networks, client workstations have the option of sending a print job to a local printer or to a networked printer (Figure 18.4). Often the local printer is an inexpensive printer that is adequate for short, draft-quality print jobs, while the networked printer (or printers) is both faster and more effective for large print jobs and finished-quality documents. The networked printer is typically controlled by a print server that performs **print services.**

Sending a print job to a networked computer is similar to printing to a local client-side printer. When the user issues a print command, the client-side operating system routes the job to the local printer or to the print server. Jobs that are routed to the print server are stored temporarily on a print queue (Figure 18.5). Some time later when the printer is free and can service the job, the print server sends the print job to the networked printer. The print queue acts as a buffer and allows multiple clients to share the same networked printer.

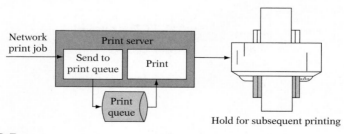

FIGURE 18.5

The print queue.

Many print servers also support bi-directional communication with the networked printers, allowing users to access the print queue to find the status of their jobs. Once printing is complete, the print server might send a confirmation message to the client machine. On some systems, users can request notification when certain events (such as low toner) occur.

E-Mail Services

E-mail services predate Web services. Think of an e-mail server as an electronic post office that accepts and stores messages, notifies clients when their mailboxes contain mail, and distributes the mail on request. Additional e-mail services might allow a user to look up the addresses of other users, broadcast messages, and so on. The user reads, writes, and replies to the messages through a client-side mail program.

File Services

File services enable a user to create, retrieve, and update data on the network file server, often by accessing a virtual disk. For example, in addition to the usual A (diskette), C (local hard disk), and D (CD-ROM) drives, a student or faculty member accessing a workstation connected to the Miami University's School of Business Administration's local area network can access a virtual G drive. Faculty members post course materials to the G drive, and students (who have read-only access) can retrieve those materials twenty-four hours a day, seven days a week. To a user, there is no apparent difference between accessing the G drive and accessing the C drive, even though the G drive is physically stored on a central host and accessed via a file server. In addition to supporting centralized sharable files, a file server can be used to provide backup for both private and shared files, specify access and control information, and provide file compression and data migration utilities.

Like print services, modern file services are designed to make the physical location of a file largely irrelevant, ignoring transmission time of course. On the client side, the user requests access to a file as though the file was stored on a local, client-side hard disk (Figure 18.6). If the file is available on the client-side (for example, on drive C), the client's operating system simply calls the local file system, which returns the file. If, however, the file is located on a remote computer, (virtual drive G, for example) the request is directed to the client's network interface (TCP/IP), which sends the request to the file server. The file server then retrieves the file and returns it to the client.

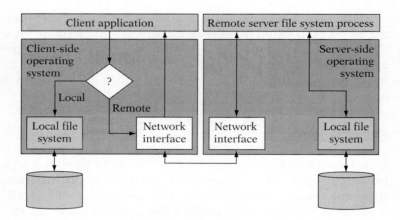

FIGURE 18.6

File services.

Directory Services

Modern business organizations and other large organizations have offices and users all over the world. Ideally, all these users should be able to access such network resources as files, databases, applications, and information without worrying about where a given service is physically located or through which server it is accessed. In other words, the users expect the network's resources to be location independent.

A **directory service** is a database of objects and users that organizes the network resources and makes them available to all the users. In effect, directory services help to manage interpersonal and internetwork relationships, network devices, network applications, and other network-based information by providing a single logical view of the network's resources and services. The directory database might be distributed over several nodes, with different portions stored on different servers. An alternative is to replicate the directory database, storing identical copies on multiple servers for faster access.

For example, imagine that a user working at a client workstation in Cincinnati wants to route a document to a laser printer located in a Los Angeles branch office. By working through directory services, the user can select the proper printer and send a print job to that printer as though the printer was directly connected to his or her computer. Directory services make the details associated with transporting the document across the network transparent to the user.

Management Services

For many modern organizations, the network has become a mission-critical resource. For example, a large business concern simply cannot tolerate network downtime because downtime means that employees lose access to applications, the central database, print services, e-mail, and other services essential to performing their jobs. Even worse, network downtime means that customers cannot access the system, and that can mean lost business. **Management services,** a collection of modules that support system management, play a crucial role in reducing network downtime by helping the system manager maintain the network and recover from service interruptions quickly and with minimal disruption.

Typically, management services allow the responsible administrator to access and manage all the desktop (client) services without leaving his or her office. For example, a system administrator might use management services to electronically distribute a software upgrade from a central source, which is significantly more efficient than individually installing the upgrade on each client machine. Other management services allow the system administrator to manage and monitor the use of licensed software to ensure that no violations of licenses take place, track software usage, and shut down and start services remotely. Additionally, management services sometimes support load balancing algorithms designed to spread the workload over multiple servers. For example, if a given server's processor is fully utilized, management services can shift work to another server.

Updating Application Software

One of the first reasons why many organizations (including many schools) installed a client/server LAN was to simplify the task of maintaining application software. Imagine, for example, that your academic division's computer lab has 100 workstations. In the pre-LAN days, application programs such as Word or Excel were independently installed on each of those 100 workstations, so when a bug was discovered, it had to be patched 100 times. When the supplier released an updated version of the software, the technical support group faced a difficult decision: install the new software 100 times or stay with the old version. As you can imagine, the decision was often to stay with the old version, so the students who used the lab were stuck with outdated software.

Contrast the old system with a LAN-based system. Key applications are still installed on each of the 100 workstations. However, when an update or a patch is received, the system administrator updates the server copy and then sets up a program that copies the update from the server to the user's machine the next time the user logs onto the network. Using a LAN significantly reduces software maintenance costs.

Content Management Services

Content management services allow the responsible individuals to add, delete, modify, and generally maintain the content of a Website. Often, three (or more) versions of the Website are maintained—the public or active version, a backup version that can be activated if the public version is corrupted, and a test or development version.

There are two common approaches to Website content management: centralized and decentralized. In the centralized approach, content experts submit updates to a technical expert who converts the information to HTML form and updates the site. As the amount of content grows, however, the technical expert can become a bottleneck. The decentralized approach shifts the responsibility for generating the HTML to the content experts. Distributing responsibility to multiple sources can introduce inconsistencies in the look and feel of a Website's pages, however, which can create navigational problems for users. In an attempt to overcome the disadvantages of both approaches, some organizations use a hybrid approach, allowing the content experts to generate the content in HTML form and assigning a centralized group the responsibility and authority to enforce consistency across the Website.

Database Services

In a distributed client/server environment, the results of a database query might be displayed in a spreadsheet, incorporated in a Web page, merged into a word processing document, and so on. **Database services** are an important key to enabling such applications. The aim of database services is to allow users to easily access, integrate, and use a system's data resources. For example, if client's query is passed to a database server, the database server responds by retrieving the requested information and passing the results back to the client (Figure 18.7). In addition to queries, a database server might allow a user to manage the contents of the database by issuing transactions to add, delete, and modify information. Report generation is another common feature.

Application Services

An application server (or application platform suite) performs a variety of **application services** that integrate many of an organization's day-to-day tasks. Additionally, most application service providers support a system development environment for client/server applications. The application services concept is still evolving so the definition remains a bit imprecise, but the intense competition among such major players as BEA (WebLogic),

FIGURE 18.7
Database services.

Hewlett-Packard (OpenView), IBM (WebSphere), Microsoft (.Net), Oracle, Rational, Sun Microsystems, and others suggests that the potential for such software is enormous.

◼ Middleware

In a basic Web information system, surfing the Web for example, a client-side application program (a browser) communicates with a single service (a Web server) on the server side. In contrast, more sophisticated Web information systems often rely on **middleware** to link multiple servers and/or custom application routines, where middleware is software that connects two dissimilar applications and allows them to exchange data or intercommunicate.

For example, consider a Web information system that involves accessing a database (Figure 18.8). The client's browser initiates the database query. A browser communicates with a Web server using HTML, so the query flows across the Internet to the Web server in HTML form. In addition to the Web server, the host computer also runs a database server that requires a database language such as SQL (structured query language), so the HTML query is converted to a form acceptable to the database server by a middleware routine. Subsequently, the database server's results are converted back to HTML form by the middleware routine before the Web server returns them to the client browser for display.

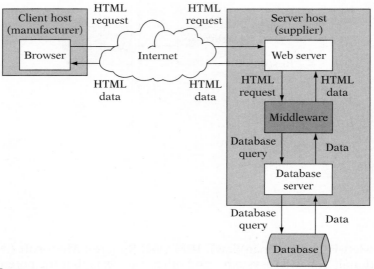

FIGURE 18.8

Middleware connects two otherwise separate applications.

Note that multiple servers can run on a single host computer (Figure 18.9). For example, one Web server might manage access to the organization's public Website, a second Web server might be available only to authorized customers and business partners who know the proper password, and access to a third Web server might be restricted to the organization's own employees. Add a file server and an e-mail server, and you have five server applications running on the same host. It is also possible to run each server on a separate host (Figure 18.10) or spread the five servers over two, three, or four hosts. Using middleware, those servers can be linked to form complex Web information systems.

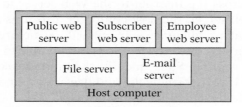

FIGURE 18.9

Multiple servers can run on the same host.

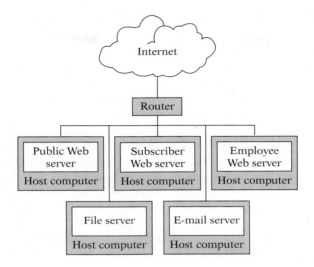

FIGURE 18.10
Multiple servers can run on multiple hosts.

◼ Security

The ability to partition a Web-based application over multiple, interconnected computers is the key to creating sophisticated Web information systems, but there are significant security implications associated with such systems. It might be possible to prevent unauthorized users from gaining physical access to a system's clients, server hosts, and other nodes by using doors, locks, guards, and other access control tools. However, once those nodes are connected to a network and begin communicating over the public Internet, logical access control is lost because both legitimate users and cybercriminals can access the Internet from virtually any computer located anywhere in the world. Usually, the advantages of using the Internet outweigh the risk, but it is dangerous to ignore the risk.

What Is Security?

According to Merriam-Webster's *Collegiate Dictionary* (the online version), **security** is "the quality or state of being secure," which includes "freedom from danger" and "freedom from fear or anxiety." Security also means "something that secures," including "measures taken to guard against espionage or sabotage, crime, attack, or escape." In an information technology context, security is a set of procedures, techniques, and safeguards designed to protect the hardware, software, data, and other system resources from unauthorized access, use, modification, or theft.

Somewhat hidden by the apparently straightforward definitions is a clear sense of security as a series of trade-offs between conflicting objectives. Users want convenience, ease of use and no downtime. Consequently, system administrators are under constant pressure from management and users to keep the system up and running, and security is essential to achieving that objective. But security adds an extra layer of overhead that makes system access more difficult and less convenient. The key to effective security is balancing those conflicting objectives.

Figure 18.11 summarizes several key security criteria. The first criterion, **access,** focuses on the user. The principle is simple: security must not interfere with the user's primary activities. The purpose of **authentication,** the act of verifying a user's credentials and confirming that the user is who he or she claims to be, is to ensure that only authorized people are allowed access to a network, a service, a system, or a facility. The purpose of the **integrity** criterion is to ensure that the message was not modified during transmission, while the purpose of the **privacy** criterion is to ensure that only the sender and the receiver know the contents of a transaction. **Nonrepudiation** prevents the sender from denying that he or she sent the message. If the message can be repudiated, it is possible for the sender or someone posing as the sender to commit fraud. The **recovery** criterion calls

FIGURE 18.11

The objectives of security.

Criterion	To ensure that:
Access	Each user has reasonable access to all the system resources he or she needs to perform a task.
Authentication	Only authorized users are allowed access to a network, a service, a system, or a facility.
Integrity	The message was not modified during transmission.
Privacy	The contents of the message are known only to the sender and the recipient.
Nonrepudiation	The sender cannot deny that he or she sent the message.
Recovery	Procedures are in place to quickly get the system back on line after a security breech has occurred.
Auditability	The security procedures can be audited.

for effective backup and recovery procedures to quickly get the system back on line after a security breech has occurred. Finally, the key to **auditability,** a measure of the extent to which a set of procedures can be audited, is consistent, accurate data collection.

Hackers and Malware

Back in the 1970s, to be called a **hacker** was a compliment. In those days, a hacker was an expert programmer with a knack for quickly creating elegant solutions to difficult problems. Today, however, the term is more commonly applied to someone who illegally breaks into computer systems.

True hackers (in the expert programmer sense) resent that characterization. They divide themselves into white-hat and black-hat categories. The white-hat hackers follow an unwritten code of ethics. They believe that a hacker should cause no harm and should not profit financially from his or her hacking activities. Black-hat or dark-side hackers, on the other hand, break into computers with malicious intent; they are the Internet's cyberterrorists, industrial espionage agents, free-lance spies, and troublemakers.

Once they gain access, hackers sometimes introduce destructive software called **malware** into a computer system. A logic bomb is a program that (symbolically) blows up in memory, often taking the contents of a hard disk, selected data, or selected software with it. A variation called a time bomb executes on a particular date or when a particular condition is met. A rabbit is a program that replicates itself until no memory is left and no other programs can run. For example, one well-known rabbit copies itself twice and then launches the copies. A few nanoseconds later there are four rabbits running. Then eight, then sixteen, then.... By the time the operator realizes what is happening, the rabbit is out of control.

A backdoor is an undocumented software routine (less frequently, a hardware trap) deliberately inserted by a system's designer or a hacker that allows undetected access to a system. Sometimes called a trap door or a wormhole, a backdoor is a legitimate programming, testing, and debugging tool, but sometimes, programmers and system administrators forget to properly close a backdoor after they finish using it. Hackers use such backdoors to gain access to a system, and they sometimes leave behind a backdoor for future use following an initial intrusion by some other means.

A Trojan horse is a seemingly harmless program that invites an unsuspecting user to try it. Trojans typically enter a system in the guise of a computer game or a cool graphic attached to an e-mail message or available for free download from a mysterious Web site. A Trojan horse is often used as a delivery vehicle for a payload that might hold a logic bomb, a time bomb, a rabbit, a backdoor, or a similar piece of destructive software.

Perhaps the biggest fear among Internet users and corporate network managers alike is the uncontrolled spread of a virus or a worm. A **virus** is a program that is capable of replicating and spreading between computers by attaching itself to another program. Viruses typically spread through infected diskettes, downloaded copies of infected programs, or e-mail attachments. They are parasites that require a host program to reproduce and survive. A **worm,** in contrast, is a viruslike program that is capable of spreading under its own power.

Network Vulnerabilities

Before a hacker can launch a piece of malware, he or she must first gain access to the target computer. Physically secure information systems, networks, and access points are an essential starting point for system security, but even the most physically secure system can be successfully attacked. Often, the easiest way to gain access to an unauthorized computer is to log in using the ID and password of someone who has the appropriate rights.

The hacker's most common source of passwords is carelessness. Obvious passwords are easy to remember, but they are also easy to guess. In the lab, a hacker might watch a student and steal a password by reading the keyboard, a technique called shoulder surfing. Often, a user writes down and then throws away a password. Unfortunately, hackers do not hesitate to hunt through the paper trash, an activity they call dumpster diving. Some users write their password on a sticky-back note and paste it to their display screen, visible to anyone who might walk by including a visitor or an insider hacker. It is surprising how many people simply tell others their password. The act of convincing someone to divulge his or her password by taking advantage of the target's apathy, courtesy, curiosity, good nature, greed, gullibility, or ignorance is a form of what hackers call social engineering. Standard patterns give the hacker another potential source of passwords and software designed to crack passwords, can be downloaded from the Internet.

Not all illegal access is the fault of a careless user, however. Many network operating systems contain well-known **vulnerabilities** that allow a hacker to gain access. For example, computers are typically shipped with default passwords (such as *system, setup, startup, sysop,* and so on) that are used by the system operator to initialize the operating system. Once the system is properly initialized and ready to use, the system operator is expected to assign new passwords and disable the defaults, but sometimes the operator forgets. Once a hacker discovers a vulnerable system, he or she can simply log on using the default password and gain system operator (sysop) or root status (a common hacker objective), giving the hacker the ability to access and change virtually anything on the system.

Other possible access points must remain open to support common applications. For example, e-mail has become an accepted way of communicating and conducting business, so the e-mail messaging port must be active. That is why hackers rely on e-mail attachments to insert Trojan horses, viruses, and worms into a system.

Instant messaging is a growing problem. The technology relies on presence detection and buddy lists to identify currently online friends, colleagues, and contacts and allows a user to send instant messages to them, thus eliminating phone tag and crossing e-mail messages and making possible an effective, ad hoc form of data conferencing. Users like instant messaging because it improves efficiency and makes their lives easier. However, the popular instant messaging services are maintained by such public domain service providers as AOL, Microsoft Network, and Yahoo, so the supporting software is outside the organization's or the user's control.

Good Passwords

Your password is your first line of defense against hackers, so pick a good one. A good password is easy to remember and difficult to guess. Longer is better—6 to 9 characters is a good target. Mix different types of characters (letters, digits, special characters) to increase the number of possibilities a cracking program must test. Give your password a challenging meaning by using an acronym formed from a phrase; for example, "my first dog's name was Spot" becomes *m1dnws,* where the second character is the digit 1. To thwart password-cracking programs, avoid dictionary words, proper nouns, and foreign words; if you can find it in a dictionary, don't use it. Incidentally, sticking a digit or two at the beginning or the end of a dictionary word or substituting ph for f will not confuse a good password cracker. Stay away from personal information, too; a determined hacker can easily locate your telephone number, your mother's maiden name, your significant other's name, your pet's name, the last four digits of your social security number, and similar information. To limit the damage caused by a cracked password, avoid using the same password on multiple accounts. Finally, it only takes a few minutes to change your password, so change it regularly. Quarterly is reasonable for most users, but people with access to sensitive information should change their passwords more frequently.

Antivirus Software

These days, it is folly to access the Internet without up-to-date **antivirus software** installed on your system. A good antivirus program protects a system in three ways. First, it scans incoming and outgoing messages and files (and files stored on disk) for code patterns called **virus signatures** that uniquely identify a given virus. When a virus is detected, the software sounds an alarm, and many antivirus programs can isolate and destroy the virus before it even enters the system. The software also incorporates heuristic logic that continuously monitors the system for abnormal activity such as an attempt to modify the Windows registry. Finally, most antivirus programs include facilities that help a system manager to recover from a virus attack. New viruses are created almost daily, so it is important to keep your antivirus software up to date by regularly downloading new virus signatures and heuristics.

Perhaps the most effective approach is to implement virus protection in layers. Placing a router between the host server and the Internet and screening incoming and outgoing messages on that router provides a measure of networkwide protection. Antivirus software running on the host server represents a second layer of protection. Personal antivirus software running on each workstation forms a third line of defense. On such defend-in-depth systems, the lower-level filters are likely to stop any virus that manages to slip by the higher layers.

Firewalls

A **firewall** isolates a private network from a public network by controlling how clients from outside can access the internal servers. Often, the firewall software runs on a router or a bastion host (a host computer that is directly linked to the Internet and thus fully exposed to attack) that sits between the host server and the Internet and blocks potentially dangerous or questionable transactions from getting in or out (Figure 18.12). Another common configuration allows unrestricted access to Web servers, FTP servers, and similar public services but restricts access to the corporate network or a local area network (Figure 18.13), and proxy servers are often firewall-protected, too. Additionally, users often install personal firewall software on their workstations.

A packet filtering firewall works by screening incoming and outgoing packets at the TCP/IP Internet level. It accepts or rejects packets based on

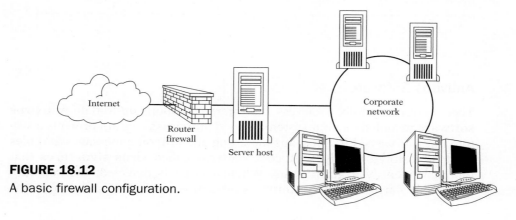

FIGURE 18.12

A basic firewall configuration.

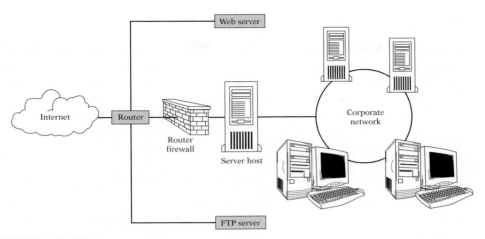

FIGURE 18.13

An alternative firewall configuration.

criteria stored in the message headers such as protocol (reject all *telnet* transactions), sending IP address, outgoing IP address, incoming port (reject all packets that do not come through port 80, the HTTP port), and so on. Most packet filtering firewalls are stateless; in other words they treat each packet as an independent entity and accept or reject it without considering related packets.

Other firewalls run at the application level and function as content filters, perhaps enforcing the organization's acceptable use policies. Sometimes called stateful firewalls, they rely on a proxy server to cache related packets, reconstruct the original message, and inspect the message content. Stateful firewalls tend to make better, more intelligent accept/reject decisions. For example, by screening content a stateful firewall can reject messages or pages with a possible sexual content by looking for such key words as breast and sex. One problem with such screens, however, is that they can reject legitimate information such as articles about breast cancer or biographical information about John Sexton, and they do cause some performance degradation. Once again, security is a series of tradeoffs.

A good firewall significantly improves security, but even a good firewall has weaknesses. They are particularly vulnerable to inside attack. Carelessness is perhaps the most serious risk, however, with system operators failing to remove default passwords, users choosing easy-to-guess passwords or writing their passwords on paper, users failing to disable Windows printer and file sharing, and users failing to update their antivirus software. One possible solution is to take responsibility away from the user and automate such tasks as software updates and regular password changes, but some tasks require human intervention.

Encryption

No matter how well a network is protected, some intrusion attempts will succeed—the question is not if but when. Consequently, it is wise to add another layer of protection to sensitive information stored on disk or while in transit. Cryptography is a potential solution.

Cryptography is the science of encrypting or otherwise concealing the meaning of a message to ensure the privacy and integrity of the information transfer. An unencrypted message is called **plain text.** The originator uses a secret code or cipher to **encrypt** the message into encoded or ciphered form. A code replaces one word or phrase with another; for example, the Secret Service assigns a code name to the President. A cipher replaces each letter or digit with another, for example substituting Q for A. On the other end of the line, the recipient reverses the process, **decrypting** the message by converting it back into plain text. Cryptographic techniques can also be used to protect the contents of a database from an intruder.

Symmetric encryption techniques such as **secret-key cryptography** use the same key to both encrypt and decrypt a message (Figure 18.14). Secret-key algorithms can be almost unbreakable, and both the encryption and decryption processes are relatively fast. However, both the sender and the receiver (at least two people) must know the key and getting the right key to both parties (the key exchange process) represents a significant security risk.

In contrast to symmetric single-key encryption, asymmetric encryption uses different keys to encrypt and decrypt a message. **Public-key cryptography** (Figure 18.15) is a good example. The encryption and decryption keys are distributed in related pairs. The receiver keeps one, the **private key,** and publishes the other, the **public key.** A message is encrypted using the *receiver's public* key (which is known to everyone) and decrypted using the *receiver's private* key (which is known only to the recipient).

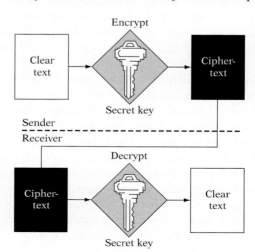

FIGURE 18.14
Secret-key cryptography.

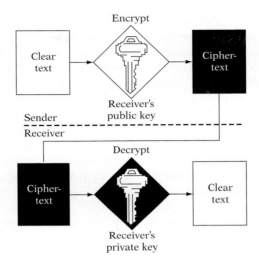

FIGURE 18.15
Asymmetric public-key cryptography.

Public-key algorithms are more complex and use longer keys than secret-key algorithms. Consequently, they are much slower (perhaps thousands of times slower) than secret key algorithms, making them unsuitable for encrypting real-time or lengthy messages. They are more secure than secret key algorithms, however, primarily because there is no need to exchange keys. Often, the solution is a hybrid approach that uses secret-key encryption to encode the message and public-key encryption to exchange the key.

The Secure Sockets Layer

The **secure sockets layer (SSL)** is a protocol that runs in the context of the standard TCP/IP protocols. It uses public-key encryption techniques to send a secret key to the recipient and then establishes a secure symmetric secret key connection between a client and a server for the duration of a session. The next time you pay for an e-commerce purchase by submitting your credit card number over the Internet, look for a closed lock icon near the bottom of your screen. It indicates that SSL is active. Check the protocol field in the URL, too; it should read *https*.

Security Services

The nature of security attacks is incredibly dynamic, with new system vulnerabilities, viruses, worms, and other malware appearing daily. Application, operating system, and security software suppliers respond to these threats by releasing a steady stream of patches, updates, new virus signatures, and similar fixes. Generally, it is the responsibility of the network administrator or system operator to ensure that these fixes are installed in a timely manner, because the failure to do so leaves the system vulnerable to attack. The problem is the sheer volume of patches, updates, virus signatures, and similar fixes that must be identified and installed. Each fix takes time, and system operators are often so overwhelmed with just keeping the system up and running that they don't have time for proper maintenance. The result can be disastrous.

A subscription model is often used to deliver patches and updates. Perhaps you have access to a service that, for an annual fee, automatically downloads at regular intervals new virus signatures and/or firewall patches to your personal computer, and similar subscription services are available at the server level.

The problem with the subscription model is that each service typically provides patches and updates for a single supplier. A user might find it relatively easy to deal with two or three subscription services to obtain patches and updates for an operating system, an application suite, and a security suite, but a system operator responsible for a large network might have dozens, even hundreds of software suppliers.

An important trend on modern network operating systems is to install a set of **security services** that help to automate all or part of the security maintenance task. For example, Opsware, a product of Loudcloud Corporation and the latest brainchild of Marc Andreessen, the creator of Netscape, is designed to monitor and track changes to numerous servers, in effect automating server operation and maintenance. Other security services monitor key Web sites and file servers for new patches and automatically download and install them.

◼ Summary

Today's state of the art in information technology features sophisticated interactive Web information systems that rely on communication between asynchronous client-side and server-side application routines. A Web information system can be partitioned so that some of the logic is implemented on the client and some on the server. A server is an application program that runs on the server side and performs services, such as Web services, print services, e-mail services, file services, directory services, management services, content management services, and database services. A Web information system's application programs are linked by middleware.

Security involves balancing conflicting objectives. Hackers use a variety of malware tools to attack computer systems and networks. E-mail, instant messaging, and Web surfing are considered potential sources of network vulnerability because access to those tools cannot be fully controlled. Antivirus software works by scanning for virus signatures, monitoring for viruslike patterns of activity, and supporting recovery. Firewalls are commonly used to help minimize the risk of intrusion. Symmetric, secret-key cryptography requires that both the sender and the receiver share the same secret key, but it is relatively fast and the algorithms are difficult to break. With asymmetric public-key encryption, two different keys are used for encryption and decryption—the public key (known to everyone) and a companion private key (known only to the key holder). Public-key encryption is relatively slow, but it solves the key exchange problem.

◼ Key Words

access	partition
antivirus software	plain text
application services	print services
auditability	privacy
authentication	private key
client/server information system	public key
content management services	public-key cryptography
cryptography	recovery
database services	secret-key cryptography
decrypt	Secure Sockets Layer (SSL)
directory services	security
e-mail services	security services
encrypt	service
file services	virus
firewall	virus signature
hacker	vulnerability
integrity	Web-based
malware	Web-enabled
management services	Web information system
middleware	Web services
nonrepudiation	worm

◼ Review Questions

1. What is a Web information system?

2. Distinguish between Web-based and Web-enhanced applications.

3. Explain the concept of partitioning a Web information system's logic between the client and the server.

4. What is a service? What is a server?

5. What functions are performed by a Web server?

6. What are print services?

7. What functions are performed by a file server? How does a file server make the physical location of a file transparent to the user?

8. What are directory services?

9. What are management services? Why are management services necessary?

10. What are database services?

11. What is middleware? Explain how middleware enables complex Web applications.

12. What is a hacker? Describe several common hacker tools.

13. What is a vulnerability? How do hackers find vulnerabilities?

14. What is security? List and define seven key security criteria.

15. Why are e-mail, instant messaging, and Web surfing considered potential sources of network vulnerability?

16. How does antivirus software work?

17. What is a firewall? What is a stateful firewall?

18. What is cryptography? Distinguish between symmetric and asymmetric cryptography.

19. What are the primary advantages of symmetric, secret-key cryptography? What is the biggest weakness of this technique?

20. What is the primary advantage of asymmetric public-key encryption? Distinguish a public key, a private key, and a secret key.

▌ Exercises

1. Investigate your school's network and determine how the technical support people update software.

2. Determine what services are available on your school's (or your company's) network.

3. Why do you suppose that an active Web site's content must be carefully managed?

4. Discuss the relative advantages and disadvantages of centralized and decentralized Web site content management.

5. What are the characteristics of a good password?

6. A good password is easy to remember and difficult to guess, but those two criteria conflict. How do you balance those criteria when you define your own passwords? In your experience, how do other people balance those criteria?

7. Security is a series of tradeoffs between conflicting objectives. What does that statement mean? Why is it important?

8. Do you have antivirus software installed on your personal computer? If not, install some; free versions are available for download via the Internet. If you do, how often do you update your virus signatures?

9. The intelligence community tried to keep public-key encryption secret. Why? Do you agree with the intelligence agencies or with the people who decided to take public-key encryption public? Why?

10. Figure 18.8 is a useful template for organizing many of this chapter's nonsecurity key terms. Study Figures 18.11, 18.13, 18.14, and 18.15 to review the security concepts.

CHAPTER 19

Windows 2003 Server

When you finish reading this chapter you should be able to:

▶ Briefly explain the functions performed by the protocols that operate at each level of the Windows 2003 network model.

▶ Define domain, domain tree, and forest.

▶ Describe the purpose of the Windows 2003 Active Directory.

▶ Describe the functions performed by the Windows 2003 Common Internet File System (CIFS).

▶ Explain the purpose of a shared folder.

▶ Identify the purpose of the Distributed file system (Dfs).

▶ Describe the primary components of the Windows 2003 Internet Information Services (IIS).

▶ Identify the tasks performed by clustering services.

▶ Identify several common features for managing Windows 2003 Server.

▶ Describe several Windows 2003 features and services you can access from a client computer.

Introduction

In Chapters 8 and 12 you studied Windows XP Professional running on a workstation in a client environment. This chapter focuses on the server features incorporated in Windows 2003, an enhanced, highly robust version of Windows XP. There are several different Windows 2003 Server editions, including: (1) the small business Standard Edition, (2) the Enterprise Edition, which is generally used as a departmental or enterprise server in a client/server network, (3) the Data Center Edition, which is designed to support mission critical applications that require a high degree of availability and scalability, and (4) the Web Edition, which is designed to host Web application services. The examples in this chapter feature the Enterprise edition.

Unless stated otherwise, the term server will be used to refer to software. Clearly, there is a hardware component called a server in a client/server network, but what makes a server host computer (hardware) a server is the software that runs on it, and given other software that computer could just as easily be used as a client.

The Windows 2003 Network Architecture

The network architecture supported by Windows 2003 (Figure 19.1) is based on the seven layer OSI model you encountered in Chapter 17 (Figure 17.12). Rather than having each of the seven layers implemented as distinct modules, Windows 2003 is divided into broad interfaces, with each interface straddling multiple layers of the OSI model.

The topmost layer, the application interface layer, runs in user mode. Some of the standard application programming interfaces (APIs) are implemented through user mode dynamic link libraries and others utilize both user mode libraries and kernel mode drivers.

Network APIs must use transport protocols such as TCP/IP to communicate information across the network. Other transport protocols such as Novell's IPX/SPX and Apple's AppleTalk are also widely used, so Windows 2003 must support multiple protocols. The network APIs use the **transport driver interface (TDI)** to provide a protocol-independent way for applications to communicate over the network. A transport driver implements a specific protocol such as TCP/IP and exposes the TDI interface to the network API clients.

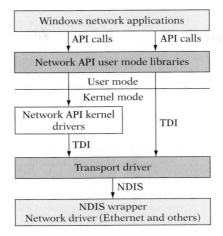

FIGURE 19.1

Windows 2003 network architecture.

The transport driver is independent of the underlying network hardware and communicates with the network card using the **network driver interface specification (NDIS).** NDIS describes the interface used to communicate with underlying hardware or network interface card. NDIS drivers are responsible for interfacing TDI transports to a particular network adapter and allow network card vendors to ensure that their drivers are compatible with Windows.

Domains

In most organizations, groups of users require access to shared resources. For example, students at a university might want access to a faculty member's PowerPoint presentations, and they might need to share printers and disk space to perform group work. In this example, different groups require different access rights. The faculty member must have read/write access to the PowerPoint files, but students must be restricted to read-only access. In contrast, all the students in a given workgroup require read/write access to their shared disk space, but they must not be able to access other workgroups' shared workspaces.

Windows uses the notion of a **domain** to manage the user workgroups, where a domain is a group of computers that share an **Active Directory** database and have a common security policy (Figure 19.2). The Active Directory is a hierarchical database that holds information about all the objects on the network, such as servers, users, shared volumes, printers, domains, applications, services, and security policies. The domain controller is a computer running Windows 2003 Server that hosts the Active Directory. The Active Directory is replicated across all domain controllers, so if the main **domain controller** fails the directory is not lost. Servers that are in the same domain but do not host an Active Directory are called member servers.

Each domain has a name. The Windows naming scheme resembles the Internet domain name system, so a university might have a domain name such as *university.edu*. The **namespace** is the set of all names that are unique within a network. In a contiguous namespace, each child object contains the name of its parent object; for example, the business school domain within the university might be named *business.university.edu*.

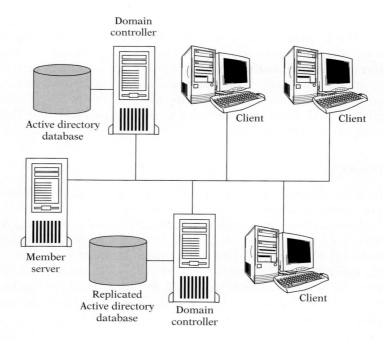

FIGURE 19.2

The basic unit of a Windows 2003 client/server network is a domain.

A **domain tree** is a hierarchical organization of different domains. For example, the business school and the engineering school might each have a domain and those two domains might be integrated to form a domain tree. A domain tree is characterized by a shared Active Directory database and a shared contiguous namespace. For example, the university might use *university.edu* as its Internet name, the business school might use *business.university.edu*, and the engineering school might use *eng.university.edu*. Additionally, each domain within the tree has a trust relationship with other domains; in other words each trusts the other to authenticate users within their domains, allowing users to access any network resource within the tree for which they have rights.

A domain tree is associated with a contiguous namespace, while a **forest** (a group of one or more domain trees) is associated with a noncontiguous (disjointed) namespace. Imagine, for example, that company X purchases or merges with company Y. Prior to the merger, both companies have their own, independent domain trees, *X.com* and *Y.com*. After the merger, employees at Y must be able to access and use resources on X's domain tree, and vice versa. A forest is used to bring together and link the independent domain trees of such disjointed namespaces and enable communication across the entire organization. All domains in a forest share a common global catalog. Each domain tree within the forest has a trust relationship with the other domain trees that allows authentication in one tree to carry over to the other trees.

Active Directory Service

A service is a specific task, often a system task that supports another program. A **network service** is a service that supports a system task over a network. A **directory service** is a network service that makes a directory available to users, system administrators, and applications.

Under Windows 2003 Server, all objects exist within a domain and Active Directory is a directory service installed on a Windows 2003 domain controller. The main Active Directory object is the **domain component (DC).** Network resources (such as users, printers, files, and applications) are found at the end of the hierarchical tree structure and are called **leaf objects.** Organizational units, such as companies, divisions, and departments are **container objects;** they contain other containers and leaf objects and are used to divide and organize the tree structure into branches. **Access control lists** are permissions assigned to the resource that identify which users have access to the object and the specific actions each user can perform on the object. Active Directory associates an access control list with each container, object, and object attribute within the directory.

Every object has a **distinguished name (DN)** that uniquely identifies the object. The DN includes the common name associated with the object and its ancestors in the tree. For example, in Figure 19.3, user *DavisW* is in the container *Users,* which is in the container *Business School,* which is in the *University* domain. Hence, its DN might be

/DC=University/OU=Business School/OU=Users/CN=DavisW

where *DC* means domain component, *OU* means organization unit, and *CN* means common name.

Since users are objects, logon authentication is provided by Windows using the information in the Active Directory. Each user has a single logon name within the domain and has access to all the network resources to which he or she has rights. Active Directory user objects can also be mapped to their corresponding Passport identification, if it exists. Passport is a Microsoft service that allows users to log on once on the Web and use that logon and profile information at multiple participating Web sites. All user account and security information is stored centrally in the Active Directory.

Active Directory provides a **global catalog** that allows users to find any object for which they have access rights. A user can use the global catalog to search for objects within the Active Directory; for example, a user can find the e-mail address of another user using the global catalog. The catalog is also the primary mechanism by which a user logs onto the network.

◼ File Services

File services allow users to share files stored on the server and access a single point of backup. Windows 2003 uses the **Common Internet File System (CIFS)** to share files. CIFS defines a standard remote file system access protocol for use over the Internet, enabling groups of users to share documents (files). Standard network functions, such as read, write protection, and so on, are implemented within CIFS. Generally, servers that provide file services are installed as member servers rather than domain controllers (in other words, they do not store a copy of the Active Directory).

Shared Folders

To share files on the server, you create **shared folders.** When a folder is shared, users (with the appropriate permissions) can read, create, and modify the files in the shared folder. Shared application folders hold applications installed on the server. The client computers download and use these applications, so they need not be installed on every client computer. Client computers store configuration information for the shared applications on their own machines. Shared data folders are created when users wish to

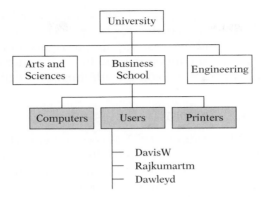

FIGURE 19.3

Active Directory is a directory service installed on a Windows 2003 domain controller.

Net and Passport

Windows 2003 is the first Windows operating system to integrate Microsoft's .Net framework. In fact, for a few months before it was released, .NET was called *.net-server.*

A major benefit of .Net is that it facilitates the development of Web services, applications that can be used over the Web. Businesses use these Web services as building blocks to help develop applications. At the heart of .Net is the Common Language Runtime (CLR). Programs written in languages such as Visual Basic, C, and C# are first compiled into the Microsoft Intermediate Language (MSIL), which defines instructions for the CLR. The CLR then translates the MSIL code into machine language before it is executed. The advantage of this approach is that objects from different languages can be mixed and combined to create a single application. For example, a program can have a Windows form written in Visual Basic call a service from a C# object. The CLR also provides memory management and security features. In addition to the CLR, .Net contains a library of classes that provide a variety of reusable components such as buttons, list boxes used by Windows forms, database connections, tools to help build applications that can talk to databases and html-form elements, image objects, and other Web application tools.

Many Web sites require users to register and log in with a user ID and a password to access services, and remembering multiple user IDs and passwords is difficult. Incorporated within .NET is a Web service called Passport that provides a single login service that makes signing in to Web sites fast and easy. Passport uses encrypted cookies on the client machine to allow authentication credentials to travel with the user to other Web sites that participate in Microsoft's passport system.

exchange data. Working data folders are created for small work teams. Public data folders are created for large groups within the organization.

The system administrator has special rights and privileges on a shared folder. The users who are connected to a computer can be monitored and disconnected if necessary, and the administrator can close files.

Distributed File System

Distributed file system (Dfs) allows a network administrator to link together files that exist on physically different servers to form a single namespace (Figure 19.4). Defining a single namespace simplifies user access because all the files appear to be on a single server and the user need not know where the file is located or how to specify access.

Using Dfs, Windows 2003 can link files managed by servers that are not necessarily Windows-based. The Dfs client and server both use the Common

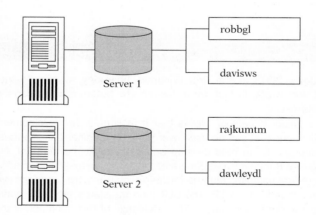

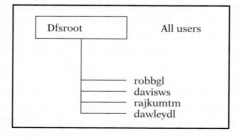

FIGURE 19.4

Distributed file system (Dfs) allows a network administrator to link together files that exist on physically different servers to form a single namespace.

Internet File System (CIFS) to decide which file server the client is accessing. Once the non-Windows server has been identified, that server's protocol (for example, UNIX file system) is used to access the file.

Shadow Copy

Windows 2003 uses **shadow copies** to maintain previous versions of files. With the appropriate client, users can see all previous versions of their files and restore a previous version if necessary. Windows 2003 provides a volume shadow copy service for backup applications. Once the service receives a backup request, it temporarily freezes the programs/applications that are writing to the file, performs the backup, and restarts the programs/applications. Thus Windows 2003 ensures consistent data on backups.

■ Print Services

As the name implies, a **print server** is server program running under Windows 2003 Server that manages printers. A printer can be connected to a server computer, a client computer, or directly to the network. The print server software makes the printer visible on the network and accepts and schedules print jobs from client computers. Windows 2003 Server supports plug and play, which simplifies printer installation. Active printers are defined as objects in Active Directory.

Windows 2003 supports print pools, allowing a print job to be submitted to a logical printer that connects to a set of physical printers. The job is then printed on the first available printer. Additionally, print priorities can be enabled and administrators can specify user permissions and priorities.

■ Web Services

An **application service** is a network service that provides a computing platform on which day-to-day applications can run smoothly. As the term implies, a **Web service** is an application service that utilizes the World Wide Web.

Under Windows 2003, the key Web services component is a Web server named **Internet Information Services (IIS)** (Figure 19.5). One key kernel-mode IIS component, **http.sys**, responds to http connection requests that arrive via port 80 and places each request on a queue for subsequent processing. In a simple two-tier Web surfing application, IIS returns to the queue a static (predefined) Web page. In an n-tier application, IIS might activate a middleware routine responsible for consolidating information from a file server or database server into a template page, creating a dynamic (constructed in real time) page, and placing the dynamic page on the queue. Http.sys subsequently returns the dynamic page to the client.

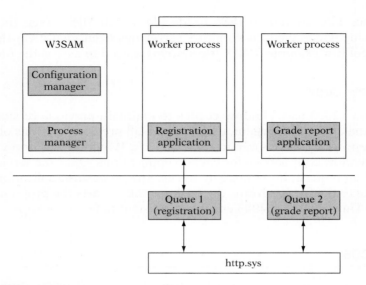

FIGURE 19.5
IIS architecture.

When http.sys receives a request that requires a middleware routine to be run, a second IIS component, World Wide Web Service Administration and Monitoring (W3SAM) starts a **worker process** that hosts and executes the middleware routines. Since different middleware routines can be assigned to run within a worker process, IIS allows the administrator to name the worker process and associate it with a specific middleware routine or application. A named worker process is called an application pool. Note that each application pool services a single queue (a single application).

Http.sys places different application requests in different queues. For example, a student registering for a course at a university might be serviced by a process associated with queue 1, while a student checking his or her grades might be serviced by a process associated with queue 2. It is also possible for a given queue to be serviced by more than one worker process. For example, at registration time multiple students are likely to be registering simultaneously and multiple processes might serve the single registration queue to improve response time and share the workload.

Application pools work in isolation and are separated from other application pools by process boundaries. Thus, if a faulty Web application runs in the application pool, it crashes only that application pool and not the entire Web server. Each worker process also runs in a default account with very few privileges and has no access to command line tools, thus reducing the potential for security violations or break-ins. These features improve the stability, security, and reliability of Web services in Windows 2003.

W3SAM allows the Web administrator to determine which applications will run and helps configure those applications. For example, by default an application pool has only one process, but the administrator can configure the number of processes within an application pool. Additional parameters such as memory usage, scheduled process run times, caching, and so on can be configured using W3SAM.

■ Media Services

An optional module called **media services** can be used to configure Windows 2003 Server as a streaming server. In contrast to a Web server, which delivers the contents of a file, a **streaming server** is designed to broadcast live information (music, sound, video) in real time, encoding, compressing, and transmitting the information at a constant, predictable rate so that playback glitches (like dropped phrases and broken or frozen images) can be minimized. Streaming servers often use UDP (User Datagram Protocol) rather than TCP at the transport layer. Because the UDP protocol skips some of the TCP protocol's error checks, a streaming server effectively sacrifices quality for speed. On the client side of the connection, the user's media player application offers such controls as pause and rewind, and the streaming server must have the ability to respond to such commands. Also, a streaming server must be able to transmit information at different bit rates to accommodate both broadband and dial-up clients.

A Windows server using Media Services establishes publishing points to link clients to the server. A broadcast publishing point is used to stream live content to the client, and an on-demand publishing point is used respond to such client commands as rewind and pause. Server side play lists containing a list of contents and advertisements are specified for each publishing point using a variation of XML. Such information as content security and the maximum number of clients that can connect to a given publishing point are configured and set by the system operator, and additional plug-ins can be used to provide such services as authentication and logging.

▪ Clustering Services

A **cluster** is a group of computers (hardware) that act like a single system to provide services to clients (Figure 19.6). The computers in the cluster are connected using high-speed network links and run server software such as the Windows 2003 operating system. To the clients or users who log on to the cluster, the computers that form the cluster appear as though they are a single unified resource. Each computer in the cluster is referred to as a node or host.

Note that a cluster links several computers—hardware. The word "server" generally implies software, but it is sometimes applied to the host computer that runs a server program, and you'll encounter that second meaning in the next paragraph. To help avoid confusion, we'll selectively use the term "server host" or "host" to make clear that we are talking about hardware. Note, however, that if you read Microsoft's source documentation, the term "server" is used without qualification.

When one of the hosts in the cluster goes down, a client request is routed automatically to another host without the client being aware of the switch, thus increasing reliability and availability. Under Windows, each server host in the cluster operates independently on its copy of the data and shares nothing with the other hosts. Devices that can be shared, such as a disk, are selectively owned and managed by a single server host. Windows provides load balancing so that each server host performs similar amounts of work. For example, the first request for a Web page might go to server host 1, the second to server host 2, and so on. However, once an application is assigned to a given host, further service requests from the client go to the same host. Windows 2003 can handle up to eight server hosts in a cluster.

One benefit of the World Wide Web is that customers can use self-service twenty-four hours per day, seven days per week rather than relying on the Web site's employees to complete work for them. Applications calling for such high availability are well suited to clustered services. In fact, many popular Web sites such as *cnn.com, ibm.com,* and *microsoft.com* use clustered Web servers called Web farms to share the load among computers and keep the system available. For example, if you issue the command

nslookup cnn.com

from the command line, multiple IP addresses will be returned reflecting different computers working together to provide a single Web service.

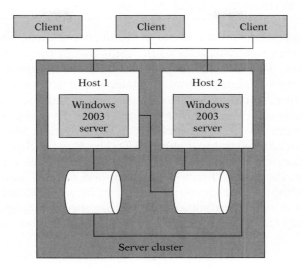

FIGURE 19.6

A cluster consists of two or more host computers running Windows 2003 Server.

▮ Peer-to-Peer Networks

Although client/server networks are much more common, both Windows 2003 Server and Windows XP Professional can be used to support a peer-to-peer network. A peer-to-peer network is called a **workgroup** in Windows terminology. Each computer maintains its own **security database** that contains information on users and resource security. All network administration is decentralized, and a user who wants access to multiple machines must have accounts and permissions on each machine. The advantages of running a peer-to-peer network include ease of setup and the ability to share such resources as files and printers. Such networks are effectively limited to connecting perhaps twenty-five computers, however.

◼ Managing Windows 2003 Server

Organizations must control the total cost of ownership, and administration contributes significantly to the total cost of ownership as a network grows in size. Windows 2003 provides numerous administrative aids such as security templates, remote installation of software on the client's desktop machine, software update services, command line controls, and elimination of duplicate copies of files to reduce storage costs.

Windows 2003 provides a *Start* menu option, *Manage Your Server,* for the system administrator (Figure 19.7). The *Manage Your Server* option is a single location from which the administrator can manage a file server, an application server, the Active Directory, security, and so on (Figure 19.8). For example, if the administrator chooses *Manage this file server* (from the right panel), a new window will open showing other file server management options such as *Backup File Server, Configure Shadow Copies,* and so on (Figure 19.9).

FIGURE 19.7

Select *Manage Your Server.*

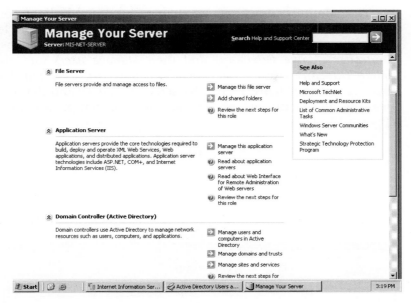

FIGURE 19.8

The *Manage Your Server* option.

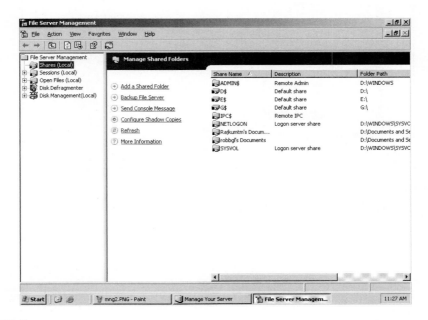

FIGURE 19.9

The *File Server* window.

The administrator can also manage users and client computers by accessing the information in the Active Directory. Click the left-pointing arrow to return to Figure 19.8. If the administrator chooses *Domain Controller (Active Directory)* and then *Manage users and computers in Active Directory* (right panel, near the bottom), a screen displaying all users is shown (Figure 19.10). By selecting a user and that user's properties, the administrator can change the information for any given user (Figure 19.11).

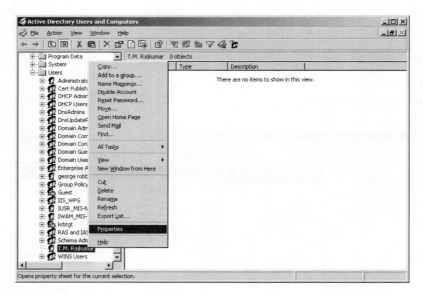

FIGURE 19.10

The *Active Directory Users and Computers* screen.

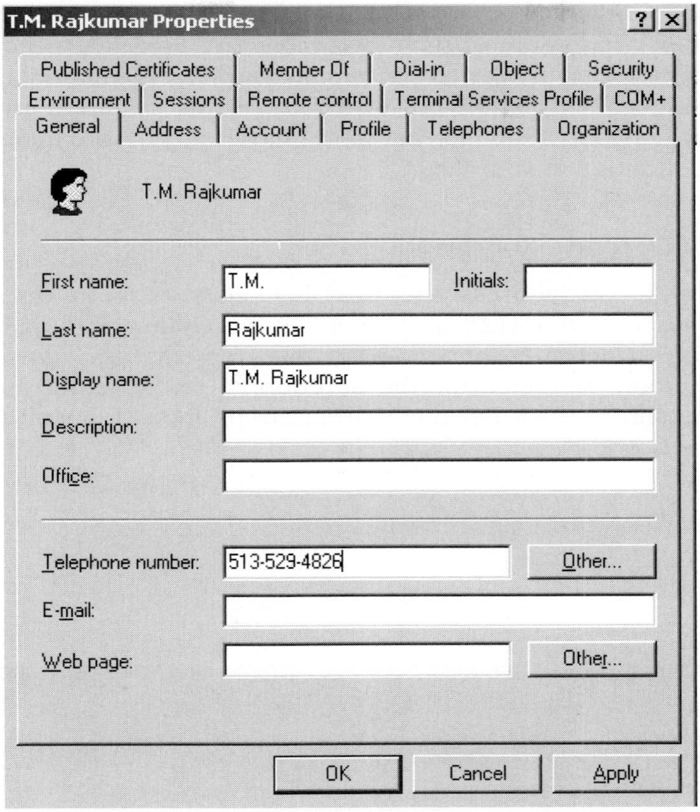

FIGURE 19.11
The administrator can change the information for any given user.

Using Windows 2003 Server from a Client Computer

The preferred client for Windows 2003 Server is the Windows XP Professional product. In this section, you will use the Windows XP client to perform some simple and standard operations with the Windows 2003 Server. Most users log in to the network, retrieve and manipulate network files, and use network printers. The network is transparent to the user and regular Windows tools such as *Explorer* are used when accessing network resources such as files or printers. As you read the material, try (with your instructor's permission) to work through the examples given here. Since every network is unique, you might have to adapt the material to the specific situation in your lab.

Logging onto the Network

Simultaneously press the *Ctrl+Alt+Delete* keys to display the login screen (Figure 19.12), and click on the Options button to reveal your choices. Choose *Logon to Servername* from the drop down menu; check with your instructor for the appropriate server name. Enter your user name and password at the appropriate prompts. Click on *OK* to log onto the network.

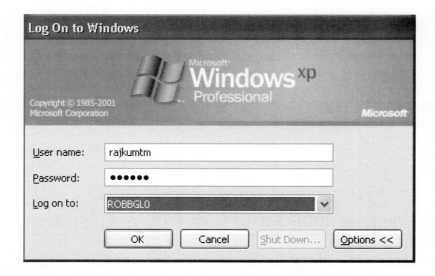

• Some commands available on Windows XP

• Access logon window by pressing *ctrl-alt-del*

FIGURE 19.12

The logon window.

Browsing Network Resources

Since the Windows XP client is integrated within the Windows interface, you can use Windows features such as *My Network Places* and *Explorer* to browse the resources on the network. *My Network Places* allows you to browse the resources of all networks to which your computer is connected. *Explorer* allows you browse through folders in a hierarchical fashion.

Accessing Network Resources Using My Network Places

Click on Start and select *My Network Places* (Figure 19.13). Choose *Entire Network* from the next screen (Figure 19.14) and double click *Microsoft Windows Network* (Figure 19.15) to reveal the domains available on your network (Figure 19.16). Depending on your environment, your domains and choices will almost certainly be different. Check with your instructor for the correct domain name and double click on the domain where your server is located (it's *robbgl0* in Figure 19.16) to open it. You will see a list of computers within the selected domain (Figure 19.17).

FIGURE 19.13

Select *My Network Places.*

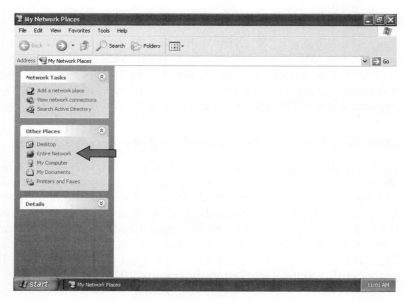

FIGURE 19.14

Choose *Entire Network.*

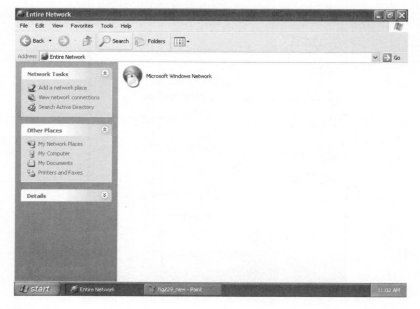

FIGURE 19.15

Double click *Microsoft Windows Network.*

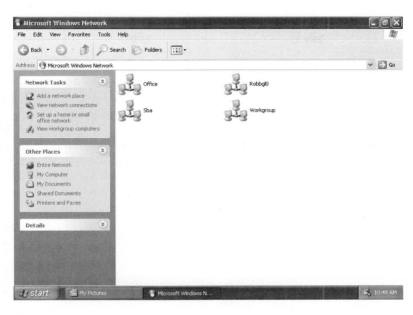

FIGURE 19.16

The domains available on the author's network.

FIGURE 19.17

A list of computers within the selected domain.

Check with your instructor for the correct choice on your system (it's *Mis-net-server* in Figure 19.17) and double click the icon to open your server. You will see the list of shared folders that are available on the server (Figure 19.18). By default, certain shared folders (such as *NETLOGON* and *SYSVOL)* are always available, and other shared application and data folders might be listed. Check with your instructor for the name of the shared data folder you are to use and double click the folder name (the example in the book uses *rajkumtm's documents)*. You should see the contents of the shared folder (Figure 19.19); note that the author's shared folder is currently empty. You can now access or add to the contents of this folder as you would any other folder.

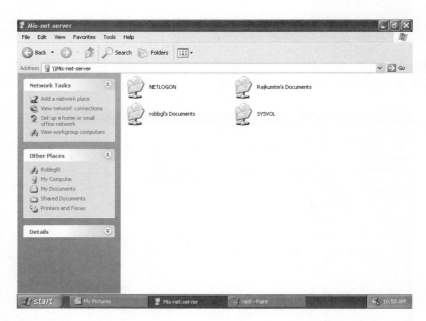

FIGURE 19.18
A list of shared folders.

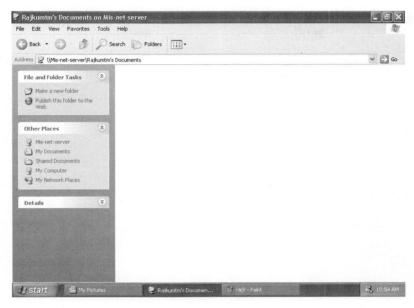

FIGURE 19.19

The contents of the author's (currently empty) shared folder.

Mapping a Folder

If you want repeated access to a shared folder, you can map the folder to a drive on your system. Mapping makes the shared folder on the server appear to your system as though it were a local drive. Once you map it to a drive (for example the G drive), the shared folder can be accessed from within *Explorer* by referencing the drive letter.

To map a shared folder, click on *Tools/Map Network Drive* (Figure 19.20) to start a wizard (Figure 19.21). Choose G on the first pull down list box *(Drive)* and enter the server address or browse to the shared folder (Figure 19.22) in the second pull down list box *(Folder)*. Check the *Reconnect at logon* box to ensure that every time you log onto the system the shared folder will be available as the G drive. Click on *Finish* to map the drive. Once the mapping takes place you can reference the G drive much as you reference your C drive.

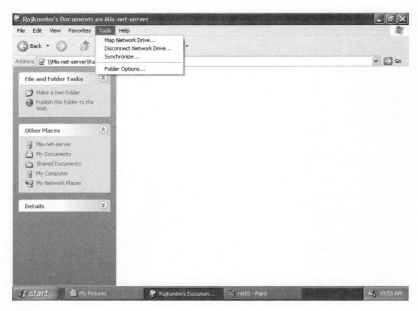

FIGURE 19.20
Mapping a network drive.

FIGURE 19.21
The mapping wizard.

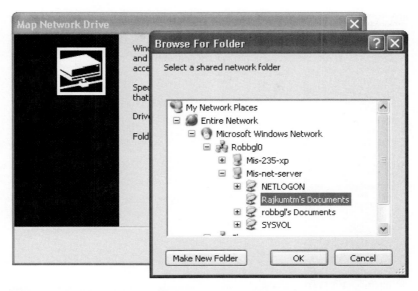

FIGURE 19.22
Browsing for the folder.

Windows *Explorer* and Mapped Shared Folders

Open Windows *Explorer* and select the drive G to make the files within the shared folder visible (Figure 19.23). Provided you have the appropriate rights, you can create files, rename files, delete files, or execute files from the shared folder. In other words, all normal file operations can be performed.

Using the Mapped Drive

A mapped drive can be opened and used to read and write files. To test this facility, create a file with Notepad and store it on the network drive. Click on *Start/Programs/Accessories/Notepad* to open *Notepad* and enter the text shown in Figure 19.24. Click on *File/Save* as and save the file on the G drive (your mapped drive) as *test.txt*. You can copy, rename, and perform other normal operations on the file using the techniques you learned in Chapter 8.

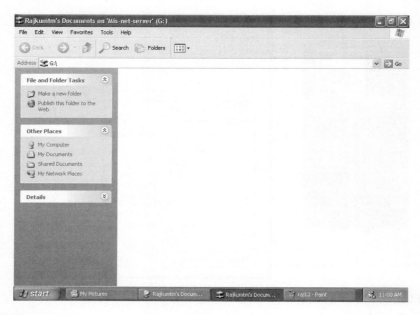

FIGURE 19.23

The files within the shared folder accessed via drive G.

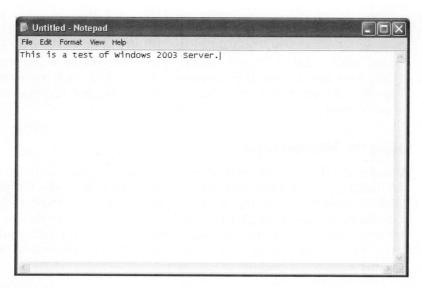

FIGURE 19.24

A test file.

Printing with a Network Printer

Printing within the network is seamless as long as the printer driver is installed on your machine. To print a file, simply return to *Explorer*, choose the *test.txt* file on the *G* drive, right click on the file name, and choose *Print* (Figure 19.25).

Disconnecting a Mapped Drive

To disconnect from a mapped drive, open Windows *Explorer* and choose *Tools/Disconnect Networked drive* (Figure 19.26) to access a screen that lists all networked drives (Figure 19.27). Select drive G, and click on *OK*. The mapping will be removed.

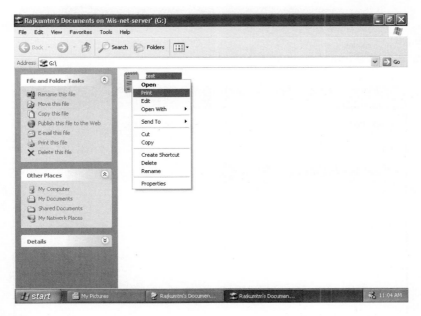

FIGURE 19.25
Printing the test file.

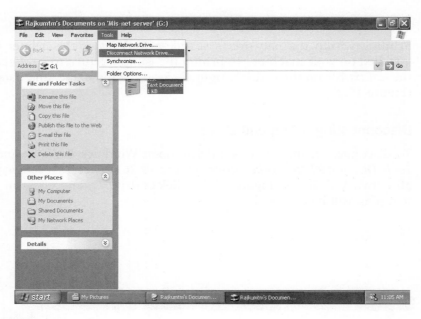

FIGURE 19.26

Disconnecting from a mapped drive.

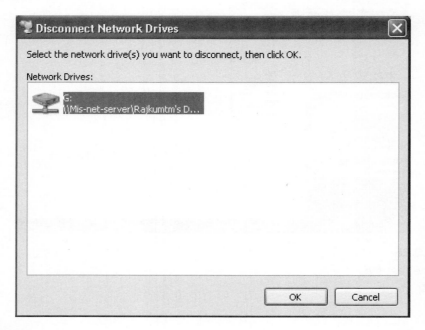

FIGURE 19.27

A list of all networked drives.

Creating a Shared Folder

You may or may not have the appropriate rights to create a shared folder. Unless your instructor tells you to perform the following tasks, please read this subsection and do not follow the step-by-step instruction.

Open *My Computer (Start/ My Computer)* and click on *Shared Documents* to select the default shared documents folder. Select *File/New Folder* from the menu and create a new folder. Name the folder *testsharing*. Your screen will resemble Figure 19.28.

Highlight testsharing, right click the mouse, and select *Sharing and Security* to access the *Sharing* window (Figure 19.29). Click on *If you understand the security risks* option under *Network sharing and security* to display the screen shown in Figure 19.30. Choose *Just enable file sharing,* click on *OK,* and the screen shown in Figure 19.31 appears. Check the *Share this folder on the network* option, leave the *Allow network users to change my files* box unchecked, and click on OK. You have now created a shared folder that other users on the network can see and use. However, they cannot modify the files on the folder. Accessing this shared folder is similar to accessing a shared folder on the server.

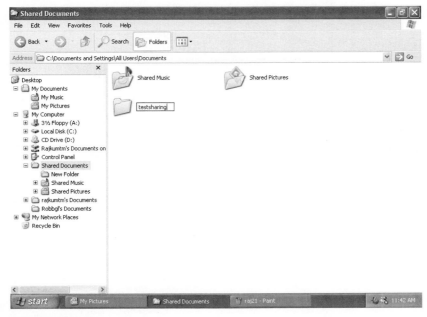

FIGURE 19.28

Name the new folder *testsharing*.

- Highlight *testsharing*

- Right click icon

- Select *Sharing and Security*

- Click *If you understand ...*

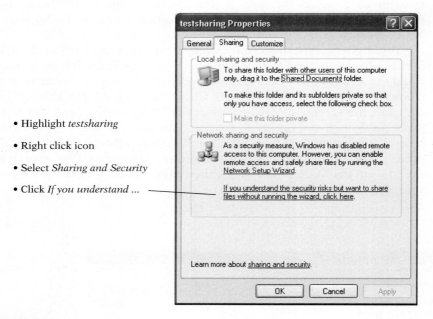

FIGURE 19.29

The *Sharing* window.

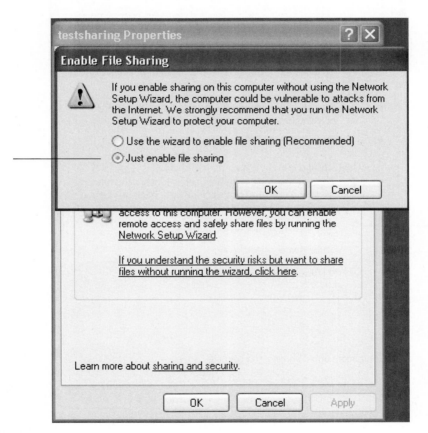

FIGURE 19.30
Enabling file sharing.

FIGURE 19.31

Check *Share this folder on the network.*

Shared Files

You can use Windows XP to share files with other users on your computer (such as your family members) by storing the files within shared folders. By default, there are two standard shared folders, *Shared Music* and *Shared Pictures,* under *Shared Documents* and, as you discovered in Figures 19.29 through 19.31, you can make any folder a shared folder. To share a file, simply drag it to the appropriate folder.

In contrast to sharing files on a single computer with people you know, the files under the shared folder option in this section enable you to share files with other users on your entire network, whether or not they hold an account on your Windows XP machine. Unless you trust everyone who has access to your network, be careful about providing network access to your files.

File sharing provides numerous benefits including the ability to read and modify one another's work and perform other group tasks. There are risks, however. You must ensure that only authorized users have access to your files. Most networks are connected to the Internet and it is possible for some unknown person to stumble onto your files and change them without your knowledge. It is also important to realize that when you access a file from someone else's computer, you run the risk of acquiring a virus. Thus, it is essential that you protect the shared folders with strong passwords, share those passwords only with those you trust and who need access to the files, and always use virus scanning software on all files downloaded from other computers.

Logging Off a Client

When you are finished with this brief tutorial, log off by choosing *Start/Log off*. Click *Log off* to complete the process (Figure 19.32).

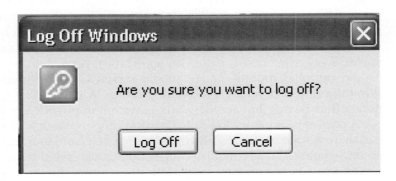

FIGURE 19.32
Logging off.

▪ Summary

Windows 2003 supports a number of network transport protocols, including TCP/IP. The Network Device Interface Specification (NDIS) communicates with network card drivers. All transport protocols use the transport driver interface (TDI) to expose their services to the upper layer. Application programs use application interfaces to access services.

The basic unit of a Windows 2003 client/server network is a domain. A domain controller is a computer running Windows 2003 Server that contains the Active Directory database. Servers that are in the same domain but do not have an Active Directory are called member servers. A domain tree is a hierarchical organization of different domains. A forest consists of one or more domain trees.

Active Directory is a directory service installed on a Windows 2003 domain controller. A directory service is a network service that makes the directory available to users, administrators, and applications. Every object has a distinguished name (DN) that uniquely identifies it. Active Directory provides a global catalog that allows users to find any object for which they have access rights.

Windows 2003 uses the Common Internet File System (CIFS) to share files by creating shared folders. Shared application folders hold applications. Shared data folders are created when users wish to exchange public and working data. Windows 2003 provides Distributed file system (Dfs) to let the network administrator link files that exist on physically different servers to form a single namespace. A print server is a computer running Windows 2003 Server that manages printers. Windows 2003 supports print pools.

A Web service is an application service that utilizes the World Wide Web. Under Windows 2003, the key Web services component is a Web server named Internet Information Services (IIS). One key kernel-mode IIS component, http.sys, responds to http connection requests and places each request on a queue for subsequent processing. When http.sys receives a request that requires a middleware routine to be run, a second IIS component, World Wide Web Service Administration and Monitoring (W3SAM) starts a worker process that hosts and executes the middleware routines. A named worker process is called an application pool.

An optional module called media services can be used to configure Windows 2003 Server as a streaming server. A cluster is a group of computers (hardware) that act like a single system to provide services to clients.

A peer-to-peer network is called a workgroup in Windows terminology and can share resources such as files or printers. Each computer maintains its own security database that contains information on users and resource security.

The rest of the chapter consisted of examples illustrating the management and client-level use of Windows 2003 Server.

◼ Key Words

access control list
Active Directory
application service
cluster
Common Internet File System
  (CIFS)
container object
directory service
distinguished name (DN)
Distributed file system (Dfs)
domain
domain component (DC)
domain controller
domain tree
forest
global catalog
http.sys

Internet Information Services (IIS)
leaf object
media services
namespace
network device interface specification (NDIS)
network service
print server
security database
shadow copy
shared folder
streaming server
transport driver interface (TDI)
Web service
worker process
workgroup

◼ Review Questions

1. Briefly explain the functions performed by the protocols that operate at each level of the Windows 2003 network model.

2. What is a domain? What is a domain tree? What is a forest?

3. What is the Active Directory? What is its purpose?

4. What is a distinguished name? Distinguish between leaf objects and container objects.

5. What functions are performed by the Windows 2003 Common Internet File System (CIFS)?

6. What is a shared folder? What is its purpose? Distinguish between a shared data folder and a shared application folder.

7. What is the purpose of the Distributed file system (Dfs)?

8. Why are shadow copies useful?

9. What functions are performed by a print server? What is a print pool?

10. What are Web services?

11. Describe the primary components of the Windows 2003 Internet Information Server (IIS).

12. What functions are performed by media services?

13. What is a cluster? What tasks are performed by clustering services? What is a Web farm?

14. Distinguish between a client/server network and a peer-to-peer network. Briefly describe a peer-to-peer network under Windows 2003.

15. Identify several common features for managing Windows 2003 Server.

16. Describe several Windows 2003 features and services you can access from a client computer.

▍Exercises

1. With your instructor's permission, complete the brief tutorial starting with the header "Using Windows 2003 Server: A Client's Perspective."

2. Turn back to Figure 17.12 and review the seven-layer OSI model. Then relate the OSI model to the Windows 2003 network architecture.

3. Cite at least two benefits associated with Microsoft's .NET and Passport services.

4. Would you be willing to sign up for Microsoft's Passport service? Why or why not?

5. What are some of the risks associated with sharing files? What can you do to minimize those risks?

6. Figures 19.1, 19.5, and 19.6 are useful templates for organizing many of this chapter's key terms.

Linux Networking

When you finish reading this chapter you should be able to:

▶ Identify the services performed by *inetd*.

▶ Explain how file sharing is achieved by Linux/UNIX.

▶ Discuss the Linux/UNIX Network File System (NFS).

▶ Identify the purpose of Server Message Block (SMB).

▶ Identify the functions performed by *smbd* and *nmbd,* the two primary Samba daemons.

▶ Distinguish between Postscript and Ghostscript.

▶ Distinguish between *lpd,* the line printer daemon, and the Common UNIX Printing System (CUPS).

▶ Explain how a kernel-based Web server such as *khttpd* and a user-mode Web server such as Apache work together to fill page requests.

▶ Explain the Apache pre-forking model.

▶ Distinguish between a single system image and a Beowulf cluster.

▣ Introduction

Traditionally, UNIX and Linux systems have dominated enterprise networking, providing file services, remote printing, mail services, Web services, and a wide variety of other services. For example, Apache, a popular Web server that runs under Linux/UNIX, powers more than half the Web sites in the world[1], and popular mail services such as Hotmail and Yahoo mail started on UNIX systems. Key reasons for this dominance include the configurability (the ability to customize a system to fit a unique set of needs), scalability (the ability to serve an increasing number of users without increasing response times), and stability (the ability to avoid system crashes) of UNIX applications and systems. This chapter will consider some common network services that are available under Linux.

Although Linux/UNIX enjoys a significant server-side presence, most client computers run Windows. Consequently, because few students have access to a server-side host, this chapter will not feature a tutorial.

▣ Network Services

Services are programs that run on Linux/UNIX machines and wait for clients to connect using specific network ports. For example, most Web servers use the *http* protocol that generally connects at port 80. These services run with little or no human intervention.

Daemons

Within the UNIX world, services that run in the background are known as **daemons,** and the names of these programs traditionally end with *d* (for daemon). For example, the *http* service is enabled by a daemon program named ***httpd.*** Generally, daemons are started when the system starts, stop when the system is shut down, find the information they need in configuration files, and record error information in an error log file. Daemons usually sit idly until a client connects, consuming computing resources only when they are active.

---

[1]Netcraft.com, *http://news.netcraft.com/archives/2003/05/05/may_2003_web_server_survey.html*.

In a typical Linux system there may be many such daemons waiting and listening for client connections. Rather than have each of these daemons wait for connections, Linux provides a superserver daemon named ***inetd*** (Internet services daemon) that functions as an intermediary, listens for connection requests for certain ports, and starts the appropriate service program when a request reaches a port (Figure 20.1). The *inetd* daemon maintains a configuration file that links port numbers to the associated server daemon. For example, if a Web page is requested by a client via port 80, *inetd* checks the configuration table to find the daemon associated with port 80 and starts *httpd*, which handles the Web page transfer and stops on completion of the transfer of the Web page data. If, in contrast, a file transfer is requested via port 21, *inetd* starts *ftpd*, the file transfer daemon, to handle the file transfer request. Using a superserver such as *inetd* insures that less memory is consumed because there is only one listener running. Also, *inetd* helps improve system security by supporting filters for incoming requests.

Since, *inetd* must start and stop the other server daemons there is a slight delay inherent in the Linux/UNIX approach. Thus, *inetd* is often not used for high demand daemons. For example, a university Web site that gets numerous page hits might not run the *http* service daemon under *inetd*. However, an individual faculty member's Web server is likely to get relatively few hits per day, making the *inetd* option more efficient.

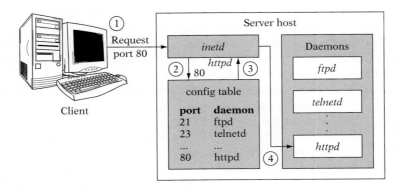

FIGURE 20.1

Linux provides a super-server daemon named *inetd*.

UNIX Naming Conventions

UNIX line commands tend to be quite cryptic, which can be intimidating to a beginner. Remember, however, that UNIX was not designed with beginners in mind. It was designed to simplify the work of professionals, such as system administrators, system operators, and system programmers. For example, UNIX line commands are typed all lowercase because typing all lowercase simplifies typing.

If you look carefully at a UNIX line command, its meaning is actually quite clear. Generally, the commands are acronyms composed of a few key letters or the first letter of each word in the command. Thus, *cd* means change directory, cp means copy, *http* is the hypertext transfer protocol, *httpd* is the hypertext transfer protocol daemon, *ftp* is the file transfer protocol, and *ftpd* is the file transfer protocol daemon. If you use such cryptic commands on an everyday basis (as system professionals do), they soon become second nature.

Even words like daemon begin to make sense when you think about them. "Daemon" is an archaic spelling of the word "demon" that often appears in swords and sorcery games. In mythology, a demon is a dark-side being that does negative things. Primitive, text-based computerized swords and sorcery games were very popular among the computing pioneers and hackers who helped UNIX evolve back in the late 1960s and 1970s, so they were familiar with daemons. Service programs (usually) perform useful functions, but sometimes they misbehave. A misbehaving service program can literally crash a system, so it makes perfect sense to call it a daemon.

Improving Security

Many Linux distributions install numerous server daemon programs by default. To reduce security exposure, before they complete the system initialization process, system administrators are urged to review the *inetd* configuration file (typically stored in */etc/inetd.conf*) and remove any unnecessary daemons.

Linux systems also place a program named TCP Wrappers between the *inetd* server and the other server daemons (Figure 20.2) by modifying the *inetd* configuration file to refer to the TCP Wrappers application instead of the server daemons. The TCP Wrappers application daemon *(tcpd)* examines each request and either grants or denies access to the server daemon based on a set of criteria that the system administrator specifies. The criteria for each network service typically include a set of allowable clients *(/etc/hosts.allow)* and a set of clients to which the service is denied *(/etc/hosts.deny)* and can be defined separately for each network service. TCP *Wrappers* can also log (in a system log file) every network request, recording the date/time stamp, the service that was requested, the client address and name, and the decision (grant or deny service).

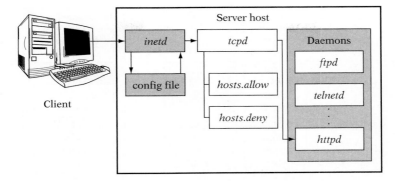

FIGURE 20.2

TCP Wrappers sits between *inetd* and the other server daemons.

■ Linux File Services

File sharing is the process of making available one or more of the directories (or folders) on a local computer to a user on a remote computer. The directories that a client might want to share, such as the */home/sharedfolder* directory, are **exported** by creating an entry in the */etc/exports file*. When a directory is exported, all the files and any folders inside it are also exported. Exported folders are made available to other clients over the network, appearing as though they were available locally to each participating client subject to the limitations imposed by UNIX file system permissions and ownerships.

Linux/UNIX file sharing is achieved either by using an FTP program (Chapter 17) or by using the **Network File System (NFS).** You can use NFS when you want to share files with other Linux/UNIX systems. For example, in an enterprise that supports only Linux/UNIX servers, a user might be able to use NFS to access all his or her files from virtually any computer in the organization.

Under Linux, the NFS server daemon *knfsd* and NFS client tools can run in kernel mode (the leading k on the daemon name), improving response time to clients. As you discovered in Chapter 13 (Figure 13.17), Linux uses the virtual file system to direct read or write requests from applications to the appropriate file system. The NFS client is a virtual file system (Figure 20.3). When a client application requests a read (or write) operation for an NFS file, the NFS client uses the network to contact the NFS server daemon *(knsfd)*. The NFS server then sends the request to the virtual file system on the server, which uses the server's file system to retrieve the file from the disk. The NFS server then returns the file to the client.

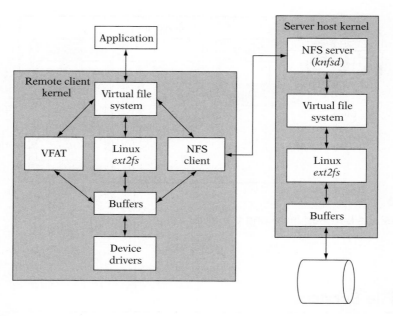

FIGURE 20.3

NFS client server is a virtual file system.

The system administrator specifies the folders to be exported in the */etc/exports* file by recording for each file such information as the folder name, its read and/or write permissions, and an optional list of hosts that are allowed to access the specified folders. NFS restricts the hosts from which connections can be made but relies on the client operating system to authenticate the user.

A Linux/UNIX file is owned by the file's creator. Each Linux user account has a numeric user ID (UID) in addition to a user name, and file ownership is defined by the UID. File ownership in NFS follows standard UNIX techniques and is based on the UIDs of each file and directory in the path name. Thus it is important that the user IDs associated with the user names on the client and server be coordinated so that a file that belongs to one user is not erroneously associated with a different user.

For example, Figure 20.4 lists a set of users and their user IDs on two Linux hosts named *os6e* and *mis*. On *os6e,* user *bill's* files are associated with the UID 1002, but on the *mis* host *bill's* files are associated with UID 1003. Assume *bill* is working on the *os6e* host. If he tries to access a file stored on host *mis,* he will erroneously access user *don's* files because the UID 1002 is associated with user *don.* The system administrator can correct this problem by issuing the appropriate *usermod* (user modify) commands on the *mis* host or by setting up a map file that associates each remote user with his or her correct UID.

User	User ID *os6e*	User ID *mis*
george	1001	1001
bill	1002	1003
don	1003	1002

FIGURE 20.4

Three users' IDs on two Linux hosts.

A client computer that wants to access a file via NFS must run the NFS client and be listed in the NFS server host's */etc/exports* file. A user must know where the shared folder is located in order to be able to mount it by issuing a *mount* command at the line prompt. (In other words, the user cannot browse or search for the shared folder on the network.) Once the shared folder is mounted, the files in the server's exported folder can be accessed by the client from the mount point like any other local directory.

NFS differs from many other types of file sharing in that, like the *http* protocol, it is stateless. Each NFS request is completely self-contained and need not refer to prior connections or requests. The stateless nature of NFS allows it to survive server crashes. For example, assume a client had previously sent a request to read file X on the server, but the server crashed. Because the server is down, the client does not receive a response. Rather than crashing, the client responds by intermittently repeating the request to the server. Once the server comes back up, it can handle the request as though all those independent, unanswered requests never happened. Thus, while the client might experience a delay, the data will eventually be delivered.

◼ Windows Interconnectivity

NFS is useful for sharing files with other UNIX or Linux systems. However, in most enterprises most of the client workstations run Windows.

Server Message Block (SMB) is a client/server protocol for file sharing, printing, and login services that is commonly found in Windows. SMB corresponds to the application and presentation level protocol within the OSI model and runs on most transport and network protocols such as TCP/IP. A number of commands within the SMB protocol support file sharing, printer sharing, authentication, and authorization services. In the mid-1990s, Microsoft updated their SMB protocol and called it Common Internet File System (CIFS) (Chapter 19). However, in the Linux world what Microsoft calls CIFS is still widely known as SMB.

Windows XP (Chapter 19) includes CIFS clients and servers that enable a user to create shared folders. The SMB server for the UNIX and Linux world is called **Samba,** and the client is known as *smbclient*. Samba and *smbclient* allow Windows and UNIX clients to access shared files as though they were stored locally. In other words, Samba allows Windows clients to access UNIX files.

A **share** is a server resource such as a file or printer that is made available to SMB clients for network sharing. The system administrator can place security restrictions on access to shares, and users might be asked to enter a user name and password before they can access the share. (This is also the level of security prevalent in Windows XP.) File services are created by setting up file or folder shares. You can access files and folders from a server over a share as though the files were stored locally.

Figure 20.5 shows an example of a server host running Linux server software. Stored on the server is a shared directory resource named *server**group*. The client machines can use SMB to map this resource to their file directories as a virtual drive (for example, the G drive). To the applications that run on the clients, the files on the G drive are accessed just like a file stored on the local hard drive (C). When the client needs a file on the server, the client sends an SMB request and receives an SMB response containing the file.

Samba Components

Under Samba, the *smbd* daemon is responsible for file and print services (Figure 20.6). In addition, *smbd* implements user authentication and access to the shares; note that Windows domains might provide additional authentication. Samba and *smbd* can work with the Windows domain controller (Chapter 19) so that once a user logs into the Windows domain, he or she can also access Samba shares. Samba can also perform the functions of a Windows domain controller.

The second primary Samba daemon, *nmbd*, implements name resolution and browsing. The *nmbd* daemon resolves names such as *server* to their corresponding IP (Internet protocol) address and keeps track of which names correspond to which IP address. Clients can then use the *nmbd*

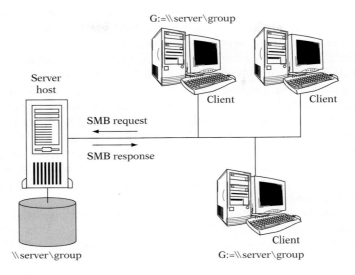

FIGURE 20.5
Samba share mapping.

mappings to open an SMB request directly with the server. Note that *smbd* and *nmbd* are linked by a shared routine named *libsmb* that implements the *smb* protocol routines.

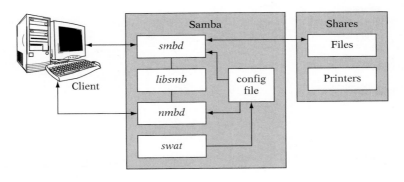

FIGURE 20.6
Samba's architecture.

Under Windows, users can use the *My Network Places* application to browse a domain list (note, not the Internet) for shared resources. When a Linux host runs a Samba server, the Linux machine appears to a Windows client as a resource within the *My Network Places* application (Figure 20.7), and clicking on an option can take you to the exact resource you need (Figures 20.8). Depending on how the Samba share is set up, a username and password may or may not be required to reach Figure 20.8. Otherwise, the Windows user sees little or no difference between the Linux machine and the Windows system. For example, the only hint that *os6e* in Figures 20.7 and 20.8 is a Linux machine can be gleaned from the title bar near the top of Figure 20.8. The *nmbd* daemon implements the service announcements that make the Linux machine available for browsing with the SMB protocol.

Samba Web Administration Tool (SWAT) can be used to administer and manage Samba using a Web browser. SWAT allows the system administrator to easily change the Samba configurations, designate shares, set authentication requirements (user name and password) for the shares and so on. Configuration information is stored on a *config* (configuration) file that is accessed by *smbd* and *nmbd*.

FIGURE 20.7

A Windows client can browse the Linux system like a network resource.

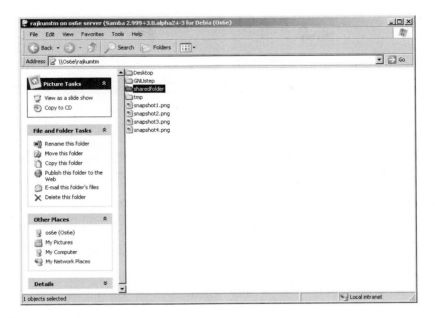

FIGURE 20.8

The Linux system's shared folder.

Samba Clients

SMB file sharing works both ways. If you are using a Windows client, you can mount on a file share that is stored on a Linux/UNIX server. Similarly, you can make a shared folder that is stored on a Windows system available to a Linux client. *Smbclient* works like an *ftp* client and allows you to transfer files to and from a Windows server. *Smbfs* is a Linux/Unix driver that allows you to mount the remote file share as a local mount point in Linux. Once the file share is mounted, files can be read and written as though the file share were local. Two command line utility programs, *smbmount* and *smbumount,* make it simple to mount and dismount (the *umount* command means unmount in UNIX) the file share.

Konqueror, the KDE file manager (Chapter 9), allows you to view the file share graphically using the SMB protocol (Figure 20.9). In order to use Konqueror, you must know the location of the file share. In contrast, *LinNeighborhood* is a graphical utility similar to *My Network Places* in Windows that allows users to browse for SMB resources (Figure 20.10). *LinNeighborhood* uses the *smbfs* and *smbmount* programs.

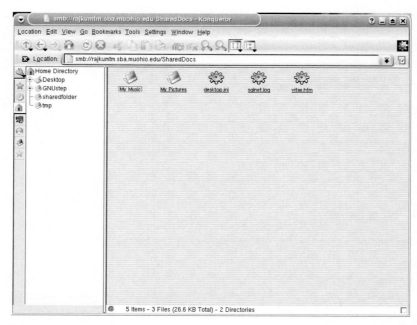

FIGURE 20.9

Viewing a Windows shared folder with Konqueror.

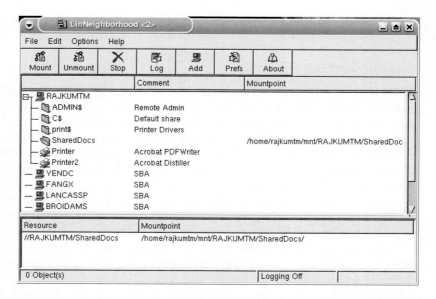

FIGURE 20.10

Browsing with LinNeighborhood.

Print Services

Under Linux/UNIX, when you choose the print option from an application program the program generates a Postscript file. **Postscript** is a device independent page description language that specifies the layout of the text and graphics on the page. Most modern printers print a raster image composed of pixels or dots. Page description languages are abstract and must be converted to a raster image before they can be printed. A Postscript printer's raster image processor (RIP) is a Postscript interpreter that converts the Postscript language to a raster image.

Not all printers are Postscript compatible; for example, most common inkjet printers do not understand Postscript. In such cases, Linux uses a software filter that converts one print format to another. Typically, a filter called **Ghostscript** is used to convert the Postscript document to a raster image for use by a specific, non-Postscript printer. Figure 20.11 outlines the flow of a typical printing operation in Linux.

Postscript is *not* a Windows standard, so a Windows client that sends output to a printer server on a Linux system must ensure that a Postscript printer driver is installed on the Windows client. On demand, Samba 3 (the latest version of Samba) allows the necessary printer driver to be downloaded from the server to a Windows client and installed before the output is sent to the SMB print share.

The Line Printer Daemon

Typically, when an application program issues a print command, a client-side operating system routine named lpr (line printer) transfers the file to a

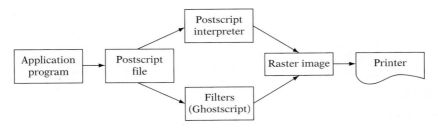

FIGURE 20.11
Postscript is the Linux/UNIX page description language.

local (client-side) print server (Figure 20.12). (Yes, it is possible to have a print server residing on the client. Remember the client/server concept.) Each active printer is identified by a queue name and has an associated spool subdirectory that specifies whether the printer associated with the print queue is local or networked. The line printer daemon (lpd) watches this directory and listens on port 515 for requests from lpr clients. Every time lpd receives a request, it finds the file on the spool subdirectory and either passes the print job to a local Postscript printer, through a filter such as Ghostscript to a local non-Postscript printer, or, if the request is for a remote printer, to the lpd server running on the remote (networked) computer to which the printer is attached.

CUPS

Linux's default printing system is *lpd*, but it has drawbacks. For example, *lpd* does not use printer drivers, which means the user cannot take advantage of such printer-specific features as printing on both sides of the paper. Consequently, **Common UNIX Printing System (CUPS)** (Figure 20.13) is a recommended replacement for traditional lpd-based print servers.

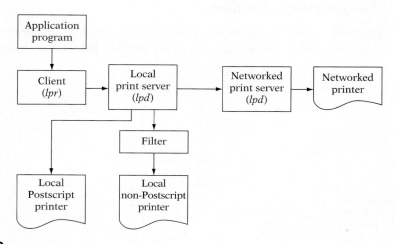

FIGURE 20.12

The line printer daemon is *lpd*.

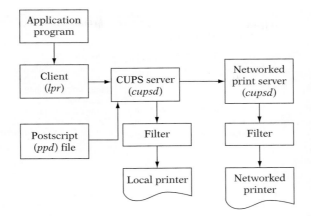

FIGURE 20.13

CUPS is a replacement for *lpd* print services.

CUPS can work with **Postscript printer description (PPD)** files, which are simple text files that describe the device-dependent features and contain commands that a Postscript printer understands. The CUPS server, *cupsd,* incorporates a raster image processor based on Ghostscript filters that allows non-Postscript printers to print documents initially formatted in Postscript using PPD.

CUPS also supports the **Internet printing protocol (IPP),** a protocol that runs on top of *http* and allows for bi-directional communication between client and server. Using IPP allows clients to browse for available printers on the network (Figure 20.14) and to get status and other detailed information about a printer. A Web-based interface available at port 631 (Figure 20.15) allows the system administrator to configure every aspect of CUPS. IPP supports access control and authentication using the CUPS configuration file *(/etc/cups/cupsd.conf)* that specifies which clients are allowed to access a given server host. CUPS can also be configured to store usage logs for specific printers and provides accounting capabilities. Finally, CUPS offers a compatibility layer called *cups-lpd* to support work with older *lpd*-style clients and provides the *cupsadsmb* utility to share CUPS printers using Samba. Because CUPS can work with most UNIX facilities, it is the recommended Linux/UNIX printing system.

FIGURE 20.14

IPP allows a client to browse the network for available printers.

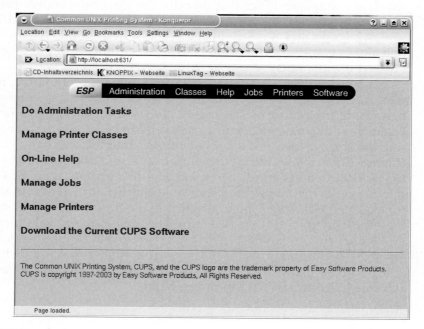

FIGURE 20.15

The CUPS Web interface for system administration.

Samba Print Shares

In Samba, print shares behave very much like file shares. In order to print to a network printer, the client sends the file to the print share. The server then treats the file as though it originated locally and passes it through its (the server's) print system. Many features, such as access control, work equally on both file and print shares.

Apache Web Server

Linux/UNIX systems are frequently used as Web server platforms. **Apache,** a freely available, open source Web server, is a popular software choice.

A Web server is an application-layer program that runs on the host server computer in a client/server network. As you read earlier in this chapter, under Linux/UNIX a Web server daemon called *httpd* listens for connections at port 80 (Figure 20.16). Apache is a Web server daemon, a specific version of *httpd*. When a client makes a connection, httpd responds by serving a static or dynamic (created on demand by middleware) HTML file back to the client. The client's browser then receives and displays the page.

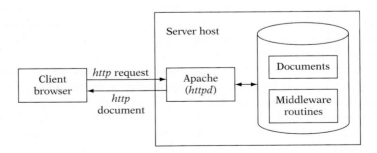

FIGURE 20.16
Apache is a Web server daemon *(httpd)*.

So You Want to Host a Web Site?

DSL and cable modems provide different speeds for transferring data upstream (from your computer) and downstream (to your computer). In general, downstream speeds are faster, which is fine for browsing the Internet. If you want to host a Web site on your computer, however, you must run a Web server, and Web servers spend most of their time uploading files to clients. In other words, if you want to host a Web site, you'll need fast upstream speeds. You'll also need a domain name such as *yourcompany.com* mapped to your Web site and to a static IP address.

Security is another consideration. Opening any port for service can create system vulnerabilities. Security holes are occasionally found in Web server software and, in addition to maintaining the system and the Web site, you'll find it necessary to spend time installing patches and fixes. (Security issues were discussed in Chapter 18.) If you are serving only a few pages, you might consider renting space and service from an Internet service provider rather than running your own Web server.

Kernel-Based Web Servers

Most *httpd* daemons such as Apache run in user mode. However, user mode processes carry considerably more overhead than processes that run inside the kernel. For example, kernel mode processes can be started and stopped much more quickly.

Many user mode Web servers actually perform a significant part of their work in kernel mode. For example, an *http* request on port 80 is initially sensed by the kernel and not by the user mode *httpd* process (Figure 20.17). The kernel then forwards the request to the user mode process. Assuming the requested page is static, the *httpd* daemon sends a request for the *html* file to the kernel. The kernel returns the *html* file to the daemon, which creates the *http* response (the page), and forwards it to the kernel. Finally, the kernel returns the page to the client.

The overhead and communication that takes place between the user process and the kernel can be significantly reduced by running a kernel-based Web server such as *khttpd,* a kernel mode Linux daemon that provides Web services. Note, however, that kernel-mode Web servers can only provide static pages. Dynamic pages are created by user mode middleware routines.

Kernel-based Web servers such as *khttpd* (for kernel *http* daemon) can run in conjunction with other Web servers such as Apache. In such systems, khttpd is configured to monitor port 80 for *http* requests and the Apache

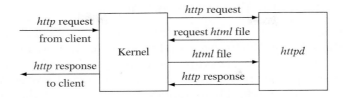

FIGURE 20.17

The Web server *(httpd)* must communicate with the kernel to fill a request for a static Web page.

httpd listens on a different port such as 8080. If the request is for a static page, then *khttpd* serves the page back to the client (Figure 20.18) without involving the user mode Web server. If, however, the request is for a dynamic page, then *khttpd* forwards the request to the user mode daemon (Apache), which responds.

While kernel mode Web servers can speed up the serving of static pages, they have drawbacks. If there is a bug in the kernel mode server, it can bring the entire system down. In contrast, user based processes are inherently more stable because an error will bring down only a single user process (the Web server) and not the entire system.

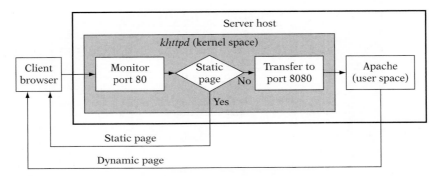

FIGURE 20.18

A kernel mode Web server *(khttpd)* passes dynamic page requests to a user mode Web server (Apache).

The Apache Pre-Forking Server Model

Apache supports a particularly robust server model called the **pre-forking model** (Figure 20.19). New UNIX processes are created via calls to *forks* (Chapter 13), but it takes time for a child process to be created. To speed the process, Apache creates in advance a main parent process and several child processes to handle client requests. Note that all the processes share a common pool of memory.

A child process can serve either a static page or a dynamic page, but serving a dynamic page calls for a middleware routine that runs within the child process. If the middleware routine fails, then only that child process fails, and the Web server and the other child processes remain unaffected and stable. Isolating errors in this way is what makes the pre-forking model robust.

Figure 20.20 is a screen capture that shows the Apache processes in use on the authors' system. The main Apache process has a process id *(pid)* of 13603, and the eight child processes have *pids* ranging from 13604 to 13612. Each of the child processes also references (in the column labeled PPID) the parent process, 13603. Note also (in the STIME column) that all the child processes were started immediately after the main process was started.

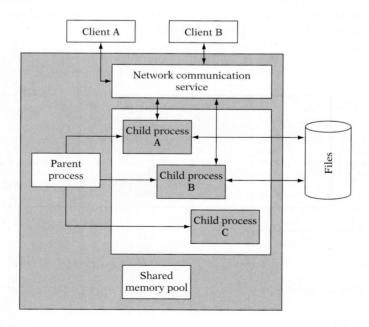

FIGURE 20.19

The Apache pre-forking model.

```
UID        PID  PPID  C  STIME TTY           TIME  CMD
root      13603    1  0  08:36 ?         00:00:00  /usr/sbin/apache
www-data  13604 13603  0  08:36 ?         00:00:00  [apache]
www-data  13605 13603  0  08:36 ?         00:00:00  [apache]
www-data  13606 13603  0  08:36 ?         00:00:00  [apache]
www-data  13607 13603  0  08:36 ?         00:00:00  [apache]
www-data  13608 13603  0  08:36 ?         00:00:00  [apache]
www-data  13610 13603  0  08:37 ?         00:00:00  [apache]
www-data  13611 13603  0  08:37 ?         00:00:00  [apache]
www-data  13612 13603  0  08:37 ?         00:00:00  [apache]
```

FIGURE 20.20

A screen capture showing Apache pre-forking in use.

Each child process has one thread and can service only one request at a time. When all the child processes are busy, the main parent process creates an additional child process to handle a new request. When a system administrator shuts down the service, the parent process uses signals to shut down the child processes.

Apache Multiprocessing Model

Apache is a cross-platform Web server that runs on UNIX/Linux, Windows, and numerous other platforms. A number of different processing models can be substituted for the pre-forking model on non-Linux/UNIX systems, and the system administrator can choose and configure the model that works best on his or her system.

Apache provides the *winnt* model for Windows platforms. The *winnt* model is multithreaded and runs as a single task or process that creates child threads (rather than child processes) to handle client requests. Threads are faster and less demanding, and consume fewer resources than processes, so *winnt* is the default processing model for Windows.

Apache Modules

The Apache daemon uses a modular architecture (Figure 20.21). A core module provides basic *http* functionality and other modules are incorporated to provide additional functionality. For example, the code that performs process/thread management is provided as a platform-specific multiprocessing module. If the platform is Linux, the pre-fork model is present. If, on the other hand, the platform is Windows, then the *winnt* model is present.

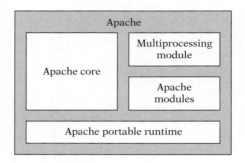

FIGURE 20.21
Apache's architecture.

Other modules can be incorporated statically (compiled along with the server) or dynamically, on demand. Apache supports dynamic shared objects that permit the loading of external modules at run time, and modules can be specified for inclusion at startup or re-start or added or removed without recompiling the server. Many different dynamic modules are available. For example, if you need encryption, the secure sockets layer (Chapter 18) is available as a module. Middleware routines that run applications might be written in such languages as perl, php, and so on, and each of these languages is available as a module that links the language's run-time libraries to Apache.

Like an operating system, Apache provides an application programming interface implemented in the Apache portable run-time layer. For example, Windows and Linux/UNIX handle files, locking, processes, and threads differently. The Apache portable run-time layer provides file input/output, network input/output, its own memory management routines, and so on. Using the Apache API allows a system administrator or a programmer to fully customize the version of Apache that runs on a given platform, and if programs are written to be consistent with the Apache API, the modules can be easily ported from one platform to another.

Apache Filters

When an Apache thread or process receives a request, it delegates the request to a single content handler module that sends the data back to the client. Based on the type of request, different content handlers are invoked. For example, if the request is for an image, an image-handler module transmits the image to the client. If, on the other hand, the request is for a middleware routine, a corresponding middleware module transmits the output to the client.

Generally, the modules work independently of each other, but it is sometimes necessary for one module's output to be modified by another module. For example, it is common for a middleware routine to generate a dynamic page that incorporates server-side *include* tags, template directives included within the html such as the date and time that are processed and filled by a server-side *include* module. Apache takes advantage of the UNIX filters concept (Chapter 9) to support such applications. The output of the first middleware module (the dynamic page generator) is sent to the second module (the server-side *include* module) using the same mechanism UNIX uses to send the output of a line command to the *sort* filter. The server-side *include* module then sends the finished dynamic page to the client. Apache can be configured to specify the sequence of modules that support different types of requests.

◘ Clustering

A **cluster** consists of multiple computers, each with its own operating system, working together over a high speed network. The network interconnections are typically gigabit Ethernet connections that are specifically configured for the cluster. The goals of clustering are high performance, high availability, load balancing, scalability, and manageability. For example, Google, the Internet search engine, uses a cluster of 4000 Linux systems to support its Web services. Linux/UNIX clustering is similar to Windows clustering (Chapter 19).

Beowulf Clusters

High performance clustering refers to a tightly connected network of computers all dedicated to the solution of a single problem. A **Beowulf cluster** links multiple inexpensive computers in an effort to achieve the performance of a conventional supercomputer at a much lower price.

For example, to find all the prime numbers between 1 and 1,000,000, you might divide the problem into ten groups (1 through 100,000, 100,001 through 200,000, and so on), give a portion of the task to each of ten different computers, and assign one computer responsibility for coordinating and merging the results. In such a Beowulf cluster, ten systems (nodes) might be connected via Ethernet, with each running a copy of Linux. The nodes in the cluster are usually connected to the outside world through the single master node (Figure 20.22).

On such a system, the individual nodes lose their individuality and the operating system is tuned to make a single parallel program run efficiently across the entire cluster. Multiple messages are passed between the nodes,

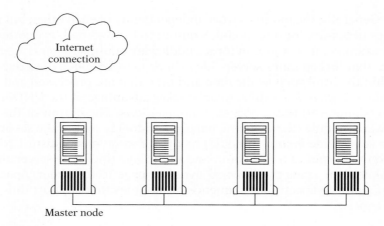

FIGURE 20.22

A four-node Beowulf cluster.

so high speed proprietary networks are typically used to link the nodes. All the programs that run inside this high performance computing environment must be modified to use message passing interface (MPI) commands.

Single System Image

A **single system image (SSI)** is a form of distributed computing in which multiple heterogeneous resources such as networks, distributed databases, or servers appear to the user as one, more-powerful, unified resource[2]. The nodes in an SSI cluster are linked to form a peer-to-peer network and do not share a client-server relationship. In an SSI cluster, it does not matter with which node a given resource is physically associated, because to the user the entire cluster appears as one global resource managed by the operating system's kernel.

The goal of an SSI cluster is to provide better performance for both sequential and parallel applications. The operating system is modified to support group scheduling of parallel programs by identifying global unused resources such as processors and memory and by managing access to those resources. Processes are automatically moved from one node to another, so the load is balanced across multiple machines. Unlike the Beowulf clusters,

---

[2]Based on *http://www.webopedia.com/TERM/S/single_system_image.html*.

it is not essential for the programs to be modified to use MPI. Regular programs can be run without any modification, and they need not be cluster-aware to take advantage of the cluster's benefits.

▪ Summary

The *http* service is run by a daemon named *httpd*. Linux provides a super-server daemon named *inetd* (Internet services daemon) that functions as an intermediary between client requests and the daemons. Linux systems also place a program named TCP Wrappers *(tcpd)* between the *inetd* server and the other server daemons.

Linux/UNIX file sharing is achieved either by using an FTP program or by using the Network File System (NFS). Server Message Block (SMB) is a client/server protocol for file sharing, printing, and login services that is commonly found in Windows. A share is a server resource such as a file or printer that is made available to SMB clients for network sharing. Windows XP includes SMB clients and servers that enable a user to create shared folders. The SMB server for the UNIX and Linux world is called Samba. Two daemons named *smbd* and *nmbd* implement most of Samba's key features.

Under Linux/UNIX, the default page description language is Postscript. A filter called Ghostscript is used to convert the Postscript document to a raster image for use by a specific, non-Postscript printer. When an application program issues a print command, a client-side operating system routine named *lpr* (line printer) transfers the file to a local (client-side) print server. The line printer daemon *(lpd)* either passes the print job to the appropriate local printer or to the remote (networked) computer to which the appropriate printer is attached. Common UNIX Printing System (CUPS) is a recommended replacement for traditional *lpd*-based print servers. In SMB, print shares behave very much like file shares.

Apache is a user-mode Web server daemon, a specific version of *httpd*. The overhead and communication that takes place between the user process and the kernel can be significantly reduced by running a kernel-based Web server such as *khttpd*. Apache supports a particularly robust server model called the pre-forking model. The Apache daemon uses a modular architecture. It is sometimes necessary for one module's output to be modified by another module using the UNIX filters concept.

A Beowulf cluster links multiple inexpensive computers in an effort to achieve the performance of a conventional supercomputer at a much lower price. A single system image (SSI) is a form of distributed computing in which multiple heterogeneous resources such as networks, distributed databases, or servers appear to the user as one, more-powerful, unified resource.

▮ Key Words

Apache	Internet printing protocol (IPP)
Beowulf cluster	line printer daemon (lpd)
cluster	Network File System (NFS)
Common UNIX Printing System (CUPS)	Postscript
	Postscript Printer Description (PPD)
daemon	pre-forking model
export	Samba
Ghostscript	Server Message Block (SMB)
httpd	share
inetd	single system image (SSI)

▮ Review Questions

1. What is a daemon? What is *httpd*?
2. What is *inetd*? What services are performed by *inetd*?
3. What functions are performed by TCP Wrappers?
4. How is file sharing achieved by Linux/UNIX?
5. What is the Network File System (NFS)? What is *knfsd*? What does the *k* imply?
6. NFS requests are stateless. What does that mean? Why is it significant?
7. What is the purpose of Server Message Block (SMB)? What is Samba? What is a share?
8. What functions are performed by *smbd* and *nmbd,* the two primary Samba daemons? What functions are performed by SWAT?
9. What is Postscript? What is Ghostscript? Why is something like Ghostscript necessary?
10. What does *lpd,* the line printer daemon, do?
11. What is the Common UNIX Printing System (CUPS)? What advantages are gained by replacing *lpd* with CUPS?
12. What is the Internet Printing Protocol (IPP)?
13. What is Apache? How is Apache related to *httpd*?
14. Why are kernel-based Web servers such as *khttpd* used? How do *khttpd* and a user-mode Web server such as Apache work together to fill page requests?
15. How does the Apache pre-forking model save time?
16. Why does a modular architecture make sense for a Web server like Apache?
17. What is the purpose of an Apache filter ?
18. What is a cluster?
19. What is a Beowulf cluster? Why are Beowulf clusters used?
20. What is a single system image? Distinguish between a single system image and a Beowulf cluster.

■ Exercises

1. Apache, a popular Web server that runs under Linux/UNIX powers more than half the Web sites in the world. However, most client computers run under Windows. Why do you suppose that is true?

2. Why do you suppose so many computing professionals prefer cryptic line commands to the more user-friendly interface provided by a GUI?

3. How is it possible to have a print server running on a client computer?

4. Distinguish between downstream and upstream. Why does a Web server host require faster upstream speed than a client?

5. Why would anyone want to create a Beowulf cluster?

6. Compare file sharing under the Common Internet File System (CIFS) described in Chapter 19 and Linux/UNIX Samba file sharing.

7. Compare Windows clustering from Chapter 19 to Linux/UNIX clustering.

8. Figures 20.2, 20.6, 20.12, and 20.18 are useful templates for organizing many of this chapter's key terms.

CHAPTER 21

Novell NetWare

When you finish reading this chapter you should be able to:

▶ Identify NetWare as the operating system on a Novell network server.

▶ Identify TCP/IP as NetWare's native protocols and briefly explain SPX/IPX.

▶ List the functions performed by the NetWare control protocol (NCP).

▶ Explain how the traditional Novell file system works.

▶ List several advantages of using Novell distributed print services (NDPS).

▶ Explain the purpose of Novell's directory services (NDS).

▶ Distinguish between a leaf object and a container object.

▶ Define a distinguished name.

▶ Distinguish between object rights and property rights.

▶ Describe the purpose of a network provider or network client.

◼ NetWare

Novell's **NetWare** is a commonly used networking operating system on local area networks. It provides robust services for the general business, including file services, print services, and application services. This chapter describes NetWare Version 5 and includes a section on NetWare 6.5.

NetWare is the server's operating system (Figure 21.1). Each client computer runs its own primary operating system (Windows XP, for example). A NetWare module runs under the client's operating system and communicates with NetWare on the server.

NetWare Kernel

NetWare's kernel (filename *server.exe*) runs on the server and provides such basic operating system functions as input/output management, interrupt processing, memory management, and thread and process management. The kernel (currently) can support up to 32 processors and can run on both multiprocessor and single-processor machines. It runs in protected mode at privilege level 0 on an Intel Pentium processor. Its scheduler provides for preemptive multitasking.

Networking Protocols

NetWare is based on the TCP/IP model (Chapter 17), and uses TCP and IP as its native protocols. Previous versions of NetWare used SPX/IPX, and NetWare continues to support these two protocols.

The **IPX** protocol occupies the Internet layer of the TCP/IP model and the network layer of the OSI model (Figure 21.2). Like IP (and similar protocols at this level), IPX addresses and routes packets from one location to another. IPX uses the address information in its header to forward the packet to its destination node or to the next router that provides a path to its destination.

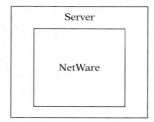
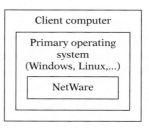

FIGURE 21.1

NetWare is the server's operating system. A NetWare module also runs on the client computer.

IPX provides a **connectionless datagram** service (as does IP). Datagram means each packet is independent of other packets and has no logical or sequential relationship with other packets. Connectionless means that when a process running on a particular node communicates with a process on another node, no connection is established between the two nodes. Consequently, when IPX packets are sent to their destination, successful delivery is not guaranteed.

Like TCP, **SPX** occupies the transport layer of both the TCP/IP model and the OSI model (Figure 21.2) and provides a virtual circuit or connection oriented service. **Connection oriented** implies that when SPX is used by a process on one node to communicate with a process on another node, a dedicated connection is established between the two nodes. Consequently, SPX guarantees delivery of packets to their destination and delivers them in their proper sequence. Since SPX carries a high overhead, NetWare avoids using it whenever possible.

Consistent with the TCP/IP model, the presentation and session layers are not present in NetWare. The data link and physical layers of the OSI model correspond to the physical layer in the TCP/IP model and are provided in the network interface cards.

The application layer is provided through the **NetWare control protocol (NCP)** (Figure 21.2), which enables NetWare clients and servers to communicate. NCP provides its own session control and sequence control, avoiding the overhead of SPX. The client issues NCP requests for file access and transfers, virtual drive mappings, directory searches, and so on. The server responds to these requests and replies to NCP. When the server finishes processing the request, the client terminates the connection. Under NetWare 5, NCP can run with either IPX or IP. If an IP connection is made, NCP uses TCP (transmission control protocol) for communication.

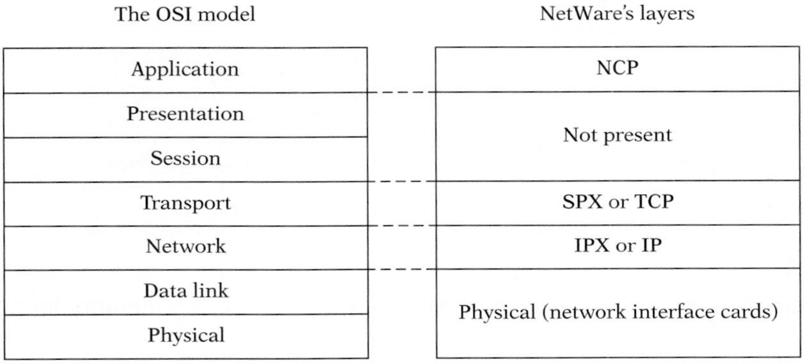

The OSI model	NetWare's layers
Application	NCP
Presentation	Not present
Session	
Transport	SPX or TCP
Network	IPX or IP
Data link	Physical (network interface cards)
Physical	

FIGURE 21.2

NetWare and the OSI model.

NetWare Loadable Modules

NetWare loadable modules (NLM) are object modules linkable at run time. They can be loaded and unloaded at will, and once loaded they become part of the network operating system. Many pieces of NetWare run as NetWare loadable modules, including software to support TCP/IP and printing services. In NetWare 5, NetWare loadable modules run in the protected address space at Pentium privilege level 3. Optionally, they can run at privilege level 0, along with the kernel.

Memory Architecture

NetWare is a 32-bit operating system and can access 4GB of address space. NetWare provides protected memory and uses Intel's logical memory addressing (Chapter 10). Page translation tables are used to translate logical addresses to physical addresses. NetWare also supports virtual memory and swaps least recently accessed pages to disk as needed.

NetWare keeps its kernel *(server.exe)* in memory and allocates the rest of the memory for cache (Figure 21.3). The cache is used for all the server's processing needs, such as creating protected address spaces, storing programs (including NetWare loadable modules), storing file and directory entries, and storing user data files. Memory is allocated from the cache when a program requires memory and is returned to the cache pool when the program releases the memory. Cache is always allocated as fixed 4KB pages called cache buffers.

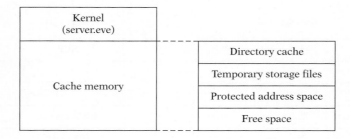

FIGURE 21.3
NetWare keeps its kernel in memory and allocates the rest of the memory for cache.

When the server receives a request for data on disk, it retrieves the data and stores it in a file cache buffer. The file cache buffers are organized to form a linked list. The most recently used buffer is placed at the head of the linked list and is stamped with the current time. As new buffers are added to the head of the list, the older buffers move down the list. Whenever the server requires a buffer, it retrieves the oldest buffer from the tail of the list, stores the new data in the buffer, and moves the buffer to the top of the list. When the server receives a request for data already in a cache buffer, it retrieves the data from the buffer, stamps the buffer with the new time, and moves the buffer to the head of the list. Consequently, the most recently used buffers are found at or near the top of the list and the least recently used buffers gather at the bottom.

A portion of the cache memory is used as the protected address space. The kernel's memory protection subsystem prevents a module in a protected address space from having direct access to anything outside its address space. All protected address spaces use virtual memory, and each one has its own page translation table to provide logical addressing. When data are moved from memory to disk they are stored in a swap file. The kernel is never swapped out of memory.

◼ File Systems

NetWare provides two compatible file systems that allow a user to store, access, retrieve, and manage data on the network using files: the traditional **NetWare file system** and **Novell Storage Services (NSS).** The basic object in either file system is a **volume,** a fixed amount of space on one or more disks. Physically, a volume is divided into segments, where a segment is an area of physical storage. The segments that make up a volume can reside on different physical devices. For example, a 32-segment volume can be physically stored on 32 different devices.

NetWare reads and writes data in blocks, where a block is the smallest number of bytes that is read from or written to the disk. The block size is determined at installation time, generally based on the size of the volume. The larger the volume size, the larger the block size.

Logically, a volume is divided (by network supervisors and users who have the appropriate rights) into directories that contain files and subdirectories (Figure 21.4). When the server is booted, the volume is mounted and becomes visible to users who log into the system.

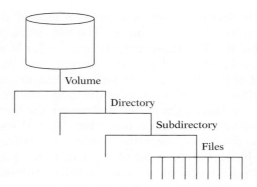

FIGURE 21.4

A volume is divided into directories that contain files and subdirectories.

The Traditional NetWare File System

Like MS-DOS (Chapter 11), NetWare maintains a file allocation table (FAT) to support allocating files on disk. The FAT is cached in RAM as long as the volume is mounted. Since the number of files on a volume can be large, NetWare caches the directory table on an as-needed basis, and caches the file entry whenever a file is opened. NetWare uses a least recently used algorithm to erase old entries from the caches. It relies on a hashing algorithm to improve initial search time through the directory table by constructing a numeric key for each file name and using the numeric key to locate the file.

A directory or a file is located by following its **path** (Figure 21.5). A fully defined path consists of the server name, the volume, the directory, any subdirectories, and the file name. Parameters are separated by backslashes, except for the volume and the directory, which are separated by a colon.

Since specifying such long names can become tedious, drive pointers or mappings are used to simplify file access. A **mapped drive** is a convenient way to reference a particular subdirectory on the network with a single letter. For example, if you map the letter Z to the MS-DOS subdirectory, instead of typing *Server\sys:Public\DOS* to fully specify the subdirectory, you can just type the letter Z followed by a colon (Z:). In effect, when you access the Z drive, you are really accessing the MS-DOS network subdirectory. Later in the chapter you will learn how to map drives.

---

servername\volume:directory\subdirectory\filename

FIGURE 21.5

A directory or a file is located by following its path.

Novell Storage Services

In addition to the traditional file system, NetWare supports Novell storage services (NSS), which enables the management of large files, volumes, name spaces, and storage devices. NSS uses a 64-bit file system and can support larger capacity disk drives than are prevalent today, with file sizes up to 8 terabytes, volumes that hold up to 8 trillion files, and up to 1 million open files per server. Free space on multiple disk drives can be combined to create a storage pool, and NSS volumes can be created within this storage pool. An additional advantage is that NSS volumes mount faster than traditional file systems while consuming less memory. For example, CD-ROMs can be mounted as NSS volumes, allowing faster access to multiple CDs in CD towers.

Disk Management

All disks on the server are managed by the NetWare operating system. Each server must contain at least one **NetWare partition** (Figure 21.6) that stores the system files using the traditional file system. Any unused space can be allocated to a **Novell storage services partition.** Additionally, at least one disk on the server must contain a **boot DOS partition.** The kernel file, *server.exe,* is stored in the boot partition. Each server must contain at least one NetWare partition that stores the system files using the traditional file system.

Fault Tolerant Features

NetWare has some built-in support for fault tolerance, the ability to recover from errors. **Disk duplexing** is the use of a redundant disk as a mirror. Everything written to the primary disk is also written to the redundant disk. If the primary disk fails, the system switches to the redundant disk. **Read after write** keeps data in the buffer after the write operation has completed. It then reads the data again and compares them against the buffer. If an error occurs, it rewrites the data. **Hot fix** detects the presence of bad sectors on the disk and moves the data from the defective area to an error-free location. These fault tolerant features must be turned on explicitly and work only in the traditional file system.

NSS partition
NetWare partition
Boot DOS partition

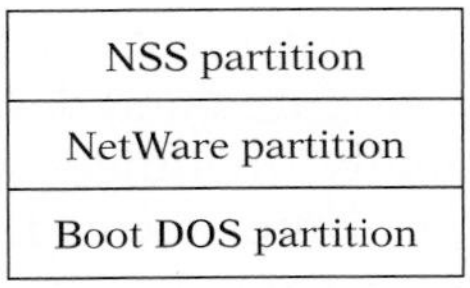

FIGURE 21.6
Hard disk partitions.

Storage Management Services

NetWare provides enhanced backup services, too. It can back up and restore files stored on the server or a client workstation to (or from) a target storage device. The files can be on a traditional NetWare file system, NSS, or client file systems. As a user, you must follow good backup practices, performing regular backups to ensure that critical data are never lost. Full backup ensures all the data are backed up. Differential (also known as incremental) backup backs up all data since the last full backup.

■ Printing Services

NetWare supports the traditional print queue-based printing and a new service called Novell distributed print services (NDPS).

Queue-Based Services

NetWare's queue-based print services use printers, print queues, and a print server. A print queue is essentially a subdirectory on a print server where the data are stored while waiting to be sent to a printer. The network administrator creates the queues and manages each individual printer separately. The user downloads and installs the driver needed for the central printer on his or her client machine. When a user prints from an application to a print queue, the data are sent directly to the queue or redirected from a local print port to a queue.

The redirection of printed data to a queue has several advantages. The user can resume working with the application without waiting for the print job to complete, print jobs can be sequenced so that higher priority jobs get routed to the printer first, and large print jobs can be stored and printed later.

Novell Distributed Print Services (NDPS)

Novell distributed print services (NDPS) allow the network administrator to manage network printing more efficiently than queue-based services. A system administrator creates a printer object as a resource on the network. Printers can be configured and designated for certain users, and drivers can be automatically installed and set up for the users. The administrator sets up a printer agent that allows a user to submit a job directly to the printer and enables bi-directional feedback between the client and the printer. Consequently, the client can check on the status of a print job, but the printer can also inform the client that toner is low, the paper tray is empty, and so on, and status messages can be routed to a third party or a printer administrator. NDPS also allows the client to schedule jobs on the printer based on time of day, job size, availability, and so on.

◼ Novell Directory Services

Novell directory services (NDS) is a method of storing and retrieving service and other information in a distributed database. Instead of keeping all the service information in the same location, each directory server contains a portion of the database. Each directory server, however, has access to all the service information in the entire directory database.

NDS is organized logically as a hierarchical database (a tree structure) and stored on the server (Figure 21.7). Network resources, such as disk volumes, printer agents, servers, users, and workstations, are represented as objects. Each of these objects has properties that define its characteristics, such as identification, login restriction, mailbox, rights to files and directories, and so on. Entries for these properties are known as values.

Network resources (such as those just identified) fall under the category of **leaf objects.** They are found at the end of the hierarchical tree structure. Organizational units, such as companies, divisions, and departments, are **container objects,** which contain other containers and leaf objects. They are used to divide and organize the tree structure into branches. Generally, the container objects mirror the business unit's organizational structure, although an exact match is not necessary.

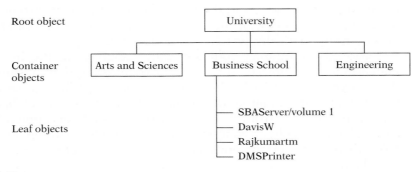

FIGURE 21.7
NDS is organized logically as a hierarchical database.

Novell directory services (NDS) objects are referenced by using their position in the tree. For example in Figure 21.7, user *DavisW* is in the container *Business School*, which is in the container *University*. Thus, users can be referenced by their **distinguished name,** such as *DavisW.Business School.University*.

Rights are associated with NDS objects. Whenever a user requests an NDS object, the system checks the user's rights before granting access. **Object rights** control what the user can do with an object, such as browse, create, rename, supervise, and so on. **Property rights** control access to information fields that define an object, such as supervise, read, write, and so on. Rights can be assigned to or denied to users, groups, or containers, and can be inherited. For example, if you specify rights at the container level, those rights flow to all the leaf objects in that container.

A **partition** is a logical division of the NDS tree that contains one or more complete branches. These partitions can be pruned and stored on different servers. The NDS tree might be partitioned on the basis of geographical location; for example, resources at the Los Angeles branch of a company might be in the Los Angeles tree and those at the Cincinnati branch might be in the Cincinnati tree. This arrangement provides better performance because Cincinnati users are most likely to use Cincinnati resources. However, because NDS is global, Cincinnati users can see and use the Los Angeles resources if needed.

Replication is the act of storing of a copy of an NDS partition on a different server. Replication provides for fault tolerance because the replicated copy can be used in case the primary server fails. Replication does not replicate the file system resources; only information about NDS is replicated.

Before a new user can access a Novell network, the network administrator must create an account for the user through Novell Directory Services. The first step is to identify the user's container and unique id (or login name) within the container. Then the login name, home directory, and additional parameters and properties are defined. The new user can also be assigned to one or more groups, and the user inherits all properties that are set for the group. For example, if the group has read access to certain folders, the new user automatically gets access to those folders.

NDS allows Internet addresses and resources on the Internet to be managed as NDS objects. It also allows each user to have a single login to the network. Once you log in at one location, you have access to all the servers and other resources to which you have rights. This global login feature saves the user from having to create multiple accounts on multiple servers. Additionally, if your network and desktop settings are stored in NDS, then your working environment can be recreated wherever you log into the network.

◾ Network Management

Zero Effort Networks (ZENworks) is the part of NetWare that supports desktop management. With ZENworks, the network administrator can use the Novell directory services to automate application management, remote management, and workstation management. These features reduce the time and effort a network administrator spends managing the network because they can solve many user problems without physically visiting the user's workstation.

Application management allows the administrator to distribute software and customize the software for each group or individual user. Applications can also be launched automatically by creating scheduled actions for users. **Workstation management** is the ability of the user's desktop to follow the user. This facility allows a user to log on at multiple clients; for example, a faculty member might log on through his or her office computer and also from a computer laboratory and see the same services at all locations. **Remote management** allows the network administrator to control the user's workstation remotely from his or her desktop to troubleshoot a problem.

◾ Novell Netware 6.5

NetWare 6.5 is the latest version of Novell NetWare. With this release, Novell addresses enterprise concerns such as strong support for Web application services, business continuity, and reliability with clusters and virtual office support.

Virtual office support provides a **portal** for end users. Using the portal, users access files and applications, print documents, and communicate with other team members via the Internet. Printing and sharing files are greatly simplified in NetWare 6.5; for example, with iPrint, users can print to any printer on the Internet. Users find their closest printer using Web pages set up by administrators, automatically download drivers and configure the printer, and print to the printer as if it were local. With iFolder, users can synchronize their files on any client device by accessing the NetWare server over the Internet. NetWare's iFolder provides a virtual centralized file repository. Every time the user logs in with the iFolder client, both client and server are checked for updates, and the data on the client device are synchronized with the server.

Novell directory services (NDS) has evolved to Novell eDirectory. NDS was originally restricted to managing users, servers, printers, print queues, and applications within NetWare. eDirectory can manage users, servers, printers, print queues, and applications not only within NetWare, but also within UNIX and Windows. It provides a single view for all the resources within an organization and provides a secure identity management that runs across multiple platforms. eDirectory provides both Web-based and wireless management capabilities, allowing all resources to be managed with a Web browser or a handheld device. The directory is physically stored as a set of database files on a server. Similar to NDS, the directory is organized in a tree structure.

In NetWare 6.5, Netware Storage Services (NSS) is robust and can recover fully after a system crash. NSS also allows storage devices to be added dynamically. NSS supports both directly attached storage (a hard disk connected to the server), and network attached storage (a dedicated data server that provides centralized storage access for users and application servers). NetWare provides preconfigured solutions for network attached storage that allow for Web-based sharing of and access to files using a variety of protocols, and browsers.

NetWare 6.5 provides Novell **cluster** services to manage clusters that combine two or more servers into a single group. If one server in the cluster should fail, another server automatically takes over for the downed server and runs in its place. The second server recovers the downed server's applications, services, IP addresses, and volumes, so users are not aware of the failure of the first server. NetWare 6.5 has the capability to cluster up to 32 Netware servers into a single high availability group. The workload can be balanced among the NetWare servers in the cluster, and resources can be dynamically allocated to any server in the cluster. Figure 21.8 shows an example of a cluster using a shared disk system.

NetWare 6.5 includes Novell Web and Application services (NWAS), a mix of open source and Novell products integrated within NetWare that uses Apache 2.0 (Chapter 20) as its basic Web server. Apache is available as a custom NetWare loadable module and is tightly integrated with eDirectory. In addition, NWAS also supports Secure Sockets Layer encryption. The integration of Apache with eDirectory and SSL provides a secure means of sharing company information over the Internet. Other supported open source products include the MySql database management system, the PHP scripting language, and the Tomcat server, which can host Java server pages. These open source products are enhanced with Novell's NetWare Web Search Server (NWSS), which lets you add search and print functionality to any Web site in your organization. Additionally, for high end application server needs (for example, complex Java API support), NetWare includes the ExteNd Application server. The Apache Web server is also used internally within NetWare to provide Web-based administration to eDirectory, Novell Storage solution, and other services.

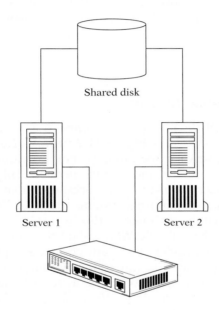

FIGURE 21.8
A shared volume cluster.

Novell and Linux

In November 2003, Novell announced plans to acquire Suse, a major Linux vendor, and to support Novell services on Linux. Earlier in the year (August 2003), Novell acquired another Linux vendor, Ximian, and ported Novell's e-mail system, Groupwise, to run on the Linux platform. The latest acquisition will allow eDirectory, Novell storage, and print solutions all to be available on the Linux platform. These acquisitions appear to be consistent with Novell's usage of high quality open source products, enhanced by the company's own products.

◼ Using NetWare

An excellent way to grasp how NetWare works is to use it to perform a few simple operations. With your instructor's permission, much of the balance of this chapter can be run as a tutorial similar to the chapters in Part 3. Note, however, that (for security reasons) many network administrators prefer that students not work directly with network commands.

The Client/Server Structure

The structure of the client/server connection that will be used to illustrate this example is shown as Figure 21.9. Novell's NetWare (as outlined in this chapter) is the server's operating system, providing print services, management services, and file and storage services, all coordinated by NetWare directory services. Your (client) workstation can run under any of several different primary operating systems, such as Windows or UNIX/Linux. Windows XP will be assumed in this example.

A subset of Novell's NetWare called the **network provider** or the **network client** runs under the client computer's primary operating system. The network provider is integrated within the desktop environment of Windows. When a user accesses a Novell NetWare network through *Explorer* or *My Computer* or *My Network Places,* the information is routed to the Novell network provider.

The network provider is a dynamic link library that uses the network redirector (Figure 21.9, client operating system) to access services from the network. The redirector is a file system driver under the I/O manager services of Windows XP. The redirector sends information to and returns information from the NetWare network to the provider. The provider and redirector together form the Novell client and provide access to the NetWare network, making it possible to perform network functions via the familiar Windows interfaces.

This section illustrates the use of the Novell client running under Windows XP to perform some simple and standard operations with the NetWare operating system. Since every network is unique, you might have to adapt the material to the specific situation in your lab. Finally, please do not perform these functions without the explicit permission of your instructor or system administrator.

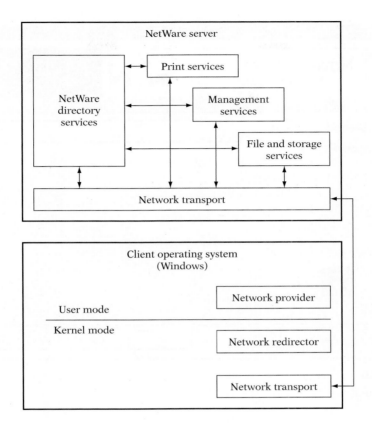

FIGURE 21.9
The client/server connection.

Logging In

In order to access the network, you must first login (Figure 21.10), generally to a Novell directory services tree rather than a specific server. The login step enables NDS to authenticate you once and use that authentication to provide access to any and all resources on the network for which you have rights. If the machine is already on, you can get to the login prompt by clicking on

Start/All Programs/Novell (Common)/Novell Login

(Figure 21.11). Enter your *userid* and *password,* and click *OK* to login to the network.

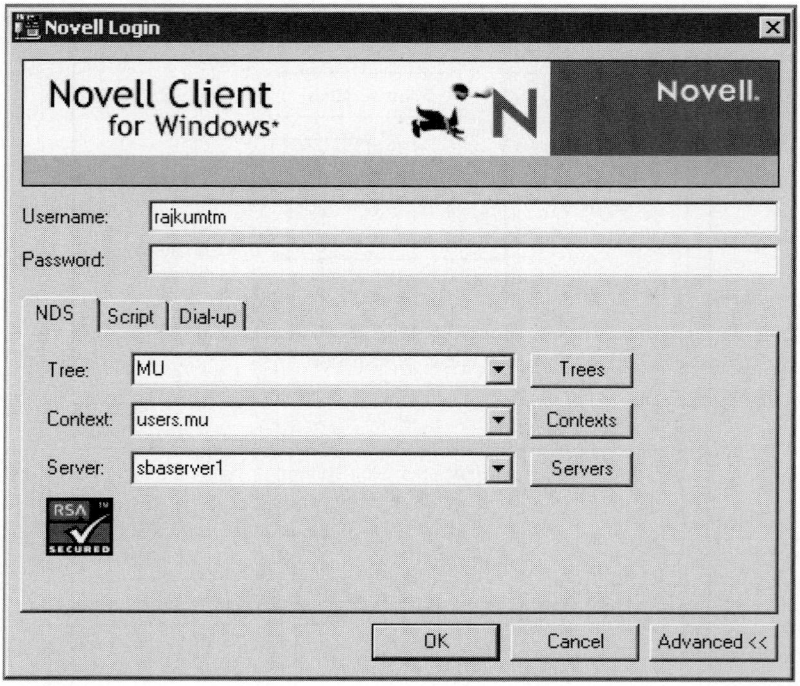

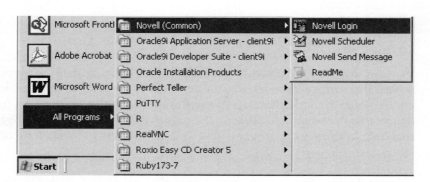

FIGURE 21.10
The login screen.

FIGURE 21.11
The path to the login screen.

Accessing Network Resources Using My Network Places

My Network Places allows you to browse resources on the entire network, be they Windows 2003 servers, Novell servers, or the Internet. Click the *Start/My Network Places* icon on the desktop (Figure 21.12) to open *My Network Places* (Figure 21.13). Open the *Tools* menu and click on the *Folder* options to bring up the *Options* window (Figure 21.14) and ensure that *Open each folder in same Window* is selected under the *Browse Folder* options. Then click *OK*.

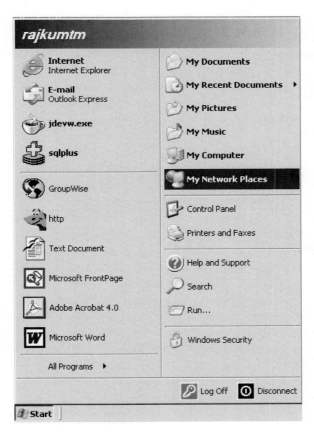

FIGURE 21.12

My Network Places.

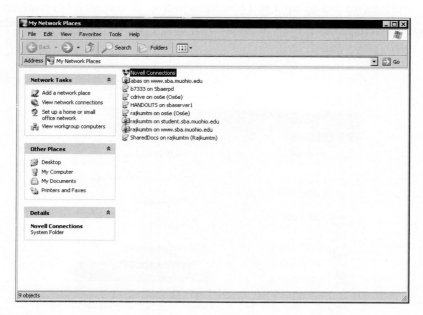

FIGURE 21.13
The *My Network Places* screen.

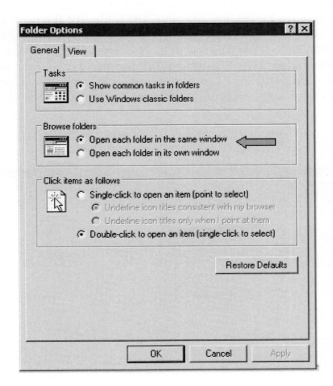

FIGURE 21.14

The *Options* window.

Double click on *Novell Connections* (Figure 21.13) to display the available trees. Select a tree that you know you have access to (Figure 21.15) and open it. (For example, the authors selected *MU* for Miami University; ask your instructor for help if necessary.) *Double click* on the organizational unit container (screen not shown) that holds your server. The authors selected SBA (for School of Business Administration). Then select your server (Figure 21.16). For example, the folder for the primary student server at Miami University is found in the SBA container and is called SBASERVER1_SYS. Your system is likely to be different, so please check with your instructor for information on what container, server, and folder to use. Generally, you can choose any sys folder for a server, because all servers have a sys folder that contains NetWare system files.

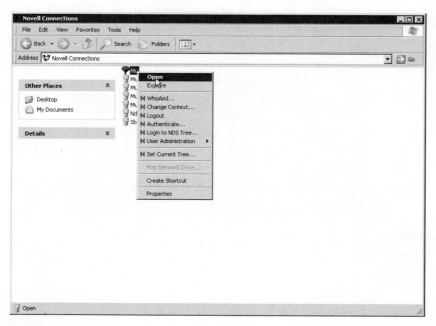

FIGURE 21.15

Novell Connections.

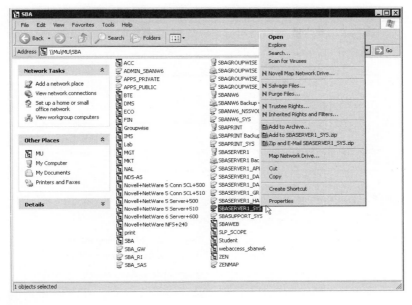

FIGURE 21.16

The authors' server.

Mapping a Network Drive

Once you have identified the server and system folder, *right click* on the folder (Figure 21.16) and you will see a variety of Novell client options. Choose *Novell Map Network Drive* and the system will allow you to map the drive (Figure 21.17). The system (by default) picks the first available letter. To be consistent, please use the pull down menu for drives and choose *O* as the drive letter to map. To add drive *O* to the search path, click on the check box *Map Search Drive*. Then click on Map, to map the drive, and the network drive *sbaserver1_sys* is available to you as your *O:* drive (Figure 21.18). You can then open folders and work with the *O* drive using *My Computer* or *Explorer*.

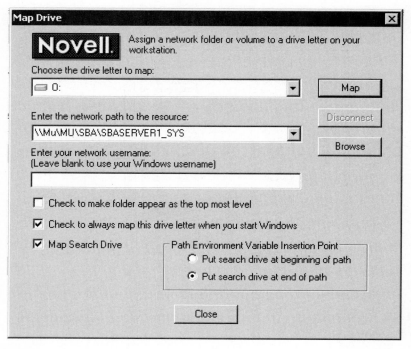

FIGURE 21.17

Mapping a drive.

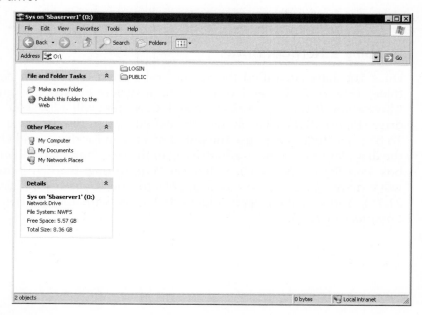

FIGURE 21.18

It is now the O drive.

Volume Information

Click on *Start/All Programs/Accessories/Windows Explorer* to open *Explorer*. Note that the mapped drive *O* created earlier is now visible on the left panel (Figure 21.19). *Right click* on the *O* drive to bring up the menu (Figure 21.20) and choose *Properties* to see the general volume information for this folder (Figure 21.21). The *General tab* shows the file system in use (NWFS) and the amount of used and available disk space. Click on some of the other tabs and browse through the information provided. Click on *Cancel* to close the properties window.

Mapping with *Explorer*

You can also map drives with Windows *Explorer*. Choose *Tools/Map Drive* from the *Explorer* menu to bring up the map screen (Figure 21.22). Note that the next drive, *P,* is selected by default. Click on *Browse* and then click on *Novell Connections* (Figure 21.23) to browse for your data folder. (If necessary, check with your instructor to identify your data folder.) In contrast, to the sys folder, you can read, write, and share files on your data folder. Click *OK* to select your data folder. Then click *Finish* to map it.

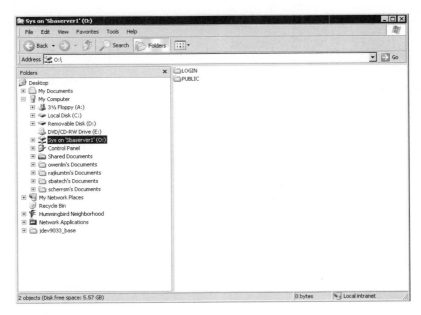

FIGURE 21.19

The mapped drive on *Explorer*.

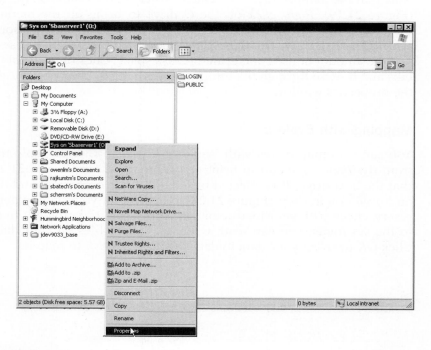

FIGURE 21.20

Select *Properties*.

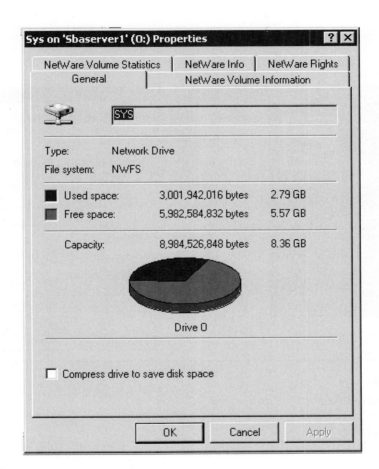

FIGURE 21.21
General information about the *O* drive.

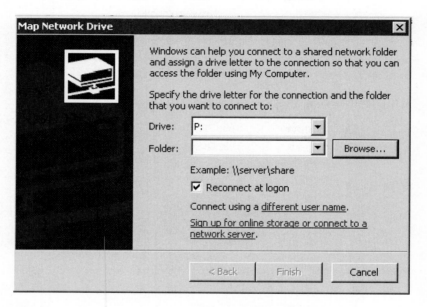

FIGURE 21.22

Mapping drives with Windows *Explorer*.

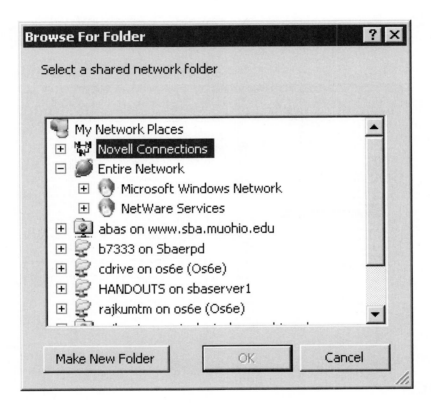

FIGURE 21.23
Browsing for your data folder.

Disconnecting a Mapped Drive

To disconnect from a mapped drive, choose *Tools/Disconnect Networked Drive* (Figure 21.24). The resulting screen lists all networked drives (Figure 21.25). Select drive *P*, and click on *OK* to remove the mapping. Choose *View/Refresh* from the *Explorer* menu to repaint the screen and show that the mapping has been removed. Repeat these steps for drive *O*.

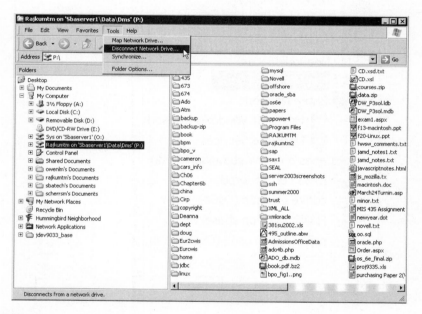

FIGURE 21.24

Disconnecting from a mapped drive.

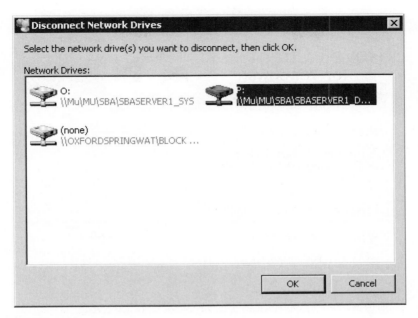

FIGURE 21.25
All networked drives.

Logging Out

To log out from the network, click on *Start/Windows Security* to bring up the Netware security window (Figure 21.26). Click on *logout* to log out of Novell and Windows. The system will ask for confirmation. Choose *OK* to close all active applications, log you out, and return you to the *Novell Login* Window.

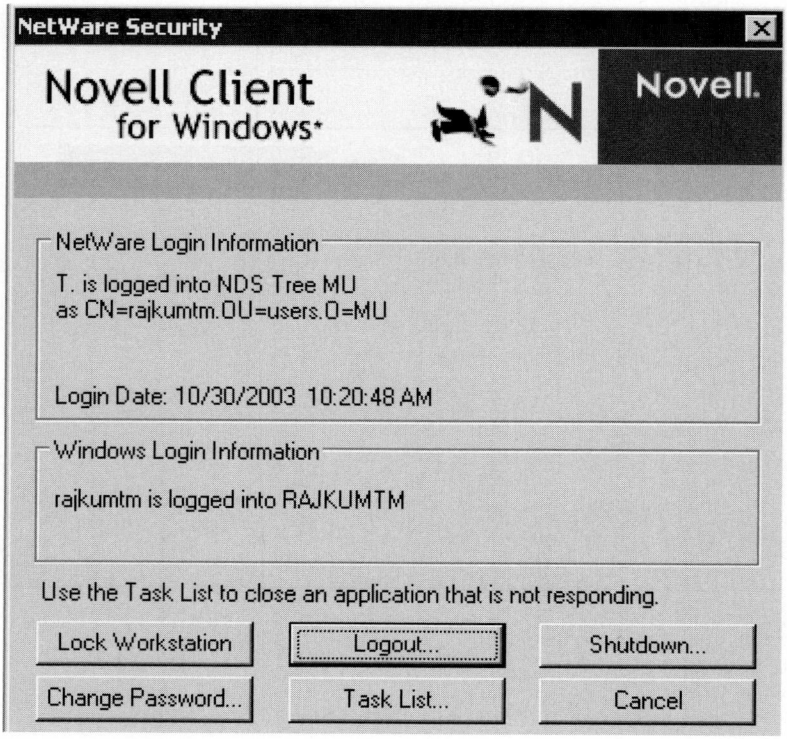

FIGURE 21.26
Logging out.

▣ Summary

Novell's NetWare is a common local area network operating system. NetWare's kernel runs on the server and provides basic operating system functions. The Internet protocols (TCP and IP) are NetWare's native protocols, but previous versions used SPX/IPX. The application layer is provided through the NetWare control protocol (NCP). NetWare loadable modules (NLM) are object modules linkable at run time. NetWare is a 32-bit operating system and can access 4GB of address space. NetWare keeps its kernel in memory and allocates the rest of the memory for cache. A portion of the cache memory is used as the protected address space.

The basic object in a Novell file system is a volume. In the traditional NetWare file system, NetWare maintains a file allocation table (FAT) to support allocating files on a disk volume and caches the directory table on an as-needed basis. A directory or a file is located by following its path. A mapped drive is a convenient way to reference a particular subdirectory on the network with a single letter. A search path is a path to a directory on another computer. Novell Storage Services (NSS) enables the management of large files, volumes, name spaces, and storage devices.

All disks on the server are managed by NetWare. NetWare's queue-based print services use printers, print queues, and a print server. Novell distributed print services (NDPS) allows the network administrator to manage network printing more efficiently than queue-based services.

Novell directory services (NDS) is a method of storing and retrieving service and other information in a distributed database. Network resources, found at the end of a hierarchical tree structure, are called leaf objects. Organizational units, such as companies, divisions, and departments, are container objects used to divide and organize the tree structure into branches. Users can be referenced by their distinguished name.

Object rights control what the user can do with an object, such as browse, create, rename, supervise, and so on. Property rights control access to information fields that define an object, such as supervise, read, write, and so on. A partition is a logical division of the NDS tree containing one or more complete branches. Replication is the act of storing a copy of an NDS partition on a different server. Before a new user can access a Novell network, the network administrator must create an account for the user through Novell Directory Services. Zero Effort Networks (ZENworks) is the part of NetWare that supports desktop management. NetWare 6.5 is Novell's latest version.

A subset of Novell's NetWare called the network provider or the network client runs under the client computer's primary operating system. The chapter ended with a brief example using NetWare.

▌ Key Words

application management
boot DOS partition
cluster
connectionless datagram
connection oriented
container object
disk duplexing
distinguished name
hot fix
IPX
leaf object
mapped drive
NetWare
NetWare control protocol (NCP)
NetWare file system
NetWare loadable module (NLM)
NetWare partition

network client, or network provider
Novell directory services (NDS)
Novell distributed print services (NDPS)
Novell storage services (NSS)
Novell storage services partition
object rights
partition
path
portal
property rights
read after write
remote management
replication
SPX
volume
workstation management
Zero Effort Networks (ZENworks)

◼ Review Questions

1. What is the operating system on a Novell network server? What operating system(s) can be used on the client computers?
2. What are NetWare's native protocols? What is SPX/IPX?
3. What functions are performed by the NetWare control protocol (NCP)?
4. Explain the purpose of cache buffers. Explain how file cache buffers work.
5. Briefly explain how the traditional Novell file system works. What is a mapped drive?
6. What is fault tolerance? Briefly explain several fault tolerance techniques.
7. Explain how queue-based print services work.
8. What advantages (over traditional queue-based print services) are gained by using Novell distributed print services (NDPS)?
9. Briefly explain the purpose of Novell directory services (NDS).
10. Distinguish between a leaf object and a container object.
11. What is a distinguished name?
12. Distinguish between object rights and property rights.
13. What is a network provider or network client?
14. What is the purpose of ZENworks?
15. Briefly outline the key differences between NetWare Version 5 and NetWare 6.5

◼ Exercises

1. Turn back to Figure 17.12 and review the seven-layer OSI model. Then relate the OSI model to the NetWare architecture.
2. Apache, a popular Web server that runs under Linux/UNIX and is available under NetWare, powers more than half the Web sites in the world. However, most client computers run Windows. Why do you suppose that is true?
3. With your instructor's permission, complete the brief tutorial at the end of the chapter. What container, server, and folder did you use? Note any interesting properties associated with the drive you mapped. What data folder did you map with *Explorer?*
4. Figure 21.9 is a useful template for organizing at least some of this chapter's key terms.

Number Systems, Data Types, and Codes

◼ Number Systems

A decimal number consists of a series of digits (0, 1, 2, 3, 4, 5, 6, 7, 8, 9) written in precise relative positions. The positions are important; for example, although they contain the same two digits, 23 and 32 are clearly different numbers because the digits are in different relative positions. The value of a given number is found by multiplying each digit by its place or positional value and adding the products. For example, 3582 represents:

$$
\begin{array}{rrr}
3 \text{ times} & 1000 = & 3000 \\
+5 \text{ times} & 100 = & 500 \\
+8 \text{ times} & 10 = & 80 \\
+2 \text{ times} & 1 = & 2 \\
\hline
& & 3582
\end{array}
$$

Generally, any number's value is the sum of the products of its digit and place values.

Take a close look at the decimal place values 1, 10, 100, 1000, 10000, and so on. The pattern is obvious. Rather than writing all those zeros, you can use scientific notation, for example, writing 10000 as 10^4. Because any number raised to the zero power is (by definition) 1, you can write the decimal place values as the base (10) raised to a series of integer powers:

$$\ldots\ 10^8\ \ 10^7\ \ 10^6\ \ 10^5\ \ 10^4\ \ 10^3\ \ 10^2\ \ 10^1\ \ 10^0$$

A few general rules can be derived from this discussion of decimal numbers. First is the idea of place or positional value represented by the base (10) raised to a series of integer powers. The second is the use of the digit zero (0) to represent "nothing" in a given position. (How else could you distinguish 3 from 30?) Third, a total of ten digits (0 through 9) are needed to write decimal values. Finally, only values less than the base (in this case, 10) can be written with a single digit.

Binary Numbers

There is nothing to restrict the application of these rules to a base-10 number system. If the positional values are powers of 2, you have the framework of a binary or base-2 number system:

$$... \quad 2^8 \quad 2^7 \quad 2^6 \quad 2^5 \quad 2^4 \quad 2^3 \quad 2^2 \quad 2^1 \quad 2^0$$

As in any number system, the digit zero (0) is needed to represent nothing in a given position. Additionally, the binary number system needs only one other digit, 1. Given these digit and place values, you can find the value of any number by multiplying each digit by its place value and adding these products. For example, the binary number 1100011 is:

$$
\begin{aligned}
& 1 \text{ times } 2^6 = 1 \text{ times } 64 = 64 \\
+\, & 1 \text{ times } 2^5 = 1 \text{ times } 32 = 32 \\
+\, & 0 \text{ times } 2^4 = 0 \text{ times } 16 = 0 \\
+\, & 0 \text{ times } 2^3 = 0 \text{ times } 8 = 0 \\
+\, & 0 \text{ times } 2^2 = 0 \text{ times } 4 = 0 \\
+\, & 1 \text{ times } 2^1 = 1 \text{ times } 2 = 2 \\
+\, & 1 \text{ times } 2^0 = 1 \text{ times } 1 = \underline{1} \\
& \phantom{1 \text{ times } 2^0 = 1 \text{ times } 1 =} 99
\end{aligned}
$$

The decimal number 2 is 10 in binary; the decimal number 4 is 100. Decimal 5 is 101 (1 four, 0 twos, and 1 one).

Octal and Hexadecimal

Other number systems, notably octal (base 8) and hexadecimal (base 16) are commonly used with computers. The octal number system uses powers of 8 to represent positional values and the digit values 0, 1, 2, 3, 4, 5, 6, and

7. The hexadecimal number system uses powers of 16 and the digits 0, 1, 2, 3, 4, 5, 6, 7, 8, 9, A, B, C, D, E, and F. The hexadecimal number FF is:

$$
\begin{array}{rl}
15 \text{ times } 16^1 = & 240 \\
+15 \text{ times } 16^0 = & \underline{15} \\
& 255
\end{array}
$$

There are no computers that work directly with octal or hex; a computer is a binary machine. These two number systems are used simply because it is easy to convert between them and binary. Each octal digit is exactly equivalent to three binary digits (Figure A.1); each hexadecimal digit is exactly equivalent to four binary digits (Figure A.2). Thus, octal and hex can be used as shorthand for displaying binary values.

Octal	Binary	Octal	Binary
0	000	4	100
1	001	5	101
2	010	6	110
3	011	7	111

FIGURE A.1

Each octal digit is exactly equivalent to three binary digits.

Hex	Binary	Hex	Binary
0	0000	8	1000
1	0001	9	1001
2	0010	A	1010
3	0011	B	1011
4	0100	C	1100
5	0101	D	1101
6	0110	E	1110
7	0111	F	1111

FIGURE A.2

Each hexadecimal is exactly equivalent to four binary digits.

◼ Data Types

The binary patterns stored inside a computer can be interpreted as several different data types.

Numeric Data

Because binary numbers are so well suited to electronic devices, computers are at their most efficient when working with pure binary values. A typical computer is designed around a basic unit of binary data called a word (usually 16, 32, or 64 bits). Normally, the high-order bit is set aside to hold a sign (0 for +, 1 for -), and the remaining bits are data bits. For example, the biggest binary value that can be stored on a 32-bit word computer is

0111 1111 1111 1111 1111 1111 1111 1111

which is 2,147,483,647 in decimal. The limit on a 16-bit machine is

0111 1111 1111 1111

or 32,767 in decimal. There is no provision for a decimal point. Decimal point alignment is the programmer's responsibility.

Binary integers are fine for many applications, but at times very large, very small, and fractional numbers are needed. With scientific notation, numbers are written as a decimal fraction followed by a power of 10; for example, the speed of light, 186,000 miles per second, is written as 0.186×10^6. Many computers can store and manipulate binary approximations of scientific numbers called real or floating-point numbers.

Certain applications, particularly business applications, demand precisely rounded decimal numbers. While any data type will do for whole numbers or integers, floating-point and binary numbers provide at best a close approximation to decimal fractions. Thus, many computers support a form of decimal data. Generally, computers are at their least efficient when processing decimal data.

String Data

Computers are not limited to storing and manipulating numbers. For example, many applications call for such data as names, addresses, and product descriptions. These string values (sometimes called character values) are typically stored as sets of individual characters, with each character represented by a code. Most modern computers use the ASCII code (Figure A.3). On many computers, a single coded character occupies one byte, so the name *Lopez* would be stored in five consecutive bytes.

It is important to note that strings and numbers are different. For example, if you type the digit 1 followed by the digit 2, each character will be stored as a 1-byte string in memory. On a computer that uses the ASCII code, these two characters would appear as:

00110001 00110010

That is *not* the number 12. On a 16-bit computer, a pure binary 12 is stored as

0000000000001100

(Try using the "digit-times-place-value" rule.)

Character	ASCII	Character	ASCII
0	0011 0000	I	0100 1001
1	0011 0001	J	0100 1010
2	0011 0010	K	0100 1011
3	0011 0011	L	0100 1100
4	0011 0100	M	0100 1101
5	0011 0101	N	0100 1110
6	0011 0110	O	0100 1111
7	0011 0111	P	0101 0000
8	0011 1000	Q	0101 0001
9	0011 1001	R	0101 0010
A	0100 0001	S	0101 0011
B	0100 0010	T	0101 0100
C	0100 0011	U	0101 0101
D	0100 0100	V	0101 0110
E	0100 0101	W	0101 0111
F	0100 0110	X	0101 1000
G	0100 0111	Y	0101 1001
H	0100 1000	Z	0101 1010

FIGURE A.3

The ASCII code for digits and uppercase letters.

Numbers and strings are different. That is why programmers and even spreadsheet users must distinguish strings from numbers. The positional value of each digit in a number is significant. In contrast, as you move from byte to byte, the positional values of the individual bits have no meaning in a string. (The order of the bits is significant, but defined by the code.)

Data normally enter a computer through an input device in string form. Most computers have special instructions to convert strings to numbers. Arithmetic operations are performed on the numbers, and the results are converted back to string form before they are sent to an output device. Most programming languages automatically perform these data type conversions for you. Assembler languages are an exception.

Images

Imagine laying a fine screen over a line drawing, chart, graph, photograph, or similar image. Each hole in the screen is one dot, or pixel, and numbers can be used to record each pixel's brightness, color, and other appearance parameters. For example, visualize an electronic scoreboard that displays the score by turning on and off selected light bulbs to form a pattern. Represent each unlit bulb as a 0 and each lit bulb as a 1, string those bits together, and you have a good mental model of a digital image.

A bitmap or raster image is a digital version of that dot pattern stored in memory. Bitmaps can be very large. For example, at one byte per pixel, a high-resolution, 1024 by 768 pixel bitmap occupies 786,432 bytes of memory. Such large files can quickly fill a hard drive and slow the download process.

To save space, bitmaps are usually compressed. Some compression algorithms, such as GIF (graphics interchange format) are lossless; in other words, following compression they retain every bit in the original bitmap. Others, such as JPEG (Joint Photographic Experts Group) are lossy—they lose some content during the compression process. Generally, lossy algorithms yield smaller files.

Rather than storing bitmaps, vector graphics relies on geometric formulas to represent images; Macromedia's Flash (SFW) format is an example. Prior to displaying or printing an image, the necessary pixel or dot values are computed from the formulas. Because the formulas require less space than an equivalent bitmap, a vector graphics file requires less memory and downloads faster than an equivalent raster graphics image. It is difficult to define a set of formulas for a complex image such as a photograph, however, so vector graphics is used primarily for lines and geometric shapes.

Figure A.4 lists several common graphics formats.

Extension	Description
AVI	Microsoft's audio video interleaved format. Used for movies and videos, with soundtrack. Access through Windows Media Player.
BMP	Microsoft Windows bitmap. No compression.
GIF	Graphics interchange format. A de facto Web standard developed by CompuServe for compressing bitmapped graphics and pictures. Lossless. Limited to 256 colors.
JPG or JPEG	Joint Photographic Experts Group. A de facto Web standard for compressing bitmapped still images and photographs. Lossy.
MOV	QuickTime movie file. The Apple Macintosh video format, now supported by Windows.
MPG or MPEG	Motion Picture Experts Group. A highly compressed format for storing movies.
PDF	Portable Document Format. Adobe Acrobat's page definition format. Download Acrobat Reader to view a PDF file.
PNG	Portable network graphics. A proposed replacement for GIF. Lossless, with better compression than GIF.
QTW	QuickTime for Windows. Movie files.
SVC	Scalable vector graphics. An open, XML-based vector graphics standard.
SWF	Macromedia Shockwave Flash file. Flash is a proprietary, scalable, vector graphics file format. Requires a downloadable plug-in.
TIF or TIFF	Tagged image (or information) file format. A bitmap format popular in desktop publishing applications. No compression.

FIGURE A.4

Some common graphics formats.

Note that AVI, MPEG, and QTM (Figure A.4) incorporate a sound track.

◼ Sounds

The idea of representing a visual image as a pattern of dots makes sense to most people, but sounds are different. By their very nature, sound waves are continuous (analog), not discrete (digital). How can sound be digitized?

Sound is digitized through a sampling process. Imagine turning a microphone on and off thousands of times per second. During the time the microphone is on, it captures a brief pulse of sound, and for each sound pulse such parameters as tone, pitch, frequency, and so on are represented as numbers. Later, playing back the sound pulses in the proper order reproduces the original samples, and as long as the time between samples is sufficiently short, a human listener hears continuous sound.

Audio files can be huge. For example, to create an audio CD, the sound is sampled 44,100 times per second. Two bytes are used to store the information generated by each sample, so one second of sound consumes 88.2 KB and each minute fills 5.292 MB (that's megabytes) of storage. Consequently, audio files are almost always compressed. Figure A.5 lists several common audio formats.

Extension	Description
AIF	Audio interchange format. An Apple Macintosh format.
AU	Audio file. An early Internet sound format.
MID or MIDI	Musical instrument digital interface. Access through Windows Media Player.
MP3	MPEG, audio layer 3. MP3 uses a compression algorithm that shrinks CD-level sound files by a factor of 12 with no loss in sound quality. A popular format for swapping audio files.
RA or RAM	RealAudio file. Used for Internet streamed audio and video.
WAV	Waveform. Sound file for Windows. Access through Windows Media Player and Sound Recorder.

FIGURE A.5

Some common audio formats.

Summary of MS-DOS Commands

◼ General

▶ Command format

```
d>COMMAND parameters
```

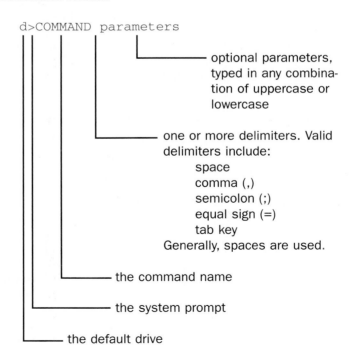

optional parameters, typed in any combination of uppercase or lowercase

one or more delimiters. Valid delimiters include:
space
comma (,)
semicolon (;)
equal sign (=)
tab key
Generally, spaces are used.

the command name

the system prompt

the default drive

▶ Rules for defining a file name

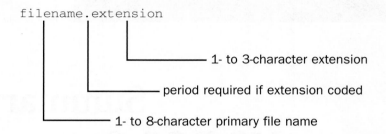

`filename.extension`

1- to 3-character extension

period required if extension coded

1- to 8-character primary file name

▶ legal characters

A-Z a-z 0-9 $ & # % ' ( ) @ ^ { } ~ ` ! _

▶ illegal characters

? . , ; : = * / \ + " < >

▶ lowercase letters converted to uppercase

▶ primary file name padded with spaces to 8 characters

▶ extension padded with spaces to 3 characters

▶ wild-card characters

? any single character

* any group of 1 to 8 characters

▶ Rules for defining path names

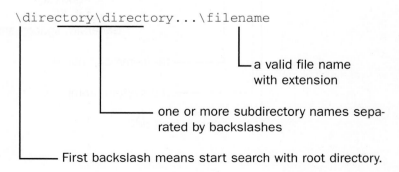

`\directory\directory...\filename`

a valid file name
with extension

one or more subdirectory names separated by backslashes

First backslash means start search with root directory.

▶ To define a subdirectory name, use the rules for defining a file name without an extension.

▶ Maximum path name length is 64 characters.

▶ If path name does not start with a backslash, search begins with current working directory.

▶ Reserved device names

CON   PRN   LPT1   AUX   COM1

LPT2   LPT3   COM2   NUL   CLOCK$

▶ Conventional file name extensions

ASM	assembler source	EXE	executable file
BAK	backup file	FOR	FORTRAN source
BAS	BASIC source	LIB	library source
BAT	batch file	LST	ASCII list file
BIN	binary file	MAP	ASCII load module
COB	COBOL source	OBJ	object module
COM	command file	OVR	overlay file
DAT	ASCII data file	REF	cross reference
DIF	difference file	TMP	temporary link
DOC	ASCII document	$$$	temporary work
DVD	device driver		

▶ Redirection parameters

Parameter	Meaning	Example
<	Change source to a specified file or device.	<MYFILE.DAT
>	Change destination to a specified file or device.	>PRN
>>	Change destination, usually to an existing file, and append new output to it.	>>HOLD.DAT
|	Pipe standard output to another command or to a filter.	DIR | MORE

■ Selected Commands

▶ CHDIR changes the current working directory.

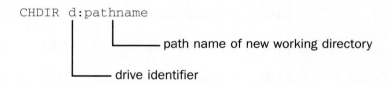

```
CHDIR d:pathname
```
path name of new working directory

drive identifier

▶ . designates the current working directory.

▶ .. is the parent of the current working directory.

▶ CHDIR with no parameters displays name of current working directory.

▶ **CHKDSK** checks a disk's directory and reports on its contents.

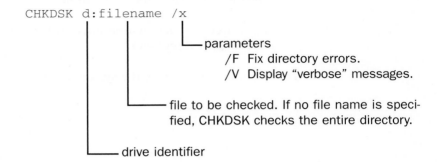

▶ **CLS** clears the screen.

CLS (no parameters)

▶ **COMP** compares two files.

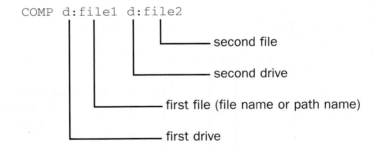

COMP is often used after **COPY** to verify results.

▶ **COPY** copies one or more files from a source to a destination.

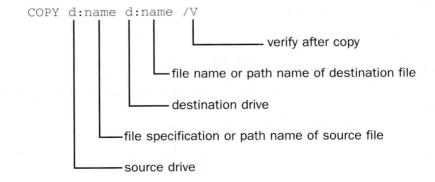

▶ If the destination file name is blank, the source file name is used and the drives must be different.

▶ The source and destination must differ in some way (file name, drive, and/or directory).

▶ DATE checks and/or sets the system date.

```
DATE

DATE mm-dd-yy
```

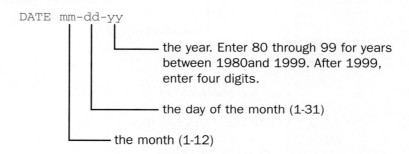

the year. Enter 80 through 99 for years between 1980and 1999. After 1999, enter four digits.

the day of the month (1-31)

the month (1-12)

▶ DIR displays a directory's contents.

```
DIR d:name /x
```

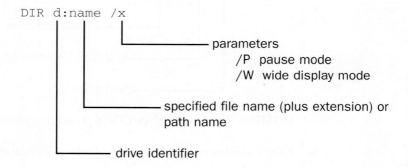

parameters
/P pause mode
/W wide display mode

specified file name (plus extension) or path name

drive identifier

▶ Default drive selection

A: selects drive **A**.
B: selects drive **B**, and so on.

▶ DISKCOMP compares the contents of two complete diskettes.

```
DISKCOMP d: d:
```

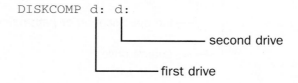

second drive

first drive

▸ Note: a /V option on a DISKCOPY command implies DISKCOMP.

▸ **DISKCOPY** copies the contents of one disk to another.

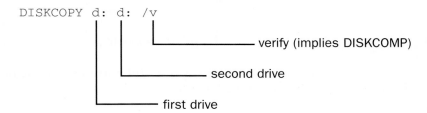

```
DISKCOPY d: d: /v
```
verify (implies DISKCOMP)
second drive
first drive

▸ **ECHO** controls the display of batch file commands and displays comments on the screen.

```
ECHO ON          commands displayed
ECHO OFF         commands not displayed
ECHO message     message displayed
```

▸ **ERASE** (or **DEL**) erases a file or files.

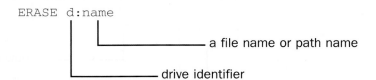

```
ERASE d:name
```
a file name or path name
drive identifier

▸ **FORMAT** formats a disk.

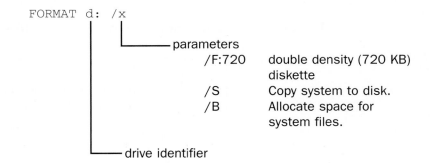

```
FORMAT d: /x
```
parameters
/F:720   double density (720 KB) diskette
/S   Copy system to disk.
/B   Allocate space for system files.
drive identifier

▶ **MKDIR** creates a new directory.

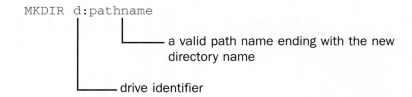

MKDIR d:pathname

a valid path name ending with the new directory name

drive identifier

▶ **RECOVER** salvages useful portions of a file or files on a disk containing bad sectors.

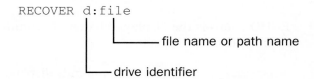

RECOVER d:file

file name or path name

drive identifier

▶ Note: if no file is specified, all files stored on the specified or default disk are recovered.

▶ **RENAME** (or **REN**) renames an existing file.

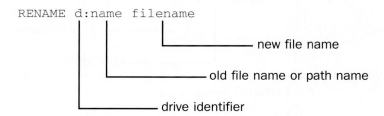

RENAME d:name filename

new file name

old file name or path name

drive identifier

▶ **RMDIR** (or **RD**) removes the specified directory.

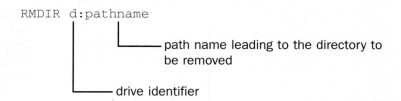

RMDIR d:pathname

path name leading to the directory to be removed

drive identifier

▶ Note: the directory to be removed must be empty.

▶ **SCANDISK** checks a disks surface, files, and directories for errors and corrects some errors.

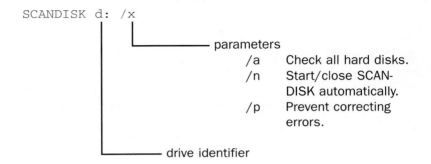

```
SCANDISK d: /x
```

parameters
/a Check all hard disks.
/n Start/close SCAN-
    DISK automatically.
/p Prevent correcting
    errors.

drive identifier

▶ **TIME** checks and/or sets the system time.

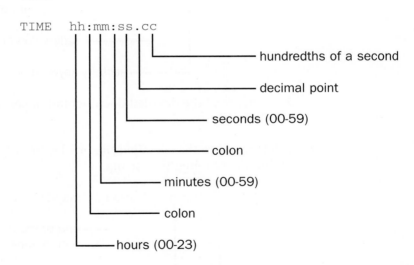

```
TIME

TIME  hh:mm:ss.cc
```

hundredths of a second

decimal point

seconds (00-59)

colon

minutes (00-59)

colon

hours (00-23)

▶ **TYPE** displays the selected file's contents on the screen.

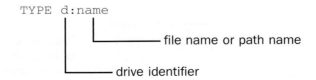

```
TYPE d:name
```

file name or path name

drive identifier

▶ VER displays the MS-DOS version number.

`VER` (no parameters)

■ Selected Filters

▶ CIPHER encrypts and decrypts files for security.

```
CIPHER keyword>d:name
CIPHER keyword<d:name
CIPHER keyword<d:name1>d:name2
```

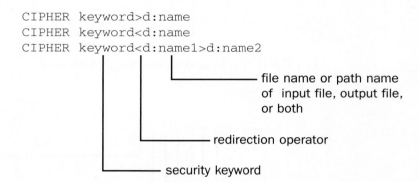

file name or path name
of input file, output file,
or both

redirection operator

security keyword

▶ Note: read the detailed documentation carefully before using **CIPHER.**

▶ FIND searches the specified file or files for a string, and displays all lines containing that string.

```
FIND /x "string" name1 name2 ...
```

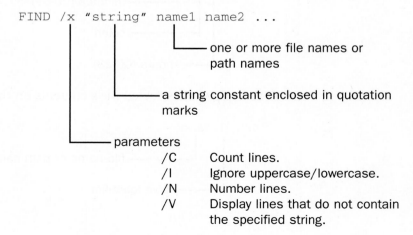

one or more file names or
path names

a string constant enclosed in quotation
marks

parameters

/C	Count lines.
/I	Ignore uppercase/lowercase.
/N	Number lines.
/V	Display lines that do not contain the specified string.

▶ **MORE** reads text from the standard input device and displays it one screen at a time.

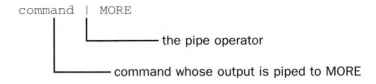

command | MORE

the pipe operator

command whose output is piped to MORE

▶ **SORT** sorts data into ascending order.

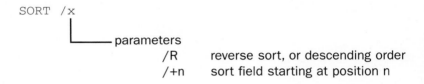

SORT /x

parameters
/R   reverse sort, or descending order
/+n   sort field starting at position n

Summary of UNIX Commands

General

▶ Format of a command

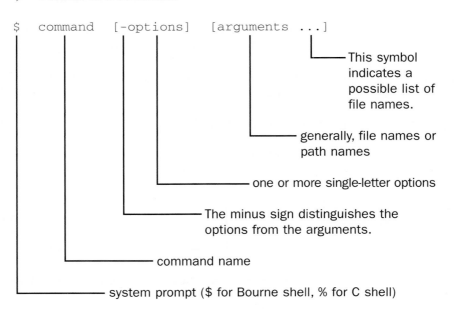

```
$   command   [-options]   [arguments ...]
```

This symbol indicates a possible list of file names.

generally, file names or path names

one or more single-letter options

The minus sign distinguishes the options from the arguments.

command name

system prompt ($ for Bourne shell, % for C shell)

▶ Fields are separated by one or more spaces.

▶ Fields enclosed in brackets [..] are optional.

▶ Rules for defining a file name

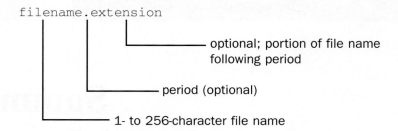

```
filename.extension
```
— optional; portion of file name following period

— period (optional)

— 1- to 256-character file name

▶ Suggested characters include A-Z, a-z, 0-9, comma (,), and underscore (_).

▶ Avoid using slash (/) characters in a file name.

▶ Don't start a file name with a minus sign (-).

▶ UNIX distinguishes between uppercase and lowercase.

▶ If you include a period in the file name, the characters following the period form the extension.

▶ The period and the extension count against the 256-character limit.

▶ You can code more than one period.

▶ Rules for defining path names

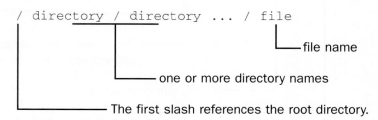

```
/ directory / directory ... / file
```
— file name

— one or more directory names

— The first slash references the root directory.

▶ A directory is a special type of file; thus the rules for defining a directory name are the same as the rules for defining a file name.

▶ If the path name starts with a directory name instead of a slash, UNIX starts searching with the working directory.

▶ Redirection parameters

Parameter	Meaning	Example
<	Change source to a specified file or device.	<myfile
>	Change destination to a specified file or device.	>tempfile
>>	Change destination, usually to an existing file, and append new output to it.	>>master.pay
|	Pipe standard output to another command or to a filter.	cat file1|sort

▶ Access Permissions

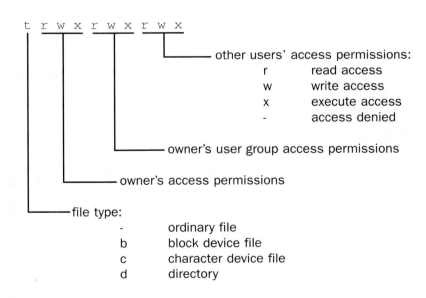

◼ Commands and Utilities

▶   cat displays the contents of a file or files.

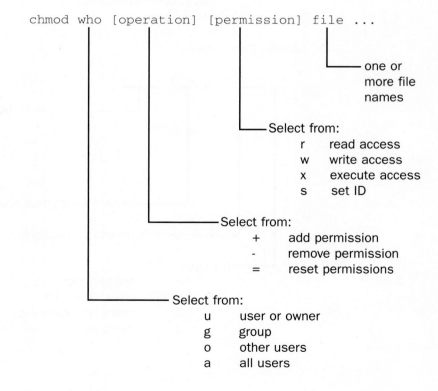

```
cat  [file ...]
```
one or more file names

▶   cd changes the working directory.

```
cd  [directory]
```
new working directory. If no directory
is coded, the home directory is assumed.

▶   chmod changes a file's access permissions.

```
chmod who [operation] [permission] file ...
```

one or
more file
names

Select from:
 r   read access
 w   write access
 x   execute access
 s   set ID

Select from:
 +   add permission
 -    remove permission
 =   reset permissions

Select from:
 u   user or owner
 g   group
 o   other users
 a   all users

▶ cp copies a file or files.

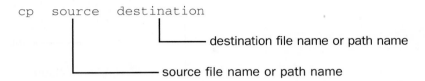

```
cp   source   destination
```

destination file name or path name

source file name or path name

▶ csh activates the C shell.

```
csh
```

no options or parameters

▶ date displays the system date and time.

```
$ date
```

no options

▶ ln creates a link.

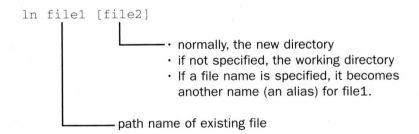

```
ln  file1  [file2]
```

· normally, the new directory
· if not specified, the working directory
· If a file name is specified, it becomes
  another name (an alias) for file1.

path name of existing file

▶ logout logs a user off the system.

```
logout
```

no options or parameters

Note: on most systems, press control-D to log off.

▶ lpr sends the contents of a file to the printer.

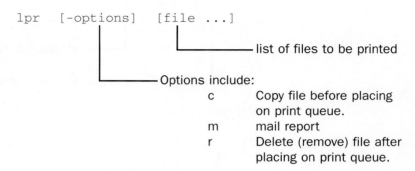

lpr [-options] [file ...]

────────── list of files to be printed

Options include:

c	Copy file before placing on print queue.
m	mail report
r	Delete (remove) file after placing on print queue.

▶ ls lists the contents of a directory or directories.

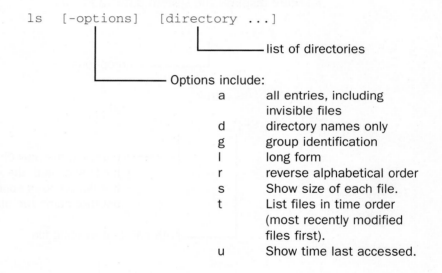

ls [-options] [directory ...]

────── list of directories

Options include:

a	all entries, including invisible files
d	directory names only
g	group identification
l	long form
r	reverse alphabetical order
s	Show size of each file.
t	List files in time order (most recently modified files first).
u	Show time last accessed.

▶ mail allows a user to send or receive electronic mail.

▶ To send mail, use:

mail user-list

────── login IDs of users to receive mail

▶ To receive mail, use:

```
mail   [-options]
```

Options include:

p	Display mail without prompts.
q	Quit.
r	View mail in reverse (chronological) order.

▶ `man` displays the UNIX manual page for the indicated command.

```
man   name
```

command or utility name

▶ `mkdir` creates one or more directories.

```
mkdir   directory ...
```

one or more directory names

▶ `more` displays a file one screen at a time.

```
more   file ...
```

list of files to be displayed

▶ `mv` moves or renames a file.

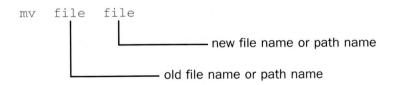

```
mv   file   file
```

new file name or path name

old file name or path name

▶ `passwd` changes a user's password.

```
passwd
```

no options

▶ `pr` prepares standard input or a file for printing.

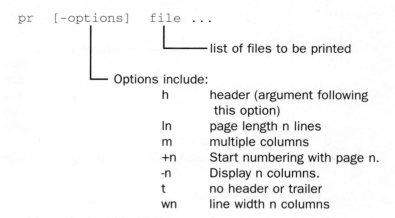

```
pr   [-options]   file ...
```
list of files to be printed

Options include:

h	header (argument following this option)
ln	page length n lines
m	multiple columns
+n	Start numbering with page n.
-n	Display n columns.
t	no header or trailer
wn	line width n columns

▶ `ps` displays the status of a process.

```
ps   [options]
```
Select from:

-a	all processes (any terminal)
-l	long form

If no options are coded, displays status of all processes controlled by user's terminal.

▶ `pwd` displays the user's current working directory.

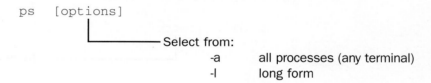

```
pwd
```
no options

▶ `rm` deletes a file by removing a link.

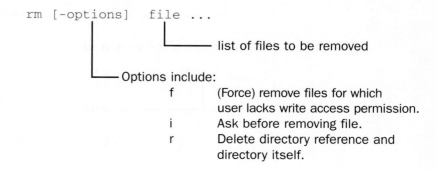

```
rm [-options]   file ...
```
list of files to be removed

Options include:

f	(Force) remove files for which user lacks write access permission.
i	Ask before removing file.
r	Delete directory reference and directory itself.

▶ `rmdir` deletes one or more directories.

```
rmdir   directory ...
```
———— path names of one or more
empty directories

▶ `sh` activates the Bourne shell.

```
sh
```
———— no options

▶ `sort` sorts the contents of a file.

```
sort [-options] [fields] [file ...]
```
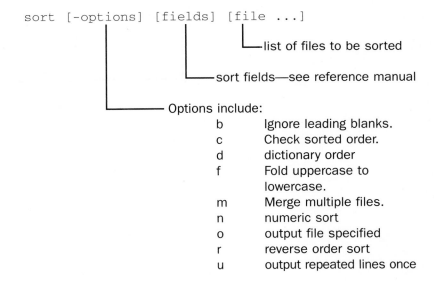

——— list of files to be sorted

——— sort fields—see reference manual

——— Options include:

b	Ignore leading blanks.
c	Check sorted order.
d	dictionary order
f	Fold uppercase to lowercase.
m	Merge multiple files.
n	numeric sort
o	output file specified
r	reverse order sort
u	output repeated lines once

▶ `spell` checks a file for spelling errors.

```
spell   [options]   file ...
```
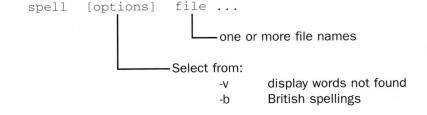

——— one or more file names

——— Select from:

-v	display words not found
-b	British spellings

▶ `vi` activates the visual editor.

`vi file`

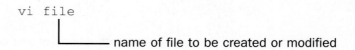

name of file to be created or modified

▶ `who` displays the names of users currently logged on the system.

`$ who    [am i]`

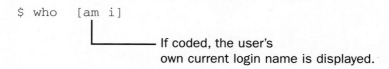

If coded, the user's
own current login name is displayed.

▶ `write` sends a message to another user in real time.

`write    login-name    [terminal]`

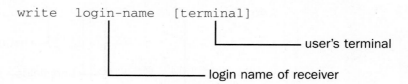

user's terminal

login name of receiver

IBM OS/JCL

Job Control Language

During the 1960s and much of the 1970s, the dominant computer applications included such accounting tasks as payroll, accounts receivable, accounts payable, and general ledger. These applications were (and still are) run on a scheduled basis, so most computer systems of that era were batch oriented. Punched cards were the standard input medium. A programmer prepared a deck of cards containing program source statements and data for a group of related application programs, arranged them to form a unit of work called a job, and submitted the job to the computer center. Instructions to the operating system for running the job were coded in a set of job control language (JCL) statements that were integrated into the job stream.

There are three basic types of IBM/OS JCL statements:

1. JOB statements separate and identify jobs. Secondary functions include passing accounting and priority information to the operating system.
2. EXEC (or execute) statements identify the programs (or job steps) to be executed.
3. DD (or data definition) statements define, in detail, the characteristics of each and every peripheral device used by each job step.

A job must begin with a JOB statement, and can contain almost any number of job steps. Each job step calls for one EXEC statement. Within a job step, one DD statement must be coded for each peripheral device accessed by the program.

JCL Statement Format

The basic format of a JCL statement is shown in Figure D.1. The first two columns must contain slash characters, and the name field must begin in position 3. The job name (the name associated with a JOB statement), step name (the name associated with an EXEC statement), or DD name (the name associated with a DD statement) is chosen by the programmer using a combination of from 1 to 8 letters, digits, or national characters (@, $, #). The first character may *not* be a digit.

Continuing to the right in Figure D.1, one or more blanks (or spaces) separate the name field from the operation field, which must be JOB, EXEC, or DD. One or more blanks separate the operation field from the operands, which consist of a series of parameters separated by commas. One or more blanks separate the operands from the optional comments. The JCL statement ends with column 71. Historically, columns 72 through 80 were reserved for sequence numbers, just in case a large deck of cards was dropped.

Note carefully that blanks are used to separate fields. Stray blanks are the beginner's most common JCL error. They *will be* interpreted as field separators. For example, coding

```
//  STEP2 EXEC COBOL
```

results in a strange error message—there is no such operation as STEP2 (only JOB, EXEC, and DD are valid). Try

```
//STEP2 EXEC COBOL
```

with no blanks between the // and the name field.

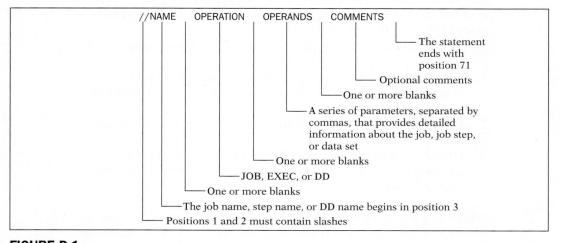

FIGURE D.1
An OS/JCL statement.

◾ JOB Statements

The function of a JOB statement (Figure D.2) is to identify and mark the beginning of a given job, thus separating it from all other jobs. The job name is required, and must be unique. It must start with a letter or a national character; otherwise, any combination of from 1 to 8 letters, digits, and national characters is legal. In many computer centers, job names are assigned by the operating system to eliminate the risk that two or more jobs might have the same name. The job name and the operation (JOB) are the only required fields.

Positional Parameters

One important secondary function of the JOB statement is passing information to an accounting routine. Accounting information is a positional parameter that (if present) is always the first parameter. The meaning of a positional parameter is determined by its relative position in the operands field. For example, the statement

```
//JOB396 JOB 1234
```

indicates that the cost of running job JOB396 is to be charged against account 1234. Often, multiple accounting subparameters are coded. For example,

```
//MU435 JOB (1234,875)
```

might mean that job MU435 is to be charged against account number 1234, user number 875. When more than one subparameter is coded, commas are used to separate them. Note also the use of parentheses. When more than one subparameter is coded, parentheses are *required*.

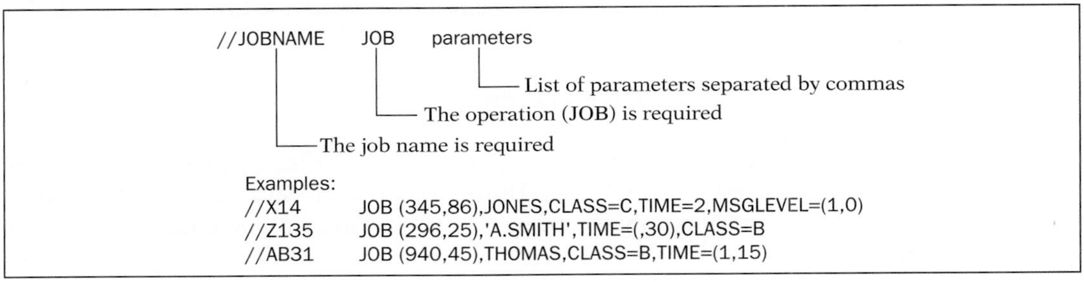

```
//JOBNAME    JOB    parameters
                            └── List of parameters separated by commas
                      └── The operation (JOB) is required
           └── The job name is required

Examples:
//X14      JOB (345,86),JONES,CLASS=C,TIME=2,MSGLEVEL=(1,0)
//Z135     JOB (296,25),'A.SMITH',TIME=(,30),CLASS=B
//AB31     JOB (940,45),THOMAS,CLASS=B,TIME=(1,15)
```

FIGURE D.2

A JOB statement.

The exact content of the accounting information parameter is up to the installation, and each computer center can define its own accounting subparameters. Note that the subparameters are also positional—in other words, they must be coded in a prescribed order.

On a batch processing system, programmers (and users) submit complete jobs and come back for the results some time later. To simplify programmer identification, the programmer's name is coded as a second positional parameter, for example,

```
//MU098 JOB (2987,235),DAVIS
```

or

```
//MU1735 JOB (2195,235),'W.S. DAVIS'
```

The programmer name parameter can contain up to 20 letters or digits, including a single period. The apostrophes (or single quotation marks) are needed when special characters, such as commas, blanks, or additional periods, are part of the programmer's name. Your computer center may have a preferred format.

Keyword Parameters

A job's class indicates the partition or region in which it runs. Another way to think of a job class is as a set of default limits on such parameters as execution time, memory space, types of peripherals accessed, and so on. For example, a simple, I/O-bound compilation job that reads source statements, compiles the code, prepares a compiler listing, and writes the object code to a library might run in a class A partition, while a complex application that requires mounting multiple disks and/or tapes might run in a less restrictive but lower priority class D partition. The various job classes supported by a given computer system are defined by the system operator at startup time.

A programmer indicates a job's class by coding a CLASS parameter, for example,

```
//MU741 JOB (3984,444),SMITH,CLASS=A
```

CLASS is a keyword parameter. It derives its meaning not from its position, but from the key word CLASS. Unlike positional parameters, which must be coded in a prescribed order, keyword parameters can be coded in any order.

Most batch systems automatically cancel a program caught in an endless loop after a reasonable time has passed. Often, an estimate of the job's likely run time is reported to the operating system in a TIME parameter. For example,

```
TIME=(5,30)
```

asks for 5 minutes and 30 seconds of processor time, while

```
TIME=5
TIME=(5)
TIME=(5,0)
```

are *all* requests for exactly five minutes. Note the use of parentheses. When the first subparameter alone is coded (minutes), they can be skipped. However, when more than one subparameter is coded, parentheses must be used.

Minutes and seconds are positional subparameters; in other words, they are defined by their relative positions. Minutes come first; seconds come second. For example, to request exactly 30 seconds, code

```
TIME=(,30)
```

The comma indicates the absence of the "minutes" positional subparameter. Because both the comma (indicating the absence of the first positional subparameter) and the second positional subparameter (seconds) are coded, parentheses are required.

CLASS and TIME are themselves keyword parameters. The key words CLASS and TIME give them meaning independent of their position. For example, the following JOB statements are all legal:

```
//X14   JOB (345,86),JONES,CLASS=C,TIME=2

//Z135 JOB (296,25),'A. SMITH',TIME=(,30),CLASS=B

//AB31 JOB (940,45),THOMAS,CLASS=B,TIME=(1,15)
```

The accounting information must come first, followed by the programmer name. They are positional parameters, and derive their meaning from their relative positions. CLASS and TIME are keyword parameters that can be coded in any order.

On some systems, a job's priority is determined, in part, by the amount of space it requires. The programmer can request space by coding a REGION parameter. For example,

```
REGION=128K
```

represents a request for a 128K region. Modern memory management systems have largely eliminated the need to prespecify a region size.

The MSGLEVEL Parameter

Programmer-coded JCL statements, the JCL statements included in a cataloged procedure, and messages indicating the operating system's actions are valuable to the programmer, but once the program is released they are meaningless to the user. The MSGLEVEL (message level) parameter (Figure D.3) allows the programmer to select which JCL and device allocation messages are to be printed. For example,

```
MSGLEVEL=(1,1)
```

means to print everything, while

```
MSGLEVEL=(0,0)
```

means print only the JOB statement unless the job fails, and

```
MSGLEVEL=(1,0)
```

tells the system to print all JCL statements but to skip allocation messages.

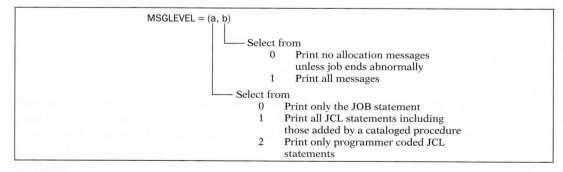

FIGURE D.3
MSGLEVEL specifies which JCL statements and messages are to be printed.

Instead of requiring the programmer to code numerous parameters each time a job is submitted, most computer centers rely on defaults. If the programmer fails, for any reason, to code a particular parameter, the system assumes a value. Often, only accounting information, the programmer's name, and the job class are required. Defaults are typically based on the job class with, for example, all CLASS=A jobs assigned a 640K region and a 30 second time limit, while CLASS=B jobs get 512K and a 2 minute time limit. To override a default, simply code the appropriate parameter.

Continuing a JCL Statement

Consider the following JOB statement:

```
//C1234567 JOB (3998,659),'A.B. JONES',CLASS=A,
//          TIME=(5,30),REGION=128K
```

It's too long to fit on a single line, and thus must be continued. The rules for continuing a JCL statement are:

1. Interrupt the field after a complete parameter or subparameter, including the trailing comma, has been coded. (In other words, stop after *any* comma in the operands field.)
2. *Optionally* code any nonblank character in position 72. Position 72 can be left blank; the continuation character is optional.
3. Code slashes (//) in positions 1 and 2 of the continuation line.
4. Continue coding in any position from 4 through 16. Position 3 must be blank and coding must be resumed no later than position 16.

In other words, just break after a comma and resume coding on the next line. The same rules hold for any type of JCL statement.

■ EXEC Statements

An EXEC statement (Figure D.4) marks the beginning of a job step. Its purpose is to identify the program or cataloged procedure (a set of precoded JCL statements stored on a library) to be executed. The step name is optional; if coded, the rules for a step name are the same as the rules for a job name. The first parameter must be a program or procedure name, for example,

```
//  EXEC  PGM=SORT6
```

or

```
//    EXEC    PROC=COBOL
```

The keyword **PROC** can be skipped, for example,

```
//    EXEC    COBOL
```

If a program is referenced, the keyword **PGM** must be coded. Often, the program or cataloged procedure name is the only parameter coded on an EXEC statement.

When a cataloged procedure is referenced, the operating system searches the procedure library and replaces the programmer's EXEC statement with a set of precoded JCL. For example, the cataloged procedure FORTRAN is replaced by all the EXEC and DD statements needed to support three job steps—compile, link edit, and go (execute the resulting load module).

If you have ever programmed in a traditional compiler language, you may have noticed something called a severity code on your compiler listing. A program containing severe errors will almost certainly not run. The compiler passes the highest severity code to the system by placing a condition code in a register. The operating system can check this condition code prior to loading and executing a job step, skipping the step if the condition code is not acceptable. The programmer sets the limits for this comparison through a COND (condition) parameter.

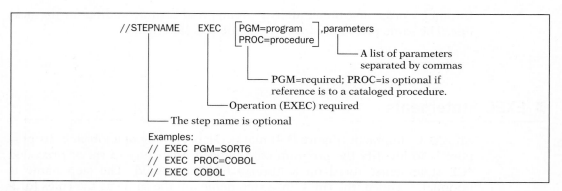

FIGURE D.4

An EXEC statement.

Other EXEC parameters allow the programmer to pass accounting information to a job step or set a dispatching priority for the step. Some parameters can be coded on the JOB statement or on an EXEC statement. For example, the programmer has the option of specifying a time limit, a region size, restart options, and other conditions for the complete job or for each job step independently.

Programmers often encounter a PARM parameter in a cataloged procedure. For example, in the FORTRAN procedure,

```
//  EXEC  FORTRAN,PARM.FORT='NODECK,LIST'
```

the PARM parameter informs the FORT job step (the compiler) that no object deck (at one time, a real deck of cards) is to be output and that a listing is to be printed. Information on the meaning of parameters for any compiler language can be found in the programmer's guide to that language.

■ DD Statements

On a traditional IBM mainframe, one data control block is coded inside the program for each external device accessed by the program. The DCB contains only those parameters that must be known before the program is loaded. The actual physical devices are defined outside the program in DD statements. A program and its peripherals are not physically linked until run (open) time.

The UNIT Parameter

The general format of a DD statement is shown in Figure D.5. The UNIT parameter specifies the physical input or output device. One option is coding an actual unit address. Every peripheral attached to a traditional IBM system is identified by a three-digit hexadecimal number. For example, if a printer is device 8 on channel 0, its unit address is 008, and the DD statement

```
//PRINTER  DD  UNIT=008
```

references it. The unit address form implies that no other device will do; given the DD statement illustrated above, if device 008 is busy, or for some other reason not available, the program must wait to be loaded. This form of the UNIT parameter is rarely used.

```
//DDNAME   DD   UNIT=device,
                DCB=(parameters),
                DSNAME=name,
                VOLUME=SER=number,
                DISP=(a,b,c),
                SPACE=(parameters)
```

FIGURE D.5

A DD statement.

If a programmer wants a 3330 disk, and any 3330 disk will do, a device type can be specified; for example,

```
//OUTS  DD  UNIT=3330
```

The program can be loaded and run as soon as any 3330 is free. If a system has more than one of a particular device, specifying a device type is less restrictive than specifying a unit address.

A third choice is referencing a group name. For example, the DD statement

```
//XYZ  DD  UNIT=SYSDA
```

might represent a request for any available disk. It is the most general form of the UNIT parameter, and thus the most frequently used.

The DCB, DSN, and VOL Parameters

DCB parameters can be coded on the DD statement or in the program DCB. Both UNIT and DCB are keyword parameters. They can be coded in any order.

In the 1960s, IBM coined the term dataset to encompass both traditional files and libraries. To simplify retrieving cataloged or passed datasets, the programmer can give a file a unique name by coding a DSNAME (or DSN) parameter. A valid dataset name consists of from one to eight letters, numbers, or national symbols and must begin with a letter or a national symbol. Temporary, life-of-job files are assigned dataset names beginning with an ampersand (&); for example,

```
DSNAME=&&TEMP
```

To avoid confusing them with assembly language macro parameters, temporary dataset names normally begin with a double ampersand.

The VOLUME (or VOL) parameter specifies a particular disk volume (or pack). Each volume has a unique serial number. To request pack number MU1234, a programmer would code

```
VOL=SER=MU1234
```

The VOLUME parameter is coded only if the application demands a specific disk or magnetic tape volume.

The DISP Parameter

The DISP (disposition) parameter (Figure D.6) tells the system what to do with a disk file after the job step is completed. The first positional subparameter describes the file's status before the job step is executed. If a file is to be created, it's NEW. An existing file is OLD. Some files (a library for example) might be concurrently accessed (but not modified) by more than one program. Such files are shared (SHR). Disposition MOD allows a program to add more data to an existing file.

The second subparameter specifies system action following *normal* job step completion. If there is no further need for the data, the programmer can DELETE the file. KEEP means that the file will be retained. If the data are needed by a subsequent step within the same job, the programmer can PASS the dataset. The file can be entered on a catalog (CATLG) and retained, or removed from a catalog (UNCATLG) and deleted.

The third DISP subparameter defines the file's disposition following *abnormal* job termination. Options include DELETE, KEEP, CATLG, or UNCATLG. If the third subparameter is not coded, the normal termination disposition is assumed.

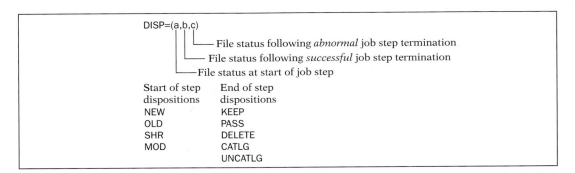

FIGURE D.6

The disposition (DISP) parameter specifies the file's status.

The SPACE Parameter

It makes little sense to load and execute a program unless adequate direct access space is available. Thus programmers are required to estimate their space requirements by coding a SPACE parameter (Figure D.7). Space can be requested in tracks, cylinders, or blocks. The first positional subparameter identifies the unit and the second positional subparameter indicates the number of units. For example,

```
SPACE=(TRK,20)
```

is a request for 20 tracks, while

```
SPACE=(CYL,14)
```

asks for 14 cylinders, and

```
SPACE=(200,10)
```

asks for ten 200-byte blocks (for a total of 2000 bytes).

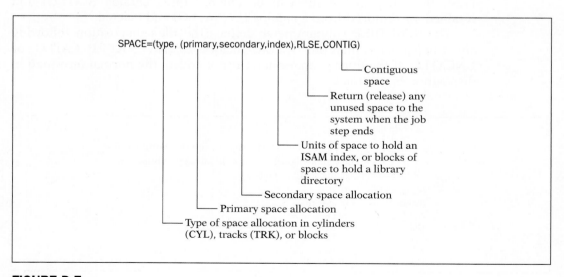

FIGURE D.7
The SPACE parameter.

Estimating space requirements can be difficult. To ensure sufficient space, a programmer might be tempted to request a bit more than the program needs, thus tying up a limited resource. Fortunately, there is another option. The parameter

```
SPACE=(TRK,(10,2))
```

requests a *primary* allocation of 10 tracks, and a *secondary* allocation of 2 tracks. Should the initial 10 tracks be filled, an additional 2 will be allocated, if available. If those 2 are filled, 2 more are allocated. The system will make a maximum of 15 secondary allocations, so the parameter coded above could represent as many as 40 tracks (10, plus 2 times 15).

The primary space allocation is made before the program is loaded. The secondary allocation is filled on an as-needed, if-available basis *after* the job step begins executing. A job step may be canceled for insufficient direct access space even though its primary and secondary requests are more than adequate if space is not available at the time of the secondary request.

Note that the primary and secondary subparameters are enclosed in parentheses. Both deal with the number of units of direct access space and thus should be treated as a single entity. (In effect, the primary and secondary allocations are *sub*parameters. When two or more subparameters are coded, a set of inner parentheses is needed.)

Requesting too much space can tie up a limited resource. The programmer can return unused space to the system at the end of a job step by coding a RLSE (release) subparameter, for example,

```
SPACE=(CYL,(5,1),RLSE)
```

RLSE is a positional subparameter that must follow the primary and secondary allocations.

To optimize disk input and output, space is sometimes requested in contiguous units. The parameter

```
SPACE=(TRK,(5,2),RLSE,CONTIG)
```

asks for 5 contiguous tracks, with a secondary request for 2 more, and returns unused space to the system at the conclusion of the job step. Without RLSE, this parameter would be coded

```
SPACE=(TRK,(5,2),,CONTIG)
```

Note the extra comma indicating the absence of a positional subparameter.

System Input and Output

A great deal of input and output takes place through relatively few devices. On some systems, a terminal keyboard and screen are the standards. On others, spooling routines create temporary disk files to insulate application programs from such slow devices as keyboards and printers. Default parameters are often used to access the standard system input and output devices.

For example, the system input device is normally defined by a statement such as

```
//SYSIN   DD   *
```

The asterisk indicates that the data follow this DD statement in the job stream. There is nothing sacred about SYSIN; it's just a DDNAME. The programmer can use any DDNAME for the system input device, as long as it matches the name coded in the program's internal data control block. Many compilers and utilities use SYSIN to reference the system input device, however, so it has become a de facto standard.

To spool data to the system output device, code

```
//SYSOUT   DD   SYSOUT=A
```

or

```
//SYSPRINT DD SYSOUT=A
```

Device A generally implies eventual printer output, but an installation can choose its own symbols to indicate the various system devices.

Job Step Qualification

Sometimes two or more DD statements, each in a different job step but still within the same job, are assigned the same DDNAME. For example, on a compile, link edit, and go job, both the compiler and the go step might get input from the system input device. Thus, both can contain a

```
//SYSIN DD *
```

statement. To distinguish these two statements, the DDNAMEs are qualified. The FORTRAN procedure contains three job steps: FORT (the compiler), LKED (the linkage editor), and GO (the program load module). FORT.SYSIN is the name of a DD statement attached to the first job step. GO.SYSIN is attached to the GO step. Qualified DDNAMES can be used only within a cataloged procedure.

■ A Complete Job

Figure D.8 lists the job control language statements needed to support a three-step assemble, link edit, and go job. The statements have been numbered to simplify reference. Statements submitted by the programmer begin with //. Statements added by the cataloged procedure begin with XX. Read through the statements one at a time and make sure you understand the purpose of each parameter.

1. The programmer's JOB statement.
2. The programmer's EXEC statement. ASMFCLG is a three-step catalogued procedure (assemble, link edit, and go).
3. This execute statement is added by the catalogued procedure. It references the assembler program, IEUASM.
4. The SYSLIB DD statement is added by the catalogued procedure. It allows the assembler program to access the system's macro library.
5. A work file added by the catalogued procedure. The assembler program uses this file to hold intermediate results as it assembles the program.
6. Another work file.
7. Another work file.
8. The SYSPRINT DD statement allows the assembler program to print a source statement listing.
9. The SYSPUNCH DD statement allows the assembler program to output the object module as a deck of punched cards. At one time this was a common option.
10. The SYSGO DD statement defines the disk file where the object module will be stored. The temporary dataset name &&LOADSET allows the linkage editor to find the object module in the next job step (see statement 15).
11. The ASM.SYSIN DD statement is coded by the programmer. It precedes the source code and is inserted into the ASM job step because the DDNAME SYSIN is qualified by ASM.
12. The programmer's source code.
13. The /* statement is an end-of-data marker coded by the programmer. It marks the end of the source code.
14. The second EXEC statement added by the catalogued procedure. This one references the linkage editor program, IEWL.
15. The SYSLIN DD statement tells the linkage editor where to find the just-created object module (see statement 10). Note the reference to dataset name &&LOADSET.
16. Note that this DD statement has no DDNAME. Consequently, it is treated as a continuation of the previous DD statement, SYSLIN. It tells the linkage editor that in addition to the object module file

1	//MU132	JOB	
2	//	EXEC	ASMGCLG
3	XXASM	EXEC	PGM=IEUASM
4	XXSYSLIB	DD	DSNAME=SYS1.MACLIB,DISP=SHR
5	XXSYSUT1	DD	...
6	XXSYSUT2	DD	...
7	XXSYSUT3	DD	...
8	XXSYSPRINT	DD	SYSOUT=A
9	XXSYSPUNCH	DD	SYSOUT=B
10	XXSYSGO XX XX	DD	DSNAME=&&LOADSET,DISP=(NEW,PASS), SPACE=(400,(100,20)),UNIT=SYSDA, DCB=(LRECL=80,BLKSIZE=400,RECFM=FB)
11	//ASM.SYSIN	DD	*
12	Source code		
13	/*		
14	XXLKED	EXEC	PGM=IEWL
15	XXSYSLIN XX	DD	DSNAME=&&LOADSET,DISP=(OLD,DELETE), DCB=(LRECL=80,BLKSIZE=400,RECFM=FB)
16	XX	DD	DDNAME=SYSIN
17	XXSYSLMOD	DD	DSNAME=&&GOSET(GO),DISP=(NEW,PASS), SPACE=(1024,(50,20,1)), UNIT=SYSDA
18	XXSYSUT1	DD	...
19	XXSYSPRINT	DD	SYSOUT=A
20	/*		
21	XXGO	EXEC	PGM=*.LKED.SYSLMOD
22	//GO.OUTPUT	DD	SYSOUT=A
23	//GO.DISK	DD	Parameters for program disk file
24	//GO.SYSIN	DD	*
25	Data		
26	/*		
27	//		

FIGURE D.8

A complete set of JCL for an assemble, link edit, and go job.

(&&LOADSET), additional input (other object modules, linkage editor commands) might be found following the DDNAME SYSIN later in the job stream. Had the programmer chosen to code an LKED.SYSIN DD * statement, he or she could have included additional linkage editor input. In this case, the SYSIN statement was not coded so there is no additional input. See the linkage editor reference manual for more information on linkage editor commands and object modules.

17. The SYSLMOD DD statement defines a temporary library named &&GOSET and adds one member named GO to that library. This is the load module. It will be referenced in the final EXEC statement (statement 21).

18. SYSUT1 is a work file used by the linkage editor to hold intermediate results.

19. The SYSPRINT DD statement allows the linkage editor to print messages.

20. The /* statement is an end-of-data marker. Technically it isn't needed because no SYSIN DD * statement was coded within the LKED step. It acts as a job step separator.

21. The final EXEC statement. The * following the key word PGM is a backward reference. Reading from left to right, the reference says to look back to the LKED step, find a DD statement named SYSLMOD (statement 17), and execute the load module stored on that dataset. The load module in question is member name GO on the temporary library &&GOSET.

22. The programmer coded this DD statement to allow the program to generate printed output.

23. The programmer coded this DD statement to define a disk file.

24. The programmer coded this DD statement to allow the program to get input data from the system input device.

25. The programmer's input data go here.

26. The /* statement is an end-of-data marker.

27. The // statement marks the end of the job.

If you can understand the purpose of each of these JCL statements, you have a pretty good grasp of job control language.

Contents

Taking from: *Operating Systems for Technicians 2004*
by Todd Meadors and Cheryl A. Schmidt

Chapter 5 Introduction to Microsoft Windows NT

Chapter 6 Introduction to Windows 2000

Chapter 7 Introduction to Microsoft Windows XP

Chapter 8 Introduction to UNIX/Linux

Chapter 9 Introduction to Networking

624   Contents

Preface

A+ Operating Systems for Technicians is written for an introductory course in operating systems software. At the beginning of each chapter is the latest CompTia A+ Operating System Technologies exam. Although this book focuses mainly on operating systems, Chapter 9 is dedicated to Networking including a section on wireless. There are numerous exercises embedded within the chapter and lab projects at the end of each chapter.

Organization of the Text

This textbook is organized in the following manner:

Chapter 1 The Operating System Environment covers basic hardware and software terminology.

Chapter 2 Basic Operating System Theory covers operating systems software in greater detail.

Chapter 3 DOS and the DOS Command Line Interface details the commands used in DOS and the DOS command line. Coverage includes the file system hierarchy, commands and batch files.

Chapter 4 Introduction to Windows 98 deals with Windows 98 from installation, managing files and folders to the boot process and troubleshooting.

Chapter 5 Introduction to Windows NT handles Windows NT installation, managing files and folders, compression, the Registry, configuring and troubleshooting.

Chapter 6 Introduction to Windows 2000 covers Windows 2000 installation, managing files and folders, compression and encryption, dual-booting, the Registry, Dr. Watson, configuring and troubleshooting.

Chapter 7 Introduction to Windows XP details Microsoft's newest desktop operating system. It covers Windows XP installation, dual-booting, the Registry, the boot process, Task Manager, Event Viewer, Performance Monitor and Dr. Watson.

Chapter 8 Introduction to UNIX/Linux covers the basic UNIX/Linux operating system commands, and concepts that are common to nearly all versions of UNIX or

Linux. Topics include understanding the tree structure, file and directory commands, redirection, filtering (piping) and wildcards (pattern matching). Also, included in a section on shell programs and security using the chmod command.

Chapter 9 Introduction to Networking highlights networking theory, protocols, topologies, access mechanisms, the OSI model, cabling, and three sections on wireless.

Appendix A Number Conversions covers how to convert numbers to and from different bases such as binary, decimal and hexadecimal. Problems are included for reinforcement.

Appendix B DOS (including DOS Command Prompt) and Linux Commands highlights the commands used by DOS and Linux discussed in this textbook.

Appendix C is the ASCII Chart with a few student problems to complete.

Appendix D includes the answers to the odd-numbered questions.

The Appendices will be on the CD included with the book.

From a pedagogical stance, if you lack the time to cover all chapters, you could go over Chapters 1, 2, 3 and then any of the Microsoft Windows chapters 4 through 7 (depending upon what you have available), Chapter 8 on UNIX/Linux and then Chapter 9, the Networking chapter.

Features
Easy-to-understand text Each chapter includes with excellent explanations of basic and advances concepts.

Hands-on exercises embedded Hands-on exercises are embedded with chapters to reinforce a concept.

A+ Operating System Technologies objectives At the beginning of each chapter is a list of the A+ Operating System Technologies objectives and the corresponding page number(s) of the topic. The UNIX/Linux chapter does not include a list because it is not on the current A+ exam.

Coverage of the major operating systems The major operating systems are discussed. These include: Windows 98, NT, 2000, XP, DOS, and UNIX/Linux.
Tech Tips Technical tips are included. A Sherlock Holmes icon precedes these tips.

Chapter Summary A chapter summary is included at the end of each chapter to highlight the chapter's main points.

Chapter Review Questions Each chapter has 20 multiple choice review questions.

Lab Projects (including Challenge) Each chapter has from 12 to 22 Lab Projects. Challenge Lab Projects are included too.

Internet Discovery Labs Each chapter has additional labs that require the student to perform Internet research as it relates to chapter content.

Soft Skills Help Desk Support This is the OTJ (On-The-Job) section of each chapter that includes real life working scenarios.

Critical Thinking Each chapter includes thought provoking questions forcing the student to stretch his or her knowledge about the subject matter.

Study Skills Each chapter includes a study skill topic followed by questions that the student should be focusing on.

Glossary A glossary of key terms.

Appendices Topics here include: number conversions, a summary of DOS and UNIX/Linux commands, the ASCII chart and answers to odd-numbered questions.

Instructor Support Ancillary materials include a Test Bank, Power Point slides and a CD with all of the answers to the Chapter Review Questions.

Acknowledgements

We would like to thank the many people who have encouraged me along the way to make this project succeed. First, we would like to thank Richard Jones of Scott Jones Publishers for giving us the opportunity to write this book. This has been the best writing experience we've ever had. We would also like to thank Audrey Anderson for managing the production process for me – she is great at what she does! We would like to thank Lois Principe, the book's proofreader and Diane DeMarco, the book's compositor.

Todd would like to thank his boss, Ernie Hensley, at DeKalb Technical College, where Todd teaches. He encouraged Todd to finish this book because no other book on the market has labs like this one. Todd also would like to thank other faculty members at DeKalb Technical College who gave him encouragement along the way: Walter Dula, William Monahan, Keith Humphrey, and Wayne Brown.

We also want to thank the real audience of this book - our students. We hope this book will enrich your working career!

Other thanks to these DeKalb Technical College colleagues: Dr. Paul Starns, President, Dr. Robin Hoffman, Vice President, Julian Wade, Dean and Fred Gibson, Assistant Dean.

Todd saves the best for last: his wife Micki for her steadfast support. She was Todd's technical reviewer and did a superb job! Todd dedicates this book to her and their two wonderful children, Zachary and Jessica.

Additionally, Todd thanks his parents, Dr. and Mrs. Lawrence H. Meadors, for the sacrifices they made for his education. "Thanks Mother for tutoring me so much in the 3rd grade – it continues to pay countless rewards".

Thanks to these reviewers for helping to make this a great textbook:

Kirk Ruby, College of Southern Idaho
Dave Bosilovatz, Bay de Noc Community College
Carol Mills, Cotton Boll Institute
Sally Douglass, Central Florida Community College
Martyns Kanu, Canada College
Gerald Sampson, Walla Walla Community College
Ross Decker, Brevard Community College
Tom Melvin, Allegany Community College
Professor M. Aghili, McNesse State College
David Oliver, Johnson Community College
Bonita A. Moyer, DeSales University
Russell Foszcz , McHenry County College
Karl Linderoth , Bay College
Roy F. Bonnett, Jr., Blue Ridge Community College
Larry Dumais, American River College
Richard Kalman, Atlantic Community College
Tom Holmes, Cotton Boll Institute
Kelly Flanagan, Brigham Young University
Kimberly A. Perez, Tidewater Community College
LaVaughn Hart, Las Positas College
Dianne Boseman, Nash Community College
Cindy Herbert, Longview Community College
Greg Stefanelli,, Carroll Community College
Connie Ivey, Robeson Community College

If you need to contact us, please feel free to point out any corrections or offer suggestions to this email address: **ltmeadors@yahoo.com**

A Note to Students
"I hear, and I forget
I see, and I remember
I do, and I understand"
　—Chinese proverb

This book is written with you in mind. We write like we teach. So, while going over this book, you will find the analogies, screen shots, tips, memory lists, projects or anything we can do to get a concept across. They are meant to help you understand.

A Note to Instructors
The real impetus for writing this book was the lack of good lab projects in any of the textbooks available. Over the years, we developed dozens of labs for different operating systems. Students were often frustrated that they were required to purchase a textbook that had virtually no lab projects with any depth. Countless times, the students have said that my labs were very useful as a resource and better than any they had seen. Now, they have a book that contains both theory and labs in one place.

Our teaching approach is to 1) discuss a topic, 2) show the topic, 3) involve the student in discussion and thought and 4) give the students lots of hands-on labs because this is where real learning occurs.

Our intent is for this book to follow that teaching style by 1) discussing a concept, 2) showing through screenshots, 3) involving through questions, critical thinking and exercises within the chapter and 4) numerous Lab Projects at the end of the chapter.

We hope you find this book a valuable resource for you and your students.

1

Chapter 1
The Operating System Environment

OBJECTIVES

The goal of this chapter is to introduce you to the operating system environment. This chapter will help you prepare and pass the following sections of the A+ Operating System Technologies Exam:

A+ Operating System Technologies Exam Objectives
covered in this chapter (and corresponding page numbers)

In this chapter, you will complete the following sections:
- 1.1 Understanding Software
- 1.2 Understanding Hardware
- 1.3 Understanding the Types of Users
- 1.4 Understanding the Operating System
- 1.5 Understanding Classifications of Operating Systems

1.1 Understanding Software

Software is defined as a set of instructions that are processed by a computer system. A software **program** is a collection of instructions that accomplish a task. Software programs are written in **programming languages** such as Pascal, C, C++, Java, Visual BASIC, COBOL, FORTRAN or Assembly. When a person writes a program, they write instructions to perform a certain function or task. This is called an **algorithm**. An **instruction** is a statement that performs an action. An example would be add or subtract. Combine instructions together in a set of logical steps and you have a software program. Programs are written in a specific programming language. Programming languages are like speaking languages. Words make up statements and there are strict syntax rules to follow.

Languages are divided into two broad categories:
- Low-level
- High-level

Low-level programming languages are hardware specific. The most common example is the Assembly, or Assembler, language native to each processor. These languages are extremely fast because they are written in the instruction set of each processor. An **instruction set** is the set of instruction statements the processor can understand and use. Look at the following Assembly language program below. This program simply adds two variables, X and Y, and places the result in the variable named T. Another name for an assembly language statement is **mnemonic**.

```
L 2,X
A 2, Y
ST 2,T
```

You can see this is not easily understandable. If you weren't told, you probably would not be able to tell what those statements do. Low-level languages are generally more difficult for humans to read and understand because their statements are close to the processor's language.

High-level languages are easier for us to read and interpret. However, this tends to cause more work for the computer because the language statements must be converted into a form the processor understands. For example, review the following instructions from a Visual BASIC program:

```
IF HOURS > 40 THEN
     CALL OVERTIME
ELSE
     CALL REGULAR_TIME
END-IF
```

In the example, if the hours for an employee exceed 40, then overtime will be calculated. If the hours for an employee are under or up to 40, then regular time will be calculated. You can clearly see how this sample Visual BASIC program is very similar to the English language. Examples of high-level programming languages include Pascal, COBOL, C, BASIC, Visual BASIC and FORTRAN.

Programming languages must be converted from the human-readable into machine-readable form. For low-level programming languages, this conversion is known as assembling. For high-level programming languages, this conversion is known as either compiling or interpreting. The compiler or interpreter is software that is written to perform the conversion.

Assembling converts the assembly language statements and data into machine-readable (known as binary code or executable code) form for a **linker**, or **linkage editor**. Part of the assembling process is to assign memory locations to the instructions and data. The linker is used to create a program that can be executed on the computer.

Compiling is the process of converting a completely written program into an **executable** program. An executable program is one that is compiled and syntax error free. It is capable of being run or executed. You can execute a program by clicking an icon representing the program or typing in the program name. For example, if you have ever double-clicked an icon or typed in the DOS **dir** command, that is executing a program. Pascal, C, C++, Java, COBOL, and FORTRAN are all complied languages.

Interpreting is the process of converting each line of the program into executable form. Interpreting differs from compiling because one line at a time is converted then immediately executed. Think of an interpretive language as being one where a mini-compile is done for each statement. Examples of interpretive languages are Visual BASIC, BASIC and the shell in the UNIX and Linux operating systems. Compiled languages tend to take more time to convert to an executable form, but are generally faster when executed because each line is not converted as it goes. Also, once the program is in machine-readable form, there is no need for the actual compiler software.

Compiled programs need to be converted only once. Interpretive languages require their interpreter software in order to execute. This makes interpreted language software more difficult to take to another operating system to execute than a compiled language. Interpreted programs need to be converted every time they are executed.

Because assembly language programs are hardware specific, generally you must rewrite, reassemble, and re-link the assembly program on a computer with an instruction set different from the one originally used. Thus, you can say that assembly programs are **proprietary** in nature. Programs written using compiled and interpreted languages can generally be copied to computers with differing instruction sets without much modification. Thus, compiled and interpretive languages are considered **portable** in nature.

Programs process data into information. **Data** are the raw facts and have no meaning to us alone. **Information** is processed data that has meaning to us. Consider the number 85. This is considered data. You cannot look at the number 85 and tell if it is someone's age, the grade on an exam, or the temperature outdoors. Only when a program processes the number will it be information.

The computer processes everything in **binary**. Binary is the system where bits are used to represent numbers and characters. You can refer to Appendix I for a discussion of number conversions including binary. The term **bit** stands for <u>bi</u>nary dig<u>it</u> and can be either a zero (0) or a one (1). Each computer system has a **character set** that maps all the letters on the keyboard to its appropriate bit sequence. A character set is the set of characters on the keyboard and their binary equivalent. For example, the letter A is represented by the binary sequence 01000001. The character set common among most computer systems is the **American Standard Code for Information Interchange** (**ASCII**). It is used on most computer environments, including all Windows operating systems and the UNIX and Linux operating systems. In the computer industry, the term **byte** to refers to eight bits taken in sequence. Letters, numbers and other special symbols are considered bytes. So, the letter A and its binary equivalent, 01000001, is considered a byte.

Now let's explore the major classifications of software. Software is divided into two major categories:

- System software
- Application software

System software includes the core components of the system that must be present in order for the computer to operate. Examples of system software are the operating system kernel, process management, memory management, and device drivers. System software will be discussed further in Chapter 2.

Application software is software used to assist users in performing typical office type work. Application software can be divided into these general areas:

- Word processing
- Spreadsheet
- Database

Word processing software allows you to create, modify, delete, save, and print documents that are office quality. They also have capabilities for spell checking, and include a dictionary and thesaurus. Word processing software has been around since the early 1980s. One of the first word processing software packages was WordPerfect. Now, Microsoft makes Word and Sun Microsystems has a word processing package called OpenOffice Writer. A screenshot of OpenOffice Writer appears in Figure 1.1. It operates similarly to Microsoft Word and comes free with Red Hat Linux.

Figure 1.1: A Screenshot of OpenOffice Writer by Sun Microsystems

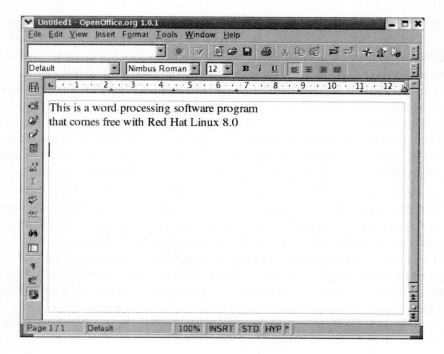

The first spreadsheet program was written in the early 1980s by college students who were taking an accounting class. Growing weary of making written changes to their accounting worksheets and having to recalculate by hand, they developed a program that automatically performed calculations and recalculated changes automatically.

Spreadsheet programs allow you to manage data in rows and columns. Spreadsheets hold data in **cells**, which is a row and column coordinate. When one cell changes, all cells referencing the original cell will change. Cells are labeled with names such as A1 or B7. Letters represent the columns and numbers represent the rows. Spreadsheet programs are extremely powerful and can include programming logic. They also include built-in functions. **Functions** are small programs where you just supply the data and the function does the work. Spreadsheet programs allow you to create your own formulas too, as shown in Figure 1.2. In Figure 1.2, you can see a spreadsheet with data and a formula.

Figure 1.2: Screenshot of the Microsoft Excel Application with Data

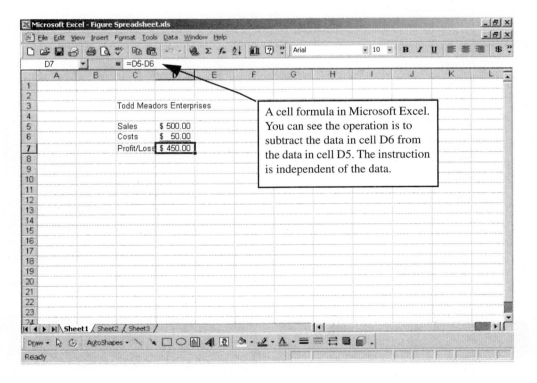

Database programs allow you to manipulate and manage data in tables. A **table** is a collection of database data stored on disk. One of the first database programs, called dBASE, was developed by the Ashton-Tate Corporation in the 1980s. Other companies such as IBM, Microsoft, Oracle and Sun Microsystems have developed database software as well. Database software allows you to create tables of data for organization. You can add, delete, or modify data in a database. You can join or combine data from multiple tables to create views or subsets of tables. Most programming languages allow you to interface with database software, letting you to create a powerful program. In Figure 1.3, an Employee database has been created. In the figure, you can see field names such as "Employee Name," "Employee Address," and so on. A **field** is a group of bytes. Multiple fields together comprise a **record**. So all of the Employee fields in Figure 1.3 make up an Employee record. The database holds the records.

Figure 1.3: A Screenshot of a Database Using Microsoft Access

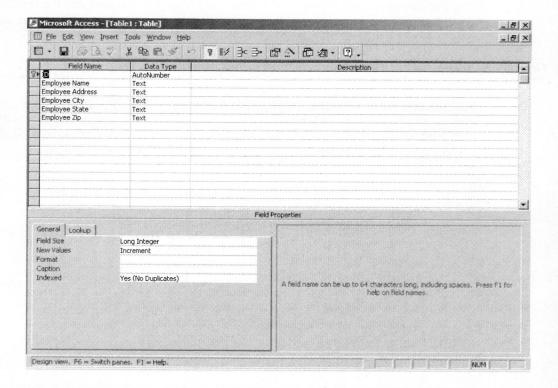

 Many software companies combine word processing, spreadsheet, and database software into a software suite. Microsoft has done this with Microsoft Office. Software that is combined in such a manner is called **integrated** software.

1.2 Understanding Hardware

If you are going to work with operating systems in the Information Technology industry, you need to understand a little about hardware. Hardware can generally be classified as follows:

- Input
- Processing
- Output

Input devices provide for data and instructions to be input into the computer system. Examples of devices that are strictly used for input are the keyboard, the mouse, a digital camera, and a scanner. After the data is input by the input device, it travels along a **bus** and is temporarily stored in **Random Access Memory (RAM)**. The bus is a set of wires on the **motherboard** that carry data and instructions. The motherboard is the main system board in the Personal Computer that interconnects the other hardware components.

The data is processed by the **Central Processing Unit (CPU)**. The CPU, or **processor**, is considered the "brains" of the computer system because it performs action on the data. The most important measure of a CPU is its speed. The speed of a processor is measured in **hertz**, or cycles per second. A **cycle** is made up of two stages known as the **Instruction time**, or **I-time**, and the **Execution time**, or **E-time**. During the I-time, these two events occur:

1. The instruction is fetched from RAM by the processor to the processor's own memory. Actually, the instruction is stored into a storage unit called a **register**. There are several different register types. For example, the **Accumulator** is a register that stores data. The **Instruction Register** stores the instruction.
2. The instruction is decoded and addresses for the data are generated.

During the E-time, these two events occur:

1. The instruction is actually executed by the processor.
2. The results of the execution are stored back into RAM.

Processors handle many of these instructions in a second. Common measurements are **MHz**, for mega (million) hertz, or **GHz** for giga (billion) hertz. A 3.0 GHz processor can perform 3 billion cycles per second. That is analogous to 3 billion addition operations in a second.

Let's look at general components of the CPU. The CPU is comprised of two main parts:

- Control Unit (CU)
- Arithmetic Logic Unit (ALU)

The **Control Unit (CU)** is the heart of the CPU. It governs all actions of the CPU.

The **Arithmetic Logic Unit (ALU)** function is particularly important to the topic of programming because this is where all the arithmetic and logic functions of the computer are done. Arithmetic functions include Multiply (*), Divide (/), Add (+) and Subtract (-), Exponential (**), and Parentheses. Refer to the following sample code for an arithmetic operation:

```
X = 5 * (4 + 2) / (6 + (1 / 10) - 50)
PRINT X
```

The Logic portion of the ALU performs comparisons. The types of comparisons performed by the Logic function are: AND, OR, EQUAL TO, NOT EQUAL TO, GREATER THAN, and LESS THAN. An example of a logic operation is in the calculation of the Dean's List in college. Let's assume you must have a GPA greater than 3.80 and carry 12 hours in a given semester. The logic for this operation would be an AND operation as in the following sample code:

```
IF GPA >= 3.80 AND HOURS >= 12.0 THEN
      PRINT "Dean's List"
END-IF
```

If you took 15 hours but have a GPA of 3.65, you would not be on the Dean's List. Or, if you had a GPA of 4.00 but only took a three-hour semester course, you would not be on the Dean's List.

Output devices receive the data that are processed by the CPU. Examples of output devices are the monitor, the printer, and a plotter.

Some devices are considered both input and output. Disk drives, tapes, and memory are all both input and output devices. They are called **Input/Output (I/O)** devices. The hard disk drive is a common example of an I/O device. When you save a document from within an application program, the document is output to disk for permanent storage. Later, when you need to retrieve the document, it is input from the disk into the application you are using.

Some hardware devices store data permanently and others store data temporarily. **Random Access Memory**, or **RAM**, is temporary. RAM is also shortened to "memory." Disk drive and tape storage units are permanent. However, memory is like the rough draft version of the data that will be written to the hard disk drive. Accessing memory is faster than accessing disk drives, but if you were to lose power to your computer, the contents of memory would be lost. Under the same conditions, the contents of the hard disk would remain intact.

Figure 1.4 shows a diagram of the flow of data through a computer system.

Figure 1.4: A Diagram Representing the Flow of Data

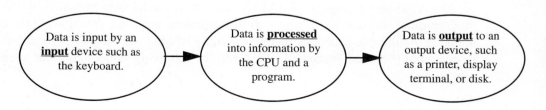

Memory and the hard drive store data in units. If you've ever heard the term megabyte or gigabyte, then you are hearing references to storage capacities. Generally, the more memory you have, the faster your computer will be. For a reference list of storage terms, see Table 1.1.

Table 1.1: Some Units of Storage in a Computer System

Term	Storage
Bit	Either a 0 or 1.
Byte	8 bits—for example the letter A (ASCII 01000001) would be considered a byte. A byte is also known as a character.
Kilobyte (KB) or thousand	1,024 bytes—typically stated as 1,000 bytes.
Megabyte (MB) or million	1,024 KB—typically stated as 1,000,000 bytes
Gigabyte (GB) or billion	1,024 MB—typically stated as 1 billion bytes.
Terabyte (TB) or trillion	1,024 GB—typically stated as 1 trillion bytes.

Processors are compared by their speed (hertz). Memory and disk drives are compared by their capacity (bytes).

1.3 Understanding the Types of Users

You need to understand the types of users that exist in an operating system environment so you can know how to best serve and interact with them. Their jobs also govern the type of access they need to the system. Here are the typical user types in an operating system setting:
- Standard User or user
- Programmer Analyst
- System Administrator
- Help Desk Support Representative

The **Standard User**, or **user**, is the person who uses the system on a daily basis in support of his or her job. They use the system to access an application. The application they need depends upon their function in the organization. For example, a Payroll Manager may need access to the Payroll application, whereas an Engineer may only need access to a Computer Aided Design/Computer Aided Manufacturing (CAD/CAM) program, and a Travel Agent may need access to the Travel Booking application. Users normally have limited access to the system.

The **Programmer Analyst** is the person responsible for analyzing the business needs of the user and writing the programs for users. This person must learn the programming language being used, as well as the business processes so they can write programs effectively for users. Normally, Programmer Analysts write programs using an editor. They need to be skilled problem-solvers and they need to be able to think logically.

The **System Administrator** is the person responsible for the operations of the computer systems and network. The System Administrator may have to work a varying work schedule depending upon the nature of the business. Many are on call 24 hours a day, seven days a week, called 24/7. Also, depending upon the size of the operation, there may be more than one System Administrator in an organization. They are completely responsible for ensuring that the computer systems, the networks, and the applications are available to the users during the hours needed by the users.

In larger organizations, the System Administrator's job may be divided between a **Network Administrator**, who is responsible for the network, and an **Operating System Specialist**, who is responsible for the operating system. They perform duties such as installs, upgrades, adding users, and so on. These people usually have complete access to the system, or at least more than the typical user. On a Windows NT and 2000 system, the user with complete access to the system is called **Administrator**. On a Novell system, this user is called **Supervisor** or **Admin**, depending upon the version of operating system. On Linux systems, this user is called **root**.

The **Help Desk Support Representative**, or Help Desk Technician, typically works in a telephone support environment where users of all types call in with problems. Help Desk people must be able to learn quickly, listen carefully, and have technical skills and patience. They learn a great deal in a short period of time. They must be able to resolve problems for users when called. One of the first questions Help Desk Support Representatives should politely ask users is, "What changed?"

1.4 Understanding the Operating System

An **operating system (OS)** is a set of software instructions that allows your computer system to operate. Operating systems are written in programming languages like application programs. For example, the Linux operating system is written in both Assembly and C. The operating system interacts with the hardware allowing the computer system to function. Nearly all computer systems require an operating system to run. This includes computer systems as small as your laptop and those as large and powerful as a supercomputer. The computer system needs both the software and the hardware to operate the computer successfully; a computer system cannot operate without either.

The operating system interfaces with the hardware for the application. For example, if you were using Microsoft Word to create a word processing document and you needed to save the document, you would click File and Save As and enter a file name to save. The operating system would intercept the request to save the document to disk for Microsoft Word. The operating system also retrieves files from disk. If you have ever clicked File, then Open and entered a file name, you have experienced the operating system retrieving a file from disk.

In Figure 1.5 you can see how an operating system fits within a computer environment. In the figure, you can see that users interact with an application that in turn interacts with the operating system. The operating system interacts with hardware on behalf of the user.

Figure 1.5: The Placement of the Operating System within a Computer Environment

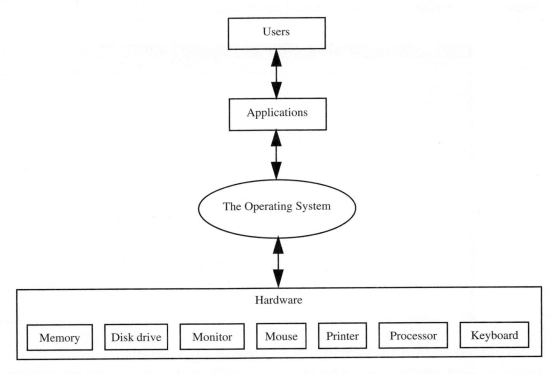

Now, let's perform a short exercise. The goal of this exercise is to help you understand how to open an application, create data in a file, and save the file. Because most all Windows operating systems have the Notepad application, this will be used. For this exercise, Windows 2000 will be assumed. Follow these steps:

1. Power on your computer. The Windows desktop should appear.
2. Click **Start**, and then click **Run**. The Run dialog box displays.
3. In the Open text box, type **notepad** and press Enter. The Notepad application opens in a separate window.
4. Refer to Figure 1.6 for a screenshot of Notepad. Enter the lines shown in Figure 1.6 replacing my name with yours.
5. In order to save the data, you will need a disk storage location. Insert a formatted floppy into the floppy drive. The floppy is referenced as A: drive.

6. You must enter a file name to save. Click **File** and then click **Save As**. The Save As window appears.
7. In the Save In drop-down box, select A: Floppy drive.
8. In the File name text box, enter **Exercise1** and click **Save**. The file will be saved with a .txt extension. File names and extensions will be discussed in Chapter 2. The point is the OS interacted with the hardware for the application and you.
9. To close Notepad, click **File** and then click **Exit**.

Figure 1.6: A Screenshot of the Notepad Application

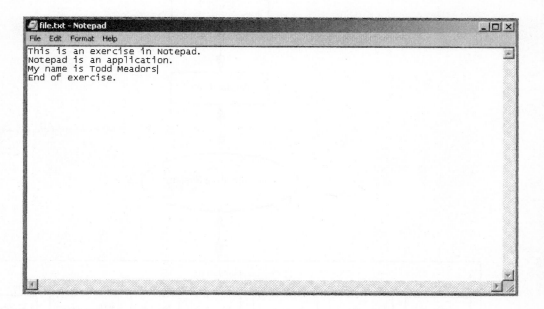

1.5 Understanding Classifications of Operating Systems

There are quite a few operating systems on the market today. There are operating systems for mainframe computers, PCs, laptops, and even hand-held computers. Let's look at a few of the operating system (OS) types.

Mainframe operating systems are designed to handle the Input/Output (I/O), processing and storage requirements for a lot of users. Mainframe operating systems run mainframe computers and are generally used in large organizations to handle the volume of work. Mainframe computers are usually centralized in a computer room with **terminals** connecting to it from remote locations. A terminal is a device that has no computing ability and is strictly dependent upon the processing power of another, such as the mainframe. It is merely a display monitor and a keyboard with wires connecting to the mainframe. Applications are accessed on the mainframe itself. You can also use a Personal Computer (PC) with software to act like a terminal to connect to a mainframe;

this software is called terminal **emulation** software. The term emulate means imitate. An example of a mainframe operating system is IBM's Multiple Virtual Storage (MVS).

When you access the UNIX or Linux OS from a Windows PC using the **telnet** command, then your computer is acting as a terminal for that session. The telnet command allows you to remotely connect to another computer. In Figure 1.7, you can see a screenshot of the telnet command in action. The very last line tells the story. Here you can see that a Linux command, **echo $TERM**, is issued and returns a terminal type of "**ansi**" on the screen. Note that "ansi" is just a terminal type—there are many more. Don't be too concerned about this Linux command or its output for now, just understand that terminal emulation is occurring here. Linux commands will be covered in a later chapter.

Figure 1.7: A Screenshot of a Terminal Emulation Session

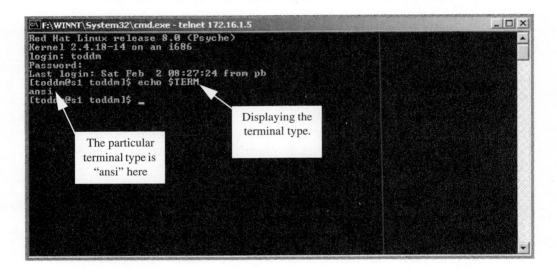

A mainframe computer has the same general components, such as processor, memory, and disk drive storage, as your own **Personal Computer**, or **PC**. They are usually physically larger and spread out over the area of a room. For example, your PC has a disk drive physically located in your **system unit**, or **chassis**. A mainframe computer may have multiple disk drive units spread out in a computer room, but these units would be connected to the mainframe computer.

Midrange operating systems have the same properties of mainframe operating systems. However, they are generally used for medium-sized organizations. They operate in a centralized manner with terminals and PCs using emulation software, accessing applications remotely. An example of a midrange operating system is IBM's OS/400, which runs on an AS/400.

A **Network Operating System (NOS)** allows computers to share resources in a network. A NOS and mainframe/midrange operating system differ in one main respect.

Where mainframe and midrange operating systems utilize centralized processing and storage capabilities, a NOS allows you to decentralize your operations. This is because instead of using terminals, a NOS relies on PCs, which have their own processing power, memory, and storage capabilities. With a NOS, you can distribute the processing load over multiple computers. For example, one computer could be a web server, another could be an e-mail server, and another could be an application server.

Which came first—the mainframe or the NOS? From an historical perspective, the use of mainframes dates back to the 1940s when they were used in military applications during World War II. Utilization of Network Operating Systems is a more recent innovation with the development of PCs in the 1980s.

A **resource** is a hardware device, a software program, or a file needed by users. A **shared resource** is a resource that is capable of being used on other computers. A printer that can be used by multiple users is an example of a shared resource. An application stored on a computer that is used by multiple users is another example of a shared resource. Let's see this in an exercise. For this exercise, Windows 2000 will be assumed. You will also use Windows Explorer to access the floppy drive. Follow these steps:

1. Power on your computer. The Windows desktop should appear.
2. Right-click **Start** then click **Explore**. A separate Explorer window appears.
3. Insert a formatted floppy into the floppy drive.
4. Scroll until you see the Floppy (A:) drive.
5. Right-click the floppy drive and click Sharing. The Properties page of the floppy appears. Refer to Figure 1.8 for a screenshot of this page.
6. Click the **Sharing** tab.
7. Click **Share this folder**. Notice the share name is "A," for the floppy.
8. Click **OK**. Now the floppy can be access from another computer remotely over the network.
9. Close the floppy's Properties page by clicking the **X** in the upper right-hand corner. This means to close the window.

Figure 1.8: A Screenshot of Sharing a Resource

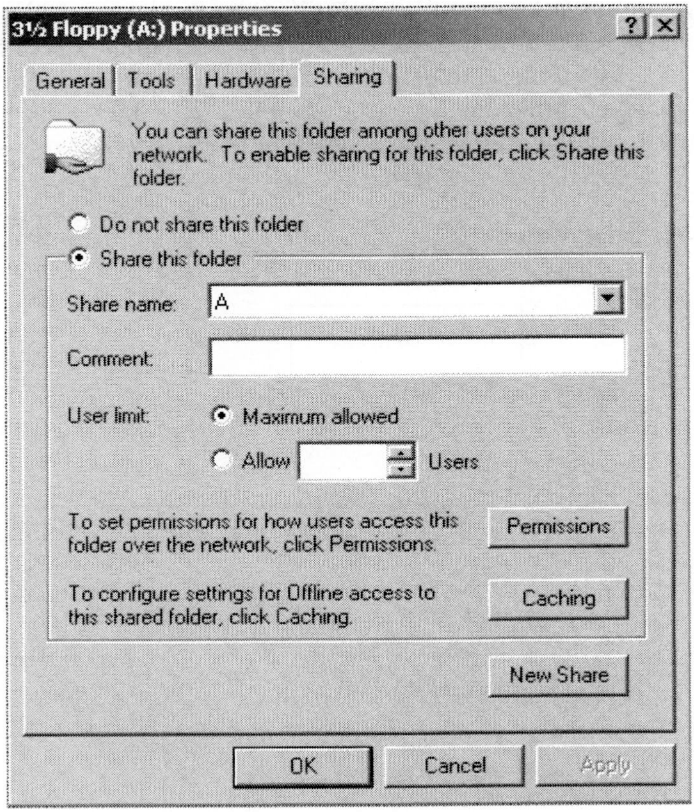

A network is a group of computers and printers connected by cables or some wireless media. Network operating systems use **protocol** software to facilitate the communication among other computers in a network. The term **Local Area Network**, or **LAN**, generally refers to a collection of computers, printers, and other networking components, such as cable, hubs, switches, and routers, which are physically close together. For example, computers interconnected in the same room or building would generally be considered a LAN.

In a LAN, **servers** are computers that allow other computers to connect to the server's shared resources. **Clients** are the computers that use the resources made available by the servers. In the **client/server** model, a server computer handles the requests made by the client computer. There are usually more clients than servers in a network. The server usually has additional memory, hard drive capacity, and processing capability because the server has to handle numerous client requests. The computers generally use a **Network Interface Card**, or **NIC**, to connect to the server in either a wire or wireless configuration.

Examples of operating systems that run on servers are Novell NetWare, Microsoft Windows NT Server, 2000 Server, and UNIX/Linux. DOS, Windows 3.x, Windows 95, Windows 98, Windows NT Workstation, Windows 2000 Professional, and Windows XP are examples of client operating systems. The UNIX/Linux operating system can also be used as a client. Servers and clients are required to use the same protocol in order to communicate with one another. Although it can be a complicated process, the use of a common protocol can even allow different operating systems to communicate with one another. In Figure 1.9, you can the client/server LAN environment.

Figure 1.9: The Client/Server LAN Environment

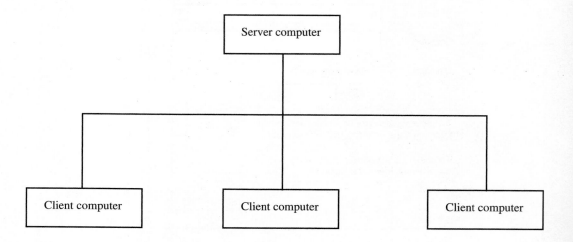

Centralized processing occurs when the processing and storage resources are performed at a central site. There may be multiple processors and storage units, however they are usually in one physical location. Access to these resources occurs locally over communication wires, or links, and remotely via terminals or terminal emulation. Mainframes and midrange operating systems are examples of centralized processing.

Distributed processing occurs when the processing and storage resources are spread out, hence distributed, over multiple computers. Instead of terminals, PCs are used to share the load. The advent of Network Operating Systems in a client/server LAN environment has brought about the use of distributed processing.

The **Transmission Control Protocol/Internet Protocol (TCP/IP)** is the most commonly used protocol today. It was developed by the United States Department of Defense. TCP/IP is what allows you to connect to the Internet and browse web sites, take college courses, perform searches, or buy products. Actually, the first use of the Internet was an electronic mail (e-mail) message sent from one user to another on different coasts of the United States. Each computer, called a **host**, must have an IP (Internet Protocol) address to communicate with other computers on the network. Note that each host must also have an operating system that supports TCP/IP. The host may also have a **Domain Name Service (DNS)** name such as www.meadors.org. This is sometimes called the host's "user friendly name." The DNS name keeps us from having to remember the IP address. Networking technologies will be discussed in more detail in a later chapter.

DNS is what allows you to enter a name such as http://www.scottjonespub.com or http://www.meadors.org in the address line of your web browser software and view a web page on your computer.

Let's view your IP address settings in an exercise. This exercise assumes Windows 2000 running on a PC. Follow these steps:

1. Connect to the Internet from home, work, or school.
2. Click **Start**, then click **Run**. The Run dialog box displays.
3. In the Open text box, type **command** and press Enter. The DOS command line interface displays. (On Windows 2000, you could also have entered **cmd** to display the command line interface.)
4. In order to display your IP configuration, enter **ipconfig** and press Enter. (If you happen to be on Windows 95, the command is **winipcfg**.) The IP configuration of your PC displays.
5. Refer to Figure 1.10 for a sample screenshot. The Internet connection for the PC shown in Figure 1.10 has an IP address of 67.30.192.18.
6. Close the window. The command line interface window closes.

Figure 1.10: Displaying the TCP/IP Properties of a Computer

```
F:\WINNT\System32\command.com                                    _ □ ×
(C)Copyright Microsoft Corp 1990-1999.

F:\>ipconfig

Windows 2000 IP Configuration

Ethernet adapter Local Area Connection:

        Connection-specific DNS Suffix  . :
        Autoconfiguration IP Address. . . : 169.254.254.251
        Subnet Mask . . . . . . . . . . . : 255.255.0.0
        Default Gateway . . . . . . . . . :

Ethernet adapter Local Area Connection 2:

        Media State . . . . . . . . . . . : Cable Disconnected

PPP adapter NetZero:

        Connection-specific DNS Suffix  . :
        IP Address. . . . . . . . . . . . : 67.30.192.18
        Subnet Mask . . . . . . . . . . . : 255.255.255.255
        Default Gateway . . . . . . . . . : 67.30.192.18

F:\>
```

Traditionally, mainframe computers have not supported the TCP/IP. This is because mainframe computers were around before TCP/IP was developed. Mainframe manufacturers such as IBM had to develop their own communications software, such as IBM's System Network Architecture (SNA), so the terminals could connect with the mainframe. However, with the advent of the Internet, many mainframe manufacturers began to provide products allowing Internet connectivity. Thus, mainframe computers and midrange computers now allow connectivity using TCP/IP.

The use of the Internet is so pervasive that with the release of Windows 95, Microsoft incorporated its own web browser, Internet Explorer, with its operating system. This was an issue in litigation during the 1990s. Now, products released by Microsoft come with Internet Explorer for Internet connectivity. Other operating systems, such as Red Hat's Linux, also come with Internet browser software ready to use. Connecting your computer to the Internet involves **Wide Area Network (WAN)** technologies. A WAN refers to computers connected remotely. While LANs usually connect many devices in physical proximity, WANs generally connect devices in remote locations.

A telecommunications carrier such as AT&T, Sprint, or Bell South provides WAN technologies, such as Dial-up, DSL, T1, or ISDN. WANs sometimes connect separate LANs that are spread over geographic distances. For example, if a company had a LAN in Jacksonville, Florida, and another LAN in Lawrenceville, Georgia, a WAN could be configured to allow these two separate LANs to communicate.

To help you understand this concept, Figure 1.11 represents the Internet as "the cloud." Typically you connect to the Internet using your **Internet Service Provider (ISP)**, such as AT&T, Sprint, or Bell South, and they provide remote access. The "lightning bolts" refer to a WAN type connection.

Figure 1.11: Your Home Connection Along with LAN Connections to the Internet Cloud

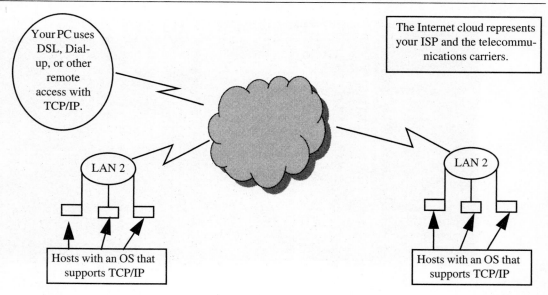

Table 1.2 provides a summary of the more common operating systems used on PCs. Note that each of these operating systems supports TCP/IP for Internet access.

Table 1.2: A Few of the More Common Operating Systems Used on PCs Today

Operating System	Description
DOS	One of the first operating systems developed commercially by Microsoft in the early 1980s. It is a text-based, single-tasking operating system.
Windows 3.1	Microsoft Windows 3.1 was not really an operating system but is a Graphical User Interface (GUI) for managing DOS. Windows 3.1 was developed after DOS and is executed after DOS is up and running.
Windows 9x	The Windows 9x class of operating systems include Windows 95 and 98. Windows 95 is the first true GUI operating system developed by Microsoft. Windows 95 and 98 are multi-tasking operating systems with a DOS shell component allowing you to run DOS commands. These operating systems have many GUI tools as well as Internet Explorer.
Windows NT	Microsoft developed Windows NT Workstation and Server to compete in the server-based networking market. Users typically use the Workstation product and the Server product performs network functionality for the Workstations. NT is a GUI operating system with DOS command line access.
Windows 2000	Microsoft developed Windows 2000 Professional and Server as upgrade paths to Windows NT Workstation and Server. Windows 2000 includes more administrative tools and functionality than NT. These are also GUI operating systems with DOS command line access.
UNIX	AT&T developed the UNIX operating system in the 1960s. There were two main original versions of UNIX: AT&T System V (Five) and Berkeley Source Distribution (BSD). UNIX is a multi-tasking, multi-user text-based operating system. DOS has many similar characteristics to UNIX.
Linux	Linux is a version of UNIX that runs on PCs and includes both a GUI and text interface to the operating system. It usually runs as a server-based product and was developed in the 1990s.

| NetWare | Novell developed its network operating system, called NetWare, in the 1980s as a server-based product. NetWare runs in a DOS-based partition. |
| Mac OS | Apple developed the Mac operating system. |

A **platform** is comprised of <u>both</u> the hardware and software that a given system runs on. For example, Linux version 8.0 is the software running on an Intel-based hardware system. The two combined are called the platform. Another example would be Windows 2000 on an Intel-based system.

Chapter Summary

- Software is a set of instructions processed by the computer. Software programs are written in programming languages. Programs are either compiled or interpreted. Programs are converted from programming languages to the processor's machine language. Data is defined as raw facts that are processed into information. Software is divided into two categories: system software and application software.
- Hardware is the tangible part of the computer system. Hardware devices are classified as input, processing, or output. Input devices facilitate data coming into the computer system. The Central Processing Unit (CPU) performs the processing activity for the computer. The CPU is comprised of the Arithmetic Logic Unit and the Control Unit. Output devices receive data processed by the CPU. Some devices are considered I/O devices. They perform either input or output functions. Examples of I/O devices are the hard disk, tape, and memory.
- The Standard User utilizes the operating system to perform their daily duties. The Programmer Analyst is responsible for analyzing business needs of users and writes the programs for them. The System Administrator is responsible for all operating systems functions. The Network Administrator ensures the network is up and running. The Help Desk Support Representative provides telephone support for customer problems.
- The operating system is a set of software instructions allowing your computer system to operate. It works with the hardware, users, and the applications.
- Mainframe operating systems handle I/O, processing and storage requirements for many users. Midrange operating systems have similar properties as mainframes except they are typically used in medium-sized organizations. A Network Operating System (NOS) allows you to share resources in a network environment.

Review Questions

1. Which of the following is defined as a set of instructions that are processed by a computer system?
   a) Firmware
   b) Software
   c) ASCII
   d) Low-level programming language

2. Which of the following is a collection of instructions that accomplish a purpose?
   a) Program
   b) Hardware
   c) ASCII
   d) I-time

3. A (n) _____ is a statement that performs an action.
   a) Program
   b) Instruction
   c) CPU
   d) Compiler

4. A (n) _____ is hardware specific.
   a) Application software program
   b) High-level programming language
   c) Low-level programming language
   d) Compiler

5. A (n) _____ is the set of instruction statements the processor can understand and use.
   a) Application software program
   b) High-level programming language
   c) Low-level programming language
   d) Instruction set

6. A (n) _____ is a program that is compiled and syntax error-free.
   a) Executable program
   b) Record
   c) Hardware device
   d) Piece of data

7. What is data processed into?
   a) I-time
   b) ASCII
   c) Information
   d) Compiled language

8. The character set common to most PCs is called _____.
   a) I-time
   b) ASCII
   c) Information
   d) System software

9. With _____ software, you can create and modify office-quality documents.
   a) Spreadsheet
   b) ASCII
   c) Word processing
   d) Database

10. With _____ software, you can manage data in cells and perform calculations on the data.
    a) Spreadsheet
    b) ASCII
    c) Word processing
    d) Database

11. With _____ software, you can manipulate and manage data in tables.
    a) Spreadsheet
    b) ASCII
    c) Word processing
    d) Database

12. A _____ is a group of bytes.
    a) RAM
    b) Table
    c) File
    d) Field

13. During the _____, an instruction is fetched from RAM.
    a) MHz time
    b) E-time
    c) CPU time
    d) I-time

14. A _____ is either a 0 or a 1.
    a) MHz
    b) MB
    c) Bit
    d) Byte

15. A _____ utilizes the computer system on a daily basis in support of his or her job function.
    a) System Administrator
    b) Programmer Analyst
    c) Standard User
    d) Help Desk Support Representative

16. A _____ writes instructions to accomplish a task.
    a) System Administrator
    b) Programmer Analyst
    c) Standard User
    d) Help Desk Support Representative

17. A _____ is responsible for operations of the computer systems.
    a) System Administrator
    b) Programmer Analyst
    c) Standard User
    d) Help Desk Support Representative

18. A _____ mainly provides telephone support for customer problems.
    a) System Administrator
    b) Programmer Analyst
    c) Standard User
    d) Help Desk Support Representative

19. Which of the following is defined as software that facilitates communication among computers within a LAN?
    a) Protocol
    b) Server
    c) Client
    d) NIC

20. Which of the following best describes when processing and storage resources are spread over multiple computers?
    a) Centralized
    b) Distributed
    c) DNS
    d) TCP/IP

Lab Projects

Lab Project 1

In this project you will need to visit an organization that uses a computer system and discuss the type of hardware and software it uses. You can use your school, work, library, or church.

1. Locate an organization that uses a computer system.

2. Record the name of the organization.

   _____

3. Interview someone with System Administrator responsibility and record the classification of computer system, the operating systems, and versions used.

   _____

   _____

   _____

4. Interview a user and record the type of applications used.

   _____

   _____

   _____

5. If they use the Internet, record how it is used.

   _____

   _____

   _____

6. Politely thank the users and leave.

Lab Project 2

In this project you will go through the process of purchasing a computer system to help you understand the terminology of an operating system environment. You are to identify the computer make and model, vendor, the total price, and your source of information.

1. With a fictitious budget of $2,500, you will purchase an operating system and hardware for a computer meeting these requirements:

Hardware:

    256 MB RAM
    800 MHz or higher CPU
    60+ GB Hard disk drive
    Floppy drive
    DVD/CD-ROM (50 X speed)
    100 Mbps Network Interface Card
    Video card
    17" monitor
    ink jet printer
    modem card

2. Record the operating system you chose.

    _____

3. Record the reason for choosing this operating system.

    _____

4. Present your findings to the class.

5. Turn in all documentation to your instructor.

Lab Project 3

The goal of this project is to help you understand how to view additional TCP/IP settings on your computer. This exercise assumes Windows 2000 Professional as the operating system on a running computer. Follow these steps:

1. Connect to your Internet Service Provider (ISP).

2. While connected, click **Start**, and then click **Run**. The Run dialog box displays.

3. In the **Open** text box, type **command** and press Enter. The DOS command line interface displays.

4. Type **ipconfig /all** to display your TCP/IP properties with information about your remote connection.

5. Record the settings for the following:
   IP address: _____
   Subnet mask: _____
   Default gateway: _____
   DNS server: _____

6. Record two additional settings.

   _____

   _____

7. Refer to Figure 1.12 for a sample screenshot. In the figure, you'll notice the "PPP adapter NetZero" connection. This is the WAN connection going to the Internet. Notice the IP address information. This was sent to the computer from the ISP.

8. Close your window. The command line interface window closes.

Figure 1.12: Internet Connectivity Showing IP Address Settings Using the WAN Protocol (Point-to-Point, or PPP)

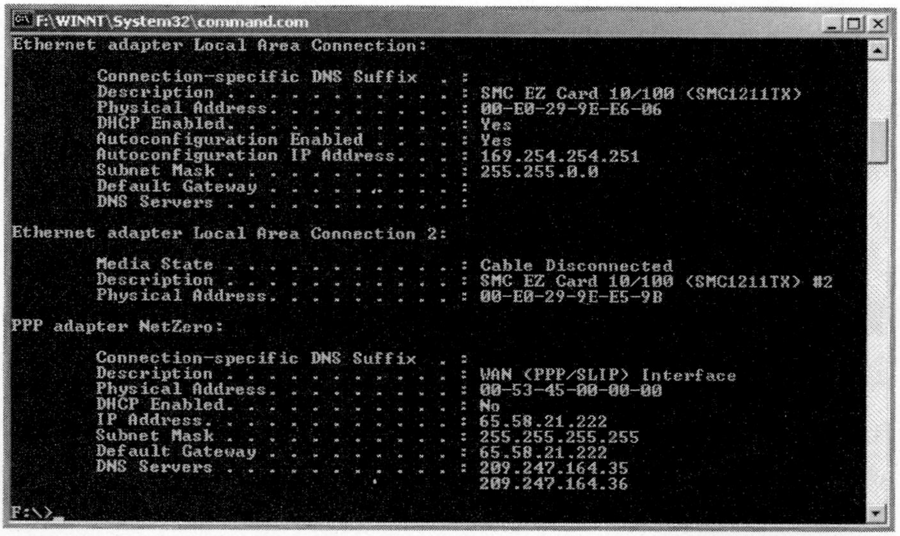

Lab Project 4

The goal of this project is to help you understand how to convert storage capacities.

1. Convert 10 MB to KB. Record your answer.

_____

2. Convert 5 GB to MB. Record your answer.

_____

3. Convert 1,700 KB to GB. Record your answer.

_____

4. Convert 1 KB to bits. Record your answer.

_____

5. Record how many 1.5 KB files will fit on a 1.44 MB floppy.

_____

Lab Project 5—Challenge

The goal of this project is to help you understand how to create a file, share it, and view it from another computer in a network. This project assumes at least two computers are connected. The project also assumes Microsoft 2000. If you don't have two computers, you can simulate a second one just by viewing the network icon on the same computer you create the file on.

1. Create a folder on your hard drive, C:.

2. Share the folder.

3. List the steps you took to share the folder.

_____

4. From a second computer (or the same one if you don't have a second computer), go to the **My Network Places** icon until you see the share name of the folder on the other computer. Refer to Figure 1.13 for a sample screenshot. In the figure, the folder that is shared is named Shared Folder.

5. List the steps you took to view the folder on the second computer.

_____

6. Close all windows of all computers and logout.

Figure 1.13: A Screenshot of Viewing a Shared Folder from Another Computer

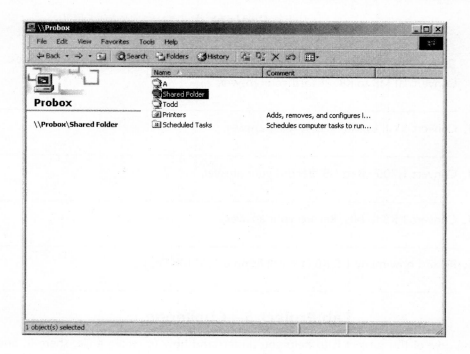

Internet Discovery

Internet Discovery Lab 1

The goal of this Internet Discovery Lab is to help further your knowledge of chapter terms by accessing the Webopedia web site.

1. Connect to the Internet.

2. Open your web browser.

3. In the address box, type **http://www.webopedia.com** and press Enter.

4. Locate the search box, enter the following terms, search for them, and write a brief synopsis of each term. Close your browser when complete.

    a. Firmware

_____

_____

_____

    b. Compiler

_____

_____

_____

    c. Instruction

_____

_____

_____

Internet Discovery Lab 2

The goal of this Internet Discovery Lab is to have you determine the minimum hardware needed for installing Red Hat Linux 8.0.

1. Connect to the Internet.

2. Open your web browser.

3. In the address box, type **http://www.redhat.com** and press Enter.

4. Locate the search box and type **minimum** and press Enter.

5. Record the CPU type, amount of memory, disk drive capacity, and any other necessary hardware requirements for installing Red Hat Linux 8.0.

   _____

   _____

   _____

6. Close your browser.

Internet Discovery Lab 3

The goal of this Internet Discovery Lab is to have you determine the minimum hardware needed for installing Microsoft operating systems.

1. Connect to the Internet.

2. Open your web browser.

3. In the address box, type **http://www.microsoft.com** and press Enter.

4. Browse the web site until you find the minimum hardware requirements for these operating systems:

   a. Windows 98

   _____

   _____

   b. Windows 2000

   _____

   _____

   c. Windows XP

   _____

   _____

5. Close your browser.

Internet Discovery Lab 4

The goal of this Internet Discovery Lab is to help further your knowledge of chapter concepts by accessing the Howstuffworks web site.

1. Connect to the Internet.

2. Open your web browser.

3. In the address box, type **http://www.howstuffworks.com** and press Enter.

4. Search for "operating system."

5. Review any related articles.

6. Record your findings. Find an example of an operating system not discussed in this chapter and record the name and manufacturer.

_____

_____

_____

7. Close your browser.

Soft Skills: Help Desk Support

1. A user calls and tells you they are having trouble saving a file to disk. What type of questions do you ask? What steps do you tell the user to take to successfully save the file?

2. You are working the help desk for your company and a user calls and says they would like to delete a payroll file on the system. What types of issues should you consider?

Critical Thinking

1. Discuss how an operating system environment is like a human body.

2. Oppose or defend the statement: All computer systems require some type of operating system to operate.

3. Defend what you think is more important—software or hardware. Which do you think came first?

 # Study Skills

Obtaining Success in Your Technical Studies

Technical courses can be quite challenging. Not only are you learning new skills but also you are exposed to a wide range of terms and acronyms. However, attaining these new skills will help you on your first job. Listed below are the Study Skills for Chapter 1. In future chapters, you will be introduced to additional Study Skills to help you to a rewarding and exciting computer career. Following these will put you on the right path to improving your success in class and on the job!

- Attend class **on time every day!** Attending all class sessions is one of the best habits you can get into towards your goal of **obtaining success**. Missing class will put you behind. Get to class 10 minutes early. At the very least, you can review the chapter material or work on a Lab Project. If you have to be out, contact your instructor via telephone or e-mail as soon as you can.
- Take complete and accurate notes—Taking notes will help reinforce your knowledge when preparing for a test.
- Listen to your instructor and ask questions when you don't understand. You instructor has a wealth of knowledge and experience. Listen to his or her directions and pay attention to their rules! Don't be afraid to ask questions. There are probably others that have a similar question so you'll help them too.
- Bring all necessary materials. Many students go to class with the idea that the instructor will provide everything. If your instructor asks you to bring floppy disks, bring them each class session. Always bring your textbook, notebook paper, pen or pencil and a positive attitude!
- Get a Study Skills Partner. Contact a classmate who you can count on when you get into trouble. This is particularly useful for Lab Projects where one mistake can cost you time.

Study Skills: Self-Study Question(s)
1. Identify at least one Study Skill you did today to "Obtain Success in Your Technical Studies".
2. Who is your Study Skills Partner?

2

Chapter 2
Basic Operating
System Theory

OBJECTIVES

The goal of this chapter is to introduce you to basic operating system theory. This chapter will help you prepare and pass the following sections of the A+ Operating System Technologies Exam:

A+ Operating System Technologies Exam Objectives
covered in this chapter (and corresponding page numbers)

Domain 1 Operating System Fundamentals

1.1 Identify the major desktop components and interfaces, and their functions. Differentiate the characteristics of Windows 9x/Me, Windows NT 4.0 Workstation, Windows 2000 Professional, and Windows XP.

1.4 Identify basic concepts and procedures for creating, viewing, and managing disks, directories and files. This includes procedures for changing file attributes and the ramifications of those changes (for example, security issues).

Domain 2 Installation, Configuration, and Upgrading

2.4 Identify procedures for installing/adding a device, including loading, adding, and configuration device drivers, and required software.

In this chapter, you will complete the following sections:
- 2.1 Understanding the User Interface
- 2.2 Understanding Application Management
- 2.3 Understanding File System Management
- 2.4 Understanding Hardware Management
- 2.5 Understanding the Operating System Kernel

2.1 Understanding the User Interface

One goal of the operating system is to interface with the user. There are two major classifications of user interfaces that are available with operating systems. They are:

- Command Line Interface (sometimes generically called CLI)
- Graphical User Interface (GUI)

The most common operating systems using a **Command Line Interface (CLI)** are Microsoft DOS (MS-DOS or just DOS) and UNIX/Linux. To use a command line interface, you must be able to type and learn the command line syntax and structure. Figure 2.1 shows a screenshot of the DOS command line displaying a list of files on the floppy drive. The command being executed is the DOS **dir** command. It includes an option, **/a**, to show all files. This command and its options will be covered in detail in Chapter 3 on DOS and the DOS command line. For now, just understand that the command line exists and it is not graphical.

Figure 2.1: The MS-DOS Command Line Interface

```
A:\>dir /a

 Volume in drive A has no label
 Volume Serial Number is 2156-18E8
 Directory of A:\

IO       SYS       222,390  05-11-98  8:01p IO.SYS
MSDOS    SYS             9  05-11-98  8:01p MSDOS.SYS
COMMAND  COM        93,880  05-11-98  8:01p COMMAND.COM
DRVSPACE BIN        68,871  05-11-98  8:01p DRVSPACE.BIN
         4 file(s)        385,150 bytes
         0 dir(s)       1,071,104 bytes free

A:\>_
```

In UNIX/Linux terminology, the command line interface is called a **shell**. Figure 2.2 contains a screenshot of the Red Hat Linux shell. In this figure, two commands are executed to show you how the shell works. The **who** command is executed first and displays users currently logged into the system. Next, the **pwd** displays the current directory location. These commands will be covered in detail in Chapter 8 on the UNIX/Linux operating system.

Figure 2.2: The Red Hat Linux Command Line Interface (Shell)

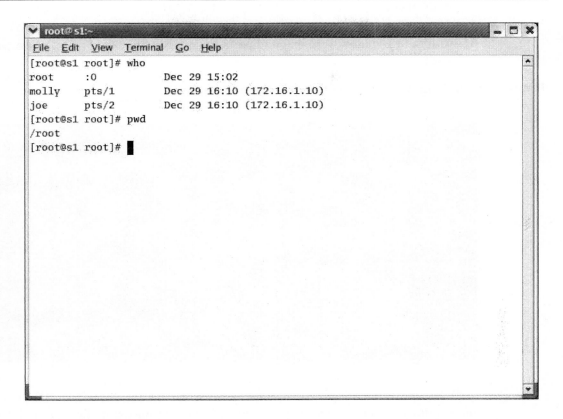

To help you understand the user command line interaction, you will perform an exercise in the DOS command mode of a Windows operating system. You will display the version of the operating system and the memory statistics. Understanding the version of the operating system and the amount of memory available is important because you may have to install an application that requires a specific operating system level and a minimum amount of memory. These commands will assist you in determining if the application you plan to install will run. This exercise assumes a PC is up and running with the Windows 98 (or higher) operating system. Follow these steps:

1. Click **Start**; then click Run. The Run dialog box displays.
2. In the Open text box, type **command** and press Enter. The DOS command line interface displays. Note that you could enter **cmd** instead of **command** for Windows NT, Windows 2000, and Windows XP. Either command will work on those operating systems.
3. In order to display the current version of the operating system, type **ver** and press Enter. The operating system version displays.

4. In order to display memory statistics, type **mem** and press Enter. The memory statistics display.

5. Refer to Figure 2.3 for a screenshot of this exercise.

6. To close the window, type **exit** and press Enter. The command line interface window closes.

Figure 2.3: Working with the DOS Command Line Interface

```
F:\WINNT\System32\command.com
Microsoft(R) Windows DOS
(C)Copyright Microsoft Corp 1990-1999.

F:\>ver

Microsoft Windows 2000 [Version 5.00.2195]

F:\>mem

    655360 bytes total conventional memory
    655360 bytes available to MS-DOS
    629792 largest executable program size

   1048576 bytes total contiguous extended memory
         0 bytes available contiguous extended memory
    941056 bytes available XMS memory
           MS-DOS resident in High Memory Area

F:\>_
```

Today most operating systems have a **Graphical User Interface (GUI)** where a pointing device, such as mouse, is used to navigate, or **point and click**, around the operating system. The area on the screen where the user interacts with the operating system is called the **desktop**. Users click on **icons**, which are pictures that represent items such as programs and folders. Both Windows and Linux operating systems have a GUI interface.

Refer to Figure 2.4 for a screenshot of the Windows 98 Explorer program displaying the same files that are shown in Figure 2.1. On the left hand side of the screen you see folders and on the right you see the contents of the folders. Notice the horizontal bar at the top of a window. This is called the **Title Bar** and indicates the name of the program that is running. In the upper right hand corner of the Title Bar are three buttons. These are the **Minimize**, **Maximize,** and **Close** buttons. Notice how the same files from Figure 2.1 show up as icons here instead of simply file names. You can view most of the same information using the command line or the GUI with a given system.

Figure 2.4: Microsoft Windows 98 GUI Operating System Explorer Program

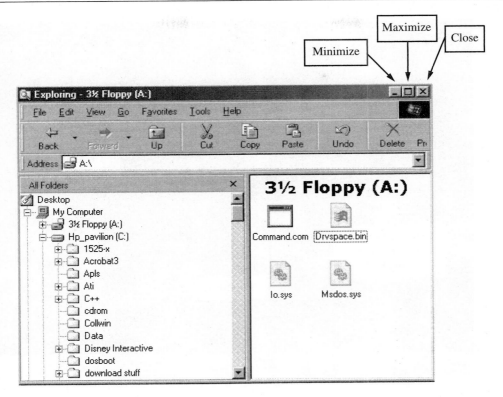

Because you have most likely seen a GUI desktop in Windows but not in Linux, Figure 2.5 shows a screenshot of the Red Hat Linux 8.0 operating system GUI. You can see the icons on the desktop, the Panel at the bottom of the screen, and the Internet browser software.

Figure 2.5: A Screenshot of a Red Hat Linux 8.0 Operating System Graphical Desktop

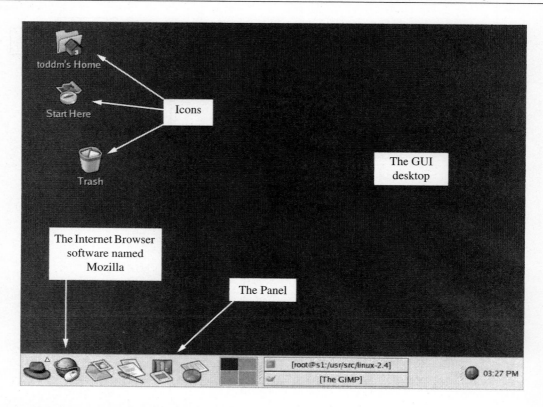

2.2 Understanding Application Management

Operating systems provide application management in the following ways:

- Access the hardware for applications
- Facilitate installing and uninstalling of applications
- Provide a consistent interface among applications through an Application Program Interface (API)

One role of the operating system is to perform hardware **Input/Output (I/O)** for applications. Some examples of I/O operations are reading from the hard drive, writing to the hard drive, printing to the printer, storing data in memory, or displaying data on the screen. In some older operating systems, applications were able to access hardware directly. When this occurred, a **General Protection Fault (GPF)** could occur causing the computer to halt, or crash. A GPF occurs when a program tries to use the same area of memory as another program. GPFs occur less often in more current operating systems such as Windows 2000 and Windows XP because they don't allow applications direct access to the hardware. The operating system calls upon device drivers when performing I/O operations. **Device drivers** are software programs that tell the device how to operate. They will be discussed further in a later section of this chapter.

Another role the operating system performs is to allow users to install and uninstall applications on their computer system. This allows the user to customize his or her system for maximum personal benefit. On many Windows operating systems, this is performed using the Add/Remove Programs software tool. On Red Hat Linux you can run a command called **rpm**, Red Hat Package Manager, to install and uninstall software programs.

Additionally, the operating system provides consistency among applications. For example, in both Microsoft Word and Excel, you save a file by clicking File and then Save, or Save As. This similarity makes learning a new application quicker. Application consistency is provided through a set of software routines and tools for building software called an **Application Program Interface (API)**. APIs are designed for programmers and guarantee all programs, sharing a common API, have similar interfaces.

Many operating system manufacturers encourage programs be written to conform to the **Common User Access (CUA)** standard developed by IBM and Microsoft. The CUA makes sure Windows programs are consistent. Programmers use an API to implement the CUA. Having a common interface makes it easier for the user to navigate Windows applications. Microsoft operating system tools and applications support CUA. This standard is also supported on X Windows, which is the GUI for UNIX/Linux operating systems.

An API is a programming standard. The CUA is a Windows standard facilitated by the use of a standard API.

Microsoft Windows applications consist of executable files and **Dynamic Link Libraries (DLLs)**. A DLL is an executable file that contains smaller programs, called functions, and data. They allow applications to be loaded, unloaded, and reused easily. An application that is currently running is known as a **process** or job. A process has system resources allocated to it, such as the processor, memory, and environment variables. A process will be given a **Process Identification** number, called a **PID**, which is used by the operating system to reference the process. You can change the amount of processor time a process has or terminate a process by its PID. Figure 2.6 shows a screenshot of Task Manager in Windows 2000. Notice the columns for each process such as Image Name, PID, CPU (percentage used), CPU Time (used), and Mem Usage (Memory Usage).

Figure 2.6: A Display of Process Information Using Task Manager in Windows 2000 Professional

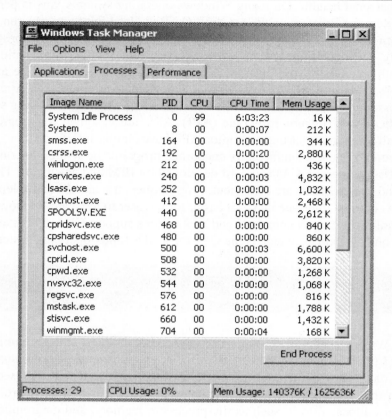

Figure 2.7 is a screenshot of the Linux System Monitor. To access this menu under Linux Red Hat 8.0, you would follow these steps:

1. Log in as a user.
2. Click the Red Hat icon on the taskbar. A list of tools appears.
3. Click **System Tools**. Additional tools appear.
4. Click **System Monitor**. System monitor appears.
5. Click **Process Listing**.
6. Once you are through reviewing System Monitor, click **x** to close the window.

This program is the equivalent of Windows 2000 Task Manager. It shows that Linux displays a column for the user running the process in addition to the ID, %CPU, and memory used. This is because Linux is a multi-user OS. The far right column, labeled "ID," is the PID.

Figure 2.7: System Monitor in Linux Displaying Process Information

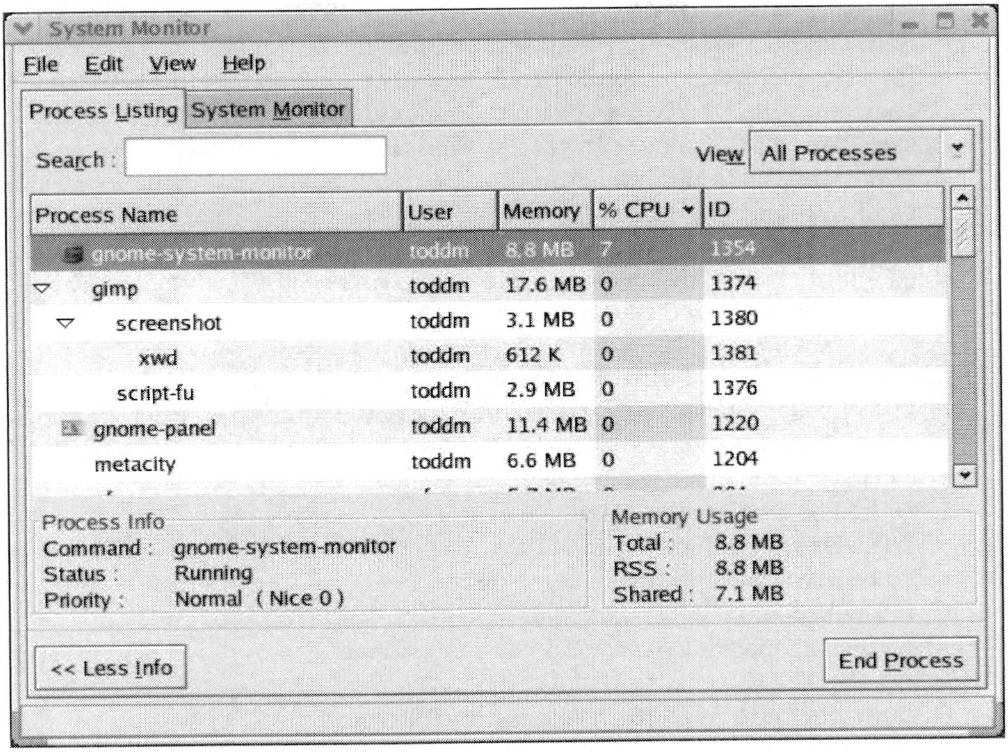

A **thread** is a basic unit of instruction that is allocated processor time by the operating system. Think of a process as being made up of many threads. The threads of a process execute the process code. A thread can execute any part of the code, which includes portions that are currently run by another thread. Threads synchronize with each other to coordinate resource access. This prevents one thread from interrupting another. Operating systems supporting **multithreaded** applications allow threads to be executed concurrently. Most Windows and Linux operating systems support multithreaded applications. For example, multithreading occurs anytime you are using products like Microsoft Excel or OpenOffice.org Writer and save a large file while printing another file concurrently.

On computers with multiple processors and an operating system that supports multiple processors, you can set which processor actually runs a process. Although more costly, having multiple processors speeds up your computer system because the processes can be divided among available processors. Microsoft server products support multiple processors.

Let's look at an analogy to help you understand the concepts of a process and threads. Everyone has purchased a product at one time or another that has been made using an assembly line production process. Suppose TM Industries, Inc., produces a product known as Product Z. Product Z has to be created on the assembly line. When an order comes in from a customer, a Production Number is assigned to the order so the product can be made for the customer. The Production Number is like the <u>PID</u> of a process. Once the Production Number is created for Z, then resources are allocated to it. In the computer system, resources are processor time and memory, but resources in the company will be time, parts, and labor. Manufacturing product Z is divided into several steps. When an employee makes Part A for Product Z, this step is analogous to a <u>thread</u>. If this step takes more than one shift, it may involve a shift turnover meeting where employees meet to discuss the status of Product Z. The next shift knows to continue where the employee on the previous shift left off. Shift turnover is like the thread <u>synchronization</u>. If TM Industries had multiple assembly plants, that would be like having multiple processors on the system.

2.3 Understanding File System Management

File system management is a complex issue covering a variety of major topics. The topics covered here are:
- Overview of File System Access and Storage
- The File System Hierarchy
- The Drive Specification and Files
- The File Allocation Table
- Fragmentation
- Specific Operating System File System Formats

Overview of File System Access and Storage

The operating system also manages the **file system** for users and applications. The file system defines how files and folders are stored on disk. The file system is created when you **format** a **partition**. Formatting is the process of preparing the disk for use. A partition is a logical division of a hard disk drive. In DOS, you use the **fdisk** command, short for Fixed Disk, to create partitions. Linux has an fdisk program, which accomplishes the same thing.

You can install multiple operating systems on your PC. This is called **multibooting**. However, you can only boot one operating system at a time. You can install multiple operating systems on the same partition but it is recommended to place them on separate partitions.

The **primary partition** contains your operating system and is the first partition on a drive. In order to boot your operating system, you must have a primary partition and it must be marked as the **active partition**. Microsoft assigns letters to partitions. In DOS, your primary partition is the C: partition. An **extended partition** type can be further divided into multiple **logical** partitions, called logical drives. Here, you could have a drive D:, E:, all the way up to Z:. Note that A: and B: both represent your floppy drive and C: typically represents your hard drive. A primary partition cannot be further divided.

Under DOS and Windows 95/98, you can have only two partitions: one primary and one extended. Windows NT, 2000, and XP use the terms **system partition** and **boot partition**. The system partition is where the load files are located. The system partition must be marked as active in order for these operating systems to load. The boot partition is where the operating system itself is located. The system and boot partitions can be on the same or different partitions in NT/2000/XP. On Windows NT, 2000, and XP, you can have up to

- four primary partitions, or
- three primary partitions and one extended (with multiple logical) partitions.

The **Master Boot Record (MBR)** is a record that tells the operating system about the partitions. The MBR looks for the active partition and boots it. If the MBR becomes corrupt, you can run the **fdisk /mbr** command to fix it.

You can see the partitions, labeled as C:, E:, F:, and so on, in Windows XP by using the Disk Management tool. Disk Management is located in Administrative Tools under Control Panel. For a screenshot of the partitions on a computer, refer to Figure 2.8. To access this menu, follow these steps:

1. Log on as Administrator.
2. Click **Start**, point to **All Programs**, point to **Administrative Tools** and click **Computer Management**. The **Computer Management** window appears.
3. In the left window pane, click **Disk Management**.
4. View and then close the window by clicking **x**.

Figure 2.8: Displaying the Partitions Using the Disk Management Tool

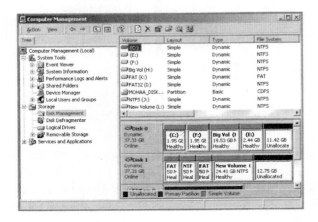

In Windows products, the file system stores a file in units called **clusters**, or **allocation units**. A cluster is equal to a specific number of sectors on disk. A **sector** is equal to 512 bytes. A hexadecimal number references a cluster location. Refer to Appendix A for a discussion of hexadecimal numbers. A cluster is the smallest amount of space the operating system reserves for a file. The size of the partition determines the cluster size. If you have a file that increases in size, it may need additional clusters. If the file does not occupy all of the space in a cluster, the excess is wasted and cannot be used for additional file storage.

Let's compare large and small cluster sizes. While a large cluster size is typically more efficient than a small cluster size, it generally wastes more disk space. Large cluster sizes are more efficient because the file system has a fewer number of clusters to access when compared to small cluster sizes. Large cluster sizes potentially waste more space because more sectors would be allocated for each file. On the other hand, a small cluster size tends to waste less space because fewer sectors are allocated for each file. However, a small cluster size is generally less efficient than a large cluster size because of the greater number of clusters the operating system must manage.

File systems with large cluster sizes are best for data intensive applications like database systems, while small cluster size file systems are best for e-mail systems, which typically contain small file sizes.

Data is magnetically stored on disk in **sectors** and **tracks**. As you can see in Figure 2.9, a sector is a slice, or section, of the disk while a track is a concentric circle running around the center of the disk.

Figure 2.9: Sectors and Tracks on a Disk Surface

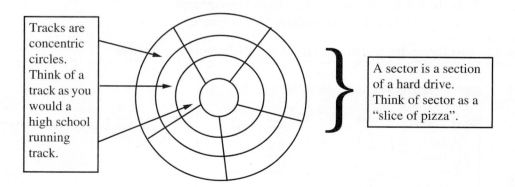

Figure 2.10 shows the effect of waste in a cluster. Let's suppose you had a file named **filename.dat** that completely occupied the first two clusters, 1 and 2, but only a portion of cluster 3 (about two-thirds of cluster 3). The remaining one-third of space has already been allocated to the file and cannot be used. It is considered waste in file system terminology. This waste occurs naturally when storing data on disk because cluster sizes are

specific sizes and not all files are the same size as the cluster size. Later in the chapter, you will see the cluster sizes for the file system types. These sizes vary depending upon the size of the partition.

Figure 2.10: Wasted Cluster Space

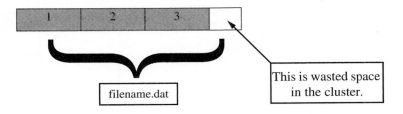

Linux use the term **block** instead of cluster.

The File System Hierarchy

A **file** is the lowest unit of storage within the file system. A **folder**, or **directory**, can contain other folders or a folder can contain files. Placing files within folders is useful for organizational purposes. It is easier to locate a file if it is stored in a related folder. For example, you could create a folder called Personal for documents such as your resume. Or, you could use the system created folder called My Documents. The file system is also hierarchically represented in most GUI tools, such as Microsoft Explorer. The hierarchical design makes referring to file and folders easier.

The term **folder** is used when in the GUI and the term **directory** is used when referring to the command line of an OS. The terms are synonymous.

Figure 2.11 shows a hierarchical representation of the file system. Note in the figure that we are referring to a Windows operating system. The drive is C:, or the hard drive, and the forward slash, \, is the root, or top level directory.

Figure 2.11: Hierarchical Representation of the File System

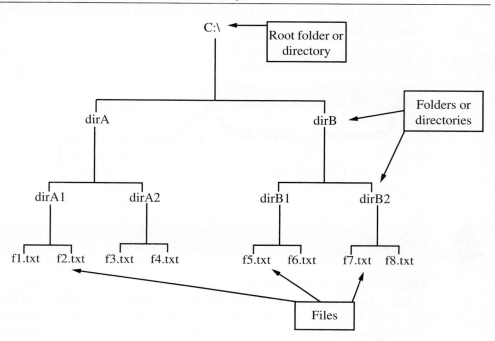

 In Windows, the root symbol is \. In Linux, the root symbol is /. So in Figure 2.11, if you changed C:\ to /, you would have a Linux hierarchy.

Let's explore this hierarchy concept by using an analogy. The file system hierarchy is analogous to an actual tree you might buy at a garden store that has its root system bundled up in a burlap bag. If you turn that tree upside down, you have the concept of the file system hierarchy. The root system is now on top, just like the <u>root</u> directory is at the top of the file system. The branches and leaves stem from the root. A <u>directory</u> is analogous to a branch on the garden tree. A leaf is analogous to a <u>file</u>. Just as a leaf on the tree cannot contain branches or other leaves, a file in the file system hierarchy cannot contain directories or other files. Just as a branch on the tree can contain other branches and leaves, a directory in the file system hierarchy can contain other subdirectories and files.

Let's follow up with an exercise. The goal of this exercise is to help you understand the hierarchical relationship that exists on Windows operating systems by creating a few folders and files. This exercise assumes the Windows 2000 operating system is up and running. Follow these steps:

1. Right-click **Start**; then click **Explore**. A separate Explorer window appears.
2. Insert a formatted floppy disk in the floppy drive.

3. Scroll until you see the Floppy (A:) drive.
4. Right-click the floppy drive and click **Open**. Another window with the floppy's contents appears.
5. To create a folder, click **File**, then point to **New**, and then click **Folder**. A folder icon appears prompting you to enter a folder name.
6. Name the folder **Chapter1** and press Enter. The folder is created.
7. Double-click the folder named **Chapter1**. The folder's contents appear.
8. To create a subfolder within Chapter1, click **File**, then point to **New**, and then click **Folder**.
9. Press Enter to accept the name, **New Folder**.
10. To create a file within Chapter1, click the Chapter 1 folder, then click **File**, point to **New**, and click **Text Document**.
11. Press Enter to accept the name, **New Text Document.txt**. Notice the extension. Notepad uses the .txt extension for files. So, this is a Notepad compatible file.
12. To create another file within Chapter1, repeat the previous step. Notice the file name is different from the one in the previous step.
13. Close all windows.
14. Go back into Windows Explorer and open up all the folders on the floppy until you see the hierarchical relationship similar to the one shown in Figure 2.12.
15. Close Windows Explorer.

Figure 2.12: Display of Windows Explorer's Hierarchical View

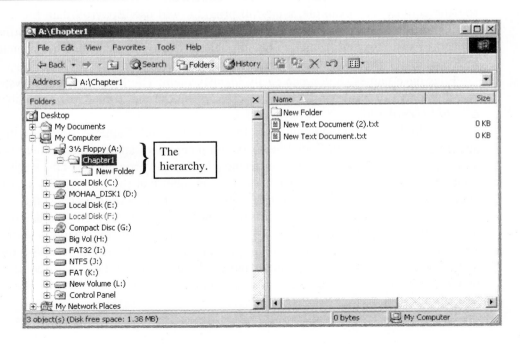

The Drive Specification and Files

When referencing a drive in DOS or the DOS command line in Windows, you <u>must</u> include the drive letter and the colon. Collectively, this is known as the **drive specification**, or **drive spec** for short. If you leave out the colon, DOS will display an error message. UNIX and Linux also have a hierarchical view of their file system; however, they do not refer to drives using drive letters. They refer to a file system by its **mount point**. A mount point is a directory name that is associated with a partition.

 Remember that the file system is logical not physical. The view of the file system that we see in Windows Explorer is hierarchical and for our use only. The operating system does not store files and folders in the same hierarchical fashion that we see in Explorer.

Data and programs are stored in files within folders on disk. There are two major types of data that a file can contain. They are:
• Executable or binary
• Non-executable (including text, pictures, graphics, and motion picture files)

Executable or **binary** programs are ones that have been **compiled** and perform some type of operation or task. They are written using text editors following the strict syntax of the language, and then they are compiled. The compilation process creates the executable code.

Non-executable, or data, files are files that are used by the executable programs for a specific activity. For example, a payroll program will use a payroll data file to process checks. A game program will use where you last saved in the game as the starting point data for the next round. Finally, your digital camera software will use the picture you took as data when displaying the image to you on the screen.

Files have names so you can easily identify them. The Linux operating system uses an index node, or **inode**, number when referencing the file. It is a unique number Linux uses to locate the file.

Let's look at a quick analogy to help you understand. Suppose you are a <u>file</u> in this analogy, the <u>inode</u> is your Social Security Number (SSN), and the government is the <u>OS</u>. You may go by your name with your friends, but the government (the OS) knows you by your SSN (inode). So just as your SSN is the number that the government uses to reference you, the inode is the number the operating system uses to reference a file.

In DOS file names follow the **8.3** rule. There can be up to eight characters in a file name, followed by a dot, and a three-character extension. The **extension** is a set of characters used to associate the file to an application. You can run most DOS-based commands by entering the file name and leaving off the extension. DOS will see files ending in .com, .exe, and .bat, as programs it can execute. These are also known as **file types**.

In Windows, the extension is what allows you to open the application and the file, as data, by double-clicking on the file name. This is also known as **file type association.**

Not all characters are allowed in a DOS file name. For example, the space is not allowed and you can only use uppercase characters. DOS converts all characters to uppercase. Chapter 3 discusses illegal DOS file name characters in detail. For now be aware that a DOS file name must conform to the 8.3 standard. Microsoft Windows operating systems, from Windows 95 and up, allow you to store file names up to 255 characters and allow you to use a space in a file name. The Linux operating system allows up to 255 characters in a file name and does not require an extension.

To help you remember the 8.3 rule for DOS file names, just think "filename.ext." There are 8 characters in the word "filename" (with no space), followed by a dot, and the 3-character extension, "ext" in this case. In other words, "filename.ext" contains the maximum letters that are allowed for the name of the file and the extension.

One other aspect about files and directories is the concept of a **path**. The path is the location of the file, or directory. The two types of paths are **full** and **partial**. A full path always begins from the root directory of a partition and a partial path is simply the file name without any reference to the root directory. Think of the full path as your full name and the partial path as the name you go by. Your full name can usually be used to uniquely identify you. But a first name, such as Joe, does not uniquely identify you because there could be several people with the same first name.

The term "full path" is also called the **fully qualified path** or **absolute path** (the path is absolutely defined). The "partial path" is also called a **relative path** (the path is relative to your current position in the directory tree structure).

The File Allocation Table

Files and folders are accessed through the use of a table. A Windows operating system keeps track of files and folders on disk by using a file system format called the **File Allocation Table**, or **FAT**. Table 2.1 shows the operating systems and the specific file system formats they support on their hard drives. The specific formats will be discussed later in this section.

Table 2.1: File System Formats Supported by Various Operating Systems

Operating System	File System Format
Windows XP	FAT16, FAT32 and NTFS
Windows 2000	FAT16, FAT32 and NTFS
Windows NT	FAT16 and NTFS
Windows 98	FAT16 and FAT32
Windows 95 OSR2	FAT16 and FAT32
Windows 95 (before OSR2)	FAT16
DOS	FAT16

One file system format not mentioned in Table 2.1 is VFAT. Microsoft developed VFAT (Virtual FAT) with Windows 95 to allow file names to exceed the 8.3 rule. VFAT allows up to 255 characters in a file name, including spaces. These file names are called **Long File Names**, or **LFNs**. These FAT types will be discussed further in a later section.

If you have ever seen a file name on a Windows 95 operating system with a tilde (~) in the name, you are looking at an LFN. Figure 2.13 is a listing of the **dir** command displaying file names with their 8.3 and LFN equivalents. (On Windows 2000, you can use the **dir /x** command to display the Long File Name of a file name.) The two rightmost columns display the file names. The first file name column shows the 8.3 file name, while the last column shows the LFN equivalent. Because DOS can have only 8.3 uppercase characters, how does it fit a file name of potentially 255 characters into 8.3? The 8.3 format uses the same first six legal characters as the LFN, but reserves the last two for uniqueness. If you have several LFN file names with the same first eight characters, then the last two file name characters of 8.3 notation would be ~1 for the first occurrence, ~2 for the second, ~3 for the third, and so on as shown in Figure 2.13.

Figure 2.13: A Directory Listing of 8.3 and LFN File Names

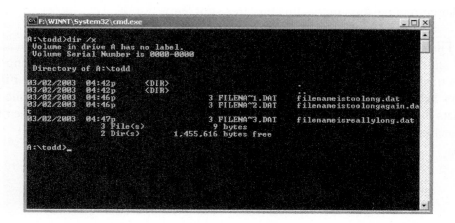

The operating system does not store all of the files you have on disk in memory. The operating system only stores the disk address locations of the files. The FAT is usually **cached**, or stored, in memory for speedy access. Caching is the concept of storing frequently used files or tables in memory. Accessing memory is faster because memory access is electronic and disk access is mechanical. But not everything is cached. If a file or program is not heavily used, it does not need to be cached. It can still be accessed on disk when needed.

It would be impossible for the operating system to store all files from disk in memory anyway. Computer disk capacity far exceeds the memory capacity. For example, it is common to have a computer system with an 80 GB (gigabytes) hard drive and only 512 MB (megabytes) of RAM.

Let's see how the operating system uses the FAT to access a file. Suppose you have a file named Payroll.dat located on the C:\ drive in the Apps directory. The full path of the file is C:\Apps\ Payroll.dat. A partial path would be simply Payroll.dat. You need to perform a File Open to open the file. How does the operating system retrieve the file? Refer to Figure 2.14 while you read through this section to help your understanding. Although these steps assume a Microsoft operating system, the same general theoretical concept applies to how many other operating systems retrieve their files and folders (directories).

Because a file is stored in a directory, the operating system first looks to the directory for the location of the file. The location is specified as a cluster number. The directory has the starting cluster location of the actual file. In Figure 2.14, this is cluster 4. The operating system then goes into the FAT at cluster location 4 to retrieve the data. Once the data from this cluster is retrieved, the operating system goes to the next cluster and retrieves the data there. You can see in the figure that the next cluster, after cluster 4, is cluster 5. The data located in cluster 5 is retrieved, but the next cluster listed is cluster 10. How did it skip clusters 6 through 9? Disk access is random as shown in this figure. Another file could be located in clusters 6 though 9. Eventually, cluster 10's data is retrieved, and it points to cluster 11 as the next location of data. Cluster 11's data is retrieved and a special set of characters representing an **End Of File (EOF)** tells the operating system file retrieval is complete.

Think of End Of File (EOF) as "The End" in a movie.

Figure 2.14: The Logical Representation of the File System Table

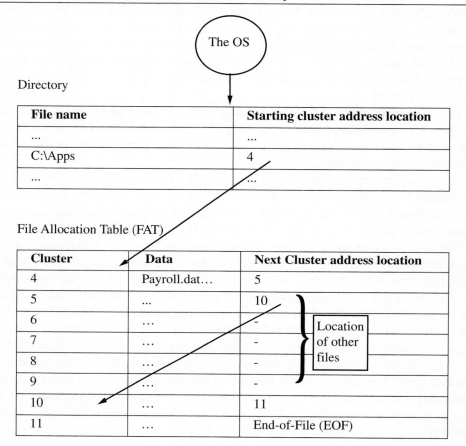

Let's look at another analogy. When trying to understand the FAT, it may help to think of it as an index in the back of a book. When you want to locate a term, you go to the index. To the right of the term is the page number for the associated term. You then turn to the page for an explanation of the term. The page number is a location for the term in the book, just like a <u>cluster address</u> is a location for the file or directory on disk. The explanation of the term is analogous to the data within the file. Without the book's index, you would have to sequentially read the entire book starting from page 1. Without the FAT, the operating system would have to sequentially start reading the entire disk starting from the first cluster until it found the file. That would take far too long.

There are two important overall concepts to remember about an OS. They are:
- The operating system stores files and directories logically in a hierarchical fashion for organization.
- The operating system relies on tables for quick access and lookup capabilities. When you think of a table, think about an index in the back of a book. You use the index to locate the page reference for a term you don't understand.

Fragmentation

Because the file C:\Apps\Payroll.dat shown in Figure 2.14 is not located in **contiguous**, or adjacent, cluster locations, it is considered **fragmented**. A fragmented file is one that is physically spread over non-contiguous areas of the disk. The disadvantage of fragmentation is that it increases the time to locate a file because the file is spread out on different parts of the disk.

Files become fragmented because they change over time. For example, assume you created a document named Resume.doc and you store your resume information in it. At the time it takes up several contiguous clusters. Sometime later, you gain new experience and decide to update your resume to reflect this fact, but another file named File2.doc occupies the clusters immediately after Resume.doc. The operating system cannot place the changes to Resume.doc immediately after the original because File2.doc is stored there. It uses cluster locations after File2.doc. Resume.doc now occupies clusters that are not contiguous. The file is spread out on the disk in fragments, which increases the time it takes to retrieve it.

In Figure 2.15, you can see fragmentation. Notice cluster 3 is about two-thirds full. The document did not take up the entire cluster, but the rest of it cannot be used so it is considered wasted disk space.

Fragmentation on a system increases over time. If the files on your system have been modified over a period of time, it has probably become fragmented. Before the days of defragmentation tools, System Administrators would back up all of the data to tape, reformat the hard drive, then restore the hard drive from the tape backup. By backing the data up to tape, the file's fragments were adjacent to one another. It could take hours to perform this operation, but it sped up system performance for the users in the long run.

Figure 2.15: Diagram of Fragmentation

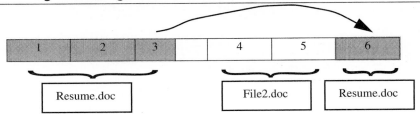

Defragmenting is the process of placing a file into contiguous areas of the disk. This speeds access to the file because there is less mechanical movement of the read/write mechanism in the drive. Microsoft includes a Disk Defragmenter tool to help you analyze and defragment your disk. Microsoft recommends you click Analyze to analyze your disk before you actually try to defragment it. It is possible that you would not save enough disk space compared to the amount of time disk defragmentation takes.

Notice what happens to Resume.doc after it has been defragmented by referring to Figure 2.16. There is still wasted space in cluster 3. However, the pieces of the file are contiguous. This translates to quicker access by the hard drive because the pieces of the file are in close proximity.

Figure 2.16: The Result of Defragmenting a Disk

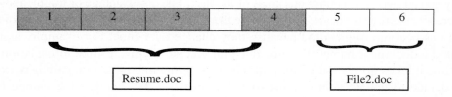

Figure 2.17 shows a screenshot of the Disk Defragmenter in Windows 2000. You can see that the C: drive has been analyzed and has fragmented files. The fragmented files will appear color-coded on an actual screen.

Figure 2.17: The Disk Defragmenter Tool Available in Windows 2000 Professional

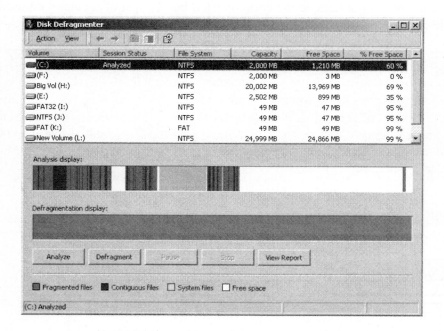

Depending upon the version of Microsoft's defragmentation tool, you should try to analyze the disk for defragmentation purposes prior to actually attempting to defragment it. There may be little to gain from spending resources performing the actual defragmentation.

Specific Operating System File System Formats

Some of the most common file system formats are FAT12, FAT16, and FAT32. The numerals in the names refer to the number of bits required for a file allocation table entry.

- **FAT12**—This is used on floppies and is supported by all operating systems allowing storage up to 1.44 MB. A floppy has 2,847 clusters of 512 bytes each. If you multiply these two numbers, you get 1,457,664 total bytes, which is where we get 1.44 MB. In Windows XP Professional, FAT12 is used only on floppy disks and on volumes smaller than 16 MB.

- **FAT16**—This is the original File Allocation Table file system used on DOS, Windows 95, 98, and NT. It is limited to 8.3 file names. One disadvantage of FAT16 is that the root directory can manage a maximum of 512 entries. FAT16 has no built-in file system security or compression scheme. In FAT16, there is a primary FAT and a copy of the primary FAT. The use of a backup copy of the FAT is for **fault tolerance**. Fault tolerance is used to describe the degree to which a system can tolerate a problem, or fault. It is much like storing a backup copy of an important document, such as your resume, taxes, or a term paper on floppy. You may have a primary copy on the hard drive, but if something happens to it, you can go to your backup on the floppy.

The size of the cluster is dependent upon the size of the partition and the file system format.

- **FAT32**—This offers improvements over FAT16. The main benefit being it supports larger partitions than FAT16.

- **VFAT**—Virtual FAT came out with Windows 95 to support file names longer than 8.3. It supports file names up to 255, lowercase characters, and spaces in the file names.

- **NTFS**—New Technology File System, provides performance and reliability not present in FAT. Some of the features provided by NTFS are:
  - Disk quotas, which allow you to limit the amount of storage a user can utilize on a partition.
  - Encryption, which allows you to encrypt the contents of a file for security purposes. **Encryption** is the process of disguising data to hide its true value.
  - Compression, which allows you to compress a whole partition and saves disk space. **Compression** is the process of removing redundant data thereby saving disk space.
  - Dynamic disks, which allow you to extend a partition from unallocated free space on the disk.

- Auditing, which allows you to track changes to files and folders by users in order to track usage of files.
- Bad-cluster remapping, which allows the system to mark physical locations on disk that are bad and not use them in the future.
- File level security, which allows you to set permissions for a user on a file.

   Although FAT only allows you to set permissions on a folder, NTFS allows you to set permissions on both folders and files.

   NTFS uses a **Master File Table** (**MFT**), which is analogous to the table used by FAT16 and FAT32. The MFT is the first file on an NTFS volume that contains information about each file and folder on each volume.

   Table 2.2 compares the default cluster sizes for FAT16, FAT32, and NTFS on varying partition sizes. You can see that NTFS is more efficient in terms of disk space usage due to its smaller cluster sizes. For example, if you have a 1,000-byte partition, FAT16 would allocate a cluster size of 16,000 (16 KB), FAT32 would allocate a cluster size of 4,000 (4 KB), and NTFS would allocate a cluster size of 1,000 (1 KB). A 1-byte file would occupy 16 KB on the 1,000-byte FAT16 partition, 4 KB on the 1,000-byte FAT32 partition, and 1 KB on the 1,000-byte NTFS partition.

   Typically, the larger the partition size, the larger the cluster size. For example, on FAT16, a 50 MB partition uses a cluster size of 1 KB, a 100 MB partition uses a cluster size of 2 KB, and a 150 MB partition uses a cluster size of 4 KB.

Table 2.2: Cluster Sizes for Various Partition Sizes

Partition Size	FAT16 Cluster Size	FAT32 Cluster Size	NTFS Cluster Size
7 MB–16 MB	2 KB	Not supported	Not supported
17 MB–32 MB	512 bytes	Not supported	512 bytes
33 MB–64 MB	1 KB	512 bytes	512 bytes
65 MB–128 MB	2 KB	1 KB	512 bytes
129 MB–256 MB	4 KB	2 KB	512 bytes
257 MB–512 MB	8 KB	4 KB	512 bytes
513 MB–1,024 MB	16 KB	4 KB	1 KB
1,025 MB–2 GB	32 KB	4 KB	2 KB
2 GB–4 GB	64 KB	4 KB	4 KB
4 GB–8 GB	Not supported	4 KB	4 KB
8 GB–16 GB	Not supported	8 KB	4 KB
16 GB–32 GB	Not supported	16 KB	4 KB

- **CDFS**—Used on read-only CD-ROM drives.
- **UDFS**—Universal Disk Format, is primarily used for read-only DVD/CD-ROM media.

- **ext2**—The file system supported by the Linux operating system.
- **ext3**—A newer version of ext2 that uses an on-disk journal to keep track of changes thereby keeping the file system in a consistent state. The ext3 file system allows for a power outage without having to clean the file system.
- **NFS**—Network File System, developed by Sun Microsystems, is a file system accessible from a network connection. With NFS, you don't have to have the disk physically attached to your computer.

You should go through the shutdown process for your operating system. This will write any necessary system information from memory to disk safely. If you have ever experienced a power outage while using your system, the operating system may need to fix the file system. This is because the table in memory may become corrupt due to the abrupt loss of power. Many versions of Linux are particularly susceptible to this problem. With the ext3 file system, this problem is less severe. The tool to fix the disk is CHKDSK or SCANDISK on most Microsoft operating systems. The Linux command is **fsck** (file system check).

Let's perform a short exercise to help you understand file systems. You will run a file system check on a floppy disk. This exercise assumes Windows 2000 is up and running. Follow these steps:

1. Right-click **Start** then click **Explore**. A separate Explorer window appears.
2. Insert a formatted floppy disk in the floppy drive.
3. Scroll until you see the Floppy (A:) drive.
4. Right-click the floppy drive and click **Properties**. Another window with the floppy's properties appears.
5. Click the **Tools** tab and click **Check Now**. The **Check Disk** window appears. A window such the one shown in Figure 2.18 appears. Notice you can elect to automatically fix file system errors or scan for bad sectors. Otherwise, the Check Disk procedure simply displays the status of the disk.
6. Click **Start** to check the disk.
7. Close all windows when complete.

Figure 2.18: Running the Check Disk Command

2.4 Understanding Hardware Management

Another function of the operating system is hardware management. Hardware devices connect to the computer either through **expansion slots** located inside the computer or **ports** located externally. For example, a Network Interface Card (NIC) usually fits into an expansion slot that is housed on the motherboard itself. Devices such as your printer, mouse, keyboard, display monitor, CD-Writer, speakers, Digital Camera, and scanner use a cable to connect to the computer system. Figure 2.19 shows a view of external ports.

Figure 2.19: External Ports Available on PCs

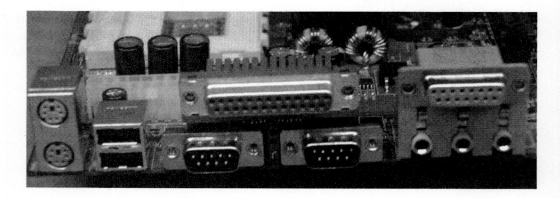

The **BIOS (Basic Input/Output System)** is an important function for the computer system from the standpoint of most operating systems. The **BIOS** is a set of instructions permanently stored on a chip that directs basic input and output operations such as the keyboard. This is an example of **firmware**. Firmware is a set of instructions permanently stored on **Read-Only Memory (ROM)** chips. You cannot simply delete the contents of the ROM firmware by shutting down the computer. The BIOS has basic functionality for your keyboard, display adapters, serial ports, and other functions.

Firmware is "software on hardware." The software is "firmly" (permanently) coded on the chip.

The operating system uses the ROM firmware for booting, or starting, the computer. When you power on your computer system, it goes through a Power On Self Test (POST) to ensure the basic components such as memory, keyboard, mouse, and the hard drive are available. Once this occurs, the Master Boot Record (MBR) is used to locate the address of the operating system stored on disk. Next, the operating system is loaded into RAM for your use.

The term booting comes from the phrase "pull yourself up by your bootstraps", as in the boots that go on your feet.

Devices need software in order to communicate. If the software is not included in the BIOS, then you will need a device driver for the device. You must configure the correct driver for the type of hardware you install. It's not uncommon to install a device driver incorrectly. For example, if you install the wrong printer driver for a given printer, output on the printer may be garbled and unreadable.

Let's look at memory addressing before we delve into additional hardware management topics. Random-Access Memory (RAM) is a physical piece of hardware. However, data and programs are stored in RAM and accessed logically using memory addresses. The necessary portions of the operating system are loaded into RAM during the boot process and stored in memory address locations. These addresses are given in hexadecimal notation like disk addresses. The operating system, other programs, and data are referenced using their memory address location. RAM is considered volatile because its contents are constantly changing as programs are loaded and unloaded and data is modified. When you double-click to run a program or you key in the program's name in the CLI of an operating system, the command will be loaded in vacant memory. Any data you enter will also be placed into memory. The contents of memory are lost during a shutdown— this is normal. So the data must be saved from memory to disk in order for you to keep a permanent copy of it.

In Figure 2.20, you can see an example of how memory address locations contain programs and data. Memory is comparable to the rows and columns of Post Office (P.O.) boxes. The P.O. boxes have an address. The contents of the P.O. boxes are constantly changing just like memory.

Figure 2.20: The Contents of Memory Address Locations

Memory Address Location	Contents
A100	OS
A101	OS
A102	Software instructions for other programs.
…	Software instructions for other programs.
FFFE	Data

When thinking of data and instructions being stored in memory, just visualize a spreadsheet. The cells are like memory address locations. These cells store data and instructions to be performed.

System resources are features that control how devices on a computer system work. System resources are set either manually or within software when installing the device. The manual method is the older form of setting system resources. Typically, there was a series of little switches that could be turned on or off. Their combination created a numeric setting.

A new, improved method of setting system resources is **Plug and Play (PnP)**. Plug and Play, developed by Intel, is a standard that allows a computer to automatically detect and configure the installed device. Both the operating system and the device must be Plug and Play compliant for this method to work. Windows 95/98/2000/XP are PnP compliant, but Windows NT is not. During configuration, the PnP operating system will assign a unique set of system resources to a device. If you have ever plugged or unplugged a device on your system that is PnP compliant, the operating system will typically display a message indicating the change. In the case of a new device, the PnP operating system will install the associated driver and allocate necessary system resources.

On PnP systems, you should not manually change the system resources. If you change them improperly, it can disable your hardware and cause your computer to malfunction. Resource settings should only be changed if you are sure the new settings won't conflict with other hardware. On many older systems called "legacy" computers, you have to manually set system resources by setting jumpers or switches on the particular board itself. However, some legacy boards came with configuration software allowing you to accomplish the same task.

The system resources used by devices are as follows:
• Interrupt Request (IRQ)

- Input/Output ports
- Base memory address range
- Direct Memory Access (DMA)

The operating system and devices communicate using **interrupts**. An **Interrupt Request (IRQ)** occurs when a signal is sent by a device to the processor when it needs attention. For example, each time you press the Enter key on the keyboard, you are interrupting the processor.

There are two types of interrupts. A **hardware interrupt** is an interrupt requested by a hardware device such as a disk drive or printer. A **software interrupt** occurs when application software requests use of a device. The IRQ numbers do not change for either type of interrupt. For example, when you want to print or save a file from within an application such as MS-Excel, a software interrupt occurs. Interrupts are sent over hardware lines, or wires, that interconnect the components. There are 16 such lines that are labeled 0 through 15. Table 2.3 lists the IRQs and the devices that use them.

Table 2.3: TIRQ and Device Assignments

IRQ	Device
0	System timer
1	Keyboard
2	Cascade, or bridge, to IRQs 8–15
3	COM2 and COM4 (serial ports)
4	COM1 and COM3 (serial ports)
5	LPT2 (parallel port)
6	Floppy
7	LPT1 (parallel port)
8	Real-time clock
9	Available
10	Available
11	Available
12	Mouse
13	Math coprocessor
14	Primary hard drive
15	Secondary hard drive

When an interrupt occurs, an **interrupt handler** goes to work. The interrupt handler is software that takes care of the processor interruption. The interrupt handler uses an **Interrupt Vector Table** to locate the software, whether it is the BIOS or a device driver stored in memory.

Think of the Interrupt Vector Table as a table that has pointers to memory locations for the driver needed. This table is also known as the **dispatch table**.

Let's look at an example. Suppose you have a printer connected to your parallel port, LPT1. You have your resume opened within an application on your computer and you want to print it. This will trigger an interrupt to occur. Referring back to Table 2.3, LPT1 uses IRQ 7. Once the interrupt occurs, the interrupt handler refers to the Interrupt Vector Table to locate the address of the device driver for the printer. You can see this in Figure 2.21. In the first table of Figure 2.21, you can see that memory address A7 is the location of the driver for IRQ 7. In the second table of the figure, the actual memory location is referenced and the appropriate driver is executed for the device.

Figure 2.21: How the Interrupt Handler Uses Interrupt Vector Table to Locate Device Instruction

IRQ	Memory Address Location
0	A0
1	A1
…	…
7	A7
…	…
15	AF

Interrupt Vector Table

Memory Address Locations	Contents
A0	…
A1	…
…	…
A7	Software instructions for printer.
…	…
AF	…

Snapshot of Memory

Let's look at an analogy to help you understand IRQs. Imagine the President of the United States with 16 telephones next to his desk. Each phone number is like an IRQ number, the President is like the processor and the heads of state of other countries are like devices. Assume the heads of state have a particular number they use. For example, the Prime Minister of Great Britain uses phone number 1, which is like IRQ 1. When the Prime Minister calls the President, phone 1 rings, interrupting the President. The President knows who it is because phone number 1 is associated with the Prime Minister of Great Britain. The President stops his business and handles the call. Once over, the President resumes his previous duties. This is similar to how devices use IRQs and how the processor responds.

Devices also use **Input/Output port** (**I/O ports**) to transfer data. An I/O port is really a memory address through which data is transferred between a device and the microprocessor. Think of the I/O port as a channel. The I/O port addresses are reserved for each device and are given in hexadecimal values. Table 2.4 contains the most common I/O ports.

Table 2.4: Common I/O Port Addresses for Devices

I/O Port Address	Device
040–043	System Timer
060 and 064	Keyboard
03F8–03FF	COM1
02F8–02FF	COM2
03E8–03EF	COM3
02E8–02EF	COM4
0378–037F	LPT1
0278–027F	LPT2
01F0–01F7	Primary Disk Controller
0170–0177	Secondary Disk Controller
03F0–03F7	Floppy Disk Controller

A device driver needs to be loaded into memory in order to be utilized. Each device is allotted an area of memory known as a **memory address range**. These memory addresses are given in hexadecimal. Figure 2.22 shows a screenshot of the System Information tool containing memory address ranges for devices.

Figure 2.22: Memory Address Ranges for Devices

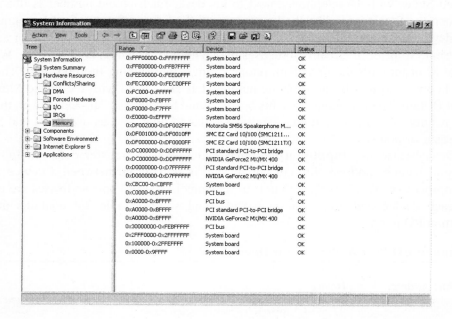

The CPU takes charge and directs the flow of traffic in and out of memory for most devices on Windows platforms. But some devices can access memory directly. This is called **Direct Memory Access** (**DMA**). DMA is most often used for data transfer directly between memory and a device such as a hard disk drive. The use of DMA improves the performance of a device.

Let's perform an exercise in to help you understand system resources. You will use the Device Manager tool in Windows 2000 to view system resources for your keyboard. The Device Manager tool is used to manage devices in Windows. This exercise assumes Windows 2000 is up and running. Follow these steps:

1. Right-click the My Computer icon on the Windows desktop and then click **Properties**. The System Properties page appears.
2. Click the **Hardware** tab and click **Device Manager**. The Device Manager page appears with your computer name.
3. Double-click your computer name until you see the keyboard icon listed.
4. Double-click the keyboard icon until you see a specific keyboard beneath the main keyboard icon. For example, the one used in this exercise is the **Standard 101/102-Key or Microsoft Natural PS/2 Keybaord**.
5. Double-click the icon for the specific keyboard type. The properties page appears.
6. Click the **Driver** tab and then click **Driver Details**. A Driver Details window appears.
7. Review the details and click **OK** to close the Details window.

8. Click the **Resources** tab.
9. Review the resource settings. Figure 2.23 contains a sample screenshot of system resources.
10. Compare the Interrupt Request value to the one in Table 2.3. It should be the same.
11. Compare the I/O Port Address to the one in Table 2.4. It should be the same.
12. Close all windows when complete.

Figure 2.23: Viewing System Resources of the Keyboard Using Device Manager

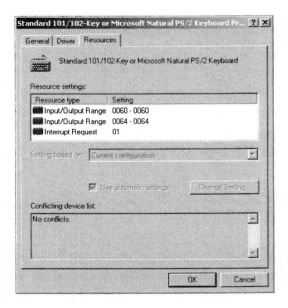

2.5 Understanding the Operating System Kernel

The kernel is the "heart" of the operating system. When any computer system boots, a set of instructions is loaded from the hard drive and kept in memory. Many of these instructions are discarded from memory after being used. The **kernel** however is the core of any operating system, and it occupies memory as long as the computer remains on. The kernel controls all other software activity. Only the most important and widely used programs are part of the kernel. The kernel calls upon programs that are held on disk or in memory by interfacing with other operating system programs and the hardware of the computer system. Most operating systems have a kernel that remains in memory. Examples include Linux, Novell NetWare, Windows NT, Windows 2000, and Windows XP.

As the kernel boots up, it looks in certain locations on disk to determine what to load. On Windows platforms, the kernel looks to the Registry. The **Registry** is a hierarchical database that contains values for specific computer settings. Figure 2.24 shows a screenshot of the Registry on a Windows 2000 computer using the **regedt32** command. The folders in the left hand pane are called **keys**. The items in the right hand pane are the

value entries with data. For example, the "Identifier" entry in Figure 2.24 has a value of "AT/AT COMPATIBLE." The term **hive** is used to represent a set of keys and values. So, in Figure 2.24, HKEY_LOCAL_MACHINE is considered a hive.

Figure 2.24: A Screenshot of the Registry Editor, regedt32

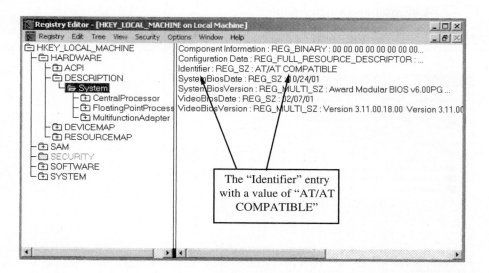

It is not advisable to change the Registry unless you are sure about the change. Setting a key entry to an incorrect value could make your system malfunction.

The Linux operating system uses configuration files stored in various system directories to inform the kernel how and what to boot. Some of these are located in the Linux system directory named /etc. Figure 2.25 shows the Linux kernel configuration screen for changing kernel values.

Figure 2.25: The Kernel Configuration Screen for Red Hat Linux 8.0

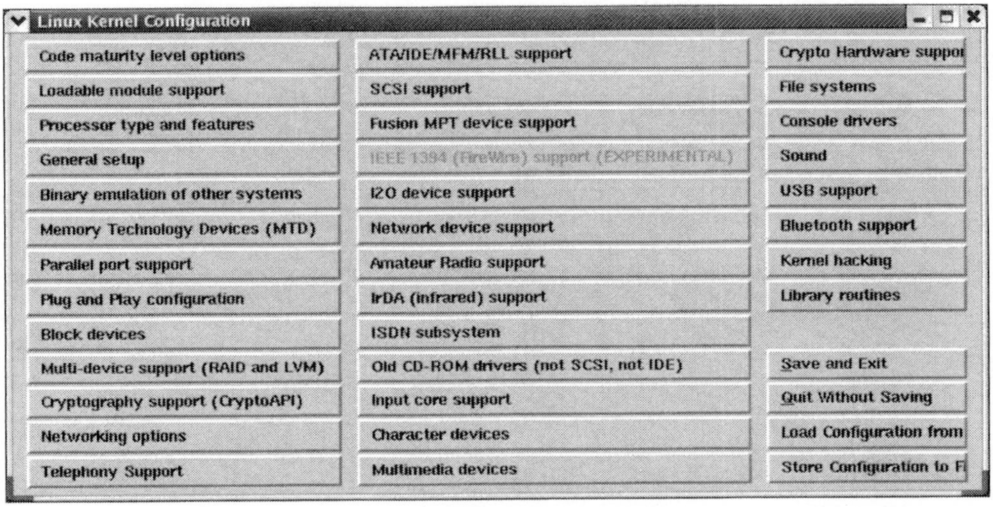

An operating system kernel that can utilize several processors concurrently is called a **multi-processor** operating system. Many UNIX and Linux operating systems versions, and Windows NT/2000/XP, can utilize multiple processors. Use of multiple processors improves the performance of processor intensive applications. For example, programs that perform mathematical computations on large amounts of data for the government or engineering firms would benefit from multiple processors. The ability of a computer system to use multiple processors that can execute different portions of a program is called **Symmetrical Multi-Processing** or **SMP**. Windows and Linux operating systems support SMP.

If the operating system can support multiple users at the same time, then the operating system is a **multi-user** operating system. Mainframe, midrange, UNIX, and Linux operating systems are multi-user operating systems.

A **multitasking** operating system kernel is one that appears to handle multiple tasks at the same time. A **task** is a program that is running. A task is also known as a **job** or **process**. The operating system actually does one task at a time, but using something called time slicing the operating system gives each task a little bit of CPU time. The tasks take turns being processed in a round-robin fashion. A **time slice** is a unit of time allocated to a task.

For example, assume an operating system gives each task two minutes of CPU time—which is actually quite a bit. If a job exceeds the two-minute time slice, the job and its data are placed into the virtual memory page file. **Virtual memory** uses RAM and a section of the hard disk to accommodate multitasking and multiple users. The **page file**, or **swap file,** is the section of the hard disk used for virtual memory. Figure 2.26 shows the Virtual Memory settings on Windows 2000.

Figure 2.26: A Screenshot of the Windows 2000 Virtual Memory Settings

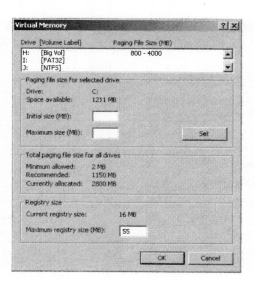

Once the job is moved to the page file, the next task in line will be processed. If this job finishes in less than two minutes, then the system can retrieve the first task from the swap area to continue processing. This is done for all jobs until there is no more work to be done. The advantage of multitasking is one large task won't bottleneck jobs requiring less time.

 On Windows 2000, the page file is named Pagefile.sys. The minimum size of the file is 2 MB and the recommended page file size is 1.5 times memory.

There are two variations of multitasking—preemptive and cooperative. With **preemptive multitasking**, the operating system has the ability to take control of the computer system from an application. With **cooperative multitasking**, the application takes control of the system resources. Preemptive multitasking is much more effective because if an application fails, the system won't necessarily crash. In cooperative operating systems, a failed application can cause the whole computer to freeze or crash.

 People multitask using time slicing all the time. For example, you may be busy studying at home when the phone rings. While you are on the phone, the doorbell rings and the dryer shuts off with a beep. You manage each of these processes by putting the person on the phone on hold, going to the door, checking the dryer, etc., and continuing to give little slices of time to each process until they are all handled.

Let's briefly discuss real and protected mode operating systems and software. An operating system can operate its application software in one of two modes: **real** (also called 16-bit mode) or **protected** (also called 32-bit mode). The term 16-bit means the software was developed using a 16-bit processor such as the Intel 80286. The term 32-bit means the software was developed using faster 32-bit processor such as an Intel Pentium processor. The features of real mode are as follows:

- The single application can access hardware directly—"real" access.
- It supports only single-task (one application) execution.
- The processor can only access up to 1 MB of memory (it can access more than 1 MB with Extended Memory Specification or XMS (this will be discussed in Chapter 3.)
- The failure of a single application can cause the whole system to fail.
- It is slower than 32-bit processors and operating systems.
- It is written for 16-bit processors (processors with 16 physical bus lines), such as the Intel 8088.

Some of the features of protected mode are as follows:

- The failure of a single application does not necessarily cause the other applications (or system) to fail—they are "protected" from one another.
- It supports multi-tasking (multiple applications).
- The processor can access up to 4 GB of memory.
- It is faster than 16-bit processors and operating systems.
- It is written for 32-bit processors (processors with 32 physical bus lines), such as the Intel 80286, 80386, 80486, and Pentium class of processors.
- The applications cannot access hardware directly.

In real mode, the application software has direct (hence the term "real") access to the hardware (such as memory). In real mode, the failure of a single application can cause the whole computer to fail. The reason is the application can access hardware directly and could potentially overwrite the memory address space occupied by operating system programs. Native DOS runs in real mode.

In protected mode, the application software does not have direct access to the hardware. Also, multiple applications are assigned their own memory address space and are "protected" from one another. Thus, the failure of one application does not necessarily mean another will fail. So, other applications are protected and so is the hardware. Windows 98, NT, 2000, and XP boot into real mode and then run in protected mode. This is why you can end one task without affecting another while in those operating systems.

Application software and device drivers are written for either a 16-bit or a 32-bit operating system. The 16-bit applications and device drivers run on DOS and Windows 3.1 (16-bit operating systems). These applications operate in real mode and could potentially fail causing complete system failure. The 32-bit applications and device drivers run under Windows 98, NT, 2000, and XP (32-bit operating systems). These applications operate in protected mode. A 16-bit operating system cannot run 32-bit software. The 32-bit operating systems can run a 16-bit application in an **emulated** environment, which means that the 16-bit application "thinks" it is running on a 16-bit operating system. However, a 32-bit program actually runs the 16-bit application.

Chapter Summary

- Operating systems facilitate user interaction with a Command Line Interface (CLI) or a Graphical User Interface (GUI). For most users, the GUI is user-friendlier than the CLI. You must learn the command syntax when executing commands in the CLI. In the GUI, you point and click on programs you want to execute.

- Operating systems provide application management by accessing hardware for applications, allowing applications to be installed or uninstalled, and providing a consistent interface among applications with an Application Programmer Interface (API). Microsoft and IBM developed the Common User Access (CUA) standard, which makes applications consistent for users.

- The operating system manages the file system for both users and applications. The file system defines the organization of the files and folders on disk and is created when you format a partition. The file system on Windows and Linux operating systems are hierarchical.

- The operating system also manages the hardware. The Basic Input/Output System (BIOS) is firmware that guides basic input and output functions of the PC. Booting the operating system means loading the operating system into memory so you have a functional system. System resources control how the devices on a computer work. Examples of system resources are: Interrupt Requests (IRQs), I/O ports, base memory address, and Direct Memory Access (DMA).

- The operating system kernel is the core set of instructions that remain in memory once the system is booted. On Windows, the kernel looks at the Registry for information on how and what to load. On Linux, the kernel looks to configuration files for this information.

Review Questions

1. What is the CLI called in the Linux operating system?
   a) DOS
   b) Shell
   c) ASCII
   d) Compiler

2. What is the name of the program to get to the command line on Windows 98/NT/2000/XP?
   a) Command
   b) Firmware
   c) COBOL
   d) Desktop

3. What is the area on the screen where a user interacts with the GUI of an operating system?
   a) Thread
   b) Firmware
   c) Desktop
   d) ASCII

4. What occurs when a program tries to occupy the same area of memory as another program?
   a) Thread
   b) Firmware
   c) BIOS
   d) GPF

5. Which of the following is an executable file that consists of functions and data?
   a) Kernel
   b) JAVA
   c) BIOS
   d) DLL

6. Which of the following is a standard written by Microsoft and IBM to make Windows programs consistent?
   a) CUA
   b) Firmware
   c) BIOS
   d) API

7. Which of the following is used to guarantee similar interfaces among programs?
   a) CUA
   b) Firmware
   c) BIOS
   d) API

8. Which of the following is a number used to reference a process?
   a) PID
   b) CUA
   c) BIOS
   d) API

9. Which of the following is a basic unit of instruction allocated processor time by the operating system?
   a) CUA
   b) Thread
   c) BIOS
   d) API

10. Operating systems supporting _____ allow threads to be executed at the same time.
    a) Virtual memory
    b) Multitasking
    c) Multithreading
    d) APIs

11. The _____ defines the organization of the files and folders stored on disk.
    a) File system
    b) Active partition
    c) Boot partition
    d) System partition

12. The _____ contains your operating system and is the very first partition on the drive.
    a) File system
    b) Active partition
    c) Primary partition
    d) System partition

13. On Windows NT/2000/XP, you can have up to _____ primary partitions.
    a) 1
    b) 2
    c) 3
    d) 4

14. What is the name of the record that tells the operating system about the partitions?
    a) System partition
    b) MBR
    c) CUA
    d) API

15. On Windows operating systems, the file system stores a file in _____.
    a) Clusters
    b) Other files
    c) CUA
    d) API

16. _____ are the concentric circles on disk.
    a) Clusters
    b) Tracks
    c) Sectors
    d) Allocation units

17. The drive letter and the colon are known as the _____.
    a) Drive specification
    b) Extension
    c) Folder
    d) Cluster

18. What is used to associate a file to an application?
    a) Extension
    b) Tracks
    c) Folder
    d) CUA

19. In DOS, file names must follow the _____ rule.
    a) Extension
    b) 255
    c) 8.3
    d) Fragment

20. A file that is stored in non-adjacent clusters is _____.
    a) Extended
    b) Multithreaded
    c) Fragmented
    d) Paged

Lab Projects

Note that these projects assume the PC is powered on. Although you can perform these projects in other versions of Microsoft Windows with minor changes, the assumed operating system is Windows 2000 unless otherwise specified. You are logged in as the Administrator user.

Lab Project 1

The goal of this project is to help you understand how to view system information. In this project, you will view both hardware and software information.

1. Click **Start** and point to **Programs**, **Accessories**, and **System Tools**. Then click **System Information**. The System Information window opens.

2. In the left hand windowpane of System Information, click the **System Summary** folder. Note: This folder may already be opened. In the right hand windowpane Item names and their Values appear in columns.

3. Record the operating system Name, Version and System Manufacturer.

   _____

4. Choose two other Items and Values and record them.

   _____

5. In the left hand windowpane of System Information, double-click the **Hardware Resources** folder. Additional folders appear.

6. Click the **IRQs** folder. The list of IRQs on the computer appear.

7. Click the **IRQ Number** column to sort the IRQ numbers from lower to higher.

8. Record the IRQs for COM1, COM3, and the Primary IDE controller.

   _____

9. Choose two other devices and record their IRQs.

   _____

10. Double-click the **Hardware Resources** folder to close it.

11. Double-click the **Software Environment** folder. Additional folders appear beneath the Software Environment folder.

12. Click **Loaded Modules**. A list of modules appears. Notice some of the modules are DLLs due to the .dll extension. Refer to Figure 2.27 for a screenshot.

Figure 2.27: Viewing Loaded Modules in System Information

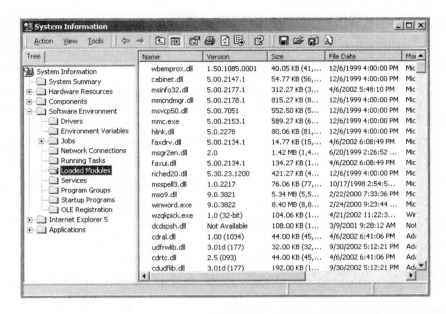

13. Record the name, version, size, file date, and path of three modules. Note you may have to scroll to the right to locate the path.

_____

_____

_____

14. Close System Information.

Lab Project 2

The goal of this project is to help you understand how a task impacts hardware resources. In this project you will use Task Manager on Windows 2000 to view process information of the Calculator program. Because the Calculator program is processor intensive, you will perform calculations causing the CPU usage to increase.

1. Click **Start** and then click **Run**. The Run dialog box appears.

2. Type **calc** and press Enter (or click **OK**).

3. The Calculator program window appears. Keep the window open.

4. Execute Task Manager by pressing Ctrl + Alt simultaneously and then Del. The Windows Security dialog box appears.

5. Click the **Task Manager** button. The Windows Task Manager program appears.

6. Click the **Processes** tab. Scroll until you locate the calc program in the Image Name column. It should be named calc.exe.

7. Record the PID, the CPU, CPU Time, and Mem Usage values for calc.

_____

8. Click the **Performance** tab in Task Manager.

9. Go back to the Calculator program by clicking its name in the Title Bar of the Window. Click **View** and the click **Scientific**. To view both windows on the screen, you may have to move them around.

10. In order watch the CPU Usage increase, click the number **9** and then click the **x^3** key 10 times.

11. Notice the CPU Usage in Task Manager reaches 100% as shown in Figure 2.28.

12. To end the calculator program within Task Manager, click **Applications**.

13. Locate the Calculator and click **End Task**.

14. Close Task Manager.

Figure 2.28: Viewing CPU Usage Reaching 100%

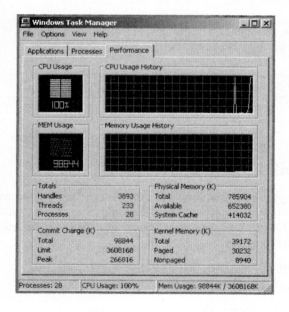

Lab Project 3

The goal of this project is to help you understand how to analyze and defragment a disk partition. In this project you will use the Disk Defragmenter in Windows 2000 to analyze and defragment a disk. An analysis is performed to determine if defragmenting the drive is cost-effective.

1. Click **Start** and point to **Programs**, **Accessories**, and **System Tools**. Then click **Disk Defragmenter**. The Disk Defragmenter program opens.

2. Click the C: drive and click **Analyze**. The analysis occurs. When the analysis is done an Analysis Complete window appears.

3. Click **View Report**. Analysis Report opens.

4. Record whether your drive needs to be defragmented.

   _____

5. In the Volume Information section of the report, record the total fragmentation and file fragmentation percentages. You may need to scroll up and down to locate these.

   _____

6. In the Most fragmented files section, record the file name with the most fragments, its size, and total number of fragments. You can click the Fragments column name to sort the listing from higher to lower.

   _____

7. Close the Analysis Report.

8. Whether recommended or not, defragment your drive.

   _____

9. Record the total fragmentation now.

   _____

10. Record the difference in fragmentation before and after.

   _____

11. Close all windows.

Lab Project 4

The goal of this project is to further your understanding of the file system hierarchy. In this project you will create folders and files. Although the figure in this project is taken from a Windows 2000 PC, you could perform this project on Windows 95 or higher.

1. Insert a formatted floppy in the floppy drive.

2. Create the file system hierarchy shown in Figure 2.29. You will have to use the **File**, **New** command to create the folders and files. The MIS, Payroll, and Sales folders are immediately beneath the floppy (the root folder). MIS contains two files: Project1.txt and Project2.txt. Payroll contains two folders: Paychecks and Managers, which are empty. Sales contains these folders: Eastern and Western. The Eastern folder contains these files: Jan.txt, Feb.txt, and Mar.txt. The Western folder is empty.

3. Close all windows.

Figure 2.29: A Screenshot of the Partial Hierarchy for Project 4

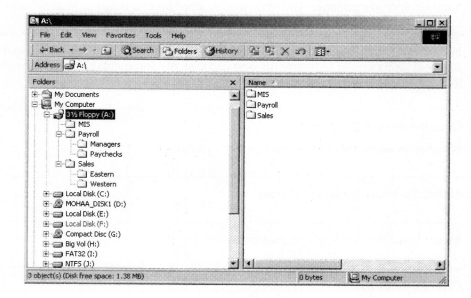

Lab Project 5

The goal of this project is to help you understand file system formats. In this project, you will view disk property information and convert the FAT file system to NTFS. The drive letter used in this project is K: but another drive letter will suffice as long as it is FAT. Once you change the drive to NTFS, you cannot change it back to FAT.

1. Double-click the **My Computer** icon on your desktop. The My Computer window appears with various devices and folders on the system.

2. Right-click on the K: drive or another driver spec as long as it is FAT.

3. Record the file system format (although you know it is FAT) and the used and free space on the partition.

   DESKTOP C: USED 116.7GB FREE 57.7GB

4. To access the command line in order to convert the drive using the **convert** command, click **Start**, and then click **Run**. In the Run dialog box, type **cmd** and press Enter or click **OK**. The Windows command line prompt appears.

5. At the prompt, enter **convert *drive_spec:* /fs:ntfs** and press Enter. Note that you will supply your own specific drive letter in the place of the drive specification. The option **/fs:ntfs** indicates to convert to the NTFS file system.

6. Figure 2.30 shows a sample screenshot. In the figure, drive k: is converted.

Figure 2.30: A Screenshot of Converting FAT to NTFS

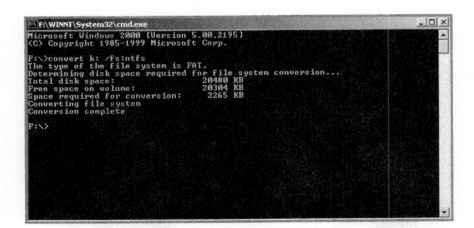

7. View the file system format again.

8. Now record the file system format and the used and free space on the drive.

9. Close all windows.

Lab Project 6

The goal of this project is to help you understand Device Manager in Windows 2000. In this project, you will scan for Plug and Play (PnP) devices and view device information.

1. Right-click the **My Computer** icon on your desktop and click **Properties**. The **System Properties** window appears with various tabs. The **General** tab is selected by default.

2. Record the System information.

      _____

3. Record the Computer information.

      _____

4. Click the **Hardware** tab. Additional command buttons appear.

5. Click **Device Manager**. The Device Manager window appears.

6. To scan for Plug and Play devices, right-click the computer's name icon and click **Scan** for hardware changes. Another box appears indicating it is scanning.

7. Record whether or not it found any new PnP hardware.

      _____

8. View three devices other than the keyboard (because it was viewed in a chapter exercise).

9. Record whether the device is working properly, driver details, and any resource information.

      _____

      _____

      _____

10. Close all windows.

Lab Project 7

The goal of this project is to help you understand how to view and modify performance settings on your computer.

1. Right-click the **My Computer** icon on your desktop and click **Properties**. The System Properties window appears with various tabs.

2. Click the **Advanced** tab. Additional command buttons appear.

3. Click **Performance Options**. The Performance Options screen appears.

4. Record the Application Response setting.

   _____

5. Click **Change**. The Virtual Memory window opens.

6. Scroll in the top portion of the window until you see a drive letter with a paging file.

7. To highlight the drive spec with a page file, click the driver letter for a drive that has a page file. If you only have one partition, it may already be highlighted. The initial and maximum size entry values appear in the middle of the screen.

8. Record the initial and maximum size of the paging file.

   Desktop   384 / 768

9. Record the Registry's current size and maximum.

   _____

10. Now, let's increase the paging file size. Add 5 to the maximum page file size.

11. In the Maximum size, enter the new value.

12. To set the new maximum, click Set.

13. Record the new maximum.

   _____

14. Click OK three times. Restart your computer, if prompted to do so. You have increased your page file size.

Lab Project 8

The goal of this project is to help you understand the Registry on Windows 2000. In this project, you will see what happens when you change a Registry setting.

1. Click **Start** and then click **Run**. The Run dialog box appears.

2. To open the Registry Editor, type **regedt32** and press Enter (or click **OK**). The Registry Editor opens.

3. Double-click **HARDWARE**. The HARDWARE key opens.

4. Double-click **DESCRIPTION**. The DESCRIPTION key opens.

5. Double-click **System**. The System key opens with values in the right hand windowpane.

6. Double-click the **Identifier** item. A box appears with the value.

7. In order to change the value entry, type *your_name* and press **OK**, where *your_name* is your own name.

8. Refer to Figure 2.31 for a sample screenshot.

Figure 2.31: A Screenshot of the Registry After Changing the Identifier Key

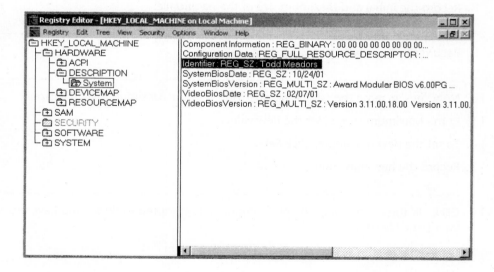

9. Close the Registry Editor.

10. To verify the change, right-click the **My Computer** icon on your desktop and click **Properties**. The **System Properties** window appears with various tabs. The **General** tab is selected by default.

11. Record the Computer information.

12. Notice how this differs from the Computer information you recorded in Step 3 of Project 6.

13. Close all windows.

Lab Project 9 Challenge

The goal of this project is to further your understanding of the file system hierarchy. In this project, you will implement a file and folder hierarchy in Linux.

1. Repeat Project 4 using the Linux operating system GUI.

2. Close all windows when complete.

Lab Project 10 Challenge

The goal of this project is to help you understand how cluster sizes vary on partitions for various file system types. You will need Windows 2000 and between 4 and 6 GB of unallocated free disk space.

1. Open Disk Management located in Administrative Tools under Control Panel.

2. Create three 1,000-byte partitions and format them as FAT (for FAT16), FAT32, and NTFS.

3. Create a 1-byte file in each partition named a.dat.

4. View the properties of the file on the FAT16 partition.

5. Refer to Figure 2.32 for a sample screenshot of the Properties page for the file named a.dat.

Figure 2.32: A Screenshot Showing File Size and Size on Disk

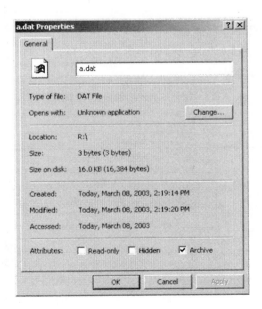

6. Notice the Size and Size on Disk amounts in Figure 2.32. The Size amount for the FAT16 partition is 3 bytes. Although there is only 1 byte in the file, the extra 2 bytes are overhead. Included in this overhead is the EOF character sequence. The Size on Disk amount

for the FAT16 partition is 16 KB. Note the Size on Disk amount is the cluster size. There is quite a bit of wasted disk space (16, 384 − 3 = 16,381 bytes wasted).

7. Record the Size and Size on Disk amounts for a.dat on the FAT32 partition.

_____

8. Record the Size and Size on Disk amounts for a.dat on the NTFS partition.

_____

9. Compare the Size on Disk values to Table 2.2.
10. Record how they relate.

_____

_____   _____

11. Delete the partitions.
12. Create three 1,025-byte partitions and format them as FAT (for FAT16), FAT32, and NTFS.
13. Create a 1-byte file in each partition named a.dat.
14. Record the Size and Size on Disk amounts for a.dat on the FAT16 partition.

_____

15. Record the Size and Size on Disk amounts for a.dat on the FAT32 partition.

_____

16. Record the Size and Size on Disk amounts for a.dat on the NTFS partition.

_____

17. Compare the Size on Disk values to Table 2.2.
18. Record how they relate.

_____

_____

19. Close all windows.

Internet Discovery

Internet Discovery Lab 1

The goal of this Internet Discovery Lab is to help further your knowledge of chapter terms by accessing the Webopedia web site.

1. Connect to the Internet.
2. Open your web browser.
3. In the address box, type **http://www.webopedia.com** and press Enter.
4. Locate the search box, enter the following terms, and write a brief synopsis of each term.

    a. Multitasking

_____

_____

_____

    b. Partition

_____

_____

_____

    c. Fragmentation

_____

_____

_____

    d. Cluster

_____

_____

_____

Internet Discovery Lab 2

The goal of this Internet Discovery Lab is to have you obtain a copy of the Linux operating system that boots on a CD. This version is called Knoppix.

1. Connect to the Internet.
2. Open your web browser.
3. In the address box, type **http://www.knoppix.com** and press Enter.
4. Download the Knoppix version or order a copy. Ordering a copy costs under $30.00. Downloading is free but you will need a CD Writer and a 700 MB CD.
5. Once you obtain the operating system, boot the CD and try out the GUI. Notice the differences and similarities between Linux and Windows.

Soft Skills: Help Desk Support

1. A user calls you and indicates that opening files takes longer than it used to take. What suggestions do you offer them as to what could be happening?
2. You receive an e-mail from a user asking you to compare the FAT and NTFS file systems because his or her manager wants to know the benefits. Summarize the differences.
3. A user wants to add a new device to his or her system and calls you for assistance. What solution do you suggest?
4. You get paged in the middle of the night from a user because the MBR on his or her computer has become corrupt. What do you tell the user to do?

Critical Thinking

1. If a file can become fragmented, do you think a folder can become fragmented? Why or why not?
2. Assuming the file system table was not present yet everything else still functioned normally, how do you think the operating system would go about locating a file you wanted to open?
3. Referring to Table 2.2, why do you think the minimum cluster size is equal to 512 bytes?
4. Explain the pros and cons of a fictitious cluster size of 1 byte.

Study Skills

Reinforcements are on the way!

- Read your textbook—again! This provides wonderful reinforcement of the content of a chapter.
- Summarize the chapter in your own words. By doing this, you will go over the material at least twice. This also provides great reinforcement of the material.
- Do all homework assignments. Doing your homework will improve your test score results.
- Do all Lab Projects because that is where learning really occurs. Plus, you'll have fun doing them.
- Repeating Lab Projects provides invaluable reinforcement.
- Understand the analogies. Your instructor may come up with good everyday analogies that help "hook" the material in your brain. An example of an analogy is the garden store tree analogy discussed in this chapter. You can also come up with your own analogies to help you understand a topic.
- Review the tips embedded within a chapter to further your understanding of the finer points of a topic.
- Search the Internet for study questions on the A+ test. Again, reinforcement!
- Ask the instructor questions about material that you don't understand. If you are afraid to ask in class, ask your question in private. Your instructor is there to help!

Study Skills: Self-Study Question(s)
1. Identify at least one reinforcement technique you performed today!
2. Identify at least one analogy that reinforced your knowledge. (You **cannot** use the garden store tree analogy.)

3

Chapter 3
DOS and the DOS
Command Line
Interface

OBJECTIVES

The goal of this chapter is twofold:

- To introduce you to DOS and the DOS Command Line Interface (CLI)
- To help you prepare and pass the following sections of the A+ Operating System Technologies Exam:

A+ Operating System Technologies Exam Objectives
covered in this chapter (and corresponding page numbers)

Domain 1 Operating System Fundamentals

1.2 Identify the names, locations, purposes, and contents of major system files.

1.3 Demonstrate the ability to use command-line functions and utilities to manage the operating system, including the proper syntax and switches.

In this chapter, you will complete the following sections:
- 3.1 Understanding DOS and the DOS Command Prompt in Windows
- 3.2 Understanding the DOS Tree Structure
- 3.3 Understanding the Types of DOS Commands
- 3.4 Understanding Drive Related Commands
- 3.5 Learning about Wildcard Characters
- 3.6 Learning about Redirection and Filtering
- 3.7 Learning about Batch Files
- 3.8 Learning about Additional Commands

3.1 Understanding DOS and the DOS Command Prompt in Windows

Microsoft developed the Microsoft Disk Operating System or MS-DOS in the early 1980s for the IBM PC. **MS-DOS**, sometimes called DOS, is a single-user, single-tasking operating system. This means only one user can do only one task at a time. If you printed a document in DOS, you can't do anything else until the document is through printing. You cannot load several applications at once like you can on Windows-based platforms.

DOS is an operating system comprised of various programs that help it control the overall operation of the PC. The basic categories of DOS software are:

1. **System programs and files**—used to start DOS during the boot process. Examples include IO.SYS, MSDOS.SYS, and COMMAND.COM. These are sometimes called the **boot files**.
2. **File system management programs**—used to manage the directories and files. Examples include COPY, DIR, and CD.
3. **Utilities**—used to augment the operating system. Examples include FDISK and FORMAT.

Let's look at system programs in more detail. File system management programs and utilities will be discussed in later sections.

As the PC is powered on and passes its Power-On Self Test (POST), it begins to load the operating system into memory. MS-DOS uses three system files for booting. The files are:

IO.SYS
MSDOS.SYS
COMMAND.COM

The first two, IO.SYS and MSDOS.SYS, are hidden to prevent accidental deletion. Without these files, DOS won't boot. These two files provide generic input/output and file management functionality. You cannot even see the files without doing a little extra work. However, if you run the DOS ATTRIB command you will be able to see that they do exist. Figure 3.1 shows a screenshot of the ATTRIB command displaying these files. The ATTRIB command is used to view and set file attributes. In DOS, a file can have these four attributes: Read-Only, Archive, System, and Hidden. You will learn about more attributes and the ATTRIB command later in this chapter. In Figure 3.1, you also see another hidden file named DRVSPACE.BIN commonly used for disk drive compression to save disk space.

The system program named **COMMAND.COM** is known as the **command interpreter**. It is the last boot file listed in Figure 3.1. It gives you the DOS prompt and is responsible for processing every command typed into the computer. In Figure 3.1 the prompt **A:\>** appears to the left of the ATTRIB command. Remember from Chapter 2, this references the floppy.

Figure 3.1: Viewing the System Program Files on a DOS Disk

```
A:\>attrib
A    SHR        A:\IO.SYS
A    SHR        A:\MSDOS.SYS
A    SHR        A:\DRVSPACE.BIN
A               A:\COMMAND.COM

A:\>_
```

You can create a DOS boot disk by running the SYS command. The SYS command transfers the DOS system program files and command interpreter to the drive specified. So SYS A: makes a floppy bootable. You can also create a DOS boot disk by running the FORMAT command using the /S option. The command FORMAT A: /S will format the floppy and make it bootable. The difference between SYS and FORMAT /S is the SYS command does not format the disk. So, if you have a floppy that has files you want to keep on it, and you want to make it bootable, use the SYS command.

If COMMAND.COM is missing from your disk, you will receive an error on the screen. The error displays a message such as **"Bad or missing Command Interpreter"** during the boot process. This indicates that COMMAND.COM is either corrupt or indeed missing. To fix this problem, you need to get a copy of COMMAND.COM on the boot disk. You can do this by typing the SYS command or using the /S option on the FORMAT command.

There are two other optional system files. They are called **AUTOEXEC.BAT** and **CONFIG.SYS**. The AUTOEXEC.BAT file is a batch file. A batch file contains DOS commands and its last three characters are BAT for "batch." When creating batch files, you are creating a program that is interpreted. This file is used to customize your boot process. Because it is a batch file, it can be executed anytime. The following is a partial AUTOEXEC.BAT file:

PROMPT PG
PATH C:\DOS;C:\WINDOWS

The first line sets the prompt and the second line allows DOS commands to be executed anywhere in the tree structure. If you had Windows 3.1 installed, you could load it into memory by placing the statement WIN (to load WIN.COM) as the last statement in the AUTOEXEC.BAT file.

The CONFIG.SYS file is a configuration file that has entries for device drivers such as memory, the mouse, and the CD-ROM. The CONFIG.SYS file is read only during the boot process. If you change it, you must reboot for the changes to take effect. A partial CONFIG.SYS file looks like this:

DEVICE=C:\DOS\HIMEM.SYS
DOS=HIGH
FILES=30

The first line allows use of Extended Memory, the second line loads DOS into High Memory and the last line sets the number of concurrent open files to 30. These types of memory will be discussed next.

If the statement has an equal sign, it generally goes in CONFIG.SYS. Device driver and other variable references go in CONFIG.SYS. Commands go into AUTOEXEC.BAT. You must reboot your system in order to use the changes made to CONFIG.SYS. You can simply enter AUTOEXEC to implement changes made to AUTOEXEC.BAT.

You need to be aware of the DOS system file load order for troubleshooting purposes and to help you with the A+ OS Technologies exam. The MS-DOS system files are loaded in the following order:

1. IO.SYS
2. MSDOS.SYS
3. CONFIG.SYS
4. COMMAND.COM
5. AUTOEXEC.BAT

During the boot sequence, you can press the **F5** key to bypass executing CONFIG.SYS and AUTOEXEC.BAT. You can press the **F8** key and DOS will prompt you to confirm executing each line of CONFIG.SYS and AUTOEXEC.BAT. The use of these keys allows you to test different configurations on your PC when running DOS.

For example, pressing **F8** would show a confirmation line such as the following:

MS-DOS will prompt you to confirm each CONFIG.SYS command.

DOS=HIGH [Y,N]?

You would then enter Y to load DOS high. If you entered N, DOS would not be loaded high.

During the boot process, DOS is loaded into **conventional memory**. Conventional memory, or base memory, is memory in the range of 0 to 640 KB. This is where MS-DOS and other applications reside. Figure 3.2 shows a diagram of the types of memory used by DOS.

Figure 3.2: The Memory Ranges Used by MS-DOS

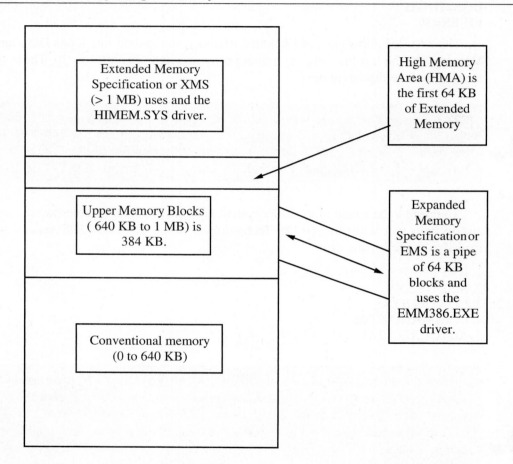

DOS uses **upper memory** for the system BIOS, video BIOS, and other functions. Upper memory is addressed in blocks known as **Upper Memory Blocks** or UMBs and is sometimes called reserved memory. This is the 384 KB of memory from 640 KB to 1 MB. You can make UMBs available to DOS by placing this line in CONFIG.SYS:

DOS=UMB

If you ever get the following message, then check your floppy drive. You may have placed a non-system disk in the drive. Remove or replace it and press any key to continue booting.

Invalid system disk

Replace the disk, and then press any key

Over time, software demanded that hardware run more effectively. With the release of MS-DOS Version 5.0, the use of **Extended Memory Specification** or XMS was developed to break the 640 KB barrier. (You can determine the version of your operating system by running the VER command.) With XMS, DOS uses additional memory in the PC. Applications and data can now be loaded in the memory range made available by XMS. XMS requires a device driver named HIMEM.SYS to use it. You place the following in the CONFIG.SYS file:

DEVICE=C:\DOS\HIMEM.SYS

Lotus, Intel, and Microsoft developed a standard called **Expanded Memory Specification** or EMS. This standard is called the LIM (the initials of Lotus, Intel, and Microsoft) EMS. EMS uses a technique where 16 KB blocks of data are transferred in and out of a reserved 64 KB section of upper memory. If you think back to Chapter 2, this is similar to how virtual memory swaps programs and data between memory and the page file on disk. In order to use EMS, you have to use a device driver named EMM386.EXE and place the following in the CONFIG.SYS file:

DEVICE=C:\DOS\EMM386.EXE ON

The option **ON** following the device driver name activates it.

Another type of memory called the **High Memory Area** or HMA is the first 64 KB block of memory in extended memory. HMA actually came about as a result of a software bug. Once it was discovered, DOS was retrofitted to utilize it. DOS can be loaded into HMA thus freeing conventional memory for use by applications and programs. Extended memory will generally activate HMA, but you could do it by placing the following in CONFIG.SYS:

DOS=HIGH

You can combine the HIGH and UMB option on the DOS= statement by adding this entry to CONFIG.SYS to load DOS high and create UMBs:

DOS=HIGH, UMB

Programs such as HIMEMS.SYS, EMM386.EXE, COMMAND.COM, and IO.SYS are called **Terminate and Stay Resident** or TSR programs. This means they execute, terminate normally, and then stay resident in memory until needed by the operating system.

You can think of a TSR as executing and then "going to sleep" until needed. When an activity they perform is required, they "wake up" and go to work. Once the activity is completed, they "go back to sleep" until the next time they are needed. Other programs such as DIR or ATTRIB execute, terminate, and do not stay resident.

Originally Microsoft did not think users would need more than 1 MB of memory. Nowadays, many GUI operating systems need a minimum of 32 MB just to run properly.

Table 3.1 summarizes the types of memory used by MS-DOS as discussed in this section.

Table 3.1: Types of Memory Used by MS-DOS

Type of Memory	Description
Conventional Memory	The range of memory from 0 to 640 KB used by DOS and applications.
Upper Memory Blocks (UMB)	The range of memory is reserved for video memory and other needs.
High Memory Area (HMA)	The first 64 KB of extended memory used by DOS.
Extended Memory Specification (XMS)	Extended memory is memory above 1 MB used by applications.
Expanded Memory Specification (EMS)	Blocks of data are swapped in and out of a 64 KB section of memory between UMBs and EMS.

There are two different modes where you can execute DOS commands at a command line prompt. They are:
- Within the DOS operating system—the PC is booted using DOS.
- Within the DOS command prompt of a Windows operating system—the PC is booted using a Microsoft Windows operating system such as Windows 95/98/2000/XP.

Using the first method, DOS is booted and there is no Graphical User Interface. With the second method, you enter the name of the command interpreter to go into DOS mode. It is called COMMAND.COM on Windows 95/98. On Windows NT/2000/XP, it is called COMMAND.COM or CMD.EXE.

You must learn the DOS commands and command line syntax regardless of version used. Most commands, such as CD and DIR, work across all operating systems revisions. But not all commands exist in all revisions of DOS. Likewise, not all commands exist in all versions of the DOS command prompt mode provided by each Windows operating system revision. For example, the TREE command exists in DOS 6.22, but not in Windows 98. Microsoft included it in Windows XP.

You may be wondering why you need to spend time learning MS-DOS. After all, using the GUI of an operating system is so much easier than learning DOS commands. Besides laying the fundamental groundwork, an actual experience may offer you a good reason. Recently, one of the author's PCs would not boot. A backup had not been performed in about a week—not a good situation. Pressing F8 during the boot process of Windows 2000 to go to Safe Mode did not work. Finally, the author booted Windows 2000 to "Safe Mode with Command Prompt" and used the DOS COPY command to copy important files to the floppy, A:, and then to another system. The PC had to be completely reinstalled. Although the data was intact after reinstalling, without understanding how the DOS commands and command line worked, the important data files on the PC might have been lost.

Note: The remaining sections in this chapter will cover commonly used DOS-related commands available to most of the Microsoft operating systems. Discussion includes use of commands actually within DOS or at the DOS command prompt mode of Windows 98/2000/XP. It does not really matter how you get to the command prompt; what matters is understanding the purpose of the commands and topics discussed. Additionally, because the command prompt can be changed, it is assumed that the prompt is the default prompt in all exercises and lab projects throughout this chapter. Thus, the current drive and directory is assumed for the command prompt.

Let's perform an exercise to get you started with DOS. This exercise assumes a PC is up and running a Microsoft operating system with access to DOS or the DOS command prompt.

Because there are several methods you can use to get to the DOS command prompt, choose an appropriate method for the operating system you are using.

A. DOS: You are already at the command prompt.

B. Windows 98:

Method 1: Click Start, point to Programs, and then click the MS-DOS Prompt option.

Method 2: Click Start, click the Run option, and type in COMMAND at the dialog box and press Enter.

Method 3: During start-up, hold down either the Ctrl key or press the F8 key to access the Command-Prompt-Only mode.

C. NT Workstation:

Method 1: Click Start, point to Programs, and then click on the Command Prompt option.

Method 2: Click Start, click the Run option, type in either CMD or COMMAND (either command works), and click on the OK button.

D. Windows 2000 or Windows XP:
Click Start, click the Run option, type in CMD or COMMAND (both commands work) in the dialog box, and click the OK button.

1. Notice your prompt. Your prompt should look something like this: C:\WINDOWS> or C:\>. It will have a drive letter specification followed by the root, \, symbol.
2. At the command prompt, type **FORMAT A:**. A message appears indicating you need to insert a new diskette for drive A: and press Enter.
3. Insert your floppy in the drive.
4. The disk is formatted. If you receive a message indicating the disk has an unusable track, replace the disk and begin again with step 1.
5. Once the disk is formatted, you can enter a volume label. It is a good practice to include your last name as the volume label. However, you are limited to 11 characters. The volume label is like a "software version" of a sticker on the front of your disk with your name on it.
6. When prompted for formatting another disk, enter **N**.
7. Refer to Figure 3.3 for a sample screenshot taken using the FORMAT command under Windows XP.
8. Shut down your PC and operating system by following one of these methods:

A. DOS: Press **Ctrl+Alt** at the same time and while you are holding these down, press **Del**. This is known as the Ctrl+Alt Del key sequence.

B. Windows 98, **NT Workstation,** or **Windows 2000:** Click Start and then click Shut down. When the **Shut Down Windows** dialog box appears, click **Shut down** and then click **OK**. Your PC turns off**.**

C. Windows XP: Click Start then point to **Turn Off Computer**. When the **Turn Off Computer** dialog box appears, click **Turn Off**. Your PC turns off.

9. Insert the newly formatted floppy in the drive.
10. Power up your PC.
11. During the boot process, press the appropriate key to enter the BIOS Setup. You will need to watch the screen as the PC goes through its POST to determine the appropriate key to press to enter the Setup. Typically it is the Del key, but it depends upon the BIOS manufacturer.
12. In the BIOS Setup, locate the option to change the boot sequence.
13. Change it to boot the floppy (A:) if it is not already set. Make sure that the hard drive (C:) is the next boot device.
14. Save the changes. The system boots to the floppy.
15. You receive an error message indicating that the disk is not a system disk.
16. In order to fix this problem, remove the disk and press Enter.
17. The system boots normally.

Figure 3.3: A screenshot of Formatting a Floppy Under Windows XP

```
C:\>format a:
Insert new disk for drive A:
and press ENTER when ready...
The type of the file system is FAT.
Verifying 1.44M
Initializing the File Allocation Table (FAT)...
Volume label (11 characters, ENTER for none)? Meadors
Format complete.

    1,457,664 bytes total disk space.
        5,120 bytes in bad sectors.
    1,452,544 bytes available on disk.

        512 bytes in each allocation unit.
      2,837 allocation units available on disk.

         12 bits in each FAT entry.

Volume Serial Number is 285D-A969

Format another (Y/N)? n

C:\>_
```

3.2 Understanding the DOS Tree Structure

DOS files can be organized like chapters in a book. However, DOS files are grouped into **directories**. The starting point for all directories is the **root directory**. From the root directory, other directories can be made. The garden tree analogy discussed in Chapter 2 applies to the DOS tree. Figure 3.4 shows how a hard disk's file structure might be organized.

Figure 3.4: The DOS Tree Hierarchy

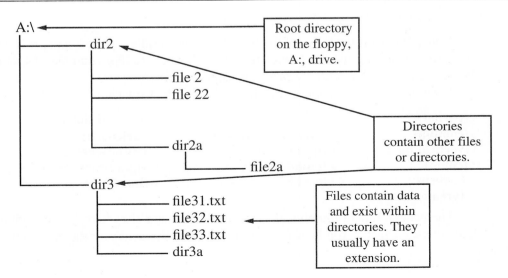

Figure 3.5 shows the TREE command output of the same structure. The TREE command normally shows only directories, but with the /F option, it shows files too.

Figure 3.5: The DOS TREE Command of the Tree Structure in Figure 3.4.

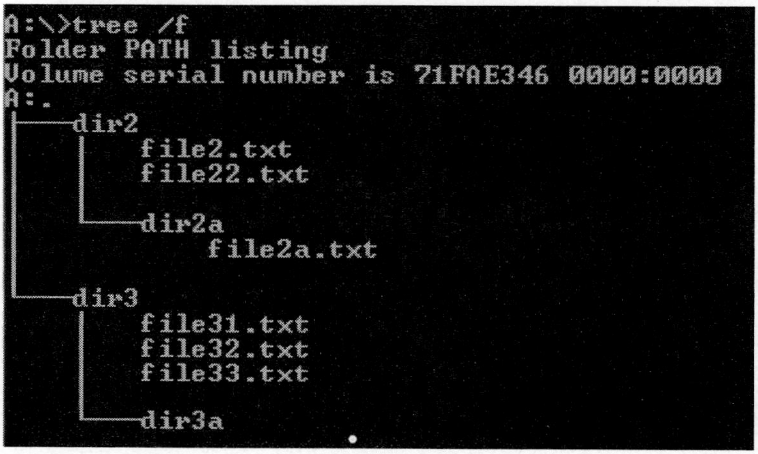

```
A:\>tree /f
Folder PATH listing
Volume serial number is 71FAE346 0000:0000
A:.
├───dir2
│       file2.txt
│       file22.txt
│   └───dir2a
│           file2a.txt
├───dir3
│       file31.txt
│       file32.txt
│       file33.txt
│   └───dir3a
```

A hierarchy is useful because it helps with organization and that translates to quick access for the user.

Notice in Figure 3.4 how each directory has a unique name. A **file name** in DOS can be a maximum of eight characters followed by a dot, then a three-character extension. However, the DOS command mode that comes with most Windows products can support additional characters in the file name.

The general format is as follows:

filename.ext

Note *filename* is the name of the file, the dot is literally a period, and *ext* is the extension. Extensions are used to associate files with software. For example, .DOC are MS-Word documents and .XLS are MS-Excel spreadsheets.

In DOS, a file name *cannot* contain the following characters:

. (period)	**; (semicolon)**	**/ (forward slash)**
, (comma)	**" (quotation marks)**	**\ (backslash)**
| (vertical bar)	**? (question mark)**	**[(left bracket)**
: (colon)	**= (equal sign)**	**] (right bracket)**
* (asterisk)	**(space)**	**< (less than)**
> (greater than)		

The general rule of thumb is if you use the character elsewhere, you cannot use it for a file name character. You need to be aware of these characters for the A+ exam.

Let's discuss navigating the tree structure. Assume the tree structure shown in Figure 3.4 has already been created and the current directory is root, or \. In DOS, there is a command prompt that is set to your current directory path location by default. This is useful because you can just look on your screen and tell where you are located.

In order to change directory locations to dir2, you would issue this command: **CD dir2** and press Enter. Now let's navigate to the directory beneath dir2 named dir2a. By the way, any directory beneath another directory is called a subdirectory, but they'll just be referred to as directories in this chapter.

In Figure 3.4, the directories named dir2 and dir3 are children of root. Or said another way, root is their parent. A **parent directory** is the directory that holds a given file or directory. It is up one level from the current directory. A **child directory** is a directory contained within its parent. It is down one level. The parent directory is represented by two dots, **..**, commonly called dot-dot. The current directory is represented by a single dot.

To help you remember that two dots represent the parent directory in the tree, just remember that you have two parents. So, one dot represents mom and one dot represents dad and collectively, they are called **..** in DOS.

You can issue the **CD ** to always take you to the root directory of the current drive. You can use the **CD ..** command to take you to the parent directory of your current directory. Notice in Figure 3.4 that dir2a is a child of dir2 and dir2 is a child of the root directory. The root directory is a grandparent of dir2a. If you wanted to change to root from dir2a, you would issue either one **CD ** command or two **CD ..** commands.

To change to root by name, you would issue the single command: **CD **. However, to change to any parent directory, you would enter the **CD ..** command. To change to a parent directory going up one level, you must use two dots, or dot-dot. To change to a parent's parent (grandparent), you would enter **CD ..** twice. Or, you can combine levels on one command. For example, you could issue the **CD ..\..** command to go back up two levels.

Each directory and file in the tree has a location called its **path**. There are two types of paths: full path and partial path. The **full path** identifies the directory or file location beginning from root. It is called an **absolute path** because it <u>absolutely</u> refers to the file or directory from root. A command employing the full path <u>always</u> begins at root.

A **partial path** identifies the directory or file location relative to your current location. A partial path does <u>not</u> begin at root. The partial path is also called the **relative path** because you are referring to a file or directory <u>relative</u> to where you are. Refer to Table 3.2 for a few examples. Notice how each full path has the root symbol as the very first character. Each of these paths can also be used with most any command.

Table 3.2: Examples of Full and Partial Paths

Path	Path Type
\	Full
\dir2	Full
\dir2\dir2a	Full
\dir3\file33.txt	Full
..	Partial
..\..	Partial
dir2	Partial
..\dir3	Partial

3.3 Understanding the Types of DOS Commands

In the past, many manufacturers created their own DOS version. IBM developed a version known as PC-DOS and Novell has licensed DR-DOS. Microsoft controls the operating system market today. Microsoft's DOS is known as MS-DOS. While there are many commands, only some of them will be discussed in this chapter. You can type the HELP command in the Windows 2000 and XP command mode to find the available commands for those operating systems.

DOS commands are classified as either internal or external. **Internal commands** are not visible when viewing files on a disk or hard drive but after you enter the commands, they will execute. Internal commands are built into the COMMAND.COM file and execute much faster than external. This is because COMMAND.COM is loaded into memory, which is faster than disk. Table 3.3 lists some of the more common internal commands. DOS and the command mode in Windows 98, Windows 2000, and Windows XP support all of these commands.

Table 3.3: DOS Internal Commands

Command	Description
CD or **CHDIR**	Change directory locations in the tree structure.
MD or **MKDIR**	Create a directory.
DIR	Display a listing of both files and directories.
TYPE	Display the contents of a file.
RD or **RMDIR**	Remove a directory.
COPY	Copy a file to another file.

CLS	Clears your screen.
DATE	Displays the date and allows you to change it.
PATH	Display the current search path.
PROMPT	Display or set your prompt.
REN	Change the name of a file.
ECHO	Displays text on the screen.
TIME	Displays the time and allows you to change it.
DEL	Delete a file.
VER	Displays the current DOS version.

External commands can be seen when viewing files on a disk or a hard drive. External commands execute slower than internal commands because the external commands must be retrieved and loaded from the disk or hard drive. External commands are usually stored in one of the following directories, depending upon the version of the operating system you are using:

- C:\WINDOWS—used by Windows 98 and Windows XP
- C:\WINDOWS\SYSTEM—used by Windows 98
- C:\WINDOWS\COMMAND—used by Windows 98
- C:\WINDOWS\SYSTEM32—used by Windows NT, 2000, and XP
- C:\WINNT\SYSTEM32—used by Windows NT and Windows 2000
- C:\DOS—used by MS-DOS

External commands have an extension of .EXE or .COM. Table 3.4 lists some of the more common external commands. The third column indicates which command is supported under which operating system for DOS, Windows 98, Windows 2000, and Windows XP. Although the FORMAT command is supported among these operating systems, the /S on the FORMAT command is not supported under Windows 2000 and Windows XP.

Table 3.4: Some Common DOS External Commands and Their Operating System Availability

Command	Description	OS Version Availability
ATTRIB	View or change the attributes of a file or directory.	DOS, Windows 98, Windows 2000 and XP command mode.
CHKDSK	Check the status of a disk.	DOS, Windows 98, Windows 2000 and XP command mode.
DELTREE	Remove a tree, which includes files and directories.	DOS and Windows 98 command mode. In Windows 2000 and XP, you use the **rd /s** command.

DOSKEY	Allows you to scroll up and down through the list of commands that you've entered. Think of DOSKEY as keeping a history of the commands you've entered.	DOS, Windows 98, Windows 2000 and XP command mode
EDIT	The DOS editor.	DOS, Windows 98, Windows 2000 and XP command mode
FDISK	Partition a hard disk.	DOS and Windows 98 command mode. Windows 2000 and XP have GUI tools.
FIND	Search for text within a file.	DOS, Windows 98, Windows 2000 and XP command mode.
FORMAT	Prepare a drive for use by DOS.	DOS, Windows 98, Windows 2000 and XP command mode. **Note:** The /S option is not available in Windows 2000 and XP.
LABEL	Change the label on a disk. Think of the label as a software version of a sticker you physically place on your floppy identifying it as being yours.	DOS, Windows 98, Windows 2000 and XP command mode.
MOVE	Used to move a file from one directory location to another.	DOS, Windows 98, Windows 2000 and XP command mode.
MEM	Display a listing of commands and processes in memory.	DOS, Windows 98, Windows 2000 and XP command mode.
SYS	Transfer system files to a device.	DOS and Windows 98 command mode.
SORT	Sort data in a file.	DOS, Windows 98, Windows 2000 and XP command mode.
TREE	Display a tree listing of a directory.	DOS and Windows 2000 and XP command mode. Not available in Windows 98.
XCOPY	Copy a whole tree, which includes files and directories.	DOS, Windows 98, Windows 2000 and XP command mode.

Commands are further classified into two broad categories:
- Directory commands
- File commands

Some commands deal only with directories and some commands deal only with files. Internal or external commands can deal with either files or directories. There are a few exceptions. For example, the DOS DIR command displays both files and directories. Most commands use the following syntax:

command options

Note *command* is the name of the command and *options* are either file and directory names or actual options that alter the command in some way. You can enter the command in upper- or lower-case. Almost all commands use options to enhance the way they operate. The symbol for using options is the forward slash, /.

Let's discuss some of the basic commands you would use in DOS. Let's say you wanted to create a directory. In order to create a directory, you would use the MD, or MKDIR, command. Assuming your current directory is the root directory on the floppy (A:\), if you wanted to create a directory named DirTM you would enter **MD DirTM**. You could issue the DIR command to see that the directory was created. If you wanted to put a file or directory within DirTM, you would first change to that directory using the **CD DirTM** command. Figure 3.6 shows a screenshot of these steps. Because the default prompt is used, your prompt changes as you change directory locations.

Figure 3.6: A Screenshot of Creating a Directory, Taking a Directory Listing, and Changing to a Directory

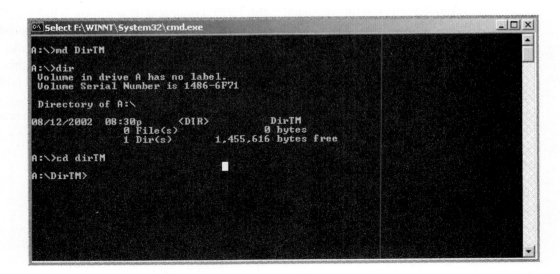

Command options modify the command in some way. For example, DIR /W displays the files and directories in column form. DIR /P pauses the listing. The most useful option for all commands is the question mark symbol, ?. It allows you to question DOS as to what a command does. Think of it as "help" on the command. Figure 3.7 shows a screenshot of DIR /?. You could use this option with most any command. Try CLS /?, CD /? and MD /? at the prompt.

Figure 3.7: A Screenshot of the DIR /? Command

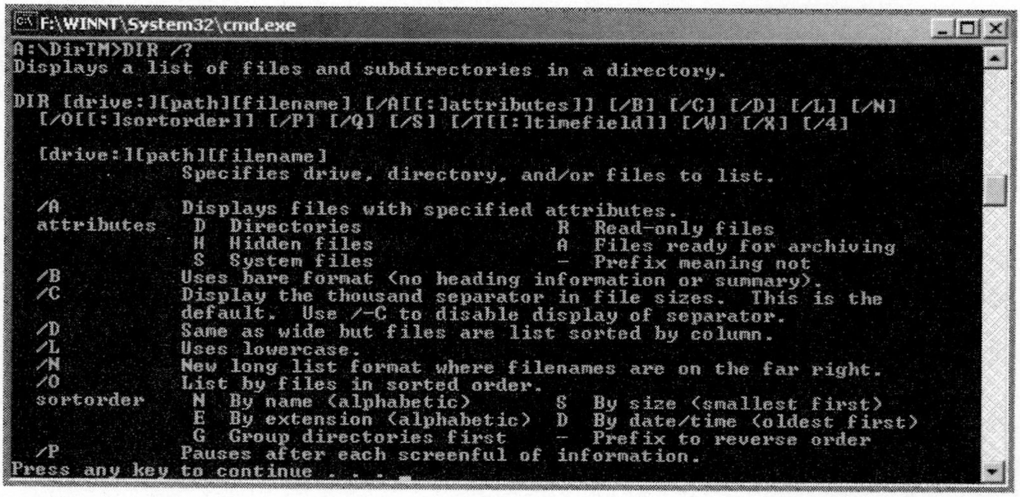

Another very useful command is the TREE command. It works on Windows 2000 but not on Windows 98. The TREE command gives you a directory listing of all subdirectories in a directory. You can use the /F option to include all files in the listing. So, if you wanted to see a tree listing of a directory named A:\PAYROLL, you would enter TREE A:\PAYROLL. If you wanted to see the files as well as directories, you would add the /F option as in TREE /F A:\PAYROLL.

Figure 3.8 shows a sample tree directory for a fictitious organization named The Firm.

Figure 3.8: A Screenshot of Using the TREE /F Command

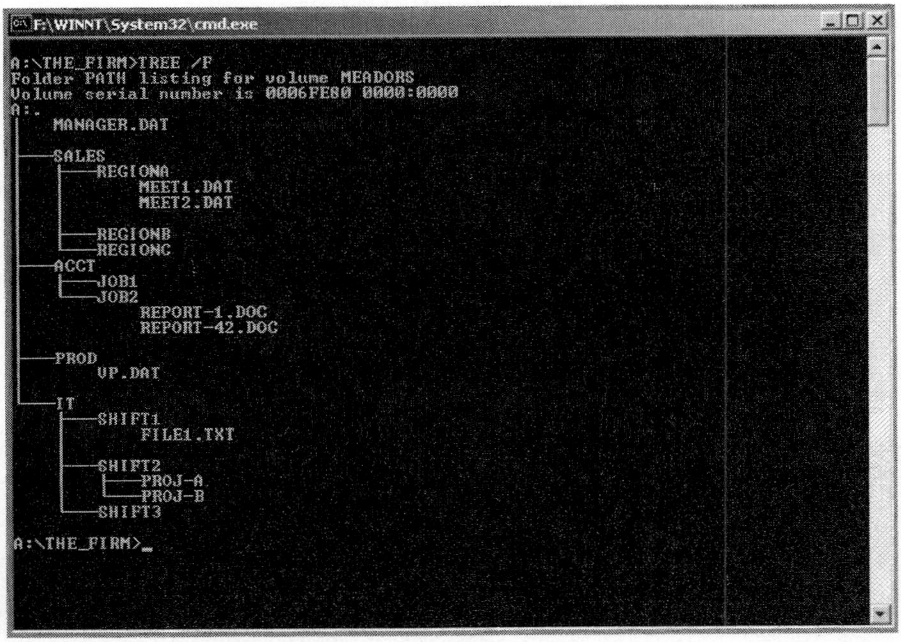

```
F:\WINNT\System32\cmd.exe                                            _|□| x|
A:\THE_FIRM>TREE /F
Folder PATH listing for volume MEADORS
Volume serial number is 0006FE80 0000:0000
A:.
    MANAGER.DAT

    ─SALES
    │    ┌──REGIONA
    │    │      MEET1.DAT
    │    │      MEET2.DAT
    │    │
    │    ┌──REGIONB
    │    └──REGIONC
    ─ACCT
    │    ┌──JOB1
    │    └──JOB2
    │           REPORT-1.DOC
    │           REPORT-42.DOC
    │
    ─PROD
    │      UP.DAT
    │
    └─IT
         ┌──SHIFT1
         │      FILE1.TXT
         │
         ┌──SHIFT2
         │    ┌──PROJ-A
         │    └──PROJ-B
         └──SHIFT3

A:\THE_FIRM>_
```

Creating and Removing Directories

In order to create a directory, you would use the MD or MKDIR command. Although it has been discussed, here is the format for the MD command:

> MD *directory-name*
> MKDIR *directory-name*

To create a directory named Payroll, you would enter **MD Payroll**. Notice that the directory Payroll is a partial path. You really don't know what parent directory it is located in. You can use the MD command with either the partial path or full path name of a directory. For example, you could enter **MD \Acct\General** to create a directory using a full path. Or, you could use a partial path, as in these examples: **MD ..\dir5, MD dir6\dir6a\dir6b**, or **MD dirTM**. Also, you could create a directory on a drive other than your current drive. For example, if your current drive and directory is A:\ (the floppy) and you wanted to make a directory on the C: (hard disk) drive, named Sales, you could enter: **MD C:\Sales**.

Next, you need to understand how to remove directories. The command to remove a directory is RD or RMDIR. Here is the format:

> RD *directory-name*

When using the RD or RMDIR command there are two things to remember:
1. The directory must be empty.
2. Your current directory cannot be the directory you want to remove.

If you get an error indicating you cannot remove the directory, try looking at your prompt or running the CD command. Typing in the CD command with no options will display your current directory. Looking at your prompt will also show your current directory as long as it has not been changed. If your current directory is the one you are trying to delete, then go to the parent using the **CD ..** command. Retry the failed RMDIR command and it should work.

Figure 3.9 shows a sample session of attempting to remove a directory while in the directory. Only when you change directory locations to somewhere higher in the tree will you be able to delete the directory.

Figure 3.9: A Screenshot of the Using the RD (or RMDIR) Command

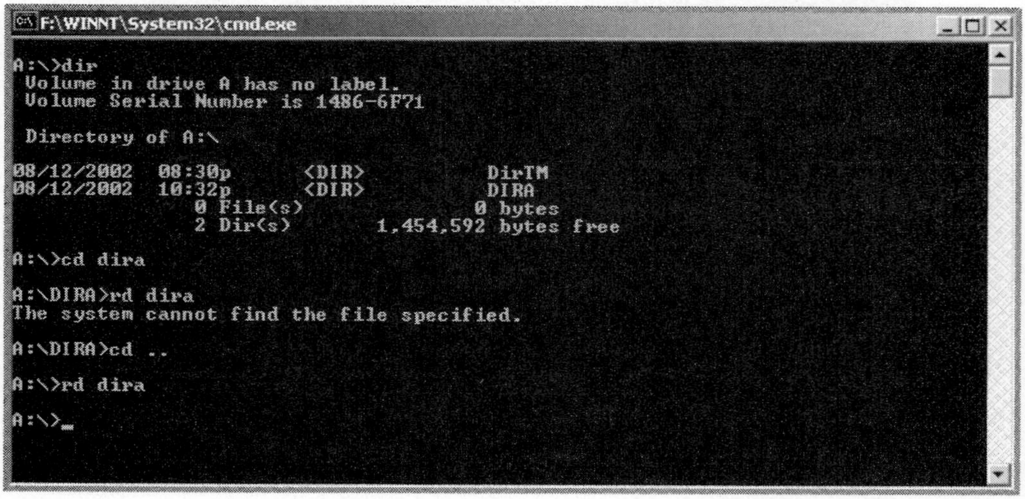

Let's perform an exercise. This exercise assumes a PC is up and running with a Microsoft operating system with access to DOS or the DOS command prompt. A formatted floppy is in the floppy drive. Choose the operating system you are using to access DOS command mode.
1. To change your prompt to the floppy drive, type **A:**.
2. To create a directory, type **MD dira** and press Enter.
3. To change directory locations, type **CD dira** and press Enter.
4. Let's make a directory within the directory named "dira." Type **MKDIR diraa** and press Enter. Remember either MD or MKDIR will work.
5. To change locations to "diraa," type **CD diraa** and press Enter.

6. To change directory locations to the parent directory, type **CD ..** at the command prompt.
7. To remove the "diraa," type **RD diraa**. Remember either RD or RMDIR will work.
8. To change directory locations to the root directory, type **CD ** at the command prompt.
9. To create a directory, type **MD DIRB**.
10. To create a directory, type **MD DIRC**.
11. To verify, type **DIR**.
12. To change to DIRC, type **CD DIRC**.
13. To create a directory, type **MD DIRC1** and press Enter.
14. To create a directory, type **MD DIRC2** and press Enter.
15. To verify, type **DIR.**
16. To change to DIRC2, type **CD DIRC2**.
17. To create a directory, type **MD DIRC2-1** and press Enter.
18. To create a directory, type **MD DIRC2-2** and press Enter.
19. To change directory locations to the root directory, type **CD ** at the command prompt.
20. If your operating system supports the TREE command, type **TREE** and press Enter. It is <u>not</u> supported by Windows 98. To verify whether your operating system supports a command, simply type the command. If it works, it is supported; otherwise, you will see a message indicating the command was not found.
21. Exit the system appropriately.

Managing Files

You need to know how to create, delete, modify, copy, and move files. In this section, we will learn how to do that. In terms of creating files, there are several ways. We are not concerned about all the methods, nor are we really concerned about the data that is in the files. We just need to create files so we can manipulate them within the tree structure.

Let's explore the methods to create files in greater detail. To create a file you could use the COPY command. Although this is not the typical use of the COPY command, it can be used to quickly make files.

The COPY command allows you to copy from a source file (the file name immediately following COPY) to a destination file (the very last file name). Here is the general form:

COPY *source-file destination-file*

For example, **COPY FILEA.DAT FILEB.DAT** will copy FILEA.DAT to FILEB.DAT. Using the COPY command to copy files will be explored more a bit later. It is included here because it can be used to create a new file, as you'll see next.

The COPY command allows you to use the special name CON, which stands for Console Keyboard, to enter text directly into a file. The source in this case is the keyboard. The format is:

COPY CON *filename.txt*

The TYPE command can be used to display the contents of a file. It takes this general form:

TYPE *filename.txt*

Figure 3.10 shows a screenshot of using the COPY CON command to create a file and the TYPE command to display the contents. Notice the case of the letters does not matter.

Figure 3.10: A Screenshot of Using the COPY CON and TYPE Commands

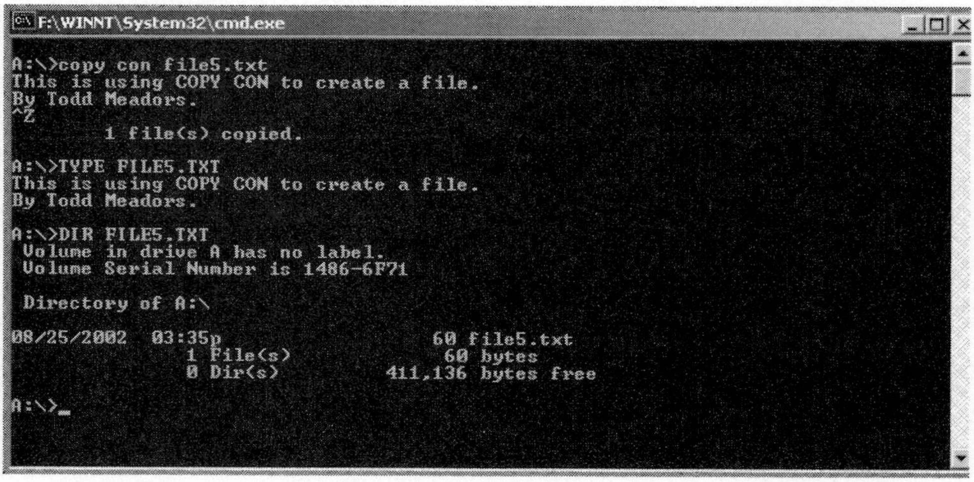

Now let's perform an exercise to help you understand the COPY CON and TYPE commands.

1. Use the appropriate steps to get to the DOS prompt on your floppy.
2. In order to create a file using the COPY CON command, type **COPY CON file2.txt**. The cursor will move to the beginning of the next line. There will be no prompt on that line.
3. Type the following, pressing **Enter** after each line of text is typed. If you make a mistake on a line and press Enter, you cannot change it using the COPY CON method. You would have to use EDIT to modify a previous line.

Computers are powerful devices.
DOS is fun and will come in handy on the job.
The End

4. Press **F6**. A caret (^) and a Z (representing Shift + Z) appear on the screen. Press Enter. A message appears stating that one file copied. This is how you save the file. Note that F6 signifies an End-of-File (EOF).
5. To display the contents of the file using the TYPE command, type **TYPE file2.txt** and press Enter.
6. Create another file using the COPY CON method.
7. Use the TYPE command to display its contents.
8. Exit the system appropriately.

The COPY CON command is ideal for creating small files quickly. However, if EDIT is available, you should consider using it.

The EDIT Command

You can also create a file with the DOS EDIT command. This tool allows you to modify files as well. The COPY CON command will not allow you to change or delete text within a file, but the EDIT command will. To edit a file, type the EDIT command followed by a file name. If the file is present, it will be displayed on the screen. If it is not present, a new file will be created and a blue screen will appear. Figure 3.11 shows a screenshot of text created using the EDIT command.

Once the editor opens, you can begin typing your text. You need to press the Alt key to activate the menu commands. For example, you would press Alt + F + Save to save the file. Within EDIT, you can use either Save to save to the current file name that is opened, or Save As to a different file name. You can also search, cut and copy text, and perform other menu commands.

Figure 3.11: A Screenshot of Using the EDIT Command

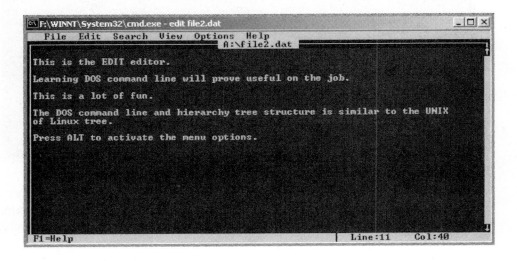

The COPY, REN, and MOVE Commands

You need to understand how to copy, rename, and move a file. To make a duplicate of a file, you would use the COPY command.

For example, if you wanted to copy a file named PAY4.DAT to one named PAY5.DAT, you would enter **COPY PAY4.DAT PAY5.DAT** at the command prompt. The source file name must be present. The destination file name is a name you determine. If it is present, DOS will ask you if you want to overwrite. You can use full or partial paths in conjunction with the source and destination. So if you wanted to copy a file from C:\SALES\MONTHLY\SALES1.DAT to A:\BACKUP\SALES1.DAT, you would enter:

COPY C:\SALES\MONTHLY\SALES1.DAT A:\BACKUP\SALES1.DAT.

Figure 3.12 shows a screenshot of using the COPY command to make a backup of a file named GAME1.DAT. The first DIR listing displays only GAME1.DAT. Then the file is copied to GAME2.DAT. Both files exist in the second DIR listing.

Figure 3.12: A Screenshot of the COPY Command

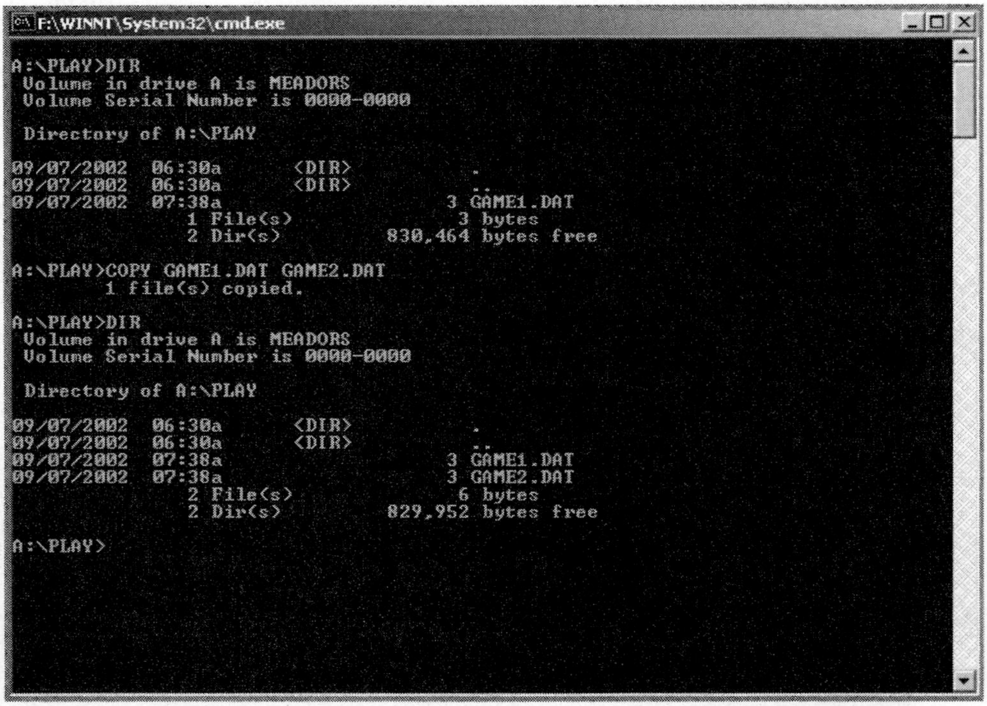

```
F:\WINNT\System32\cmd.exe                                              _ □ ×

A:\PLAY>DIR
 Volume in drive A is MEADORS
 Volume Serial Number is 0000-0000

 Directory of A:\PLAY

09/07/2002  06:30a      <DIR>          .
09/07/2002  06:30a      <DIR>          ..
09/07/2002  07:38a                  3 GAME1.DAT
               1 File(s)             3 bytes
               2 Dir(s)        830,464 bytes free

A:\PLAY>COPY GAME1.DAT GAME2.DAT
        1 file(s) copied.

A:\PLAY>DIR
 Volume in drive A is MEADORS
 Volume Serial Number is 0000-0000

 Directory of A:\PLAY

09/07/2002  06:30a      <DIR>          .
09/07/2002  06:30a      <DIR>          ..
09/07/2002  07:38a                  3 GAME1.DAT
09/07/2002  07:38a                  3 GAME2.DAT
               2 File(s)             6 bytes
               2 Dir(s)        829,952 bytes free

A:\PLAY>
```

The REN command allows you to rename a file, but the destination directory must be the same as the source. In other words, you can only rename a file to another name within the same directory. The REN command cannot be used to rename a file to another directory. The syntax is:

> REN *source-filename destination-filename*

For example to rename a file named PAY7.DAT to PAY8.DAT, you would enter:

REN PAY7.DAT PAY8.DAT

The source file, PAY7.DAT, must present in this case. Figure 3.13 shows a screenshot of the REN command. The first DIR listing shows GAME1.DAT and GAME2.DAT. Next, the command **REN GAME1.DAT PLAYTIME.DAT** is used to rename the file. In the last DIR listing, the file is renamed. The old name no longer exists.

Figure 3.13: Using the REN Command

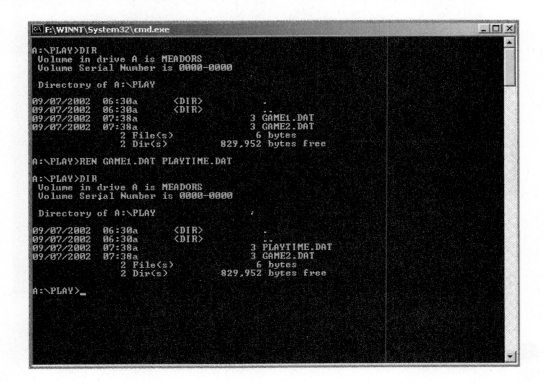

To move a file to another directory you would use the MOVE command. The syntax is:

> MOVE *source-filename destination-filename*

For example to move a file named SALES5.DAT to SALES6.DAT, you would enter:

MOVE SALES7.DAT SALES8.DAT

The source file, SALES7.DAT, must present in this case. Figure 3.14 shows a screenshot of using the MOVE command to move a file to another directory. The command DIR PLAYTIME.DAT displays the file. Next, **MOVE PLAYTIME.DAT A:\BEACH\PLAY TIME.DAT** moves the file to another directory. The command DIR PLAYTIME.DAT is run again to show you it not longer exits in the current directory. The command **DIR A:\ BEACH\PLAYTIME.DAT** shows you it does indeed exist in the A:\BEACH directory where it was moved.

Figure 3.14: Using the MOVE Command to Move a File to Another Directory

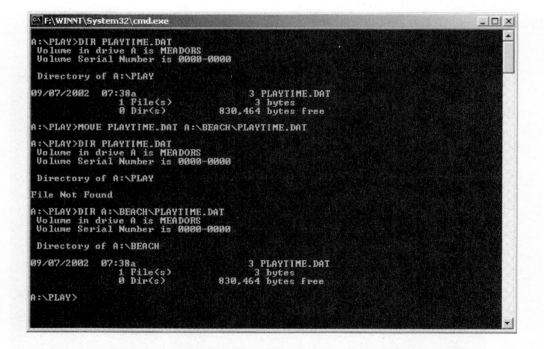

 The difference between the REN and MOVE commands is that with REN, the source and destination directory must be the current directory. With the MOVE command, the source and destination directory can be the same or different. When in doubt, use MOVE.

The DEL Command
In order to delete a file, you would use the DEL command. The syntax is:

DEL *filename*

One of the most useful options the DEL command allows is the /P option. With this option, you are prompted before the file is deleted. Without this option, DEL goes ahead and deletes the file. Think of the /P option as a safety switch. It gives you a chance to keep the file. Figure 3.15 shows a screenshot of the DEL command. You can see in the figure that **DEL /P FOOTBALL.DAT** prompts you to delete the file named FOOTBALL.DAT.

Figure 3.15: Using the DEL Command and the /P Option to Prompt Before Deleting

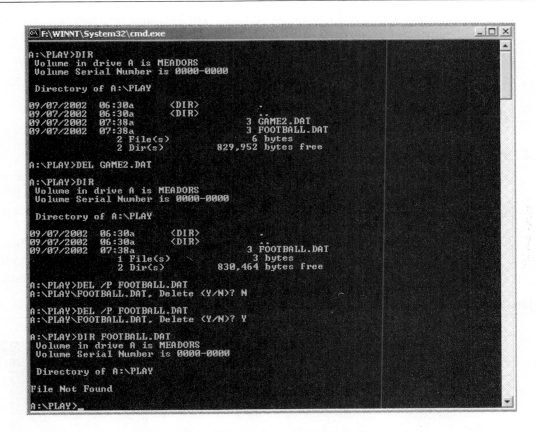

Now let's perform an exercise to help you understand EDIT, COPY, and MOVE.

1. Use the appropriate steps to get to the DOS prompt.
2. Go to the floppy drive.
3. Type **EDIT FILE4.TXT**.
4. Insert the following text:

Learning about DOS.
Having a lot of fun!

5. Press the Alt key and then the F key for File. Then press the S key for Save. This saves your file.

6. Press the Alt key and then the F key for File. Then press the X key for Exit. This exits DOS EDIT.

7. To copy the file to FILE4B.TXT, type **COPY FILE4.TXT FILE4B.TXT**.

8. To verify, type **DIR**.

9. To rename FILE4B.TXT, type **REN FILE4B.TXT FILE4Z.TXT**.

10. To verify, type **DIR**.

11. To move FILE4Z.TXT to another directory, first create a directory named DIR4 by typing **MKDIR A:\DIR4**.

12. Now move it. Type **MOVE FILE4Z.TXT A:\DIR4\FILE4Z.TXT**.

13. To verify, type **DIR A:\DIR4**

14. To delete FILE4.TXT, type **DEL FILE4.TXT.**

15. To verify, type **DIR**.

16. Exit the system appropriately.

3.4 Understanding Drive Related Commands

Drive letters are assigned to hardware devices when a computer boots. For example, the first floppy drive gets the drive letter A:. The colon is part of the device's drive letter. The first hard drive in a system gets the drive letter C:. The devices detected by the operating system can use drive letters A: through Z:.

The LABEL command allows you to change the label on a drive letter. It is like a software version of a sticker you would place on your floppy, with your name, to indicate the floppy is yours. Figure 3.16 shows a sample screenshot of the LABEL command.

Figure 3.16: Using the LABEL Command to Change the Label on the Floppy

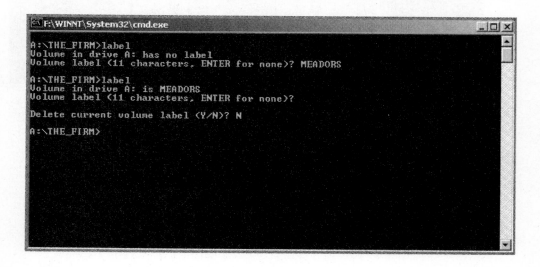

Another useful command is the CHKDSK command. It allows you to check the disk's status and reports statistics about the disk. Some statistics are the amount of space on the disk, the amount used, and any unused areas on the disk. You can use the /F option to fix errors. Figure 3.17 shows a sample screenshot of the CHKDSK command run on a floppy.

Figure 3.17: The CHKDSK Command

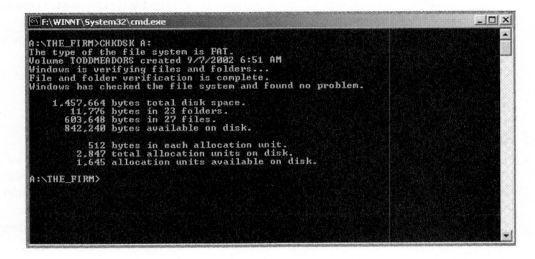

You can change how your prompt appears by running the PROMPT command. Figure 3.18 shows the options available to change your prompt.

Figure 3.18: A Screenshot of the PROMPT Command Displaying Its Options

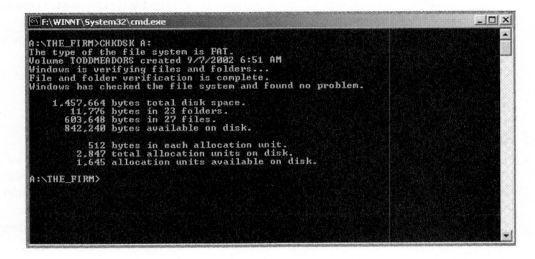

Let's do a brief exercise using the PROMPT command.

1. Use the appropriate steps to get to the DOS prompt.
2. Go to the floppy drive.
3. To change your prompt to include the text "Hi" followed by the date, type **PROMPT Hi $D** and press Enter.
4. To change your prompt to include text, the date, the time, and the greater than symbol, type **PROMPT Hi $D $T $G** and press Enter.
5. To change your prompt to "Enter command: >" type **PROMPT Enter command: $G** and press Enter.
6. To change your prompt to include the DOS version, the current drive and path, and the less than symbol, type **PROMPT $V $P $L** and press Enter.
7. To change your prompt back to its original state, type **PROMPT PG** and press Enter.
8. Exit the system appropriately.

3.5 Learning about Wildcard Characters

The DOS operating system allows for pattern matching of files. This means you can use certain symbols to match characters following a certain pattern. Suppose you want to see all of the files that begin with an S or all of the files that end in .DAT. How would you do this?

The operating system provides two pattern matching mechanisms, sometimes called "wildcarding," to accomplish this. These wildcard characters are:

- The asterisks symbol (*), which matches all characters.
- The question mark symbol (?), which matches a single character position.

You use the * symbol when you want to match all character positions. For example, if you wanted to display all files that begin with the letter S, then you would enter **DIR S*** at the prompt. If you wanted to display all the files that had DAT after the dot in the file name, then you would enter **DIR *.DAT**.

If you wanted to display all files that had a 5 in the fourth character position, and you didn't care about the previous or following characters, you have to use the question mark. To do this, you would type **DIR ???5*** at the command line prompt. You could not use the asterisks before the 5 in this case, because it would display all files with a 5 anywhere in the file name—not just in the fourth character position.

Figure 3.19 shows the use of wildcards. In the figure, the DIR T*.* command displays all files beginning with a T regardless of the remaining characters in the file name or extension. The next command, DIR *.TXT displays those files with a .TXT extension.

Figure 3.19: Working with Wildcards

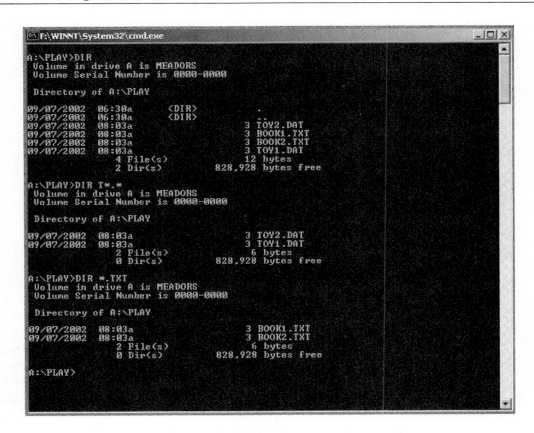

3.6 Learning about Redirection and Filtering

When you run a command, the output generally goes to the screen. The input for most commands is usually the keyboard. With redirection, you change the normal input or output locations.

These are the redirection symbols:
- A single less-than symbol (<) to redirect input
- A single greater-than symbol (>) to redirect output
- Two greater-than symbols (>>) to redirect and append output

The syntax of redirecting input is:

> *command < filename.ext*

For example, the SORT command will accept input from the command line. However, you can redirect input from a file by typing **SORT < UNSORT.DAT** at the command line prompt. This command will read input from the file named UNSORT.DAT and display the sorted results on the screen.

The syntax of redirecting output is:

> *command > filename.ext*

You would redirect the output of a command if you wanted to keep it in a file to print or view it later. For example, to redirect the output of the DIR command from the screen to a file named LISTING.TXT, type **DIR > LISTING.TXT**.

The output would be redirected to a file named LISTING.TXT. When you redirect standard output to a file using the > symbol, the contents of the file are deleted. If you wanted to add standard output from another command to the same file name, you would issue the redirect and append output symbols, >>.

The syntax of redirecting and appending output is:

> *command >> filename.ext*

For example, the command **DIR >> LISTING.TXT** means to append the directory listing to the file named LISTING.TXT. If you had issued **DIR > LISTING.TXT**, you would have written over the previously redirected listing of the DIR command.

The filter symbol is the pipe symbol (|). It appears as the broken vertical bar (it is located on the same key as the backslash symbol) on your keyboard but it prints as a solid vertical bar. The command on the left side of the pipe symbol sends its output as input to the command on the right side of the pipe symbol. Think of the pipe as a physical pipe beneath your kitchen sink. Water flows through the pipe and out the other end some-where. For example, the DIR command displays files and directories, and the MORE command allows you to scroll through a page of data at a time. If the output of the DIR command scrolled several pages, how would you be able to see all of the files and directories? One answer is to use the pipe symbol.

The syntax of commands using the pipe symbol is:

> *command1 | command2*

The command **DIR | MORE** will display a list of file and directories one page at a time. You could also use the pause switch option /P on the DIR command.

Many users think the pipe symbol can only be used with the MORE command because they are frequently used together, but you can use the pipe symbol with other commands too. If you wanted to sort the directory listing, you could enter **DIR | SORT**. If this command displayed too many lines, then you could put several pipes together, such as **DIR | SORT | MORE**. This will allow you to scroll through the sorted listing. Several pipes can go on one command line. For example, you could have the following:

> *command1 | command2 | command3 | command4*

The way this works is that *command1's* output is pipe as input to *command2*. Then, that filtered output is piped to *command3* and then the filtered output of *command1*, *command2,* and *command3* is piped as input into *command4*.

Figure 3.20 shows a screenshot of redirecting output, redirecting and appending output, redirecting input, and using the pipe symbol. In the figure, the first ECHO command redirects output to the file named GREETING.TXT. The contents are displayed using the TYPE command. Next, the file is appended using the >> redirection symbols and the file's contents are displayed again. To redirect input, the command **SORT < UNSORT.DAT** is used. It simply sorts a file and displays the output to the screen. The command **TYPE UNSORT.DAT | SORT** is another version of sorting a file. It sends the output of the TYPE UNSORT.DAT command, which is the file's contents, to the SORT command for processing. The SORT command then sorts the data and displays the results on the screen. The command **TYPE UNSORT.DAT | SORT | MORE** displays the same information one screen at a time if there is more than one screen of data.

Figure 3.20: Using Redirection and Pipe Symbols

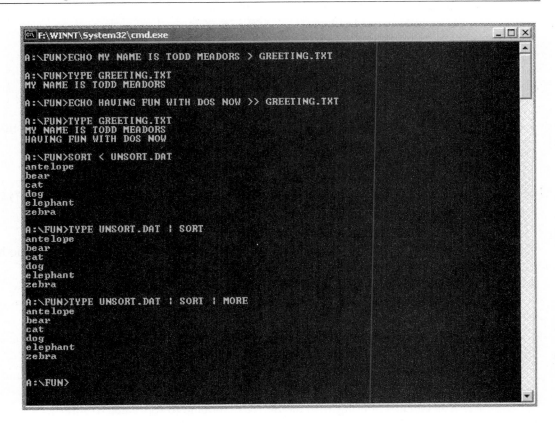

Let's do an exercise to help you understand the concepts of wildcarding, redirection, and filtering.

1. Use the appropriate steps to get to the DOS prompt.
2. Go to the floppy drive.
3. You will need to create some files to work with. Create the files named ZOO1.DAT, ZOO2.DAT, ZOO3.DAT, FUN1.TXT, and FUN2.TXT.
4. To display only the files beginning with an F, type **DIR F*.*** and press Enter.
5. To display only the files with an extension of .DAT type **DIR *.DAT** and press Enter.
6. To display only the files with a 2 in the fourth position, regardless of other characters, type **DIR ???2.*** and press Enter.
7. To redirect output, type **ECHO HI > ZAC12.DAT**.
8. To display the contents of the file, type **TYPE ZAC12.DAT**.
9. To redirect and append output, type **ECHO BYE >> ZAC12.DAT**.
10. To display the contents of the file, type **TYPE ZAC12.DAT**.
11. In order to redirect input, let's create a file named UNSORT.BAT using DOS EDIT. Type the following lines that contain a number ID (in column 1) followed by a Name (in column 3) and Phone Number (in column 25):

4 Todd Meadors	**555-555-5551**
2 Micki Meadors	**555-555-5552**
5 Zac Meadors	**555-555-5553**
3 Jessie Meadors	**555-555-5554**
1 Larry Meadors	**555-555-5555**

12. Save the file.
13. To sort the data, type **SORT < UNSORT.DAT**. By default, SORT sorts on the first column of data, although you can change which column it sorts on. So in UNSORT.DAT, the SORT command will sort on the ID. To sort on the first name column (column 3), you would enter **SORT /+3 <UNSORT.DAT**.
14. To sort the data and redirect the sorted output to another file named SORT.DAT, type **SORT < UNSORT.DAT > SORT.DAT**.
15. To view the contents of SORT.DAT, type **TYPE SORT.DAT**.
16. To reverse sort the data in reverse order and redirect the sorted output to another file, type **SORT /R < UNSORT.DAT > SORTR.DAT**.
17. To view the contents of SORTR.DAT, type **TYPE SORTR.DAT**.
18. To find Todd's phone information type **FIND "Todd" < UNSORT.DAT**. The ID, Name, and Phone Number for "Todd" are displayed on the screen.
19. To find Micki's phone number and redirect it to a file type **FIND "Micki" < UNSORT.DAT > Micki.dat**.
20. To view the contents of the file, type **TYPE MICKI.DAT**. The ID, Name, and Phone Number appear in the file.
21. You can use filtering with the SORT command to sort data. To sort the UNSORT.DAT file using the pipe filter symbol, type **TYPE UNSORT.DAT | SORT**.

22. To perform sort in reverse order using the pipe filter, type **TYPE UNSORT.DAT |
    SORT /R**.

23. To further understand filtering, you will need to create a file with about 30 lines of
    text. So create a file named LOTSA.DAT and place the numbers 1 to 30 on separate
    lines.

24. Type **TYPE LOTSA.DAT**. The data scrolls off the screen before you can view it all.

25. Type **TYPE LOTSA.DAT | MORE**. This time the data is displayed a page at a time.
    You can press the Spacebar or Enter key to continue viewing the contents of the file
    and return to your command prompt.

26. Exit appropriately.

3.7 Learning about Batch Files

Batch files are a specific type of file that contain other DOS commands. In effect, you are
creating your own program. A batch file must have an extension of .BAT. However, you
can leave off the .BAT extension when you execute it. Let's get started with an exercise to
help you understand batch files.

1. Use the appropriate steps to get to the DOS prompt.

2. Go to the floppy drive.

3. Create a file named BATCH1.BAT using DOS EDIT with the following lines:

CLS
DIR /P
DATE
VER

4. Save the file.

5. To run the batch file, type **BATCH1**. The batch file runs.

6. Exit appropriately.

The commands you place in a batch file are executed sequentially from the top to the
bottom, so you need to consider where you place your commands in order to get the
output you desire. For example, in BATCH1.BAT, the first command is CLS for clearing
the screen. If you place it last in the batch file, then it will be executed last and your
output will scroll off the screen. A few additional DOS commands that augment batch
files are listed in Table 3.5. These commands allow you to utilize conditions and loops in
your batch files. A **condition** allows you to test for criteria and perform commands based
upon it. A **loop** occurs in a program when commands are executed repeatedly. Table 3.5
shows a sample of these additional commands.

Table 3.5: Other Batch File Related Commands

Command	Description	Example
CALL	Calls one batch program within another.	CALL BATCH2
CHOICE	Waits for the user to choose one of a set of choices. The /C option allows you to specify allowable keys for the user to enter. Note: CHOICE is not available in Windows 2000 or in Windows XP.	CHOICE /C 123 Press a Number
FOR	Runs a specified command for each file in a set of files.	FOR %a IN (*.BAT) DO ECHO %a is a batch file.
GOTO	Directs the batch file to a label in a batch program.	GOTO LabelA
IF	Performs conditional processing in batch programs.	IF EXIST x.dat echo xx.dat exists >> yes.txt
PAUSE	Suspends processing in a batch file and displays the message "Press any key to continue…."	PAUSE
REM	Records a comment or remark.	REM This batch file copies files.
SHIFT	Allows you to shift parameters that are passed to a batch file at the command prompt. You can normally pass up to nine at one time on the command line following the batch file name.	SHIFT

Let's look at a few of these now. The CALL command is used to call a batch file program from another. The basic syntax follows:

CALL *filename*

For example, the following statement will call or run the SALES.BAT file from REPORTS.BAT batch file:

REM This is REPORTS.BAT
CALL SALES.BAT

The REM statement is used for placing comments or remarks in a file. Remarks should include the author's name, how the batch file is to be executed, and a general description as to what the batch file accomplishes. For batch file troubleshooting, you can place REM in front of a command when you are testing your batch file. See the partial batch file below using the REM command:

REM Author: Joseph Sunday
REM To run: MYBATCH file1 file2
REM This batch file will copy file1 to file2

The FOR command allows you to run a specified command for every file that is in a set of files. The syntax follows:

> FOR *%variable* IN *(set)* DO command

The *%variable* is a variable name such as %a, %b, or %c. It will contain the contents of the files in the *set*. For example, the following statement will display the message that a given file is a batch file for all batch files (*.BAT). If the file is not a batch file, no message will be displayed.

FOR %a IN (*.BAT) DO ECHO %a is a batch file.

The GOTO command is used to cause the batch file to branch to another portion of the batch file. So, if you wanted the batch file to branch to another location to perform a different set of commands, you would use GOTO. The basic syntax is:

> GOTO *label*

This is where *label* is a user-defined label. For example, in the following partial batch file the GOTO command is used to branch to a label named LabelA, thus creating a loop. During execution of this batch file, the label, LabelA, is the first command statement but the command interpreter ignores it. Next, commands following the label are executed. When they are finished, the GOTO command moves processing back to LabelA. Again, the commands following the label are executed.

> :LabelA
> *commands...*
> GOTO LabelA

Note that the name of the label must be preceded with a colon.

The IF command can be used for conditional processing. There are several variations of the IF command depending upon the operating system. For more information about the IF command, type IF /? or HELP IF. The following syntax will test whether a file exists (using EXIST) and if it does, then the command specified, as *command* will execute.

> IF EXIST *filename command*

For example, the following command will test if the file named x.dat exists and if so, its contents is displayed.

IF EXIST x.dat TYPE x.dat

Note that Windows XP supports the use of an ELSE clause to perform a command if the condition is false. However DOS and the DOS command mode in Windows 98 do not support the ELSE clause. Thus, the following would work in Windows XP to display the contents of the file if it exists and display "File not found" if it does not exist:

IF EXIST x.dat (type x.dat) ELSE echo File not found

The use of parentheses is required when using the ELSE clause.

The PAUSE command allows you to suspend processing in a batch program by displaying a message "Press any key to continue...". To use it, simply enter the command as follows:

PAUSE

One very useful concept with batch files is the ability to execute a batch file and add variables after its name on the command line. These variables are called **positional parameters**. You can pass up to nine positional parameters on the command line after the batch file name. The positional parameters are named %1 though %9. You can add more than nine but you must use the SHIFT command to shift or move the data one position to the left. For example, to give the batch file named PAYDATA.BAT three variables, "001" for Employee ID, $25.00 for Rate, and 35 for Hours, you would enter:

PAYDATA 001 $25.00 35

So, "001" is referenced in the batch file as %1, $25.00 is %2, and 35 is %3. To display these three positional parameters in a batch file, you would enter the following:

ECHO %1 %2 %3

Let's look at a practical example using positional parameters. In this next batch file PARAM1.BAT, the COPY command will copy the file name specified as the first parameter %1 to the file name specified as the second parameter %2. The TYPE command will be used to display the contents of the file name specified as %1.

COPY %1 %2
TYPE %1

Figure 3.21 shows a screenshot of PARAM1.BAT and the output of its execution.

Figure 3.21: A Batch Program File Using Positional Parameters

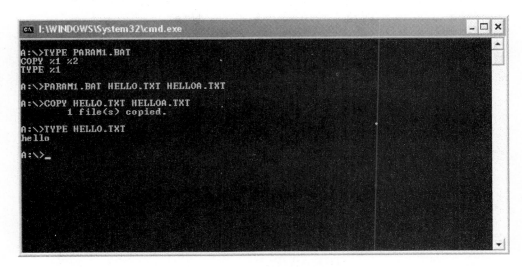

The CHOICE command allows you to create a menu in your batch file, but it is not available in Windows 2000 or Windows XP. The basic syntax is:

CHOICE /C *choices text*

The /C option lets you specify letters that are allowed. The default is Y for Yes or N for No.

The CHOICE command works by testing the key that was pressed. It uses the IF command to accomplish this. You use an option on the IF command called ERROR-LEVEL for testing the key that is pressed as in this example:

IF ERRORLEVEL *number command*

The *number* represents the key the user presses. Once the user presses a key, the *command* is executed.

Let's look at an example. In the following batch file a menu is created. The first command, @ECHO OFF turns off echo, which means that commands are not displayed on the screen as they are executed. The next few ECHO commands create the menu list that will be displayed on the screen. Next comes the CHOICE command. The /C options allows you to specify the letters ABC as valid keys the user can press. The first key assigned returns an ERRORLEVEL value of 1 when entered by the user. The second returns an ERRORLEVEL of 2 and so on. For example, if the user pressed A for a directory listing, because A is the first item number, then the ERRORLEVEL of 1 is set. Hence, the batch file causes execution to GOTO LabelA. You need to place the IF ERRORLEVEL commands in decreasing order. As you can see in the batch program, ERRORLEVEL 3 is tested first. Once the commands after the label name are executed, the GOTO TOP command causes processing to branch to the beginning of the batch file where :TOP is the second command in the batch file. This is the loop process in action. Ultimately pressing C causes ERRORLEVEL 3 to be set and the batch file ends.

```
@ECHO OFF
:TOP
CLS
ECHO              --------- MENU ---------
ECHO.
ECHO              A. DIR LISTING
ECHO              B. MEM LISTING
ECHO              C. EXIT
ECHO.
CHOICE /C:ABC SELECT A KEY
IF ERRORLEVEL 3 GOTO END
IF ERRORLEVEL 2 GOTO LabelB
IF ERRORLEVEL 1 GOTO LabelA
:LabelB
                 MEM /C/P
                 PAUSE
                 GOTO TOP
:LabelA
                 DIR A:\ /W/P
                 PAUSE
                 GOTO TOP
:END
```

You can terminate a batch file program by pressing Ctrl + C.

Figure 3.22 shows a screenshot of the execution of the batch file and running the first option, A, for a directory listing.

Figure 3.22: Screenshot of the Menu Batch File

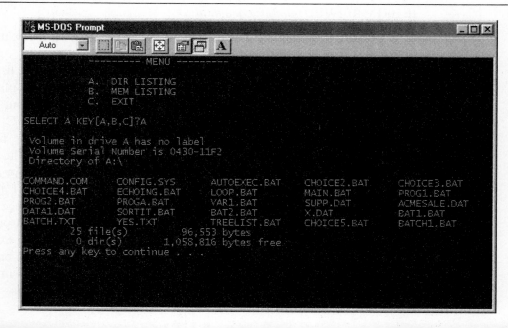

3.8 Learning about Additional Commands

The XCOPY command is more powerful and faster than the COPY command. The XCOPY command allows the copying of directories, subdirectories, and files. The syntax of the XCOPY command is:

> XCOPY *source-file destination-file*

If the destination is omitted, the XCOPY command copies the source files to the current directory. If you have a disk containing files in subdirectories to be copied to a different capacity disk, the XCOPY is a great command to use.

Two useful options the XCOPY allows are /S and /E. The /S option copies subdirectories except empty ones. The /E copies only empty subdirectories. Used together, you get all files and subdirectories in a directory. Figure 3.23 shows the XCOPY command with both the /S and /E options.

Figure 3.23: Using the XCOPY with the /S and /E Options

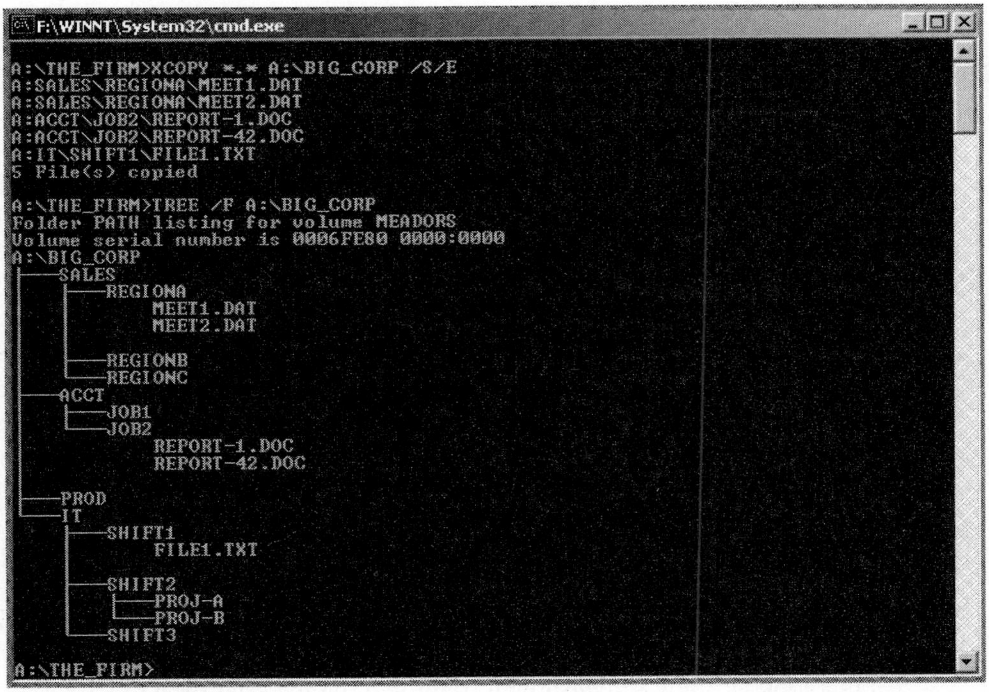

```
F:\WINNT\System32\cmd.exe                                          _ □ ×
A:\THE_FIRM>XCOPY *.* A:\BIG_CORP /S/E
A:SALES\REGIONA\MEET1.DAT
A:SALES\REGIONA\MEET2.DAT
A:ACCT\JOB2\REPORT-1.DOC
A:ACCT\JOB2\REPORT-42.DOC
A:IT\SHIFT1\FILE1.TXT
5 File(s) copied

A:\THE_FIRM>TREE /F A:\BIG_CORP
Folder PATH listing for volume MEADORS
Volume serial number is 0006FE80 0000:0000
A:\BIG_CORP
├───SALES
│   ├───REGIONA
│   │       MEET1.DAT
│   │       MEET2.DAT
│   │
│   ├───REGIONB
│   └───REGIONC
├───ACCT
│   ├───JOB1
│   └───JOB2
│           REPORT-1.DOC
│           REPORT-42.DOC
│
├───PROD
├───IT
│   ├───SHIFT1
│   │       FILE1.TXT
│   │
│   ├───SHIFT2
│   │   ├───PROJ-A
│   │   └───PROJ-B
│   └───SHIFT3
A:\THE_FIRM>
```

In Figure 3.23, you can see that the command **XCOPY *.* A:\BIG_CORP /S /E** copies everything from the current directory, which is THE_FIRM, to the directory named BIG_CORP. The command **TREE /F A:\BIG_CORP** displays the tree showing you the command worked.

The **ATTRIB** command sets, removes, or shows the attribute of a file or a directory. Attributes change how a file or directory displays on the screen or what can be done with the file or directory. Possible attributes include read-only, archive, system, and hidden. The **read-only attribute** protects files so they cannot be accidentally changed or deleted. For example, the AUTOEXEC.BAT and CONFIG.SYS files start and configure a computer. The **archive attribute** marks files that have changed since they were last backed up by a backup program. The XCOPY and MSBACKUP commands use the archive attribute as well as any other backup software program. The **system attribute** designates a file as a system file. Files with this attribute do not show in directory listings. The **hidden attribute** allows file hiding and even directory hiding. If someone has hidden files, and you need to see all files without having to change the attributes, the DIR /AH or ATTRIB commands display the files no matter what attributes they possess.

The syntax of the ATTRIB command is:

ATTRIB *options filename*

Set each attribute using the +options where the +R option adds the read-only attribute, the +S option adds the system attribute, the +H adds the hidden attribute, and the +A adds the archive attribute. Remove each attribute using the -R, -S, -H, or -A option with the ATTRIB command. One command can set more than one attribute on files or directories. For example, to make the file PAY.TXT hidden and read-only, type **ATTRIB +R +H PAY.TXT**.

An excellent use of the archive attribute is to copy multiple files onto a disk. Normally, there is no warning when copying too many files to a disk that cannot hold them, until it is too late and the disk runs out of room. The BACKUP and RESTORE commands are traditionally used to get around this problem. However, the ATTRIB command (with the +A option) and the XCOPY command (with the /M option) together can copy files across multiple disks. For example, copying all the DOS files requires multiple disks. When copying all these files to a disk, the operating system copies as many files as possible, then produces an error saying the destination disk is full. To prevent this problem, use the ATTRIB command and assign all the files the archive attribute. Enter **ATTRIB +A C:\TESTDIR*.***, then insert a disk into the A: drive and enter **XCOPY C:\TESTDIR*.* A: /M**. When the XCOPY command stops to display the error message saying the destination disk is full, insert a new floppy into the A: drive and repeat the command. The /M option tells XCOPY not to copy the same files again. The /M option only copies files that have the archive attribute set. Once the files are copied, they no longer have the archive attribute.

Let's look at a few screenshots to reinforce the material on ATTRIB. In Figure 3.24 the command **ATTRIB +R MANAGER.DAT** is used to set the read-only attribute. You cannot modify a file with this attribute; the file is protected. You can see the DEL MANAGER.DAT is used to attempt to delete it; however, an error message denying you access is displayed, indicating you cannot delete it. Only after the command **ATTRIB –R MANAGER.DAT** is used to turn off the read-only attribute can the file be deleted.

Figure 3.24: Using the ATTRIB Command with the +R and –R Options

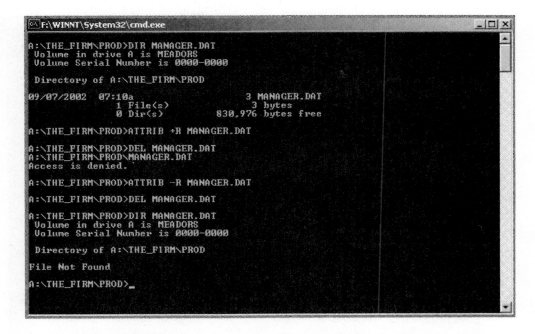

In Figure 3.25, the **ATTRIB +H VP.DAT** command is used to hide the file VP.DAT. With this attribute set you cannot even see the file with a DIR command, much less delete it as attempted in the figure. When the **DEL VP.DAT** command is attempted with the hidden attribute set, a "Could Not Find" message appears.

If a file is hidden, how do you unhide it? If you type ATTRIB command with no options, you will see all attributes for all files, hidden or not. This is done in Figure 3.25.

To unhide the VP.DAT file, type **ATTRIB –H VP.DAT**.

Figure 3.25: Using the ATTRIB Command with the +H and –H Options

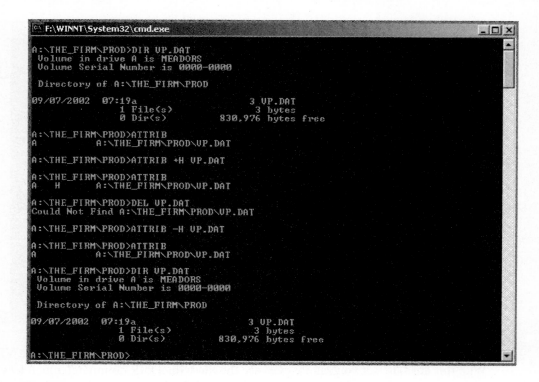

Chapter Summary

- All computers need an operating system to function. The Disk Operating System (DOS) runs on most PCs and was commercialized by Microsoft. There are two methods of accessing the DOS commands. You can boot up the DOS operating system or you can go into the DOS command prompt in the GUI of the Windows operating systems.

- The DOS file system is hierarchical (tree-like) in nature. The file system uses a directory to store files or other directories. A file cannot store another file or directory. The root directory (\), is the top level directory.

- DOS commands are either internal to COMMAND.COM or external, residing individually on the computer's disk. The two basic categories of commands are file and directory commands.

- In order to navigate the DOS tree, you use the CD command. A full path begins from root, \, and a partial path does not.

- You use the MD or MKDIR command to create directories. The RD or RMDIR command removes directories.

- The COPY command makes a copy of a file. The MOVE command allows you to change a file's location to another directory. The REN command renames a file. The

TYPE command is used to display the contents of a file. The DEL command deletes a file.
- The command prompt is where all commands are entered. When you get C:\> that is your command prompt. The C: drive is your hard drive. The A: drive is your floppy drive. Your prompt can be changed with the PROMPT command.
- You can manage a subset of the files by using wildcard characters. The * symbol matches all characters. The ? symbol matches a single character position.
- Redirection is the idea of changing a command's normal location for accepting input or displaying output. The > symbol redirects output. The >> symbols redirect and append output. The < symbol redirects input. Filtering uses the pipe symbol (|) to process data between commands.
- The AUTOEXEC.BAT is a boot file that will be executed during the system's boot sequence. The CONFIG.SYS file contains configuration information that enhances your PC's capabilities. Batch files have an extension of .BAT.

Review Questions

1. You want to make a duplicate of a file named data3.dat. The new file is to be named data4.dat located in the same directory. What command will do this for you?
   a) COPY data3.dat data4.dat
   b) COPY data4.dat data3.dat
   c) COPY data4.dat data4.dat
   d) MOVE data3.dat data4.dat

2. Which of the following is considered a full path?
   a) ..\.
   b) fun2\file2.txt
   c) \
   d) dir4

3. What symbol is used to redirect and append output to a file?
   a) >
   b) >>
   c) |
   d) ?

4. Which of the following will wildcard a single character position?
   a) ?
   b) *
   c) |
   d) >

5. Zac wants to display all the files that have a 0 for the fourth position and a 7 for the fifth position in their file name regardless of the characters in other positions. What command will accomplish this?
a) DIR *05?
b) DIR ?05*
c) DIR 4 and 5
d) DIR ???07*

6. Which of the following commands is used to display the contents of a file named FunA.dat?
a) DIR FunA.DAT
b) TYPE FunA.DAT
c) MEM /C /P > FunA.DAT
d) CD FunA.DAT

7. Which of the following will wildcard multiple character positions?
a) ?
b) *
c) |
d) <

8. Which of the following will delete all files with an extension of .DAT?
a) DIR *.DAT
b) DEL *.BAT
c) DEL ?.DAT
d) DEL *.DAT

9. Which of the following will create a directory?
a) DIR
b) FDISK
c) MOVE
d) MKDIR

10. Which of the following allows you to partition a hard disk drive?
a) FDISK
b) MKDIR
c) SYS
d) FORMAT

11. Which of the following allows you to transfer system files to the floppy?
a) FDISK
b) SYS C:
c) SYS A:
d) FORMAT A:

12. Which of the following is the correct load order for the DOS system files?
    a) MSDOS.SYS, IO.COM, CONFIG.SYS, COMMAND.COM, AUTOEXEC.BAT
    b) IO.SYS, MSDOS.SYS, CONFIG.SYS, COMMAND.COM, AUTOEXEC.BAT
    c) IO.SYS, MSDOS.SYS, COMMAND.COM, CONFIG.SYS, AUTOEXEC.BAT
    d) AUTOEXEC.BAT, IO.SYS, MSDOS.SYS, CONFIG.SYS, COMMAND.COM

13. Which of the following commands will run a batch program within a batch program?
    a) IF
    b) CHOICE
    c) CALL
    d) REM

14. Which of the following commands is a comment in a batch program?
    a) IF
    b) CHOICE
    c) CALL
    d) REM

15. What symbol is used to redirect but not append output to a file?
    a) >
    b) >>
    c) |
    d) ?

16. What command is used to sort a file named data1.dat in column 10 in reverse order and redirect and append the output to a file named data2.dat?
    a) TYPE data1.dat | SORT \+10 \R >> data2.dat
    b) TYPE data1.dat | SORT /+10 /R > data2.dat
    c) TYPE data2.dat | SORT /+10 /R >> data1.dat
    d) TYPE data1.dat | SORT /+10 /R >> data2.dat

17. What command is used to copy all the files that begin with an A, regardless of the middle characters with an extension of .TXT from A:\Prod to C:\Backup?
    a) COPY A?.TXT BACKUP
    b) COPY A:\Prod\A*.TXT C:\Backup\A*.TXT
    c) COPY C:\BACKUP\A*.TXT A:\A*.TXT
    d) COPY A:/A*.TXT C\Backup\A*.TXT

18. What key saves a file when using COPY CON?
    a) F5
    b) F6
    c) F8
    d) F7

19. What key bypasses the AUTOEXEC.BAT and CONFIG.SYS files after the POST during boot-up?
    a) F5
    b) F7
    c) F8
    d) F9

20. What key performs step-by-step confirmation of the lines in the AUTOEXEC.BAT and CONFIG.SYS files after the POST during boot-up?
    a) F5
    b) F7
    c) F8
    d) F9

Lab Projects

Note that these projects assume the PC is powered on. Although you can perform these projects in other versions of Microsoft Windows or DOS with minor changes, the assumed operating system is Windows 2000 unless otherwise specified.

Lab Project 1

The goal of this lab is to create a tree structure on the floppy.

1. Go to the DOS command prompt.

2. In order to change drive locations to your floppy, type **A:** and press Enter.

3. Type **MD Project1** and press Enter.

4. Type **CD Project1** and press Enter.

5. Type **MD dir2** and press Enter.

6. Type **MD dir3** and press Enter.

7. Type **CD dir2** and press Enter. Notice your prompt changes.

8. Type **CD** and press Enter.

9. Record the directory location.

   _____

10. Type **MD dir2a** and press Enter.

11. Type **CD dir2a** and press Enter.

12. Type **CD** and press Enter.

13. Type **COPY CON FILE2A.TXT** and press Enter. The prompt moves to the beginning of the next line.

14. Insert the following:

    This is DOS.
    I'm having fun!

15. Press **F6** and press Enter.

16. Record what happens when you press F6.

    _____

17. Type **CD ..** and press Enter.

18. Record the new directory location.

    _____

19. Type **COPY CON FILE2.DAT** and press Enter. The prompt moves to the beginning of the next line.

20. Insert the following:

This is FILE2.DAT.
Bye
The End!

21. Press **F6** and press Enter.

22. Type **COPY FILE2.DAT FILE22.DAT** and press Enter.

23. Record another way you could have created file22.txt.

_____

24. Type **CD ..** and press Enter. This should take you to A:\ Project1.

25. Type **CD** and press Enter.

26. Record the output.

_____

27. Type **MD dir3** and press Enter.

28. Type **ECHO Hello! > file32.txt** and press Enter. This is another method to create a file.

29. Type **COPY file32.txt file33.txt** and press Enter.

30. Exit appropriately.

Lab Project 2

In this lab project, you will review a list of commands and then draw the tree based upon the commands.

1. Review the list of commands below. Pay careful attention to the order of the commands listed. Create them on the floppy.

> **A:**
> **MKDIR Project2**
> **CD Project2**
> **MKDIR payroll**
> **MKDIR general**
> **MKDIR fun**
> **CD payroll**
> **MKDIR paychecks**
> **MKDIR payday**
> **CD payday**
> **ECHO Howdy, Todd Meadors > pay1.dat**
> **ECHO Hi, Zac, Jessie and Micki >> pay1.dat**
> **COPY pay1.dat pay2.dat**
> **CD ..\\..\\general**
> **ECHO Hi ya'll > gen1.dat**
> **COPY gen1.dat gen2.dat**
> **COPY gen2.dat \\Project2\\gen3.dat**
> **CD \\Project2\\payroll**
> **COPY payday\\pay1.dat paychecks\\payC.dat**
> **CD A:**

2. Draw the tree structure. You have been given a starting point, A:\\. The rest is up to you.

>   A:\\
> | (Draw the tree here!)

Lab Project 3

The goal of this lab project is to have you gain additional practice creating tree structures in DOS. Note: Files have an extension and directories do not have an extension.

1. Go to the command prompt, create a directory named Project3, and then change locations to it.

2. Create the tree shown in Figure 3.26.

Figure 3.26: Sample Tree Structure to Be Created

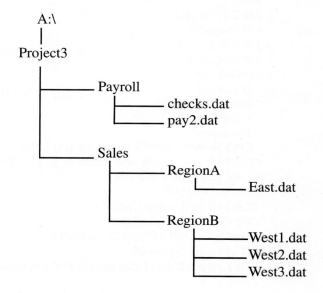

Lab Project 4

The goal of this lab project is for you to be able to distinguish between navigating to a parent, a child, and a sibling directory. A sibling directory is defined as a directory that is on the same hierarchical level as another. This lab project is dependent upon completion of Lab Project 3.

1. Go to the DOS command prompt.

2. Insert the floppy with the tree structure from Lab Project 3.

3. Change directory locations to A:\. Your prompt will reflect the change.

4. Type **CD Project3** and press Enter.

5. Type **CD Sales** and press Enter. Your prompt will reflect the change.

6. In order to change to a child directory, you must use the child directory's name.

   Type **CD RegionA** and press Enter. Your prompt will reflect the change.

7. In order to change to a sibling directory, type **CD ..\RegionB** and press Enter. The format is CD ..*sibling-name* where *sibling-name* is the name of a sibling directory. In Figure 3.26, RegionA and RegionB are sibling directories.

8. Answer this question: There is another sibling relationship in the Figure 3.26. What are the sibling names?

   _____

9. In order to change back to RegionA, type **CD ..\RegionA** and press Enter.

10. Record what this command accomplishes.

    _____

11. In order to change to the parent directory, type **CD ..** and press Enter.

12. Record what this command accomplishes.

    _____

13. Exit.

Lab Project 5

The goal of this lab project is to utilize some of the features of the DOS editor.

1. Go to the DOS command prompt.

2. Type **MD Project5** and press Enter.

3. Type **CD Project5** and press Enter.

4. Type in **EDIT file27.txt** and press Enter.

    Computers are exciting to learn.
    DOS is fun but I need to brush up on my keyboarding skills.
    See ya!
    Todd Meadors

5. Press Alt + F to access the File menu.

6. Press S to Save the file.

7. Move your cursor to the first letter of the first line.

8. To search for a word, press Alt + S to access the Search menu.

9. Press F for Find. The Find dialog box appears.

10. To search for the text **exciting**, type **exciting** and press Enter. The text **exciting** highlights.

11. Press Alt + E to access the Edit menu.

12. Press t for Cut.

13. Type the word **fun**. The text **exciting** was just replaced with the text **fun**.

14. Press Alt + F to access the File menu.

15. Press S to Save the file.

16. Explore some of the other EDIT commands.

17. List the ones you find most useful.

    _____

    _____

18. Press Alt + F and then X to Exit.

19. Exit.

Lab Project 6

The goal of this lab project is to help you correctly use the XCOPY, RD, and DEL commands.

1. Go to the command prompt.

2. Insert a disk into the A: drive and create two files, one called **FRIEND.TXT** and another called **FOE.TXT**, and place the files in the A: drive's root directory. Use an editor to create the two files. Type two lines of text in each file.

3. From the C:\> prompt, type **XCOPY A:\F*.* A:\TEST1**. A message might appear asking if TEST1 is a file or a directory. If so, press **D** for directory. A message appears stating the number of files copied. If the message does not appear, redo steps 2 and 3.

4. From the C:\> prompt, type **DEL A:\TEST1*.*** and press Enter.

5. From the C:\> prompt, type **RD A:\TEST1**.

6. Verify that the directory is gone by typing **DIR A:\TEST1**.

7. Type the following commands:

> **MD \TEST2**
> **CD \TEST2**
> **MD SUB1**
> **MD SUB2**
> **MD SUB3**

8. Using an editor, create three files called **FILE1**, **FILE2**, **FILE3** and place the files in the SUB1 subdirectory. Verify that the files are created and in the current directory before proceeding.

9. Using the XCOPY command, copy all of the files located in SUB1 subdirectory to the SUB2 and SUB3 subdirectories on the floppy disk.

10. Exit.

Lab Project 7

The goal of this lab project is to help you correctly use the ATTRIB command.

1. Go to the DOS command prompt.

2. Create a directory name Project7.

3. Change directory locations to Project7.

4. Create two files, Secret1.DAT and Secret2.DAT.

5. To make the Secret1.DAT read-only, use the ATTRIB command with the +R switch. Type **ATTRIB +R A:\PROJECT7\Secret1.DAT**.

6. To prove that the +R switch works, attempt to delete the files. Type **DEL A:\PROJECT7\Secret1.DAT**.

7. Record the message.

_____

8. Try to modify the file with the DOS EDIT command.

9. Record the message.

_____

10. To make Secret1.DAT readable, type **ATTRIB –R A:\PROJECT7\Secret1.DAT**.

11. Attempt to modify the file by using the DOS EDIT command.

_____

12. Record whether or not you could edit the file.

13. To hide the file named Secret2.dat, type **ATTRIB +H A:\PROJECT7\Secret2.DAT**.

14. To verify that the file is hidden, type **DIR A:\PROJECT7\Secret2.DAT**. The file should not appear.

15. View the file named Secret2.dat by typing **ATTRIB**.

16. Record the output and identify each column.

_____

17. View the file named Secret2.dat by typing **DIR /AH**.

18. Record the output and identify each column.

_____

19. Unhide Secret2.dat.

20. Record the command used.

_____

21. Use the DIR command to view the file.

22. Record whether or not you could view it with the DIR command (with no options).

_____

23. Exit.

Lab Project 8

The goal of this lab project is for you to utilize the SORT command to sort data in ascending (lower to higher) and descending (higher to lower) order.

1. Get to the DOS command prompt.

2. Type **MD Project8** and press Enter.

3. Type **CD Project8** and press Enter.

4. Type **EDIT INPUT.DAT** and press Enter. The DOS editor opens.

5. Enter the following text making sure you press the Enter key at the end of each line. Each row is considered a Part Record and contains four fields. The first field is the Part Number and begins in column 1. The second field is the Part Name and begins in column 14, the third field is the Part Cost and begins in column 35, and the last field is the Part Quantity and begins in column 43. You are required to place the fields in the correct columns.

102A	Wrench	12.00	76
105T	Drill	99.00	17
103F	Saw	55.00	38
101A	Hammer	35.00	64

6. Save the file and exit the editor.

7. Your prompt will return.

8. Sort the data in ascending order. Type **SORT < INPUT.DAT** and press Enter.

9. Record the output.

   _____

10. Sort the data in descending order. Type **SORT /R < INPUT.DAT** and press Enter.

11. Record the output.

    _____

12. Sort the data in descending order and redirect the output to another file.
    Type **SORT /R < INPUT.DAT > REVERSE.DAT** and press Enter.

13. Record the output.

    _____

14. To sort the file by the Part Name, type **SORT /+14 < UNSORT.DAT**.

15. Record the output.

    _____

16. Sort by the Part Cost name column in reverse order.

17. Record the command you used.

    _____

18. Sort by the Part Quantity column reverse order and redirect the output to a file.

19. Record the command you used.

20. Exit.

Lab Project 9

The goal of this lab project is to create an AUTOEXEC.BAT file using COPY CON.

1. Get to a DOS prompt.

2. Create a bootable floppy.

3. Note that when Enter is pressed after each line, NO messages appear!

4. Go to A:\.

5. Create an AUTOEXEC.BAT file using either the COPY CON method or EDIT method. Type **COPY CON AUTOEXEC.BAT** or **EDIT AUTOEXEC.BAT.**

6. Insert the following text:

   REM The AUTOEXEC.BAT file.
   ECHO This is the AUTOEXEC.BAT file executing...
   VER
   DATE
   PAUSE
   TIME
   PROMPT My DOS Prompt: $G

7. Reboot the computer and watch the screen as the AUTOEXEC.BAT file automatically executes.

8. Close your DOS command prompt.

Lab Project 10

The goal of this lab project is to understand DOSKEY.

1. Get to the DOS prompt.
2. To install the DOSKEY program from the prompt, type **DOSKEY**.
3. Insert the floppy disk into the floppy drive.
4. From the command prompt, type

    A:
    MD \SPECIAL

5. The DOSKEY program allows use of the arrow keys and function keys (the F1 through F12 keys on the keyboard). Press the **up arrow** once. The last typed command appears at the prompt. If the last command does not appear, then DOSKEY is not loaded properly. Perform Steps 1 through 6 again.
6. Press the **up arrow** until the MD\SPECIAL command appears at the command prompt. *Do not press Enter* when the command appears.
7. Press the **left arrow** key 3 times until the blinking cursor is under the *I* in SPECIAL. *DO NOT PRESS ENTER*. The arrow keys, when used with DOSKEY, allow movement through the command line.
8. While the cursor is blinking under the letter I, type the letter **T**. *DO NOT PRESS ENTER*. The command should now read MD\SPECTAL. DOSKEY is automatically in the type over mode.
9. Press **Ins** (Insert), but *DO NOT PRESS ENTER*. The cursor changes to a blinking box.
10. While the cursor is a blinking box over the letter A, type the letter **R**. The command changes to SPECTRAL, because pressing the Ins key causes DOSKEY to go into the insert mode.
11. Press Enter to create a directory named SPECTRAL.
12. Press the **up arrow** key once. The last command typed appears on the screen.
13. Press **Esc** (Escape) once. Esc erases the current command from the command prompt.
14. Press **F7** once. A list of all typed commands appears on the screen.
15. Press **F9** once. The Line Number prompt appears. While in DOSKEY, F9 allows you to enter a specific command based on a line number (that showed when you pressed F7).
16. Type the number corresponding to the **A:** command, then press **Enter**. The A: command appears at the command prompt.
17. Press **Esc** to clear the command.
18. Press and *hold down* **Alt**. While holding Alt down, press **F7** once, then release both keys. DOSKEY uses Alt + F7 to clear the list of commands DOSKEY tracks. Sometimes, pressing the F7 key is cumbersome to use because the command list is so long. Clearing the command list allows DOSKEY to start over tracking commands.
19. Press **F7** to verify the command list is clear.
20. Exit.

Lab Project 11

The goal of this lab project is for you to be able to utilize the redirection and pipe symbols.

1. Get to a DOS command prompt.

2. Type **MD Project11** and press Enter.

3. Type **CD Project11**and press Enter.

4. Create 10 files and five directories within Project11. Use appropriate names.

5. Record the name of the command you used to create one of the files.

_____

6. Record just the name of the command you used to create one of the directories.

7. In order to redirect output and create a new file, type **ECHO Directory Listing > DIRL-IST.DAT** and press Enter.

8. In order to redirect and append output, type **DIR >> DIRLIST.DAT** and press Enter.

9. In order to redirect and append output again, type **ECHO All Done! >> DIRLIST.DAT** and press Enter.

10. Verify the contents of the file named DIRLIST.DAT.

11. Record the command used.

_____

12. In order to overwrite the contents of the file named DIRLIST.DAT, type **ECHO > DIRL-IST.DAT** and press Enter.

13. Issue another command to redirect output.

14. Record the command used.

_____

15. Issue another command to redirect and append output.

16. Record the command used.

_____

17. To use the pipe symbol, type **SORT /? | MORE**. The listing is displayed one screen at a time.

18. Issue another command to filter using the pipe symbol.

19. Record the command used.

_____

20. Close the DOS command prompt.

Lab Project 12

The goal of this lab project is for you to be able to utilize the wildcard symbols.

1. Go to the DOS command prompt.

2. Change directory locations to A:\. Your prompt will reflect the change.

3. Type **MD Project12** and press Enter.

4. Type **CD Project12** and press Enter.

5. Create the following 12 files in Project12. These represent payroll files with the three-character month followed by the two-digit day of the month.

JAN07.DAT	**DEC04.DAT**	**JUL04.DAT**
JAN02.DAT	**DEC21.TXT**	**JUN06.DAT**
JAN03.DAT	**JUL04.TXT**	**JUL13.TXT**
JAN04.TXT	**FEB07.DAT**	**DEC07.DAT**

6. In order to display all files ending in .DAT, type **DIR *.DAT** and press Enter.

7. Record the output.

_____

8. Issue a command to display all files ending in .TXT.

9. Record the command.

_____

10. Record the output.

_____

11. In order to display all files that begin with a J and end with .DAT, type **DIR J*.DAT** and press Enter.

12. Record the output.

_____

13. Issue a command to display all files that begin with a D and end in .DAT.

14. Record the command.

_____

15. Record the output.

_____

16. In order to display all files for January, type **DIR JAN*** and press Enter.

17. Record the output.

_____

18. Issue a command to display all files for July.

19. Record the command.

    _____

20. Record the output.

    _____

21. In order to display files for the fourth day of the month (a 0 in the fourth position and a 4 in the fifth position), type **DIR ???04*** and press Enter.

22. Record the output.

    _____

23. Issue a command to display just the files for the seventh day of each month.

24. Record the command.

    _____

25. Record the output.

    _____

26. Exit.

Lab Project 13

The goal of this lab project is to help you understand batch files.

1. Get to a DOS command prompt.

2. Open the DOS editor and create a file named Project13.dat with the following data: Employee ID in column 1, Employee Name in column 6, and Pay Rate in column 20.

0006	Zelda, Jack	44.20
0001	Smith, Zac	40.25
0003	Brown, Mike	29.50
0009	Smith, Zoe	35.00
0008	Addams, Al	24.00
0002	Cook, Jim	20.01
0004	Cook, Jinny	22.01
0005	Adams, Art	17.50
0007	Meade, Timmy	16.11

3. Save the file and close the editor.

4. Open the DOS editor and create a file named PROJ13.bat.

5. Enter the following commands. Replace the remarks with appropriate comments.

```
REM "YOUR NAME"
REM "PROGRAM NAME"
REM "PROGRAM DESCRIPTION"
@ECHO OFF
ECHO COPYING THE FILE TO MAKE A BACKUP:
COPY %1 %2
ECHO SORTING THE DATA:
TYPE %2 | SORT | MORE
ECHO REVERSE SORT:
TYPE %2 | SORT /R | MORE
ECHO SORTING THE DATA BY PAY RATE:
TYPE %2 | SORT /+20 | MORE
ECHO SORTING THE DATA BY LAST NAME:
TYPE %2 | SORT /+6 | MORE
ECHO SORTING BY PAY RATE AND REDIRECTING TO A NEW FILE:
TYPE %2 | SORT /+20 > PAY.DAT
ECHO CONTENTS OF PAY.DAT:
TYPE PAY.DAT | MORE
```

6. Save the file and close the editor.

7. Run the batch program by typing **PROJ13 PROJ13.DAT PROJ13C.DAT**. The parameter %1 is PROJ13.DAT and %2 is PROJ13C.DAT. Watch the screen as the batch file executes.

8. Create another batch program file named PROJ13A.BAT with the following:

   ECHO RUNNING PROJ13A.BAT
   SORT PAY.DAT

9. Modify PROJ13.BAT and append these two statements:

   CALL PROJ13A.BAT
   ECHO RETURNED TO PROJ13.BAT

10. Rerun the batch program by typing **PROJ13 PROJ13.DAT PROJ13C.DAT**. This time PROJ13A.BAT is called from PROJ13.BAT.

11. Exit.

Lab Project 14

The goal of this lab project is to combine your understanding of the DOS tree structure and batch files. You will write a batch file that will be used to create the tree structure from Project 3.

1. Create a directory named Proj14 and change to it.

2. Create a batch file named TREEMAKE.BAT to create the tree structure in Figure 3.26 of Project 3.

3. On a separate piece of paper record your batch file.

Lab Project 15 Challenge

The goal of this lab challenge project is to have you create a bootable floppy disk and add an AUTOEXEC.BAT and CONFIG.SYS file.

1. Format a floppy and make it bootable.

2. In the AUTOEXEC.BAT file, do the following:

   a. Turn echoing of command off.
   b. Place an appropriate PATH command that includes the references to the external commands depending upon your operating system.
   c. Display the version of the operating system.
   d. Enable DOSKEY.
   e. Set the PROMPT to include the current drive path and the greater than symbol.

3. In the CONFIG.SYS file do the following:

   a. Enable XMS.
   b. Enable EMS.
   c. Place DOS into HMA.
   d. Enable UMBs.
   e. Set concurrent files to 28.

4. Boot the floppy.

5. Immediately after the POST, press F5 to bypass AUTOEXEC.BAT and CONFIG.SYS.

6. Record the amount of all types of memory.

   _____

   _____

   _____

7. Boot the floppy again.

8. This time press F8 to perform the step-by-step confirmation. This gives you the chance to decide whether or not you want to execute a particular command within AUTOEXEC.BAT and CONFIG.SYS. This time do not load XMS and EMS.

9. Record the amount of all memory.

   _____

   _____

   _____

10. The amounts in step 6 and step 9 should differ. Record why.

   _____

   _____

   _____

11. Exit appropriately.

Lab Project 16 Challenge

The goal of this lab challenge project is to create a batch file menu. You will need to use either DOS or the Windows 98 command prompt mode.

1. Create a menu on the floppy that does the following:
   Allows the user to enter:

   - The number 1 for a directory listing of files on the floppy with an extension of
   - .BAT and redirect the output to a file named Proj15.dat.
   - The number 2 for changing the date.
   - The number 3 for changing the time.
   - The number 4 for formatting the floppy.
   - The number 5 for transferring system files.
   - The number 6 for running another batch file that contains this command:
         FDISK
   - The number 7 for exiting the menu.

2. Include appropriate remarks.

3. Run and test your menu batch program.

Internet Discovery

Internet Discovery Lab 1

The goal of this Internet Discovery Lab is to help you use the Internet to discover batch file samples and concepts.

1. Connect to the Internet.

2. Open your web browser

3. Access the **www.google.com** web site.

4. Search for DOS Batch files.

5. Visit at least three sites that discuss batch files.

6. Record the web site addresses.

_____

_____

_____

7. Look for a batch file under 10 lines in length. Record the commands in it and explain each line.

8. Exit.

Internet Discovery Lab 2 Challenge

The goal of this Internet Discovery Lab is to use the Internet to download a free copy of DOS.

1. Connect to the Internet.

2. Open your web browser

3. Access the **www.freedos.org** web site.

4. Download a copy of the free DOS.

5. Install and run it.

Soft Skills: Help Desk Support

1. A user passes you in the hall and asks you how to make a floppy bootable and keep the current files that are already on it. How do you handle this situation?
2. You are working the midnight help desk when a user calls and asks you for assistance. They user wants to partition a floppy with the FDISK command. What assistance do you offer the user?
3. You are the Team Leader for the second shift help desk for Arbornomics, Inc. A user calls and asks you and your team members for assistance. There is a mix of DOS, Windows 98, Windows NT, Windows 2000, and XP operating systems on the PCs. The user wants to create a batch file that contains the TREE command. The user wants to be able to run this on any operating system. What do you tell the user?

Critical Thinking

1. Prove why the **CD ..** command issued at the root directory of a drive changes you to root.
2. Compare the DOS file system to a company's organization chart.
3. Explain the difference between the COPY, MOVE, and REN commands.
4. Why does each directory have a dot (.) directory except the root directory?

 *Study Skills*

Relying on Your Textbook and Notes

- Do you read your textbook? You should. If you read your textbook, your test scores will improve. Although reading technical information such as a textbook can be difficult, it is important that you spend time each day reading your textbook. Allocate at least one to two hours a day!

- As you read your textbook, use a brightly colored (such as yellow) marker to highlight definitions, facts, explanations of statements, and any other information that you feel is important. This will provide a great "summary" of facts because the important ones will be highlighted.

- Make sure you answer the questions at the back of the book—at least twice. This will improve your score on a test. The first time, try to do them on your own. Then, if you have trouble, research the chapter. Additionally, go through the Soft Skills: Help Desk Support and the Critical Thinking sections in each chapter to further your understanding of material.

- Do **not** wait until the night before a test to do your major studying. If you've read your textbook chapters all along, you should not have to cram the night before. Get a good night's rest the night before the test and eat a good breakfast the morning of the test. Review the Chapter Summary right before the test, to help you get the most important facts.

- Take good lecture notes. Your lecture notes should include any class discussion that is relevant to the chapter. If the instructor says something more than once, it is probably important so write it down.

- Rewrite the chapter, page by page, in your own words. Although this takes a little time, it proves invaluable for test preparation. By rewriting the chapter in your own words, you are going over it at least twice—once for reading and again for rewriting. So, when it comes time for a test, you've already gone over the material. So, at this point, you can simply review your notes. Plus, some instructors allow you to use your notes (but not your textbook) for a test!

Study Skills: Self-Study Question(s)

1. Identify at least one Study Skills item from this section that you performed prior to a test.
2. Did you read your textbook today?

4

Chapter 4 Introduction to Microsoft Windows 98

OBJECTIVES

The goal of this chapter is twofold:
- To introduce you to Windows 98.
- To help you prepare and pass the following sections of the A+ Operating System Technologies Exam:

A+ Operating System Technologies Exam Objectives
covered in this chapter (and corresponding page numbers)

1.1 Identify the major desktop components and interfaces, and their functions. Differentiate the characteristics of Windows 9x/Me, Windows NT 4.0 Workstation, Windows 2000 Professional, and Windows XP.

1.2 Identify the names, locations, purposes, and contents of major system files.

Domain 3 Diagnosing and Troubleshooting

3.3 Recognize common operational and usability problems and determine how to resolve them.

In this chapter, you will complete the following sections:
- 4.1 Understanding Microsoft Windows 98
- 4.2 Managing Files and Folders
- 4.3 Understanding the Windows 98 Registry
- 4.4 Understanding the Pre-Installation Steps of Windows 98
- 4.5 Understanding How to Install and Upgrade Windows 98
- 4.6 Troubleshooting the Windows 98 Installation
- 4.7 Understanding the Dual-Boot Feature of Windows 98 Systems
- 4.8 Configuring Windows 98
- 4.9 Understanding the Boot Process
- 4.10 Troubleshooting Application Problems

4.1 Understanding Microsoft Windows 98

Microsoft's Windows 98 is a popular operating system normally used by home users and small businesses. It is a 32-bit operating system that supports plug and play, DVD drives, TV tuner adapters, multitasking, 16-bit applications, and 32-bit applications. Windows 98 supports older (16-bit) applications better and takes less hard drive space and memory than NT Workstation and 2000 Professional, but it does <u>not</u> have the built-in security capabilities that NT and 2000 offer.

With Windows 98, Microsoft introduced **Internet Explorer** or **IE**. IE is a web browser for connecting to the Internet. It is integrated into Windows 98. Windows 98 also supports **Internet conferencing** and **Internet Connection Sharing** or **ICS**. With Internet conferencing, you can use your computer and the Internet to communicate with others around the world. With ICS, multiple computers can connect to the Internet via a computer using Windows 98. The Windows 98 computer is connected to both the Internet and the other computers.

With Internet Connection Sharing, you are able to share an Internet connection using your Windows 98 computer. This is a very useful feature of Windows 98 because it allows you to have one connection to an Internet Service Provider (ISP). The only downside is if the Windows 98 computer that is connected to the Internet crashes, you lose access to the Internet for the other computers.

The file systems that Windows 98 supports for hard drive partitions are FAT16 and FAT32. A FAT16 partition can be converted to a FAT32 partition using a command called CVT1.EXE. Once a partition is converted to FAT32, it cannot be reconverted to FAT16.

When a computer's drive has been formatted with an NTFS partition, a FAT16 partition must be created before installing Windows 98.

The Windows 98 Desktop

After booting Windows 98 the desktop appears. The **desktop** is the area where all work in Windows 98 begins. Refer to Figure 4.1 for a screenshot of the Windows 98 desktop. It is the interface between the user and the computer files, applications, and hardware. The desktop is part of the operating system's **GUI (Graphical User Interface)** environment. The desktop consists of icons and shortcuts. An **icon** is a graphical representation of an application, file, folder, or utility. A **shortcut** is a special type of icon created by the user to quickly access a file or application.

Figure 4.1: The Windows Desktop

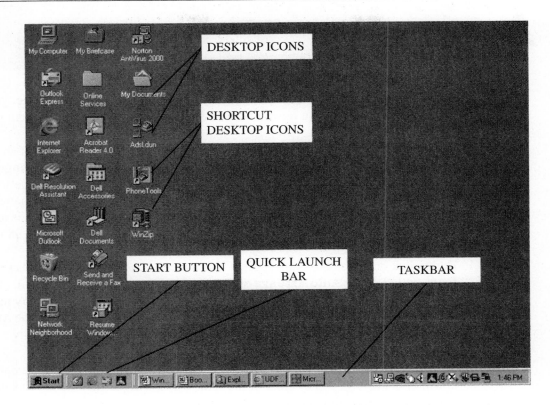

When you double-click on an icon or shortcut, you open an application, file, or window that allows you to interface with various devices installed or connected to the computer. A **window** is a part of the screen that belongs to a specific application or utility. Windows are a normal part of the working environment through the desktop.

A **shortcut** icon looks like any other desktop icon except that it has a bent arrow in the lower left corner. A shortcut represents a path (location on the drive) to a file, folder, or program. It is a link to where the file or application resides on a disk. When you double-click on a shortcut icon, the shortcut icon tells Windows where to find the specific file that the icon represents. If the shortcut represents an application, the application opens. If the shortcut represents a document, the application used to create the document appears along with the document. A shortcut offers faster access to an application or file than going through the Start button or through the My Computer icon. Users frequently place shortcuts on the desktop and you must know how to create one. Users create shortcuts to their favorite applications or to documents used frequently.

Your Windows 98 desktop is like your own desk where you study or work. The icons represent your tools such as your pens, staplers, paper clips, etc. Think of a shortcut as a yellow sticky note with a commonly called phone number on it. You store the phone number on the sticky note so you can access the number quickly.

Sometimes the desktop is cluttered with things you put on it. For example, you may clutter you desktop when you download files from the Internet and place them on your desktop.

Let's go through a brief exercise to help you understand how to maintain an uncluttered Windows 98 desktop. In this exercise, you will work with the **Auto Arrange** option to force your icons on your desktop to be automatically arranged towards the left hand side of the desktop. When you attempt to relocate an icon, it will automatically be arranged back to its original position—on the left hand side of the desktop. It is assumed that Windows 98 is installed and running on a computer with the Windows 98 desktop displayed on your screen.

1. Right-click on a blank desktop space. Once a menu appears, point to the **Arrange Icons** option. If the **Auto Arrange** option does have a check mark beside it, click on an **empty portion of the desktop** to cancel because Auto Arrange is already in use. If the **Auto Arrange** option does not have a check mark beside it, click on the **Auto Arrange** option to add the check mark and enable **Auto Arrange** capability.
2. Note the position of the icons on the desktop.
3. Click on the **My Documents** icon and while continuing to hold the mouse button down, drag the icon to the center of the screen. You will see that the My Documents icon moves to its original position.
4. Click on the **Recycle Bin** icon and while continuing to hold the mouse button down, drag the icon to the top right portion of the screen. This icon moves to its original position too.
5. Right-click on a **blank desktop space.** A menu appears.
6. Using step 1 as a guide, set Auto Arrange back to its original setting.

One of the Windows 98 features you can set for the desktop is Auto Arrange. When the **Auto Arrange** option is enabled, the desktop icons cannot be moved. When it is not enabled, the desktop icons can be moved but this setting may clutter your desktop.

One way to modify the desktop appearance is by changing the wallpaper scheme. A **wallpaper scheme** is a background picture, pattern, or color. Other changes to the desktop are altering the **color scheme** (which is used in displaying folders), and enabling a

screen saver (which is the picture, color, or pattern that displays when the computer is inactive).

Let's go through an exercise to help you understand how to modify or view your desktop appearance. It is assumed that Windows 98 is installed and running on a computer with the Windows 98 desktop displayed on your screen.

1. Right-click on an **empty desktop area.** A menu appears.
2. Click on the **Properties** option. The Display Properties window appears. (Note: this screen can also be accessed by clicking on the **Start** button, point to the **Settings** option, click on the **Control Panel** option, and double-click on the **Display** control panel icon.)
3. Click on the **Background** tab. This tab controls how the background color and pattern appears.
4. To change your wallpaper to Black Thatch, click on the **Black Thatch** option.
5. Click on the **Apply** button.
6. To view the **Screen Saver** tab settings, click on the **Screen Saver** tab. This tab controls what screen saver, if any, loads and is used to control monitor power settings. A screen saver password can also be applied.
7. Click on Screen Saver down arrow.
8. To view the **Appearance** tab settings, click on the **Appearance** tab at the top of the window. This tab is good to use when people with vision problems need adjustments.
9. Click **Cancel** to close the Display Properties window.

As mentioned before, icons are an important part of the Windows 98 desktop. The desktop consists of various icons such as My Documents, My Computer, Recycle Bin, Internet Explorer, the Start button, the Quick Launch bar, and the taskbar. These can be seen in Figure 4.1. The **My Documents** icon is used to quickly access the My Documents folder on the hard drive. The My Documents folder is the default location for files the user saves. The **My Computer** icon is used to access the hardware, software, and files located on the computer.

The **Recycle Bin** is used to hold files and folders that the user deletes. When a file or folder is deleted, it is not really gone. Instead, it goes into the Recycle Bin. The deleted file or folder can be removed forever from the Recycle Bin, just as a piece of trash can be removed from a real trash can. The deleted files and folders in the Recycle Bin take up hard drive space.

The **Internet Explorer** icon is used to start the Internet Explorer application, which is used when communicating across the Internet. Internet Explorer is Microsoft's Internet communications package.

Other common desktop items include the Start button, Quick Launch bar, and the taskbar. The **Start button** is located in the lower left corner of the desktop and is used to launch applications and utilities, find files and other computers, get help, and add/remove hardware and software.

The **Quick Launch bar** is a set of icons to the right of the Start button that allows you to launch applications with one click on a Quick Launch icon. The Quick Launch bar is a great addition to the GUI operating system for those people who have many windows open at one time. An important icon on the Quick Launch bar is the **Show Desktop** icon. This icon looks like a desk with a pencil touching a piece of paper. A click on the Show Desktop icon reduces all windows and displays the desktop. Another Quick Launch icon is the **Internet Explorer** icon. Click once on this icon and the Internet Explorer application opens. If a user does not prefer the Quick Launch bar, right-click on an empty task-bar space, point to the Toolbars option, and click on Quick Launch.

An important desktop item is the taskbar. The **taskbar** is the bar that runs across the bottom of the screen. The taskbar holds buttons that represent applications or files currently loaded into memory. The taskbar also holds icons that allow access to system utilities. These utilities can include a clock icon for the date and time, an icon of a speaker for volume control, and an icon for a virus utility. Look back to Figure 4.1 to identify the taskbar.

The Start Button

Now let's look at an important tool used by Windows 98—the Start button. The Start button contains additional buttons. They will be discussed next. The **Shut Down** Start button option is used to shut down the computer, restart the computer, restart the computer in MS-DOS mode, and possibly put the computer in standby mode. The **Restart the computer in MS-DOS mode** option restarts the computer and boots to a command prompt. From there, you can shut off the computer and type commands at the prompt, or type WIN to start the GUI Windows 98 environment. The **Standby** option is available on computers that support power-saving features. Standby is helpful on laptop computers to save on battery life.

The **Log Off Start button** option stops the current environment and brings up a dialog box for a user name and password. This is so others can log into a network or onto the computer with a user name and password and display their own customized desktop. Press the Esc key to bypass this dialog box. The **Run** button (sometimes called the Run command) option starts an application or brings up a command prompt window. The **Help** option is for Windows 98 general usage and troubleshooting assistance. The **Find** button option helps to locate files and remote network devices.

The Settings Option

The **Settings** option is used to access various sub-options that allow computer configuration. This is one of the most commonly used Start menu options. Refer to Figure 4.2 for a sample screenshot. The **Control Panel** option is used to access various utilities that customize the Windows 98 environment, such as the display, mouse, and CD-ROM. You get to Control Panel by going through the Settings option. The **Printers** selection is used to install, configure, or monitor a printer. The **Taskbar** and **Start Menu** item is used to customize the taskbar or Start button menu. **Folder Options** brings up a dialog box that allows you to change how files and folders appear on the screen. The **Active Desktop** option allows enabling, disabling, or customizing the Active Desktop environment. The

Windows Update submenu item is used to connect to the Microsoft web site to access the most recent drivers and operating system updates.

The **Documents** selection contains the 15 most recently used files (provided the application supports this option). The **Favorites Start** menu item is a list of preferred web sites. The **Programs** choice allows access to applications installed in the computer.

Figure 4.2: The Windows 98 Start Button

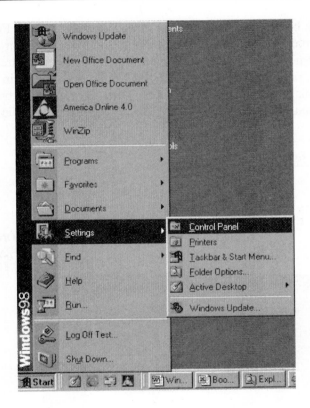

Frequently you will interact with the Windows 98 operating system through a dialog box. A **dialog box** is used by the operating system and with Windows applications and allows you to configure application or operating system preferences. The most common features found in a dialog box are a text box, tabs, a Help button, a Close button, a check box, a radio button, a drop-down menu, an OK button, a Cancel button, and an Apply button.

A **text box** is an area where you can type a specific parameter. When you click inside a text box, a vertical line appears, which is the insertion point. Any typed text is placed to the right of the insertion point. Notice in Figure 4.3 how the Top, Bottom, Inside, Outside, etc., options are text boxes. Text boxes sometimes have up or down arrows that can be used to select a preset option or you can simply type your own parameter.

Tabs normally appear across the top of a dialog box. Each tab normally holds a group of related options. Click once on the tab to bring that particular major section to the window forefront. The tabs in Figure 4.3 are Margins, Paper Size, Paper Source, and Layout.

The **Close button**, which is an X located to the right of the Help button, is used to close the dialog box. When the Close button is used, changes that have been made in the dialog box are not applied.

When checked, a **check box** option is enabled or turned on. As shown in Figure 4.3, clicking inside the check box enables the Mirror margins option. When an option is enabled, a check mark appears in the check box. A **radio button** is a round circle, which behaves in the same way. A radio button is enabled when a solid dot appears in the radio button. Click once on a blank radio button and a solid dot appears in the radio button center. Click once on a radio button with a dot in it, and the dot disappears and the option is disabled.

Figure 4.3: The Windows 98 Dialog Box Components

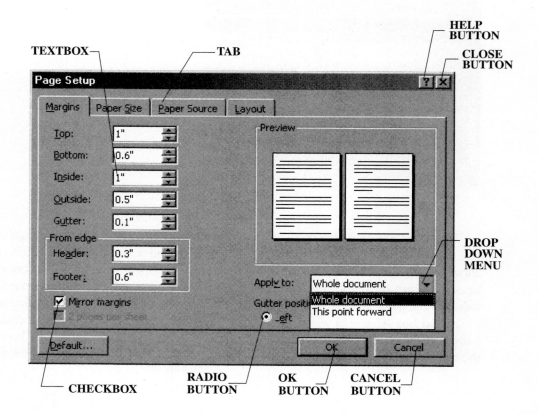

Drop-down menus are presented when you click on a down arrow. The example in Figure 4.3 shows a drop-down menu that appears when you click on the down arrow in the section marked Apply to. Clicking on the Preferred option in the drop-down menu causes that option to appear in the drop-down window.

The **OK button** and the **Cancel button** are standard in a dialog box. When you click on the OK button, all options selected or changed within the dialog box are applied. When you click on the Cancel button, all changed options in the dialog box are not applied; the options are left in their original state.

Another related button that can be found in a dialog box, but is not shown in Figure 4.3, is the Apply button. The **Apply button** is used to make changes immediately (before clicking on the OK button). One example is when changes are made to the desktop's background. New operating system specialists often make the mistake of clicking on the Close button (the button with an X). When a dialog box is closed with the Close button, no changes in the dialog box window are saved or applied.

4.2 Managing Files and Folders

Users are always creating, deleting, and moving files and folders. It is important that you are able to do these tasks quickly and without error. The important thing to remember is to think about what file and folder you want to work with, where the files and folders are located now, and where you want the files or folders to be eventually.

A drive letter followed by a colon represents every drive in a computer. For example, the floppy drive is represented by A: and the first hard drive partition is represented by C:. Disks or drives hold files. A **file** is an electronic container that holds computer code or data. Another way of looking at it is thinking of a file as a box of bits. A file is kept on some type of media, such as a floppy disk, hard drive, tape, or CD. Each file is given a name called a **file name**. An example of a file name is 98CHAP.DOC.

Files are kept in folders. A **folder** holds files and can also contain other folders. In older operating systems, a folder was called a directory. Every file and folder is given a name. It is easier to understand file and folder names if we look at how older operating systems named files and folders and then look at how Windows 98 names differ.

With Windows 95/98/NT/2000, the application normally adds an extension to the end of the file name. In most windows, Windows 98 does not automatically show the extensions. To view the extensions in Windows Explorer, click on the View menu option. Click on the View tab and on the Hide file extensions for known file types check box, which will remove the check from the box. Click on the OK button.

When Windows recognizes an extension, it associates that extension with a particular application. File name extensions can tell you a lot about a file, such as which application created the file or what purpose the file has. Table 4.1 lists the most common file extensions, their purposes, and which application typically creates the extension.

Table 4.1: Common File Extensions

Extension	Purpose or Application
AI	Adobe Illustrator
BAT	Used in DOS environments for batch files. Combines executable commands into one file and uses one command to start the batch file.
BMP	Bitmap file
CAB	Cabinet file—a compressed file that holds operating system or application files.
COM	Command file or executable file that opens an application or tool.
DLL	Dynamic Link Library file contains executable code that can be code already running.
DOC	Microsoft Word
DRV	Device driver—a piece of software that enables an operating system to recognize a hardware device.
EPS	Encapsulated postscript file
EXE	Executable file that opens an application
GIF	Graphics Interchange File
HLP	Windows-based help file
INF	Information or setup file
INI	Initialization file—Used in Windows 3.x environment to control applications and the operating environment. Used in 95, 98, NT, and 2000 to be backward compatible with Windows 3.x.
JPG or JPEG	Joint Photographic Experts Group file format graphics file
MPG or MPEG	Movie clip file
PCS	Microsoft Paintbrush
PDF	Adobe Acrobat portable document format
PPT	Microsoft PowerPoint
RTF	Rich Text Format
TIF or TIFF	Tag Image File Format

TXT	Text file
VXD (also VxD)	Virtual device driver
WPS	Microsoft Works file
WRI	Microsoft WordPad
XLS	Microsoft Excel
ZIP	Compressed file

Windows 98 Files

File names in Windows 98 can be up to 255 characters in length. These extended file names are commonly called **long file names**. Folders and file names can contain all characters, numbers, letters, and spaces *except* the following:

/ (forward slash) " (quotation marks) \ (backslash)
| (vertical bar) ? (question mark) : (colon)
*** (asterisk)**

As you can see, the list is much shorter (which means more characters are allowed) in Windows 98 when compared to a similar list for DOS file name characters in Chapter 3.

An example of a long file name is WINDOWS 98 CHAPTER.DOC. Any time a document has been saved with one of these long file names and is taken to an older computer with an operating system that does not support long file names, the file name is shortened to a maximum of eight characters. Windows does this by using the first six characters of the file name, deleting any spaces, and using two special characters—a tilde (~) and a number. For example, WINDOWS 98 CHAPTER.DOC would be shortened to WIN-DOW~1.DOC. If there were two files named WINDOWS 98 CHAPTER.DOC and WINDOWS 98 INDEX.DOC, the two files would be saved as WINDOW~1.DOC and WINDOW~2.DOC, respectively.

When saving a file in a Windows application, the application automatically saves the file to a specific folder. This is known as the **default folder**. With Windows 98, this folder is the My Documents folder.

A file's **path** is like a road map to the file and includes the drive letter plus all folders and subfolders, as well as the file name and extension. For example, if the CHAP1.DOC file is in the MY DOCUMENTS folder on the first hard drive partition, the full path is C:\MY DOCUMENTS\CHAP1.DOC. The first part is the drive letter where the document is stored, C:. The C: represents the first hard drive partition. The name of the document is always at the very end of the path. In the example given, CHAP1.DOC is the name of the file. Everything in between the drive letter and the file name is the name of one or more folders where the CHAP1.DOC file is located. The folder in this example is the MY DOCUMENTS folder.

If the CHAP1.DOC file is located in a subfolder called COMPUTER BOOK, which is located in the folder called MY DOCUMENTS, then the full path is C:\MY DOCU-MENTS\COMPUTER BOOK\CHAP1.DOC. Notice how the backslashes in the path are always used to separate the folder names as well as separate the drive letter from the first folder name.

Windows Explorer is the most common application used to create, copy, or move files or folders; however, the My Computer window can also be used in a similar fashion. When you are copying a file or folder, use the Copy and Paste functions. When you are moving a file or folder, use the Cut and Paste functions.

Let's go through an exercise to help you understand how to manipulate files and folders. It is assumed that Windows 98 is installed and running on a computer with the Windows 98 desktop displayed on your screen.

1. Insert your floppy in the floppy drive.
2. Right-click **Start** and then click **Explore**. Windows Explorer opens with left and right windowpanes.
3. Click the icon associated with the floppy.
4. Click **File**, click **New,** and then click **Folder**. The name of the folder appears as **New Folder**. Type **My Folder** and press Enter.
5. In the left windowpane, expand the floppy by clicking the plus sign to the right of it. If you see a minus sign to the right, it already is expanded.
6. Click **My Folder**.
7. To create a folder within **My Folder**, click **File**, click **New,** and then click **Folder**. The name of the folder appears as **New Folder**. Enter your own name for the name of the folder and press Enter.
8. To create a file within **My Folder**, click **File**, click **New,** and then click **New Text Document**. The name of the text document appears as **New Text Document**. Press Enter to keep this name.
9. To rename the new text document, right-click the document and click **Rename**. The document name is highlighted. Type **My Document** and press Enter. Note if the extension (.txt) appears, then the folder is set to show extensions. In this case, leave it otherwise you will receive a message that changing the file extension may cause the file to become unusable.
10. To delete the text document, right-click the document (note its name has changed) and click **Delete**. A confirmation message will appear.
11. Click **Yes** to delete. The file is deleted.
12. Close Windows Explorer.

A text document <u>is</u> a file.

When you delete a file or folder from a floppy, the file or folder is permanently deleted. When you delete a file or folder from a hard drive, the file or folder is automatically sent to the Recycle Bin. The contents of the Recycle Bin take up hard drive space and many users do *not* realize that they are not really deleting the file, but simply moving it to the Recycle Bin. To delete a file permanently from the hard drive, hold down the Shift key while pressing the Delete key on the keyboard. Otherwise, you will have to remember to empty the Recycle Bin periodically. An exercise at the end of the chapter illustrates how to copy, move, and delete files and folders. Figure 4.4 shows how the A+ COMPLETE BOOK.DOC long file name looks in graphical form using the Windows Explorer application.

Figure 4.4: Windows Explorer Document

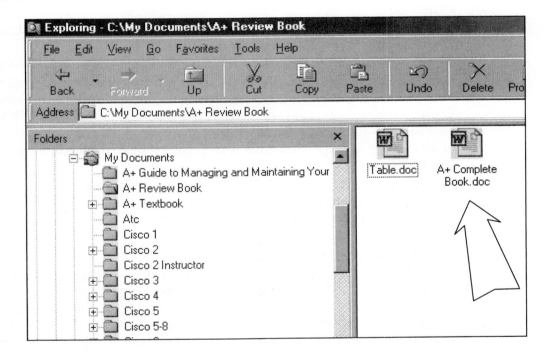

File Attributes

My Computer and **Windows Explorer** can be used for setting attributes for a file or folder. The file and folder attributes are read-only, hidden, archive, and system. The read-only attribute marks a file or folder so that it cannot be changed. The hidden attribute marks a file or folder so that it is not visible through My Computer or Windows Explorer unless someone changes the default view for the window. Some applications use the archive attribute to control which files or folders are backed up. The system attribute is placed on certain files used to boot Windows 98.

Let's perform an exercise to help you understand a file's attributes. It is assumed that Windows 98 is installed and running on a computer with the Windows 98 desktop displayed on your screen.

1. Insert your floppy in the floppy drive.
2. Right-click **Start** and then click **Explore**. Windows Explorer opens with left and right windowpanes.
3. Click the icon associated with the floppy.
4. To create a file, click **File**, click **New,** and then click **New Text Document**. The name of the text document appears as **New Text Document**. Press Enter to keep this name.
5. To set the file's attributes, right-click the new text document and click **Properties**. The Properties window for the file opens.
6. In the **Attributes** section of the page, check **Read-only** and click **OK**. The Properties window closes.
7. Next, you will attempt to modify the file. Remember it is set to read-only. Double-click the document. The document opens.
8. On the document screen, type your name and press Enter. This is considered text.
9. Attempt to save the document. Click **File** then click **Save**. The **Save As** window opens. Normally, this window does not appear—the file is simply saved. However, because the file has the read-only attribute, you cannot save the text to this file. Windows 98 wants you to enter a new file name.
10. To see the error message, click **Save**. A message is displayed indicating you cannot save this file.
11. Click **OK** and then click **Cancel**. The document screen remains.
12. Close the document. Do not save changes if prompted.
13. Close Windows Explorer.

Determining the Windows 98 Version

The operating system version is very important to you as an operating system specialist. With Windows 95, 98, NT, and 2000, upgrades or patches to the operating system are provided by way of service packs. A **service pack** fixes problems with the operating system. You must determine what version of operating system is on the computer so you can research whether or not a service pack is needed. There are two ways to determine what version of 98 is loaded on a computer. They are listed below.

• Click on the Start button. Point to the Programs option. Point to the MS-DOS Prompt option. At the command prompt, type **ver.** The 98 version appears on the screen.
• Right-click on the My Computer desktop icon. Click on the Properties option. A window appears. On the General tab under the System section, the version of Windows 98 appears.

It is important to know how to determine the version of your operating system. The reason is that many applications require a specific operating system version in order to run properly.

4.3 Understanding the Windows 98 Registry

All Windows 98 software and hardware configuration settings are stored in a set of files collectively called the registry. The **registry** contains such things as folder and file property settings, application preferences, and user profiles. A **user profile** contains a user's specific configuration settings, such as what applications the user has access to, desktop settings, user preferences, and the user's network configuration. The registry loads into memory during the boot process but once in memory, the registry is updated continuously by changes made to software and hardware. Many times when you make a change to the registry, you must reboot in order to make the changes take effect. The new registry settings will then be "seen" by the operating system kernel and stored in memory.

 Be careful when modifying the registry. You could make a change that could render your system useless. Because most of the things you do on the system ultimately change the registry, when in doubt, simply use the graphical method to change a setting.

The registry is made up of two files—**SYSTEM.DAT** and **USER.DAT**. The registry files are stored in the folder where the Windows 98 files are located, which is normally the C:\WINDOWS folder. The SYSTEM.DAT holds computer-specific hardware settings, plug and play configurations, and application settings. USER.DAT holds user-specific files (the user profile settings) such as log-on names, desktop settings, and Start button settings. Both files have the hidden attribute set by default. If the system is configured for multiple users (user profiles), a USER.DAT file is built for each user and is normally kept in the C:\WINDOWS\PROFILES*USER*\USER.DAT (where *USER* is the user name).

In the Windows 3.x environment, initialization files (having an extension of .INI) were used instead of the registry. They were called initialization files because they were read by the system during the initial boot stages of the operating system. Each .INI file contained application-specific data, hardware configuration information, the computer environment configuration, and so forth. Windows 98 still has the SYSTEM.INI, PROTOCOL.INI, and WIN.INI files located in the default Windows 98 folder (normally C:\WINDOWS) as well as the C:\COMMAND.COM, C:\AUTOEXEC.BAT, and C:\CONFIG.SYS files so that older 16-bit applications can operate under Windows 98. To see the contents of these files in Windows 98, click on the Start button, click on the Run option, and type **SYSEDIT** in the dialog box. The System Configuration Editor opens with the SYSTEM.INI, WIN.INI, PROTOCOL.INI, AUTOEXEC.BAT, and CONFIG.SYS files open in separate windows.

The registry is divided into five subtrees. **Subtrees** are like folders and are also sometimes called branches or hives. Think of the hive as a collection of folders. The five standard subtrees are as listed in Table 4.2. Each of these subtrees has **keys** that contain values related to hardware and software settings.

Table 4.2: TWindows 98 Registry Subtrees

Registry Subtree	Function
HKEY_LOCAL_MACHINE	Holds global hardware configuration. Included in the branch is a list of hardware components installed in the computer, the software drivers that handle each component, and the settings for each device. This information is not user-specific.
HKEY_USERS	Keeps track of individual users and their preferences.
HKEY_CURRENT_USER	Holds a specific user's configuration such as software settings, how the desktop appears, and what folders the user has created.
HKEY_CURRENT_CONFIG	Holds information about the hardware profile that is used when the computer first boots.
HKEY_CLASSES_ROOT	Holds file associations and file links. The information held here is what allows the correct application to start when you double-click on a filename in Explorer or My Computer (provided the file extension is registered).

Editing the Windows 98 Registry

Most changes to Windows 98 are made through various control panels, but sometimes the only way to make a change is to edit the registry directly. Windows 98 comes with a registry editor called REGEDIT. Some technical problems can only be corrected by editing the registry. The registry editor is not a tool for average users, but it is a tool for use by operating system specialists; thus it is not readily available through the Start menu or through System Tools. In Figure 4.5, you can see that the subtree HKEY_LOCAL_MACHINE\Hardware\Description\System\CentralProcessor\0 has an Identifier value of x86 Family 6 Model 8 Stepping 3. An exercise will not be given here due to the potential danger of accessing the registry. Lab Project 6 at the end of the chapter is available but ask your instructor for permission before performing this lab project.

Figure 4.5: The Windows 98 REGEDIT Window

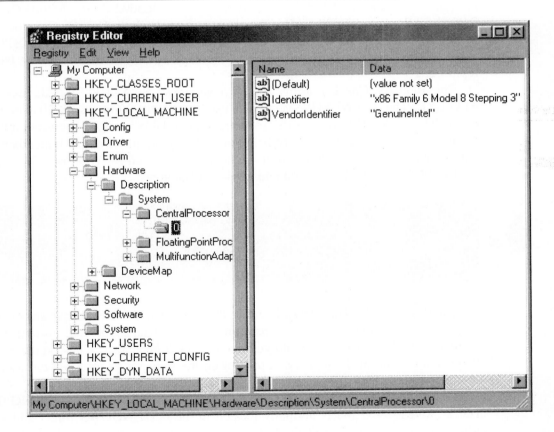

Backing Up and Restoring the Windows 98 Registry

The registry should be backed up whenever the computer is fully functional and when any software or hardware changes are made. The registry should be backed up and stored on a different working computer <u>before</u> disaster hits. The time to learn how to restore the registry is <u>not</u> when the computer is down.

The registry can be backed up and restored these different ways:

- SCANREG Registry Checker utility
- REGEDIT utility
- Backup utility

Using the SCANREG Registry Checker Utility

The most common method used is the SCANREG Registry Checker utility. The Windows 98 Registry Checker utility automatically starts every time the computer starts. The Registry Checker automatically scans the registry for any problems. If no errors are found, the Registry Checker backs up the registry once a day. By default, five backups are kept in a hidden folder, which is normally located in C:\WINDOWS\SYSBCKUP. The backups are labeled RB000.CAB, RB001.CAB, RB002.CAB, RB003.CAB, and RB004.CAB where RB000.CAB is the oldest registry backup. These backup files contain a compressed version of USER.DAT, SYSTEM.DAT, WIN.INI, and SYSTEM.INI. When a new backup is created and five backups already exist, the oldest backup is replaced.

The Registry Checker utility has two versions—SCANREGW.EXE and SCANREG.EXE. The SCANREGW version is used when the Windows 98 GUI interface is active. The SCANREG.EXE is the 16-bit real mode DOS version. The version that runs during startup is SCANREGW. To help you differentiate the two, just remember the one with a "W," as in SCANREGW, in its name is the one used for Windows. The one without the "W" is for the DOS command line—not Windows.

The command SCANREGW can be executed from the Run dialog box if you want to make your own registry backup. This would be important if you are going to install new software, install hardware, remove software, or before editing the registry.

The Registry Checker runs and verifies that the registry does not have any errors, displays a message that the registry has already been backed up that current day, and prompts with the question, "Would you like to back it up again?" Click on the *Yes* button to make a backup of the registry. A prompt on the screen appears when the backup has completed successfully.

You can customize the Registry Checker utility by editing the SCANREG.INI file. The SCANREG.INI file is normally located in the C:\WINDOWS folder and you can edit it by opening the SCANREG.INI file in any text editor program such as Notepad or WordPad. Table 4.3 lists the SCANREG.INI file entries and possible values.

Table 4.3: TWindows 98 SCANREG.INI Entries

Entry	Explanation and Values
Backup=	0 = disables registry backup 1 = registry is backed up the first time the computer is started on a specific day
BackupDirectory=	Default is blank, which means that backups are saved to the WINDOWS\SYSBCKUP hidden folder.
Files=	By default, this value does not exist, but is used to add the registry CAB backup file.
MaxBackupCopies=	Default is 5 and valid values are 0 to 99.
Optimize=	Default is 1, which means that the Registry Checker utility automatically optimizes the registry if it contains 500 KB or unused space. Value of 0 means the Registry Checker utility does not automatically optimize unused space in the Registry.

The SCANREG.EXE program has several options that can be used to customize the way it works. Table 4.4 lists the switches that can be used with the SCANREG command.

Table 4.4: Windows 98 SCANREG Switches

Switch	Explanation
/"comment=*text*"	*text* is a descriptive comment that is added to the Registry backup.
/autoscan	The Registry is automatically scanned and backed up without displaying any prompts.
/backup	Backs up the Registry.
/fix	Repairs the Registry and optimizes it by removing unused space.
/opt	Optimizes the Registry by removing unused space.
/restore	Brings up the Registry Checker window and allows a specific Registry backup file to be selected for repairing a system that will not boot or operate correctly.
/scanonly	Checks the Registry for errors and displays a message if problems are found.

You need to be familiar with the information in Table 4.3 and Table 4.4 because you are likely to see this on the A+ Operating System exam.

Using the REGEDIT Command

The second method of backing up the registry is to use the REGEDIT command. The REGEDIT program allows you to export the registry to a file that has an extension of .REG. The backed up file can be edited with a text editor, if necessary. The file can also be imported back into the computer. Because accessing the registry is potentially dangerous, an exercise will not be given here. As stated earlier in this chapter, Lab Project 6 at the end of the chapter deals with the registry. However, you should ask your instructor before performing the lab project.

Using the Backup Utility

The Backup utility is accessed through Start button, Programs, Accessories, System Tools, Backup. With the Backup utility, you can either back up the entire computer, or just back up the registry.

4.4 Understanding the Pre-Installation Steps of Windows 98

Windows 98 can be installed from a central location or locally. Because this book focuses on the A+ Certification exam, only local installation is covered. The pre-installation of any operating system is more important than the installation process. If you grab a disk or CD and load a new operating system without going through a logical process, you are asking for trouble. The overall steps to take before installing Windows 98 are as follows:

1. Decide whether the installation will be an upgrade or a clean install.
2. Decide whether the computer will have more than one operating system installed.
3. Scan the computer for viruses.
4. Determine if the hardware is compatible.
5. Obtain necessary software drivers.
6. Back up any data files necessary.
7. Disable any unnecessary TSRs before upgrading to Windows 98.

The first decision to make when planning to install Windows 98 is whether you are upgrading from another operating system or performing a clean install. A **clean install** is when you install an operating system on a computer that does not have one, or the existing operating system has been removed (the hard drive is formatted). If the decision is to do an upgrade, then determine what operating system is already installed. Windows 98 supports upgrading from DOS 5 and higher, Windows 3.x, and Windows 95. When Windows 98 is installed as an upgrade from Windows 3.x or Windows 95, the user's applications and data are preserved if the operating system is installed in the same folder (directory) as the original operating system. If Windows 98 is installed in a different folder, then all applications must be reloaded.

A related issue, if upgrading to 98, is whether or not to convert the hard drive partition to FAT32. Once a partition is converted to FAT32, the partition <u>cannot</u> be changed. If you are unsure whether or not to convert the partition, leave it unchanged and later use the Drive Converter wizard to upgrade. You would want to convert the partition to FAT32 for these reasons:

- Use of cluster space is more efficient.
- FAT32 supports larger hard drive partition sizes.
- Supports larger hard drives (up to 2TB).
- With FAT32, the root folder can be relocated and a backup copy of the FAT can be used.
- FAT32 is more flexible than FAT16 because the root folder is an ordinary cluster that can be located anywhere on the drive instead of the outer hard drive track. This also means that the previous root folder entries limitation is no longer an issue.

Sometimes a clean install is the best choice, especially if the current operating system is DOS or Windows 3.x. Because a clean install involves formatting the hard drive, the user's data must be backed up and all applications reinstalled once the Windows 98 installation is complete. In addition, all user-defined settings are lost if Windows 98 is installed into a different folder.

The second decision that must be made is whether or not Windows 98 will be installed along with one or more other operating systems. This is often called a dual-boot or multi-boot scenario. **Dual-boot** means that the computer can boot from two (or more) different operating systems. Windows 98 can be dual-booted with DOS 5 and higher, Windows 3.x, NT, and 2000. If this is desired, a separate hard disk partition should be created and used for each operating system. Dual booting is discussed in further detail in Section 4.7.

The third pre-installation step is to scan the drive for viruses. The next section covers viruses in detail.

The fourth step when installing Windows 98 is to determine what computer hardware is installed and whether it is compatible with Windows 98. Table 4.5 lists the minimum and preferred hardware requirements for installing Windows 98.

Table 4.5: Windows 98 Minimum Requirements

Component	Minimum
CPU	Intel 486 (or compatible) 33 MHz
RAM	16 MB
Free hard drive space	120 MB
Input Device	Keyboard, mouse, or other pointing device
Multimedia Drive	CD-ROM
Floppy drive	3.5" 1.44 MB
Video	VGA

An upgrade from Windows 95 or Windows 3.x takes a minimum of 120MB free hard disk space. If you are doing a new installation to a FAT16 file system, 165MB of free hard disk space is the minimum. If you are doing a new installation to a FAT32 file system, 140MB is the minimum free hard disk space. If you are installing Windows 98 to a partition or drive other than the C:, the C: drive still needs a minimum of 25MB free hard disk space for Windows 98 system and log files.

The Windows 98 CD contains a document called HCL (Hardware Compatibility List). Use this list to see compatible hardware. The most current list is on Microsoft's web site. Once you have verified all hardware, you may have to get Windows 98 device drivers (step 5) from the hardware device manufacturer or its web site. There are also notes about hardware in the Windows 98 README and SETUP.TXT files contained on the 98 Setup disks.

The fifth step involves obtaining any necessary software drivers that are compatible with Windows 98. At a minimum, you may need a modem driver that is compatible with Windows 98. That way, if you have to load other drivers, such as a video driver, you will be able to download it from the Internet. A **modem** is a device that allows you to access the Internet.

The sixth step involves backing up your data. As with any upgrade, hardware change, or software change, data should be backed up. A user's data is very valuable to him or her. Whether you are doing a clean install or an upgrade, if the user has data on the computer, it must be backed up before starting the installation process. Also, before backing up data, remove any unwanted files and/or applications to free up hard drive space.

The final step is to disable old TSRs no longer needed. If Windows 98 is being upgraded, disable any unnecessary TSR (Terminate and Stay Resident) programs and device drivers loaded through CONFIG.SYS, AUTOEXEC.BAT, or the STARTUP folder. Windows 98's SETUP.TXT file on the CD-ROM contains information about TSRs that are incompatible with the upgrade.

Viruses

When installing a new operating system on a computer that already has an operating system loaded, it is a good time to run a virus scan. A **virus** is a computer program that is designed to do something to your computer that changes the way the computer operates. The virus could infect the computer so it does not boot, infect a particular application so it operates differently, or erase files. Some viruses are written to cause mischief rather than harm. An example of this could be a program that puts a picture on the screen. Some people think that they can eliminate viruses by high-level formatting their hard drive. This is a mistake. Do not take a chance; take a few moments and scan the hard drive for viruses! Common types of viruses include the boot sector virus, the file virus, the macro virus, and the Trojan horse virus.

A **boot sector virus** is a program placed in the computer's boot sector. Because the computer loads boot sector code into memory, the virus loads into RAM at the same time. Once in memory, the virus can take control of computer operations and spread to other drives, such as floppy drives, hard drives, and drives located on a network.

A **file virus** replaces or attaches itself to a file that has a COM or EXE extension. COM or EXE files are commonly known as executable files. Executable files are used to start applications. By attaching itself to this type of file, a virus can cause the program to not start or operate properly as well as load into RAM and affect other COM or EXE files.

A **macro virus** is written for a specific application such as Microsoft's Excel or Word. A macro virus is written in a specific language and attaches itself to a document that was created in the application. Once the document is opened and loaded into memory (along with the virus), the virus can attach itself to other documents.

A **Trojan horse virus** pretends to be a normal application. When the virus executes, the computer does something that the user does not expect such as put a message or a picture on the screen or put a new screen saver up. A Trojan horse virus does not replicate (copy itself somewhere else). The virus can be used to gather information such as user names and passwords that can be later used to hack into your computer.

Three other types of viruses that infect computers are the stealth virus, polymorphic virus, and a worm virus. A **stealth virus** is a program written to avoid being detected by anti-virus software. When an anti-virus program executes, the stealth virus provides the anti-virus program with a fake image that makes the anti-virus program believe that no virus is present. A **polymorphic virus** is a virus that constantly changes its own program to avoid detection by an anti-virus program. A **worm virus** makes a copy of itself from one drive to another and can use a network to replicate itself. The most common types of worm viruses today are in the form of an e-mail message. Once the e-mail is opened, the worm virus is sent to every other user that is in an address book. Common symptoms of a virus are as follows:

- Computer does not boot.
- Computer hard drive space is reduced.
- Applications will not load.
- An application takes longer to load than necessary or longer than normal.
- Hard drive activity increases, especially when nothing is being done on the
- computer.
- An anti-virus software message appears.
- The number of hard drive sectors marked as bad steadily increases.
- Unusual graphics or messages appear on the screen.
- Either files are missing or files are created (taking up excessive hard disk space).
- A message appears that the hard drive cannot be detected or recognized.
- Strange sounds come from the computer.

If a virus is detected or even suspected, run an anti-virus program. Follow the program's directions for installing and executing. The time to get an anti-virus program is *before* a virus infects the computer, because the damage may be irreversible, especially if backups are not performed. Back up data often! Always back up data files before upgrading to a new operating system. Backups are an important part of any computer support plan.

Maintaining the anti-virus program and keeping it up-to-date with the latest virus signatures is also very important. New viruses are constantly created, so the virus software must be kept current as well. Some anti-virus software can be set to load into memory when the computer boots and runs continuously. Make sure you disable this feature when installing an operating system patch (called a **Service Pack** or **SP** by Microsoft). The anti-virus software can prevent the upgrade or patch from installing. Other types of software that can prevent an operating system from being upgraded are power management and disk management software/tools. Disable these utilities and applications before attempting an operating system installation or upgrade.

4.5 Understanding How to Install and Upgrade Windows 98

Once all of the pre-installation checklist steps are complete, you are ready to install Windows 98. The installation process is easy if you performed the pre-installation steps. The program to install Windows 98 is called Setup or **SETUP.EXE**. The Setup program can be run from a Windows 95 GUI environment, from a Windows 3.1x GUI environment, or from a command prompt. If you are upgrading from Windows 95 and keeping the current configuration, run the Setup program from the Windows 95 interface by closing all programs including any anti-virus programs. Insert the Windows 98 CD into the CD-ROM drive. Normally, the Setup program automatically starts. If the Setup program does not automatically start, click on the **Start** button, click on the **Run** option, and type the drive letter for the CD-ROM followed by a colon and **\setup** in the text dialog box and press **Enter.** An example of the command is **D:\setup**. The Windows 98 Setup wizard starts.

During the installation process, you are asked to enter a Product Key. The Product Key is located either on the certificate found on the back of the Windows 98 book (that shipped with the computer) or on the back of the 98 CD. In addition, during the setup process, you are prompted for the type of setup. The installation types are listed below.

- The **Typical** option installs the most common components for Windows 98. This is the most frequently chosen option.
- The **Portable** option is used for laptop computers and installs Windows 98 components used on portable computers.
- The **Compact** option is the smallest possible number of Windows 98 files that can be loaded and Windows 98 still work.
- The **Custom** option allows you to select the components to install.

The SETUP.EXE file can be used with various switches that control the setup process. Table 4.6 lists some of the switches that can be used. If networking is installed, an Identification window appears prompting for the computer name, workgroup name, and a description of the computer. The computer name prompt is used to uniquely identify the computer across a network. The name can be up to 15 characters long and should not contain blank characters. The workgroup name can also be up to 15 characters and must be the same for all computers networked together. Contact the network administrator for what to type in this dialog box. The computer description box can contain up to 48 characters and contain spaces to describe the computer or the computer's location.

Table 4.6: Some Windows 98 SETUP.EXE Switches

Switch or Option	Purpose
/?	Displays switches available
/c	Bypasses SmartDrive (used for drive caching)
/d	Bypasses using the existing Windows configuration
/ie	Skips the Startup Disk screen
/is	Skips the disk check (ScanDisk)
/it	Bypasses checking for TSRs
/nr	Skips the Registry check

The A+ Operating System exam will test your knowledge of these switches. So learn them.

4.6 Troubleshooting the Windows 98 Installation

The key to troubleshooting the Windows 98 installation is to get the operating system installed as best you can and troubleshoot the problem with the tools provided with Windows 98. Windows 98 ships with a feature called **Safe Recovery** that allows the installation to continue after a failure. Installation problems can be caused by a number of factors. The following are the most common causes and their associated solutions during the installation process:

- **Incompatible drivers**—Obtain Windows 98 drivers from the hardware manufacturer.
- **Existing drivers are incompatible or halt the installation/upgrade process**—Obtain Windows 98 drivers from the hardware manufacturer. If upgrading from a previous operating system, edit the AUTOEXEC.BAT and CONFIG.SYS and put the REM command before each line so the drivers do not load.
- **Incompatible TSRs**—Remove TSRs or obtain updated ones from the software manufacturer. Make sure to remove power management and anti-virus programs.
- **Minimum hardware requirements have not been met**—Upgrade the hardware. The top items to check are the CPU (486DX 66MHz minimum), RAM (16MB minimum), and hard drive space (120MB minimum).
- **A virus is on the hard drive**—Run a virus-checking program and remove the virus.
- **Pre-installation steps have not been completed**—Go back through the list!
- **The Windows 98 boot disk or CD is corrupted** (not as likely as the other
- causes)—Try the disk in another machine and see if you can see the contents. For the CD, check to see if any scratches or dirt are on the surface. Clean the CD as necessary.
- **Incorrect Product Key**—Type in the correct CD key to complete the Windows 98 installation. The Product Key is located either on the certificate found on the back of the Windows 98 book (that shipped with the computer) or on the back of the 98 CD.

Several text files can be helpful in determining the installation problem. Table 4.7 lists the text files and a description of each. You can view the contents of a file to determine what occurred at various stages of the installation.

Table 4.7: Windows 98 Startup Log Files

Log File	Description
BOOTLOG.TXT	Hidden text file in the root directory that is created when Windows 98 boots for the first time. Contains a list of Windows 98 components and drivers that load during the boot process.
DETCRASH.LOG	Hidden text file in the root directory that is used when Setup fails during the installation process.
DETLOG.TXT	Hidden text file in the root directory that contains a chronological list of hardware devices found during the hardware detection phase.
NETLOG.TXT	Text file stored in the root directory that chronologically lists network components found during the network detection phase.
SETUPLOG.TXT	Hidden text file stored in the root directory that chronologically lists what happens during the installation process.

If Windows 98 gets an error message that states "Invalid System Disk" after the system reboots the first time, a virus may be present; an anti-virus program is running and has not been disabled either through AUTOEXEC.BAT, STARTUP folder, or CMOS; or disk management software is enabled.

4.7 Understanding the Dual-Boot Feature of Windows 98

Sometimes users would like to try a new operating system, but keep their old operating system loaded as well. If this is the case, two operating systems can reside in one system and it is called dual-booting. Windows 98 can be dual-booted with DOS, Windows 3.x, Windows 95, NT, and 2000 Professional, but care must be taken. NT supports and uses either NTFS or FAT16 and Windows 98 supports and uses either FAT16 or FAT32. NT cannot read FAT32 partitions and Windows 98 cannot read NTFS4 partitions. If Windows 98 is to access the files stored when using NT, both operating systems need to use FAT16 (but the FAT32 and NTFS features are lost). It is best if the two operating systems are placed on different hard drive partitions and Windows 98 loaded before NT is installed. If the computer currently dual-boots with NT from another operating system or environment such as DOS, Windows 3.x, or Windows 95, the Windows 98 Setup program can be executed from the other operating system.

The dual-booting feature is a misnomer. You cannot boot more than one operating system. What it really means is that you can install multiple operating systems (yes, more than two). However, you can only boot one operating system at a time. For the most part, in business, it is not practical to dual-boot because only one operating system can be booted. For home use, dual-booting is a good idea because you can learn different operating systems simply booting to the one you want.

4.8 Configuring Windows 98

One of the most common windows in Windows 98 is the Control Panel window. A **control panel** is a method for configuring various Windows 98 components. The Add New Hardware, Add/Remove Programs, and Printing control panels are used when installing or removing hardware and software. Each control panel icon represents a Windows utility that allows you to customize a particular part of the Windows 98 environment. The number of control panels displayed depends on the type of computer and the components contained within the computer. Figure 4.6 shows some of the more common Windows 98 control panels.

Figure 4.6: The Windows 98 Control Panel

You must know which control panel to use for changing a computer's configuration. Table 4.8 shows some common Windows 98 control panels and the function of each.

Table 4.8: Common Windows 98 Control Panel Functions

Control Panel	Function
Accessibility	Controls keyboard, sounds, display, and mouse behavior for people with vision, hearing, or mobility disabilities.
Add New Hardware	Used when installing new hardware devices.
Add/Remove Programs	Used to install or uninstall software applications.
Display	Used to install a monitor driver and configure monitor settings.
Keyboard	Used to install a keyboard driver and configure keyboard.

Multimedia	Used to install multimedia device drivers, configure properties for audio and video, and configure settings for playing audio CDs.
Network	Used to install NIC drivers, add network software, and configure network connections.
Passwords	Used to configure user preferences and passwords.
Power Management	Used to reduce electrical power use in devices such as a monitor or hard drive.
Printers	Used to add, remove, and modify printer settings.
Regional Settings	Used to set the time zone and set the format for numbers and currency.
System	Allows viewing system information and changing parameters related to system performance such as virtual memory. It also allows access to Device Manager where you can manage devices.
Users	Used to configure the computer for more than one person.

Operating system specialists must frequently add new hardware and software using the operating system. Windows 98 has specific tools for these functions. Using the correct procedure is essential for success on the job. The following sections handle many of the tasks an operating system specialist must perform:

- Adding Plug and Play Devices
- Adding Non-Plug and Play Devices
- Adding a Printer
- Removing Hardware Devices
- Installing and Removing Software

Hardware devices are physical components that connect to the computer. Hardware devices can be either plug and play or non-plug and play. A device driver is a piece of software that allows hardware to work with a specific operating system. Some device drivers are automatically included with Windows 98. An operating system specialist must be aware of what hardware is installed into a system so that the latest Windows 98-compatible drivers can be downloaded and installed.

Adding Plug and Play Devices
Plug and play devices are hardware and software designed to be automatically recognized by the operating system. The key to a successful plug and play device installation includes the following:

- Possessing the most up-to-date device driver

• Following the directions provided by the device manufacturer

Always make sure that the computer is turned off when installing any new hardware component. Some plug and play devices can be inserted into the computer without restarting. These include a PC Card, a laptop into a docking station, and a Universal Serial Bus (USB) device. However, devices such as internal modems or network cards require the computer to be turned off during installation.

Install the device according to the device manufacturer's instructions. Once installed, power on the computer. The Windows 98 Found New Hardware wizard appears. Windows 98 attempts to find a driver for the new device. If Windows 98 detects the plug and play device, the device gives Windows 98 a device ID. Windows 98 uses this device ID to look for the appropriate .INF file. A .INF file contains information used to install and configure the device. If a driver cannot be found, a dialog box appears. The best policy with any operating system is to use the latest driver even if the operating system detects the device.

Adding Non-Plug and Play Devices

Legacy devices are also called **non-plug and play** devices. For devices that are not plug and play, use the Add New Hardware control panel. The Add New Hardware wizard allows hardware configuration and is used for hardware that is not automatically recognized by Windows 98. It is also used for plug and play devices that do not install properly with Windows 98's automatic detection. Windows 98 prompts with the question asking if you want Windows 98 to search for non-plug and play devices. Select the *Yes* option. If Windows 98 finds the device, follow the rest of the prompts to install a driver for the device. If Windows 98 does not find the device, you must select the type of device that is being installed. Then, you must select the device manufacturer and device model from a list. A generic device or "other" option is available for most device categories. Have the Windows 98-compatible device driver ready, click on the **Have Disk** button and specify the drive and path to the driver.

You should let Windows 98 automatically detect any new hardware you add to your system. As a result, you won't need to do locate the correct driver—unless, of course, Windows 98 cannot locate an appropriate driver for the hardware.

Adding a Printer

Printers can be connected to a computer through the printer's parallel or USB port through a local area network. Only local printers (printers directly connected to a computer port) will be covered in this chapter. Networked printers will be explained in the Chapter 9. Windows 98 can automatically detect printers. If Windows 98 detects the printer, the operating system installs the drivers, updates the registry, and allocates system resources to the printer. Most printer are automatically detected by Windows 98.

To install a printer, connect the printer to the appropriate computer port with the appropriate cable. Power on the computer, and the Windows 98 wizard normally detects it and leads you through the installation process. However, if it does not, have the Windows 98-compatible printer driver ready, click on the **Start** button, point to the **Settings** selection, and click on the **Printers** option. When the Printers window opens, click on the **Add Printer** icon. Click on the **Next** button and select the **Local Printer** selection. When prompted for the printer driver, insert the CD or disk that contains the printer driver and use the Browse button to locate the driver. Continue through the Add Printer wizard until the printer is installed.

Removing Hardware Devices

When a plug and play hardware device is removed, Windows 98 automatically detects this and removes the resources and registry entries assigned to the device. When removing most non-plug and play hardware devices (all but printers), use Device Manager. Right-click on the **My Computer** desktop icon to access Device Manager, then click on the **Properties** option, and then click on the **Device Manager** tab. Through Device Manager, a device can either be removed or disabled. When a non-plug and play device is removed, the driver does not load and any resources assigned to the device are now free. When a non-plug and play device is disabled, the resources assigned to the device are kept, but the device's driver does not load when the computer restarts.

To remove a device, click on the plus sign located beside the appropriate device category, then click on the name of the device being removed, and then click on the **Remove** button. To disable a device, click on the plus sign located beside the appropriate device category, then click on the device name, and then click on the **Properties** button. On the **General** tab in the Device Usage section is a check box that allows you to disable the device for a specific hardware profile. Click once in this check box to disable the device.

If you are removing a printer from the system, use the **Printers** control panel. Access this control panel by clicking on the **Start** button. Point to the **Settings** option and click on the **Printers** option. Right-click on the printer you want to delete and choose the **Delete** option.

Installing and Removing Software

No computer is fully functional without software and Windows 98 supports 16-bit and 32-bit applications. Most software today is 32-bit and comes on CD and includes an **Autorun** feature. If the CD has the Autorun feature, an installation wizard steps you through installing the software when the CD is inserted into the drive. If there is not an Autorun feature on the CD or if the software is on a disk, then the Add/Remove Programs control panel is normally used to install or remove the software.

Remember to always to consult the application documentation for installation procedure.

To access the Add/Remove Programs control panel, click on the **Start** button and point to the **Settings** option. Click on the **Control Panel** option and then double-click on the **Add/Remove Programs** control panel icon. To install an application, click on the **Install/Uninstall** tab, click on the **Install** button, insert the application disk or CD, and click on the **Next** button. Windows 98 searches the floppy drive and CD for a Setup program. If one is found, continue the installation process. If one is not found, type the drive letter and path for the application's Setup program. Use the **Browse** button if necessary. Click on the **Finish** button to complete the process.

Close all active applications before starting the installation process. This will eliminate some complications. The computer must frequently be rebooted after an application or Windows component has been installed.

To remove a software application, use the same Add/Remove Programs control panel; however, instead of clicking on the **Install** button, select the application to be removed and click on the **Add/Remove** button. Do not forget to check the application's documentation for specific removal procedures.

The Add/Remove Programs control panel can also be used to add operating system components, add programs across your network, and add or remove Windows components. The Windows Setup tab is used to add or remove operating system components. The Startup Disk tab is used to create a Windows 98 disk that can be used when Windows 98 does not boot properly.

4.9 Understanding the Boot Process

Every operating system needs specific files that allow the computer to boot. These files are known as system files or startup files. The common **system files** and their specific location on the hard drive are listed in Table 4.9. The locations listed in Table 4.9 assume that Windows 98 is loaded in the default folder (WINDOWS). If Windows 98 is loaded in a different folder, substitute the location WINDOWS for the name of the folder in which Windows 98 was initially loaded.

Table 4.9: Common Windows 98 Startup Files

Startup File Name	File Location and Purpose
AUTOEXEC.BAT	Root directory—used to load TSRs not designed to run under Windows 98
BOOT.INI	Root directory—used when multiple operating systems are present
CONFIG.SYS	Root directory—used to load 16-bit drivers not designed to run under Windows 98
DRVSPACE.BIN	WINDOWS\COMMAND—supports compressed drives

GDI.EXE	WINDOWS\SYSTEM—provides support for the graphical environment; one of the Windows 98 core files
GDI32.DLL	WINDOWS\SYSTEM—provides support for the graphical environment
HIMEM.SYS	WINDOWS—driver for extended memory
IFSHELP.SYS	WINDOWS—driver for 32-bit Installable File System Manager
IO.SYS	Root directory—boot file for real mode that loads drivers and TSRs listed in CONFIG.SYS and AUTOEXEC.BAT
KERNEL32.DLL	WINDOWS\SYSTEM—loads the main Windows components
KRNL386.EXE	WINDOWS\SYSTEM—loads Windows device drivers
MSDOS.SYS	Root directory—contains boot parameters and provides backwards compatibility for applications
SYSTEM.DAT	WINDOWS—part of the Registry
SYSTEM.INI	WINDOWS—only exists to be backward compatible with older applications
USER.EXE	WINDOWS\SYSTEM—provides the user interface
USER32.DLL	WINDOWS\SYSTEM—provides user interface code
WIN.COM	WINDOWS—the file that starts Windows
WIN.INI	WINDOWS—only exists to be backward compatible with older applications

The boot process is actually quite involved, but the major steps are as follows:

1. The computer powers on.
2. POST executes.
3. If the computer has a plug and play BIOS, plug and play adapters and devices are configured. If the computer does not have a plug and play BIOS, all ISA bus devices are enabled.
4. BIOS searches for an active partition on the hard drive.
5. BIOS reads the Master Boot Record, then locates and loads the information into sector 0 of the system partition. The contents of sector 0 define the type of file system and the location of the boot files, then start loading the file system.
6. Real mode starts.
7. MSDOS.SYS boot configuration loads.
8. DRVSPACE.BIN loads if it is needed for compressed drives.
9. Prompts for a hardware profile if multiple profiles exist.

10. Bitmap image stored in LOGO.SYS loads.
11. SYSTEM.DAT loads.
12. DOS drivers and TSRs needed for backward compatibility load as specified by the CONFIG.SYS and AUTOEXEC.BAT files.
13. Initializes static VxDs in real mode specified by VMM32.VXD and the registry.
14. Starts protected-mode and loads WIN.COM.
15. Loads protected-mode VxDs as specified by VMM32.VXD, the registry, and the settings in the SYSTEM.INI file.
16. Loads KRNL386.EXE, GDI files, user libraries, Explorer shell, and network support (if needed).
17. Executes any programs located in the Startup folder and those referred to in the registry.

The only reason the AUTOEXEC.BAT, CONFIG.SYS, WIN.INI, and SYSTEM.INI files load is to make Windows 98 backward compatible with older operating systems, 16-bit TSRs, and 16-bit drivers.

The IO.SYS File

Windows 98's IO.SYS file is responsible for loading key files that were previously loaded through the CONFIG.SYS file. Table 4.10 lists the files that are automatically loaded through IO.SYS and the default setting. If the computer needs a setting change, modify the setting by adding the line in the CONFIG.SYS file.

Table 4.10: Windows 98 Default IO.SYS Settings

Setting	Default Parameter and Purpose
buffers=	30 — sets the number of file buffers to create for 16-bit programs
dos=high	No default setting—loads part of the operating system into the HMA
fcbs=	4 — sets the file control blocs that can be open
files=	60 — the number of concurrent open files
himem.sys	No default setting—enables access to XMS
ifshlp.sys	No default setting—used to load device drivers
lastdrive=	Z: — specifies the last drive letter available to be assigned by the operating system
server.exe	No default setting—included for DOS compatibility
shell=	No default setting—sets the default command interpreter

| stacks= | 9,256 — specifies the number and size of data stacks to handle hardware interrupts. For example, the default setting of 9,256 indicates that 9 stacks are available and they are 256 bytes in size. |

The MSDOS.SYS File

Windows 98 has a hidden, read-only system file called MSDOS.SYS that is located in the root directory. MSDOS.SYS enables backward compatibility with older DOS applications. The file holds multiple operating system boot options as well as the paths to important Windows 98 files such as the registry. There are lines of Xs in the MSDOS.SYS file. Do not remove the Xs. Table 4.11 lists some of the more common options found in the MSDOS.SYS file.

Table 4.11: Windows 98 MSDOS.SYS Settings

Section	*Setting*	*Default Setting and Purpose*
[Options]	AutoScan=	1 — enables a prompt to run ScanDisk; a value of 0 disables it; a value of 2 runs ScanDisk without prompting
[Options]	BootDelay=	2 — seconds delayed after the "Starting Windows" message appears; a value of 0 disables the delay
[Options]	BootGUI=	1 — enables the GUI interface; a value of 0 boots to a prompt
[Options]	BootKeys=	1 — enables startup function keys; a value of 0 prevents startup keys from functioning and overrides the BootDelay= setting
[Options]	BootMenu=	0 — enables/disables Startup Menu automatically appearing; a value of 1 displays the Startup menu
[Options]	BootMenuDefaults=	3 or 4 — the number of the menu item to automatically start; a value of 3 is the default for a computer without networking installed; a value of 4 is the default for a computer with networking installed
[Options]	BootMulti=	0 — enables dual-booting; a value of 1 enables the F4 key (for DOS) or the F8 key (for the Windows 98 Startup menu)

[Options]	BootWin=	1 — enables Windows 98 as the default operating system; a value of 0 makes another operating system the default; this setting is only useful with DOS-dual booted with Windows 98
[Options]	LoadTop=	1 — enables loading COMMAND.COM or DRVSPACE.BIN at the top of conventional memory; a value of 0 disables this feature
[Paths]	HostWinBootDrv=	C — the drive letter for the boot drive root directory
[Paths]	WinBootDir=	Varies — defines the location of the startup files
[Paths]	WinDir=	Varies — specifies the folder where many of the Windows 98 files are located

Troubleshooting the Boot Process

Windows 98 has a wealth of tools to help you when troubleshooting the boot process. One of the more common startup problem solving tools is the **Startup menu**. This menu is used to determine how to boot Windows 98. Access the Windows Startup menu by pressing the Ctrl key when you boot the computer. If this does not work, press the **F8** key during the boot process. Each item in the Startup menu is used in different situations. The Startup menu options are listed in table 4.12.

Table 4.12: Windows 98 Startup Menu Options

Mode	Purpose
Normal	Used to boot Windows normally.
Logged	Used to track the boot process and log each event in a file located in the root directory called BOOTLOG.TXT; used to determine where the boot failure occurs.
Safe	Prevents the CONFIG.SYS and AUTOEXEC.BAT files from loading, prevents the [Boot] and [386enh] sections of the SYSTEM.INI file from loading, prevents the Load= and Run= parameters of the WIN.INI file from loading, prevents the items found in the Startup folder from loading, prevents portions of the registry from loading, prevents all device drivers except for the keyboard and mouse from loading, and loads a standard VGA driver.
Step-by-Step confirmation	Allows performing the boot process one step at a time to see where the problem occurs.

Command Prompt Only	Used to troubleshoot DOS applications (only CONFIG.SYS, AUTOEXEC.BAT, COMMAND.COM, and the Registry are loaded; the GUI does not load).
Safe Mode with Command Prompt Only	Used if the computer does not boot to Safe Mode; does not load the HIMEM.SYS or IFSHLP.SYS files, and does not execute WIN.COM to start the GUI. Various switches can be used at the command prompt with the WIN.COM file to troubleshoot the problem.
Previous Version of MS-DOS	Used to perform a DOS function that does not operate correctly under Windows 98.

Other tools that can be used for startup problems include the System Configuration utility, Microsoft System Information tool, Automatic Skip Driver, System File Checker, Startup and Shutdown Troubleshooter, and Registry Checker. Determining which tool to use and how to access the tool is the challenge.

The **System Configuration** utility is used when you suspect a problem with old device drivers or TSRs especially on a computer that has been upgraded to Windows 98. The System Configuration utility allows you to enable or disable entries in the AUTOEXEC.BAT, CONFIG.SYS, SYSTEM.INI, and WIN.INI files. The order in which the file entries load can also be controlled. These files are available in Windows 98 to be compatible with older operating systems and older applications. Access the System Configuration utility by clicking on the **Start** button | **Programs** | **Accessories** | **System Tools** | **_System Information**. Click on the **Tools** menu option and select the **System Configuration Utility** from the drop-down menu. The easiest way to determine if one of the four files is causing the problem is to click on the **Diagnostic startup** radio button and click on the **OK** button. When the Windows 98 Startup menu appears, press the number corresponding to the **Step-by-Step Confirmation** setting. The command that starts the System Configuration utility is MSCONFIG.EXE located in the WINDOWS\SYSTEM subfolder. Figure 4.7 shows the System Configuration Utility.

Figure 4.7: Windows 98 System Configuration Utility

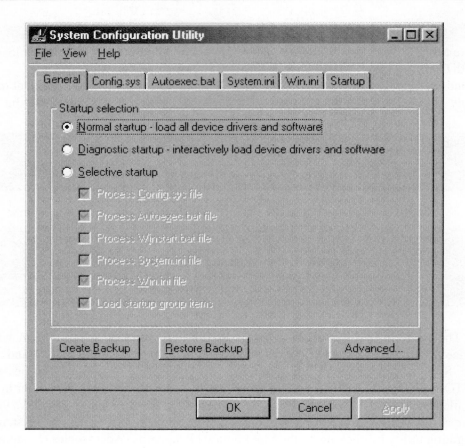

The **MSINFO (Microsoft System Information)** tool is used to display information about system resources and can be used to detect conflicts between devices. Follow the steps below to access MSINFO from a fully operational Windows 98 computer:

1. To access the MSINFO tool, click the **Start** button, point to **_Programs**, point to **Accessories**, point to **System Tools**, and click **System Information**. The System Information window opens.
2. Click on the plus sign beside the **Hardware Resources** option in the left window. The option expands.
3. Click on the **Conflicts/Sharing** setting to see resource conflicts between devices and resources.
4. To view the software environment, click **Software Environment** to expand it.
5. Click **16-bit modules loaded** to view the 16-bit programs that are currently loaded into memory.

6. Click **32-bit modules loaded** to view the 16-bit programs that are currently loaded into memory.
7. Close the System Information window.

Another popular option is the **Forced Hardware** view that lists devices that have been assigned resources manually. The Problem Devices selection allows you to view any devices that have problems and the History option shows seven days of driver history. The command to execute MSINFO tool is MSINFO32.EXE. Figure 4.8 shows the Microsoft System Information tool.

Figure 4.8: Windows 98 System Information Utility

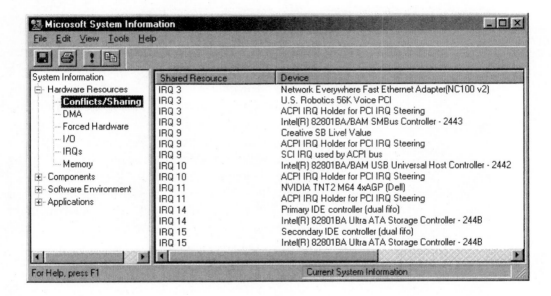

The MSINFO and the Windows Report tools update a file called HWINFO.DAT every time these tools execute. The HWINFO.DAT file is created during the installation process and holds a record of the computer's current hardware configuration, device drivers, and system resources. The MSINFO tool can be used to open the HWINFO.DAT file at any time.

The **ASD.EXE (Automatic Skip Driver Agent)** program is found in the same folder as where Windows 98 is installed. The Automatic Skip Driver tool determines which drivers fail to load during startup. After two failed attempts, ASD marks the device as defective and turns off the device driver. Clicking the Tools menu in System Information accesses ASD. If no problems are found, a dialog box appears on the screen.

Sometimes applications overwrite system files or files become corrupt. The **System File Checker (SFC.EXE)** is located in the WINDOWS\SYSTEM subfolder and protects your system files by checking them and repairing them if necessary. A prompt appears before the original files are restored.

Many error messages can appear in Windows 98. Some of them are listed in Table 4.13.

Table 4.13: Windows 98 Troubleshooting

Error Message	Solution
A device referenced in SYSTEM.INI, WIN.INI, or registry could not be found	1)Edit SYSTEM.INI and WIN.INI and look for all references to the device. Put a semicolon before the line. For Windows 9x, see if there is a 9x driver for the device. If so, leave the semicolon before the SYSTEM.INI line and reload the 9x driver if necessary. After rebooting the computer, if an application displays a message that it cannot find this file, the file needs to be recopied (usually to the WINDOWS SYSTEM folder) and the semicolon removed from the SYSTEM.INI line. 2) To see which file caused the error, use MSCONFIG to choose Selective Startup and step through the startup process. 3) If a Registry error occurs, back up the Registry, use a Registry Editor to locate the driver in the HKLM \System\Current\ControlSet\Services\Vxd key. If you know the driver is no longer needed, highlight the Open subkey and delete it. If any application needs the missing file, a message appears that the file is missing. Reload the file the application disk or CD.
Bad or missing COMMAND.COM	The COMMAND.COM file is missing. Replace the boot disk or CD.
Error in CONFIG.SYS line xx	Edit CONFIG.SYS and look at the line referenced in message. Check if the referenced file is in the listed folder. Check for typing errors on the line. Replace file in appropriate folder if necessary.
Error loading kernel. You must reinstall Windows.	Extract the KERNEL32.DLL file from Windows disk or CD and copy it to the WINDOWS\SYSTEM folder.
HIMEM.SYS not loaded or missing or corrupt HIMEM.SYS	Check the WINDOWS folder for the HIMEM.SYS file. Reload file from original disk, boot disk, or CD if the file is missing or corrupt.

Incorrect DOS version	The command or utility is from a different system version than the command interpreter loading during startup. Replace the command or COMMAND.COM and system files with the appropriate version or use the SETVER command to fool the application into using the command interpreter installed.
No operating system found	Boot from the appropriate boot disk and replace the operating system files by typing SYS C:.

Another error resulting from different causes is the Windows Protection Error. A **Windows Protection Error** is usually caused by a virtual device driver being loaded or unloaded. Sometimes the specific device driver (VxD) is mentioned in the error message. The following list cites the most common causes of a Windows Protection Error:

• Real mode driver conflicting with a protected mode driver
• Corrupt registry
• A virus has infected WIN.COM or COMMAND.COM or one of the files is corrupt
• Driver referenced in the registry has initialized and a conflicting SYSTEM.INI driver loads
• I/O or DMA address conflict (use Device Manager or MSINFO)
• Motherboard has been replaced. (Sometimes Windows 98 must be reinstalled to recognize the new motherboard capabilities.)

Windows 98 comes with many troubleshooting wizards. One that relates to the boot process is the Startup and Shutdown troubleshooter. Access this troubleshooting wizard follow these steps on a fully operational Windows 98 computer:

1. Click the **Start** button and then click the **Help** button. The Help window opens.
2. Click on the **Index** tab.
3. Type **startup** in the text box.
4. Double-click on the **troubleshooting** option in the left windowpane.
5. In the right window, click on the **Click here** option to start the wizard.
6. Go through the various screens by clicking a radio button for a problem and then clicking **Next**.
7. When finished, click **Close**.

Sometimes, when the computer will not boot, a startup disk (boot disk) is needed. Another time to use a startup disk is when the computer has a virus. Create a Windows 98 startup disk by following these steps on a fully operational Windows 98 computer:

1. Click the **Start** button, point to Settings, and then click Control Panel.
2. Double-click **Add/Remove Programs**. The Add/Remove Programs window opens.
3. Click **Startup Disk**.
4. Insert a floppy that you don't mind formatting. CAUTION: All data will be lost because the disk will be formatted!

5. Click **Create Disk**. The disk is created.
6. When finished, close the window.

4.10 Troubleshooting Application Problems

Most computer problems occur when installing an operating system or a new hardware component, but applications can cause problems too. Application problems can occur when a new application is installed, a new operating system is installed, an operating system service pack or upgrade is installed, and during normal computer operation. The way in which an application problem is tackled depends on whether the application is 16-bit or 32-bit. This is because Windows 98 uses two types of multitasking—preemptive and cooperative. **Preemptive multitasking** is the operating system determining which application gets the microprocessor's attention and for how long. Preemptive multitasking is used with 32-bit applications. **Cooperative multitasking** relies on the application to relinquish control of the CPU and is the type of multitasking that 16-bit applications use.

An important concept when dealing with applications is the virtual machine. A **virtual machine** is a way for the operating system to appear as a separate computer to each application. Each 32-bit application runs in its own virtual machine. Each 16-bit DOS application runs in its own virtual machine. However, every 16-bit Windows application (an application designed for Windows 3.x) runs in one virtual machine. When a 16-bit Windows application crashes, all 16-bit applications that are loaded into memory crash as well.

Another important concept to remember is that 16-bit applications were not designed to interact with the registry. DOS applications are designed to interact and update the AUTOEXEC.BAT and CONFIG.SYS files. 16-bit Windows applications are designed to interact and update the AUTOEXEC.BAT, CONFIG.SYS, and various .INI files such as SYSTEM.INI and WIN.INI. Windows 98 still contains and supports these files in order to be backward compatible with older applications.

General Protection Fault (GPF)

When an application error occurs, a **GPF (General Protection Fault)** error message appears. When a Windows 16-bit application GPF occurs, all other 16-bit Windows applications are halted until you exit the application that caused the error. In most cases, the other 16-bit applications must be closed as well. When a 32-bit application GPF occurs, no other application is affected. Sometimes when the GPF occurs, you are allowed to terminate the application from the GPF error window, but sometimes you must use a different method to quit the application. In that case, press the Ctrl + Alt + Del keys and the Close Program window appears. Click on the offending application and then click on the **End Task** button.

Dr. Watson

Another useful utility to help with application problems is Dr. Watson. **Dr. Watson** has the ability to take a snapshot of the computer system when a fault occurs. For software applications, Dr. Watson can provide information about the problem cause. The Dr. Watson utility does not load by default in Windows 98. To start Dr. Watson on a fully operational Windows 98 computer, follow these steps:

1. To access the MSINFO tool, click the **Start** button, point to **Programs**, point to **Accessories**, point to **System Tools**, and click **System Information**. The System Information window opens.

2. From the System Information window, click on the **Tools** menu option and choose the **Dr. Watson** menu item. A Dr. Watson icon appears in the taskbar system tray in the bottom right corner.

3. To view Dr. Watson, double-click the Dr. Watson icon on the taskbar. It builds information about the system and opens.

4. When finished, close the window.

On the Diagnosis tab is information relating to the system snapshot. Figure 4.9 illustrates the Dr. Watson window. The Dr. Watson window also has blank space at the bottom so you can insert notes.

Figure 4.9: The Dr. Watson Window

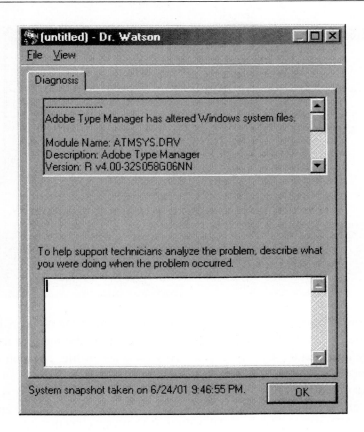

Dr. Watson also includes an advanced view that provides detailed information about the computer system. Click on the **View** menu option and select **Advanced view**. The Advanced view has many tabs across the top. To view more tabs, click on the right or left arrows located to the right of the tabs. Several important tabs include the Kernel drivers, User Drivers, MS-DOS drivers, and 16-bit Modules. These tabs separate the various drivers that can be used on Windows 98. Figure 4.10 illustrates the Dr. Watson Advanced view.

Figure 4.10: Dr. Watson Advanced View Window

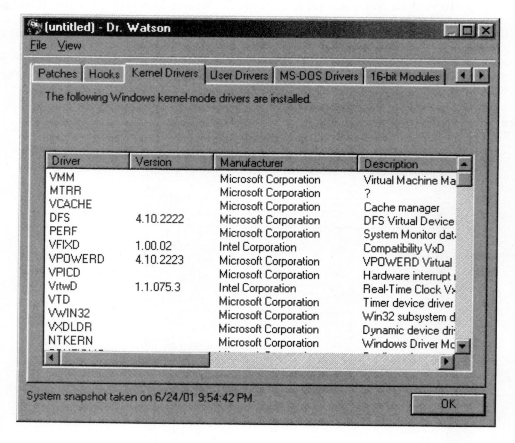

When Dr. Watson is running and an application error occurs, Dr. Watson logs the information into a file called WATSON*xx*.WLG file. The *xx* in the file name is a number that is automatically incremented by Dr. Watson. To view a saved file, click on the *File* menu option and select the Open Log File menu item. Any system snapshot can also be saved using the **Save** or **Save As File** menu options. To have Dr. Watson start every time the computer boots, create a shortcut to the WINDOWS\DRWATSON.EXE file and place the shortcut in the WINDOWS\START MENU\PROGRAMS\STARTUP folder.

System Monitor

Many tools have already been covered that help with resource management, but two new ones are System Monitor and Resource Meter. **System Monitor** is a utility that tracks performance of individual system components, such as disks, file system, operating system kernel, and memory manager. Under each category are numerous individual selections. System Monitor helps identify where performance bottlenecks are located. To access System Monitor, click on the **Start** button, point to **Accessories** and **System Tools**, and click on the **System Monitor** option.

System monitor has three views—ine chart, bar chart, and numeric chart. Figure 4.11 shows System Monitor using a bar chart. An exercise at the end of this chapter demonstrates System Monitor usage.

Figure 4.11: System Monitor Bar Chart

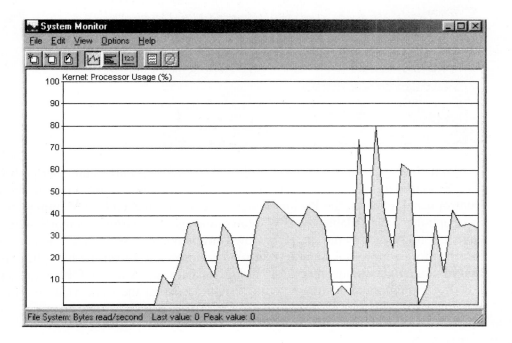

Resource Meter is a very simple graphical display of how Windows 98 is using memory. To access Resource Meter, click on the **Start** button, point to **Programs**, **Accessories**, and **System Tools** options, and click on the **Resource Meter** selection. A window with a Resource Meter description appears on the screen and then the Resource Meter becomes an icon on the taskbar system tray. Double-click on the icon that looks like a set of stairs with a colored bar across the bottom to display Resource Meter. Keep in mind that Resource Meter consumes system resources just like any utility. After viewing Resource Meter, right-click on the Resource Meter icon in the taskbar system tray and click on the **Exit** option.

The three Windows 98 core components—Kernel (system), User, and GDI—are shown with individual lines. The **System line** represents the Windows 98 kernel, which is the part of the operating system that supports input/output, task scheduling, and virtual memory management. The **User line** represents how much memory is being used to manage user input such as mouse usage, window sizing, etc. The **GDI (Graphics Device Interface) core component line** represents the amount of memory being used for screen and printer graphics. Figure 4.12 shows the Resource Meter window.

Figure 4.12: Resource Meter

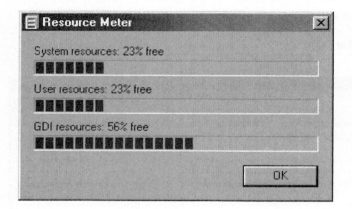

Sometimes you must adjust the paging file size for optimum computer performance. The **System** control panel is used to set the virtual memory size. Once in the System control panel, click on the **Performance** tab. Click on the **Virtual Memory** button and two options are available—Let Windows manage my virtual memory settings (the default setting) and Let me specify my own virtual memory settings. Click on the **Let me specify my own virtual memory settings** radio button, select the hard drive partition and minimum/maximum amount of hard drive space. Click on the **OK** button when finished. The minimum/maximum settings should contain the same value for maximum computer performance.

Chapter Summary
- Windows 98 is a 32-bit operating system used by home users and businesses. It supports Plug and Play, USB, and both 16-bit and 32-bit applications.
- Windows 98 provides a hierarchical file system allowing you to create folders and store files within them.
- The Registry is a database, which stores the hardware and software information installed on your computer.
- As part of the pre-installation steps of Windows 98, you should decide whether or not to perform a clean installation or an upgrade. You should consider installing virus protection software, which can detect and remove common software viruses.

- The SETUP.EXE program allows you to install Windows 98. It has numerous switches that can be uses for various purposes.
- Troubleshooting your Windows 98 installation includes entering the wrong Product Key and having incompatible hardware or hardware drivers.
- You can dual-boot Windows 98 and Windows NT or Windows 2000. However, it is advisable to install each on separate partitions. It is recommended to install Windows 98 before you install the other operating systems.
- Configuring Windows 98 involves using Control Panel to change the look and feel of your Windows 98 system. Examples include: changing mouse, keyboard, and sound settings. You can also add and remove devices.
- You need to understand the boot process of Windows 98 so you know how to troubleshoot when problems occur.

Review Questions

1. What Microsoft browser software allows you to connect to the Internet?
   a) Internet Connection Sharing
   b) Internet Explorer
   c) Windows Explorer
   d) Control Panel

2. What Microsoft feature allows you to connect to the Internet through another Windows 98 computer?
   a) Internet Connection Sharing
   b) Internet Explorer
   c) Windows Explorer
   d) Control Panel

3. The _____ is the area where all of your work in Windows 98 begins. This area contains icons and shortcuts.
   a) Desktop
   b) Window
   c) Control Panel
   d) Long File Names

4. What Windows feature prevents you from moving icons on your desktop?
   a) Auto Unclutter
   b) Auto Arrange
   c) Arrange Order
   d) Automatically Detect

5. Where are files held when they are deleted from the hard disk drive?
   a) Trash Can
   b) They are not held anywhere because they are permanently deleted.
   c) Recycle Bin
   d) Quick Launch Bar

6. Where is the name of the horizontal bar the runs across the bottom of your screen?
   a) Recycle Bin
   b) Taskbar
   c) Quick Launch Bar
   d) Task Manager

7. A file with an extension of _____ is a compressed cabinet file.
   a) COM
   b) TXT
   c) CAB
   d) DLL

8. A file with an extension of _____ is a command file or executable.
   a) COM
   b) TXT
   c) CAB
   d) DLL

9. Which of the following are invalid Windows 98 long file names? Choose all that apply.
   a) Payroll.txt
   b) F/Le:100.tx*t
   c) Sales.dat
   d) X.DOC

10. Which of the following commands will display the Window 98 version?
    a) ver
    b) version
    c) update
    d) vers

11. Which of the following commands allows you to install Windows 98?
    a) SETUP.COM
    b) SETUP.BAT
    c) SETUP.XLS
    d) SETUP.EXE

12. Which Windows 98 registry files contain computer-specific hardware settings?
    a) SETUP.DAT
    b) SYSTEM.DAT
    c) SYSTEM.BAT
    d) USER.DAT

13. Which Windows 98 registry files contain user profile settings?
    a) PROFILE.INI
    b) SYSTEM.DAT
    c) SYSTEM.BAT
    d) USER.DAT

14. Which registry subtree contains global hardware configuration?
    a) HKEY_USERS
    b) HKEY_CURRENT_USER
    c) HKEY_CLASSES_ROOT
    d) HKEY_LOCAL_MACHINE

15. Which registry subtree contains user preferences?
    a) HKEY_USERS
    b) HKEY_CURRENT_USER
    c) HKEY_CLASSES_ROOT
    d) HKEY_LOCAL_MACHINE

16. Which command allows you to backup the registry from the 16-bit real mode (DOS mode)?
    a) REGEDIT
    b) SCANREGW
    c) SCANREG
    d) SCANREG.INI

17. Which term is used to define the capability to install more than one operating system on your computer?
    a) Dual-boot
    b) Partitioning
    c) Formatting
    d) TSR

18. Which hidden startup log file is stored in the root directory and chronologically lists what occurred in the installation process?
    a) DETLOG.TXT
    b) SETUPLOG.TXT
    c) NETLOG.TXT
    d) DETCRASH.LOG

19. Which Control Panel function allows you to install a new software application?
    a) Add New Hardware
    b) Add/Remove Programs
    c) Regional Settings
    d) Printers

20. Which Windows 98 Startup file is located in the WINDOWS\SYSTEM directory and provides support for the GUI environment?
    a) HIMEM.SYS
    b) GUI.SYS
    c) GDI.SYS
    d) WIN.COM

Lab Projects

Unless otherwise indicated, all projects assume the computer is powered on, you are logged in, and your desktop appears on the screen.

Lab Project 1

The goal of this lab is to help you determine system and disk information.

1. To determine CPU type, operating system and version, and RAM capacity, right- click the **My Computer** icon and click **Properties**. The System Properties screen appears with your system information.

2. Record the operating system type and level, the processor type, and RAM.

   _____

3. Click **OK** when complete.

4. In order to determine disk capacity and file system type, double-click **My Computer**. The My Computer screen appears with icons. Note the drive icons.

5. Right-click on the C: drive and then click **Properties**. Make sure the **General** tab is selected. The Properties page for the C: drive appears.

6. Record the used space for drive C:.

   _____

7. Record the free space for drive C:.

   _____

8. Record the file system type for drive C:.

   _____

9. Draw the pie chart representing how the space is used.

10. Insert a floppy in the floppy drive.

11. Repeat steps 6 through 9 for the floppy. Write your answers on a separate piece of paper.

12. Log out.

Lab Project 2

The goal of this lab is to help you understand Task Manager.

1. First you will start a task. Press Start in the lower right-hand corner. Next, click **Run** and in the Open dialog box, type **calc** and press Enter. The calculator program appears on the screen.

2. To see the **calc** task (along with other jobs), press Ctrl + Alt + Del.

3. Record three other tasks.

   _____

4. You can scroll up and down this list and click **End Task** to delete a task. Be careful because ending a task will terminate it and you do not want to terminate a system task.

5. Highlight **calc** and press End Task.

6. Now, see what happens when you remove a system task. Terminate the **explorer** task. Follow the steps that appear on the screen. Hint: The shutdown screen will appear.

7. Record what happens.

   _____

8. Log out.

Lab Project 3

The goal of this project is to associate a file extension with a file type.

1. Click on the **Start** button and point to the **Programs** selection.

2. Point to the **Accessories** option.

3. Click on the **Notepad** menu selection.

4. Type in the following:

   However far modern science and techniques have fallen short of their inherent possibilities, they have taught mankind at least one lesson: Nothing is impossible.
   —Lewis Mumford

5. Click on the **File** menu option.

6. Click on the **Save** option from the drop-down menu.

7. Insert a formatted disk into the floppy (A:) drive.

8. Click on the **down arrow** in the **Save in** textbox.

9. Click on the **3_ Floppy (A:)** option.

10. In the File name text box, type **Junk**.

11. Click on the **Save** button.

12. Click the Notepad application by clicking on the **Close** button (which is a button in the upper right corner with an X).

13. Right-click on the **Start** button.

14. Click on the **Explore** option.

15. Click on the **View** menu option.

16. Click on the **Folder Options** drop-down menu option.

17. Click on the **View** tab in the Folder Options dialog box.

18. If the **Hide file extensions for known file types** check box contains a check mark, click inside the check box to remove the check mark. If the check box is empty, ignore this step.

19. Click on the **OK** button.

20. In the left Explorer window, use the vertical scroll bar to locate the A: drive. Click on the **3_ Floppy (A:)** drive option.

21. Locate the **Junk.txt** file in the right window and double-click on the icon.

22. Record what happened. Did Notepad open with the Junk file open?

_____

23. Close the Notepad application by clicking on the **Close** button (which is a button in the upper right corner with an X).

24. In the right Explorer window, right-click on the **Junk** file name.

25. Click on the **Rename** option. The name of the file, Junk.txt, is highlighted.

26. Type in **junk.abc** and press the **Enter** key. Junk.txt is renamed to junk.abc. A Rename warning box appears stating that if you change a file name extension, the file may become unusable. It also asks, "Are you sure you want to change it?" Click on the **Yes** button.

27. What does the junk.abc file icon look like now?

   _____

28. Double-click on the **junk.abc** file icon.

29. What happened when you double-clicked on the junk.abc file icon?

   _____

30. In the Choose the program you want to use section, scroll down until you reach the Notepad icon. Click on the **Notepad** icon and then click on the **OK** button.

31. What happened when you clicked on the OK button?

   _____

32. In the Notepad application, click on the **File** menu option. Then click on **New** from the drop-down menu.

33. Type in the following:

   Technology is dominated by two types of people: Those who understand what they do not manage, and those who manage what they do not understand.
   —Source Unknown

34. Click on the **File** menu option.

35. Click on the **Save** option from the drop-down menu.

36. Click on the **down arrow** in the **Save in** text box.

37. Click on the **3_ Floppy (A:)** option.

38. In the File name text box, type **Junk2**.

39. Click on the **Save** button.

40. Close the Notepad application by clicking on the **Close** button (which is a button in the upper right corner with an X).

41. Using Explorer, rename the **Junk2.txt** file to **Junk2.abc**. Notice the file icon after the change.

42. How is the JUNK2.ABC icon different from before?

   _____

43. Double-click on the **Junk2.abc** icon.

44. What happened when you double-clicked on the Junk2.abc icon?

   _____

Lab Project 4

The goal of this project is to help you understand how to create a tree structure from a screenshot.

1. Using Windows Explorer, create the following tree structure in Figure 4.13 on your floppy. To get to Explorer, right-click Start and then click Explore.

Figure 4.13: A Sample Tree Hierarchy

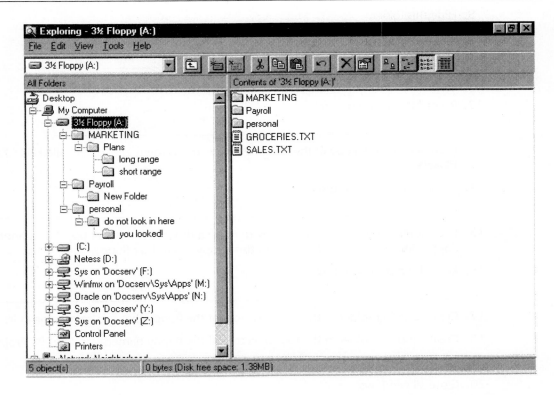

2. Using Notepad, create the following files as Text Documents in the **long range** folder. Place your name in each file.
   Monday.txt
   Tuesday.txt
   Wednesday.txt
   Thursday.txt
   Friday.txt

3. Record the steps you took to create them.

4. Rename the **New Folder** to **Weekly**.

5. Record the steps you took.

_____

6. Create a **Medium Range** folder in **Plans**.

7. Record the steps you took.

_____

8. In the **personal** folder, create a file called **resume.txt**.

9. Hide this folder.

10. Record the steps you took.

_____

11. View all files.

12. Record the steps you took.

_____

13. Make a complete copy of the files in **Plans** and put them in a folder called **BACKUP of PLANS**.

14. Record the steps you took.

_____

15. In Explorer, right-click on the floppy to make a disk copy of the floppy. Insert another floppy disk and make a disk copy of this floppy to another floppy.

16. Record the steps you took.

_____

17. Create another folder in the root directory of the floppy that has your name in it.

18. Create another folder in the root directory of the floppy named Windows 98 Project 4.

19. Show your instructor.

20. Close all windows.

Lab Project 5

The goal of this project is to reinforce your understanding of how to create a tree structure. You will also work with attributes to help you understand how they work.

1. Using Windows Explorer, create the following tree structure in Figure 4.14 on your floppy.

Figure 4.14: A Sample Tree Hierarchy

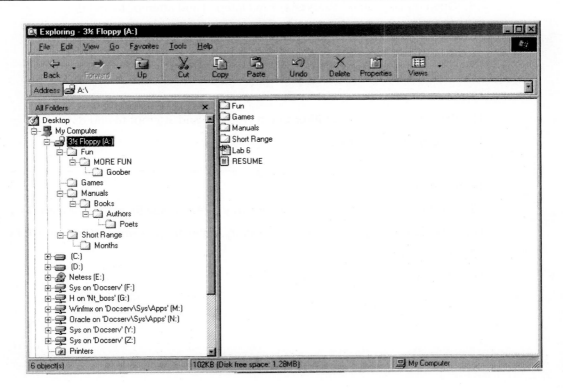

1. Using Notepad, place these files in the **Poets** folder:
   Poe.txt
   Walker.txt
   Smith.txt

2. In Explorer, click **View**, then **Folder Options**, and then **View**. The **Folder Options** window opens. In the **Advanced Settings** box, activate the setting so hidden and system files are not displayed.

3. Right-click on **Poe.txt** and click **Properties**. The Properties page appears. Click **Hidden** and then click **OK**. The files are hidden.

4. In Explorer, click **View**, then **Folder Options**, and then **View**. The **Folder Options** window opens. In the **Advanced Settings** box, activate the setting to show all files. This will display hidden files.

5. Record whether or not you can now see **Poe.txt**.

_____

6. Using the previous step as a guide, make the file **Walker.txt** read-only.

7. Record the steps you took.

_____

8. Open the file named **Walker.txt** in Notepad and attempt to add data.

9. Record what occurred.

_____

10. Close Notepad.

11. Make **Walker.txt** readable.

12. Open the file named **Walker.txt** in Notepad and attempt to add data.

13. Record what occurred.

_____

14. Close Notepad.

15. Create another folder in the root directory of the floppy that has your name in it.

16. Create another folder in the root directory of the floppy named **Windows 98 Project 5**.

17. Show your instructor.

18. Close all windows.

Lab Project 6 (Caution!)

The goal of this project is to familiarize you with the REGEDIT registry editing utility.

CAUTION: Editing the registry can cause your computer to run erratically, or not run at all! When performing any registry editing, follow ALL directions carefully, including spelling, syntax use, etc. Failure to do so may cause your computer to fail. _Ask your instructor for permission before proceeding!_

1. From the Start menu, choose **Run**, type **REGEDIT**, and click **OK**. The REGEDIT utility opens.

2. In the left window, expand **HKEY_LOCAL_MACHINE, Hardware**, and **Description, System, CentralProcessor**, and then select the **0** folder.

3. In the right window, the **Identifier** and **VendorIdentifier** information display.

4. Record the CPU identifier.

_____

5. In the left window, expand **HKEY_LOCAL_MACHINE, Software**, and **Microsoft**.

6. List three Microsoft applications loaded under the Microsoft folder.

7. In the left window, expand **HKEY_USERS, .DEFAULT, Control Panel, Appearance**, and then select the **Schemes** folder.

8. Name three schemes available to be chosen from the Display control panel as listed in the right window.

9. When finished viewing the information, close the **REGEDIT** utility.

Lab Project 7

The goal of this project is to use the Windows 98 Registry Checker utility to back up the registry.

1. Click on the **Start** button.

2. Point to the **Programs** option.

3. Point to the **Accessories** option.

4. Point to the **System Tools** option.

5. Click on the **System Information** option. The Microsoft System Information window opens.

6. Click on the **Tools** menu option and select **Registry Checker**. The Registry Checker tool opens. Click on the **Yes** button. A window appears with a message that the backup was successful. Click on the **OK** button.

7. Notice the system data and time by double-clicking on the time display on the taskbar. Write the system date and time in the space below.

   _____

8. Using Windows Explorer, locate the WINDOWS\SYSBCKUP folder. In the left Explorer window, click on the **WINDOWS\SYSBCKUP** folder.

9. In the right window, locate the RB000.CAB, RB001.CAB, RB002.CAB, RB003.CAB, and RB004.CAB files.

10. Right-click on each of these file icons and determine when the backup file was created.

11. Record the backup file name that was used to manually back up the registry.

    _____

12. Close the **System Information** window.

Lab Project 8

The goal of this project is to install an updated driver under the Windows 98 operating system. You will need the latest Windows 98 driver for the hardware device.

Note: The installation process outlined below may differ due to computer differences. If the process is different, follow the directions on the screen. Contact your instructor or a lab assistant if you are unsure of the step.

1. Turn the computer on and verify that the operating system loads. If necessary, log in to Windows 98 using the userid and password provided by the instructor or lab assistant.

2. Click on the **Start** button, point to **Settings**, and click on the **Control Panel** menu option.

3. When the Control Panel window opens, scroll down to the **System** icon and double-click on it.

4. Click on the **Device Manager** button.

5. Click on the **+ (plus sign)** beside the class of device you want to upgrade.

6. Right-click on the specific device you want to upgrade.

7. Click on the **Properties** option.

8. Click on the **Driver** tab.

9. Click on the **Update Driver** button. The Upgrade Device Driver wizard appears.

10. Click on the **Next** button.

11. Click on the **Display a list of the drivers in a specific location, so you can select the driver you want** radio button. Click on the **Next** button.

12. Click on the **Have Disk** button.

13. Insert the media that contains your updated driver into the floppy drive, CD-ROM, or DVD drive.

14. In the **Copy manufacturer's files from** box, type in the drive letter for the device that contains the updated driver followed by a colon and click on the **OK** button. An example of a driver device is A:. The Browse button can be used to locate a device driver as well.

15. Click on the **Next** button and follow the instructions on the screen to complete the upgrade.

Lab Project 9

The goal of this project is to use the Windows 98 System Information tool to troubleshoot device conflicts.

1. Turn on the computer and verify that Windows 98 loads.

2. If necessary, log on to Windows 98 using the userid and password provided by the instructor or lab assistant.

3. Click on the **Start** button and point to the **Accessories** and **System Tools** selections.

4. Click on the **System Information** option. If the System Information item is not highlighted, click on it.

5. Record the percentage of free system resources.

   _____

6. Click on the + (**plus sign**) next to the **Hardware Resources** item.

7. Click on the **Conflicts/Sharing** item.

8. Are any devices sharing an IRQ (for Interrupt Request)? If so, list two that are sharing an IRQ and the IRQ they are sharing.

   _____

9. Click on the **IRQs** item located under the Hardware Resources folder in the left window.

10. List any IRQ that is available for use by a new device.

    _____

11. Click on the **Memory** item located under the Hardware Resources folder in the left window.

12. List one memory address range used by a device.

    _____

13. In the left window, click on the + (**plus sign**) next to the **Components** item.

14. In the left window, click on the **Problem Devices** item. Any devices with hardware conflicts are listed in the right window. Keep in mind that you use the Device Manager program to correct any problems with resource allocation.

15. Record whether any devices have conflicts. If a device conflict exists, record the devices in conflict.

    _____

16. Close the System Information window by clicking on the **Close** button (the one with the X) in the upper right corner of the window.

Lab Project 10

The goal of this project is to create a boot disk that can be used when the computer does not boot properly. You will need a blank floppy disk.

1. Click on the **Start** button.

2. Point to the **Settings** option.

3. Click on the **Control Panel** option.

4. Double-click on the **Add/Remove Programs** control panel.

5. Click on the **Startup disk** tab.

6. Click on the **Create disk** button. The Insert Disk window opens. Insert a floppy disk into the A: drive. Click on the **OK** button.

7. Record when you think the startup disk would be useful.

_____

8. When the boot disk is created, use Explorer to examine the contents of the disk, the items in the AUTOEXEC.BAT file, and the items in the CONFIG.SYS file.

9. Does the CONFIG.SYS include commands for CD-ROM support? How do you know?

_____

Lab Project 11

The goal of this project is to use Windows 98 tools effectively when problems occur. Dr. Watson, System File Checker, and Registry Checker should be installed.

1. Click on the **Start** button, point to the **Accessories** and **System Tools** option, and click on the **System Information** selection.

2. Click on the **Tools** menu item and select the **Dr. Watson**. A new icon appears on the right end of the taskbar next to the clock icon.

3. Double-click on the **Dr. Watson** taskbar icon. Dr. Watson records a snapshot of the system. The Diagnosis tab displays any problems found during the analysis.

4. Click on the **View** menu item and select **Advanced view**. Ten tabs appear across the top.

5. Click on the **System** tab. The System tab shows an overall view of the computer including operating system version, amount of RAM installed, amount of resources available, amount of free space for the swap file, etc.

6. How much RAM does the computer have?

   _____

7. Click on the **Startup** tab. The Startup tab shows the applications that run every time the computer boots.

8. List three applications that load when the computer boots as found on the Startup tab.

9. Click on the **MS-DOS Drivers** tab. The MS-DOS Drivers screen displays a list of 16-bit drivers that load when the computer boots.

10. List three MS-DOS drivers.

    _____

11. Close the Dr. Watson tool by clicking on the **OK** button. Notice that the Dr. Watson utility is still active because the icon is still located on the taskbar. Right-click on the **Dr. Watson** icon located on the taskbar. Select the **Exit Dr. Watson** item. Dr. Watson closes.

12. Click on the **Microsoft System Information** button located on the taskbar. The Microsoft System Information window reappears on the screen.

13. Click on the **Tools** menu item and select the **System File Checker** option. The System File Checker window opens.

14. Ensure the **Scan for altered files** radio button is selected and click on the **Start** button. The system takes about a minute to scan the system files. When the scan is finished, a message displays. Click on the **OK** button. Click on the **Close** button to exit from the System File Checker window.

15. Click on the **Tools** menu item and select the **System File Checker** option again.

16. Click on the **Settings** button. The Settings window allows you to customize how the System File Checker tool works by allowing you to add or remove files to be checked,

prompt before restoring system files, determine the default location for the good system files are stored, etc.

17. Click on the **View Log** button on the Settings tab. You may be prompted that the file is too big for Notepad and asked if it is okay to open the document in WordPad. If so, click on the **Yes** button. The default name of the log file is SFCLOG.TXT and it is stored in the WINDOWS folder by default. Close the **SFCLOG.TXT** file window.

18. Click on the **Search Criteria** tab. The Search Criteria tab lists files and folders that are checked through the System File Checker tool.

19. Locate the folder that contains the Windows 98 operating system (normally C:\WINDOWS). Are subfolders located in the WINDOWS folder checked by the System File Checker tool?

_____

20. Click on the **Advanced** tab. The Advanced tab is where you can define the verification data file's default location.

21. What is the default location for the verification data file?

_____

22. Click on the **Cancel** button to leave the System File Checker Settings window. Click on the **Close** button to exit the System File Checker utility.

23. Click on the **Close** button to exit the Microsoft System Information window.

Lab Project 12 Challenge

The goal of this project challenge is to install Windows 98 on a computer that does not have an operating system or one on which the old operating system will be replaced (removed). You will need a Windows 98 CD, a blank floppy disk, and a computer with a formatted hard drive. You can refer to Chapter 3 for a discussion on partitioning and formatting your hard disk. The installation process outlined below may differ due to computer differences. If the process is different, follow the directions on the screen. Contact your instructor or a lab assistant if you are unsure of the step.

1. Insert the Windows 98 setup disk into the floppy drive and boot the computer. The Startup menu appears.

2. Insert the Windows 98 CD into the CD-ROM and type **1** and press the **Enter** key.

3. At the prompt, type **x:setup**, where **x:** is the drive letter of the device containing the Windows 98 CD, and press **Enter.**

4. A message appears that ScanDisk is going to be performed. After the ScanDisk check, press the **X** key.

5. The Welcome to Windows 98 Setup screen appears. Click on the **Continue** button.

6. The licensing agreement appears on the screen. Read the agreement and click on the **I accept the Agreement** radio button and click the **Next** button. The Product Key window appears.

7. Enter the product key provided by the instructor or lab assistant, or located on the registration certificate or CD case. Click the **Next** button to continue. The Select Directory window appears.

8. The default Windows 98 folder is C:\WINDOWS. Contact the instructor or lab assistant to see if the default or a different drive/folder is to be used. If a different drive/folder is to be used, click on the **Other directory** radio button and click **Next.** If the default directory is to be used, simply click on the **Next** button. The Preparing Directory screen appears.

9. What is the path where Windows 98 is to be installed?

10. Setup checks the computers hardware and then displays the Setup Options screen. The default is Typical. Ensure the **Typical** radio button is selected and click on the **Next** button.

11. The User Information window appears. Type a name and a company in the text boxes and click on the **Next** button.

12. The Windows Components window appears. Ensure the **Install the most common components** radio button is selected and click on the **Next** button.

13. When the Identification screen appears, contact an instructor or lab assistant for the Name and Workgroup. The computer name must be unique and can be up to 15 characters. Spaces are not allowed. The workgroup name must be the same for all computers on the same network (if the computer is networked) and can be up to 15 characters; spaces are not allowed.

14. What computer name and workgroup name is to be used on this computer? Fill in the information below:

    Computer name _____

    Workgroup name _____

15. The Establishing Your Location window appears. Select the appropriate country and click on the **Next** button.

16. The Startup Disk screen appears. Click on the **Next** button. A prompt appears; insert the blank floppy disk into the A: drive and click on the **OK** button.

17. The Start Copying Files window appears. Click on the **Next** button and the Windows 98 files are copied to the computer hard drive. After copying, you are prompted to restart the computer.

18. Click on the **Restart Now** button. After the computer reboots, Windows 98 configures hardware and restarts again. The Welcome to Windows 98 screen appears.

Internet Discovery

Internet Discovery Lab 1

The goal of this lab is to obtain specific information on the Internet regarding Windows 98.

1. What is the URL for the Microsoft Windows 98 on-line help?

2. Locate a magazine article on the Internet that describes how to automatically log a user into a Windows 98 computer.

3. Locate a description of IRQ steering on the Internet and write the URL and basic description in the space below.

4. Find three different locations on the Internet that have the *Microsoft Windows 98 Resource Kit* book for sale. Find the lowest price on these three sites. Write the cost and the site in the space below.

_____

_____

_____

_____

_____

_____

_____

_____

_____

_____

_____

_____

_____

_____

_____

_____

5. Locate a site on the Internet that has Windows 98 troubleshooting tips that is not the Microsoft web site. Write the URL of this location in the space below.

6. At the Frank Condron's World O'Windows web site, he has Easter eggs listed for Windows 98. What panel is used to discover the Windows 98 Easter egg?

Soft Skills: Help Desk Support

1. A customer calls you in the middle of the night and is attempting to install Windows 98 on a PC that crashed. The PC had been running Windows 98. It seems that the boot sector is infected with a virus. What do you tell the customer?
2. A user from Accounting e-mails you about installing a printer. What steps do you give them to install this printer?
3. You receive a call from a user interested in setting up a dual-boot PC. How do you tell the user to proceed?

Critical Thinking

1. How do viruses infect Windows 98?
2. Compare and contrast a DLL file, a DRV file, and a CAB file.
3. When would you use System Monitor?
4. Explain how dual-booting works.

Have You Done Your Homework?

Homework is work but it can be fun because you are learning valuable skills. The only way you can really learn a technical topic such as operating systems is by doing the homework assignments and lab projects.

- Are you doing all of your homework? You should complete all homework assignments as soon as you can once they are assigned. This way, the material is still fresh in you brain and you'll tend to remember it better.
- Are you doing your homework in a quiet place? You should complete your homework where you can be free of outside noises. Don't play the radio, television, or your favorite music CD while you study. If necessary, go to the library because it'll be quiet there.
- Do you have a complex problem that you can't answer? If you get stuck on a problem, look for a similar situation in the textbook or your notes. Instructors will often choose problems for homework assignments that are similar in nature to ones that have already been discussed.
- Try to work through problems before asking another person. If you figure it out, it will build your confidence in the material. If you still run into trouble, ask your study partner or your instructor.
- Store you homework in a separate three-ring binder for later access. This will be a good source of information for test preparation.

Self-Study Question(s)

1. Have you done your homework today?
2. Identify at least one problem you had trouble answering and list the steps as they relate to the above Study Skills that helped you figure out the problem.

5

Chapter 5
Introduction to
Microsoft
Windows NT

OBJECTIVES

The goal of this chapter is twofold:
- To introduce you to Windows NT.
- To help you prepare and pass the following sections of the A+ Operating System Technologies Exam:

$A+$ Operating System Technologies Exam Objectives
covered in this chapter (and corresponding page numbers)

1.2 Identify the names, locations, purposes, and contents of major system files.

Domain 2 Installation, Configuration and Upgrading

2.1 Identify the procedure for installing Windows 9.x/Me, Windows NT 4.0 Workstation, Windows 2000 Professional, and Windows XP and bringing the operating system to a basic operational level.

2.2 Identify steps to perform an operating system upgrade from Windows 9.x/Me, Windows NT 4.0 Workstation, Windows 2000 Professional, and Windows XP. Given an upgrade scenario, choose the appropriate next steps.

Domain 3 Diagnosing and Troubleshooting

In this chapter, you will complete the following sections:
- 5.1 Understanding Microsoft Windows NT
- 5.2 Managing Files and Folders
- 5.3 Understanding NTFS Compression
- 5.4 Understanding the Windows NT Registry
- 5.5 Understanding the Pre-Installation Steps of Windows NT
- 5.6 Understanding How to Install and Upgrade Windows NT Workstation
- 5.7 Troubleshooting the Windows NT Installation
- 5.8 Configuring Windows NT Workstation
- 5.9 Understanding the Boot Process
- 5.10 Understanding Task Manager, Event Viewer, and Windows NT Diagnostics
- 5.11 Troubleshooting a Service that Does Not Start
- 5.12 Monitoring System Performance

5.1 Understanding Microsoft Windows NT

Microsoft created NT Workstation for business computers operating in a networked environment. There are actually two major versions of NT: NT Server and NT Workstation. This chapter covers NT Workstation because it is on the A+ exam.

NT Workstation has two versions: Windows NT 3.5.1 and Windows NT 4.0. NT Workstation 4.0 offers many enhancements to prior operating systems such as Window NT Workstation 3.5.1, Windows 3.x, Windows 95, and Windows 98. The NT Workstation enhancements are listed below.

- More efficient use of memory than NT Workstation 3.5.1.
- Improved graphics performance.
- True 32-bit operating system.
- Supports SMP (Symmetric Multiprocessing), which is the ability to run multiple processes on multiple CPUs.
- Better network security.
- Support of long file names.
- More reliable than Windows 3.x and Windows 95.
- Better application reliability.
- NT can be installed on **RISC (Reduced Instruction Set Computer)** systems as well as **CISC (Complex Instruction Set Computer)** systems.

RISC computers have fewer instructions (or reduced) in their instruction set than CISC computers. Because RISC computers have fewer instructions, they rely on additional hardware to perform the operations lacking from the instruction set. This makes them faster yet more expensive. Your PC is a CISC system. IBM makes a RISC system called an IBM RS (RISC System) 6000. It operates a version of the UNIX operating system. The UNIX operating system will be discussed in Chapter 8.

The file systems NT Workstation 4 supports are FAT16 (File Allocation Table) and NTFS (New Technology File System). For CD media, NT Workstation supports **CDFS (Compact Disk File System)**. NT Workstation 4 does not support DVD (Digital Versatile Disk) media.

When NT Workstation boots, a log-in screen appears. A user can log in to a network server or the user can log in locally to the local workstation. After logging in, the desktop appears. The **desktop** is the area where all work is performed. The desktop is the interface between you and the applications, files, and computer hardware. The desktop is part of a **GUI (Graphical User Interface)** environment. Figure 5.1 shows the NT Workstation desktop.

Figure 5.1: Windows NT Workstation Desktop

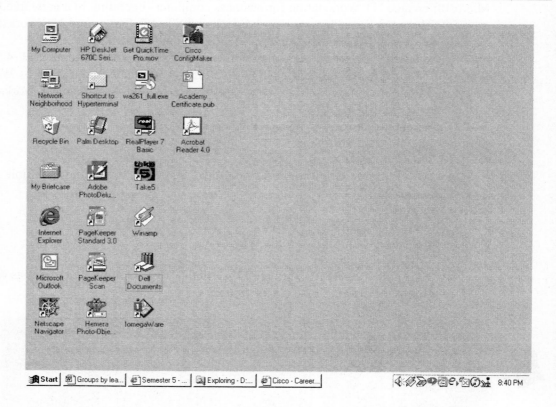

On the desktop are icons. **Icons** are graphics that can represent applications, files, the computer and its hardware devices, and shared network resources. In Figure 5.1, examples of icons include the My Computer icon, the Network Neighborhood icon, and the Recycle Bin icon. The desktop can be modified to have a background or desktop pattern. This can include a graphic or a specific color.

Let's go through a short exercise to help you understand how to maintain an uncluttered Windows NT desktop. In this exercise, you will work with the **Auto Arrange** option to force your icons on your desktop to be automatically arranged towards the left hand side of the desktop. When you attempt to relocate an icon, it will automatically be arranged back to its original position—on the left hand side of the desktop. It is assumed that Windows NT is installed and running on a computer with the Windows NT desktop displayed on your screen and you are logged in.

1. Right-click on a blank desktop space. Once a menu appears, point to the **Arrange Icons** option. If the **Auto Arrange** option does have a check mark beside it, click on an **empty portion of the desktop** to cancel because Auto Arrange is already in use. If

the **Auto Arrange** option does not have a check mark beside it, click on the **Auto Arrange** option to add the check mark and enable **Auto Arrange** capability.

2. Note the position of the icons on the desktop.

3. Click on the **My Documents** icon and while continuing to hold the mouse button down, drag the icon to the center of the screen. You will see that the **My Documents** icon moves to its original position.

4. Click on the **Recycle Bin** icon and while continuing to hold the mouse button down, drag the icon to the top right portion of the screen. This icon moves to its original position too.

5. Right-click on a **blank desktop space.** A menu appears.

6. Using step 1 as a guide, set Auto Arrange back to its original setting.

Notice in Figure 5.1 how part of the desktop includes the Start button and the taskbar. The **Start button,** located in the lower left corner of the desktop, is the most commonly used desktop item. The Start button is used to access applications, files, help, and utilities.

The **taskbar** is the bar that runs across the bottom of the desktop. The taskbar holds buttons that represent applications or files currently loaded into memory. The taskbar also holds icons that allow access to system tools. These tools can include an icon for changing or viewing the date and time, a speaker icon for adjusting speaker volume control, and an icon for a virus utility. In Figure 5.1, the files currently loaded into memory and displayed on the taskbar as a button are a Word document called **Groups by lea...**, an Internet Explorer session opened to **Semester5...**, the Explorer application as shown by the **Exploring-D...** button, and another Internet Explorer session opened to **Cisco-Career....** On the right portion of the taskbar in Figure 5.1 is the speaker icon, which is used to adjust speaker volume.

Other common desktop icons include My Computer, Internet Explorer, Network Neighborhood, and Recycle Bin. The **My Computer** desktop icon is used to access hardware, software, applications, and files located on or in the computer. To use the My Computer icon, simply move the mouse pointer to the icon and double-click on it. The same is true for all desktop icons.

The **Internet Explorer** icon is used to start the Internet Explorer application. The **Network Neighborhood** icon only appears if the computer has a network card installed and is used to display and access all networked computers and networked devices in your workgroup or domain. The **Recycle Bin** is used to hold files and folders that the user deletes. When a file or folder is deleted, it is not immediately discarded; instead, it goes to the Recycle Bin. Once a file or folder is in the Recycle Bin, it can be removed. This is similar to the fact that a piece of trash can be retrieved from an office trash can.

Let's go through an exercise to help you understand how to modify or view your desktop appearance on Windows NT. It is assumed that Windows NT is installed and running on a computer with the Windows NT desktop displayed on your screen and you are logged in.

1. Right-click on an **empty desktop area.** A menu appears.

2. Click on the **Properties** option. The Display Properties window appears. (Note: this screen can also be accessed by clicking on the **Start** button, pointing to the **Settings** option, clicking on the **Control Panel** option, and double-clicking on the **Display** control panel icon.)
3. Click on the **Background** tab. This tab controls how the background color and pattern appears.
4. To change your wallpaper to the **WINNT** option, click on the **WINNT** option.
5. Click on the **Apply** button.
6. To view the **Appearance** tab settings, click on the **Appearance** tab at the top of the window. This tab controls the color scheme and size of the letters. This tab is good to use when people with vision problems need adjustments.
7. Click Cancel to close the window.

An operating system specialist must remember that the files and folders in the Recycle Bin take up hard drive space and that users often forget to empty the files and folders from the Recycle Bin.

5.2 Managing Files and Folders

Managing files and folders is an important part of NT Workstation. You must be able to create, delete, and move files and folders regularly. The easiest way to learn about files and folders is to start with the drive letter. A drive letter followed by a colon represents every drive in the computer. The first floppy drive in a system receives the drive letter A:. The first hard drive partition gets the drive letter C:. Other partitions receive consecutive drive letters (D:, E:, F:, etc.), usually before other devices.

Computer drives hold files and folders. A **file** is an electronic container that holds data or computer code. An example of a file is NT CHAPTER.DOC. A **folder** holds files and can also contain other folders. This is similar to an office folder that has memos and paper documents as well as other folders. A folder was called a **directory** in older DOS operating systems.

In DOS, in addition to naming a file or a folder, you frequently would have to add an extension to a file name. An **extension** is part of the file name and it can be up to three characters in length. The extension is separated from the first part of the file name by a period (.). Most people consider the extension to be part of the file name. An example of a file name (with an extension) is NTCHAP.DOC where *.DOC* is the extension. The good part about extensions today is that the applications normally add an extension automatically to the end of a file name. In most windows, NT Workstation does not automatically show the extensions.

Next, you will perform an exercise to help you understand how to view extensions on Windows NT. It is assumed that Windows NT is installed and running on a computer with the Windows NT desktop displayed on your screen and you are logged in.

1. Right-click Start and click Explore. Windows Explorer opens.

2. To view the extensions in Windows NT Explorer, click on the **View** menu option.
3. Click on the **Folder Options** menu option. Click on the **View** tab and click on the **Hide file extensions for known file types** check box (which will remove the check from the box).
4. Click on the **Apply** button. Windows Explorer displays the extension for all files.
5. Close Explorer.

When NT Workstation recognizes an extension, it associates that extension with a particular application. This means that NT Workstation assigns a known graphical icon to that file. Extensions work the same as they do in Windows 98 so you can refer to Chapter 4 for a discussion of extensions.

File names in NT Workstation can be up to 255 characters. These extended file names are commonly called **long file names**. Folder names and file names can have all characters, numbers, letters, and spaces except for the following:

/ (forward slash) " (quotation marks) \ (backslash)
| (vertical bar) ? (question mark) : (colon)
* (asterisk)

An example of an NT Workstation long file name is NT WORKSTATION CHAPTER.DOC. Any time a document has been saved with one of these long file names and is taken to an older computer with an operating system that does not support long file names, the file name is shortened to a maximum of eight characters. Windows does this by using the first six characters of the file name, deleting any spaces, and using two special characters—a tilde (~) and a number. For example, NT WORKSTATION CHAPTER.DOC would be shortened to NTWORK~1.DOC. If there were two files named NT WORKSTATION CHAPTER.DOC and NT WORKSTATION INDEX.DOC, the two files would be saved as NTWORK~1.DOC and NTWORK~2.DOC, respectively.

Any time a file is saved on a disk, the reference for what drive and folder the file is saved to is known as the file's **path.** A path is like a roadmap of how to get to the file. An example of an NT path is as follows: C:\MY Documents\A+ Book\NT WORKSTATION CHAPTER.DOC

To understand a path statement, look at the items in small chunks. In the previous example, C: is the drive letter where the document is stored. The C: represents the first hard drive partition. The name of the document is always at the very end of the path. In the example given, the name of the document is **NT WORKSTATION CHAPTER.DOC**. Everything in the middle of these two items is the name of the folders one must go through to find the NT WORKSTATION CHAPTER.DOC file.

For example, the first folder listed in the example is **My Documents**. The My Documents folder is on the C: drive and is separated from the drive letter by a backslash (\). The next folder (which is a subfolder within the My Documents folder) is called **A+**

Book. The **A+ Book** folder is separated from the parent folder (My Documents) by another backslash (\). The A+ Book folder is also separated from the name of the document by a backslash (\).

NT Workstation comes with an application called Windows NT Explorer. **Windows NT Explorer** is the most common application used to copy or move files and folders. Figure 5.2 shows Windows NT Explorer. You can see how the document A+ Book hardware from Pagemaker.doc looks.

Figure 5.2: Windows NT Explorer

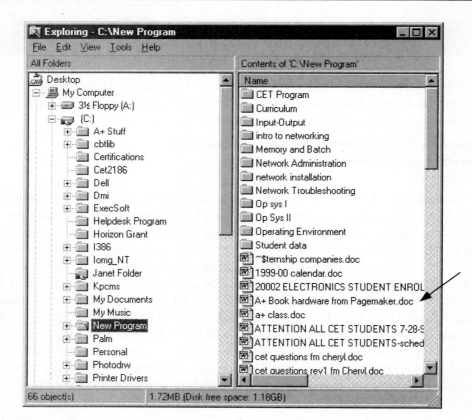

The My Computer desktop icon can be used in a similar fashion to copy or move files and folders. Even though the graphical form is nice, you must thoroughly understand a file's path written in long format. Frequently, technical directions, advisories, support documents, etc., have the path written in long format, such as the example given earlier.

My Computer and NT Explorer can be used for setting attributes for a file or folder. The file and folder attributes are read-only, hidden, archive, and system. The **read-only attribute** marks a file or folder so that it cannot be changed. The **hidden attribute** marks a file or folder so that it is not visible through My Computer or NT Explorer, unless someone changes the default view for the window. Some applications use the **archive attribute** to control which files or folders are backed up. The **system attribute** is placed on certain files used to boot NT Workstation.

Let's perform an exercise to help you understand a file's attributes. It is assumed that Windows NT is installed and running on a computer with the Windows NT desktop displayed on your screen and you are logged in.

1. Insert your floppy in the floppy drive.
2. Click the **Start** button, point to the **Programs** option, and click on the **Windows NT Explorer**.
3. Click the icon associated with the floppy.
4. To create a file, click **File**, click **New,** and then click **New Text Document**. The name of the text document appears as **New Text Document**. Press Enter to keep this name.
5. To set the file's attributes, right-click the new text document and click **Properties**. The Properties window for the file opens.
6. In the **Attributes** section of the page, check **Read-only** and click **OK**. The Properties window closes.
7. Next, you will attempt to modify the file. Remember it is set to read-only. Double-click the document. The document opens.
8. On the document screen, type your name and press Enter. This is considered text.
9. Attempt to save the document. Click **File** and then click **Save**. The **Save As** window opens. Normally, this window does not appear—the file is simply saved. However, because the file has the read-only attribute, you cannot save the text to this file. Windows NT wants you to enter a new file name.
10. To see the error message, click **Save**. A message is displayed indicating you cannot save this file.
11. Click **OK** and then click **Cancel**. The document screen remains.
12. Close the document. Do not save changes if prompted.
13. Close Windows Explorer.

5.3 Understanding NTFS Compression

NT Workstation can use the NTFS and FAT16 file systems. In the NTFS file system, file and folder compression are supported. In NT Workstation, when you click on an NTFS compressed file, the file automatically uncompresses. After all work on the file is complete, the file recompresses when it is saved or the document is closed. Even though a compressed file or folder takes less space on the hard drive, the file or folder takes longer to access when it is compressed. Each file and folder in NTFS has a compression state of either compressed or uncompressed. Just because a folder is in a compressed state, does not mean that all files in the folder are compressed.

 Think of compression as "squeezing" redundant data from file and creating a new smaller file. The smaller file will take up less room so you save disk space.

Let's run through a short exercise to help you understand compression. It is assumed that Windows NT is installed and running on a computer with the Windows NT desktop displayed on your screen and you are logged in.

1. Insert your floppy in the floppy drive.
2. Click the **Start** button, point to the **Programs** option, and click on the **Windows NT Explorer**.
3. Right-click **Start** and then click **Explore**. Windows Explorer opens with left and right windowpanes.
4. Click the icon associated with the floppy.
5. Right-click the document you created earlier: **New Text Document**. The Properties window for the file opens.
6. Click once in the **Compressed** check box.
7. Close Windows NT Explorer.

The compression on Windows NT Workstation can only be accomplished if the partition has been formatted as NTFS—not FAT16.

The operating system version is important to you when troubleshooting a computer. With NT Workstation, upgrades or patches to the operating system are provided with service packs. A **service pack** contains fixes for known operating system problems. Some application installation requirements list the minimum service pack that has to be installed before the software will install and/or operate properly. There are several ways to determine what version and service pack are installed with NT Workstation. They are listed below.

• When NT Workstation boots and the blue screen appears, the version and service pack level display.
• Click on the **Start** button. Click on the **Run** option. In the **Open** text box, type **WINVER** and press **Enter.**
• Open Windows NT Explorer. Click on the **Help** menu item. Click on the **About** option. The version appears.

5.4 Understanding the Windows NT Registry

With NT Workstation, every hardware and software configuration is stored in a database called the **registry.** The registry contains such things as folder and file property settings, application preferences and settings, driver files, environment settings, and user profiles. A **user profile** is all settings associated with a specific user including what application the user has access to, desktop settings, and the user's network configuration. The registry loads into RAM during the boot process. As changes are made to the computer's hardware and software settings, the registry updates continuously.

Be careful when modifying the Windows NT registry. You could make a change that could render your system useless. Because most of the things you do on the system ultimately change the registry, when in doubt, simply use the graphical method to change a setting.

The registry consists of five subtrees. Subtrees are also called branches or hives. In Chapter 4, which covered Windows 98, you learned that **subtrees** are like folders and are also sometimes called hives. Think of the hive as a collection of folders. The five standard subtrees are HKEY_LOCAL_MACHINE, HKEY_USERS, HKEY_CURRENT_USER, KEY_CURRENT_CONFIG, and HKEY_CLASSES_ROOT. Each of the subtrees has keys and subkeys containing values.

The registry can contain other subtrees depending on what software (applications, device drivers, or services) are added to the computer. A **service** is a process running on NT that provides a specific function to the computer. Examples of services include: DHCP (Dynamic Host Configuration Protocol) client, computer browser, event log, net logon, and remote access connection manager.

DHCP is a service that allows computers on a network to obtain an IP address. The computers need an IP address to access the Internet.

The registry is located in the %SYSTEMROOT%\SYSTEM32\CONFIG folder, where %SYSTEMROOT% is the boot partition and the name of the folder under the folder where NT Workstation is installed (normally C:\WINNT). Table 5.1 lists the five major subtrees and the function of each.

Table 5.1: Windows NT Workstation Registry Subtrees

Registry Subtree	Function
HKEY_LOCAL_MACHINE	Holds global hardware configuration. Included in the branch is a list of hardware components installed in the computer, the software drivers that handle each component, and the settings for each device. This information is not user-specific.
HKEY_USERS	Keeps track of individual users and their preferences.
HKEY_CURRENT_USER	Holds a specific user's configuration such as software settings, how the desktop appears, and what folders the user has created.

HKEY_CURRENT_CONFIG	Holds information about the hardware profile that is used when the computer first boots.
HKEY_CLASSES_ROOT	Holds file associations and file links. The information held here is what allows the correct application to start when you double-click on a file name in Explorer or My Computer (provided the file extension is registered).

Editing the NT Workstation Registry

Most changes to the registry are accomplished through the various control panels, but some changes can only be done through the registry editor. By default, only users who log on as the Administrator user can edit the registry, but all users can view the registry. Before making changes to the registry, make sure you make a backup of the registry.

With Windows NT, users log on using a user account. The user account with the greatest control over the computer is called **Administrator**. The Administrator user can do just about anything. For example, if you are logged on as this user, you can add other users, add groups, add and remove hardware, and perform other system administration functions. Microsoft distinguishes between a local Administrator user account and a network Administrator user account. A local user account exists on the local system (or the one you are logging on to). A network user account exists on a server. An example of Microsoft server is a computer that is installed with Microsoft Windows NT Server. Its purpose it to "serve" resources to client computers; Windows NT Workstation could be the client it serves.

NT Workstation ships with two registry editors—**REGEDIT** and **REGEDT32.** Either editor can be used to change the registry. For most technicians, it is simply a matter of which view he or she prefers. However, there are some differences between the two. Table 5.2 shows some of the more important differences.

Table 5.2: REGEDIT and REGEDT32 Differences

REGEDIT	*REGEDT32*
Provides more powerful search capabilities.	Can display and edit values larger than 256 characters.
All of the subtrees are shown in one window.	The subtrees are shown in individual windows.
Allows exporting the registry to a text file.	Can look at and apply access permissions to the subtrees, keys, and subkeys.
Allows importing the registry from the command line.	Can work with multiple registry files simultaneously.

Backing Up and Restoring the NT Workstation Registry

The registry should be backed up once a computer is initially configured and operating properly. The registry should also be backed up when any software or hardware changes are made.

The registry should be backed up and restored on a different working computer *before* disaster strikes.

There are several ways to back up the registry; they are listed below.
• Use the NT Backup program.
• Use the RDISK (Repair Disk) utility.
• Use the REGEDIT registry editor.

The **NT Backup** program is accessed by first clicking on the **Start** button. Point to **Programs**, point to **Administrative Tools**, and click on the **Backup** option. The Backup dialog box appears. Select the **Windows** menu option and then click on the **Drives** option. Double-click on the drive letter that represents the boot drive (normally C:). In the bottom window, click on a check box to enable at least one file on this drive. At least one file must be chosen in order to back up the registry. Click on the **Backup** button. In the Backup Information dialog box, click once in the **Backup local registry** check box to enable the option. Click on the **OK** button.

The **RDISK (Repair Disk)** utility is used to create an **ERD (Emergency Repair Disk)** after NT is installed. When using the RDISK utility, two options are available: **Update Repair Info** and **Create Repair Disk**. The **Update Repair Info** button updates the emergency repair directory, which is a folder called Repair. The system then prompts you to create an ERD (Emergency Repair Disk). After NT is installed for the first time, the emergency repair folder is updated only using this **Update Repair Info** option. It is especially important to use the **Update Repair Info** option when making an updated ERD.

The **Create Repair Disk** button is used to create an ERD and use the information stored in the Repair folder. This option does not back up the current options to the Repair folder. Since the **Update Repair Info** option creates an ERD anyway, it is best to use the **Update Repair Info** option. An exercise at the end of the chapter details how to create an ERD.

One limitation of the RDISK program is that it does not update the default, security, or SAM files in the Repair folder. This means none of the user account information or changes are backed up. To do a complete update, use the **RDISK /S** command from the command prompt. This takes a bit of time. That is why most people prefer using some type of backup program to back up the registry. The BACKUP utility that ships with NT Workstation is a better method once the Repair folder has been updated using the RDISK program.

The REGEDIT program can also be used to back up or export the registry to back up media. To start the REGEDIT utility, click on the **Start** button. Click on the **Run** option and in the text box type in **REGEDIT** and press **Enter**. In the REGEDIT window, click on the **Registry** menu item. Click on the **Export Registry File** option from the drop-down menu. Select the drive location where the registry will be saved. In the **File name** text box, type in the name for the registry file backup. Click on the **Save** button. Figure 5.3 illustrates the REGEDIT utility.

Figure 5.3: REDEDIT Window

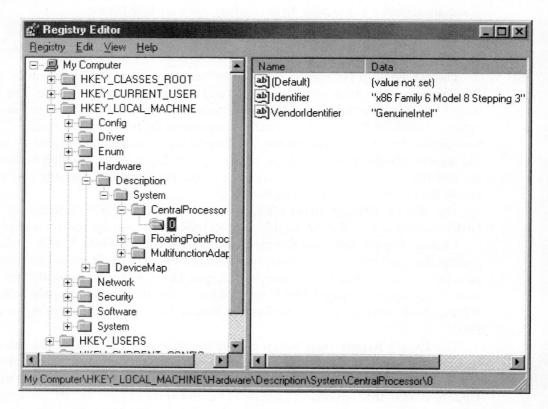

The subtrees in Figure 5.3 are in the left window. Click on the plus sign (+) beside each subtree and more subkeys appear. Click on a folder and the folder values appear in the right window. For example, in Figure 5.3, the Hardware folder has a subfolder called Description. The Description folder has a subfolder called System. The System folder has a subfolder called CentralProcessor. The CentralProcessor folder has a subfolder called 0. Once the 0 subfolder is double-clicked, the values appear in the right window. The value names for the 0 subfolder are (Default), Identifier, and VendorIdentifier. The value data for the 0 subfolder is on the far right side of the right window. These values must be changed sometimes to repair technical problems.

5.5 Understanding the Pre-Installation Steps of Windows NT

Skipping the installation planning is a bad habit for you to get into, especially when installing an operating system. The planning stages save time (and time is money to any business). If you skip the pre-installation steps, you many find yourself troubleshooting the installation process unnecessarily. The following steps outline the various stages of NT Workstation pre-installation.

1. Decide whether the installation will be an upgrade or clean install.
2. Decide whether the computer will have more than one operating system installed.
3. Decide how you want to partition the hard drive.
4. Determine which type of file system NT Workstation will use.
5. Determine if the hardware is compatible.
6. Obtain any drivers, upgrades, or hardware replacements.
7. Determine if the software applications are compatible.
8. Obtain any patches, upgrades, or software replacements.
9. Scan the computer for viruses.
10. Remove any power management or disk management tools.
11. Delete any unwanted files and uninstall any unwanted applications.
12. Back up any data files necessary.
13. Determine the local administrator password.

A **clean install** places an operating system on a computer that does not already have an operating system installed. An operating system **upgrade** is when an operating system already exists on the computer and NT Workstation 4 will be installed on top of this operating system. Windows 3.x and a previous version of NT Workstation (such as 3.5.1) can be upgraded to NT Workstation 4; however, a computer that already has Windows 3.x will probably not have enough hardware to load NT Workstation 4.

When NT Workstation 4 is installed to a different folder than the existing operating system, the computer will automatically be configured to be a dual-boot system. **Dual-boot** means that the computer has two operating systems installed and you can boot from either one. If Windows 95 or 98 is already installed, remove the operating system or install NT to a different folder. The default installation folder for NT is **C:\WINNT**.

If you decide that you are going to install NT on a machine that already has Windows 95/98, first check to see that all applications are supported by NT Workstation 4.0. Then, install NT into a separate directory on the hard drive. The system now has two operating systems and can boot from either of them. Reinstall all Windows 9x applications through NT. If Windows 95/98 is no longer desired, manually delete the folder that contains the Windows 95 or 98 operating system files.

There are two types of NT Workstation partitions: system partition and boot partition. The **system partition** is the active hard drive partition that contains hardware-specific files used to load the operating system. The system partition is normally located on the C: hard drive partition. The **boot partition** is the hard drive partition that holds the majority of the NT Workstation operating system files. What is confusing is that the two types of

NT partitions can be located on the same hard drive partition, or they can be on different partitions. For example, take a hard drive that has one partition, C:. The files needed to boot the system are on C:, and the NT files, located in the folder, are also on the C: partition. Therefore, in this example, both the system partition and the boot partition are on the same hard drive partition (C:).

Another example is a computer that has two partitions, C: and D:. The active partition that the computer boots from is C:. An extended partition with one logical drive is D:. The C: partition already has Windows 95 installed. This computer will be able to dual-boot from either Windows 95 or NT Workstation. When NT Workstation is installed, the files needed to load and boot NT are put on the C: partition (the NT system partition). The NT files are loaded to the folder on the D: partition (the NT boot partition).

NT Workstation can use either the FAT16 or the NTFS file system. The FAT16 file system should only be used if NT is to be dual-booted with an older operating system and there is only one hard drive partition formatted as FAT16. With the FAT16 file system, there is no file or folder compression. Nor are there as many permissions for individual files and folders. Also, the partition does not support large hard drive volumes greater than 2 GB. The NTFS file system supports security options and long file names.

The FAT16 partition can be converted to NTFS after the installation by using the **CONVERT program**. CONVERT *partition letter*: /FS:NTFS will convert a FAT16 partition to NTFS with no data loss. Take the example of the C: hard drive partition that is currently FAT16. The command used to convert the partition to NTFS is CONVERT C: / FS:NTFS. This command would be executed from a command prompt or by using the Run option from the Start menu.

The hardware requirements for NT Workstation are very important in the pre-installation checklist. If you omit this, you may find that you have to troubleshoot when actually there is nothing wrong except that the hardware requirements are not met. Table 5.3 lists the minimum requirements for NT Workstation.

Table 5.3: NT Workstation Minimum Hardware Requirements

Component	Minimum Requirements
CPU	Intel 486 (or compatible) 33 MHz
RAM	12 MB
Free hard drive space	120 MB
Input Device	Keyboard, mouse, or other pointing device
Multimedia Drive	CD-ROM
Video	VGA

On the NT Workstation CD in the Support folder, there is a file called HCL.HLP. This is the hardware compatibility list that contains hardware devices compatible with NT Workstation. If a computer device is not listed here, check Microsoft's web site at www.microsoft.com for the latest listing. Also check the device manufacturer's web site to see if it offers an NT driver for the device or if the driver is compatible with NT.

Microsoft provides a utility called **NTHQ (NT Hardware Qualifier)** that identifies what hardware is installed in the system. The NTHQ program is executed from a special floppy disk that you must make. To make this disk, insert a blank floppy disk into the computer. Run the **MAKEDISK.BAT** command, (which is located on the NT Workstation CD in the SUPPORT\HQTOOL folder). After this program executes, reboot the computer from this special disk. If your computer will not boot from the disk, check BIOS settings to make sure the A: drive is the first boot device. The NTHQ program automatically executes. Once hardware has been verified, obtain the appropriate NT driver for the device. If the device is incompatible with NT, replace the hardware device with a compatible one *before* installing NT.

DOS applications, 16-bit, and 32-bit Windows-based applications can all operate under NT. However, any older application that tries to access hardware directly will not operate properly in the NT environment. One way you can know whether an application is compatible with NT is to try it. Some application manufacturers provide software upgrades (for a fee) so that the application can be run on NT. Contact the software manufacturer for any software compatibility issues. Microsoft also has some application compatibility notes on their web site.

When upgrading an operating system to NT Workstation, it is wise to free up hard drive space and clean off unwanted files and applications. Hard drive space is an important commodity to an operating system. As applications and operating systems increase in size, it is very important to have enough free hard drive space and enough RAM installed.

The last preparation steps before installing or upgrading NT Workstation are to determine what the name of the computer will be and what the local administrator passwords will be. NT Workstation was designed for a corporate networked environment. In a network, every computer must have a unique name. The company may have a standard for naming computers. Gather this information before starting an NT upgrade or installation.

A local administrator has full power over the NT Workstation computer. When someone logs in as the local administrator, he or she can create and delete user accounts, create and delete hard drive partitions, and use all of the administration tools that ship with NT Workstation. Some companies have standards for the local administrator account password.

Check with the network administrator or desktop support supervisor to see if this is the case. Otherwise, determine what password will be set during the installation process. The password can be blank (not advised), or it can be up to 14 characters in length. Also, the password is case-sensitive (unlike the user name, such as Administrator).

Don't forget about checking for viruses. Viruses were discussed in the Virus section in Chapter 4. Review that section if necessary.

5.6 Understanding How to Install and Upgrade Windows NT Workstation

After all pre-installation steps are completed, you can start the installation process. NT Workstation uses the **Setup** program to install the operating system files. There are three ways to start the Setup program: (1) from an NT Workstation CD, (2) by launching the installation program from a local hard drive partition, and (3) across a network. When installing NT across a network, one of two files is used to start the Setup program: WINNT.EXE or WINNT32.EXE. **WINNT.EXE** is used to install NT Workstation to a computer that currently has DOS, Windows 3.x, Windows 95, or Windows 98 installed. The **WINNT32.EXE** file is used to upgrade from a previous version of NT Workstation.

There are two major parts of the installation process—the text mode (otherwise known as DOS mode) and the GUI mode (also known as Windows mode). In **text mode**, characters are shown on a plain blue background. During text mode, the hard drive is partitioned and formatted for either FAT16 or NTFS, the location of where to install the NT files is chosen, hardware is checked for minimum requirements, hard drives are detected, and some of the installation files are copied. During the **GUI mode**, the setup logs are created, the computer is named, the administrator password is entered, and the rest of the operating system files are copied. You may also create an Emergency Repair Disk, as well as install networking components.

5.7 Troubleshooting the Windows NT Installation

Various problems can cause the NT Workstation installation process to halt. If the computer halts during text mode and displays a STOP message, there is probably an incompatible piece of hardware or software installed in the computer, or a virus is present. If no error messages appear, but the computer halts during text mode, check the BIOS settings, especially on older ISA devices. If an error message appears during text mode that indicates the HAL.DLL is missing or corrupt or a similar HAL.DLL message, then the incorrect HAL (Hardware Abstraction Layer) is being loaded. This is a layer between the operating system and hardware devices. The **HAL** allows NT to run with different hardware configurations and components without affecting (or crashing) the operating system. To correct this, restart the Setup program. When the message appears that NT is examining your hardware configuration, press the **F5** key. Select the correct computer type from the list that appears. If the computer type is not listed there, obtain a HAL from the computer manufacturer. Then, select **Other** from the list and load the HAL provided by the computer manufacturer. Another indication that the HAL is incorrect is if the Setup program hangs while copying files to the hard drive.

If the computer halts during the GUI portion of Setup, restart the computer. The installation process attempts to continue from the place it left off. Incompatible hardware devices normally cause this. You can troubleshoot the device once Windows is installed. Also, if the system hangs at random intervals, an IRQ (Interrupt Request) conflict, I/O (Input/Output) port address conflict, or video setting is probably the culprit. IRQ and I/O ports were discussed in Chapter 2 entitled *Basic Operating System Theory*. Incompatible hardware devices are the most common problem during the installation process because they can cause both the text and GUI modes to halt. If the system hangs after the final reboot, the problem is most likely caused by incorrect information in the BOOT.INI file or an incorrect hardware configuration. The **BOOT.INI** file is a Windows NT file that instructs the operating system as to which partition to boot.

Installation problems can be caused by a number of factors. The following list shows the most common causes and their associated solution during the installation process.

- **Incompatible BIOS**—Obtain compatible BIOS, upgrade to a compatible BIOS, replace motherboard with one that has a compatible BIOS, or do not upgrade/ install NT Workstation.
- **BIOS needs to be upgraded**—Upgrade the BIOS.
- **Incompatible hardware**—Replace the hardware or do not upgrade/install NT Workstation.
- **Incompatible drivers**—Obtain NT drivers from the hardware manufacturer.
- **Existing drivers are incompatible or halt the installation/upgrade process**—Obtain NT drivers from the hardware manufacturer.
- **Incompatible TSRs**—Remove TSRs or obtain updated ones from the software manufacturer; otherwise, disable the TSR until after NT has been installed and then try re-enabling the TSR.
- **Incompatible applications**—Obtain upgrades from software manufacturer.
- **Minimum hardware requirements have not been met**—Upgrade the hardware. The number one thing to check is the CPU (486 33 MHz minimum) and RAM (12 MB minimum).
- **A virus is on the hard drive**—Run a virus-checking program to remove the virus.
- **Pre-installation steps have not been completed**—Go back through the list!
- **The installation floppy disks or CD is corrupted** (not as likely as the other causes)—Try the disk in another machine and see if you can see the contents. For the CD, check to see if any scratches or dirt are on the surface. Clean the CD as necessary.
- **Incorrect CD key**—Type in the correct CD key to complete the NT Workstation installation. The key is located on the CD case.
- **Hard drives are not configured correctly**—If a message appears that Setup did not find any hard drives on your computer and this is a new computer, check that the cable(s) are properly connected and that power connects to the drive.

- **Existing FAT32 partition**—If a message appears that there is no valid partition on the hard drive and a previous operating system has been (or is) on the hard drive, there is a good possibility that the drive has been partitioned to FAT32. NT Workstation does not support FAT32. Back up the data and create a new partition (FAT16 or NTFS) if NT Workstation is to be installed.
- If Setup hangs while files are copying to the hard drive, the wrong HAL is installed (see previous section that describes the HAL file) or some BIOS settings are interrupting the copy process. Go into the computer's BIOS and disable video shadow RAM and the 32-bit enhanced file throughput settings.

You need to know the installation steps for the A+ Operating System exam.

5.8 Configuring Windows NT Workstation

Technicians must frequently add new hardware and software using the operating system. NT Workstation has specific tools for these functions. Using the correct procedure is essential for success. The following sections handle many of the tasks a technician must perform.

- Adding and Removing Hardware Components
- Installing and Removing Software
- Adding a Printer

Adding and Removing Hardware Components

All hardware devices must have NT drivers in order to operate with NT Workstation. An important thing to remember is that the only type of user who can install hardware components by default is the Administrator. The Administrator uses various control panels to add hardware components in NT Workstation.

To access the control panels, click on the **Start** button. Point to the **Settings** option and then click on the **Control Panel** menu option. The number of control panels is determined by what hardware is installed in the computer. Table 5.4 lists a few of the control panels and their functions.

Table 5.4: A Few NT Control Panel Functions

Control Panel	Function
Devices	Used to start and stop device drivers; used to control how the device driver loads.
Display	Used to install a monitor driver and configure monitor settings.
Keyboard	Used to install a keyboard driver and configure keyboard.

Network	Used to install NIC drivers, add network software, and configure network connections.
SCSI Adapters	Used to add and configure SCSI device drivers.
Tape Devices	Used to add tape device driver and configure tape device parameters.

Knowing what control panel to use and what specific control panel tab to use to install a hardware device driver is sometimes confusing in NT. The following procedures are provided to help with the most common NT hardware installations.

- To load a monitor device driver, use the **Display** control panel, click on the **Settings** tab, and click on the **Change** button.
- To load a keyboard driver, use the **Keyboard** control panel, click on the **General** tab, and click on the **Change** button.
- To load a modem driver, use the **Modem** control panel, click on the **Add** button.
- To load a multimedia device driver such as a CD-ROM, or joystick driver, use the **Multimedia** control panel, click on the **Devices** tab, and click on the **Add** button.
- To install a NIC driver, use the **Network** control panel, click on the **Adapters** tab, and click on the **Add** button.
- To install a SCSI adapter device driver, use the **SCSI Adapter** control panel, click on the **Drivers** tab, and click on the **Add** button.
- To install a tape drive device driver, use the **Tape Devices** control panel, click on the **Detect** button.

Two important things to remember about NT Workstation: (1) you must have Administrator rights to install a hardware driver and (2) the driver needs to be compatible with NT. Administrator rights means you log on the Windows NT system as the Administrator user account.

Installing and Removing Software

No computer is complete without software. Various types of applications can be used with NT including DOS applications, 16-bit Windows applications, and 32-bit Windows applications. Not all older applications are compatible with NT, but the only way you can know is to load the application and try it. 16-bit applications are installed using the directions from the software manufacturer. 32-bit applications are installed using the **Add/Remove Programs** control panel. To access this control panel, click on the **Start** button. Point to the **Settings** option and click on the **Control Panel** menu option. When the Control Panel window appears, click on the **Add/Remove Programs** control panel. Follow the directions on the screen or the directions from the software manufacturer.

DOS applications run in a special environment called **NTVDM** (NT Virtual DOS Machine). NTVDM simulates a DOS environment inside NT Workstation. Each DOS application loaded into RAM (started), loads into one NTVDM. The environment the DOS application runs in can be customized through NT Workstation. Using My Computer or Explorer, right-click on the EXE file or shortcut that starts the DOS application. Select the **Properties** option from the drop-down menu. A Properties screen appears with tabs across the top. All of the settings made through this window are collectively known as the DOS application's **PIF** (**Program Information File**).

The two most common tabs used with DOS applications are Memory and Screen. The **Memory tab** allows setting memory parameters for the NTVDM that the DOS application is using. With this tab, you can specify a specific amount of expanded and extended memory. Figure 5.4 shows the Memory tab for the DOS application executable file called SHERLOCK.EXE.

Figure 5.4: Memory Tab for a DOS Application

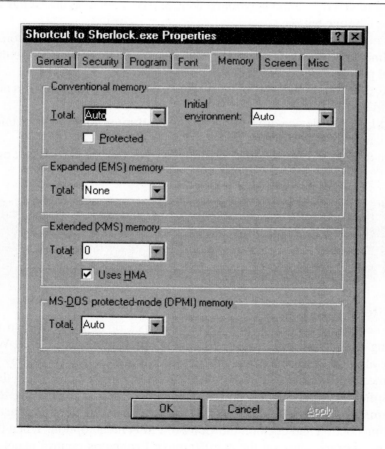

The other commonly used tab for a DOS application is the Screen tab. The **Screen tab** allows the DOS application to run in full-screen mode (the application takes up the entire screen and has no common Windows buttons) or in a window mode (the application runs inside a window that has common Windows buttons to control the window).

> Not all DOS applications are compatible with NT Workstation. The only way to know is to install the software and attempt to execute it. If it doesn't work, try adjusting the memory settings described above for the specific amount and type of memory the DOS application requires. DOS applications frequently try to directly access hardware and NT has a built-in feature called HAL (Hardware Abstraction Layer) that prevents direct access to hardware.

A 16-bit Windows application runs in a **Windows On Windows** (or **WOW**) environment. WOW is a WIN16 environment simulator running inside a NTVDM. All 16-bit Windows applications run in a single NTVDM, which means that when one 16-bit Windows application fails, they all fail. You can configure each 16-bit Windows application to operate in its own NTVDM. Create a shortcut for the icon that starts the program. (Use Explorer to create the shortcut. Click and drag the executable file that starts the program to the desktop and a shortcut is automatically created.) Right-click on the shortcut icon. Click on the **Shortcut** tab. Click on the **Run in Separate Memory Space** check box to enable starting the application in its own NTVDM and preventing other 16-bit applications from crashing if this application fails.

> Not all 16-bit Windows applications are compatible with NT Workstation. This is because some 16-bit Windows applications use a VxD (virtual device driver) that accesses hardware directly. NT Workstation has a built-in feature called HAL (Hardware Abstraction Layer) that prevents direct access to hardware.

A 32-bit Windows application has its own memory space allocated—2 GB for the operating system files that all applications share and 2 GB for the application. This means that if a 32-bit application crashes, no other 32-bit application will fail because it does not use the same memory space.

Adding a Printer

Printers normally connect to a computer through the parallel port, a USB port, or through a local area network. Only local printers (printers directly connected to the computer) will be covered in this chapter.

To install a printer under NT, use the **Add Printer wizard**. To access the Add Printer wizard, click on the **Start** button. Point to the **Settings** option and then click on the **Printers** option. Double-click on the **Add Printer** icon. Figure 5.5 shows this concept.

Figure 5.5: NT Workstation Printers Option

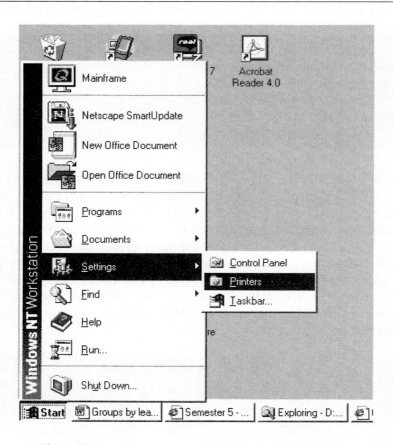

If multiple printers are available to an NT Workstation computer, one printer is marked as the default printer. A default printer is the one to which a computer prints unless a different one is chosen. To set the default printer, click on the **Start** button, point to the **Settings** option, and click on the **Printers** drop-down menu option. The Printers folder opens. Right-click on the printer that will be the default printer. From the drop-down menu, click on the **Set As Default** option.

5.9 Understanding the Boot Process

With NT Workstation and Windows 2000, two types of partitions are important during the boot process—the system partition and the boot partition. The **system partition** is the active drive partition that has the files needed to load the operating system. The system partition is normally the C: drive (the active partition). The **boot partition** is the partition or logical drive where the NT operating system files are located. One thing that people sometimes forget is that the system partition and the boot partition can be on the same partition. These partitions are where certain files needed to boot are located.

Every operating system needs specific files that allow the computer to boot. These files are known as **system files** or startup files. The system files and their specific location on the hard drive are listed in Table 5.5.

Table 5.5: Windows NT Boot Files

Startup File name	File Location
BOOT.INI	Root directory of system partition.
BOOTSECT.DOS (needed if dual or multi-boot system	Root directory of system partition.
HAL.DLL	%systemroot%\SYSTEM32 (%systemroot% is a variable representing the folder where Windows NT is installed. This is normally C:\WINNT.)
NTBOOTDD.SYS (used with SCSI drives that have the SCSI BIOS disabled)	Root directory of system partition.
NTDETECT.COM	Root directory of system partition.
NTLDR	Root directory of system partition.
NTOSKRNL.EXE	%systemroot%\SYSTEM32 (%systemroot% is a variable representing the folder where Windows NT is installed. This is normally C:\WINNT.)

Information from Microsoft can be confusing at times because of the *%systemroot%* and *%systemdrive%* entries. This is because computers can be partitioned differently. If you install Windows NT Workstation onto a drive letter (a partition or logical drive) other than the active partition (normally C:), the startup files can be on two different drive letters. Also, you do not have to take the default folder name to install NT. To account for these different scenarios, Microsoft uses the *%systemroot%* to represent the boot partition—the partition and folder that contains the majority of the NT Workstation files. On a computer with a single operating system, this would be C:\WINNT. The *%systemdrive%* represents the root directory of the same drive letter. On a computer with a single operating system, this would be C:\.

The boot process is actually quite involved, but the major steps are as follows:

1. The computer is powered on.
2. POST executes.
3. BIOS searches for an active partition on the hard drive.
4. BIOS reads the Master Boot Record, then locates and loads the information into sector 0 of the system partition. The contents of sector 0 define the type of file system

and the location of the bootstrap loader file, then start the bootstrap loader. With NT Workstation, this file is NTLDR.

5. NTLDR starts the file system.

6. NTLDR reads the BOOT.INI file and displays the various operating system choices. If something other than NT Workstation is chosen, the BOOTSECT.DOS file takes over. If NT Workstation is chosen, the NTDETECT.COM file executes.

7. NTDETECT.COM detects the computer's hardware. A message appears on the screen saying "**NTDETECT V4.0 Checking Hardware...**"

8. NTLDR passes the hardware information to the NTOSKRNL.EXE file and displays the Startup screen. The message on the screen is "**OS Loader V4.0.**" Press **Spacebar** now to invoke Hardware Profile/Last Known Good menu. This menu stays on the screen three to five seconds.

9. The operating system kernel, NTOSKRNL.EXE, executes and the HAL.DLL file loads. The message on the screen displays "**Microsoft® Windows NT™ Version 4.0 (Build 1381) 1 System Processor (x MB Memory).**" This is where x is the amount of memory on your system.

10. The registry key HKEY_LOCAL_MACHINE\SYSTEM loads. This registry key is located in the *%SYSTEMROOT%*\SYSTEM32\CONFIG\SYSTEM folder. This key has information found during the hardware detection process.

11. The WINLOGON.EXE file executes and the log-on screen appears.

Troubleshooting the Boot Process

Various problems exist that cause NT Workstation to not boot, but boot problems can usually be narrowed down to two main areas: (1) missing or corrupted boot files, or (2) configuration problems. When boot files are missing or corrupted, different error messages can appear. Table 5.6 shows some of the most common error messages seen with missing or corrupt boot files.

Table 5.6: Windows NT Workstation Boot Problems

Symptom	Cause
Message "Boot: Couldn't find NTLDR. Please insert another disk."	NTLDR file is missing or corrupt.
Message "Error opening NTDETECT. Press any key to continue."	Timeout option for the boot loader located in the BOOT.INI file is set to 0 or the path of the operating system in the boot loader section of the BOOT.INI file is not the same as a path listed in the [operating systems] section of BOOT.INI.

Message "The system did not load because of a computer disk hardware configuration problem. Could not read from selected boot disk. Check the boot path and disk hardware. Please check the Windows NT documentation about hardware disk configuration and your hardware reference manuals for additional information. Boot failed."	The device or partition information regarding a path in the [operating systems] section of BOOT.INI is wrong.
Message "multi(0)disk(0)rdisk(0)partition(1)\winnt\system\ntoskrnl.exe The system did not load because it cannot find the following file: C:\ \SYSTEM32\NTOSKRNL.EXE. Pease reinstall a copy of the above file."	The path information in the BOOT.INI file's [operating systems] section is wrong or NTLDR and/or BOOT.INI files are not in the root directory of the system partition.
Message "I/O error accessing boot sector file multi(0)disk(0)rdisk(0)partition(1) \bootsect.dos."	The BOOTSECT.DOS file is missing or corrupted. Restore the file from a backup copy.
When you select an operating system from the operating system selection screen, the selected operating system does not load.	Corrupted BOOT.INI file. The path information in the [operating systems] section of BOOT.INI is wrong.
Message "Invalid Partition Table."	A virus is on the hard drive or there is an error in the BOOT.INI file.
Blue screen appears after a power failure.	The boot files are missing or corrupt.

When any of these error messages appear, the most common tool used is the ERD (Emergency Repair Disk). The **ERD** is a disk that can be made during the installation process and after NT Workstation is installed. An entire section is devoted to the ERD immediately following this section.

Other problems that can occur during the boot process are POST errors, STOP errors, and blue screens. **POST errors** are normally caused by an invalid/incorrect hardware configuration or a faulty piece of hardware. If NT Workstation has booted correctly prior to this POST error, press the **spacebar** on the keyboard when the message, "**OS Loader V4.0. Press spacebar NOW to invoke Hardware Profile/Last Known Good menu**" appears on the screen. By default, this message stays on the screen for approximately five seconds. Once you press the spacebar, a menu appears. Press the letter **L** to access the **Last Known Good Configuration** option. This allows you to change the configuration of the new device or disable it until you can determine the exact problem or get an NT driver for the device.

The same process of accessing the **Last Known Good Configuration** is used if you get a **blue screen** (commonly called the "**Blue Screen of Death**") after a configuration change. If a blue screen appears after a power failure, there is a good chance that the boot files are missing or corrupt. Use the ERD or copy over the boot files to the correct location on the hard drive. If a **STOP message** appears, the registry may be corrupt. The registry can be reinstalled using a current ERD for the computer or you can reinstall the registry from a backup.

In older operating systems, a startup disk was used to begin the troubleshooting process. With NT Workstation, the startup disk is actually the set of three installation disks that came with the NT Workstation CD. If you cannot find these, you can go to any computer that has the same version of Windows NT Workstation loaded and make a set. To do this, insert the NT Workstation CD, click on the **Start** button, and click on the **Run** option. In the dialog box, type *drive***:\i386\winnt32.exe /ox** where *drive* is the drive letter that represents the CD-ROM. Click on the **OK** button and follow the prompts on the screen. You will need three floppy disks to complete this procedure. The installation disks are used when repairing a system using the ERD.

Creating an Emergency Repair Disk

The **ERD** (**Emergency Repair Disk**) is used to fix system file problems, the partition boot sector, and startup environment settings, all of which can cause a computer to not boot properly. The ERD is unique to a specific computer. The ERD should be recreated any time changes are made to the computer's configuration. An ERD can also be created during the installation process but it still needs to be recreated whenever changes are made.

To create an ERD, click on the **Start** button and click on the **Run** menu option. In the dialog box, type **RDISK /S**. If an error occurs, type the correct path for the **RDISK** program. By default, RDISK is located in the SYSTEM32 subfolder under C:\WINNT. The RDISK program creates a disk that can be used for emergency repairs. The **/S** switch causes a backup of the Security Accounts Manager (SAM) database as well as the entire registry in a subfolder under called **Repair**. When prompted to create the ERD, click on the **Yes** button if you are simply updating the existing ERD.

If the computer system will not work and you want to use the ERD, you must actually start the NT Workstation installation process and get to the Welcome to Setup screen. Use the NT Workstation setup disks. Once presented with the Welcome to Setup screen, press the **R** option, which is the To repair a damaged Windows NT version 4.0 installation. Once you press **R**, a menu appears. The menu has four selections that are all enabled. Press **Enter** to start the process. A prompt appears telling you to insert the ERD. The CHKDSK program runs and verifies the hard disk clusters. Each operating system file is checked and reinstalled if the file is missing or corrupt. The system and security portion of the registry is replaced (if you confirm that you want them replaced), and the boot sector and boot files are replaced. An exercise at the end of the chapter illustrates how to create an ERD.

Windows Scripting

A Windows **script** can automate desktop shortcuts for users and set or restrict access for the desktop, Start menu, network share mapping, network printer mapping, setting default printer, and launching applications. In Windows scripts can be executed three different ways:

- By double-clicking on an icon associated with a particular file.
- By running a script from the Run dialog box.
- By typing WSCRIPT.EXE *script_name* (where *script_name* is the path and name of the previously created script) from the Run dialog box.

In a DOS environment, a batch file can provide how the operating system loads, how a particular application loads, a menu-driven environment, and other environment settings.

With Windows 98, NT, and Windows 2000, Microsoft provides a Windows-based scripting tool called WSCRIPT.EXE. When the WSCRIPT tool is executed, a Windows-based dialog box appears and allows you to configure script properties.

The Windows scripting host is sometimes known as WSH. The scripting host is integrated into Windows 2000 and the NT option pack and can be downloaded from Microsoft's web site. Microsoft also provides sample scripts and a tutorial.

5.10 Understanding Task Manager, Event Viewer, and Windows NT Diagnostics

Task Manager is a Windows-based utility that displays applications currently loaded into memory, processes that are currently running, microprocessor usage information, and memory usage data. To activate the Task Manager utility, press the **Ctrl + Alt + Delete** keys. From the window options that appear, click on the **Task Manager** button. Two other ways to access Task Manager are:

- Press **Ctrl + Alt + Esc.**
- Right-click on the **taskbar** and then click on the **Task Manager** option.

One of the common uses of Task Manager is to exit from an application that is "hung" or not responding. Task Manager can help with exiting the program. To exit from a 32-bit application, access the Task Manager window and click on the **Applications** tab. Locate the name of the troublesome application and click on it. Normally, the status shows the application as "not responding." Click on the **End Task** button. Close the Task Manager window.

To exit from a DOS or 16-bit Windows applications, access the Task Manager window and click on the **Processes** tab. Locate the appropriate NTVDM.EXE file that contains the program. Note that there may be more than one application running within the NTVDM if they are 16-bit Windows programs that have not been configured to run in separate NTVDMs. Click on the **End Process** button. Close the Task Manager window.

Event Viewer is a Windows tool used to monitor various events in your computer, such as when a driver or service does not start properly. One of the most common reasons a technician uses the Event Viewer is when he or she encounters the message "One or more services failed to start. Please see the Event Viewer for details." (As a side note, the individual administrative tool that controls the service or the Services control panel is used to manage the event. The Event Viewer is used to determine which service had the problem.)

The **EventLog** service starts automatically every time a computer boots. This service is what allows events to be logged. Event Viewer is then used to see the log. Event Viewer is a great troubleshooting tool because, even when a user cannot remember exactly what happens when a problem occurs, Event Viewer tracks the problems.

Event Viewer tracks three different categories of events: system events, security events, and application events. **System events** log events regarding system components. An example would be a driver that does not load during startup. **Security events** are only accessible to system administrators and contain information such as valid and invalid log on attempts and whether someone tried to access a protected file. An administrator can set what security events are logged and tracked by Event Viewer. **Application events** are associated with a specific program. The programmers that design the software decide which events to display in the Event Viewer's application log. All users can view the system log and the application log, but only a member of Administrators can view or enable security log information. The most commonly used log is the system log.

Let's go through an exercise to help you understand Event Viewer.

1. Access the Event Viewer by clicking on the **Start** button, pointing to the **Programs** option, pointing to the **Administrative Tools** option, and clicking on **Event Viewer**.
   Event Viewer opens and the system events appear by default in the Event Viewer window.
2. Double-click on any event that is shown in Event Viewer to see more information.
3. Click the **Close** button to return to the full Event Viewer screen.
4. Select the **Security** option. All Security events display.
5. To access application events, click on the **Log** menu option.

6. Select the **Applications** option. All Application events display.
7. To clear the System log, right-click **System** and click **Clear All Events**. You are prompted to save the log file.
8. Click on the **No** button when asked if you want to save the log. Note: Once events are cleared from the log, they cannot be retrieved. Save the events when prompted if you want to keep the events that are currently logged before clearing the log. You will need to supply a file name.
9. To exit Event Viewer, click on the **Close** box in the upper right corner or click on the **Log** menu option and select the **Exit** option.
10. Click on the **Yes** button when asked if you are sure that you want to clear the log. This process clears all prior logged events in the System log and will only displays events that occur from this point forward.
11. Press the **F5** key to refresh the Event Viewer.

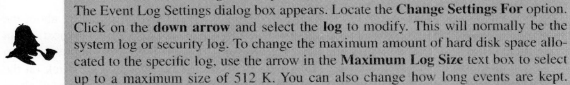

If an error message appears stating that the Event Viewer log is full, start the **Event Viewer.** Click on the **Log** menu option and then click on the **Log Settings** selection. The Event Log Settings dialog box appears. Locate the **Change Settings For** option. Click on the **down arrow** and select the **log** to modify. This will normally be the system log or security log. To change the maximum amount of hard disk space allocated to the specific log, use the arrow in the **Maximum Log Size** text box to select up to a maximum size of 512 K. You can also change how long events are kept. Locate the **Event Log** Wrapping section. Click on one of the following: **Overwrite events as needed, Overwrite events older than 0 days,** or **Do not overwrite events**. Figure 5.6 shows what the settings screen looks like.

Figure 5.6: Event Viewer Full Settings

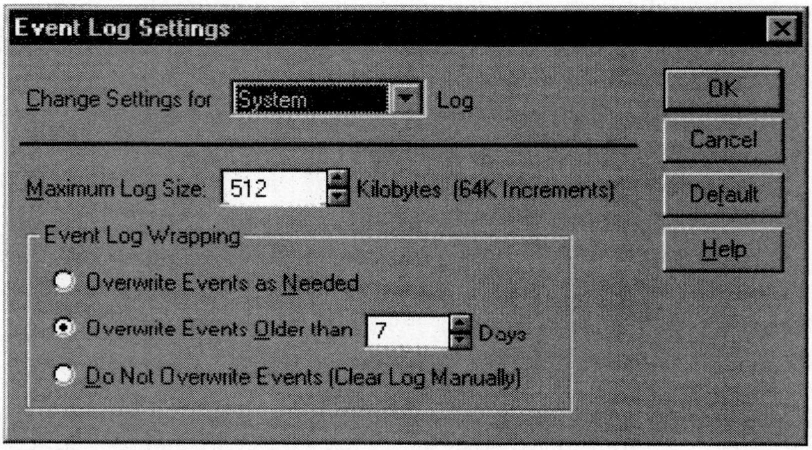

NT Diagnostics is a utility that allows viewing configuration information about the computer's hardware, installed device drivers, and installed services. NT Diagnostics can help when troubleshooting configuration problems. The utility does not really perform any diagnostics; it simply displays information. To access NT Diagnostics, click on the Start button, point to Programs, point to Administrative Tools (Common), and click on the Windows NT Diagnostics option. The tabs across the top of the window include Version, System, Display, Drives, Memory, Services, Resources, Environment, and Network.

The Version NT Diagnostics tab displays the version, service pack version, and NT serial number. A Print button on this screen allows a comprehensive listing of all NT Diagnostic information (from all of the various tabs). The System NT Diagnostics tab displays the installed HAL type, BIOS manufacturer and date, and the type of processor(s) installed in the computer. The Display tab lists video adapter information including chip type, BIOS date, driver, driver version, and amount of video memory. The Drives NT Diagnostics tab displays information about any drives connected to the computer, including hard drive partitions. The window also displays network connected drives (shares). Double-click on any drive and the amount of used space, number of bytes per sector, number of sectors per cluster, and available space is shown. The Memory NT Diagnostics tab displays physical memory and information about the paging file. This tab is useful in determining if the computer has enough physical memory or if the paging file needs to be adjusted.

The back row of NT Diagnostic tabs includes Services, Resources, Environment, and Network. The Services tab displays the current status of all services and device services. Double-click on any service to see detailed information such as the path name to the service or device and any dependencies. There are two types of dependencies, service and group. Service dependencies are the services or drivers that must run before the particular service can start. **Group dependencies** are groups of services that must be running before the particular service can start.

The **Resources tab** is probably the most common tab used by technicians. On this display, IRQs, I/O port addresses, DMA channels, memory addresses, and devices can be shown by clicking on the appropriate button at the bottom of the tab. Figure 5.7 illustrates the Resources tab.

The **Environment tab** lists the path to the command interpreter, how many processors are installed, and the directory where the majority of NT files are located. The **Network tab** shows the domain or workgroup name and what user is currently logged onto NT. Other buttons located on the bottom of the tab are Transports, Settings, and Statistics. The Statistics button is helpful when troubleshooting network problems because you can see the number of bytes transmitted, bytes received, network errors, failed sessions, server disconnects, hung sessions, etc.

Figure 5.7: NT Diagnostics Screen

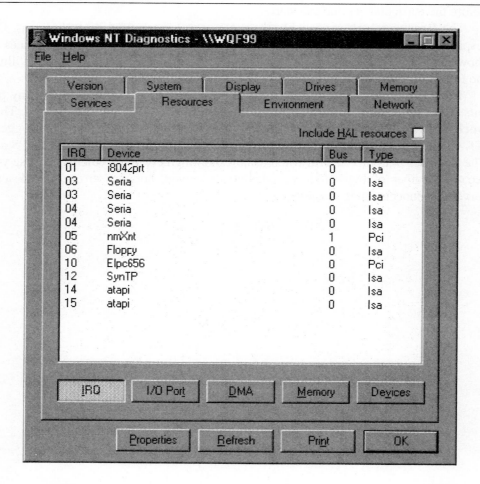

5.11 Troubleshooting a Service that Does Not Start

Some Windows NT services start automatically each time the computer boots. If one of these services has a problem, an error message normally appears during the boot sequence. You can use Event Viewer to see what particular service did not start. To control the service, use the individual administrative tool or the Services control panel.

To access the Services control panel, click on the **Start** button. Point to the **Settings** menu option. Click on the **Control Panel** option. A window appears with all the control panels displayed. Double-click on the **Services** icon. To start or stop a service manually, click on its name. Click on the **Start** or **Stop** button as appropriate.

Shutdown Problems

To shut down Windows NT Workstation properly, click on the **Start** button, click on the **Shut Down** option, click on the **Shut down the computer** radio button, and click on the **Yes** button. A shortcut is to press the **Alt + F4** keys after all applications are closed. If applications are open when you try to shut down NT, the operating system will attempt to close the applications and, if successful, it will shut down. If any documents have not been saved, you are prompted to save changes.

Before NT Workstation can shut down, the operating system sends a message to all devices, services, and applications. Each device that is running sends a message back saying it is okay to shut down. Any active application saves data that has not been previously saved and sends a message back to the operating system. Active system services also respond that it is okay to shut down. If the system has trouble shutting down, it is due to one of these three things. The most common problem is an application that is not responding. When this happens, press Ctrl + Alt + Del to access Task Manager. Click on the **Task Manager** button. Click on the **Applications** tab. Click on the application that has the words "not responding" in the Status column. Click on the **End Task** button. If a single application continually prevents NT Workstation from shutting down, contact the software manufacturer to see if there is a fix.

For services problems, boot the computer into Safe Mode and then shut down the computer. Take note as to whether or not the computer had any problems shutting down. If the process works, access the BOOTLOG.TXT file that is located in the root directory of the drive containing NT Workstation. Inside the file, take note of each service that is disabled because of booting into Safe Mode. Boot the computer normally. Stop each service one at a time to see which service is causing the problem. Before troubleshooting non-responding devices, eliminate services and applications. A device usually does not cause a shutdown problem. While working on the computer, take notice of which devices you are using. Common ones are video, hard drive, CD-ROM, keyboard, and mouse. Verify that all of your devices have the most up-to-date drive loaded and that the driver is compatible with Windows NT.

5.12 Monitoring System Performance

Another utility used to monitor the computer is the Performance Monitor tool. **Performance Monitor** allows creation of graphs, bar charts, and text reports. Specific resources such as memory and CPU usage can be tracked through Performance Monitor. An exercise at the end of the chapter shows how to use the Performance Monitor utility.

To access the Performance Monitor utility, click on the **Start** button, point to **Programs**, point to **Administrative Tools (Common)**, and click on the **Performance Monitor** option. The utility can be customized to show different counters. The button with a + (plus sign) is used to add various counters on the display. Some of the most important memory counters are Available Bytes and Pages/sec. The Available Bytes counter shows the amount of RAM available for running program processes. The Pages/sec counter shows the number of times per second that the information requested could not be found in RAM, and the data had to be retrieved from the hard drive. Since memory is a potential bottleneck for many computers, a technician should familiarize himself or herself with this technique. Sometimes you must adjust the paging file size for optimum computer performance. Note that the paging file is known by various terms including swap file, paging file, or virtual memory.

The **System** control panel is used to set the virtual memory size. Once in the System control panel, click on the **Performance** tab. Click on the **Change** button and the Virtual Memory window appears. Two values are selectable: Initial size and Maximum size. Both of these values should be the same for maximum computer performance. Once you change the values, click on the **Set** button. The Virtual Memory window may also be used to change the amount of space reserved for the registry.

Another potential bottleneck is the hard drive. The hard drive and memory work together because NT makes use of the paging file. The Performance Monitor charts you should watch are the Page Writes/sec and Pages Output/sec for memory and the Disk Writes/sec, Disk Write Bytes/sec, and Avg. Disk Write Queue Length for the logical disk option. You should practice working with the Performance Monitor utility before a problem occurs or the computer slows down.

The Task Manager utility may also be used to monitor your current systems performance. Sometimes a computer starts slowing down. A baseline is needed before the slowdown occurs. A **baseline** is a snapshot of your computer's performance during normal operations (before it has problems).

Start the Task Manager utility and click on the **Performance** tab to see the CPU usage and memory usage statistics. The first window on the left shows the CPU usage percentage. It is actually a percentage of time the processor is running a thread. A thread is a type of Windows object that runs application instructions. This percentage relates directly to the System Monitor's (Processor) %Processor Time counter. The first window on the right displays the CPU usage history, which is a graph of how busy the processor has been over a period of time.

The second window on the left shows the amount of virtual memory being used. The amount shown is in kilobytes as evidenced by the K after the number. The number displayed directly relates to the System Monitor's (Memory) Committed Bytes counter. The second window on the right is a graph of the virtual memory used over time. Memory is a frequent bottleneck for computer performance issues. Task Manager can also be used to see the total amount of RAM installed and how much RAM is available. Task Manager is an invaluable tool for technicians when a computer is slowing down.

Chapter Summary

- Windows NT is a true 32-bit operating system that has better security due to the support of the NTFS file system. It also supports FAT. Its GUI is similar to Windows 98.
- Windows NT provides a hierarchical file system allowing you to create folders and store files within them.
- Windows NT supports compression when using the NTFS. Compression saves disk space by "squeezing" redundant data from a file.
- The Registry is a database, which stores the hardware and software information installed on your computer.
- As part of the pre-installation steps of Windows NT, you should decide whether or not to perform a clean installation or an upgrade. You should consider installing virus protection software, which can detect and remove common software viruses.
- When installing Windows NT, the setup program named WINNT.EXE is used to install Windows NT on a system that currently has DOS, Windows 3.1, Windows 95/98 loaded. The WINNT32.EXE is used to upgrade from a previous version of Windows NT Workstation.
- Troubleshooting your Windows NT installation involves verifying BIOS and driver compatibility, inserting the correct CD key, ensuring you have a minimum CPU that is a 486 33 MHz, and having at least 12 MB of RAM.
- Configuring Windows NT involves using Control Panel to add and remove hardware components such as a mouse or a printer. It also includes adding and removing additional software.
- You need to understand the boot process of Windows NT so you know how to troubleshoot when problems occur. For example, if the NTLDR file is missing or corrupt, Windows NT will not boot.
- Windows Task Manager allows you view the applications that are running on your system. You get to Task Manager by pressing Ctrl + Alt + Del. Event Viewer contains a log of events that have occurred on your system. The Windows NT Diagnostic utility aids in troubleshooting by displaying system information.
- When Windows NT boots, various services are started. You can see the status of a service by checking the Services program in Control Panel. If a service fails to start, consider pressing F8 and booting to Safe Mode during the boot sequence.
- You can use Performance Monitor to monitor the performance of your Windows NT system through the use of objects and counters. It is useful to take a baseline of your system for comparative purposes.

Review Questions

1. Which type of computer system contains a relatively small number of instructions, and is fast and expensive?
   a) CISC
   b) IRQ
   c) RISC
   d) I/O port

2. What icon allows you to view networked computers when a network card is installed?
   a) Internet Connection Sharing
   b) Internet Explorer
   c) Network Explorer
   d) Network Neighborhood

3. The _____ is the area where all of your work in Windows NT begins. This area contains icons and shortcuts.
   a) Desktop
   b) Window
   c) Control Panel
   d) Long File Names

4. What Windows feature prevents you from moving icons on your desktop?
   a) Auto Unclutter
   b) Auto Arrange
   c) Arrange Order
   d) Automatically Detect

5. Where are files held when they are deleted from the hard disk drive?
   a) Trash Can
   b) They are not held anywhere because they are permanently deleted.
   c) Recycle Bin
   d) Quick Launch Bar

6. Where do you view file extensions?
   a) Under the Folder Options menu, which is beneath the View menu.
   b) Under the Folder View menu, which is beneath the Options menu.
   c) Under the View Options menu, which is beneath the Folder menu.
   d) Quick Launch Bar

7. How many characters can you have in a Windows NT file name?
   a) 128
   b) 255
   c) 256
   d) 8

8. Which of the following are invalid Windows NT long file names? Choose all that apply.
   a) PayrollQ.txt
   b) Fo/Le:100.tx*t
   c) Salary.dat
   d) TEXAS.DOC

9. Which NTFS feature allows you to save file disk space by reducing a file's size?
   a) Clustering
   b) Compression
   c) Partitioning
   d) Attributes

10. Which feature allows you make a file hidden?
    a) Clustering
    b) Compression
    c) Partitioning
    d) Attributes

11. Which feature allows you make a file read-only?
    a) Clustering
    b) Compression
    c) Partitioning
    d) Attributes

12. Which partition does Windows NT Workstation compress require?
    a) NFS
    b) NTFS
    c) FAT16
    d) FAT32

13. What is the database of folder and file property settings, and application and user preferences?
    a) REGEDIT
    b) Registry
    c) Backup
    d) DHCP

14. A _____ is a process running on Windows NT.
    a) Function
    b) Process
    c) DLL
    d) CAB file

15. Which registry subtree contains global hardware configuration?
    a) HKEY_USERS
    b) HKEY_CURRENT_USER
    c) HKEY_CLASSES_ROOT
    d) HKEY_LOCAL_MACHINE

16. Which registry subtree contains user preferences?
    a) HKEY_USERS
    b) HKEY_CURRENT_USER
    c) HKEY_CLASSES_ROOT
    d) HKEY_LOCAL_MACHINE

17. The _____ command is used to change the file system type from FAT to NTFS.
    a) CONVERT
    b) COMPRESS
    c) COMPACT
    d) FAT_TO_NTFS

18. What is the name of the special environment where a DOS application runs on a Windows NT computer?
    a) Partition
    b) PIF
    c) NTVDM
    d) Control Panel

19. Which Control Panel function allows you to install a new software application?
    a) Add New Hardware
    b) Add/Remove Programs
    c) Regional Settings
    d) Printers

20. The _____ directory is the default location where Windows NT is installed.
    a) C:\WINNT
    b) C:/WINNT
    c) C:\SETUP
    d) C:\SYSTEM32\WINNT

Lab Projects

Unless otherwise indicated, all projects assume the computer is powered on, you are logged in, and your desktop appears on the screen. Windows NT is up and running.

Lab Project 1

The goal of this project is to help you understand how to create a tree structure from a screenshot.

1. Using Windows Explorer, create the tree structure shown in Figure 5.8 on your floppy. To get to Explorer, right-click Start and then click Explore.

Figure 5.8: A Sample Tree Hierarchy

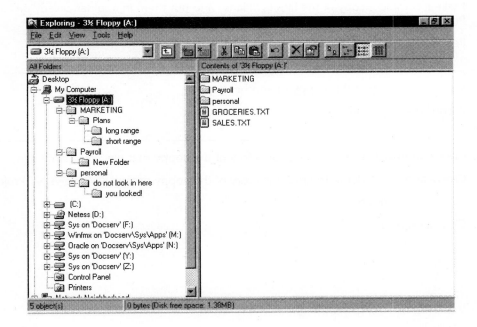

2. Using Notepad, create the following files as Text Documents in the "long range" folder. Place your name in each file.

   Monday.txt
   Tuesday.txt
   Wednesday.txt
   Thursday.txt
   Friday.txt

3. Record the steps you took to create them.

4. Create a "Medium Range" folder in "Plans."

5. Record the steps you took.

   _____

6. In the "personal" folder, create a file called "resume.txt."
7. Hide this folder.
8. Record the steps you took.

   _____

9. View all files.
10. Record the steps you took.

    _____

11. Make a complete copy of the files in "Plans" and put them in a folder called "BACKUP of PLANS."
12. Record the steps you took.

    _____

13. Make a disk copy of this floppy to another floppy.
14. Record the steps you took.

    _____

15. Create another folder in the root directory of the floppy that has your name in it.
16. Create another folder in the root directory of the floppy named "Windows NT Project 1."
17. Show your instructor.
18. Close all windows.

Lab Project 2

The goal of this project is to reinforce your understanding of how to create a tree structure. You will also work with attributes to help you understand how they work.

1. Using Windows Explorer, create the tree structure shown in Figure 5.9 on your floppy.

Figure 5.9: A Sample Tree Hierarchy

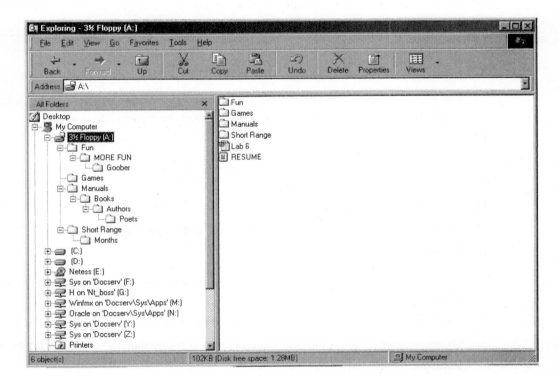

2. Using Notepad, place these files in the "Poets" folder:

   Poe.txt
   Walker.txt
   Smith.txt

3. Activate the setting so hidden and system files are not displayed.

4. Record the steps you took.

5. Hide "Smith.txt."

6. Record the steps you took.

7. Record whether or not you can now see "Smith.txt."

_____

8. Activate the setting to show all files.
9. Record the steps you took.

_____

10. Record whether or not you can now see "Smith.txt."

_____

11. Make the file "Walker.txt" read-only.
12. Record the steps you took.

_____

13. Open the file named "Walker.txt" in Notepad and attempt to add data.
14. Record what occurred.

_____

15. Close Notepad.
16. Make "Walker.txt" readable.
17. Open the file named "Walker.txt" in Notepad and attempt to add data.
18. Record what occurred.

_____

19. Close Notepad.
20. Create another folder in the root directory of the floppy that has your name in it.
21. Create another folder in the root directory of the floppy named "Windows NT Project 2."
22. Show your instructor.
23. Close all windows.

Lab Project 3

The goal of this project is to help you understand how to use the Windows NT Recycle Bin.

1. Turn the computer on and verify that Windows NT Workstation loads.

2. Log on to Windows NT Workstation using the userid and password provided by the instructor or lab assistant.

3. Double-click the **My Computer** desktop icon and then double-click the **C: Drive**. The C: Drive directory structure displays in the My Computer window.

4. Right-click on an empty space in the window, choose New, and then select Text Document. A new text document file appears in the window with the name highlighted.

5. Type **TESTDOC** and press **Enter.** You have now created a blank text file on the C: drive.

6. Record the file extension of TESTDOC.

_____

7. Right-click the **TESTDOC** file and choose **Delete**. Confirm the file deletion by clicking **Yes**. The TESTDOC file has now been sent to the Recycle Bin.

8. Double-click the **Recycle Bin** desktop icon. The Recycle Bin window opens with the **TESTDOC** file appearing in the window.

9. Highlight the **TESTDOC** file and select the **File** menu option.

10. Record which option you would select to return the TESTDOC file to its previous location.

_____

11. Choose the **Empty Recycle Bin** option, and then click **Yes** to confirm the deletion. The TESTDOC file has been permanently deleted.

Lab Project 4

In this lab, you will use REGEDIT to modify how Windows NT Workstation participates in the Browser process.

CAUTION: Editing the registry can cause your computer to run erratically, or not run at all! When performing any registry editing, follow ALL directions carefully including spelling, syntax use, etc. Failure to do so may cause your computer to fail!

1. Turn on the computer and verify that the NT Workstation loads.

2. Log on to NT Workstation using the userid and password provided by the instructor or lab assistant.

3. Click on the **Start** button. Click on the **Run** option.

4. In the text box, type in **REGEDIT** and press **Enter.** The REGEDIT utility appears.

5. In the left window, click on the + **(plus sign)** by the **HKEY_LOCAL_MACHINE** folder.

6. In the left window, click on the + **(plus sign)** by the **System** folder.

7. In the left window, click on the + **(plus sign)** by the **CurrentControlSet** folder.

8. In the left window, click on the + **(plus sign)** by the **Services** folder.

9. In the left window, click on the + **(plus sign)** by the **Browser** folder.

10. In the left window, click on the **Parameters** folder. The values contained in the Parameters folder list in the window on the right side.

11. In the right window, locate the MaintainServerList value.
    Note: The MaintainServerList value controls how the local computer participates in Browser selections. It has three possible DATA values:

    A. Yes: Will always participate as a Browser
    B. No: Will not participate as a Browser
    C. Auto: Can be a Browser if necessary

    Record the DATA value for your computer's **MaintainServerList** value.

    _____

12. Double-click the **MaintainServerList** value. The **Edit String** window opens.

13. If the current DATA value is **Auto**, change the value to **Yes**. If the current DATA value is **Yes**, change the value to **Auto**. If the current DATA value is **No**, change the value to **Auto**.

    What effect will the change made have on the computer's Browser status?

    _____

14. Click on the **OK** button to close the **Edit String** window. The new DATA value appears in the REGEDIT window.

    When will the new registry setting take effect?

    _____

15. Close the **REGEDIT** utility and reboot the computer.

Lab Project 5

In this lab, you will use REGEDT32 to create and configure a new registry setting to resize the desktop icons from the default of 32 pixels to 20 pixels.

CAUTION: Editing the registry can cause your computer to run erratically, or not run at all! When performing any registry editing, follow ALL directions carefully including spelling, syntax use, etc. Failure to do so may cause your computer to fail!

1. Turn on the computer and verify that the NT Workstation loads.

2. Log on to NT Workstation using the userid and password provided by the instructor or lab assistant.

3. Click on the **Start** button. Click on the **Run** option.

4. In the text box, type in **REGEDT32** and press **Enter.** The REGEDT32 utility appears.

5. Click on the **HKEY_CURRENT_USER** window.

6. Expand the **Control Panel** folder by clicking on the **+ (plus sign)** beside it.

7. Expand the **Desktop** folder.

8. Select the **WindowMetrics** option.

9. Form the **Edit** menu item, click on the **Add Value** option. The Add Value window opens.

10. In the Value Name field, type **Shell Icon Size**.

11. In the Data Type field, choose **REG_SZ** and then click on the **OK** button. The String Editor opens.

12. From the String Editor window, enter the value of **20**, (the default number of pixels in a desktop icon is 32) and click on the **OK** button. The new value displays.

    How is the new value displayed in REGEDT32?

    _____

13. Close the **REGEDT32** utility and reboot the computer for the new registry setting to take effect.

    After the computer reboots, are your desktop icons smaller or larger than before? If not, perform the exercise again.

    _____

Lab Project 6

The goal of this project is to help you understand the proper use of the Windows NT Backup utility to back up and restore files. This project assumes you will back up all files from the C: drive to a tape backup unit. If you don't have one, then choose three files to back up to floppy instead.

To back up files, follow these steps:

1. Turn the computer on and verify that Windows NT Workstation loads.

2. Log on to Windows NT Workstation using the userid and password provided by the instructor or lab assistant.

3. From the **Start** menu, point to the **Programs** selection, then the **Administrative Tools** option, and double-click on the **Backup** menu selection. The Windows NT Backup utility starts.

4. From the **Drives** window, select the **C: drive check box** to enable it. This action selects all files and folders on the C: drive for back up.
   Note: To select specific files only, double-click the drive, then browse to and select specific files and/or folders.

   How many drives list in the Drives window?

   _____

5. After choosing the files to be backed up, click on the **Backup** button to begin the backup process. The Backup Information window opens.

6. From the Backup Information window, type **TESTTAPE** in the Tape Name field, choose **Verify After Backup**, select **Normal** for the backup type, and click on the **OK** button.

   What types of backups are available?

   _____

   What does the setting Verify After Backup mean?

   _____

7. Windows NT Backup begins backing up the selected files and folders. The status of the backup can be monitored from the Backup Status window. When Windows NT Backup completes the backup process, a summary report displays. Click on the **OK** button to close the Backup Status window.

   To restore files and/or folders, follow these steps:

8. Verify that the tape with the needed files is inserted into the tape drive.

9. From within the Windows NT Backup utility, open the **Tapes** window. Browse to and select the files to be restored, and then click on the **Restore** button. The Restore Information window opens.

10. Click on the **OK** button to begin the restore process.

    Can the files be restored to an alternate location?

    _____

11. Confirm any file replacement messages by selecting **Yes to all**.

12. When the restore process is completed, a summary report displays in the Restore Status window.

13. Click on the **OK** button to close the Restore Status window and then exit the Windows NT Backup utility.

Lab Project 7

The goal of this project is to help you understand the proper installation of devices using Windows NT Workstation.

Most devices installed on a Windows NT Workstation are installed using the device icons within Control Panel. Each device type has its own specific installation steps, and you must follow the device-specific on-screen prompts and instructions for proper installation.

To install a device on a Windows NT Workstation, follow these general steps:

1. With the computer turned off and following proper ESD precautions, install the device into the appropriate BUS slot or external port.

2. Turn the computer on and verify that Windows NT Workstation loads.

3. Log on to Windows NT Workstation using the userid and password provided by the instructor or lab assistant.

4. From the **Start** menu, point to the **Settings** option, and then select **Control Panel**.

   How else can you open the Control Panel?

   _____

5. From the Control Panel window, double-click on the **Control Panel** icon that represents the device you are installing. Follow the appropriate device-specific instructions and steps to install the device.

Modems

6. Double-click the **Modems** control panel icon.

7. Click on the **Next** button to allow NT to detect the modem.

8. When the modem is detected, click on the **Next** button and follow the on-screen prompts to complete the installation.

Sound Cards

9. Double-click the **Multimedia** control panel icon.

10. Select the **Devices** tab.

11. Click on and highlight **Audio Devices**, click on the **Add** button, and then follow the on-screen prompts to complete the device installation.

Network Adapters

12. Double-click the **Network** control panel icon and select **Adapters**.

13. Click **Add** and then follow the on-screen prompts to complete the device installation.

Ports

14. Double-click the **Ports** control panel icon.

15. Click on the **Add** button and follow the on-screen prompts to complete the device installation.

Printers

16. Double-click the **Printers** control panel icon.

17. Double-click **Add Printer** icon and follow the on-screen prompts to complete the device installation.

SCSI Adapters

18. Double-click the **SCSI Adapters** control panel icon and select **Drivers**.

19. Click on the **Add** button and follow the on-screen prompts to complete the device installation.

Tape Devices

20. Double-click the **Tape Devices** control panel icon and select **Drivers**.

21. Click on the **Add** button and follow the on-screen prompts to complete the device installation.

Note: If the device cannot be installed through a control panel, follow the device manufacturer's specific installation instructions.

Lab Project 8

The goal of this project is to help you understand how to view memory usage statistics in Windows NT Workstation.

At times, it is beneficial to view memory usage statistics to troubleshoot resource conflicts. NT provides two utilities that can be used for this: Task Manager and NT Diagnostics. Task Manager allows you to view the memory usage for individual processes whereas NT Diagnostics allows you to view overall memory usage statistics.

To use Task Manager, follow these steps:

1. Turn the computer on and verify that Windows NT Workstation loads.

2. Log on to Windows NT Workstation using the userid and password provided by the instructor or lab assistant.

3. Press **Ctrl , Alt, and Delete** simultaneously. The Windows Security window opens.

4. Choose **Task Manager** and then select the **Processes** tab.

5. The currently running processes display along with each process's CPU and Memory usage statistics.

   How much memory are the Winlogon.exe and the Taskmgr.exe processes using?

   _____

   To use the Windows NT Diagnostics utility, follow these steps:

6. Click on the **Start** button, point to **Programs, Administration Tools**, and then click on the **Windows NT Diagnostics** option.

   What other method can be used to start Windows NT Diagnostics?

   _____

7. When the Windows NT Diagnostics window opens, select the **Memory** tab. The memory statistics display.

   How much memory is set aside for file caching?

   _____

Lab Project 9

The goal of this project is to help you understand the proper use of the NT Diagnostics utility.

Windows NT provides a diagnostic utility that can be used to view system information. This is especially useful for diagnosing and troubleshooting system errors and conflicts.

1. Turn on the computer and verify that the Windows NT Workstation loads.

2. Log on to NT Workstation using the userid and password provided by the instructor or lab assistant.

3. From the **Start** menu, choose **Programs, Administrative Tools**, and then select **Windows NT Diagnostics**. The Windows NT Diagnostics utility starts.

   How else can you start Windows NT Diagnostics?

   _____

4. Click on the **Version** tab. From the Version tab, you can view the version, service pack, registration key, and registration information for the computer.

5. Select the **System** tab. From the System window, you can view system, HAL, BIOS, and CPU information.

   What type of processor is installed in the computer?

   _____

6. Select the **Display** tab. From the Display window, you can view video adapter and display information.

   What type of video adapter is installed in the computer?

   _____

7. Select the **Drives** tab. From the Drives window, you can view the hard drives and CD-ROM drives.

8. Select the **Memory** tab. From the Memory window, you can view memory statistics for the system.

   How much total physical memory is installed in the system?

   _____

9. Select the **Services** tab. From the Services window, you can view installed services and their status, as well as installed devices and their operational state.

10. Select the **Resources** tab. From the Resources window, you can view IRQ, I/O port, DMA, memory, and device statistics for your system.

    Are any devices using DMA channels? If so, which devices?

    _____

11. Select the **Environment** tab. From the Environment window, you can view the system and local user environment variables.

12. Select the **Network** tab. From the Network window, you can view the network environment settings and statistics.

    Is your workstation a member of a domain, or a workgroup?

    _____

13. Close the Windows NT Diagnostics utility.

Lab Project 10

The goal of this project is to use the Windows NT Diagnostics tool to troubleshoot device conflicts.

1. Turn on the computer and verify that the Windows NT Workstation loads.

2. Log on to NT Workstation using the userid and password provided by the instructor or lab assistant.

3. Click on the **Start** button.

4. Point to the **Programs** option.

5. Point to the **Administrative Tools (Common)** option.

6. Click on the **Windows NT Diagnostics** option. The Windows NT Diagnostics window opens. The tab that opens by default is the Version tab.

    What version of NT Workstation is running and what, if any, service pack is installed?

    _____

7. Click on the **Resources** tab.

    What IRQs are not used?

    _____

8. Click on the **I/O Port** button.

    What device uses 03F7 I/O address space?

    _____

9. Click on the **DMA** button.

    What device uses DMA channel 2?

    _____

10. Click on the **Memory** button.

    What device uses the memory range 000A0000—000AFFFF?

    _____

11. Close the **NT Diagnostics** window.

Lab Project 11

The goal of this project is to help you understand the installation of a local printer on a Windows NT Workstation. You will need a computer with NT Workstation loaded and a printer physically attached to a printer port. Before an NT Workstation can send a print job to a local printer, the driver for that printer must be installed and configured.

1. Turn the computer on and verify that NT Workstation loads.

2. Log on to NT Workstation using the userid and password provided by the instructor or lab assistant.

3. Double-click on the **My Computer** desktop icon and then double-click on the **Printers** folder. The Printers folder opens.

4. Double-click the **Add Printer** icon, and the Add Printer wizard starts.

5. Select **My Computer** and then click on the **Next** button and the Ports window opens.

   How many LPT and COM ports are listed in the Ports window?

   _____

6. Choose the printer **Manufacturer** of your printer and then select the printer **Model**. If the attached printer is not listed, click on the **Have Disk** button, insert the print driver disk or CD, enter a path to the driver files (such as A: or the drive letter for the CD-ROM), and click on the **OK** button.

7. Select the appropriate printer mode and click on the **Next** button.

8. Enter a **name** for the printer in the **Printer Name** field and click on the **Next** button.

   The Sharing and Additional Drivers window opens.

   What name did you assign to the printer?

   _____

9. Select the **Not Shared** option, leave the Share Name field blank, and click on the **Next** button.

10. Select the **Yes** option to print a test page and click on the **Finish** button.

11. If prompted, insert the Windows NT Workstation CD-ROM or enter a path to the installation files.

12. The printer installation process finishes and returns to the Printers Folder. If the installation is successful, a printer test page prints.

    Did a test page print successfully? If not, redo the exercise. Take special precautions when selecting the appropriate print driver.

    _____

Lab Project 12

The goal of this project is to create an ERD on an NT Workstation computer.

1. Turn on the computer and verify that the NT Workstation loads.

2. Log on to NT Workstation using the userid and password provided by the instructor or lab assistant.

3. Click on the **Start** button.

4. Click on the **Run** option.

5. In the Open: text box, type, **RDISK** and press **Enter.** The Repair Disk Utility appears on the screen.

6. Click on the **Update Repair Info** button. A prompt may appear that states that the repair information that was previously saved will be deleted. If this prompt appears, click on the **Yes** button.

   What is the difference between using the Update Repair Info button and the Create Repair Disk options?

   _____

7. A prompt appears asking if you want to create an Emergency Repair Disk. Click on the **Yes** button to create an Emergency Repair Disk.

8. Insert a floppy disk into the A: drive and click on the **OK** button.

9. When finished, remove the disk, label it with the current date and store in a safe location.

10. Click on the **Exit** button to close the Repair Disk program.

Lab Project 13

The goal of this project is to help you understand the proper use of the Performance Monitor utility in monitoring system performance in Windows NT Workstation. Windows NT provides the Performance Monitor utility that can be used to monitor system performance.

1. Turn the computer on and verify that Windows NT Workstation loads.

2. Log on to Windows NT Workstation using the userid and password provided by the instructor or lab assistant.

3. From the **Start** menu, point to **Programs, Administrative Tools**, and then select **Performance Monitor**. The Performance Monitor utility starts.

4. Before Performance Monitor can be used to monitor system performance, you must configure the system counters to monitor. To add counters to Performance Monitor, click the **+ (plus)** button on the Performance Monitor toolbar. The Add To Chart window opens.

5. From the Object drop-down menu, select **Processor**.

   How many objects are available for adding system counters?

   _____

6. From the Counter window, hold the **Ctrl** key down while selecting the following:

   %Processor Time, %User Time, %Interrupt Time, and **%Privileged Time**. Click on the **Add** button, and then click on the **Done** button to return to the Performance Monitor window.

7. Each of the selected counters will be represented on the Performance Monitor chart by different color. Minimize the **Performance Monitor utility** window by clicking on the icon with the line symbol in the top right corner of the window.

8. From the **Start** menu, choose **Programs, Accessories,** and then select **Notepad**.

9. Maximize the **Performance Monitor utility** window by clicking on the Performance Monitor icon located on the taskbar.

   Did starting the Notepad application cause any activity with the selected counters in Performance Monitor?

   _____

10. Move the mouse cursor across the Performance Monitor screen.

    Did moving the mouse cursor cause any counter activity?

    _____

    If moving the mouse cursor caused counter activity, which of the selected counters show the most activity?

    _____

11. When finished with monitoring the selected counters, close the **Performance Monitor** utility.

Lab Project 14

The goal of this project is to create a computer baseline report that can be used when the computer does not function properly.

1. Turn on the computer and verify that the Windows NT Workstation loads.

2. Log on to NT Workstation using the userid and password provided by the instructor or lab assistant.

3. Click on the **Start** button.

4. Point to the **Programs** option.

5. Point to the **Administrative Tools (Common)** option.

6. Click on the **Event Viewer** option.

   What log is opened by default?

   _____

   If any events list on the screen, write the two most recent events in the space below.

   _____

7. Scroll down through the events and note the different symbols that precede events.

   How many different event symbols show in the Event Viewer system log?

   _____

   What does each symbol mean?

   _____

8. Double-click on an **event** in the system log.

   What information does the Event Detail window give you that was not available on the original screen?

   _____

9. Click on the Event Detail **Help** button.

   What happens to event data if you archive the event log in a TXT file?

   _____

10. Click on the **Close** button in the Event Viewer Help window.

11. Click on the **Close** button in the Event Detail window.

12. Click on the **Log** menu item and select the **Security** option.

    What types of events are kept in the security log?

    _____

13. Click on the **View** menu option.

What is an alternative to viewing the newest information first?

_____

14. Click on the **Log** menu item and select the **Log Settings** option.

What is the current setting for the Maximum Log Size option?

_____

15. Click on the **Change Settings for Security** down arrow. The Maximum Log Size option is applicable to each type of event log.

How many types of logs are available in the drop-down menu and what are the names of the logs?

_____

16. Click on the **Cancel** button.

17. Click on the **Log** menu item and select the **System** option.

18. Click on the **View** menu item and select the **Filter Events** option. The Filter Events option is a dialog box that allows you to define the event time period, event type, and event category. When filtering is enabled, the word Filtered appears in the title bar.

What types of events are filtered by default?

_____

19. Click on the **Cancel** button in the Filter window.

20. Click on the **Close** button in the Event Viewer window.

Lab Project 15

The goal of this project is to use Task Manager to halt an application.

At times, it may become necessary to halt a hung or stalled application. Windows NT Workstation provides a method to accomplish this through the Task Manager utility.

1. Turn on the computer and verify that Windows NT Workstation loads.

2. Log on to Windows NT Workstation using the userid and password provided by the instructor or lab assistant.

3. From the **Start** menu, point to **Programs, Accessories,** and then click on the **Notepad** option. The Notepad utility runs.

4. To access Task Manager, simultaneously press the **Ctrl, Alt**, and **Del** keys and then select **Task Manager**.

   What things can you view from Task Manager?

   _____

5. Select the **Applications** tab.

   What applications are listed as open?

   _____

6. Highlight the **Notepad.exe** application and select **End Task**. The Notepad.exe application closes.

7. Close the **Task Manager** utility.

Lab Project 16 Challenge

The goal of this challenge project is to install the Windows NT Workstation operating system on a computer. For this project, you will need a computer without an operating system and a Windows NT Workstation installation CD-ROM along with the setup disks.

The method used to start the Windows NT Workstation installation process depends on whether or not your system supports booting from a CD-ROM.

If your computer supports booting from a CD-ROM, follow these steps:

1. Insert the Windows NT Workstation CD-ROM into the CD-ROM drive and start the computer. The computer boots from the CD and begins the installation process.

2. At the Welcome to Setup screen, press **Enter** to begin Windows NT Setup.

3. Setup detects the mass storage devices installed on your computer and displays a list of the detected devices. Press **Enter** to continue. Continue with Step 5 below.

If your computer does NOT support booting from a CD-ROM, follow these steps:

1. Insert the Windows NT Setup Disk 1 into the floppy drive and start the computer.

   Note: If you do not have the Windows NT Setup floppy disks, you can create them from the installation CD. Insert the installation CD in a computer that has been booted with CD-ROM support. From a command prompt, change to the I386 directory on the CD.

   Type /OX and press Enter when upgrading from DOS, WIN 3.x, or WIN9x, or type 32 /OX and press Enter to upgrade an older version of NT or install a new version of NT. You are prompted to label and insert three floppy disks.

2. When prompted, change the floppy disks.

3. At the Welcome to Setup screen, press **Enter.** Windows prompts to detect the mass storage devices. Press **Enter** to continue.

4. Setup detects the mass storage devices installed and displays a list of the detected devices. Press **Enter** to continue.

From this point on, setup for both types of installations is identical:

5. Page down through the Licensing Agreement and press **F8** to agree.

6. At the Hardware Components page, verify that the listed components match what is installed in the computer and press **Enter.**

7. Highlight the **un-partitioned disk space** where you want to install Windows NT and press **Enter**.

8. Choose to format the partition as **NTFS** and press **Enter**.

9. Press **Enter** to install Windows NT into the default directory.

10. Press **Enter** to have Windows Setup examine the hard disks. After the examination is complete, Setup begins copying files to the hard drive.

11. When prompted, remove all floppy disks and CDs from the drives and press **Enter** to restart the computer.

12. The computer restarts and Setup enters the graphical (GUI) Setup mode. If you chose to use the NTFS file system format, Setup converts the partition to NTFS and restarts the computer a second time.

13. When prompted, re-insert the **Windows NT Installation CD-ROM** and click **OK**.

14. At the Gathering Information about your Computer window, click on the **Next** button.

15. Choose **Typical** installation and click **Next**.

16. Enter the **Name** and **Organization** information provided by the instructor or lab assistant, and click **Next**.

17. Enter the **CD-key** (found on the back of the CD case or provided by the instructor or lab assistant) and click **Next**.

18. Enter the **computer name** (provided by the instructor or lab assistant) and click **Next**.

19. Enter and confirm the **Password** (provided by the instructor or lab assistant) and click **Next**.

20. Select **No, Do not create an Emergency Repair Disk** and click on the **Next** button.

21. Select **Install the most common components**, and click on the **Next** button.

22. Click on the **Next** button to begin installing Windows NT Networking.

23. Choose **This computer will participate on a network**, select **Wired to the Network**, and click **Next**.

24. Select **Start Search**, and Setup searches for network adapters. When the network adapter is detected, click on the **Next** button.

25. Select the **TCP/IP Protocol**, click on the **Next** button, and click on the following **Next** button.

26. If directed by the instructor or lab assistant to use DHCP, choose **Yes** at the TCP/IP Setup window. If not using DHCP, choose **No**. Setup installs the selected networking components.

27. If you are NOT using DHCP, enter an IP address and subnet mask provided by the instructor or lab assistant and click **OK**.

28. Click on the **Next** button to start the network.

29. At the Make this computer a member of window, enter the workgroup or domain information (provided by the instructor or lab assistant) and click on the **Next** button.

30. Click on the **Finish** button to complete Windows NT setup.

31. Select the appropriate **Time Zone** information and click on the **Close** button.

32. Test the selected video settings by selecting the **Test** button. If the settings are correct, click **Yes**, and then click **OK** twice.

33. When prompted, remove all floppy disks and CDs from the drives and select **Restart Computer**. The computer restarts using the newly installed Windows NT Workstation operating system.

Internet Discovery

Internet Discovery Lab 1

The goal of this project is to access the Internet to obtain specific information regarding a computer or its associated parts.

1. List two web sites that have information about troubleshooting the NT Workstation installation.

2. You have just loaded Norton AntiVirus and now NT Workstation does not boot. Find a web site that details what to do.

3. How do you create boot floppies for NT Workstation? Find a web site that describes how and write the URL in the space below.

4. What is Paged Pool Memory as it relates to NT Workstation? Find a definition for this term on the Internet and write the URL and the definition in the space below.

5. On the Microsoft Internet site, find a description of how to install NT Workstation unattended. Write the URL in the space below.

6. An internal 100 MB Iomega Zip Drive is installed in an NT Workstation computer. The computer displays the error, "ASPI for Win32 not initialized." Find a URL that details the resolution process. Write the URL in the space below.

Soft Skills: Help Desk Support

1. A customer calls and asks you how to install a Network Interface Card (NIC). What do you tell them?

2. You receive a page from a Technical Support Engineer. She is receiving this message when booting Windows NT: "Couldn't find NTLDR. Please insert another disk." What is the problem and what suggestions do you offer her for correcting the problem?

3. You attempt to install Windows NT Workstation on a computer that is an Intel 80386 running at 33 MHz with 16 MB of RAM and 100 MB of hard disk space free. What potential issues do you see with this configuration before you install the operating system?

Critical Thinking

1. What is the difference between the system partition and the boot partition?
2. Explain the terms NTVDM and WOW.
3. Define the purpose of the BOOT.INI file.

Study Skills

The "Do" in "Hear, See, Do, Say"

Key to learning are these four points: hear, see, do, say. You need to <u>hear</u> the topic, <u>see</u> it, <u>do</u> and then <u>say</u> it. The "hear" is the easy part. You just simply need to listen to the instructor's lecture in class and take good notes. You can "see" a topic by the instructor writing on the board, showing a video. or presenting PowerPoint slides to you. The "do" part is doing the work and in this case, it means doing the Review Questions and Lab Projects. You complete the "say" point when you are asked a question in class or when you must give answers on a test. Instructors may use traditional pen and paper tests combined with hands-on lab tests. This Study Skills section focuses on the "Do" which translates into doing the Lab Projects."

- Before you begin a Lab Project, read the lab over quickly to get a sense of what is being asked.
- Once you have read it quickly, carefully read it over again. This time, you are reading for content. At this point, you may need to go through the chapter again to help you understand some specific point in the Lab Project.
- Make sure you have the necessary materials to do the Lab Project. For example, if you need a floppy disk, then make sure you have one. Always be prepared. If you need additional paper to complete additional tasks, bring it.
- If you have a hands-on test, practice the Lab Projects, practice the Lab Projects, and then practice the Lab Projects again. Ask the instructor for additional Lab Projects if you want additional help.
- Always bring your textbook and notebook to class. Sometimes instructors will give open book hands-on tests but time the test to simulate a real-world business situation. By all means, bring your material for that type of test. Otherwise, you could fail the test.
- If you are having trouble doing a Lab Project, do a little research first. Dig into your textbook, search the Internet, use the online help available on the computer, and ask your partner. Of course, you can ask your instructor but they will be impressed at the amount of research you've done.

Self-Study Question(s)

1. What Lab Projects did you complete this week?
2. Which Study Skill(s) listed above helped you this week in completing your Lab Projects?

6

Chapter 6
Introduction to
Windows 2000

OBJECTIVES

The goal of this chapter is twofold:
- To introduce you to Windows 2000 Professional.
- To help you prepare and pass the following sections of the A+ Operating System Technologies Exam:

A+ Operating System Technologies Exam Objectives
covered in this chapter (and corresponding page numbers)

1.1 Identify the major desktop components and interfaces, and their functions. Differentiate the characteristics of Windows 9x/Me, Windows NT 4.0 Workstation, Windows 2000 Professional, and Windows XP.

1.2 Identify the names, locations, purposes, and contents of major system files.

1.4 Identify basic concepts and procedures for creating, viewing, and managing disks, directories and files. This includes procedures for changing file attributes and the ramifications of those changes (for example, security issues).

1.5 Identify the major operating system utilities, their purpose, location, and available switches.

Domain 2 Installation, Configuration and Upgrading

2.1 Identify the procedure for installing Windows 9.x/Me, Windows NT 4.0 Workstation, Windows 2000 Professional, and Windows XP and bringing the operating system to a basic operational level.

2.3 Identify the basic system boot sequences and boot methods, including the steps to create an emergency boot disk with utilities installed fro Windows 9.x/Me, Windows NT 4.0 Workstation, Windows 2000 Professional, and Windows XP.

2.4 Identify procedures for installing/adding a device, including loading, adding, and configuration device drivers, and required software.

In this chapter, you will complete the following sections:
• 6.1 Understanding Windows 2000 Professional
• 6.2 Managing Files and Folders on Windows 2000
• 6.3 Understanding Compression and Encryption on Windows 2000 Professional
• 6.4 Understanding the Windows 2000 Registry
• 6.5 Understanding the Pre-Installation Steps of Windows 2000
• 6.6 Understanding How to Install and Upgrade Windows 2000 Professional
• 6.7 Troubleshooting the Windows 2000 Professional Installation
• 6.8 Understanding How to Dual-Boot Windows 2000 Professional and Windows NT
• 6.9 Configuring Windows 2000 Professional
• 6.10 Understanding the Windows 2000 Professional Boot Process
• 6.11 Understanding Task Manager, Dr. Watson, and Event Viewer
• 6.12 Troubleshooting a Service that Does Not Start
• 6.13 Monitoring System Performance

6.1 Understanding Windows 2000 Professional

There are several versions of Windows 2000—Windows 2000 Professional, Windows 2000 Server, Windows 2000 Advanced Server, and Windows 2000 Data Center Server. Windows 2000 Professional is an operating system designed for a computer workstation.

Windows 2000 Professional is an operating system designed for business workstations—computers in the workplace that are connected to a network. Windows 2000 is easy to install and you can upgrade from Windows 95, Windows 98, or NT Workstation. The installation can also be done across a network. In addition, Windows 2000 is more robust and more stable than previous workstation operating systems. Windows 2000 supports plug and play. The operating system supports many new hardware devices including DVD, video capture devices, speakers, USB, multiple monitor support, removable storage drives, infrared devices, and digital cameras. One important change is that with Windows 2000, the computer does not have to be restarted after every change, as it did with Windows 95/98. This feature is only available if the drivers being installed are Windows 2000 certified.

Windows 2000 Professional is based on a 32-bit architecture. This operating system provides better performance than NT Workstation and Windows 95/98. Every 32-bit application under Windows 2000 and NT runs in its own memory space. When an application freezes or crashes, other 32-bit applications loaded into memory are not affected. Like NT Workstation, all 16-bit applications run in a single process called **NTVDM (NT Virtual DOS Machine)**. If one 16-bit application crashes, any other 16-bit applications loaded into memory crash too. However, Windows 2000 Professional offers the option of running a 16-bit application in its own memory space to prevent this from happening. To allow a 16-bit application to run in its own memory space, go to a command prompt and type **start /separate** *process_name*, where *process_name* is the name of the 16-bit application process.

Windows 2000 Professional can use up to 4 GB of RAM and support **SMP (Symmetric Multiprocessing)**. SMP is the ability to support two processors that operate simultaneously. Each process being run by an application or the operating system is distributed equally across two microprocessors and makes sure that one processor does not become a bottleneck for the system.

A new Windows 2000 Professional feature is **WFP (Windows File Protection)**, which is a program that protects system files. WFP is a program that runs in the background. It detects whether a system file has been altered or deleted. In previous operating systems, applications or users changed the system files and thus made the operating system unstable. WFP detects when a system file has been altered, deleted, or overwritten.

The file systems that Windows 2000 Professional supports include FAT16, FAT32, and NTFS.

After a user logs on to Windows 2000, the desktop appears. The log-in screen cannot be bypassed as it can in Windows 95/98. A user can log in to a network server, log in to a network workgroup (peer-to-peer network), or log in locally (as a stand-alone computer not participating in a network). Figure 6.1 shows the Windows 2000 desktop.

Figure 6.1: The Windows 2000 Professional Desktop

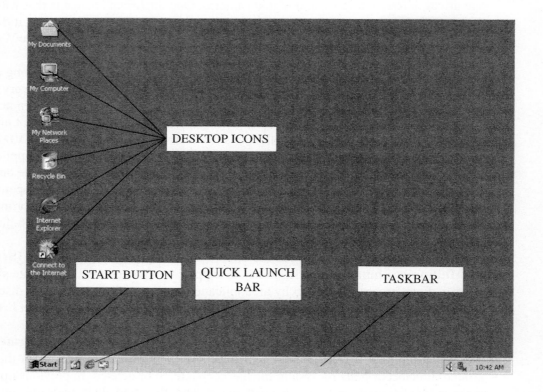

The desktop consists of many icons. Icons are pictures on the desktop. When you double-click on them, you interface with various devices, files, and applications on your computer. The desktop sometimes is cluttered with things the user puts on it.

Let's go through a brief exercise to help you understand how to maintain your Windows 2000 desktop. In this exercise, you will work with the **Auto Arrange** option to force your icons on your desktop to be automatically arranged towards the left hand side of the desktop. When you attempt to relocate an icon, it will automatically be arranged back to its original position—on the left hand side of the desktop. It is assumed that Windows 2000 is installed and running on a computer with the Windows 2000 desktop displayed on your screen.

1. Right-click on a blank desktop space. Once a menu appears, point to the **Arrange Icons** option. If the **Auto Arrange** option does have a check mark beside it, click on an **empty portion of the desktop** to cancel because Auto Arrange is already in use. If the **Auto Arrange** option does not have a check mark beside it, click on the **Auto Arrange** option to add the check mark and enable **Auto Arrange** capability.

2. Note the position of the icons on the desktop.

3. Click on the **My Documents** icon and while continuing to hold the mouse button down, drag the icon to the center of the screen. You will see that the **My Documents** icon moves to its original position.

4. Click on the **Recycle Bin** icon and while continuing to hold the mouse button down, drag the icon to the top right portion of the screen. This icon moves to its original position too.

5. Right-click on a **blank desktop space.** A menu appears.

6. Using step 1 as a guide, set Auto Arrange back to its original setting.

The desktop can also be modified to have a wallpaper scheme (which is a background picture, pattern, or color), a color scheme (which is the color scheme used in displaying folders), and a screen saver (which is the picture, color, or pattern that displays when the computer is inactive).

Let's perform an exercise on the desktop properties. Again, it is assumed that Windows 2000 is running on a computer.

1. Right-click on an **empty desktop area.** A menu appears.

2. Click on the **Properties** option. The Display Properties window appears. (Note: this screen can also be accessed by clicking on the **Start** button, pointing to the **Settings** option, clicking on the **Control Panel** option, and double-clicking on the **Display** control panel icon.)

3. Click on the **Background** tab. This tab controls how the background color and pattern appears.

4. To change your wallpaper to the **Chateau** option, click on the **Chateau** option.

5. Click on the **Apply** button.

6. To view the **Appearance** tab settings, click on the **Appearance** tab at the top of the window. This tab controls the color scheme and size of the letters. This tab is good to use when people with vision problems need adjustments.

7. Click Cancel to close the window.

Whenever you open an application or utility, a window appears. Windows are a normal part of the desktop. The desktop consists of icons, the Start button, the Quick Launch bar, and the taskbar. Common icons include: My Documents, My Computer, My Network Places, and Recycle Bin.

The **My Documents** icon is used to quickly access the My Documents folder (directory) on the hard drive. The My Documents folder is the default location for files the user saves. The **My Computer** icon is used to access the hardware, software, and files located on the computer. The **My Network Places** icon is used to access network resources such as computers, printers, scanners, fax machines, and files. The **Recycle Bin** is used to hold files and folders the user deletes. When a file is deleted from a folder, it is not immediately discarded; instead, it goes into the Recycle Bin. Once a file or folder is in the Recycle Bin, it can be removed. This is similar to a piece of trash being retrieved from an office trash can. You must remember that these files and folders in the Recycle Bin take up hard drive space and that users frequently forget to empty the files and folders from the Recycle Bin.

The **Internet Explorer** icon is used to start the Internet Explorer application. This application allows Internet connectivity. The **Connect to the Internet** icon is a Windows 2000 wizard that steps you through setting up an Internet connection. The Connect to the Internet icon is actually a common type of desktop icon called a shortcut. A **shortcut** is an icon that looks like any other icon except that it has a bent arrow in the lower left corner. A shortcut represents a path (location on the drive) to a file, folder, or program. It is a link (a pointer) to where the file or application resides on a disk. When you double-click on a shortcut icon, the shortcut icon tells Windows where to find the specific file that the icon represents. If the shortcut represents an application, the application opens. If the shortcut represents a document, the application used to create the document appears along with the document. A shortcut offers faster access to an application or file than going through the Start button or through the My Computer icon. Users frequently place shortcuts on the desktop and it is important that you know how to create one. Users create shortcuts to their favorite applications or to documents used frequently.

The **Start button** is located in the lower left corner of the desktop and is used to launch applications and utilities, search for files and other computers, get help, and add or remove hardware and software. Figure 6.2 shows the Start button.

Figure 6.2: The Windows 2000 Start Button

The **Shut Down Start button** option is used to shut down the computer, log off from the network, restart the computer, and possibly put the computer in standby or hibernate. The standby and hibernate options are available on computers that support power saving features. Standby is helpful on laptop computers to save on battery life. Hibernate is available on computers that support Windows 2000 power options and is similar to the shutdown option except that it can be scheduled. At a specific time, the computer is shut down and when the computer restarts, the active components on the desktop at the time of hibernation are still there.

The **Run Start button** option is used for starting an application or bringing up a command prompt window. The Help option is used for Windows 2000 general usage and troubleshooting assistance. The **Search Start button** option is used to locate files, remote network devices, web sites on the Internet, and people in the Windows address book. The Settings option is used to access various suboptions that allow computer configuration. The Documents selection contains the 15 most recently used files (provided the application supports this option). The Programs choice allows access to applications installed in the computer. The Windows Update option is used to connect to the Microsoft web site to access the most recent drivers and operating system updates.

The **Quick Launch bar** is a set of icons to the right of the Start button and allows you to launch applications with one click on a Quick Launch icon. An important icon on the Quick Launch bar is the **Show Desktop** icon. This icon looks like a desk with a pencil touching a piece of paper. Single-click on the Show Desktop icon to reduce all windows on the screen and display the desktop. If you click on the icon a second time, the original document (that was on the screen when you clicked the Show Desktop icon) reappears. Another Quick Launch icon is the Internet Explorer icon. Click once on this icon and the Internet Explorer application opens.

The **taskbar** is the bar that runs across the bottom of the screen. The taskbar holds buttons that represent applications or files currently loaded into memory. The taskbar also holds icons that allow access to system utilities. These utilities can include a clock icon for the date and time, an icon of a speaker for volume control, and an icon for a virus utility. Look back to Figure 6.1 to identify the taskbar.

One type of window used with Windows operating systems is a dialog box. A **dialog box** allows you to set application or operating system preferences. The most common features found in a dialog box are a check box, a text box, tabs, a drop-drown menu, a Help button, a Close button, an OK button, and a Cancel button.

A **text box** is an area where you can type a specific parameter. When you click inside a text box, a vertical line appears, which is the insertion point. Any typed text is placed to the right of the insertion point. Notice in Figure 6.3 how the Top, Bottom, Inside, Outside, etc. options are text boxes. Text boxes sometimes have up or down arrows that can be used to select a preset option, or you can simply type your own parameter.

Tabs normally appear across the top of a dialog box. Each tab normally holds a group of related options. Click once on the tab to bring that particular major section to the window forefront. The tabs in Figure 6.3 are Margins, Paper Size, Paper Source, and Layout.

The **Help button** is used to provide context-sensitive assistance and is the question mark located in the upper right corner of the dialog box. When you click on the Help button (the question mark), the cursor turns into an arrow with a question mark attached. Click on any item you want basic information on and a pop-up window appears on the screen. To close the pop-up window, click anywhere on the screen.

The **Close button**, which is located to the right of the Help button and is an "X," is used to close the dialog box. When the Close button is used, no changes that have been made in the dialog box are applied.

A **check box** is an option that, when checked, is enabled or turned on. In Figure 6.3, clicking inside the check box enables the Mirror Margins option. When an option is enabled, a check mark appears in the check box.

A **radio button** is a round circle, but it operates the same way a check box does. A radio button is enabled when a solid dot appears inside it. Click once on a blank radio button and a solid dot appears. Click once on a radio button that has a dot in it, and the dot disappears. The option is disabled when no dot appears.

Drop-down menus are presented when you click on a down arrow. In Figure 6.3, the drop-down menu appears when you click on the down arrow in the section marked Apply to. Once presented with the drop-down menu, click on the preferred option and that option appears in the drop-down window.

Figure 6.3: Windows 2000 Dialog Box Components

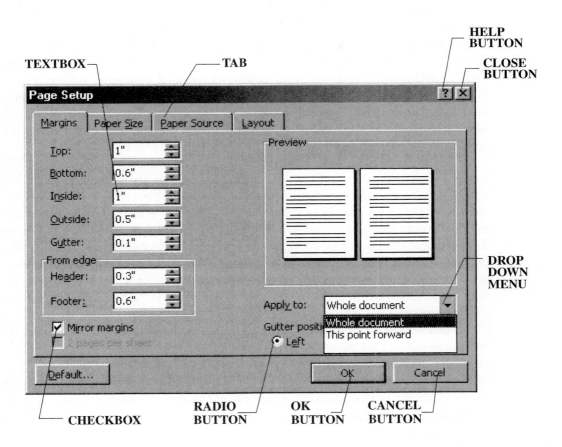

The **OK button** and the **Cancel button** are standard buttons in a dialog box. When you click on the OK button, all options selected or changed within the dialog box are applied. When you click on the Cancel button, all changed options in the dialog box are not applied; the options are left in their current state.

Another related button that can be found in a dialog box, but is not shown in Figure 6.3, is the Apply button. The **Apply button** is used to make changes immediately (before clicking on the OK button). This is useful when you want to see the results of your selection, such as when you are making changes to the desktop's background.

One of the most frequent mistakes users make is clicking on the Close button without first applying or clicking OK for changes. When a dialog box is closed with the Close button, no changes in the dialog box window are saved or applied.

6.2 Managing Files and Folders on Windows 2000

Users are always creating, deleting, and moving files and folders. It is important that you are able to do these tasks quickly and without error. The important thing to remember is to think about what file and folder you want to work with, where the files and folders are located now, and where you want the files or folders to be eventually.

A drive letter followed by a colon represents every drive in a computer. For example, the floppy drive is represented by A: and the first hard drive partition is represented by C:. The CD-ROM drive, or DVD drive, is also represented by a letter followed by a colon. Disks or drives hold files. A **file** is an electronic container that holds computer code or data. Another way of looking at it is thinking of a file as a box of bits. A file is kept on some type of media such as a floppy disk, hard drive, tape, or CD. Each file is given a name called a file name. An example of a file name is 2000CHAP.DOC.

Files are kept in folders. A **folder** holds files and can also contain other folders. In folder operating systems, a folder was called a directory. Every file and folder is given a name. It is easier to understand file and folder names if we look at how older operating systems named files and folders and then look at how Windows 2000 names differ. An **extension** is an addition to the file name and it can be up to three characters in length. The file name and the extension are separated by a period. An example of a file name with an extension is BOOK.DOC where BOOK is the name of the file and DOC is the extension.

Normally with Windows 95/98/NT/2000, the application automatically adds an extension to the end of the file name. In most windows, Windows 2000 does not automatically show the extensions.

In this next exercise, you will learn view the extensions of files. Be default, Windows 2000 does not display the extension of files.

1. Right-click **Start** and then click **Explore**. Windows Explorer opens.
2. To view the extensions in Windows NT Explorer, click on the **View** menu option.
3. Click on the **Folder Options** menu option. Click on the **View** tab and click on the
4. **Hide file extensions for known file types** check box (which will remove the check from the box).
5. Click on the **Apply** button. Windows Explorer displays the extension for all files.
6. Close Explorer.

Windows 2000 Files

File names in Windows 2000 Professional can be up to 255 characters. These extended file names are commonly called long file names. Folders and file names can have all characters, numbers, letters, and spaces _except_ the following:

/ (forward slash) " (quotation marks) \ (backslash)
| (vertical bar) ? (question mark) : (colon)
* (asterisk)

An example of a long file name is WINDOWS 2000 CHAPTER.DOC. Any time a document has been saved with one of these long file names and is taken to a computer with an older operating system that does not support long file names, the file name is shortened to a maximum of eight characters. Windows does this by using the first six characters of the file name, deleting any spaces, and using two special characters—a tilde (~) and a number. For example, 2000 PROFESSIONAL CHAPTER.DOC would be shortened to 2000PR~1.DOC. If there were two files named 2000 PROFESSIONAL CHAPTER.DOC and 2000 PROFESSIONAL INDEX.DOC, the two files would be saved as 2000PR~1.DOC and 2000PR~2.DOC, respectively.

When a file is saved in a Windows application, it automatically goes to a specific folder. This is known as the default folder. With Windows NT and 2000, this folder is the **My Documents** folder. In documentation, installation instructions, and when writing down the exact location of a file, the full path should be used. A file's **path** is like a road map to the file and includes the drive letter plus all folders and subfolders as well as the file name and extension. For example, if the CHAP1.DOC file is in the MY DOCU-MENTS folder on the first hard drive partition, the full path is C:\MY DOCU-MENTS\CHAP1.DOC. The first part is the drive letter where the document is stored, C:. The C: represents the first hard drive partition. The name of the document is always at the very end of the path. In the example given, CHAP1.DOC is the name of the file. Everything in between the drive letter and the file name is the name of one or more folders where the CHAP1.DOC file is located. The folder in this example is the MY DOCU-MENTS folder.

If the CHAP1.DOC file is located in a subfolder called COMPUTER BOOK, which is located in the folder called MY DOCUMENTS, then the full path is C:\MY DOCU-MENTS\COMPUTER BOOK\CHAP1.DOC. Notice how the backslashes in the path are always used to separate the folder names as well as separate the drive letter from the first folder name.

Explorer is the most common application used to create, copy, and move files or folders; however, the My Computer window can be used in a similar fashion. When you are copying a file or folder, use the Copy/Paste functions. When you are moving a file or folder, use the Cut/Paste functions.

Let's go through an exercise to help you understand how to manipulate files and folders. It is assumed that Windows 2000 is installed and running on a computer with the Windows 2000 desktop displayed on your screen.

1. Insert your floppy in the floppy drive.
2. Right-click **Start** and then click **Explore**. Windows Explorer opens with left and right windowpanes.
3. Click the icon associated with the floppy.
4. Click **File**, click **New,** and then click **Folder**. The name of the folder appears as **New Folder**. Type **My Folder** and press Enter.
5. In the left windowpane, expand the floppy by clicking the plus sign to the right of it. If you see a minus sign to the right, it already is expanded.
6. Click **My Folder**.

7. To create a folder within **My Folder**, click **File**, click **New,** and then click **Folder**. The name of the folder appears as **New Folder**. Enter your own name for the name of the folder and press Enter.

8. To create a file within **My Folder**, click **File**, click **New,** and then click **New Text Document**. The name of the text document appears as **New Text Document**. Press Enter to keep this name.

9. To rename the new text document, right-click the document and click **Rename**. The document name is highlighted. Type **My Document** and press Enter. Note if the extension (.txt) appears, then the folder is set to show extensions. In this case, leave it otherwise you will receive a message that changing the file extension may cause the file to become unusable.

10. To delete the text document, right-click the document (note its name has changed) and click **Delete**. A confirmation message will appear.

11. Click **Yes** to delete. The file is deleted.

12. Close Windows Explorer.

When you delete a file or folder from a floppy disk, the file or folder is permanently deleted. When deleting a file or folder from a hard drive, the file or folder is automatically sent to the Recycle Bin. The contents of the Recycle Bin take up hard drive space. Many users do not realize that they are not really deleting the file, but simply moving it to the Recycle Bin. To delete a file permanently from the hard drive, hold down the **Shift** key while pressing the **Delete** key on the keyboard and the file is permanently removed. Otherwise, you will have to remember to empty the Recycle Bin periodically. Figure 6.4 shows how the A+ COMPLETE BOOK.DOC long file name looks in graphical form using the Explorer application.

Figure 6.4: Windows 2000 Explorer

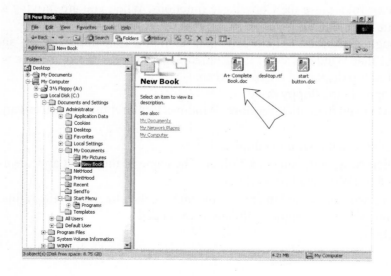

File Attributes

My Computer and Explorer can be used for setting attributes for a file or folder. The file and folder attributes are read-only, hidden, archive, and system. The **read-only attribute** marks a file or folder so that it cannot be changed. The **hidden attribute** marks a file or folder so that it is not visible through My Computer or Explorer unless someone changes the default view for the window. Some applications use the **archive attribute** to control which files or folders are backed up. The **system attribute** is placed on certain files used to boot Windows 2000 Professional.

Let's perform an exercise to help you understand a file's attributes. It is assumed that Windows 2000 is installed and running on a computer with the Windows 2000 desktop displayed on your screen.

1. Insert your floppy in the floppy drive.
2. Right-click **Start** and then click **Explore**. Windows Explorer opens with left and right windowpanes.
3. Click the icon associated with the floppy.
4. To create a file, click **File**, click **New,** and then click **New Text Document**. The name of the text document appears as **New Text Document**. Press Enter to keep this name.
5. To set the file's attributes, right-click the new text document and click **Properties**. The Properties window for the file opens.
6. In the **Attributes** section of the page, check **Read-only** and click **OK**. The Properties window closes.
7. Next, you will attempt to modify the file. Remember it is set to read-only. Double-click the document. The document opens.
8. On the document screen, type your name and press Enter. This is considered text.
9. Attempt to save the document. Click **File** then click **Save**. The **Save As** window opens. Normally, this window does not appear—the file is simply saved. However, because the file has the read-only attribute, you cannot save the text to this file. Windows 2000 wants you to enter a new file name.
10. To see the error message, click **Save**. A message is displayed indicating you cannot save this file.
11. Click **OK** and then click **Cancel**. The document screen remains.
12. Close the document. Do not save changes if prompted.
13. Close Windows Explorer.

Refer to Figure 6.5 for a sample screenshot of a file's attributes.

Figure 6.5: The Attributes of the File named "Todd Meaders.doc"

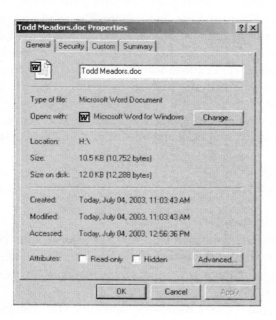

Determining the Windows 2000 Version

The operating system version is very important to you. With Windows 95, 98, NT, and 2000, upgrades or patches to the operating system are provided through **service packs**, which fix problems within the operating system. You must determine what operating system version is on the computer so that he or she can research whether or not a service pack is needed. Several ways to determine what version of 2000 is loaded on a computer are listed below.

• Right-click on the **Start** button. Click on the **Explore** option. Windows Explorer opens. Click on the **Help** menu option. Click on the **About Windows** option from the drop-down menu.

• Click on the **Start** button. Click on the **Run** option. In the Open text box, type **winver** and press Enter. A window appears with the version.

• Click on the **Start** button. Point to the **Programs** option. Point to the **Administrative Tools** option. Click on the **Computer Management** option. Right-click on the **Computer Management (Local)** option and then click on the **Properties** option.

• Click on the **Start** button. Click on the **Run** option. In the Open text box, type **winmsd** and then press Enter.

Refer to Figure 6.6 for a sample screenshot of the WINVER program.

Figure 6.6: The WINVER Program Displaying the Windows Version

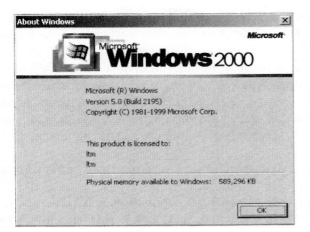

Refer to Figure 6.7 for a sample screenshot of the WINMSD program.

Figure 6.7: The WINMSD Program Displaying the Windows Version and Other Information

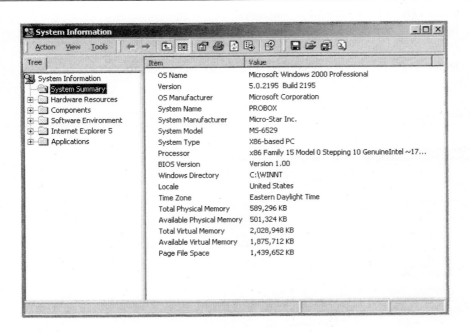

6.3 Understanding Compression and Encryption on Windows 2000 Professional

If the hard drive is partitioned for the NTFS file system, files and folders can be compressed or encrypted with Windows 2000. **Compression** is where a file or folder is compacted to take up less disk space. However, with compression enabled, the computer's performance can degrade. This is because, in order to open a compressed file, that file must be uncompressed, copied, and then recompressed. Degradation can also occur if a compressed file is transferred across a network because the file must be uncompressed before it is transferred. You can enable file compression by using Windows Explorer.

In this next exercise, you will learn how to compress a file on a computer running Windows 2000.

1. Right-click **Start** and then click **Explore**. Windows Explorer opens with left and right windowpanes.
2. Click the local disk (C:) icon. Note that this partition must be NTFS.
3. To create a file, click **File**, click **New,** and then click **New Text Document**. The name of the text document appears as **New Text Document**. Press Enter to keep this name.
4. Right-click the document, and click **Properties**. The Properties window opens.
5. Click **Advanced**. The **Advanced Attributes** window opens.
6. Click **Compress contents to save disk space**.
7. Click **OK** twice to close the windows.
8. Notice the attribute is now set to compressed.
9. Close all windows.

Refer to Figure 6.8 for a sample screenshot of the Compress check box. It is located in the lower half of the screen.

Figure 6.8: Compressing a File

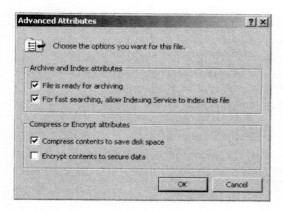

When working with compressed files and folders, users like them to appear in a different color than other files and folders. The color will be blue. To set this option, click on the **View** Windows Explorer menu option. Click on the **Options** selection. Click in the **Display compressed files and folders with alternate color** radio button. Click on the **OK** button. Refer to Figure 6.9 for a sample screenshot. Note this is the first check box selected.

Figure 6.9: Screenshot of Folder Options

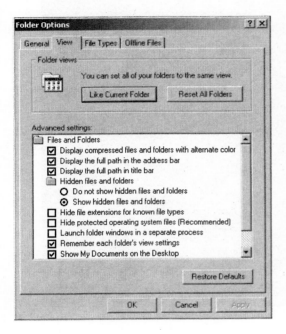

Files and folders can also be compressed or uncompressed from the command line using the **COMPACT** command. The COMPACT command can also be used to view the compression state of folders. The COMPACT command automatically compresses or uncompresses all the files and subfolders when you change a folder's compression state. Refer to Figure 6.10 for the information on the COMPACT command.

Figure 6.10: The COMPACT Command

```
C:\WINNT\System32\cmd.exe                                    _ 5 X

C:\>
C:\>compact /?
Displays or alters the compression of files on NTFS partitions.

COMPACT [/C | /U] [/S[:dir]] [/A] [/I] [/F] [/Q] [filename [...]]

    /C          Compresses the specified files. Directories will be marked
                so that files added afterward will be compressed.
    /U          Uncompresses the specified files. Directories will be marked
                so that files added afterward will not be compressed.
    /S          Performs the specified operation on files in the given
                directory and all subdirectories. Default "dir" is the
                current directory.
    /A          Displays files with the hidden or system attributes. These
                files are omitted by default.
    /I          Continues performing the specified operation even after errors
                have occurred. By default, COMPACT stops when an error is
                encountered.
    /F          Forces the compress operation on all specified files, even
                those which are already compressed. Already-compressed files
                are skipped by default.
    /Q          Reports only the most essential information.
    filename    Specifies a pattern, file, or directory.

Used without parameters, COMPACT displays the compression state of
the current directory and any files it contains. You may use multiple
filenames and wildcards. You must put spaces between multiple
parameters.

C:\>
```

You can compress a file or folder only on an NTFS partition.

Encryption is a method of securing data from unauthorized users. Windows 2000 has a new encryption feature called **EFS (Encrypting File System)**. When a file or folder is encrypted with EFS, only the authorized user can view or change the file. Administrators have the ability to recover encrypted files if necessary. EFS is not compatible with any prior version of Windows.

In this next exercise, you will learn how to compress a file on a computer running Windows 2000. This exercise assumes you performed the previous exercise on compression because that is where you created the file used in this next exercise.

1. Right-click **Start** and then click **Explore**. Windows Explorer opens with left and right windowpanes.
2. Click the local disk (C:) icon.

3. Right-click the **New Text Document** document you created in the previous exercise, and click **Properties**. The Properties window opens.
4. Click **Advanced**. The **Advanced Attributes** window opens.
5. Click **Encrypt contents to secure data**. Notice the check box that was selected for compression is removed.
6. Click **OK** twice to close the windows.
7. Notice the attribute is now set to compressed.
8. Close all windows.
Refer to Figure 6.11 for a sample screenshot.

Figure 6.11: Encrypting a File

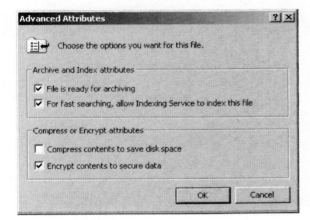

You can encrypt a file or folder only on an NTFS partition.

The **CIPHER** command line utility can be used to encrypt and decrypt files. The command can also be used to encrypt and decrypt folders. If you type **CIPHER** from the command prompt without any switches, current file/folder encryption states are displayed on the screen. Type **CIPHER /?** to view the various switch options available with this command. Refer to Figure 6.12 for a sample screenshot of this command.

Figure 6.12: The CIPHER Command

```
C:\WINNT\System32\cmd.exe                                    _ 8 X
Microsoft Windows 2000 [Version 5.00.2195]
(C) Copyright 1985-1999 Microsoft Corp.

C:\>cipher /?
Displays or alters the encryption of directories [files] on NTFS partitions.

  CIPHER [/E | /D] [/S:dir] [/A] [/I] [/F] [/Q] [/H] [/K] [pathname [...]]

    /E        Encrypts the specified directories. Directories will be marked
              so that files added afterward will be encrypted.
    /D        Decrypts the specified directories. Directories will be marked
              so that files added afterward will not be encrypted.
    /S        Performs the specified operation on directories in the given
              directory and all subdirectories.
    /A        Operation for files as well as directories. The encrypted file
              could become decrypted when it is modified if the parent directory

              is not encrypted. It is recommended that you encrypt the file and
              the parent directory.
    /I        Continues performing the specified operation even after errors
              have occurred. By default, CIPHER stops when an error is
              encountered.
    /F        Forces the encryption operation on all specified objects, even
              those which are already encrypted. Already-encrypted objects
              are skipped by default.
    /Q        Reports only the most essential information.
    /H        Displays files with the hidden or system attributes. These
              files are omitted by default.
    /K        Create new file encryption key for the user running CIPHER. If thi
s
              option is chosen, all the other options will be ignored.
    pathname  Specifies a pattern, file or directory.

  Used without parameters, CIPHER displays the encryption state of
  the current directory and any files it contains. You may use multiple
  directory names and wildcards. You must put spaces between multiple
  parameters.

C:\>
```

The compression and encryption attributes cannot both be checked. In other words, you cannot compress and encrypt a folder or file. You can either compress or encrypt, but not both.

6.4 Understanding the Windows 2000 Registry

Every software and hardware configuration is stored in a database called the **registry**. The registry contains such things as folder and file property settings, port configuration, application preferences, and user profiles. A **user profile** contains a user's specific configuration settings such as what applications the user has access to, desktop settings, and the user's network configuration. The registry loads into memory during the boot process. Once in memory, the registry is updated continuously through changes made to software and hardware. The registry is divided into five subtrees. **Subtrees** are sometimes called branches or hives. The five standard subtrees are as follows:

HKEY_LOCAL _MACHINE, HKEY_USERS, HKEY_CURRENT_USER, HKEY_ CURRENT _CONFIG, and HKEY_CLASSES_ROOT. Each of these subtrees has keys and subkeys that contain values related to hardware and software settings.

Table 6.1 lists the five subtrees and each function.

Table 6.1: Windows 2000 Registry Subtrees

Registry Subtree	Function
HKEY_LOCAL_MACHINE	Holds global hardware configuration. Included in the branch is a list of hardware components installed in the computer, the software drivers that handle each component, and the settings for each device. This information is not user-specific.
HKEY_USERS	Keeps track of individual users and their preferences.
HKEY_CURRENT_USER	Holds a specific user's configuration such as software settings, how the desktop appears, and what folders the user has created.
HKEY_CURRENT_CONFIG	Holds information about the hardware profile that is used when the computer first boots.
HKEY_CLASSES_ROOT	Holds file associations and file links. The information held here is what allows the correct application to start when you double-click on a file name in Explorer or My Computer (provided the file extension is registered).

The registry can contain other subtrees that are user-defined or system-defined depending on what hardware and software is installed in the computer.

Most changes to Windows 2000 are made through the various control panels, but sometimes the only way to make a change is to edit the registry directly. However, be careful, because if you make an incorrect registry change, you could cause your system to become inoperable.

Windows 2000 has two registry editors called **REGEDIT** and **REGEDT32**. Both registry editors can be used to change the registry; however, there are some differences between the two. Table 6.2 shows some of the more important differences.

Table 6.2: REGEDIT and REGEDT32 Differences

REGEDIT	REGEDT32
Provides more powerful search capabilities.	Can display and edit values larger than 256 characters.
All of the subtrees are shown in one window.	The subtrees are shown in individual windows.
Allows exporting the registry to a text file.	Can look at and apply access permissions to the subtrees, keys, and subkeys.
Allows importing the registry from the command line.	Can work with multiple registry files simultaneously.

With the REGEDIT program, subtrees are listed in the left window. Figure 6.13 shows the REGEDIT utility.

Figure 6.13: Windows 2000 REGEDIT Window

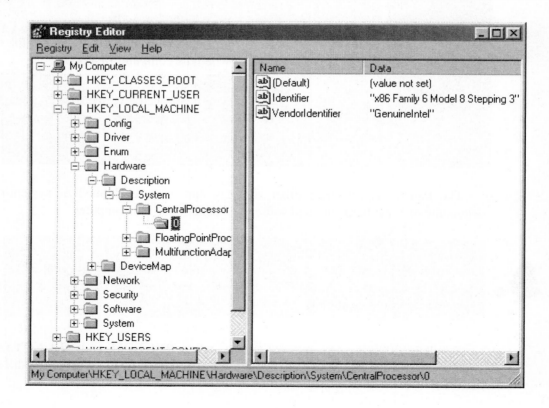

Notice in Figure 6.13 how the subtrees show up in the left window. When you click on the + (plus) symbol beside each subtree, more subkeys appear. After several layers, when you click on a folder in the left window, values appear in the right window. These values are the ones you must sometimes change to fix a problem.

In REGEDT32, each registry hive appears in a separate window inside the Registry Editor window. Each subtree has individual folders with a + (plus) symbol beside them. Click on the plus symbol to view subkeys. Values appear in the right window as they do in the REGEDIT program. Each hive, or even part of a subtree, can be backed up individually.

Backing Up and Restoring the Windows 2000 Registry

The registry should be backed up whenever the computer is fully functional and when any software or hardware changes are made. The registry can be backed up and restored several different ways. The two most common methods used are the REGEDIT and the Backup utilities. The REGEDIT program allows you to export the registry to a file that has the .REG extension. The backed up file can be modified with a text editor if necessary. The file can also be imported back into the computer.

The registry should be backed up and restored on a working computer *before* disaster hits. The time to learn how to restore the registry is *not* when the computer is down.

The Backup utility is accessed through Start button, Programs, Accessories, System Tools, Backup. The Backup utility is the preferred method for backing up the Windows 2000 registry. The Backup option to look for is the System State, which is discussed in the next section. Refer to Figure 6.14 for a sample screenshot of backing up the System State. In the left-hand pane, notice that "System State" is checked (in blue).

Figure 6.14: Screenshot of Backing Up the System State

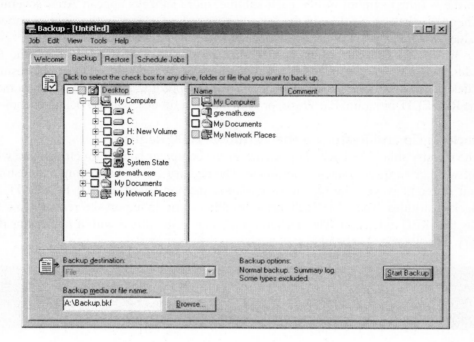

One option available in the Backup utility is the System State. The **System State** is a group of important Windows 2000 files including the registry, the system files, the boot files, and the COM+ Class Registration database. With the Backup utility, you cannot back up or restore these items individually. They are all needed because they depend on one another to operate properly. The Backup utility is accessed through Start button, Programs, Accessories, System Tools, Backup. Click on the **Backup** tab. Click in the box next to **System State**. Select the destination and click on the **Start Backup** button. Once you click on the Start Backup button, the Backup Job Information dialog box appears. The **Advanced** option has a setting: **Automatically backup system protected files with the System State**. This option, when selected, backs up all system files in the *%systemroot%* folder (which is normally C:\WINNT). Click on the **OK** button to start the backup. Refer to Figure 6.15 for a screenshot of selecting the automatic backing up of system protected files.

Figure 6.15: Automatically Back Up System Protected Files with System State

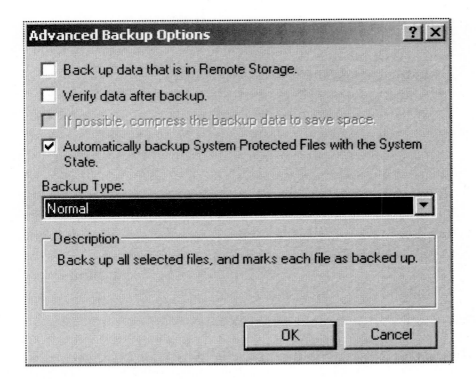

The registry files are located in a folder normally labeled *%systemroot%*\Reg-backup (which is normally C:\WINNT\REPAIR\REGBACKUP). The registry can be restored without having to restore the other System State files. In order to use the Backup program, you must be an administrator or a member of the Backup Operators group.

Restoring the System State After a Failure

In order to correct a problem with the system files, registry, or Windows 2000 boot failure, you must restore the registry. You may also have to restore the System State files (which include the registry) to make the system operational again. To start the restoration process, install a copy of Windows 2000 to the same folder in which it was installed originally. When you are prompted to format the hard drive volume or leave it, select the **Leave the current file system intact** option. Use the Backup utility to restore the System State and/or the registry, (Programs, Accessories, System Tools, Backup). Click on the **Restore** tab and select the device that holds the backed up files.

Refer to Figure 6.16 for restoring the System State. Notice it is selected in the right-hand pane.

Figure 6.16: Restoring the System State Data

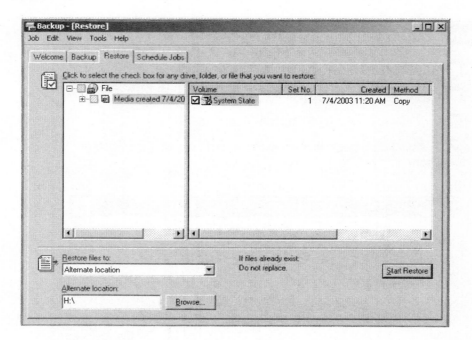

6.5 Understanding the Pre-Installation Steps of Windows 2000

Windows 2000 Professional can be installed from a central location or locally. Because this book focuses on the A+ Certification exam, only local installation is covered. The pre-installation of any operating system is more important than the installation process. The steps to be taken before installing Windows 2000 Professional are outlined below.

1. Decide whether the installation will be an upgrade or a clean install.
2. Determine the file system(s) to be used.
3. Decide whether the computer will have more than one OS installed.
4. Scan for viruses.
5. Determine if the hardware is compatible.
6. Obtain any drivers, upgrades, or hardware replacements.
7. Decide if the software applications are compatible.
8. Obtain any patches, upgrades, or software replacements.
9. Back up any data files necessary.
10. Remove any power management or disk management tools.

The first decision to make when planning to install Windows 2000 Professional is whether to upgrade from another operating system or perform a clean install. A **clean install** puts an operating system on a computer without an operating system, or reformats the hard drive so that the computer's existing operating system is removed.

If the decision is to do an upgrade, then determine which operating system is already installed. Windows 2000 Professional supports upgrading from Windows 95, Windows 98, NT Workstation 3.51, and NT Workstation 4. When Windows 2000 Professional is installed as an upgrade, the user's applications and data are preserved if the operating system is installed in the same folder (directory) as the original operating system. If Windows 2000 Professional is installed in a different folder, then all applications must be reloaded.

Another decision you must make if upgrading to Windows 2000 Professional is whether or not to convert the hard drive partition to NTFS. Once a partition is converted to NTFS, the partition cannot be changed back. If you are unsure whether or not to convert the partition, leave it unchanged and later use the CONVERT.EXE program to upgrade. Most people want to convert the partition to NTFS for the following reasons:

• Security (individual files can be protected with NTFS).
• More efficient use of cluster space (the cluster size can be defined based on the user's needs with NTFS).
• NTFS supports file compression.
• NTFS supports larger hard drive partition sizes.

Actually there are two versions of NTFS: NTFS4 and NTFS5. Windows 2000 supports and uses NTFS5 and NT Workstation supports and uses NTFS4. In NTFS5, a new type of encryption called Encryption File System (EFS) is supported. Additionally, disk quotas can be set to monitor and limit user disk space. If upgrading from a prior version of NTFS, the drive is automatically configured for NTFS5. If any NTFS4 volumes are not powered during the installation process, the volume is automatically upgraded when the drive is mounted. If you want to dual-boot between Windows NT 4 and Windows 2000 Professional (have both operating systems loaded), make sure that NT Workstation Service Pack 4 or higher is installed because some of the features in NTFS5 change the data structure on disks.

In order to take advantage of Windows 2000 Professional's reliability, enhancements, and security features, sometimes a clean installation is the best choice, especially if the current operating system is Windows 95 or Windows 98. Because a clean installation involves formatting the hard drive, the user's data must be backed up and all applications reinstalled once the Windows 2000 Professional installation is complete. Also, all user-defined settings are lost. Another important point to remember is that not all Windows 3.x, 95, and 98 applications are compatible with Windows 2000 Professional.

If the computer already has NT Workstation 3.5 or 4, then a Windows 2000 Professional upgrade is recommended. However, if there are hardware drivers for such devices as a DVD player, power management software, or network utilities loaded on the computer, a clean installation may be a better choice. Whichever is the case, the user's data

Microsoft has a web site that addresses application compatibility and you should check at this site before making your decision: http://windows.microsoft.com/ windows2000/reskit/webresources. You can also contact the company that developed your application and see if the application is compatible with Windows 2000.

and applications should be backed up and restored once the Windows 2000 Professional installation is complete.

The third decision that must be made is whether or not Windows 2000 Professional will be installed with one or more other operating systems. This situation is often called a dual-boot scenario. **Dual-boot** means that the computer can boot from more than one operating system. Windows 2000 Professional can be dual-booted with DOS, Windows 3.1 or higher, Windows 95, Windows 98, and Windows NT Workstation. If this is desired, a separate hard disk partition should be created and used for each operating system. When doing a dual- or multi-boot configuration, make sure that Windows 2000 Professional is installed *after* the other operating systems. Multi-booting is beyond the scope of this chapter. See the Microsoft web site for more details.

The fourth step is to scan the system for viruses. Viruses were covered in Chapter 4, *Introduction to Windows 98*.

The fifth thing to do when installing Windows 2000 Professional is to determine what computer hardware is installed. Table 6.3 lists the minimum and preferred hardware requirements for installing Windows 2000 Professional.

Table 6.3: Windows 2000 Professional Hardware Requirements

Component	Minimum	Preferred
CPU	Intel Pentium (or compatible) 33 MHz	Intel Pentium II (or compatible) 300 MHz or higher
RAM	32 MB	64 MB
Free hard drive space	650 MB	2 GB
Input Device	Keyboard, mouse, or other pointing device	Keyboard, mouse, or other pointing device
Multimedia Drive	CD-ROM or DVD	CD-ROM or DVD 12x or faster

The sixth decision relates to obtaining drives, upgrades, or hardware replacements. Once you have verified all of your hardware, you may have to get Windows 2000 device drivers from the hardware device manufacturer or its web site. You may also need to upgrade the hardware device, which usually means replacing it. This is sometimes the

Microsoft has a tool called **Readiness Analyzer** that checks your system for hardware and software compatibility issues. This tool can be downloaded from Microsoft's web site at http://www.microsoft.com/windows2000/upgrade/compat/default.asp. Be aware that the Readiness Analyzer might not be able to detect all hardware devices or software applications.

cost of going to a bigger and better operating system. You may also decide at this point not to upgrade, but to buy a computer with Windows 2000 already installed.

The seventh determination you must make before installing Windows 2000 Professional is whether or not any existing software applications are compatible. The preparation for installing a new operating system is usually more work than the actual installation process, but any omitted step will cost you more time in the long run. Use the Readiness Analyzer or contact the developer of each software application to determine if it is compatible. You may also go to the software developer's web site. The information may be posted there. A list of compatible software is also listed on Microsoft's web site.

The eighth decision is as follows: Once you have determined whether the software is compatible with Windows 2000, you may have to obtain software patches, upgrades, or buy a new version. This is best done before you install Windows 2000. Be proactive, not reactive—solve any problems you can _before_ upgrading or installing any operating system.

The ninth decision deals with backing up your data. As with any upgrade, hardware change, or software change, data must be backed up. It is almost funny that the worst people in the world for backing up data are operating system specialists—the very ones who are entrusted with the clients' data and computer. Since Windows 2000 is really designed for the corporate/small business environment, backing up data is an essential step. Whether you do a clean install or an upgrade, if the user has data on the computer, it must be backed up before starting the installation process. Also, before backing up data, remove any unwanted files and/or applications that are no longer needed in order to free up hard drive space.

The last step in the pre-installation checklist is to remove any power or disk management tools loaded on your computer. Computer manufacturers for older operating systems frequently provide these types of tools. Power or disk management tools can interfere with the new tools provided with Windows 2000. Disable these utilities and applications before attempting an operating system installation or upgrade. One important note about disk drives is that you cannot install Windows 2000 on a compressed hard drive partition. Uncompress the partition before starting the Windows 2000 installation process.

6.6 Understanding How to Install and Upgrade Windows 2000 Professional

After all the pre-installation checklist steps are completed, you are ready to install Windows 2000 Professional. The installation process is easy if you performed the pre-installation steps. An exercise at the end of the chapter guides you through both a clean installation (one where no other operating system is on the machine) and an upgrade to Windows 2000. The number one piece of advice you need to follow when installing any operating system is this: Do your homework first. The number of possible problems will be greatly reduced.

There are two major portions of the installation process the text mode (otherwise known as the DOS mode) and the GUI mode (also known as the Windows mode). In **text mode**, the monitor only shows characters with a blue background. The text mode portion of Setup checks for the proper minimum hardware requirements; detects plug and play devices and adapters; locates hard drives; creates the registry; partitions and formats the hard drive for the file system you select; copies most of the Windows 2000 installation files to begin the installation process; and restarts the computer to begin the Windows mode. During the **GUI mode** portion of Setup, hardware devices are detected, installed, and configured; the Setup logs are created; the operating system starts; and you are allowed to create an Administrator password.

6.7 Troubleshooting the Windows 2000 Professional Installation

Various problems can cause the Windows 2000 installation process to halt. There are two major places the installation stops—during the text mode portion of Setup or during the GUI mode portion of Setup. If the computer halts during text mode and displays a text message, there is probably an incompatible piece of hardware installed in the computer. If the computer halts during the GUI portion of Setup, restart the computer. The installation process attempts to continue from the place it left off. Incompatible hardware devices normally cause this. You can troubleshoot the device once Windows is installed.

An incompatible hardware device is the most common problem during the installation process because it can cause both the text and GUI modes to halt. Installation problems can be caused by a number of factors. The following list shows the most common causes and their associated solution during the installation process.

- **Incompatible BIOS**—Obtain compatible BIOS, replace motherboard with one that has a compatible BIOS, or do not upgrade/install Windows 2000 Professional.
- **BIOS needs to be upgraded**—Upgrade the BIOS.
- **Incompatible hardware**—Replace the hardware or do not upgrade/install Windows 2000 Professional.
- **Incompatible drivers**—Obtain Windows 2000 drivers from the hardware manufacturer.
- **Existing drivers are incompatible or halt the installation/upgrade process** Obtain Windows 2000 drivers from the hardware manufacturer.
- **Incompatible TSRs**—Remove TSRs or obtain updated ones from the software manufacturer.
- **Incompatible applications**—Obtain upgrades from software manufacturer.
- **Minimum hardware requirements have not been met**—Upgrade the hardware. The primary things to check are the CPU (133 MHz minimum) and RAM (32 MB minimum).

- **A virus is on the hard drive**—Run a virus-checking program and remove the virus. One of the tools that comes on the 2000 Professional CD is the InoculateIT anti-virus program (sometimes called the AV boot disk). To make a bootable disk that has the anti-virus program on it, insert the 2000 Professional CD into the CD-ROM drive and a 1.4 MB disk in the floppy drive. Click on the **Start** button and then click on the **Run** option. Click on the **Browse** button; locate and double-click on the drive letter that represents the CD-ROM. Locate the VALUEADD folder, the 3RDPARTY subfolder, and the CA_ANTIV subfolder. Double-click on the CA_ANTIV subfolder. In the right window, double-click on the **MAKEDISK.BAT** file. Click on the **OK** button. To use the disk and run the anti-virus program, make sure the BIOS is set to boot from the floppy drive. Insert the disk into the floppy drive and boot the computer. When the menu appears, press **1** and follow the directions on the screen. Refer to Figure 6.17 for a sample screenshot.

Figure 6.17: Screenshot of the MAKEDISK.BAT Anti-Virus Program

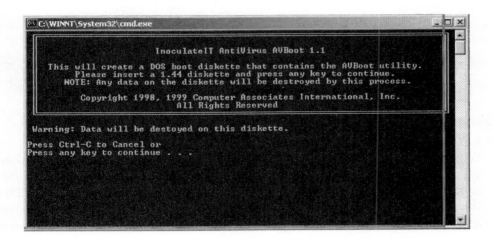

- **Pre-installation steps have not been completed**—Go back through the list!
- **The installation floppy disks or CD are corrupted** (not as likely as the other causes)—Try the disk in another machine and see if you can see the contents. For the CD, check to see if any scratches or dirt are on the surface. Clean the CD as necessary.
- **Incorrect CD key**—Type in the correct CD key to complete the 2000 installation. The key is located on the CD case.

    Several text files can be helpful in determining the installation problem. WINNT.LOG and WINNT32.LOG are created during the installation process. SETUPLOG.TXT logs information detected during the text mode portion of Setup and includes device drivers that are copied. SETUPERR.LOG lists errors logged during the installation. SETUPACT.LOG and SETUPAPI.LOG are located in the folder that contains most of the Windows 2000 files (normally C:\WINNT). SETUPACT.LOG displays information about the files copied during the installation and SETUPAPI.LOG contains information about device driver files copied during installation. The NBTLOG.TXT is used when the Enable Boot Logging boot option is chosen and lists the drivers loaded during the boot process. BOOTLOG.TXT is located in the root directory and lists boot-logging messages when booting from Safe Mode.

Different function keys can also help when troubleshooting the Windows 2000 installation process, as well as troubleshooting boot problems. Table 6.4 shows a list of keystrokes that can be used.

Table 6.4: Windows 2000 Professional Startup Keystrokes

Keystroke	Purpose
F5	System hangs at "Setup is inspecting your computer" screen. Select Standard PC from the list.
F6	Used when you need to go back and load third-party drivers.
F7	Loads the normal HAL instead of ACPI HAL.
F8	Brings up the Advanced Options menu.
Shift + F10	Displays a command prompt during the GUI mode portion of installation.

6.8 Understanding How to Dual-Boot Windows 2000 Professional and Windows NT

Sometimes users would like to try a new operating system, but keep their old operating system loaded as well. If this is the case, two operating systems can reside in one system and it is called **dual-booting**. Because Windows 2000 supports and uses NTFS5, and NT Workstation supports and uses NTFS4, it is best if the two operating systems are placed on different hard drive partitions. As soon as Windows 2000 is installed onto a partition formatted as NTFS, Windows 2000 upgrades the partition to NTFS5 without any prompting.

NT Workstation should be installed first. Service Pack 4 or later should also be installed. Install Windows 2000 to a different hard drive partition by inserting the Windows 2000 Professional CD. The CD normally starts automatically. A dialog box appears, asking if you want to install Windows 2000 Professional. Another dialog box appears asking if you want to install a new operating system or upgrade your old one. For a dual-boot situation, make sure you select that you want to install a new copy.

After installing all files and rebooting, a menu appears with the Microsoft Professional option, NT Workstation option, and NT Workstation (VGA Mode) option. To select which option is the default operating system, right-click on the **My Computer** desktop icon and click on the **Properties** option from the drop-down menu. Click on the **Advanced** tab and select the **Startup and Recovery** button. Select the default boot option. Refer to Figure 6.18 for a sample screenshot of selecting an operating system. In the **Default operating system** drop-down box, you'll notice in the figure there are several operating system choices. This means this system is dual-booted.

Figure 6.18: Selecting an Operating System in the Startup and Recovery Options

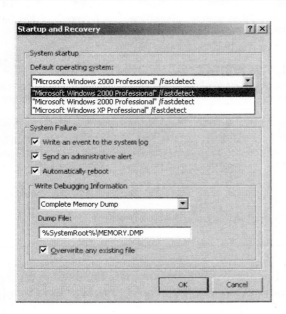

6.9 Configuring Windows 2000 Professional

One of the most common windows used by operating system specialists is the Control Panel window. A **control panel** is a method for configuring various Windows 2000 components. The Add/Remove Hardware, Add/Remove Programs, and Printing control panels are used when installing or removing hardware and software. Each control panel icon represents a Windows utility that allows you to customize a particular part of the Windows 2000 environment. The number of control panels displayed depends on the type of computer and the components contained within that computer. Figure 6.19 shows some of the more common Windows 2000 Professional control panels.

Figure 6.19: Windows 2000 Control Panels

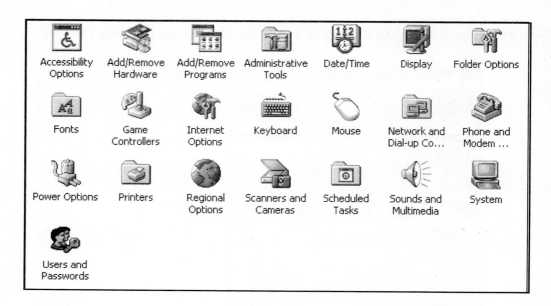

You must know which control panel to use for changing a computer's configuration. Table 6.5 shows a few of the common Windows 2000 control panels and the function of each.

Table 6.5: A Few Windows 2000 Control Panel Functions

Control Panel	Function
Devices	Used to start and stop device drivers; used to control how the device driver loads
Display	Used to install a monitor driver and configure monitor settings
Keyboard	Used to install a keyboard driver and configure keyboard
Network	Used to install NIC drivers, add network software, and configure network connections
Tape Devices	Used to add tape device driver and configure tape device parameters

Operating system specialists frequently must add new hardware and software using the operating system. Windows 2000 Professional has specific tools for these functions. Using the correct procedure is essential for success. Here are some tasks you are likely to perform:

- Adding plug and play devices
- Adding non-plug and play devices
- Adding a printer
- Removing hardware devices
- Installing and removing software

Hardware devices are physical components that connect to the computer. Hardware devices can be either plug and play or non-plug and play. A device driver is a piece of software that allows hardware to work with a specific operating system. Some device drivers are automatically included with Windows 2000 Professional. You must be aware of what hardware is installed into a system so that the latest 2000-compatible drivers can be downloaded and installed.

Adding Plug and Play Devices

Plug and play devices are hardware and software designed to automatically be recognized by the operating system. These include: USB devices, FireWire devices, SCSI devices, PC Card and CardBus devices, VL bus devices, PCI, ISA, and EISA devices, and printers. In order for Windows 2000 to fully support plug and play devices, the computer should have a BIOS that supports ACPI. Successful plug and play device installation involves the following:

- Possessing the most up-to-date device driver
- Following the directions provided by the device manufacturer

Always make sure that the computer is turned off when installing any new hardware component. Some plug and plug devices can be inserted into the computer without restarting. These include a PC card, a laptop into a docking station, and a USB device. However, devices such as internal modems or network cards require that the computer be turned off during installation.

Install the device according to the manufacturer's instructions. Once it is installed, power on the computer. The Windows 2000 Found New Hardware wizard appears. Windows 2000 attempts to find a driver for the new device. Plug and play devices make use of a special .CAB (cabinet) file called DRIVER.CAB, which is located in *%systemroot%*\DriverCache\i386 folder (where *%systemroot%* is normally C:\WINNT). This file is over 50 MB and contains more than 3,000 compressed files. If Windows 2000 detects new hardware, it will automatically search DRIVER.CAB for a driver. If a driver cannot be found, a dialog box appears. The best policy with any operating system is to use the latest driver, even if the operating system detects the device. An exercise at the end of this chapter outlines how to install a new hardware driver.

Remember that if the Windows 2000 Professional operating system cannot configure a plug and play device and prompts for a device driver, you must have administrator rights to install the driver.

Adding Non-Plug and Play Devices

Devices known as **legacy** devices are also called non-plug and play devices. For devices that are not plug and play, Windows 2000 has a tool (wizard) called Add/Remove Hardware. The Add/Remove Hardware wizard allows hardware configuration and is used for hardware that is not automatically recognized by Windows 2000 Professional. It is also used for plug and play devices that don't install properly with Windows 2000's automatic detection. You must have administrator privileges in order to load device drivers for new hardware. Refer to Figure 6.20 for a screenshot of adding/removing hardware.

Figure 6.20: The Add/Remove Hardware Screen

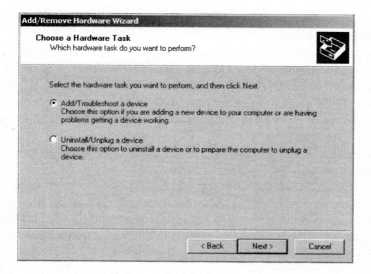

Adding a Printer

Printers can be connected to a computer through the printer's parallel port or through a local area network. Only local printers (printers connected to the computer's parallel port) will be covered in this chapter. Windows 2000 can automatically detect printers. If Windows 2000 detects the printer, the operating system automatically installs the drivers, updates the registry, and allocates system resources to the printer. Automatically detected printers are normally USB, or infrared printers.

To install a printer, connect the printer to the appropriate computer port with the appropriate cable. Power on the computer and the Windows 2000 wizard normally detects and leads you through the installation process. However, if it does not, have the Windows 2000 printer driver ready, click on the **Start** button, point to the **Settings** selection, and double-click on the **Printers** option. When the Printers window opens, click on the **Add Printer** icon. Click on the **Next** button and select the **Local Printer** selection. When prompted for the printer driver, insert the CD or disk that contains the printer driver and use the Browse button to locate the driver. Continue through the Add Printer wizard until the printer is installed.

To configure a printer as a default printer (the printer that applications normally use), locate the printer in the Printers folder. Access the Printers folder by clicking on the **Start** button, pointing to the **Settings** option, and clicking on the **Printers** selection. Once you locate the appropriate printer icon, right-click on the icon. Click on the **Set as Default Printer** option. In the Printers folder, the default printer has a check mark next to (above) the icon. Refer to Figure 6.21 for a screenshot of adding a printer using the Add Printer Wizard.

Figure 6.21: Adding a Printer Using the Add Printer Wizard

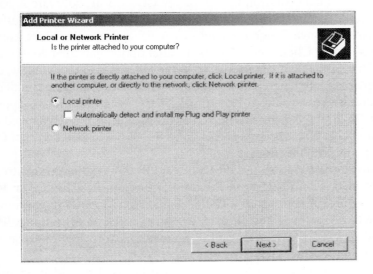

Removing Hardware Devices

When removing most hardware devices (all but printers), use the Add/Remove Hardware tool (wizard). To access this wizard, click on the **Start** button. Point to the **Settings** option and then click on the **Control Panel** option. Start the wizard by double-clicking on the **Add/Remove Hardware** icon located in the Control Panel window. Click on the **Uninstall/Unplug a device** radio button. Click on the **Next** button. Click on the **Uninstall a device** option and click on the **Next** button. Click the **Yes, I want to uninstall this device** option and click on the **Next** button. Click on the **Finish** button to complete the hardware removal.

If you are removing a printer from the system, use the Printers control panel. Access this control panel by clicking on the **Start** button. Point to the **Settings** option and click on the **Printers** option. Right-click on the **printer** you want to delete and choose the **Delete** option.

Be careful when deleting anything! One of the textbook authors was attempting to delete a print job associated with a printer and accidentally deleted the printer itself. Needless to say, it took a few minutes to reinstall the printer drivers.

Installing and Removing Software

No computer is functional without software. One thing you should know about Windows 2000 is that it does not support some of the older 16-bit software. Most software today is 32-bit and comes on CD that includes an Autorun feature. If there is no Autorun feature, an installation wizard steps you through installing the software when the CD is inserted into the drive. If there is not an Autorun feature on the CD or if the software is on a disk, then the Add/Remove Programs control panel is used to install or remove the software.

To access the Add/Remove Programs control panel, click on the **Start** button and point to the **Settings** option. Click on the **Control Panel** option and then double-click on the **Add/ Remove Programs** control panel icon. In the left panel in the window, click on the **Add New Programs** icon. Click on the appropriate **CD** or **Floppy** button depending on the type of media. Make sure the software disk or CD is inserted in the appropriate drive. If Add New Programs cannot find a SETUP.EXE file on the designated disk, it prompts with a dialog box. Use the **Browse** button to locate the installation file. Click on the **Finish** button to complete the process.

To remove a software application, use the same Add/Remove Programs control panel; however, instead of clicking on Add New Programs, click on the **Change or Remove Programs** icon in the left panel. A list of installed applications appears in the right panel. Locate the software to be removed and click on its **name**. Click on the **Change/Remove** button. When asked if you are sure you want to remove this software, click on the **OK** button and close the Control Panel window.

The Add/Remove Programs control panel can also be used to add programs from Microsoft, add programs across your network, and add/remove Windows components. The **Add Programs from Microsoft** icon automatically opens a web browser to the Microsoft web site. There you can locate, download, and install software upgrades, patches, and service releases. The **Add Programs from Your Network** icon is used to install software from a network share on another computer. The **Add/Remove Windows Components** icon is used to add or remove standard Windows applets, games, accessibility options, and communication components. Refer to Figure 6.22 for a screenshot of adding and removing programs.

Figure 6.22: The Add/Remove Programs Screen

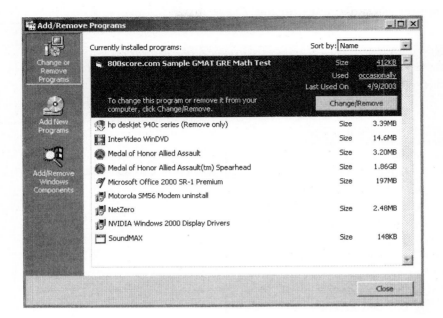

Once an application is installed, launch the application by clicking on the **Start** button and pointing to the **Programs** option. Locate the application name and click on it. If the application does not appear on the list, do not panic. Windows 2000 has a feature that only shows the most commonly used programs in the Programs list. If the application name does not appear, point to the double down arrows at the bottom of the **Programs** submenu. The less frequently used program names appear on the screen.

The Computer Management Console

The **Computer Management Console** is a large group of Windows 2000 tools displayed on one screen. The tools are called snap-ins and the 2000 Professional CD contains additional snap-ins that you can add to your system.

To add the Administrative tools to the Start button Programs option, right-click on an empty space on the taskbar. Click on the Properties option and click on the Advanced tab. Click in the Display Administrative Tools check box and click on the OK button.

The Computer Management Console allows you to manage shared folders, manage disk drives, start and stop services, look at performance logs and system alerts, and access Device Manager to troubleshoot hardware problems.

Figure 6.23 shows a partial listing of a Computer Management Console screen.

Figure 6.23: Computer Management Console

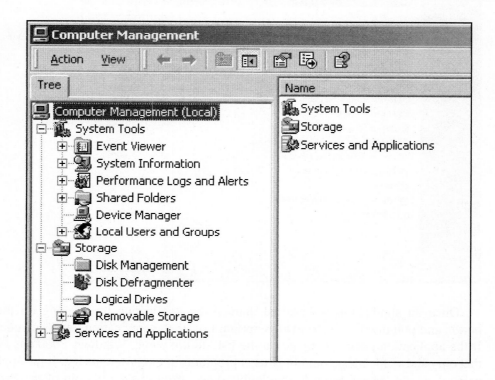

The three major tool categories found in the Computer Management Console include: System Tools, Storage, and Services and Applications. Let's perform an exercise with the Computer Management Console tool. Again, it is assumed that Windows 2000 is running on a computer.

1. Click **Start**, point to the **Settings** option and then click on the **Control Panel**. The Control Panel window opens.
2. Double-click on the **Administrative Tools** icon. The Administrative Tools window opens.
3. Double-click **Computer Management**. The Computer Management window opens.
4. To get an idea of what is in Computer Management, open a few of the tools and then close them.
5. When finished, close Computer Management.

6.10 Understanding the Windows 2000 Professional Boot Process

With NT Workstation and Windows 2000, two types of partitions are important during the boot process—the system partition and the boot partition. The **system partition** is the active drive partition that contains the files needed to load the operating system. The system partition is normally the C: drive (the active partition). The **boot partition** is the partition or logical drive where the Windows 2000 operating system files are located. People sometimes forget that the system and boot partitions can be on the same partition.

Every operating system needs specific files that allow the computer to boot. These files are known as **system files** or startup files. The system files and their specific location on the hard drive are listed in Table 6.6.

Table 6.6: Windows 2000 Boot Files

Startup File Name	File Location
BOOT.INI	Root directory of system partition
BOOTSECT.DOS (needed if dual- or multi-boot system)	Root directory of system partition
CDLDR	Root directory of system partition
HAL.DLL	%systemroot%\SYSTEM32 (%systemroot% is a variable representing the folder where Windows 2000 is installed. This is normally C:\WINNT.)
HYBERFIL.SYS	%systemdrive% (%systemroot% is the root directory on the drive where Windows 2000 boot files are located, which is normally C:\.)
NTBOOTDD.SYS (used with SCSI drives that have the SCSI BIOS disabled)	Root directory of system partition
NTDETECT.COM	Root directory of system partition
NTLDR	Root directory of system partition
NTOSKRNL.EXE	%systemroot%\SYSTEM32
System Key	%systemroot%\SYSTEM32\CONFIG

The table can be confusing because of all of the *%systemroot%* and *%systemdrive%* entries. This is because computers can be partitioned differently. If you install Windows 2000 onto a drive letter (a partition or logical drive) other than the active partition (normally C:), the startup files can be on two different drive letters. Also, you do not have to take the default folder name of WINNT to install Windows 2000. To account for these different scenarios, Microsoft uses the *%systemroot%* to represent the boot partition, the partition and folder that contains the majority of the Windows 2000 files. On a computer with a single operating system, this would be C:\WINNT. The *%systemdrive%* represents the root directory of the same drive letter. On a computer with a single operating system, this would be C:\.

If Windows 2000 is installed onto the C: drive and the C: drive is the active partition, then the BOOT.INI, BOOTSECT.DOS, HYBERFIL.SYS, NTBOOTDD.SYS, NTDE-TECT.COM, and NTLDR files would all be in the root directory of C:. The HAL.DLL and NTOSKRNL.EXE files would be located in the SYSTEM32 folder (that is located under the WINNT folder) on the C: drive. The system key would be in the CONFIG folder (that is located under the SYSTEM32 folder that is located under the WINNT folder) on the C: drive.

Another example: If you installed Windows 2000 onto the D: drive, but the C: drive is the active partition, the BOOT.INI, BOOTSECT.DOS, HYBERFIL.SYS, NTBOOTDD. SYS, NTDETECT.COM, and NTLDR files would all be in the root directory of C:. The HAL.DLL and NTOSKRNL.EXE files would be located in the SYSTEM32 folder (that is located under the WINNT folder) on the D: drive. The system key would be in the CONFIG folder (that is located under the SYSTEM32 folder that is located under the WINNT folder) on the D: drive.

The **system key** is a protection feature for Windows 2000 passwords. By default, the system key is stored on the local computer, but it can also be stored on a floppy disk used to boot Windows 2000. An algorithm secures the system key and it is stored in various locations through the registry. The boot process is actually quite involved, but the major steps are as follows:

1. The computer is powered on.
2. POST executes.
3. BIOS searches for an active partition on the hard drive.
4. BIOS reads the Master Boot Record, then locates and loads the information into sector 0 of the system partition. The contents of sector 0 define the type of file system, the location of the bootstrap loader file, and start the bootstrap loader. With Windows 2000, this file is NTLDR.
5. NTLDR starts the file system.
6. NTLDR reads the BOOT.INI file and displays the various operating system choices contained within the BOOT.INI file. If something other than Windows 2000 is chosen, the BOOTSECT.DOS file takes over. If Windows 2000 is chosen, the NTDE-TECT.COM file executes.
7. NTDETECT.COM detects the computer's hardware.
8. NTLDR passes the hardware information to the NTOSKRNL.EXE file and displays the startup screen.
9. The operating system kernel, NTOSKRNL.EXE, executes and the HAL.DLL file loads. HAL stands for Hardware Abstraction Layer. This is a layer between the operating system and the hardware devices. The HAL allows Windows 2000 to run with different hardware configurations and components, without affecting (or crashing) the operating system.

10. The registry key HKEY_LOCAL_MACHINE\SYSTEM loads from the registry key located in *%systemroot%*\System32\Config\System. This key has information found during the hardware detection process.
11. The Windows 2000 Professional screen appears.
12. The Starting Up process bar displays.
13. The WINLOGON.EXE file executes and the log-on screen appears.

Troubleshooting the Windows 2000 Boot Process

When Windows 2000 has startup problems, the Emergency Repair Disk, Recovery Console, and the Advanced Options menu are used. Many times startup problems are due to a virus. The AVBoot disk can be used to check the computer for a virus. The procedure for creating this is in the Troubleshooting the Windows 2000 Professional Installation section of this chapter. Other utilities that can be used within Windows 2000 to help with MBR, boot sector, and system files are FIXBOOT, FIXMBR, System File Checker, and the Advanced Options menu.

To use FIXBOOT, type **FIXBOOT** *x:* command where *x:* is the drive letter of the volume that has the problem. To use FIXMBR, type **FIXMBR** from a command prompt. Both the FIXBOOT and FIXMBR commands are covered in the Recovery Console section later in the chapter. The System File Checker program can be run from the Run dialog box by typing *x:***\WINNT\SYSTEM32\SFC.EXE /scannow** where *x* is the drive letter where 2000 is installed.

Indications that there is a problem with the Master Boot Record or the system files are as follows:
• Invalid partition table
• Error loading operating system
• Missing operating system
• A disk read error has occurred
• NTLDR is missing
• NTLDR is corrupt

When Windows 2000 has startup problems due to incompatible hardware or software, or a corrupted installation process, the Windows 2000 Advanced Options menu can help. This option can be selected by pressing the **F8** key when the **For troubleshooting and advanced startup options for Windows 2000, press F8** message appears on the screen during the boot process. Also, look back to Table 6.4 for a review of keystrokes that can be used to bring up different start options used in troubleshooting Windows 2000 Professional.

The most commonly used boot option is **Safe Mode**. In prior Windows operating systems, when the system had a problem it automatically booted into Safe Mode. This is not the case with Windows 2000. You must use the Advanced Startup Options to select Safe Mode.

Safe Mode is used when the computer stalls, slows down, does not work right, video is not working properly, intermittent errors appear, or new hardware/software installation causes problems. When the computer boots in Safe Mode, the mouse, keyboard, CD-

ROM, and VGA video device drivers are all that are loaded. After the computer boots to Safe Mode, you can disable or delete a system service; delete, reload, or upgrade a device driver, and disable or delete a shortcut in the Startup folder, any of which can cause the computer to hang during startup. The bottom line is that Safe Mode puts the computer in a "bare bones" (or minimum) mode so you can troubleshoot problems.

Another menu item that is useful when troubleshooting device drivers is Boot Logging. This option creates a file called NTBTLOG.TXT that is placed in the *%systemroot%* folder, (which is normally C:\WINNT). The NTBTLOG.TXT file contains a list of the drivers that load and the drivers that do not load. If you suspect a problem with a driver, use the **Enable Boot Logging** option from the Advanced Options menu to see if Windows 2000 loaded the driver. An exercise at the end of the chapter explains how to take advantage of this feature.

The other menu items are also used for troubleshooting and Table 6.7 shows the function of each menu option.

Table 6.7: Windows 2000 Advanced Options Menu

Menu Option	Function
Safe Mode	Loads the bare minimum device drivers needed to boot the system.
Safe Mode with Networking	Loads the bare minimum device drivers needed to boot the system plus the network services and drivers needed for the computer to participate in a network.
Safe Mode with Command Prompt	Loads the bare minimum device drivers needed to boot the system but does not load the GUI interface (EXPLORER.EXE).
Enable Boot Logging	Creates a log file called NTBT in the *%systemroot%* folder. This file contains all drivers that load during startup and shows each driver's status.
Enable VGA Mode	Used when an incompatible or corrupted video driver has been loaded. It boots the system with a generic VGA driver so you can troubleshoot.
Last Known Good Configuration	Used to load a previous configuration that worked (as long as you don't log on).
Debugging Mode	Used to debug the OS kernel.
Boot Normally	Boots Windows 2000 with normal device drivers, registry, and startup folders.

In older operating systems, a startup disk was used to begin the troubleshooting process. With Windows 2000, the startup disk is actually the set of four installation disks that came with the Windows 2000 Professional CD. If you cannot find these, you can go to any computer that has the same version of Windows 2000 Professional loaded and make a set. Insert the Windows 2000 Professional CD, click on the **Start** button, and click on the **Run** option. In the dialog box, type *x:\bootdisk\makeboot.exe a:* where *x* is the drive letter that represents the CD-ROM. Click on the **OK** button and follow the prompts on the screen. You will need four floppy disks to complete this procedure.

Creating an Emergency Repair Disk for Windows 2000 Professional

The **ERD (Emergency Repair Disk)** is used to fix system file problems, the partition boot sector, and startup environment settings, all of which can prevent a computer from booting properly. By default, the ERD does not contain a backup copy of the registry. Use the Backup utility to back up and restore the registry. You should make a new ERD whenever hardware or software changes are made to the computer. Store the disk in a safe place. The ERD contains the following files: AUTOEXEC.NT, CONFIG.NT, SETUP. LOG, NTLDR, NTDETECT.COM, BOOT.INI, NTBOOTDD.SYS, and HAL.DLL. The **AUTOEXEC.NT** and **CONFIG.NT** files are used to initialize the DOS environment. The **SETUP.LOG** lists the files installed by the Setup program. **NTLDR** is the file used to load Windows 2000; **BOOT.INI** is used to tell the computer which hard drive and which hard drive partition to use to boot Windows 2000. The **NTBOOTDD.SYS** is only used when the computer has a SCSI hard drive installed. The **HAL.DLL** file is used by Windows 2000 to keep hardware problems from crashing the operating system. An exercise at the end of this chapter illustrates how to make an ERD.

If the computer system will not work and you want to use the ERD, start the Windows 2000 installation process and get to the Welcome to Setup screen. Use the Windows 2000 Professional Setup disks (you must get through Disk 4 before you see the Welcome to Setup screen) or boot your computer from the Windows 2000 Professional CD. Once presented with the Welcome to Setup screen, press the **R** option, which is the **To repair a Windows 2000 installation by using the emergency repair process** option that allows you to use the ERD to fix the computer. Once you press **R**, you are asked if you want a manual repair or a fast repair. The manual repair allows you to select what portions of the operating system are repaired. The fast repair will check and try to repair system files, the partition boot sector, or the startup environment settings. Most people select the fast repair option. After making a selection, you are prompted to insert the ERD. Follow the instructions on the screen to complete the repair process. The computer must reboot after the repairs have been done.

Using Recovery Console

Another useful tool to use when Windows 2000 crashes or does not boot properly is the Recovery Console. The **Recovery Console** boots the computer to a command prompt and allows access to the hard drive no matter what type of file system is being used (FAT,

FAT32, or NTFS). From the command prompt, the administrator can manipulate files and folders, start and stop services, repair the Master Boot Record, repair the boot sectors, or format the hard drive. You must have the administrator password to access the full potential of this option.

The Recovery Console can be loaded to the hard drive and added to the Start menu, but it is not loaded by default. Refer to Figure 6.24 for a sample screenshot of how to add the Recovery Console. To do so, you must run **winnt32.exe** with the **/cmdcons** option. Note it requires an additional 7 MB of disk space.

Figure 6.24: Adding the Recovery Console

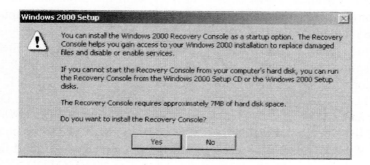

Recovery Console is started from the Windows 2000 CD or the Setup floppy disks. Start the computer from the Setup disks or CD. (If you do not have the Setup disks, go to a working 2000 computer and make some.) When the Setup program begins, press **Enter** at the **Setup Notification** screen. At the **Welcome to Setup** screen, press **R** (Repair a Windows 2000 installation). On the next screen, press **C** to access the Recovery Console. A screen appears that shows all of the Windows 2000 installations that are detected. Press the number corresponding to the Windows 2000 installation you want to work with. You are prompted for the local administrator password. Type the password to continue.

If the registry is corrupt or has been deleted, you are not prompted for an administrator password. Instead, the system boots to a prompt where you can use basic commands like CHKDSK, FIXBOOT, and FIXMBR to repair the system. However, you cannot access any folders on the hard drive.

The drive letters available at the Recovery Console command prompt might not be the same ones you used in the GUI environment. Use the MAP command to see the drive letters (and the volumes that do not have drive letters). The syntax for the MAP command is covered later in this chapter.

In order to work in the Recovery Console, you must be able to work from a command prompt. You may want to go through Chapter 3 entitled *DOS and the DOS Command Line Interface* in this book to understand the process and procedures needed when working from a command prompt. Some of the most frequently used commands at the Recovery Console command prompt are outlined below.

- **DISABLE**—Used to disable a system service or hardware driver.
- **DISKPART**—Used to manage and manipulate the hard drive partitions.
- **ENABLE**—Used to enable a system service or hardware driver.
- **EXIT**—Exits the Recovery Console and restarts the computer.
- **EXPAND**—Used to uncompress a file from the Windows 2000 CD.
- **FIXBOOT**—Used to rewrite the hard drive's boot sector.
- **FIXMBR**—Rewrites the startup partition's Master Boot Record.
- **FORMAT**—Used to format a disk and can be used to format it for a particular file system.
- **LISTSVC**—Lists all of the services, hardware drivers, and their start-types. The **listsvc** command is useful to use before using the **disable** or **enable** command.
- **MAP**—Used to list the computer's drive letters, types of file systems, volume sizes, and physical device mappings.

To receive help on any of the commands listed above, go to the Recovery Console prompt and type the command followed by /?. For example, to find out all about the FIXBOOT command, type FIXBOOT /? (while in Recovery Console mode).

6.11 Understanding Task Manager, Dr. Watson, and Event Viewer

Task Manager is a Windows-based utility that displays applications currently loaded into memory, processes that are currently running, microprocessor usage information, and memory usage data. To activate Task Manager press the **Ctrl + Alt + Del** keys and from the window options that appear, click on the **Task Manager** button. Two other ways of accessing this utility are (1) by pressing **Ctrl + Alt + Esc** and (2) by right-clicking on the **taskbar** and then clicking on the **Task Manager** option.

One of the common uses of Task Manager is to exit from an application that is "hung up" or not responding. Task Manager can help with exiting the program. Once inside the Task Manager window, click on the **Applications** tab. Locate the name of the troublesome application and click on it. Normally, the status shows the application as "not responding." Refer to Figure 6.25 for a screenshot of ending a process in Task Manager.

Figure 6.25: Using Task Manager to End a Process

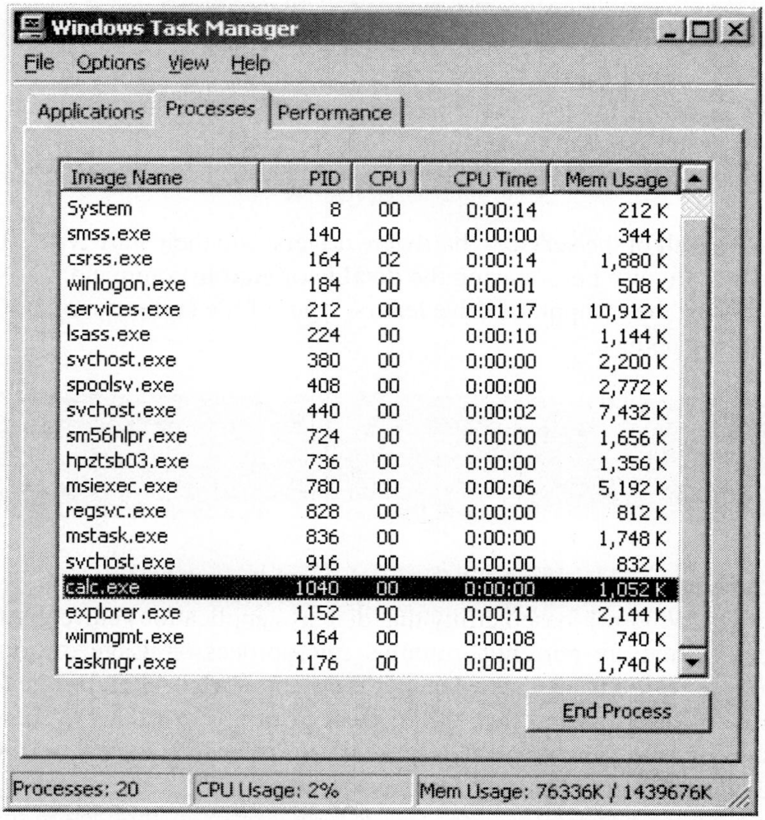

Dr. Watson is a utility that automatically loads when an application starts. Dr. Watson can detect and display troubleshooting information as well as create a text log file when a system or application error occurs. You might need this information when communicating with Microsoft or the application developer's technical support. Make notes of any messages that appear on the screen when any type of problem occurs. To start Dr. Watson in Windows 2000, click on the **Start** button, click on the **Run** option, type **drwtsn32**, and press **Enter**. Click on the **application error** and click on the **View** button. The default location for the log file is C:\Documents and Settings\All Users\Documents\DrWatson. The name of the log file is drwtsn32.log. When an error occurs, Dr. Watson appends information to the end of this log file. Refer to Figure 6.26 for a screenshot of Dr. Watson.

Figure 6.26: Running Dr. Watson

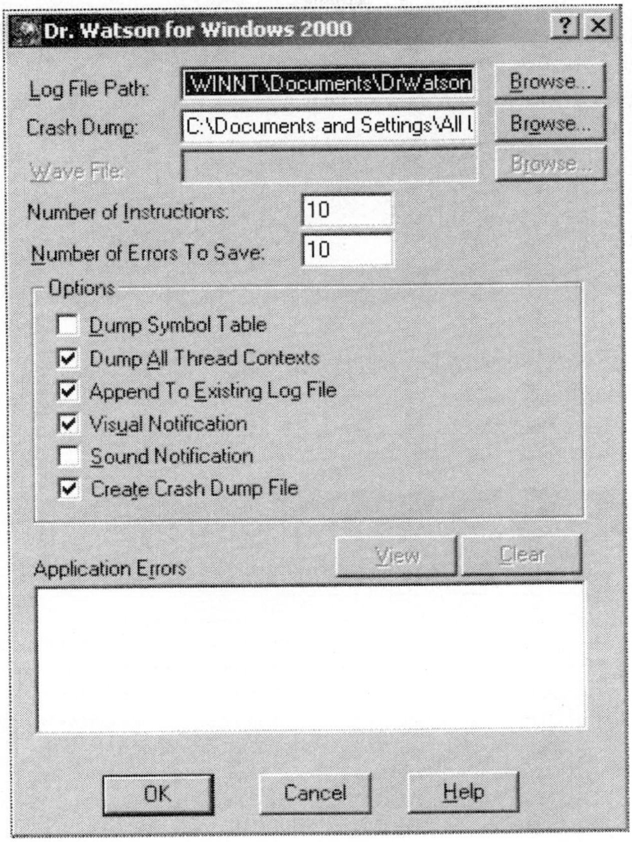

Event Viewer is a Windows tool used to monitor various events in your computer such as when a driver or service does not start properly. The EventLog service starts automatically every time a computer boots to Windows 2000. This service is what allows the events to be logged and then Event Viewer is used to see the log.

Let's perform an exercise to demonstrate the use of Event Viewer.

1. Click **Start**, point to the **Settings** option and then click on the **Control Panel**. The Control Panel window opens.
2. Double-click on the **Administrative Tools** icon. The Administrative Tools window opens.
3. Double-click **Event Viewer**. The Event Viewer window opens.
4. Click on the **System Log** option in the left panel. The system log events are displayed in the right window.
5. Close Event Viewer.

The **System log** displays events that deal with various system components, such as a driver or service that loads during startup. The type of system log events cannot be changed, added, or deleted. The **Security Log** can display events, such as when different users log in to the computer (both valid and invalid log ins). You can pick which events are displayed in the security log. The **Application Log** displays events associated with a specific program. The programmers that design the software decide which events to display in the Event Viewer's application log. All users can view the system log and the application log, but only a member of Administrators can view or enable security log information. The most commonly used log is the system log.

Refer to Figure 6.27 for a screenshot of Event Viewer.

Figure 6.27: Event Viewer

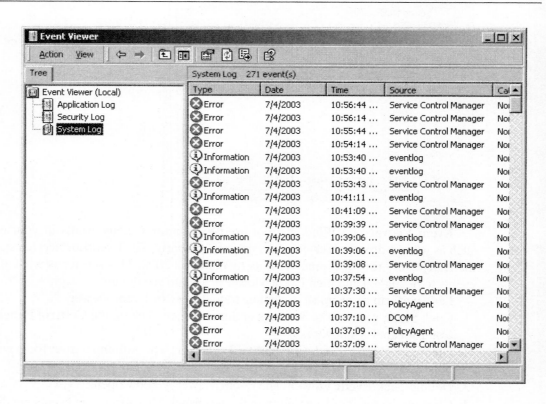

If an error message appears stating that the Event Viewer log is full, start the Event Viewer. Note that you must be an administrator or a member of the administrators group to perform this procedure. Click on the **Action** menu option and then click on the **Properties** selection. Click on the **General** tab. Click in the **Clear log** option. The Log Size option may need to be changed to one of the following: Overwrite events older than 0 days, Maximum log size, or Overwrite events as needed.

6.12 Troubleshooting a Service that Does Not Start

Some Windows 2000 services start automatically each time the computer boots. If one of these services has a problem, an error message normally appears during the boot sequence. You can use Event Viewer also as previously discussed or use the Services and Application tool available through the Computer Management administrative tool.

Before Windows 2000 can shut down, the operating system sends a message to all devices, services, and applications. Each device that is running sends a message back saying it is okay to shut down now. Any active application saves data that has not been previously saved and sends a message back to the operating system. Active system services also respond that it is okay to shut down. If the system has trouble shutting down, it is due to one of the following three things:

- The most common problem is an application that is not responding. When this happens, press **Ctrl + Alt + Del** to access Task Manager. Manually stop any applications from running to see if that is causing the problem. If a single application continually prevents Windows 2000 from shutting down, contact the software manufacturer to see if there is a fix.
- For services problems, boot the computer into Safe Mode and then shut the computer down. Take note as to whether or not the computer had any problems shutting down. If the process works, access the BOOTLOG.TXT file that is located in the root directory of the drive that contains Windows 2000. Once inside the file, take note of each service that is disabled because of booting into Safe Mode. Boot the computer normally. Stop each service one at a time to see which service is causing the problem.
- To troubleshoot devices not responding, eliminate services and applications first. A device frequently does not cause a shutdown problem. Then, while working on the computer, take notice of what devices you are using—common ones are video, hard drive, CD-ROM, keyboard, and mouse. Verify that all of your devices have the most up-to-date driver loaded and that the driver is compatible with Windows 2000.

6.13 Monitoring System Performance

Another utility used to monitor the computer is the Performance Logs and Alerts snap-in tool. **Performance Logs and Alerts** allows creation of graphs, bar charts, and text reports. An exercise at the end of the chapter shows how to use the Performance Logs and Alerts utility. This utility can also be customized to show different counters. The button with a + (plus sign) is used to add various counters to the display. Some of the most important memory counters are Available Bytes, Pages/sec, and Paging file\%Usage. The **Available Bytes** counter shows the amount of RAM available for running program processes. The **Pages/sec** counter shows the number of times per second the information requested could not be found in RAM, and the data had to be retrieved from the hard drive. The **Paging file\%Usage** counter shows what percentage of allocated space for the paging file is in use.

Sometimes you must adjust the paging file size for optimum computer performance. The System control panel is used to set the virtual memory size. Once in the System control panel, click on the **Advanced** tab. Click on the **Performance Options** button and two sections appear in the window: Application Response and Virtual Memory. Click on the **Change** button in the Virtual Memory section and the Virtual Memory window appears. Refer to Figure 6.28 for a screenshot of Performance Monitor. In the figure, the CPU time is being monitored.

Figure 6.28: Using Performance Monitor

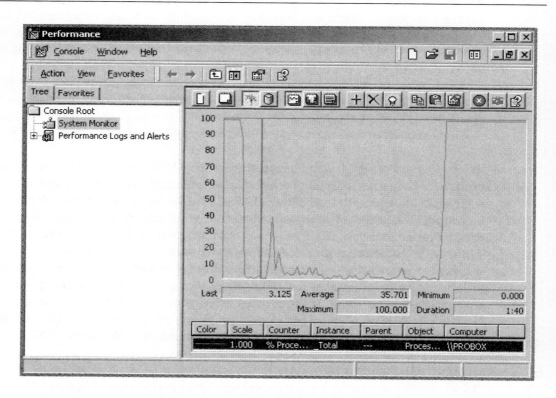

Two values are selectable: Initial size and Maximum size. Both of these values should be the same for maximum computer performance. Once you change the values, click on the **Set** button. The default amount of virtual memory is 1.5 times the amount of RAM installed in the computer. The Virtual Memory window can also be used to change the amount of space reserved for the registry.

The Task Manager utility can be used to monitor your current system's performance. Sometimes a computer can start slowing down. A baseline report is needed before the slowdown occurs. A **baseline** report is a snapshot of your computer's performance during normal operations (when it does not have any problems).

Start the Task Manager utility by pressing **Ctrl + Alt + Del** and clicking on the **Task Manager** button (or right-clicking on an empty space on the taskbar and clicking on the **Task Manager** option). Click on the **Performance** tab to see the CPU usage and memory usage statistics. The first window on the left shows the CPU usage percentage. Actually, it is a percentage of time the processor is running a thread. A thread is a type of Windows object that runs application instructions and was discussed in Chatper Two entitled *Basic Operating System Theory*. The first window on the right displays the CPU usage history, which is a graph of how busy the processor has been over a period of time.

The second window on the left shows the amount of memory being used. The amount shown is in kilobytes as evidenced by the K after the number. The second window on the right is a graph of the memory used over time.

Refer to Figure 6.29 for a screenshot of the Performance tab in Task Manager.

Figure 6.29: The Performance Tab in Task Manager

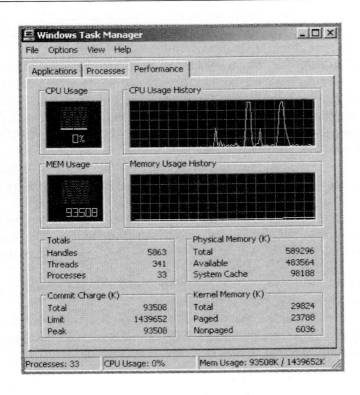

Memory is a frequent bottleneck for computer performance. Task Manager can also be used to see the total amount of RAM installed and how much RAM is available. Task Manager is an invaluable tool when a computer is slowing down.

Chapter Summary

- Windows 2000 Professional is a 32-bit operating system that provides better performance than Windows NT Workstation and Windows 95/98. Every 32-bit application runs in its own memory space meaning that if that application fails, other applications are not affected.
- Windows 2000 Professional provides a hierarchical file system allowing you to create folders and store files within them.
- Windows 2000 Professional supports both compression and encryption on files and folders. Compression saves disk space. Encryption provides security.
- The Windows 2000 Professional Registry is a database, which stores the hardware and software information installed on your computer.
- As part of the pre-installation steps of Windows 2000 Professional, you should decide whether or not to perform a clean installation or an upgrade.
- There are two modes of the Windows 2000 Professional installation—text mode and GUI mode. A few tasks done in text mode are as follows: the installation process checks for minimum hardware requirement and Plug and Play devices are installed. During GUI mode, other components are installed and configured.
- You can dual-boot Windows 2000 with other Microsoft operating system. When dual-booting, you should create a separate partition for each operating system. Install Windows 2000 Professional after installing the other operating systems.
- Troubleshooting your Windows 2000 installation includes verifying BIOS and driver compatibility, inserting the correct CD key, ensuring you have a minimum CPU that is a 486 33 MHz, and having at least 12 MB of RAM.
- Configuring Windows 2000 involves using Control Panel to add and remove hardware components such as a mouse or a printer. It also includes adding and removing additional software.
- You need to understand the boot process of Windows 2000 so you know how to troubleshoot when problems occur. The system partition is the active partition containing the operating system boot files. The boot partition is where the operating system files are located. They can be on the same partition.
- When Windows 2000 boots, various services are started. You can see the status of a service by checking the Services program in Control Panel.
- You can use Performance Monitor to monitor the performance of your Windows 2000 system through the use of objects and counters. It is important to take a baseline of your system for comparative purposes over time.

Review Questions

1. A _____ is an electronic container that holds data; you can open a _____ using an editor.
   a) Folder
   b) File
   c) Tab
   d) Taskbar

2. What is the maximum number of characters in a Windows 2000 file name?
   a) 8
   b) 256
   c) 255
   d) 512

3. What attribute allows you to only view the contents of a file?
   a) Hidden
   b) Archive
   c) Read
   d) System

4. How would you run a 16-bit application named programA in its own separate memory space?
   a) start /separate programA
   b) start programA \separate
   c) start \separate programA
   d) start /memory_space programA

5. What feature of Windows 2000 allows you to run multiple processors to operate on a task at the same time?
   a) WFP
   b) PnP
   c) SMP
   d) XMS

6. What feature of Windows 2000 runs in the background and protects system files from alteration?
   a) WFP
   b) PnP
   c) SMP
   d) XMS

7. With _____ the contents of the file are altered as a means of securing the data.
   a) Compression
   b) Encryption
   c) WFP
   d) XMS

8. What do you select to view the file names of compressed files in blue?
   a) **Select** Display compressed files and folders with alternate color
   b) **Select** Display noncompressed files and folders with alternate color
   c) **Select** Display compressed files and folders in blue color
   d) **Deselect** Display compressed files and folders with alternate color

9. The _____ is a group of important Windows 2000 files including the registry, the system files, the boot files, and the COM+ Class Registration database.
   a) System State
   b) REGEDT32
   c) SMP
   d) WFP

10. _____ is the most common application used to create, copy, or move files or folders.
    a) System State
    b) Registry
    c) Explorer
    d) Internet Explorer

11. Which of the following are considered issues related to a Windows 2000 installation?
    a) Incompatible BIOS
    b) BIOS needs to be upgraded
    c) Incompatible hardware
    d) All of the above

12. The system variable named *%systemroot%* is normally
    a) C:/WINNT
    b) C:/WINNT
    c) C:/Windows
    d) A:/WINNT

13. The _____ command line utility can be used to encrypt and decrypt files.
    a) COMPACT
    b) ENCRYPT
    c) SECRET
    d) CIPHER

14. The _____ command line utility can be used to compress files.
    a) COMPACT
    b) ENCRYPT
    c) COMPRESS
    d) SQUEEZE

15. Which of the following commands will display the Windows version?
    a) COMPACT
    b) COMPRESS
    c) WINDOWS_VERSION
    d) WINVER

16. Which file system does compression require?
    a) NTFS
    b) EXT2
    c) FAT16
    d) FAT32

17. With Windows 95, 98, NT, and 2000, upgrades or patches to the operating system are provided through _____, which fix problems within the operating system.
    a) WFP
    b) SMP
    c) Baseline
    d) Service Packs

18. A _____ report is a snapshot of your computer's performance during normal operations when it does not have any problems.
    a) Baseline
    b) Service Pack
    c) Task manager
    d) Performance

19. Which key do you press during the installation to load third party drivers?
    a) F8
    b) F2
    c) F6
    d) F13

20. Which registry subtree holds file associations and file links?
    a) HKEY_LOCAL_MACHINE
    b) HKEY_USERS
    c) HKEY_CURRENT_USER
    d) HKEY_CLASSES_ROOT

Lab Projects

Unless otherwise indicated, all projects assume the computer is powered on, you are logged in, and your desktop appears on the screen. Windows 2000 is up and running and you are logged on.

Lab Project 1

The goal of this lab is to help you determine system and disk information.

1. To determine CPU type, operating system and version, and RAM capacity, right-click the **My Computer** icon and click **Properties**. The System Properties screen appears with your system information.

2. Record the operating system type and level, the processor type, and RAM.

   _____

3. Click **OK** when complete.

4. In order to determine disk capacity and file system type, double-click **My Computer**. The My Computer screen appears with icons. Note the drive icons.

5. Right-click on the C: drive and then click **Properties**. Make sure the **General** tab is selected. The Properties page for the C: drive appears.

6. Record the used space for drive C:.

   _____

7. Record the free space for drive C:.

   _____

8. Record the file system type for drive C:.

   _____

9. Draw the pie chart representing how the space is used.

10. Insert a floppy in the floppy drive.

11. Repeat steps 6 through 9 for the floppy. Write your answers on a separate piece of paper.

12. Log out.

Lab Project 2

The goal of this lab is to help you understand *Task Manager*.

1. First, you will start a task. Press **Start** in the lower right-hand corner. Next, click **Run** and in the Open dialog box, type **calc** and press Enter. The calculator program appears on the screen.

2. To see the **calc** task (along with other jobs), press **Ctrl + Alt + Del**.

3. Record three other tasks.

   _____

4. You can scroll up and down this list and click End Task to delete a task. Be careful because ending a task will terminate it and you do not want to terminate a system task.

5. Highlight **calc** and press **End Task**.

6. Now, see what happens with you remove a system task. Terminate the **explorer** task. Follow the steps that appear on the screen. *Hint*: The shutdown screen will appear.

7. Record what happens.

   _____

8. Log out.

Lab Project 3

The goal of this project is to help you understand how to create a tree structure from a screenshot.

1. Using Windows Explorer, create the tree structure shown in Figure 6.30 on your floppy. To get to Explorer, right-click **Start** and then click **Explore**.

Figure 6.30: A Sample Tree Hierarchy

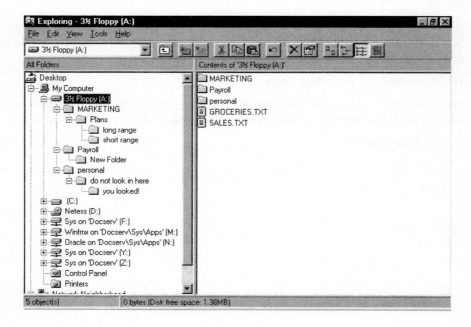

2. Using Notepad, create the following files as Text Documents in the "long range" folder. Place your name in each file.

   Monday.txt
   Tuesday.txt
   Wednesday.txt
   Thursday.txt
   Friday.txt

3. Record the steps you took to create them.

   _____

4. Rename the "New Folder" to "Weekly."

5. Record the steps you took.

   _____

6. Create a "Medium Range" folder in "Plans."

7. Record the steps you took.

   _____

8. In the "personal" folder, create a file called "resume.txt."

9. Hide this folder.

10. Record the steps you took.

    _____

11. View all files.

12. Record the steps you took.

    _____

13. Make a complete copy of the files in "Plans" and put them in a folder called "BACKUP of PLANS."

14. Record the steps you took.

    _____

15. In Explorer, right-click on the floppy to make a disk copy of the floppy. Insert another floppy disk and make a disk copy of this floppy to another floppy.

16. Record the steps you took.

    _____

17. Create another folder in the root directory of the floppy that has your name in it.

18. Create another folder in the root directory of the floppy named "Windows 2000 Project."

19. Show your instructor.

20. Close all windows.

Lab Project 4

The goal of this project is to reinforce your understanding of how to create a tree structure. You will also work with attributes to help you understand how they work.

1. Using Windows Explorer, create the tree structure shown in Figure 6.31 on your floppy.

Figure 6.31: A Sample Tree Hierarchy

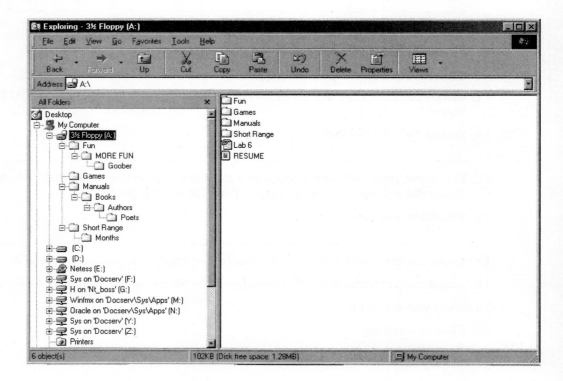

2. Using Notepad, place these files in the "Poets" folder:

 Poe.txt
 Walker.txt
 Smith.txt

3. In Explorer, click **Tools**, then click **Folder Options** and then click **View**. The Folder Options window opens. In the Advanced Settings box, activate the setting so hidden and system files are not displayed.

4. Right-click on "Poe.txt" and click **Properties**. The Properties page appears. Click **Hidden** and then click **OK**. The files are hidden.

5. In Explorer, click **Tools**, then click **Folder Options** and then click **View**. The Folder Options window opens. In the Advanced Settings box, activate the setting to show all files. This will display hidden files.

6. Record whether or not you can now see "Poe.txt."

_____

7. Using the previous step as a guide, make the file "Walker.txt" read-only.

8. Record the steps you took.

_____

9. Open the file named "Walker.txt" in Notepad and attempt to add data.

10. Record what occurred.

_____

11. Close Notepad.

12. Make "Walker.txt" readable.

13. Open the file named "Walker.txt" in Notepad and attempt to add data.

14. Record what occurred.

_____

15. Close Notepad.

16. Create another folder in the root directory of the floppy that has your name in it.

17. Create another folder in the root directory of the floppy named "Windows 2000 Project 4."

18. Show your instructor.

19. Close all windows.

Lab Project 5

The goal of this project is to work with Windows 2000 taskbar options.

1. Turn on the computer and verify that the operating system loads.

2. Log on to Windows 2000 using the userid and password provided by the instructor or lab assistant.

3. Locate the taskbar on the bottom of the screen. If it is not showing, move the mouse to the bottom of the screen and the taskbar pops up.

4. To modify or view the taskbar settings, right-click on a **blank area** of the taskbar. A menu appears. Note: You can also use the **Start** button, point to the **Settings** option, and click on the **Taskbar and Start Menu** option.

5. Click on the **Properties** option. The Taskbar and Start Menu Properties window appears.

6. Click on the **General** tab.

7. The five options available on this screen relate to how things are shown on the taskbar. The items with a check in the check box to the left are active. The **Always on top** option puts the taskbar visible on the screen at all times (even if a window is full size or maximized). The **Auto hide** option hides the taskbar during normal operation. Press **Ctrl + Esc** or the **Start** button on the keyboard (the one with the Windows emblem on it) to make the taskbar reappear. If both the Always on top and Auto hide options are checked, then the taskbar appears when you are in a window that is full size (maximized). The **Show small icons in Start menu** option reduces the size of the Start menu words. The **Show clock** option displays the clock icon in the right corner of the taskbar. The **Use Personalized Menus** option allows you to hide menu items that you rarely use. Make sure the **Always on top** and **Show clock** options are the only ones with check marks in the check boxes. To remove a check mark, click in the **check box** that already contains a check in it. To put a check mark in a box, click once in an **empty box.**

8. Click on the **Apply** button.

9. Click on the **OK** button.

10. Right-click on an **empty space** on the taskbar.

11. Point to the **Toolbars** option. A submenu appears.

12. Ensure that there is a check mark beside the **Quick Launch** option. This setting allows the Quick Launch icons to appear on the desktop by the Start button.

13. Using the skills you just learned, access the **Taskbar Settings** window.

   List the steps you performed to do step 13.

14. Click on the **Properties** option. Click on the **Question mark** icon in the upper right corner of the window. The question mark is an interactive help system. The pointer on the screen changes to an arrow with a question mark attached. Click on the **Always on top** option. A description of the option appears with the on-line help active.

    What text does the help balloon display?

    _____

15. Click on the **Advanced** tab. The Advanced tab is used to customize the Start button and to delete files that list under the Start button's Documents option or previously accessed web sites.

16. Click on the **Cancel** button.

Lab Project 6

The goal of this project is to work with Windows 2000 REGEDIT editor.

REGEDIT is a utility used for editing the Windows registry. With REGEDIT, you can view existing registry settings, modify registry settings values, or create new registry entries to change or enhance the way Windows operates. In this lab, you will use REGEDIT to view the System BIOS and Video BIOS information on your computer.

CAUTION: Editing the registry can cause your computer to run erratically, or not run at all! When performing any registry editing, follow ALL directions carefully, including spelling, syntax use, etc. Failure to do so may cause your computer to fail!

1. From the Start menu, choose **Run**, type **REGEDIT**, and click **OK**. The REGEDIT utility opens.

2. In the left window, expand **HKEY_LOCAL_MACHINE**, **HARDWARE**, and **DESCRIPTION**, and then select **System**.

3. In the right window, the System BIOS and Video BIOS information display.

    What is the System BIOS date?

    _____

    Who is the manufacturer of your System BIOS?

    _____

    When was your Video BIOS manufactured?

    _____

4. When finished viewing the System and Video BIOS information, close the **REGEDIT** utility.

Lab Project 7

The goal of this project is to work with Windows 2000 REGEDT32 editor.

REGEDT32 is a utility used for editing the Windows registry. With it, you can find and view existing registry settings, modify registry settings values, or create new registry entries to change or enhance the way Windows operates. In this lab, you will use REGEDT32 to create and configure a new registry setting to control how many document entries appear in Documents on the Start menu.

CAUTION: Editing the registry can cause your computer to run erratically, or not run at all! When performing any registry editing, follow ALL directions carefully, including spelling, syntax use, etc. Failure to do so may cause your computer to fail!

1. From the Start menu, click on the **Run** option, type **REGEDT32** in the textbox, and click **OK**. The REGEDT32 utility opens.

2. From HKEY_CURRENT_USER on Local Machine window, expand the following options: **Software, Microsoft, Windows, CurrentVersion,** and **Policies,** and then select the **Explorer** option.

3. From the Edit menu option, choose **Add Value**. The Add Value window opens. Editor opens.

4. The default number of documents that appear in the Start menu's Document folder is 15. From the **DWORD Editor** window, select the **Decimal** radio button, enter the value of **20** in the Data textbox, and click **OK**. The new DATA value displays in Hexadecimal format.

   What is the Hexadecimal value of the new DATA value?

   _____

5. Close the **REGEDT32** utility and reboot the computer for the new registry setting to take effect.

   After the computer reboots, how many documents can be displayed in the Start menu's Documents folder?

   _____

Lab Project 8

The goal of this project is to use the Windows 2000 Backup Utility to back up the registry.

1. Turn on the computer and verify that Windows 2000 Professional loads.

2. Log on to Windows 2000 using the userid and password provided by the instructor or lab assistant. Make sure that the userid is an Administrator userid or a userid that is a member of the Backup Operators group.

3. Click on the **Start** button.

4. Point to the **Programs** option.

5. Point to the **Accessories** option.

6. Point to the **System Tools** option.

7. Click on the **Backup** option. The Backup Utility window opens.

8. Click on the **Backup** tab.

9. Click once in the **System State** check box to enable this option. A check mark appears in the check box.

10. At the bottom of the window, click on the **Browse** button to select a hard drive or any other type of media. Contact your instructor for the location to put the backed up files.

11. Type a **name** for the backup and click on the **Open** button.

    What name did you assign for the backup file?

    _____

12. Click on the **Start Backup** button to begin the backup procedure. The Backup Job Information dialog box appears.

13. Click on the **Advanced** option.

14. Click on the **Automatically backup system protected files with the System State** option.

15. Click on the **OK** button.

16. Click on the **Start Backup** button. A Backup Progress window appears.

    How many estimated files will be backed up?

    _____

17. Click on the **Close** button.

18. Close the **Backup** window.

Lab Project 9

The goal of this project is to install an updated driver under the Windows 2000 operating system.

Note: The installation process outlined below may differ due to computer differences. If the process is different, follow the directions on the screen. Contact your instructor or a lab assistant if you are unsure of the steps.

1. Turn the computer on and verify that the operating system loads. Log in to Windows 2000 using the userid and password provided by the instructor or lab assistant.

2. Click on the **Start** button, point to **Settings**, and click on the **Control Panel** menu option.

3. When the Control Panel window opens, scroll down to the **System** icon and double-click on it.

4. Click on the **Hardware** tab.

5. Click on the **Device Manager** button.

6. Click on the **+ (plus sign)** beside the class of device you want to upgrade.

7. Right-click on the **specific device** you want to upgrade.

8. Click on the **Properties** tab.

9. Click on the **Driver** tab.

10. Click on the **Update Driver** button. The Upgrade Device Driver wizard appears.

11. Click on the **Next** button.

12. Click on the **Display a list of known drivers for this device so that I can choose a specific driver** radio button. Click on the **Next** button.

13. Click on the **Have Disk** button.

14. Insert the media that contains your updated driver into the floppy drive, Zip drive, CD-ROM, or DVD drive.

15. In the Copy manufacturer's files from box, type in the drive letter for the device that contains the updated driver followed by a colon and click on the **OK** button. An example of a driver device is A:. The Browse button can be used to locate a device driver as well.

16. Click on the **Next** button and follow the instructions on the screen to complete the upgrade.

Lab Project 10

The goal of this project is install a non-plug and play device into a computer running Windows 2000 and load the proper driver for it. Additionally you will need the following:

• Non-plug and play device
• Latest Windows 2000 driver for the hardware device

Note: The installation process outlined below may differ due to computer differences. If the process is different, follow the directions on the screen. Contact your instructor or a lab assistant if you are unsure of the steps.

1. Turn the comsuter off and install the piece of hardware according to the manufacturer's directions.

2. Turn the computer on and verify that the operating system loads. Log in to Windows 2000 using the userid and password provided by the instructor or lab assistant. The Found New Hardware window should not appear if the device is truly non-plug and play.

3. Start the Add/Remove Hardware wizard by clicking on the **Start** button.

4. Point to the **Settings** option and then click on the **Control Panel** menu option.

5. When the Control Panel window appears, double-click on the **Add/Remove Hardware** icon. The Add/Remove Hardware wizard initializes. Click on the **Next** button to continue.

6. Ensure the Add/Troubleshoot a device radio button is selected, and then click on the **Next** button. A list of installed devices appears.

7. Click on the **Add a new device** option from the window and click on the **Next** button.

8. Click on the **No, I want to select the hardware from a list** option and then click on the **Next** button.

9. Select the type of hardware you want to install and then click on the **Next** button.

10. Insert your device driver into the floppy drive, Zip drive, CD-ROM, or DVD drive.

11. Click on the **Have disk** button. In the Copy manufacturer's files from box, type in the **drive letter** for the device that contains the updated driver followed by a colon. An example of this would be A:. Click on the **Browse** button if you don't know where the file is located. Click on the **OK** button. You may be required to select your specific device or model from a list on the screen. If so, select the device and click the **Next** button. Contact an instructor or lab assistant if you don't know what to select.

12. Click on the **Finish** button.

Lab Project 11

The goal of this project is to install a printer attached to the computer running Windows 2000 and load the proper driver for it. Additionally you will need the following:

• Printer (with appropriate cabling if necessary)
• Latest Windows 2000 driver for the printer

Note: The installation process outlined below may differ due to printer differences. If the process is different, follow the directions on the screen. Contact your instructor or a lab assistant if you are unsure of the steps.

1. Turn the computer off and install the printer according to the manufacturer's directions. If you do not have the correct driver, go on the printer manufacturer's web site and download the driver or obtain it from the instructor or lab assistant.

2. Turn the computer on and verify that the operating system loads. Log on to Windows 2000 using the userid and password provided by the instructor or lab assistant. The Found New Hardware wizard should appear. Follow the instructions on the screen to install the printer. When prompted for the printer driver, insert the CD or disk that contains the printer driver, and use the Browse button to locate the driver. Continue through the Add Printer wizard until the printer is installed.

3. If the Found New Hardware wizard does not appear, have the Windows 2000 printer driver ready, click on the **Start** button, point to the **Settings** selection, and double-click on the **Printers** option.

4. When the Printers window opens, click on the **Add Printer** icon.

5. Click on the **Next** button and select the **Local Printer** selection.

6. When prompted for the printer driver, insert the CD or disk that contains the printer driver, and use the Browse button to locate the driver. Continue through the Add Printer wizard until the printer is installed.

7. Print a test page to test the printer. If the page did not print, troubleshoot the printer.

Lab Project 12

The goal of this project is to use the Windows 2000 System Information tool to troubleshoot device conflicts.

1. Turn on the computer and verify that Windows 2000 Professional loads.

2. Log on to Windows 2000 using the userid and password provided by the instructor or lab assistant.

3. Click on the **Start** button and point to the **Settings** selection.

4. Point to the **Control Panel** option.

5. Double-click on the **Administrative Tools** control panel icon.

6. Double-click on the **System Information** icon.

7. Click on the + **(plus sign)** next to the **Components** folder.

8. Click on the **Problem Devices** folder. Any devices with hardware conflicts list in the right window. Keep in mind that you use the Device Manager program to correct any problems with resource allocation.

   Do any devices have conflicts listed in the Problem Devices window? If so, write them below.

   _____

9. Another good check for hardware conflicts is through the Hardware Resources option. Click on the + **(plus sign)** next to the Hardware Resources folder.

10. Double-click on the **Conflicts/Sharing** folder. Any device that lists under this folder has a resource conflict or is sharing a system resource. Do not forget that PCI devices can legitimately share system resources.

    List two devices that are sharing system resources in the space below.

    _____

11. Click on the **IRQs** folder located under the Hardware Resources folder in the left window.

    List any IRQ that is available for use by a new device.

    _____

    Are any IRQs shared by two devices? If so, write them in the space below.

    _____

12. Click on the **Memory** folder located under the Hardware Resources folder in the left window.

13. Close the System Information window by clicking on the **Close** box (the one with the **X**) in the upper right corner of the window.

Lab Project 13

The goal of this project is to create an Emergency Repair Disk (ERD) that can be used when the computer does not boot properly.

1. Turn on the computer and verify that Windows 2000 Professional loads.

2. Log on to Windows 2000 using the userid and password provided by the instructor or lab assistant.

3. Click on the **Start** button.

4. Point to the **Programs** option.

5. Point to the **Accessories** option.

6. Point to the **System Tools** option.

7. Click on the **Backup** option. The Backup window appears.

8. Click on the **Tools** menu option.

9. Click on the **Create an Emergency Repair Disk** option.

   Give one situation where an Emergency Repair Disk is useful.

   _____

10. Insert a blank formatted floppy disk when prompted.

11. Click on the **OK** button.

12. When the ERD creation is complete, close the **Backup** window.

Lab Project 14

The goal of this project is to use the Performance utility to track individual computer components.

1. Turn on the computer and verify that Windows 2000 Professional loads.

2. Log on to Windows 2000 using the userid and password provided by the instructor or lab assistant.

3. Click on the **Start** button, point to the **Settings** option, and click on the **Control Panel** selection.

4. Double-click on the **Administrative Tools** control panel icon.

5. Double-click on the **Performance** icon. The Performance utility allows you to track individual computer component's performance. This is done through individual counters.

6. In the left window, click on the **System Monitor** item.

7. Click on the **Add button** (the button that has a plus sign on it) or right-click in the right window and click on the **Add Counters** option. The Add Counters dialog box opens.

8. Click on the **Performance object** down arrow. A list of system components appears such as Processor, physical disk, paging file memory, etc. Select the **Memory** performance object.

9. Once a system component has been selected, individual counters for that component can be selected and monitored. In the Select counters from list window, click on the **Available Bytes** counter. Click on the **Add** button.

10. Click on the **Performance** object down arrow. Select the **Paging File** performance object.

11. In the Select counters from list window, click on the **%Usage** counter. Click on the **Add** button.

    Using the Explain button, find out for what the %Usage counter is used. Write the explanation in the space below.

    _____

12. Using the method outlined in steps 7 through 9, select two more counters to be monitored.

    What two counters did you add?

    _____

13. Click on the **Close** button. The right window in the Performance window displays a graph of the various counters. You may need to start some applications, do some cutting and pasting, or surf the Internet to see some of the counter activity. When finished, close the **Performance** window.

Lab Project 15

The goal of this project is to help you understand how to encrypt and decrypt files at the command prompt. You must complete this lab project on an NTFS partition. This lab project is a bit more advanced because you are expected to determine many of the steps in the lab. If you have trouble with the command prompt mode, refer to Chapter 3 on DOS and the DOS command prompt.

1. Go to a command prompt.

2. At the command prompt, create a directory named C:\Project15.

3. Record the command used.

   _____

4. Create two files named File15A.txt and File15B.txt in Project15.

5. Record the command used.

   _____

6. To make sure you are at the root directory of the C: drive, type **CD C:** and press Enter.

7. To encrypt a directory, type **CIPHER /E Project15** and press Enter. The directory and new files will be encrypted.

8. To verify the encryption status, type **CIPHER** and press Enter. The status of the directories and files are displayed. If an "E" is beside the directory or file name, then the item is encrypted. If there is a "U," the item is not encrypted.

9. Change directory locations to Project15.

10. Create a new file named File15E.txt.

11. To verify the encryption status, type **CIPHER** and press Enter.

12. Record the output.

    _____

    _____

    _____

13. Record the reason for the output.

    _____

    _____

    _____

14. To make sure you are at the root directory of the C: drive, type **CD C:** and press Enter.

15. To decrypt a directory, type **CIPHER /D Project15** and press Enter. The directory and new files will not be encrypted.

16. Create a new file in Project15.

17. Check the encryption/decryption status now.

18. Record the output and reason for the output.

_____

_____

_____

19. Close the command prompt window.

Lab Project 16

The goal of this project is to help you understand how to compress and uncompress files at the command prompt. You must complete this lab project on an NTFS partition. This lab project is a bit more advanced because you are expected to determine many of the steps in the lab. If you have trouble with the command prompt mode, refer to Chapter 3 on DOS and the DOS command prompt.

1. Go to a command prompt.

2. At the command prompt, create a directory named C:\Project16.

3. Record the command used.

   _____

4. Create two files named File16A.txt and File16B.txt in Project16.

5. Record the command used.

   _____

6. To make sure you are at the root directory of the C: drive, type **CD C:** and press Enter.

7. To encrypt a directory, type **COMPACT /C Project16** and press Enter. The directory and new files will be compressed.

8. To verify the compression status, type **COMPACT** and press Enter. The status of the directories and files are displayed. If a "C" is beside the directory or file name, then the item is compressed. Otherwise, the item is not compressed.

9. Change directory locations to Project16.

10. Create a new file named File16C.txt.

11. To verify the compression status, type **COMPACT** and press Enter.

12. Record the output.

    _____

    _____

    _____

13. Record the reason for the output.

    _____

    _____

    _____

14. Close the command prompt window.

15. To make sure you are at the root directory of the C: drive, type **CD C:** and press Enter.

16. To uncompress a directory, type **COMPACT /U Project16** and press Enter. The directory and new files will not be compressed.

17. Create a new file in Project16.

18. Check the compression/uncompression status now.

19. Record the output and reason for the output.

_____

_____

_____

20. Close the command prompt window.

Lab Project 17 Challenge

The goal of this project is to upgrade an existing operating system to Windows 2000 Professional. Other requirements are :

• Computer with Windows 95 or 98 installed
• Windows 2000 Professional installation CD

Note: The installation process outlined below may differ due to computer differences. If the process is different, follow the directions on the screen. Contact your instructor or a lab assistant if you are unsure of the steps.

1. Turn the computer on and verify that the operating system loads.

2. Insert the Windows 2000 Professional CD into the CD-ROM or DVD drive.

3. The CD may automatically start. If it does, click on the **Setup** icon. If the CD does not automatically start, click on the **Start** button. Click on the **Run** option. Type in **x:setup** where x: is the drive letter of the device containing the Windows 2000 Professional CD.

4. A message appears on the screen that a newer operating system is being installed and asks if you want to continue. Click the **Yes** button.

5. The Welcome to Windows 2000 Setup wizard appears. Make sure the **Upgrade to Windows 2000** radio button is selected. Click on the **Next** button.

6. The licensing agreement appears on the screen. Read the agreement and click on the **I accept this agreement** radio button and then click on the **Next** button if you agree with the terms.

7. The Your Product Key screen appears. Enter the **product key** provided by the instructor or located on the CD case. Click the **Next** button to continue.

8. The Preparing to Upgrade to Windows 2000 screen appears. Click the **Next** button.

9. The Provide Upgrade Packs screen appears. Click on the **No, I don't have any upgrade packs** radio button. Click the **Next** button to continue.

10. If you have a file system other than NTFS, you will be prompted to upgrade to NTFS. Ask your instructor whether or not to upgrade to NTFS.

    If an upgrade to NTFS is desired, click on the **Yes, upgrade my drive** radio button and then click on the **Next** button.

11. An Upgrade Report screen appears. If there was any incompatible hardware or software found by Windows 2000, it displays on the screen. Go back to the pre-installation steps listed at the beginning of the chapter for more assistance. Print the report or save it if the instructor tells you to. Click the **Next** button to continue.

12. After some files are copied, the computer restarts several times.

13. After the final restart, you must type in the **username and password** entered during the setup process.

Lab Project 18 Challenge

The goal of this project is to install Windows 2000 Professional on a computer without an operating system or on a computer on which the old operating system will be replaced (removed). Other requirements are:

- Computer appropriate hardware
- Four Windows 2000 Professional installation disks
- Windows 2000 Professional installation CD

Note: The installation process outlined below may differ due to computer differences. If the process is different, follow the directions on the screen. Contact your instructor or a lab assistant if you are unsure of the steps.

1. Turn the computer on and verify that the BIOS is set to boot from the floppy drive first, and the hard drive second (A,C sequence). Contact an instructor or lab assistant for assistance on entering the BIOS SETUP program.

2. Insert the Windows 2000 Professional Disk 1 into the floppy drive.

3. Restart the computer. If the computer does not boot from the floppy disk, go back to step 1.

4. Hardware detection starts and then you are prompted to insert Disk 2. Insert the Windows 2000 Professional floppy Disk 2 into the drive and press **Enter**. You will later be prompted for Disks 3 and 4. Follow the directions on the screen.

5. After all files from the floppies have been copied, the Welcome to Windows 2000 Professional Setup screen appears. Press **Enter** to continue with the installation process.

6. The licensing agreement appears on the screen. Read the agreement and press the **F8** key if you agree to the terms.

7. The partitioning options appear next. Contact an instructor or lab assistant to find out if you are to create a partition, use an existing partition, or delete a partition.

8. Follow the directions on the screen and partition the hard drive.

   What type of partitioning will you be doing on this computer? Write the instructions in the space below:

   _____

9. After the hard drive partition is created, more files are copied and the computer restarts.

10. After the computer restarts, a more graphical Setup wizard displays. Click the **Next** button to continue.

11. The regional options such as language and time zone appear. Select the **appropriate option** for your area of the world. Click on either **Customize** button that appears on the screen to change the regional settings. Click on the **Next** button to continue.

12. When the Personalize Your Software screen appears, contact an instructor or lab assistant for the Name and Organization to type.

Name _____

Organization _____

13. The Product Key screen appears. Type in the **product key** that is located on the CD case or type in a **key** provided by your instructor. Click the **Next** button to continue.

14. The Computer Name and Password screen appears. Contact an instructor or lab assistant for the Name and Administrator password.

Name _____

Password _____

15. The Date and Time screen appears. Enter the **correct date and time** and click on the **Next** button.

16. The Network Settings screen appears. Click on the **Typical Settings** button.

17. The Workgroup or Computer Domain screen appears. Click on the **No, this computer is not on a network or is on a network without a domain** radio button. Click on the **Next** button to continue.

18. Setup continues to copy more files. When instructed to, remove the installation CD and click on the **Finish** button.

Lab Project 19 Challenge

The goal of this project is to verify any errors that occurred during the Windows 2000 installation.

1. Turn on the computer and log in to Windows 2000 using the userid and password provided by the instructor or lab assistant.

2. Right-click on the **Start** button. Click on the **Explore** option.

3. In the left window, locate the drive letter on which Windows 2000 was loaded. (Normally this is the C: drive.) Contact the instructor or a student assistant if you are unsure. Click on the **+ (plus sign)** beside the drive letter. If there is no plus sign by the drive letter, but instead it is a minus sign, skip this step.

4. In the left window, locate the folder in which Windows 2000 was loaded. (Normally this is WINNT.) Contact the instructor or a student assistant if you are unsure. Double-click on this folder.

5. In the left window, locate the folder called WINDIR and click on the **+ (plus sign)** beside this folder.

6. Click on the **Tools** menu option.

7. Click on the **Folder options** selection.

8. Click on the **View** tab.

9. Locate the Hidden files and folders option and ensure the radio button beside the Show hidden files and folders option is selected. If it is not, click in the **radio button** to enable it. Click on the **OK** button.

10. In the right window, if files and folders do not appear, click on the **Show files** option. Locate the **SETUPACT.LOG** file and double-click on it. Notepad opens with this file. This file contains a listing of all installation actions performed.

    What was the first listing shown in the SETUPACT.LOG of what was done during the installation process?

    _____

11. Close the SETUPACT.LOG file by clicking on the **Close** button (**X**) located in the upper right corner of the window.

12. In the right Explorer window, locate the **SETUPERR.LOG** file and double-click on it. Notepad opens with this file. The SETUPERR.LOG file contains a listing of any errors that occurred during the Windows 2000 installation process.

    Were any errors logged during the Windows 2000 installation? If so, write one of the errors in the space below.

    _____

13. Close the SETUPERR.LOG file by clicking on the **Close** button (**X**).

Internet Discovery

Internet Discovery Lab 1

1. What is the URL for the Microsoft Windows 2000 Professional on-line help?

2. When Windows 2000 Professional is in Standby mode, a stop 0x9F error appears. What should you do? Write the URL and the answer in the space below.

3. Frank Condron has a web site for Windows 2000. On this web site, Frank describes what to do if you get a blue screen of death with the stop error of DATA_BUS_ERROR. What is Frank's solution and what is the URL where you found the solution?

4. ZD, Inc. has a web site for Windows 2000. Write the URL for this site.
   Locate one book on the Internet that deals with troubleshooting Windows 2000 Professional. Write the name of the book, the author, and the URL in the space provided.

5. How many Service Packs are currently available for Windows 2000 Professional? Write the number and URL where you found the answer in the space below.

Soft Skills: Help Desk Support

1. A customer named Marsha Weng calls you and says that her Windows 2000 Professional computer system is running very slowly. It had been working fine prior to today. Identify at least three problems and resolutions.

2. You attempt to install Windows 2000 Professional on a computer that is a Pentium running at 300 MHz with 24 MB of RAM and 10 GB of hard disk space free. What potential issues, if any, do you see with this configuration before you install the operating system?

3. A customer named Matilda Ayers in Sydney, Australia calls you with a problem. She needs to load third party disk drivers on a computer during the installation process. What do you tell her?

4. You work as a consultant for a large international firm and you are currently assigned to a customer in Madrid, Spain. You are working on the Windows 2000 Professional computer for the Vice President of Production. When booting the computer, you receive a message that NTLDR is missing or corrupt. What should you do?

Critical Thinking

1. What is the difference between *%systemroot%* and *%systemdrive%*?

2. What do you do if you forget the password for the Administrator account?

3. If you can only boot one operating system at a time, what is the purpose of dual-booting and multi-booting?

4. How could you fix a corrupt Master Boot Record in Windows 2000?

5. Explain how encryption works.

6. Discuss the pros and cons of compression.

Study Skills

The "See" in "Hear, See, Do, Say"

Remember the key to learning are these four points: hear, see, do, say. This section focuses on the visual part or the "see" study skill.

- One of ways we learn and get input into our brain is through our senses. Consider your eyes as an "input device," allowing sensory data to enter the "processor" or brain.
- Your instructor may use visual aids on the overhead such as a PowerPoint presentation or demonstrating a lab activity. You learn a great deal in the computer industry by using your eyes.
- Make sure you can "see" the classroom chalkboard or white board. You may see this again on a test.
- Make sure you can "see" the classroom overhead screen. You could see this material on a test as well.
- Make sure you can "see" the computer screen in front of you.
- Pay attention to the output in front of you. The computer is telling you something whether it is good or bad.
- If you have to move closer to the board, do so. Ask your instructor for assistance.
- If you cannot see the screen in front of you, you may need to get your eyes checked.
- "Seeing" does _not_ involve using another person's answers (known as **cheating**).

Self-Study Question(s)
1. Can you clearly see the necessary screens or boards in the classroom?
2. Identify at least two "see" Study Skills you did this week.

7

Chapter 7
Introduction to
Microsoft
Windows XP

OBJECTIVES

The goal of this chapter is twofold:
- To introduce you to Windows XP.
- To help you prepare and pass the following section of the A+ Operating System Technologies Exam:

A+ Operating System Technologies Exam Objectives
covered in this chapter (and corresponding page numbers)

1.1 Identify the major desktop components and interfaces, and their functions. Differentiate the characteristics of Windows 9x/Me, Windows NT 4.0 Workstation, Windows 2000 Professional, and Windows XP.

1.2 Identify the names, locations, purposes, and contents of major system files.

1.4 Identify basic concepts and procedures for creating, viewing, and managing disks, directories and files. This includes procedures for changing file attributes and the ramifications of those changes (for example, security issues).

In this chapter, you will complete the following sections:
- 7.1 Understanding Microsoft Windows XP
- 7.2 Understanding the Pre-Installation Steps of Windows XP
- 7.3 Understanding How to Install and Upgrade Windows XP
- 7.4 Troubleshooting the Windows XP Installation
- 7.5 Understanding How to Dual-Boot Windows XP
- 7.6 Backing Up and Restoring the Windows XP Registry
- 7.7 Configuring Windows XP
- 7.8 Understanding the Boot Process
- 7.9 Understanding Task Manager, Dr. Watson, and Event Viewer
- 7.10 Monitoring System Performance

7.1 Understanding Microsoft Windows XP

Windows XP is a 32-bit operating system but a 64-bit version is also available. Microsoft created Windows XP in two different versions: Home and Professional. Windows XP Home is for personal computers and Windows XP Professional is for a business environment. The following list shows you the features available in both versions.

- Supports disk quotas to limit users on storage space.
- Core reliability and stability like Windows 2000.
- Enhanced support for movies, pictures, and music.
- Contains Windows Messenger that is a collaboration tool for instant messaging and video conferencing.
- Supports **Internet Connection Firewall** (**ICS**), which can help prevent attacks to your computer from hackers when connected to the Internet.
- Improved boot and power resume performance.
- Can automatically configure 802.1x wireless networks—to be discussed in Chapter 9, *Introduction to Networking.*
- Allows you to view output on multiple monitors—this is called **DualView.**
- CDs can be made using drag-and-drop or the CD Writing Wizard.
- Supports **WIA** (**Windows Image Acquisition**), which allows communication between software application and image-capturing devices. The Scanner and Camera wizard is used to retrieve images from any WIA-enabled device.
- Can switch between users without rebooting.

There are quite a few differences between Windows XP Professional and Windows XP Home. Here is a list of specific features available on the Professional edition:

- Supports two CPUs.
- Supports roaming profiles.
- Supports Remote Desktop and Remote Assistance.
- Has Computer Management and Performance Monitor.
- Supports joining a Windows-based server domain.
- Allows Group Policies with users, which allow you to customize user and computer accounts.
- Provides Encrypting Files System (EFS) as discussed in Chapter 6, *Introduction to Windows 2000.*
- Supports dynamic disk support allowing you to increase the size of a partition.
- Supports **IPSec** (**IP Security**), which allows you to secure and encrypt TCP/IP data.
- Upgradeable from Windows 98, Windows NT, Windows ME, or Windows 2000 Professional.

Here is a list of specific features available on the Home edition:

- Supports only one CPU.
- Supports only Remote Assistant.
- Upgradeable from Windows 98 and Windows ME.

Windows XP Professional supports 32-bit Windows applications, 16-bit Windows applications, and some DOS applications (only those that do not access hardware directly). Every 32-bit application runs in its own 2 GB memory space. All 16-bit Windows applications run in a single virtual machine. A virtual machine simulates a single computer with its own memory, hardware devices, and software configuration.

DOS and 16-bit Windows applications run in a single 2 GB memory space. The Windows XP **VMM (Virtual Memory Manager)** handles allocating memory to applications. A single block called a **page** is 4 KB in size. A page is used to store files and may also retrieve a file located on a disk. This file is called a **paging file**.

Windows XP supports **WFP** (**Windows File Protection**). WFP protects system files (files critical to the operating system). WFP runs in the background. When WFP detects that a file has been altered or deleted, it copies a replacement file from the WINDOWS \SYSTEM32\DLLCACHE folder, from the Windows XP CD, or from a network share (a shared folder that contains a copy of the XP CD).

Windows XP uses the same file system hierarchy concept to store files and folders as Windows 2000. So, a section covering file and folder management will not be covered here. For review, refer to Section **6.2 entitled Managing Files and Folders on Windows 2000** in Chapter 6, *Introduction to Windows 2000.*

With Windows XP, the first screen to appear when you boot the computer is the Welcome screen. The Welcome screen allows users to log in. A user can log in to the local computer, to a workgroup (peer-to-peer network), or to a domain (a network with a server). See Chapter 9, *Introduction to Networking,* for more information on network types. Note that the log-in screen cannot be bypassed as it could in Windows 9x.

To log in, click on a user account icon and enter a password (if necessary) or press **Ctrl + Alt + Del** to go to the Log On to Windows box.

Note that the local Administrator account (the master account that is allowed to change everything on the local machine) is not a user icon. You must press **Ctrl + Alt + Del** *twice* and enter the correct userid and password to use the Administrator account.

7.2 Understanding the Pre-Installation Steps of Windows XP

Windows XP can be installed from a central location or locally. The pre-installation of any operating system is more important than the installation process. Technicians that grab a disk or CD and load a new operating system without going through a logical process are just asking for trouble. There are two major portions of any new operating system installation—hardware and software. The hardware and software already installed in the system must be compatible with the operating system and researched before any installation steps are taken. The steps to be taken before installing Windows XP are outlined next.

- Decide whether the installation will be an upgrade or clean install and which version of XP is to be loaded.
- Determine the file system(s) to be used.
- Decide whether the computer will have more than one operating system installed.
- Scan for viruses.
- Determine if the hardware is compatible.
- Obtain any drivers, upgrades, or hardware replacements.
- Decide if the software applications are compatible.
- Obtain any patches, upgrades, or software replacements.
- Delete any unwanted files and uninstall any unwanted applications.
- Back up any data files necessary.
- Remove any power management or disk management tools.

The first decision to make when planning to install Windows XP is whether to upgrade from another operating system or perform a clean install. A **clean install** puts an operating system on a computer without one, or the computer's existing operating system is removed (the hard drive is formatted). Three reasons exist to perform a clean install:

- The computer does not have an operating system already installed.
- The computer's current operating system is not upgradeable to Windows XP.
- The computer's current operating system is upgradeable to Windows XP, but the existing files and applications are going to be reloaded.

If the decision is made to upgrade, then determine what operating system is already installed. Windows XP Professional supports upgrading from Windows 98, Windows ME, NT Workstation 4, 2000 Professional, and XP Home Edition. Windows XP Home edition only supports upgrades from Windows 98 and Windows ME. When Windows XP is installed as an upgrade, the user's applications and data are preserved if the operating system is installed in the same folder (directory) as the original operating system. If Windows XP is installed in a different folder, then all applications must be reloaded.

If any of the following situations exist, Windows XP Professional should be used.

- The computer contains multiple processors. Windows XP Professional supports two processors. Multiple processors are normally used on a database or web server. If the computer runs an application that does intense computations such as financial or scientific applications or graphic rendering such as a game uses, then Windows XP Professional is the best choice.
- The computer is in a networked environment and remote access to the computer as if you were there is desired.
- File system encryption is needed.
- The computer is in a networked office environment.

Another decision you must make if upgrading to Windows XP is whether or not to convert the hard drive partition to NTFS. Once a partition is converted to NTFS, the partition cannot be changed. If you are unsure whether or not to convert the partition, leave it unchanged and later use the CONVERT.EXE program to upgrade. Most people want to convert the partition to NTFS for the following reasons:

- Security (individual files can be protected with NTFS).
- More efficient use of cluster space (the cluster size can be defined based on the user's needs when using NTFS).
- NTFS supports file compression.
- NTFS supports larger hard drive partition sizes.

The information in Table 7.1 helps when making the file system decision.

Table 7.1: FAT32 and NTFS Comparison

FAT32	NTFS
Hard drive is < 32 GB	Hard drive is > 32 GB and only one OS is installed
XP is dual-booted with Windows 95, 98, or 2000 and the existing OS uses FAT32 and files need to be shared between the two operating systems	File security is needed
	Disk compression is needed
	Upgrading from Windows NT or 2000 and the partition is already formatted as NTFS
	Disk quotas are needed
	File encryption is needed

If a FAT32 partition is desired but the FAT32 partition option is not available, the partition is most likely greater than 32 GB. Make the partition less than 32 GB or use NTFS as a file system.

If upgrading from a prior version of NTFS, the drive is automatically configured for XP's NTFS. If any older NTFS volumes are not powered during the installation process, the volume is automatically upgraded when the drive is mounted. If you want to dual-boot between Windows NT 4 and Windows XP (have both operating systems loaded), make sure that NT Workstation Service Pack 4 or higher is installed because some of the features in XP's NTFS change the data structure on disks. The CONVERT command can be used to change a FAT16 or FAT32 partition to NTFS5. The format of the command is CONVERT *x:* /fs:ntfs (where *x:* is the drive to be converted to NTFS).

In order to take advantage of Windows XP's reliability, enhancements, and security features, sometimes a clean installation is the best choice especially if the current operating system is Windows 98 or Windows ME. Because a clean installation involves formatting the hard drive, the user's data must be backed up and all applications reinstalled once the Windows XP installation is complete. Also, all user-defined settings are lost. Another important point to remember is that not all Windows 3.x, 95, and 98 applications are compatible with Windows XP. You can contact the company that developed your application and see if the application is compatible with Windows XP.

If the computer already has NT Workstation 4 or Windows 2000 Professional, then a Windows XP upgrade is recommended. However, if there are hardware drivers for such devices as a DVD player, power management software, or network utilities loaded on the computer, a clean installation may be a better choice. Whichever the case, the user's data and applications should be backed up and restored once the Windows XP installation is complete.

The third decision that must be made is whether or not Windows XP will be installed with one or more other operating systems. This situation is often called a dual-boot or multi-boot scenario. **Dual-boot** means that the computer can boot from two operating systems. **Multi-boot** means the computer can boot from two or more operating systems. Windows XP can be dual-booted with DOS, Windows 95 (SR2), Windows 98, NT Workstation, or Windows 2000 Professional. If this is desired, a separate hard disk partition should be created and used for each operating system. When doing a dual or multi-boot configuration, make sure that Windows XP is installed *after* the other operating systems. The fourth step in planning for a Windows XP installation is to scan the system for viruses. Viruses can cause havoc on a new upgrade. Viruses are covered in section A4.4 Understanding the Pre-Installation Steps of Windows 98 of Chapter 4 entitled *Introduction to Microsoft Windows 98*.

The fifth thing to do when installing Windows XP is to determine what computer hardware is installed. Table 7.2 lists the minimum and preferred hardware requirements for installing Windows XP Professional.

Table 7.2: Windows XP Professional Requirements

Component	Minimum	Preferred
CPU	Intel Pentium (or compatible) 233 MHz	Intel Pentium II (or compatible) 300 MHz or higher
RAM	64 MB	128 MB
Free hard drive space	1.5 MB	> 1.5 MB
Input Device	Keyboard, mouse, or other pointing device	Keyboard, mouse, or other pointing device
Multimedia Drive	CD-ROM or DVD	CD-ROM or DVD 12x or faster

Microsoft has a tool called the Upgrade Advisor that checks your system for hardware and software compatibility issues. This tool can be downloaded from Microsoft's web site at http://www.microsoft.com/windowsxp/pro/howtobuy/upgrading/advisor.asp. Be aware that the tool might not be able to detect all hardware devices or software applications.

Do *not* download a BIOS update unless you are sure it is compatible with your computer. Installing an invalid update can damage your computer system and cause it not to operate.

Once you have verified all of your hardware, you may have to get Windows XP device drivers from the hardware device manufacturer or their web site. This is the sixth step. You may also need to upgrade the hardware device which usually means replacing the device. This is sometimes the cost of going to a more powerful operating system. You may also decide at this point not to upgrade but to buy a computer with Windows XP already installed.

The seventh determination you must make before installing Windows XP is whether or not any existing software applications are compatible. The preparation for installing a new operating system is usually more work than the actual installation process, but any omitted step will cost you more time in the long run. Use the Upgrade Advisor or contact the developer of each software application to determine if it is compatible. You may also go to the software developer's web site and the information may be posted there. Microsoft also has a list of compatible software on their web site.

Windows XP has a help function that can check for software compatibility after XP is loaded. To access this tool, click on **Start** button, select **Help and Support**, and in the search box type **Program Compatibility wizard**.

Once you have determined whether the software is compatible with Windows XP, you may have to obtain software patches, upgrades, or buy a new version. This is best done before you install Windows XP. Be proactive, not reactive—solve any problems you can *before* upgrading or installing any operating system.

An installation option is the **Check Upgrade Only Mode**, which does not install Windows XP but checks whether your hardware and software are compatible. At the end of the check there is a report generated that lists potential issues.

As with any upgrade, hardware change, or software change, data needs to be backed up. It is really funny that the worst people in the world for backing up data are technicians, but a user's data is very valuable to them. Backing up data is an essential step. Whether you do a clean install or an upgrade, if the user has data on the computer, it must be backed up before starting the installation process. Also, before backing up data, remove any unwanted files and/or applications that are no longer needed in order to free up hard drive space.

The last step in the pre-installation checklist is to remove any power or disk management tools that are loaded. Computer manufacturers for older operating systems frequently provide these types of tools. Power or disk management tools can interfere with the new tools provided with Windows XP. Sometimes software such as this can prevent an operating system from installing whether it is an upgrade or a clean installation.

7.3 Understanding How to Install and Upgrade Windows XP

Once all the pre-installation checklist steps are completed, you are ready to install Windows XP. The installation process is easy if you performed the pre-installation steps. The number one piece of advice to give you when installing any operating system is to do your homework first. The number of possible problems will be greatly reduced.

During the installation process, the computer must be restarted three times. During the first phase, a selection must be made whether to upgrade or perform a clean installation, the product key must be entered, and a basic hardware check including available disk space is accomplished. The computer restarts. After the restart, the second phase begins and setup runs in text mode. During this process, a partition to install XP can be chosen and setup files are copied to the partition. The computer restarts and the third phase begins. During this portion, devices are installed, the Administrator password is entered, and the operating system is created. The system restarts a final time and the log-on screen is presented.

Microsoft requires activation of the Windows XP operating system within 30 days. No name or personal information is required, but activation must occur. You can activate XP over the phone or the Internet. Most new computers that have XP pre-loaded do not require activation.

7.4 Troubleshooting the Windows XP Installation

Installation problems can be caused by a number of factors. The following list shows the most common causes and their associated solution during the installation process.

- **Incompatible BIOS**—Obtain compatible BIOS, replace the motherboard with one that has compatible BIOS, or do not upgrade/install Windows XP.
- **BIOS needs to be upgraded**—Upgrade the BIOS.
- **Incompatible hardware**—Replace the hardware or do not upgrade/install Windows XP.
- **Incompatible hardware drivers**—Obtain Windows XP drivers from the hardware manufacturer.
- **Incompatible TSRs**—Remove TSRs or obtain updated ones from the software manufacturer.
- **Incompatible applications**—Obtain upgrades from software manufacturer.

- **Minimum hardware requirements have not been met**—Upgrade the hardware. The most likely things to check are the CPU (233 MHz minimum) and RAM (64 MB minimum).
- **A virus is on the hard drive**—Run an anti-virus program and remove the virus.
- **Pre-installation steps have not been completed**—Go back through the list!
- **The installation floppy disks or CD is corrupted** (not as likely as the other causes)—Try the disk in another machine and see if you can see the contents. For the CD, check to see if any scratches or dirt are on the surface. Clean the CD as necessary.
- **Incorrect CD Key**—Type in the correct CD key to complete the installation. The key is located on the CD case.
- If a **STOP message occurs** when installing a dual boot system, boot from the Windows XP installation CD rather than the other operating system.
- If the **installation halts**, try removing any nonessential hardware such as network cards, modems, and USB devices and start the installation again. Reinstall the hardware once XP is loaded.
- If the **computer locks up** during setup and shows a blue screen, check the BIOS and hardware compatibility.
- If a message appears during setup that **a device driver was unable to load**, obtain the latest device drivers that are XP-compatible and restart the setup program.
- When upgrading from Windows 98 or ME to XP and **setup displays an error that states it has disabled the upgrade option**, clean boot the computer and try to run setup again. If that does not work, copy the I386 folder from the Windows XP CD and run setup manually by locating the folder and double-clicking on the **WINNT32.EXE** file.
- If **setup hangs during the file copy phase**, the SMARTDRV command in the AUTOEXEC.BAT file has switches that interfered with the installation. Modify the AUTOEXEC.BAT file to remove SmartDrive switches.
- After the file copying has been completed, if **setup displays the message that it cannot set the required XP configuration information**, a hardware conflict is normally the cause.
- If a **STOP: 0x0000001E (0x800000003, 0xBFC0304, 0X0000000, 0x0000001) error occurs**, there is either not enough disk space to load XP, an incompatible or outdated driver is installed, or the motherboard BIOS needs updating.

Several text files located in whatever folder Windows XP was loaded can be helpful in determining the installation problem—SETUPLOG.TXT and SETUPAPI.LOG. These two files can be opened with any word processor including Notepad.

7.5 Understanding How to Dual-Boot Windows XP

Sometimes users like to try a new operating system and keep the old operating system loaded with the new operating system installed too.

Any time a dual-boot situation is desired, the oldest operating system should be installed first. The operating systems need to be in separate hard disk partitions.

If Windows XP is installed on an NTFS partition, only Windows 2000 and NT Workstation (with Service Pack 4 or higher) can access the XP partition. In the situation where Windows XP is loaded on a FAT32 partition, only Windows 95 (SR2), Windows 98, and Windows ME can access the partition. One solution to this scenario is to create three partitions—one for XP using NTFS; one for Windows 95 (SR2), Windows 98, or Windows ME using FAT32; and a third partition for shared data that is FAT32 (a partition type that both operating systems can access).

After installing all files and rebooting, a menu appears with the Microsoft Professional option, NT Workstation option, and NT Workstation (VGA Mode) option. To select which option is the default operating system, right-click on the **My Computer** desktop icon and click on the **Properties** option from the drop-down menu. Click on the **Advanced** tab and select the Startup and Recovery **Settings** button. In the System Startup section, select the **Default Operating System** drop-down menu.

7.6 Backing Up and Restoring the Windows XP Registry

The registry is a database that contains information about the Windows XP environment including installed hardware, software, and users. The registry should be backed up whenever the computer is fully functional and when any software or hardware changes are made.

The registry should be backed up and restored on a working computer *before* disaster hits. The time to learn how to restore the registry is *not* when the computer is down.

The registry can be backed up and restored several different ways. The two most common methods used are the REGEDIT and the Backup tools. The **REGEDIT program** allows you to export the registry to a file that has an extension of .REG. The file can be imported back into the computer if the computer fails. The REGEDIT program and the **Backup utility** both back up the entire registry. Refer to Figure 7.1 for a sample screenshot.

Figure 7.1: The Windows XP Registry

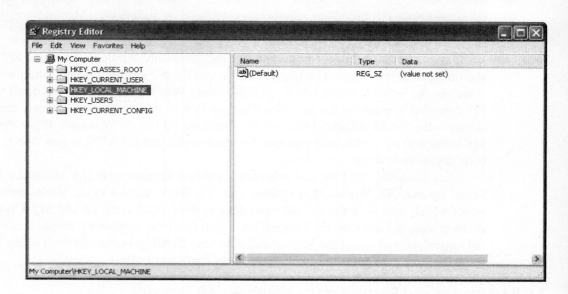

Backing Up the System State

One option available in the Backup utility is the System State. The **System State** is a group of important Windows XP files including the registry, the system files, the boot files, and the COM+ Class Registration database. With the Backup utility, you cannot back up or restore these items individually. They are all needed because they depend on one another to operate properly. The registry files are located in a folder normally labeled *%systemroot%*\Repair\Regbackup, which is normally C:\WINNT (or WINDOWS, depending on the type of installation) \REPAIR\BACKUP. The registry can be restored without having to restore the other System State files.

In order to use the Backup program, you must be an Administrator or a member of the Backup Operators group.

Refer to Figure 7.2 for a sample screenshot of the Backup and Restore Wizard program.

Figure 7.2: The Backup and Restore Wizard

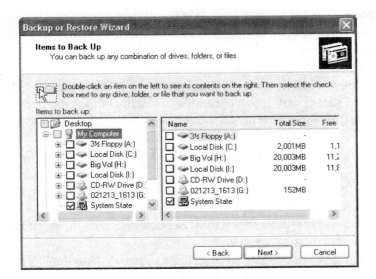

Restoring the System State After a Failure

In order to correct a problem with the system files, registry, or Windows XP boot failure, you must restore the registry. You may also have to restore the System State files (which includes the registry) to make the system operational again. To start the restoration process, install Windows XP to the same folder that it was installed in originally. When you are prompted to format the hard drive volume or leave it, select the **Leave the current file system intact** option. Use the Backup utility to restore the System State and/or the registry (All Programs, Accessories, System Tools, Backup). Click on the **Restore** tab and select the device that holds the backed up files.

Let's perform an exercise to help you understand the registry. Make sure you ask your instructor before performing this exercise. The goal of this exercise is to familiarize you with the REGEDIT registry editing utility. You will need a computer with Windows XP installed and a formatted 3.5″ floppy disk.

REGEDIT is a utility used for editing the Windows registry. With REGEDIT, you can view existing registry settings, modify registry settings values, or create new registry entries to change or enhance the way Windows operates.

In this lab, you will use REGEDIT to view the System BIOS and Video BIOS information on your computer.

CAUTION!: Editing the registry can cause your computer to run erratically or not run at all! When performing any registry editing, follow ALL directions carefully including spelling, syntax use, etc. Failure to do so may cause your computer to fail!

1. From the **Start** menu, choose **Run**, type **REGEDIT**, and click **OK**. The REGEDIT utility opens.

2. In the left window, expand **HKEY_LOCAL_MACHINE**, **HARDWARE**, and **DESCRIPTION** by clicking on the + (plus) symbol located to the left of the name. Click on the **System** option located under DESCRIPTION. The system BIOS and video BIOS information display in the right window.

3. REGEDIT can be used to back up and restore part or all of the registry. To illustrate this point, a portion of the registry will be exported to disk and then imported into the registry. Ensure the following option is still selected in the Registry window: HEKY_LOCAL_MACHINE\Hardware\Description\System

4. Click on the **File** menu option and select **Export**. The Export Registry File window opens.

5. Insert a blank formatted disk into the A: drive. Click on the **Save in** down arrow and select the **3_ Floppy (A:)** option.

6. In the File name text box, type **Registry System Section** and click on the **Save** button. The specific registry key is saved to disk.

7. To restore the registry (or a portion of it as in this exercise), click on the **File** menu option and select **Import**. The screen should list the file located on the A: drive, but if it does not, select the 3_ Floppy (A:) option from the Look in drop-down menu.

8. Click on the **Registry System Section** file name and click on the **Open** button. A message appears when the section is successfully inserted into the registry. Show this message to the instructor or lab assistant.

9. Close the REGEDIT utility and properly power off the system.

7.7 Configuring Windows XP

One of the most common windows used by technicians is the control panel window. A **control panel** is a method for configuring various Windows components. Each control panel icon represents a Windows utility that allows you to customize a particular part of the Windows environment. The number of control panels displayed depends on the type of computer and the components contained within the computer. Windows XP has two control panel views—classic and category. Figure 7.3 shows the Windows XP control panel category view.

Figure 7.3: Windows XP Control Panels

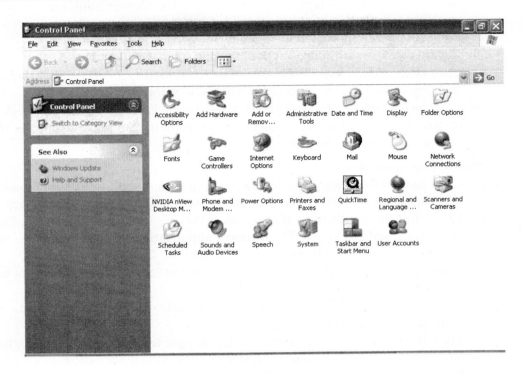

The following exercises will help familiarize you with several control panel categories. The goal of this exercise is to be able to use the appropriate control panels to configure a mouse, keyboard, and enable disabilities options. A computer with Windows XP installed is required.

1. Turn on the computer and verify that the operating system loads.
2. Log on to Windows XP using the userid and password provided by the instructor or lab assistant.
3. Click on the **Start** button and select the **Control Panel** option. **Pick a Category** should display in the right window. If it does not, click on the **Switch to Category View** option in the left pane.

Keyboard Configuration

4. Click on the **Printers and Other Hardware** control panel category. Click on the **Keyboard** icon. The Keyboard Properties window appears.
5. Click on the **Speed** tab. The Keyboard Properties window contains two tabs—Speed and Hardware. The Speed tab has three settings: repeat delay, repeat rate, and cursor blink rate.
6. The **Repeat delay** option configures the duration of wait time before a key starts repeating. This is especially important for people who do not type well or who have to

use a device such as a pencil to press keys down. The **Repeat rate** is an adjustment for how fast characters repeat across the screen. The **Cursor blink rate** controls how many times the cursor blinks per second. Adjust each of these settings and test them using the **Click here and hold down a key to test repeat rate** area.

7. Configure the keyboard settings back to their original configuration.
8. Click on the **Hardware** tab. The Hardware tab is used to access the keyboard trouble-shooting wizard and the keyboard driver. Click on the **Properties** button.
9. Click on the **Driver** tab. The **Update driver** button is used to load a new keyboard driver. Click on the **Cancel** button twice and return to the Printers and Other Hardware control category window.

Mouse Configuration

10. Click on the **Mouse** icon. The Mouse Properties window appears. The options available depend on the mouse manufacturer, but some of the settings are standard.
11. On the Buttons tab, there are three standard options—Button configuration, Double-click speed, and ClickLock. The **Button Configuration** section is where the mouse buttons can be reversed for left-handed people.
12. Adjust the **Double-click speed** and test it using test folder located in the right window of this section.
13. Reset the **Double-click speed** setting to its original configuration. Refer to the answer in the previous question.
14. The **ClickLock** setting is so you can select an option and drag the mouse without holding the left mouse button down. Once a click is made for more than a second, the button locks and the icon can be dragged. When a second click is made, the mouse unlocks.
15. The mouse troubleshooter and driver is accessed through the Hardware tab. Click on the **Hardware** tab. Click on the **Troubleshoot** button. The Mouse Troubleshooter window appears. Close the Mouse Troubleshooter.
16. Access the Mouse control panel's Hardware tab. Click on the **Properties** button.
17. Click on the **Driver** tab. Just like with the keyboard, the **Update Driver** button is used to load a new mouse driver.
18. Click on the **Cancel** button twice to return to the Printers and Other Hardware control panel category. Click on the **Back** button to return to the control panel categories.

Accessibility Options

19. Accessibility options are not just for people with disabilities. The settings can be applicable to any computer user to make their computer environment more comfortable. Click on the **Accessibility Options** category. Click on the first task, **Adjust the contrast for text and colors on your screen**. The Accessibility Options window opens with the Display tab active.

20. The two configuration sections are High Contrast and Cursor Options. Click on the **Use High Contrast** check box to enable it and click on the **Apply** button. A "Please wait" message appears and then the screen changes.

21. Click on the **Use High Contrast** check box to disable it and click on **Apply**. The screen returns to normal. Click on the **Cancel** button and the Accessibility Options control panel category window reappears.

22. Click on the second task, **Configure Windows to work for your hearing, vision, and mobility needs**. The Accessibility Wizard appears. This wizard steps through visual, auditory, and motor skills settings. Click on the **Next** button. The Text Size window appears.

23. Click on the **Next** button and the Display Settings window appears.

24. Click on the **Next** button and the Set Wizard Options window appears.

25. The option that is probably the most vague is **Administrative options**. This option is used to turn certain accessibility features off if the computer sits idle and make the accessibility features available to one user or all users. Click on the **Cancel** button. A Save Changes message box appears. Click on the **No** button so that all configuration changes are not kept.

Controlling Sound

26. Access the **Sounds and Audio Devices** control panel category. Select the **Adjust the system volume** task.

27. The Volume tab is used to control the volume for the entire computer system and speaker configuration. The **Mute** check box is used to mute all of the computer's sound. The **Place volume icon in the taskbar** is used to add a volume control icon in the taskbar in the notification area. The Device Volume slide bar sets the computers value settings. Click on the **Advanced** button located in the Device volume section. The Volume Control window opens.

28. Click on the **Mute all** check box to enable it. If it is already enabled, leave the setting turned on (enabled). Close the Volume Control window. Return to the Sounds and Audio Devices Properties window. You will have to reaccess the control panel category.

29. Return all Volume Control settings back to their original settings and return to the Sounds and Audio Devices Properties window.

30. Click on the **Speaker Volume** button. The Speaker volume screen has a left and right speaker volume. This setting does not affect speakers that simply plug into the Line out connection on the sound adapter or built into the motherboard. Click on the **Cancel** button.

31. The **Advanced** button in the Speakers settings section is used to configure speakers for such things as headphone usage and surround sound. Click on the **Advanced** button in the Speakers settings section and click on the **Speakers** tab. The Speakers setup list is used to specify external speakers. Computers such as ones in a business environment or a lab can be configured for no speakers.

32. To disable speakers, click on the **Speaker setup down arrow** and select the **No Speakers** option. Click on the **Cancel** button twice and close the control panel window.

33. Power off the computer properly.

Operating system specialists must frequently add new hardware and software using the operating system. Windows XP has specific tools for these functions. Using the correct procedure is essential for success. The following sections highlight many of the tasks a technician must perform:

- Adding Plug and Play Devices
- Adding Non-Plug and Play Devices
- Adding a Printer
- Removing Hardware Devices
- Installing and Removing Software

Hardware devices are physical components that connect to the computer. Hardware devices can be either plug and play or non-plug and play. A device driver is a piece of software that allows hardware to work with a specific operating system. Some device drivers are automatically included with Windows XP. A technician must be aware of what hardware is installed into a system so that the latest XP-compatible drivers can be downloaded and installed.

Adding Plug and Play Devices

Plug and play devices are hardware and software designed to automatically be recognized by the operating system. In order for Windows XP to fully support plug and play devices, the computer should have a BIOS that supports **ACPI** or **Advanced Configuration and Power Interface**. ACPI allows the computer's motherboard and operating system to control power needs and modes of operation of various devices. The key to a successful plug and play device installation includes the following:

- Possessing the most up-to-date device driver
- Following the directions provided by the device manufacturer

Install the device according to the device manufacturer's instructions. Once installed, power on the computer. The Windows XP **Found New Hardware** wizard appears. Windows XP attempts to find a driver for the new device. Plug and play devices make use of a special .CAB (cabinet) file called DRIVER.CAB located in *%winroot%*\Driver Cache\i386 folder (where *%winroot%* is normally C:\WINNT or C:\WINDOWS). This file is almost 75 MB and contains more than 2,500 compressed files. If Windows XP detects new hardware, it will automatically search DRIVER.CAB for a driver. If a driver cannot be found, a dialog box appears. The best policy with any operating system is to use the latest driver even if the operating system detects the device. An exercise at the end of the chapter outlines how to install a new hardware driver.

In XP Professional, remember if the operating system cannot configure a plug and play device and prompts for a device driver, you must have Administrator rights to install the driver.

Adding Non-Plug and Play Devices

Devices, known as legacy devices, are also called non-plug and play devices. For devices that are not plug and play, Windows XP has a control panel called **Add Hardware**. If using control panel categories, select the **Printers and Other Hardware** category and then select **Add Hardware** from the left pane. The Add Hardware wizard allows hardware configuration and is used for hardware that is not automatically recognized by Windows XP. It is also used for plug and play devices that don't install properly with Windows XP's automatic detection. You must have Administrator privileges in order to load device drivers for new hardware. An exercise at the end of the chapter explains how to do this.

With both plug and play and non-plug and play devices, the Device Manager tool is used to view installed hardware devices, enable or disable devices, troubleshoot a device, view and/or change system resources such as IRQs and I/O addresses, update drivers, and access the driver roll back option. The **driver roll back** option is a new feature in Windows XP. It allows an older driver to be reinstalled when the new driver causes problems.

You must have Administrator privileges to access or use the driver roll back option.

If the device driver has not been updated, driver roll back will not be possible and a message screen displays stating this fact. The troubleshooting tool should be used instead to troubleshoot the device. An exercise follows that details how to use this feature.

Place older adapters closest to the power supply because XP checks expansion slots in order starting with the closest to the power supply. By putting the older adapters in these slots, XP will allocate system resources to the older adapters first and there is less chance of system resource conflicts.

Sometimes XP can install the wrong driver for an older device or adapter. From Device Manager, right-click on the device and you can uninstall the device driver or disable it. Sometimes the computer must reboot and XP will reinstall the wrong driver (again). The solution to this is to disable the device and then manually install it. The following exercise illustrates how to disable a device on a computer running Windows XP. To manually install new hardware, use the following steps:

1. Log on to the computer.

2. Click on the **Start** button and select the **Control Panel** option.

3. If in Category View, click on **Printers and Other Hardware** and select **Add Hardware** from the left pane. If in Classic View, double-click on the **Add Hardware** icon. The Add Hardware wizard starts.

4. Make sure the new hardware is physically connected and select the **Yes, I have already connected the hardware** option and click on the **Next** button.

5. Use the Installed hardware scroll bar to find and select the **Add a new hardware device** checkbox and click on **Next**.

6. Select the manual option and select the type of hardware being installed. Scroll through the manufacturer list or have an XP-compatible driver ready and click on the **Have Disk** button to install the appropriate driver. Click on the **Next** button to finish the device driver installation.

Adding a Printer

Printers can be connected to a computer through the printer's parallel port, USB port, or through a local area network. Only parallel printers (printers connected to the computer's parallel port) and USB printers will be covered in this chapter. Networked printers will be in Chapter 9, *Introduction to Networking*.

Windows XP can automatically detect printers. If Windows XP detects a printer, the operating system automatically installs drivers, updates the registry, and allocates system resources to the printer.

To install a printer, connect the printer to the appropriate computer port with the appropriate cable. First, power the computer on. The Windows XP wizard normally detects and leads you through the installation process. However, if XP does not detect the printer and it is a printer attached to the parallel port, have the Windows XP-compatible printer driver ready and perform the following steps on a computer running Windows XP:

1. Log on to the computer.

2. Click on the **Start** button and select **Control Panel**.

3. If in Category View, click on **Printers and Other Hardware**. If in Classic View, double-click on the **Printers and Faxes** icon.

4. Access the **Add a printer** icon or selection. The **Add Printer** wizard begins. Click on the **Next** button.

5. Ensure the **Local printer attached to this computer** radio button is enabled and click on **Next**. Windows XP tries to detect a plug and play printer. If it cannot detect it, you are advised of this fact and that a manual installation is required. Click on the **Next** button.

6. Ensure the **Use the following port** radio button is enabled, select the correct port (usually LPT1), and click **Next**.

7. In the Install Printer Software window, click on the **Have Disk** option, insert the XP-compatible driver, and click on **Next**. Select the appropriate model and click on **Next**.
8. Name the printer and select whether the printer will be the default printer.
9. Click **Next**.
10. When prompted if the printer is to be shared, select the appropriate response. If shared, the printer must have a share name and optionally list the location and enter comments. Click **Next**.
11. Select the option to print a test page and click **Next**.
12. Click on the **Finish** button.

If a printer has a TCP/IP connection, manually install the printer using the steps above except instead of selecting the Local printer option, select the **Standard TCP/IP Port** option and click **Next** twice. Enter the printer name or IP address, the port name, and click **Next**. The Install Printer Software window appears and the same steps are used as a local printer.

To configure a printer as a default printer (the printer that applications normally use), locate the printer in the Printers folder. Access the Printers folder by clicking on the **Start** button and clicking on the **Printers and Faxes** selection. Once you locate the appropriate printer icon, right-click on the icon. Click on the **Set as Default Printer** option. In the Printers folder, the default printer has a check mark next to the icon.

Removing Hardware Devices

Windows XP normally detects when hardware has been removed and the operating system automatically removes the device's driver(s). If Windows XP does not automatically detect the device removal, you must manually remove the drivers. An exercise follows that describes how to remove the driver.

If you are removing a printer from the system, use the **Printers** control panel. Access this control panel by clicking on the **Start** button. Point to the **Settings** option and click on the **Printers** option. Right-click on the printer you want to delete and choose the **Delete** option.

Let's perform an exercise.

The goal of this exercise is to install an updated driver under the Windows XP operating system. You will need a computer with Windows XP installed and Internet access. In this lab a new driver is loaded, but then the old driver is reinstalled with the driver roll back feature. The student must be logged in as a user with local Administrator rights to perform this lab.

1. Turn the computer on and verify that the operating system loads. Log in to Windows XP using the userid and password provided by the instructor or lab assistant.
2. Pick an installed hardware device and locate an updated driver using the Internet and download the driver to the hard drive. Note that some drivers may come in a compressed file and must be uncompressed before continuing the procedure.
3. Click on **Start** button, point to **Settings**, and click on the **Control Panel** menu option.

4. When the Control Panel window opens, click on the **Switch to Category View** option if necessary. Select the **Printers and Other Hardware** category. In the left *See also* pane, select the **System** option. The System Properties window opens.
5. Click on the **Hardware** tab and select the **Device Manager** button.
6. Click the **+** (plus sign) beside the hardware category that contains the device being upgraded.
7. Right-click on the device name and click on the **Properties** selection.
8. Click on the **Update Driver** button. The Update Hardware wizard screen appears.
9. Select the **Install from a list or specific location (Advanced)** radio button and click **Next**.
10. Click on the **Don't search. I will select the driver to install** radio button and click **Next**.
11. Click on the **Have Disk** button, use the **Browse** button to locate the downloaded file, and click on **OK**. A list of models might appear. If so, select the correct model and click on **Next**. Finish the driver update.
12. Use Device Manager and right-click on the device name again and select **Properties**.
13. Click on the **Driver** tab and click on the **Roll Back Driver** button. Click on the **Yes** button to roll back the driver. If the device driver has not been updated, driver roll back will not be possible and a message screen displays this fact.
14. Close all windows and power off the computer properly.

Installing and Removing Software

No computer is fully functional without software. One thing you should know about Windows XP is that it does not support some of the older 16-bit software. Most software today is 32-bit and comes on CD and includes an autorun feature. If the CD has the autorun feature, an installation wizard steps you through installing the software when the CD is inserted into the drive. If there is not an autorun feature on the CD or if the software is on a disk, then the Add or Remove Programs control panel is used to install or remove the software.

To access the Add or Remove Programs control panel, click on the **Start** button and click on the **Control Panel** option and then double-click on the **Add or Remove Programs** control panel. Click on the **Add New Programs** icon in the window's left panel. Click on the **CD or Floppy** button and ensure the software disk or CD is inserted in the appropriate drive. If a SETUP.EXE file cannot be found on the designated disk, the system prompts with a dialog box. Use the **Browse** button to locate the installation file. Click on the **Finish** button to complete the process.

To remove a software application, use the same **Add or Remove Programs** control panel; instead of clicking on Add New Programs, click on the **Change or Remove Programs** icon in the left panel. A list of installed applications appears. Locate the software to be removed and click on its name. Click on the **Remove** button. When asked if you are sure you want to remove this software, click on the **OK** button and close the control panel window. Some applications have their own uninstall program. Refer to the application's help file or look in the application's folder where the application was installed for an uninstall icon. The Add or Remove Programs control panel can also be used to update operating system components. An exercise follows that illustrates this concept.

Once an application is installed, launch the application by clicking on the **Start** button and pointing to the **All Programs** option. Locate the application name and click on it. If the application does not appear on the list, do not panic. The most frequently used program names appear in the left Start button panel. Let's perform an exercise to help you understand how to install software.

The goal of this exercise is to be able to install Administrative Tools to Windows XP. You will need a computer with Windows XP installed, the Administrator password and a Windows XP CD.

In this lab, if Administrative Tools is already loaded, it will be removed and reinstalled.

1. Turn the computer on and verify that the operating system loads. Log in to Windows XP using the userid and password provided by the instructor or lab assistant. Ensure the userid is one that has Administrator rights.
2. Click on the **Start** button, point to **All Programs** and look for an Administrative Tools item. Does the Administrative Tools item appear in the All Programs list? If so, proceed with the exercise. If it does not appear, skip to step 5 below.
3. Right-click on the **Start** button and select the **Properties** option. Click on the **Start Menu** tab.
4. Click on the **Customize** button. The Customize Start Menu window opens. In the Start Menu items section, locate the **System Administrative tools** section and click in the **Don't display this item** radio button. Click on the **OK** button. Click on the **OK** button again. Verify that the Administrative Tools no longer displays in the All Programs list.
5. Right-click on the **Start** button and select the **Properties** option. Click on the **Start Menu** tab.
6. Click on the **Customize** button. The Customize Start Menu window opens. In the Start Menu items section, locate the **System Administrative tools** section and click in the **Display on the All Programs menu** radio button. Click on the **OK** button. Click on the **OK** button again. Verify that the Administrative Tools displays in the All Programs list.

7.8 Understanding the Boot Process

With NT Workstation, Windows 2000, and Windows XP, there are two types of partitions that are important during the boot process—the system partition and the boot partition. The **system partition** is the active drive partition that has the files needed to load the operating system. The system partition is normally the C: drive (the active partition). The **boot partition** is the partition or logical drive where the operating system files are located. One thing that people sometimes forget is that the system partition and the boot partition can be on the same partition. These partitions are where certain boot files are located.

Every operating system needs specific files that allow the computer to boot. These files are known as **system files** or startup files. The system files and their specific location on the hard drive are listed in Table 7.3.

Table 7.3: Windows XP Boot Files

Startup File Name	File Location
BOOT.INI	Root directory of system partition.
BOOTSECT.DOS (needed if dual- or multi-boot system)	Root directory of system partition.
CDLDR	Root directory of system partition.
HAL.DLL	%systemroot%\SYSTEM32 (%systemroot% is a variable representing the folder where Windows 2000 is installed. This is normally C:\WINNT.)
HYBERFIL.SYS	%systemdrive% (%systemroot% is the root directory on the drive where Windows 2000 boot files are located which is normally C:\.)
NTBOOTDD.SYS (used with SCSI drives that have the SCSI BIOS disabled)	Root directory of system partition.
NTDETECT.COM	Root directory of system partition.
NTLDR	Root directory of system partition.
NTOSKRNL.EXE	%systemroot%\SYSTEM32
System Key	%systemroot%\SYSTEM32\CONFIG

Reading about Windows XP files can be confusing because the file locations frequently have the entries *%systemroot%* and *%systemdrive%*. This is because computers can be partitioned differently. If you install Windows XP onto a drive letter (a partition or logical drive) other than the active partition (normally C:), the startup files can be on two different drive letters. Also, you do not have to take the default folder name of WINNT or WINDOWS (depending on the type of installation) to install XP. To account for these different scenarios, Microsoft uses the *%systemroot%* to represent the boot partition, the partition and folder that contains the majority of the Windows XP files. *%systemdrive%* represents the root directory and on a computer with a single operating system, this would be C:\.

If Windows XP is installed onto the C: drive and the C: drive is the active partition, then the BOOT.INI, BOOTSECT.DOS, HYBERFIL.SYS, NTBOOTDD.SYS, NTDE-

TECT.COM, and NTLDR files would all be in the root directory of C:. The HAL.DLL and NTOSKRNL.EXE files would be located in the SYSTEM32 folder (located in either the WINNT or WINDOWS folder) on the C: drive.

Another example would be if you installed Windows XP onto the D: drive, but the C: drive is the active partition. The BOOT.INI, BOOTSECT.DOS, HYBERFIL.SYS, NTBOOTDD.SYS, NTDETECT.COM, and NTLDR files would all be in the root directory of C:. The HAL.DLL and NTOSKRNL.EXE files would be located in the SYSTEM32 folder (that is located under the WINNT or WINDOWS folder) on the D: drive.

The boot process is actually quite involved, but the major steps are as follows:
- Power on the computer.
- POST executes.
- BIOS searches CMOS for the boot device order and checks for a boot sector. If the boot device is a hard drive, BIOS reads the Master Boot Record (MBR), and locates and loads the information into sector 0 of the system partition. The contents of sector 0 define the type of file system, the location of the bootstrap loader file, and start the bootstrap loader. With Windows XP, this file is NTLDR.
- NTLDR starts in real mode so that 8- and 16-bit software can be loaded. Then XP is switched to 32-bit mode and the file system begins to load.
- NTLDR reads the BOOT.INI file and displays the various operating system choices contained within the BOOT.INI file. If something other than Windows XP is chosen, the BOOTSECT.DOS file takes over. If Windows XP is chosen, the NTDETECT.COM file executes.
- NTDETECT.COM detects the computer's hardware and ACPI tables are read so that XP can detect power management features.
- NTLDR passes the hardware information to the NTOSKRNL.EXE file.
- The operating system kernel, NTOSKRNL.EXE, executes and the HAL.DLL file loads. **HAL (Hardware Abstraction Layer)** is a layer between the operating system and the hardware devices. The HAL allows Windows XP to run with different hardware configurations and components without affecting (or crashing) the operating system.
- The registry key HKEY_LOCAL_MACHINE\System loads. This registry key is located in the *%systemroot%*\System32\Config\System file. This key has information found during the hardware detection process and is used to determine which device drivers to load.
- The operating system kernel initializes and NTLDR passes control to it. The Starting Up process bar displays. During this time, a hardware key is created, device drivers load, and services start.
- The WINLOGON.EXE file executes and the log-on screen appears. While the log-on process is occurring, XP detects plug and play devices.

Troubleshooting the Boot Process

Quite a few things can cause XP to not boot properly. XP has a wealth of tools and start modes that can be used to troubleshoot the system. If XP boots, but still has a problem, try to solve the problem without booting into one of these special modes. For example, if one piece of hardware is not working properly and the system boots properly, use Device Manager and the troubleshooting wizards to troubleshoot the problem. Another problem can be caused by an application that loads during startup.

To disable startup programs, hold the **Shift** key down during the log-on process and keep it held down until the desktop icons appear. For a permanent change to an application starting automatically, move or delete the startup shortcuts from the one of the following places:

%systemdrive%\Documents and Settings*Username*\Start Menu\Programs\Startup
%systemdrive%\Documents and Settings\All Users\Start Menu\Programs\Startup
%windir%\Profiles*Username*\Start Menu\Programs\Startup
%windir%\Profiles\All Users\Start Menu\Programs\Startup

Four major tools can be used to troubleshoot Windows XP boot problems: Last Known Good Configuration, Safe Mode, Recovery Console, and Automated System Recovery wizard.

The Last Known Good Configuration

Last Known Good Configuration is used when XP has been just changed by adding hardware or software that is incompatible with XP, has configuration settings that conflict with XP or other hardware/software, or an important service such as the one used to initialize SCSI (Small System Computer Interface) hard drives has been accidentally disabled. It reverses the most recent changes that have been made since the last successful XP boot. Whenever XP boots successfully (without any problems), a copy of the Clone control set is made to be used if the Last Known Good Configuration options is chosen. A control set is a registry subkey located under HKEY_LOCAL_MACHINE\System and contains information about devices and services. To access Last Known Good Configuration, press the **F8** key during the boot process and select the **LastKnownGood Configuration** option from the Windows Advanced Options menu.

Whenever the **Last Known Good Configuration** option is used, all configuration changes made since the last successful boot are lost! However, since the changes are the most likely cause of XP not booting correctly, **Last Known Good Configuration** is a useful tool when installing new devices and drivers that do not work properly. If Last Known Good Configuration does not work properly, boot the computer into Safe Mode, which is covered in the next section.

If Windows XP works, but a hardware device does not work and a new driver has been recently loaded, use the driver roll back option for the device.

Safe Mode

Safe Mode is used when the computer stalls, slows down, does not work right, improper video, intermittent errors, or new hardware/software installation causes problems. Safe Mode is used to start XP with minimum device drivers and services. Software that automatically loads during startup is disabled in Safe Mode and user profiles are not loaded. When the computer boots in Safe Mode, the mouse, keyboard, CD-ROM, and VGA video device drivers are all that are loaded. Safe Mode allows you to access configuration files and make necessary changes, troubleshoot installed software and hardware, disable software and services, and adjust hardware and software settings that may be causing XP from starting correctly. The bottom line is that Safe Mode puts the computer in a "bare bones" mode so you can troubleshoot problems.

Another option similar to this is **Safe Mode with Networking** that operates the same as Safe Mode except that it allows network drivers and services to load. **Safe Mode with Command Prompt** is used to start the system with the minimum files and drivers and a command prompt where you must use commands instead of a graphic interface. Access Safe Mode by pressing the **F8** key during the boot process and selecting **Safe Mode** from the Windows Advanced Options menu.

The Windows Advanced Options menu contains other options used to troubleshoot Windows XP which are Enable Boot Logging, Enable VGA Mode, Directory Services Restore Mode, and Debugging Mode. **Enable Boot Logging** is used to create a log file, NTBTLOG.TXT, that records drivers and services loaded during the boot process. This text file is located in the folder that contains the operating system, which is normally C:\WINNT or C:\WINDOWS. The file can be used to identify problems that occurred during the boot process and that relates to a driver or service. Each loaded driver or service file is marked as loaded or not loaded and this information can be used to narrow suspect problems. Boot logging is enabled for every Windows Advanced Options menu selection except for Last Known Good Configuration.

Enable VGA Mode is used to start XP with a standard VGA video driver instead of the one currently installed. This option is used when the current video driver will not load or loads in such a way that it is hard to reconfigure XP. With this option enabled, XP loads and the desktop can be seen and used to load a newer driver or adjust the current video settings. All Windows Advanced Options menu selections except for Last Known Good Configuration load the standard VGA driver.

Directory Services Restore Mode is for server operating systems and is used to restore the SYSVOL directory and Active Directory service on a network domain controller. The **Debugging Mode** option is used by programmers and engineers to send debugging information through a serial cable to another computer. Other options may be available on the Windows Advanced Options menu if you are using or have installed and have used the remote installation service.

Recovery Console

Recovery Console is used when Safe Mode and other startup options do not solve a problem. Recovery Console allows access to hard drive volumes without starting the GUI (Graphical User Interface). In other words, the Recovery Console allows you access to a command prompt from which you use commands to start and stop services, repair and access hard drive volumes, replace corrupt files, and perform a manual recovery.

You must have the administrator password to access the full potential of this option.

Recovery Console is not loaded onto the system by default, but it can be installed from the XP CD and then loaded through the boot menu or executed from the XP CD. Normally technicians run Recovery Console from the CD because Recovery Console is needed when there is a problem and is not preloaded.

To run Recovery Console from the Windows XP CD, use the XP CD to start XP. If the CD is unavailable or the computer does not support booting from CD, use XP setup boot disks (obtained from Microsoft). Press **R** at the Welcome to Setup screen to select the repair the installation option and the Recovery Console window appears. Press the number that corresponds to the partition where XP is loaded. An Administrator password prompt appears. Type the Administrator password and press **Enter**. A command prompt appears.

To install Recovery Console, insert the XP CD into the CD drive. If the welcome screen appears, close it. Click on the **Start** button, click on the **Run** option, and type in the appropriate path to access the **i386** folder and the **WINNT32 /CMDCOMS** command. An example is F:\I386\WINNT32 /CMDCOMS. This starts the Recovery Console installation process. When asked if you want to install Recovery Console, click on the **Yes** button and follow the prompts on the screen. Once Recovery Console is installed, restart the computer and Recovery Console appears as a boot option. Use the arrow keys to select the Recovery Console option and press **Enter**. A command prompt appears.

You must sometimes work from the command prompt when the system is not working properly. That is what the Recovery Console tool is all about. You may want to go through the Chapter 3, *DOS and the DOS Command Line Interface*, to understand the process and procedures needed when working from a command prompt.

If the registry is corrupt or has been deleted, you are not prompted for an Administrator password. Instead, the system boots to a prompt where you can use basic commands like CHKDSK, FIXBOOT, and FIXMBR to repair the system. However, you cannot access any folders on the hard drive.

The drive letters available at the Recovery Console command prompt might not be the same ones you used in the GUI environment. Use the MAP command to see the drive letters (and the volumes that do not have drive letters). The syntax for the MAP command is covered later in this chapter.

There are several ways to access a command prompt when the computer is functional. These methods are listed below.

- Click on the **Start** button, click on the **Run** option, and type **cmd** in the dialog box.
- Click on **Start** button, click on the **Run** option, and type **command** in the dialog box. Note that when this option is used, the keyboard arrow keys do not bring up previously used commands as the CMD command does.
- Click on **Start** button, point to the **All Programs** option, point to the **Accessories** option, and click on the **Command Prompt** option.

Some of the most frequently used commands used from the Recovery Console command prompt are outlined in Chapter 6, *Introduction to Windows 2000*. Some commands have different options when used within Recovery Console. To get help from a command prompt running within Windows XP or from within Recovery Console, type **Help** to see a list of commands; type *Help command-name* (where *command_name* is the command itself); or type *command_name /?*.

If using FAT, the Recovery Console is installed, and the partition is converted to NTFS, Recovery Console will have to be reinstalled.

The copy command can be used through Recovery Console to restore the two important files, system and software, that are used to build two important registry keys, HKEY_LOCAL_MACHINE \System and HKEY_LOCAL_MACHINE \Software. If the unresolved problem relates to hardware, try replacing the System file first. If the problem relates to software, replace the software file first. Do not replace both files at the same time because the System or Software files may not be current, which means that drivers or service packs may have to be reinstalled after replacement.

Recovery Console has four default limitations of which a technician should be aware. They are as follows:

- No text editor is available in Recovery Console by default.
- Files cannot be copied to removable media such as floppy disks while in Recovery Console. Write access is disabled.
- The Administrator password cannot be changed from Recovery Console.
- Some folders such as Program Files and Documents and Settings are inaccessible from the Recovery Console prompt.

Automated System Recovery

Automated System Recovery replaces the Emergency Repair Disk used by NT and 2000 Professional and it uses the Backup tool to backup up important system files used to start Windows XP. Automated System Recovery does not backup data files (although the Backup program can be used to back data up too).

To create an Automated System Recovery disk, you will need a 1.44 MB floppy disk and media such as a CD (if the machine has a CD-RW drive) or tape (for a tape drive). The floppy is used to boot the system and then you can restore the files if the hard drive crashes or operating system is inoperable.

To access the Backup tool, which is used to back up the system files, click on the **Start** button, point to the **All Programs** option, point to **Accessories**, point to **System Tools**, and click on the **Backup** option. The Backup wizard begins. On the initial screen, click on the words **Advanced Mode**. The words are underlined in the window. Click on the **Tools** menu option and select **ASR Wizard**. The Automated System Recovery wizard starts.

To use the disk and media created with Automated System Recovery, you will need the floppy disk created when the system was backed up, the backup media written to when the system was backed up, and the original Windows XP CD. Start the computer using the Windows XP CD. During the Setup process, press the **F2** key. A prompt appears to insert the Automated System Recovery floppy disk into the floppy drive. Insert the disk and follow the screen directions to restore the system.

System Configuration Utility

The **System Configuration utility** is used to disable startup programs and services selectively one at a time or several at once. This graphical utility reduces the chances of possible typing errors, deleting files, and other misfortunes that occur when technicians work from a command prompt. Only an Administrator or a member of the Administrators group can use System Configuration utility.

To start System Configuration utility, click on the **Start** button, click on the **Run** option, type in **msconfig** and press **Enter**. Figure 7.4 shows the System Configuration utility's General tab.

Figure 7.4: System Configuration Utility General Tab

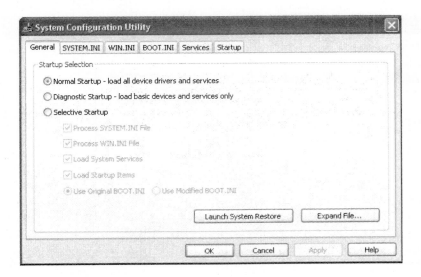

The **General** tab has three radio buttons: Normal Startup, Diagnostic Startup, and Selective Startup. **Normal Startup** is the default option and all device drivers and services load normally when this radio button is selected. The **Diagnostic Startup** radio button is selected when you want to create a clean environment for troubleshooting.

When **Diagnostic Startup** is chosen and Windows XP restarts, the system boots to Safe Mode and only the most basic device drivers and services are active. The Selective Startup radio button is the most common troubleshooting tab on the General tab. When **Selective Startup** is chosen, you can selectively pick which startup options load.

You can narrow down the startup file that is causing boot problems. Start with the first check box, **Process SYSTEM.INI File**, and deselect the check box. Click on the **OK** button and restart the computer. Once you determine which file is causing the problem (the problem reappears), click on the **System Configuration Utility** tab that corresponds to the problem file and deselect files until the exact problem file is located.

The System Configuration Utility Services and Startup tabs are also quite useful when troubleshooting boot problems. Certain applications, such as an anti-virus program, run as services and many services are started during the boot process. The Services tab can be used to selectively disable and enable these boot services. Enabling the **Hide All Microsoft Services** option allows you to view and manipulate third-party (non-Microsoft) services. The Startup tab allows you to enable and disable Windows-based startup programs. Figure 7.5 shows a sample Startup tab screen.

Figure 7.5: System Configuration Utility Startup Tab

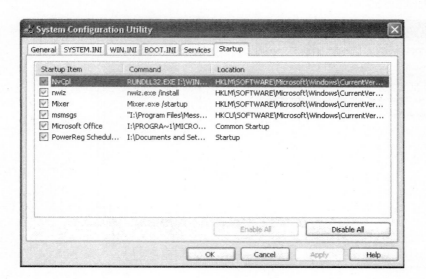

Windows XP does not support creating an Emergency Repair Disk (ERD) in the same way that NT Workstation and Windows 2000 Professional do. A set of installation disks can be obtained from Microsoft and would only be needed if the computer does not support booting from CD.

Let's perform an exercise to help you understand the System Configuration Utility.

The goal of this exercise is to be able to use the System Configuration utility to troubleshoot boot problems. You will need a computer with Windows XP installed and you will need Administrator rights.

1. Turn the computer on and verify that the operating system loads. Log in to Windows XP using the userid and password provided by the instructor or lab assistant. Ensure the userid is one that has Administrator rights.

2. Right-click on the **Start** button and click on the **Explore** option.

3. Locate the **Documents and Settings** folder and expand it if necessary. Locate the **All Users** folder (located under Documents and Settings) and expand it if necessary. Locate the **Start Menu** subfolder (located under All Users) and expand it if necessary. Locate the **Programs** subfolder (located under the Start Menu folder) and expand it if necessary. Click on the **Startup** folder located under the Programs folder.

4. Use the **Search** Start button option to locate the original Notepad application (notepad.exe). Create a shortcut to the Notepad application and place it in the Startup

folder located under the Programs folder (see step 3). A previous exercise explains how to create a shortcut.

Have a classmate verify your shortcut (especially that it is a shortcut and not a copy of the application or the application itself). Is the icon in the STARTUP folder a shortcut icon?

Classmate's printed name: _____

Classmate's signature: _____

5. Restart the computer and verify that the Notepad program starts automatically when the computer boots. If it does not, re-do step 4.

6. Click on the **Start** button, click on the **Run** option, type in **msconfig** and press Enter. The System Configuration utility window opens.

7. Click on the **Diagnostic Startup—load basic devices and services only** radio button. Click on the **Apply** button and then click on the **Close** button. A System Configuration message box appears. Click on the **Restart** button. When the computer restarts, log in with the same userid used previously.

What is different about the way Windows XP loads?

Did the Notepad application automatically start?

8. Click on the **OK** button. Click on the **Selective Startup** radio button found on the General tab. Check boxes are now available that you can select the startup files that are to be loaded the next time the computer boots. Click in the **Load Startup Items** check box. Click on the **Apply** button and then click on **Close**. Click on the **Restart** button and the system restarts. Log in using the same userid and password.

Did the Notepad application automatically start? Why or why not?

9. Click on the **OK** button. Click on the **Normal Startup—load all device drivers and services** option located on the General tab.

10. Click on the **Startup** tab. Click on the **Shortcut to notepad** check box to disable it.

11. Click on the **Apply** button and then click on **Close**. Click on the **Restart** button. When the computer restarts, log in using the same userid and click on **OK**.

Did the Notepad application automatically start? Why or why not?

What is different about the System Configuration Utility's General tab?

12. Click on the **General** tab and select the **Normal Startup** radio button. Click on the **Apply** button and then **Close**. Click on the **Restart** button. Log in using the same userid.

13. Once the computer reboots, remove the shortcut to the Notepad application from the Startup folder.

7.9 Understanding Task Manager, Dr. Watson, and Event Viewer

Task Manager is a Windows-based utility that displays applications currently loaded into memory, processes that are currently running, microprocessor usage information, and memory usage data. To activate the Task Manager utility, press the **Ctrl + Alt + Del** keys. Another way of accessing Task Manager is to right-click on the taskbar and then click on the Task Manager option.

One of the common uses of Task Manager is to exit from an application that is "hung up" or not responding. Task Manager can help with exiting the program. Once inside the Task Manager window, click on the **Applications** tab. Locate the name of the troublesome application and click on it. Normally, if an application is causing a problem, the status shows the application as "not responding." Select the problem application and click on the **End Task** button. Figure 7.6 shows a sample Task Manager's Applications tab.

Figure 7.6: A Screenshot of Task Manager

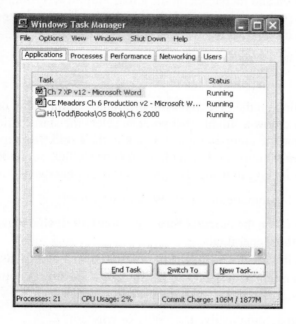

Let's perform a few exercises to help you understand Windows XP Task Manager and Event Viewer.

The goal of this exercise is to use Task manager to halt an application. You need a computer with Windows XP installed.

1. Turn the computer on and verify that the operating system loads. Log in to Windows XP using the userid and password provided by the instructor or lab assistant. Ensure the userid is one that has Administrator rights.

2. From the **Start** menu, choose **All Programs, Accessories,** and then select **Notepad**. The Notepad utility opens.

3. To access Task Manager, simultaneously press **Control, Alt**, and **Delete**. The Task Manager window opens.

4. Select the **Applications** tab.

5. Click on the **Untitled—Notepad** option and click on the **End Task** button. Notepad closes.

6. Close the Task Manager window.

Dr. Watson is a utility that automatically loads when an application starts. Dr. Watson can detect and display troubleshooting information as well as create a text log file (DRWTSN32.LOG) when a system or application error occurs. A technician might need this information when communicating with Microsoft or the application developer's technical support. Make notes of any messages that appear on the screen when any type of problem occurs.

To start Dr. Watson in Windows XP, click on the **Start** button, click on the **Run** option, and type **drwtsn32** and press Enter. Click on the application error and click on the View button. The default location for the log file is C:\Documents and Settings\All Users \Application Data\Microsoft\DrWatson. When an error occurs, Dr. Watson appends information to the end of this log file.

Event Viewer is a Windows tool used to monitor various events in your computer such as when a driver or service does not start properly. The EventLog service starts automatically every time a computer boots to Windows XP. This service is what allows the events to be logged and then Event Viewer is used to see the log.

Access the Event Viewer by clicking on the **Start** button, then click on the **Control Panel** option, and if in Category view, click on the **Performance and Maintenance** category, click on **Administrative Tools** icon, and double-click on the **Event Viewer** icon. If in Classic Control Panel view, double-click on the **Administrative Tools** control panel icon. Then, double-click on the **Event Viewer** icon. The left window contains the type of Event Viewer logs such as the application log, the security log, and the system log. The application log displays events associated with a specific program. The programmers who design software decide which events to display in the Event Viewer's application log. The security log displays events such as when different users log in to the computer (both valid and invalid log ins). A technician can pick which events are displayed in the security log. All users can view the system log and the application log, but only a member of Administrators can enable security log information.

The most commonly used log is the system log. The system log displays events that deal with various system components such as a driver or service that loads during startup. The type of system log events cannot be changed, added, or deleted. Click on the system log option in the left panel. The system log events displays in the right window. Figure 7.7 shows an example of Event Viewer's system log.

Figure 7.7: A Screenshot of Event Viewer

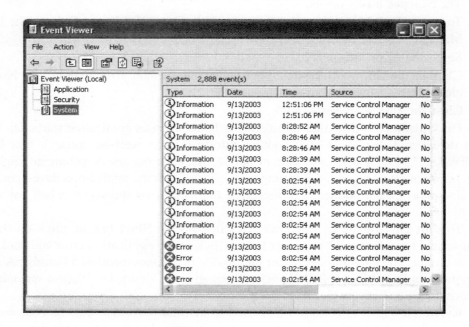

Double-click on an Event Viewer event to see more information about it.

Event viewer logs can be saved as files and viewed later. This is especially useful with intermittent problems. Use the **Action** menu item to save and retrieve saved event viewer log files. Let's perform a few exercises to help you understand Windows XP Task Manager and Event Viewer.

The goal of this exercise is to use Event Viewer. You need a computer with Windows XP installed.

1. Turn the computer on and verify that the operating system loads. Log in to Windows XP using the userid and password provided by the instructor or lab assistant. Ensure the userid is one that has Administrator rights.

2. Event Viewer is used to monitor various events such as when drivers and services load (or fail to load and have problems). Click on the **Start** button, click on the **Control Panel** option. If in Control Panel Category view, click on **Performance and Maintenance** category, and click on **Administrative Tools**. If in Classic view, double-click on **Administrative Tools** control panel icon, and then double-click on the **Event Viewer** icon. The Event Viewer window opens.

3. Click on the **Application** log located in the left pane. Application events list in the right pane.

4. Double-click on any application event.

5. Close the Event Properties window. Click on the **System** log located in the left plane. System events list in the right pane.

6. Double-click on any of the individual events. Click on the button that looks like two pieces of paper. It is the button directly under the up and down arrow buttons.

7. Click on the **Start** button. Click on the **Run** option. Type **clipbrd** and press Enter. The event is copied to the Clipboard and the **clipbrd** command opens the Clipboard Viewer.

8. Open Notepad by clicking on the **Start** button, pointing to **All Programs**, pointing to **Accessories**, and clicking on the **Notepad** option.

9. Click on the **Edit** menu option and select **Paste**.

10. The event information can be saved as a text file and referenced later especially when there is a problem. Close Notepad without saving the document.

11. Close Event Viewer.

Shutdown Problems

Windows XP should be shut down properly when all work is finished. Before Windows XP can shut down, the operating system sends a message to all devices, services, and applications. Each device that is running sends a message back saying it is okay to shut down now. Any active application saves data that has not been previously saved and sends a message back to the operating system. Active system services also respond that it is okay to shut down. If the system has trouble shutting down, it is due to one of the following three things. The most common problem is an application that is not responding back. When this happens, press **Ctrl + Alt + Del** to access Task Manager. Manually stop any applications that show a status of not responding. You can also click on any applications and stop them to see if they are causing the problem. Sometimes a program will not show a status of not responding until you try to manually stop the application from within Task Manager. If a single application continually prevents Windows XP from shutting down, contact the software manufacturer to see if there is a fix.

For services problems, boot the computer into Safe Mode and then shut the computer down. Take note as to whether or not the computer had any problems shutting down. If the process works, access the BOOTLOG.TXT file that is located in the root directory of the drive that contains Windows XP. Once inside the file, take note of each service that is disabled from booting into Safe Mode. Boot the computer normally. Stop each service one at a time to see which service is causing the problem.

To troubleshoot devices not responding, eliminate services and applications first because a device frequently does not cause a shutdown problem. Then, while working on the computer, take notice of what devices you are using. Common ones are video, hard drive, CD-ROM, keyboard, and mouse. Verify that all of your devices have the most up-to-date drive loaded and that the driver is compatible with Windows XP.

If you cannot stop the problem application or determine if the problem is a service or hardware, try restarting the computer instead of shutting down. Once the computer restarts, try shutting down again. As a last resort, use the computer's power button to power the computer off.

7.10 Monitoring System Performance

It is important for a technician to understand how a computer is performing and be able to analyze why a computer might be running slow. In order to do that, a technician must know what type of applications are being run on the computer and the effect of these applications on the computer resources. A technician must also be able to monitor the computer's resource usage when problems occur, change the configuration as needed, and observe the results of the configuration change.

Three utilities are commonly used to monitor system performance: Task Manager, Performance tool's System Monitor, and Performance tool's Performance Logs and Alerts. **Task Manager** is used to monitor your current system's performance. **System Monitor** is used to monitor real-time data about specific computer components. **Performance Logs and Alerts** allows you to create logs about the computer's performance and create alerts that notify you when a specific instance being monitored reaches a threshold that you define. It includes a summary graph of processor and memory usage.

Task Manager has been discussed in a previous section. How to use it to monitor your computer's performance is as follows. Access Task Manager and click on the Performance tab. Task Manager immediately starts gathering CPU and memory usage statistics and displays them in graph form in the window. Figure 7.8 shows the Task Manager graphs.

Figure 7.8: A Screenshot of Task Manager Showing the Performance Tab

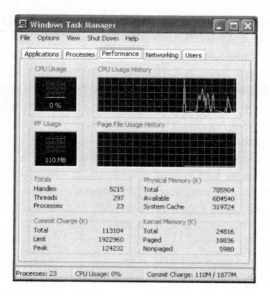

The first window on the left, **CPU Usage**, shows the CPU usage percentage or what percentage of time the processor is working. Actually, it is a percentage of time the processor is running a thread. A thread is a type of Windows object that runs application instructions. The first window on the right, **CPU Usage History**, is a graph of how busy the microprocessor is over a period of time.

The second window on the left (**PF Usage**) shows the amount of virtual memory (the paging file) being used. The amount shown is in megabytes as evidenced by the M after the number. If the display shows that the paging file is near the maximum, you can adjust the page file size. The following steps allow you to set the paging file size:

1. Click on the **Start** button and select **Control Panel**.
2. If in category view, select **Performance and Maintenance** followed by the **System** control panel icon. If in classic control panel view, double-click on the **System** control panel icon.
3. Click on the **Advanced** tab, locate the Performance section, and click on the **Settings** button.
4. Click on the **Advanced** tab, locate the Virtual Memory section, and click on the **Change** button.

The default paging file size is 1.5 times the total amount of physical RAM installed in the computer. Two values are selectable—Initial size and Maximum size. Both of these values should be the same for maximum computer performance. Once you change the values, click on the **Set** button. The Virtual Memory window can also be used to change the amount of space reserved for the registry.

The second window on the right, **Page File Usage History**, is a graph of the virtual memory used over time.

Memory is a frequent bottleneck for computer performance issues. Task Manager can also be used to see the total amount of RAM installed and how much RAM is available. Look in the Physical Memory information section in the Task Manager window to see this.

If you determine that memory is a problem, there are several things you can do including increasing the amount of RAM installed in the system, create multiple paging files when multiple hard drives are installed in the system, manually set the paging file size, run applications that require a lot of memory with all other applications closed, close any unnecessary windows, avoid having too many applications open, upgrade the hard drive or add another hard drive, and run the disk defragmenter program provided with XP.

Task Manager also has the Networking tab that is useful to technicians. The **Networking** tab shows a graph of network performance. The information shown can also be changed by selecting the **View** menu option, clicking on the **Select Columns** option, clicking in the available check boxes, and clicking on the **OK** button. Figure 7.9 shows this window.

Figure 7.9: A Screenshot of Task Manager Showing the Networking Tab

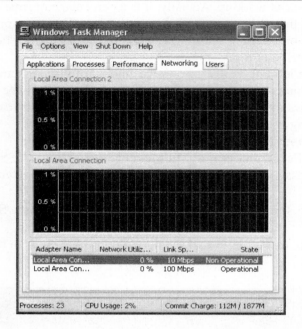

Sometimes a computer can start slowing down. The most common cause of slowdowns are that the computer's resources are insufficient or an application is monopolizing a particular resource such as memory. Other causes of slowdowns include a resource that is not functioning properly or is outdated such as a hard drive, the resource is not configured for maximum performance and needs to be adjusted, or resources such as hard drive space and memory are not sharing workloads properly. They need to be adjusted.

A baseline report is needed before the slowdown occurs. A **baseline** is a snapshot of your computer's performance during normal operations (before it has problems). Task Manager can be used to get an idea of what normal performance is, but the System Monitor and Performance Logs and Alerts tools are better suited to capturing and analyzing specific computer resource data.

To access the Performance tool (which contains System Monitor and Performance Logs and Alerts), perform the following steps:

1. Click on the **Start** button and access **Control Panel**.
2. If in category view, click on **Performance and Maintenance**, click on the **Administrative Tools** control panel icon, and double-click on the **Performance** icon. If in classic control panel view, double-click on the **Administrative Tools** control panel icon, and double-click on the **Performance** icon.

The Performance tool can also be accessed from a command prompt by clicking on the **Start** button, clicking on **Run**, typing **perfmon.msc** and pressing Enter.

The Performance window opens and System Monitor and Performance Logs and Alerts list in the left pane. Click on the **System Monitor** option and the tool starts collecting and displaying real-time data about the local computer or, if configured, from remote computers. A previously captured log file can also be loaded. Data can be displayed in graph, histogram, and report views. Figure 7.10 shows the System Monitor default screen (graph view).

Figure 7.10: A Screenshot of System Manager Showing the Networking Tab

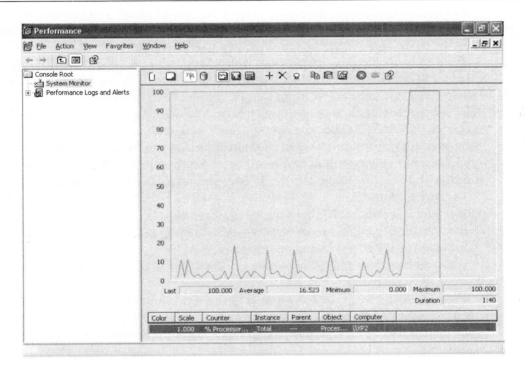

Notice in Figure 7.10 at the bottom of the window is the legend for interpreting the graph including what color is used for each of the performance measures and what counter is being used. A counter is a specific measurement for an object. Common objects include cache, memory, paging file, physical disk, processor, system, and thread.

Running System Monitor also affects your computer's performance especially when you are using the graph view and are sampling large amounts of data. The following helps when running System Monitor or Performance Logs and Alerts:

- Turn off any screen saver.
- Use report view instead of graph view to save on resources.
- Keep the number of counters being monitored to a minimum.
- Sample at longer intervals such as 10 to 15 minutes rather than just a few seconds or minutes apart.

Chapter Summary

- Microsoft Windows XP is a 32-bit operating system that comes in two variations: Home and Professional.
- Before you install Windows XP, you need to run through a pre-installation checklist that includes the file system used, determining hardware compatibility, and virus checking.
- The installation of Windows XP is performed in three phases. During the first phase, you determine whether you are upgrading or performing a clean install. You also enter the Product Key during this phase. During the second phase, you partition the hard drive and enter the Administrator password. The operating system is loaded during this phase. In the final phase, the log-on screen is displayed to you.
- You may be required to troubleshoot your Windows XP installation. Some type of problems you may encounter are: incompatible hardware, hardware drivers and TSRs, incorrect Product Key, a virus, or the BIOS needs to be upgraded.
- Dual-booting allows other operating system to be installed on the same hard drive. Of course, you can only boot one operating system at a time.
- Because the registry is the database containing system information, you need to back it up whenever changes occur to the computer. You use the REDEDIT tool to backup and restore the registry. To backup the registry you would use the backup utility to back up the System State data.
- Configuring Windows XP involves using Control Panel to change the look and feel of your Windows XP system. Examples include: changing mouse, keyboard, and sound settings. You can also add and remove devices.
- You need to understand the boot process of Windows XP so you know how to troubleshoot when problems occur.
- Windows Task Manager allows you view the applications that are running on your system. You get to Task Manager by pressing Ctrl + Alt + Del. Dr. Watson is an application debugging tool and Event Viewer contains a log of events that have occurred on your system.
- You can use System Monitor to monitor the performance of your Windows XP system through the use of objects and counters.

Review Questions

1. Which of the following is not a reason to perform a clean install of Windows XP?
   a) The computer does not have an operating system already installed.
   b) The computer's current operating system is not upgradeable to Windows XP.
   c) The computer's current operating system is upgradeable to Windows XP, but the existing files and applications are going to be reloaded.
   d) You have a new printer and need to add a printer driver.

2. Which product helps protect your Windows XP computer from Internet hacker attacks?
   a) DualView
   b) WIA
   c) ICS
   d) Windows Messenger

3. Which Windows XP software provides for instant messaging and video conferencing?
   a) DualView
   b) WIA
   c) ICS
   d) Windows Messenger

4. Which Windows XP software allows you to view output on multiple monitors?
   a) DualView
   b) WIA
   c) ICS
   d) Windows Messenger

5. Which Windows XP software allows communication between software application and image-capturing devices?
   a) DualView
   b) WIA
   c) ICS
   d) Windows Messenger

6. Which Windows XP software allows you view the applications that are running on your system?
   a) Task Manager
   b) DualView
   c) WIA
   d) NTFS

7. You get to Task Manager by pressing _____.
   a) F8
   b) F2
   c) Alt + Del
   d) Ctrl + Alt + Del

8. _____ is an application debugging tool.
   a) Task Manager
   b) WIA
   c) Dr. Watson
   d) DualView

9. _____ contains a log of events that have occurred on your system.
   a) DualView
   b) Event Viewer
   c) Dr. Watson
   d) WIA

10. _____ is used to monitor the performance of your Windows XP system through the use of objects and counters.
    a) WIA
    b) DualView
    c) Performance Monitor
    d) System Monitor

11. During the boot sequence, _____detects the computer's hardware.
    a) NTLDR
    b) NTDETECT.COM
    c) NTOSKRNL.EXE
    d) HAL.DLL

12. The name of the Windows XP bootstrap loader is _____.
    a) NTLDR
    b) NTDETECT.COM
    c) NTOSKRNL.EXE
    d) HAL.DLL

13. During the boot sequence, the _____ file is read and is used to display the various operating system choices.
    a) NTLDR
    b) NTDETECT.COM
    c) BOOT.INI
    d) HAL.DLL

14. The operating system kernel is called _____.
    a) NTLDR
    b) NTDETECT.COM
    c) BOOT.INI
    d) HAL.DLL

15. The bootstrap loader file starts in _____ mode so 8-bit and 16-bit software can be loaded.
    a) Protected
    b) Real
    c) WFP
    d) WIA

16. The _____ allows Windows XP to run with different hardware configurations and components without affecting (or crashing) the operating system.
    a) NTFS
    b) Real mode
    c) HAL
    d) WIA

17. The _____ is a group of Windows XP files that includes the registry, system files, and boot files.
    a) HAL
    b) IPSec
    c) ICS
    d) System State

18. The _____ utility is used for editing the Windows registry.
    a) HAL
    b) REGEDIT
    c) DualView
    d) System State

19. Which file system should you use if your hard drive is dual-booted with Windows 95?
    a) FAT32
    b) NTFS
    c) HAL
    d) Explorer

20. The _____ feature allows an older driver to be reinstalled when the new driver causes problems.
    a) ACPI
    b) Disk quota
    c) System State
    d) Driver roll back

Lab Projects

The following projects assume Windows XP is installed and running on a computer unless otherwise noted.

Lab Project 1

The goal of this project is for you to be able to use the Task Manager program to evaluate basic computer performance. You will need a computer with Windows XP installed and you need Administrator rights.

1. Turn the computer on and verify that the operating system loads. Log in to Windows XP using the userid and password provided by the instructor or lab assistant. Ensure the userid is one that has Administrator rights.

2. Press the **Ctrl + Alt + Del** keys to bring up Task Manager. Click on the **Performance** tab. The Performance tab is used to view CPU and page file usage.

3. Open Notepad, access the Internet if possible, open a game if possible, and start other applications.

   What happens to the CPU usage as displayed in Task Manager?

   _____

   What is the page file usage (PF Usage)?

   _____

   What is the total physical memory?

   _____

   How much RAM is available?

   _____

4. Close the Task Manager window.

Lab Project 2

The goal of this project is to use the System Monitor utility to track individual computer components. You need a computer with Windows XP and Administrative Tools loaded.

1. Turn the computer on and verify that the operating system loads. Log in to Windows XP using the userid and password provided by the instructor or lab assistant. Ensure the userid is one that has Administrator rights.

2. Click on the **Start** button, click on the **Control Panel** option. If in Control Panel Category view, click on **Performance and Maintenance** category, and click on **Administrative Tools**. If in Classic view, double-click on **Administrative Tools** control panel icon, and then double-click on the **Performance** icon. The Performance window opens. The Performance utility allows you to track individual computer component's performance. This is done through individual counters.

3. In the left window, click on the **System Monitor** item.

4. Click on the **Add button** (the button that has a plus sign on it) or right-click in the right window and click on the Add Counters option. The Add Counters dialog box opens.

5. Click on the **Performance object** down arrow. A list of system components appears such as Processor, physical disk, paging file memory, etc. Select the **Memory** performance object.

6. Once a system component has been selected, individual counters for that component can be selected and monitored. In the **Select counters from list** window, click on the **Available Bytes** counter. Click on the **Add** button.

7. Click on the Performance object **down arrow**. Select the **Paging File** performance object.

8. In the **Select counters from list** window, click on the **%Usage** counter. Click on the **Add** button.

   Using the Explain button, find out for what the %Usage counter is used. Write the explanation in the space below.

   _____

9. Close the Explain text message box. Using the method outlined in Steps 5 through 8, select two more counters to be monitored.

   What two counters did you add?

   _____

10. Click on the **Close** button. The right window in the Performance window displays a graph of the various counters. You may need to start some applications, do some cutting and pasting, or surf the Internet to see some of the counter activity. When finished, close the Performance window.

Lab Project 3

The goal of this project is to use the System Monitor utility to track individual computer components.

1. Turn the computer on and verify that the operating system loads. Log in to Windows XP using the userid and password provided by the instructor or lab assistant. Ensure the userid is one that has Administrator rights.

2. Click on the **Start** button, click on the **Control Panel** option. If in Control Panel Category view, click on **Performance and Maintenance** category, and click on **Administrative Tools**. If in Classic view, double-click on **Administrative Tools** control panel icon, and then double-click on the **Performance** icon. The Performance window opens. The Performance utility allows you to track individual computer component's performance. This is done through individual counters.

3. Click on the **Performance Logs and Alerts** option in the left pane. Click on the + (plus sign) if necessary to expand the Performance Logs and Alerts category.

   What are the three types of logs tracked by this utility?

   _____

4. Counter logs are used to create a log file using objects and counters you select. Click once on the **Counter logs** option in the left pane.

5. Click on the **Action** menu item and select **New Log Settings**.

6. In the name text box, type **Memory Usage** and click on the **OK** button.

7. Click on the **Add Counters** button. Click on the **Performance object** down arrow and select **Memory**. In the Select counters from list window, click on the **Available bytes** counter, and click on the **Add** button. In the Select counters from list window, click on the **Cache bytes** counter, and click on the **Add** button. Click on the **Close** button. The counters appear in the Counters window.

8. Click on the **Log Files** tab. The Log Files tab is used to select what type of file is created. The default type of file is a binary file, but a text file can be selected. Click on the **Log file type** down arrow and select the **Text File (Comma delimited)** option.

9. The Configure button is used to specify the location of the log file. Click on the **Configure** button.

   What is the default location (folder) for the log file?

   _____

10. Click on the **Cancel** button. Click on the **Schedule** tab. The Schedule tab is used to define the start and stop time for the log file. The default is to start the log and keep going until it is manually stopped. In the Stop log section, click on the **At** radio button. Change the time to two minutes after the current time. Make sure the date is today's date. (The default is one day later.) In other words, you will only be logging for two minutes. Click on the **Apply** button and click on the **OK** button. The Memory Usage log file appears in the right pane.

11. After two minutes, access the **WordPad** accessory. Click on the **File** menu option and select **Open**. Click on the **Files of type** down arrow and select **All Documents**. Use the Look in drop-down box or the icons on the left to locate the Memory Usage file. Reference your answer to the previous question for the name of the folder and drive letter. Click once on the file name and click on the **Open** button. The Memory Usage log file appears. The first set of numbers is the date followed by the time. The next two numbers are the counters that were requested: Available bytes and Cache bytes.

On the first logged event line, what is the number of available bytes and cache bytes?

_____

12. Return to the Performance window and click once on the **Memory Usage** counter log that you created earlier. Click on the **Red X** (delete) icon. An alternative method for doing the same thing is to click on the **Action** menu item and click on the **Delete** option.

13. Click once on the **Alerts** log in the left pane. Click on the **Action** menu item and select **New Alert Settings**. In the Name text box, type **Memory Alert** and click on the **OK** button. The Alerts option is used to set a counter that triggers an alert event to be sent to **Event Viewer**.

14. Click on the **Add** button. In the Performance object drop-down menu, select **Memory**. In the Select counters from list window, use the scroll bars to locate the **Available Bytes** counter. Click on the **Explain** button.

What does the Available Bytes counter log?

_____

15. Close the Explain Text window. Click on the **Add** button. Click on the **Close** button. On the General tab, type in a **1** in the Limit text box. (Note that this is not a value you would normally pick, but is used for illustration purposes.) Click on the **Action** tab. The Action tab is used to specify what happens when an alert is generated. The default is to send an alert into the application event log.

16. Click on the **Schedule** tab. The Schedule tab is used to define the start and stop time for the log file. The default is to start the log and keep going until it is manually stopped. In the Stop log section, click on the **At** radio button. Change the time to two minutes after the current time. Make sure the date is today's date. In other words, you will only be logging for two minutes. Click on the **Apply** button and click on the **OK** button. The Memory Alert log file appears in the right pane.

17. Open Event Viewer (see previous exercise if necessary) and open the Application event log by clicking on **Application** in the left pane. Look in the right pane. The first few application events should have event code 2031. Double-click on one of these events.

Write the event description in the space below.

_____

18. Close Event Viewer and return to the Performance window. Click on the **Alerts** Performance Logs and Alerts category. Click once on the **Memory Alert** log. Click on the **Red X** (delete) icon. An alternative method for doing the same thing is to click on the **Action** menu item and click on the **Delete** option.

Have a classmate verify that the counter log and alert log you created in this exercise are deleted. Have both the Memory Usage counter log and the Memory Alert alert log been deleted?

Classmate's printed name: _____

Classmate's signature: _____

19. Close the Performance window.

Lab Project 4

The goal of this project is for you to be able to back up the Windows XP system state using the Backup utility. You will need a computer with Windows XP installed and a formatted 3.5" floppy disk.

Note: In order to do this exercise, the student must have local Administrator privileges. The system state can be quite large (a common size is 400 MB), so adequate hard drive space must be available.

1. Turn on the computer and verify that the operating system loads.

2. Log on to Windows XP using the userid and password provided by the instructor or lab assistant. Note that the userid must have local Administrator privileges to do this exercise.

3. Click on the **Start** button and point to the **All Programs** selection. Point to the **Accessories** option, point to **System Tools** and click on the **Backup** menu selection. The Backup Wizard starts.

4. Click on the **Advanced Mode** option (which is an underlined option in the words appearing in the window).

5. Click on the **Backup** tab and select the **System State** check box to enable it.

6. Select where the backup is to be stored by clicking on the **Browse** button.

   What hard drive and folder is being used to store the system state backup?

   _____

7. Click on the **Start Backup** button. The Backup Job information dialog box appears. Click on the **Start** button located in the window to start the backup.

8. When the backup finishes, the Backup Progress window shows that the backup is complete. Show this to your instructor.

9. Click on the **Close** button. Close the Backup Utility window.

10. Use Windows Explorer to locate the BACKUP.BKF file and permanently delete it.

   Have a classmate verify the BACKUP.BKF file is *permanently* deleted. Has the BACKUP. BKF file been deleted?

   Classmate's printed name: _____

   Classmate's signature: _____

Lab Project 5

The goal of this project is to disable a driver under the Windows XP operating system.

Note: The student must be logged in as a user with local Administrator rights to perform this lab. In this lab, a driver is disabled and then re-enabled. The purpose of this is to demonstrate disabling a driver because sometimes XP can install the wrong driver. Drivers must sometimes be disabled and then manually reinstalled.

1. Turn the computer on and verify that the operating system loads. Log in to Windows XP using the userid and password provided by the instructor or lab assistant.

2. Using Device Manager, expand the **Network adapters** category.

   What network adapter is installed in the computer?

   _____

3. Right-click on a network adapter and click on the **Disable** selection.

   What message displays on the screen?

   _____

4. Click on the **Yes** button.

   In Device Manager, how is a device that has its driver disabled displayed differently from any other device?

   _____

5. In Device Manager, right-click on the same network adapter and click on the **Enable** option. The device is enabled and appears normally in the window.

6. Close the Device Manager window and all other windows. Log off and power down the computer properly.

Lab Project 6

The goal of this project is to install a new hardware component under the Windows XP operating system. You will need a new device to install and Internet access.

Note: The student must be logged in as a user with local Administrator rights to perform this lab. In this lab, the Internet is used to obtain the device's installation instructions and latest device driver, and then the new hardware device is installed.

1. There are four installation procedures depending on what type of hardware device is being installed. (1) A plug and play external device is normally installed when the computer is powered on. (2) A plug and play internal device is normally installed with the computer powered off and the device is installed according to the manufacturer's instructions. However, with PC Cards, the computer can be usually turned on and they can be inserted. (3) PCI and ISA cards are installed with the computer powered off. When the computer is powered on, Windows XP normally detects the device and starts the installation procedure. **Note:** PCI and ISA are interfaces that cards such as video cards, network cards, and modem cards use to "talk" with the motherboard. (4) Non-plug and play devices are installed with the computer powered off. When the computer powers on, the Add Hardware control panel is used to install the device.

   Of the four types of hardware devices, which one are you installing?

2. Using the Internet, locate the manufacturer's instructions for installing the device.

   Who is the device manufacturer?

   _____

3. Using the Internet, locate the latest device driver that is compatible with XP.

   Does the device have an XP driver?

   What is the device driver version being downloaded?

   _____

4. Connect the device to the computer using the proper installation procedures.

5. Boot the computer. Usually Windows XP automatically detects the new hardware and begins the Found New Hardware wizard. If it does not present this wizard, look to see if the hardware device vendor supplied an installation program. If so, use this program to install the device. If no vendor-supplied installation program is available, use the Add Hardware control panel to install the device. Install the device driver based on the device type and manufacturer's instructions.

   Did the Found New Hardware wizard begin?

   _____

6. Test the device installation either by using the device.

Lab Project 7

The goal of this project is for you to be able to install and remove Windows XP components. In addition to a computer with Windows XP installed, you need the Administrator password and about 18 MB of free hard disk space.

Note: In this lab, Windows XP's Accessories and Utilities component is removed, if already installed, and reinstalled. If the Accessories and Utilities component is not installed, it will be installed, removed, and reinstalled. The Accessories and Utilities component requires about 17.5 MB of hard disk space. The final objective of this lab is to have Accessories and Utilities installed.

1. Turn the computer on and verify that the operating system loads. Log in to Windows XP using the userid and password provided by the instructor or lab assistant. Ensure the userid is one that has Administrator rights.

Verifying if Accessories and Utilities Are Already Loaded

2. Click on the **Start** button and click on the **Control Panel** option. Access the **Add or Remove Programs** control panel by clicking on the category view or double-clicking on the Classic View control panel icon.

3. Click on the **Add/Remove Windows Components** icon located on the left portion of the Add or Remove Programs window. The Windows Components window opens.

   Is the Accessories and Utilities option enabled (checked)?

   _____

   If so, proceed to the **Removing Accessories and Utilities** section. Remove the components and then proceed to the **Installing and Utilities** section to reinstall the components. If the Accessories and Utilities option is not installed (unchecked), proceed to the **Installing and Utilities** section, install the components, then go to the **Removing Accessories and Utilities** section, and uninstall the components, then finally, reinstall the components again. When this lab is complete, the Accessories and Utilities component should be installed.

4. You can double-click on any component to view the subcomponents. Try this procedure on your own. Close all windows and proceed to the appropriate section based on the previous answer.

Removing Accessories and Utilities

5. Click on the **Start** button and click on the **Control Panel** option. Access the **Add or Remove Programs** control panel by clicking on the category view or double-clicking on the Classic View control panel icon.

6. Click on the **Add/Remove Windows Components** icon located on the left portion of the Add or Remove Programs window. The Windows Components window opens.

7. Click on the **Accessories and Utilities** check box to deselect (uncheck) it and click on the **Next** button. The files are deleted.

8. Click on the **Finish** button and verify that Accessories and Utilities are uninstalled using previously described procedures.

   Has the Accessories and Utilities component been removed? Have a classmate verify.

   Classmate's printed name: _____

   Classmate's signature: _____

Installing Accessories and Utilities

9. Click on the **Start** button and click on the **Control Panel** option. Access the **Add or Remove Programs** control panel by clicking on the category view or double-clicking on the classic view control panel icon.

10. Click on the **Add/Remove Windows Components** icon located on the left portion of the Add or Remove Programs window. The Windows Components window opens.

11. Click on the **Accessories and Utilities** check box to select (enable) it. If the box is already checked, go to the **Removing Accessories and Utilities** section. Click on the **Next** button. A prompt appears to insert the Windows XP CD. Insert the CD and the files copy.

12. Click on the **Finish** button, close all Add/Remove Components control panel windows, and verify that Accessories and Utilities are installed using previously described procedures.

    Is the Accessories and Utilities Windows XP component installed? Show this component to your instructor.

Lab Project 8

The goal of this project is for you to be able to access various Windows XP boot options that are used to troubleshoot startup problems. In addition to a computer with Windows XP installed, you need the Administrator password and about 18 MB of free hard disk space.

Note: In this lab, the students boot without startup programs loaded, boot to Safe Mode, boot to Safe Mode with Command Prompt, boot to Enable Boot Logging and examine the NTBTLOG.TXT file, and boot to Recovery Console and examine commands using the command prompt.

1. Turn the computer on and verify that the operating system loads. Log in to Windows XP using the userid and password provided by the instructor or lab assistant. Ensure the userid is one that has Administrator rights.

Verifying Startup Folder Contents

2. Right-click on the **Start** button and click on the **Explore** option.

3. Locate the **Documents and Settings** folder and expand it if necessary. Locate the **All Users** folder (located under Documents and Settings) and expand it if necessary. Locate the **Start Menu** subfolder (located under All Users) and expand it if necessary. Locate the **Programs** subfolder (located under the Start Menu folder) and expand it if necessary. Click on the **Startup** folder located under the Programs folder.

   Are there any program shortcuts listed in the Startup folder? If so, write at least one of the programs in the space below. If there is no program shortcut, create a shortcut to the Notepad application and place it in the Startup folder. A previous exercise explains how to create a shortcut. Have a classmate verify your shortcut.

   Classmate's printed name: _____

   Classmate's signature: _____

4. Restart the computer and verify that the program listed in the Startup folder starts *automatically* when the computer boots. If it does not, re-do step 3.

Preventing Startup Programs from Loading

5. Restart the computer and while the computer boots and while the log-in process occurs, hold the **Shift key** down until the desktop icons appear. Holding the Shift key down stops startup programs from loading automatically. This technique works when any program that starts automatically is causing problems. If this does not work for you, shut down the computer properly, power off, power back on, log in and hold the Shift key down during the log-in process.

   What indication do you have that holding the Shift key down while booting stopped the application from loading?

   _____

6. Using Windows Explorer, delete the *shortcut* located in the Startup folder.

Have a classmate verify that you only deleted the shortcut and not the application. Has the *shortcut* been deleted?

_____

Classmate's printed name: _____

Classmate's signature: _____

Using Boot Options

7. Restart the computer and press the **F8** key as the computer boots. The Windows Advanced Options Menu appears. If it does not, repeat this procedure until it does. Select the **Safe Mode** option and press Enter.

   What is different about the Windows XP log-in screen?

   _____

   Why do you think the Administrator user icon appears in Safe Mode and not during the regular boot sequence?

   _____

8. Log in as Administrator.

   What indication appears letting you know that the computer is running in Safe Mode?

   _____

9. Click on the **Yes** button.

   Did your program in the startup folder automatically start?

   _____

   Are Administrative Tools available through the Start button's All Programs list?

   _____

   To what Control Panel view does the system default?

   _____

10. Double-click on the **Administrative Tools** control panel. Double-click on the **Computer Management** icon. Access the **Services** folder. Refer to the Computer Management exercise if you forgot how to access it.

    List two automatic services that have a status of _started_.

    _____

11. Notice how there are quite a few services that are automatic services that did not start in Safe Mode. Close the Computer Management screen and the Administrative Tools window.

12. Restart the computer and press the **F8** button to see the Windows Advanced Options menu.

List the boot options available.

_____

Match the following definitions to the appropriate boot option.

_____ Safe Mode

_____ Safe Mode with Command Prompt

_____ Enable Boot Logging

_____ Last Known Good Configuration

      A. Starts the system with minimum files and drivers and only typed commands can be used.

      B. Records the boot process into a text file that can later be viewed and used for troubleshooting.

      C. Starts the system with minimum file and drivers including VGA video drivers.

      D. Used when a newly installed piece of hardware or software causes the system not to boot properly.

13. Select the **Safe Mode with Command Prompt** option and log in as Administrator.

    What is different about the desktop appearance?

    _____

14. Click on the **Minimize** button, which is the left-most button in the upper right corner of the cmd.exe window.

    What does the screen look like now?

    _____

15. The Safe Mode with Command Prompt option is used to start the system with minimum files and drivers and a command prompt where you must type commands instead of working through a graphical interface. Type **exit** at the command prompt.

    What happened to the screen?

    _____

16. Press **Ctrl + Alt + Del** and the Task Manager window appears. Click on the **Shut Down** menu option and select **Restart**. Restart the computer, press the **F8** key to see the Windows Advanced Options Menu. Select the **Enable Boot Logging** option.

    Does the Administrator userid appear as a log-in choice?

    _____

17. Log in to Windows XP.

    How does the desktop appear when using the Enable Boot Logging option?

    _____

18. Using Windows Explorer, locate the file **NTBTLOG.TXT** and double-click on the file icon to open the file.

    List two drivers that loaded properly.

    _____

19. Close the NTBTLOG.TXT window and close all Windows Explorer windows.

Recovery Console

20. Shut the computer down and power off. Insert the Windows XP CD into the drive and power on the computer. The Welcome to Setup screen appears. If the computer does not boot from the Windows XP CD, the BIOS settings probably need to be adjusted. Press **R** at the Welcome to Setup screen. The Recovery screen appears.

21. Press the number that corresponds to the partition that contains XP.

22. Type the Administrator password. Contact a lab assistant or the instructor if the password is unknown. The Recovery Console loads.

    Write down what the prompt looks like.

    _____

23. The Recovery Console is used as a last resort—when other boot options are used and you are not able to solve the problem with these options. At the prompt, type **copy** and press Enter. An error message appears. Command prompt usage must be very precise and exact commands with proper switches must be used.

24. Type **help copy** and press Enter. Help information on the Copy command appears.

25. Type **copy /?** and press Enter. Again, help information appears.

26. Type **help** and press Enter. A list of Recovery Console commands appears. Press the **space bar** to see the rest of the command list.

27. Remove the XP CD and type **exit**. The system boots normally.

Lab Project 9

The goal of this project is to have you create a tree structure on the floppy.

1. Turn the computer on and verify that the operating system loads. Log in to Windows XP using the userid and password provided by the instructor or lab assistant.

2. Create the tree structure shown in Figure 7.11.

Figure 7.11: A Sample Tree Hierarchy

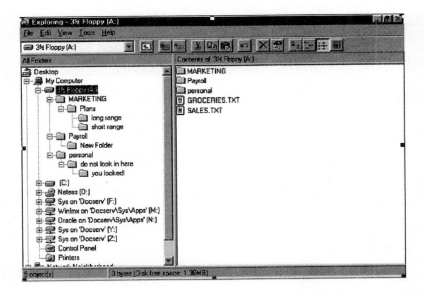

3. Create another folder in the root directory of the floppy that has your name in it.

4. Create another folder in the root directory of the floppy named "Windows XP Project 9."

5. Show your instructor.

Lab Project 10

The goal of this project is to have you create a tree structure on the floppy.

1. Turn the computer on and verify that the operating system loads. Log in to Windows XP using the userid and password provided by the instructor or lab assistant.

2. Create the tree structure shown in Figure 7.12.

Figure 7.12: A Sample Tree Hierarchy

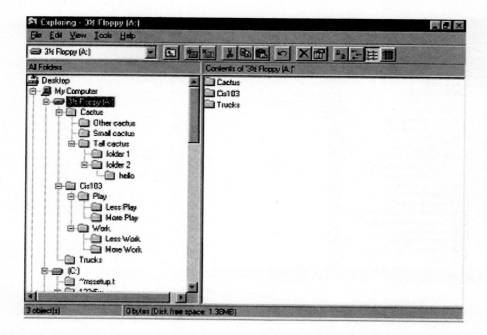

3. Create another folder in the root directory of the floppy that has your name in it.

4. Create another folder in the root directory of the floppy named "Windows XP Project 10."

5. Show your instructor.

Lab Project 11

The goal of this project is to help you understand how to encrypt and decrypt files at the command prompt. You must complete this lab project on an NTFS partition. This lab project is a bit more advanced because you are expected to determine many of the steps in the lab. If you have trouble with the command prompt mode, refer to Chapter 3 on DOS and the DOS command prompt.

1. Go to a command prompt.

2. At the command prompt, create a directory named C:\Project11.

3. Record the command used.

   _____

4. Create two files named File11A.txt and File11B.txt in Project11.

5. Record the command used.

   _____

6. To make sure you are at the root directory of the C: drive, type **CD C:** and press Enter.

7. To encrypt a directory, type **CIPHER /E Project11** and press Enter. The directory and new files will be encrypted.

8. To verify the encryption status, type **CIPHER** and press Enter. The status of the directories and files are displayed. If an "E" is beside the directory or file name, then the item is encrypted. If there is a "U," the item is not encrypted.

9. Change directory locations to Project11.

10. Create a new file named File11E.txt.

11. To verify the encryption status, type **CIPHER** and press Enter.

12. Record the output.

    _____

    _____

    _____

13. Record the reason for the output.

    _____

    _____

    _____

14. To make sure you are at the root directory of the C: drive, type **CD C:** and press Enter.

15. To decrypt a directory, type **CIPHER /D Project11** and press Enter. The directory and new files will not be encrypted.

16. Create a new file in Project11.

17. Check the encryption/decryption status now.

18. Record the output and reason for the output.

_____

_____

_____

19. Close the command prompt window.

Lab Project 12

The goal of this project is to help you understand how to compress and uncompress files at the command prompt. You must complete this lab project on an NTFS partition. This lab project is a bit more advanced because you are expected to determine many of the steps in the lab. If you have trouble with the command prompt mode, refer to Chapter 3 on DOS and the DOS command prompt.

1. Go to a command prompt.

2. At the command prompt, create a directory named C:\Project12.

3. Record the command used.

_____

4. Create two files named File12A.txt and File12B.txt in Project12.

5. Record the command used.

_____

6. To make sure you are at the root directory of the C: drive, type **CD C:** and press Enter.

7. To encrypt a directory, type **COMPACT /C Project12** and press Enter. The directory and new files will be compressed.

8. To verify the compression status, type **COMPACT** and press Enter. The status of the directories and files are displayed. If a "C" is beside the directory or file name, then the item is compressed. Otherwise, the item is not compressed.

9. Change directory locations to Project12.

10. Create a new file named File12C.txt.

11. To verify the compression status, type **COMPACT** and press Enter.

12. Record the output.

_____

_____

_____

13. Record the reason for the output.

_____

_____

_____

14. Close the command prompt window.

15. To make sure you are at the root directory of the C: drive, type **CD C:** and press Enter.

16. To uncompress a directory, type **COMPACT /U Project12** and press Enter. The directory and new files will not be compressed.

17. Create a new file in Project12.

18. Check the compression/uncompression status now.

19. Record the output and reason for the output.

_____

_____

_____

20. Close the command prompt window

Lab Project 13 Challenge

The goal of this exercise is for you to be able to install Windows XP on a hard drive that does not have an operating system installed nor any partitions. You will need a computer with a hard drive without any partitions and you will need the Windows XP CD. If your hard drive has partitions, delete them.

1. Insert the Windows XP CD into the CD-ROM drive and turn on the computer. Some computers require you to press a key to boot from the CD or require special BIOS settings to boot from the CD. Perform the appropriate steps required on the computer to allow the computer to boot from CD. The Setup screen displays. If the CD is an evaluation copy of XP, **Enter** must be pressed. Press **Enter** to display the licensing agreement.

2. Press **F8** to accept the licensing agreement. The hard drive partitioning screen appears.

3. Check with the instructor on how much space is desired for the partition. The partition must be a minimum of 2 GB in size. Record the partition size you chose.

   _____

4. Select a hard drive area that is not partitioned and press **C** to create a partition. A prompt appears asking for the partition size. Use the answer obtained in the previous question and enter this information. Note that **Enter** can be pressed to use all available space for the partition. Press **Enter** to install Windows XP on the partition just created.

5. A screen appears prompting to format the newly create partition. Select **NTFS** as the type of file system used on the formatted partition. The drive is formatted and setup files are copied to the drive.

6. When prompted to restart the computer, **remove the CD from the drive** and press **Enter**.

7. When prompted to insert the CD into the drive, reinsert the Windows XP CD into the drive and click on the **OK** button.

8. Accept the default path for the Windows XP installation by clicking on the **OK** button. After copying more files, you are prompted for regional settings. Set the appropriate language and click **Next**.

9. The Personalize Your Software page appears. This is what applications use for product registration and document identification. Leave this information blank and click on the **Next** button. The Product Key page appears.

10. Enter the product key located on the back of the Windows XP case, on the CD, or provided by the student assistant or instructor. Click on the **Next** button. Check with the lab assistant or instructor for the name that will be given to the computer as well as the Administrator password. Write this information in the space below:

    Computer name: _____

    Administrator password: _____

11. The setup program prompts for the computer name and Administrator password. Type the computer name and Administrator password that were written in the previous step. Click on the **Next** button.

12. If a modem is installed, the modem dialing information is displayed. The correct country, area code, number to access an outside line, etc., are required. Contact the lab assistant or instructor for this information (if displayed), enter it and click on the **Next** button. If a modem is not installed (or after this information is entered), the date and time page appears. Set the **date** and **time** as appropriate and click on the **Next** button.

13. If a network card is installed in the computer, the network settings page displays. If this is the case enter the appropriate networking information as provided by the lab assistant or instructor and click on **Next**. The setup process continues copying files and installing the operating system and then restarts the computer. After the restart, the Welcome to Microsoft Windows screen appears. Does the welcome screen appear? Show this screen to the instructor.

_____

14. Click on the **Next** button and the Internet Connection screen appears. Select to skip this step.

15. When asked if you want to activate Windows, select the **wait until later** option.

16. When prompted, do not select to set up user accounts. This process is covered in another lab.

17. Click on the **Finish** button. Does Windows boot properly after the installation process?

Lab Project 14 Challenge

The goal of this project is for you to be able to install Windows XP on a hard drive that already has an operating system installed. You will need a computer with a hard drive that has Windows 98, Windows ME, NT Workstation 4, or Windows 2000 installed and that has a CD drive installed. You will also need the Windows XP CD.

1. Power on the computer and log on as necessary. Contact the instructor or lab assistant for the userid and password if necessary. Insert the Windows XP CD into the CD-ROM drive. The Welcome to Microsoft Windows XP screen should appear. Click on **Install Windows XP**. The setup process collects information about the computer to ensure it is upgradeable.

2. When asked what type of installation to use, select **Upgrade** and click on the **Next** button.

3. Click on the radio button to accept the licensing agreement and click **Next**.

4. Enter the product key located on the back of the CD case, written on the CD, or provided by the instructor or lab assistant and click on the **Next** button.

5. The Dynamic Update is optional and can only be used if an Internet connection is available. The Dynamic Update updates installation files. Contact the instructor or lab assistant to determine if the Dynamic Update is necessary.

   Was the Dynamic Update performed?

   _____

6. The setup process copies installation files and restarts. When prompted to choose a Windows installation, ***do not select anything***. Windows automatically selects the correct version. The XP logo appears, more files are copied, and the computer reboots again.

7. You may be asked to enter a computer name if the old computer name is not appropriate. If necessary, type an appropriate computer name and click on the **Next** button. The Tour Windows screen appears.

8. When asked to activate the product, select the option to bypass this step. Click the **Finish** button.

9. When asked to setup user accounts, contact the instructor or lab assistant to verify if any are to be created.

   Were any user accounts created? If so, list them below.

   _____

10. Click the **Next** button and the XP desktop appears.

Internet Discovery

Internet Discovery Lab 1

Access the Internet to obtain specific information regarding a computer or its associated parts.

1. Find a web site that offers Windows XP freeware tools. Write the URL in the space below.

2. What is the latest service pack available from Microsoft for Windows XP Professional? Write the answer and the URL where you found the answer in the space below.

3. Find a web site that details how to set up DualView. Write the web address in the space below as well as the steps to configure DualView.

4. Microsoft always has minimum requirements for any of its operating systems. Find a web site that tells you what your system should really have to run Windows XP efficiently. Write the name of the company that posts the recommendation as well as the URL.

5. You are upgrading a computer from Windows 2000 Professional to XP Professional. After the installation, Device Manager is showing that the Windows Sound System Compatible (WDM) drive is having a problem. When you view the device properties, the description shows a code 28 error and states that the drivers are not installed. Find a web site that describes this error and write the cause and URL in the space below.

6. Find one book that prepares you for the Microsoft Windows XP Professional exam. Write the name of the book and the URL in the space below.

Soft Skills: Help Desk Support

1. A customer calls you and wants to install Windows XP. They have a Pentium II running at 233 MHz with 32 MB of RAM and a 2.0 GB hard disk drive. What do you tell them?

2. A user named Tom Smith calls and tells you that he gets some strange data in his spreadsheet. How do you help him? List possible problems.

3. You receive a call from a Support Engineer working for your same company. He wants to be able to pull up specific Administrative Tools easily. How do you help him?

Critical Thinking

1. How large is the System State data?
2. Why is the term "dual-boot" used when you cannot boot but one operating system at a time?
3. What is the purpose of disabling hardware?

 Study Skills

The "Say" in "Hear, See, Do, Say"

Remember the key to learning are these four points: hear, see, do, say. This section focuses on the visual part or the "say" study skill.

- If your eyes are considered input and your brain is considered processes, then what would your mouth (used for saying) be considered?
- When you say or repeat something, you are reinforcing your understanding of the topic.
- Your instructor may call on you in class to answer a question. If you have prepared well, you should have no problem with the answer. And, you don't want to be embarrassed because you don't know the answer.
- Your instructor may assign a classroom research paper and presentation. When you present your paper, you are "saying" your work to the class. Who knows, you may teach a classmate something.
- When you have a test, you are "saying" what you know on paper.
- When studying, you can actually make some note cards of key points and definitions and have someone go over them with you. You can have the question on one side and the answer on the other. Have them ask the question and you can "say" the answer. It will really help you to retain the chapter material.
- Go to a place where you cannot disturb others. Read key points and definitions out loud. Again, this will help you remember the material.
- "Saying" does _not_ involve telling someone an answer on a test (known as **cheating**).

Self-Study Question(s)
1. Have you gone over your note cards out loud this week?
2. Identify at least two "say" Study Skills you did this week.

8

Chapter 8
Introduction to
UNIX/Linux

OBJECTIVES

Although the contents of this chapter do not apply directly to the A+ Operating System Technologies Exam, the Linux operating system is becoming increasingly popular and should be included in an Operating Systems Concepts book.

In this chapter, you will complete the following sections:
- 8.1 Understanding the Linux Operating System
- 8.2 Learning about the Linux Hierarchy
- 8.3 Understanding the Types of Commands
- 8.4 Navigating the Tree Structure
- 8.5 Creating and Removing Directories
- 8.6 Managing Files
- 8.7 Learning about Additional Commands
- 8.8 Learning about Pattern Matching (Wildcard Characters)
- 8.9 Learning about Redirection and Filtering
- 8.10 Learning to Write Shell Script Programs

8.1 Understanding the Linux Operating System

AT&T developed the UNIX operating system in the early 1960s. It was based on the C language with some code written in the Assembler language. That version was called AT&T System Release V, or "SR5" for short. At the time, the operating system code was given out to major universities and the employees and students made modifications to it. The University of California at Berkley developed a version named Berkley Source Distribution, or BSD. The UNIX operating system became more commercialized over time. Multiple vendors bought rights to it and made changes to it in hopes of carving a niche in the market. There have been numerous versions of the original UNIX operating system. One such version is Linux.

Linus Torvalds, a student at the University of Helsinki, is credited with being instrumental in the development of Linux. He wrote Linux to be PC-based so anyone could use it at home. It comes with many built-in features with a full array of programming languages, compilers, and system administration tools at a very reasonable cost. Although there are differences between the many versions of UNIX, the term "Linux" is used throughout this chapter. This is because most of the concepts and lab exercises apply to most versions of UNIX and Linux. The screenshots in this chapter were done with Red Hat Linux 8.0.

8.2 Learning about the Linux Hierarchy

Like many operating systems, Linux is hierarchical in nature. This hierarchy is sometimes called a tree structure. Let's look at an analogy. Think of a tree that you buy at a garden store. There is the ball root with branches and leaves. Now, turn it upside down. The root is at the top with branches and leaves flowing from it. A branch can have other branches or leaves. However, a leaf cannot contain a branch or another leaf—it is an endpoint.

The Linux file system hierarchy is identical to the DOS file system hierarchy. However, there are a few differences. As you know from Chapter 3, the root symbol in DOS is \; however, the root symbol in Linux is /. Branching from the root are directories or files. As in DOS, a directory is analogous to a branch and a file is analogous to a leaf. A directory can contain other directories or files. A file cannot contain a directory or another file—like a leaf, it is an endpoint. However, a file does have contents. For example, a file can contain payroll data used for processing paychecks, or a file can contain a picture of someone (like a JPEG file), or it can contain executable code (like a command). Figure 8.1 shows an example of the Linux file system.

Figure 8.1: The Linux Hierarchical File System

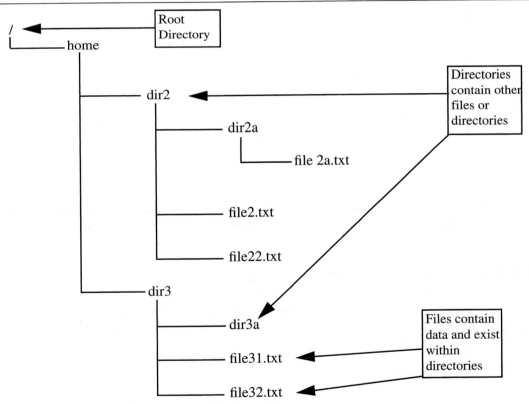

You can see in Figure 8.1 that the root symbol, "/" is at the very top of the hierarchy, or tree. Below the root directory is a directory named home and below that are two directories named "dir2" and "dir3." Each of these directories can contain other directories and files. Figure 8.2 shows a similar tree structure in Linux using the **tree** command.

**Figure 8.2: A Screenshot Showing the Tree Structure of Figure 8.1
Using the Linux Tree Command**

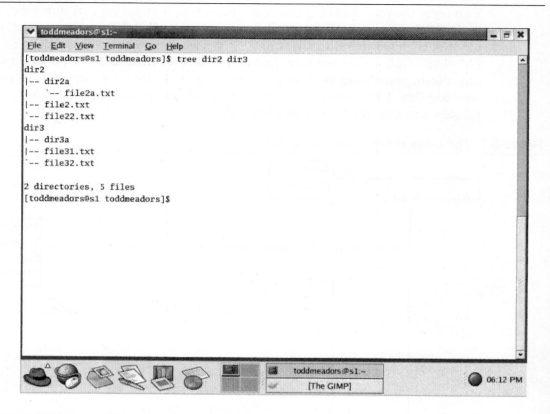

8.3 Understanding the Types of Commands

Commands are classified into two broad categories: 1) directory commands, or 2) file commands. In other words, some commands deal only with directories and some commands deal only with files. There are a few exceptions. For example, the **ls** command displays both files and directories. Most commands use the following generic syntax:

> *command options*

Note *command* is the name of the command and *options* are either file and directory names or actual options that alter the command in some way.

Almost all commands use options to alter the way the command operates. The symbol for using options is the hyphen (-). Refer to Table 8.1 for a list of a few basic commands, a brief description of them, and their DOS/DOS command prompt equivalents. Linux and DOS have commands that operate similarly. Of the commands in the table, the **cd, ls,** and the **pwd** commands are the most common.

Table 8.1: A Listing of a Few Basic Linux Commands

Command	Description	DOS and DOS Command Line Equivalent
cd	Allows you to change directory positions, or location, within the tree.	CD
mkdir	Allows you to create a directory.	MD or MKDIR
rmdir	Allows you to remove a directory.	RD or RMDIR
pwd	Allows you to display your current working directory.	CD or look at your prompt
ls	Allows you to see directories and files in a given directory.	DIR

8.4 Navigating the Tree Structure

Before discussing tree structure navigation, let's discuss the concept of command prompts and user accounts. The Linux operating system is a multi-user and multitasking operating system. It acts like a small mainframe in that users can connect to it remotely using the **telnet** command, or they can log in locally as they would on a Microsoft Windows operating system. Because it is a multi-user environment, all users can potentially see the same directories and files.

One specific user account exists that has complete control over the system. That user is the **root** user. This is not the same as the root directory. With the root user account, you actually log in using the user name of "root." If you don't have root user access you can still log in with a standard user account. The root user can create standard user accounts. The standard user account used in this chapter is "toddmeadors." You can do many of the same commands as the root user account. However, the root user account has access to additional system administration commands and tools. If you have root access, it is not a good practice to log in as the root user on a routine basis. You should create a standard user account and log in using that account. You should only use the root user account when you cannot do what you need to do using your standard user account. The author of this chapter worked in UNIX technical support and has seen System Administrators accidentally delete all of the files on their system as the root user using a single command. The command they executed was **rm –r *** in the / directory as the root user. This will remove all of the software on your system. Fortunately, most of us don't have complete access to the root user account and the root directory.

Be careful using the root user account on a daily basis! Log in as a user and only log in as root when you need to do something that the standard user account cannot accomplish. For this chapter, you will only need a standard user account.

Linux provides a command prompt for users to enter their commands. The root user and standard user accounts have different prompts. The root user's prompt includes the # sign. The standard user account includes the $ sign. If you don't have root access, then you'll see a dollar sign as part of your prompt. In Figure 8.3, you can see the differences. Notice that the user name is included in the command prompt.

Figure 8.3: A Screenshot Displaying the Root User and Standard User Prompts

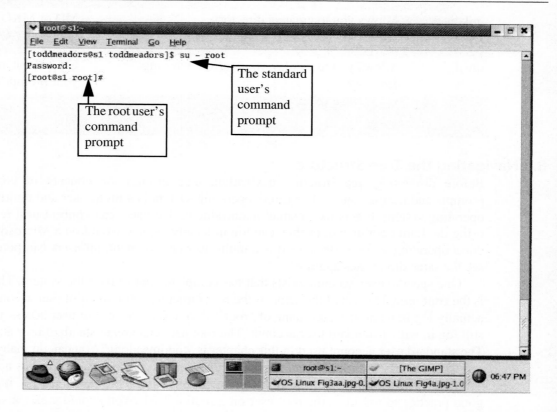

Each user has a home directory represented by the variable **$HOME**. The home directory is the default path, from the root directory, where your files and directories are stored. Generally the home directory begins in /home. Each users home directory ($HOME) is unique. For example, the $HOME variable for the user "toddmeadors" is /home/toddmeadors. The $HOME variable for the user "mickimeadors" is /home/mickimeadors. When you first log in to the Linux system your current directory is your home directory ($HOME). You can **cd** to **$HOME** and that will take you to your own home directory. The home directory will be used for storing your directories and files in this chapter.

Now let's discuss navigating the tree structure. For now, assume the tree structure shown previously in Figure 8.2 has already been created in a user's home directory.

Assume the current directory is root, or /. In order to change directory locations to dir2, you would issue this command: **cd dir2** and press Enter. You can follow up the **cd** command with the **pwd** command. Figure 8.4 shows for a sample screenshot. Notice the prompt changes to reflect the current directory.

Figure 8.4: A Sample Screenshot Displaying the Results of the cd and pwd Command for dir2

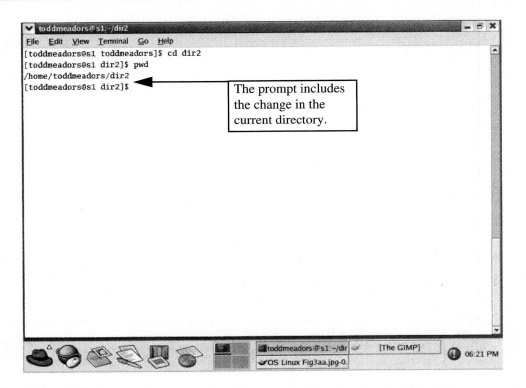

You must watch the case of the letters as you type in a command. Most Linux commands are lowercase, and the operating system is case-sensitive. In other words, entering **CD dir2** would generate an error. This is easy to fix, just toggle the Caps Lock key. The Linux operating system can use uppercase characters for file and directory names. For example, dirTM, is valid and is different from dirtm, which is also valid. The rule is if you use an uppercase when you create a file or directory, you must use an uppercase when using the file or directory. Also, most versions of Linux allow you to use most characters in a file name as long as you place double quotes around the file name. For example, the file name, "Payroll Data for June.dat" would be valid. Notice the use of spaces within the name itself. If double quotes surround the name, it should work. We'll discuss file name characters later.

Now let's navigate to the directory beneath dir2 named dir2a. Any directory beneath another directory is called a **subdirectory**, but they will simply be referred to as directories in this chapter. Figure 8.5 is a screenshot of the change to dir2a. Notice that the command prompt has changed to reflect the change.

Figure 8.5: A Screenshot Displaying the Results of the cd and pwd Command for dir2a

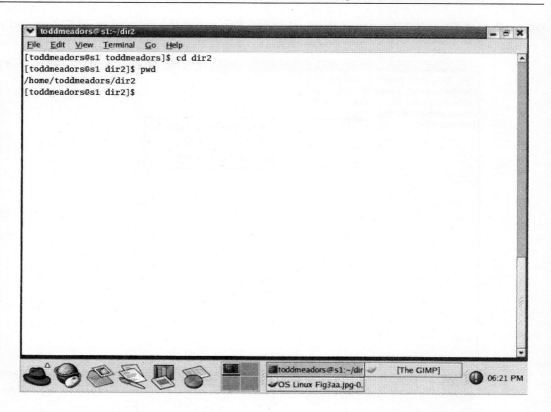

Now let's use the **ls** command to take a directory listing. By entering in just **ls** you will see any directories and files in the current directory. You can also use options with the **ls** command. Options modify the command in some way. For instance, the **ls –l** command performs a long listing. This gives you more information about the file or directory. This information will be discussed later. The **ls –a** command displays all files and directories. This includes files or directories that are classified as hidden. The **ls** command by itself won't show you hidden files or directories. We'll discuss creating hidden files and directories later too. You can combine options on some commands. For example, the **ls –la** command gives you a long listing of all files. Or, interchangeably, **ls –al** gives the same result. Figure 8.6 shows a screenshot of the **ls** command. The **ls, ls –a,** and **ls –al** commands are shown.

Figure 8.6: Results of the ls Command and Some of Its Options

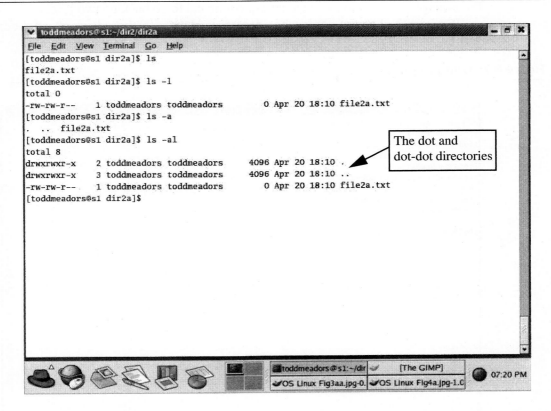

Referring back to Figure 8.1, the directories named dir2 and dir3 are children of root. Or said another way, root is their parent. A **parent directory** is the directory that holds a given file or directory. It is up one level in the hierarchy from the current directory. A **child directory** is a file or directory contained within its parent. It is down one level. The parent directory is represented by two dots, .., commonly called dot-dot. The current directory is represented by a single dot. Notice the dot and dot-dot displayed in Figure 8.6.

Let's use this knowledge of the parent and child relationship to change directory locations. If you wanted to change to the root directory, you could type the **cd /** command. If you want to change to your parent directory, you can type **cd ..** command.

Notice in Figure 8.1 that dir2a is a child of dir2 and dir2 is a child of the root directory. The root directory is a grandparent of dir2a. If you wanted to change to root from dir2a, you would issue either one **cd /** command or two **cd ..** commands. You might ask why would you change to the root directory with two commands instead of one? To change to root by name, you would issue the single command: **cd /**. However, to change to any parent directory, you would enter the **cd ..** command. To change to a parent directory going up one level, you must use two dots, or dot-dot. To change to a parent's parent (grandparent), you would enter **cd ..** twice. Or, you can combine levels on one command. For example, you could issue the **cd ../..** command to go back up two levels.

Figure 8.7 shows a screenshot demonstrating both the **cd ..** and **cd /** command variations.

Figure 8.7: Using the cd .. and cd / Commands

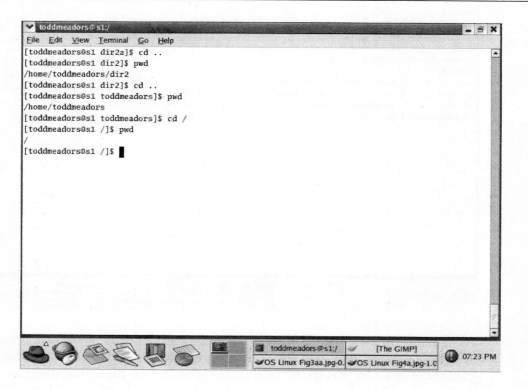

Each directory and file in the tree has a location called its **path**. There are two types of paths. There is a **full path**, sometimes called an absolute path, which identifies the directory or file location beginning from root. A command employing the full path always begins at root. There is a **partial path**, sometimes called the relative path, which identifies the directory or file location relative to your current location. A command employing the partial path depends upon your present location in the tree. Table 8.2 shows a few examples. Notice how each full path has the root symbol as the very first character. Also, each of these paths can be used with most any command.

Table 8.2: Examples of Full and Partial Paths

Path	Path Type
/	Full
/dir2	Full
/dir2/dir2a	Full
/dir3/file31.txt	Full
..	Partial
../..	Partial
dir2	Partial
../dir3	Partial

8.5 Creating and Removing Directories

In order to create a directory, you would use the **mkdir** command. For example, to create a directory named Payroll, you would enter **mkdir Payroll**. Notice that the directory Payroll is a partial path. You really don't know what parent directory it is located in. You can use the mkdir command with either the partial path or full path name of a directory. For example, you could enter **mkdir /Acct/General** to create a directory using a full path. Or, you could use a partial path, as in these examples: **mkdir ../dir5, mkdir dir6/dir6a/ dir6b.** or **mkdir dirTM**. You can also create multiple directories using one mkdir command. To create three directories in the current directory, you could enter **mkdir a b c**. They will be siblings.

Next, you need to understand how to remove directories. The command to remove a directory is **rmdir**. In order to remove a directory, it must be empty and your current directory location cannot be in the directory. Refer to Figure 8.2 from earlier in the chapter. You would enter the **rmdir dir3a** command. If you get an error indicating you cannot remove the directory, try doing a **pwd** command. If your current directory is the one you are trying to delete, then go to the parent, with the **cd ..** command. Retry the failed **rmdir** command and it should work.

Let's do an exercise to get you started. You may have telnet access to the computer. If so, get the necessary information from your instructor on how to telnet to the school's Linux computer. Because the login steps are the same for all the exercises and hands-on projects in this chapter (at the end), subsequent exercises and hands-on projects will use to step 1 of this exercise in this chapter. This step will be presented only once—in this exercise.

1. Based on your situation, choose the appropriate method to get to get to a login prompt.
   a) **Remote access using telnet:** Telnet to the computer that has Linux loaded. For example, if your computer's IP address is 160.100.100.1, then enter TELNET

160.100.100.1. If you know the name of the computer, then issue the name instead of the IP address. For example, if the computer's name is xxx.yyy.edu, then enter TELNET xxx.yyy.edu.

b) **Local access with Windows running Red Hat Linux:** On the taskbar located at the bottom of the screen, locate the **Terminal emulation program** by moving your cursor along the icons. A new window will open with a prompt.

3. Log in to your Linux computer and get to the command prompt. In order to make sure you are in your HOME directory, type **cd $HOME** and press Enter.

4. To create a directory, type **mkdir dira** and press Enter. The directory is created and your prompt returns.

5. Now we need to change directory locations to it. Type **cd dira** and press Enter. Your current directory changes to dira.

6. Let's make a directory within the directory named dira. Type **mkdir diraa** and press Enter. The directory is created and your prompt returns.

7. Type **cd diraa** and press Enter. Your current directory changes to dira.

8. In order to remove the directory, type **rmdir diraa** and press Enter. You receive an error message because you cannot remove your current directory.

9. In order to change to the parent directory, type **cd ..** and press Enter. Your prompt changes to your parent directory.

10. In order to display a listing of files, type **ls** and press Enter. The listing displays.

11. Type **rmdir diraa** again and press Enter. This time it works because you are at the parent directory.

12. Type **pwd** and press Enter. Your current directory displays.

13. Type **cd ..** and press Enter. Your prompt changes to your parent directory.

14. Refer to Figure 8.8 for a sample screenshot.

15. Close your window.

Figure 8.8: A Screenshot of the Previous Exercise

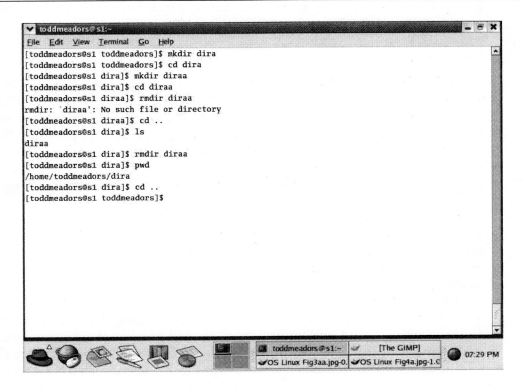

8.6 Managing Files

In this section, we will learn how to create, delete, modify, copy, and move files. There are several ways to create files. We are not concerned about all the methods, nor are we really concerned about the data within the files. We just need to have files created so we can manipulate them within the tree structure. Table 8.3 highlights a few ways to create a file.

Table 8.3: A Few Methods Used to Create a File

Command	Description	Example
echo	Displays text on the screen. Can be used to create a file.	echo "hi" > file1.txt
touch	Used to update the modification time of a file. It will create an empty file if the file does not exist.	touch pay4.dat
cat	Displays the contents of a file to the screen. Can be used to create a file.	cat > sales2.dat
vi	The most common text editor available on most Linux computers.	vi marketing.txt

You need to know that a file name in the Linux operating system is typically comprised of characters making up the name, followed by a dot, and then a three- character extension. The general format is as follows:

> *filename.ext*

Note *filename* is the name of the file, the dot is literally a period, and *ext* is the extension. For example, these file names are valid: **pay5.dat**, **file5.txt**, **Paychecks03.txt** and **Acct.doc**. The extension is not required and it can also be more than three characters. File names are case-sensitive. For example, **Pay5.dat** is not the same as **pay5.dat**. There are several characters that you generally don't use in a file name. They are: / \ > < * . | and space. The general rule of thumb is if you use the symbol elsewhere, don't use it for a character in a file name. If you stick to letters and numbers, you will be fine. Rules about file names also apply to directory names.

Let's explore the methods used to create files in greater detail. In order to create a file with the echo command, you would enter **echo "Text" > filename**. The echo command normally displays text to the screen. However, you can place a greater-than symbol after the text, followed by a file name and the echo command will put the text in the file name instead. We will discuss the use of the > symbol later in this chapter.

The touch command simply updates the modification time for an existing file. You would use the **ls –l** command to verify that the time has changed. However, if there is no file, the touch command creates a new empty file with an updated time. This command is quick for creating files when practicing because you usually don't care if it is empty.

The **cat** command is usually used for displaying the contents of a file. However, it can be used to create a file with some text in it. Let's try an exercise using the **cat** command. Follow these steps:

1. Log in to Linux and access the command prompt.
2. Go to your home directory.
3. In order to create a file using the cat command, type **cat > file2.txt** and press the **Enter** key. The cursor will move to the beginning of the next line. There will be no prompt on that line.
4. Type the following and press **Enter** after each line of text is typed. Note, if you make a mistake on a line and press Enter, you cannot change it using the **cat >** method. You would have to use **vi** to modify a previous line.

Working with Linux is fun!
I like ice cream - chocolate.
My birthday is in February.

5. Press **Ctrl + D** to send an End-of-File (EOF) character to the cat command. This is how you save the file.
6. In order to display the contents of the file using **cat**, type **cat file2.txt** and press Enter.
7. Close your window.
8. Refer to Figure 8.9 for a screenshot.

Figure 8.9: A Screenshot of the Previous Exercise

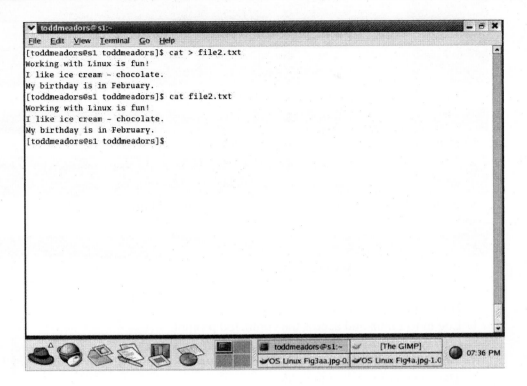

Most Linux computer systems come with the **vi** (VIsual) Editor. Although there are other editors around, and it is a bit tricky to use, you should become familiar with it because it's widely used. Not all versions of Linux use those other editors. So there's no guarantee that one editor specific to one version will be on another version of the operating system.

There are two modes of **vi**: **command mode** and **text mode**. In command mode you tell the **vi** editor what you want to do by issuing various commands. In text mode you actually type in the text you want to appear in the file. The **Escape** key is used to toggle back and forth between command mode and text mode. You must issue a command before you enter the text. Table 8.4 lists some of the more common **vi** commands.

Table 8.4: Common vi Commands

Command	Description
i	The vi editor will insert text at the current location of the cursor.
o	The vi editor will open a new line below the current line.

a	The vi editor will allow you to append text immediately after the current location of the cursor.
Shift + G	Move the cursor to the end of the file.
N followed by Shift + G	Move the cursor to the Nth line in the file. For example, 3 and Shift + G, takes you to the third line.
d followed by d	Delete the current line.
u	Undo the previous command.
y followed by y	Yank, or copy, one line into the **vi** buffer.
p	Put lines previously yanked from the **vi** buffer. Using yank and put is like copy and paste in MS Windows.
N followed by y and y	Yank, or copy, N lines into the **vi** buffer.
x	Delete one character.
:wq!	Write and quit **vi**.

Now you will use **vi** to create a file.
1. Log in to Linux and access the command prompt.
2. Change directory locations to your home directory.
3. Type in **vi file27.txt** and press **Enter**. The **vi** editor opens the file named file27.txt. The ~ symbol is called the tilde.
4. In order to insert text, press **Escape** and then **i**.
5. Enter the following text, pressing the **Enter** key at the end of each line:

   This is line 1.
   This is line 2.
   This is line 3.
   Last line of the file.

6. In order to save the file, press **Escape** followed by the colon symbol, **:**, and the cursor will move to the bottom of the screen with a colon to its left.
7. In order to write the file, press the **w**, then **q**, then **!**, and then press **Enter**. Your prompt returns.
8. Close your window.
9. Refer to Figure 8.10 for a screenshot.

Figure 8.10: A Screenshot of the Previous Exercise

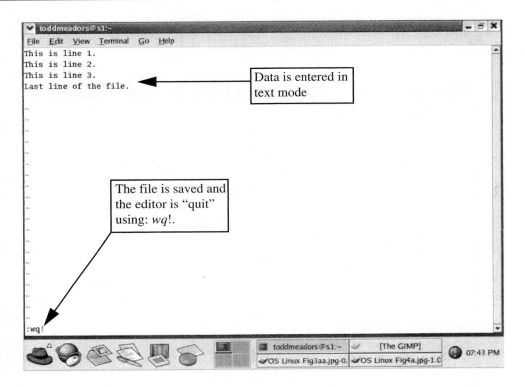

There are more hands-on projects using the **vi** editor in the Lab Projects section near the end of this chapter. Let's look at creating hidden files and directories.

You can create hidden files in the Linux operating system by preceding the file name with a dot. For example, the file named **.resume.txt** is considered a hidden file. In order to see a hidden file using the **ls** command, you must use the –a option. This shows all files including those starting with a dot. You can also create a hidden directory by simply placing a dot in front of the name when you create the directory using the **mkdir** command. Let's go through an exercise to create hidden files and directories.

1. Log in to Linux and access the command prompt.
2. Change directory locations to your home directory.
3. In order to create a hidden file, type **touch .salesreport.dat** and press Enter.
4. Type **ls** and press Enter. A listing displays.
5. Type **ls –a** and press Enter. A listing of all files and directories displays.
6. To create a hidden file using the **echo** command, type **echo "hello" > .secret.txt** and press Enter. The file is created and your prompt returns.
7. To create a hidden directory, type **mkdir .secretdir** and press Enter. The directory is created and your prompt returns.

8. Type **ls –a** and press Enter. A listing of all files and directories displays.
9. Close your window.
10. Refer to Figure 8.11 for a screenshot.

Figure 8.11: A Screenshot of the Previous Exercise

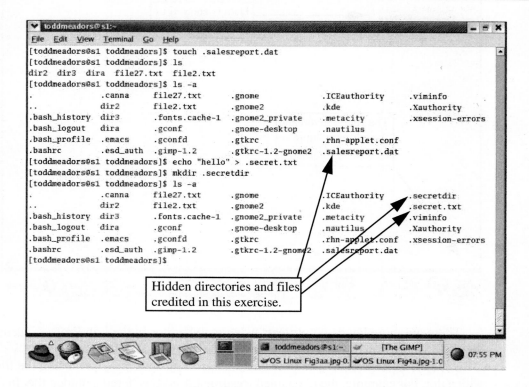

Now you will learn how to copy and move files. The Linux command to copy a file is **cp**, and the Linux command to move a file is **mv**. Use caution because these two commands are very different. The **cp** command will make a duplicate of an existing file. Two files will exist once the **cp** command completes. The move command will actually change to name of an existing file. Only one file will exist once the **mv** command completes. The **cp** command would be used to create a backup file whereas the mv command would be used to move a file from one directory to another or to rename a file.

If you wanted to copy a file named Sales.rpt to SalesBackup.rpt, you would enter **cp Sales.rpt SalesBackup.rpt** at the command prompt. In Figure 8.12, the first **ls** command shows the presence of Sales.rpt, but not SalesBackup.rpt. Then the **cp** command is executed. Finally, the **ls** command is executed again to show you that SalesBackup.rpt was created. Also, you notice that Sales.rpt is still present.

Figure 8.12: Using the cp Command to Make a Copy of a File

If you wanted to move or rename the file named Sales.rpt to MonthlySales.rpt, you would enter **mv Sales.rpt MonthlySales.rpt** at the command prompt. In Figure 8.13, the first **ls** command shows the presence of Sales.rpt, but not MonthlySales.rpt. Next, the **mv** command is executed. Finally, the **ls** command is executed again to show you that MonthlySales.rpt was created, but Sales.rpt is no longer present.

Figure 8.13: Using the mv Command to Move or Rename a File

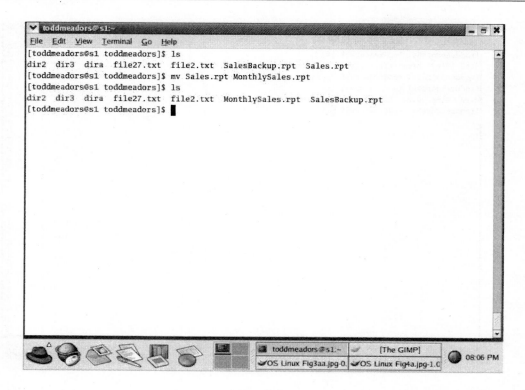

The **cp** and **mv** commands have two useful options. The **–i** (for interactive) option is used to prompt before you overwrite the destination file. The **–v** (for verbose) option will display a message indicating action taken. So, to copy, verify, and prompt before overwriting fileA.txt to fileB.txt, you would enter **cp –iv fileA.txt fileB.txt**. To move the file, enter **mv –iv fileA.txt fileB.txt**. You can use either option alone. For example, **cp –i fileA.txt fileB.txt** and **cp –v fileA.txt fileB.txt** would work as well.

Let's go through an exercise to copy and move files.

1. Log in to Linux and access the command prompt.
2. Change directory locations to your home directory.
3. Create a file named Pay1.rpt so you can copy and move it. Type either **touch Pay1.rpt** or **echo "data" > Pay1.rpt**. The file is created.
4. To copy the file to Pay2.rpt, type **cp Pay1.rpt Pay2.rpt** and press Enter. The file is copied and your prompt returns.
5. Run the **ls** command. The output displays.
6. To move or rename the file, type **mv Pay2.rpt PayOld.rpt** and press Enter. The file named Pay2.rpt will be renamed to PayOld.rpt and your prompt will return.
7. Run the **ls** command. The output displays.

8. To copy using the verbose and prompt options, type **cp –iv Pay1.rpt PayOld.rpt**. Because PayOld.rpt exists (from the are previous move), you are prompted whether you want to overwrite the file.

9. Enter **y** to overwrite.

10. Next, due to the verbose setting a line displays with an arrow point from Pay1.rpt to PayOld.rpt indicating the file was copied.

11. To move using the verbose and prompt options, type **mv –iv Pay1.rpt PayOld.rpt**. Because PayOld.rpt exists, you are prompted.

12. This time enter **n** so the file will not be overwritten. Your prompt returns and no message appears because you entered **n**.

13. Close your window.

14. Refer to Figure 8.14 for a screenshot.

Figure 8.14: A Screenshot of the Output of the cp and mv Commands

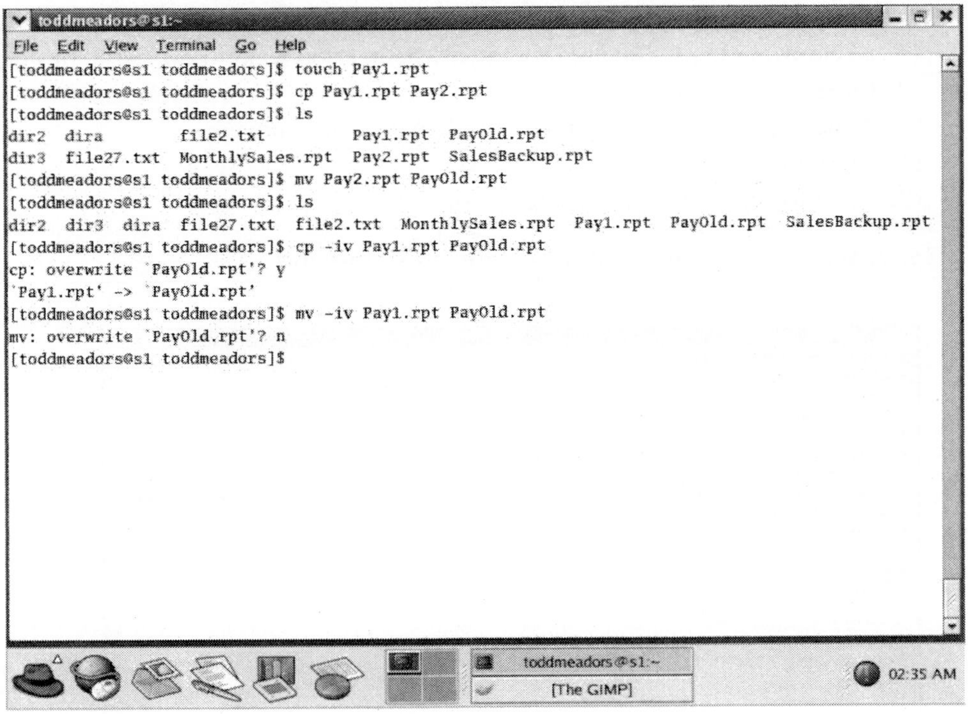

In order to remove a file, you use the **rm** command. For example, to remove the file named resume2.txt, you would enter **rm resume2.txt** and press Enter. On some versions of Linux, the **rm** command will go ahead and remove the file. On others, it will prompt you with an "Are you sure?" type message.

Use caution when executing the **rm** command. There is no way to get a removed file back.

Let's go through an exercise to remove a file.

1. Log in to Linux and access the command prompt.
2. Change directory locations to your home directory.
3. First you need to create a file so you can remove it. Create a file named Accounting2.rpt. Type **touch Accounting2.rpt**. The file is created.
4. Run the **ls** command. The listing shows files and directories including the one just created.
5. Type **rm Accounting2.rpt** and press Enter. The file is removed.
6. Run the **ls** command. It is not in the listing.
7. Create a new file to use. Type **touch Accountin3.rpt**.
8. To use the interactive and verbose options on the **rm** command, type **rm –iv Accounting3.rpt**. You are prompted whether you want to overwrite or not.
9. Enter **y** to remove.
10. A message displays indicating the file has been removed.
11. Close your window.
12. Refer to Figure 8.15 for a screenshot.

Figure 8.15: A Screenshot of the Output of the rm Command

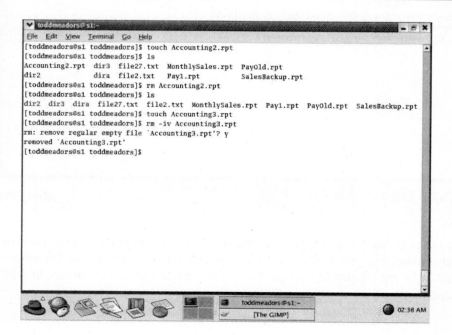

The "-l" option on the **ls** command displays additional information about a file or directory. Look at Figure 8.16 and you'll see additional information using the **ls –l** command.

Figure 8.16: A Screenshot of the Output of the ls –l Command

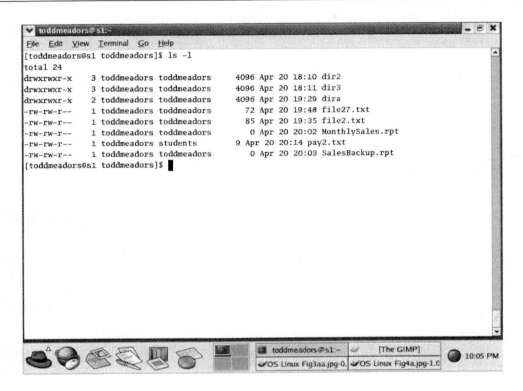

Each row of information deals with either a file or directory. Take a look at the file named pay2.txt. Its name is in the last column. The row for pay2.txt is as follows:

-rw- rw - r - - 1 toddmeadors students 9 Apr 20 20:14 pay2.txt

The first character is a dash. This means that pay2.txt is a file. A "d" in place of the dash would indicate a directory instead of a file. Next, you have "rw- rw- r - -." These are the file permissions. An "r" means you can read the contents of the file. A "w" means you can write to the file, and an "x" means the file is executable. If there is a dash, then the permission is not allowed. The permissions are taken in sets of three. The first set of three permissions is for the owner; the second set is for members of the group; and the last set of permissions is for everyone else, called the world. So, the owner has read and write but not execute (the first set: r w-), the members of the group have read and write (the middle set: r w -), and the world has read only (the last set: r - -).

The number after the permissions is the number of links, or shortcuts, to the file. In our case, there is only one. The name after the links is the owner of the file. In our case the owner is "toddmeadors." Next, you see the group member name as "students." This means that members of the group "students" have the middle set of permissions on the file. The number to the right of the group name is the file size in bytes. Next, you have the date and time, and finally you have the file name.

You can change permissions with the Linux **chmod** command. You can change permissions of a file you own. When a file is first created, it has certain default permissions. For the root user, the permissions are read and write for the owner and read for the group and others. For standard users, the default file permissions are read and write for the owner and group members, and only read for others. The **chmod** command uses numbers to set permissions. Table 8.5 shows the permission numbers for the different permissions along with their binary equivalent.

Table 8.5: Permission Numbers Used by the chmod Command

Permissions	Permission Number	Binary Equivalent
---	0	000
--x	1	001
-w-	2	010
-wx	3	011
r--	4	100
r-x	5	101
rw-	6	110
rwx	7	111

Here's how you use this table. Look for the permission you want to assign and then look to the right to find the appropriate number. The three permission columns represent a 4, 2, and 1 for read (r), write (w), and execute (x), respectively for the user owner, group, and other users. You add up the numbers for the permissions you want.

For example, if you want read only, you simply need 4 for the permission. If you want read and write, you would add 4 and 2 to get the number 6. If you want read, write, and execute, you add up 4, 2, and 1 to get the number 7. If you want read, write, and execute for the owner; read and execute for the group; and only read for all others for a file named SalesA.dat, you would enter **chmod 754 SalesA.dat**.

Let's go through an exercise to help you understand how this works.
1. Log in to Linux and access the command prompt.
2. Change directory locations to your home directory.
3. Type **echo "secret" > secure.dat**. The file is created.

4. Type **ls –l secure.dat**. A long listing appears.
5. Type **cat secure.dat**. The contents are displayed.
6. To remove all permissions and prevent the file from being changed, type **chmod 000 secure.dat**. The permissions change to no permission.
7. Type **ls –l secure.dat** to prove the permissions changed.
8. Attempt to open the file. Type **cat secure.dat**. A permission denied message appears because the **cat** command cannot read the contents of the file.
9. Type **chmod 740 secure.dat**. The permissions change to read, write, and execute for the owner; read for the group members; and no permissions for everyone else.
10. Type **ls –l secure.dat** to prove the permissions changed.
11. Attempt to open the file. Type **cat secure.dat**. This time you can.
12. Type **chmod 444 secure.dat**. The permissions change to read only for all.
13. Attempt to write to the file. Type **echo "data" > secure.dat**. You receive a permission denied message because you are attempting to write to the file.
14. Type **chmod 664 secure.dat** to set the permissions to the default of read and write for owner and group members, and read for all others.
15. Type **ls –l secure.dat** to prove the permissions changed.
16. Close your window.
17. Refer to Figure 8.17 for a sample screenshot of these steps.

Figure 8.17: A Screenshot of the Previous Exercise Using the chmod Command

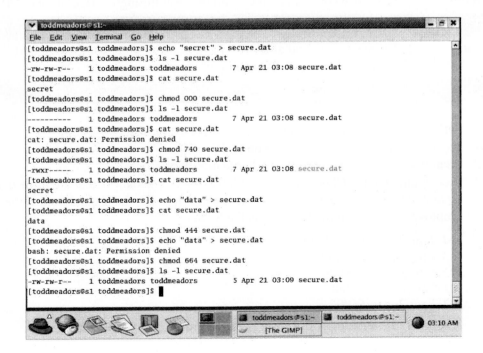

8.7 Learning about Additional Commands

Table 8.6 lists a few other commands with which you should become familiar.

Table 8.6: Additional Commands

Command	Description
awk	The **awk** command is a pattern scanning and processing language.
cal	The **cal** command is used to display a calendar.
cut	The **cut** command allows you to take text out of files. It is useful for extracting columns from a file.
date	The **date** command displays the current date and time.
df	The **df** command displays the amount of free disk space you have available.
diff	The **diff** command displays the differences between two files. This is useful for verifying the integrity of a file against a master file.
find	The **find** command allows you to search for files.
grep	The **grep** command allows you to search for text within files.
man	The **man** command displays help on a command.
more	The **more** command allows you to scroll through a page of text at a time.
passwd	The **passwd** command allows you to change your password.
sort	The **sort** command allows you to sort the contents of a file in both ascending field and descending field order.
who	The **who** command displays the list of current users on the system.

Let's go through an exercise using some of these commands.
1. Log in to Linux and access the command prompt.
2. Change directory locations to your home directory.
3. Create a file named Checks.txt, which holds employee data. There are three fields separated by a colon. The first field is the Employee ID, the second field is the Employee Name, and the last field is the Salary.

   104:Tina Brownlee:55000
   103:Roger Avery:45060
   105:Mary Davis:78000
   101:Sue Smith:45000
   102:Tom Jones:56000

4. In order to view the **man** pages for the **cut** command type **man cut**.

5. Review the **man** pages on **cut**. You can press the Spacebar to move down a page or press Enter to move down one line.

6. Press **q** (for quit) when finished.

7. In order to use the cut command to select the Employee Name column, you would type **cut –d: -f2 Checks.txt** and press Enter. The **–d:** option means to use the colon as the delimiter (separator). The **–f2** option means to cut field 2, or the Employee Name. The command displays all the names of the Employees.

8. In order to view the **man** pages for the **sort** command type **man sort**.

9. Review the **man** pages on **sort**.

10. Quit when finished.

11. In order to sort the data in ascending order, type **sort Checks.txt** and press Enter.

12. In order to sort the data in descending order, type **sort –r Checks.txt** and press Enter. In order to search for the name "Tom" in the file, type **grep Tom Checks.txt** and press Enter.

13. View **man** pages on **grep** if necessary.

14. In order to display users logged on the system, type **who** and press Enter.

15. In order to display the amount of free disk space, type **df** and press Enter.

16. In order to display the current system date and time, type **date** and press Enter.

17. In order to display the calendar for the current month, type **cal** and press Enter.

18. In order to display help about the **diff** command, type **man diff** and press Enter.

19. Review the **man** pages for **diff**.

20. Quit when finished.

21. The **awk** command is really a complete programming language, and fully discussing it is beyond the scope of this book. However, a few of its options will be discussed here. In order to use **awk** to display the fields in the Checks.txt file in different order, type **awk –F: '{print $2, $1, $3}' Checks.txt**. The –F option means to use the following character, which is the colon, as a field separator. Look back at the file and you'll see that a colon separates each field. The $1 equates to field 1, which is Employee ID, $2 equals field 2, which is the Employee Name and $3 is the Salary. So, in this case, the Employee Name is displayed first, followed by the Employee ID and then Salary.

22. View the **man** pages on **awk** if necessary.

23. To display just the Employee Name and Salary, type **awk –F: '{print $2, $3}' Checks.txt**. The Employee Name and Salary are displayed for each employee.

24. Close your window.

8.8 Learning about Pattern Matching (Wildcard Characters)

The Linux operating system allows for pattern matching of files. You use certain symbols to match characters following a certain pattern. Suppose you wanted to see all of the files that began with an uppercase S or all of the files that ended in .dat. How would you do this? Or, what if you wanted to see all files that began with either a lowercase t or an uppercase T?

The answer to these questions is pattern matching, sometimes called wildcarding. The operating system provides three pattern matching mechanisms:

- The asterisks symbol (*), which matches all characters.
- The question mark symbol (?), which matches a single character positions.
- The square brackets ([...]), which match one of several characters positions listed between the brackets. The dots in [...] represent characters.

Let's look at the asterisks symbol. You can use the * symbol to match all character positions. For example, if you wanted to display all files that begin with the letter m, then you would enter **ls m*** at the prompt. If you wanted to display all the files that had **dat** after the dot in the file name, then you would enter **ls *.dat**.

Let's take a look at the use of the question mark to wildcard a single character position. Suppose you wanted to display all files that had a 5 in the fourth character position, and you didn't care about the other characters. You would have to use the question mark. You would type the command **ls ???5*** at the command line prompt. You could not use the asterisks prior to the 5 in this case, because it would display all files with a 5 anywhere in the file name—not just in the fourth character position.

Let's look at the use of the square brackets as a wildcard technique. If you wanted to display all files that began with either an uppercase L or a lowercase l, you would need to use the square brackets. You would type **ls [Ll]*** in this case. If you wanted to display all files that began with either an S or an s followed by the letters pa, then you would enter **ls [Ss]pa*** at the command line prompt. An example of some of the files that would be displayed using this command are: Spanish, Spaniel, sparkle, sparkling, and spa.

Figure 8.18 shows a screenshot of the wildcard symbols in use. First the **ls** command displays the files. The second command, **ls t***, displays all files that begin with the letter t. The third command, **ls ?3***, displays all files with a 3 in the second position. The last command, **ls [Tt]***, displays all files that begin with a T or t.

Figure 8.18: A Screenshot of Using Wildcard Characters

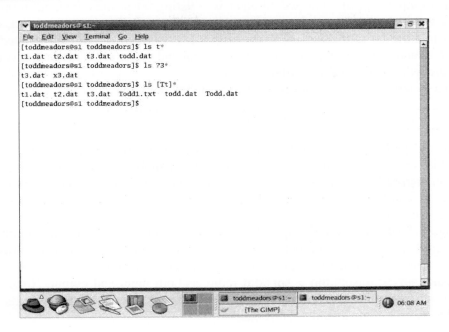

8.9 Learning about Redirection and Filtering

Let's look at the concept of redirection. These are the redirection symbols:

- A single less-than symbol (<) to redirect input.
- A single greater-than symbol (>) to redirect output.
- Two greater-than symbols (>>) to redirect and append output.

With redirection, you change the direction of the normal input and output locations for a file. When you run a command, the output normally displays on the screen. This is called **standard output** (or **stdout**). **Standard input** (or **stdin**) is the normal input that a command will get data from—which is the keyboard. With redirecting, you are indicating that you want to change standard output or standard input to be some other device, usually a file.

The general format of redirecting input is

> *command < filename.ext*

For example, the sort command will accept input from the command line. However, you can redirect input from a file by typing **sort < unsort.dat** at the command line prompt. This command will read input from the file named "unsort.dat" and display the sorted results on the screen.

Let's look at redirecting output. The general format of redirecting output is

> *command > filename.ext*

The standard output for the ls command is the display screen. If you wanted to redirect that output to a file, you would enter **ls > listing.txt** at the command prompt. The output would be redirected to a file named "listing.txt." When you redirect standard output to a file using the > symbol, the ***original contents of the file are deleted***. If you wanted to add standard output from another command to the same file name, you would issue the redirect and append output symbols, >>.

The general format of redirecting and appending output is

> *command >> filename.ext*

Now, if you wanted to display the output of the who command and append it to the same file, you would need to use two greater-than symbols. For example, the command **who >> listing.txt** means to append the list of current users to the file named "listing.txt." If you had issued **who > listing.txt**, you would have written over the listing of the ls command.

Figure 8.19 shows an example of redirecting input and output. The command **cat unsort.dat** displays the data before it is sorted. The next command **sort < unsort.dat** redirects input but notice the output is on the screen following the command. The next command **sort < unsort.dat > sort.dat** redirects both input and output. Notice that no output appears from this command. Finally, the command **cat unsort.dat** demonstrates that the original contents did not change.

Figure 8.19: A Screenshot of Redirecting Input and Output

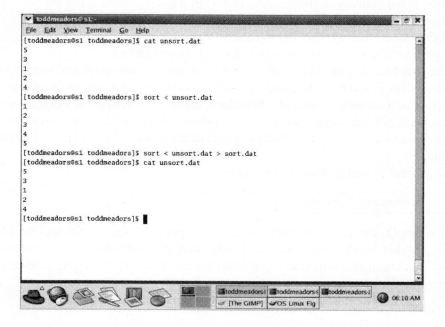

You can use filtering to modify the output of a command in some way. The filter symbol is the pipe symbol (|). It is the broken vertical bar on your keyboard but prints as a solid vertical bar. It is located on the same key as the backslash symbol. The general format of commands using the pipe symbol is

> *command1 | command2*

The command on the left side of the pipe symbol will have its output sent as input to the command on the right side of the pipe symbol. For example, the ls command displays files and directories, and the more command allows you to scroll through a page of data at a time. If the output of the ls command scrolled several pages, how would you be able to see all of the files and directories? The answer is to use the pipe symbol. The command **ls | more** will display a list of file and directories one page at a time.

If you wanted to sort the listing, you could enter **ls | sort**. If this command displayed too many lines, then you could enter **ls | sort | more** command instead. This will allow you to scroll through the sorted listing. You can have several pipes going on one command line. For example, you could have the following:

> *command1 | command2 | command3 | command4*

The way this works is that command1's output is pipe as input to command2. Then, that filtered output is piped to command3 and then the filtered output of command1, command2 and command3 is piped as input into command4.

Refer to Figure 8.20 for a sample screenshot of the pipe symbol in action. The command **ls | sort | more** displays a sorted directory listing and shows you a page at a time. Notice the text **---More---** at the bottom of the screen. If you press the Spacebar or the Enter key, you can scroll forward through the list of files and directories.

Figure 8.20: A Screenshot Displaying the Use of the Filtering (Pipe) Symbol

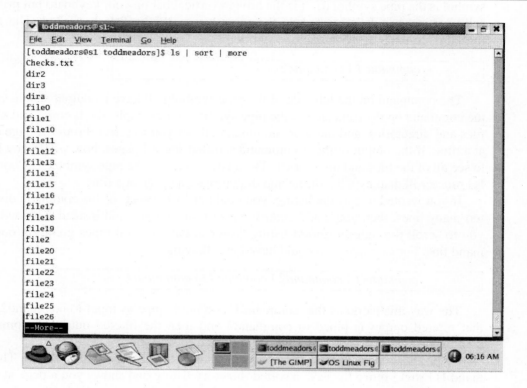

Just remember, redirection occurs to or from a file. Filtering (piping) occurs from one command to another command.

8.10 Learning to Write Shell Script Programs

The shell is the Linux program that interprets the command you enter on the command line. The default shell on Linux is called **bash** for Bourne-Again SHell. The bash program is like the DOS COMMAND.COM program. The bash program gives you your command prompt. A shell script program is similar to a DOS batch program. A **shell script** is a file containing Linux operating system commands and programming structures such as conditional processing and looping. Shell scripts execute their statements sequentially beginning from the first line in the file. We'll give you a general overview of the process here. Learning all aspects of shell script programming is beyond the scope of this book.

Let's learn shell scripts by performing an exercise. In this exercise, you will use operating system commands to create your own shell script.

1. Log in to Linux and access the command prompt.
2. Change directory locations to your home directory.
3. Open a file named **script1** using the **vi** editor.

4. Insert the following text. Note that the # sign is like the DOS REM statement and is used for a comment. Change *Your-Name* to your actual name. Make sure to save the file and quit the editor before executing it.

 # Author: *Your-Name*
 # Script Name: **$HOME/script1**
echo My first shell script:
pwd
who

5. To execute the shell script, type **bash script1** and press Enter. The script executes. With this command, you are giving the bash shell the name of your script called script1 and the script executes.

6. Let's create another shell script. Open a file named **script2** using the **vi** editor.

7. Insert the following:

 # Author: *Your-Name*
 # Script Name: **$HOME/script2**
echo Shell script to create a small tree structure:
mkdir scriptsA scriptsB scriptsC
touch scriptsA/fileA1.dat
touch scriptsB/fileB1.dat
touch scriptsC/fileC1.dat
touch scriptsC/fileC2.dat
tree –f $HOME/scripts*

8. To execute the script, type **bash script2** and press Enter.

9. For a challenge, create a script on your own that removes the directories and files created in **script2**.

10. Log out.

Chapter Summary

- The Linux file system is hierarchical (tree-like) in nature. The file system uses a directory to store files or other directories. A file cannot store another file or directory. The root directory (/), is the top level directory.
- The two basic categories of commands are file and directory commands.
- The **ls** command displays files and directories. The **cd** command changes directory locations. The **mkdir** command creates a directory. The **rmdir** command removes a directory.
- The **vi** editor is used to create a file. The **cp** command is used to copy or duplicate a file. The **mv** command is used to rename a file.
- You create a hidden file by placing a dot (period) as the first character in the file name.
- You can use wildcard characters to match on certain patterns. The * symbol matches all character positions. The **?** matches a single character position. The use of **[…]** matches one of several character positions.

- You can redirect standard output by using the > symbol. You can redirect and append output by using the >> symbols. You can redirect input by using the < symbol.
- You can filter command output by using the pipe symbol, which is | .
- You can write shell script programs to automate your operating system commands. Shell scripts allow you to combine commands with programming structures such as conditions and loops.

Review Questions

1. Which of the following is not a valid Linux command?
   a) cd
   b) mkdir
   c) md
   d) dir

2. Which of the following are full paths?
   a) ../..
   b) fun2/file2.txt
   c) /
   d) /sales/southern/regionA/sales.dat

3. You are working as a Technical Support Specialist. A customer named Consuela Gomez calls and asks you how to copy a file named /monthly/jan1.dat to her home directory. A pwd shows her current directory is /tmp. What command do you give Consuela to accomplish this goal?
   a) mv /monthly/jan1.dat $HOME/jan1.dat
   b) rm /monthly/jan1.dat
   c) move /monthly/jan1.dat $HOME/jan1.dat
   d) cp /monthly/jan1.dat $HOME/jan1.dat

4. What symbol is used to redirect and append output to a file?
   a) >
   b) >>
   c) |
   d) ?

5. You want to make a duplicate of a file named data3.dat. The new file is to be named data4.dat located in the same directory. What command will do this for you?
   a) copy data3.dat data4.dat
   b) cp data4.dat data3.dat
   c) cp data3.dat data4.dat
   d) mv data3.dat data4.dat

6. Which of the following will wildcard a single character position?
   a) ?
   b) *
   c) […]
   d) >

7. A customer calls while you are carrying the beeper for the weekend. She is having trouble accessing a file in a certain directory. She cannot recall the exact name of it but she knows it begins with a dot. She runs the **ls** command with no options and she cannot see the file. What command should you suggest to her in order for her to see the file name on the screen?
   a) ls –l
   b) ls –a
   c) ls *
   d) dir

8. Which of the following will redirect input?
   a) >
   b) >>
   c) *
   d) <

9. You want to change the name of a file named data3.dat. The new file is to be named data4.dat located in the same directory. What command will do this for you?
   a) copy data3.dat data4.dat
   b) cp data4.dat data3.dat
   c) cp data3.dat data4.dat
   d) mv data3.dat data4.dat

10. You want to remove the file named data3.dat and no other file. What command will do this for you?
   a) del data3.dat
   b) rm data3.dat
   c) rm data3.*
   d) rm *.*

11. Which of the following will create a directory named /Spooling?
   a) mkdir Spooling
   b) mkdir \Spooling
   c) md /Spooling
   d) mkdir /Spooling

12. Which of the following will write and quit a file in the vi editor?
    a) :W
    b) :Q
    c) :q
    d) :wq!

13. The name of the command that will display your current working directory is
    _____.
    a) mkdir
    b) cd
    c) pwd
    d) ls

14. Which of the following will allow you to display file permissions?
    a) ls
    b) ls –l
    c) ls –a
    d) pwd

15. You are working for a small consulting firm. A customer, George Patel, calls you and has a problem with the **ls** command. He wants to review the online help for this command. What command do you tell him to run?
    a) ls
    b) man ls
    c) ls *
    d) ls ???

16. Jessie wants to determine the names of the users currently logged onto the system. What command will do this for her?
    a) ls
    b) pwd
    c) who
    d) cd

17. Zac wants to display all the files that have a 0 for the fourth position and a 7 for the fifth position in their file name regardless of the characters in later positions. What command will accomplish this?
    a) ls *05?
    b) ls ?05*
    c) ls 4 and 5
    d) ls ???07*

18. Sue Weng wants to make sure that the permissions of a file are set as follows: owner has read and execute, the group has read, and the world has no access. Choose the correct answer that meets this requirement in the order as they would appear on the **ls –l** command.

    a) -r - - r x - r - -
    b) -r - - r - - r - x
    c) -r - - r - x r - -
    d) -r - x r - - - - -

19. What command will allow you to change to the root directory?

    a) cd \
    b) cd /
    c) cd ..
    d) cd .

20. What of the following would allow you to change to the parent directory?

    a) cd \
    b) cd /
    c) cd ..
    d) cd .

Lab Projects

Lab Project 1

In this lab project you will create the tree structure displayed in Figure 8.1. However, instead of building it starting in the root directory, we will build it starting from your own home directory, $HOME.

1. Log in to Linux and access the command prompt.

2. In order to change directory locations to your home directory, type **cd $HOME** and press Enter. Make sure you specify the HOME directory in uppercase and precede the text with a dollar sign, $. The dollar sign, $, refers to the contents of the variable named HOME. It's just the Linux syntax.

3. Type **mkdir Project1** and press Enter.

4. Record what this command accomplishes.

_____

5. Type **cd Project1** and press Enter.

6. Record what this command accomplishes.

_____

7. Type **mkdir dir2** and press Enter.

8. Type **mkdir dir3** and press Enter. **Note:** You could have typed **mkdir dir2 dir3** on the same line to create both directories. This would have replaced the previous two **mkdir** commands.

9. Type **cd dir2** and press Enter. Notice your prompt changes.

10. Type **pwd** and press Enter.

11. Record what the command accomplishes.

_____

12. Record the output of the **pwd** command.

_____

13. Type **mkdir dir2a** and press Enter.

14. Type **cd dir2a** and press Enter.

15. Type **pwd** and press Enter.

16. Record the output.

_____

17. Type **touch file2a.txt** and press Enter.

18. Type **cd ..** and press Enter.

19. Record what this command accomplishes.

_____

20. Type **pwd** and press Enter.
21. Record the output.

_____

22. Type **touch file2.txt** and press Enter.
23. Type **touch file22.txt** and press Enter.
24. Record another way you could have created file22.txt.

_____

25. Type **cd ..** and press Enter. This should take you to $HOME\Project1.
26. Type **pwd** and press Enter.
27. Record the output.

_____

28. Type **echo "hi" > file32.txt** and press Enter. This is another method to create a file.
29. Type **cp file32.txt fil33.txt** and press Enter.
30. Type **cp $HOME/Project1/dir2/dir2a/file2a.txt $HOME/Project1/dir3/file3a.txt** and press Enter.
31. Record the output.

_____

32. Log out of your account.

Lab Project 2

In this lab project you will review the commands given and then draw the tree based upon the commands.

1. Review the list of commands below. Pay careful attention to the order of the commands listed. Your instructor may allow you to enter the commands on the computer. If so, log in and run them.

   cd $HOME
   mkdir Project2
   cd Project2
   mkdir payroll
   mkdir general
   mkdir fun
   cd payroll
   mkdir paychecks
   mkdir payday
   cd payday
   touch pay1.dat
   cp pay1.dat pay2.dat
   cd ../../general
   echo "Hi" > gen1.dat
   cp gen1.dat gen2.dat
   cp gen2.dat $HOME/Project2/gen3.dat
   cd $HOME/Project2/payroll
   cp payday/pay1.dat paychecks/payC.dat
   cd $HOME

2. Draw the tree structure. You have been given a starting point, $HOME. The rest is up to you.

   $HOME
   | (Draw the tree here!)

Lab Project 3

In this lab project you will reinforce your understanding of the tree structure. As with Lab Project 2, you will review the commands given and then draw the tree based upon the commands.

1. Review the list of commands below. Pay careful attention to the order of the commands listed and the case (lower vs. upper) of the files and directories. Your instructor may allow you to enter the commands on the computer. If so, log in and run them.

   ```
   cd $HOME
   mkdir Project3
   cd Project3
   mkdir DirA
   mkdir DirB
   mkdir DirC
   mkdir DirA/DirAA
   mkdir DirA/DirAB
   mkdir DirA/DirAC
   mkdir DirB/DirBB
   cd DirA/DirAA
   mkdir Fun5
   cd Fun5
   mkdir MoreFun
   cd MoreFun
   touch fileT.dat
   touch fileM.dat
   cp MoreFun/*.dat $HOME/Project3/DirC
   touch $HOME/Project3/DirB/DirBB/Games.dat
   ls >> $HOME/listing.txt
   cd $HOME
   ```

2. Draw the tree structure. You have been given a starting point, $HOME. The rest is up to you.

   $HOME

   | (Draw the tree here!)

Lab Project 4

In this lab project you will review a tree structure and create it using Linux commands. Note that directories do not have an extension, but files do have an extension so use the appropriate command. Notice that checks.dat is hidden (initial character is a dot).

1. Log in to Linux and access the command prompt.

2. Type **cd $HOME** and press Enter.

3. Type **mkdir Project4** and press Enter.

4. Type **cd Project4** and press Enter.

5. Review and create the following tree structure.

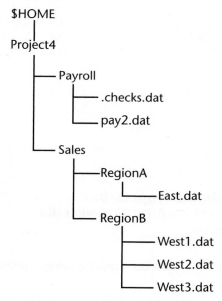

6. List the exact steps you took to create this tree.

Lab Project 5

In this lab project you will review a tree structure and create it using Linux commands. Note that directories do not have an extension, but files do have an extension so use the appropriate command.

1. Log in to Linux and access the command prompt.

2. Type **cd $HOME** and press Enter.

3. Type **mkdir Project5** and press Enter.

4. Type **cd Project5** and press Enter.

5. Review and create the following tree structure.

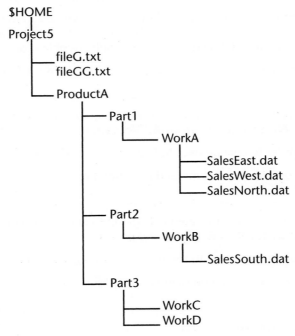

6. List the exact steps you took to create this tree.

Lab Project 6

The goal of this lab project is for you to be able to distinguish between navigating to a parent, a child, and a sibling directory. A sibling directory is defined as a directory that is on the same hierarchical level as another. You must complete Lab Project 4 before beginning this project.

1. Log in to Linux and access the command prompt.

2. Change directory locations to $HOME. Your prompt will reflect the change.

3. Type **cd Project4** and press Enter. (Yes, it is Project4!)

4. Type **cd Sales** and press Enter. Your prompt will reflect the change.

5. In order to change to a child directory, you must use the child directory's name. Type **cd RegionA** and press Enter. Your prompt will reflect the change.

6. In order to change to a sibling directory, type **cd ../RegionB** and press Enter. The format is cd ../*sibling-name* where *sibling-name* is the name of a sibling directory. In the tree structure in Project 4, RegionA and RegionB are sibling directories.

7. Record at least one other sibling relationship in the tree structure in Project 4.

_____

8. To copy West1.dat from RegionB to RegionA using the sibling concept, type **cp West1.dat ../RegionA/West1.dat** and press Enter. The file is copied.

9. In order to change back to RegionA, type **cd ../RegionA** and press Enter.

10. Record what this command accomplishes.

_____

11. To move East.dat located in RegionA to RegionB using the sibling concept, type **mv East.dat ../RegionB** and press Enter.

12. In order to change to the parent directory, type **cd ..** and press Enter.

13. Record what this command accomplishes.

_____

14. Log out of your account.

Lab Project 7

The goal of this lab project is to be able to utilize the vi editor to append, insert, yank, put, and delete text in a file.

1. Log in to Linux and access the command prompt.

2. Change directory locations to $HOME. Your prompt will reflect the change.

3. Type **mkdir Project7** and press Enter.

4. Type **cd Project7** and press Enter.

5. Type in **vi file27.txt** and press Enter. The tilde (~) symbol appears. The vi editor opens the file named file27.txt.

6. In order to insert text, press **Escape** and then the **i**.

7. Enter the following text and make sure you press the Enter key at the end of each line:

   This is the first line of the vi editor.
   This is the second line of the vi editor.
   Last line of the vi editor.

8. In order to save the file, press **Escape** followed by the colon symbol, **:**. The cursor moves to the bottom of the screen with a colon to its left.

9. In order to write the file, press the **w**, then **q,** then **!,** and then press Enter. Your prompt returns.

10. Do not close your terminal window because we'll use it in the next step.

11. In order to open the file again, type in **vi file27.txt** and press Enter. The vi editor opens file27.txt.

12. Now you will work with the yank and put commands to copy and paste text. In order to copy the first three lines and place them at the end of the file, move your cursor to the first character on the first line.

13. Next, press the number **3**, and then press the letter **y** twice. This will yank, or copy, the three lines and place them in the vi buffer.

14. Move your cursor to the end of the file by pressing **Shift + G**. The cursor moves to the first character on the last line.

15. Now you will paste the three previously yanked lines by pressing the letter **p**. This will place a copy of the three lines at the end of the file.

16. Now, let's delete the first two lines. Move the cursor to the first character on the first line by pressing the number **1** followed by **Shift + G**. Your cursor moves to the first character of the first line in the file.

17. Press the letter **d** twice to delete the first line of text.

18. Repeat the previous step to delete the second line of text. When this step is complete, the file will look like this:

Last line of the vi editor.
This is the first line of the vi editor.
This is the second line of the vi editor.
Last line of the vi editor.

19. Now you will change the word "Last" in the very first line to "First." Press **Escape**, followed by pressing the number **1** and then by **Shift + G**. Your cursor moves to the first character of the first line in the file.

20. To delete each letter in the word "Last," press **x**, to delete a single character, four times (one for each letter). The word is deleted.

21. To insert the word "First," press **i**, for insert. Type **First**. The word "First" appears.

22. To append a line of text at the end of the file, use the **a** command in vi. Press **Escape**, then press **Shift + G**. Your cursor moves to the first character of the last line in the file.

23. Press **Escape**, followed by **o** and then Enter. The cursor drops down to a blank line. Type **The End!** and press Enter. The completed file will appear as follows:

First line of the vi editor.
This is the first line of the vi editor.
This is the second line of the vi editor.
Last line of the vi editor.
The End!

24. Press **Escape**, followed by **:wq!** and then Enter. The file is saved and your prompt is returned.

25. Log out of your account.

Lab Project 8

The goal of this lab project is to create files and directories and identify the columns of the output of the **ls -l** command.

1. Log in to Linux and access the command prompt.

2. Change directory locations to $HOME. Your prompt will reflect the change.

3. Type **touch pay1.dat** and press the **Enter** key.

4. Repeat the previous step five additional times. Change the number within the file name each time. You should end up with six files you created.

5. Create four directories. You decide upon the names.

6. Issue a long listing of the directory. Type **ls –l** and press Enter.

7. On a separate piece of paper, label and identify each column. Refer to the man pages on the **ls** command if necessary.

8. Log out of your account.

Lab Project 9

The goal of this lab project is for you to be able to utilize the **sort** command to sort data in ascending (lower to higher) and descending (higher to lower) order.

1. Log in to Linux and access the command prompt.

2. Change directory locations to $HOME. Your prompt will reflect the change.

3. Type **mkdir Project9** and press Enter.

4. Type **cd Project9** and press Enter.

5. Type **vi inputfile.dat** and press Enter. The **vi** editor opens.

6. In order to insert text, press **Escape** and then the **i**.

7. Enter the following text and make sure you press the Enter key at the end of each line. Each row is considered a Part Record with the colon separating the fields. The first field is the Part Number. The second field is the Part Name, the third field is the Part Amount, and the last field is the Part Quantity.

   102A:Wrench:$12.00:56
   105T:Drill:$129.00:7
   103F:Saw:$55.00:18
   101A:Hammer:$35.00:24

8. In order to save the file, press **Escape** followed by the colon symbol, **:wq!** and press Enter. Your prompt will return.

9. Sort the data in ascending order. Type **sort inputfile.dat** and press Enter.

10. Record the output.

    _____

11. Sort the data in descending order. Type **sort –r inputfile.dat** and press Enter.

12. Record the output.

    _____

13. Sort the data in descending order and redirect the output to another file. Type **sort –r inputfile.dat > sorted_reverse.dat** and press Enter.

14. Sort the data in ascending order and redirect the output to another file.

15. Record the command you used.

    _____

16. Record the output of the command you executed in the previous step.

    _____

17. Log out.

Lab Project 10

The goal of this lab project is for you to be able to utilize the **cut** and **diff** commands to manipulate text in a file.

1. Log in to Linux and access the command prompt.

2. Change directory locations to $HOME. Your prompt will reflect the change.

3. Type **mkdir Project10** and press Enter.

4. Type **cd Project10** and press Enter.

5. Copy **inputfile.dat** from the Project9 directory to the Project10 directory.

6. Record the command you used.

   _____

7. To cut the first field, type **cut -d: -f1 inputfile.dat** and press Enter. The cut command does not remove the data from the file it simply displays the requested information on the screen.

8. Record the result.

   _____

9. To cut the second field, type **cut -d: -f2 inputfile.dat** and press Enter.

10. Record the result.

   _____

11. Cut the last field in the file and record the command you used.

12. Record the result.

   _____

13. To cut both the Product Name and Product Price, type **cut -d: -f2, f3 inputfile.dat** and press Enter.

14. Record the result.

   _____

15. To cut both the Product Name and Product Price and redirect the output to a file name **outfile.dat**, type **cut -d: -f2, f3 inputfile.dat > outfile.dat** and press Enter.

16. Record the result.

   _____

17. Cut the first and last fields of **inputfile.dat** and redirect the output to a new file named **outfile2**.

18. Record the command you used.

   _____

19. Record the result.

_____

20. Now, let's look at the **diff** command. First, you'll need to make a copy of the input file and add some additional records. To make a copy of inputfile.dat, type **cp inputfile.dat inputfile2.dat** and press Enter.

21. Open the file named inputfile2.dat and add three additional records.

22. To display the differences between the two files, type **diff inputfile.dat inputfile2.dat** and press **Enter**. Refer to the man pages on the **diff** command if necessary.

23. Record the output.

_____

24. Close the window.

25. Log out of your account.

Lab Project 11

The goal of this lab project is for you to be able to utilize the **grep** to search for data within a file and to use the **find** command to search for file names.

1. Log in to Linux and access the command prompt.

2. Change directory locations to $HOME. Your prompt will reflect the change.

3. Type **mkdir Project11** and press Enter.

4. Type **cd Project11** and press Enter.

5. Copy **inputfile.dat** from the Project9 directory to the Project11 directory.

6. Record the command you used.

   _____

7. In order to search for the record with the text "Drill" in the file named inputfile.dat, type **grep Drill inputfile.dat** and press Enter.

8. Record the output.

   _____

9. Issue the command to search for the record with the text "Saw" in the file named **inputfile.dat**.

10. Record the command.

   _____

11. Record the output.

   _____

12. If you type the text "Drill" using a lowercase "d," the **grep** command would not find a match. It is case-sensitive. However, you can use an option on the **grep** command to ignore the case. Type **grep –i drill inputfile.dat** and press Enter.

13. Record the output.

   _____

14. Issue the command to search for the text "saw" in the file named inputfile.dat.

15. Now let's look at the **find** command. In order to locate a file somewhere in the tree, you can issue the **find** command. To find the file named inputfile.dat, type **find inputfile.dat** and press Enter. The file name should be displayed.

16. The **find** command really comes in handy when you are in one directory and a file is in another part of the tree but you don't know where it is. Let's say you want to find a file, in this case inputfile.dat, that is somewhere in your home directory but you aren't sure where. You would type **find $HOME –name inputfile.dat** and press Enter. The file name should be displayed. The $HOME variable tells the **find** command to start the search in that directory. You could start the search from another directory. The "-name"

option tells the **find** command to look for the name that follows; in our example it would be **inputfile.dat**.

17. Create another file in the Project11 directory.

18. Record the name.

_____

19. Change to the parent directory.

20. Record the command used.

_____

21. Issue the **find** command to search for the location of the file you just created. Instead of using the $HOME variable, use the dot (.) for your current directory.

22. Record the command used.

_____

23. Log out of your account.

Lab Project 12

The goal of this lab project is for you to be able to utilize the redirection and pipe symbols.

1. Log in to Linux and access the command prompt.

2. Change directory locations to $HOME. Your prompt will reflect the change.

3. Type **mkdir Project12** and press Enter.

4. Type **cd Project12** and press Enter.

5. Create 10 files and five directories within the Project12 directory. You decide upon their names.

6. Record the name of the command you used to create one of the files.

   _____

7. Record just the name of the command you used to create one of the directories.

   _____

8. In order to redirect output, type **ls > listing.dat** and press Enter.

9. In order to redirect and append output, type **date >> listing.dat** and press Enter.

10. In order to redirect and append output again, type **who >> listing.dat** and press Enter.

11. Verify the contents of the file named listing.dat.

12. Record the command used.

   _____

13. In order to remove the contents of the file named listing.dat, type **echo > listing.dat** and press Enter.

14. Issue another command to redirect output.

15. Record the command used.

   _____

16. Issue another command to redirect and append output.

17. Record the command used.

   _____

18. To redirect input to a command, type **cat < listing.dat** and press **Enter**. In reality, you could leave off the less-than symbol. You don't redirect input that often, hence there are very few practical examples. You redirect output more often.

19. Issue another command to redirect input.

20. Record the command used.

   _____

21. To use the pipe symbol, type **ls | more**. The listing is displayed one screen at a time.

22. To use the pipe symbol again, type **who | more**. The list of current users is displayed one screen at a time.

23. Issue another command to redirect output.

24. Record the command used.

_____

25. Log out of your account.

Lab Project 13

The goal of this lab project is for you to be able to utilize wildcard symbols.

1. Log in to Linux and access the command prompt.

2. Change directory locations to $HOME. Your prompt will reflect the change.

3. Type **mkdir Project13** and press Enter.

4. Type **cd Project13** and press Enter.

5. Create the following 12 files within the Project13 directory using the **touch** command. These represent payroll files with the three-character month followed by the two-digit day of the month.

jan07.dat	**dec04.dat**	**jul04.dat**
jan02.dat	**dec21.txt**	**jun06.dat**
jan03.dat	**jul04.txt**	**jul13.txt**
jan04.txt	**feb07.dat**	**dec07.dat**

6. In order to display all files ending in .dat, type **ls *.dat** and press Enter.

7. Record the output.

   _____

8. Issue a command to display all files ending in .txt.

9. Record the command.

   _____

10. Record the output.

    _____

11. In order to display all files that begin with a j and end with .dat, type **ls j*.dat** and press Enter.

12. Record the output.

    _____

13. Issue a command to display all files that begin with a d and end in .dat.

14. Record the command.

    _____

15. Record the output.

    _____

16. In order to display all files for January, type **ls jan*** and press Enter.

17. Record the output.

    _____

18. Issue a command to display all files for July.

19. Record the command.

_____

20. Record the output.

_____

21. In order to display files for the fourth day of the month (a 0 in the fourth position and a 4 in the fifth position), type **ls ???04*.*** and press Enter.

    Note: ls ???04* would work too.

22. Record the output.

_____

23. Issue a command to display files for the seventh day of each month.

24. Record the command.

_____

25. Record the output.

_____

26. Log out of your account.

Lab Project 14

The goal of this lab project is to help reinforce your knowledge of the tree structure. Additionally, you will list the exact commands you used to create the tree structure.

Optionally, you will write a shell script of the commands you used, delete the existing tree structure and then run the shell script to recreate the tree structure. Because this is optional, ask your instructor before proceeding with this.

1. Log in to Linux and access the command prompt.

2. Change directory locations to $HOME. Your prompt will reflect the change.

3. Create a directory named **Project14** and change locations to it.

4. Create the tree structure shown in Figure 8.21.

5. List the exact steps used to create it.

6. **(Advanced Optional Step—ask your instructor before doing this step!)** Using the **vi** editor, create a shell script with the exact commands you listed in step 5. Make the script executable. Delete the existing tree structure you just created and run your script. The shell script should recreate the tree structure.

7. Log out of your account.

Figure 8.21: A Screenshot of the Tree Structure for Project 14

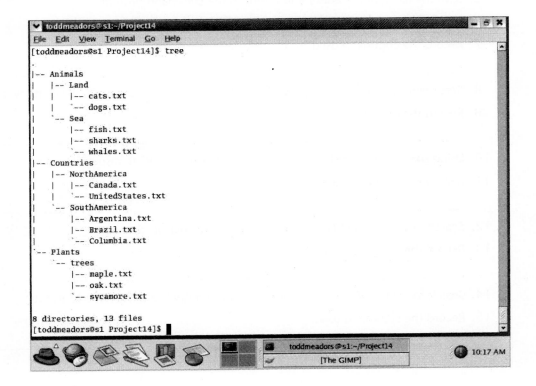

Lab Project 15

The goal of this lab project is to further your understanding of **sort**, **grep** and **awk** commands will be used.

1. Log in to Linux and access the command prompt.

2. Change directory locations to your home directory.

3. Create a directory named Project15 and change locations to it.

4. Create a file named Parts.txt, which holds part data. There are four fields separated by a colon. The first field is the Part ID, the second field is the Part Name, the third field is the Part Quantity on Hand and the last field is the Part Price.

   1009:Hammer:10:15.99
   1006:Saw:4:39.99
   1005:Tool Kit:3:99.99
   1004:Anvil:1:399.99
   1008:Pipe Wrench:50:5.49
   1002:Drill:14:12.49
   1001:Chain Saw:15:100.00
   1003:Box of Nails:40:4.99
   1000:Hack Saw:6:5.99
   1007:Box of Tacks:53:2.00

5. Save the file, quit the editor and return to the command prompt.

6. Sort the file in reverse order.

7. Record the command used.

   _____

8. Sort the file in reverse order and redirect the output to a file named PartsSortReverse.txt.

9. Record the command used.

   _____

10. Using **grep**, search for the Product Name of "Chain Saw" to display its data.

11. Record the command used.

    _____

12. Search for the Product Name of "Hammer" to display its data.

13. Record the command used.

    _____

14. Search for all the Saw records and redirect the output to a file named Saw.txt.

15. Record the command used.

    _____

16. Display just the second and last fields.

17. Record the command used.

   _____

18. Display just the Product ID and Product Name.

19. Record the command used.

   _____

20. Display just the Product Name, Product Quantity on Hand and Part Price and redirect the output to a file named PartsA.txt

21. Record the command used.

   _____

22. Type **grep Anvil parts.txt | awk –F: '{print $2, $4}'** and press Enter.

23. Record what this command does.

   _____

   _____

   _____

24. Type **grep Saw parts.txt | sort | awk –F: '{print $2, $4}'** and press Enter.

25. Record what this command does.

   _____

   _____

   _____

26. Type the following and press Enter when complete:

   grep Saw parts.txt | sort | awk –F: '{print $2, $4}' > SawsSortedNamePrice.txt

27. Record what this command does.

   _____

   _____

   _____

28. Close your window.

29. Logout.

Lab Project 16 Challenge

You have been hired by ZJ Industries to design its tree structure. The company has four departments: Accounting, Sales, Manufacturing, and IT (Information Technology). The Accounting Department has these three work groups: Accounts Receivable, Accounts Payable, and Payroll. The Sales department has regional offices located in the West, East, North, and South. The Manufacturing department runs three shifts. The IT department is currently working on three projects.

1. You need to design the Linux file system hierarchy on paper. Each department, work group, shift, region, and project will become directories. Keep the tree structure on the Linux file system just as you would have an organizational chart for the company. In other words, create a directory named East under Sales, not Accounting. The first part has been done for you to get you started.

$HOME
|

ZJ_Industries
|

2. You need to create this tree structure within the Linux system. Create at least one empty file in each directory. Use the department, work group, shift, region, or project name as the file name.

Lab Project 17 Challenge

1. Create a directory in your home directory named Project17.

2. Change to Project17.

3. Create a shell script that creates the tree you designed for ZJ Industries in Project 16 Challenge.

4. On a separate piece of paper, record your script.

5. Using one command, list all of the files and directories.

6. Log out.

Internet Discovery

Internet Discovery Lab 1

1. Go to a computer with Internet access. Open a web browser.

2. In the **Address** text box, type **http://www.redhat.com** and press the Enter key. The Red Hat web site appears.

3. In the **Search Red Hat:** text box, enter **find** and click **Go**. The screen displays a listing of the links to documents utilizing the **find** command.

4. Click one of the documents and review it.

5. Based on your findings, briefly discuss the **find** command in the space provided.

6. Repeat the search for the **ls** command.

7. In the space provided, discuss something new you've learned about this command by visiting this web site.

8. Browse the web site.

9. In the space provided, discuss something new you've learned by visiting this web site.

Internet Discovery Lab 2

1. Using your browser, search the Internet for any scripts using the **awk** command.

2. Identify at least three new features of the **awk** command.

3. Locate and record an **awk** script.

4. Close your browser.

Soft Skills: Help Desk Support

1. A customer calls you and is very upset. He used the **mv** command to move a file but he thought it would keep the original. The file has been moved but he wants a duplicate of the file instead. What do you tell him?

2. Explain to a customer how you would navigate to a sibling directory.

3. You receive a call in the middle of the night. A customer has deleted a file and wants to get it back. How do you proceed?

Critical Thinking

1. Compare the Linux file system to your family tree. Go back as far as your great-grandparents if you can.

2. Explain why you cannot issue the **cd ..** command at the root directory.

3. Compare and contrast the DOS and Linux file system hierarchy.

The "Hear" in "Hear, See, Do, Say"

Remember the key to learning are these four points: hear, see, do, say. This section focuses on hearing, or listening to your instructor.

- Listen, listen and listen again. Make sure you listen to your instructor at every class meeting to know what you must do for the day and week.
- Good listening habits include focusing on the instructor's lecture. If the instructor gives hand-outs, review them as the instructor reads over them.
- Although you should listen during every class session, listen very carefully the first week of class. The tone of the class is usually set during this first week and you don't want to miss anything.
- Pay attention to detail. If the instructor says do **NOT** begin a lab yet, then do not begin the lab yet—the instructor may have good reason. The lab project could entail formatting a disk or deleting a file that the instructor needed to see before you you're your data.
- Listening does include being attentive and asking questions when you don't understand. However do _not_ waste time over issues the instructor covered but you didn't get because you were not listening!
- Listening does _not_ include searching the Internet while the instructor is lecturing.
- Listening does _not_ include talking to fellow students while the instructor is lecturing.
- Listening does _not_ include asking questions over material you just heard!
- Listening does _not_ include being disruptive! Just because you are in a class that you might pay for, does not give you license to participate in disruptive behavior. This simply wastes time. Remember, you are only hurting yourself but more importantly, you are hurting fellow students. You could be interviewing for a job one day and the interviewer might be a fellow student—how would that job interview turn out?
- Finally, did we mention to listen? Listen and you will learn something!

Self-Study Question(s)
1. Did you hear your instructor's lecture today?
2. Identify at least two listening Study Skills you did this week.

9

Introduction to Networking

OBJECTIVES

The goal of this chapter is twofold:

- To introduce you to networking concepts.
- To help you prepare and pass the following sections of the A+ Operating System Technologies Exam:

A+ Operating System Technologies Exam Objectives
covered in this chapter (and corresponding page numbers)

Domain 4 Networks

4.1 Identify the networking capabilities of Windows. Given configuration parameters, configure the operating system to connect to a network.

4.2 Identify the basic Internet protocols and terminologies. Identify procedures for establishing Internet connectivity. In a given scenario, configure the operating system to connect to and use Internet resources.

In this chapter, you will complete the following sections:
- 9.1 Understanding Networking
- 9.2 Understanding Network Topologies
- 9.3 Understanding Network Cabling
- 9.4 Understanding Access Methods
- 9.5 Understanding Network Standards
- 9.6 Understanding the OSI Model
- 9.7 Understanding Network Protocols
- 9.8 Configuring Networking
- 9.9 Troubleshooting Networks
- 9.10 Configuring a Networked Printer
- 9.11 Understanding Dial-Up Networking (DUN)
- 9.12 Learning about Internet Software
- 9.13 Understanding Wireless Networks
- 9.14 Installing and Configuring a Wireless Network Card
- 9.15 Understanding Wireless Access Points
- 9.16 Troubleshooting Wireless Networks

9.1 Understanding Networking

A **network** is two or more devices that can communicate with one another and share resources. A network allows computer users to share files; communicate via e-mail; browse the Internet; share a printer, modem, or scanner; and access applications and files. Networks can be divided into two major categories—LANs and WANs. A **LAN** (**Local Area Network**) is a group of devices that can share resources in a single area, such as a room or a building. A **WAN** (**Wide Area Network**) is communication between LANs. The Internet is an example of a WAN as are two networks located in two cities.

Networks are vital to businesses today. They can even be found in many homes. You must have a basic understanding of the devices that make up networks (computers, printers, modems, etc.) and then learn network devices. You cannot bypass computer repair and go straight into networking.

Types of Local Area Networks

There are two basic types of LANs: a server-based network and a peer-to-peer network. With a **server-based network**, computer users log in to a main computer called a server where they are authenticated (authorized to use the network). The server is a more powerful computer than a normal workstation. The server contains information about who is allowed to connect to the network, and to what network resources (files, printer, and applications) the network user is allowed access. A **peer-to-peer network** does not have a central server. Instead, each computer is its own server. The computer user sets up passwords to allow others access to the resources. A user uses the network to access the remote files, printer, applications, and so forth, from their own workstation. Server-based networks are more common in businesses, whereas peer-to-peer networks are more common in homes and very small businesses. A server-based network can consist of 10 or more computers; in contrast, a peer-to-peer network usually has fewer than 10 computers.

A server-based network is more secure than a peer-to-peer network. This is because the server is normally located in a locked network room or wiring closet. Also, the network users and what they are allowed to do (their network rights and permissions) are configured and stored on the network server. Servers have a special operating system loaded on them called a **NOS** (**Network Operating System**). Examples of network operating systems are Novell's NetWare, Microsoft's NT Server, 2000 Server, and 2003 Server. A network operating system has utilities that allow computer user management (who is allowed onto the network), resource management (what network applications, files, printers, etc. a user can use), and security management (what a user is allowed to do with a resource, such as read, write, read and write, etc.). One userid and password is all a remote user needs to access many network resources located throughout the business organization. A network user can sit down at any computer in the organization, log on to the server, and start working with the network resources.

Figure 9.1 shows how a server-based network can be configured. The network has one server in the center, four workstations, and two laser printers labeled LP1 and LP2. The server has a database of users, CSchmidt, RDevoid, and MElkins, and their associated passwords. The server also has three applications loaded—Microsoft Excel, Microsoft Project, and Microsoft Word. These applications and associated documents are stored on the server. Whether or not the users can access these applications and documents and what they can do within each document is also stored on the server. In the Permission column of the table located in Figure 9.1 is either R for Read or R/W for Read/Write. This is an indication of what the user can do in a particular application. For example, user CSchmidt has read and write access to Excel, Project, and Word. User MElkins can only read Excel and Word documents, but she can read and write Microsoft Project documents. User CSchmidt can print to either of the laser printers, but user RDevoid prints only to the LP1 laser printer.

Another benefit of server-based networks is that a user can sit down at any workstation, log in to the server with his or her userid and password, and have access to all of the network resources. For example in Figure 9.1, computer user RDevoid can sit down at any workstation and have access to her Excel and Word documents and print to laser printer LP1.

Figure 9.1: A Server-Based Network

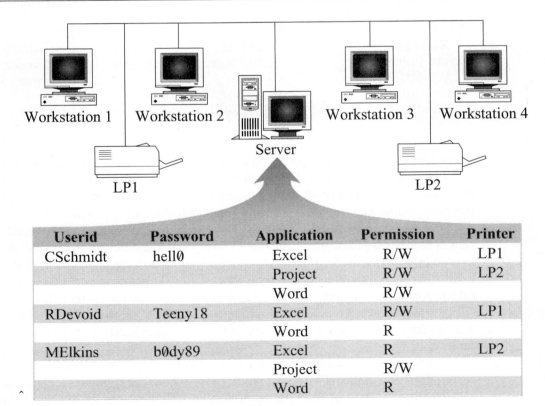

Userid	Password	Application	Permission	Printer
CSchmidt	hell0	Excel	R/W	LP1
		Project	R/W	LP2
		Word	R/W	
RDevoid	Teeny18	Excel	R/W	LP1
		Word	R	
MElkins	b0dy89	Excel	R	LP2
		Project	R/W	
		Word	R	

A peer-to-peer network is not as expensive, nor as secure as a server-based network. A server is more expensive than a regular workstation plus it requires a network operating system. Since peer-to-peer networks do not use a dedicated server, costs are reduced. Instead of a network operating system, each workstation uses a regular operating system such as Windows 95, 98, NT Workstation, 2000 Professional, or XP. A peer-to-peer network is not as secure as a server-based network because each computer must be configured with individual userids and passwords. Figure 9.2 shows how a peer-to-peer network is configured.

Figure 9.2: A Peer-to-Peer Network

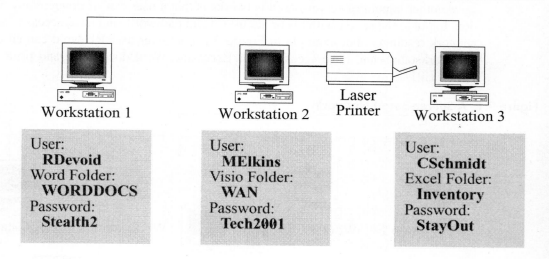

In Figure 9.2, there are three workstations labeled Workstation 1, 2, and 3. Workstation 2 has a shared printer. A shared printer is a printer connected to the computer that has been configured so that other network users can print to it. There are three people in this company, Raina Devoid, Cheryl Schmidt, and Melodie Elkins. Raina Devoid normally works at Workstation 1 and Raina has shared a folder on the hard drive called WORDDOCS that has a password of Stealth2. Cheryl and Melodie can access the documents located in WORDDOCS from their own workstations as long as they know the password is Stealth2. If Raina (who is sitting at Workstation 1) wants to access Melodie's WAN folder, Raina must know and remember that the password is Tech2001. If Melodie changes the password on the WAN folder, Melodie must remember to tell the new password to anyone who needs access. The password is only used when accessing the WAN folder documents.

A peer-to-peer network password is only effective across the network. The password is not effective if someone sits down at the workstation. For example, if a summer intern, Ken Tinker, sits down at Workstation 3, Ken has full access to the Inventory folder and documents. Even though the folder is passworded for the peer-to-peer network, Ken is not using the network to access the folder so the password is useless.

Management of network resources is much harder to control on a peer-to-peer network than on a server-based network. Each user is required to manage the network resources on one computer and password management can become a nightmare. Remember with peer-to-peer networks, anyone who has the password can access the folder across the network. Server-based networks are normally more secure because (1) passwords are managed centrally at the server and (2) the server is normally locked in a wiring closet.

The problem of having access to a workstation and all its resources simply by sitting down at a computer is not as much of a threat today because of the newer operating systems' features. NT Workstation and 2000 Professional cannot be accessed without a userid and password.

In order to have a network, the following are required: network adapters (NICs), network cabling, and an operating system with network options enabled. The following sections explore these concepts.

9.2 Understanding Network Topologies

Network topology is how network devices connect together. The three major types of network topologies are star, ring, and bus. Keep in mind that a large business may have combinations of these topologies. A topology that combines other topologies is known as a hybrid topology.

The most common network topology used today is the **star topology** because it is used with Ethernet networks. Each network device connects to a central device, normally a hub or a switch. Both the **hub** and the **switch** contain two or more RJ-45 network jacks. The hub is not as intelligent as a switch. The switch takes a look at each data frame as it comes through the frame. The hub is not able to do this. Figure 9.3 illustrates a hub or switch.

Figure 9.3: A Hub/Switch

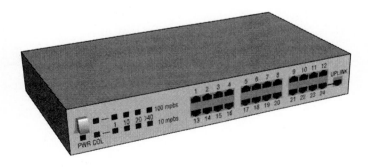

In a star topology, each network device has a cable that connects between the device and the hub or switch. If one computer or cable fails, all other devices continue to function. However, if the hub or switch fails, the network goes down. The hub or switch is normally located in a central location such as a network wiring closet. Figure 9.4 shows how a star topology is cabled. By looking at how each device connects to a central location, you can easily see why it is called a star.

What is the difference between a hub and a switch? Bottom line: A switch is faster than a hub! A switch is considered a "smart" device because it "learns" what computers are attached to it and forward data packets to the correct port on the switch. (A **port** is a receptacle on a hub or switch where one end of a network cable connects; the other end connects to your computer's network card.)

A hub on the other hand does not "learn" where the computers are. It simply checks each port to determine if the data packet should be sent to the computer attached to it. A switch may sometimes take longer to become operable after it boots because it is learning what ports contain what computers. However, after it is up, it is faster than a hub for network operations. Memory tip: "S" for Switch, "S" for "Smart" and "S" for "Speed."

More cable is used in wiring a star topology than with the bus topology, but the type of cable used is cheap and this is not an issue for today's network managers. Star topologies are easy to troubleshoot. If one network device goes down, the problem is in the device, cable, or port on the hub/switch. If a group of network devices go down, the problem is most likely in the device that connects them together (hub or switch). Look at Figure 9.4. If Workstation 1, Workstation 2, Workstation 3, Workstation 4, and Workstation 5 cannot communicate with one another, the problem is the switch in the middle. If only Workstation 3 cannot communicate with the other network devices, the problem is in Workstation 3, the cable that connects Workstation 3, or in port 13 on the switch.

Figure 9.4: A Star Topology

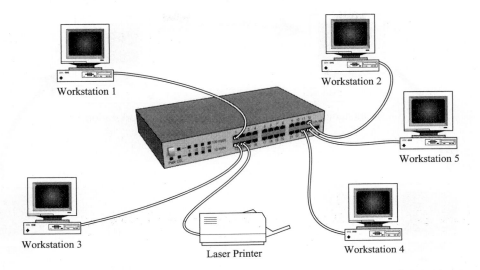

Workstation 1
Workstation 2
Workstation 5
Workstation 3
Laser Printer
Workstation 4

The **ring topology** is physically wired like a star, but operates differently. The ring topology is used in Token Ring networks. A token (a special network packet) passes from one network device to the next in a continuous fashion. Token Ring networks are wired like a star, but they operate like a logical ring. Figure 9.5 shows how the Token Ring network appears to be a ring.

The token passes from one workstation to another in a continuous loop. When the token does not contain data, it is known as a free token. As the free token is passed around the ring, any workstation wishing to transmit data takes the token and adds data. The data is sent around the ring until it reaches its destination. No other workstation can accept the data except for the destination network device. Once the data has been transmitted, a free token is placed on the ring again. No workstation can transmit until the free token comes back around the ring.

Figure 9.5: A Ring Topology

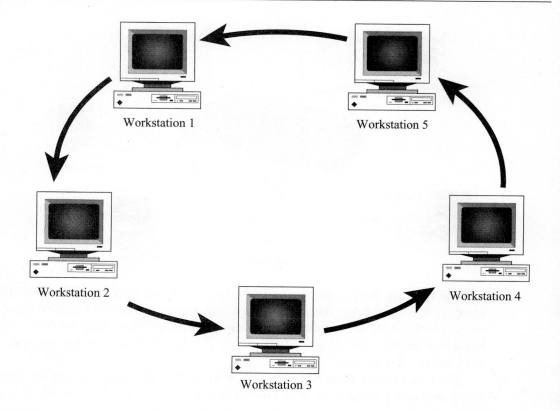

Workstation 1

Workstation 5

Workstation 2

Workstation 4

Workstation 3

Think of a Token Ring topology like an Olympic relay race. In the relay race, several racers pass a baton, or "token," to the next racer down the line. This racer in turn races to the next racer and gives the "token" to that racer. This continues until the race is won. Token ring topologies operate similarly with a token being passed to each computer. The computer wiith the token is the one that can "talk" on the network. IBM developed Token Ring networks.

The **bus topology** is one of the oldest network topologies. All network devices connect to a single cable. If the cable has a break, the entire network is down. Bus topologies are also difficult to troubleshoot when there is a network problem. Figure 9.6 depicts a bus topology.

Figure 9.6: A Bus Topology

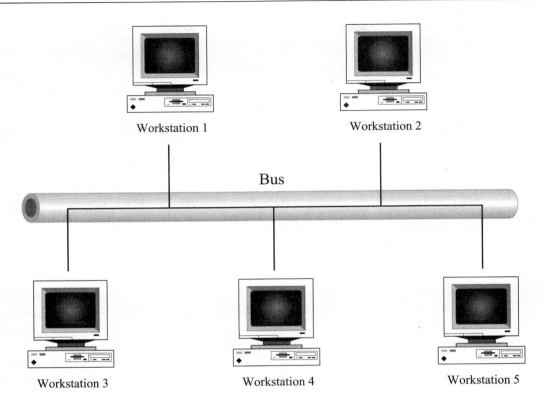

A mesh topology is not as common as other topologies, but it is used when all network devices connect to each other. Mesh topology is more likely to be used in a WAN (Wide Area Network) rather than a LAN (Local Area Network). Mesh topologies take a lot of cabling, but if a cable breaks, the network still continues to function.

An example of a mesh topology is a college that has three main campuses—North, South, and West. Each campus has a connection to the other two campuses. For example, the North campus has a connection to the South and the West campuses. Each campus has important servers to which the other campuses need access. If the North campus to South campus connection breaks, the North campus can still reach the South campus by going through the West campus. Whenever a network can still function after a cable break, the network is said to be fault tolerant. A mesh topology provides the most fault tolerance of any network topology. Table 9.1 summarizes network topologies.

Table 9.1: A Comparison of Network Topologies

Topology	Advantage	Disadvantage
Bus	Takes less cable (cheaper)	If a break in the bus, network is down
Mesh	If a break in the cable, network still works (fault tolerant)	Expensive and complex (hard to reconfigure)
Ring	Easy to install	Expensive parts
Star	Easy to install; most common; if a break in workstation cable, network still works (fault tolerant)	More expensive than bus

9.3 Understanding Network Cabling

Networks require some type of medium to transmit data. This medium is normally some type of cable or air (when using wireless networking). The most common types of cable are twisted-pair and fiber-optic, although some very old networks have coax cable.

Twisted-pair cable comes in two types: shielded and unshielded. The acronyms used with this type of cable are **STP** for shielded twisted-pair and **UTP** for unshielded twisted pair. The most common is UTP. With twisted-pair cable, all network devices connect to one central location such as a patch panel, hub, or switch. If one cable breaks, only the one device fails. Most people are familiar with twisted-pair cable because this type of cable is used in homes for telephone wiring. The type used with networking has eight copper wires. The wires are grouped in colored pairs. Each pair is twisted together to prevent crosstalk. **Crosstalk** occurs when a signal on one wire interferes with the signal on an adjacent wire. The wires are wrapped in a vinyl insulator. Figure 9.7 shows unshielded twisted-pair cable.

UTP cabling is measured in gauges. The most common measurements for UTP cabling are 22,- 24-, or 26-gauge unshielded twisted-pair cables. UTP cables come in different specifications called categories. The most common are categories 3, 4, and 5. People usually shorten the name Category 3 to CAT 3, or Category 5 to CAT 5. The categories determine, in part, how fast the network can run. Category 3 was mainly installed for telephone systems in many office buildings. CAT 3 is called a voice grade cable, but it has the ability to run up to 10 Mbps Ethernet or 16 Mbps Token Ring topologies. Networks that run 10 Mbps are known as 10BaseT networks. 100 Mbps Ethernet networks are known as Fast Ethernet, 100BaseT4, and 100BaseT8. The 100BaseT4 networks use two pairs (four wires) of the UTP cable whereas the 100BaseT8 networks use all four pairs (8 wires). The most common type of UTP is CAT 5. Fairly new categories of UTP cable include CAT 5e, which is designed for 100 Mbps on UTP and STP; CAT 6, which is designed for 1000 Mbps on UTP and STP; and CAT 7, which is designed for 1000 Mbps on UTP, STP, and fiber. UTP and STP cable are used in star and ring topologies.

Figure 9.7: UTP Cabling

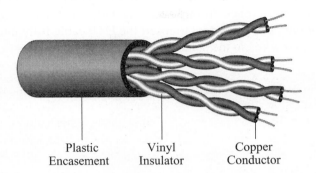

Plastic Encasement   Vinyl Insulator   Copper Conductor

In order to avoid extra troubleshooting time, most businesses install their network cabling according to the ANSI/TIA/EIA-568-A or 568-B standard. This standard specifies how far the cable can extend, how to label it, what type of jack to use, and so forth. Figure 9.8 illustrates the common cabling standards used in industry.

Figure 9.8: UTP Wiring Standards

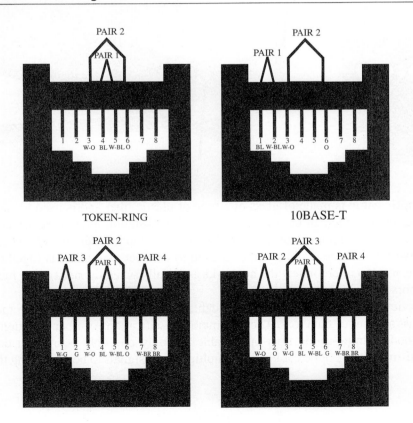

STP (**Shielded Twisted-Pair**) cable has extra foil shielding that provides more shielding. Shielded twisted-pair cable is used in industrial settings where extra shielding is needed to prevent outside interference from interfering with the data on the cable. When installing network cabling, it is important to insert the UTP cable fully into the RJ-45 jack and to insert the colored wires in the standardized order.

One common mistake that you might make when putting an RJ-45 connector on UTP cable is they put the cable into the RJ-45 connector backwards. Figure 9.9 shows the location of pin 1 and pin 8 on an RJ-45 connector. Another common mistake is not pushing the wires to the end of the RJ-45 connector. Before crimping the wires into the connector, look at the end of the RJ-45 connector. You should see each wire jammed against the end of the RJ-45 connector.

Figure 9.9: RJ-45 Pin 1 and Pin 8 Assignments

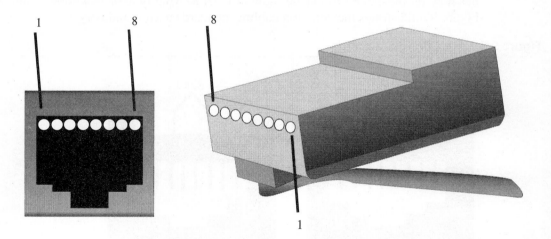

Fiber-optic cable is made of glass or a type of plastic fiber and is used to carry light pulses. Fiber-optic cable can be used to connect a workstation to another device, but in industry, the most common use of fiber-optic cable is to connect networks together forming the network backbone. Copper cable is used to connect workstations together. Then fiber cable is used to interconnect the networks especially when the network is located on multiple floors or multiple buildings.

Fiber-optic cable is the most expensive cable type, but it also handles the most data with the least amount of data loss. The two major classifications of fiber are single-mode and multi-mode. **Single-mode** fiber-optic cable has only one light beam sent down the cable. **Multi-mode** fiber-optic cable allows multiple light signals to be sent along the same cable. Multi-mode fiber is cheaper than single-mode fiber and is good for shorter distance applications. But, single-mode fiber can transmit a signal farther than multi-mode.

Fiber-optic cabling has many advantages including security, long distance transmission, and bandwidth. Fiber-optic cabling is used by many government agencies because of the high security it offers. Light signals that travel down fiber are impossible to detect remotely, unlike signals from other cable media. Also, because light is used instead of electrical signals, fiber-optic cable is not susceptible to interference from EMI or RFI-producing devices.

Each fiber-optic cable can carry signals in one direction, so an installation normally has two strands of fiber-optic cable in separate jackets. Fiber is used in the ring and star topologies. Figure 9.10 shows a fiber-optic cable.

Figure 9.10: Fiber-Optic Cable

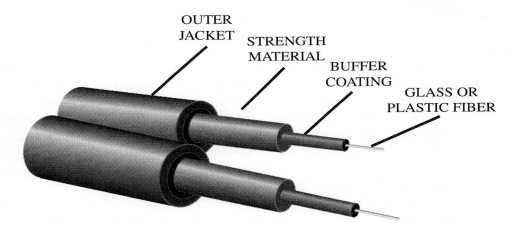

The last type of cable is **coaxial cable** (usually shortened to **coax**). Coax cable is used in older Ethernet 10Base2 and 10Base5 networks as well as mainframe and minicomputer connections. Most people have seen coax cable in their homes. The cable used for cable TV is coax cable, but is a different type than network cabling. Coax cable has a center copper conductor surrounded by insulation. Outside the insulation is a shield of copper braid, a metallic foil, or both, that protects the center conductor from EMI. Figure 9.11 shows a coax cable. Coax is used in star and bus topologies.

Figure 9.11: Coax Cable

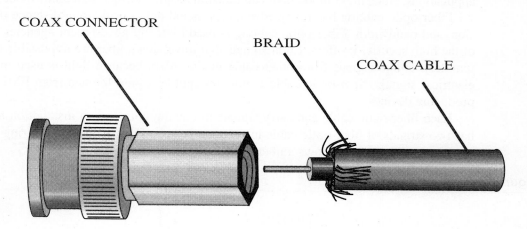

9.4 Understanding Access Methods

Before a computer can communicate on a network it must adhere to a set of communication rules to which all computers on the network comply. This set of communication rules is known as a **common access method**. Ethernet uses a common access method known as **CSMA/CD** (Carrier Sense Multiple Access/Collision Detect), whereas fiber networks and Token Ring use **token passing** as the common access method. Wireless networks and Apple networks use **CSMA/CA** (Carrier Sense Multiple Access/Collision Avoidance). The purpose of the common access method is to ensure that each workstation has an opportunity to communicate with the other workstations.

With CSMA/CD, each workstation can place data onto the network cable at any time, but the network adapter checks the network cable to ensure that no other workstation is already transmitting. In the acronym CSMA/CD, the CS stands for "Carrier Sense," which means that it is checking the network cable for other traffic. "Multiple Access" means that multiple computers can access the network cable simultaneously. "Collision Detect" provides rules for what happens when two computers access the network at the same time. One point to remember is that collisions are common and normal on Ethernet networks.

Take an example of a busy highway. The highway represents the network cable and cars on the highway represent data traveling down the cable. Each intersection that crosses the highway is simply a computer wanting to connect onto the major highway. Using CSMA/CD, the workstation checks that no other traffic is traveling down the highway (cable). If the way is clear, data is allowed to go onto the highway. If two workstations happen to transmit at the same time, a collision occurs. Both workstations have to stop transmitting data for a specified amount of time and then try transmitting again.

A Token Ring adapter uses token passing as the common access method. This method differs from CSMA/CD because there are no collisions in the Token Ring environment. With token passing, a **token** (a small packet of data) is passed from one workstation to another. Only the workstation that possesses the token is allowed to transmit data. The token is passed around the ring from one workstation to another with each workstation receiving a turn. When a workstation wants to transmit, it changes one bit inside the token data frame, adds data, and then places the data frame onto the cable. If a workstation does not want to transmit any data, the token is passed to the next workstation.

CSMA/CA is used with wireless LANs and Apple networks. Network devices listen on the cable for conflicting traffic just like CSMA/CD; however, with CSMA/CA, a workstation that wants to transmit data sends a jam signal onto the cable. The workstation then waits a small amount of time for all other workstations to hear the jam signal and then the workstation begins transmission. If a collision occurs, the workstation does the same thing as CSMA/CD—the workstation stops transmitting, waits a designated amount of time, and then retransmits.

Ethernet Issues and Concepts

Since Ethernet is the most common type of network, more time needs to be spent on some issues that deal directly with Ethernet. Some of these issues are full duplex and half duplex transmissions, network slowdowns, and increasing bandwidth.

Ethernet networks were originally designed to support either half duplex or full duplex data transmissions. **Half duplex** transmission is data transmitted in both directions on a cable, but not at the same time. Only one network device can transmit at a time. One example of half duplex transmission is using a walkie-talkie. **Full duplex** transmission is data transmitted in both directions on a cable simultaneously. This is similar to a phone conversation. Both people can talk at the same time if they want to do so. Ethernet networks were originally designed for half duplex transmission. Ethernet was also designed for a 10 Mbps bus topology and still performs as if it is connected in a bus network. Due to CSMA/CD, each workstation has to listen to the cable to see if any other transmission is occurring. Then, if no other network device is transmitting, the workstation starts transmitting data. In a request for a web page, for example, data would travel back to the workstation from the web server. With half duplex transmission, the workstation transmits and then later the web server transmits. The transmission could not occur simultaneously in both directions. The more workstations on the same network, the more collisions occur and the more the network slows down. In addition, with half duplex Ethernet, less than 50 percent of the 10 Mbps available bandwidth could be used because of collisions and the time it takes for a network frame to transmit across the wire.

Today's Ethernet networks support speeds of 10 Mbps, 100 Mbps, and 1000 Mbps. Most Ethernet NIC cards are 10/100, which means they can run at either 10 Mbps or 100 Mbps. Ethernet networks are also known as 10Base2, 10Base5, 10BaseT, 100BaseT, and 1000BaseT. When considering the term 10Base2, the 10 means that the network runs at 10 Mbps. Base means that the network uses baseband technology. The 2 in 10Base2 means that the maximum coax cable length is 185 meters (which is close to 200 meters). A 10Base2 network has terminators at both ends of the coax cable bus network. The T at the end of 10BaseT means that the computer uses twisted-pair cable. The 100 in 100BaseT means that the network supports 100 Mbps and the 1000 in 1000BaseT means that 1000 Mbps is supported.

Ethernet networks now support full duplex transmissions. With full duplex implemented, collisions are not a problem. This is because full duplex takes advantage of the two pairs of cables, one for receiving and one for transmitting. Full duplex Ethernet creates a direct connection between the transmitting station at one end and the receiving circuits at the other end. Full duplex allows 100 percent of the available bandwidth to be used in each direction. In order to implement full duplex Ethernet, both network cards in the devices must have the ability and be configured for full duplex.

Another way to speed up the network is to use a switch instead of a hub when connecting network devices together. Full duplex Ethernet works great, but replacing hubs with switches also improves network performance. A switch has more intelligence than a hub. When a workstation sends data to a hub, the hub broadcasts the data out all ports except for the port the data came in on. This is inefficient. A switch, on the other hand, keeps a table of addresses. When a switch receives data, the switch forwards the data out the port for which it is destined. A switch looks very similar to a hub and it is sometimes hard to distinguish between the two. Switches are very common devices in today's business network environment.

A classroom setting is much like CSMA/CD. Many times students will simply blurt out questions and answers and interrupt one another (and sometimes the instructor) in a classroom—that is the "multiple access" part. The instructor senses the communication—the "carrier sense" part. And, the instructor decides who will go first—the "collision detect" part.

9.5 Understanding Network Standards

The **IEEE (Institute for Electrical and Electronics Engineers)** committee created network standards called the **802 standards**. Each standard is given an 802.x number and represents an area of networking. Standardization is good for the network industry because different manufacturers' network components work with other manufacturers' devices. Table 2 lists the various 802 standards.

For more information about the 802 standards, access the IEEE web site at http://standards.ieee.org/getieee802/index.html.

Table 9.2: IEEE 802 Standards

802 Standard	Purpose
802.1	Bridging and Management
802.2	Logical Link Control
802.3	CSMA/CD Access Method
802.4	Token-Passing Bus Access Method
802.5	Token Ring Access Method
802.6	DQDB (Distributed Queue Dual Bus) Access Method
802.7	Broadband LAN
802.8	Fiber Optic
802.9	Isochronous LANs
802.10	Security
802.11	Wireless
802.12	Demand Priority Access
802.15	WPANs (Wireless Personal Area Networks)
802.16	Broadband Wireless Access
802.17	Resilient Packet Ring

The number 802 comes from the month (02 for February) and the year (80 for 1980) that the standards where first developed.

9.6 Understanding the OSI Model

The **International Standards Organization (ISO)** has developed a model for network communications known as the OSI (Open Systems Interconnect) model. The **OSI model** is a standard for information transfer across the network. The model sets several guidelines including (1) how the different transmission media are arranged and interconnected, (2) how network devices that use different languages communicate with one another, (3) how a network device goes about contacting another network device, (4) how and when data gets transmitted across the network, (5) how data is sent to the correct device, and (6) how it is known if the network data was received properly. All of these tasks must be handled by a set of rules and the OSI model provides a structure into which these rules fit.

Can you imagine a generic model for building a car? This model would state that you need some means of steering, a type of fuel to power the car, a place for the driver to sit, safety standards, and so forth. The model would not say what type of steering wheel to put in the car or what type of fuel the car must use, but is just a blueprint for making the car. In networking, the OSI model is such a model. The OSI model divides networking into different layers so that it is easier to understand (and teach). Dividing up the network into distinct layers also helps manufacturers. If a particular manufacturer wants to make a network device that works on layer 3, the manufacturer only has to be concerned with layer 3. This division makes networking technologies emerge much faster. Having a layered model also helps to teach network concepts. Each layer can be taught as a separate network function.

The layers of the OSI model (starting from the top and working down) are application, presentation, session, transport, network, data link, and physical. Refer to Figure 9.12.

Each layer of the OSI model uses the layer below it (except for the physical layer which is on the bottom). Each layer provides some function to the layer above it. For example, the data link layer cannot be accessed without first going through the physical layer. If communication needs to be performed at the third layer, (the network layer), then the physical and data link layers must be used first.

Figure 9.12: OSI Model Layers

7	Application
6	Presentation
5	Session
4	Transport
3	Network
2	Data Link
1	Physical

Certification exams contain questions about the OSI model and knowing the levels is a good place to start preparing for the exams. A mnemonic to help remember the OSI layers is: **A Person Seldom Takes Naps During Parties.** Each first letter of the mnemonic phrase is supposed to remind you of the first letter of the OSI model layers. For example, *A* in the phrase is to remind you of the application layer. The *P* in Person is to remind you of the Presentation layer, and so on. Another mnemonic is All People Seem To Need Data Processing. Or, from the bottom to the top: Programmers Do Not Throw Sausage Pizza Away.

Each layer of the OSI model from the top down (except for the physical layer) adds information to the data being sent across the network. Sometimes this information is called a header. Figure 9.13 shows how a header is added as the packet travels down the OSI model. When the receiving computer receives the data, each layer removes the header information. Information at the physical layer is normally called bits. When referring to information at the data link layer, use the term **frame**. When referring to information at the network layer, use the term **packet**.

Each of the seven OSI layers performs a unique function and interacts with the layers surrounding it. The bottom three layers handle the physical delivery of data across the network. The **physical layer** (sometimes called layer 1) defines how bits are transferred and received across the network media without being concerned about the structure of the bits. The physical layer is where connectors, cable, and voltage levels are defined. The **data link layer** (sometimes called layer 2) provides the means for accurately transferring the bits across the network and it groups (encapsulates) the bits into usable sections called frames. The **network layer** (sometimes called layer 3) coordinates data movement between two devices. This layer provides path selection between two networks. Most companies and even some homes have a router that they use to connect to the Internet through their **ISP (Internet Service Provider)**. An ISP is a vendor who provides Internet access.

Figure 9.13: OSI Peer Communication

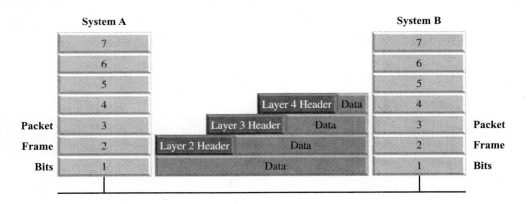

The top four layers handle the ins and outs of providing accurate data delivery between computers and their individual processes, especially in a multi-tasking operating system environment. The **transport layer** (sometimes called layer 4) provides a service to the upper layers so they do not have to worry about the details of how data is sent. The transport layer provides such services as whether the data should be sent "reliably" or not. This is similar to getting a return receipt for a package at the post office.

The **session layer** manages the communication and synchronization between two network devices. The **presentation layer** provides a means of translating the data from the sender into data the receiver understands. This allows all types of computers to communicate with one another even though one computer may be using one language (such as EBCDIC) and another computer using a different language (such as ASCII). Note EBCDIC is a character set developed by IBM for use on mainframe computers. The **application layer** provides network services to any software applications running on the network. The application layer provides network services to a computer. This allows the computer to participate or enter the OSI model (the network). Some of the services the application layer provides include negotiating authentication (what type of authentication will be used in the communication), negotiating who has responsibility for error recovery, and negotiating quality of service across the network.

Certain network devices or components work at a specific OSI layer. For example, cables, connectors, repeaters, hubs, and patch panels all reside at layer 1 of the OSI model, the physical layer parts of the network card reside at layer 1, and part of the OSI model resides at layer 2. A switch also resides at layer 2, the data link layer. A **router**, a network device that determines the best path to send a packet, works at layer 3, the network layer.

The OSI model is very confusing when you are first learning about networking, but it is very important. Understanding the model helps when troubleshooting a network. Knowing where the problem is occurring narrows the field of what the solution may be. For example, if a computer has problems communicating with a computer on the same network, then the problem is most likely a layer 1 or a layer 2 problem because layer 3 takes care of communication between two networks. Check the cabling and NIC settings.

Table 9.3 summarizes the OSI model for you.

Table 9.3: OSI Model

OSI Model Layer	Purpose
Application	Provides network services (file, print, and messaging services) to any software application running on the network.
Presentation	Translates data from one character set to another.
Session	Manages the communication and synchronization between devices.
Transport	Provides the mechanisms for how data is sent, such as reliability and error correction.
Network	Provides path selection between two networks. Routers reside at the network layer. Encapsulated data at this layer is called a packet.
Data Link	Encapsulates bits into frames. Can provide error control. MAC address and switches are at this layer.
Physical	Defines how bits are transferred and received. Defines the network media, connectors, and voltage levels. Data at this level is called bits.

9.7 Understanding Network Protocols

A **network protocol** is a data communication language. There are three primary network protocols used: TCP/IP, NetBEUI, and IPX/SPX. **TCP/IP (Transport Control Protocol/ Internet Protocol)** is the most common network protocol and is used when accessing the Internet. Most companies (and homes) use TCP/IP as their standard protocol. **IPX/SPX (Internetwork Packet Exchange/Sequenced Packet Exchange)** is used when connecting to a Novell network, but Novell networks now use TCP/IP as its standard protocol. **NetBEUI (NetBIOS Enhanced User Interface)** is a non-routable network protocol. This means that it can only be used on simple networks, not on multiple networks that are tied together. A common place for NetBEUI is on a peer-to-peer network.

Network Addressing

Network adapters normally have two types of addresses assigned to them—a MAC address and an IP address. The **MAC address** is used when two network devices on the same network communicate with one another. The MAC address is a 48-bit unique number that is burned into a ROM chip located on the NIC and is represented in hexadecimal. A MAC address is unique for every computer on the network. However, the MAC address has no scheme to it except that the first three bytes represent the manufacturer. The MAC address is known as a layer 2 address.

The **IP address** is a much more organized way of addressing a computer than a MAC address and it is sometimes known as a layer 3 address. The IP address is a 32-bit number that is entered into a NIC's configuration parameters. The IP address is used when multiple networks are connected together and when accessing the Internet. The IP address is shown using dotted decimal notation, such as 192.168.10.4. Each number is separated by periods and represents eight bits, and the numbers that can be represented by eight bits are 0 to 255.

IP addresses are grouped into classes. It is easy to tell which type of IP address is being issued by the first number shown in the dotted decimal notation. Class A addresses have any number from 0 to 127 as the first number; Class B addresses have any number from 128 to 191 as the first number; and Class C addresses have numbers 192 through 223. For example, if a computer has an IP address of 12.150.172.39, the IP address is a Class A address because the first number is 12. If a computer has an IP address of 176.10.100.2, it is a Class B IP address because the first number is 176.

An IP address is broken into two major parts—the network number and the host number. The **network number** is the portion of the IP address that represents which network the computer is on. All computers on the same network have the same network number. The **host number** is the portion of the IP address that represents the specific computer on the network. All computers on the same network have unique host numbers or they will not be able to communicate.

The number of bits that are used to represent the network number and the host number depends on which class of IP address is being used. With Class A IP addresses, the first eight bits (the first number) represent the network portion and the remaining 24 bits (the last three numbers) represent the host number. With Class B IP addresses, the first 16 bits (the first two numbers) represent the network portion and the remaining 16 bits (the last two numbers) represent the host number. With Class C IP addresses, the first 24 bits (the first three numbers) represent the network portion and the remaining eight bits (the last number) represent the host number. Figure 9.14 illustrates this point.

Figure 9.14: IP Addressing

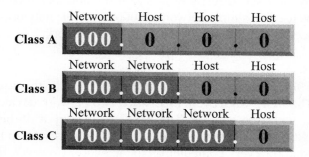

In order to see how IP addressing works, it is best to use an example. A business has two networks connected together with a router. On each network, there are computer workstations and printers. Each of the networks must have a unique network number. For this example, one network has the network number of 193.14.150.0, and the other network has the network number of 193.14.151.0. Notice how these numbers represent a Class C IP address because the first number is 193.

With a Class C IP address, the first three numbers represent the network number. The first network has a network number of 193.14.150 and the second network has a network number of 193.14.151. Remember that each network has to have a different number than any other network in the organization. The last number of the IP address will be used to assign different network devices their IP address. On the first network, each device will have a number that starts with 193.14.150 because that is the network number and it stays the same for all devices on that network. Each device will then have a different number in the last portion of the IP address, for example, 193.14.150.3, 193.14.150.4, or 193.14.150.5.

On the second network, each device will have a number that starts with 193.14.151 because that is the network number. The last number in the IP address changes for each network device, for example, 193.14.151.3, 193.14.151.4, 193.14.151.5, and so forth. No device can have a host number of 0 because that number represents the network and no device can have a host number of 255 because that represents something called the broadcast address. A **broadcast address** is the IP address used to communicate with all devices on a particular network. So, in the example given, no network device can be assigned the IP addresses 193.14.150.0 or 193.14.151.0 because these numbers represent the two networks.

Furthermore, no network device can be assigned the IP addresses 193.14.150.255 or 193.14.151.255 because these numbers represent the broadcast address used with each network. An example of a Class B broadcast is 150.10.255.255. An example of a Class A broadcast is 11.255.255.255. Figure 9.15 shows this configuration.

Figure 9.15: IP Addressing with Two Networks

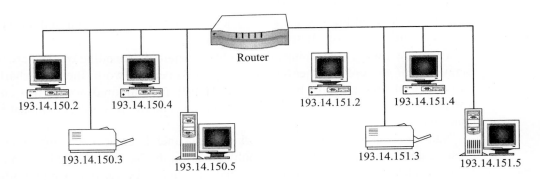

In addition to assigning a computer an IP address, you must also assign a subnet mask. The **subnet mask** is a number that the computer uses to determine which part of the IP address represents the network and which portion represents the host. The subnet mask for a Class A IP address is 255.0.0.0; the subnet mask for a Class B IP address is 255.255.0.0; the subnet mask for a Class C IP address is 255.255.255.0. Table 9.4 recaps this important information.

Table 9.4: IP Address Information

Class	First Number	Network/ Host Number	Standard Subnet Mask
A	0-127	N.H.H.H *	255.0.0.0
B	128-191	N.N.H.H *	255.255.0.0
C	192-222	N.N.N.H *	255.255.255.0

Note: * N= Network number; H=Host number

9.8 Configuring Networking

When you install a NIC card in a computer, there are four things that must be configured before connecting to the network:

1. An appropriate driver for the NIC must be installed. The type of driver needed depends on which operating system is being used.

2. You must give the computer a unique name and either a workgroup name (the same name must be used, and this is implemented on a peer-to-peer network), or a domain name (the same name must be used, and this is implemented on a server-based network).

3. You must select the appropriate protocol being used (TCP/IP, IPX/SPX, or Net-BEUI). Contact the network administrator for this information. The majority of businesses and homes use TCP/IP.

4. A network client must be installed. The most common client used in industry is Microsoft's client for Microsoft networks.

There are always other things that could be required depending on the network environment. For example, if the system is a peer-to-peer network, then file sharing (and possibly print sharing) must be enabled. If TCP/IP is configured, some other configuration parameters may be necessary. Exercises at the end of this chapter demonstrate these concepts.

Name a computer using the Network control panel. Each device on the same network must be a unique name. When you double-click on the Network Neighborhood desktop icon, you can view the network device names. It can also be viewed by typing **nbtstat –n** from a command prompt. The command prompt can also be used to access network shares by using the **UNC (Universal Naming Convention)**. For example, a computer called CSchmidt has a network share called TESTS. By typing **\\CSchmidt\TESTS** at the Run prompt, you can access the network share.

To share a folder, use My Computer or Explorer. Locate the folder to be shared and right-click on it. Click on the **Sharing** option. Click on the **Sharing** tab and click in the **Shared As** radio button to enable sharing. In the Share Name text box, type a name for the network share. This name appears in other computers' Network Neighborhood or My Network Places when accessed across the network. In the Access Type section of the window, click on the **appropriate radio button** for the type of access remote users have to the folder. If a password is to be assigned, type it in the text box. Click on the **OK** button and test from a remote computer.

In a network, it is common to map a drive letter to a frequently used network share. To map a drive letter to a network share, right-click on the **Network Neighborhood** or **My Network Places** (Windows 2000) desktop icon. Select the **Map Network Drive** option. Select a drive letter in the **Drive** box by clicking on the down arrow. In the **Folder** or **Path** box (depending on the operating system), type the **UNC** for the network share or use the **Browse** button or **Shared Directories** window (depending on the operating system) to select the network share. The Reconnect at Logon check box allows you to connect to the mapped drive every time you log on.

When configuring TCP/IP, an IP address and subnet mask must be assigned to the network device. The IP address is what makes the network device unique and what allows it to be reached by other network devices. There are two ways to get an IP address:
• Statically define the IP address and mask.
• Use Dynamic Host Configuration Protocol (DHCP).

When an IP address is **statically defined**, that means that someone manually enters an IP address into the computer. This is done through the Network control panel. The appropriate mask must also be entered. The correct IP address and mask can be obtained from the company's network administrator. Entering an IP address that is a duplicate of another network device renders the new network device inoperable on the network. Most support people do not statically define IP addresses unless the device is an important network device such as a web server, database server, network server, router, or switch. Instead, you would use DHCP.

DHCP (Dynamic Host Configuration Protocol) is a method of automatically assigning IP addresses to network devices. A DHCP server (software configured on a network server or router) contains a pool of IP addresses. When a network device has been configured for DHCP and it boots, the device sends out a request for an IP address. A DHCP server responds to this request and issues an IP address to the network device. DHCP makes IP addressing easier and keeps network devices from being assigned duplicate IP addresses.

Another important concept that relates to IP addressing is a default gateway (or gateway of last resort). A **default gateway** is an IP address assigned to a network device that tells the device where to send a packet that is destined for a remote network. The default gateway address is the IP address of the router that is directly connected to that immediate network. A router's job is to find the best path to another network. A router has various network numbers stored in memory. Consider Figure 9.16.

Figure 9.16: A Network with a Default Gateway (or Router)

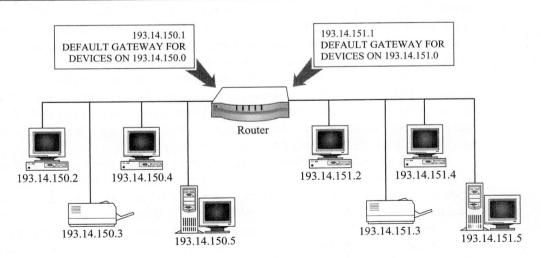

Network devices on the 193.14.150.0 network use the router IP address of 193.14.150.1 as a default gateway address. When a network device on the 193.14.150.0

network wants to send a packet to the 193.14.151.0 network, it sends the packet to the router's IP address that is on the same network (the gateway address). The router, in turn, looks up the destination address (193.14.151.x) in its routing table and sends it out the other interface (193.14.151.1) to the remote network device on the 193.14.151.0 network.

The default gateway address for all network devices on the 193.14.151.0 network is 193.14.151.1, the router's IP address on the same network. Any network device on 193.14.151.0 sending information to the 193.14.150.0 sends it to the default gateway address. For network devices on the 193.14.151.0 network, the gateway address is 193.14.151.1.

Network devices can receive their default gateway address from the DHCP server just like they can an IP address. The DHCP server must be configured for the appropriate default gateway address to give to network devices. An important note is that a DHCP server can give out IP addresses to network devices on remote networks as well as the network to which the DHCP server is directly connected. Default gateway addresses are important for network devices that need to communicate with network devices on other networks. The default gateway address is configured using the Network control panel under the TCP/IP section.

Other elements of TCP/IP information that may need to be configured are one or more DNS server IP addresses and one or more WINS server IP addresses. A **DNS (Domain Name System) server** is an application that runs on a network server that provides translation of Internet names into IP addresses. DNS is used on the Internet, so you do not have to remember the IP address of each site to which you connect. For example, DNS would be used to connect to Scott/Jones Publishing by translating the **URL (Universal Resource Locator)** www.scottjonespub.com into the IP address 167.160.239.173. A computer can receive the DNS server's IP address from DHCP if the DHCP server has been configured for this. You can also manually configure the system for one or more DNS server IP addresses through the Network control panel.

If a DNS server does not know a domain name (it does not have the name in its database), the DNS server can contact another DNS server to get the translation information. Common three-letter codes used with DNS (three letters used at the end of a domain name) are com (commercial sites), edu (educational sites), gov (government sites), net (network-related sites), and org (miscellaneous sites).

A **WINS (Windows Internet Naming Service) server** keeps track of IP addresses assigned to a specific computer name. When connecting to another computer, a user types in a computer's name and not the computer's IP address. The WINS server translates the name to an IP address. The WINS server's IP address can be configured under the Network control panel. WINS is very important especially on computers that receive their IP addresses from DHCP. The IP address can change each time the computer boots because with DHCP, you can configure the DHCP server to issue an IP address for a specific amount of time. In addition, the DHCP server can send the WINS server's IP address to a network device just like the server sends the default gateway address and the DNS address. Another important fact about WINS is that newer DNS servers can now provide the computer name as well as the domain name to IP address translation.

Think of DHCP as a "distributor" of IP addresses and other information. Think of DNS as the phone book. In a phone book, you look up a person's name to get his or her phone number. With DNS, a computer's name, such as **www.somewhere.com**, is looked up and DNS returns its IP address (phone number).

9.9 Troubleshooting Networks

One way to troubleshoot a network is to determine how many devices are affected. For example, if only one computer cannot communicate across a network, it will be handled differently than if several (or all) computers on a network cannot communicate. The easiest way to determine how many devices are having trouble is by using a simple test. Since most computers use TCP/IP, one tool that can be used for testing is the ping command. **Ping** sends a packet to an IP destination (that you determine) and a reply is sent back from the destination device (when everything is working fine). The ping command can be used to determine if the network path is available, if there are delays along the path, and whether the remote network device is reachable.

The ping utility can be used to test the NIC as well as the TCP/IP protocol running on the NIC with the command **ping 127.0.0.1**. The 127.0.0.1 IP address is what is known as a private IP address, which means it cannot be used by the outside world. The 127.0.0.1 is also known as a loopback address. A **loopback address** is not used to check connections to another computer, but is used to test a NIC card's own basic network setup.

If the ping is successful (a message that a reply was received from 127.0.0.1), then the TCP/IP protocol stack is working correctly on the NIC. If the ping responds with a no answer or 100% packet loss error, TCP/IP is not properly installed or functioning correctly on that one workstation.

The ping command can be used to check connectivity all around the network. Figure 9.17 shows a sample network that is used to explain how ping is used to check various network points.

Submarines use a sonar ping to determine if another submarine is in the vicinity. The network **PING** stands for **P**acket **IN**ternet **G**roper.

Figure 9.17: A Sample Network Configuration

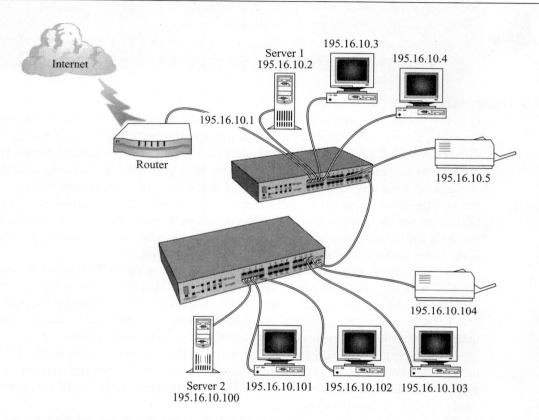

In Figure 9.17, the network consists of various network devices including two servers and two laser printers. The devices connect to one of two switches that are connected together using the uplink port. This port allows two similar devices to be connected together with a standard Ethernet cable or fiber cable. A router connects to the top switch and the router connects to the Internet.

The 195.16.10.3 workstation cannot access a file on Server2 (195.16.10.100). The first in troubleshooting is to ping Server2. If this is successful (the destination reachable), the problem is in Server2 or the file located on the server. If the ping is unsuccessful, there is a problem elsewhere. Right now, the ping is unsuccessful, so ping another device that connects to the same switch. From workstation 195.16.10.3, ping Server1 (195.16.10.2), which connects to the same switch. This ping is successful and tells you the connection between the 195.16.10.3 workstation and the switch is good, the switch is working, the cable connecting to Server1 is fine, and Server1 is functioning. If the ping is unsuccessful, one of these things is faulty.

Now ping workstation 195.16.10.101 (a device other than the server on the remote switch), If the ping is successful, (1) the uplink cable is operational, (2) the second switch is operational, (3) the cable that connects workstation 195.16.10.101 to the switch is good, and (4) the 195.16.10.101 workstation has been successfully configured for TCP/IP. If the ping is unsuccessful, one of these four items is faulty. If the ping is successful, the problems could be (1) Server2's cable, (2) the switch port to which the server connects, (3) server NIC, (4) server configuration, or (5) the file on Server2.

To see the current IP configuration, use the WINIPCFG or IPCONFIG command from a DOS prompt. The **WINIPCFG** command is used with Windows 95 and Windows 98. The **IPCONFIG** command is used with Windows 98, NT Workstation, NT Server, 2000 Professional, and 2000 Server. To access the DOS prompt on Windows 9x, click on the **Start** button, point to the **Programs** option, and click on the **MS-DOS Prompt** option. In NT Workstation or Server, click on the **Start** button, point to the **Programs** option, and click on the **Command Prompt** option. When using Windows 2000 Professional or Server, click on the **Start** button, point to **Programs**, point to the **Accessories** option, and click on the **Command Prompt** option. Figures 9.18 and 9.19 show the switches and output of each command.

Figure 9.18: The WINIPCFG Command

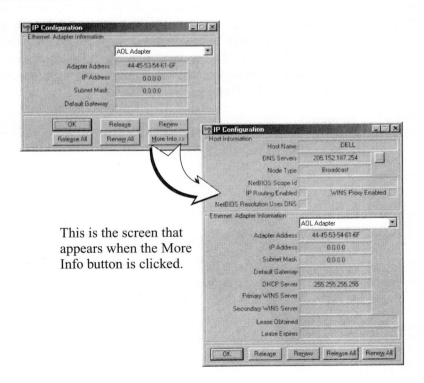

This is the screen that appears when the More Info button is clicked.

Make sure when using WINIPCFG, that you click on the down arrow to select the appropriate NIC.

Use the ping command followed by the name of the device being tested, for example, ping **www.scottjonespub.com**. A DNS server translates the name to an IP address. If the site can be reached by pinging the IP address, but not the name, there is a problem with the DNS server.

A program that helps with DNS server troubleshooting is a tool called **NSLOOKUP**. NSLOOKUP is available on NT Server and 2000 Server. NSLOOKUP allows you to see domain names and their associated IP addresses. When an Internet site (server) cannot be contacted by its name, but can be contacted using its IP address, there is a DNS problem. NSLOOKUP can make troubleshooting these types of problems easier.

The **tracert** command is also a commonly used tool. The tracert command is used to display the path a packet takes through the network. The benefit of using the tracert command is that you can see where a fault is occurring in a larger network.

The **NET command** is also useful in network troubleshooting and configuration. NET DIAG can be used in Windows 98 and 2000 to run a hardware diagnostic program between two computers. Windows 98 and 2000 also have a utility called NET LOGOFF, which breaks the connection between the computer and its connected network resources. The NET USE command can be used to connect or disconnect the computer from a network resource and can be used to display information about network connections. For example, to view all the network connections currently in use, type **NET USE** and press **Enter**. In Windows 98 and 2000, the NET VER command displays the type and version of the network redirector. The NET VIEW command displays a list of computers in a workgroup or a specific computer's shared network resources. A good web site for the NET command is **http://www.computerhope.com/nethlp.htm**.

Figure 9.19: The IPCONFIG Command

```
C:\WINDOWS> ipconfig

Windows 98 IP Configuation

0 Ethernet adapter :

        IP Address . . . . . . . . . : 0.0.0.0
        Subnet Mask. . . . . . . . . : 0.0.0.0
        Default Gateway. . . . . . . :

1 Ethernet adapter :

        IP Address . . . . . . . . . : 0.0.0.0
        Subnet Mask. . . . . . . . . : 0.0.0.0
        Default Gateway. . . . . . . :

2 Ethernet adapter :

        IP Address . . . . . . . . . : 192.168.10.10
        Subnet Mask. . . . . . . . . : 255.255.255.0
        Default Gateway. . . . . . . :

C:\WINDOWS>ipconfig /?
Command line options:
 /All - Display detailed information.
 /Batch [file] - Write to file or ./WINIPCFG.OUT
 /renew_all   - Renew   all adapters.
 /release_all  - Release all adapters.
 /renew   N   - Release adapter N.
 /release N   - Release adapter N.
```

9.10 Configuring a Networked Printer

There are three ways to network a printer:

- Connect a printer to a port on a computer that is connected to the network and share the printer.
- Set up a computer that is designated as a print server. Connect the print server to the network.
- Connect a printer with a network connector installed directly to the network.

Printers can also be password protected on the network. A networked printer is very common in today's home and business computing environments. Networking expensive printers such as laser printers and color printers is cost-effective.

A printer that is connected to a workstation can be shared across the network by enabling File and Print Sharing. An exercise at the end of the chapter explains how to do this. Once File and Print Sharing is enabled, a printer is shared simply by clicking on the **Start** button, pointing to the **Settings** option, clicking on the **Printer** option, right-clicking on the printer to be shared, selecting **Properties**, and clicking on the **Sharing** option.

With Microsoft operating systems, networked printers are much easier to configure than they used to be. To connect and use a networked printer, use the Add Printer wizard. A prompt is available that asks whether the printer is local or networked. A local printer is one that is directly attached to the computer and a networked printer is one attached to another workstation, a print server, or directly connected to the network.

Even though print drivers normally automatically download, sometimes they cause printing problems. The best way to tackle this situation is to manually load the print driver for the networked printer.

9.11 Understanding Dial-Up Networking (DUN)

DUN (Dial-up Networking) is a remote computer that dials into the Internet or a corporation using a modem. Another technology using dial-up networking is virtual private networking. **VPN (Virtual Private Networking)** is a remote computer connecting to a remote network by "tunneling" over an intermediate network such as the Internet or a LAN. Once connected, the remote user can make use of network devices as if they were directly connected to the network. Figure 9.20 illustrates these concepts.

Figure 9.20: DUN and VPNs

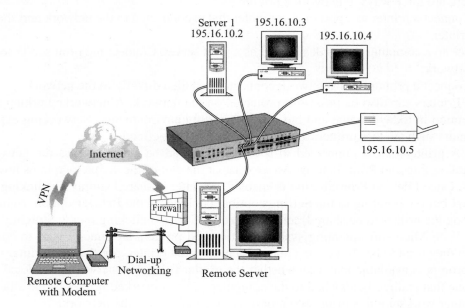

The type of connection, protocol, and settings that you configure on the remote computer depends on the company to which you are connecting. The most commonly used protocol is TCP/IP, but Microsoft operating systems do support IPX/SPX and NetBEUI. A connection protocol used with dial-up networking is PPP. **PPP** (**Point-to- Point Protocol**) is a connection-oriented, layer 2 protocol that encapsulates data for transmission over phone lines. An older protocol that was used with dial-up networking and was the predecessor to PPP is SLIP (Serial Line Internet Protocol).

In Windows 98, to make a dial-up networking connection, make sure a modem is properly installed. Then access the dial-up networking wizard by double-clicking on the **My Computer** desktop icon, double-clicking on the **Dial-up Networking** folder, and then double-clicking on the **Make New Connection** icon. If the Dial-up Networking folder is not there, you can install the required components using the Add/Remove Programs control panel.

In Windows 2000, click on the **Start** button, access the **Settings** option, and click on the **Network and Dial-up Connections** folder. The Make New Connection wizard is used to setup dial-up networking or configure a VPN connection.

In Windows XP, click on the **Start** button, select **Control Panel**, point to **Network and Internet Connections**, and select **Network Connections**. Under Network tasks, select **Create a new connection**. An area code may have to be entered. Click on the **Next** button.

Select the appropriate type of network connection and click on the **Next** button. Type in a name for the connection and select **Next**. Enter the remote modem's phone number and click on the **Next** button. Ensure the Add a shortcut to this connection to my desktop check box is enabled and click on the **Finish** button.

Before creating a remote connection, you should always determine what parameters are to be entered *before* starting the configuration. Contact the network administrator for exact details on how to configure the remote connection. If the connection is to the Internet via an ISP, detailed instructions are available on the ISP's web site and/or with the materials that come with the Internet package from the ISP.

There are many types of network connections. Dial-up networking normally uses POTS (Plain Old Telephone Service) or ISDN. Businesses use various types of network connections leased from the local phone company or a provider. Table 9.5 shows the types of network connections and speeds.

Table 9.5: Network Connections

Connection Type	Speed
POTS (Plain Old Telephone Service)	2400 bps to 115 Kbps analog phone line
ISDN (Integrated Services Digital Network)	64 Kbps to 1.544 Mbps digital line
Frame Relay	56 K to 1.544 Mbps
56 K point to point	56 K guaranteed bandwidth between two points
T1	1.544 Mbps guaranteed bandwidth between two points
T3	44 Mbps guaranteed bandwidth between two points
DSL (Digital Subscriber Line)	256 Kbps and higher; shares data line with voice line
ATM (Asynchronous Transfer Mode)	Up to 2 Gbps

9.12 Learning about Internet Software

Once a dial-up networking configuration or the LAN configuration tasks have been completed, you can connect to the Internet. Most people use a web browser when connecting to the Internet. A **browser** allows you to view web pages across the Internet. The two most common Internet browsers are Internet Explorer (also known as IE) and Netscape Navigator. Other web browsers include Opera Software's Opera and NeoPlanet, Inc.'s NeoPlanet. Internet Explorer comes with Microsoft operating systems. Netscape Navigator is available from Netscape Communications Corporation (http:// home.netscape.com/)

or free from some ISPs when you enroll with their service. If Internet Explorer is not loaded on the computer, add it using the Add/Remove Programs control panel or go to Microsoft's web site at **www.microsoft.com** to download the latest version.

Keeping the web browser current is important. Internet hackers frequently target Internet browsers and constant updates are provided that help with these attacks. Before upgrading, you should determine the web browser's current version. With any software application, the version is determined by starting the application, clicking on the **Help** menu item, and clicking on the **About** *x*, where *x* is the name of the application. With Internet Explorer, the first two numbers listed are the software version numbers. There is another value called Cipher Strength that is a bit value for encryption. Encryption is the process of changing your transmitted files into data so it cannot be recognized. In the United States, 128-bit encryption is the best.

Internet browsers frequently need plug-ins. A **plug-in** is an application designed to work with the browser. Common plug-ins include Macromedia Flash, Macromedia Shockwave, RealNetwork's RealPlayer, Apple QuickTime, Adobe Acrobat Reader, and WinZip. Macromedia Flash allows web animations to be played. Macromedia Shockwave is for interactive multimedia graphics and audio applications. RealPlayer is for playing streaming audio and video, QuickTime is used for playing video clips. Acrobat Reader is for displaying PDF documents. WinZip is used for compressing and expanding ZIP files.

Another common tool for a web browser is an accelerator. An **accelerator** speeds up downloads and Internet browsing (surfing). Some accelerators are plug-ins for the web browser software and others are standalone applications. Various download and browsing accelerators are available on the Internet. One example is SpeedBit's Download Accelerator Plus; it's available at www.speedbit.com. Two other popular ones are Go!Zilla available from www.gozilla.com and NetSonic available from www.netsonic.com.

Another common Internet software application is an e-mail package. This software allows you to send messages across the Internet. Microsoft operating systems come with Windows Messaging (Inbox). Another popular freeware e-mail software program is Eudora Light. Many Internet providers also have their own e-mail package.

The e-mail service has to be configured. Many settings are configured through the Mail control panel. Two common settings are POP and SMTP server addresses. POP stands for Post Office Protocol and a POP3 server is a server used for retrieving e-mail. **SMTP (Simple Mail Transport Protocol)** is used for sending e-mail. These settings for the e-mail service are available from the network administrator or the ISP in their instructions for configuring dial-up networking.

You must be familiar with troubleshooting browser and e-mail applications. A good place to start is with the userid and password, POP3, and SMTP settings. In Internet Explorer, you need to be familiar with the settings that can be configured under the Internet Options section of the Tools menu item. The Connections tab is a great place to start.

9.13 Understanding Wireless Networks

Wireless networks are networks that transmit data over air using either infrared or radio frequencies. Wireless networks operate at layers 1 and 2 of the OSI model. Most wireless networks in home and businesses use radio frequencies. Wireless networks are very popular both in the home and business computer environments and are great in places that are not conducive to running cable such as an outdoor center, convention center, bookstore, coffee shop, hotel, between buildings, and in between non-wired rooms in homes. You must be familiar with this technology for installation, configuration, and troubleshooting.

The standard for wireless is IEEE 802.11.

There are two main types of wireless networks: ad hoc and infrastructure. An **ad hoc mode** wireless network is also known as a peer-to-peer or IBSS (Independent Basic Service Set) mode or simply IBSS (Independent Basic Service Set). An ad hoc wireless network is when at least two devices such as two computers have wireless NICs (Network Interface Cards) installed. The two devices transmit and receive data.

There are three major types of wireless NICs: PC Card, USB, and PCI (Peripheral Component Interconnect). Note PCI is a type of interface for computer cards, such as video, network and modem, to connect to your computer's motherboard. Figure 9.21 shows a D-link Systems, Inc.'s wireless NIC that could be installed in a laptop computer.

Figure 9.21: D-Link's Wireless PC Card NIC

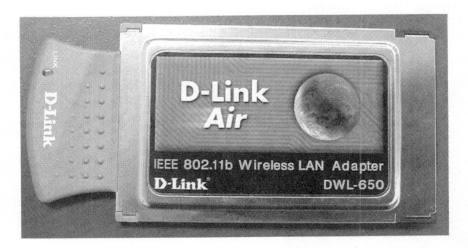

PCI wireless NICs allow desktop or tower computers to access a wireless network. Figure 9.22 shows D-Link Systems Inc.'s PCI wireless NIC.

Figure 9.22: PCI Wireless NIC PCI Wireless NIC

The third most popular type of wireless NIC attaches to the USB port and is quite popular in home networks. Figure 9.23 shows a USB wireless NIC.

Figure 9.23: Linksys USB Wireless NIC

An ad hoc mode wireless network is used when two people want to play a network-based game, two or more computers need to transfer data, or one computer connects to the Internet and the other computer(s) are not wired into the same network. Figure 9.24 shows an ad hoc mode wireless network that consists of two laptops communicating over airwaves.

Figure 9.24: Ad Hoc Wireless Network

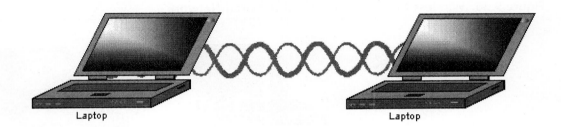

The **infrastructure mode** wireless network connects multiple wireless network devices through an access point. An **access point** is a device that receives and transmits data from multiple computers that have wireless NICs. The easiest way to describe an access point is to think of it as a network hub—it connects the wireless network. Network Figure 9.25 shows an infrastructure mode wireless network with an access point and multiple wireless devices.

Figure 9.25: Infrastructure Mode Wireless Network

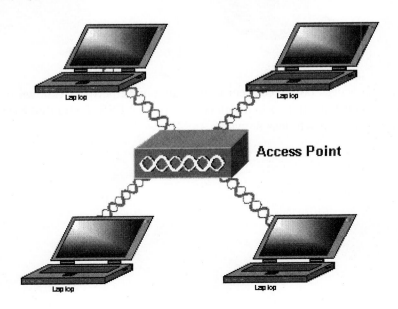

The access point can also be wired to another wireless network or a wired network. The access point can then relay the transmission from a wireless device to another network or to the Internet through the wired network. When multiple devices connect to an access point (whether that access point is wired to a LAN or not), the configuration is known as a **BSS (Basic Service Set)**. Figure 9.26 shows an infrastructure mode and an access point. The access point connects to a wired network and gives the wireless devices access to the Internet.

Figure 9.26: Wireless Network Connected to Wired Network

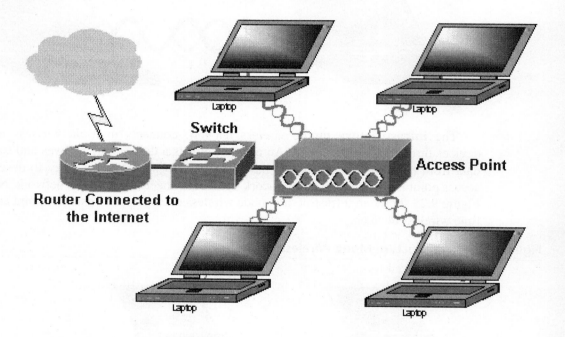

When multiple access points connect to the same main network (known to some as the distribution system), the network design is known as an **ESS (Extended Service Set)**. Figure 9.27 shows an ESS wireless network.

Figure 9.27: Extended Service Set Wireless Network

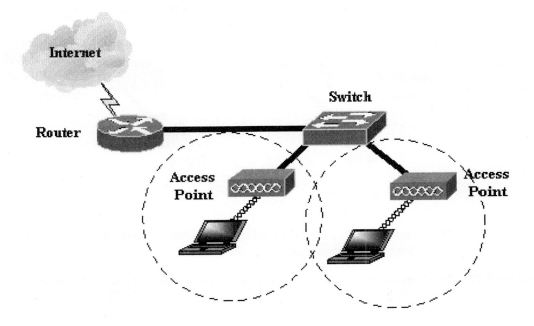

Each access point can handle 60 to 200 network devices depending on vendor, wireless network environment, amount of usage, and the type of data being sent. Each access point is assigned an **SSID (Service Set Identifier)**. An SSID is a set of 32 alphanumeric characters used to differentiate between different wireless networks. Wireless NICs can automatically detect an access point or be manually configured with the access point's SSID. Some manufacturers refer to the SSID in infrastructure mode as the **ESSID (Extended Service Set Identifier)**, but this is the same concept as SSID. In situations such as a wireless café, bookstore, or convention center, no SSID may be required on the wireless NIC. However, in a home or business environment, an SSID may be required.

If two access points are used and they connect two different wireless networks, two different SSIDs would be used. Figure 9.28 shows this concept.

Figure 9.28: Two Separate Wireless Networks with Two SSIDs

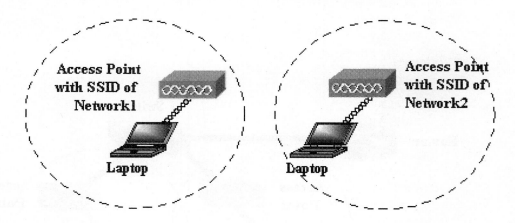

If two access points connect to the same wireless network, the same SSID is used. Figure 9.29 shows this concept.

Figure 9.29: One Extended Wireless Network with the Same SSID on Both Access Points

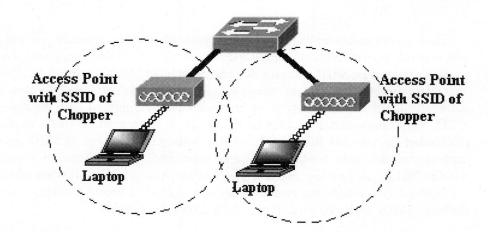

9.14 Installing and Configuring a Wireless Network Card

Before any wireless adapters are installed, the basic configuration parameters should be determined. The following list helps with these decisions.

• Will the wireless adapter be used in an ad hoc environment or infrastructure mode?
• What is the SSID?
• Is WEP enabled? **WEP (Wireless Equivalent Privacy)** encrypts data being transmitted.
• If WEP is enabled what is the key length?
• Is authentication open or shared key?

- If shared key authentication is being used, what is the shared key?
- What is the most current driver for the operating system being used?

Wireless network adapters can be USB, PCI, ISA, or a PC Card. Each of these adapters install like any other adapter of the same type. Not all computers in the wireless network have to have the same type of wireless NIC. For example, a desktop computer could have a PCI wireless NIC installed, a laptop computer in a cubicle office would have an integrated wireless NIC, and another laptop in another cubicle has a PC Card wireless NIC. All three can access the same wireless network and access point.

With most wireless NICs, the manufacturer's software is normally installed before the NIC is installed or attached to the computer. With all wireless NICs, the latest driver for the particular version of Windows should be downloaded from the manufacturer's web site before the card is installed. Once the adapter is inserted or attached and the computer powered on, Windows recognizes that a new adapter has been installed and prompts for the driver, browse to the location of the new downloaded driver. Another method that can be used is to install the driver that comes with the adapter and then upgrade it once installed.

Once the wireless adapter is installed, the options such as SSID and security options can be installed. These parameters are normally configured through a utility provided by the wireless NIC manufacturer or through Windows network control if Windows XP is installed. Figure 9.30 shows the wireless NIC properties screen that is accessible through the Windows XP Network Connections control panel.

Figure 9.30: General Tab of the Wireless NIC Properties Window

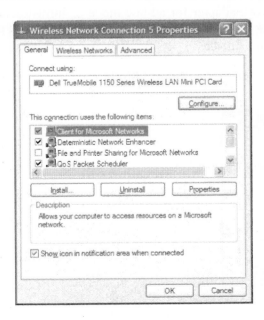

To access the configuration for the wireless network, click on the **Wireless Networks** tab. Figure 9.31 shows this window.

Figure 9.31: Wireless Networks Tab of the Wireless NIC Properties Window

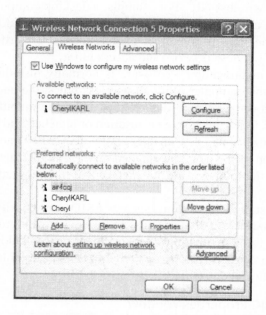

To configure the wireless network adapter for ad hoc mode or infrastructure mode, click on the **Advanced** button at the bottom of the window. Figure 9.32 shows the screen that appears where the selection can be made.

Figure 9.32: Window to Select Ad Hoc Mode or Infrastructure Mode

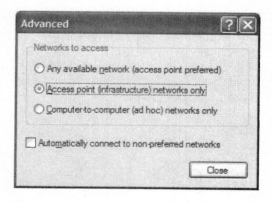

On the Wireless Networks tab, select the **Add** button to configure the wireless NIC for a wireless network. On this screen, the SSID can be input, WEP enabled, and the shared key input. Figure 9.33 shows this window.

Figure 9.33: Windows XP's Wireless NIC Configuration Screen

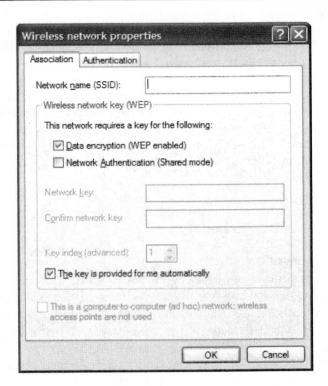

Wireless NICs are very easy to install. The utilities that are provided with the NICs are quite sophisticated and easy to use. Always follow the manufacturer's instructions. All of the screens and configuration utilities have the same type of information. Understanding what the configuration parameters means is important. The hardest part about configuring wireless NICs is obtaining the correct parameters *before* installation begins. Incorrectly inputting any one of the parameters will cause the wireless NIC to not associate with the access point or remote wireless device and not transmit. Planning is critical for these types of cards.

9.15 Understanding Wireless Access Points

Many of the parameters needed for wireless NIC configuration are also needed for access point installation. However, an access point is more involved because it is the central device of the wireless network. The following list of questions help with access point installation. These questions should be answered *before* the access point is installed.

- What is the SSID to be used?
- Is WEP enabled?
- If WEP is enabled what is the key length?
- Is authentication open or shared key?
- If shared key authentication is being used, what is the shared key?
- Is there power available for the access point? Note that some access points can receive power through an in-line switch.
- How will the access point be mounted? Is mounting hardware provided with the access point or does extra equipment have to be purchased?
- Where should the access point be mounted for best coverage of the wireless network area? Perform a site survey to see best performance. Temporarily mount the access point. With a laptop that has a wireless NIC and site survey software, walk around the wireless network area to see the coverage range. The site survey can also be conducted by double-clicking on the network icon on the taskbar; the signal strength is shown in the window that appears. Move the access point as necessary to avoid attenuation and obtain the largest area coverage.
- What Channel ID will be used?
- Will the access point connect to the wired network and, if so, is there connectivity available where the access point will be mounted?

9.16 Troubleshooting Wireless Networks

Troubleshooting wireless networks is sometimes easier than a wired network because of the mobility factor. A laptop with a wireless NIC installed can be used to troubleshoot connectivity, configuration, security, etc. Most wireless network problems stem from inconsistent configuration. The standards deployed must be for the lowest common denominator. For example, if a wireless NIC only supports 64-bit WEP encryption, then that must be what is used even if 128-bit WEP encryption is available on some of the cards. The list that follows are some general wireless networking tips designed to get you started. Most of these tips have been discussed in their previous sections, but it is nice to have a troubleshooting list in one spot.

- Is the SSID correct?
- Is the type of wireless network (ad hoc or infrastructure) correctly configured?
- Is the wireless NIC seen by the operating system? Use Device Manager to check.
- Is WEP enabled? If so, is the WEP key correctly configured? Is the WEP key length correct?
- Is open or shared key authentication being used? Check configuration.
- Can any devices attach to the access point? If not, check the access point.
- Is anything causing interference or attenuation? Check antenna placement.
- Is there a Channel ID overlap problem?
- If a manufacturer's utility is being used and Windows XP is installed, does the Network Properties window have the **Use Windows to configure my wireless network settings**

check box unchecked? If not, uncheck this check box to allow the utility to configure the wireless NIC.

Wireless networking is an emerging technology and will continue to grow in size, technology, and support issues. Today you must be familiar with this technology as corporations and home users install these types of products. Because the technology is reasonably priced, you may want to install your own wireless network for the experience. Enjoy this technology because more wireless technologies are evolving.

Chapter Summary

- A network is comprised of two or more devices that can communicate with one another and share resources.
- The three major types of network topologies are star, ring, and bus.
- Networks require some type of medium to transmit data. This medium is normally wire or wireless. The most common types of cable are twisted-pair and fiber-optic, although some very old networks have coax cable.
- Before a computer can communicate on a network, it must adhere to a set of communication rules to which all computers on the network comply. This set of communication rules is known as a common access method. Ethernet uses a common access method known as CSMA/CD whereas fiber networks and Token Ring use token passing as the common access method.
- The IEEE committee created network standards called the 802 standards. Each standard is given an 802.x number and represents an area of networking.
- ISO has developed the OSI model. The OSI model is a standard for information transfer across the network.
- A network protocol is a data communication language. There are three primary network protocols used: TCP/IP, NetBEUI, and IPX/SPX. TCP/IP is the most common network protocol and is used when accessing the Internet. The most commonly used protocol is TCP/IP.
- When you install a NIC card in a computer, you need to supply an appropriate driver, a unique computer name, a workgroup or domain name, the appropriate protocol, and network client software.
- You can troubleshoot a network by using the ping command. It is the most commonly used networking tool to determine the status of other devices on your network. You can connect a network printer in one of several ways. You can connect a printer to a port on a computer that is connected to the network. You can set up a computer that is designated as a print server. You can then connect the print server to the network. You can connect a printer with a network connector installed directly to the network.
- If you want to access a computer remotely, you can use DUN to dial the Internet or an organization that has a computer connected to a mode. You can also create a VPN to secure your data by implementing a secure "tunnel" through the Internet or an intranet.
- A browser allows you to view web pages across the Internet. Browsers frequently need plug-ins. A plug-in is an application designed to work with the browser. Common plug-

ins include Macromedia Flash, Macromedia Shockwave, RealNetwork's RealPlayer, Apple QuickTime, Adobe Acrobat Reader, and WinZip.
- Another common Internet related software tool is e-mail. It uses the SMTP protocol for sending and receiving e-mail messages.
- Wireless networks are networks that transmit data over air using either infrared or radio frequencies. Wireless networks operate at layers 1 and 2 of the OSI model. Most wireless networks in home and businesses use radio frequencies.
- WEP is used to encrypt data transmitted over wireless networks.

Review Questions

1. A _____ is a group of devices that can share resources in a single area such as a room or a building.
   a) WAN
   b) LAN
   c) IEEE 802.11 standard
   d) OSI

2. A _____ is communication between Local Area Networks.
   a) WAN
   b) LAN
   c) IEEE 802.11 standard
   d) OSI

3. The standard for wireless networks is _____.
   a) WAN
   b) LAN
   c) IEEE 802.11 standard
   d) OSI

4. The IEEE standard for Token Ring is _____.
   a) 802.2
   b) 802.3
   c) 802.4
   d) 802.5

5. The IEEE standard for CSMA/CD is _____.
   a) 802.2
   b) 802.3
   c) 802.4
   d) 802.5

6. A _____ defines how network devices connect.
   a) Protocol
   b) OSI Model
   c) Topology
   d) IEEE 802 standards

7. The most common network topology used today is the _____ .
   a) Ring
   b) Bus
   c) Star
   d) OSI

8. A _____ topology passes a special network packet from one device to another.
   a) Ring
   b) Bus
   c) Star
   d) OSI

9. _____ transmission is data transmitted in both directions but not at the same time.
   a) Full duplex
   b) Duplex
   c) Half duplex
   d) Simplex

10. _____ transmission is data transmitted in both directions but at the same time.
   a) Full duplex
   b) Duplex
   c) Half duplex
   d) Simplex

11. In a _____ topology all devices connect to one cable.
   a) Star
   b) Bus
   c) Ring
   d) Half duplex

12. A _____ server is used for retrieving e-mail.
   a) SMTP
   b) POP
   c) HTTP
   d) TCP/IP

13. A _____ server is used for sending e-mail.
    a) SMTP
    b) POP
    c) HTTP
    d) TCP/IP

14. A _____allows you to view web pages across the Internet.
    a) Web site
    b) Browser
    c) IPX/SPX protocol drive
    d) POP3 Server

15. In wireless communication, when multiple access points connect to the same main network, the network design is known as _____.
    a) BSS
    b) Infrastructure mode
    c) WEP
    d) ESS

16. The _____ is a standard for information transfer across the network.
    a) Half duplex transmission
    b) Topology
    c) BSS
    d) OSI Model

17. A _____, a network device that determines the best path to send a packet, works at layer 3, the network layer.
    a) Hub
    b) Switch
    c) Router
    d) Ethernet

18. A _____ of data is transmitted at the network layer of the OSI Model.
    a) Frame
    b) Bit
    c) Packet
    d) Byte

19. The _____ defines how the bits are transferred and retrieved across the network media. This layer is where connectors, cable, and voltage levels are defined.
    a) Presentation
    b) Session
    c) Network
    d) Physical

20. A _____ is guaranteed to be 1.544 Mbps bandwidth between two points.
    a) T1
    b) T2
    c) T3
    d) DSL

Lab Projects

Lab Project 1

The goal of this project is for you to be able to install and configure a NIC in a Windows 9x computer. You will need a computer with Windows 9x installed, and a NIC card with driver. The method used to install a NIC in Windows 9x depends on whether the NIC is a plug and play device or a non-plug and play or legacy device.

Installing a Plug and Play NIC

1. With the computer turned off, remove the **computer cover**.

2. Using proper ESD precautions, insert the **NIC** in a compatible bus slot and secure with a screw.

3. Turn the computer on and verify that Windows 9x loads.

4. Log on to Windows 9x using the userid and password provided by the instructor or lab assistant.

5. Windows 9x automatically detects and installs the NIC. If Windows 9x does not detect a driver for the NIC, you will be prompted for a driver location. If this is the case, insert the driver disk and enter the path to the driver. Proceed to the **Checking the Installation** section.

Installing a Non-Plug and Play or Legacy NIC

6. Using jumpers or a software configuration utility, configure the NIC so it will use system resources that do not conflict with any other device.

7. With the computer turned off, remove the **computer cover**.

8. Using proper ESD precautions, insert the **NIC** in a compatible bus slot and secure with a screw.

9. Turn the computer on and verify that Windows 9x loads.

10. Log on to Windows 9x using the userid and password provided by the instructor or lab assistant.

11. Click on the **Start** button, point to the **Settings** option, and double-click on the **Control Panel** option. The Control Panel window opens.

12. Double-click on the **Add/Remove Hardware** icon. The Add/Remove Hardware wizard opens. Select the **Next** button twice.

13. Windows searches for new plug and play devices. When Windows does not find any, you are given the option to allow Windows to search for non-plug and play devices or you can select the hardware from a list. Choose **No, I want to select the hardware from a list** and click on the **Next** button.

14. Scroll down and select **Network Adapters** and then click on the **Next** button.

15. Select the **NIC Manufacturer and Model** from the list. If the NIC is not listed, select **Have Disk**, enter a path to the driver files, and click on **OK**.

16. After selecting the proper NIC, click on the **Next** button.

17. Select **Finish** to continue the installation. If prompted, enter the proper configuration information for the NIC and click on **OK**.

18. Restart the computer.

Checking the Installation

19. From the **Start** menu, point to **Settings,** and then click on the **Control Panel** option.

20. From the Control Panel window, double-click on the **System** icon, and then select **Device Manager**.

21. Expand **Network Adapters**, select the **network adapter** installed in the computer, and then click on **Properties**.

22. Click on the **General** tab.

    What is the device status of your NIC?

    _____

23. Select the **Driver** tab.

    What is the driver version number of the NIC?

    _____

24. Select the **Resources** tab.

    What resources are being used by the NIC?

    _____

    Are any devices conflicting with your NIC? If so, list them below.

    _____

25. Click on **OK** to close the Network Adapters Properties window.

Lab Project 2

The goal of this project is for you to be able to properly install and configure a NIC using Windows NT Workstation. You will need a computer with Windows NT Workstation loaded, a NIC card, and a NIC driver disk. Installing a NIC using NT Workstation is different from using Windows 95, 98, or 2000 Professional because NT Workstation is not a plug and play operating system.

1. With the computer turned off, remove its cover.

2. Using proper ESD precautions, insert the **NIC** in a compatible bus slot and secure with a screw.

3. Turn the computer on and verify that Windows NT Workstation loads.

4. Log on to NT Workstation using the userid and password provided by the instructor or lab assistant.

    What rights are required to be able to install a NIC in Windows NT Workstation?

    _____

5. Right-click on the **Network Neighborhood** desktop icon and select **Properties**. The Network window opens.

    What alternate method can be used to open the Network window?

    _____

6. Select the **Adapters** tab, the Adapters Installation and Configuration window opens.

7. Click on the **Add** button and the Select Network Adapter window opens.

8. If the NIC that is installed in the computer is listed, click on it from the list. If the proper NIC is not listed, insert the NIC driver disk, click on the **Have Disk** button, and enter the path to the driver.

9. If prompted, insert the Windows NT Workstation CD, or enter the path to the installation files, and click on the **Continue** button.

10. If prompted, enter configuration information such as Ethernet ID, bus type, and slot number and click on the **OK** button.

11. Windows NT Workstation copies and installs the NIC driver files.

12. Click on the **Close** button to exit the Adapter Installation and Configuration window.

Lab Project 3

The goal of this project is for you to be able to properly install and configure a NIC using Windows 2000 Professional. You will need a computer with Windows 2000 Professional installed, a NIC card, and a NIC driver. The method used to install a NIC in Windows 2000 Professional depends on whether the NIC is a plug and play device or a non-plug and play device (also known as a legacy device).

What type of NIC is to be installed into the computer: plug and play or non plug and play?

_____

Contact your instructor or lab assistant if unsure. Once the type of NIC is determined, follow the directions appropriate for the type of NIC: Installing a Plug and Play NIC or Installing a Non-Plug and Play or Legacy NIC.

Installing a Plug and Play NIC

1. With the computer turned off, remove the **computer cover**.

2. Using proper ESD precautions, insert the **NIC** in a compatible bus slot and secure with a screw.

3. Turn on the computer and verify that Windows 2000 Professional loads.

4. Log on to Windows 2000 Professional using the userid and password provided by the instructor or lab assistant.

5. Windows 2000 Professional automatically loads the drivers and configures the NIC. If Windows 2000 Professional does not have a driver for the NIC, you will be prompted for a driver location. If this is the case, insert the driver disk into the floppy drive and enter the path to the driver (A:).

6. Go to the section labeled **Checking the Installation**.

Installing a Non-Plug and Play or Legacy NIC

7. With the computer turned off, remove the **computer cover**.

8. Using proper ESD precautions, insert the **NIC** in a compatible bus slot and secure with a screw.

9. Turn on the computer and verify that Windows 2000 Professional loads.

10. Log on to Windows 2000 Professional using the userid and password provided by the instructor or lab assistant.

11. Click on the **Start** button.

12. Point to the **Settings** option.

13. Click on the **Control Panel** option. The Control Panel window opens.

14. Double-click on the **Add/Remove Hardware** icon. The Add/Remove Hardware wizard opens.

15. Click on the **Next** button.

16. Choose the **Add/Troubleshoot a device** option and select **Next**.

17. Windows searches for plug and play devices. When the search is over, select the **Add a new device** option from the **Choose a Hardware Device** window, and then click on the **Next** button.

18. Choose the **Yes, search for new hardware** option and click on the **Next** button.

19. Windows searches for non-plug and play hardware and displays devices found. Choose your NIC from the list and select **Next**.

20. In the **Found New Hardware** wizard window select the **Resources** button.

21. Ensure the resources assigned to the NIC are correct. Make any necessary changes and click on the **OK** button to return to the Found New Hardware Wizard window.

22. Select the **Finish** button twice to complete the installation.

23. Continue to the **Checking the Installation** section.

Checking the Installation

24. Click on the **Start** button.

25. Point to the **Programs** option.

26. Point to the **Administrative Tools** option.

27. Click on the **Computer Management** option. The Computer Management window opens.

28. In the left window, select **Device Manager**.

29. In the right window, select the **+ (plus sign)** next to **Network adapters**.

30. Right-click on the NIC you just installed and select the **Properties** option from the menu. The Properties page opens.

31. Click on the **General** tab.

    What is the device status of the NIC selected?

    _____

32. Select the **advanced** tab (if available).

    Are any properties listed? If so, list one property and its value.

    _____

33. Select the **Driver** tab.

    What is the driver version number of your NIC's driver?

    _____

34. Select the **Resources** tab.

    What resources are being used by your NIC?

    _____

    Are any devices conflicting with your NIC? If so, list them below.

    _____

35. Click on **OK** to close the Properties page.

Lab Project 4

The goal of this project is to install the Microsoft Client on a Windows 9x computer. You will need a Windows 9x computer with NIC installed and configured. The Microsoft Client for Windows 9x enables a client computer to take advantage of the built-in Microsoft networking services in a Microsoft peer-to-peer network. It also allows a Windows 9x computer to access a Windows domain.

1. Turn on the computer and verify that Windows 9x loads.

2. If necessary, log on to Windows 9x using the userid and password provided by the instructor or lab assistant.

3. From the Start menu, point to the **Settings** option, click on the **Control Panel** option, and then double-click on the **Network** icon. The Network Properties window opens.

4. Click on the **Add** button. The Select Network Component Type window opens.

5. From the Select Network Component Type window, choose **Client** and then select **Add**. The Select Network Client window opens.

6. Highlight the **Microsoft** option, select **Client for Microsoft Networks**, and then click on the **OK** button.

   Which Microsoft network clients appear as available in the Select Network Client window?

   _____

7. From the Network Properties window, verify that **Client for Microsoft Networks** appears in the Installed Components window, and then click on the **OK** button.

8. If prompted, insert the Windows 9x CD-ROM in the drive or enter a path to the installation files.

9. When the Client for Microsoft Networks installation finishes, reboot the computer for the new client to take effect.

Lab Project 5

The goal of this project is to install networking on a computer that uses NT Workstation. You will need an NT Workstation computer with NIC installed and configured. The instructor or lab assistant must be prepared to answer questions such as these:

• Should the student select Workgroup or Domain network model?

• Is DHCP being used in the lab?

You must configure NT networking a bit differently than the other operating systems. The Network Setup wizard takes you through the installation process.

1. Turn on the computer and verify that NT Workstation loads.

2. Log on to Windows using the userid and password provided by the instructor or lab assistant.

3. From the **Start** menu, point to the **Settings** option, click on the **Control Panel** option, and then double-click on the **Network** icon. A dialog box appears stating that networking is not installed and asks if you want to install it. Click on the **Yes** button.

4. The next prompt asks if you are wired to the network or if you are going to use a modem to connect. In a lab environment, you are probably wired to the network. Look at the back of the computer and see if a NIC is installed and a network cable connects to the NIC. If so, click on the **Wired to the network** check box and click on the **Next** button.

5. On the next screen, click on the **Start Search** button so the operating system looks for the installed NIC. This exercise assumes the NIC is installed, but if it hasn't been, you can click on the **Select from list** button and install the NIC drivers and then continue. The NIC appears in the window. Click on the **Next** button.

6. A list of protocols appears. Ensure the **TCP/IP Protocol** is selected and click on the **Next** button.

7. The Network Services screen appears. These default services are what allow your computer to participate in a peer-to-peer network or in a server-based network. Ensure that **RPC Configuration, NetBIOS Interface, Workstation,** and **Server** are all checked and click on the **Next** button.

8. A message appears that NT is going to install the components. Click on the **Next** button. Another screen appears that allows you to change your binding order. Simply click on the **Next** button. You may be asked to insert the NT installation CD or be prepared to type in the path to where the programs are stored. Contact your instructor or lab assistant if you are unsure what to do.

9. Since TCP/IP was selected, you will be asked if there is a DHCP server connected to the network. This is lab-dependent. Most schools have a DHCP server, but contact the instructor or student assistant if you are unsure. If you select **No**, you must enter the IP address, mask, and default gateway information. If you select **Yes**, the computer will be assigned this information by the DHCP server.

10. Click on the **Next** button to start the NT networking services.

11. You are asked to give the computer a name and determine if the computer participates in a peer-to-peer network (Workgroup option) or a server-based network (Domain option); either way, you will have to enter either a workgroup name or a domain name. Contact the instructor or lab assistant for the correct names if you are unsure. Click on the **Next** button after all information has been entered.

What is the network name of your computer?

_____

Is the computer participating in a peer-to-peer network or a server-based network?

_____

Is DHCP being used?

_____

12. Click on the **Finish** button to complete the installation.

13. The computer must reboot in order for the setting to take effect. Click on the **Yes** button to restart the computer.

14. After restarting and logging in, double-click on the **Network Neighborhood** desktop icon.

How many other computers do you see on the network?

_____

Lab Project 6

The goal of this project is to correctly install Microsoft Client on a Windows 2000 Professional computer. You will need a computer with Windows 2000 Professional Workstation with a NIC installed and configured (Client for Microsoft Networks is not installed.)

Microsoft Client enables a computer to take advantage of the built-in Microsoft networking services in a Microsoft peer-to-peer network. It also allows a computer to access a Windows NT domain.

1. Turn on the computer and verify that Windows 2000 Professional loads.

2. Log on to Windows 2000 Professional using the userid and password provided by the instructor or lab assistant.

3. Right-click on the **My Network Places** desktop icon, and select the **Properties** option. The Network and Dial-up Connections window opens.

4. Right-click on the **Local Area Connection** icon and select the **Properties** option. The Local Area Connections window opens.

   Which installed network components are being used by this connection?

   _____

5. Select the **Install** button. The Select Network Component Type window opens.

6. Choose the **Client** option, and then click on the **Add** button. The Select Network Client window opens.

   What network clients are listed as available?

   _____

7. Select the **Client for Microsoft Networks** option, and click on the **OK** button.

8. If prompted, insert the Windows 2000 Professional installation CD-ROM or enter a path to the installation files.

9. When prompted, reboot the workstation for the new network settings to take effect.

Lab Project 7

The goal of this project is for you to be able to install and configure the TCP/IP protocol on a Windows 9x computer. You will need a Windows 9x computer with a NIC installed and configured. The TCP/IP protocol is a routable protocol. It is the protocol that powers the Internet, so it is important that you understand how it is installed and configured.

1. Turn on the computer and verify that Windows 9x loads.

2. If necessary, log on to Windows 9x using the userid and password provided by the instructor or lab assistant.

3. Right-click on the **My Network Places** desktop icon, and then select **Properties**. The Network Properties window opens.

   What other method can be used to access Network Properties?

   _____

4. Click on the **Add** button, and the Select Network Component Type window opens.

   What network component types are listed as available?

   _____

5. Click on the **Protocol** item, and then click on the **Add** button. The Select Network Protocol window opens.

6. Click on the **Microsoft** option in the left window. In the right window, click on the **TCP/IP** option and then click on the **OK** button.

7. From Network Properties, scroll down and choose **TCP/IP** and then select **Properties**.

8. If you are using DHCP on your network, choose **Obtain an IP address automatically**. If you are not using DHCP on your network, choose **Specify an IP address**, and enter an **IP address** and **subnet mask**. Contact the instructor or a lab assistant if you are unsure which option to use.

9. If needed, select **DNS configuration** and enter DNS information, select **Gateway** and enter gateway information, and select **WINS configuration** and enter WINS information. Again, contact the instructor or lab assistant if you are unsure which option to use.

   Which of the following is responsible for host name to IP address resolution: DNS, gateway, or WINS?

   _____

   Which of the following is responsible for NetBIOS name to IP address resolution: DNS, gateway, or WINS?

   _____

10. Click on the **OK** button and if prompted, insert the Windows 9x CD-ROM or enter the path to the installation files.

11. Reboot the computer for the new settings to take effect.

Lab Project 8

The goal of this project is for you to be able to install and configure the TCP/IP protocol on a Windows NT Workstation computer. You will need a Windows NT Workstation computer with a NIC installed and configured. The TCP/IP Protocol is a routable protocol. It is the protocol that powers the Internet, so it is important that you understand how it is installed and configured.

1. Turn on the computer and verify that NT Workstation loads.

2. Log on to NT Workstation using the userid and password provided by the instructor or lab assistant.

3. From the Start menu, point to the **Settings** option, click on the **Control Panel** option, and then double-click on the **Network** icon. The Network Installation and Configuration window opens.

   What alternate method can be used to access the Network Installation and Configuration window?

   _____

4. Click on the **Protocols** tab. The Protocols window opens.

   Which protocols are already installed on your computer?

   _____

5. Click on the **Add** button. The Select Network Protocol window opens.

   List the protocols that are available for installation.

   _____

6. Select the **TCP/IP Protocol** option and click on the **OK** button.

7. If DHCP is used on the network, select **Yes** to use DHCP, otherwise select **No**. Contact the instructor or lab assistant if you are unsure which option to select.

8. If prompted, insert the Windows NT Workstation CD-ROM or enter the path to the installation files and click on the **Continue** button. When TCP/IP finishes installing, select **Close**. The TCP/IP Properties page opens.

9. If DHCP is used on the network, select **Obtain an IP address from a DHCP server**. If DHCP is not used, select **Specify an IP address** and enter the **IP address**, **subnet mask**, and **default gateway** information provided by the instructor or lab assistant.

   When DHCP is not used, which one of the following is optional: IP address, subnet mask, or default gateway?

   _____

10. If directed by the instructor, click on the **DNS** tab and enter the provided DNS information. Click on the **WINS** tab and enter the provided WINS information.

11. When all TCP/IP configuration information has been entered, click on the **OK** button. NT Workstation goes through a bindings process, and you will be prompted to restart the computer. Restart the computer for the new settings to take effect.

Lab Project 9

The goal of this project is for you to be able to install and configure the TCP/IP protocol on a Windows 2000 Computer. You will need a Windows 2000 Professional computer with a NIC installed and configured. The TCP/IP protocol is a routable protocol. It is the protocol that powers the Internet, so it is important that you understand how it is installed and configured.

1. Turn on the computer and verify that Windows 2000 Professional loads.

2. Log on to Windows 2000 Professional using the userid and password provided by the instructor or lab assistant.

3. Right-click on the **My Network Places** desktop icon, and then select **Properties**. The Network and Dial-up Connections window opens.

4. Right-click on the **Local Area Connection** icon, and then select **Properties**. The Local Area Connections page opens.

5. Choose **Install.** The Select Network Component Type window opens.

   What types of network components are available?

   _____

6. Choose **Protocol** and then select **Add**. The Select Network Protocol window opens.

   Which network protocols are available for installation?

   _____

7. Choose the **TCP/IP** protocol and then select **OK**.

8. If prompted, insert the Windows 2000 Professional CD-ROM into the drive, or enter the path to the installation files.

9. From the Local Area Connection window, highlight **TCP/IP**, and then select **Properties**. The TCP/IP Properties window opens.

10. If you are using DHCP, select the **Obtain an IP Address Automatically** option. If you are not using **DHCP,** select the **Use the Following IP Address** option and enter an **IP address**, a **subnet mask**, and the **default gateway** information provided by the instructor or lab assistant.

    Which of the following is optional: IP address, subnet mask, or default gateway?

    _____

11. When you are finished entering TCP/IP configuration information, click on the **OK** button and close the Local Area Connections Properties window.

Lab Project 10

The goal of this project is to create a functional CAT 5 UTP network cable. You will need the following parts:

- Category 5 UTP cable
- RJ-45 connectors
- CAT 5 stripper/crimper tool
- UTP cable tester

Note: Standard Ethernet networks are cabled with either CAT 5 UTP cable or RG-58 coaxial cable. In this exercise, you create a standard CAT 5 cable for use with either 10BaseT or 100BaseT networks connected through a central hub or switch.

1. Category 5 UTP cable consists of four twisted pairs of wires, color-coded for easy identification. The color-coded wires are as follows:

    Pair 1: White/Orange and Orange

    Pair 2: White/Blue and Blue

    Pair 3: White/Green and Green

    Pair 4: White/Brown and Brown

2. Using the **stripper/crimper tool**, strip approximately **1/2 inch** of the protective outer sheath to expose the four twisted pairs of wires. Most strippers have a strip gauge to ensure stripping the proper length. (See Figure 9.34.)

    Note: In order to make it easier to sort the wire pairs, the sheathing can be stripped further than 1/2 inch, then the wires can be sorted properly and trimmed to the proper length.

Figure 9.34: Using a Stripper/Crimper Tool

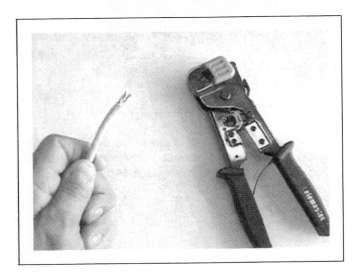

3. Untwist the exposed wire pairs. Be careful that you do not remove more twist than necessary. Sort the wires according to the following:

Wire 1: White/Orange Wire 5: Blue

Wire 2: Orange Wire 6: Green

Wire 3: White/Green Wire 7: White/Brown

Wire 4: White/Blue Wire 8: Brown

Ethernet cabling utilizes wires 1, 2, 3, and 6. Using the above wiring scheme means that the cable will use the White/Orange-Orange and White/Green-Green wire pairs. (See Figure 9.35.)

Will both ends of the cable need to follow the same wiring schematic?

Figure 9.35: Creating the Correct Cable Scheme

4. Insert the sorted and trimmed **cable** into an **RJ-45 connector**. The RJ-45 connector's key should face downward. Verify that all eight wires fully insert into the RJ-45 connector and that they are inserted in the proper order. (See Figure 9.36.)

Figure 9.36: The Inserted Cable Ends

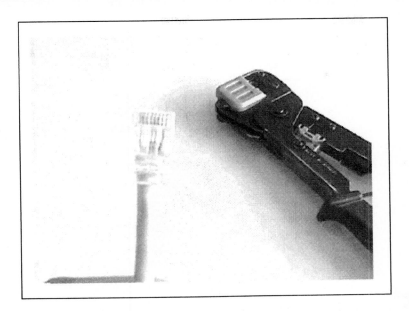

5. Insert the **cable-connector assembly** into the **stripper/crimper tool** and crimp the connector firmly. (See Figure 9.37.)

Figure 9.37: Crimping the Cable

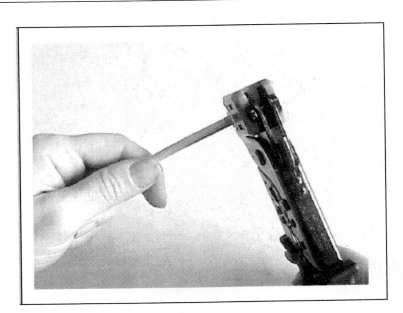

6. Remove the **cable/connector assembly** from the **stripper/crimper tool** and verify that the wires fully insert into the connector and that they are in the proper order. (See Figure 9.38.)

Figure 9.38: Removing the Cable

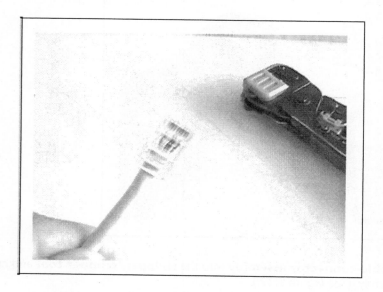

7. Repeat steps 2 through 6 for the other end of the CAT 5 UTP cable. (See Figure 9.39.)

Figure 9.39: The Newly Created Cable

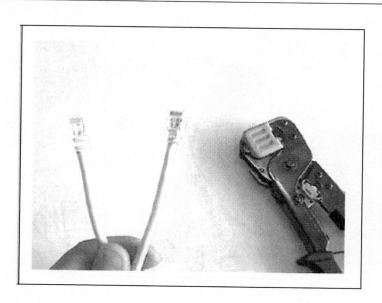

Can the cable be used at this point?

_____

8. Before using the cable, it should be tested with a cable tester. This verifies that you have end-to-end continuity on individual wires and proper continuity between wire pairs. Insert the **RJ-45 connector** into the proper **cable tester receptacle** and verify that the cable is functional. (See Figure 9.40.)

Figure 9.40: Testing the Cable

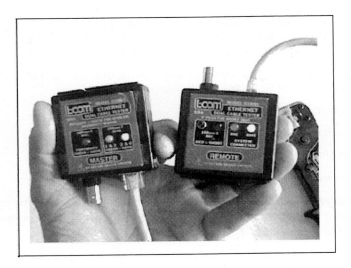

Lab Project 11

The goal of this project is to create a functional CAT 5 UTP crossover cable. You will need the following parts:

• Category 5 UTP cable

• RJ-45 connectors

• Stripper/crimper tool

• UTP cable tester

Note: In normal situations, straight-through CAT 5 UTP cabling is used to connect to a central hub or switch. In this exercise, you create a crossover CAT 5 cable for use when connecting two network devices—computers without using a central hub or switch.

1. Category 5 UTP cable consists of four twisted pairs of wires that are color-coded for easy identification. The color-coded wires are as follows:

   Pair 1: White/Orange and Orange

   Pair 2: White/Blue and Blue

   Pair 3: White/Green and Green

   Pair 4: White/Brown and Brown

2. Using the **CAT stripper/crimper tool**, strip approximately **1/2 inch** of the protective outer sheath to expose the four twisted pairs of wires. Most tools have a strip gauge to ensure stripping the proper length.

   Note: In order to make it easier to sort the wire pairs, the sheathing can be stripped further than 1/2 inch. The wires can then be sorted properly and trimmed to the proper length.

3. Untwist the exposed wire pairs. Be careful that you do not remove more twist than necessary. Sort the wires as follows:

   Wire 1: White/Orange Wire 5: Blue

   Wire 2: Orange Wire 6: Green

   Wire 3: White/Green Wire 7: White/Brown

   Wire 4: White/Blue Wire 8: Brown

   Ethernet networks utilize wires 1, 2, 3, and 6. Using the above wiring scheme means the cable will use the White/Orange-Orange and White/Green-Green wire pairs.

   When making a crossover cable, will both ends of the cable need to follow the same wiring schematic?

   _____

4. Insert the sorted and trimmed **cable** into a **RJ-45 connector**. The RJ-45 connector's key should face downward. Verify that all eight wires fully insert into the RJ-45 connector, and that they are inserted in the proper order.

5. Insert the **cable-connector assembly** into the **CAT 5 stripper/crimper tool** and crimp the connector firmly.

6. Remove the **cable/connector assembly** from the **CAT 5 stripper/crimper** tool and verify that the wires are fully inserted into the connector and that they are in the proper order.

7. To create the crossover cable, the wire pairs must be put in a different order. To accomplish this, repeat steps 2 through 6 on the opposite end of the cable, but when sorting the wire pairs, use the following color codes:

Wire 1: White/Green Wire 5: Blue

Wire 2: Green Wire 6: Orange

Wire 3: White/Orange Wire 7: White/Brown

Wire 4: White/Blue Wire 8: Brown

Can the crossover cable be used at this point?

8. Before using the crossover cable, it should be tested with a cable tester. This verifies that you have end-to-end continuity on individual wires and proper continuity between wire pairs. Insert the **RJ-45 connector** into the proper **cable tester receptacle** and verify that the cable is functional.

Note: Your cable tester must have the capability to test crossover cables.

Lab Project 12

The goal of this project is for you to be able to share a local printer on a Windows 9x computer so it will be available to other workstations. You will need a Windows 95 or 98 computer with a NIC installed and configured, and a printer physically attached and configured.

Note: A printer that is physically attached (local) to a networked workstation can accept and process print jobs from other workstations on the network. Before this can happen, the local printer must be shared on the network. Before a printer can be shared in Windows 9x, Printer Sharing must be installed.

Installing Printer Sharing

1. Turn on the computer and verify that Windows 9x loads.

2. If necessary, log on to Windows 9x using the userid and password provided by the instructor or lab assistant.

3. Right-click on the **Network Neighborhood** desktop icon and select the **Properties** option. The Network Properties window opens.

4. Choose **File and Print Sharing**, select **I want to be able to allow others to print to my printers**, and then click on the **OK** button.

   What will this setting allow you to share?

   _____

5. From the Network Properties window, click on the **OK** button.

6. If prompted, insert the Windows 9x installation CD-ROM or enter a path to the installation files.

7. Reboot the computer when prompted.

Sharing a Windows 9x Printer

8. From the **Start** menu, point to **Settings**, and then click on the **Printers** option. The Printers folder opens.

9. Right-click on a specific printer that is attached to the computer, and then select the **Sharing** option. The Printer Sharing window opens.

10. Select the **Shared As** radio button, and enter a share name of **TESTPRINT** in the Share Name field.

11. In the **Comment** field, enter a user-friendly description of this printer.

12. In the Password field, type the word **password**.

    What effect will setting a password have?

    _____

13. Click on the **Apply** button to save your sharing settings, re-enter the password **(password)** when prompted, and then click on the **OK** button.

14. Click on the **OK** button to exit the Printer Sharing window. Your printer is now shared and available on the network.

Lab Project 13

The goal of this project is for you to be able to share a local printer on a Windows NT Workstation so it will be available to other workstations on the network. You will need a Windows NT Workstation with a NIC installed and configured, and a printer physically attached and configured.

Note: A printer that is physically attached (local) to a networked workstation can accept and process print jobs from other workstations on the network. Before this can happen, the local printer must be shared on the network.

1. Turn on the computer and verify that NT Workstation loads.

2. Log on to NT Workstation using the userid and password provided by the instructor or lab assistant.

3. Click on the **Start** button, point to **Settings**, and then click on the **Printers** option. The Printers folder opens.

   What other method can be used to access the Printers folder?

   _____

4. Right-click on the name of the printer that is attached to the workstation. Select the **Sharing** option. The Printer Sharing window opens.

   What other method can be used to access the Printer Sharing window?

   _____

5. Click on the **Shared** radio button and enter a name in the Share Name field.

   What name did you assign to the printer?

   _____

6. Click on the **OK** button to return to the Printers folder. The printer is now shared.

   How can you verify that the printer has been shared?

   _____

Lab Project 14

The goal of this project is for you to be able to share a local printer on a Windows 2000 Professional Workstation so it will be available to other workstations. You will need a Windows 2000 Professional Workstation with a NIC installed and configured, and a printer physically attached and configured.

Note: A printer that is physically attached (local) to a networked workstation can accept and process print jobs from other workstations on the network. Before this can happen, the local printer must be shared on the network.

1. Turn on the computer and verify that Windows 2000 Professional loads.

2. Log on to Windows 2000 Professional using the userid and password provided by the instructor or lab assistant.

3. Click on the **Start** button, point to the **Settings** option, and then click on the **Printers** option. The Printers folder opens.

4. Right-click on the local printer attached to the workstation and select the **Properties** option. The printer's Properties window opens.

5. Click on the **Sharing** tab. From the Sharing window, you can share the printer, give it a share name, and install additional drivers for each type of Windows operating system connected to the network that will use the printer. You can also publish the printer in Active Directory if the workstation is part of a Windows 2000 domain.

6. Choose the **Shared as** option and type **TestShare** in the Share Name field.

7. Choose **Apply** and then click on the **OK** button. The printer's Properties window closes and then returns to the Printers folder. The local printer is now shared and is available to other workstations on the network.

   How can you tell the printer has been shared?

Lab Project 15

The goal of this project is for you to understand how to connect to and use a networked printer on a Windows 9x Computer. You will need a Windows 9x computer with a NIC installed and configured, and local printer installed and shared on the network.

Note: A printer that is physically attached (local) to a networked computer and shared on the network can accept and process print jobs from remote computers on the network. Before this can happen, the remote computers must connect to the shared printer and install the proper printer driver.

1. Turn the computer on and verify that Windows 9x loads.

2. Log on to Windows 9x using the userid and password provided by the instructor or lab assistant.

3. Click on the **Start** button, point to the **Settings** option, and then click on the **Printers** option. The Printers folder opens.

4. Double-click on the **Add Printer** icon and the Add Printer wizard runs.

5. Click on the **Next** button, select the **Network printer** option, and then click on the **Next** button.

6. Locate the shared printer, highlight the printer, and then click on the **OK** button. Contact the instructor or lab assistant if you cannot locate the shared printer. The printer's UNC name appears in the Network path or Queue Name field.

   What does UNC stand for?

   _____

7. Choose **No** to the Do you print from MS-DOS based programs prompt, and click on the **Next** button.

8. Enter the name **LABTEST** for this printer in the Printer Name field.

   Where does this printer name appear?

   _____

9. Select the **Yes** option in order to have Windows use this printer as the default printer and then click on the **Next** button.

10. Choose **Yes** to print a test page and then select **Finish**.

11. The printer driver downloads and installs on your local computer.

12. To complete the connection, type **password** for the printer share password and then click on the **OK** button.

    Can the printer be used across the network without a network user supplying the password?

    _____

13. If the printer connection and driver installation were successful, a printer test page prints.

Lab Project 16

The goal of this project is for you to be able to connect to and use a networked printer in Windows NT Workstation. You will need a Windows NT Workstation with a NIC installed and configured, and a local printer installed and shared on the network.

Note: A printer that is physically attached (local) to a networked computer and shared on the network can accept and process print jobs from remote computers on the network. Before this can happen, the remote computers must connect to the shared printer and install the proper printer driver.

1. Turn the computer on and verify that Windows NT Workstation loads.

2. Log on to Windows NT Workstation using the userid and password provided by the instructor or lab assistant.

3. Click on the **Start** button, point to the **Settings** option, and then click on the **Printers** option. The Printers folder opens.

4. Double-click on the **Add Printer** icon and the Add Printer wizard runs.

5. Choose **Network Printer Server** and then click on the **Next** button. The Connect to Printer window opens.

6. From the Connect to Printer window, browse through the available computers and shared printers until you locate the appropriate shared printer. After several minutes of browsing, contact the instructor or lab assistant if you cannot locate the shared printer.

7. Click on the **appropriate shared printer**. The printer's UNC name appears in the Printer field. Click on the **Next** button.

   The UNC name is made up of two parts. What do these two parts represent?

   _____

8. Choose **Yes** for Windows applications to use this printer as the default printer, and then click on the **OK** button.

9. The printer driver downloads and installs. Click on the **Finish** button to exit the Add Printer wizard. You have now connected to and installed the driver for a networked printer.

   How can you tell the printer has been connected to a shared printer?

   _____

Lab Project 17

The goal of this project is to connect to and use a networked printer in Windows 2000 Professional. You will need a Windows 2000 Professional computer with a NIC installed and configured, and a local printer installed and shared on the network.

Note: A printer that is physically attached (local) to a networked workstation and shared on the network can accept and process print jobs from remote workstations on the network. Before this can happen, a remote workstation must connect to the shared printer and install the proper printer driver.

1. Turn the computer on and verify that Windows 2000 Professional loads.

2. Log on to Windows 2000 Professional using the userid and password provided by the instructor or lab assistant.

3. From the **Start** menu, point to **Settings**, and then click on the **Printers** option. The Printers folder opens.

4. Double-click on the **Add Printer** icon and the Add Printer wizard opens.

5. Click on the **Next** option, and the Local or Network Printer window opens.

6. Choose **Network Printer** and then select **Next**. The Locate Your Printer window opens.

7. If the workstation is part of an Active Directory domain, you could choose the **Find a printer in the directory** option or select the **Connect to a printer on the Internet or on your intranet** option and enter the URL for the printer. Contact the instructor or lab assistant if you are unsure about which option to choose.

   What does the acronym URL stand for?

   _____

8. Choose the **Type the printer name or click on Next to browse for a printer** option and then click on the **Next** button. The Browse for Printer window opens.

9. From the Browse for Printer window, browse through the available computers and shared printers until you find the appropriate shared printer. Contact the instructor or lab assistant if you are unsure about which printer to choose.

10. Highlight the **shared printer**. The printer's UNC name displays in the Printer Name field. Click on the **Next** button.

    The UNC name is made up of two parts. What do these two parts represent?

    _____

11. From the Default Printer window, choose **Yes** for Windows to use this printer as your default printer, and then select **Next**.

12. From the Completing the Add Printer Wizard window, review the settings and click on **Finish**.

13. The printer driver automatically downloads from the host workstation and you return to the Printers folder after the driver downloads. You have now connected to and installed the driver for a networked printer.

How can you tell the printer has been connected to a shared printer?

_____

Lab Project 18

The goal of this project is for you to understand how to create a dial-up connection using Windows 98. You will need a Windows 98 computer with a modem and Dial-up Networking installed and configured. You will also need a phone number of a dial-up server.

Note: The Windows Dial-up Networking (DUN) utility allows you to create and configure dial-up connections to dial-up access servers. In this exercise, you create a dial-up connection using Windows 98.

1. Turn the computer on and verify that Windows 98 loads.

2. Log on to Windows 98 using the userid and password provided by the instructor or lab assistant.

3. Double-click on the **My Computer** desktop icon and then double-click on the **Dial-up Networking** folder. The Dial-up Networking folder opens.

   Can you create a new connection if a modem has not been installed?

   _____

4. Double-click on the **Make New Connection** icon. The **Make New Connection** window opens.

5. Type **Test** in the Connection Name field and from the **Select a device** drop-down menu select the modem to use for this connection. Click on the **Next** button.

6. Enter the **area code** and **phone number** of the remote dial-up server to be dialed, select the **Country or Region code** from the drop-down menu, and click on the **Next** button. Contact the instructor or lab assistant for this number.

7. Click on the **Finish** button to create the Test connection.

8. Close the **Make New Connection** window. The Test Connection icon appears in the Dial-up Networking folder.

   Can you modify the dialing properties of the Test connection after it has been created?

   _____

   To use the Test connection, follow these steps:

9. Double-click on the **My Computer** desktop icon and then double-click on the **Dial-up Networking** folder. The Dial-up Networking folder opens.

10. Double-click on the **Test Connection** icon. The Connect to window opens.

11. Enter a **username** and **password** for the connection, verify the proper **phone number** is listed, and click on the **Connect** button. The Dial-up Networking utility will complete the connection to the remote dial-up server.

Lab Project 19

The goal of this project is to use the Dial-up Networking utility to create a dial-up connection in Windows NT Workstation. You will need a computer with Windows NT Workstation and a modem and Dial-up Networking installed.

Note: Windows NT Workstation comes with Dial-up Networking to enable you to create a dial-up connection to a remote dial-up access server.

1. Turn the computer on and verify that Windows NT Workstation loads.

2. Log on to NT Workstation using the userid and password provided by the instructor or lab assistant.

3. Double-click on the **My Computer** desktop icon and then double-click on the **Dial-up Networking** icon. The Dial-up Networking window opens.

4. To create a new dial-up connection, select **New**. The New Phonebook Entry wizard starts.

5. Type **Test** in the **Name the phonebook entry** field and click on the **Next** button.

6. From the Server window, select the type of dial-up connection you are configuring.

   Which type of connection would you choose for browsing the web?

   _____

7. Choose **I am calling the Internet** and click on **Next**.

8. Enter the phone number of the Internet Service Provider (ISP) you are calling and click on **Next**.

9. Click on **Finish** to complete the creation of the Test connection.

   Where will the new connection appear?

   _____

10. To use the Test connection, double-click on the **My Computer** desktop icon and then double-click on the **Dial-up Networking** icon.

11. From the Phonebook Entry drop-down menu, select the **Test** connection.

12. Select **Dial**, enter a **user name**, **password**, and **domain** (if required), and click on **OK**. Dial-up Networking dials the Internet Service Provider and completes the connection.

Lab Project 20

The goal of this project is to use the Dial-up Networking utility to create a dial-up connection in Windows 2000 Professional. You will need a computer with Windows 2000 Professional and a modem installed and a phone number of a dial-up server.

Note: Windows 2000 Professional comes with Dial-up Networking to enable you to create a dial-up connection to a remote dial-up access server.

1. Turn the computer on and verify that Windows 2000 Professional loads.

2. Log on to Windows 2000 Professional using the userid and password provided by the instructor or lab assistant.

3. From the Start menu, choose **Settings**, and then select **Network and Dial-up Connections**.

   What other method can be used to access Network and Dial-up Connections?

   _____

4. Double-click on the **Make New Connection** icon. The Network Connection wizard starts.

5. Click on the **Next** button.

6. From the Network Connection Type window, you can select the **type of connection** you are making.

   Which connection type would you select to allow your computer to act as a Remote Dial-up Access Server?

   _____

7. Select **Dial-up to Private Network** and click on the **Next** button.

8. Enter the **Phone number** of the Remote Dial-up Access Server. Contact the instructor or lab assistant for the number. Click on the **Next** button.

9. Select **Create this connection for all users** and click on the **Next** button.

10. Enter **Test in the Connection Name** field and click on the **Finish** button.

11. A new Dial-up connection appears in the Network and Dial-up Connection window.

12. Double-click on the **Test connection** icon, enter a User name and Password, and click on **Dial**. Dial-up Networking places the call and completes the connection to the remote dial-up access server.

Lab Project 21

The goal of this project is to have you share a folder within Windows XP and view the results of this shared folder.

1. Boot the Windows XP computer.

2. Create a folder on the hard drive or floppy drive named "OS Book."

3. Right-click on the folder, click **Properties,** and then click **Sharing**. The Sharing properties for the folder appear.

4. Click **Share this folder** and then click **OK**. Note that the folder name and the share name are the same in this case but can be different.

5. Refer to Figure 9.41 for a sample screenshot.

Figure 9.41: Sharing a Folder

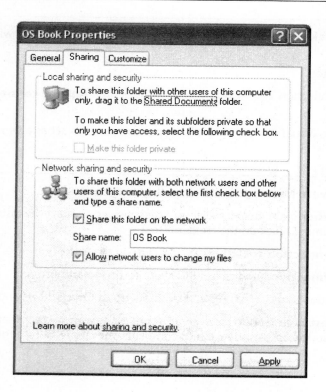

6. To verify the folder is shared, click **Start** and then click **Run**. The Run dialog box appears.

7. In the Run dialog box, type *computer-name**share-name,* where *computer-name* is the name of your computer and *share-name* is the share name. For example, in Figure 9.42, you can see that the computer name is XP2 and the share name is OS Book.

8. Close all windows.

Figure 9.42: Results of Sharing a Folder

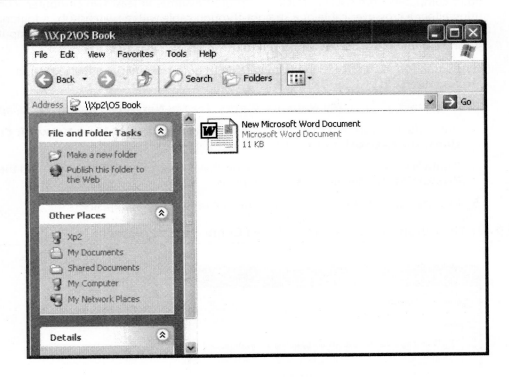

Lab Project 22 Challenge

The goal of this project is to set up a Windows XP computer as a firewall to protect it and other computers from hacker attack. This project assumes at least two computers connected using either a crossover cable or a straight-through cable with a switch/hub. Additionally, the XP computer will be the only one connected to the Internet and to the other computer. The second computer will not be connected to the Internet.

1. Boot the XP computer (the one connected to both the Internet and the second computer).

2. Click **Start**, point to **My Network Places**. The **My Network Places** window appears.

3. Under the Network Tasks section in the left windowpane, click **View Network Connections**. The **Network Connections** window appears.

4. Right-click the Local Area Connection icon that is connected to another PC and then click **Properties**. The **Properties** page appears.

5. Click **Advanced**. A window such as the one in Figure 9.43 appears.

Figure 9.43: The Advanced Page of a Local Area Connection's Properties

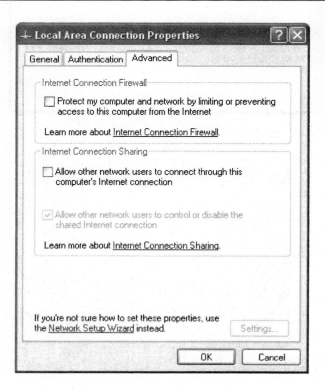

6. Attempt to ping the second computer.

   Did it work? (It should!)

   _____

7. To protect your computer and network by limiting or preventing access, check **Protect my computer and network by limiting or preventing access to this computer from the Internet**.

8. Once you check this box, the Settings button is highlighted.

9. Click the **Settings** button.

10. List the services that can be blocked.

11. Attempt to ping from the second computer.

    Did it work? (It should not due to firewall protection!)

    _____

12. To allow other users to use this computer to connect to the Internet, check **Allow other network users to connect through this computer's Internet connection**.

13. What IP address was selected for this connection?

    _____

14. Close all windows.

Lab Project 23 Challenge

The goal of this Challenge Lab Project is to connect two computers together using a CAT 5 crossover network cable. You will need to have completed Lab 11 prior to beginning this Challenge Lab Project. You will also need two Windows 9x computers with network cards installed and configured.

Note: In normal situations on Ethernet networks, all networked computers connect to a central hub or switch using CAT 5 straight-through cables. In this exercise, you connect two Windows 9x computers using a CAT 5 crossover cable.

1. Plug the **CAT 5 crossover cable** directly into the network cards' RJ-45 ports on the two Windows 9x computers.

   Can you connect more than two computers together using a CAT 5 crossover network cable?

   _____

   Why or why not?

   _____

2. Turn the computers on and verify that Windows 9x loads.

3. Log on to both Windows 9x computers using the userid and password provided by the instructor or lab assistant.

4. Right-click on the **Network Neighborhood** desktop icon and select **Properties**. The Network Properties window opens.

5. From the General tab, select the **File and Print sharing** button. Verify that the **I want to be able to give others access to my files** check box is selected, and click on **OK**.

6. Select the **Identification** tab. Verify that both computers are members of the same **workgroup**.

7. Click on **OK** to close the Network Properties window.

8. If prompted, insert the Windows CD into the CD-ROM and restart the computers.

9. From the My Computer desktop icon, right-click on the **C:** drive and select **Sharing**.

10. From the Sharing window, select **Shared as**, enter a share name, and click on **OK.**

    What is the significance of a share name?

    _____

11. After finishing sharing both C: drives, double-click on the **Network Neighborhood** desktop icon.

12. If the crossover cable connection is working, both computers should appear in the Network Neighborhood browser window. If it is not working, check the NIC configuration settings, the crossover cable, or redo the steps in this exercise. Show the instructor or lab assistant the two computer names in the Network Neighborhood browser window.

Internet Discovery

Internet Discovery Lab 1

The goal of this Internet Discovery Lab is to access the Internet to obtain specific information regarding a computer or its associated parts. You will need access to the Internet.

1. On an HP BRIO computer and after installing a 10/100 BT PCI Ethernet adapter, NT Workstation displays the error message, "At least one service failed to start." What is the problem, solution, and at what Internet address did you find the solution?

2. What does the term "Wake on LAN" mean and at what URL did you find the answer?

3. On a clone computer running Windows 95 and with a 3Com 3C359B adapter installed, the "Divide by zero error R6003" error appears. The computer is upgraded to Windows 98 and the problem does not change. What is the solution? List the URL where the answer was found.

4. How can you tell if an infrared device is within range on a Windows 2000 Professional computer? Write the answer and the URL in the space below.

5. Find an Internet site that explains the differences between CAT 5 and CAT 5E UTP cable. Write one difference and the URL in the space below.

Internet Discovery Lab 2 Challenge

The goal of this Internet Discovery Lab is to access the Internet to obtain specific information regarding networking. You will need access to the Internet.

1. Research the Internet and locate two companies that sell T1 technology. Compare their prices. You may have to call the companies.

2. Research the Internet and locate at least three companies, including their web sites, that produce the following:

   a) routers
   b) switches
   c) hubs
   d) fiber

3. Research the Internet, locate and download pictures of the following in use:

   a) star topology
   b) bus topology
   c) ring topology
   d) mesh topology

Soft Skills: Help Desk Support

1. A customer calls you and says she cannot access the Internet. What types of questions do you ask to help troubleshoot the problem?
2. A user is attempting to download a file and it seems to be taking too long. What types of issues could be causing this apparent slowness?

Critical Thinking

1. Discuss the differences between a crossover cable and a regular straight-through cable. Prove why they cannot be interchanged.
2. Research the Internet or other sources for information on what the uplink toggle switch is used for on a switch/hub. Can you interchange a crossover and straight-through cable by toggling this switch?
3. Discuss the benefits of using a star topology over a mesh topology. Now, discuss the benefits of the mesh topology over a star topology.
4. How long will it take to transfer a 2 GB file over a T1 assuming you have the maximum transfer rate for your file transfer?
5. How long will it take to transfer the same 2 GB file over POTS assuming the low end of the speed range?

 *Study Skills*

Test Preparation

Test preparation occurs over time—not the night before the test.
- Know what you will be tested on.
- Know what time the test begins.
- Bring all necessary test materials such as pencils and paper. If the test is open book and open note, bring those to class.
- Review all necessary material particularly instructor lecture notes, labs, and chapter highlights such as the summary.
- Go over the material at least three times.
- Get a good night's rest before the test.
- Eat something before the test.
- Get to the testing area on time.
- Do not cheat off another's test paper.
- Study daily! Spend at least 30 minutes a day reviewing material.
- When you get the test, do a "brain dump" of key terms so they will be readily accessible when you need them.
- Have confidence—if you have kept up with your studies, you should have no surprises on the test.

Self-Study Question(s)
1. Did you prepare for a test today? You should prepare a little each day.
2. Identify at least two test preparation Study Skills you did this week.

Instructor's Answers

Chapter 1

1. B
2. A
3. B
4. C
5. D
6. A
7. C
8. B
9. C
10. A
11. D
12. D
13. D
14. C
15. C
16. C
17. A
18. D
19. A
20. B

Chapter 2

1. B
2. A
3. C
4. D
5. D
6. A
7. D
8. A
9. B
10. C
11. A
12. C
13. D
14. B
15. A
16. B

17. A
18. A
19. C
20. C

Chapter 3

1. A
2. C
3. B
4. A
5. D
6. B
7. B
8. D
9. D
10. A
11. C
12. B
13. C
14. D
15. A
16. D
17. B
18. B
19. A
20. C

Chapter 4

1. B
2. A
3. A
4. B
5. C
6. B
7. C
8. A
9. B
10. A
11. D
12. B

13. D
14. D
15. A
16. B
17. A
18. A
19. B
20. D

Chapter 5

1. C
2. A
3. A
4. B
5. C
6. A
7. C
8. B
9. B
10. D
11. D
12. B
13. B
14. B
15. D
16. A
17. A
18. C
19. B
20. A

Chapter 6

1. B
2. B
3. C
4. A
5. C
6. A
7. B

8. A
9. A
10. B
11. D
12. A
13. D
14. A
15. D
16. A
17. D
18. A
19. C
20. D

Chapter 7

1. D
2. C
3. D
4. A
5. B
6. A
7. D
8. C
9. B
10. C
11. B
12. A
13. C
14. A
15. B
16. C
17. D
18. B
19. A
20. D

Chapter 8

1. D
2. C and D
3. D
4. B
5. C
6. A
7. B
8. D
9. D
10. B
11. D
12. D
13. C
14. B
15. B
16. C
17. D
18. D
19. B
20. C

Chapter 9

1. B
2. A
3. C
4. D
5. B
6. C
7. C
8. A
9. C
10. A
11. B
12. B
13. A
14. B
15. D
16. D
17. C
18. C
19. D
20. C

Glossary

. Under MS-DOS, a reference to the active directory.

.. Under MS-DOS, a reference to the active directory's parent directory.

% The character used for passing positional parameters to a batch file.

The prompt for the UNIX/Linux root user.

$ The prompt for a UNIX/Linux user.

$HOME A variable that represents a user's home directory.

%systemdrive% A variable within Microsoft Windows operating systems that represents the root directory. For example C:\.

%systemroot% A variable within Microsoft Windows operating systems that represents the boot partition. For example C:\WINNT.

* The wildcard character used to match all characters.

. Represents the current directory.

.. Represents the parent directory.

? The wildcard character used to match specific character positions.

[...] A wildcard technique used in UNIX/Linux where wildcarding occurs on multiple characters. For example [abc] would match on the characters a, b or c.

| The pipe symbol used to filter output from one command as input to another.

< The redirection symbol used to redirect input.

> The redirection symbol used to redirect output and a new file is created.

>> The redirection symbol used to redirect output and append to a file.

16-bit mode Also known as real mode. See real mode.

32-bit mode Also known as protected mode. See protected mode.

8.3 rule The rule used by DOS for creating files. There can be a maximum of 8 characters in the file name followed by 3 characters in the extension.

Absolute Address A physical address defined relative to the first byte in memory.

Absolute Path Another name for full path.

Abstraction A simplified view of an object that ignores the internal details.

Access Control List A list of permissions assigned to a resource that identifies which users have access to the object and the specific actions they can perform on the object.

Access Method A subroutine that performs application-dependent portions of the logical to physical I/O translation process.

Access Point An access point is a device that receives and transmits data from multiple computers that have wireless NICs.

Access The security criterion that each user has reasonable access to all the system resources required to do his or her task.

Accumulator A register that contains the accumulated value of operations such as addition.

Active Directory A directory service installed on a Windows 2003 domain controller.

Active Partition A partition that has been designated as "active" is one that will be booted. A partition is made active by using the FDISK command.

Ad Hoc Mode An ad hoc wireless network is when at least two devices such as two computers have wireless NICs (Network Interface Cards) installed.

Add Printer An icon allowing you to add a printer to your computer.

Add/Remove Hardware A Microsoft Windows control panel icon allowing you to manage hardware.

Add/Remove Programs A Microsoft Windows control panel icon allowing you to manage programs.

Address A number that represents the physical location of a unit of memory.

Address Resolution Protocol (ARP) An Internet protocol that operates at the network layer and is used to find the data link layer's hardware address; also known as the media access control (MAC) address, for a known IP address.

Administrative Tools A Microsoft Windows program allowing you access to administrative programs.

Algorithm A set of instructions to perform a task.

Allocation File A file on an HFS+ volume that uses a bitmap (a bit for every block on disk) to indicate whether each block has or has not been used.

Allocation Unit The Microsoft suggested term for a cluster. An allocation unit is equal to a specific number of sectors on disk.

American Standard Code for Information Interchange (ASCII) The character set used on PC based computer systems.

Antivirus Software Software that can recognize certain code patterns (called virus signatures) or heuristically recognize viruslike activity and sound an alarm when a virus is detected.

Apache A freely available, open source Web server popular on Linux/UNIX platforms.

Application Environment Under Mac OS X, one of four environments (Classic, Carbon, Cocoa, or Java) for running application programs.

Application Layer (1) The highest OSI layer. Users interact with the application layer by executing application programs to fetch and transmit data. (2) In the TCP/IP model, the layer that supports application programs.

Application Management A Novell network management tool that allows the administrator to distribute software and customize the software for each group or individual user.

Application Program Interface (API) A standard used by programmers to guarantee standards among applications.

Application Programming Interface (API) A set of routines, protocols, and other tools that programmers, writing in a variety of languages, can use to build applications consistent with the underlying operating environment.

Application Service(s) (1) A network service that provides a computing platform on which day-to-day applications can run smoothly. (2) A set of Web-based services that integrates many of an organization's day-to-day tasks. (3) In the system software view of Mac OS X, the layer that supports the Carbon, Cocoa, and Java application environments.

Application Software Software used to perform office work. Examples include word processing, spreadsheet and database software.

Application Starter In the Linux K-Desktop Environment, an icon that opens a menu that lists all available programs.

Apply Button A Microsoft Windows button that applies changes immediately to an option once it is clicked.

Aqua The Mac OS X graphical user interface.

Architecture The interconnections and relationships between a computer's components.

Archive Attribute A Microsoft DOS and Windows attribute that indicates a file needs to be backed up the next time a backup is scheduled. All new files and modified files will have this attribute set by the operating system.

Arithmetic and logic unit (ALU) The processor component that executes instructions.

Arithmetic Logic Unit (ALU) The ALU is the portion of the CPU where all the arithmetic and logic functions of the computer are done.

Assembler Language A prog ramming language in which the programmer codes one source statement for each machine-level statement.

Assembling The process of converting the assembly language statements and data into machine-readable (known as binary code or executable code) form.

Assembly Language The computer language that uses mnemonic statements and is native to each processor (CPU).

Asynchronous Mode An operating mode in which an I/O request is handed off to an operating system routine and the process or thread that made the request continues to execute while the request is being processed.

AT&T System Release V (SR5) A version of UNIX developed by AT&T.

ATTRIB A Microsoft DOS and Windows command that allows you to change the attributes of a file or directory (folder).

Auditability The security criterion that requires that security procedures can be audited.

Auditing A technique allowing you to track changes to files and folders.

Authentication The process of identifying users or network components to each other and ensuring that they are who they say they are.

Auto Arrange A Microsoft Windows option forcing your icons on your desktop to be automatically arranged towards the left hand side of the screen.

AUTOEXEC.BAT A Microsoft Windows and DOS customizable batch file. The commands in this file will be executed upon system boot.

AUTOEXEC.NT A file on the ERD that emulates AUTOEXEC.BAT.

Automated System Recovery (ASR) This software is used in Windows XP and replaces the ERD used in Windows NT and 2000.

Automatic Skip Driver Agent (ASD) A Microsoft Windows program that helps determine which drivers failed to load during startup.

Autorun A Microsoft Windows feature that allows a software program on a CD to be automatically started when inserted into the CD drive.

Awk A UNIX/Linux command that allows you to perform pattern matching on text within a file.

Backbone A network of high-speed communication lines that carries the bulk of the traffic between major segments of the Internet.

Background A region of memory that holds a low priority program.

Backup A copy used to recover data or software in case the original is lost. The act of producing such a copy.

Bad-cluster Remapping A technique where bad clusters on a disk are marked so they won't be used in the future.

Bandwidth A measure of the speed of a communication line, usually the number of bits the line can transmit in a fixed amount of time.

Base Address The absolute address of a routine's, or set of data's entry point. Typically, the base address is stored in a register.

Base Memory Address Range An area of memory allocated to a device for its device drivers.

Baseband A communication mode in which the line carries one message at a time.

Baseline A snapshot of your computer's performance during normal operations.

Bash Shell A UNIX/Linux command that provides the shell prompt.

Basic Input/Output System (BIOS) A set of instructions permanently stored on a chip that handles the basic input and output functions of the computer. Examples include keyboard and video functionality.

Basic Service Set (BSS) When multiple devices connect to an access point (whether that access point is wired to a LAN or not), the configuration is known as a BSS.

Batch File A Microsoft DOS and Windows file that contains other commands.

Batch File A set of commands saved in a file that can subsequently be executed by typing the file name.

Beowulf Cluster A type of cluster that links multiple inexpensive computers in an effort to achieve the performance of a conventional supercomputer at a much lower price.

Berkeley Source Distribution (BSD)
A version of UNIX developed by The University of California at Berkeley.

Binary Program Also known as an executable program, a binary program is a set of instructions in computer form that can be executed, or run, by the computer.

Binary The language of the computer consisting of zeroes and ones.

Bit A binary digit, either a zero or a one.

Black Box A component whose contents are unknown.

Block A block is also known as a cluster. Linux uses the term block to represent a collection of sectors on disk.

Blue Screen or Blue Screen of Death The blue colored screen you receive when a Microsoft Windows operating system crashes.

Boot DOS Partition A Novell NetWare disk management partition.

Boot Partition Under Microsoft Windows NT, 2000 and XP, the boot partition is where the operating system itself is located.

Boot The program that loads the operating system into memory.

BOOT.INI A file used to determine which operating system is loaded during boot up.

Booting The process of starting the computer. This includes loading the operating system into memory.

BOOTSECT.DOS A Microsoft Windows NT file used for dual-booted systems.

Bridge A computer that links two or more similar networks.

Broadband A communication mode in which the medium is divided into distinct channels that act much like independent wires and transmit simultaneous messages in parallel.

Broadcast A communication technique in which a message is sent to every node on the network.

Broadcast Address A special IP address used to communicate to all hosts on a specific network.

Browser An application program such as Internet Explorer or Netscape that runs on the client computer and requests and displays Web pages.

BSD (Berkeley Software Design) UNIX
A popular open-source version of UNIX. Under Mac OS X, Darwin's second layer.

Buffer Temporary memory or storage used to adjust for the speed differential between adjacent devices.

Bus A ribbonlike set of parallel electrical lines or wires that can carry several bits at a time. Used to physically link a computer's internal components.

Bus Network A network in which the server, the workstations, and various peripheral devices all share a common bus.

Bus Topology A topology where each devices is connected by a single cable.

Byte A unit of memory that contains enough bits (usually eight) to represent a single character. On many computers, the basic addressable unit of memory.

C:\WINDOWS The default installation folder for Windows 2000 and XP.

C:\WINNT The default installation folder for Windows NT.

Cable A physical connectivity medium such as a wire, a coaxial cable, or a fiber-optic cable.

Cable Modem A modem that links a computer to a high-speed, broadband communication line such as cable.

Cache A form of high speed memory. Programs and data that are frequently used are held in cache memory.

Caching A technique for increasing performance by holding information in memory (rather than on disk) in case the information is needed a second time.

Cal A UNIX/Linux command that allows you to display a calendar.

CALL A Microsoft DOS and Windows command that calls one DOS batch program within another.

Cancel Button A Microsoft Windows button that returns options to their original state when it is clicked.

Carrier Sense Multiple Access/Collision Avoidance (CSMA/CA) A technique used by wireless networks and Apple networks allowing devices to communicate.

Carrier Sense Multiple Access/Collision Detect (CSMA/CD) A technique used by Ethernet networks allowing devices to communicate.

Cat A UNIX/Linux command that allows you to display the contents of a file.

Catalog File A file on an HFS+ volume that describes the volume's folder/file hierarchy, holds vital information about those files and folders in the files' data and resource forks, and enables quick searches for the files in the hierarchy.

CD .. A Microsoft DOS and Windows command that allows you to change to your parent directory in DOS.

CD .. A UNIX/Linux command that allows you to parent directory.

CD / A UNIX/Linux command that allows you to change to the root directory.

**CD ** A Microsoft DOS and Windows command that allows you to change to the root directory in DOS.

CD A Microsoft DOS and Windows command allowing you to change directory positions within the directory tree structure.

CD A UNIX/Linux command that changes directory locations within the directory structure.

CDFS A file system used for CD-ROMs.

Cells A combination of rows and columns used in a spreadsheet to identify data.

Central Processing Unit (CPU) The part of the computer system used perform arithmetic, logic and control functions of the computer system.

Centralized Processing This term is typically used when discussing the operations of a mainframe computer. With centralized processing, the processing and storage of a computer system is performed in a central location.

Change Directory (CHDIR or CD) Command An MS-DOS command that changes the current working directory.

Channel A device that handles device-independent I/O functions, usually on a mainframe computer.

Channel Address Word (CAW) On an IBM mainframe, a fixed memory location that holds the address of the channel program.

Channel Command Word (CCW) On an IBM mainframe, one instruction (or command) in a channel program.

Channel Program A series of channel commands executed by a channel's processor.

Channel Status Word (CSW) On an IBM mainframe, a fixed memory location through which the channel passes status information to the computer.

Character Set The set of characters on the keyboard and their binary equivalent.

Chassis Also known as the system unit.

CHDIR The same as the Microsoft DOS and Windows command CD command. See CD.

Check Box A Microsoft Windows box where you can turn on or off an option.

Child A UNIX process that is created by another process (the parent).

Child Directory A directory contained within a parent.

CHKDSK A DOS and Microsoft Windows command that checks the status of a disk.

Chmod A UNIX/Linux command that allow you to modify permissions of a file or directory.

CHOICE A Microsoft DOS and Windows command that waits for the user to choose one of a set of choices in a batch file.

CIPHER The Microsoft Windows command allowing you to encrypt and decrypt a file.

Clean Install Installing an operating system on a computer that does not have an existing operating system.

Client In a network environment, a computer that uses resources on a server.

Client In client/server mode, the module or node that requests a service.

Client/Server Information System Another name for a Web information system, an application system that relies on communication between asynchronous client-side and server-side application routines.

Client/Server Mode An operating mode in which each server module performs a single service such as file service, memory service, and so on. A client module requests a service by sending a message to the server module. The server module executes the request and sends the reply to the client module.

Client/Server Model In networking, the client server model, is where a few server computers serve many client computers.

Client/Server Network A network in which a dedicated machine acts as the network server and all the other computers (the clients) request services from the server.

Clock A processor component (or an independent chip linked to the processor) that generates precisely timed electronic pulses that synchronize the other components.

Clone A Linux utility similar to *fork* that gives a process a new identity but does not call *exec*.

Close Button A Microsoft Windows button, located in the upper right hand corner of a window, allowing you to close a window.

Close The act of terminating a link to a file. In response to a close command, the file system updates the directory to indicate such information as the file's length and ending address.

CLS A Microsoft DOS and Windows command used to clear the screen.

Cluster (1) On an MS-DOS system, the basic unit of disk space allocation. (2) One or more (generally, a power of 2) contiguous sectors. (3) Under Windows 2003 Server, a group of computers (hardware) that act like a single system to provide services to clients. (4) Multiple computers, each with its own operating system, working together over a high speed network.

Cluster A cluster is equal to a specific number of sectors on disk.

Cluster Address The hexadecimal address of a disk cluster.

Cmd The command that allows you to access the DOS command line in Microsoft Windows NT, 2000 and XP.

Coaxial Cable (or coax) Coax cable has a center copper conductor surrounded by insulation. Outside the insulation is a shield of copper braid, a metallic foil, or both, that protects the center conductor from EMI.

Collision Detection A network management technique that allows the workstations to send messages whenever they want. Collisions are detected electronically and the affected messages are retransmitted.

Collision The condition that occurs when simultaneous (or nearly simultaneous) messages interfere with each other and are rendered unreadable.

Command A request to the operating system for a service.

Command Interface, or Command Line interface A user interface that requires the user to type brief, cryptic commands or acronyms.

Command Language A set of available commands and their syntax rules.

Command Line A Windows interface that provides access to all the features of MS-DOS.

Command Line Interface (CLI) A text area when commands are entered and processed by a command processor.

Command Processor Another name for the user interface or shell.

Command Prompt The prompt, such as C:\ in DOS or $ in UNIX/Linux, that allows you enter commands.

Command The command that allows you to access the DOS command line.

COMMAND.COM The DOS command interpreter. This is what gives you the A:\> or C:\> prompt and either executes a command or displays an error.

COMMAND.COM The MS-DOS command processor or shell, consisting of a command interpreter and a number of resident operating system routines.

Commit The time when a process first uses a unit of memory it was allocated.

Common Carrier An organization that provides the public communication services that define the higher levels of the communication infrastructure.

Common Internet File System (CIFS) A standard remote file system access protocol that enables groups of users to share documents (files) over the Internet.

Common UNIX Printing System (CUPS) A recommended replacement for traditional lpd-based print servers on Linux/UNIX systems.

Common User Access (CUA) A standard developed by IBM and Microsoft. The CUA makes sure Microsoft Windows programs are consistent.

Communication Services A set of operating system routines that support intercomputer communication.

Communication Vector Table, (CVT) An IBM MVS table that holds system constants and pointers to most of the key control blocks.

COMPACT A Microsoft Windows command allowing you to compress or uncompress files.

Compiler A program that converts each source instruction into one or more machine-level instructions.

Compiling The process of converting the programming language statements and data into machine-readable (known as binary code or executable code) form.

Complex Instruction Set Computer (CISC) A computer that contains a large number of instructions in its instruction set. Your PC is a CISC computer.

Compression A technique where redundant data is removed from a file thereby making a smaller file. Compression allows a file to occupy less disk space. Compression also reduces the amount of time a file will transfer or download.

Computer Management Console A Microsoft Windows program allowing you to manage shared folders, disk drives, stop and start services, view performance logs and system alerts and troubleshoot hardware.

Condition A technique used to test criteria and then perform commands based upon the criteria.

CONFIG.NT A file on the ERD that emulates CONFIG.SYS.

CONFIG.SYS A DOS configuration file that has entries for device drivers such as memory, the mouse, and the CD-ROM.

Configuration Table A UNIX table that lists all the devices attached to the system, including their major device number and minor device number.

Connection Oriented A communication protocol in which, when a process on one node communicates with a process on another node, a dedicated connection is established between the two nodes, thus guaranteeing delivery of packets to their destination in their proper sequence.

Connectionless Datagram A communication protocol in which each packet is independent of other packets and has no logical or sequential relationship with other packets. Consequently, when a process running on a particular node communicates with a process on another node, no connection is established between the two nodes.

Connectivity The ability of a device or a program to communicate with other devices or software.

Container Object In a horizontal directory structure, an organizational unit, such as a company, a division, or a department, that contains other containers and leaf objects.

Content Management Services A set of service routines that allow the responsible individuals to add, delete, modify, and generally maintain the content of a Web site.

Context Switching A multitasking technique in which a thread executes until it is interrupted by the operating system or must wait for resources. When a thread is interrupted, the system saves the context of the thread, loads the context of another thread, and executes the new thread.

Contiguous The term contiguous means adjacent and is typically used to refer to how a file is stored on disk. If a file is stored in contiguous sectors, retrieval of the file is usually faster than if the file were not stored in contiguous sectors.

Control Block A set of data that holds a partition's key control flags, constants, variables, and other information required to resume executing the program following an interrupt.

Control Panel A Microsoft Windows method of configuring various Microsoft Windows components.

Control Unit (CU) The CU is the part of the CPU, which handles the main activity.

Control unit (I/O) A device that handles device-dependent I/O functions, usually on a mainframe computer.

Controller A chip that controls the information transfer process between a bus and memory, a bus and a peripheral, and so on.

Conventional Memory Also known as base memory, conventional memory is in the range of 0 to 640 KB. DOS and applications reside here.

CONVERT A Microsoft DOS and Windows command allowing you to convert from FAT16 to FAT32.

Cooperative Multitasking A form of multitasking where an application takes control of the system resources.

Coprocessor A special-purpose processor that assists the main processor on certain operations. For example, a math coprocessor performs mathematical computations, and a graphics coprocessor manipulates graphic images.

COPY Command An MS-DOS command that copies a file or files.

Copy-on-write A form of delayed copy used by Mach 3.0 (Mac OS X) when a task modifies a portion of shared memory.

Core Services A layer that provides nonwindowing and nongraphical services that

are common to all the application environments except BSD, giving Mac OS X the ability to share code and data across environments.

Cp A UNIX/Linux command that allows you to copy files.

Crosstalk A problem that occurs when signals on wires interfere with one another.

Cryptography The science of encrypting or otherwise concealing the meaning of a message to ensure the privacy and integrity of the information transfer.

Current Directory The directory on the default drive in which the user is currently working.

Current PSW On an IBM mainframe, the register that holds the address of the next instruction.

Cut A UNIX/Linux command that allows you remove text from files.

Cycle A unit of measure for CPU speed.

Daemon A UNIX service routine that runs in the background.

Darwin The OS X kernel.

Data Communication The process of transferring data, information, or commands between two computers or between a computer and a terminal.

Data Element A single, meaningful unit of data, such as a name, a social security number, or a temperature reading.

Data Raw facts.

Data Segment A segment of a UNIX image that holds data.

Data Structure A rule (or set of rules) for organizing data. A set of data elements that are stored, manipulated, or moved together.

Database A set of integrated, related files.

Database A storage area for data.

Database Services A set of Web-based services that allows users to easily access, integrate, and use a system's data resources.

DATE A Microsoft DOS and Windows command used to display or change the date.

Date A UNIX/Linux command that allows you to display the current date.

Deadlock A problem that occurs when two (or more) programs each control a resource needed by the other. Neither program can continue until the other gives in, and if neither is willing to give in, the system, almost literally, spins its wheels.

Decrypt To convert a message from encoded or ciphered form back into plain text.

Default Drive The working or current drive.

Default Gateway A device that forwards a packet to a remote network.

Defragmentation The process of placing a file into contiguous areas of a disk for quick retrieval.

DEL A DOS command used to delete a file.

Delimiter A character (often a space) that separates a command from its parameters and (if there are several) the parameters from each other.

DELTREE A Microsoft DOS and Windows command used to remove a tree, which includes files and directories. This is not available in Microsoft Windows XP and 200. In Microsoft Windows 2000 and XP, you use the **Rd /s** command.

Demand Paging Bringing pages into memory only when they are referenced.

Descriptor Table In the Intel architecture, a table that holds the segment descriptors for all the segments.

Desktop The area of a Microsoft Windows screen where users interact with the operating system.

Device Driver Software that allows a device to operate.

Device Driver, or Driver A special file that defines the linkage to a physical device.

Device Management A set of operating system services responsible for communicating with the system's peripheral devices, such as the keyboard, the display screen, the printer, and secondary storage.

Device Manager A Microsoft Windows software program allowing you to manage devices.

Device Number On a UNIX system, a number that uniquely identifies a device.

Device Port An access point for attaching a peripheral device (hardware) to an interface card or board.

DEVICE The DOS command allowing you to specify a device driver. For example DEVICE=mouse.sys.

Df A UNIX/Linux command that allows you display the amount of free disk space on a partition.

Dialog Box A Microsoft Windows box that allows you to interact with the operating system when configuring software.

Dial-up Networking (DUN) A Microsoft product where a computer dials the Internet using a modem.

Diff A UNIX/Linux command that allows you display the difference between two files.

DIR A Microsoft DOS and Windows command that displays both files and directories.

Direct Access Processing data without regard for their physical order. Also known as random access.

Direct Memory Access (DMA) A technique where devices bypass the CPU and access memory directly.

Directory (DIR) Command An MS-DOS command that lists the contents of a directory.

Directory A list of the files stored on a disk or other device. Often used to convert a file name to a physical address.

Directory A storage location for other directories and files. A directory is also known as a folder.

Directory Management A set of functions and routines for managing directories.

Directory Service(s) (1) A database of objects (network resources) and users that organizes the network resources and makes them available to the users. (2) A network service that makes a directory available to users, system administrators, and applications.

Dirty The state of a buffer to which data has been written.

Disk A thin circular plate coated with a magnetic material and used to store and retrieve data. See also diskette and hard disk.

Disk Duplexing The use of a redundant disk as a mirror.

Disk Operating System (DOS) A Microsoft operating system that is disk based and command oriented.

Disk Quotas A technique where users are given a limited amount of disk storage space.

Diskette A thin circular piece of flexible polyester coated with a magnetic material and used to store and retrieve data.

Dispatch Table A dispatch table is also known as an Interrupt Vector Table. It is used to point to where device drivers are stored in memory.

Dispatcher The operating system routine that determines which application routine or task the processor will execute next.

Displacement A location relative to a base address.

Distinguished Name A complete name for a file or other object, similar to a path name or a URL.

Distributed File System (Dfs) A Windows 2003 Server facility that lets network administrators link together files that exist on physically different servers to form a single namespace.

Distributed Processing A technique used in a computer environment where process is spread over multiple computers. The advent of the PC facilitated distributed processing.

Domain (1) A set of nodes administered as a unit; for example, all the networked computers belonging to Miami University form one domain and all the networked computers belonging to Microsoft Corporation form another. (2) Under Windows 2003 Server, a group of computers that share an Active Directory database and have a common security policy.

Domain Component (DC) The main object in Windows 2003 Active Directory.

Domain Controller A computer running Windows 2003 Server that contains the directory database.

Domain Name A logical name consisting of two or more (generally up to four) words separated by dots that equates to an IP address.

Domain Name Service (DNS) A technique where TCP/IP names are resolved to IP addresses.

Domain Name System (DNS) (1) An Internet protocol that runs at the application layer and converts domain names to IP addresses. (2) The Internet's facility for converting domain names to IP addresses.

Domain Tree A hierarchical organization of different domains.

DOSKEY A Microsoft DOS and Windows command that allows you to scroll up and down through the list of commands that you've entered.

Dr. Watson A Microsoft Windows program that assists with debugging applications.

Drive Specification A DOS term comprised of a drive letter followed by a colon. Examples include A:, C: and D:.

Driver Roll Back A feature in Windows XP where you can reinstall on old driver when a new driver causes problems.

Driver *See* device driver.

Drop-down Menu A Microsoft Windows box that contains a down arrow allowing you to select from a list of choices for an option.

DRVSPACE.BIN A Microsoft DOS and Windows command used for disk compression.

DSL A technique used to transfer data over a WAN.

Dual-boot A technique where multiple operating systems are installed on a computer and a choice is made as to which one to boot.

DualView A feature where you can display output on multiple monitors.

Dynamic Address Translation The process of converting a relative address (e.g., a segment/displacement address) to an absolute address as a program is executed.

Dynamic Disks An NTFS technique allowing you to extend a partition from unallocated free space.

Dynamic Host Configuration Protocol (DHCP) DHCP is a method of automatically assigning IP addresses to network devices.

Dynamic Link Library (DDL) A library that contains frequently used executable routines and data. From the programmer's perspective, the application program interface defines the rules for calling the dynamic link library's functions.

Dynamic Memory Management A memory management technique in which the transient area is treated as a pool of unstructured free space and a region of memory just sufficient to hold a program is allocated from the pool when the program is loaded.

Dynamic Storage A feature that allows a user to resize a disk without restarting Windows XP.

ECHO A Microsoft DOS and Windows command used to display text on the screen.

Echo A UNIX/Linux command that allows you to display text.

EDIT The Microsoft DOS and Windows command editor.

Electronic Magnetic Interference (EMI) Electronic noise generated by electrical devices.

E-mail Services An electronic post office that accepts and stores messages, notifies clients when their mailboxes contain mail, and distributes the mail on request.

Emergency Repair Disk (ERD) A disk used to repair a Microsoft Windows operating system.

Emulated Environment When a 32-bit application can run a 16-bit application.

Emulation Software Software that emulates (or imitates) characteristics of a device.

Encapsulation Hiding implementation details by requiring other objects to obtain an object's data through one of that object's methods.

Encrypt, or Encryption A process that ensures the privacy of an information transfer by converting the original, plain text message into encrypted text by using a key.

Encryption File System (EFS) A Microsoft Windows 2000 and XP feature where you can encrypt files.

End Of File (EOF) A special character indicating to the operating system that a file contains no more data.

Environment Subsystem A Windows XP subsystem that emulates different operating systems.

Escape Key The key you use in the UNIX/Linux vi command that toggles between command and text mode.

Ethernet A network access mechanism used in star and bus topologies.

E-time, or Execution Time The time during which the current instruction is executed by the arithmetic and logic unit.

Event In UNIX, an occurrence (such as the death of a process) that produces a signal.

Event Viewer A Microsoft Windows program allowing you to manage events.

Event-wait A UNIX routine that responds to an event by searching the process table and waking (setting to a ready state) every process waiting for that event.

Exception A synchronous event that is generated when the processor detects a predefined condition, such as division by 0.

Exec A UNIX routine, called by fork, that overlays the child's text and data segments with the contents of a new file.

Executable Program A binary program is a set of instructions in computer form that can be executed, or run, by the computer.

Execute Permission For a directory, this UNIX/Linux permission allows you to list files and directories in the directory with this permission. For a file, this UNIX/Linux permission allows you to execute (or run) a program or shell script.

Execution Time (E-time) The second part of the two-part instruction cycle where an instruction is executed.

Executive, or Executive Services Windows XP's top kernel mode layer.

Exit A UNIX routine that marks the death of a process.

Expanded Memory Specification (EMS) EMS uses a technique where 16 KB blocks of data are transferred in and out of a reserved 64 KB section of upper memory.

Expansion Slot A hardware component where devices connect to the computer.

Explorer A Windows tool that provides a hierarchical view of the directories on a system.

Export Under Linux/UNIX, the act of making a file or folder available for sharing.

Ext2 A Linux file system.

Ext2fs The native Linux file system,

Ext3 A newer version of the ext2 file system that includes an on-disk journal that keeps track of changes.

Extended Memory Specification (XMS) XMS is memory that can exceed the 640 KB memory limit.

Extended Partition An extended partition is a partition that can be further divided into multiple logical partitions, called logical drives.

Extended Service Set (ESS) When multiple access points connect to the same main network (known to some as the distribution system), the network design is known as an ESS.

Extended Service Set Identifier (ESSID) Some manufacturers refer to the SSID in infrastructure mode as the ESSID, but this is the same concept as SSID.

Extension An optional addition to a file name. The extension usually follows a period and often identifies the type of file.

External Bus A bus that links several external peripheral devices to a system through a single port.

External Commands External commands can be seen when viewing files on a disk or a hard drive. External commands execute slower than internal commands because the external commands must be retrieved and loaded from the disk or hard drive. External commands reside in a system directory such as C:\WINDOWS.

External Interrupt On an IBM mainframe, an interrupt that comes from the operator's console, another processor, or the timer.

External Paging Device On a virtual memory system, the disk space that holds application programs and transient operating system pages that will not fit or are not currently needed in real memory.

Family Under the Mac OS X I/O Kit, an object that provides a software abstraction common to all devices of a particular type.

FAT The original MS-DOS file system. See file allocation table.

FAT12 A File Allocation Table type used for floppies.

FAT16 A File Allocation Table type used for file storage.

FAT32 A File Allocation Table type used for file storage.

FAT32 An enhancement of FAT that allocates the disk space in smaller units, creating a more efficient file system.

Fault Tolerance The ability of a computer system to recover following errors.

FDISK A Microsoft DOS and Windows command to create primary, extended and logical partitions.

Fiber-optic Cable A type of cable that uses glass or plastic fiber to carry light pulses.

Field A set of related characters. For example, Social Security Number or Employee Name are considered fields.

File A set of related records.

File A storage area for data.

File Allocation Table (FAT) On an MS-DOS system, a linked list that links the clusters that make up a file. The FAT contains one node for each cluster on the disk.

File Attributes File settings such as Read, Archive and Hidden.

File Descriptor On a UNIX system, a small, nonnegative integer number that identifies an open file to the user's process.

File Extension A three character part of a file name that is used to associate an application to a file.

File Level Security The capability of setting security permissions, such as Read or Write, upon files.

File Management *See* file system.

File Name A logical name assigned to a file.

File Services Network services that enable a user to create, retrieve, and update data on the network file server, often by accessing a virtual disk.

File System A set of operating system services that allows the user or programmer to create, delete, modify, and manipulate files and programs by name.

File Transfer Protocol (ftp) A protocol that enables the transfer of files between two computers.

File Type Association A technique where a file's extension is associated with a program.

FILES A Microsoft DOS and Windows command allowing you to specify the number of concurrent open files.

Filter A command that accepts input from the standard input device, modifies (or filters) the data in some way, and sends the results to the standard output device.

FIND A Microsoft DOS and Windows command allowing you to search for text within a file.

Find A UNIX/Linux command that allows you to search for files or directories within the directory tree structure.

Firewall A set of hardware and software that controls how clients from outside can access an organization's internal servers.

Firmware A hardware component that contains specific software instructions.

FIXBOOT A Microsoft Windows program that will fix the boot sector.

Fixed-partition Memory Management A memory management technique that divides the available space into fixed-length partitions, each of which holds one program.

FIXMBR A Microsoft Windows program that will fix the MBR.

Flat Memory Model A single continuous address space called the linear address space. Generally used to model real memory. The base address is always 0. Hence, the offset is the actual physical address and is called a linear address.

Folder A storage location for other folders and files.

Folder A subdirectory.

FOR A Microsoft DOS and Windows command used to perform looping.

Forest A group of one or more domain trees.

Fork The UNIX system primitive that creates a process.

FORMAT A Microsoft DOS and Windows command that allows you to format a drive.

FORMAT Command An MS-DOS command used to format a disk.

Format The process of preparing a disk for use by the operating system.

Fragmentation A concept where a file is spread over non-contiguous areas of disk.

Fragmentation A problem that occurs over time when little chunks of unused space are spread throughout memory.

Frame Data at the Data Link layer of the OSI model.

Fsck The UNIX/Linux command to verify a file system. This is similar to the DOS CHKDSK or SCANDISK command.

Full Duplex Full duplex transmission is data transmitted in both directions on a cable simultaneously.

Full Path A full path always begins from the root directory of a partition.

Functions Small programs that perform a specific purpose.

Gateway A computer that links dissimilar networks

GDL.EXE A Microsoft Windows system file that provides support for the GUI environment.

General Protection Fault (GPF) An error that occurs when a program tries to access the same area of memory as another program.

Ghostscript Under Linux/UNIX, a filter used to convert a Postscript document to a raster image for use by a specific, non-Postscript printer.

Gigabyte (GB) 1 billion bytes.

Global Catalog A catalogue that allows users to find any object located anywhere on the network for which they have access rights.

GOTO A Microsoft DOS and Windows command that directs processing to a specific location in a batch program.

Graphical User Interface (GUI) A user interface that presents the user with a selection of windows, icons, menus, and pointers.

Graphics Subsystem The Mac OS X subsystem responsible for screen rendering, controlling what appears on the display and ensuring that type fonts are smooth and not jagged.

Grep A UNIX/Linux command that allows you to search for text within files.

Hacker A person who illegally breaks into computer systems.

Half Duplex Half duplex transmission is where data transmitted in both directions on a cable, but not at the same time.

Hard Disk One or more thin circular plates coated with a magnetic material and used to store and retrieve data. A hard disk is faster and has a higher storage capacity than a diskette.

Hardware Abstraction Layer (HAL) A layer of a Microsoft Windows operating system between the operating system and the hardware.

Hardware Abstraction Layer (HAL) A Windows XP layer that hides the underlying hardware and provides a virtual machine interface to the other processes, thus supporting portability to different hardware environments by implementing functions such as interrupt controllers and I/O interfaces that are processor specific.

Hardware Interrupt An interrupt originating from hardware.

Hardware/Software Interface The point where hardware and software communicate. A function often performed by the operating system.

Help Desk Representative The Help Desk Support Representative, or Help Desk Technician, typically works in a telephone support environment where users of all types call in with problems.

Hertz A measure of processor speed.

HFS+ (Hierarchical File System Plus) The standard Mac OS file system before OS X was released.

Hidden Attribute A Microsoft DOS and Windows attribute that indicates a file is hidden for normal view. You can see a hidden file in DOS if you enter the ATTRIB command. You can change the File Options to see a hidden file in Windows Explorer.

High Memory Area (HMA) The first 64 KB of extended memory used by DOS.

High-level Programming Language A language such as COBOL, C or Visual BASIC that is "English-like" in nature.

HIMEM.SYS A device driver used for extended memory.

Hive A Registry term used to represent a set of keys and values.

Home Directory A user's initial working directory.

Home Page A starting page that serves as a table of contents or index for navigating a Web site.

Host (1) In a wide area network (such as the Internet), a computer that performs end-user tasks. (2) A node on a wide area network.

Host In TCP/IP terms, a computer that has an IP address. In mainframe terms, a device that has a keyboard, terminal and a link to a mainframe for processing.

Host Number The portion of an IP address that represents a specific computer on the network.

Hot Fix A fault tolerant feature that detects the presence of bad sectors on a disk and moves the data defect to an error-free location.

HTML (Hypertext Markup Language) The standard markup language used to define Web pages.

HTTP (Hypertext Transfer Protocol) A TCP/IP application layer protocol that defines the format of World Wide Web requests from a browser and replies by the server.

Http.sys Under Windows 2003 Server, a key kernel-mode Internet Information Services (IIS) component that responds to http connection requests that arrive via port 80 and places each request on a queue for subsequent processing.

Httpd The Linux/UNIX http daemon.

Hub A device that connects other devices, such as computers or printers, on a network.

Hyperlink A logical pointer that links to a Web page. Typically, a URL lies behind the hyperlink.

Hyperthreading Executing tasks in parallel.

I/O Catalog Under Mac OS X, a library of the system's available device drivers.

I/O Kit The Mac OS X device driver subsystem.

I/O Registry Under Mac OS X, a dynamic database that keeps track of active nubs and drivers and tracks the relationships between them.

I/O Request Packet (IRP) A request for service from the Windows XP I/O manager.

Icon A graphical representation of items such as programs, files or folders.

IEEE 802 Standards Standards developed in February of 1980 by the IEEE.

IF A Microsoft DOS and Windows command allowing you to perform conditional processing. Typically used in a batch file.

IF ERRORLEVEL A Microsoft DOS and Windows command used in a DOS batch file to test if a key was pressed.

IIS. *See* Internet Information Services.

I-list A UNIX table of i-nodes.

Image On a UNIX system, an execution environment that consists of program and data storage, the contents of general-purpose registers, the status of open files, the current directory, and other key elements.

Independent Self-governing.

Inetd The Internet services daemon. Under Linux/UNIX, a superserver daemon that functions as an intermediary, listens for connection requests for certain ports, and starts the appropriate service program when a request reaches a port.

Information Data that has been processed.

Infrastructure Mode The infrastructure mode wireless network connects multiple wireless network devices through an access point.

Init A UNIX utility that creates one system process for each terminal channel. For example, if the system supports twenty concurrent terminals, twenty processes are created.

Initiator/terminator An IBM job management routine that starts and ends tasks.

Inode A unique number representing a file in the Linux operating system.

I-node On a UNIX system, a 64-byte file definition that lists the disk addresses of blocks associated with a single ordinary file and the major and minor device numbers of a special file.

I-node Table A UNIX table that holds the i-nodes of all open files. Also known as the system file table.

Input Device A device that facilitates input into the computer system.

Input Output Manager (I/O manager) A Windows XP module that manages the file systems, the cache, hardware drivers, and network drivers, works with the virtual memory manager (VMM) to provide memory-mapped file I/O, and manages the buffers for requests to the installed file system.

Input The act of sending data into a computer. Data ready to be entered to a computer.

Input/output (I/O) Interrupt On an IBM mainframe, an interrupt sent by a channel to the main processor to signal the completion of an I/O operation.

Input/output Control System (IOCS) The operating system module that communicates directly with the computer's peripherals.

Input/Output device (I/O) The term used to describe input and output devices such as keyboards, disk drives, and monitors.

Input/Output Port A memory address through which data is transferred between a device and the processor.

Input/Output The term used to describe the input and output functions in a computer system.

Institute for Electrical and Electronics Engineers (IEEE) The IEEE committee created network standards called the 802 standards.

Instruction Address A field in an IBM mainframe PSW that holds the address of the next instruction to be executed.

Instruction Control Unit (ICU) The processor component that fetches and decodes instructions from memory.

Instruction One step in a program that tells the computer to perform one of its basic functions.

Instruction Register A register that contains the current instruction that is being executed by the CPU.

Instruction Set The set of instruction statements a processor can understand and use.

Instruction Time (I-time) The first part of the two-part instruction cycle where an instruction is fetched from memory to the processor's registers.

Integral Subsystem A Windows XP subsystem that provides protection and system services.

Integrity The security criterion that requires that the message not be modified during transmission.

Interface (1) A component that translates the signals moving from one device to another. (2) The point of linkage between two electronic devices and/or software routines.

Internal Commands Microsoft DOS and Windows commands that exist in the file named COMMAND.COM.

International Standards Organization (ISO) ISO has developed a model for network communications known as the OSI (Open Systems Interconnect) model.

Internet A vast network of networks layered on top of the global data communication network.

Internet Conferencing Software allowing you to communicate with other users on the Internet.

Internet Connection Sharing (ICS) Software allowing multiple computers to access the Internet via one computer.

Internet Explorer (IE) A web browser for connecting to the Internet.

Internet Information Services (IIS) The Web server under Windows 2003.

Internet Layer In the TCP/IP model, the layer responsible for routing and delivering packets to their destinations. The Internet layer roughly corresponds to the OSI model network layer and is typically implemented using the Internet protocol (IP). Sometimes called the network layer.

Internet Model *See* TCP/IP model.

Internet Printing Protocol (IPP) A protocol that runs on top of http and supports bi-directional communication between client and server. Using IPP allows a client to browse for available network printers and to get status and other detailed information about a printer.

Internet Protocol (IP) The protocol responsible for routing packets of data over the Internet.

Internet Service Provider (ISP) A service that provides Internet connectivity.

Internetwork Packet Exchange/Sequenced Packet Exchange (IPX/SPX) IPX/SPX is used when connecting to a Novell network, but Novell networks now use TCP/IP as their standard protocol.

Internetworking The process of linking two or more networks.

Interpreter A program that works with one source statement at a time, reading it, translating it to machine level, executing the resulting binary instructions, and then moving on to the next source statement.

Interpreting The process of converting programming language statements to executable code and then executing them.

Interrupt An electronic signal that is sensed by hardware. The hardware responds by saving the control information needed to resume processing the current program and starting an operating system routine that responds to (or handles) the interrupt.

Interrupt Descriptor Table (IDT) An Intel Pentium table that associates each interrupt vector with an interrupt descriptor.

Interrupt Handler An operating system routine that processes interrupts.

Interrupt Handler Software that handles processor interrupts.

Interrupt Request (IRQ) A signal sent by a device to the processor indicating that the device needs the processor's assistance.

Interrupt Vector Table An MS-DOS table that occupies the first 1K bytes of memory and holds the addresses (interrupt vectors) of up to 256 different interrupt processing modules, most of which are found in MSDOS.SYS or IO.SYS. See also interrupt descriptor table.

I-number On a UNIX system, an i-node's offset from the beginning of the i-list.

Invalid Page A page that does not reside in physical memory because it has been swapped out to disk or has not yet been swapped into memory.

IO.SYS The hardware dependent MS-DOS module that issues physical data transfer commands.

IP Address A 32-bit, dotted format number that indicates the address of a device or a node on the Internet.

IP Security (IP Sec) A method of encrypting IP packets.

IPCONFIG Command A Microsoft command that displays IP settings on Windows 98, NT, 2000 and XP.

IPV4 The current Internet protocol standard.

IPV6 The new proposed Internet protocol standard that increases the number of address bits to 128, significantly increasing the number of unique addresses that can be used.

IPX A Novell NetWare protocol that occupies the Internet layer of the TCP/IP model and the network layer of the OSI model. IPX addresses and routes packets from one location to another.

Is The UNIX/Linux command that displays files and directories.

ISA (industry standard architecture) A standard I/O bus that links slower devices such as the keyboard and the mouse to many microcomputer systems.

ISDN A technique used to transfer data over a WAN.

Itanium The Intel 64-bit architecture.

I-time, or Instruction Time The time during which an instruction is fetched by the instruction control unit.

Job A unit of work consisting of one or more job steps or tasks.

Job Control Language (JCL) A batch, command-based user interface that allows a programmer to identify a job, specify to the operating system the programs to be run, and specify the peripheral devices to be allocated in support of those programs.

Job Management Under IBM's MVS, the routines that dispatch, queue, schedule, load, initiate, and terminate jobs or tasks.

Journaling File System A file system that uses a log to keep track of changes to the metadata in an effort to improve recoverability.

KDE (K-Desktop Environment) A popular Linux graphical user interface.

Kernel Mode A Windows operating mode in which kernel mode processes have access to the entire system memory and all processor instructions and can bypass Windows security to access objects.

Kernel The core of the operating system that remains in memory.

Kernel-space Driver Under Mac OS X, a device driver that resides in kernel space.

Key (1) A value that identifies a specific record in a file. (2) A value that converts a general encryption algorithm into a specific rule for encrypting and decrypting a particular message.

Keys Registry folders.

Kilobyte (KB) 1 thousand bytes.

Konqueror The KDE file system.

Konsole The KDE shell, a line command interface.

LABEL A Microsoft DOS and Windows command allowing you to change the disk label.

Last Known Good Configuration A setting you can choose during the Startup menu that allows you to access the last known good configuration of the operating system. Commonly used when you load a device driver that does not work.

Last Mile Problem The problem associated with linking a home or office to the telephone service provider's local central office. The problem is caused by the enormous speed disparity between a local line and a long distance line.

Layering The process of adding onto or tapping into an existing infrastructure.

Leaf Object A network resource that is defined at the end of a hierarchical tree structure.

Legacy Device A non-Plug and Play device.

Library An organized collection of data or software.

Line Command A cryptic command that is typed on a single line.

Line Printer Daemon (*lpd*) The standard Linux/UNIX printer server.

Linear Address Space A byte addressable address space in a flat memory model.

Linear Address The offset (from 0) in a flat memory model address. The actual physical address.

Linkage Editor A transient system routine that prepares a complete load module and copies it to a load module library for immediate or eventual loading.

Linked List A list in which each node contains data plus a pointer to the next node.

Linker Software used to create a program. Once a program is assembled, it is then linked.

Linux A version of UNIX developed by Linus Torvald. The source code is posted on the Internet, making Linux an example of open-source software. Over the years, it has been refined and modified and today incorporates contributions from hundreds of software developers around the world.

List A data structure in which each entry is called a node, and each node holds a single data element or data structure.

Load Module A complete, ready-to-execute program with all subroutines in place.

Local Area Network (LAN) A set of computers located in close proximity, for example within the same building.

Log File A file that records message information about events that have occurred on the system.

Logical Address A relative address that consists of a base address and an offset from the base address.

Logical I/O (1) The programmer's view of I/O. (2) The set of data that supports a single iteration of a program. (3) A request from an application program for a single logical record.

Logical Partition A logical partition is where drive specifications, such as A: or C:, refer to a physical partition.

Logical Record The unit of data requested by a logical I/O operation.

Logical Volume Manager A Linux service that allows a user to combine two or more physical disks to create a volume group, a virtual disk that can be partitioned into logical volumes upon which file systems can be built.

Login Name A series of characters that uniquely identifies a user.

Long File Name (LFN) A Microsoft Windows file name that can contain up to 255 characters.

Loop A technique used when program statements are repeated.

Loopback Address The address, 127.0.0.1, of the local NIC in a computer.

Low-level Programming Language A language such as Assembly that is the language of the CPU.

Ls, or List Directory A UNIX command that lists the contents of a directory.

MAC OS An operating system developed by Apple Computer.

Mac OS X Release X (10) of Apple's Macintosh platform operating system.

Mach 3.0 Under Mac OS X, the Darwin kernel's lowest layer.

Machine Check Interrupt On an IBM mainframe, an interrupt that occurs when the computer's self-checking circuitry detects a hardware failure.

Machine Cycle The process of fetching and executing a single instruction.

Machine Language The binary instructions the processor actually executes.

Main Memory *See* memory.

Mainframe Operating System Operating systems that are designed to handle the Input/Output (I/O), processing and storage requirements for a lot of users.

Make Directory (MKDIR or MD) Command An MS-DOS command that creates a directory.

MAKEDISK.BAT A Microsoft Windows batch file that allows you to create an anti-virus disk.

Malware Intentionally destructive software.

Man A UNIX/Linux command that allows you to display the manual help pages on a command.

Management Services A set of services that support network management.

Mapped Drive A convenient way to reference a particular subdirectory on the network with a single letter.

Master Boot Record (MBR) The Master Boot Record (MBR) is a record that tells the operating system about the partitions. The MBR looks for the active partition and boots it.

Master File Table (MFT) On a Windows XP system, a master directory that contains information about each file on the volume.

Master Scheduler The IBM MVS dispatcher.

Maximize Button A Microsoft Windows button, located in the upper right hand corner of a window, allowing you to maximize your window.

MD A Microsoft DOS and Windows command allowing you to create a directory.

Media Access Control (MAC) address The physical hardware address associated with a NIC. A MAC address is 48 bits and is unique.

Media Services An optional module that can be used to configure Windows 2003 Server as a streaming server.

Medium The path over which a message flows. Sometimes called a line, a channel, or informally a pipe.

Megabyte (MB) 1 million bytes.

MEM A Microsoft DOS and Windows command that displays memory statistics.

Member Server A server that is in the same domain as a domain controller but does not have an active directory database.

Memory Address Range A section of memory address.

Memory Management A set of operating system services concerned with managing the computer's available pool of memory, allocating space to application routines and making sure that they do not interfere with each other.

Memory Mapping A technique for minimizing the number of physical I/O operations by (in effect) storing an image of the file in virtual memory.

Memory Object Under Mac OS X, a specific source of data, such as a file. Logically, a repository for data upon which various operations (read and write) can be performed.

Memory Protection An operating system routine that intervenes if a program attempts to modify (or, sometimes, even to read) the contents of memory locations that do not belong to it and (usually) terminates the program.

Memory, or Main Memory The computer component that holds currently active programs and data.

Menu A list of available options.

Menu Bar A bar at the top of a window that displays key words that activate pull-down menus.

Menu Interface A user interface that presents the user with a list of available options.

Mesh Topology A topology where all devices connect to each other for redundancy.

Message (1) A unit of communication consisting of a header, a body, and a trailer. (2) In object-oriented software, a communication between objects. (3) Under Mac OS X, the unit of task-to-task communication.

Message (or Messaging) Port The endpoint of a logical (program-to-program) connection. A port (usually implemented in memory) that links two logical software routines.

Method A process that accesses and manipulates an object's data.

Microcode A layer of circuitry that lies between memory and the processor. Instructions are converted to microinstructions, which are executed in microcode. Sometimes called firmware.

Microkernel A compact version of a kernel that implements a limited number of specific tasks and serves as a base for supporting any of several operating systems.

Microsoft DOS A Microsoft operating system that is disk based and command oriented.

Microsoft System Information (MSINFO) A Microsoft Windows program allowing you to display information about system resources and can be used to detect conflicts between devices.

Microsoft Windows 2000 A Microsoft operating system that is graphically oriented.

Microsoft Windows 3.1 A Microsoft application used to interact with the operating system. Microsoft Windows 3.1 required an actual operating system such as MS-DOS.

Microsoft Windows 98 A Microsoft operating system that is graphically oriented.

Microsoft Windows Explorer A Microsoft application used to create, copy, and move files and folders.

Microsoft Windows NT A Microsoft desktop and server operating system.

Microsoft Windows XP A Microsoft desktop operating system.

Middleware (1) A class of software that helps with the translation of messages and communications between a client and a server or between two servers. (2) Any set of routines or functions that allow two dissimilar programs to interoperate.

Midrange Operating System Midrange operating systems are handle the Input/Output (I/O), processing and storage requirements and are generally used for medium-sized organizations. They operate in a centralized manner with terminals and PCs using emulation software, accessing applications remotely.

Minimize Button A Microsoft Windows button, located in the upper right hand corner of a window, allowing you to minimize your window.

Mkdir A UNIX/Linux command that allows you to create a directory.

MKDIR The Microsoft DOS and Windows command that is the same as the MD command. See the MD command.

MMX Technology A set of extensions built on top of the Intel Architecture that enhance the performance of multimedia applications such as video, audio, and 3D graphics.

Mnemonic Another name for an assembly language statement is mnemonic.

Modem A device that converts (or modulates) digital signals to analog and then demodulates the analog signals back to digital. A modem allows you to connect to a computer with another modem, say one at your Internet Service Provider. Modem comes from the terms "modulate/demodulate".

Module A software component that provides a set of services to the rest of the system.

MORE A Microsoft DOS and Windows command that allows you to display a screen of text at once.

More A UNIX/Linux command that allows you to display a screen of text.

MORE Filter An MS-DOS filter that sends output to the terminal one screen at a time.

Motherboard A metal framework that contains a series of slots linked through a bus to a processor. Memory and interface boards are plugged into the slots.

Mount Point In the UNIX and Linux operating systems, a mount point is a directory name that is associated with a partition.

MOVE A Microsoft DOS and Windows command used to move a file from one directory location to another.

MS-DOS A command-driven operating system that allows users to issue cryptic, single-line commands through a command interface.

MSDOS.SYS The hardware independent MS-DOS module that implements logical I/O.

Multi-boot The capability of a computer to boot multiple operating systems.

Multi-mode Fiber-optic A type of fiberoptic that carries multiple light signals down the cable.

Multiple-bus Architecture A design in which a computer system's primary components are linked by multiple buses.

Multiprocessing Two or more processors that share the same memory and are capable of executing instructions simultaneously.

Multi-processor An operating system kernel that can utilize several processors concurrently is called a multi-processor operating system.

Multiprogramming A processor management technique that takes advantage of the speed disparity between a computer and its peripheral devices to load and execute two or more programs concurrently.

Multitasking A multitasking operating system kernel is one that appears to handle multiple tasks at the same time. A task is a program that is running. A task is also known as a job or process.

Multithread Operating systems supporting multithreaded applications allow threads to be executed concurrently. Also, see thread.

Multithreading Concurrently executing more than one thread.

Multi-user The capability of an operating system to support multiple users at the same time.

Mv A UNIX/Linux command that allows you to move or rename files or directories.

MVS Acronym for multiple virtual systems. A traditional IBM mainframe operating system.

My Computer An icon that is used to access hardware, software and files located on the computer.

My Documents icon A Microsoft Windows icon allowing you to quickly access the My Documents folder.

My Network Places A Microsoft Windows icon allowing you to view network computers. This icon is available only on Windows 2000 and XP. On Windows 98 and NT, the Network Neighborhood icon is used for the same purpose.

Namespace The set of all names that are unique within a network.

Navigation Panel *Konqueror's* left panel, which displays a hierarchical view of the directory structure.

NET A Microsoft DOS and Windows command used for network troubleshooting and configuration.

NetBIOS Enhanced User Interface (NetBEUI) NetBEUI is a non-routable network protocol.

NetWare A commonly used networking operating system on local area networks. A product of Novell.

NetWare Control Protocol (NCP) A Novell NetWare protocol that runs at the application layer.

NetWare File System Novell's traditional file system.

NetWare Loadable Module (NLM) An object module linkable at run time.

NetWare Partition A disk partition that stores the system files using the traditional file system.

NetWare The network operating system developed by Novell.

Network A connection of two or more devices that can communicate.

Network Access Layer Under TCP/IP, the physical connection between two nodes. Equivalent to the OSI physical layer.

Network Access Point (NAP) An Internet backbone node at which the network service providers are interconnected and exchange data.

Network Administrator A technical specialist responsible for all aspects of a network.

Network Client, or Network Provider A subset of Novell's NetWare that runs under the client computer's primary operating system.

Network Device Interface Specification (NDIS) A Windows 2003 Server protocol that communicates with network card drivers, translating between the drivers and the transport protocol. NDIS allows network card vendors to ensure that their drivers are compatible with Windows.

Network Driver A file system driver that redirects an I/O request from a client to the appropriate server machine and receives data from the remote machine.

Network File System (NFS) Under Linux/UNIX, a virtual file system that directs read or write requests from applications to the appropriate file system.

Network Interface Card (NIC) A hardware device allowing you to connect to other computers.

Network Layer (1) The OSI layer just above the data-link layer that routes packets. (2) Another name for the TCP/IP Internet layer.

Network Neighborhood A Microsoft Windows icon allowing you to view network computers.

Network Number The portion of an IP address that represents which network segment a computer is on.

Network Operating System A set of system software routines that help to manage a network.

Network Server (1) The computer that controls a client/server network. (2) A computer that controls a resource needed by a client in the client/server model.

Network Service A service that supports a system task over a network.

Network Service Provider (NSP) An organization that maintains and leases access to one or more of the high-speed communication links that define the Internet's backbone.

Network Two or more computers linked by communication lines.

New PSW On an IBM mainframe, a permanent storage location that holds the address of an interrupt handling routine in the operating system.

New Technology File System (NTFS) New Technology File System, provides performance and reliability not present in FAT. NTFS allows for disk quotas, compression, encryption, file level security, bad-cluster remapping, auditing and dynamic disks.

Node A single computer, router, or terminal on a network.

Non-executable Program A file such as a document, text file or graphics file that cannot be run, or executed, by the operating system.

Nonprocedural Language A programming language in which the programmer simply defines the logical structure of the problem and lets the language translator figure out how to solve it. Sometimes called a fourth-generation or declarative language.

Nonrepudiation The security criterion that requires that the sender cannot deny that he or she sent the message.

Notepad A text processing Microsoft Windows application.

Notification Area A portion of the bottom bar on a Windows XP desktop that displays important information such as the current time.

Novell Directory Services (NDS) A method of storing and retrieving service and other information in a distributed database.

Novell Distributed Print Services (NDPS) A set of print services that allow a Novell network administrator to manage network printing more efficiently than queue-based services.

Novell NetWare A networking operating system developed by Novell.

Novell Storage Services (NSS) A Novell storage service that enables the management of large files, volumes, name spaces, and storage devices.

Novell Storage Services Partition A Novell disk management partition.

NT Diagnostics A Microsoft Windows program that allows you to view configuration information about the computer's hardware, installed device drivers, and installed services.

NT Hardware Qualifier A Microsoft program that identifies what hardware is installed on a computer system.

NT Virtual DOS Machine (NTVDM) A software program that simulates a DOS environment inside NT.

NTBOOTDD.SYS A Microsoft Windows file used on a system with SCSI drives that have the SCSI BIOS disabled.

NTDETECT.COM A Microsoft Windows system command that detects the hardware on a PC.

NTFS The Windows/NT file system. NTFS not only manages files, handles large disk spaces, and so on, but also incorporates robustness features required by corporations and businesses.

NTLDR The Microsoft Windows operating system bootstrap loader.

NTOSKRNL.EXE The Microsoft Windows operating system kernel.

Nub Under Mac OS X, an object that acts as a bridge or communication channel between two drivers (hence two families).

Nucleus The resident operating system.

Object A thing about which data are stored and manipulated.

Object Manager The Windows XP executive service responsible for creating, destroying, and granting access to an object's services or data.

Object Module A machine-level version of a programmer's code that can be loaded into memory and executed.

Object Rights A set of rights that control what the user can do with an object, such as browse, create, rename, supervise and so on.

Object-oriented An approach to software development in which the software is designed and written as a set of independent objects linked by signals.

OK Button A Microsoft Windows button that applies all changes when it is clicked.

Old PSW On an IBM mainframe, a permanent storage location that holds the PSW that was active at the time an interrupt occurred.

Open Source Software, such as an operating, system, that features open, published source code that can be modified by anyone.

Open Systems Interconnect (OSI) A seven-layer model for computer-to-computer communication proposed by the International Standards Organization (ISO).

Open The act of establishing a link with a physical device or file. For example, when a file is opened, the file system reads the directory, finds the file's directory entry, extracts the file's start address, and (sometimes) reads all or part of the file.

Operand (1) The portion of an instruction that specifies the memory locations or registers holding the data to be manipulated. (2) On a JCL statement, a field that specifies a detail about the job, job step, or data definition, one of a series of parameters separated by commas.

Operating System An operating system (OS) is a set of software instructions that allows your computer system to operate. Operating systems are written in programming languages like application programs.

Operation An external view of the object that can be accessed by other objects.

Operation Code The portion of an instruction that specifies the function to be performed.

Ordinary File On a UNIX system, a data file.

OS X Release X (10) of Apple's Macintosh platform operating system.

Output (1) The act of sending data or information out from a computer. (2) The results of that action.

Output Devices A device that facilitates output from the computer system.

Overlay A memory management technique in which a program is broken into logically independent modules and only the active modules are loaded into memory. When a module not yet in memory is referenced, it replaces (or overlays) a module already in memory.

Packet Data at the Network layer of the OSI model.

Packet Internet Groper (PING) A TCP/ IP command that tests connectivity of a host computer.

Packet Switching A communication technique in which a message is divided into a set of small blocks called packets. The packets are transmitted independently and reassembled at the receiving end of the line.

Page Directory Entry (PDE) A page directory value that specifies the address of the appropriate page table.

Page Directory On an Intel Pentium (or Windows) system, a table containing entries that point to a page table.

Page Fault An event that occurs when a virtual address points to a page that is not in real memory (an invalid page).

Page File The page file, or swap file, is the section of the hard disk used for virtual memory.

Page Pool On a virtual memory system, the transient program area in real memory.

Page Table A table that lists the (absolute) entry point address of each of a program's pages.

Page Table Entry (PTE) A page table value that contains the actual physical address of the page that holds the referenced code or data.

Pager A task that is used to move data between the backing store (usually disk) and physical memory.

Paging A memory management technique in which a program is broken into fixed-length pages and the pages are loaded into noncontiguous memory.

Panel Under KDE, a window that displays system information.

Parallel Port A connection point for a parallel device such as a printer.

Parameter A field in a JCL statement, a command, or an instruction that specifies a relevant detail.

Parent A UNIX process that creates another process (the child).

Parent Directory A directory that contains another directory or a file.

Partial Path A partial path is simply the file name without any reference to the root directory.

Partition (1) A fixed length unit of memory defined when the operating system is first generated or loaded. (2) The act of distributing application logic over two or more computers. (3) Under Novell NetWare, a logical division of the NDS tree that contains one or more complete branches.

Partition A section of a hard disk.

Passwd A UNIX utility that allows a user to change his or her password.

Password A series of characters used to authenticate a logon ID.

Path A list of all the subdirectories (and, possibly, other elements) one must navigate to get to a specific file.

PATH Command The DOS command that contains the directory path of available commands.

Path Name, or Pathname A name that identifies the directory and all the subdirectories one must navigate (the path) to get to a specific file.

Path The path is the location of the file, or directory. The two types of paths are full and partial.

Pattern Matching A technique where symbols are used to represent characters in a file name. Also called wildcarding.

PAUSE A Microsoft DOS and Windows command allowing you to pause the execution of a batch file. You can enter the PAUSE command at the command prompt but it is typically used in a batch file. The user can press ENTER to continue when this statement is used.

PCI (Peripheral Component Interconnect) A local I/O bus that links high-speed peripherals, such as a disk, to many personal computer systems.

Peer-to-peer (Peer-peer) Network A network in which there is no dedicated server, every computer can be a server and a client, and each user can decide to share his or her hard disk files or printer with any other user.

Performance Monitor A Microsoft Windows program allowing you to monitor the performance of your computer.

Personal Computer (PC) A computer for personal use.

Personality Identifier A Linux feature that allows Linux to emulate the behavior of other versions of UNIX (such as System V Release 4) and allows these other versions to run under Linux without modification.

Physical Address A memory address defined by counting the bytes sequentially, starting with zero (0). Also known as an absolute address and a real address.

Physical I/O The act of physically transferring a unit of data between memory and a peripheral device.

Physical Layer (1) In the OSI model, the medium of transmission. (2) In the TCP/IP model, another name for the network access layer.

Physical Record The unit of data transferred by a physical I/O operation.

Pipe An operator that causes one command's standard output to be used as the standard input to another command.

Pipelining A processor technique that allows multiple instructions to be processed simultaneously to obtain an overall execution rate of one instruction per clock cycle.

Plain Old Telephone Service (POTS) The traditional, wire-based telephone network.

Plain Text The form of an unencrypted message.

Platform A platform is comprised of both the hardware and software that a given system runs on. For example, Microsoft Windows XP running on an Intel Pentium would be considered a platform.

Plug and Play (PnP) Plug and Play, developed by Intel, is a standard that allows a computer to automatically detect and configure the installed device. Both the operating system and the device must be Plug and Play compliant for this method to work.

Plug-in An application designed to be used with a browser such as Macromedia Flash or Shockwave.

Point and Click A method whereby the mouse is used to navigate and manipulate Microsoft Windows.

Pointer (1) A symbol, often an arrow, that shows the current position of the mouse. (2) An address, often stored in a register or on a stack, that points to a specific unit of data or a specific software routine.

Point-to-Point Protocol (PPP) PPP (Point-to-Point Protocol) is a connection-oriented, layer 2 protocol that encapsulates data for transmission over phone lines.

Polling (1) A network management technique in which the network server sends a signal to each workstation in turn and messages are transmitted only in response to the signal. (2) A dispatching technique in which the dispatcher checks a priority table to determine which program the processor will execute next.

Port (1) An access point for attaching a peripheral device to an interface card or board.

(2) The endpoint of a logical (program-to-program) connection. (3) Under Mac OS X, a secure channel for intertask or interprocess communication.

Portability The ability to run a program on multiple platforms.

Portable This term is used to mean that an operating system can be fairly easily carried to a computer of another type and execute correctly.

Portal An access point to the Internet or a private network.

Positional Parameters Data that can be passed (or given) to a batch file. You can pass up to 9 positional parameters. You can use the SHIFT command to allow more to be passed.

POSIX The acronym for Portable Operating System Interface for UNIX, a standard application programming interface.

Post Office Protocol (POP) A protocol that allows a user to download messages from or upload messages to a server.

Postscript A device independent page description language that specifies the layout of the text and graphics on the page.

Postscript Printer Description (PPD) A simple text file that describes device-dependent features and contains commands that a Postscript printer understands.

Power On Self Test (POST) Part of the boot sequence where components such as memory, the keyboard, the mouse and the disk drive are verified.

Preemptive Multitasking A form of multitasking in which each thread or process is given a set amount of time called a quantum to access the processor. Once the quantum has expired, the thread is interrupted to let another thread with the same priority access the processor. Additionally, if a second thread with a higher priority is ready to execute, the operating system interrupts the currently executing thread to let the higher priority thread run.

Preemptive Multitasking With preemptive multitasking, the operating system has the ability to take control of the computer system from an application.

Pre-forking Model A robust Apache server model that creates in advance a main parent process and several child processes to handle client requests.

Prepaging Predicting the demand for a new page and swapping it into memory before it is actually needed.

Presentation Layer The second highest OSI layer, which is concerned with differences in data representation or syntax.

Primary Partition The primary partition contains your operating system and is the first partition on a drive. In order to boot your operating system, you must have a primary partition and it must be marked as the active partition.

Primitive A low-level operation that tells a peripheral device to perform a single task.

Print Queue A subdirectory on a print server where the data are stored while waiting to be sent to a printer.

Print Server A network computer that manages printers.

Print Services A set of services that support network printing.

Priority A value that specifies a task's execution order.

Priority Bands Under Mac OS X, a set of the four priority levels. Each thread is classified into one of those four bands.

Privacy The security criterion that requires that the contents of the message be known only to the sender and the recipient.

Private Key In public key encryption, the key that is kept private.

Privilege Level A number that indicates a program's memory protection rights. A program executing at a lower privilege level cannot access a segment or page associated with a higher privilege program.

Privileged Instruction On an IBM mainframe, an instruction that can be executed only by an operating-system routine.

Problem State The state of an IBM mainframe that is executing an application program.

Process (1) On a Windows XP system, an object that consists of an executable program. (2) On a UNIX system, the execution of an image.

Process File Table A list of open files stored within a process's system data area. The process file table entry points, in turn, to an i-node in the system file table.

Process Id (pid) A process number assigned by UNIX when the process is created.

Process Identification (PID) Number A process will be given a Process Identification number, called a PID, which is used by the operating system to reference the process.

Process Manager The Windows XP module responsible for creating and deleting processes and threads.

Process Table A UNIX table created by *fork* that contains one entry for each process. Each entry contains all the data needed by UNIX when the process is not active.

Processor or Process Management A set of operating system services concerned with efficiently managing the processor's time.

Processor The computer component that manipulates data. Also known as the central processing unit (CPU) or main processor.

Program A series of instructions that guides a computer through a process. Each instruction tells the computer to perform one of its basic functions: add, subtract, multiply, divide, compare, copy, start input, or start output.

Program Interrupt On an IBM mainframe, an interrupt that results from an illegal or invalid instruction.

Program Request Block (PRB) An IBM MVS control block that holds information to support an active task.

Program Status Word (PSW) An IBM mainframe's instruction counter.

Programmer Analyst The Programmer Analyst is the person responsible for analyzing the business needs of the user and writing the programs for users. This person must learn the programming language being used as well as the business processes so they can write programs effectively for users.

Programming Language Software programs are written in programming languages such as Pascal, C, C++, Java, Visual BASIC, COBOL, FORTRAN or Assembly. When a person writes a program, they write instructions to perform a certain function or task.

Prompt A symbol or symbols displayed by the operating system to indicate that the command processor is ready to accept a command.

Property Rights A set of rights that control access to information fields that define an object, such as supervise, read, write, and so on.

Proprietary Closed. Made, sold, and/or licensed by an entity that retains exclusive rights to do so.

Protected Mode In protected mode, the application software does not have direct access to the hardware. Also, multiple applications are assigned their own memory address space and are "protected" from one another. Microsoft Windows 98, NT, 2000, and XP boot into real mode and then run in protected mode. Protected mode is also called 32-bit mode.

Protection Key Under MFT, a 4-bit key stored in the PSW that uniquely identifies a partition or region.

Protocol A set of rules for initiating a connection and exchanging information.

Proxy Server An intermediate server located on the client side of the connection that accepts a transaction from a user, forwards it to the appropriate server, and returns the response to the originator.

Pseudocomputer On a UNIX system, an imaginary, private personal computer running under control of a simulated command-driven operating system on which it appears an image is executed.

Public Key In public key encryption, the key that is published.

Public-key Cryptography An encryption algorithm that uses two keys, a public key to encrypt and a private key to decrypt a message. Also called asymmetric encryption.

Pwd A UNIX and Linux command that displays your present working directory.

Queue A type of linked list in which insertions occur at the rear and deletions occur at the front. Access to a queue is controlled by two pointers.

Queuing Routine An operating system routine that places programs on a queue as they enter the system.

QuickTime The Mac OS X multimedia component that allows a user to play back audio, video, graphics, and animation.

Radio Button A Microsoft Windows round circle where you can select an option.

Radio Frequency Interference (RFI) A specific type of EMI noise that occurs in the radio frequency range.

Random Access Memory (RAM) Random Access Memory, or RAM, is temporary. RAM is also shortened to "memory."

Random Access Processing data without regard for their physical order. Also known as direct access.

RD /S A Microsoft DOS and Windows command used to remove a tree, which includes files and directories.

RD A Microsoft DOS and Windows command allowing you to remove a directory.

RDISK A Microsoft utility used to create the Emergency Repair Disk (ERD).

Read After Write A fault tolerant technique in which data are kept in the buffer after a write operation has completed. The data are then read again and compared against the buffer. If an error occurs, the data are rewritten.

Read Memory A nondestructive operation that extracts the contents of memory but does not change them.

Read Permission A UNIX/Linux file permission allowing you to read the contents of a file.

Readiness Analyzer A Microsoft Windows tool allowing you to check your system for hardware and software compatibility issues.

Read-only Attribute A Microsoft DOS and Windows attribute allowing you to only read the contents of a file. You cannot change the contents of the file if the read-only attribute is set.

Read-only Memory (ROM) Firmware is a set of instructions permanently stored on Read-Only Memory (ROM) chips. You cannot simply delete the contents of the ROM firmware by shutting down the computer.

Ready State The state of a program that is in memory and ready to resume processing.

Real Address Mode An Intel Pentium execution mode in which the processor is treated as a high speed 8086.

Real Computer A physical computer.

Real Memory Main memory, directly addressable by the processor.

Real Mode In real mode, the application software has direct (hence the term "real") access to the hardware (such as memory). In real mode, the failure of a single application can cause the whole computer to fail. Native DOS runs in real mode. Real mode is also known as 16-bit mode.

Receiver The destination or recipient of a message.

Record Multiple fields together comprise a record. For example, a record could include these five fields: Employee ID, First Name, Last Name, Pay Rate, and Hours Worked.

Recovery Console A boot method for Microsoft Windows operating systems that allows you to boot to a command prompt. Here, you can start and stop services, repair the MBR with the FIXMBR command, repair boot sectors with the FIXBOOT command or format the disk drive with the FORMAT command. It takes up about 7 MB and is installed with the WINNT32 / CMDCONS command.

Recovery The security criterion that requires that procedures are in place to quickly get the system back on line after a security breech has occurred.

Recycle Bin An icon used to hold files and folders that have been deleted. Note that files and folders deleted from a floppy will not be held in the Recycle Bin.

Redirection The act of changing the default input or output device by adding parameters to a command.

Reduced Instruction Set Computer (RISC) A computer that contains few instructions in its instruction set and relies on hardware to handle the instructions not specifically contained within the instruction set.

Reentrant A program or program module that does not modify itself.

REGEDIT A Microsoft Windows command to modify and view Registry components.

REGEDT32 A Microsoft Windows command to modify and view Registry components.

Region A variable length unit of memory allocated when the application program is first loaded.

Regional ISP A service that operates a statewide or regional backbone and (typically) connects to the Internet by leasing bandwidth from a network service provider.

Register Temporary storage located in the processor that holds control information, key data, or intermediate results.

Registry The Registry is a hierarchical database that contains values for specific computer settings. Microsoft Windows 95, 98, NT, 2000 and XP all have a Registry.

Relative Address An address expressed relative to some base location.

Relative Path Another name for partial path.

Relative Record Number The location of a record relative to the beginning of a file.

REM A Microsoft DOS and Windows command used as a remark in a DOS batch file.

Remote Management A network management technique that allows the network administrator to control the user's workstation remotely from his or her desktop to troubleshoot a problem.

Remote Procedure Call (RPC) A facility that allows structured data to be passed between application processes.

Remove Directory (RMDIR or RD) command An MS-DOS command that deletes a directory.

REN A Microsoft DOS and Windows command used to rename a file.

Replication The act of storing of a copy of a file or a partition on a different server.

Request Block An IBM MVS control block, spun off the task control block, that describes the contents of a given partition or region.

Reserve The act of setting aside a block of memory for a process to use. Generally, the reserved memory does not count against the process until commit time.

Resident A routine that occupies memory at all times.

Resource A resource is a hardware device, a software program, or a file needed by users.

Restart Interrupt On an IBM mainframe, an interrupt that allows an operator or another processor to start a program.

Ring Network A network in which the connections form a ring and messages move around the ring from machine to machine.

Rm A UNIX/Linux command that allows you to remove a file.

Rmdir A UNIX/Linux command that allows you to remove a directory.

RMDIR The Microsoft DOS and Windows command that is the same as the RD command. See the RD command.

Roll-in/roll-out A memory management technique in which a given user's workspace can be rolled out to secondary storage, making room for another application in memory. Later, when the first user's next transaction arrives, his or her workspace is rolled back into memory. A common memory management technique on time-sharing systems.

Root Directory The lowest-level directory on a secondary storage device. Often created by the format routine.

Root User The name of the UNIX and Linux user account that has full control of the operating system commands and files.

Router A device that forwards a packet to a remote network.

Routing The process of selecting the next node or set of nodes for transmitting a message.

Rpm The Linux command to manage software applications.

Safe Mode A boot method for Microsoft Windows operating systems that loads the mouse, keyboard, CD-ROM and VGA drivers. This mode is useful for troubleshooting hardware problems.

Safe Recovery A Microsoft Windows feature allowing an installation to continue after a failure in the middle of the installation.

Samba The SMB (Server Message Block) server for the UNIX and Linux world.

Scalar A chip that uses a single pipeline.

SCANDISK A Microsoft DOS and Windows command that checks the status of a disk.

SCANREG A command line based Registry Checking utility.

SCANREG.INI An initialization file for SCANREG.

SCANREGW A GUI line based Registry Checking utility.

Scheduler An operating system routine that selects a program from the queue and loads it into memory.

Screen Saver A picture, color or pattern that displays when the computer is inactive.

SCSI (Small Computer System Interface) An external bus for linking such parallel devices as printers and external disk drives to a personal computer system.

Secondary Storage A fast, accurate, inexpensive, high-capacity, nonvolatile extension of main memory; e.g., disk.

Secret-key Cryptography A symmetric technique that uses the same key to both encrypt and decrypt a message.

Sector A sector is equal to 512 bytes.

Secure Sockets Layer (SSL) A protocol that runs in the context of the standard TCP/IP protocols, uses public-key encryption to

exchange the secret key, and establishes a secure symmetric secret key connection between a client and a server for the duration of a session, thus ensuring the integrity and privacy of the messages.

Security Database A Windows 2003 Server database that contains information on users and resource security.

Security Hardware, software, and procedures designed to protect system resources from unauthorized access, use, modification, or theft.

Security Services A set of services that support or enable system security.

Segment Descriptor A value in a segment table that holds a segment's base address.

Segment Selector A pointer in a segmented memory model that identifies the segment.

Segment Table A table that lists the (absolute) entry point address of each of a program's segments.

Segmentation A memory management technique in which programs are divided into independently addressed segments and stored in noncontiguous memory

Segmentation *and* Paging A memory management technique in which addresses are divided into a segment number, a page number within that segment, and a displacement within that page. Normally, pages are loaded into noncontiguous memory.

Segmented Model A memory model in which memory is pictured not as a continuous address space but as a group of independent address spaces called segments.

Sequential Access Processing data in physical order.

Serial Line Internet Protocol (SLIP) An older protocol that was used with dial-up networking and was the predecessor to PPP.

Serial Port A connection point for a serial device such as a mouse.

Server In a client/server network, the computer or software routine that controls access to a resource and services client requests.

Server Message Block (SMB) A client/server protocol for file sharing, printing, and login services that is commonly found in Windows.

Server Process A server-side process that is run as a service.

Server-based Network With a server-based network, computer users log in to a main computer called a server where they are authenticated (authorized to use the network).

Service (1) A specific task, often a system task, that supports another program. (2) Under Windows XP, a Win32 program (such as event log, spooler, and so on) that is run automatically at startup.

Service Pack (SP) A software or set of software that fixes a problem. Microsoft uses the term SP.

Service Set Identifier (SSID) An SSID is a set of 32 alphanumeric characters used to differentiate between different wireless networks.

Session A relatively brief series of related transactions with a clear beginning and a clear end.

Session Layer The OSI layer just below the presentation layer that establishes a connection with another computer, keeps the line open for the entire session, recovers the connection if necessary, and terminates the session.

SETUP.EXE A Microsoft Windows software program allowing you to install the operating system.

Shadow Copy A backup facility that allows users to see all previous versions of their files and restore a previous version if necessary.

Share A server resource such as a file or printer that is made available to SMB clients for network sharing.

Shared Folder A folder that is shared by multiple users on a network.

Shared Resource A shared resource is a resource that is capable of being used on other computers. A printer that can be used by multiple users is an example of a shared resource. An application stored on a computer that is used by multiple users is another example of a shared resource.

Shell (1) A set of services that provides a mechanism for the user and application programs to communicate with the operating system and request operating system support. Also known as the user interface. (2) The line command interface.

Shell Mode The UNIX system user interface state when the shell is active.

Shell Script A file that consists of a series of shell commands. A shell script is executed by entering the file name.

Shielded Twisted-Pair (STP) A type of twisted-pair cabling with additional insulation.

SHIFT A Microsoft DOS and Windows command used to shift positional parameters.

Shortcut An icon or button that provides quick access to files that are accessed frequently.

Signal (1) A response to an event that activates an object. (2) The form in which a message is transmitted over a communication line.

Simple Mail Transfer Protocol (SMTP) A protocol that transfers mail from the sender's host computer and delivers it to the receiver's mailbox on a different machine using a standard TCP connection.

Simple Network Management Protocol (SNMP) A popular network management protocol.

Single System Image (SSI) A form of distributed computing in which multiple heterogeneous resources such as networks, distributed databases, or servers appear to the user as one, more-powerful, unified resource.

Single-bus Architecture A design in which all a computer's components are linked to a common bus.

Single-mode Fiber-optic A type of fiberoptic that carries only one light beam down the cable.

Slot A connector for plugging a memory card or an interface board into the system bus.

Small Computer System Interface (SCSI) An interface standard that connects multiple small devices to the same adapter via a SCSI bus.

Software Interrupt An interrupt originating from software.

Software Software is defined as a set of instructions that are processed by a computer system.

SORT A Microsoft DOS and Windows command used to sort, or arrange, data in a file.

Sort A UNIX/Linux command that allows you sort, or arrange, data in a file.

SORT Filter A filter that accepts data from the keyboard, sorts the data into alphabetical or numerical sequence, and outputs the sorted data to the screen.

Sort The UNIX sort filter.

Source Code Instructions written by a programmer in a programming language.

Spanned Record A single logical record that extends over two or more physical records.

Special File On a UNIX system, a file that represents a block or character device.

Spooling The act of copying input data to a high speed device such as disk for subsequent input or writing output data to a high speed device for eventual output.

Spreadsheet Spreadsheet programs allow you to manage data in rows and columns.

SPX A Novell NetWare protocol that occupies the transport layer of both the TCP/IP model and the OSI model and provides a virtual circuit or connection oriented service.

Stack A type of linked list in which all insertions and deletions occur at the top. Access to the stack is controlled by a single pointer.

Stack Segment A segment of a UNIX image that holds a memory stack. The stack segment holds addresses, pointers, and so on.

Standard User The Standard User, or user, is the person who uses the system on a daily basis in support of their job. They use the system to access an application. The application they need depends upon their function in the organization.

Star Network A network in which each host is linked to a central "star" machine.

Star Topology A topology where each device connects to a hub or switch.

Start Button The button located in the lower left hand corner of a Microsoft Windows desktop used to launch application and utilities, find files and other computers, get help, and add/ remove hardware and software.

Startup Menu A Microsoft Windows menu that determines how the operating system will boot. Pressing the F8 key during the boot sequence will display the Startup menu.

State Status. The state of an executing program is often defined by a snapshot of essential operating information such as the values of key control variables, a list of open files, a list of active print jobs, and so on.

Streaming Server A server designed to broadcast live information (music, sound, video) in real time, encoding, compressing, and transmitting the information at a constant, predictable rate so that playback glitches (like dropped phrases and broken or frozen images) can be minimized.

Structured Program A program that consists of a series of logical modules linked by a control structure.

Subdirectory A special file that holds pointers to other files. Think of a subdirectory as a file folder that allows a user to group related files and thus organize the disk.

Subnet Mask A 32-bit number that is used to determine which part of the IP address represents the network and which part represents the host.

Subtree A Registry folder that contains hives.

Super Block On a UNIX disk, a region that identifies the disk, defines the sizes of the disk's regions, and tracks free blocks.

Superpipelining A processor chip that uses more than four stages to complete an instruction and thus support additional levels of pipelining.

Superscalar A processor chip that uses more than one pipeline and thus allows more than one instruction to be executed simultaneously.

Supervisor Call (SVC) Interrupt On an IBM mainframe, an interrupt that originates when a program executes an SVC instruction.

Supervisor Request Block (SVRB) An IBM MVS request block that indicates that a supervisory routine is active in support of a task.

Supervisor The resident operating system.

Supervisor User A user with a great deal of access on a computer system.

Supervisory State The state of an IBM mainframe that is executing a supervisor routine.

Swap File The swap file, or page file, is the section of the hard disk used for virtual memory.

Swapping The process of moving program instructions and data between memory and secondary storage as the program is executed.

Switch A switch is an intelligent hub.

Switched Line A temporary communication link that is established for the life of a single message or a series of related messages.

Symmetrical Multi-Processing (SMP) The ability of a computer system to use multiple processors that can execute different portions of a program is called Symmetrical Multi-Processing or SMP.

SYS A Microsoft DOS and Windows command used to transfer system files to a device.

SYSEDIT A Microsoft Windows program allowing you to modify system files.

System Administrator A person responsible for the operation of a computer system.

System Configuration Utility (MSCONFIG) A Microsoft Windows program allowing you to disable or enable entries in AUTOEXEC.BAT, CONFIG.SYS, SYSTEM.INI or WIN.INI.

System Data Segment On a UNIX system, a process segment that holds data needed by the operating system when the process is active.

System File Checker (SFC) A Microsoft Windows program that protects system files.

System File Table A UNIX table that holds the i-nodes of all open files. Also known as the i-node table.

System Files A set of Microsoft Windows operating system files.

System Key A protection feature for Windows 2000 and XP passwords.

System Management Mode An Intel Pentium execution mode used primarily for system security and power management.

System Monitor A Microsoft Windows program that assists with monitoring system performance.

System Partition Microsoft Windows NT, 2000, and XP use the terms system partition to refer to the location of the load files. The system partition must be marked as active in order for these operating systems to load.

System Process A process (such as the logon facility that accepts user logons and authenticates them) that does not run as a service and requires an interactive logon.

System Resources System resources are features that control how devices on a computer system work.

System Software System software includes the core components of the system that must be present in order for the computer to operate. Examples of system software are the operating system kernel, process management, memory management, and device drivers.

System State A group of Microsoft Windows 2000 and XP files that consist of the Registry, system files, boot files and the COM+ Class Registration database.

System Unit Also known as the computer system chassis. See chassis.

SYSTEM.DAT A Registry file that holds computer-specific hardware settings, PnP configurations and application settings.

T1 A type of WAN connection.

Table A table is a collection of database data stored on disk.

Task (1) A unit of work that the processor can dispatch, execute, and suspend. (2) A single program or routine that has been loaded on the computer and is ready to run. (3) The basic Mac OS X resource allocation unit.

Task A running program. Also known as a job or process.

Task Control Block (TCB) An IBM MVS control block that holds key control information for a task.

Task Execution Space On an Intel Pentium system, a unit of memory space that holds a program's code, stack, and data segments.

Task Management Under IBM's MVS, the routines that support a program it as it runs, primarily by handling interrupts.

Task Manager A Microsoft Windows utility allowing you to manage processes.

Task State Segment (TSS) An Intel Pentium control block with entries that point to the segments in the task execution space.

Taskbar A bar at the bottom of a Windows or KDE screen that displays one button for each active program.

TCP/IP Model The model that defines the Internet's standard protocols. Also known as the Internet model.

Telnet A program that allows a user to connect to another computer (host) and enter commands as though he or she were on the host system.

Terabyte (TB) 1 trillion bytes.

Terminals A terminal is a device that has no computing ability and is strictly dependent upon the processing power of another, such as the mainframe.

Terminate and Stay Resident (TSR) A TSR is a program that executes, terminates normally, and then stays resident in memory until needed by the operating system. Examples include HIMEM.SYS, EMM386.EXE and COMMAND.COM.

Text Box A Microsoft Windows area where you can type a specific parameter (or value).

Text Mode A mode where characters are entered on the screen. DOS and Linux have a text mode.

Text Segment A segment of a UNIX image that holds executable code.

Text Table A UNIX table that lists each current text segment, its primary and secondary addresses, and a count of the number of processes sharing it.

The Cloud A graphical representation of the Internet.

Thrashing A problem that occurs when a virtual memory system finds itself spending so much time swapping pages into and out from memory that little time is left for useful work.

Thread A thread is a basic unit of instruction that is allocated processor time by the operating system. Think of a process as being made up of many threads. The threads of a process execute the process code. A thread can execute any part of the code, which includes portions that are currently run by another thread.

Thread Synchronization Threads synchronize with each other to coordinate resource access. This prevents one thread from interrupting another.

Thunk A piece of coding that provides an address.

TIME A Microsoft DOS and Windows command used to display or change the time.

Time Slice A time slice is a unit of time allocated to a task

Time-sharing A processor management technique in which multiple, concurrent, interactive users are assigned, in turn, a single time-slice before being forced to surrender the processor to the next user.

Time-slicing A processor management technique in which each program is limited to a maximum slice of time.

Title Bar The horizontal bar at the top of a window that indicates the name of the program that is running.

Token A packet of data passed between computers in a ring topology.

Token Passing A network management technique in which an electronic signal (the token) moves continuously around the network and a computer is allowed to transmit a message only when it holds the token.

Token Ring A topology, developed by IBM, that is wired like a star topology but the computers are logically accessed in a ring where a "token" is passed to each computer. The computer with the "token" can use the network.

Topology The arrangement of devices in a network.

Touch A UNIX/Linux command that allows you to update the modification time stamp on a file or directory.

Tracert Command A TCP/IP related command used to trace the route a packet takes from source to destination.

Track A track is a concentric circle running around the center of the disk.

Transient A routine that is stored on disk and loaded into memory only when needed.

Transient Area The portion of memory where application programs and transient operating system routines are loaded.

Transmission Control Protocol (TCP) The Internet protocol that guarantees delivery of the complete message to the destination.

Transmission Control Protocol/Internet Protocol (TCP/IP) The protocol used to access the Internet.

Transmitter The sender or originator of a message.

Transparent Hidden. Not visible.

Transport Driver Interface (TDI) A Windows 2003 layer that provides a common interface that file system drivers and network redirectors use to communicate with network protocols.

Transport Layer (1) The OSI layer just below the session layer that ensures successful end-to-end transmission of the complete message, from start to finish. (2) The TCP/IP layer that performs the same function.

TREE A Microsoft DOS and Windows command allowing you to view the file system hierarchy.

Twisted-pair cable Cable used in a star topology.

TYPE A Microsoft DOS and Windows command allowing you to display the contents of a file.

UFS (UNIX file system) One of the Mac OS X primary file systems.

Uniform Resource Locator (URL) A World Wide Web page's unique address.

Universal Disk Format (UDFS) Universal Disk Format, is primarily used for read-only DVD/CD-ROM media.

Universal Naming Convention (UNC) A Microsoft naming convention for a shared resource. The UNC is comprised on the computer and shared device name.

UNIX An operating system developed at Bell Laboratories designed to provide a convenient working environment for programming. Today, it is an important standard that has influenced the design of many modern operating systems.

Unshielded Twisted-Pair (UTP) A type of twisted-pair cabling with no additional insulation.

Upgrade The process of installing an operating system with a higher version on a computer with an operating system that contains a lower version operating system. For example, if Windows 2000 existed on a PC, you could upgrade it to Windows XP.

Upper Memory or Upper Memory Block (UMB) Upper memory is used for the system BIOS, video BIOS and other functions and is the 384 KB from 640 KB to 1 MB.

USB (Universal Serial Bus) An external bus used to connect such serial devices as a scanner, a mouse, and a modem to a personal computer system.

User Datagram Protocol (UDP) A connectionless Internet protocol that works at the transport layer. Faster than but not as reliable as TCP.

User Interface A set of services that provides a mechanism for the user and application programs to communicate with the operating system and request operating system support.

User Mode A Windows operating mode in which user applications and a collection of subsystems execute.

User Profile A Registry setting that contains a user's specific configuration settings.

User The Standard User, or user, is the person who uses the system on a daily basis in support of their job. They use the system to access an application. The application they need depends upon their function in the organization.

USER.DAT A Registry file that holds user-specific settings such as logon name, desktop setting and Start button settings.

User-space Driver Under Mac OS X, a device driver that occupies user space.

Utility A system software routine that performs a specific support function but is not part of the resident operating system.

Valid Page A page that resides in physical memory.

Value Entries Fields within the Registry that contain data.

Vector On an Intel Pentium system, an identification number associated with an interrupt.

VER A Microsoft DOS and Windows command used to view the operating system version.

Vi A UNIX/Linux command that allows you to create, edit and modify text in a file.

Virtual 8086 Mode An Intel Pentium execution mode in which an 8086 processor is simulated in a separate protected memory space, which allows 8086 applications to execute while still enjoying the full benefits of the protection mechanism.

Virtual Cluster Number (VCN) A number that is mapped to a logical cluster number to identify a file on disk.

Virtual Desktop Under KDE, one of several concurrently active desktop environments.

Virtual Device Driver (VxD) A device driver that operates in protected mode and can access hardware directly.

Virtual FAT (VFAT) Microsoft developed VFAT (Virtual FAT) with Microsoft Windows 95 to allow file names to exceed the 8.3 rule. VFAT allows Long File Names, or LFNs.

Virtual File System (VFS) A Linux kernel feature that allows processes to access all file systems uniformly.

Virtual Machine A simulated computer with its own virtual operating system and its own virtual peripherals that runs on a real computer. Often, two or more virtual machines are run concurrently on a single real computer.

Virtual Machine Concept The act of multiprogramming or time-sharing at the operating system level.

Virtual Memory (VM) Module A machine independent module that runs in the Mac OS X kernel and is responsible for processing page faults, managing address maps, and swapping pages.

Virtual Memory A model that simplifies address translation. The resident operating system is stored in real memory. Application programs are stored on the external paging device and selected pages are swapped into real memory as needed.

Virtual Memory Manager (VMM) Software that manages virtual memory.

Virtual Memory Manager (VMM) The Windows XP module that allocates memory to processes and manages system memory.

Virtual Memory Virtual memory uses RAM and a section of the hard disk to accommodate multitasking and multiple users.

Virtual Private Networking (VPN) A VPN is a remote computer connecting to a remote network by securely "tunneling" over an intermediate network such as the Internet or a LAN.

Virus A program that is capable of replicating and spreading between computers by attaching itself to another program. A common carrier for malware.

Virus Signature A code pattern that uniquely identifies a particular virus.

VM Object An object associated with each region in the virtual address space by the Mac OS X kernel.

Vnode Under Mac OS X, a file representation structure used to support operations on a file within the virtual file system. There is a unique vnode for each active file or folder.

Voice-activated Interface A user interface that utilizes natural-language processing. Key elements include voice recognition and voice data entry.

Volume (1) A physical disk pack or reel of tape. (2) A portion or portions of one or more physical disks.

Volume Header A header stored on an HFS+ volume that contains information about the entire volume, including the number of files stored on the volume, the date and time the volume was created, and the location of other key structures.

Vulnerability A weakness in a system that allows a hacker to gain access.

Wait A UNIX utility that suspends execution of a process until a particular event occurs.

Wait State The state of a program that has been loaded into memory but is unable to continue executing until some event occurs.

Wallpaper Scheme A Microsoft Windows background picture, pattern, or color.

Wasted Space Unused space in a disk cluster caused by a file not completely occupying the cluster.

Web Information System An information system that relies on communication between asynchronous client-side and server-side application routines.

Web Page The basic unit of information on the World Wide Web.

Web Server A server-side application that manages, retrieves, and serves Web pages.

Web Services A set of services that support retrieving Web pages in response to a request from a client, running scripts on both the client side and the server side, and similar tasks.

Web Site A set of closely related Web pages that are interconnected by hyperlinks.

Web-based A Web application designed and built specifically to take advantage of the Internet and the World Wide Web.

Web-enabled A non-Web application, often a legacy application, to which a Web interface has been added, thus enabling a level of Web interactivity.

Web-form Interface A user interface that follows the metaphor established by the Internet and the World Wide Web.

Who A UNIX and Linux command that displays the current users logged on.

Wide Area Network (WAN) A network that links geographically disbursed computers. Generally, at least some of the communication takes place over long distance lines.

Wild Card A character (usually * or ?) that represents one or more characters in a file name.

Wildcard Characters Characters, such as * and ?, which are used to represent (or match) other characters.

WIN.COM The DOS command that loads Microsoft Windows 3.1.

Window A box that occupies a portion of the desktop and displays information associated with a program or file.

Window Part of the screen that belongs to a specific application or utility.

Windows A family of Microsoft operating systems that allows a user to access a computer through a graphical user interface.

Windows File Protection (WFP) A Microsoft Windows program that protects system files.

Windows Image Acquisition (WIA) Software allowing communication between applications and image-capturing devices.

Windows Internet Naming Service (WINS) A Microsoft program that resolves Microsoft computer names to IP addresses.

Windows On Windows (WOW) An environment simulator for 16-bit applications that runs inside of an NTVDM.

Windows Protection Error A Microsoft Windows error caused by a virtual device driver being loaded or unloaded.

Windows Script A Microsoft Windows method of automating shortcuts for users and set or restrict access for the desktop, Start menu, and applications.

Windows Script Host (WSH) The Microsoft Windows scripting host computer.

Windows Scripting Host (WSH) A Windows tool that allows users to take advantages of scripting languages to exploit the functionality of Windows.

WINIPCFG A Microsoft command that displays IP settings on Windows 95 and 98.

WINNT.EXE The Microsoft Windows NT installation program. It is used to install to a computer that currently has DOS, Windows 3.x, Windows 95 or Windows 98 installed.

WINNT32.EXE The Microsoft Windows NT installation program. It is used to upgrade from a previous version of Microsoft Windows NT.

WINVER A Microsoft DOS and Windows command that displays operating system version.

Wireless A communication medium in which there is no physical connection between the transmitter and the receiver. Examples include radio, television, cellular telephone, WiFi, microwave links, satellite links, and infrared beams.

Wireless Equivalent Privacy (WEP) WEP encrypts data being transmitted.

Word A group of bytes that is treated as a unit of memory. Often holds a number or an address. Word size is a key element in computer design.

Word Processing Word processing software allows you to create, modify, delete, save, and print documents that are office quality. They also have capabilities for spell checking, and include a dictionary and thesaurus.

Worker Process Under Windows 2003 Server's World Wide Web Service Administration and Monitoring (W3SAM) feature, a process that hosts and executes the middleware routines.

Workgroup A peer-to-peer network in Windows 2003 Server terminology

Working Directory The user's current default directory.

Workstation An end-user computer through which people access a local area network.

Workstation Management The ability of the user's desktop to follow the user.

World Wide Web, or Web A client/server application layered on top of the Internet that provides simple, standardized protocols for naming, linking, and accessing virtually everything on the Internet.

Worm A program that is capable of spreading under its own power. A common carrier for malware.

Write Memory A destructive operation that records new values in memory, replacing the old contents.

Write Permission A UNIX/Linux file permission allowing you to write to a file.

WSCRIPT.EXE The Microsoft Windows scripting tool.

XCOPY A Microsoft DOS and Windows command used to copy a whole tree, including files and directories.

Zero Effort Networks (ZENworks) The part of NetWare that supports desktop management.

Index